HARTLEY H. T. JACKSON

MAMMALS
OF
WISCONSIN

THE UNIVERSITY OF WISCONSIN PRESS

The University of Wisconsin Press
114 North Murray Street
Madison, Wisconsin 53715

3 Henrietta Street
London WC2E 8LU, England

10   9   8   7   6   5

Printed in the United States of America

ISBN 0-299-02150-5; LC 61-5186

DEDICATED TO MY WIFE

WHO TAKES THE BAD WITH THE GOOD

AND WIN OR LOSE

KEEPS TRYING

FOREWORD

Our earliest knowledge of Wisconsin mammals is due to the missionaries and fur traders. Jean Nicolet, the first European to set foot in Wisconsin, landed at Green Bay in 1634, where "at least sixscore beavers" were served at feasts given by the Indians. Information on the fur-bearers increased rapidly following the discovery of the Mississippi River, via the Fox-Wisconsin waterway, by Joliet and Marquette in 1673.

In keeping with the times, it was long before any scientific interest in the mammals was shown. Increase A. Lapham, in 1852, published *A Systematic Catalogue of the Animals of Wisconsin*. This was followed by the check lists of Moses Strong (1883), H. H. T. Jackson (1908), Ned Hollister (1910), and N. R. Barger (1952 and 1958). The only work giving any detailed information is *The Mammals of Illinois and Wisconsin*, by Charles B. Cory, published in 1912. However, Cory had little opportunity to study Wisconsin mammals at first hand and the information is quite limited.

Wisconsin is one of the few northern states without a comprehensive treatise on its mammals and birds. Fortunately, the mammalian gap is being filled admirably by the present work. The author, born and educated in Wisconsin, knows the state thoroughly. The knowledge gained as a resident has been supplemented by field trips to Wisconsin while a member of the U. S. Biological Survey, and the Fish and Wildlife Service. Being a skilled taxonomist, he has added many new races to the Wisconsin fauna. The extensive life histories and photographs in the present work extend its value far beyond the limits of our commonwealth.

May, 1959   A. W. SCHORGER

PREFACE

The present study may have sprouted from my own early interests in mammals: The germ may have been latent when as a six-year-old lad I chased a long-tailed weasel away from a duckling it had captured in our backyard. Or the seed may have burst the next autumn when I made observations on a chipmunk storing hazelnuts and wrote illegible notes on the great event. Or possibly it was in the fall of 1891 when I insisted on making a "scientific specimen" out of a gray squirrel my brother had shot. As I recall, that was my first mammal skin and the beginning of my private mammal collection. The collection later became a part of the University of Wisconsin Zoology Department Collection.

In reality, however, the study in its entirety had its making in a series of informal personal conferences between the late Professor George Wagner and myself in the years 1912 to 1916. We hoped to have coverage of a general survey of the land vertebrates of Wisconsin, to be made coöperative between the U. S. Biological Survey (now the U. S. Fish and Wildlife Service) and the University of Wisconsin. Professor Wagner and myself formulated a program of work. The beginnings of this informal and congenial coöperation are clarified by three letters that passed between the two institutions.

STATE OF WISCONSIN
Geological and Natural History Survey
Madison, Wisconsin

June 7, 1917

Mr. E. W. Nelson,
   Chief, Biological Survey,
      U. S. Department of Agriculture,
      Washington. D. C.

Dear Sir:

I have had on my desk for some time a letter from Mr. H. H. T. Jackson of your Survey to Professor Wagner of the University of Wisconsin, asking informally whether the Wisconsin Geological and Natural History Survey would be able to cooperate with the Department of Agriculture in the proposed Biological Survey of Wisconsin.

The preparation of the budget of this Survey for the year beginning July 1, 1917, has been delayed so long that I think it best to write you directly in the matter without waiting for the official communication from you which Mr. Jackson suggested. I find that our finances are such that we shall be able to cooperate with your Survey, if mutually satisfactory arrangements for cooperation can be made. We can expend during the coming year an amount not exceeding $500. This, I believe, will cover the amount of cooperation which Mr. Jackson suggested. At all events, it is as far as funds of the Survey will permit us to go during the coming year.

I trust that it will be possible to continue cooperation in the future, but for the present I can make no positive statement in regard to this aspect of the matter.

I shall be glad to hear from you officially with regard to plans and conditions of cooperation.

Very truly yours,
/s/ E. A. Birge
Director.

June 13, 1917.

Bi
Survey

Dr. E. A. Birge,
  Wisconsin Geological and Natural History Survey,
    Madison, Wisconsin.

Dear Dr. Birge:

Your letter of the 7th instant, in regard to cooperation between the U. S. Biological Survey and the Wisconsin Survey in carrying on a study of the fauna of your State, is received. I am pleased to learn that you will be able to contribute toward the undertaking. Our funds are rather limited, and the $500 which you can expend during this coming year will be of material help and will insure a more exhaustive study than might otherwise have been possible.

Dr. Jackson will be in Madison early in July, and from there will work mostly in northeastern Wisconsin during this summer. I would suggest that you hire a competent man to accompany Dr. Jackson, you to pay this assistant's salary and expenses out of the $500. In case your allotment of $500 falls short for the season, we can take over the assistant at our expense for the remaining few weeks.

The other conditions and plans as outlined in a letter from Professor Wagner to Dr. Jackson are

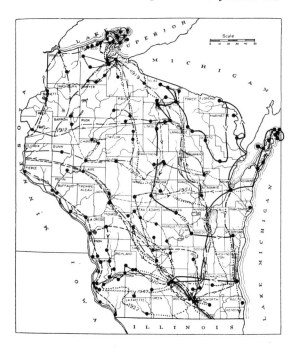

Map 1. Routes of field men and work stations.

satisfactory to me. These conditions are in general: that collections be made of mammals, birds, reptiles, and amphibians; that, during the actual time when we cooperate, mammal specimens go to the U. S. Biological Survey, except insofar as it may see fit to furnish the Wisconsin Survey a representative collection with cleaned skulls; that reptiles and amphibians go to the Wisconsin Survey on a similar basis; that birds collected during actual cooperation be divided in general equally, reserving for the U. S. Biological Survey any possible types and critical specimens; that reports on mammals, birds, and life zones be prepared by the U. S. Biological Survey, while you be privileged to report on the reptiles and amphibians; that publication be as later agreed upon.

If these conditions are entirely satisfactory to you, I shall be very pleased to have your official approval of them. Any suggestions you may have to offer will be gratefully received.

Trusting that our work will prove mutually pleasant and helpful, I am

Very sincerely yours,
/s/   E. W. Nelson
Chief, Biological Survey.

STATE OF WISCONSIN
Geological and Natural History Survey
Madison, Wisconsin

June 15, 1917

Mr. E. W. Nelson,
  Chief, Biological Survey,
    U. S. Department of Agriculture,
      Washington, D. C.

Dear Mr. Nelson:

In reply to your letter of June 13 I would say that I approve the conditions of cooperation between the United States Biological Survey and the Wisconsin Geological Survey, as indicated in that letter.

I have turned over the practical adjustment of cooperation to Professor George Wagner, who will act with Mr. Jackson of your Survey in this matter.

Very truly yours,
/s/   E. A. Birge
Director.

At the time the coöperative study began there were several private and public collections of Wisconsin mammals, but it was felt that a fairly complete coverage of the state was desirable. Plans were outlined for such coverage. Routes of fieldmen and major collecting or observation stations are shown on Map 1. The author supervised all mammal field activities and studied at each station. A chronological list of field work done in the state follows. The list includes work done both by the U. S. Biological Survey (1947 and 1951, U. S. Fish and Wildlife Service) and the state of Wisconsin, that by the state being so indicated. During this field work about 1,250 mammal specimens were collected.

1898—Vernon Bailey, one week.
1912—Hartley H. T. Jackson, six weeks.
1917 Hartley H. T. Jackson, thirteen weeks.
1917—F. Gregory Hall, twelve weeks (paid by state of Wisconsin).
1918—Hartley H. T. Jackson, sixteen weeks.
1918—Arthur J. Poole, thirteen weeks.
1918—Arthur I. Ortenburger, ten weeks (paid by state of Wisconsin).
1919—Hartley H. T. Jackson, eighteen weeks.
1919—Harry H. Sheldon, eighteen weeks.
1919—Arthur J. Poole, seventeen weeks (paid by state of Wisconsin).
1919—George Wagner, two weeks (beaver stud-

ies, paid by state of Wisconsin).
1920—Hartley H. T. Jackson, ten weeks.
1920—Arthur J. Poole, sixteen weeks (paid by state of Wisconsin).
1921—Vernon Bailey, five weeks (beaver studies).
1922—Hartley H. T. Jackson, twelve weeks.
1922—Arthur J. Poole, ten weeks.
1923—Vernon Bailey, three weeks (beaver studies).
1930—Vernon Bailey, four weeks.
1930—Oliver L. Austin, Jr., one week.
1947—Hartley H. T. Jackson, two weeks (personal expense).
1951—Hartley H. T. Jackson, two weeks.

There are many problems yet to be solved about Wisconsin mammals. It is hoped that this descriptive account will stimulate a more active interest in studies of one of the most important groups of animals.

Acknowledgments

One of the real pleasures of doing the research and preparing this volume has been the friendly and generous coöperation and help of so many institutions and individuals. The author makes grateful acknowledgment to all of these, so numerous that each cannot be named individually. Particular mention should be made of those who encouraged and sponsored the work in its initial stages, among whom were Dr. E. A. Birge and Professor George Wagner of the University of Wisconsin, W. E. Barber, director of the Wisconsin Conservation Commission, and Dr. E. W. Nelson, chief of the U. S. Biological Survey, all now deceased. Loyal and industrious student assistants enhanced the field studies, among them being Dr. F. Gregory Hall, now of Duke University; Dr. Arthur I. Ortenburger, retired; Arthur J. Poole, deceased, then of the Smithsonian Institution; and Harry H. Sheldon, then of the U. S. Biological Survey. My wife, Anna M. Adams Jackson, accompanied the field party on occasions and aided in many ways, particularly in botanical collections and in procuring information from personal contacts. Valuable help was offered by many residents of Wisconsin, including guides, hunters, summer resort owners, farmers, and others, whose interest and aid is appreciated.

Acknowledgment is due to the many institutions and individuals who extended permission to use their facilities and collections. Staff members of institutions include, among others: Dr. H. E. Anthony, American Museum of Natural History; Dr. Howard K. Gloyd, Chicago Academy of Sciences; Dr. R. M. Anderson and Austin W. Cameron, National Museum of Canada; Dr. J. Kenneth Doutt and Miss Caroline A. Heppenstall, Carnegie Museum; Dr. C. C. Sanborn, Chicago Natural History Museum; Miss Lucille Drury, Cleveland Museum of Natural History; the late Edward R. Warren, Colorado College; Dr. W. C. McKern, the late S. A. Barrett, Owen J. Gromme, and Walter K. Pelzer, Milwaukee Public Museum, and Herbert L. Stoddard, formerly with the Milwaukee Public Museum; the late Earl G. Wright, Neville Public Museum; the late G. M. Allen, Museum of Comparative Zoology, Cambridge, Mass.; Dr. Donald. F. Hoffmeister, University of Illinois; Dr. David H. Johnson, U. S. National Museum; Dr. W. H. Burt, University of Michigan Museum of Zoology; the late E. L. Moseley, Bowling Green State University; Drs. John T. Emlen, Jr., A. W. Schorger, L. E. Noland, H. R. Wolfe, and James R. Beer, and others, University of Wisconsin; and W. E. Scott, N. R. Barger, and George J. Knudsen, Wisconsin Conservation Department. I wish also to express my thanks and appreciation to the owners of the private collections of mammals I had the privilege of studying, among whom are Dr. A. W. Schorger, Frederick and Frances Hamerstrom, Harold C. Hanson, James R. Beer, the late John N. Clark, Wallace B. Grange, the late Frank J. W. Schmidt, Wayne H. Davis, and the late W. E. Snyder.

The author's sincere thanks are extended to a host of individuals who have graciously coöperated and assisted in many and various ways in the research and preparation of this monograph. Most of these must be left unmentioned. Especially helpful were Walter E. Scott, N. R. Barger, George J. Knudsen, Cyril Kabat, C. W. Lemke, Harold J. Mathiak, Ruth L. Hine, and many others in the Wisconsin Conservation Department. At the University of Wisconsin they include John T. Emlen, Jr., A. W. Schorger, and the late John J. Davis, as well as James R. Beer, Frank A. Iwen, and several other graduate students. The author was aided by many citizens of the state who offered useful information, provided specimens, or assisted in other ways. Among these were Ned Hollister, Mrs. Polly Bent Fisher, Charles F. Carr, Victor Kutchin, and Benjamin R. Twombly, all deceased. Other citizens include C. G. Conley, Cayuga; Rev. Francis F. Dayton, New London; Wallace B. Grange, Babcock; L. G. Sorden, Rhinelander; Hartley E. Summers, Milton; and Francis Zirrer, Hayward. Various observations and notes have been contributed, all of which are acknowledged in the text.

The author appreciates the help and coöperation of many of his fellow workers, particularly that of Dr. John W. Aldrich, Stanley P. Young, Dr. Richard H. Manville, Dr. Daniel L. Leedy, Charles H. M. Barrett, Miss Viola S. Schantz, Miss Emma M. Charters, and others of the U. S. Fish and Wildlife Service, and also that of Dr. David H. Johnson, Dr. Henry W. Setzer, John L. Paradiso, and Mrs. Helen S. Gaylord of the U. S. National Museum. For routine help in the preparation of the manuscript I am grateful to Mrs. Blanche M. Mahlman, Mrs. Grace Green, and others of the U. S. Fish and Wildlife Service.

Photographs of scientific specimens, whether skulls or skins, with very few exceptions were made by the photograph laboratory of the Smithsonian Institution. The photograph of the skull of the type specimen *Felis concolor schorgeri* was made by the University of Wisconsin Photographic Laboratory. Other photographs have been procured from various sources, but chiefly from the files of the Wisconsin Conservation Department and the U. S. Fish and Wildlife Service. Source of procurement when known is acknowledged in the legend to the picture. Most of the drawings in the book, particularly those of bats, lagomorphs, rodents, carnivores, and ungulates, were made by Mrs. Bess O' Melveny MacMaugh. Several drawings, especially those of marsupials and insectivores, and a few others, were made by Mrs. Katheryne C. Tabb. Credit is given to Mrs. Roxie Collie Laybourne for technical assistance in these drawings. Initials or names on the drawings identify the individual's work. Effort is made to indicate who did the work in all other drawings, but in a few the artist is unknown. The few sketches made by the author are not initialed. All of the distribution maps have been made originally in the rough by the author. The small insert maps were redrawn on the base maps of North America by Mrs. Tabb. The large Wisconsin base maps were drawn by the late Mrs. Jane S. Elliott. Original plotting of the distribution of the species on a map of Wisconsin was made by the author. The final state distribution maps were all drawn by Mrs. MacMaugh.

CONTENTS

Foreword, vii
Preface, ix
Acknowledgments, xi
Introduction, 3

Mammals: Class Mammalia
Early Mammalogy in Wisconsin, 5
Wisconsin's Physiographic Features, 5
Type Localities for Wisconsin Mammals, 7
State Ecological Areas and Life Zones, 8
Key to the Orders of Recent
  Wisconsin Mammals, 11
Hypothetical List of Wisconsin Mammals, 11
The Study of Mammals, 11
Plan of the Book, 12

Bibliography, 435
Index, 483

Order **MARSUPIALIA**, Marsupials, 17
Family **Didelphidae**, Opossums, 17

Order **INSECTIVORA**, Insectivorous
  Mammals, 26
Family **Soricidae**, Shrews, 26
Family **Talpidae**, Moles, 61

Order **CHIROPTERA**, Bats, 74
Family **Vespertilionidae**, Common Bats, 74

Order **LAGOMORPHA**, Hares and Allies, 103
Family **Leporidae**, Hares and Rabbits, 103

Order **RODENTIA**, Rodents or
  Gnawing Mammals, 121
Family **Sciuridae**, Squirrels, 122
Family **Geomyidae**, Pocket Gophers, 184
Family **Castoridae**, Beavers, 191
Family **Cricetidae**, 203
Subfamily **Cricetinae**, Deer Mice and Allies, 203
Subfamily **Microtinae**, Voles and Allies, 220
Family **Muridae**, Old World Rats and Mice, 253
Family **Zapodidae**, Jumping Mice, 261
Family **Erethizontidae**, Porcupines, 270

Order **CARNIVORA**, Carnivorous Mammals, 279
Family **Canidae**, Dogs and Allies, 279
Family **Ursidae**, Bears, 311
Family **Procyonidae**, Raccoons, 321
Family **Mustelidae**, Weasels and Allies, 328
Family **Felidae**, Cats and Allies, 389

Order **ARTIODACTYLA**, Even-toed
  Hoofed Mammals, 407
Family **Cervidae**, Deer and Allies, 407
Family **Bovidae**, Bison, 427

MAMMALS OF WISCONSIN

INTRODUCTION

Mammals: Class Mammalia

The term "mammal" is the vernacular English for the Latin *Mammalia*, a technical name invented by the Swedish naturalist Carolus Linnaeus in 1758 when he proposed his classification of living organisms both animal and vegetable. The term has not come into general use, yet it has no satisfactory equivalent. "Animal" is sometimes erroneously used, but flies, beetles, worms, corals, fishes, snakes, and birds are all animals. In years past the term "quadruped" was used, but it does not include such mammals as bats, whales, and man. Nor does the term "beast" include such mammals as, for example, bats, shrews, and some of the rodents. We must accustom ourselves to the word mammal for accurate popular English designation. Mammal is derived from the Latin *mamma,* the breast. Other languages have words more expressive for the Mammalia.

Mammals are classified as one of the five groups of vertebrate animals—that is animals with an internal skeleton consisting of a backbone with a skull articulated to it, and an anterior and a posterior pair of limbs more or less correlated or connected with the vertebral column. In a few instances the limbs have become degenerate or lacking. The five classes of existing vertebrates, from the lowest to the highest, are fishes, amphibians, reptiles, birds, and mammals.

A mammal is a warm-blooded, air-breathing animal that produces milk for feeding its young and has more or less hairy skin at some period of its existence. The blood cells are nonnucleated and generally round. The blood circulation is double, as with birds; that is, the circulation through the lungs is entirely separate and distinct from that through the rest of the body. In mammals the aorta or large artery carrying blood from the heart to the body turns to the left; in birds it turns to the right. Mammals include such diverse forms as the duck-billed platypus, which lays eggs; the opossum, which gives premature birth to its young and carries them attached to its teats in an abdominal pouch; the bat, which flies; the whale, which lives in the sea and has limbs modified into flippers for swimming; the deer and the buffalo, which feed exclusively on vegetation; the weasel and the lynx, which almost as exclusively feed on animals; and the shrew and mole, insect eaters. There are between 17,000 and 18,000 forms of mammals known in the world, of which about 3,700 occur in North and Central America.

Mammals are found nearly everywhere from the Arctic to the Antarctic, but are more plentiful in tropical and temperate regions. They exhibit not only great diversification of form, but also of habitat. We speak of mammals as being either aquatic or terrestrial. Habitat groupings, however, can easily be further divided, the aquatic forms being either marine, as the whale, sea otter, and most seals, or freshwater as the muskrat, beaver, and river otter. The whale and dolphin tribes and the manatee group are the only ones that can be called strictly aquatic, since they are the only mammals that die upon removal from water. Terrestrial mammals may be truly terrestrial in dwelling chiefly on the surface of the ground, as the deer, elk, rabbit, and many of the rodents. Others are fossorial, in that they live underground and seldom come to the surface, such as the mole and the pocket gopher. Still others are arboreal, in that they spend most of their time in trees, such as the sloth, monkey, and tree squirrel. Bats are aerial, except when at rest.

The whale and its relatives and the manatees are the only mammals that cannot progress on land. Progression on land, however, is extremely awkward with certain other aquatic forms such as the seal, with many arboreal forms like the sloth, and with the bat. Adaptations for various types of locomotion are represented in different groups of mammals, as, for example, in seals and beavers for swimming; in moles and badgers for digging; in bats for flying; in flying squirrels for gliding; in raccoons and opossums for climbing; in rabbits for leaping; in deer and foxes for running; and in bears and skunks for walking.

The Mammalia of the world are classified into

two well-marked groups or subclasses. The most primitive group constitutes the subclass Prototheria, of which there are only two existing representatives, both of the order Monotremata, the duck-billed platypus of Australia and Tasmania, and the spiny anteaters of Australia, Tasmania, and New Zealand. Members of the order Monotremata differ from all other mammals by laying eggs, in having a very simple mammary gland without external mammae, and in certain skeletal peculiarities of the breast and shoulder bones. The second subclass, the Theria, includes all living mammals except the egg-laying monotremes. The subclass Theria is divided into two infraclasses, Metatheria and Eutheria. Metatheria is represented by only one order, the Marsupialia, and differs from other mammals in that it possesses an external marsupium or pouch found in the females of most of the group, in

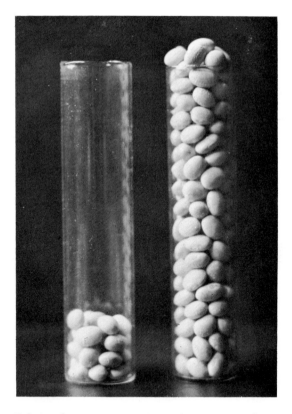

Relative brain case capacities of two mammals of about the same body and skull size. Left, the metatherian (opossum) with 26 small navy beans; right, the eutherian (raccoon) with 139 navy beans. Photograph by the author.

which the young are suckled and raised. Other important characters of the Metatheria are: typically more than forty-four teeth; angular process of lower jaw bent inward; brain case and cerebrum small; no true placenta; and epipubic bones present. Marsupials are confined mainly to Australia, Tasmania, New Zealand, and New Guinea, a few forms are found in South and Central America, and one (the genus Didelphis) ranges into North America and is found in Wisconsin. The other group of Mammalia, the infraclass Eutheria, contains all the ordinary mammals. Members of this group are provided with a true placenta, and the young are born in a more or less mature state. Other characters: never more than forty-four teeth present; angular process of lower jaw not bent inward; brain case and cerebrum comparatively large; and no epipubic bones. Eutheria comprise most of the mammals of the world and are widely distributed.

External features and the skulls of mammals offer important characteristics for indentification. The teeth of mammals especially are very important from the standpoint of classification. There are four distinct types of teeth in any typical mammal, such as the opossum or the coyote:

1. The incisor teeth, the three small teeth on both sides in front of the larger tusks.

2. The canine teeth, the tusks, immediately after the incisors.

3. The premolar teeth, the next four teeth immediately behind the canines.

4. The true molar teeth, the last two teeth in each upper jaw, and the last three teeth in each lower jaw.

The complete dentition is indicated by a formula and obvious abbreviations. In the opossum, a marsupial, the dental formula is:

$$I\frac{5-5}{4-4}, \; C\frac{1-1}{1-1}, \; P\frac{3-3}{3-3}, \; M\frac{4-4}{4-4} = 50.$$

In the coyote, which has nearly complete dentition of a Eutherian mammal, the dental formula is:

$$I\frac{3-3}{3-3}, \; C\frac{1-1}{1-1}, \; P\frac{4-4}{4-4}, \; M\frac{2-2}{3-3} = 42.$$

In man, the dental formula is:

$$I\frac{2-2}{2-2}, \; C\frac{1-1}{1-1}, \; P\frac{2-2}{2-2}, \; M\frac{3-3}{3-3} = 32.$$

Individual teeth are designated, in the coyote for example,

upper jaw I ^{1}, I ^{2}, I ^{3}, C ^{1},
P ^{1}, P ^{2}, P ^{3}, P ^{4}, M ^{1}, M ^{2},
lower jaw I $_1$, I $_2$, I $_3$, C $_1$,
P $_1$, P $_2$, P $_3$, P $_4$, M $_1$, M $_2$, M $_3$.

The incisors, canines, and last three premolars are all preceded by deciduous or milk teeth which fall out before the mammal reaches maturity, and are followed by the permanent dentition. Any of the teeth may be lacking, depending upon the genus or species of mammal. The dental formula for each genus will be found (*postea*) in its proper place.

Early Mammalogy in Wisconsin

Exploratory observations and notes on the mammals of Wisconsin were made by explorers, trappers, and missionaries as early as the middle of the seventeenth century. Jean Nicolet in 1634 and Louis Joliet in 1673 made occasional observations on mammals. Often the description of an animal was not detailed enough to permit allocation to any species. At other times the kind of animal was clear. The earliest available record of a puma in Wisconsin is that of Joliet, who saw one in what is now Grant County in 1673. Trappers followed the explorers, and many trading posts were established in the region, more especially at Green Bay, Lac du Flambeau, and Prairie du Chien. By about 1850 not less than forty fur-trading stations existed throughout the state. Many of these left accurate records of sales and receipts that included the name of the fur, number of items, price, and often place of capture. From these bookings by careful scrutiny and elimination have been derived valuable records as to probable numbers and distribution of such species as the beaver, marten, fisher, otter, black bear, Canada lynx, deer, and others. In the vouchers and bills-of-lading were often indicated the usages of the various mammal products, not only of fur, but of horns, fat, bristles, and every conceivable part of the anatomy of a mammal.

Pioneering in the study of the mammals of Wisconsin began about the year 1850. During the next forty or fifty years several naturalists were interested in the fauna of the state, and a few not only made notes on habits and distribution of mammals but in some instances acquired a collection or collected specimens for others. A more general interest, however, then as now, seemed to prevail in birds. Among naturalists of that period were Charles F. Carr, editor of the *Wisconsin Naturalist*, Madison; John N. Clark, Meridean; Dr. P. R. Hoy, Racine; F. H. King, Madison; Thure Kumlien, Busseyville; I. A. Lapham, Milwaukee; John Muir, "Fountain Lake," Marquette County; Henry Nehrling, Milwaukee; Moses Strong, Madison; and others. The work of most of these men is recognized throughout the text of this book.

Toward the end of the pioneering era a number of Wisconsin young men became seriously interested in mammals, collected specimens, and made careful and copious notes on mammals. About this time also a number of events happened that aided and abetted the study of mammals. Possibly foremost among the causes that brought on the modern era of mammal study was the organization of the U. S. Biological Survey and the influence and stimulus of its leaders (C. Hart Merriam, Vernon Bailey, A. K. Fisher, T. S. Palmer, and E. W. Nelson). Other factors that enhanced the modern era of mammalogy were the development of traps and collecting guns, particularly of those suitable for procuring small mammals; improved techniques of preparing specimens; better instruments and apparatus for use in laboratory and field; and more efficient methods of care, storage, and study of specimens. During the present era many Wisconsin naturalists have done commendable research in many phases of mammalogy. Cognizance of them and their work is frequently given throughout the text that follows and in the bibliography.

Wisconsin's Physiographic Features

Wisconsin is one of the larger states east of the Mississippi River. It has a total area of 56,154 square miles, of which 54,715 are land area and 1,439 inland water. It is approximately 318 miles in north and south dimension, measured from Devils Island, Apostle Islands, Lake Superior, south to the Illinois boundary line. The widest place, approximately 295 miles east and west along latitude 45° 25′ includes Rock Island off the tip of Door Peninsula. The narrowest east and west width, less than 145 miles, is along the Illinois boundary. The state has no outstanding physiographic features such as high mountains or arid plains, but is endowed with many other features influencing the fauna, mostly as a result of glaciation. Twice during the Pleistocene period Wisconsin was covered with great ice sheets. The first and older of these was the Illinoian Glacial Stage which extended farther south than the second, the Wisconsin, which was less extensive but probably more prolonged. Neither of these glaciations covered an extensive area in central and southwestern Wisconsin, now known as the Driftless Area. Both of these glaciations had a tremendous effect on the fauna and flora. The Driftless Area, although submitted to a severe climate during glaciation, apparently served as a reserve habitat for relict species, some of which ingressed the territory toward the north after the glaciers retreated. Many glacial lakes and gentle hills, termed moraines, now occupy the glacial drift region. Bogs and marshes have filled numbers of the shallower hollows. The Driftless Area is occupied by more rugged hills, not infrequent caves, sandy loam plains from glacial silt outwash, and small prairies. Altitudes in the state range from 579 feet at the low water surface of Lake Michigan at Milwaukee, to 1,940.76 feet at Rib Hill, T 28 N, R 7 E, near Wausau, Marathon County. The only other place in the state with an altitude of more than 1,900 feet is Sugarbush Hill, T 36 N, R 13 E, near Laona, Forest County, altitude 1,939.3. In southwestern Wisconsin the surface of low water of the Mississippi River opposite Dubuque, Iowa, is about 595 feet altitude. The effect of these comparatively slight altitudinal variations on the

Entrance to Eagle Cave, Richland County. Many bats inhabit this cave. Fish and Wildlife Service photograph by the author.

Entrance to Bogie's Cave, Richland County, in which was found the only specimen record of the wolverine from Wisconsin. Fish and Wildlife Service photograph by the author.

distribution and ecology of the mammals of the state has not been studied. It probably in itself is not an important factor in the general distribution of mammals except as it affects slope exposure, drainage, soil composition, and moisture. Extensive information on the physiography of Wisconsin may be found in *The Physical Geography of Wisconsin,* by Lawrence Martin (1916).

The climate of the state is somewhat variable and subject to sudden changes as in many parts of the Middle West. Cyclonic storms are not infrequent in summer, especially in the southern half of the state. Rainfall is about 30 inches annually. The low mean winter temperature under 12 degrees occurs in northern Vilas and southern Iron counties; the high winter mean of 22 degrees is in the extreme southeastern corner of the state. A mean summer temperature of less than 60 degrees is found in the Apostle Islands, Ashland County; a mean summer temperature of more than 70 degrees occurs in Rock County and in the Mississippi River bottom lands north to the mouth of the Chippewa River. The highest temperature recorded in the state was 111 degrees at Broadhead, Green County. The lowest temperature was 50 degrees below zero at Hayward, Mauston, and Sun Prairie in different years. The length of the growing season, the season between the last killing frost in the spring and the first killing frost in the fall, has an effect on both animal and plant life. The length of the growing season ranges from 170 days in extreme southeastern Wisconsin to about 100 days in Vilas and southern Iron counties. Lake Superior, cold as it may be, has a modifying effect, and we find a growing season of 150 days or more on the outermost of the Apostle Islands. Additional information on the climate of Wisconsin can be found in A. R. Whitson and O. E. Baker (1912) and in papers of Eric R. Miller (1927, 1930, 1931).

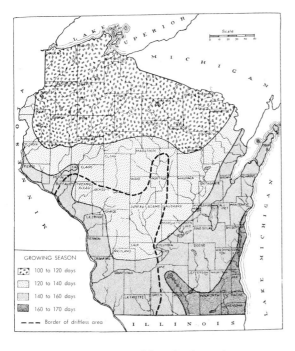

Map 2. Driftless Area and length of growing seasons

Type Localities for Wisconsin Mammals

Every scientific name should be based primarily on the description of a single specimen which is designated as the type or type specimen. The locality from which the type specimen came is known as the type locality. Frequently early naturalists paid little attention to types of races or to the exact localities from which they came. This often led to confusion. There are many old mammalian names that cannot be used because the authors neglected to give information necessary to fix them on designated specimens or localities. Nowadays the designation of a type specimen, type locality, and date of collection are considered essential in the description of any new form. Wisconsin is the type locality of fifteen species or subspecies of mammals, twelve of them being recognized as valid in the present report.

Ashland County.—Basswood Island, Apostle Islands: *Canis latrans thamnos* Jackson, 1949.

Clark County.—Withee: *Sorex palustris hydrobadistes* Jackson, 1926 a. Worden Township: *Pitymys pinetorum schmidti* Jackson, 1941 b (=*Microtus pinetorum schmidti*).

Columbia County.—West Point Township: *Reithrodontomys megalotis pectoralis* Hanson, 1944 a.

Grant County.—Platteville: *Urocyon cinereoargenteus ocythous* Bangs, 1899.

Iowa County.—Blue Mounds: *Cervus whitneyi* Allen, 1876 a (described from bones of assumed Pleistocene deposit, but usually considered as a synonym of *Cervus canadensis* Erxleben).

Oconto County.—Lakewood: *Microsorex hoyi intervectus* Jackson, 1925 b.

Oneida County.—Crescent Lake: *Eutamias minimus jacksoni* Howell, 1925; *Napaeozapus insignis frutectanus* Jackson, 1919 a.

Outagamie County.—Near Appleton: *Felis concolor schorgeri* Jackson, 1955.

Racine County.—Racine: *Sorex hoyi* Baird, 1858 (=*Microsorex hoyi hoyi*); *Arvicola austerus* Le Conte, 1853, a synonym of *Hypudaeus ochrogaster* Wagner (=*Microtus ochrogaster ochrogaster*).

Richland County.—Lone Rock: *Geomys bursarius wisconsinensis* Jackson, 1957 a.

Rock County.—Milton, four miles east of: *Taxidea taxus jacksoni* Schantz, 1946.

No exact locality—*Cariacus wisconsinensis* Belitz, Wisconsin Conservation, vol. 1, no. 5, p. 1, November, 1919 (name proposed as a substitute for *virginianus* because the author believed that the species originated in Wisconsin and not in Virginia).

State Ecological Areas and Life Zones

Various authors have recognized ecological areas in the state, more especially regarding their importance and influence on the distribution of plant life. Considerable ecological research has been applied to individual mammalian species, especially to game and pest animals. Very little area ecological research has been done on Wisconsin mammals. Possibly this is because the problem does not appear to be complex. Actually it is. Some effort has been made in the present work to recognize environmental and ecological preferences of the mammalian species under the heading "Habitat."

During the field work of the present research particular attention was given to zoogeographical areas and species complexes. This practice was followed not only in regard to land vertebrates, but also in their environmental relationship to other animals and to the flora. Dr. C. Hart Merriam in 1892 proposed a classification of the distribution of life in North America and issued a map of the life zones of North America. The same general classification and map, with modifications and slightly different terminology, have been followed by many biologists. Merriam's conclusions were based on collections of specimens and research in the field by many biologists in an area that ultimately included many regions of North and Central America between Panama and the Arctic Ocean. His earlier publications might give the impression that the only limiting factor in animal distribution is average annual temperature. Actually he believed that life zones are the expression of the influence of climate in the broadest sense, including not only temperature, but moisture, light and shade, evaporation, and many associated factors. Merriam's plan divided the whole of North America into three chief regions.

1. The Boreal Region comprises three zones, from north to south, the Arctic, Hudsonian, and Canadian. This region is circumpolar and has a similar fauna and flora in northern Europe, northern Asia, and North America. The united circumpolar region is called the Holarctic Region.

2. The Sonoran (or Austral) Region comprises three zones, from north to south, the Transition, Upper Austral, and Lower Austral. The Austral Zones, termed Sonoran Zones by some students,

as they were by Merriam, constitute a clearly marked biogeographic region. The Transition Zone is an area in which there is a mixture or overlapping of both Boreal and Austral kinds of life.

3. The Tropical Region is confined in the United States to the southern tip of Florida.

The life zone concept of Merriam is not accepted by all biologists. It is particularly objectionable to some ecologists who endeavor to accept life zones as ecological rather than biogeographical. Ecology is dynamical and a study of processes. Biogeography is structural and a study of materials. Biogeography is to ecology as anatomy is to physiology. Too often life zones or zoogeography has been based only on plant zones, they being visually more evident. The result then often is that the Canadian Zone becomes a coniferous tree area and the Transition Zone a deciduous tree area. Yet the deciduous mountain ash, mountain maple, and beaked hazel are as truly Canadian Zone indicators as the coniferous balsam fir, white spruce, black spruce, and northern white cedar. The coniferous southern red cedar is as typically Upper Austral as the black walnut. Comparatively recent life zone classifications have made many and diverse changes from Merriam's original. Both plants and animals over periods of time shift ranges. The tendency for most species in the Middle West is to move northward, following possibly the retreat of the Glacial Ice Sheet or the northward trend of forest clearing and land cultivation. Some species, however, such as the Canada lynx and the porcupine, are apparently moving southward again, thus tending to re-establish some Canadian Zone species.

The present author recognizes three life zones in Wisconsin, namely, from north to south, Canadian, Transition, and Upper Austral (Map 3). He has diverged considerably from early maps of Merriam and others. He cannot follow the logic of Dice (1943), who discards the Transition Zone entirely and includes most of Wisconsin in a "Canadian Biotic Province," leaving only a strip along the southern border in his "Illinoian." Nor does he agree with his respected colleague, Dr. John W. Aldrich, who deletes the Canadian Zone from Wisconsin and extends the Alleghanian (Transition) northward to the north shore of Lake Superior in Canada (Aldrich, 1957:3, fig.

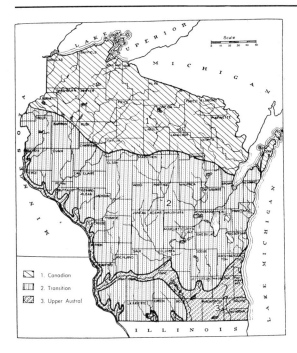

Map 3. Life zones of Wisconsin.

1). A map of "General Life Zones of Wisconsin Avifauna" (W. E. Scott in Barger, Bussewitz, Loyster, Robbins, and Scott, 1942) is well executed and could with little modification be used in the present report for the mammals of the state. The whole subject of animal ecology and zoogeography of Wisconsin is open for intensive research.

The Canadian Zone in Wisconsin is characterized among others by such plants as balsam fir (*Abies balsamea*), white spruce (*Picea glauca*), black spruce (*Picea mariana*), northern white cedar (*Thuja occidentalis*), beaked hazel (*Corylus rostrata*), speckled alder (*Alnus rugosa*), mountain ash (*Pyrus americana*), mountain maple (*Acer spicatum*), and Labrador tea (*Ledum groenlandicum*). Characteristic breeding birds include common loon (*Gavia immer*), goshawk (*Accipiter gentilis atricapillus*), spruce grouse (*Canachites canadensis canace*), northern three-toed woodpecker (*Picoides arcticus*), Canada jay (*Perisoreus canadensis canadensis*), hermit thrush (*Hylocichla guttata faxoni*), myrtle warbler (*Dendroica coronata coronata*), red crossbill (*Loxia curvirostra minor*), and white-

throated sparrow (*Zonotrichia albicollis*). Mammals include the water shrew (*Sorex palustris hydrobadistes*), varying hare (*Lepus americanus phaeonotus*), northern flying squirrel (*Glaucomys sabrinus macrotis*), woodland deer mouse (*Peromyscus maniculatus gracilis*), Hudsonian jumping mouse (*Zapus hudsonius hudsonius*), woodland jumping mouse (*Napaeozapus insignis frutectanus*), and moose (*Alces alces andersoni*).

The Transition Zone (eastern humid or Alleghanian Area) as the name implies is a transition or mixture between the Canadian Zone and the Upper Austral Zone species. It is marked as much by the absence of species as by the presence of them. Its northern limits are marked by the southern limits of the Canadian Zone. All Canadian species listed (*antea*) seldom extend southward into the Transition Zone. Similarly the southern limits of the Transition Zone are marked by the northern limits of the Upper Austral Zone. All Upper Austral Zone species listed (*postea*) seldom extend into the Transition Zone. There are a few herbaceous plants that appear to be characteristic of the Transition Zone. One mammalian subspecies, *Microtus pinetorum schmidti*, is known only from the Transition Zone.

Canadian Life Zone at Spring Lake, Vilas County, June 18, 1918. Photograph by the author.

The Upper Austral Zone (Carolinian Area) in Wisconsin is characterized among others by such plants as red cedar (*Juniperus virginiana*), black walnut (*Juglans nigra*), pecan (*Carya illinoensis*), river birch (*Betula nigra*), pin oak (*Quercus palustris*), hackberry (*Celtis occidentalis*), red mulberry (*Morus rubra*), lotus (*Nelumbo lutea*), Kentucky coffee tree (*Gymnocladus dioica*), and honey locust (*Gleditsia triacanthos*). Among characteristic breeding birds of the Upper Austral Zone in Wisconsin are the turkey vulture (*Cathartes aura septentrionalis*), barn owl (*Tyto alba pratincola*), red-bellied woodpecker (*Centurus carolinus zebra*), Acadian flycatcher (*Empidonax virescens*), tufted titmouse (*Parus bicolor*), Bewick's wren (*Thryomanes bewickii*), blue-gray gnatcatcher (*Polioptila caerulea caerulea*), Bell's vireo (*Vireo bellii bellii*), prothonotary warbler (*Protonotaria citrea*), and Kentucky warbler (*Oporornis formosus*). Mammals include Indiana cinereous shrew (*Sorex cinereus lesueurii*), Harlan's little mole-shrew (*Cryptotis parva harlani*), eastern woodchuck (*Marmota monax monax*), harvest mouse (*Reithrodontomys megalotis pectoralis*), Goss lemming mouse (*Synaptomys cooperi gossii*), and woodland pine mouse (*Microtus pinetorum nemoralis*).

Upper Austral Life Zone in Mississippi Valley and along bluffs looking northwest from east of Lynxville, Crawford County, July 26, 1930. Photograph by Oliver L. Austin, Jr.

Key to the Orders of Recent Wisconsin Mammals

a. Female with external abdominal pouch in which young are carried; innermost toe of hind foot thumb-like and without claw, brain case small; teeth 50. *Infraclass Metatheria* . . . . *Marsupialia,* p. 17
aa. No external abdominal pouch; innermost toe of hind foot never thumb-like; brain case well developed; teeth less than 50. *Infraclass Eutheria.*
  b. Fingers greatly elongated and connected by membrane attached to the body and hind limb to form wing . . . . *Chiroptera,* p. 74
  bb. Fingers not greatly elongated and not connected by membrane to form wing.
    c. Toes provided with claws; upper incisors present.
      d. Eyes minute or rudimentary; snout elongate; neither canines nor incisors conspicuously developed; molars with distinct W-shaped pattern. . *Insectivora,* p. 26
      dd. Eyes not rudimentary and snout normal; either canines or molars highly developed; molar pattern not W-shaped.
        e. Canine teeth absent; front teeth (incisors) long and chisel-shaped, and separated from cheek teeth by wide gap.
          f. Upper incisors 2-2. . . . . *Lagomorpha,* p. 103
          ff. Upper incisors 1-1. . . . . *Rodentia,* p. 121
        ee. Canine teeth conspicuously developed, adopted for seizing prey, projecting far beyond other teeth . . . . *Carnivora,* p. 279
    cc. Toes provided with hoofs; no upper incisors. . . . . . *Artiodactyla,* p. 407

Hypothetical List of Wisconsin Mammals

In a hypothetical list of the mammals of Wisconsin, Hollister (1910: 30–31) reported ten species. Since then, evidence of the occurrence of six of these in the state has been established. The records of the four other species as having occurred in Wisconsin are still unsubstantiated.

1. *Nycticeius humeralis* Rafinesque, Evening Bat.—Recorded under the name *Scotophilus carolinensis,* Carolina Bat, by Strong (1883: 438), who apparently listed as occurring in Wisconsin all the bats known to northeastern United States at that time. This bat has not been taken in Wisconsin. It may occur in the state inasmuch as it has been collected as near by as Cook County, Illinois.

2. *Microtus xanthognathus* (Leach), Yellow-cheeked Vole.—Recorded under the name *Arvicola xanthognathus,* Yellow-cheeked Meadow Mouse, by Lapham (1853: 340). The locality given as Racine would indicate the record was based on Hoy's notes. The species is unknown from Wisconsin and probably does not occur there.

3. *Rattus rattus* (Linnaeus), Black Rat.—Listed under "*Mus rattus* Linn., Black Rat (introduced), Racine" (Lapham, 1853: 340) and by Strong (1883: 438). There are no specimen records of *Rattus rattus* from Wisconsin, nor any recent records of the species from anywhere near the state. The Lapham and Strong statements are probably based on melanistic individuals of *Rattus norvegicus* misidentified by Hoy.

4. *Antilocapra americana* (Ord), Pronghorn Antelope.—Under the name *Antilope Americana,* included with Wisconsin mammals by Lapham (1852: 44; 1853: 340), who cites only "N. W. Territory, (Mr. Say)," which is extralimital. Hoy concluded that the "wild goats" of Hennipin, Joliet, and other early explorers in Wisconsin were *Antilocapra americana* and that the species "did, two hundred years ago, inhabit Wisconsin as far east as Lake Michigan" (Hoy, 1882: 255). There is no evidence that the prong-horned antelope ever occurred in Wisconsin. The "wild goats" reported by Hennipin, Joliet, and others were probably white-tailed deer with spike antlers. Their "stags" were antlered deer or elk, and their "oxen," of course, were bison.

The Study of Mammals

Taxonomy, or classification and identification, can only be done by means of well-prepared study skins and skulls. Before a serious effort is made to collect specimens the collector should approach the State Conservation Department or a like organization in order to clearly understand laws and regulations about making a collection. Most states are reasonable and lenient about legitimate collecting. The Wisconsin Conservation Department, Madison, encourages such educational activities. With practice anyone with an urge for natural history or zoology can learn to collect specimens, make satisfactory study skins, and clean skulls or even entire skeletons for study purposes. The appearance of study skins and cleaned skulls is illustrated in several figures in this book. Literature on collecting, preparing, and preserving mammal specimens has been included in the bibliography (Anderson, R. M., 1949; Anthony, H. E., 1925; Bailey, V., 1921, 1932; Burt, W. H., 1946: 28–44; Cockrum, E. L., 1955; Jackson, H. H. T., 1926 b; 1926 c). The most important data about any specimen are the actual locality of its capture and the habitat where it was found; the date; its sex, indicated by the sign ♂ for male and ♀ for female; its total length, tip of nose to tip of tail, exclusive of hair; length of tail, from its root to its tip (exclusive of hair); and the length of its hind foot, from end of heel to end of longest toe, including to tip of claw. It is often desirable to take the weight of the fresh specimen, and to measure the length of the ear. Many other notes may be taken about a specimen, such as food contents in the cheek pouches or in the stomach; number of mammae; number of embryos; condition of fur; parasites or even their preservation in 2 per cent Formalin. Each specimen should be assigned a number used for both skin and skull, and any information about the mammal should be given a number corresponding to that of the specimen.

Most people like to observe birds because they are usually attractive in appearance, many of them sing, and they are easily seen. Mammals may not be so beautiful and variant in color, yet to many persons their behavior is more interesting than that of birds. It is more like our own. Though many are wary, most mammals can be attracted by the same devices one uses to attract birds. Several calls and whistles on the market are very effective in attracting different mammals. Some of them will attract several kinds, particularly carnivores. Often an ordinary whistle with the lips or a squeak will attract a mammal. Tracking mammals may become a most interesting and instructive game. Catching mammals alive and studying them under confinement may bring out many unknown facts. Population or migration studies may be made, possibly through banding or some other marking system. Many suggestions for studies of habits, behavior, and life histories of mammals are available (Allen, A. A., 1921; Murie, O. J., 1954; Stebler, A. M., 1940; Taylor, W. P., 1948). Anyone seriously interested in mammals should have access to the *Journal of Mammalogy*, published quarterly by the American Society of Mammalogists.

Plan of the Book

The text is broken into a discussion of all Recent mammals of the state, grouped respectively under the order, family, genus, species, and subspecies. The order of arrangement follows closely that presented in *List of North American Recent Mammals* by Gerrit S. Miller, Jr., and Remington Kellogg (U. S. National Museum Bulletin 205, March, 1955). Artificial keys for identification purposes are given down to the family, in some instances to the genus, and in a few even to the species. Keys apply only to mammals found in the region under discussion, and characters as given are not necessarily diagnostic for other regions.

The account of each species or subspecies is headed by the currently recognized scientific name, followed by the common name. In the titular common names of species, I have endeavored to employ such as are more frequently and consistently applied over a considerable geographical region in which Wisconsin is included and which have had frequent and long usage. I am fully aware of considerable literature on vernacular names, including the recent list resulting from the conscientious efforts of a subcommittee of the committee of nomenclature of the American Society of Mammalogists (Hall, editor, 1957). I have independently used many names recommended by the committee. Many other names I have not accepted for various reasons: some are too bookish, others are inapplicable, and several are verging on the technical and are employed only by professional mammalogists. The first item under the headings is a citation of the original description. Then follows a series of citations of names with references. To cite every reference where a name has been applied to a mammal from Wisconsin would make an intolerable list. Therefore, only Wisconsin state lists or lists of near county coverage have been included. This work includes, chronologically, Lapham, 1852; Lapham, 1853; Hoy, 1882; Strong, 1883; Snyder, 1902; Jackson, 1908; Hollister, 1909; Hollister, 1910; Jackson, 1910; Cory, 1912; Schmidt, 1931; Komarek, 1932; and Barger, 1952. The paragraph on vernacular names results from the author's special interest in this field.

Descriptions of species under "Identification marks" may vary in extent and detail with different groups or species. Members of the orders Insectivora (shrews and moles), Chiroptera (bats), and Carnivora (flesh-eating mammals) particularly have been treated in more detail because of the difficulty in making identifications in these groups. Often actual comparisons and study with named specimens will be necessary to make a satisfactory identification. Often, too, the most eager and brilliant student will find difficulty in making identifications in some groups. The Department of Zoology, University of Wisconsin, Madison; the Milwaukee Public Museum, Milwaukee; the U. S. Fish and Wildlife Service, Washington 25, D. C.; or any of the large museums in Chicago, New York, or Washington will be glad to help in identifying difficult material. As a courtesy the collector should offer the consultant museum part of the material in exchange for the information.

Certain phases which are too involved for a book of this type have not been covered under identification marks. Among items not included are hair and hair structure and penis-bone characters and descriptions. Hair structure in general is of limited taxonomic value. It may serve a purpose in identification of fragmentary material needed in research, such as identification of food material in stomach contents or as clues in crimes or law violations. Molting, seasonal colors, variations, mutations, and abnormalities are treated in paragraphs under identification marks. Under the heading "Measurements" will be found not only the standard measurements but also a variance to make easier identification in the case of some species. Measurements and weights are given usually in the metric system, the one regularly employed in scientific work. Frequently, however, weights are given in pounds or ounces, and most metric measurements have also been transposed to English units

that follow the metric measurements in the text. English measurements can be converted to approximate metric equivalents, and vice versa, as follows:

1 inch = 25.4 millimeters
1 mile = 0.6 kilometer
1 acre = 4047 square meters
1 acre = 43,560 square feet
1 ounce = 28.4 grams
1 millimeter = 0.04 inches
1 meter = 39.4 inches
1 kilometer = 3281 feet
1 hectare = 2.47 acres
1 gram = 0.04 ounce
1 kilogram = 2.2 pounds

Distribution in Wisconsin and habitat have each been given paragraph headings. One or more maps for each species depict localities from which specimens have been examined and authentic records procured. Sometimes these maps include other information, such as population trends, present and past distribution, and hunter kills. Under the heading "Status and Habits" are included in the first paragraphs an account of the present and former numbers, fluctuation in numbers, estimates and populations per unit area, and home range of the species. Then follows in order a series of topics including means of detecting presence, times of activity, movements, intercommunication, special behavior characteristics, breeding, nests and shelters, feeding and drinking, enemies, and economics.

In the lists under "Specimens examined from Wisconsin," localities are arranged alphabetically by counties, and by places under each county. When the county only has been indicated on the label the specimen is listed under the known county as "No locality." More than 6,300 specimens from Wisconsin of the 84 kinds of mammals found in the state were examined during this study. Several thousand specimens from elsewhere were utilized as comparative material. They consisted principally of conventional scientific skins with skulls which are in institutional and private mammal collections. A personal study visit was made to each of the institutional collections, and with two exceptions private collections were examined at the owner's home. Many specimens were borrowed, sometimes for restudy. Approximately 2,018 of the specimens were in the University of Wisconsin Zoological Collection, 1,529 in the Milwaukee Public Museum, and 1,350 in the U. S. Biological Surveys Collection. In the lists of specimens examined the source of the material is indicated by appropriate letter symbols listed below. Specimens for which the source is not mentioned are in the U. S. Biological Surveys Collection, accessioned in the U. S. National Museum

AMNH.—American Museum of Natural History, New York City.
AWS.—Collection of A. W. Schorger, Madison, Wisconsin.
BG.—Bowling Green State University, Bowling Green, Ohio.
CAS.—Chicago Academy of Sciences, Chicago, Illinois.
CC.—Museum of Colorado College, Colorado Springs, Colorado.
CM.—Carnegie Museum, Pittsburgh, Pennsylvania.
CMNH.—Cleveland Museum of Natural History, Cleveland, Ohio.
CNHM.—Chicago Natural History Museum, Chicago, Illinois.
CU.—Cornell University, Ithaca, New York.
F&FH.—Collection of Frederick and Frances Hamerstrom, Plainsfield, Wisconsin.
HCH.—Collection of Harold C. Hanson, Urbana, Illinois.
HHTJ.—Collection of Hartley H. T. Jackson, Chevy Chase, Maryland.
JNC.—Collection of John N. Clark, Meridean, Wisconsin.
JRB.—Collection of James R. Beer, Oregon, Wisconsin.
MC.—Milton College Collection, Milton, Wisconsin.
MCZ.—Museum of Comparative Zoology, Cambridge, Massachusetts.
MM.—Public Museum of City of Milwaukee, Milwaukee, Wisconsin.
MVZ.—Museum of Vertebrate Zoology, Berkeley, California.
NPM.—Neville Public Museum, Green Bay, Wisconsin.
UI.—University of Illinois, Museum of Natural History, Urbana, Illinois.
UM.—University of Michigan, Museum of Zoology, Ann Arbor, Michigan.

UND.—University of Notre Dame, South Bend, Indiana.
USNM.—United States National Museum, Washington, D. C.
UWDEZ.—University of Wisconsin, Department of Economic Zoology, Madison, Wisconsin.
UWW.—University of Wisconsin, Wildlife School Collection, Madison, Wisconsin.
UWZ.—University of Wisconsin Zoological Collection, Madison, Wisconsin.
WBG.—Collection of Wallace B. Grange, Babcock, Wisconsin.
WCD.—Wisconsin Conservation Department, Madison, Wisconsin.
WCDG.—Wisconsin Conservation Department, Poynette, Wisconsin.
WES.—Collection of W. E. Snyder, Beaver Dam, Wisconsin.
WHD.—Collection of Wayne H. Davis, Middlebury, Vermont.

It is the intention under "Selected references" to list the six most important publications with reference to that particular mammal. Scant literature on a species in a few instances has limited references to less than six. In other species with an abundance of literature more than six references have been given. In any case, additional useful references can be found in the more nearly complete bibliography at the end of the book.

This book includes not only mammals actually living in the wild within Wisconsin today but also those that have been extirpated. It does not include accidental introductions that could not survive. Introductions of small mammals such as small murine opossums and Central American mice sometimes occur in shipments of tropical fruits, particularly in bunches of bananas. Domestic ferrets, escaped from captivity, have been killed as wild animals in the state, but fortunately the species has never become established in any area. Mammals likewise may occasionally escape from small traveling shows and temporarily become a part of the fauna. Other mammals may be purposely transplanted by sportsmen, yet not survive because the environment is not suitable for them, or for other reasons.

Few Pleistocene or other truly fossil mammals are known from Wisconsin. The ancient mammals of the state might offer interesting research, but these are not included in the present list. The term "fossil" has been mentioned in reference to specimens in some parts of this report. Any such specimen, however, was not truly fossil, but was a neoteric remnant of a Recent mammal. Such remains are usually found as deposits in caves, bogs, or marshes, or in accumulated soil. Remains of mammals found in Indian mounds in Wisconsin generally have been assignable to Recent species.

Illustrations have been selected to aid in identification of mammals, or to clarify phases of the ecology, habits, or economics of the species. Wherever practicable, illustrations of specimens, whether skins, skulls, or skeletal parts, are natural size; otherwise the comparative size is indicated in the legend. All specimens illustrated are in the Biological Surveys Collection, U. S. National Museum, unless otherwise specified.

ORDER **MARSUPIALIA**

Opossums, Kangaroos, and Allies

Mammals of this order constitute the infra-class Metatheria (described and their geographic range given on page 4).

The Marsupialia embrace eight living families, of which one, Didelphidae, is represented in Wisconsin.

Family **Didelphidae**

American Opossums

The family Didelphidae ranges throughout most of the tropical and temperate regions of North, Central, and South America. It is composed of eleven genera exclusive of fossil forms, of which one occurs in Wisconsin.

the base and for a few scattered hairs, prehensile; legs relatively short; five toes to each foot, the first (inside) one on the hind foot is large, nailless, and more or less opposable to the other toes, after the manner of the human thumb. The pelage is long and rather coarse, particularly the guard hairs; underfur soft and woolly; vibrissae (whiskers) moderately long.

Genus **Didelphis** Linnaeus

Common Opossums

Dental formula:

$$\text{I}\ \frac{5-5}{4-4},\ \text{C}\ \frac{1-1}{1-1}:\ \text{P}\ \frac{3-3}{3-3},\ \text{M}\ \frac{4-4}{4-4}=50.$$

Didelphis marsupialis virginiana Kerr

Virginia Opossum

Didelphis virginiana Kerr, Animal Kingdom, p. 193, 1792.
Didelphus Virginiana Lapham, p. 337, 1853.
Didelphis Virginiana Hoy, p. 256, 1882.
Didelphys Virginiana Strong, p. 440, 1883.
Didelphis virginiana Jackson, p. 14, 1908; Hollister, p. 137, 1909; Hollister, p. 22, 1910; Cory, p. 51, 1912.
Didelphis virginiana virginiana Barger, p. 10, 1952.

Vernacular names.—In Wisconsin commonly called the opossum. Other names include American opossum, common opossum, m'possum, opassom or opassum (original Indian name first mentioned by John Smith in Virginia), o'possum, oppossum, possum, Tennessee possum, Virginia opossum, Virginia possum, woolly shoat.

Identification marks.—About the size of a domestic cat; an external abdominal pouch (marsupium) in the female where the young are carried during the nursing period; somewhat conically shaped head, with pointed snout; prominent rounded, thin, leathery ears, not furred; long tapering scaly tail, naked except at

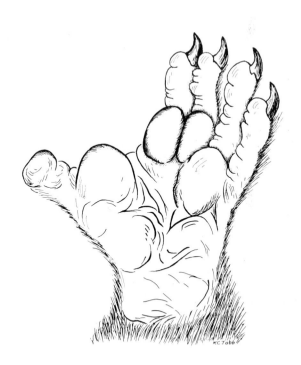

Left hind foot of opossum. About 1½×.

The normal general color tone is light gray, produced by the whitish underfur with its blackish-tipped hairs and the long whitish or grayish guard hairs; head, throat, and cheeks whitish, the eyes usually narrowly ringed with dusky; top of head dark gray; ears black, usually with a slight whitish or flesh-colored edge or tip; tail dark, almost black, basally, the apical two-thirds flesh-colored or whitish; legs and feet dark brown, nearly black; toes mostly whitish; under parts usually darker then upper parts because dark tips of underfur show and overlying guard hairs are few.

The skull is relatively narrow, pointed, greatly constricted through cranium behind orbits, exceedingly small brain case relative to skull size; sagittal crest well developed; sutures comparatively open even in old animals; nasal bones broadly expanded posteriorly and covering more than two-thirds of the distance between the orbits. Teeth 50, upper jaw 26, lower jaw 24, the greatest number in any Wisconsin mammal; teeth small and weak, except for upper canines which are greatly enlarged, curved, and sharp.

The female opossum will average only a trifle larger than the male, and individuals more than one year old tend to be more brownish in color. Fully furred young opossums up to about three months old are dark, the white-tipped guard hairs being undeveloped, and the ears are wholly whitish. Young that have developed guard hairs average paler and more whitish then adults up to about one year old. There is little seasonal variation in color, the fur, however, frequently becoming denser in winter. There appears to be two molts annually, one late in spring (April or May) and one late in summer (August or September). During freezing weather the opossum frequently gets its ears frozen, and often the tip of its tail may become frozen. Individual variation may occur in which the long guard hairs are black, giving the animal a dark and almost black appearance. In other instances the underfur may be tipped with brown and the guard hairs also brownish or the normal white, in which case the animal has a brownish appearance. Often the tips of the guard hairs are worn, which gives the animal a dusky appearance. There are records of cinnamon mutations and albinos in other states (Missouri, Oklahoma, Texas).

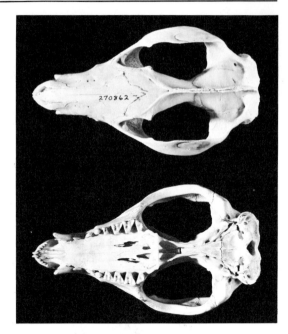

Skull of DIDELPHIS M. VIRGINIANA, ♂, *Laurel, Maryland.* ½×.

Measurements.—Total length of adults, 26 to 33 inches (650 to 825 mm.); tail, 11 to 14 (275 to 350 mm.); hind foot, 2½ to 3 inches (62 to 75 mm.); weight, 6 to 12 pounds, occasionally an excessively fat old individual may weigh to 13½ pounds. Skull length, 115 to 130 mm.; width, 60 to 70 mm.

Distribution in Wisconsin.—The southern half of the state from Sheboygan, Shawano, and Clark counties southward; more common in the southern three tiers of counties. Occasional extralimital records as far north as Bayfield, Iron, and Oneida counties.

Habitat.—The opossum is rather closely confined to deciduous swamps, woodlands, wastelands, and hedgerows having dense cover, and particularly along streams or near lakes. Sometimes it comes around farm buildings and even into towns during its meanderings.

Status and Habits.—Opossums have greatly increased in number in Wisconsin since about 1920 or 1925 and have extended their range northward in the state. They have been present in warm parts of extreme southern Wisconsin since the arrival of the early settlers and were recorded by Lapham (1853) on the authority of

Dr. Hoy as occurring in Green County. Hoy (1882) himself mentioned the species as being "not uncommon in Racine and Walworth counties as late as 1848," as having been caught as far north as Waukesha, "one near Madison in 1872," and as being found in Grant County. Opossums probably were at no time extirpated in any of the southern tier of counties, although they were undoubtedly scarce and not always recognized as opossums. The one reported (Jackson, 1908: 14) captured in Green County, January 24, 1902, was found in a hole in frozen ground in a cemetery near the village of Juda, and although well described in some of the newspapers was unrecognized as to species and created such fantastic headlines as "Unknown Grave Digger Captured" and "Cemetery Ghost Caught." Opossums began to increase in Wisconsin about 1920, and later as their population increased they extended their range northward. There can be anticipated fluctuation in their abundance, perhaps correlated with weather conditions, because, as previously mentioned, they are not adapted to withstand severely cold winters. In parts of the state where opossums may be considered fairly plentiful they prob-

ably seldom average in occurrence more than one to a square mile, and the total population of opossums in the state is normally probably less than twenty-five or thirty thousand. The normal home range of the opossum appears to be between 20 and 40 acres. Individuals may wander a mile or more from the homesite in search of food. The opossum tends to be nomadic, and over a period of time an individual may wander some distance. H. C. Reynolds (1925: 375) records an individual that was trapped seven miles from point of release nine months afterwards.

An opossum may live in a neighborhood and leave little evidence of its presence. It makes no distinctive runways other than to follow the trails of other animals; its claw marks on trees are few, indistinct, and difficult to identify; and tooth marks are almost void. Sometimes it wallows in the soil and leaves footprints. Its footprints are one of the surest ways to determine the presence of an opossum, inasmuch as the footmarks are comparatively easy to identify by the offset position of the first toe of the hind foot and the wide spread of the toes of the forefoot. In many places where the tracks are invisible the feces or scats may be found. Opossum scats are quite characteristic, being usually of grayish trend in coloration and always irregular and broken in outline as if tending to form pellets, but never becoming actually pellet form. The length of each full feces is about two and one-half inches, and the diameter of the wider parts one-half to three-fourths of an inch.

The opossum is as near strictly nocturnal as any Wisconsin mammal, which accounts in part for its frequently being undetected in places where it is common. It spends the daylight hours hidden in hollows in logs or trees, in woodchuck burrows (or it may even dig its own burrow), under brushpiles or woodpiles, in small culverts under roads, in hollows under rocks, stumps, or roots, in drain pipes and tiles, in sheltered crannies about buildings, and, proper shelter not being available when daylight strikes, may even sleep on the ground among the leaves in dense shrubbery. It rarely rests exposed in trees. The opossum does not relish winter weather, and although it does not hibernate, it often remains inactive during severe winter cold until hunger drives it forth in search of a diminished food supply. Its body temperature at such times may re-

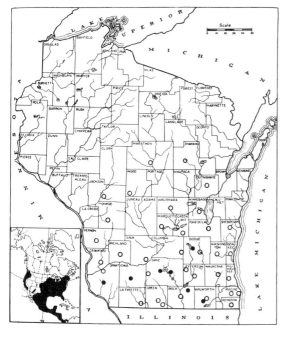

Map 4. Distribution of DIDELPHIS MARSUPIALIS. ● = specimens examined. ○ = authentic records.

*Opossum in act of "playing possum." Fish and Wild-
life Service photograph by Viola McColm.*

main as high as 75° F. Males appear to be more
active than females during cold winter weather.

The gait of the opossum is slow, heavy, plodding, and awkward. It is an ambling pace, the
two legs on the same side working in unison.
The entire foot—heel, sole, and toes—rests on the
ground; in other words the opossum is plantigrade. When chased the opossum may develop
a speed of nearly eight miles an hour, and easily
could be captured by man or dog save for its
habit of sneaking away and hiding or climbing
a tree to escape its pursuers. In such cases it
usually selects a small tree or sapling, and seldom
climbs to a height of more than 15 or 20 feet,
where it hides in a crotch until the enemy has
retired. The opossum is both terrestrial and
arboreal, spending probably at least as much of
its existence on the ground as in trees. It can
climb fairly well, however, using its prehensile
tail as a help in its arboreal activities. It can
hang by the tail and thus have use of all four
feet, although it is awkward sometimes in so
doing.

Content to live alone and associating with its
own kind only during the breeding season, the

opossum has little use for intercommunication.
So far as known it has no signals or calls, and
is one of the most silent of our larger mammals.
It may on occasion when disturbed or annoyed
give a low growl, and at other times hisses while
displaying its teeth in an angry sneer. I have
heard an opossum utter a series of low weak
grunts while it was eating. The courting male
makes a metallic clicking sound with the teeth
or tongue.

Those familiar with the opossum all agree on
its seeming stupidity and lack of intelligence.
Its low brain structure suggests this. It is a quiet,
sleepy animal, solitary in habits, the only companionship coming between the mating pair and
mother and young. Two males in friendly company of one another are unknown. It displays
little fear. It is not aggressive, although a breeding female is often pugnacious. When it is chased
by man or beast it tries to escape by climbing
a small tree or crawling in a hole. Its eyes shine
red when reflecting a flashlight. If it is suddenly
surprised on the ground or overtaken in the
chase it falls into a coma known commonly as
"playing 'possum" or "feigning death." Its body
is limp and its eyes closed. This response is undoubtedly caused by a nervous reaction and
probably is not a deliberate and willful action.
When in this condition an opossum will endure

*Opossum hanging by its tail. Photograph by Vernon
Bailey.*

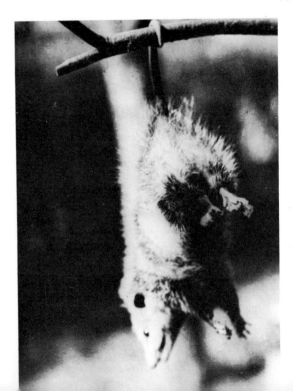

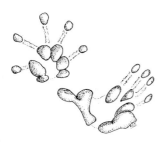

Opossum tracks. About ½×.

almost any abuse and torture, and limp and motionless, without showing any indication of suffering or concern, may be kicked and tumbled around, lifted by the tail, mauled, pummeled, and bitten by dogs, sometimes to the point of death, without giving any signs of life or suffering. An opossum may as suddenly come out of its coma as it went into it. One should not trust it too much, because once "awakened" the animal can administer a severe bite with its sharp teeth and is adept in using its front claws. The opossum is not an animal of exceptional strength, and makes little use of its muscles. Its vitality, however, is extraordinary, and it is difficult to kill.

The opossum is a rather stoical animal that indulges little if any in play of any kind. When attacked, when reviving from its stupor, or sometimes even in its coma, it bares its upper teeth in what has been called a broad or silly smile, but which to me appears more like a cynical grin. It is the same fear, anger, or defense reaction of many mammals in "showing its teeth."

Few observations have been made on the length of life of the opossum, but such records as are available indicate for it a normal longevity of five to seven years and a potential longevity

of eight or nine years. Many of the animals kept in captivity have lived only a year or two.

Superstition, weird legends, and misinformation have been current in regard to the breeding of the opossum. One of the common queries asked is, "does the opossum breed through the nose?" Of course the notion is entirely erroneous. Breeding habits are in general similar to those of mammals on the whole, except that it has been observed by some that copulation takes place with both male and female lying on their sides. The nostril idea originated from the fact that the male reproductive organ is two-forked and the only double opening visible in the female is the two nostrils. Hence it was surmised by the uninformed that intercourse took place through the nose and that the semen was afterwards blown into the vagina, or even that the young were transferred from the nose to the pouch. Stimulus might also be given to this legend by the fact that just before she gives birth to her young the mother thoroughly cleans the inside of her pouch by licking it. *Didelphis*, the generic name given to the opossum by Linnaeus, refers to the two separate uteri in the opossum, a distinctive feature of all marsupials. The two uteri enter two lateral vaginal canals, which in turn enter the vagina. There is but one external opening visible, the cloacal orifice.

In Wisconsin the opossum has as a rule but one litter of young annually, possibly in very rare instances two litters, and the breeding season may begin as early as March. In the average wild population there are normally about 20 per cent more males than females. It breeds when about one year old, and rears from 5 to 13 young in a litter, the average being about 9. Litters of as high as 18 newly born may reach the pouch, but only those that can attach themselves to teats survive; the others starve to death. As many as 22 foetuses have been found in an opossum. Apparently about one-half of the embryos of each litter become young opossums.

Dr. Carl G. Hartman, who has conducted extensive research on the breeding habits, embryology, development, and birth of the opossum, describes the manner of birth of the young as follows (Hartman, 1920):

The animal showed signs of restlessness, and soon began cleaning out the pouch, which she did about four times. Then began a short series of spasmodic contractions of the abdominal wall, after which she came to a sitting posture with legs extended. . . .

After assuming the sitting posture our specimen bent her body forward, and licked the vulva; however, her position at this time was such that we could not see the embryos, which very likely passed into the pouch with the first licking of the genital opening. Hence, we went to the outside where we could plainly hear her lap up the chorionic fluid; then suddenly a tiny bit of flesh appeared at the vulva, and scampered up over the entanglement of hair into the pouch, to join the other foetuses, which now could be seen to have made the trip without our having observed them. Unerringly, the embryo travelled by its own efforts. Without any assistance on the mother's part, other than to free it of the liquid on its first emergence into the world, this 10-day-old embryo, in appearance more like a worm than a mammal, is able, immediately upon release from its liquid medium, to crawl a full 3 inches over a difficult terrain. Indeed it can do more. After it has arrived at the pouch, it is able to find the nipple amid a forest of hair. This it must find—or perish.

. . . the pouch contained a squirming mass of 18 red embryos, of which 12 were attached though 13 might have been accommodated. The remainder were, of course, doomed to starvation. Even some of these unfortunates, however, held on with their mouths to a flap of skin, or to the tip of a minute tail, while several continued to move about.

With the mother under the influence of ether, we now gently pulled off a number of embryos from the teats in order to test their reactions. The teats had already been drawn out from about a millimeter in height to double that length, doubtless by the traction of the embryo itself, for the bottom of the pouch certainly presented a busy scene with each member of the close-pressed litter engaged in very active breathing and sucking movements.

One detached young, placed near the vulva, crawled readily back into the pouch. Two or three others regained the teats after some delay; and one wanderer, which lost out in the first scramble, found a vacant teat and attached itself even after 20 minutes' delay showing that the instinct to find the teats persists for some time. . . .

For locomotion, the embryo employs a kind of "overhand stroke", as if swimming, the head swaying as far as possible to the side opposite the hand which is taking the propelling stroke. With each turn of the head, the snout is touched to the mother's skin as if to test it out; and if the teat is touched, the embryo stops, and at once takes hold.

The teats of the opossum are more or less in horseshoe arrangement with the closed end pos-

terior. They are usually 13 in number, but may be as few as 11 or as many as 17. They are irregularly placed, one or two of them usually being toward the center within the horseshoe alignment. Usually the anterior two to four are functionless. Normally 11 mammae function, rarely 12 or 13.

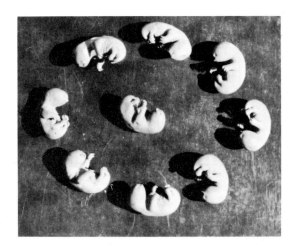

A litter of embryo opossums just before birth. About 1½×.

A baby opossum at birth is about 10 mm. (0.4 inch) long and about 2.5 mm. (0.1 inch) in diameter. It weighs about 0.13 gram (0.0046 ounce), or in other words it would take some 3,500 to weigh a pound, or about 220 to weigh an ounce. It is about the size of small navy bean. A litter of 16 very easily could be placed in an ordinary tablespoon. It grows rapidly, however, and at the end of the first week in the pouch has increased its weight tenfold. It remains attached to the teat for 60 to 70 days, when it grows to about the size of a small house mouse (25 grams, or about 0.9 ounce). Shortly afterward it may leave the pouch occasionally, but returns to it for food and protection. The young opossum is weaned when between 75 and 85 days old, but remains with its mother for three or four months. Once weaned it spends little time in the pouch, but rides on the back of the mother, its small tail entwined on its mother's tail or more often partly around her body, and its feet clinging tenaciously to the fur of the parent.

The opossum's nest or bed is rather loosely constructed though warmly made and is composed almost entirely of leaves. It is open at the top, and usually is placed in a hollow tree, stump, or log in a crevice among rocks or in a cliff, in a sheltered cranny in outbuildings or porches, or even in a woodpile or brush heap. At times, though rarely, the nest may be in the open in the crotch of a tree. The male is more nomadic than the female, and although he seems to build nests also, he frequently crawls into holes and crannies for shelter where there is no regular nest.

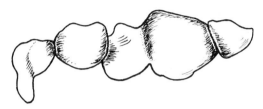

Opossum feces. Drawn from specimen near Norris, Tennessee, by the author. 1×.

The opossum is in general a cleanly animal, but so far as known has no habitual sanitary procedure. Like many mammals, it usually deposits its feces anywhere on the ground, but makes no effort to cover them nor to seek a seclusive place. It deposits some feces in the nest, and apparently does not remove them. They soon dry, however, and do not create a filth.

Leon L. Pray (1921) was one of the first to describe the opossum's method of carrying leaves with its tail. Further observations on its nest-building behavior have been given us by Luther Smith (1941), who writes the following:

Early in the morning of August 4, 1938, I had an opportunity to watch at close range an opossum in the act of gathering and transporting leaves presumably for an underground nest. I was hunting squirrels in the woods of Bollinger County, in southeastern Missouri, when my attention was attracted by a rustling in the dry leaves close by. The noise was made by a young opossum slightly more than half grown. The animal came out of a hole in the ground about eight feet from where I stood and proceeded to select small mouthfuls of two or three leaves each. The leaves were taken out of the mouth with the forepaws and passed back along the abdomen to a position in front of the thighs. There they remained momentarily while the front feet were placed on the ground and the hind feet were brought up to take them and slide them along the tail into a loop in that member, which is ordinarily thought

Mother opossum with young. Patuxent Research Refuge, Maryland. Fish and Wildlife Service photograph by Frank N. Blake.

of as a means of support by suspension but which in this case was sustaining the hind quarters above the ground while the hind feet were being used to place the leaves in the loop.

About six or eight mouthfuls were handled in this way. The action was rapid, and the leaves were in almost continuous motion from the time they were picked up from the ground until they came to rest in the coil of the tail. After the loop was filled, the opossum chose a last mouthful and, with its tail extended almost horizontally except for the loop which held the bundle of leaves, proceeded into the hole in the ground.

Soon the animal returned, and when it first came up the tail was nearly straight with the end dragging on the ground. When the first leaves were picked up, the loop was formed in the tail, and the process of gathering a bundle of leaves was repeated. The opossum made four trips in about ten minutes. It paid no attention to me, although it faced me in returning to the hole. At no time was the animal more than fifteen feet away.

During its fifth trip for leaves, I walked over and put my foot in the hole from which it had emerged. The animal dropped the unfinished roll of leaves, bristled, and advanced to attack, snarling and showing its teeth. It snapped my shoe, which I extended, and after more snarling turned and ran clumsily though quite rapidly away, presumably to another burrow.

The opossum eats almost anything, and thus has little trouble in finding food except during severe winter weather. It is normally a flesh eater, however, and consumes more animal matter than vegetable, sometimes as much as 90 per cent by volume of its food being animal, though usually it is less. Of mammal food, a considerable proportion may be opossum flesh, eaten from dead animals found by the opossum, or it may kill and eat a young one now and then. Cottontail rabbits are an important item, meadow voles and other mice rate well, and many other mammals are eaten, probably often in the condition of carrion. Birds and birds' eggs, including domestic fowl, are a smaller item in its diet. On occasion it may catch a chicken or raid a hen's nest for the eggs, particularly in winter months. The opossum consumes quantities of insects, particularly grasshoppers, stink bugs, squash bugs, and ground beetles. It at times eats frogs, snakes, crayfish, and snails. Fruit, both wild and cultivated, is an important food and may at times constitute a third or more of its diet. In the Southland the opossum is a prover-

bial consumer of persimmons and pawpaws, as well as of other fruits. In Wisconsin it eats grapes, blackberries, raspberries, hackberries, mulberries, pokeweed berries, ground cherries, and elderberries. Acorns, particularly if sprouting, are relished. It is also fond of apples and pears, the former being an important food in the autumn. It drinks by lapping, much like a dog does.

Although the opossum eats almost anything, it is very prim about its dining. It usually sits up and holds the food in a front paw. Always after a meal it washes its paws by licking them, and frequently washes its face and body, sometimes by using one paw, sometimes using both.

The opossum has few natural enemies, its worst ones being man and hunting dogs. Coyotes occasionally kill opossums, and more rarely foxes and badgers prey on them. There are also records of opossums as food of the great horned owl, their remains having been found in the owls' pellets. Not a few are killed by automobiles, the sluggish and nocturnal habits of the opossum making it especially vulnerable.

Records of diseases and parasites in the opossum are scarce. It has been reported infected with tularemia (Mease, 1929). It is comparatively free from parasites, particularly external ones. Reynolds (1945), in speaking of opossums in Missouri, says: "The American dog tick (*Dermacentor variabilis*) occurred on the ears of 19 of the 143 individuals and a flea (*Opisodasys* sp.) was found on 5.

"The nematode *Physaloptera turgida* was found in the stomach and the nematode *Cruzia tentaculata* in the caecum. Every stomach and caecum examined contained six or more of these worms."

On credit and debit in the ledger the opossum seems to about strike a balance. It is neither seriously injurious nor highly beneficial. It probably receives more condemnation than it deserves for its destruction of small game and birds' eggs, and its raids on chicken coops are infrequent. The fruit it eats is of no particular value. On the credit side it consumes many harmful insects. It is an interesting mammal, representing an old lineage, the marsupials, the opossum being the only representative in the United States. It wears a pelt of little value. The annual take of opossum skins in Wisconsin since 1930 has been between fifteen hundred and twelve thousand. The prime skin, however, has a sale value of only fifty cents to one dollar, so the total catch is insignificant as a state income. There is at present no closed season on the opossum in Wisconsin. In the Southland, the opossum is prized as a food and game animal. It usually is hunted with dogs on dark, cloudy nights. The animal seldom plays possum on such occasions, but takes to a small tree where it is retrieved by the hunters. Roasted with sweet potatoes or yams, it is considered a great delicacy by many. The meat is pale, tender, and fine-grained, somewhat like tender pork. It is very fat, and in cooking it excess fat should be removed, although the fat is of good flavor.

The opossum can be kept as a pet, but is not particularly attractive as such, sleeping as it does in the daytime and coming forth only in the dark. It becomes surly and ugly when more than a year old. The opossum could be raised in captivity for its fur and meat, but the low return would not warrant the effort and expense.

An observation made near Washington, D. C., in 1944 on a use of opossum hair that is economically unimportant but intensely interesting is reported by Fred M. Packard (1949) as described by Devereux Butcher:

Approaching a chestnut snag in the woods last spring, I looked up and saw three full-grown possums (*Didelphis v. virginiana*) peering down. It would have been a treat to see one, but three at a time was a show. I sat on the ground nearby to watch. The limbs of the chestnut had been broken off and were hanging in the tops of the surrounding smaller trees. Two of the possums were close together on one limb, while the third was alone on another. Remaining very still they gave me the impression that they were trying to escape notice. But the possums were destined for trouble anyway, and this presently came to them in the form of a scolding titmouse. Flitting about this titmouse became very bold, always coming closer to the pair. Soon the bird alighted for an instant on an outstretched tail. Unthreatened he eventually alighted on the animal's rump, pecking vigorously—or so I thought—and causing the possum to jump a little with pain. After a few moments I discovered that what was happening was that the titmouse was pulling out hair for nest lining. Upon acquiring a beakfull the bird disappeared. In a short while he returned for more, this time attacking the lone possum. Now he became so bold as to stand on the possum's back and uninterruptedly pull out hair for all he was worth.

Specimens examined from Wisconsin.—Total 9, as follows: *Dane County:* Madison, 3 (UWZ); Waubesa Beach, 1 (UWZ). *Grant County:* Lancaster, 1 (UWZ). *Iowa County:* Mineral Point, 1 (UWZ). *Rock County:* Milton, 2 (1 MC; 1 UWZ). *Walworth County:* Delavan, 1.

Selected references.—Fox, C. P., 1955; Hartman, C. G., 1923; 1952; Knudson, G. J., 1953; Reynolds, H. C., 1945; Sheak, W. H., 1926.

ORDER INSECTIVORA

Insectivores or Insect Eaters

As the name implies, most mammals of this order are essentially insect eaters, although some consume quantities of other animal matter and a few at times eat considerable vegetation. Insectivores are found in general throughout the world, except in the polar regions, in Australia, and in the southern half of South America. Members of this order are mostly small mammals characterized by a long pointed snout that extends well beyond the anterior end of the skull, five clawed toes on each of the four feet, and small eyes and ears. The skull is simple, the orbital and temporal parts not separated from one another, with the zygomata frequently lacking. The teeth have well developed cusps, those of the molariform teeth usually arranged in the form of a W; the canines are always present, but small and inconspicuous.

The Insectivora embrace eight living families, two of which are represented in Wisconsin.

Key to the Families of Living Wisconsin Insectivora

    a. Forefeet normal, width less than 10 mm.; ear conch present, sometimes very slight; head and body length less than 100 mm.; audital bullae absent; zygomata lacking; first upper incisor flat, without elongated crown . . . . *Soricidae*

   aa. Forefeet broad, width more than 10 mm.; no ear conch present; head and body length more than 100 mm.; audital bullae present, complete or incomplete; zygomata present; first upper incisor not flat, with very elongated crown . . . . . *Talpidae*

Family Soricidae

Shrews

The family Soricidae ranges throughout North America, extreme northern South America, and tropical and temperate regions of Europe, Asia, and Africa. It is composed of some 24 genera exclusive of fossil forms, of which four occur in Wisconsin.

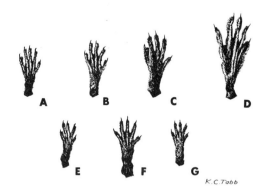

Dorsal views of left hind feet of shrews. About 1×. A. SOREX C. CINEREUS, B. SOREX F. FUMEUS, C. SOREX A. LARICORUM, D. SOREX P. HYDROBADISTES, E. MICROSOREX H. INTERVECTUS, F. BLARINA B. BREVICAUDA, G. CRYPTOTIS P. PARVA.

K.C.Tabb

Skulls of shrews. 1×. A. SOREX C. CINEREUS, Mamie Lake, Vilas County, Wisconsin, B. SOREX C. LESUEURII, Delavan, Wisconsin, C. SOREX F. FUMEUS, Bittinger, Maryland, D. SOREX A. LARICORUM, Lake St. Germain, Vilas County, Wisconsin, E. SOREX P. HYDROBADISTES, Iron River, Wisconsin, F. MICROSOREX H. INTERVECTUS, Lakewood, Wisconsin, G. BLARINA B. BREVICAUDA, ♂, Cassville, Wisconsin, H. BLARINA B. KIRTLANDI, Green Lake, Wisconsin, I. CRYPTOTIS P. PARVA, ♀, Blair, Nebraska.

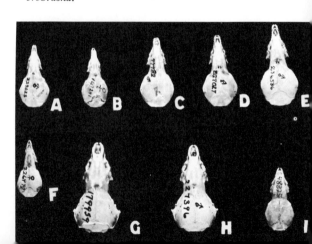

Genus **Sorex** Linnaeus
Long-tailed Shrews

Dental formula:

$$\text{I } \frac{3-3}{1-1}, \text{ C } \frac{1-1}{1-1}, \text{ P } \frac{3-3}{1-1}, \text{ M } \frac{3-3}{3-3} = 32.$$

Skins of long-tailed shrews. ½×. A. SOREX C. CINEREUS, *Mamie Lake, Wisconsin,* B. SOREX C. LESUEURII, *Delavan, Wisconsin,* C. SOREX F. FUMEUS, *Bittinger, Maryland,* D. SOREX A. LARI-CORUM, *Lake St. Germain, Wisconsin,* E. SOREX P. HYDROBADISTES, *Iron River, Wisconsin.*

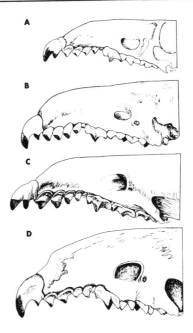

Above, lateral view of rostra and upper teeth of SOREX, *drawn from specimens indicated. A.* SOREX C. CINEREUS, ♂, *Elkhart Lake, Wisconsin, No. 227, 412, B.* SOREX F. FUMEUS, ♀, *Peterboro, New York, No. 111,123, C.* SOREX A. ARCTICUS, ♂, *South Edmonton, Alberta, No. 69,163, D.* SOREX P. PALUSTRIS, ♀, *Robinson Portage, Manitoba, No. 107,044. All about 5×. Below, lateral view of lower teeth of* SOREX, *drawn from same specimens indicated in above figure. All about 5×.*

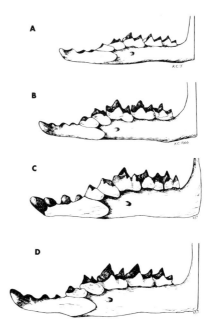

Sorex cinereus cinereus Kerr
Cinereous Shrew

Sorex arcticus cinereus Kerr, Animal Kingdom, p. 206, 1792.
[   ] *Cooperi* Lapham, p. 43, 1852.
Sorex Forsteri Lapham, p. 338, 1853.
Sorex Cooperi Lapham, p. 338, 1853; Strong, p. 438, 1883.
Sorex platyrhinus Strong, p. 438, 1883.
Sorex personatus Snyder, p. 123, 1902; Jackson, p. 30, 1908: Hollister, p. 29, 1910; Cory, p. 411, 1912.
Sorex cinereus cinereus Schmidt, p. 106, 1931; Komarek, 204, 1932; Barger, p. 10, 1952.

Vernacular names.—In Wisconsin if recognized at all usually called long-tailed shrew or shrew mouse. Other names include bill-mouse, common shrew, Cooper or Cooper's shrew, Forster's shrew, long-tailed shrew, long-tailed shrew-mouse, masked shrew, *oke-pa-ku-kue* (Chippewa), sharp-nosed mouse, shrew, and shrew-mouse.

Identification marks.—The cinereous shrew in general appearance is like a tiny slender mouse with a long sharply pointed snout, tiny beadlike eyes, and small ears almost concealed in the soft fur; the tail is relatively long, about as long as the body without head, fully haired and more or less bicolorous, paler below; feet both fore and hind delicate and weak, five toes on each foot, the claws weak, slender, and sharp; the fur is fine, soft, and silky.

Cinereous shrew, SOREX C. CINEREUS, *Burntside Lake, Minnesota. About ⅞×. Courtesy Vernon Bailey.*

The color tone of the cinereous shrew is somewhat variable, particularly in summer, when the color of the upper parts usually varies from fuscous black to mummy brown, extending well down on the sides and gradually blending with the smoke gray of the under parts. Winter pelage is somewhat darker and more grayish (less brown) than summer. The transition from winter to summer pelage may occur any time between the first of April and the last of June. Winter fur is usually acquired during October.

The skull is weak and fragile, with narrow rostrum and weak dentition; zygomatic arches incomplete, essentially absent; no auditory bullae, delicate tympanic rings replacing them; teeth dark chestnut color on the tips; incisor (front) teeth both upper and lower rather hooked and projecting forward (not vertical and chisel-like as in the mouse); posterior to the upper incisor are the five small unicuspidate teeth, the fourth

generally smaller than the third, sometimes about equal to it, both smaller than the first and second unicuspids, and the fifth minute.

So far as known there is no sexual variation of color, size, or proportions. Adult males have a relatively long and narrow gland on the flank. There is considerable variation in the skull as age advances (Jackson, 1928: 13, 21), wherein the brain case flattens and broadens, the crests develop, and the incisors gradually grow anteriorly, then inferiorly, producing an entirely different appearance in old age. Younger animals as a rule appear slenderer than adults and their tails are a trifle more hairy and sometimes slenderer. The winter pelage of the cinereous shrew is longer than in summer. Color mutations are rare in this species. A specimen collected August 5, 1933, near Marcellus, New York, is described by Pearce (1934: 67) as having a broad white band encircling about one-third of the body length in the region of the forequarters.

This shrew externally can be confused among Wisconsin species only with *Microsorex hoyi,* which is smaller on the average, with relatively shorter tail and smaller foot; the cranium of *S. cinereus* is higher and broader than in *M. hoyi,* the rostrum longer and narrower; the five unicuspid teeth in *S. cinereus* are clearly visible, whereas in *M. hoyi* the third is small and disklike, and the fifth minute. The race *Sorex cinereus lesueurii* recorded from extreme southeastern Wisconsin is smaller and darker, and has a relatively shorter tail than *S. c. cinereus.* The cinereous shrew resembles superficially the smoky shrew (*Sorex fumeus*), but is smaller, particularly the feet, and its tail is shorter; the skull is decidedly smaller and weaker, with distinctly weaker rostrum and dentition. The cinereous shrew differs from the saddle-backed shrew in being of smaller size, having a shorter and weaker hind foot and paler coloration, lacking the tricolor effect, and possessing distinctive skull differences. Comparison of *cinereus* with the large, slate-gray, long-tailed, and fringe-footed *S. p. hydrobadistes* is hardly necessary.

Measurements.—Total length of adults, 95 to 109 mm. (3.7 to 4.3 in.); tail, 37 to 44 mm. (1.5 to 1.7 in.); hind foot, 11 to 12.5 mm. (0.4 to 0.5 in.). Flank gland, 2 to 3 mm. long. Weight, 3.5 to 5.6 grams (0.12 to 0.2 oz.). Skull length, 16 to 17.2 mm.; width, 7.4 to 8.2 mm.

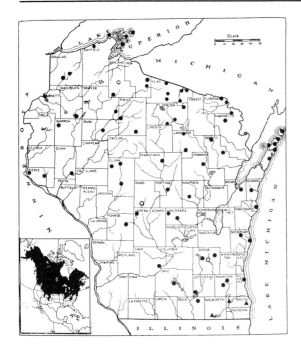

Map 5. Distribution of SOREX CINEREUS. *Solid symbols = specimens examined. Open symbols = authentic records.* ●, ○ = S. C. CINEREUS. ▲ = S. C. LESUEURII.

Distribution in Wisconsin.—All of the state in favorable habitats except that part of extreme southeastern Wisconsin (Racine and Walworth counties) inhabited by *Sorex cinereus lesueurii* and that part of southwestern Wisconsin from which no long-tailed shrews are known.

Habitat.—The cinereous shrew prefers a moist or damp but not necessarily watery habitat, preferably in woods either coniferous or deciduous, or sometimes marshes or grassy bogs, such as damp mossy woods, spruce-cedar swamps, alder thickets along brooks, mossy banks, and spruce, tamarack, or leatherleaf sphagnum bogs, and rarely are found in dry woods or even fields.

Status and Habits.—This species has probably maintained a fairly stable population in the state over many years except for disturbances caused by reduction of its habitat, such as drainage of marshes and reforestation. Both floods and drought probably affect the shrew population, but there are few data that would show population cycles. Under favorable conditions and in a limited area the cinereous shrew population may reach an intensity of more than forty per acre, but over large areas of choice environment it

seldom exceeds eight or ten to an acre, and may average only three or four. At Connors Lake, Sawyer County, nine were caught the night of August 8, 1919, and twelve the night of August 10, in the same line of forty traps. This species has a small home range that so far as known does not exceed one-fourth acre or twelve hundred square yards.

This tiny mammal leaves little evidence of its presence, its runways usually being those occupied also by other small mammals, and not often clearly diagnostic. Sometimes tiny tracks in the muddy bottom of a runway along a log or bank, or on the snow, may be suspected to be that of a long-tailed shrew, and occasionally a twisted or corkscrew-shaped feces about one-fourth inch long may indicate where a long-tailed shrew defecated. It is active both summer and winter, and does not hibernate or migrate. Its period of greatest activity is during the crepuscular hours, on cloudy days, and at night, but it continues its energetic life with little abatement during full daylight hours.

So quick in movement is this tiny phantom that one seldom gets more than a glimpse of it. It moves with a queer, jerky, trotlike run, starting and stopping abruptly. I saw one about 9:30 A.M., August 8, 1919, in the hemlock woods east of Connors Lake, Sawyer County. The sun was shining brightly, though it was shady in the deep woods where the shrew was seen only for an instant as it ran in a semi-trot-gallop gait along the base of a log into a hole under another log. It is almost strictly terrestrial, although at times it may climb small branches of very low bushes, fallen trees, or herbs. It can jump at least six inches from a still position, and with a running start will often jump eight inches. It is a good swimmer, but seldom goes into water voluntarily. No accurate records of its speed are available.

The cinereous shrew is a comparatively silent animal, and since it is not of a sociable or gregarious disposition, has little need for communication. "The shrews have been heard to use three distinct types of vocal or other sounds. When angry or fighting, a rapid series of rather staccato squeaks can be heard. While eating or in search of food they uttered a succession of faint twittering notes. These notes are so very soft and are produced so rapidly that they give to the voice a quality intermediate between a purr and a soft twitter. At times a slow gritting of the teeth is heard. This would seem to be associated with inactivity, for this sound is frequently produced when the shrew is resting" (Blossom, 1932: 137). So high-pitched are the squeaks of this shrew that it is probable that many of its notes are not audible to man.

The cinereous shrew is an active, vicious, voracious, high-strung, and restless little imp. Its restless impulse is always evident, most of its energy being devoted to the search for food, and even when the body is resting the head and snout are in continual motion, searching the air for possible scent of food or enemy. A mated pair may live together without much fighting, but put two or three others together and they fight savagely. Merriam's account of how he confined three of them under a tumbler is familiar to many: "Almost immediately they commenced fighting, and in a few minutes one was slaughtered and eaten by the other two. Before night one of these killed and ate its only surviving companion, and its abdomen was much distended by the meal. Hence in less than eight hours one of these tiny beasts had attacked, overcome, and ravenously consumed two of its own species, each as large as itself" (Merriam, 1884 a, p. 76; 1884 b, p. 174). Although the cinereous shrew is pugnacious and physically strong in proportion to its size, it at times seems unusually sensitive to any external stimulus, and individuals that show no signs of injury are not infrequently found dead on the surface of the ground, apparently the victims of shock. An interesting account of sensitiveness in a shrew (undoubtedly *Sorex cinereus*) has been described by Gilman (1876) as follows:

In the heavily timbered forest in the neighborhood of Cheboygan, Mich., on a cold day in October, 1875, I caught a characteristic full-grown specimen of Thompson's shrew (*Sorex Thompsoni* Baird). [This name is a synonym of *Microsorex hoyi thompsoni* (Baird), but Gilman's animal was probably *Sorex cinereus cinereus* Kerr.] The pretty little creature had been busy about an old decayed stump, where it seemed to have its home. It uttered no audible cry, though at first it made several hostile demonstrations, endeavoring to escape, and, seizing my fingers in its mouth tried to bite them, but the delicacy of its teeth made the attempt futile. Having no suitable place in which to deposit it, I carefully wrapped it in paper, allowing its head to protrude, and held it in my hand.

Some sportsmen were out shooting on the bay about a mile off, and the reports of their guns came to us from time to time, generally so much muffled by the distance as to be barely distinguishable, yet the shrew invariably responded to each detonation with a quick, spasmodic movement, evidently of alarm. Holding the animal as I did the movement was immediately perceptible. Though aware that the acuteness of the auditory organs of the animals and their allied genera is most wonderful, I was hardly prepared for so unequivocal a proof of its extreme sensitiveness, which, under the circumstances, I was enabled to test repeatedly in this individual *Sorex*.

It was my intention to preserve the animal alive, and take it with me on my return home for further experiment and study of its habits; but, to my regret, on unfolding the paper on my way to the house at which I was staying I found the shrew had died. I have little doubt that its death was caused by fright, as I handled it most carefully so as not to hurt it.

On the other hand, Blossom (1932: 137) experimented with the effect of various types of sound on cinereous shrews and found little reaction in the animals other than a tendency to seek cover. The sense of touch is acute, but those of smell and sight are poor. Although physically strong for its size, its excessively active life burns up its energy, and the normal longevity or life expectancy is believed to be less than two years.

We know little concerning the breeding habits of the long-tailed shrew. The male stays with the female before and after pregnancy and during the early development of the young. In sex ratio the females are more abundant than the males, and Manville (1949: 60) over a three-year period found 68 per cent of the shrews examined to be females. The gestation period is probably about 18 days. The cinereous shrew is born blind, hairless, and, relatively speaking, but slightly developed, and weighs about one-tenth of a gram. Following birth, however, it would seem that its development and growth are comparatively rapid, although it remains in the nest until well along toward maturity. There may be as many as three broods in a season. Specimens containing embryos have been collected in all months from March to September. The number of young varies from four to ten, the usual number being seven. At about ten days the young shrew is covered with very short hair and is fully half the size of the adult, with proportionately shorter tail. Ten or twelve days later it begins to shift for itself.

The nest is composed mainly of leaves, though sometimes coarse grass is used, and is located on or very near the surface of the ground in a cavity under a log, stump, rock, or other protection. In shape it is a flattened sphere some three inches in diameter, with the actual nesting cavity scarcely more than one-half inch in diameter. There is usually but one entrance, and that from the side. Surface runways often made by the shrew itself, and subterranean runways made by mice or decaying roots are also used as shelters. This shrew displays no sanitation instinct, and its small coiled droppings may be found in little piles or scattered anywhere in its runways.

Stomach examinations of this shrew have shown the following among the contents: bugs, beetles, moths, flies (both larvae and adults), caterpillars, crickets, spiders, hair and flesh of shrews and mice, and traces of moss, seeds, and other vegetable matter. Hamilton (1930: 36) "made 62 stomach examinations of this species, taken in 5 states and in Nova Scotia. Practically all were summer specimens, so little can be said of the food other than at this season. In all probability it is about the same as that of *Blarina* in winter. The percentage of the food by bulk follows: Insects, 65.3 per cent; Vertebrates, 7.1 per cent; Centipedes, 6.8 per cent; Worms, 4.3 per cent; Molluscs, 1.4 per cent; Sowbugs, 1.2 per cent; Vegetable matter, 1.1 per cent; Inorganic matter, .9 per cent; Arachnida, .9 per cent; Undetermined, 10.9 per cent. The insects include 5 determined orders, Coleoptera, Diptera, Lepidoptera, Hymenoptera, and Orthoptera, but consisted chiefly of adult beetles and the larvae of all the other orders. Only 2 contained mammalian hair, and I strongly suspect that these had eaten trapped animals. Two had salamander remains. Worms, as with *Blarina,* form a very small part of the diet. Vegetable matter was likewise rarely encountered in an analysis of these stomachs." The teeth of this tiny mammal are weak, and thus it is not able to crush the heavier chitinous parts of insects or the bones of small mammals, but cleans such flesh as it can from the bones. When not too hungry it sometimes plays with its food, much as a cat plays with a mouse. No observations have been made on its drinking, but it may possibly obtain sufficient water from its food.

This species is preyed upon by numerous animals, although comparatively few of its enemies will eat it except in case of extreme hunger. It is well known that domestic cats kill numbers of shrews but seldom eat them, and in olden times it was believed that shrews were poisonous to cats. Fragments of shrew skulls or bones are frequently found in owls' pellets. Hawks also are known to prey upon the shrew occasionally. Aside from the number killed by natural enemies, the long-tailed shrew seems to have an unusually high mortality rate compared with most mammals, as many of them are accidentally trapped in ditches, springs, wells, and post holes. It is not unusual to find several dead shrews in an uncovered well or spring. Floods and high water also are the cause of many deaths. Individuals are not infrequently found dead on the surface of the ground, some of them having been killed by other animals and abandoned, but many of them showing no signs of injury and appearing to have perished merely from nervous shock, extreme temperature, or possibly old age.

Ticks, chiggers, and other mites are not uncommon among the ectoparasites of this shrew, and more rarely fleas. The flea most frequent is *Doratopsylla blarinae,* but *Ctenophthalmus pseudogyrtes* also occurs. The ticks include *Ixodes angustus* (Moore, J. C., 1949: 236). Mites recorded have been *Protomyobia claparedei, Myobia simplex,* and *Amorphacarus hengererorum* (Jameson, 1948).

Inasmuch as this shrew feeds principally upon insects, with an occasional dessert of young mice, it is of considerable economic value in tending to hold down certain pests of agriculture and forestry. Unfortunately it is usually mistaken for a mouse by the layman and killed on sight. In parts of the north it may become a nuisance by getting into storages of meat or fish, some of which it eats and the remainder of which it ruins with its filth. In the same regions it may also become a nuisance in houses during winter. On the whole it is among the most beneficial mammals. If it becomes necessary to eliminate shrews they may be trapped with a lightly set snap mousetrap. A good bait is a mixture of ground English walnut meat (three parts) and finely chopped liver (two parts). The bait is best used one to three days old.

There is much to learn about the habits of

shrews, and it is not too difficult to keep them in captivity for observation purposes. Fill a large glass bowl or globe half full of sandy woods soil, with a handful of leaves for nest material, and use a fine wire screen for a cover. Sink a small tumbler in the earth to the rim, and keep it full of water. Feed the animal insects, grubs, raw meat or liver, nut meats, and rolled oats. In warm weather let flies in to lay eggs on raw meat to develop maggots for shrew food. Maggots can be made the main food of shrews, and they do well on it.

Specimens examined from Wisconsin.—Total 316, as follows: *Ashland County:* Bear Lake, 2 (UWZ); Madeline Island, 3; Outer Island, 12; Sand Island, 1; Stockton Island, 1. *Barron County:* Big Sand Lake, 1 (F&FH). *Bayfield County:* Herbster, 4. *Burnett County:* Danbury, 1. *Brown County:* Allouez, 7 (NPM). *Clark County:* Hewett Township, 8 (3 UWZ); Withee, 2; Worden Township, 1. *Dane County:* Blooming Grove, 1 (UWZ); Madison, 10 (UWZ). *Dodge County:* Beaver Dam, 23 (1 CAS; 1 CNHM; 21 UWZ); Horicon National Wildlife Refuge, 4. *Door County:* Clark Lake, 2; Ellison Bay, 1; Fish Creek, 1; Newport, 1 (MM); State Game Farm, 1 (UWZ); Washington Island, 3. *Douglas County:* Moose and Saint Croix rivers (junction), 8 (MM); Solon Springs, 14 (13 CNHM). *Dunn County:* Meridean, 2. *Florence County:* Florence, 3; Spread Eagle Lake, 3 (CNHM). *Iron County:* Fishers Lake, 7 (UWZ); Mercer, 8 (5 MM). *Jefferson County:* Sumner, 2. *Juneau County:* Mather, 1. *Kewaunee County:* Luxemberg, 1 (NPM). *Langlade County:* Antigo, 1 (UWZ); Elcho, 2 (UWZ). *Manitowoc County:* Point Beach State Forest, 1 (UWZ); T 20 N, R 25 E, 1 (UWZ). *Marathon County:* Rib Hill, 7. *Marinette County:* Cataline, 4 (MM); McAllister, 2; Timms Lake, 1 (UWZ). *Milwaukee County:* Milwaukee 2, (1 MM; 1 USNM). *Monroe County:* Tomah, 1 (UWZ). *Oconto County:* Kelley Brook, 2 (MM); Kelley Lake, 11; Lakewood, 10. *Oneida County:* Crescent Lake, 8; Rhinelander, 8 (2 UWZ); Three Lakes, 1 (UWZ). *Pierce County:* Ellsworth, 1 (USNM); Prescott, 4 (MM). *Portage County:* Stevens Point, 1. *Price County:* Ogema, 6; T 37 N, R 2 W, 1 (F&FH). *Rock County:* Milton, 1 (CNHM). *Rusk County:* Ladysmith, 1 (UWZ). *Sauk County:* Prairie du Sac, 4 (MM). *Sawyer County:* Connors Lake, 12 (4 F&FH). *Shawano County:* Keshena, 2 (CAS). *Sheboygan County:* Elkhart Lake (Sheboygan Bog), 6; Terry Andrae State Park, 1 (UWZ). *Vilas County:* Conover, 1 (CNHM); Eagle River, 2 (USNM); Lac Vieux Desert, 4 (CNHM); Lake St. Germain, 6; Mamie Lake, 15; Sayner, 22 (CNHM). *Washburn County:* Long Lake, 13. *Waukesha County:* Dousman, 1; Nashotah, 1 (USNM). *Waupaca County:* Saint Lawrence Township, 6 (UWZ). *Waushara County:* T 20 N, R 8 E, 1 (F&FH); Wild Rose, 3.

Selected references.—Blossom, P. M., 1932; Hamilton, W. J., Jr., 1930; Jackson, H. H. T., 1928; Manville, R. H., 1949; Moore, J. R., 1949; Seton, E. T., 1909, pp. 1106–8.

Sorex cinereus lesueurii (Duvernoy)
Indiana Cinereous Shrew

Amphisorex lesueurii Duvernoy, Mag. de Zool., d'Anat. Comp. et de Palaeont., series 2, vol. 4, Monog. du Genre Musaraigne, p. 33, November, 1842.

Identification marks.—Similar in general to *Sorex cinereus cinereus* but slightly smaller with shorter tail; darker and more richly colored; skull and teeth smaller.

Measurements.—Total length of adults, 88 to 95 mm. (3.4 to 3.7 in.); tail, 34 to 40 mm. (1.3 to 1.6 in.); hind foot, 10 to 12 mm. (0.4 to 0.5 in.). Skull length, 15 to 16 mm.; width, 7.2 to 7.7 mm.

Distribution in Wisconsin.—Known only from extreme southeastern part of the state (Racine and Walworth counties).

Habitat and Habits.—So far as known essentially like those of *Sorex cinereus cinereus.*

Specimens examined from Wisconsin.—Total 13, as follows: *Racine County:* Racine, 3 (USNM); Tichigan Lake, 1 (UWZ). *Walworth County:* Delavan, 9 (2 MM; 5 USNM).

Selected references.—Bole, B. P., Jr., and P. N. Moulthrop, 1942, pp. 90–95; Burt, W. H., 1943; Jackson, H. H. T., 1928; Lyon, M. W., Jr., 1936, pp. 39–43; Pruitt, W. O., Jr., 1954 b.

Sorex fumeus fumeus Miller
Smoky Shrew

Sorex fumeus Miller, North Amer. Fauna no. 10, p. 50, December 31, 1895.
Sorex fumeus Hollister, p. 142, 1909; Hollister, p. 29, 1910; Cory, p. 415, 1912.
Sorex fumeus fumeus Barger, p. 10, 1952.

Identification marks.—The smoky shrew in general is quite similar to the cinereous shrew, but is larger and considerably darker—particularly ventrally—more grayish, and has distinctive skull characteristics. It is about the size of *Sorex arcticus laricorum* or slightly smaller, usually paler and more grayish, never displaying the tricolor pattern of *arcticus,* and showing easily separable skull characteristics in its lower cranium, and broader rostrum.

In winter pelage (unknown from Wisconsin specimen) it is distinctly grayish, near mouse gray to dark mouse gray, the under parts only slightly paler, frequently silvery in certain lights; tail indistinctly bicolorous—fuscous above, chamois beneath—nearly to tip. Summer pelage decidedly more brownish than winter pelage.

The skull is relatively broad and short, with a rather broad interorbital region; cranium somewhat flattened; infraorbital foramen large and situated well posteriorly. Dentition moderate, the molariform teeth rather deeply emarginate posteriorly; unicuspid teeth broader (exterointerior diameter) than long, the third larger than the fourth; internal ridge extending from apex of unicuspid to about one-half the distance toward internal edge of cingulum, moderately pigmented near apex. Compared with that of *S. arcticus* the skull of *S. fumeus* is flatter throughout, with brain case considerably less deep, relatively narrower, and less angular; less attenuate rostrum, anteroposterior diameter of unicuspids relatively less, molariform teeth more deeply emarginate posteriorly, and cusps of i^1 narrower than in *arcticus*, the secondary cusp relatively smaller. Skull decidedly larger and heavier than that of *S. cinereus* in all proportions, and unicuspids lack the pigmented ridge extending from apex of tooth to interior edge of cingulum (ridge is incomplete and only partly pigmented, near apex of tooth, in *fumeus*).

In latitude approximating that of southern Wisconsin there are two molts annually, the transition from winter to summer fur usually occurring in May or early in June. Early in the autumn the winter pelage begins to appear, and is usually acquired in full by the middle of October, though sometimes as late as the first of November.

Measurements.—Total length of adults, 115 to 124 mm. (4.5 to 4.9 in.); tail, 41 to 48 mm. (1.6 to 1.9 in.); hind foot, 13 to 15 mm. (0.5 to 0.6 in.). Flank gland, 6 to 7 mm. long. Weight, 5.8 to 10 grams (0.2 to 0.35 oz.). Skull length, 18.4 to 19.2 mm.; width, 8.5 to 9.1 mm.

Distribution in Wisconsin—Known in Wisconsin only from a single specimen collected in 1853 by Dr. P. R. Hoy at Racine, and entered as number 830/4430 in the U. S. National Museum catalog, October 1, 1855. The specimen consists of a skin in faded and much worn summer pelage and a broken skull, of which the anterior part, lower jaws, and teeth are in good condition. It was misidentified by Baird (1857, p. 24) as *Sorex richard-*

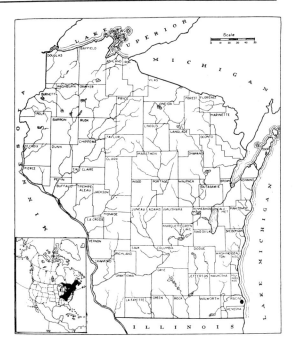

Map 6. *Distribution of* SOREX FUMEUS. ● = *specimen examined.*

soni [= *Sorex arcticus*], but later was correctly placed with *Sorex fumeus* by Miller (1895, pp. 38 and 50).

Habitat.—Apparently a woodland species, favoring both deciduous and coniferous—especially beech-hemlock—forests that have deep leaf mold, tending to be more abundant near water. Bailey (1933: 58) found it to be "fairly common among the rocks in the mouth of Mammoth Cave [Kentucky] where spring water from the roof trickles down in several little cold streams and keeps the stones beneath wet and cold and moss-covered for most of the year."

Status and Habits.—In regions where the smoky shrew is of established occurrence it is usually of more or less local and scattered distribution, but it seems to be almost gregarious where it does occur; in a favorable habitat it may reach a normal population of ten or fifteen to the acre, and has been known to number as many as 50 per acre in New York State (Hamilton, 1940 d: 487) and 58 per acre in Ohio (Bole, 1939: 65).

The smoky shrew is active both winter and summer, at any time of day or night. Like any shrew, its movements are quick and jerky, though its actual speed does not seem to be as fast as that of some of the other shrews.

When alarmed, or approached by a larger mouse or shrew, the smoky shrew utters a high-pitched grating note, not unlike that of the smaller bats. If greatly disturbed, it will throw itself on its back, and with spread and waving legs, repeatedly utter these squeaking staccato notes. When foraging for food these little shrews utter an almost indiscernible twitter. I have twice seen these little forest mammals rooting through the leaf mold or appearing on the forest litter about rotted logs, the twitching nose and vibrissae held aloft, and this faint, almost inaudible twittering was kept up continually (Hamilton, 1940 d: 478).

The sense of touch is well developed, and the vibrissae and constantly moving snout are employed in the search for food, and in detecting other objects. The senses of smell and sight are poor, though sight is sufficient for the shrew to detect and avoid objects in its way. Hearing is moderately acute—particularly for high-pitched notes—even though weak.

Breeding in the smoky shrew begins late in March, the earlier litters appearing by the first of May. Probably in some cases as many as three litters are reared in a year, the later ones appearing late in August. The gestation period is probably about 20 days, and the young number from three to ten, five or six being the average and usual number in a litter.

The life span of the smoky shrew is short, for all the adults die of old age when they are 14 to 17 months old. This conclusion is based on the fact that no shrews breed in the year in which they are born, but pass their first winter as immature individuals. Weight, degree of hairs on the tail and tooth wear combined are infallible criteria of age, and serve readily to separate the adults from the immature shrews. Following the breeding season, the adult population of shrews die, usually in August (Hamilton, 1940 d: 489).

The smoky shrew burrows some in the soft leaf mold, but its feet are too weak to burrow to any extent. Frequently the leaf mold is intermined with burrows occupied by this shrew, but such burrows have been made by other animals.

The nests are placed at various places in these tunnels, a favorite site being beneath a stump or rotten log. I have found one nest composed almost entirely of hair of a cottontail rabbit, situated beneath a stump

from which a shrew ran when the nest was exposed. Other nests which I have examined have been made of shredded leaves, usually situated from 4 to 9 inches below the surface. These nests are roughly spherical in shape and approximate a baseball in size. They are more compact and somewhat smaller than the bulkier nests of *Blarina*. One nest which I presume had been made by a smoky shrew (a specimen was trapped in a runway leading from the nest) was situated in a punky log which crumbled apart easily. The nest was placed at one end of the log near its base and communicated with several burrows leading into the soil beneath. Another was found at the bottom of a large mass of rotten logs which had been piled by a wood cutter, and allowed to disintegrate. This nest was placed directly on the ground, between two logs which formed part of the foundation of the pile.

None of the nests contained remains of food, but piles of scats were usually found within a few inches of the nest. Captive shrews are certainly sanitary creatures, often reserving a corner of the aquaria farthest removed from the nest in which to deposit their feces. All the nests which I have examined have been free of parasites (Hamilton, 1940 d: 478).

On the basis of 168 stomach analyses made from smoky shrews taken throughout the year in New York State, Hamilton finds that insects are by far the most important food, being found in 80 per cent of the stomachs. "Vegetable matter was found in 14.9%; snails, 10.1%; spiders, 5.9%; sowbugs, 5.3%; mammals, 3.0%; salamanders, 1.8% and birds .6%. Captive shrews maintain themselves well on an assortment of natural foods equal to half their weight daily. Captive individuals seldom drink" (Hamilton, 1940 d: 489).

The smoky shrew has many enemies that would prey upon it, but because of its concealed habitat it has some natural protection. Owls frequently capture this and other species of shrews, and hawks also occasionally capture them. The weasel captures not a few, and the big short-tailed shrew (*Blarina*) is a constant threat. Some of the larger predators such as the gray fox, red fox, and bobcat also prey on shrews. The smoky shrew is not as a rule heavily parasitized but externally is subject to mites of the genera *Haemogamasus, Myobia, Protomyobia,* and *Amorphacarus.* Two species of Myobiid mites have been described for *Sorex fumeus,* namely, *Protomyobia brevisetosa* and *Amorphacarus hengererorum* (Jameson, 1948). Fleas are scarce and so far as known restricted to two common species,

Ctenophthalmus pseudagyrtes and *Doratopsylla blarinae.* Roundworms of the genus *Porrocaecum* occur (Hamilton, 1940 d: 488).

The smoky shrew is economically a very useful mammal, feeding as it does almost entirely on insects and having so far as known no habits detrimental to man's interests.

Specimens examined from Wisconsin.—Only 1, as follows: *Racine County:* Racine, 1 (USNM).

Selected references.—Bailey, V., 1933, pp. 57–58; Bole, B. P., Jr., and P. N. Moulthrop, 1942, pp. 96–97; Goodwin, G. G., 1935, pp. 38–39; Hamilton W. J., Jr., 1940 d; Jackson, H. H. T., 1928; Miller, G. S., Jr., 1895.

Sorex arcticus laricorum Jackson
Southern Saddle-backed Shrew

Sorex arcticus laricorum Jackson, Proc. Biol. Soc. Washington 38: 127, November 13, 1925.

[   ] *Richardsonii* Lapham, p. 43, 1852.

Sorex Richardsonii Lapham, p. 338, 1853; Strong, p. 438, 1883.

Sorex richardsoni Snyder, p. 123, 1902; Hollister, p. 29, 1910.

Sorex richardsonii Jackson, p. 30, 1908; Cory, p. 414, 1912.

Sorex arcticus laricorum Schmidt, p. 106, 1931; Barger, p. 10, 1952.

Vernacular names.—In Wisconsin if recognized at all usually called saddle-back shrew. Other names include black-backed shrew, Richardson's shrew, saddle-backed shrew, tamarack shrew, and tricolor shrew.

Identification marks. — The saddle-backed shrew can be distinguished from other Wisconsin shrews by its tricolor pattern and rich coloration, particularly in winter. It is decidedly larger than either the cinereous shrew or the pigmy shrew, and has longer and heavier hind feet and distinctive skull differences. It is much smaller in all proportions than the water shrew, has a much shorter tail, and is not fringe-footed. More nearly like the smoky shrew (*Sorex fumeus*) among Wisconsin mammals, but separable by its tricolor pattern, its higher skull with slenderer rostrum, and other cranial features.

In winter pelage the color pattern is clearly tricolor, the upper parts a ribbon of rich dark fuscous black extending from nose to base of tail, becoming slightly paler on face and nose; sides sharply contrasted with back, snuff brown to wood brown, extending onto sides of face;

under parts paler and more grayish than sides, the line of color demarcation usually not so sharply defined as that between the back and sides, smoke gray tinged with drab or pinkish buff; tail indistinctly bicolorous, fuscous above, buffy below, the terminal fourth nearly as dark below as above. Summer pelage is paler above and more brownish below than in winter, therefore forming less of a tricolor pattern.

The skull is moderate in all dimensions, the teeth moderately large, with the unicuspids rather heavy and swollen, the fourth smaller than the third. Skull distinctly larger than that of *Sorex cinereus* or *Microsorex hoyi* with heavier dentition, the molariform teeth being actually and relatively broader. Skull higher and wider interorbitally, rostrum more attenuate, and molar teeth less emarginate posteriorly than in *Sorex fumeus.* Skull smaller in all dimensions than that of *Sorex palustris.*

There is no sexual variation in size or color, but as in other shrews adult males have a relatively long and narrow gland on the flank, which in this species is about 7 mm. long. The clearly marked difference between winter and summer fur makes it easier to follow the time of molting. The transition from winter to summer fur apparently usually takes place late in May or during June, the change to summer pelage being complete by the last of June. Autumn molt begins in September, and by the latter part of October nearly all specimens are in full winter fur. The characteristic variations of shrews with advancing age are in general similar to other species.

Measurements.—Total length of adults, 114 to 126 mm. (4.4 to 4.6 in.); tail, 38 to 46 mm. (1.5 to 1.7 in.); hind foot, 14 to 15 mm. (0.6 in.). Flank gland, 7 mm. long. Weight, 7 to 11 grams (0.24 to 0.4 oz.). Skull length, 19 to 20.6 mm.; width, 9.1 to 9.5 mm.

Distribution in Wisconsin.—Mostly north of 45° N. latitude and chiefly in Canadian Zone; also known from Dane and Dodge counties in Transition Zone of southeastern Wisconsin.

Habitat.—The saddle-backed shrew is found chiefly in wet spruce, and tamarack swamps, or in alder or willow marshes; it rarely occurs in more or less open leatherleaf-sphagnous bogs.

Status and Habits.—The saddle-backed shrew is not an abundant animal in the state, partly

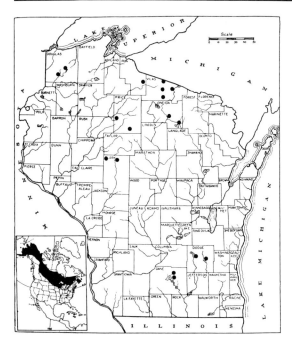

Map 7. Distribution of SOREX ARCTICUS. ● = specimens examined. ○ = authentic record.

on account of its restricted habitat. There are
probably at least twenty-five cinereous shrews in
the state to every saddle-backed shrew, but
possibly as many as five saddle-backs to each one
of the pigmy shrew or the water shrew. In a
favorable habitat it may reach a population of
eight or ten to an acre, but there are often great
areas of environment suitable to it where it apparently does not occur.

Very little is known about the habits of this
species but they are probably not essentially
different from those of other long-tailed shrews.
It is more aquatic, or at any rate lives in wetter
locations, than Sorex cinereus. It has the same
nerve tension. The writer recalls a case on August 15, 1919, at Ogema, Price County, when
one of the field men in his party chanced to
come upon a saddle-backed shrew that was
running across a road, and dropped a felt hat
over the animal. He then carefully raised the
brim of the hat, expecting to capture the shrew
alive, but to his surprise the animal was dead,
though apparently not touched by the hat.

Four females of Sorex arcticus from various
localities contained six, six, eight, and nine embryos, the dates varying from April 27 (1922)

to June 22 (1900). It would appear from this
that possibly two or more litters may be reared
a year.

The food of this shrew so far as can be determined differs little from that of the cinereous
shrew, except that its more aquatic habits might
lead to its feeding more upon aquatic insects and
other invertebrates. Economically it must be
considered beneficial, since it feeds so largely on
insects and has so far as known no harmful
habits.

Specimens examined from Wisconsin.—Total 29, as
follows: *Clark County:* Thorp Township, 1 (AMNH);
Withee, 1. *Dane County:* Burke Township, 1
(UWZ); McFarland, 1. *Dodge County:* Horicon Na-
tional Wildlife Refuge, 4. *Douglas County:* Moose
and Saint Croix rivers (junction), 1 (MM); Solon
Springs, 2 (CNHM). *Iron County:* Mercer, 1. *Onei-
da County:* Pelican Lake, 1 (CNHM); Rhineland-
er, 3 (UWZ). *Price County:* Ogema, 1; T 37 N,
R 2 W, 1 (F&FH). *Vilas County:* Conover, 1
(CNHM); Lake St. Germain, 4; Mamie Lake, 3;
Phelps, 2 (UWZ); Sayner, 1 (CNHM).

Selected references.—Bailey, V., 1927, p. 203; Burt,
W. H., 1946, pp. 94–95; Clough, G. C., 1960; Jackson, H. H. T., 1925 a; 1925 c; 1928; Seton, E. T.,
1909, pp. 1106–8.

Sorex palustris hydrobadistes Jackson
Wisconsin Water Shrew

Sorex palustris hydrobadistes Jackson, Journ. Mammalogy, 7 (2): 57, February 15, 1926.
Neosorex palustris Jackson, p. 31, 1908; Hollister, p.
29, 1910; Cory, p. 421, 1912.
Sorex palustris hydrobadistes Barger, p. 10, 1952.

Vernacular names.—In Wisconsin, when recognized, usually called water shrew. Other names
include beaver mouse, black and white shrew,
fish mouse, fish shrew, marsh shrew, muskrat
mouse, snow mole, snow shrew, and water
shrew.

Identification marks.—Largest of the Wisconsin long-tailed shrews, with long tail, nearly as
long as body and head; hind feet large, long,
and conspicuously bordered with long stiff hairs
forming a fringe adapted for swimming; third
and fourth hind toes joined by thin web at the
base for slightly more than half their length;
snout long and pointed; eyes, minute; ears small,
hidden in the fur; pelage dense, soft, and somewhat velvety, almost black above, not so dark
below with a silvery overcast.

In winter the upper parts are dark fuscous
black to nearly black, usually with a scarcely

perceptible sprinkling of whitish hair bands, sometimes with greenish or purplish iridescence; under parts paler, general tone near smoke gray, more or less glossy or silvery, occasionally stained with tawny; chin and lips near pale smoke gray; tail bicolorous (whitish beneath) nearly to tip. In summer pelage the upper parts are usually more brownish than in winter, with less tendency towards iridescence; under parts darker than in winter, scarcely paler than upper parts, occasionally as dark as upper parts; chin and lips very slightly paler, more whitish than general tone of under parts; tail as in winter.

The skull is the largest of any of the Wisconsin long-tailed shrews, but is smooth, weak, and fragile with narrow rostrum characteristic of the genus *Sorex*. The skull is nearly as long as that of the short-tailed shrew (*Blarina*), but is narrower, having a cranial breadth of less than 11.0 mm., whereas that of *Blarina* is more than 11.0 mm. The skull of *Blarina* is much more angular and ridged.

There are no sexual variations of color, size, or proportion. Adult males have the characteristic flank gland which in this species is relatively long. Age variations consist mostly of the usual skull modifications as described under *S. cinereus*. Seasonal variations are only such as appear in color. The spring molt seems to occur usually during May or early in June; the fall molt during the last half of August or early in September.

Measurements.—Total length of adults, 138 to 164 mm. (5.4 to 6.5 in.); tail, 63 to 72 mm. (2.5 to 2.8 in.); hind foot, 19 to 20 mm. (0.75 to 0.79 in.). Flank gland, 8 to 9 mm. long. Weight 12 to 18 grams (0.42 to 0.64 oz.). Skull length, 21.2 to 22.4 mm.; width, 10.0 to 10.9 mm.

Distribution in Wisconsin.—Northern part of the state, mostly in Canadian Life Zone and upper Transition Zone, south in central part of range to northern Clark County.

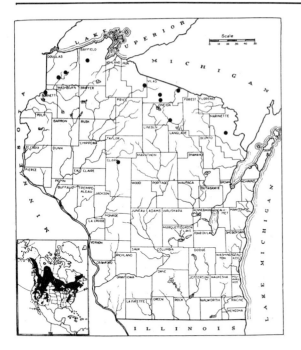

Map 8. Distribution of SOREX PALUSTRIS. ● = *specimens examined.*

Habitat.—This species, being near aquatic or at least amphibious, inhabits marshes, bogs, and wet areas near the borders of streams, lakes, or waterholes. It frequently inhabits beaver and muskrat houses, particularly in winter. It seems to prefer a more or less wooded habitat, and is rarely found in marshes devoid of bushes or trees.

Status and Habits.—Water shrews are apparently not common in the state, and, in fact, except along some of the streams in the Sierra Nevada and Rocky Mountains, are not frequently observed or collected anywhere. In Wisconsin they are possibly as plentiful as the pigmy shrew, but are outnumbered by the cinereous shrew possibly two hundred to one. Their tracks are seldom seen, but their runways may at times be recognized. One such runway has been described as follows: "I secured four specimens of *Neosorex palustris* near Rhinelander (August, 1907) in the swamp where I caught *Sorex richardsonii*. The four *Neosorex* were all trapped in the same runway, and, though the trap was in the runway over two weeks, no other species were captured there. The runway entered a mass of sphagnum which surrounded the roots of

swamp laurel (*Kalmia glauca*); within the sphagnum beneath the roots of the laurel was a dark, damp cavity, with a capacity of possibly one peck; the runway passed on through this cavity to the edge of a water hole, where I was unable to follow it further" (Jackson, 1908: 31).

The water shrew neither migrates nor hibernates, but is active all winter, even though at times its activities are curtailed. It may be primarily nocturnal, but is active also in the daytime, often in its shaded habitat on bright sunny days. In its adaptations to aquatic habits it ranks high among the best swimmers of non-marine mammals. It can swim, dive, twist and turn, float, run along the bottom of a pond or creek, or actually run on the surface of the water with the greatest ease. In a tamarack-spruce bog near Rhinelander, Wisconsin, in August, 1906, I saw one run a distance of more than five feet across a small pool, the surface of which was glassy smooth. The body and head of the animal were entirely out of the water, the surface tension of the water supporting the shrew, and at each step the animal took there appeared to be held by the hair fringe on the foot a little globule of air, which was also discernible in the shadow at the bottom of the pool, exactly as one might notice in the case of the water strider (*Gerris remigis*). In swimming it uses all four feet in the same motion and sequence as in running over the ground, and, in fact, when in the water almost imperceptibly changes from walking on the bottom to swimming without change of gait.

There are no direct observations on length of life of this shrew, but like most insectivores it probably is short-lived, possibly normally living not more than two years. In researches on *Sorex palustris navigator* in Montana it was found that "the maximum age of any specimen obtained would not be in excess of eighteen months" (Conaway, 1952: 246). This may be one factor in its rarity. Little is known of its breeding and nesting habits, though Conaway (1952) has given details of reproduction in *S. p. navigator*. It apparently has an extensive breeding season, because pregnant females have been collected in March, suckling females the first week in June, half-grown young early in July, a female with five small embryos August 2, and a male with enlarged testes August 9. Morris M. Green (in personal letter to me, November 20, 1943) says, "The only fat shrew taken by me in 55 years mammal trapping was a water shrew, trapped at Doucet, northern Quebec, on April 20, 1931. There was much snow then. My notes read 'I suspect these shrews breed in late winter. A male was taken on bank of a snow lined brook. Temperature of brook 34° F. Depth of abdominal fur 6. Dorsal fur 8. Testicles 9 mm. by 4 mm. Side Glands, inside skin, 9 mm. x 5 mm. Eye ball 1 mm. There was much fat on shoulders of this animal, which was in winter pelage.'" The number of embryos found has varied from four to eight, the usual number being five to seven. The gestation period is probably close to 21 days. More than one litter probably are produced during a season. Mammary glands are six, two pairs inguinal, one pair abdominal.

The food of the water shrew does not appear from stomach examinations to differ much from that of other long-tailed shrews, consisting chiefly of insects including adults and larvae of beetles, bugs, flies, caddis flies, and May flies. It also feeds some upon snails, leeches, and planarians, and vertebrate muscle fiber has been found in its stomach contents. It is said by some to eat small fish and is also reported to feed upon fish eggs, though there is no direct evidence. I once saw a water shrew chase a minnow in a small pool near Rhinelander, Oneida County, but it failed to capture the little fish. It seems probable that a detailed study of the food of the water shrew will show more aquatic insects consumed than by other shrews, yet Hamilton (1930: 38) is probably correct in his contention that a large part of its food probably comes from a terrestrial origin.

By nature of its habits and habitat the water shrew probably has few important enemies. It is known to have been eaten by weasels, and there is a report of a garter snake attacking one. Hawks and owls, mammalian predators such as the mink, and certain fish such as the brook and rainbow trouts, black bass, pickerel, and wall-eyed pike may account for some predation on this shrew. No detailed information is available on parasites of the water shrew, through the flea *Doratopsylla blarinae* has been reported from the New England water shrew.

Water shrews are sometimes reported to do damage in fish ponds and trout streams by destroying fish and fish eggs, but these shrews are not plentiful enough anywhere to do any serious damage. On the whole their insect destruction, their interesting and unusual nature, and their usual habitat away from man's general interests should curtail any control measures.

Specimens examined from Wisconsin.—Total 20, as follows: *Bayfield County:* Basswood Lake (10 mi. S. E. of Iron River), 1. *Burnett County:* Danbury, 2. *Clark County:* Withee, 1. *Douglas County:* Moose and Saint Croix rivers (junction), 1 (MM); Solon Springs, 4 (CNHM). *Iron County:* Mercer, 1. *Marinette County:* No locality, 1 (MM). *Oneida County:* Rhinelander, 4 (3 UWZ; 1 CC). *Vilas County:* Lac Vieux Desert, 3 (CNHM); Lake St. Germain, 1; Sayner, 1 (CNHM).

Selected references.—Burt, W. H., 1946, pp. 95–97; Cory, C. B., 1912, pp. 420–422; Jackson, H. H. T., 1908, pp. 31–32, pl. 3; 1926 a; 1928; Seton, E. T., 1909, pp. 1112–15.

Genus **Microsorex** Coues
Pigmy Shrews

Dental formula:

$$I\frac{3-3}{1-1}, \ C\frac{1-1}{1-1}, \ P\frac{3-3}{1-1}, \ M\frac{3-3}{3-3}=32.$$

Skins of pigmy shrew and mole shrews. A. MICROSOREX H. INTERVECTUS, *Lakewood, Wisconsin,* B. BLARINA B. BREVICAUDA, *Cassville, Wisconsin,* C. BLARINA B. KIRTLANDI, *Green Lake, Wisconsin,* D. CRYPTOTIS P. PARVA, *Blair, Nebraska. About* ⅗×.

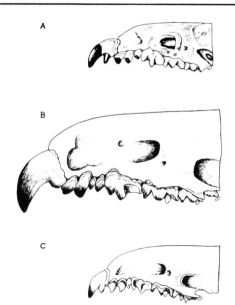

Above, lateral view of rostra and upper teeth of MICROSOREX, BLARINA, *and* CRYPTOTIS, *drawn from specimens as indicated.* A. MICROSOREX H. INTERVECTUS, *Lakewood, Wisconsin, No. 226,979,* B. BLARINA B. BREVICAUDA, *Council Bluffs, Iowa, No. 43,765,* C. CRYPTOTIS P. PARVA, *Blair, Nebraska, No. 48,817. All about* 5×. *Below, lateral view of lower teeth of* MICROSOREX, BLARINA, *and* CRYPTOTIS, *drawn from same specimens indicated in above figure. All about* 5×.

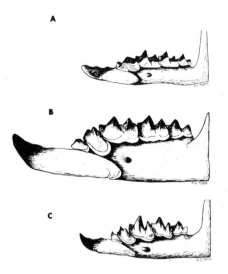

Microsorex hoyi hoyi (Baird)
American Pigmy Shrew

Sorex hoyi Baird, Rept. Pacific R. R. Survey, vol. 8, pt. 1, Mammals, p. 32, 1857.
Sorex Hoyi Strong, p. 438, 1883.
Sorex hoyi Jackson, p. 31, 1908.
Microsorex hoyi Hollister, p. 29, 1910; Cory, p. 418, 1912.
Microsorex hoyi hoyi Barger, p. 10, 1952.

Vernacular names.—Hoy's pigmy or pygmy shrew, Hoy or Hoy's shrew, pigmy shrew, and pygmy shrew.

Identification marks.—The American pigmy shrew is the smallest Wisconsin mammal. It can be confused in external characters with *Sorex cinereus cinereus* and even more so with the smaller and darker *S. c. lesueurii*, than either of which it averages smaller, with relatively and actually shorter tail and smaller feet.

In summer pelage the upper parts of *Microsorex h. hoyi* are between sepia and hair brown; the under parts smoke gray, tinged with light buff; the tail indistinctly bicolorous, mummy brown above, drabish below, darkening toward the tip. In winter pelage the upper parts are slightly duller (more grayish) than in summer; under parts and tail as in summer.

The skull of *Microsorex hoyi* is distinctive from that of *Sorex cinereus*, the cranium being flat and narrow, the rostrum short and relatively broad, and the mandible short and heavy. Dentition simple, first upper incisor large, elongate, and two-lobed, the anterior (primary) lobe relatively long and narrow, the length more than twice the width and more than twice the length of the secondary lobe; first and second unicuspid teeth (i^2 and i^3) peglike with distinct ridge from cusp to cingulum, distinctly and sharply curved caudad toward the terminus, with a pronounced secondary cusp near the terminus of the ridge of the cingulum; third unicuspid disklike, anteroposteriorly flattened; fourth unicuspid (pm^1) normal, peglike; fifth unicuspid (pm^2) minute. In lateral view of teeth in *Sorex cinereus* five unicuspids are clearly visible, whereas in *Microsorex hoyi* the third and fifth are small and indistinct.

Measurements.—Total length of adults, 80 to 98 mm. (3.1 to 3.9 in.); tail, 28 to 32 mm. (1.1 to 1.2 in.); hind foot, 9 to 11 mm. (0.35 to 0.43 in.). Flank gland, about 9 mm. long. Weight,

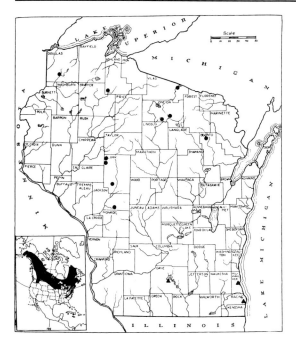

Map 9. Distribution of MICROSOREX HOYI. *Solid symbols = specimens examined.* ● = M. H. INTERVECTUS. ▲ = M. H. HOYI.

2.2 to 3.8 grams (0.08 to 0.14 oz.). Skull length, 15 to 16.4 mm.; width, 6.1 to 6.8 mm.

Distribution in Wisconsin.—Known only from the southeastern part of the state (Dane, Milwaukee, and Racine counties).

Habitat.—Under rotten logs or litter, and among roots of old stumps or other heavy vegetation in woods, clearings, and meadows, particularly those grown to high grass; sometimes on dry sandy ridges in closely grazed pastures, avoiding as a rule swampy or excessively wet areas, though at times found in cold sphagnum or tamarack bogs; occasionally around old cabins.

Status and Habits.—Very little is known about the habits of the pigmy shrew. It is scarce in Wisconsin, and probably exceeded in numbers by every other shrew except the smoky shrew (*Sorex fumeus*), the status of which is somewhat doubtful in the state. The specimen from Madison, Dane County, was turned in to Professor Lowell E. Noland at the Zoological Laboratory, University of Wisconsin, in September, 1933. Franklin Schmidt, deceased, then a student at the university, recognized it as unusual and sug-

gested that it be sent to me by Professor Noland, who did so. In general its habits probably do not vary greatly from those of the cinereous shrew. It is active in daytime but seems to be more nocturnal than some shrews, since most specimens captured are trapped during the night. Its movements are continuous and rapid, with sudden stops and starts. It can climb rough surfaces for a few feet. It sings with a weak, highpitched, rolling purr. Its food is chiefly insects. Nothing is known of its breeding habits other than that three to seven foetuses have been found in pregnant females at dates varying from June 8 to July 18 in different years.

Leslie A. Prince, while engaged in biological field work in Ontario, kept alive in a wooden cage for ten days a pigmy shrew that he captured at 6:30 A.M., August 10, 1939, in a water trap set in a dry, high-grass clearing, bordering second growth alder-poplar-birch woods. He tells us (Prince, 1940):

The shrew was continually active, its movements rapid, with many sudden stops and starts. While running the tail was held straight out from the body with a slight upward curve. It was quite adept at climbing up the sides of the cage and walking upside down on the wire mesh top. On several occasions it hung down from the cover "monkey fashion," the hind limbs clinging to the mesh, while the front limbs and body dangled below. The shrew was a very capable jumper, and once when the top was removed, it bounded from the bottom of the cage, over the rim onto the table, a height of 4½ inches.

The snout of the shrew was constantly moving and sniffing, suggesting that it depended greatly upon its sense of smell to determine direction.

The pigmy shrew did not appear to have any set period for sleeping. Observations made on a number of occasions during the night, revealed it to be just as active as during the day. During the ten days of captivity it was observed sleeping on only one occasion, in mid-afternoon. The shrew slept with the limbs drawn under the body and the head and tail curled alongside, much in the same manner as a dog would sleep.

Very audible short, sharp squeaks were emitted by the shrew as it moved about the cage. The sounds were most obvious when it was frightened or disturbed.

Food contents must have passed through the shrew's body with remarkable rapidity as the cage was continually covered with fresh droppings.

During the ten days the shrew was kept in captivity, 20 cinereous shrews, 1 white-footed mouse, 1 red-backed mouse, and the carcass of a pigmy shrew were placed in the cage. The total weight of the material was 107.5 gms. In addition 20 house flies, 22 grasshoppers, 2 crane flies, 1 beetle, and the liver of a meadow mouse were consumed by the pigmy shrew.

P. B. Saunders, Clinton, New York, also captured a *Microsorex hoyi* alive in his hands, and kept it in captivity from April 5 to May 2, 1926. His observations showed that the pigmy shrew dug a hole beneath the moss down into the earth that could easily be mistaken for that of a large earthworm. His shrew emitted a musk, especially when excited, that was very powerful and quite dominated the room in which it was kept. Saunders often saw his pigmy shrew sitting up on its hind legs like a kangaroo. Sometimes at night the shrew gave notes that "were a combination of whispering and whistling infinitely high on the musical scale." Its speed was incredibly fast; sometimes it was actually difficult for the eye to follow it. (Saunders, P. B., 1929.)

Economically *Microsorex hoyi* is so rare that it can have little effect on man's activities. It is essentially harmless in every way, feeds almost exclusively on insects, and is above all a most interesting mammal that should be given consideration as a part of our fauna.

Specimens examined from Wisconsin.—Total 3, as follows: *Dane County:* Madison, 1. *Milwaukee County:* Milwaukee, 1 (MM). *Racine County:* Racine, 1 (USNM).
Selected references.—Burt, W. H., 1946, pp. 96–99, 103; Jackson, H. H. T., 1928; Merriam, C. H., 1895 b; Miller, G. S., Jr., 1895; Prince, L. A., 1940; Sanborn, C. C., and D. Tibbitts, 1949.

Microsorex hoyi intervectus Jackson
Northwestern Pigmy Shrew

Microsorex hoyi intervectus Jackson, Proc. Biol. Soc. Washington 38: 125, November 13, 1925.
Microsorex hoyi intervectus Schmidt, p. 107, 1931; Barger, p. 10, 1952.

Vernacular name.—Intermediate pigmy shrew.
Identification marks.—Very similar externally to *Microsorex hoyi hoyi,* averaging slightly more grayish in summer pelage. Skull more angular than that of *M. h. hoyi,* with distinctly broader and higher brain case.
Measurements.—Total length of adults, 90 to 98 mm. (3.5 to 3.9 in.); tail, 28 to 32 mm. (1.1 to 1.3 in.); hind foot, 10 to 11 mm. (0.39 to 0.43

in.). Flank gland, about 10 mm. long. Weight, 2.8 to 4.0 grams (0.1 to 0.14 oz.). Skull length, 15.4 to 16.5 mm.; width, 6.8 to 7.4 mm.

Distribution in Wisconsin.—Known only from the northern half of the state north of 44° N. latitude (Jackson County), mostly in Canadian or upper Transition life zones.

Habitat.—Moist and log-strewn hemlock woods, damp grassy paper birch and aspen woods, white pine forest, sphagnaceous spruce and tamarack bogs, and aspen, and sweet fern environment on dry slopes.

Status and Habits.—So far as known like those of *Microsorex hoyi hoyi.* Although apparently a rare mammal in Wisconsin, *Microsorex hoyi intervectus* seems to be more plentiful than *M. h. hoyi.* In the Huron Mountains area of Michigan, a home range of one-half acre was assumed by Manville (1949: 68), which gave a population figure of 0.21 per acre on the plot he studied.

Specimens examined from Wisconsin.—Total 13, as follows: *Ashland County:* Bear Lake, 1 (UWZ). *Clark County:* Hewett Township, 2 (1 AMNH); Thorp Township, 1 (AMNH); Worden Township, 3 (1 AMNH, 1 UWZ). *Jackson County:* 6 mi. W. of Millston, 1 (UWZ). *Oconto County:* Lakewood, 1. *Oneida County:* Crescent Lake, 1; Rhinelander, 1 (UWZ). *Vilas County:* Lac Vieux Desert, 2 (CNHM).
Selected references.—Jackson, H. H. T., 1925 b; 1928; Schmidt, F. J. W., 1931.

Genus **Blarina** Gray
Short-tailed Shrews

Dental formula:

$$I \frac{3-3}{1-1}, \quad C \frac{1-1}{1-1}, \quad P \frac{3-3}{1-1}, \quad M \frac{3-3}{3-3} = 32.$$

Blarina brevicauda brevicauda (Say)
Giant Mole Shrew

Sorex brevicaudus Say, in S. H. Long and E. James Expedition to the Rocky Mountains, vol. 1, p. 164, 1823.
Sorex Dekayi Lapham, p. 338, 1853.
Sorex brevicaudus Lapham, p. 338, 1853.
Blarina talpoides Strong, p. 438, 1883.
Blarina brevicauda Strong, p. 438, 1883; Snyder, p. 124, 1902; Jackson, p. 32, 1908; Hollister, p. 29, 1910; Cory, p. 423, 1912.
Blarina brevicauda talpoides Schmidt, p. 105, 1931.
Blarina b. talpoides Komarek, p. 204, 1932.
Blarina brevicauda brevicauda Barger, p. 10, 1952.

Giant mole shrew BLARINA BREVICAUDA. *About* ¾ *natural size. U.S. Fish and Wildlife Service photograph.*

Vernacular names.—In Wisconsin usually called mole shrew, short-tailed shrew, or shrew mouse. Other names include baby mole, big short-tailed shrew, blarina, bob-tailed shrew, common mole shrew, common short-tailed shrew, giant blarina, giant short-tailed shrew, ground mole rat, large blarina, large bob-tailed shrew, large mole shrew, large short-tailed shrew, little mole, meadow mole, mole (particularly in localities where there are no true moles), mole mouse, mole rat, and mouse mole. The Ojibway and Cree Indians in Manitoba called this animal *Kin'-skee-sha-wah-wah-bee-gah-note-see* (sharp-nosed, short-tailed field mouse) (Seton, 1909: 1116).

Identification marks.—A large robust shrew, near the size of a small meadow mouse, with short tail (about one-fifth the total length, or one-fourth the length of head and body combined); ears small and inconspicuous, mostly concealed in the fur; eyes minute; snout sharp-pointed, somewhat proboscis-like, but comparatively shorter and heavier than that of other shrews; tail short, covered with hair; feet both fore and hind rather heavy and broad for a shrew, but not mole-like; five-toed. The hair is short and soft, producing a velvety fur.

In winter the upper parts are dark slate color or plumbeous, sometimes with a slight brownish cast; the under parts appear to be somewhat paler than the upper parts, an effect produced to some extent by the shorter, more compacted hair. Summer pelage is a shade paler than winter. Immature individuals are as a rule somewhat paler than adults, and more sleek and glossy on account of the shorter and more compacted hairs.

There are two molts annually. Transition from winter to summer fur may begin as early as April 27, as shown in a specimen of *B. b. kirtlandi* from Delavan, Wisconsin. The spring molting seems to be at its height from the last half of May through most of July, though a few molts are not completed until well into August. About one-half of the individuals have complete summer pelage by the last of July. The fall molt may, in rare instances, particularly in northern Wisconsin, begin as early as the last week of August, but usually this molt is at its height during September and the first half of October. Of ten specimens of *B. b. kirtlandi* from Wild Rose, seven are in nearly full winter pelage and three have winter fur coming in over the backs by September 16 and 17. By the last of October practically all individuals are in full winter fur. In both spring and autumn molts, the molting usually starts on the shoulders and back, and proceeds both forwards and backwards, and then downwards enveloping the under parts, though there is considerable irregularity as to the sequence of the molting. It appears to be a rather slow process in *Blarina* in most cases, though Hamilton (1931 a; 1940 a) contends that it is probably very rapid, basing his contention partly on the fact that of more than 1,000 adult shrews from New York available for study of pelage over a period of ten years, only 25 were molting. Out of 81 specimens of *Blarina brevicauda* (both subspecies *brevicauda* and *kirtlandi*) collected by the present author in various parts of Wisconsin between May and September of five different years, 30, or 37 per cent, were molting. During May and June fully half of the individuals were molting.

The skull is rather massive for a shrew, angular and with prominent ridges and processes; wider than that of any other Wisconsin shrew, both through brain case and interorbitally; lower jaw massive and angular, in keeping with general cranial characteristics. The teeth are heavier and pigmented deep chestnut at the tips; unicuspid teeth five in number in each side of upper jaw, grouped in pairs, the first two (second and third incisor) larger and subequal in size, followed by the second pair (canine and first premolar), much smaller but also subequal; the fifth unicuspid (third premolar) much smaller and invisible when the skull is viewed from the outside.

The males of *Blarina brevicauda* average a trifle larger than the females, a difference that shows more clearly in the skulls. There is no sexual variation in color. The flank gland is well developed in the male, but very small, indistinct, and usually invisible in the female. Younger animals appear paler and more slender than the adults, and the hair lies flatter and sleek against the body. The skull becomes more angular with advancing age, the tip of the rostrum tends to thicken, and the first incisors are forced downward. Winter pelage is a trifle longer than summer fur and a shade darker. Color mutations, particularly a trend towards albinism, seems to be more prevalent in this species than in other shrews. Sometimes this trend takes the characteristic of white blotches which may entirely encircle the body in a narrow ribbon. There are a few records of pure or near pure albinos, as, for example, a specimen of *Blarina brevicauda talpoides* collected April 22, 1936, at Rivière aux Chiens, Quebec, Canada, now mounted in the exhibition collection of The Provancher Society of Natural History of Canada, Quebec. Sometimes the albinistic tendency takes the form of a scattering of white hairs intermixed with the slate-colored ones over the entire animal, thus producing a peculiar pale gray effect. A few color mutations have eliminated the black and chocolate pigments and left the yellow producing a pale yellowish creamy buff color.

The species *Blarina brevicauda* can readily be distinguished from all other Wisconsin mammals

by the characters given above. It is similar in general proportions to *Cryptotis parva*, but in Wisconsin has more than three times the weight of *Cryptotis* and is more than 110 millimeters in total length, with a tail length of more than 20 millimeters, whereas *Cryptotis* is less than 85 millimeters long, with tail less than 20 millimeters long. Two subspecies occur in Wisconsin, namely, *Blarina brevicauda brevicauda* (Say) and *Blarina brevicauda kirtlandi* Bole and Moulthrop. The chief characters that distinguish *B. b. brevicauda* from *kirtlandi* are its larger size, slightly paler coloration, larger and more massive skull, and a tendency toward darker pigmentation on the teeth. Many of the specimens from the eastern part of its range in Wisconsin show intergradation with *kirtlandi,* but many of those from the Mississippi Valley are almost identical to specimens of *B. b. brevicauda* from the type region in eastern Nebraska. Some of the specimens from the south shore of Lake Superior average smaller than typical *B. b. brevicauda,* but are actually nearer to that form than to *kirtlandi.*

Measurements.—Total length of adults, 118 to 139 mm. (4.6 to 5.5 in.); tail, 23 to 32 mm. (0.9 to 1.3 in.); hind foot, 15 to 17 mm. (0.59 to 0.67 in.). Flank gland, 10.5 to 12 mm. long. Weight, 18 to 30 grams (0.64 to 1.06 oz.). Skull length, 23.6 to 24.8 mm.; width, 12.8 to 13.8 mm.

Distribution in Wisconsin.—The subspecies *brevicauda* occurs throughout western Wisconsin from Lake Superior south to the Illinois boundary, east as far as eastern Ashland County and Juneau County, and in general west of longitude 90° west.

Habitat.—The mole shrew, *Blarina brevicauda,* is about as unrestricted in habitat as any Wisconsin mammal. In times of its lower population densities it occurs more plentifully in damp brushy woodlands, bushy bogs and marshes, and weedy and bushy borders of fields, but may be taken almost any place where there is vegetative litter sufficient to offer cover. During normal or heavy populations it may be found in heavy timber of oak, spruce, white cedar, birch, or especially hemlock; in shrubby or weedy growth along brooks, lakes, sloughs, or marshes; in tamarack and spruce swamps and in sphagnum bogs; in damp grassy and willowy patches, or wet alder thickets; not infrequently in cultivated

Albino Blarina brevicauda *caught at Rivière aux Chiens, Quebec, April 22, 1936. Courtesy of Dr. D-A. Dery.*

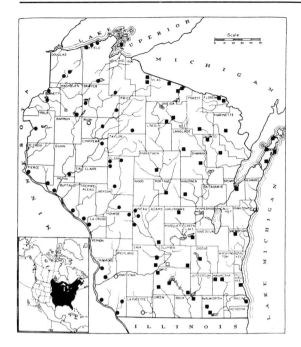

Map 10. *Distribution of* BLARINA BREVICAUDA. *Solid symbols = specimens examined. Open symbols = authentic records.* ●, ○ = B. B. BREVICAUDA. ■, □ = B. B. KIRTLANDI.

fields, and particularly in bushy borders of fields; in flower and vegetable gardens, fence rows, and beside country roads; even sometimes in the dry sand of central Wisconsin and on top of the bluffs along the Mississippi River; in the rocks and sand where there is any vegetation along the shores of Lake Superior and Lake Michigan; in winter sometimes it comes into cellars, barns, and sheds; in fact, in almost any conceivable location where it has ground or litter cover. It is slow in rehabiting forest burns.

Status and Habits.—The mammal population of any area is subject to variation, if not cycles, and this is the case with *Blarina brevicauda.* At the peak of its population there are probably more mole shrews in the state than any other one species of mammal. Its population density per acre of habitat may not be as great as that of some other mammals, such as, for example, the meadow vole (*Microtus pennsylvanicus*), or the brown rat (*Rattus norvegicus*), but its habitation in amost every ecological niche in the state gives it an aggregate of huge numbers. Assuming conservatively that three-fifths (32,829

square miles) of the total land area of 54,715 square miles in the state (Batschelet and Proudfoot, 1942: 16) is suitable habitat for *Blarina* and that there is an average of four to the acre throughout this habitat, then we would have a population of more than 84 million mole shrews in Wisconsin. This is not an exaggerated possibility of a normal population for this species, since it has had recorded populations of 4 (Shull, 1907), 8 (Hamilton, 1931 a), 48 (Bole, 1939), 50 (Seton, 1909), and 104 (Townsend, 1935: 67) per acre. In northwestern Pennsylvania it was considered that about 25 shrews per acre was near average in a normal or favorable habitat. In trapping small mammals at Milton, Wisconsin, on the night of August 30, 1922, I set 60 snap and Schuyler mouse traps 12 feet apart along a weedy and bushy fence strip 720 feet long and 10 feet wide that separated a clover-timothy field from a cornfield. My catch the following morning was 42 *Blarina b. kirtlandi*, 7 *Microtus p. pennsylvanicus*, 2 *Peromyscus m. bairdii*, 2 *Mus musculus*, and 1 *Microtus o. ochrogaster.* It can be seen that the population density of *Blarina* for this small area could be considered as 253 per acre, particularly since the traps were set in line through the middle of the strip. The estimate was made at an optimum time for a high population, in that most of the young of the year were active, and it probably was at the high point in the *Blarina* cycle. The excessive number of shrews may have accounted for the relatively small number of mice. During low populations mole shrews may be actually scarce in favorable habitats, and at such times the total population in the state is probably reduced to only a few million. The home range may depend some on food availability. When food is plentiful the shrew may not travel more than 50 feet from its home site, and thus have a range of less than one-eighth acre. Usually the home range is larger than this, in the neighborhood of one-half acre. Occasionally individuals may travel in all directions 200 feet or more from the home site, and thus have a home range of more than two acres. The ranges not only of individuals but of pairs and families often broadly overlap. J. Dewey Soper on November 13, 1943, set a single trap at a strategic point in a subsurface well-worn runway of this shrew under the leafy litter of a dry, wooded lot only 12 feet from the side of his house, one-half mile from the Red River and one mile south of the limits of Winnipeg, Manitoba. Between that date and November 25 he captured thirteen *Blarina* in the one trap at the same location (Soper, 1944).

Tracks of shrews in snow. Left, Cinereous shrew. Middle, Giant mole shrew, walking. Right, Giant mole shrew, galloping. ½×.

Excrement of BLARINA B. BREVICAUDA. *About 1½×. After A. F. Shull.*

One of the chief evidences of the presence of a *Blarina* is its characteristic runways, which are usually less than an inch in diameter and thread in a crooked and twisting line on the surface or, more often, under grass, leaves, or other vegetation, or even slightly underground, rambling hither and yon. In dry soil it usually burrows deeper than in moist soil, where it is more apt to come to the surface. Sometimes the mole shrew uses the runways of mice, particularly those of *Microtus*, which are usually made in a more nearly straight line. It also at times enters the runways of moles. At other times fragments of uneaten hard parts of insects may give a clue to its presence. Its scats or feces are quite dis-

tinctive, being about an inch long and rather slender, but always spindle-shaped, more or less twisted in a corkscrew manner. They are dark greenish-brown in color. These scats are sometimes found in the runways, or scattered here and there nearby. Scats of *Microtus* are only one-quarter inch long, not coiled, and are less spindle-shaped. The mole shrew may occasionally be seen if one has the patience to watch for it after hearing a rustling in the leaves. A slight quick movement of the vegetation shows its location, and it may dash into view momentarily. In winter it not infrequently leaves runways or tracks on the snow that are not difficult to identify. It often burrows just below the surface of soft snow and leaves a ridge of snow not unlike the ridge of soil thrown up by a mole. New snow falls and the burrows are extended until an accumulation of deep snow is often found full of its runways and tunnels. Its tracks with foot marks alternating are easily distinguished from the paired footprints of most mice, and I have often trailed mole shrews on the snow many yards in zero winter weather. Trails and runways of *Blarina* on the surface of the snow are usually not so erratic and irregular as their runways on the ground.

Neither hibernation nor migration enter the life of this shrew. It is active summer and winter, night and day. Normally it is more nocturnal than diurnal, though it is frequently very active on humid cloudy days. It seems to become active any time it has an urge to procure food, seeking shelter underground or under vegetation from bright sunlight. While it may not have accurate application, it is of interest that in 640 trap days (September 14 to 23, 1917) at Wild Rose and Green Lake, Wisconsin, when the traps were tended regularly near 6:00 A.M. and again near 6:00 P.M. each day, 55 per cent of the *Blarina* were taken in the morning (overnight) catch and 45 per cent in the evening (daytime) catch. The season of this trapping was close to the equinox. At Solon Springs, Douglas County, about 3:00 P.M., July 29, 1919, a very bright day, I caught a specimen within fifteen minutes after I had set the trap.

Although each movement of this shrew appears quick and energetic, and it is incessantly on the go during its times of activity, it actually is slow in progressing in its usual trotlike gait, and can easily be overtaken by a man walking slowly. Its normal trot on the surface of the ground seldom exceeds two miles an hour, although it could travel three miles an hour under exceptional pressure to escape. At times, when in a hurry, it bounds and lopes, but even in this stride it makes but little if any faster progress, since its short heavy legs are not built for speed. Its body is somewhat curved dorsally, back elevated, and its tail usually erect when it is running. Although almost strictly terrestrial, it will occasionally ascend trees in search of food, and has been known to climb six feet up a red oak about eight inches in diameter to partake of suet in a bird feeder. "The surprising feature was that on his trip down the tree he did not keep entirely on the upper side of the trunk, but went on a diagonal course, finishing his journey on the under side" (Carter, 1936: 285). The mole shrew digs well in loose soil, using its forefeet and nose in the operation, but once the runway or burrow is well started it digs mostly by use of its snout, forcing its way through the soil by backward movements of the feet. Through leaf mold, humus, or other loose soil it can progress at the rate of about 15 to 20 feet an hour. The *Blarina* swims well, though slowly, dog fashion, but although not particularly averse to water it is not frequently found swimming.

Not being a sociable or truly gregarious mammal, *Blarina brevicauda* has little need for communication or call signals. It may become excessively numerous in a habitat, but only from overpopulation, and not because of a herding or flocking tendency as is the case with the little mole shrew. When two individuals of the larger species meet in a runway or elsewhere they emit shrill cries or shrieks in angry protest. If the unwelcome contact continues the animals will utter sharp, shrill chatterings. This chattering usually starts with a high-pitched squeal and continues and ends with a rapid succession of short notes like *zee-zee-zee-zee-zee-zee-zee*, not dissimilar to the chatter made by some species of bats. When contented, as when feeding, this shrew frequently utters a low, continuous, and rather musical twitter.

Nervous and irritable, the short-tailed shrew is tolerant of nothing that disturbs it, not even of its own kind, with the exception of its mate during the breeding season. It is not as sensitive in some ways as certain long-tailed shrews (*Sorex*) and is not apt to die from fright or shock alone as its cousins apparently do. As with most shrews, nevertheless, whenever the animal is awake its snout and head are in constant motion, seeking out food or enemy.

My caged specimens, both male and female, exhibited great pugnacity. When I touched one several times with a stick, it would become much enraged, snapping and crying out angrily. When attacked by a meadow mouse (*Arvicola scalopsoides*) confined in a cage with it one fought fiercely; and though it did not pursue its adversary when the latter moved off, neither did it ever retreat; but the instant the mouse came close, it sprang at him, apparently not guided in the least by sight. It kept its nose and whiskers constantly moving from side to side, and often sprang forward with an angry cry, when the mouse was near, as if deceived in thinking it had heard or felt a movement in that direction. In fighting it did not spring up high, nor attempt to leap upon its adversary, as the mouse, but jerked itself along, stopping firmly, with the fore-feet well forward, and the head high. On coming in contact with the mouse, it snapped at him, and, though it sometimes rose on its hind-feet in the struggle, I did not observe that it used its fore-feet as weapons of offense, like the arvicolae. Its posture, when on guard, was always with the feet spread and firmly braced, and the head held with the snout pointing upwards, and the mouth and chin forward, in which position its eyes would have been of no use, could it have seen. The motions of this animal, when angry, are characterized by a peculiar firmness; the muscles appear to be held very rigid, while the movements are made by quick energetic jerks. Such springs, either backward, forward, or sidewise, appear to be made with equal readiness (Kennicott, 1858: 95).

In keeping with its general nervous disposition, it does not, so far as known, indulge in play as does its relative *Cryptotis*.

The sense of touch, particularly in the snout and vibrissae, is highly developed, so much so in fact that even the air vibrations caused by a slight movement of an insect or other animal are detected by the shrew. Similarly, it does not run into an obstacle in its path, but stops quickly before touching it, except possibly with the vibrissae. The eyes of the mole shrew are so poorly developed that they are of little use to the animal, except possibly to tell lightness from darkness or to distinguish a dark shadow. The sense of hearing is fairly acute, and although it does not react to sharp noises made considerable distances from it, it always reacts to a sound of almost any pitch or intensity made close to it. Inasmuch as it also reacts to almost any vibration, such as, for example, jarring of the ground, its reaction to sound may result from its response to any vibration, and thus be an accentuated tactile sense. Its sense of smell is good, though not so well developed as its tactile sense, and it depends upon smell not a little in its search for food.

When mice or beef were placed in the cage the shrew almost invariably came out of its burrow in a short time. It rarely did so when the lid was merely raised and lowered, or when other objects, as the water dish, were put in. In the case of the mouse, the response may have been due either to the trembling of the soil as the mouse ran about, or to the odor of the mouse; but with the beef, the disturbance of the ground was eliminated. When the shrew was above ground it was always going about with its nose slightly elevated and its nostrils dilated and contracting rapidly in unison with movements of the side of the body, as if sniffing the air (Shull, 1907: 512–13).

While he was trapping for weasels near Madison, Wisconsin, A. W. Schorger suspended snap-traps perpendicularly from nails on the sides of stumps so that the bait, raw beef, would be a few inches above the snow. "On the morning of December 29, 1945, I found a short-tailed shrew (*Blarina brevicauda brevicauda*) in one of the traps. The shrew had burrowed up through the snow, that was 7 inches deep, directly beneath the bait. Since the latter was 3 inches above the snow, it was necessary for the shrew to stand upon its hind legs in order to reach the bait. It would appear therefore that this species can discover food by scent at distances considerably greater than has been assumed" (Schorger, 1947: 180). The mole shrew is the most robust and probably the strongest of the Wisconsin shrews. Its body is a mass of nervous muscular energy in tense activity more than half the time. These periods of activity last from three to six or more hours, when, particularly if the shrew is well fed, it will sleep for two or more hours. Its normal temperature varies from 34.5° C. to 36.5° C., the average being 35.7° C. or 96.3° F. The potential longevity of the mole shrew is nearly three years, but the normal life span is usually less than this, probably not more than 18 or 20 months.

In Europe as far back as the seventeenth century it was a belief that the bite of a shrew was poisonous. In the first shrew-poison case known in this country, C. J. Maynard reported being bitten in January, 1889, receiving four small punctures at the base of the second finger of his left hand and then four similar ones at the base of the second finger on the right hand, by a short-tailed shrew (*Blarina*) that he had picked up in his hand.

All this occupied perhaps thirty seconds, when I began to experience a burning sensation in the first two bites, followed by a peculiar sensation . . . in the right hand. I walked to the house, only a few hundred yards away, but by this time, the pain which had been rapidly increasing, had become quite severe, and by the time I had placed the shrew in an improvised cage, I was suffering acutely.

The burning sensation, first observed, predominated in the immediate vicinity of the wounds, but was now greatly intensified, accompanied by shooting pains, radiating in all directions from the punctures but more especially running along the arm, and in half an hour, they had reached as high as the elbow. All this time, the parts in the immediate vicinity of the wounds, were swelling, and around the punctures the flesh had become whitish.

I bathed the wounds in alcohol and in a kind of liniment, but with little effect. The pain and swelling reached its maximum development in about an hour, but I could not use my left hand without suffering great pain for three days, nor did the swelling abate much before that time. At its greatest development, the swelling on the left hand caused that member to be nearly twice its ordinary thickness at the wound, but appeared to be confined to the immediate vicinity of the bites, and was not as prominent on the right hand; in fact, the first wound given was by far the most severe.

The burning sensation disappeared that night, but the shooting pains were felt, with less and less severity, upon exertion of the hand, from the elbow downward, for a week, and did not entirely disappear until the total abatement of the swelling, which occurred in about a fortnight (Maynard, 1889: 57–58).

Maynard recognized the fact that there was a poison secretion for he commented, "undoubtedly the shrew that bit me, was as poisonous as a rattlesnake in proportion to its size, and had it inflicted a wound on the tender skin of a child this would have proved serious." He minimized the incident, however, by saying that "it is a well known fact that an enraged animal, even a man is capable of inflicting a poisonous wound, and this may be the case in the present instance" (Maynard: 58–59). More than 50 years passed before Dr. Oliver P. Pearson (1942) made a study of the poison in the bite of *Blarina brevicauda,* the results of which he summarizes:

1. A poisonous extract has been prepared from the submaxillary salivary glands of the shrew, *Blarina brevicauda.*

2. A toxic material is also present in the saliva and may be introduced into wounds made by the teeth.

3. The toxic effect of the extract is characterized by a local reaction, lowering of the blood pressure, slowing of the heart, and inhibition of respiration.

4. A lethal dose for a 20 gram mouse is provided by the extract of 5.7 mg. of fresh submaxillary tissue when injected intraperitoneally, or of 0.4 mg. by intravenous injection. The lethal dose for rabbits injected intravenously is extract of approximately 7 mg. per kilogram of body weight.

5. The toxic material is soluble in water and salt solution, but not in acetone. Heating to 100° C. in neutral or acid solution does not abolish the toxic effect. Similar heating in basic solution destroys the effect.

6. Injection of large amounts of the parotid salivary glands of *Blarina* produces no serious effect on mice, cats, or rabbits (Pearson, 1942: 165).

Barbara Lawrence has further compared the poison of *Blarina* and its reaction with that of poisonous reptiles.

It has long been known that venom is useful to snakes primarily in helping them to overcome their prey and in defense. More recently it has been discovered that this secretion of the parotid glands has a digestive function. Certain ferment-like substances are present in venom in varying amounts. Among them is a strong proteolytic ferment capable of completely disintegrating muscle tissue in a very short time. Various facts suggest that such a substance may also be present in the secretions of the submaxillary gland of *Blarina.* Anyone who has trapped shrews has found that they have to be skinned almost immediately to prevent the hair on the belly from slipping. If left for any length of time, the whole ventral body wall seems to dissolve away. It is also true that *Blarina* is able to eat and digest unusually large amounts of protein food.

All the evidence available on the effect of *Blarina* poison and of reptile venom, particularly that of the cobra, suggests very strongly that these salivary secretions resemble each other closely. Since snake venom is known to have a strong digestive action on protein, it is further suggested that *Blarina* saliva, in contrast to that of other mammals, may also have this property (Lawrence, 1946: 395–96).

Sexual activity may begin as early as the last part of February, but usually does not occur until late in March or early in April. The mating behavior and reproduction have been studied by Dr. Pearson, who writes,

All shrews do not follow the same pattern of courtship and mating behavior because there are individual variations of temperament and degrees of receptivity. . . . The most important fact to be kept in mind is that shrews are nervous, ill-tempered, unsociable, and frequently blood-thirsty. Two shrews will seldom live amicably in the same cage unless they have been raised together from birth. It has been my custom to keep each shrew in a separate cage and to put two animals together when a mating is desired. . . . When he first encounters the female, both animals act as if surprised, squeak loudly, and scurry toward opposite corners of the cage. If the female is receptive subsequent meetings may be progressively less frightening to her until she finally displays a willingness to accept the male. If the male is timid, the first dozen encounters may frighten him as much as the first. Sooner or later, however, he overcomes his fear and begins to pursue the female. When this turning point in his behavior is reached, he begins to utter a stream of dry, unmusical clicks which may be described as a chitter, similar to the sound made by a twig brushing against a bicycle wheel in which the spokes are loose. This is heard only when the male is pursuing the female, and is easily distinguished from the loud squeaks and more "musical" song which is emitted by males and females at other times. When the female is not receptive, she faces the male whenever he is near and repulses his advances with lunges, loud squeaks, and sometimes a shrill chatter. The male remains a few inches away and may be excited into a similar song which only serves to excite the female further. A contest of shrill singing ensues until one of the participants retreats hastily to a distant corner of the cage. . . . If the female is totally unreceptive when the male is placed in her cage, a fight may ensue in which one of the shrews may be killed and eaten (Pearson, 1944: 48–49).

. . . Copulating pairs become locked together and, except when disturbed, are unable to separate voluntarily for a considerable time: as long as 25 minutes in one case. The mean duration of 315 timed matings was 4.7 minutes. The female is usually more active than the male while they are coupled and scurries about, dragging the male, tail-first, behind her. Withdrawal of the penis is probably hindered by small, pointed epidermal ridges encircling the glans, . . . by lateral expansion of the glans, . . . chiefly, however, by the penis becoming rigid after it has passed around one or more sharp bends of the vagina. . . . A pair may mate twenty or more times in 1 day (Pearson, 1944: 77).

The gestation period is 21 to 22 days, and usually two broods, sometimes three, are reared during the breeding season, March to September. In some cases at least, pregnant females have been captured that were still nursing young. It would appear that a pair may be mated throughout an entire breeding season, if not for life, which in this species would not be long. Young may be born as early as the first week in April, but most litters seem to be born in May or June. In Wisconsin, there appears to be a gradual tapering off in the breeding after July until it is nearly nonexistent by September, though Hamilton (1929: 128) states, "From these observations I should say that two litters are produced annually in central New York, one in spring and another in the late summer." The number of young, as indicated by embryos, varies from three to ten, though the average number of embryos is slightly below seven. The average number of young reaching an age of a few days is between five and six, and inasmuch as the mother has only six teats, rarely do more than six young survive. The young one at birth is about 25 mm. (one inch) long, weighs a little more than one gram, is void of hair except for a trace of the vibrissae, and has a wrinkled pinkish skin. Its eyes are closed and functionless. The mother is very attentive to the young, which grow rapidly, become covered with hair when ten days old, and are nearly half-grown when two weeks old. Soon afterwards, when 18 or 20 days old, they leave the nest, and when three months old they are essentially mature animals. The sex ratio is about 50:50, although some authors claim there are slightly more males than females.

Runways appear zigzagging here and there on the surface of the ground just under vegetation or vegetative litter, but longer runways appear underneath the surface, sometimes as deep as twenty inches or more, but more frequently at depths of four to eight inches. In these runways two types of nests are made, namely, a comparatively small resting nest and a larger more elab-

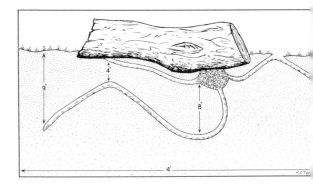

Nest of BLARINA B. BREVICAUDA *with adjoining runway. Drawn by Mrs. Tabb from rough sketches and photographs made by the author on the Mississippi River bottoms below Pepin, Wisconsin.*

orate breeding nest. The breeding nest is usually made by enlarging and adding nesting material to a resting nest occupied by the female. Ordinarily it is six to ten inches long and some four to six inches in diameter externally, enclosing a cozy globular nest cavity three or four inches in diameter. There are usually three openings, one at either end to the main runway and one at the bottom which passes downward to escape runways. Rarely, there may be more than three openings. The nest is made of whole or broken leaves, coarse grass, and plant fibers, and is not of finely shredded material as are the nests of most mice. The breeding nest is usually located under a log, stump, rock, or other object, and is apt to be nearer the surface of the ground than the resting nest, which, other than in possible location, differs from the breeding nest chiefly in its smaller size and greater numbers. Each resting nest is occupied by only one animal. At Pepin, Wisconsin, the morning of July 2, 1920, I found a nest containing seven nearly hairless young under a log near a grassy slough, along the Mississippi River. The nest was about seven inches long, three inches in diameter, and two and one-half inches deep externally, and lay lengthwise of the log and directly under it with no soil covering. Internally the nesting chamber was three and one-half inches long, two inches wide, and one and one-half inches deep. The runway extended from each end of the nest lengthwise of the log. Another entrance to the nest led perpendicularly to the principal runway and left the log at the side. I collected three of the young shrews for specimens, leaving four in the nest, but when I revisited it again that afternoon only two remained. The morning of July 3 the nest and two drowned young were submerged six inches under the rising water. Feces of the short-tailed shrew are seldom found inside the nest, it being the habit of the animal to deposit them in little piles in the runways. Dry hard food remains such as snail shells or chitinous parts of insects are often found in or near the nest.

The short-tailed shrew is a tremendous eater with an insatiable appetite and rapid digestion and assimilation. It feeds largely on insects and other invertebrates, though it consumes considerable flesh of vertebrates, particularly young mice, and a small amount of plant material. The feeding habits and food of *Blarina* have been studied by several biologists. In his studies in Michigan, Shull (1907: 519) summarizes the food and feeding thus:

1. *Blarina brevicauda* preys upon various snails of the genus Polygyra, at least in winter. 2. These snails are hoarded, and are in general moved to the surface of the ground as the temperature falls and into the burrows as it rises. 3. Empty shells which are brought to the surface are not moved back into the burrows. . . . 4. Empty shells not left at the surface are stored about the nests, along the burrows, or in special chambers. 5. Other principal foods are voles [40 per cent], insects [adult 20 per cent, immature 20 per cent], earthworms [5 per cent], and snails [15 per cent].

Vegetable foods, except nuts, he did not find employed. More detailed and recent research on the food of *Blarina* based on the examination of 244 intestinal tracts from New York state for all seasons of the year give these percentages: 78.7 per cent animal food, of which insects constitute 47.8 per cent, worms, 7.2 per cent, crustacea, 6.7 per cent, mollusks, 5.4 per cent, vertebrates (mice 4, birds 2, salamanders 3), 4.1 per cent, centipedes, 3.8 per cent, arachnids, 2.0 per cent, and millipedes, 1.7 per cent; plant material was 11.4 per cent, undetermined matter 5.2 per cent, and inorganic matter 2.3 per cent; stomachs empty, 2.4 per cent. Stomachs collected only during the winter (December 15 to March 15) showed an increase of insects to 58.6 per cent, plant remains to 25.3 per cent, and vertebrates to 7.6 per cent (Hamilton, 1930: 30–31).

Normal food for a meal may be indicated in the contents of a stomach I examined from a male *Blarina* collected at Milton, Rock County, November 7, 1909, that consisted of half a small earthworm, the remains of one fly (apparently the horsefly, *Tabanus*), flesh and a small fragment of bone of a young meadow vole, two beetle larvae, and a few grass stems and roots. The mole shrew consumes no small number of nuts, particularly beechnuts and acorns, but it is possible it is attracted to the larvae of weevils and other insects that occur therein, rather than to the nuts. It will, however, readily take peanut butter, English walnut meats, and other nuts when used as bait in traps.

Mr. Francis Zirrer, in a letter of March 25, 1942 to the author, writes that this shrew was extremely abundant at his place in northwestern Rusk County in 1935.

The place was so overrun with them that upon every turn one or two were seen. Our cats, after killing some, would let them move among them without paying the least attention. They appeared to be very hungry; they tried to devour pieces of old, porous bones; and upon more than one occasion one would tug at a bone held in my hand, apparently unable to see or realize the possible danger. In the rabbit hutch they ate potatoes, bread, oatmeal, and other grain. If one would drown in a dish of water, and, in winter, freeze in it, the others would devour it immediately. A snake (*Elaphe vulpina*) that, after it had attacked and swallowed a fledgling of the rose-breasted grosbeak was killed and thrown on the refuse pile, was shortly after save the skin and the bones entirely devoured.

Observations on the food habits of *Blarina* as observed in southern New York by Theodore Roosevelt, former president of the United States, and sent to Dr. C. Hart Merriam in December, 1888, are of interest.

Of course its food consists mainly of insects, such as ants, ground beetles, caterpillars, or earthworms, and of these it consumes enormous quantities, for it has a most insatiable appetite. But any small or weak vertebrate will be taken quite as readily. Once, while walking through the woods in the late evening, my attention was attracted by the cries of a small pair of Ovenbirds or Golden-crowned Thrushes, and on approaching I found them hovering about their domed nest in great distress. As I stooped to look into it a small animal jumped out; I caught it at once, and it proved to be a Mole Shrew, while inside the nest the torn and bloody remains of three poor little nestlings explained only too clearly the alarm of the parent birds.

I once kept one of these stout little Shrews for some weeks in a wire cage, and certainly a more bloodthirsty animal of its size I never saw. In the day it seemed rather confused by the glare, and spent most of its time in a small heap of dried grass, but with the approach of dark it became restless, running round and round the cage, and occasionally uttering a low, fine squeak. Its eyes did not seem to be very good, but its sense of smell was evidently excellent, and it seemed to rely mainly on its nose in discovering its prey. For the first few days I fed it only on insects, which it devoured greedily, holding them down firmly with its fore paws. Then one day I placed a nearly full grown Pine Mouse in the cage. The Shrew smelt it at once and rushed out. The mouse was hopping about, raising itself on its hind legs and examining the walls of its prison, when it was suddenly seized from behind by the bloodthirsty little Shrew. It squeaked piteously, and tried to use its long incisors on its antagonist; indeed I think it did inflict one bite, but in spite of this, and of its struggling and scratching, it was very soon killed and partially eaten. Two days afterward I introduced a young garter-snake, about seven inches long, into the cage. The little snake at first moved slowly about, and then coiled itself up on a piece of flannel. The Shrew had come out from its nest, but did not seem to see the snake, and returned to it. Soon afterward it came out again and quartered across the cage. While doing so it evidently struck the scent (the snake all the time was in plain sight), raised its nose, turned sharply around and ran rapidly up to the flannel. It did not attack at once, as with the mouse, but cautiously smelt its foe, while the little snake moved its head uneasily and hissed slightly, then with a jump the Shrew seized it low down, quite near the tail. The snake at once twisted itself right across the Shrew's head and under one paw, upsetting him; but he recovered himself at once, and before the snake could escape flung himself on it again, and this time seized it by the back of the neck, placing one paw against the head and the other on the neck, and pushing the body from him while he tore it with his sharp teeth. The snake writhed and twisted, but it was of no use, for his neck was very soon more than half eaten through, and during the next twenty-four hours he was entirely devoured.

Previous to President Roosevelt's account of *Blarina* attacking the pine mouse and garter snake, Merriam had conducted interesting observations on the short-tailed shrew as a mouser.

I had not previously known that the Shrew was a mouse-eater. . . . Therefore having caught a vigorous though undersized Shrew, I put him in a large wooden box and provided him with an ample supply of beechnuts, which he ate eagerly. He was also furnished with a saucer of water from which he frequently drank. After he had remained two days in these quarters, I placed in the box with him an uninjured and very active white-footed mouse. The Shrew at the time weighed 11.20 grammes, while the mouse which was a large adult male weighed just 17 grammes. No sooner did the Shrew become aware of the presence of the mouse than he gave chase. The mouse, though much larger than the Shrew, showed no disposition to fight, and his superior agility enabled him, for a long time, easily to evade his pursuer, for at a single leap he would pass over the latter's head and to a considerable distance beyond. The Shrew labored at great disadvantage, not only from his inability to keep pace with the mouse, but also, and to a still greater extent, from his defective eyesight. He frequently passed within two inches of the mouse without knowing of his whereabouts. But he was persistent and explored over and over again every part of the box, constantly putting the mouse to flight. Indeed, it was by sheer perseverance that he so harassed the mouse, that the latter, fatigued by almost continuous exertion, and also probably weakened by fright, was no longer able to escape. He was first caught by the tail; this proved a temporary stimulant, and he bounded several times across the box, dragging his adversary after him. The Shrew did not seem in the least disconcerted at being thus harshly jerked about his domicile, but continued the pursuit with great determination. He next seized the mouse in its side, which resulted in a rough and tumble, the two rolling over and over and biting each other with much energy. The mouse freed himself, but was so exhausted that the Shrew had no difficulty in keeping alongside, and soon had him by the ear. The mouse rolled and kicked and scratched and bit, but to no avail. The Shrew was evidently much pleased and forthwith began to devour the ear. When he had it about half eaten-off the mouse again tore himself free; but his inveterate little foe did not suffer him to escape. This time the Shrew clamored up over his back and was soon at work consuming the remainder of the ear. This being satisfactorily accomplished, he continued to push on in the same direction till he had cut through the skull and eaten the brains, together with the whole side of the head and part of the shoulder. This completed his first meal, which occupied not quite fifteen minutes after the death of the mouse. As soon as he had finished eating I again placed him on the scales and found that he weighed exactly 12. grammes—an increase of .80 gramme.

The Shrew was half an hour in tiring the mouse, and another half hour in killing him (Merriam, C. H., 1884: 66–68).

It would seem to be much easier for a shrew to kill a mouse confined in a cage or box than one in the open, and under normal circumstances in nature mice would not form a dominant portion of the food of *Blarina*. Nevertheless, particularly in winter, mice may form a significant part of the food, and during years of high mouse abundance may become a major food item, as at Ithaca, New York, early in 1943, where mouse remains had a frequency of 56 per cent in two hundred scats of *Blarina* examined (Eadie, 1944: 361). In Clark County, Wisconsin, F. J. W. Schmidt "heard a loud squeaking in the snow, and upon investigating found a large meadow mouse fighting a short-tailed shrew. The mouse was nearly dead from loss of blood due to cuts on the neck, but was unable to bite through the tough skin on the neck of the shrew" (Schmidt, 1931: 105). William J. Hamilton, Jr., states, "My observations with several shrews carried on for an entire spring convince me that one half the shrew's weight in food is ample for it over a 24 hour period, and more often than not, only one half of this much is daily eaten. I had a 22 gram shrew eat 20 grams of cutworms in as many hours, but this appeared to be exceptional, and the creature was sluggish after such a repast" (Hamilton, 1930: 34). Other observers, however, have claimed that a short-tailed shrew will eat more than its own weight in 24 hours. One captured in northern Indiana and observed in captivity at Northwestern University over a ten-day period had a mean daily food consumption of approximately 1.7 times its own weight, and drank a mean of 9.1 cubic centimeters of water daily during that time. Be that as it may, *Blarina* is a heavy eater and has a large food requirement. Hamilton claims *Blarina* can fast 24 and 36 hours without apparent ill effects, but does not indicate whether his animal drank water during that period. Water is quite important to *Blarina,* and animals kept in captivity frequently drink. Animals caught alive in box traps often die in the trap within a few hours. Such deaths may be caused by starvation, but more likely are usually due to thirst, temperature, fright, or nervous tension.

The mole shrew stores food, especially for winter, but may store at any season. It was found storing snails by Shull (1907: 514) in Michigan, and others have found storage material left in little piles by a mole shrew.

The habits of captive shrews would certainly indicate a propensity for storing food. When my short-tailed shrews were given more food than suited their appetite at one time, the excess food would be taken into the nest box and stored under the moss in a corner. More often than not, the greater part thus put away would turn bad before the animals were ready to eat it. Both animal and plant food was treated in this manner. Salamanders would be cut into several pieces, but raisins, sowbugs, and other small things were stored intact. The storage habit was particularly pronounced in a nursing shrew, which refused to leave her young for long at a time (Hamilton, 1930: 36).

The mole shrew is so well protected by its habits and the scent from its glands that no animals depend upon it for food. Fish, especially members of the pickerel tribe and trout, have been known to capture them, and I once took one from the stomach of a large-mouthed black bass. One was taken also from the stomach of a green sunfish (*Lepomis cyanellus*) in southern Illinois (Huish and Hoffmeister, 1947: 198). There are several records of remains of *Blarina* being found in the intestinal tract of snakes, notably the water snake (*Natrix*), pine snake, rattlesnake, and copperhead. A *Blarina* that I had caught across the shoulders in a snap mousetrap on the Big Levels Game Refuge, Augusta County, Virginia, in August, 1935, was swallowed tail first up to the trap limitation by a copperhead caught in the act. Among the birds that sometimes prey on the short-tailed shrew are most of the species of hawks and owls, and the shrikes. In Rock County I have frequently seen the body of a *Blarina* impaled on the thorn of a thornapple bush by either the migrant shrike (*Lanius ludovicianus migrans*) or the northern shrike (*L. borealis*). "Remains of shrews, mostly short-tailed (*Blarina brevicauda*), were represented in 130 (2.7 per cent) of the total pellets and stomachs" of the great horned owls examined from southern Wisconsin and Iowa (Errington, Hamerstrom, and Hamerstrom, 1940: 793). At Milton, a juvenile great-horned owl that I had in captivity in 1902 ate the bodies, both skinned and entire, of many mole shrews, and two adult screech owls that had freedom in my den in 1904 ate fresh bodies of this shrew with apparent relish. Native carnivorous mammals such as the red fox, gray fox, weasel (*Mustela erminea* and *M. frenata*), striped skunk, bobcat, possibly the coyote, and likely many other mammals kill numbers of mole shrews, but, with the exception of the weasel, seldom eat them. Even weasels sometimes are reluctant to attack shrews. In December, 1920, in Vermont, Kirk had a trap set for weasels under a brushy fence. "The place was infested with blarinas and they were attracted to the rabbit bait and caught regularly. A weasel will take almost any kind of bait in the form of flesh, but tracks in the snow showed that if a Bonaparte weasel approached the trap when it held a shrew, it kept at a distance of four inches, and refused to touch the bait. The *Blarina* was removed and the next morning the trap held a weasel" (Kirk, 1921: 111). The house cat also kills many, as does the domestic dog, but neither animal eats the shrew.

Mole shrews, in their frequent fights with one another, often kill each other, and the victor may even devour its opponent. Deaths from these fights may be the reason for dead mole shrews being found so often without any evidence of their having being killed by other enemies. Their short life span and premature senescence may also be a factor here. Floods and high water frequently play havoc by drowning many, particularly the young in the nest. The death toll from automobiles and other vehicles is probably low, but is possibly higher than known cases would indicate.

Jameson has made a study of the external parasites of *Blarina brevicauda* based on the examination of 405 specimens of the shrew collected in Welland County, Ontario, and Tompkins County, New York, and which should be fairly applicable to conditions in Wisconsin. He found represented sixteen species of mites; five species of beetles, only one of which (*Leptinus americanus*) may have been parasitic; and nine species of fleas. He found no ticks, although ticks have been collected from the mole shrew.

One flea (*Nearotopsylla genalis*) is strictly a winter species, a second species (*Doratopsylla blarinae*) is essentially a summer flea, and a third (*Ctenoph-*

thalmus pseudagyrtes) occurs throughout the year. Of the external parasites typical of the short-tailed shrew two species (*Myonyssus jamesoni* and *Myobia simplex*) are restricted to it; eight species (*Protomyobia claparedei, Euschongastia blarinae, Trombicula jamesoni, Myocoptes* sp., *Listrophorus* sp., *Hirstionyssus* sp., *Doratopsylla blarinae,* and *Nearctopsylla genalis*) are more or less restricted to, and characteristic of, soricid shrews; and four species (*Euhaemogamasus leponyssoides, Haemogamasus alaskensis, Comatacarus americanus,* and *Ctenophthalmus pseudagyrtes*) parasitize blarinas, but are also common on un-related small mammal associates (Jameson, 1950: 145).

Internal parasites include frequent cestodes in the intestines, small and large, and quantities of nematodes in the stomach, duodenum, and small intestine. Hamilton (1931 a: 103) says: "Other roundworms occur just under the integument of the rump and shoulder region, imbedded in the mesenchyme. These worms are enclosed in a tissue sheath, and always coiled. They measure 3–4 mm. in diameter when coiled and average 35 mm. in length when outstretched. There may be twenty to thirty on a single animal."

The mole shrew rates high in its economic value to man as a destroyer of insects, snails, and mice that damage crops. It is true that the shrew also eats and destroys some useful animals. The great majority that are eaten, however, are noxious animals. The only complaint I have heard against this animal was in 1912 in Rock County, where it was said by ginseng growers to be destructive to ginseng roots. Assuming that each individual consumes an average of about one-third its own weight each day (eight grams), the army of 84 million mole shrews in Wisconsin consumes more than 500 million pounds, or 250,000 tons of pests annually, an equivalent of two big truck loads a day for each county in the state. If we assume that each *Blarina* averages less than three invertebrates (insects, snails) a day and less than two mice a year then numbers consumed would reach the almost unbelievable, yet not unlikely, number of 90 billion invertebrates and 150 million mice. Meadow moles would outnumber mole shrews in the state if it were not for the "balancing" effect of predation on the mice. The mole shrew must be accepted in the class of mammals as a very useful ally to man.

Specimens examined from Wisconsin.—Total 122, as follows: *Ashland County:* Bear Lake, 1 (UWZ); Madeline Island, 4. *Bayfield County:* Herbster, 9; Namakagon Lake, 1; Orienta, 7· Port Wing, 2. *Buffalo County:* Fountain City, 1 (MM). *Burnett County:* Danbury, 2; Meenon Township, 2 (UWZ). *Chippewa County:* Holcombe, 2. *Clark County:* Hewett Township, 8 (7 AMNH; 1 UWZ); Thorp Township, 1 (AMNH); Withee, 5; Worden Township, 11 (4 AMNH; 2 UWZ). *Crawford County:* Lynxville, 2; Wauzeka, 3. *Douglas County:* Moose and Saint Croix rivers (junction), 1 (MM); Solon Springs, 8 (7 CNHM). *Dunn County:* Meridean, 2. *Grant County:* Cassville, 2 (1 UWZ); Platteville, 6 (1 AMNH); Potosi (10 mi. S. S. E.), 1. *Jackson County:* Millston, 1 (UWZ). *Juneau County:* Camp Douglas, 4; Mather, 2; T 18 N, R 3 E, 1 (F&FH). *La Crosse County:* La Crosse, 2. *Monroe County:* T 19 N, R 1 E, 1 (F&FH). *Pepin County:* Pepin, 4. *Pierce County:* Maiden Rock, 5 (MM); Prescott, 9 (8 MM). *Polk County:* Saint Croix Falls, 2. *Price County:* Ogema, 1. *Rusk County:* Ladysmith, 2 (UWZ). *Sawyer County:* Connors Lake, 1; T 39 N, R 9 W (Sand Lake), 1 (F&FH). *Trempealeau County:* Trempealeau, 1. *Washburn County:* Long Lake, 4.

Selected references.—Hamilton, W. J., Jr., 1929; 1930; Merriam, C. H., 1895 b; Pearson, O. P., 1942; Seton, E. T., 1909, pp. 1116–35; Shull, A. F., 1907.

Blarina brevicauda kirtlandi
Bole and Moulthrop
Lakes States Mole Shrew

Blarina brevicauda kirtlandi Bole and Moulthrop, Sci. Publs. Cleveland Mus. Nat. Hist. 5 (6): 99, September 11, 1942.
Blarina brevicauda kirtlandi Barger, p. 10, 1952.

Vernacular names.—Kirtland's blarina, Kirtland's mole shrew, Kirtland's short-tailed shrew, Lakes States blarina, and most of the vernacular names applied to the giant mole shrew.

Identification marks.—The chief characters that distinguish *Blarina brevicauda kirtlandi* from *B. b. brevicauda* are its smaller size, slightly darker coloration, smaller and weaker skull, and a tendency toward paler pigmentation on the teeth. Bole and Moulthrop (1942: 101) give other characters that are supposed to separate the two forms, but they are not always dependable. Many specimens from near longitude 90° west in Wisconsin are intermediate in characters between *B. b. kirtlandi* and *B. b. brevicauda* and often are difficult to identify as to subspecies.

Measurements.—Total length of adults, 110 to 137 mm. (4.3 to 5.4 in.); tail, 21 to 28 mm. (0.8 to 1.1 in.); hind foot, 14 to 16 mm. (0.54 to 0.65 in.). Flank gland, 10 to 11.5 mm. long. Weight, 14 to 22 grams (0.49 to 0.78 oz.). Skull length, 21.0 to 24.0 mm.; width, 11.3 to 12.8 mm.

Distribution in Wisconsin.—The subspecies *kirtlandi* occurs throughout eastern Wisconsin from Iron County south to the Illinois boundary, in general east of longitude 90° west.

Habitat.—Essentially the same as that of *B. b. brevicauda.*

Status and Habits.—Insofar as known the habits of *B. b. kirtlandi* are no different from those of *B. b. brevicauda,* and have been discussed under the latter subspecies.

Specimens examined from Wisconsin.—Total 271, as follows: *Adams County:* Wisconsin Dells (3 1/2 mi. N.), 2. *Brown County:* Allouez, 4 (NPM); Edgewater Beach, 1 (NPM); Preble Township, 4 (NPM). *Columbia County:* Columbus, 1(UWZ). *Dane County:* Albion, 1; Madison, 25 (UWZ); Mazomanie, 7 (5 MM; 2 UWZ); Vermont, 2 (UWZ). *Dodge County:* Beaver Dam, 64 (28 CNHM; 36 UWZ). *Door County:* Clark Lake, 3; Ellison Bay, 4; Fish Creek, 3; State Game Farm, 1 (UWZ). *Florence County:* Florence, 1; Spread Eagle, 6 (CNHM). *Forest County:* T 34 N, R 14 E, 1 (UWZ). *Green Lake County:* Green Lake, 5. *Iron County:* Fisher Lake, 1 (UWZ); Mercer, 2; Shantz Bay, 1 (UWZ). *Langlade County:* Antigo, 2 (UWZ). *Marathon County:* Rib Hill, 2. *Marinette County:* Cravitz, 1. *Milwaukee County:* Milwaukee, 5 (MM). *Oconto County:* Kelley Lake, 3; Lakewood, 3. *Oneida County:* Crescent Lake, 1; Rhinelander, 1. *Portage County:* Stevens Point, 1. *Racine County:* Racine, 3 (USNM). *Rock County:* Milton, 3 (2 UWZ). *Sauk County:* Devils Lake, 1; Prairie du Sac, 48 (MM). *Shawano County:* Keshena, 8 (CAS). *Sheboygan County:* Elkhart Lake (Sheboygan Bog), 2. *Vilas County:* Conover, 1 (CNHM); Lac Vieux Desert, 2 (CNHM); Mamie Lake, 3; Phelps, 1 (UWZ). *Walworth County:* Delavan, 17 (8 CAS; 7 MM); Turtle Lake, 2. *Waukesha County:* Chenequa, 1 (F&FH); Nashotah, 8 (7 USNM; 1 UWZ). *Waupaca County:* Saint Lawrence Township, 2 (UWZ). *Waushara County:* Wild Rose, 11.

Selected references.—Those cited under *B. b. brevicauda.* Also Bole and Moulthrop, 1942, pp. 99–113.

Genus **Cryptotis** Pomel
Little Short-tailed Shrews

Dental formula:

$$I \frac{3-3}{1-1}, \ C \frac{1-1}{1-1}, \ P \frac{2-2}{1-1}, \ M \frac{3-3}{3-3} = 30.$$

Cryptotis parva harlani (Duvernoy)
Indiana Little Short-tailed Shrew

Brachysorex harlani Duvernoy, Mag. de Zool., d'Anat. Comp. et de Paleont., ser. 2, vol. 4, Monographie du Genre Musaraigne, p. 40, pl. 53, November, 1842.
Cryptotis parva A. L. Nelson, p. 252, 1934.
Cryptotis parva parva Barger, p. 10, 1952.

Vernacular names.—Ash-colored shrew, bee mole, bee shrew, brown shrew, cryptotis, ground mole-mouse, least mole-shrew, least shrew, little bob-tailed shrew, little mole shrew, little shrew, mole mouse, oldfield shrew, pigmy or pygmy short-tailed shrew, small blarina, small brown shrew, small short-tailed shrew, small shrew, and smaller shrew.

Identification marks.—A tiny shrew, with body scarcely if any larger than a bumblebee, in total length about that of the pigmy shrew (*Microsorex*), actually averaging slightly less, but body larger and more robust and tail decidedly shorter (length of tail about one-half that of the tail of the pigmy shrew); ears inconspicuous and almost concealed in the fur; eyes minute, black, beady; snout rather long and pointed; tail relatively slender and short; feet rather heavy for

Little short-tailed shrew, CRYPTOTIS PARVA, *with young not more than 24 hours old. About 1½×. Courtesy Ernest P. Walker.*

a shrew, five-toed. The fur is dense, fine, somewhat short, and almost velvety. The genus *Cryptotis* is the only shrew, in fact the only mouse-size Wisconsin mammal, having 30 teeth.

In full winter pelage the upper parts are dark brown, fuscous or slightly darker, with practically no variation over entire dorsal surface; the under parts are mouse gray or ashy gray, sometimes faintly tinged with buffy brown. Summer pelage is a shade paler than winter fur, the upper parts near dark hair-brown or sepia; under parts ashy gray. Tail slender, somewhat bicolorous, above like back of animal, below like under parts.

The skull is small and compact, broad and relatively high interorbitally; rostrum short and broad, the anterior nares rather wide; zygomatic arches incomplete, essentially absent; mandible heavy, the ramus somewhat arched. Cusps moderately pigmented chestnut color; unicuspidate teeth four, the fourth (posterior one) minute, wedged between third unicuspid and first molariform tooth, visible only from palatal view, in outside view only three unicuspids being evident.

There is little if any sexual variation in size, color, or general appearance. Young individuals sometimes appear darker than adults. Winter pelage is also a shade darker than summer pelage. There are two molts annually, one in September or October and the other in April or May. Either molt may be delayed for several weeks. Molting usually starts on the face and progresses backward, though the rump and belly may begin to molt about the same time as the head.

This shrew (*Cryptotis*) in total length averages the smallest of Wisconsin mammals, and may be distinguished from all other shrews by its short total length of less than 85 mm. com-

bined with its slender short tail of less than 20 mm. The large short-tailed shrew (*Blarina*) is of about the same proportions, but in Wisconsin it is more than 110 mm. in total length of the adult with a tail length of more than 20 mm.

In the past the form *Cryptotis parva parva* has been considered the subspecies that occurs in Wisconsin. Comparison of the Wisconsin specimens available, however, indicates that the skulls are more nearly like those of *C. p. harlani* in size and other characters. The color of typical *harlani* is darker and more grayish than that of *C. p. parva*. We lack skin specimens from Wisconsin for color comparisons.

Measurements.—Total length of adults, 68 to 82 mm. (2.3 to 3.2 in.); tail, 13 to 18 mm. (0.5 to 0.7 in.); hind foot, 9.5 to 11 mm. (0.37 to 0.43 in.). Flank gland (flattened and weakly developed), 3 to 4 mm. long. Weight, 4.2 to 5.6 grams (0.15 to 0.2 oz.). Skull length, 16.2 to 17 mm.; width, 7.5 to 8.2 mm.

Distribution in Wisconsin.—The three records of *Cryptotis* in Wisconsin come from two localities within 18 miles of each other, both south or east of the Wisconsin River. The skull from Pine Bluff, Dane County, was recovered from the pellet of a great horned owl collected January 31, 1932, and is now No. 251113 in the Biological Surveys collection, U. S. National Museum. Another fragmentary skull, retrieved from a lot of 26 pellets of the great horned owl gathered in Columbia County, east of Prairie du Sac on February 21, 1932, is now in the Milwaukee Public Museum. Another specimen was found on the Sauk Prairie, in Sauk County, on December 15, 1942, by Albert Gastrow of Prairie du Sac. It had been killed by a red fox (Hanson, 1945: 116). In a letter of April 5, 1950, Dr. Paul L. Errington says: "Concerning the locality for the specimen of *Cryptotis parva* listed in the prey of our Family Study 9 group of horned owls at Prairie du Sac, Wisconsin, I would say that the pellet was obtained in Columbia County between three-quarters of a mile and a mile E. S. E. of the power dam across the Wisconsin River east of town. The specimen undoubtedly came from the general area from which Hanson collected his specimen." The species probably has a wider distribution in southern Wisconsin than records indicate, but whether it occurs north or west of the Wisconsin River is problematical.

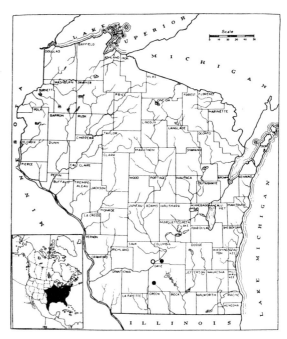

Map 11. *Distribution of* CRYPTOTIS PARVA. ● = *specimens examined.* ○ *authentic record.*

Habitat.—The little short-tailed shrew prefers dry grassy prairie, or grassy, weedy old fields, often in broom sedge or near brier patches, sometimes in hay or grain fields or grassy meadows. In some regions (Arkansas, Nebraska, New Jersey, North Carolina, and Oklahoma) it has been reported as occurring in damp situations or along streams, but always in a grassy situation. A few have been captured under logs.

Status and Habits.—So few specimens of this shrew have been taken in Wisconsin, and all by predators, that there is no clue as to the numbers present in the state. The species may not be as rare in the southern part of the state as records indicate, because it is a tiny animal, seclusive, difficult to trap or capture, and could easily be overlooked. In many localities elsewhere, though it is still difficult to trap, records from owl pellets show *Cryptotis parva* to be abundant. Thus 171 remains of this species comprised 41 per cent of the total number of mammals taken at the roost of a pair of barn owls in Colorado County, Texas (Davis, W. B., 1938), and of 25 barn owl pellets collected May 11, 1939, at Hog Island, Jefferson County, Texas, 102 of the 152 "kills" found in the pellets were of *Cryptotis parva,* indicating that more than 67 per cent of the total number of food items captured by these owls were little short-tailed shrews (Davis, W. B., 1940). Wisconsin being at the extreme northern edge of the range of *Cryptotis,* we might not expect any such heavy concentration as occurred in Texas. Its population density so far as we know is nowhere great in the northeastern United States, and six or eight to the acre over any considerable area of favorable habitat is probably a high estimate. Its home range is probably not more than one thousand square yards.

This midget shrew leaves little trace of its presence in a region. It follows the runways of mice and other small mammals, and in soft loose earth may burrow, not always by actually digging but also by using its snout and pushing and worming its way until a tunnel is made. These small tunnels may give a clue to the shrew's presence, but the burrows are so like those made by some beetles and other insects that they are difficult to identify. The feces are not easy to locate and may soon weather so as not to be distinctive. They are miniatures of the feces of *Blarina,* somewhat corkscrew in shape, but could be mistaken for small scats of some mice. The little short-tailed shrew does not hibernate or migrate, and is active both summer and winter, but in cold weather its activities are curtailed. It shows no preference for day or night, and may be either energetic or resting at any time.

Being of relatively heavier body than either the cinereous or the pigmy shrew, its movements appear to be slightly slower, yet it is quick in its movements and darts about in a trotlike run, the back raised and roundly humped, the fur fluffed, and the tail usually flat on the ground, although rarely it is carried straight out or nearly upright. It is strictly terrestrial, is not known to climb, and in meeting obstacles in its path it usually jumps over them or finds a place under which to crawl or burrow with its snout. It can swim but avoids getting into water. There are no accurately measured records of its speed, but when running in an open stretch it can be overtaken easily by a slow-running or fast-walking man, so its speed under these circumstances would be approximately five miles an hour. In its sudden dashes and darts it might more than double its straightaway speed.

It is not a noisy mammal, but some of its high-pitched notes may be inaudible to humans. When irritated it may utter a sharp squeal or shriek, or a squeaky chatter. Ordinarily, when at rest, when feeding, or in many of its activities, particularly in the presence of others of its kind, it utters a constant musical, birdlike chirping or twitter not unpleasing to the human ear. My old friend, the eminent naturalist Vernon Bailey, once told me this song of the little short-tailed shrew seemed to him not very different in character from the summer song of the winter wren, only on a smaller scale.

The little short-tailed shrew, like most of its close relatives, is active and restless. Unlike many of its tribe, however, *Cryptotis parva* is quite sociable, almost to the extent that it may be termed gregarious. In fact, although this species is usually rare over much of its range, in places where it is found it appears to be more or less colonial. Often one learns of a log, slab, or rock being overturned and there being found under it from four to eight or more of these tiny shrews. Maurice K. Brady, Washington, D. C., told me some years ago that on April 5, 1925, he found about 25 *Cryptotis* all in a pile in a leaf nest under an old log near Frustone Point, Virginia, on the Potomac River 30 miles below Washington. When he rolled the log over in search of salamanders, the shrews ran in all directions. He captured four of them in his hand. Although possessing the same helter-skelter nervous actions as the long-tailed shrew, it is not as subject to nervous shock, and can more readily be captured alive. Moreover, it is not especially difficult to keep in capitivity if given a cage with soil and cover simulating its natural environment, and proper food and atmospheric conditions. It is so far as I know the easiest shrew to keep and breed in captivity, but it does not like to be handled. Sometimes it indulges in scampering and gymnastics that would appear to be merely play. For such a mite it displays great strength, and has especially well developed muscles in its neck and shoulders, probably from its rooting activities. The animal's sight is poorly developed and apparently plays little part in its life. Its sense of smell is not highly developed, but the animal can detect food odors up to a distance of nearly two inches. Its hearing also is not well developed; the shrew can hear the movements of an insect at a distance of three inches from its ears, yet pays no attention to louder sounds such as a bell or a whistle, or the clapping of hands if there is no air movement made thereby. Possibly it can hear high-pitched notes beyond the range of human ears. The tactile sense is highly developed, particularly in the region of the snout and back, and it is upon this that it chiefly relies. When well fed it will sleep for a long period with its head, feet, and tail curled under its belly. Its normal life span in the wild is not more than two years; its potential longevity is probably less than four years.

The breeding season of *Cryptotis* in the northern part of its range is from March until November. Young born early in the spring may breed within the year. The gestation period is about 16 days, and there may be as many as four or five broods during a season. It appears that the male remains with the female during the care of the young. The parents, particularly the mother, display extreme solicitude for their offspring. Not infrequently a female may be in the early stages of pregnancy while nursing young of the preceding brood. The young vary in number from three to nine in a litter, but the usual number is four to six, with a fraction over five the average. In fact all larger broods are recorded from embryos, and it may be that the limited teats, four inguinal and two abdominal, may limit the number of young capable of being nourished. The newly born short-tailed shrew is hairless except for dark spots showing where vibrissae will develop, has the eyes closed, and weighs about one-third of a gram (five grains). After three or four days, pubescent hair begins to show dorsally, and shortly appears on the flanks, head, and under parts. The youngster develops rapidly, the eyes open at about ten days old, and by the time it quits nursing at about three weeks old it appears much like its mother except for its slightly smaller size and sleek appearance. At the time of weaning, the combined weight of a litter of young may be more than three times that of the mother, and one might well wonder how she was able to supply sufficient nourishment.

The nest is globular, about four or five inches in diameter, and is usually composed of dry grass, though sometimes dry leaves are used and one found under a log in Texas was made of shredded corn husks. The nest generally has two entrances on the side. It is most apt to be placed in a slight hollow on the surface of the ground under a flat rock or limestone slab, or sometimes under a log; rarely is it located underground, and then only at a depth of four or five inches. This shrew will also utilize for its nesting site artificial objects such as small tin cans or boxes on the surface of the ground. Writing about a specimen of *Cryptotis floridana* which he kept in captivity, Joseph C. Moore says,

> On various occasions Shivernose made nests of sphagnum moss or dried grass. At one time the shrew had only the shelter of a flimsy camouflage of bits of dry crabgrass which it had dragged together in one corner of its cage. It added to this skimpy cover whenever more material was made available, but abandoned it when a more suitable den was offered in the form of an eggshell. This dried shell of an ordinary hen's egg, into the side of which a hole 18 mm. in diameter had been broken to remove the contents, was actually large enough to have held four shrews the size of Shivernose. It had hardly been placed in the vivarium when the shrew entered it and adopted it as a rather permanent den. A bit of cotton was placed in it for nesting material, but the shrew dragged in more and also pieces of dry grass until there was barely room for the shrew (1943: 158).

The little short-tailed shrew is cleanly in its habits, and practices sanitation to the extent that it removes the feces from the nest and deposits them in one place some distance away. Like other shrews, it gets most of its natural food from insects and other small invertebrates that it captures. It is known to eat many beetles, bugs, crickets, and grasshoppers, both adults and larvae, and earthworms, millipeds, sowbugs, and snails. In captivity it seems to relish many items that it probably would not get in the wild, such as cream, cottage cheese, peanut butter, apples, pears, raw rolled oats, and cooked vegetables. When its food is of a dry nature it drinks freely. Butler (1892: 163) says that in Vigo County, Indiana, this shrew is known as the "bee shrew" from its habit of entering the hives and destroying the young brood, and Evermann (in Evermann and Butler, 1894: 133) says that a Mr. Hawley near Terre Haute, Indiana, calls it the bee mole because it gets into his bee hives and there builds its nest and feeds upon the brood. It also eats salamanders, and is believed to have a penchant for frogs.

The behavior of a *Cryptotis parva* in feeding upon frogs has been described by Robert T. Hatt as follows:

A living specimen was brought to me on November 10, 1937, by Robert R. McMath and Harold E. Sawyer, from Lake Angelus [near Pontiac, Michigan], as their observations led them to suspect that the feeding habits of the shrew might prove of interest to a mammalogist. This individual . . . was confined in a can ten inches in diameter. I introduced a medium-sized leopard frog into the container. The shrew immediately approached the frog, appeared to sniff at it from several angles, and then rushed up to nip the frog's knees. The frog responded vigorously by kicking and the shrew carefully dodged the kicks, but repeatedly attacked each knee of the frog. The frog continually cried aloud and attempted to escape, which of course it was prevented from doing by the sides of the can. After a number of attempts the shrew severed the patellar tendons and thus rendered the frog helpless. The shrew then proceeded to eat the frog.

A new-born house mouse, *Mus musculus,* was offered to the shrew before the frog was introduced, and was examined but not molested.

I am informed by Messrs. McMath and Sawyer that the shrew employed the same technique in subduing grasshoppers and crickets as it did with the frog; biting the joints of the largest legs.

Mr. McMath has kindly furnished me with his observations on the shrews at his residence, and since they are based on a more normal situation and on greater numbers, I here quote him.

"As you know my house is in the country. We have a large number of areaways built around the cellar windows. These all act as natural collecting pits. Just as the first cold weather set in this fall, each areaway collected from ten to thirty frogs.

"One night I heard a tremendous commotion in one of the areaways and took the flashlight to the window in an effort to see what was going on. I noticed three small animals chasing one frog—which frog seemed to be in great distress. Mr. Harold Sawyer was with me at the time. We killed two of the animals and damaged the third one in an endeavor to secure it alive. We also caught the frog which had been the object of the attack. The shrew was identified as *Cryptotis parva.*

"An examination of the frog showed that each shrew would dive under the frog and attempt to hamstring it at the knees. [At Cranbrook the shrew approached from the side; did not dive under the frog.] In other words the behavior of each shrew

observed was practically identical and they were not doing something unusual at the time we observed them. On subsequent evenings we found other shrews attacking the frogs in exactly the same way" (Hatt, 1938).

Although mention is made in the above accounts of the possible method of this shrew in "hamstringing" its victims, it suggests also the possibility of the employment of a poison secretion through the bite such as is mentioned in the case of *Blarina brevicauda.*

In Wisconsin the great horned owl and the red fox are the only recorded enemies of the little short-tailed shrew. In other localities several other species of owls, the barred, the long-eared, the short-eared, the screech, and particularly the barn owl are important enemies. The American rough-legged hawk as well as the red-shouldered hawk have been recorded as feeding on *Cryptotis,* and probably other hawks do so. There are records of the gray fox killing this shrew, as well as the red fox. The domestic cat also catches many. Possibly several species of snakes eat the little shrew, but records are available only for the blow viper (*Heterodon platyrhinus*) and the milk snake (*Lampropeltis doliata*) (Snyder, L. L., 1929). It is probably infested with several species of parasites, but the only one of which I have record is the flea, *Doratopsylla blarinae.* It is allergic to water and drowns easily when it falls into a well or pothole, or during floods.

This little shrew is so rare in the state as to be of no economic importance. Since it is primarily an insect feeder, if it did exist in numbers it would rate as beneficial, although it has been accused of destroying young broods of bees in Indiana and elsewhere. As a delicate, pretty, tiny mammal it deserves some credit from the esthetic viewpoint.

Specimens examined from Wisconsin.—Total 2, as follows: *Columbia County:* East of Prairie du Sac, about one mile east-southeast of dam across Wisconsin River, 1 (MM). *Dane County:* Pine Bluff, one mile N. of Klevenville, 1.

Selected references.—Hamilton, W. J., Jr., 1944; Hanson, H. C., 1944: 116; Hatt, R. T., 1938; Merriam, C. H., 1895 a; Nelson, A. L., 1934; Walker, E. P., 1954.

Family **Talpidae**
Moles

The family Talpidae ranges throughout the temperate regions of the Northern Hemisphere; exclusive of fossil forms it is composed of 17 recognized genera, of which 2 occur in Wisconsin.

Genus **Scalopus**
E. Geoffroy-Saint-Hilaire
Common Moles

Dental formula:

$$I \frac{3-3}{2-2}, \; C \frac{1-1}{0-0}, \; P \frac{3-3}{3-3}, \; M \frac{3-3}{3-3} = 36.$$

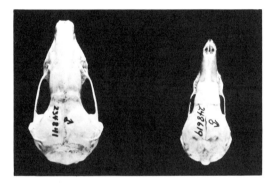

Skulls of moles. Left, SCALOPUS A. MACHRINUS, *Potosi, Wisconsin. Right,* CONDYLURA C. CRISTATA, *Delmer Township, Chippewa County, Wisconsin.*

Prairie mole, SCALOPUS A. MACHRINUS, *about* 1×. *U.S. Fish and Wildlife Service photograph by N. H. Kent.*

Scalopus aquaticus machrinus (Rafinesque)
Prairie Mole

Talpa machrina Rafinesque, Atlantic Jour. 1: 61, 1832.
Scalops aquaticus Lapham, p. 338, 1853.
Scalops argentatus Strong, p. 438, 1883.
Scalopus aquaticus machrinus Hollister, p. 142, 1909; Hollister, p. 30, 1910; Jackson, p. 90, 1910; Cory, p. 435, 1912; Schmidt, p. 107, 1931; Barger, p. 10, 1952.

Vernacular names.—In Wisconsin, commonly called the mole. Other names include common mole, common shrew-mole, eastern garden mole, garden mole, ground mole, *maulwürfe* (German), modewarp (Scotch, from the old English word "mould-warp," referring to an animal that warps or throws up the mold or soil), shrew-mole, silvery mole.

Identification marks.—Body size about that of a very small rat, robust, depressed; fore and hind legs short and stout; head short, abruptly conical, depressed; external ear conchs absent, the ears being visible only as small openings beneath the fur; eyes minute, concealed in fur; nose elongated into a snout, apical portion naked to line of anterior edge of nasals, nostrils opening upwards; crescentic, with concave side of crescent turned inward; tail short, round, indistinctly ringed, very scantily haired, in appearance naked; feet large, fleshy, scantily haired above, naked below, without tubercles. Forefeet handlike, the palms broader than long; fore toes and hind toes webbed; claws of forefeet broad, flat, and heavy;

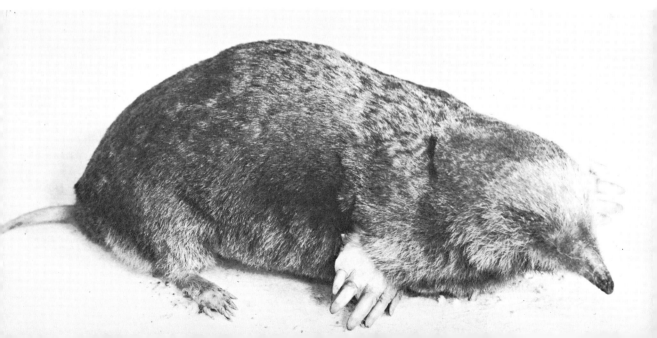

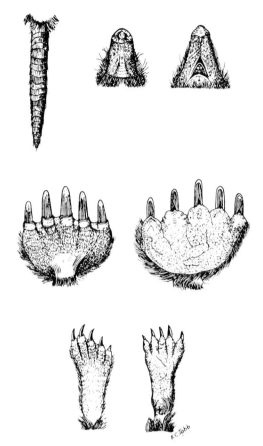

Prairie mole, SCALOPUS A. MACHRINUS. *Upper left, tail; upper right, snout above and snout below. Middle left, fore foot above; middle right, fore foot below. Bottom left, hind foot above; bottom right, hind foot below. About* 1 × .

through the orbits; mastoids rather heavy and prominent; frontal region flat, not sloping much, the frontal sinuses swollen; rostrum relatively short, the anterior ends of premaxillary bones considerably thickened and extending beyond nasals, forming an acute notch in front of nasals; anterior nares opening forward; zygomata moderately long and heavy, not curved much; audital bullae complete; horizontal ramus of mandible heavy, curved upward both at posterior and anterior ends.

The only sexual variation is that the male prairie mole averages somewhat larger than the female. The young are more grayish than adults, seldom tinged ventrally with brown. With increasing maturity there is a flattening of the skull and a broadening of the base of the rostrum. In skulls of immature specimens the roots of the molars are not infrequently exposed in places through the maxillary bones. There is little individual variation in the general color at a given season. A slight tendency towards color abnormalities shows itself occasionally in whitish, cream, orange, or ochraceous blotches on the ventral parts. Dr. A. W. Schorger (University of Wisconsin) reports receiving a completely white prairie mole taken in Marietta Township, Crawford County, in June, 1969.

Measurements.—Total length of adult males, 175 to 206 mm. (7.0 to 8.1 in.); tail, 28 to 38 mm. (1.1 to 1.5 in.); hind foot, 22 to 25 mm. (0.85 to 1.0 in.); weight, 75 to 120 grams (2.8 to 4.2 oz.). Skull length, 37.5 to 39.5 mm.; width, 19.5 to 20.7 mm. Adult females average about 5 per cent smaller than adult males.

Distribution in Wisconsin.—Western part of the state from Burnett County south and southeasterly to western Waushara and central Dane counties, and along the Mississippi River to the Illinois line. Also recorded from extreme southeastern Wisconsin (Racine. Lapham, 1853: 338).

Habitat.—The habitat of the mole seems to be determined in no small measure by soil conditions. Its normal habitat is in sandy soils and light loams in grassy prairies, meadows, pastures, cultivated fields, gardens, lawns, and woodlands. Gravelly or rocky soils, or watery swamps, are barriers to it, though moist soil is preferred by the mole. Along the Mississippi River and the lower Wisconsin River, where they are as plentiful as anywhere in the state, these moles are found both in the loam on the bottomlands and

those of hind feet relatively short and weak. The fur is dense, soft, and silky, the hairs nearly equal in length and producing a velvet-like pelage.

In full winter pelage the upper parts of the prairie mole are near sepia or hair brown, sometimes showing pinkish buff or cinnamon buff on the nose; the under parts are more grayish than the back, and usually tinged with cinnamon brown. Summer fur is slightly paler than winter pelage and usually more grayish. There are two molts annually, one early in spring and the other late in summer or early in autumn.

The skull is conoidal, flat with relatively broad brain case, and is considerably constricted in the looser soils on the uplands, as well as in suitable places on the hillsides.

Status and Habits.—Where favorable soil conditions prevail the prairie mole is often locally abundant within its range in western Wisconsin. Even in such locations its presence may go undetected unless it inhabits a lawn or a garden, and then its estimated numbers may become exaggerated. It probably has remained rather static in population in the state, and has in recent years extended its range but little. One notable extension seems to be toward the southeast from the bend of the Wisconsin River in Dane County to the center of that county (Madison). Moles are now rather common near Madison; in 1908 and 1909 I saw no trace of them in the identical spot where their ridges were common in 1946. There may also be a tendency for a northward extension of the mole's range, but the deep and long freezing of the soil during severe winter weather would tend to limit their northward progress. In areas densely populated by moles their numbers may reach as high as eight or ten to the acre, but more often in apparently well-populated areas there are only one or two to the acre. The home range of an individual mole is usually

Map 12. *Distribution of* SCALOPUS AQUATICUS. ● = *specimens examined.* ○ = *authentic records.*

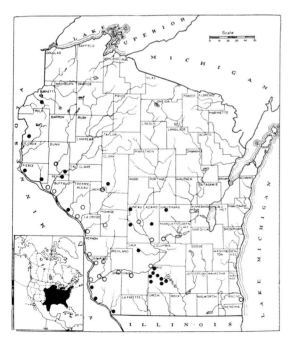

less than one acre, but at times it may extend to two or more acres.

The presence of the prairie mole in a region is usually detected by the discovery of its characteristic ridges of earth on the surface of the ground. These ridges are pushed up by the mole in its extending underground tunnels, and often form a labyrinth of wrinkles over the surface of the soil. The ridges may be very conspicuous in lawns, gardens, or clean fields, but in weedy or grassy fields and leaf-strewn woods they are discovered only as one sinks slightly into the soft ridges over the tunnels. Mole mounds or hills may also mark the work of the prairie mole. These differ from pocket gopher mounds in that they show no closed opening, the soil being pushed directly to the surface and not carried out by the animal. The runways of the prairie mole are wider and straighter than those of the star-nosed mole; the mounds are larger, flatter, and more regular in outline, and are never found in a watery or mucky soil, such as is likely with the star-nosed mole.

The prairie mole is active at any time of day or night, and if an opening is made in one of its runways the animal will repair it when next it comes that way. Such a habit could be expected in a subterranean mammal that has sight that can scarcely discern light. It does not hibernate, and is more or less active at all seasons of the year. It works at extending its surface runways at times when the soil tends to be friable, after rains or, in winter, after thaws. During droughts or when the ground is frozen it uses its old surface runways or works at depths where the soil is more pliable. It rarely exposes itself on the surface of the ground, and then chiefly during the breeding season, and on dark days or at night. This deeper series of tunnels 8 to 24 inches beneath the surface is really the more permanent home of the mole. From these tunnels it forces to the outside small piles of earth, scarcely large enough to be worthy of the name "molehills."

The burrowing habits of the mole have been studied by Dr. Frederick L. Hisaw, who tells us:

The mole excavates its burrow by antero-posterior strokes and lateral thrusts of the front feet, the vertical angle of the movements being regulated by rotating the fore part of the body.

In the excavation of shallow burrows the earth is disposed of by being pushed upward to form a ridge, while in the construction of deep tunnels, from 6 inches to 2 feet below the surface, the earth is loosened with the strong claws of the fore feet and transferred either to the surface or to some vacated part of the burrow.

Loose earth is transferred and pushed to the surface by lateral thrusts of the fore feet (the body being turned sidewise).

When the left foot is digging, the right is held either against the right or upper right side of the burrow, and the soil is loosened by lateral strokes. When the right paw is used, the reverse is true. If the inactive foot is held against the side of the tunnel, the digging strokes are almost horizontal and backward, but if held against the upper right or left sides, the strokes are directed downward and backward. At each stroke the excavated earth is thrown beneath the belly. Periodically one of the hind feet reaches forward under the body and kicks the loose earth to the rear of the animal.

After a quantity of earth is loosened and piled in the tunnel behind the mole, the animal turns about and pushes the dirt out of the burrow with one of the broad front paws.

Moles often deepen surface burrows during droughts by driving a new tunnel under an old one and the excavated earth is disposed of by being pushed up into the burrow that is being vacated (Hisaw, 1923 b).

The mole has been said to use a swimming motion in passing through the soil, but it can accomplish this motion only in very loose soil. The description by Hisaw shows clearly that as a rule it employs a digging motion. In ordinary loose garden soil it will dig at the rate of 18 feet an hour, and can during one night form a mole ridge 50 or more yards long. Its speed in these runways is not rapid, and probably seldom exceeds two miles an hour. Even that slow progress is rapid compared to its speed on a flat surface, where it normally makes about one mile an hour, although when frightened or pressed it may extend itself to one and one-half miles an hour. It can make about half this speed for a short distance swimming in water, using its hind feet as propellers, but is not aquatic like the star-nosed mole, even though it has been given the scientific name "*aquaticus.*"

A quiet mammal in all its activities, the prairie mole has no distinctive calls or warning notes. When physically irritated or tormented it utters shrill squeals. I have heard it utter a very low purring while feeding. It has a distinctive strong musky odor which may have some unknown communication significance, particularly during the mating season. The mole has been said by many to be an intolerant hermit which will fight without provocation its own kind as well as other animals, and which is pugnacious on all occasions. Such does not seem to be the case. It fights when attacked or annoyed but seldom follows as the aggressor. Frequently a single long runway may be occupied by two or three moles, and often a series of connecting runways may harbor six or eight moles. Other mammals, such as the striped ground squirrel, meadow mouse, pine mouse, and short-tailed shrew, sometimes inhabit mole tunnels, but the relationship between the mole and these intruders has not been studied carefully.

It is a powerful mammal for its size, and is especially adapted to fossorial habits in having the bones, ligaments, and muscles of the pectoral girdle strong and greatly modified. The bones of the forelegs are short, heavy, and strong, well adapted for muscle attachments. The anatomical structure is such as to enable the mole to bring its forefeet together in front of its snout, thus adapting it to excavating soil from the end of the tunnel. Prorated as to size of the animal, in order to accomplish work equal to that of a mole digging a sixty-yard tunnel in eight hours, a man would have to dig a tunnel wide enough for the passage of his body nearly one-half-mile long in the same time. A male that I trapped ten miles south-southeast of Potosi, Wisconsin, the evening of August 5, 1920, was kept alive overnight. The little animal exhibited all the strength accredited to his tribe. He would easily move the cover of my heavy telescope, weighing probably ten pounds, or 40 times the weight of the animal. His method of defense was mostly by pushing away the offender with his powerful forefeet, and in his efforts to do this he would frequently follow the point of attack around over his back, and roll entirely over. He would, of course, use his teeth occasionally, but did not do so persistently. His efforts were always to "dig down" or follow along the edge of a board, or under some object. Contact over his entire back seemed in a measure to answer the purposes of his runway, but contact at only a small part of his back acted as an irritant. I laid a mattress on the floor and he took particular delight in "digging under" it.

He could raise the mattress and crawl its entire length, and under this mattress was his favorite resting place. I placed him in a sink, and he seemed particularly attracted to the drain holes, placing his nose first in one little circular opening, then in another and at times resting for 15 or 20 minutes with his nose in one of the little holes in the drain-pipe sieve.

We have little accurate data on the life span of the prairie mole. A fully grown mole placed in the National Zoological Park, Washington, D. C., in June, 1942, died in November, 1943, probably at least two and one-half years old. Inasmuch as the life of most insectivores is comparatively short, it is probable that the normal longevity or life expectancy of the prairie mole is not more than three or four years, and the potential longevity five or six years.

In Wisconsin, mating may take place as early as the second week of March and continue well into April. The gestation period is about 45 days, and the young are usually born during the latter half of April or in May. The number of young in a litter varies from two to five, the usual number being four. The mammary glands are six in number; two latero-pectoral, two latero-abdominal, and two inguinal. Only one litter is produced each year. The young are born hairless, and are about two inches (50 mm.) long, very large compared to the size of the parent. Vibrissae very soon appear on the lips, but hair does not show until the animal is at least a week or ten days old. The fresh first pelage remains short and grows little until the animal is nearly one-third grown; it is exceedingly fine and silky, and lies close to the body, giving the animal a smooth, sleek appearance. At about a week old, the young have the same general proportions of the body as adults. The feet, both fore and hind, have much the same shape and relative size as those of adults. The claws of the forefeet are soft and weak, though thick and broad; those of the hind feet are very soft and only slightly developed. The external ear appears as a thickening of the dermis into a flat papilla 1.5 mm. in diameter. The center of this is penetrated by a minute auditory opening that seems to be closed by the contact of its sides; as an auditory organ its function is probably limited, though it may enable the mole to detect vibrations. The rudimentary eye appears as a small pigmented spot covered by dermis; a minute imperfect opening passes through the dermis to the eye proper, and may be sufficiently penetrable for the animal to distinguish between light and darkness. It seems improbable, however, that at this age the eye is sufficiently developed for form perception, and it is likely that with advancing age the sense of light perception becomes less acute. The young one grows and develops rapidly during his first weeks of life, and at the age of five weeks is more than half as large as his mother.

The prairie mole builds a nest about 5 or 6 inches in diameter, and usually 12 to 18 inches beneath the surface, though sometimes it may be only 5 or 6 inches underground. Most frequently the nest is placed under the roots of shrubs, stumps, or grass, but it may be without any such cover protection. It is made of grass and rootlets, and occasionally of leaves, and at times may be almost void of any nesting material. It is placed on the bottom of a flattened ellipsoidal enlargement of the tunnel, the length of which is about 8 inches and the diameter about 5 inches. Similar enlargements of the tunnel not utilized as a nest site are not infrequent, and are probably used as shelters or resting places.

The natural food of the mole consists chiefly of worms, insects and insect larvae, and a small amount of plants. Fully 80 per cent of its diet is animal matter. It is a prodigious eater, and at times may consume in 24 hours a quantity of food equal to its weight. Earthworms, wireworms, white grubs, cutworms, ground beetles, and the like, both in the adult and larva stage, constitute a large proportion of its diet. It consumes quantities of ants and ant pupae, and sometimes eats slugs, snails, sowbugs, May beetles, insect and mollusk eggs, spiders, centipedes, and millipedes. Even bees and hornets fall prey to it occasionally, and it has been known to burrow under a yellow jackets' nest and consume all the larvae therein. It will on occasion kill a small mouse and eat it, and there is record of a frog in its food. It seldom, however, carries its preference for animal food beyond invertebrates. Plant food eaten by the mole consists mostly of corn, potatoes, and grass, and occasionally includes wheat and oats. It also will eat tomatoes, apples, and cantaloupes. The one that I kept in captivity near Potosi, August 5, 1920, would not eat raisins, bat flesh, or cucumber rind, but would eat a little cracker

Construction of superficial tunnel, appearing as a surface ridge, by the mole, SCALOPUS AQUATICUS. *The body is rotated about forty-five degrees to right or left and the earth is pushed up by extending the front legs. Redrawn after Prince, in Hisaw. 1923:83.*

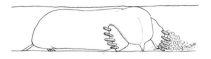

Mole, SCALOPUS AQUATICUS, *transferring earth in a deep burrow. The head and shoulders are turned abruptly to the left or right and the loose earth is pushed forward by one of the fore paws. Redrawn after Prince, in Hisaw, 1923:85.*

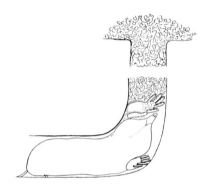

Construction of mound by the mole, SCALOPUS AQUATI-CUS. *The body is turned at an angle and the earth is pushed to the surface by extending the fore legs laterally. Redrawn after Prince, in Hisaw, 1923:85.*

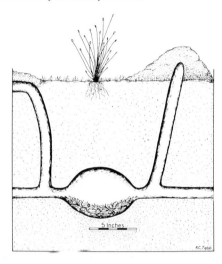

Burrows, mound and nesting site of the mole, SCALO-PUS A. MACHRINUS. *From rough sketches and photographs made by the author near Potosi, Wisconsin.*

and English walnut meat, and especially relished uncooked rolled oats, of which he ate heavily. In eating, his proboscis-like snout came into play, it being used to locate each flake of oatmeal and to draw it into his mouth, almost like an elephant would do. In its natural feeding the mole usually finds its food by direct contact. Its sense of touch and vibrations are probably better developed than those of hearing and smelling. It captures and kills active prey by crushing it with its front feet against the sides of the tunnel, or by throwing loose soil on it and then biting the prey held thereby. The mole procures most of its water from its watery food. It rarely drinks, and when it does, it laps the water like a dog.

On account of their secluded subterranean lives moles are comparatively safe from most predators. They also have a musky odor that seems to make them undesirable for food for most animals. Dogs and cats sometimes catch moles, but do not eat them. Small weasels at times cap-

ture them in their tunnels. Foxes and skunks on rare occasions capture moles, as do hawks and owls. High water and floods on their lowland habitats may drown large numbers of them; such mole reduction is not uncommon along the Mississippi and lower Wisconsin rivers.

The mole is not heavily infested with external parasites, but seems to carry an unusual quantity of internal parasites. Of the external parasites a louse, *Euhaematopinus abnormis*, is most abundant. A small parasitic beetle and a species of flea also occur. Internal parasitic worms of the genera *Filaria* and *Spiroptera* frequently occur in abundance in the intestinal tract. Hanawalt (1922: 167) in Ohio says:

Moles usually bear . . . numerous internal parasites. Nematode worms are not uncommon in the stomach. The most common internal parasite is *Moniliformis moniliformis* (Travassos). The intestines are sometimes so clogged with these parasites that one wonders how food is able to pass along the tract. Moles containing as many as three dozen of these worms give no evidence of the fact in any way unless it be by their ravenous appetites. They must have no difficulty in supplying both themselves and their parasites with food, for even the most heavily infested moles that I observed were in good condition and seemed to have as much fatty tissue as moles not infested.

The economic status of the prairie mole. has been the subject of some dispute, there being a difference of opinion whether this species is in the aggregate beneficial or harmful. Its economic status depends to a great extent on where it occurs. It consumes large quantities of earthworms, and in this it must be ruled harmful. It also consumes some vegetable matter, and has frequently been known to follow rows of recently planted corn to eat the kernels. It makes ridges in lawns, golf courses, cemeteries, and gardens. It may at times uproot bulbs and other plants, and it digs tunnels that permit incursions of rodents injurious to roots, tubers, and planted seeds. These tunnels sometimes are responsible for the weathering away of humus deposits and supersoils on hillsides, but more often serve as an erosion control agent by allowing the water to penetrate the earth instead of washing away the surface. It has been cited as a possible reservoir of poliomyelitis (Rector, 1949), but the fact that moles are entirely absent from large areas where polio is most serious lends little credence to the accusation. The mole consumes large quantities of insect pests, both adults and in larval form, as well as millipedes, slugs, and other invertebrates harmful to human welfare, and thus easily balances its credit account. Even its runways and mole hills on their lawns and grounds are considered by some people an asset of interest. The mole skin has very little value as a fur pelt, and cannot be economically procured for this purpose in the United States.

In some cultivated areas, such as small gardens, seed, flower, and nursery beds, sometimes cornfields, in hayfields where the mole ridges and mounds interfere with mowing and thus reduce the crop, and in places where the mounds and runways become a nuisance, such as on lawns and golf courses, it may be desirable to practice control measures. The mole is difficult to control. Repellents may have some effect on small areas of garden or lawn, but as a rule the mole only moves to another area temporarily. Paradichlorobenzene and naphthalene are effective, and nonharmful to plants. The movements of a mole just below the surface of the earth can usually be detected, and the mole thrown out with a spade or hoe. Where hose connections are available the mole can sometimes be drowned out by flooding its burrow. The best method of control, however, is by the use of traps. There are three efficient types of traps, the choker-loop type, the scissors-jaw type, and the harpoon type. The writer prefers the scissors-jaw type as the most effective.

Specimens examined from Wisconsin.—Total 74, as follows: *Adams County:* Friendship, 1 (MM). *Buffalo County:* Fountain City, 4 (MM). *Burnett County:* Meenon Township, 2 (UWZ). *Clark County:* Hewett, 1 (UWZ). *Dane County:* Cross Plains, 8 (UWZ); Mazomanie, 7 (UWZ); Middleton, 3 (UWZ); Roxbury, 2 (UWZ); Vermont, 2 (UWZ); Verona, 1 (UWZ). *Dunn County:* Meridean, 2 (JNC). *Grant County:* Cassville, 2 (UWZ); Potosi (10 mi. S. S. E.), 1; Rutledge, 14 (MM); Wyalusing, 4 (MM). *Juneau County:* Camp Douglas, 2 (1 AMNH; 1 USNM); Mather, 1. *Pepin County:* Durand, 1 (USNM). *Pierce County:* Maiden Rock, 3 (MM); Prescott, 8 (MM). *Saint Croix County:* River Falls (6 mi. N. E.), 1 (WHD). *Sauk County:* Reedsburg, 1 (UWZ). *Waushara County:* Plainfield, 3 (F&FH).

Selected references.—Arlton, A. V., 1936; Hisaw, F. L., 1923 a, 1923 b; Jackson, H. H. T., 1915; Scheffer, T. H., 1910; Silver, J., and A. W. Moore, 1941.

Genus **Condylura** Illiger
Star-nosed Moles

Dental formula:

$$I\frac{3-3}{3-3},\ C\frac{1-1}{1-1},\ P\frac{4-4}{4-4},\ M\frac{3-3}{3-3}=44.$$

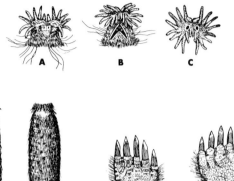

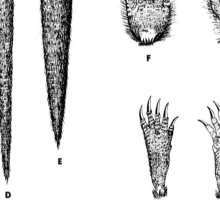

Star-nosed mole, CONDYLURA CRISTATA. *A. snout above, B. snout below, C. snout in front, D. tail in summer, E. tail in winter, F. fore foot above, G. fore foot below, H. hind foot above, I. hind foot below. About 1×.*

Condylura cristata cristata (Linnaeus)
Star-nosed Mole

Sorex cristatus Linnaeus, Systema Naturae, ed. 10, vol. 1, p. 53, 1758.

Condylura cristata Lapham, p. 43, 1852; Lapham, p. 338, 1853; Strong, p. 438, 1883; Jackson, p. 32, 1908; Hollister, p. 30, 1910; Jackson, p. 90, 1910; Cory, p. 440, 1912; Schmidt, p. 107, 1931; Komarek, p. 204, 1932; Barger, p. 10, 1952.

Vernacular names.—In Wisconsin, when recognized at all, commonly called star-nosed mole. Other names include black mole, long-tailed mole, star-nose, star-nose mole.

Identification marks.—The star-nosed mole is easily distinguished from all other mammals in having a peculiar snout fringed with 22 tentacles, thus giving the name "star-nosed." Overall length including tail about that of the prairie mole; body about three-fourths the size of that of the prairie mole, relatively less flattened and more slender, shorter girth; legs short, weaker than in *Scalopus;* head narrow, not depressed as in *Scalopus;* barely a trace of external ear conchs, the auricular openings large, much larger than in *Scalopus;* eyes small, larger than in the prairie mole, concealed in fur; snout moderately elongate, terminating in a naked disk surrounded on the margin by a fringe of 22 nasal processes symmetrically arranged, eleven on each side of a median vertical line; nostrils nearly circular, situated in anterior surface of nasal disk; tail relatively long (about equal in length to body without head), distinctly annulated, scaled, and covered with coarse blackish hairs; in summer the tail is slender, slightly depressed, gradually tapering apically, and slightly constricted proximally; in winter the tail is usually greatly enlarged, thick, and fleshy, gradually tapering apically, and much constricted at the base; feet large, not especially fleshy, scaled, scarcely haired above, naked below, not webbed; forefeet handlike, the palms as broad as long (but relatively narrower than in *Scalopus*), toes relatively long; first, second, third, and fourth toes each with three flat, triangular processes on outer inferior edge; the basal process on the first toe inconspicuous; fore claws relatively long, broad (but narrower than in *Scalopus*); hind feet relatively long, narrow basally, but broader apically; hind claws long, laterally compressed, the outer surface turned obliquely upward. The fur is dense, long, and silky (coarser than in *Scalopus,* and not so velvety); some of the hairs are longer and coarser than the major portion, which forms a distinct underfur.

In full pelage the upper parts are blackish brown to nearly black; under parts paler and more brownish; tail similar to back, sometimes indistinctly bicolored. Worn pelage, particularly summer, is paler and more brownish, the wrists frequently with a narrow ring varying from pink-ish buff to clay color. Nasal disk and processes in live animals are rose color. There are two molts annually in the star-nosed mole, the spring molt occurring late and usually being at its height during June and the first half of July; rarely, traces of winter fur may remain well into August. The autumnal molt usually takes place during October, and full winter pelage is ordinarily ob-tained before the end of that month.

The skull is long and narrow, not flattened, with relatively high and narrow brain case, not constricted through orbits, tapering anteriorly; mastoids weak and inconspicuous; frontal region sloping ventrally anteriorly, the frontal sinuses scarcely swollen; rostrum long and narrow; infero-anterior ends of premaxillae extending much be-yond nasals, the supero-anterior ends barely reaching beyond nasals; nasals in adults termi-nating anteriorly in an acute median point; ante-rior nares opening obliquely upward; zygomata short, narrow, straight, directed obliquely down-ward anteriorly; audital bullae incomplete; hori-zontal ramus of mandible weak, curved upward posteriorly, straight anteriorly. Teeth 44 (the only Wisconsin mammal having 44 teeth), upper jaw

22, lower jaw 22; upper molars W-shaped in transverse section with an interior basal shelf having an indistinctly tricuspidate edge; lower molars M-shaped in transverse section, laterally compressed, the interior shelf narrow, tricuspi-date, the mediam cusp distinctly bifid.

Males and females are essentially similar in size and color, though there seems to be a wider range in size of females than of males. Very old individuals may sometimes show scattered pale hairs throughout the pelage. Young ones are usually darker than adults. An anomalous and unique age variation is shown in the star-nosed mole in that old adults possess a distinct median longitudinal crest on the upper posterior half of the rostral part of the skull. Color mutations are rare in this species, and such color abnormalities as are known are confined to white spots which occur only rarely and usually appear to have been caused by injuries.

Measurements.—Total length of adults, 185 to 205 mm. (7.6 to 8.1 in.); tail, 65 to 84 mm. (2.6 to 3.3 in.); hind foot, 26 to 30 mm. (1.0 to 1.2 in.); weight, 40 to 75 grams (1.4 to 2.6 oz.). Skull length, 33.5 to 35.2 mm.; width, 13.0 to 14.2 mm.

Distribution in Wisconsin.—Northern Wiscon-sin from Polk County southeasterly to Portage County, south along Lake Michigan to Milwaukee County.

Habitat.—The star-nosed mole is an inhabitant of moist, wet, or even watery ground and should not be expected far from water, swamps, or marshes. It is occasionally found in upland areas where the soil is moist and loose. It prefers a soil of muck, humus, or light sandy loam, and is probably found as frequently in wooded and brushland areas as in open places.

Status and Habits.—Except where tilling and draining have lessened its habitable range, the star-nosed mole is probably as abundant as ever in the state. It is a striking animal with its star nose, and when found usually attracts consider-able attention. Rather secluded and inconspicu-ous in its habits, it may live near one's door for years unobserved. It seems to be rather local in its distribution, yet may be common in a selected small area, and, in fact, appears to be gregarious and colonial. In an established colony, probably formed largely through family lineage, there may be a population as high as thirty to

Map 13. *Distribution of* Condylura cristata. ● = *specimens examined.* ○ = *authentic records.*

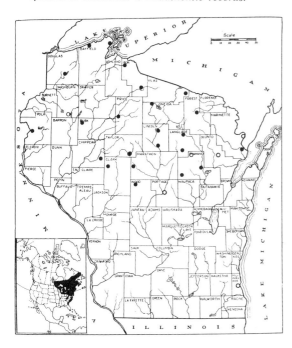

the acre over an acre or two, but as a rule ten or twelve to the acre is about normal. Such colonies are not frequent, however, and over the state as a whole the animal is rare.

Mole ridges and runways and mole hills in moist ground are usually the telltales of the star-nosed mole's presence. Moles killed by cats, dogs, or wild predators are sometimes abandoned by them in conspicuous places, and thus discovered. The surface ridges are more irregular and broken than those of the prairie mole, and usually smaller and more crooked. The burrows may be quite deep for a short distance, then appear as ridges, or even as surface runways, shortly to disappear again under ground. Sometimes, particularly in marshes and meadows, the star-nosed mole uses surface runways for long distances under and through the grass. It also frequently leaves its tunnels in winter to burrow in the snow or even travel on top of it, leaving a trail. Feces may sometimes be found in or near the runways, and are elongate, and usually curved irregularly. Frequently the tunnels enter the bank of a stream a foot or more below the water line. At Solon Springs, Douglas County, July 29, 1919, I found a small colony in a wooded moist bank of a small cold brook. The ridges were for the most part irregular in their courses, and at infrequent intervals approached the creek in open runways, only, however, for distances of eight inches or less. Apparently the animal used these as taking off points for jumping into the water. Most of the runways were from one to three feet above the water in the creek, and in the vicinity of old stumps became a veritable network. The mole ridges had an average width

Mound of star-nosed mole in moist hay meadow, Chippewa County, Wisconsin. Represents the more usual type of mound made by this species. Courtesy Frank J. W. Schmidt.

Mound of star-nosed mole in somewhat dry brushland, Worden Township, Clark County, Wisconsin. A rather unusual type of mound made by this species. Courtesy Frank J. W. and Karl P. Schmidt.

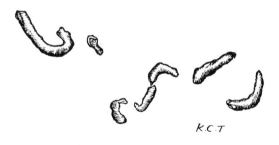

K.C.T

Excrement of star-nosed mole, Solon Springs, Wisconsin. Drawn from field sketches made by the author. About natural size.

of about one and three-fourths inches and a height of about one and one-fourth inches. The mounds which are thrown up at irregular intervals by the mole's disposing of surplus dirt may be as much as two feet wide and six inches high. On wet ground the molehill is apt to be higher. and much narrower, and shows layers and globules where each earth load was packed to the surface. Such mounds have much the appearance of large crayfish mounds. As a rule, however, in moderately moist soil the mounds are flatter and broader, and do not show the layers clearly.

The star-nosed mole is active both day and night at all seasons of the year. It neither hibernates nor migrates. In its diurnal activities it prefers cloudy and wet days, and is not so frequently active on bright days. Winter may change its habits to roaming on the snow or swimming under the ice, and the search for food at that season is more arduous. There are many records of its being exposed on the snow, and it also frequently makes runways both on the surface and beneath it. A specimen captured February 10, 1918, at Tomahawk, Lincoln County, and now in the University of Wisconsin Museum, was sent to the writer by the late Simon J. Adams, who said it was out on the snow when killed by his boys and a dog during mild weather that followed six weeks of very severe weather.

Amphibious, in fact almost aquatic, the star-nosed mole spends a good portion of its time in the water, and is an excellent swimmer and diver, though it will not dive from heights of more than a few inches above the surface. Frequently its tunnels enter the water a foot or more below the surface, and the mole enters or leaves them at will. It can remain under water for minutes, and darts swiftly hither and thither in a zigzag fashion, or sometimes crosses in a straight line under water from one submerged entrance to another. It is particularly active in winter as an underwater swimmer under the ice. Its swimming movements appear much like those of a frog except that most of its momentum is produced by the forefeet, which move alternately, as do the hind ones. The tail is not used in swimming. Not so highly modified in its fore limbs for digging as the prairie mole, it cannot make such rapid progress through the ground. It employs, however, essentially the same method of shoving the dirt ahead of it. The star-nosed mole is in contrast better adapted for surface travel than its near relative. Although it can dig its ridges at the rate of only about 8 feet an hour it can run on the surface for a short distance at four to five miles an hour and swim at nearly twice that speed.

It being a colonial and gregarious animal, one would anticipate it had methods of intercommunication, but none is known. It has a somewhat musky odor which may have use in communication, but no calls or signals have been recognized. When squeezed too tightly or physically distressed it sometimes gives a weak, husky squeak. One under study in captivity made a peculiar wheezing noise with each inhalation when sleeping (Schmidt, 1931: 110). Not in the least pugnacious, it does not attempt to bite or scratch on being handled, and appears almost friendly. When it tries to escape it shows its inherent desire to dig and probe, and tries to shove apart one's fingers with its forefeet and crawl through. The star-nosed mole is much quicker and more agile than the prairie mole, but is not as strong physically. Touching the tentacles does not bother the mole unless it be with a metallic substance, but rubbing its back may startle it. On the whole the tactile sense is highly developed, as one might expect in an animal with weak senses of sight, hearing, and smell. Short life undoubtedly faces it, and though we have little evidence, probably its normal span is not more than three or four years.

It is believed that adult star-nosed moles mate in the autumn and that the pair remain together until the young are born. Young ones breed the first year, but it is likely that they do not mate until early in the winter. Sexual activation in the males, however, does not take place until the middle of February, and may continue in some individuals up to the middle of March. Actual breeding in Wisconsin begins about the middle of March and extends to the end of April. The period of gestation is believed to be about 45 days, thus making the birth dates from the last of April to the middle of June. There is only one litter a year. Six seems to be the usual number of young in a litter, but it may vary from three to seven. At birth they are pinkish in color, void of visible hair, and show only traces of the vibrissae on the skin surface. The nasal processes, however, already are clearly marked at the tip of the snout. In fact, rudiments of the tentacles may be seen in half-developed embryos. The newly born young measures in total length 70 to 75 mm. (2.8 to 3.0 inches), of which the thick tail is about 25 mm. (1.0 inch). When it is six to eight days old a short fur growth appears over the back, and within two days later hair appears on the belly. By the time it leaves

Embryo of star-nosed mole. Eyes prominent and nasal rays visible. Lateral view, about 4×. Photograph by S. E. Simpson, 1923, pl. 20.

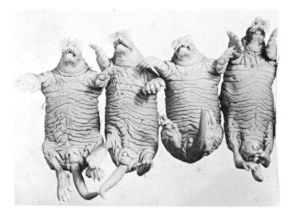

Young of star-nosed mole, four of a litter of five. Ventral view, about ⅝×. Photograph by S. E. Simpson, 1923, pl. 18.

the nest when a month or more old it is well furred with short, sleek, close-lying hair.

The nest of the star-nosed mole is loosely constructed of leaves or grass, or both, and is placed in a flattened spherical chamber five to seven inches in diameter and three to five inches high. It is always placed above high-water level, usually in or under a little hillock or knoll, and frequently beneath a stump or log. It is usually three to five inches beneath the surface of the ground, but may be as deep as ten inches. Schmidt (1931: 109) says of two nests found in hardwood forest in Worden Township, Clark County, Wisconsin: "Both nests were on knolls about one foot above water of a ditch which carried the water from the road through the woods.

The nest chambers were three or four inches from the surface and were five inches wide and three or four inches high. Both nests were placed between roots of maple trees. One nest had two horizontal and one vertical tunnel coming up from below. The tunnels measured 40 mm. by 50 mm. in diameter. . . . One nest was made of maple leaves lined with small pieces of leaves, the other, of leaves and grass." L. G. Sorden, former county agent at Rhinelander, wrote me under date of July 18, 1932, about the nest of a star-nosed mole that was found May 3, 1932, under a damp stump in the garden of Mrs. John Pollock, 218 Monico Street, Rhinelander, only a few feet from the house. The "nest was apparently similar to a mouse nest and made of dry grass and twigs," four or five inches in diameter, and placed in sandy soil. "There were five young moles in the nest and as far as they could find there was no outlet to the nest and the Pollocks could not understand how the parent moles could get in. They have never seen the parent or matured moles."

The natural food of the star-nosed mole consists chiefly of aquatic worms, insects, and other invertebrates, and less than one-fourth of its food consists of terrestrial forms. About half of its diet consists of worms, of which only a few are earthworms, and one-third consists of insects. The remaining 15 per cent is composed of crustacea (amphipods, isopods), mollusks (snails), and miscellaneous items. Little fish (minnows) and

Nest of star-nosed mole, Worden Township, Clark County, Wisconsin. The top of the mound has been removed to show the nest between the roots, Courtesy Frank J. W. Schmidt.

frog meat have appeared in its diet in insignificant quantity.

The mud in the creek bottom along a small creek which flows through a hardwood forest in Worden Township [Clark County] is heavily infested with annelid worms of the order Microdrili. When there is water in the creek one end of the worm sticks out of the mud and waves around in the water. They are so numerous in some parts of the creek bottom that they look like a waving growth of brown moss. When the creek dries up they retreat into the mud. During the summer of 1929 this creek bottom, which had partly dried up at that time was thoroughly rooted up and tunneled by star-nosed moles in search of worms (Schmidt, 1931: 107).

When it drinks, its nose and tentacles are submerged, and sometimes it completely submerges its head or even jumps into the water. On coming out of the water it scratches itself vigorously in order to fluff the fur.

On account of its seclusive habits the star-nosed mole is not the common prey of many predators, but there are records of its being captured by mink, striped skunks, red-tailed hawks, red-shouldered hawks, roughleg hawks, great horned owls, barred owls, and screech owls. It is particularly vulnerable to attack when out on the snow in winter, and is not infrequently killed by cats or dogs at such times, or by automobiles on highways. When swimming it could readily be the prey of such fish as the black bass, the pickerel, or the muskellunge.

The star-nosed mole is subject to several parasites.

Mites of the genus *Androlaelaps* are among the most abundant external parasites. Siphonaptera have been taken from half the specimens examined. . . . *Ctenophthalmus wenmanni* and *Ctenophthalmus pseudagyrtes* have been collected from the moles frequently. Less often they are afflicted with *Ceratophyllus wickhami*. Internally cestodes are occasionally found, but nematodes are often abundant. Ascarids are very common on the stomach, the walls of the intestine, just under the integument of the rump and shoulder region, and imbedded in the mesenchyme. . . . The worms are enclosed in a tissue sheath and are invariably coiled. They are 3 to 4 mm. in diameter when coiled and average 35 mm. when extended. There may be as many as a hundred in one host (Hamilton, 1931 b: 350).

A new genus and species of mite, *Eadiea condylurae*, has also been described from the star-nosed mole (Jameson, 1949: 423). No true diseases are known in *Condylura*.

The star-nosed mole, because its habitat is chiefly in non-agricultural lands, seldom interferes with man's interests. It occasionally becomes somewhat troublesome by making mounds in meadows or on golf courses, but compensates for this in the great number of insects it destroys. Moreover, it has value as a unique animal. If control procedure is necessary, the best method is by trapping. I have readily trapped star-nosed moles in Schuyler mousetraps by digging out a small portion of a runway, setting the trap across it, burying the base of the trap, and leaving the trigger across the path of the mole. The rat-trap size also will do, but not so well as the smaller trap. Some prefer the scissors-jaw trap for catching star-nosed moles. Bait seems to afford no attraction.

Specimens examined from Wisconsin.—Total 32, as follows: *Bayfield County:* Bayfield, 1 (UWZ); Herbster, 1. *Chippewa County:* Boyd, 1 (UWZ); Delmar Township, 3 (2 UWZ). *Clark County:* Worden Township, 2 (UWZ). *Douglas County:* Solon Springs, 4. *Forest County:* Newald, 1 (MM). *Iron County:* Mercer, 1 (UWZ); Upton (4 mi. N.), 1 (WHD). *Langlade County:* Antigo, 1 (UWZ); Post Lake, 1 (MM). *Lincoln County:* Merrill, 1 (MM); Tomahawk, 1 (UWZ). *Marathon County:* Colby, 1 (USNM). *Marinette County:* Peshtigo, 1 (UWZ). *Oneida County:* Minocqua, 1 (CNHM). *Polk County:* Saint Croix Falls, 1. *Price County:* T 37 N, R 2 W, 1 (F&FH). *Rusk County:* NW corner of county, 1 (MM). *Shawano County:* Keshena Falls, 1 (CAS); Whitcomb, 1 (UWZ). *Taylor County:* Medford, 2 (UWZ). *Vilas County:* Phelps, 2 (UWZ). *Wood County:* Marshfield, 1 (UWZ).

Selected references.—Hamilton, W. J., Jr., 1931; Jackson, H. H. T., 1915; Lyon, M. W., Jr., 1936, pp. 35–37; Schmidt, F. J. W., 1931, pp. 107–9; Seton, E. T., 1909, pp. 1136–44; True, F. W., 1896.

ORDER **CHIROPTERA**

Bats

Mammals of this order are the only ones with fore limbs adapted for true flight. Most of the species feed on insects which they chiefly capture while flying. The fruit-eating bats of Asian tropics are large bats whose food is indicated by their name. Bats that catch and eat small fish occur in tropical America. The vampire bat, found in Mexico and in Central and South America, acquired its name from its feeding habit of piercing with its teeth the skin of some other mammal, often a large one, and then sucking blood therefrom, usually while the victim is asleep. Bats in general range worldwide in tropical and temperate regions, and often are found on isolated oceanic islands where there is no other native mammal.

In the bat, the forearm consists of a rudimentary ulna, a long curved radius, six small bones forming the carpus, to which are attached the thumb and four greatly elongated slender digits. A thin delicate membrane, a double layer of the body integument, is stretched between the fingers and attached to the side of the body, the leg, and the tail to form the wing. The thumb is free of the membrane and bears a claw. The calcar, an elongate process, arises from the ankle, is directed inward, and supports that part of the membrane extending from the tail to the hind legs, called the interfemoral membrane. Ears usually large; tragus well developed; eyes usually small. The skull is relatively broad; zygomata complete; premaxillae, anteriorly widely separated; canines acute on posterior edge; cusps on molariform teeth W-shaped.

The Chiroptera embrace 17 living families, of which one, Vespertilionidae, is represented in Wisconsin.

Family **Vespertilionidae**

Common Bats

The family Vespertilionidae ranges nearly worldwide. It is composed of some 25 living genera, of which 5 occur in Wisconsin.

Skulls of bats. A. MYOTIS L. LUCIFUGUS, La Crosse, Wisconsin, B. MYOTIS K. SEPTENTRIONALIS, Cass Lake, Minnesota, C. MYOTIS SODALIS, Atkinson's Diggings, Grant County, Wisconsin, No. 7191 Univ. Illinois Mus. Nat. Hist., D. LASIONYCTERIS NOCTIVAGANS, Amelia Court House, Virginia, E. PIPISTRELLUS S. SUBFLAVUS, Devils Lake, Wisconsin, F. EPTESICUS F. FUSCUS, Cheat River, West Virginia, G. LASIURUS B. BOREALIS, Potosi, Wisconsin, H. LASIURUS C. CINEREUS, Kelley Lake, Wisconsin. 1×.

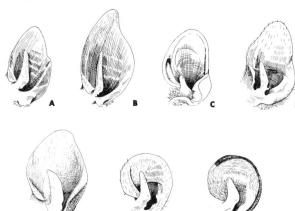

Ears of bats. A. MYOTIS L. LUCIFUGUS, B. MYOTIS K. SEPTENTRIONALIS, C. LASIONYCTERIS NOCTIVAGANS, D. PIPISTRELLUS S. SUBFLAVUS, E. EPTESICUS F. FUSCUS, F. LASIURUS B. BOREALIS, G. LASIURUS C. CINEREUS. About 1½×.

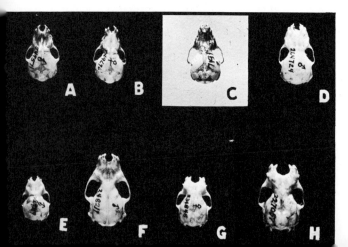

Genus **Myotis** Kaup
Mouse-eared Bats

Dental formula:

$$\mathrm{I}\,\frac{2-2}{3-3},\ \ \mathrm{C}\,\frac{1-1}{1-1},\ \ \mathrm{P}\,\frac{3-3}{3-3},\ \ \mathrm{M}\,\frac{3-3}{3-3}=38.$$

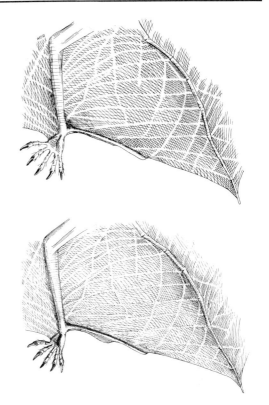

Myotis lucifugus lucifugus (Le Conte)
Little Brown Bat

V. [*espertilio*] *lucifugus* Le Conte, in H. McMurtrie,
  Cuvier. Anim. Kingdom, vol. 1, appendix of the
  American editor, p. 431, 1831. June, 1831.
V*espertilio lucifugus* Strong, p. 438, 1883.
Myotis lucifugus Snyder, p. 126, 1902; Jackson, p.
  32, 1908; Hollister, p. 30, 1910; Jackson, p. 90,
  1910; Cory, p. 455, 1912.
Myotis lucifugus lucifugus Schmidt, p. 105, 1931;
  Barger, p. 10, 1952.

Vernacular names.—Ah-pe-kwa-nah-djee or *Po-
qua-na-ge* (Chippewa Indian, applied to all
bats), big myotis, blunt-nosed bat, brown myotis,
chauvesouris (French, applied to all bats),
Fledermaus (German, applied to all bats),
mouse-eared bat, and small myotis.

*Identification marks.—*A medium-sized bat,
with body about the size of a small mouse (head
and body length about two inches); ear nearly
devoid of hair, moderately short, when laid
forward reaching barely to the tip of the nose,
its anterior edge convex, becoming nearly straight
in the upper third to the bluntly rounded tip,
its posterior edge on the lower half rather deeply convex, forming near the base a projecting
shoulder and becoming on the upper half only
slightly convex or nearly straight; tragus moderately long and pointed, nearly half the total
length of the ear, having at its outer base a small
rounded lobe marked off by a shallow notch; the
inner margin of the tragus nearly straight, the

Lower side of tail and right hind foot of MYOTIS
L. LUCIFUGUS *(upper figure) and* MYOTIS SODALIS
(lower figure), 1½×.

Skins of bats of the genus MYOTIS. *Left,* M. L. LUCI-
FUGUS, *Cassville, Wisconsin. Middle,* M. K. SEPTEN-
TRIONALIS, *Procter, Vermont. Right,* M. SODALIS,
*Atkinson's Diggings, Grant County, Wisconsin, No.
7191, Univ. Illinois Mus. Nat. Hist.*

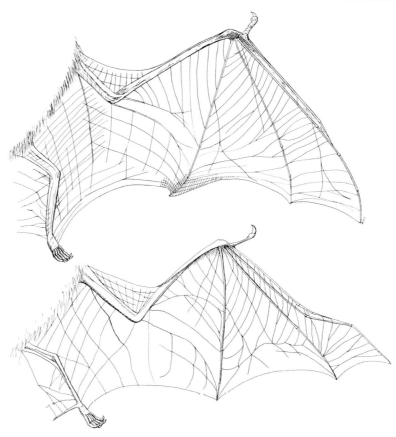

Wings, arms and legs of bats, underside. Upper,
MYOTIS LUCIFUGUS. *Lower,* PIPISTRELLUS SUBFLAVUS.
½×.

outer margin somewhat convex and faintly cren-
ulate to the narrowly rounded tip; eyes tiny,
black, and beady; nose relatively broad and
blunt; tail moderate length, the extreme tip
usually free (1 to 3 mm.); wing and interfemoral membranes essentially bare and devoid
of hair except for a few inconspicuous ones scattered along the border; foot relatively large, the
ratio of its length to that of the tibia .57 to .61;
calcar long, exceeding in length the free border
of the interfemoral membrane; fur dense, long,
and very fine, the tips of hairs, particularly dorsally, long and glossy, producing a glossy sheen.
The bat is reputed to have the finest hair of any
mammal and the greatest number of hairs per
unit area of skin surface.

The color of the upper parts is usually olive
brown, varying in some individuals to yellowish
brown, with an indistinct dusky spot on the
shoulder caused by showing of the more plumbeous basal portions of the hairs; under parts gray,
tinged with deep buff; bases of hairs of both
upper and lower parts blackish or dark plumbeous, except those at the extreme posterior of the
under parts; ears, wing, and interfemoral membranes dark brown or dark brownish plumbeous,
sometimes almost blackish, the hairs sparse and
well scattered (essentially hairless).

So far as known there are essentially no seasonal differences in color, though in some specimens there appears to be a slight paling of the
hair tips in spring following the winter period of
dormancy. Apparently there is no regular molt
or molting time, individual hairs being shed and
replaced more or less continuously.

The skull is slender and lightly built; rostrum
relatively short and narrow, the breadth across
roots of canines less than interorbital constriction;
forehead (frontal region) slightly depressed anteriorly; brain case slightly flattened; sagittal
crest seldom developed anteriorly, sometimes

Little brown bat, MYOTIS LUCIFUGUS. *Left, hanging from roof of Colossal Cave, Kentucky. Photograph by Vernon Bailey. Right, resting on tree trunk, Manitoba. Copyright by H. H. Pittman.*

sharply defined posteriorly; dentition moderate in size.

There appears to be no sexual variation in size, color, or general cranial characters. Immature individuals are more grayish and somewhat darker than adults; as growth of the hair progresses, the tips of the hairs become more brownish and glossier, until the pelage assumes the color of the adult animal. It has frequently been written that there are two color phases in *Myotis l. lucifugus,* one a "glossy yellowish brown" and the other "bronze to olive brown," but in my experience these phases simply represent extremes of a normal range of color variation. There are a few records of pied individuals (white-blotching) of this species in the United States, but I know of none from Wisconsin.

The little brown bat (*M. l. lucifugus*) is somewhat similar in general appearance and size to the eastern long-eared bat (*M. keenii septentrionalis*), but may be distinguished by its narrower and shorter ear (less than 16 mm. long) which when laid forward reaches to the nostrils but not beyond, whereas the ear of *septentrionalis* (more than 16 mm. long) when laid forward extends 2 to 4 mm. beyond the nostrils; the tragus (crest spike in the base of the ear) is less than 9 mm. long in *lucifugus*, more than 9 mm. in *septentrionalis*; the skull of *lucifugus* is relatively wider and the rostrum more robust than in *septentri-*

onalis, but actual comparison of specimens is usually necessary to determine this. *Myotis l. lucifugus* is larger than *Pipistrellus s. subflavus,* is duller and darker in color (less pale-cinnamon brown), and has relatively and actually longer forearms and larger feet, and four more teeth (three premolars above and three below on each side, instead of two).

Measurements.—Total length of adults, 80 to 100 mm. (3.1 to 3.9 in.); tail, 32 to 44 mm. (1.3 to 1.7 in.); hind foot, 9 to 11 mm. (0.3 to 0.4 in.); forearm, 36 to 42 mm. (1.4 to 1.7 in.); ear length from notch, 13 to 15 mm. (0.5 to 0.6 in.); ear width, 9 to 10 mm. (0.3 to 0.4 in.); tragus height, 7 to 8 mm. (0.27 to 0.3 in.); wing spread, 250 to 275 mm. (10 to 11 in.). Weight, 7 to 10 grams (0.25 to 0.35 oz.). Skull length, 14.2 to 15.2 mm.; width, 8.2 to 9.5 mm.

Distribution in Wisconsin.—Throughout the state in favorable habitats; apparently more abundant in southern and western Wisconsin than in northeastern.

Habitat.—In caves, caverns, abandoned mine diggings, and deep clefts in rocks; in church belfries, and towers and cupolas; about buildings,

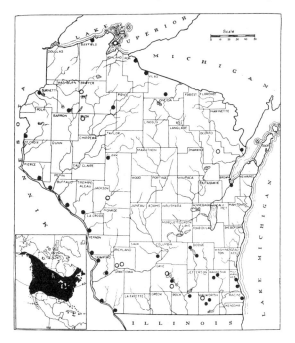

Map 14. Distribution of MYOTIS LUCIFUGUS. ● = *specimens examined.* ○ = *authentic records.*

such as behind shutters, between roofs and ceilings, in cornices or crevices near the roof, in walls, or behind loose sheathing or siding.

Status and Habits.—The little brown bat is possibly the most abundant bat in Wisconsin, although in some sections away from caves and buildings it is outnumbered by the red bat, particularly in forested or orchard areas. It is especially common along the larger streams in the southern and western parts of the state. It maintains fairly constant numbers, though it may be subject to cycles, and so far as we know may have about the same population in Wisconsin as when the first settlers arrived. Several hundred may roost in clusters in a small cave, or in a suitable steeple or cupola during daylight, and at dusk flutter out over fields, marshes, lakes, and rivers. At Cassville, Wisconsin, June 2, 1912, I estimated the concentration of little brown bats flying over many acres of Mississippi River bottoms as close to 200 per acre. Similar feeding flight concentration occurs elsewhere along the Mississippi, such as at Prairie du Chien, La Crosse, and Prescott. Estimates I made of bats flying over the shore line of Storr's Lake, town of Milton, Rock County, May 30, 1902, indicated about 110 per acre, of which possibly 60 were little brown bats. Their normal home range is probably not more than one or two miles. Bats of this species, however, have been released 76 miles from their home roost and returned to it within six nights (Hitchcock and Reynolds, 1942: 259).

Bats may inhabit some cranny unobserved for a long time. One familiar with bats, however, can usually locate a colony by the characteristic penetrating pungent odor that comes from droppings and urine of the bats. Often bats may be detected by their scratching and scrambling noises as they make their way through walls, or again, when they are disturbed by a jar or other irritation, by their metallic high-pitched chattering. They do not leave distinctive tracks or claw marks as a rule, but usually leave a brownish stain on objects upon which they have roosted for some time or rubbed frequently. Their feces are narrower than those of house mice, and are often left in measurable quantity. Sometimes bats may be seen leaving or entering the opening to their roost. At dusk they may be seen flying in search of food.

The little brown bat may rarely appear in flight in full daylight, as did one for fully five minutes in a temperature of 64° F. in bright sunlight (about 1:35 P.M.) on May 10, 1947, on Lake Mendota, Madison, while members of the Wisconsin Society for Ornithology were assembled to be photographed. Not infrequently it may appear on dark, cloudy warm days at midday, but in its usual routine it is nocturnal, leaving its roosting place at dusk and continuing active until dawn.

The little brown bat may migrate a short distance in the autumn to find suitable winter shelter for hibernating, traveling again in spring to its summer habitat. At Beaver Dam, Dodge County, "this species came with the migration of hoary bats in Sept., 1901, previous to which I had never taken one. One morning some 60 were found in a granary, having gained access through a broken window pane. They used this roost for only three nights, after which they were seen no more" (Snyder, W. E., 1902: 126). Another migration of these bats occurred at Black River Falls, Wisconsin, October 29, 1936 (Zimmerman, 1937). Only a small number of little brown bats seem to migrate, and these only for short distances to find winter shelter. Those living in locations favorable for hibernation resort to caves, mines, and sometimes crannies in buildings or in other cavities, where usually in clusters they hang suspended from the ceiling or wall by the curved claws of the hind feet. Where bats of this species are plentiful, seldom do they hang singly or in groups up to five or ten, but usually in larger assemblages numbering into the hundreds or, in rare instances, particularly in larger caves, into a thousand or more. The bats enter the caves in the autumn, usually early in November, and when insect food becomes scarce or inaccessible to them, they remain within the shelter, gradually moving deeper into the cave as the weather becomes colder, until they reach the constant cave temperature of 40° to 54°. During the last part of summer and the first part of autumn they have acquired much fat, which serves as nourishment for them during their quiescent months. Many individuals do not enter into deep hibernation and are easily brought back to some activity, and even the more stubborn cases seldom require longer than 30 minutes of warmth and light; most bats reactivate in a few seconds under such conditions. Often a bat apparently in deep hibernation when touched utters almost immediately its sharp chattering or squeaking resistance alarm, and may even attempt to nip the offending finger. Further evidence of their generally weak torpidity is that the colonies frequently change in position, location, and in number of bats during the hibernation period.

Flying is the normal and natural means of locomotion by the bat, as might be judged by its developed wing and tail membranes and its specialized arm and hand which form a wing. The shape of the bat's body, its slender limbs, and the absence of fur from its wings all aid in its adaptation to flight. The little brown bat flies relatively fast, with continuous wing strokes about fifteen a second and no soaring, and is very erratic, dodging, diving, dashing hither and thither, ofttimes, a difficult object to follow with the eye. Its normal speed in straightaway flying may not exceed 40 miles an hour, yet it seems to greatly accentuate this speed at each twist and turn. On the ground, particularly on a smooth surface, it progresses with extreme awkwardness by a series of hops, making slow or no progress, its limbs poorly adapted for such use. From such a position it is unable to launch readily into flight, which it easily does from an elevated location. The little brown bat can progress in water fairly well for a short distance by flapping around on the surface and drifting with the wind. It becomes exhausted, however, and unless fortunate enough to be lifted out of the water by wind or other agent, soon succumbs.

This species seems to most people to be a comparatively silent animal, yet much of its apparent silence may be due to the fact that its high-pitched squeaks or chirps are inaudible to many persons. In a colony of bats these chirps, as well as high-pitched chatterings, may frequently be heard. Individuals when touched will almost invariably chatter and sometimes chirp. So sensitive to sound vibrations are bats that it has been believed by some that they have a sixth sense. Certainly the experiments of Hahn (1908) and others show exceptional adaptations to vibration production and reception. Griffin has found that special cries that bats send out to locate unseen objects in their paths are similar to the radar system man uses. Sound is given out in pulses lasting only about one five-hundredth of a second. Bats may repeat cries as often as 50 times a second, but there is a relatively long silent period during which the bat listens for echoes. The frequency of the sound varies from 80 kilocycles a second at the beginning to 40 kilocycles at the end. The bat produces this sound intensity with a specialized larynx about one-fifth of an inch in its largest diameter. Ordinarily one notices no sound as a bat flies past emitting these special cries, but in a very quiet room a faint "click" may be audible (Griffin, 1950). There is an unproven theory that the special adaptation for sensory reception of these high vibrations is through the hair and skin, or the tragus. This acts as a delicate pressure gauge and probably accounts for the ability of the bat to detect objects and avoid collision with them. There appears to be no other well-developed means of intercommunication, though one might well surmise that the odor of a bat roost might aid the animal's homing instinct.

Although the little brown bat acts pugnaciously when first disturbed, and chatters saucily and threatens to bite, yet like most colonial species it is quite amicable among its kind. It sputters when nudged or bumped by its neighbor, but seldom shows real fight. While possibly not so tractable as some other bats, it can be trained to come forth when called and eat from one's hand or a spoon. It is not strong physically except in the facial, neck, and chest muscles, but can nip one's finger with its needlelike teeth. It has no evident play tendencies, as do most mammals, but is so unusual in its habits as to be always interesting. Its normal life span in the wild is near seven years, and records show a potential longevity of thirteen or fourteen years.

Copulation occurs about the middle of October or later in the autumn before the bats enter hibernation. Copulation may also occur during the winter, as recorded for this species January 3, 1948, in western Pennsylvania (Guilday, 1948). Ovulation may shortly follow these early copulations, as the record of a fetus January 30, 1949, near Uniontown, Pennsylvania (Guilday, 1950), would indicate. Normally, spermatozoa survive in the uterus throughout the winter, and fertilization by these may occur in the spring. Copulation also occurs in the spring (March or later), following which ovulation takes place after the bats leave their hibernation quarters. The gestation period is not positively known but is probably near 80 days. Spontaneous ovulation apparently correlated with a rise in temperature does not occur before late in February, and the first young are born late in May or early in June. One young at birth is usual, rarely two. Five out of six females that I dissected at Cassville, June 3, 1912, each had one well-developed fetus. Except for a few hairs on the toes and a few vibrissae, the young are naked at birth, and have the eyes closed. The sex ratio of large numbers at birth is about 51 per cent males, though in colonies of adults in winter hibernation the ratio runs from 56 to 71 per cent males (Mohr, 1945). The young one remains clinging to the mother's nipple when she is at rest, but after the first day is left hanging in the breeding cavity while she is away feeding. About four weeks after birth the youngster is on the wing feeding itself. Sexual maturity is reached in eight months. There is only one litter a year.

The little brown bat, in common with all other Wisconsin bats, makes no nest of any kind. A sheltered place in which to crawl and hang by its hind feet suffices for a home. When the mother is present, the young (until three or four weeks old) cling to her breast, but when she is away they hang by themselves.

The food of the little brown bat so far as known consists entirely of insects. Moths, beetles, and bugs, particularly nocturnal species, form a great bulk of its food. It is a gluttonous eater, and often consumes food until its stomach is distended with contents one-third its own weight. It feeds around lights to catch insects attracted thereby, and at times while pursuing its prey may enter a room through an open window or doorway, fly about with skill, and catch such insects as also may have entered. It frequently feeds over watercourses or lakes, and occasionally dips to the surface of the water, apparently to take a drink.

The little brown bat has very few enemies. There are scattered records of remains of this species found in the stomach contents of the sharp-shinned hawk, pigeon hawk, sparrow hawk, and great horned owl, and possibly other Raptores. Among mammals the mink and weasel have been known to prey on bats. There is some indication that numbers may die in a colony at times, possibly from some malady or extreme cold. A severe storm may also take its toll. It escapes almost entirely destruction by automobiles and other vehicles. The parasites of North American bats have not been thoroughly studied, but *Myotis lucifugus* is known to have external parasites that include the flea *Myodopsylla insignis*, the mite *Haemogamasus alaskensis*, and the bug *Cimex pilosellus*. Internal parasites include the tapeworm *Hymenolepis christensoni* and flukes of the genera *Lecithodendrium* and *Glyptoporus*.

Members of eight genera of bats (*Desmodus, Myotis, Lasionycteris, Eptesicus, Lasiurus, Dasypterus, Antrozous,* and *Tadarida*) are known to have been infected with rabies or hydrophobia. Representatives of *Myotis, Lasionycteris, Eptesicus,* and *Lasiurus* occur in Wisconsin. Rabid bats apparently do not often transmit rabies to humans even when the human is bitten. Development of rabies symptoms in such a victim usually is slow. Rabies in man acquired from a bat is difficult to cure, the normal rabies antitoxin seemingly being ineffective. It occurs to me that an antitoxin made from a rabid bat might be a solution.

There is record of one death from the bite of a rabid bat in Wisconsin. On the cool night of August 8, 1959, a bat flew through an open window and bit the 44-year-old Louis Ashmore on his ear as he slept in his farm house near Blue River, Wisconsin. He killed the bat. The next day he joked and laughed about the incident. On August 29, he complained of a sore ear and stiff neck, but did not connect them with the bat bite and continued to work. On September 2, he became partly paralyzed and entered the hospital. He died September 6. (Abstracted from AP report, Evening Star, Washington, D. C., Sept. 16, 1959.) The kind of bat that bit Mr. Ashmore was not determined. Since the little brown bat (*Myotis l. lucifugus*) is probably the most abundant bat around Blue River and since the genus is known to carry rabies, it might well have been this species.

All Wisconsin species of bats, including the little brown bat, are harmless and beneficial. They all feed on nocturnal flying insects, many of which are harmful to man's interests and few beneficial. Superstitions have placed a heavy load of disrepute on these animals. One of these is that they get caught in women's hair! Has any one heard of an authentic case? Another is that they bite sleeping babies! That is absurd. Still another is that they harbor bedbugs and other parasites! They do harbor parasites, as do all animals, and some of them belong to the genus *Cimex* or bedbugs, but these are peculiar to certain kinds of bats and do not infest humans. Occasionally a colony of bats becomes obnoxious on account of the odor from accumulated droppings or because of noise when it inhabits a section of a building. The surest way to control such a situation is when the bats are away, probably at night, to close with wood or metal, or by caulking, all openings through which they enter. A liberal use of napthalene flakes thrown around and into the spaces occupied by the bats will act as a repellent for several weeks, and often will permanently dislodge the colony.

The accumulated droppings of bats constitute a fertilizer of high value, the fresh manure having a composition averaging 10.9 per cent nitrogen, 7.3 per cent acid phosphate, and 2.3 per cent water-soluble potash. In caves and other coverages where large quantities may occur, at a prevailing rate of about ten dollars per hundred pounds it has an appreciable worth. Attempts have been made in Texas to colonize bats of another species by building suitable roosts, but without notable success. One of these elaborate structures was occupied by bats and yielded about two tons of guano in one year. Other attempts have failed.

Specimens examined from Wisconsin.—Total 130, as follows: *Bayfield County:* Herbster, 1. *Brown County:* Green Bay, 1 (NPM). *Buffalo County:* Alma, 1 (UWZ); Fountain City, 25 (MM). *Burnett County:* Clam River (mouth of), 1 (MM). *Clark County:* Worden Township, 5 (3 UWZ). *Crawford County:* Crystal Cave, 2 (UWZ); Ferryville, 1. *Dane County:* Madison, 9 (6 USNM; 3 UWZ). *Dodge County:* Beaver Dam, 2 (CNHM); Fox Lake, 1 (MM). *Grant County:* Cassville, 15 (1 UWZ); Potosi (10 mi. S. S. E.), 2. *Iron County:* Hurley, 5 (UWZ); Owl Lake, 1 (UWZ). *La Crosse County:* La Crosse, 6. *Marinette County:* Peshtigo, 1 (MM). *Milwaukee County:* Milwaukee, 6 (2 MM; 2 USNM; 2 UWZ); South Milwaukee, 1 (MM). *Pepin County:* Lake Pepin (lower end), 10. *Pierce County:* Maiden Rock, 12 (MM). *Polk County:* Osceola, 1 (MM). *Racine County:* Racine, 1 (USNM). *Sauk County:* Devils Lake, 6. *Sawyer County:* T 38 N, R 3 W, 1. *Trempealeau County:* Galesville, 3 (UWZ). *Vernon County:* De Sota, 1. *Vilas County:* Lake St. Germain, 1. *Walworth County:* Delavan, 2; Lanes Mill, 1 (UWZ). *Washburn County:* Long Lake, 2; no locality, 1 (UWZ). *Waukesha County:* Delafield, 1 (UWZ); Hartland, 1 (UWZ).

Selected references.—Allen, G. M., 1939; Allen, H., 1893; Cagle, F. R., and E. L. Cockrum, 1943; Dymond, J. R., 1936; Miller, G. S., Jr., 1897; Miller, G. S., Jr., and G. M. Allen, 1928.

Myotis keenii septentrionalis (Trouessart)
Eastern Long-eared Bat

Vespertilio gryphus var. *septentrionalis* Trouessart, Catalogus mammalium tam viventium quam fossilium, p. 131, 1897.
Vespertilio subulatus Lapham, p. 337, 1853; Strong, p. 438, 1883.
Myotis subulatus Hollister, p. 142, 1909; Hollister, p. 30, 1910; Cory, p. 460, 1912.
Myotis keenii septentrionalis Schmidt, p. 105, 1931; Barger, p. 10, 1952.

Vernacular names.—Acadian bat, eastern Keen's bat, eastern long-eared brown bat, eastern long-eared little brown bat, eastern long-eared myotis, Keen or Keen's bat, Keen or Keen's myotis, Say or Say's bat (mostly used by older authors), small-footed myotis, Trouessart or Trouessart's bat, and Trouessart or Trouessart's little brown bat.

Identification marks.—Externally *Myotis keenii septentrionalis* is in many respects similar to *M. l. lucifugus;* it is about the same size and color, but usually is somewhat duller and not as glossy, the bronzy tips of the hairs being shorter; the under parts also are usually duller in color and more slaty; tail rather long, forearm and hind foot moderately short; ear long for a *Myotis* (17 mm. or more), extending when laid forward about 2 to 4 mm. beyond nostrils; tragus long (10 to 12 mm.), narrow, and with acute tip; foot about half as long as tibia.

Color somewhat like that of *M. l. lucifugus,* but *septentrionalis* in series appears distinctly more slaty both dorsally and ventrally because the brown hair tips are not long enough to obscure the slate color of the base of the hairs. Young are as a rule more grayish or plumbeous than adults, and in color are quite like the young of *M. l. lucifugus.* There is little if any seasonal variation, though some specimens in spring pelage seem to be slightly paler than specimens taken later in the summer and in autumn. This may be caused by a slight paling during the hibernating period.

The skull of *M. k. septentrionalis* is relatively longer and narrower than that of *M. l. lucifugus,* and often is actually so in both dimensions; it is interorbitally more depressed and narrower; the distance from the last upper molar to the hamular process exceeds the distance between the last molars, instead of equaling it as it does in *lucifugus;* rostrum less robust than in *lucifugus,* and the width of the interorbital constriction less evidently exceeds that of the rostrum across roots of canines; small cusps of molars reduced, much more so than in *lucifugus.* There is no sexual variation in size, color, or cranial characters. Young gradually assume color of the adults as growth of the hair progresses. There are no records of color mutations in *M. k. septentrionalis.*

The eastern long-eared bat (*M. k. septentrionalis*), though similar in many features to the little brown bat (*M. l. lucifugus*), may be distinguished by its longer (more than 16 mm. long) and broader ear, which when laid forward reaches 2 to 4 mm. beyond the nostrils; the tragus is more than 9 mm. long in *septentrionalis,* less than 9 mm. in *lucifugus;* the skull of *septentrionalis* is relatively narrower and the rostrum relatively weaker than in *lucifugus.*

Measurements.—Total length of adults, 78 to 95 mm. (3 to 3.7 in.); tail, 34 to 42 mm. (1.3 to 1.7 in.); hind foot, 8 to 9.5 mm. (0.31 to 0.38 in.); forearm, 34 to 38 mm. (1.3 to 1.5 in.); ear length from notch, 17 to 19.5 mm. (0.67 to 0.77 in.); ear width, 9.5 to 10.8 mm. (0.38 to 0.42 in.); tragus height, 10 to 12 mm. (0.4 to 0.47 in.); wing spread, 250 to 275 mm. (10 to 11 in.). Weight, 7 to 8.5 grams (0.25 to 0.3 oz.). Skull length, 14.6 to 15.5 mm.; width, 8.4 to 9.2 mm.

Distribution in Wisconsin.—Probably occurs sparsely throughout the state; possibly more plentiful in the northern counties.

Habitat.—Apparently this species has about the same habitat preferences as the little brown bat, though it seems to be less attracted to buildings, and has a predilection for abandoned mines and small caves.

Status and Habits.—Very little is known of the life history and habits of this species, but they probably do not differ greatly from those of the little brown bat. It is apparently a rather scarce bat in Wisconsin. Late in August and early in September, 1947, James R. Beer and Frederick Greeley banded more than one hundred of these bats in an abandoned iron mine near Hurley, Iron County. In a personal letter to me November 14, 1947, Mr. Beer states in regard to this colony: "Items of interest from the distributional standpoint are the large numbers of *Myotis keenii* that we found in an abandoned iron mine. They were outnumbered by *Myotis lucifugus* by about 3 to 1."

Specimens examined from Wisconsin.—Total 26, as follows: *Bayfield County:* Bayfield, 1 (USNM). *Buffalo County;* Alma, 1 (UWZ). *Clark County:* Worden Township, 1 (UWZ). *Dane County:* Madison, 1 (UWZ). *Dunn County:* Meridean, 1 (JNC). *Iron County:* Hurley, 17 (9 CNHM; 8 UWZ). *Richland County:* Bogus Cave, 1; John Gray Cave, 2 (UWZ). *Sauk County:* Sumpter Township, 1 (CNHM).

Selected references.—Allen, G. M., 1939; Guthrie, Mary J., 1933; Hitchcock, H. B., 1949; Miller, G. S., Jr., 1897 b; Miller, G. S. Jr., and G. M. Allen, 1928; Rysgaard, G. N., 1942.

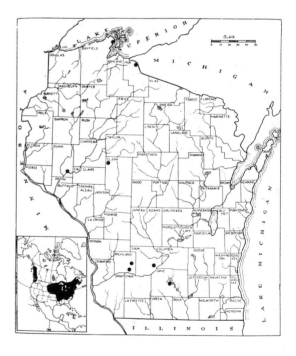

Map 15. *Distribution of* MYOTIS KEENII. ● = *specimens examined.*

Myotis sodalis Miller and G. M. Allen
Indiana Bat

Myotis sodalis Miller and G. M. Allen, U. S. Nat. Mus. Bull. 144: 128, May 25, 1928.

Vernacular names.—Cave bat, companion bat, little sooty bat, pink bat, social bat, and Wyandotte Cave bat.

Identification marks.

Size and general appearance as in *Myotis lucifugus lucifugus,* but with slightly longer tail (average ratio of tail to head and body in 10 specimens from Vermont, 80.6; in 10 from Mammoth Cave, 81.0); less enlarged foot (often not more than one-half the length of tibia, the ratio of its average length to the average length of tibia ranging from 49.3 to 51.7 instead of from 53 to 55.7), usually though not always keeled calcar, and by the pinkish-gray color and loose texture of the fur. Forearm 36 to 40.6 mm. (usually 38 to 39 mm.). Skull with a narrower brain case and more pronounced saggital crest than in *Myotis lucifugus.*

The color is distinctive. On the upper surface the basal two-thirds of the hair is fuscous-black, then comes a narrow grayish band succeeded by a cinnamon-brown tip, so that there is a distinctly tricolor effect, while the grayish band showing through the cinnamon-brown tips gives a peculiar hoary appearance at a short distance. Below, the fur is slaty basally, the hairs with grayish white tips, washed more or less heavily with cinnamon-brown, particularly at the flanks, instead of slightly yellowish as in *M. lucifugus.* The general effect is a pinkish white below and a dull chestnut gray above. The membranes and ears are blackish brown.

The skull in general resembles that of *Myotis lucifugus lucifugus* with which it agrees in length (usually 14.4 to 15 mm.). In form it differs in certain details that become evident on close comparison. The most striking of these is the smaller, narrower brain case (6.6 to 7.2 mm. instead of 7.1 to 7.6 mm.), which instead of being high and with broadly flattened top is narrower, lower (4.6 to 5.1 mm. instead of 4.9 to 5.5 mm.) and more arched transversely than in *M. l. lucifugus.* A slightly but perfectly definite sagittal crest is normally present in adults, whereas in *M. l. lucifugus* the brain case is so broad-topped that the temporal muscles rarely meet to form a sharp ridge. Correlated with this difference is the more tapering front end of the brain case, a slightly narrower interorbital constriction (3.5 to 3.9 mm. instead of 4.0 to 4.4 mm.) with more graceful lines; and a slightly larger rostrum as compared with the brain case, features

which are obvious to the eye, and consistently borne out by actual measurements (Miller and Allen, 1928: 130–33).

This species may be confused with *Myotis lucifugus lucifugus,* and it is not always easily identified. Its relationships with *lucifugus* are not clear.

Measurements.—Adult female, no. 7191, Univ. Illinois Mus. Nat. Hist., from Atkinson's Diggings, Grant County, Wisconsin: Total length, 91 mm. (3.6 in.); tail 37 mm. (1.5 in.); hind foot, 9.5 mm. (0.4 in.); ear from notch, 14.5 mm. (0.6 in.); wing stretch, 260 mm. (10.2 in.). Weight, 7.8 grams. Skull length, 14.2 mm.; width, 8.9 mm.

Distribution in Wisconsin.—Known only from a single specimen from a mine known as Atkinson's Diggings, two and one-quarter miles west of Beetown, elevation 850 feet, Grant County.

Habitat.—Most specimens collected have been hibernating animals taken in caves during winter.

Status and Habits.—This species usually occurs with *Myotis l. lucifugus* in winter hibernation. It is seldom as common as *lucifugus* and throughout its range only about one-half as many specimens have been collected as of *M. l. lucifugus.* Little is known of its general habits which are

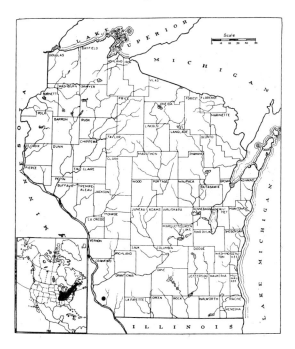

Map 16. Distribution of MYOTIS SODALIS. ● = specimen examined.

assumed to be similar to those of *M. l. lucifugus.* Vernon Bailey (1933: 74–76) has given us notes on its habits in Mammoth Cave, Kentucky. There is a longevity record of ten years.

Specimens examined from Wisconsin.—One, as follows: *Grant County:* Beetown (two and one-quarter miles west at Atkinson's Diggings, 850 ft. altitude) (UI).

Selected references.—Bailey, V., 1933: 74–76; Davis, W. H., and W. Z. Lidicker, Jr., 1955; Miller, G. S., Jr., and G. M. Allen, 1928.

Genus **Lasionycteris** Peters
Silver-haired Bat

Dental formula.

$$\text{I}\,\frac{2-2}{3-3},\ \ \text{C}\,\frac{1-1}{1-1},\ \ \text{P}\,\frac{2-2}{3-3},\ \ \text{M}\,\frac{3-3}{3-3}=36.$$

Lasionycteris noctivagans (Le Conte)
Silver-haired Bat

V[*espertilio*] *noctivagans* Le Conte, in H. M'Murtrie, Cuvier Anim. Kingdom, vol. 1, appendix, p. 431, June, 1831.
Vespertilio noctivagans Lapham, p. 337, 1853.
Scotophilus noctivagans Strong, p. 438, 1883.
Lasionycteris noctivagans Snyder, p. 126, 1902; Jackson, p. 33, 1908; Hollister, p. 30, 1910; Cory, p. 462, 1912; Schmidt, p. 105, 1931; Barger, p. 10, 1952.

Vernacular names.—Black bat, silver-black bat, silvery bat, and silvery-haired bat.

Identification marks.—The silver-haired bat is so peculiar in its color that it can readily be separated from any other Wisconsin bat by color alone. It is medium in size, averaging very slightly larger than either *Myotis lucifugus* or *Myotis keenii,* but considerably smaller than the big brown bat, *Eptesicus;* ear rather large, relatively short and broad, not pointed; tragus straight, short, broad, somewhat truncate; tail comparatively short, less than 40 per cent of total length; interfemoral membrane sparsely covered with hair basally for nearly half its length; fur long and soft. Color, sooty brown to nearly black throughout, most of the hairs on the back, flanks, and under parts tipped with ashy white, producing a frosted appearance. Young early in the first year are usually less frosted than adults, but as the bat approaches the young adult stage the silvery white tips of the hair are often more pronounced than in the older animals. The skull is broad and flat, so much so that in dorsal profile it appears nearly straight; rostrum very broad,

Skins of (left) LASIONYCTERIS NOCTIVAGANS, *Amelia Court House, Virginia. (Middle)* PIPISTRELLUS S. SUBFLAVUS, *Devils Lake, Wisconsin. (Right)* EPTESICUS F. FUSCUS, *Cheat River, West Virginia.* 1×.

concave on each side back of the nasal aperture; no sagittal crest. There seems to be little variation in this species, either sexual, seasonal, or as to age, except for the slight color variation mentioned in the young. I have no records of mutations or abnormalities.

Measurements.—Total length of adults, 95 to 115 mm. (3.7 to 4.5 in.); tail, 35 to 45 mm. (1.5 to 1.9 in.); hind foot, 8.5 to 10.5 mm. (0.33 to 0.4 in.); forearm, 40 to 42 mm. (1.6 to 1.7 in.); ear length from notch, 15 to 17 mm. (0.6 to 0.7 in.); ear width, 11 to 14 mm. (0.4 to 0.6 in.); tragus height, 6 to 8 mm. (0.24 to 0.31 in.); wing spread, 290 to 310 mm. (11.4 to 12.2 in). Weight, 7 to 10 grams (0.25 to 0.35 oz.). Skull length, 16 to 16.9 mm.; width, 9.5 to 10.3 mm.

Distribution in Wisconsin.—Probably occurs throughout the state in favorable habitats, but never abundantly.

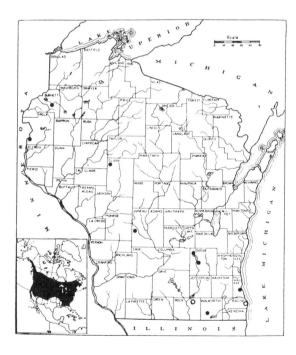

Map 17. Distribution of LASIONYCTERIS NOCTIVAGANS.
● = *specimens examined.* ○ = *authentic records.*

Habitat.—Wooded areas, parks, and orchards, especially near streams and lakes.

Status and Habits.—As based upon available records it would appear that the silver-haired

bat is rare in Wisconsin, yet part of this apparent rarity may be on account of the more or less solitary habits of this species. It is not positively known to colonize, and seldom are several found clustered together. During the daytime it remains hanging head downward sheltered among the leaves and branches, or back of loose bark, of a tree or tall shrub, although it has been found hanging in hollow trees and even in an abandoned crow's nest. It may sometimes rest in old buildings or lumber yards. W. E. Snyder (1902: 126) says of this bat:

An abundant species, particularly so about the streets of the city [Beaver Dam] in the early evening, where they may be seen in numbers, darting about among the trees. I have knowledge of several houses, where these bats roost in large numbers between the closed blinds and the windows. One of these roosts was investigated one year, during the height of the bat season, and there was an almost solid column of bats the whole length of the blind—clinging to blind and window casings—a conservative estimate being 300 bats.

Inasmuch as I have been able to locate in any of the Snyder collections only one specimen of this bat from Beaver Dam, and saw none in that collection when I personally examined it at Beaver Dam on two occasions, it would seem best to delete this record. Moreover, from my personal observation the common bat "about the streets" of Beaver Dam is *Myotis lucifugus*, followed next in abundance by *Lasiurus borealis*. In Worden Township, Clark County, "this bat was found on September 6 under the grate of the furnace in the cellar of our house" (Schmidt, 1931: 105).

There are no special means of detecting the presence of this bat except by persistent search or chance encounter. One cannot locate it by feces piles or the odor of its roost, since it is not a colonial bat. It is one of the easier bats to identify when flying.

The silver-haired bat takes wing later in the evening than many bats, possibly because it usually roosts in a place where daylight lingers later. Once on the wing it prefers the shelter of trees, and is seen less frequently over meadows and in unwooded areas. It flies over water to dip down and drink, but usually returns to the woodland. There also is proof that a few silver-haired bats hibernate, though we have no evidence of such for Wisconsin. In some other northern states there are records of this species being found dormant in winter in hollow trees cut for firewood, and back of clapboards and in crannies of old buildings. It has rarely been found hibernating in caves. This is one of the species of bats that migrates, and many, possibly most of the population, leave the state in regular migration southward about the first of October, returning in April or May. Little is known about these migrations, though many interesting observations have been made.

A granite lighthouse stands upon Mount Desert Rock, a lonely, barren dot in the ocean off the coast of Maine, twenty miles S.S.E. of Mount Desert Island, fifteen miles from the nearest island, and thirty miles from the mainland. The rock is so small and bleak that it is not inhabited by bats. Still, as I have been informed by the keeper of the lighthouse, Mr. Thomas Milan, a few small dark-colored bats visit the place during the migrations, every spring and fall. In order to identify the species Mr. Milan, at my request, was kind enough to send me several specimens procured about October 1st, 1885. They proved to be the Silver-haired Bat (*Vesperugo noctivagans*) (Merriam, 1888: 87).

It is probable that most of these migrations occur at night, though between 9:00 and 10:45 A.M., on a cloudy and mild day, September 28, 1907, at Washington, D. C., many bats, probably including this species, were seen migrating toward the southwest (A. H. Howell, 1908).

Possibly the fact that this species is our most rapid-flying bat makes it less observed in the state. It also tends to be concealed by its habit of flying among trees and not usually appearing until it is almost dark. It is as awkward trying to move on a level surface as any Wisconsin bats, but seems to be the best swimmer.

Its call and other means of communication are similar to those of *Myotis*. Its squeaks and chatterings are a trifle lower in pitch than those of *Myotis*, so that its supersonic vibrations are audible to some people. It also has the same pugnacious disposition common to other bats, chattering and scolding when touched, yet is rather easily tamed, and will respond to one's call after being kept a few days in semi-confinement.

The breeding habits of this bat are not well known. It usually has two young, sometimes only one, born blind and nearly naked the last part

of June or early in July. The young remains clinging to the breast of the mother until about three weeks old, when it is able to fly and help shift for itself. There is only one litter a year.

The silver-haired bat feeds exclusively on nocturnal insects, particularly those species that fly high in the woodlands or over the borders of watercourses with wooded banks. It has few enemies, although an owl catches one once in a while. One species of flea, *Eptescopsylla vancouverensis,* known only from British Columbia, has been recorded as a parasite. This species may have especial economic value to forests through its habit of hunting insects among the trees.

Specimens examined from Wisconsin.—Total 27, as follows: *Burnett County:* Clam River (mouth of), 1 (MM). *Clark County:* Worden Township, 2 (1 CNHM; 1 UWZ). *Dodge County:* Beaver Dam, 1 (UWZ); Fox Lake, 1 (UWZ). *Juneau County:* Camp Douglas, 4 (1 AMNH; 3 USNM). *Milwaukee County:* Milwaukee, 12 (MM). *Polk County:* Osceola, 4 (MM). *Walworth County:* Delavan, 2 (1 MM).

Selected references.—Allen G. M., 1939; Allen, H., 1893; Cory, C. B., 1912; Merriam, C. H., 1884 b; Miller, G. S., Jr., 1897 b; Miller, G. S. Jr., 1907.

Genus **Pipistrellus** Kaup
Pipistrelles

Dental formula:

$$I \frac{2-2}{3-3}, \ C \frac{1-1}{1-1}, \ P \frac{2-2}{2-2}, \ M \frac{3-3}{3-3} = 34.$$

Pipistrellus subflavus subflavus (F. Cuvier)
Georgian Bat

V[*espertilio*] *subflavus* F. Cuvier, Nouv. Ann. Mus. d'Hist. Nat., Paris, vol. 1, p. 17, 1832.
Scotophilus Georgianus Strong, p. 438, 1883.
Pipistellus [sic] *subflavus* Hollister, p. 31 (in hypothetical list), 1910.
Pipistrellus subflavus Cory, p. 465, 1912.
Pipistrellus subflavus subflavus Barger, p. 10, 1952.

Vernacular names.—Georgia pipistrelle, pigmy or pygmy bat, pipistrel or pipistrelle, pipistrelle bat, and yellowish-brown bat.

Identification marks.—The Georgian bat is distinguished from other Wisconsin bats by its small size (smallest of known Wisconsin bats), short wingspread, and peculiar yellowish-brown color. It is a relatively short-winged bat; ear moderately large, about one and one-half times as long as broad, tapering to a narrow rounded tip, and when laid forward reaching just beyond nostrils; tragus nearly straight, about half the length of ear; tail relatively long, 46 per cent or more of total length; main body of the fur of the back rather short and dense, the hairs about 6 mm. in length, intermixed with longer hairs about 10 mm. long.

Color of adults in general tone light yellowish brown on the ventral parts; on the back, shaded to a varying degree with darker brown; main part of fur of the shorter hairs are slaty or plumbeous at base to near middle, then yellowish brown to the dark brown tip; longer guard hairs clear yellowish brown from base to tip. Young of a few months are somewhat duller and more plumbeous than adults. The skull is small and lightly built; depressed interorbitally; brain case somewhat inflated; rostrum relatively broad; dentition essentially as in *Myotis* except that the third premolar is lacking.

No sexual or seasonal variations in color, size, or proportions are known. There is, however, a wide range of individual variation in color. Although in Wisconsin this variation is considerable, it is not nearly as great as in other regions, where a color mutation is indicated. For example in the series of ten specimens of *Pipistrellus* in the U. S. Biological Surveys collection from Lake George, New York, all are dusky, and two are so dark red as to suggest erythrism and one so blackish as to indicate melanism. Albinism is shown in a specimen from Texas reported as "white in appearance over most of the dorsal and ventral surfaces of the body exclusive of the head and the extreme posterior part of the body. The wings, feet, tail, interfemoral membrane, rump, and ears are normal brown" (Blair, 1848: 178).

On the basis of seven of these dark-furred skins from Lake George (Warren County), *Pipistrellus subflavus obscurus* was described as new by Miller (1897: 93), although he assigned all other specimens from the eastern United States, including 33 from Sing Sing (Ossining), New York, barely 150 miles south in the same valley, to *P. s. subflavus*. Having listed records of *Pipistrellus* from Hurley and Devils Lake, Wisconsin, as of the subspecies *obscurus*, Hall and Dalquest (1950: 600) state: "The occurrences cited above for Minnesota and Wisconsin were recorded in the literature under the specific name without indication of subspecific affinity. The reference

of specimens from these states to the subspecies *P. s. obscurus* is an arbitrary assignment on our part; we have not seen them. However, two specimens in the University of Kansas Museum of Natural History from Potosi (Snake Cave), Grant County, Wisconsin, are referable to *P. s. obscurus.*"

The present writer has not examined the two specimens in the Kansas Museum of Natural History, but has seen others from Potosi (including Snake Cave), and several specimens from other localities in southwestern Wisconsin. Comparison of these Wisconsin specimens with specimens of *Pipistrellus* from Georgia and South Carolina, the general region of the type locality of *P. s. subflavus*, shows a striking similarity in color and other characters, and none of them closely resembles any of the series of *P. s. obscurus* from Lake George, which as a series is unique in coloration.

Measurements.—Total length of adults, 78 to 86 mm. (3 to 3.4 in.); tail, 36 to 42 mm. (1.4 to 1.7 in.); hind foot, 8 to 9 mm. (0.31 to 0.37 in.); forearm, 32 to 36 mm. (1.2 to 1.4 in.); ear length from notch, 13.5 to 14.5 mm. (0.53 to 0.57 in.); ear width, 9.5 to 10 mm. (0.38 to 0.4 in.); tragus height, 6.4 to 6.8 mm. (0.25 to 0.27 in.); wing spread, 210 to 240 mm. (8.5 to 9.4 in.). Weight, 4 to 6.5 grams (0.14 to 0,23 oz.). Skull length, 12.2 to 13.2 mm.; width, 7.6 to 8.2 mm.

Distribution in Wisconsin.—May possibly occur throughout the state wherever there are caves, unworked mine shafts, or deep rock crevices, but apparently of regular occurrence only in the southwestern part of the state. Recorded for northern Wisconsin on basis of a single specimen, possibly a straggler. "A single specimen of *Pipistrellus subflavus* was taken from more than 3200 *Myotis lucifugus* and *Myotis keenii* which were trapped for banding on September 1, 2, and 3, 1948, at Hurley, Iron County, Wisconsin. The pipistrel, number 479 in the collection of James Beer, was a fat male apparently ready for hibernation. The same place was trapped during September of 1947 when nearly 1400 bats were examined without finding a single individual of this species" (Greeley and Beer, 1949: 198). The species was included in Moses Strong's "List of the Mammals of Wisconsin" (1883: 438), but Strong listed all the bats known from eastern and northern states, without having local records, and

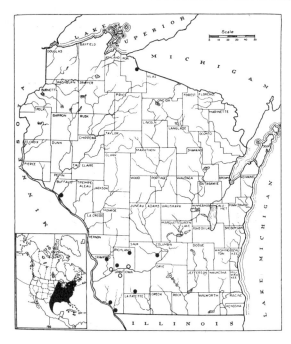

Map 18. *Distribution of* PIPISTRELLUS SUBFLAVUS.
● = *specimens examined.* ○ = *authentic records.*

this species was not entitled at that time to a place in the Wisconsin list (Hollister, 1910: 31). The first actual record for Wisconsin was a specimen (U. S. Biol. Surveys Coll., No. 229219) of an adult male collected by this writer, August 29, 1918, at Devils Lake, Sauk County (Jackson, 1919 b: 38).

Habitat.—A wide-ranging species that shows predilection for caves, abandoned mine shafts, and large deep crevices in rocks, less frequently inhabiting buildings; slight preference for wooded areas near water.

Status and Habits.—The Georgian bat is not common in Wisconsin, there apparently being fewer in the state than of any of the species of bats known to occur there except possibly the hoary bat (*Lasiurus cinereus*). There probably are fully two hundred little brown bats in the state to one Georgian bat, the total population of which cannot be expected to exceed two or three thousand in Wisconsin. There is evidence of a home feeding range for this species of at least four or five miles, and in nearby Minnesota it has been shown to have a homing instinct sufficient to bring it back 80 miles in less than 15

weeks of late fall and winter weather (Rysgaard, 1942: 263). Individuals return year after year to the same roosting cave.

The Georgian bat leaves little sign of its presence, and the only way to locate individuals is to watch for them flying in the evening or to search in caves or other likely resting places. Its period of hibernation seems to be longer than that of other Wisconsin bats, which might be anticipated since it is a more southerly species than the others. It goes into hibernation about the first or middle of October, and does not awaken to leave until the last of April or first of May. It is seldom found in groups of more than five or six, and usually hangs from the wall or ceiling of the cave either singly or in pairs or trios.

The Georgian bat, in the winter caves, remains inactive for longer periods of time than the other species; but they periodically arouse and move about. During the time they remain inactive, their bodies become clothed in droplets of condensed moisture; and in torch light they appear almost pure white. In one of the caves at Spring Valley, Fillmore County, Minnesota, I observed a Georgian bat arouse from a state of torpidity. It first showed movement by an occasional shiver, then opened its eyes and peered about with upraised head. The ears, which during the period of resting were somewhat curled or shrunken, were spread open to full size and twitched sensitively; and the wings were exercised. Before taking flight, the bat spent some moments licking the droplets of moisture from its fur, then carefully cleaned itself, scratching its fur and drawing portions of the wing membrane through its mouth (Rysgaard, 1942: 263).

This species probably does not migrate great distances in Wisconsin, but in the fall leaves the shallower and less protective rock niches utilized during summer for the deeper, warmer, more protective mine shafts and caverns. Here, in temperature ranging from 45° F. to 55° F., and humidity above 90 per cent, it spends the winter.

The Georgian bat, generally can be distinguished in flight by its small size and the weak fluttering of its wings, producing an erratic flight which to some people suggests that of a butterfly. When it first makes its appearance in the evening it usually flies high, coming down lower among the trees after dark. It is not quite so rapid a flier as the little brown bat.

Mating occurs in November, and the young are born blind and naked the last part of June or early in July. Two constitute the usual number in a litter, but rarely three are born, and occasionally only one. The young clinging to her breast are carried about with the mother for the first 12 to 14 days, but thereafter she leaves them in her roost. When four weeks old the young are able to fly, and soon thereafter begin to shift for themselves.

The food of the Georgian bat consists of insects, but inasmuch as this bat is small and weak it probably does not feed upon the larger bugs and beetles, consuming instead forms such as flies, moths, and the smaller bugs and beetles. Few enemies or parasites are known for this species. An apparent attack on a Georgian bat by a hoary bat has been reported from Canandaigua Lake, New York, at 10:20 P.M., September 9, 1946.

As we approached the spot, perhaps fifteen minutes later, I was also startled by a chattering noise and by something that seemed to bounce to a height of about 18 inches above the pavement. The beam of my flashlight revealed the "dark object" to be a hoary bat, *Lasiurus borealis,* which continued to bounce several times while exposed to the light, then settled down on the pavement, and grasped in its jaws the mutilated body of a small pipistrelle, *Pipistrellus subflavus obscurus.* When picked up by the nape of its neck, the larger bat clung momentarily to the body of its smaller relative. It was quite evident that the hoary bat resented the close approach of anything that interfered with its feeding for it twice demonstrated its displeasure by voice and actions and refused to abandon its prey (Bishop, 1947: 293).

Although Bishop used the specific name for the red bat, "*borealis*," he probably had a hoary bat.

Specimens examined from Wisconsin.—Total 17, as follows: *Buffalo County:* Alma, 3 (UWZ). *Crawford County:* Crystal Cave, 1 (UWZ); Soldiers Grove, 2 (UWZ). *Grant County:* Potosi (10 mi. S. S. E.), 1; Snake Cave (Potosi), 1 (UWZ). *Iowa County:* Mineral Point, 1 (UWZ). *Iron County:* Hurley, 1 (JRB). *Richland County:* Eagle Cave, 2 (UWZ); John Gray Cave, 4 (UWZ). *Sauk County;* Devils Lake, 1.

Selected references.—Allen, G. M., 1939; Davis, W. H., 1959; Greeley, F., and J. R. Beer, 1949; Hall, E. R., and W. W. Dalquest, 1950; Jackson, H. H. T., 1919 b; Miller, G. S., Jr., 1897; Rysgaard, G. N., 1942.

Genus **Eptesicus** Rafinesque
Serotine Bats

Dental formula:

$$I\,\frac{2-2}{3-3},\ C\,\frac{1-1}{1-1},\ P\,\frac{1-1}{2-2},\ M\,\frac{3-3}{3-3}=32.$$

Eptesicus fuscus fuscus (Beauvois)
Big Brown Bat

Vespertilio fuscus Beauvois, Catal. Raisonné Mus. de Peale, Philadelphia, p. 18 (p. 14 of English ed. by Peale and Beauvois), 1796.

Scotophilus fuscus Strong, p. 438, 1883.

Eptesicus fuscus Hollister, p. 31 (in hypothetical list), 1910; Cory, p. 467, 1912.

Eptesicus fuscus fuscus Barger, p. 10, 1952.

Big brown bat with wings spread. Ventral view. Slightly more than ½×.

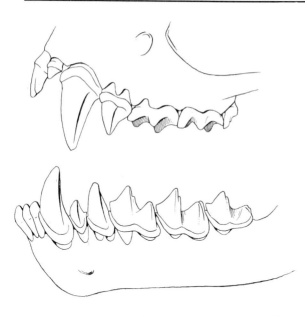

Teeth of EPTESICUS F. FUSCUS *viewed from left side.*
7½×.

Vernacular names.—Brown bat, Carolina bat, common brown bat, dusky bat, house bat, large brown bat, and scrotine bat.

Identification marks.—The big brown bat is easily distinguished from any other Wisconsin bat by its large size (exceeded in Wisconsin only by the hoary bat), its uniformly dark brown color above, and its thick, heavy, naked black or black-ish ears, wings, and interfemoral membrane. The ears are heavy, prominent, somewhat rounded, and medium in size, reaching, when laid forward, barely to the nostrils; tragus medium in size, straight, and gradually rounded at tip; fur soft, lax, and long, about 12 mm. on middle of back, and extending but slightly onto wing membranes. Color brown throughout on furred parts, always paler on the under parts than on the back; upper parts usually sepia or bister, or a shade darker, rarely almost cinnamon; under parts more vinaceous or pinkish cinnamon; base of hairs plumbeous. There appears to be no regular molting time. The skull is large and heavy, larger than that of any other Wisconsin bat except *Lasiurus cinereus*, than which it is noticeably narrower. Although *Eptesicus* has a total of 32 teeth, as does *Lasiurus*, in the former there are two upper incisors and one upper premolar on each side,

whereas *Lasiurus* has one upper incisor and two upper premolars on each side.

There is no color variation in this species that can be correlated with sexual or seasonal differences. Young of a month or two are noticeably darker and more grayish than adults, having not yet acquired the sepia color of the hair-tips. Males average very slightly larger than females. Color variations possibly of mutant origin have been described for this bat in two specimens from New Jersey and one from Pennsylvania, which consist mostly of pied pattern or slight blotching or sprinkling of paler hairs. Such variations are rare, however, and may have been caused by disease or injuries. Albinos sometimes occur.

Measurements.—Total length of adults, 110 to 118 mm. (4.3 to 4.6 in.); tail, 44 to 50 mm. (1.7 to 2.0 in.); hind foot, 9.5 to 11 mm. (0.37 to 0.43 in.); forearm, 44 to 48 mm. (1.7 to 1.9 in.); ear length from notch, 17.5 to 19.5 mm. (0.7 to 0.8 in.); ear width, 12.5 to 13.5 mm. (0.5 to 0.54 in.); tragus height, 7.8 to 8.3 mm. (0.3 to 0.34 in.); wing spread, 300 to 325 mm. (11.8 to 12.8 in.). Weight, 12 to 16 grams (0.42 to 0.56 oz.). Skull length, 18.5 to 20.6 mm.; width, 11.5 to 13.2 mm.

Map 19. *Distribution of* EPTESICUS FUSCUS. ● = *specimens examined.* ○ = *authentic records.*

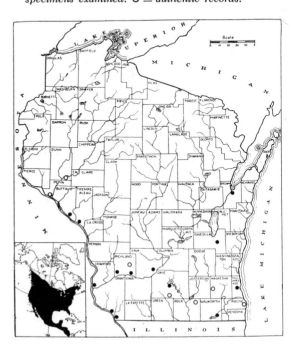

Distribution in Wisconsin.—Probably occurs throughout the state, though present records indicate it is much more common in southern Wisconsin than northern.

Habitat.—Usually found in the vicinity of buildings where during daylight hours it hangs or rests hidden in cracks and crannies in walls, roofs, or cornices, or behind doors, blinds, or awnings; occasionally in hollow trees, under bark, or in clifts of rocks; not infrequently in caves.

Status and Habits.—Records would indicate that the big brown bat is not abundant in Wisconsin, yet it undoubtedly exceeds considerably in numbers the silver-haired bat, the Georgian bat, and the hoary bat. It possibly may rate even higher than the eastern long-eared bat (*Myotis k. septentrionalis*) in its Wisconsin population, and may total roughly thirty or forty thousand individuals. It does not appear to form huge colonies as do some species of bats, yet in his bat-banding operations Frederick Greeley (ms.) found scores of these bats in winter in caves, particularly in Snake Cave, Grant County.

Occasionally one of these bats may be detected about a house by its squeaks or scratchings, but usually it gives no indication of its presence, and sallies forth each warm evening and returns with little ado. Although probably in part migratory, the big brown bat for the most part does not engage in extensive seasonal movements, other than to find a satisfactory place for hibernation. It enters hibernation rather later than other species of bats, being found flying about as late in the autumn as the middle of November, and is again on the wing sometimes as early as the first week of March. Although many big brown bats hibernate in caves, many others crawl into the cracks and walls of buildings. It apparently does not go into as intense hibernation as some species of bats. Sometimes during the coldest winter weather, when furnaces and stoves are going full blast and houses are overheated, some of these bats are aroused from hibernation in the heated walls and fly about rooms or even outdoors.

The big brown bat often makes its appearance in flight early in the evening, shortly after sunset, but at times it is well toward dusk before it takes wing. Its flight is swift, and though somewhat jerky and erratic is not so much so as with the smaller Wisconsin bats. It seldom flies low, usually maintaining a fairly steady height of 20 to 30

Big brown bat in its awkward walking posture. About ⅞ ×.

feet, and is frequently seen around city street lights. Its disposition is not in the least tolerant, and it will utter its ugly chatter and snap and bite at the least provocation. Not only does it thus react to apparent enemies, but even to its own kind. Its rather solitary habits may be either the cause or the result of this behavior. There are several records of the big brown bat living to the age of 8 or 9 years. Its life expectancy is possibly 5 to 7 years, and its life potential may be near 15 or 16 years.

The mating season is during September, and the young are born the following June. There are normally two in a litter, though occasionally only one. The young are large at birth, weighing 10 per cent or more of the parent's weight. They may cling to the breast of the mother when she flies away, or may be left hanging by their hind feet in back of a shutter or other shelter. They grow rapidly, and within three or four weeks are able to fly and shift for themselves. Males and females remain segregated during most of the post-hibernating period until after the young leave the parents.

A. Brooker Klugh has made interesting observations on a specimen of *Eptesicus fuscus* captured early in January, 1923, in a cellar in Ontario:

At first this bat was very savage, uttering a sharp "chirring" note when touched and attempting to bite when handled. In four days, during which time it was handled frequently and given food and drink, it became much more tractable, and in a week it was quite tame, never trying to bite nor squeaking, unless suddenly seized. It would lie in my hand quite contentedly and when I stroked its head it went fast asleep. At first when liberated it would always alight as far from me as possible but later it was as likely, and seemingly more likely, to alight near me than elsewhere.

At first it refused everything offered it, though unfortunately I could find no insects to offer, but after a few days it took cooked tongue, which had been moistened with water. Later it ate veal and beef, uncooked and cooked, veal jelly, ham, and cooked haddock, but refused bread or anything of a vegetable nature. It ate only very small pieces of any of these foods, and had great difficulty in handling pieces more than two millimeters in diameter. It used its long flexible tongue with considerable dexterity in getting material into its mouth.

Eptesicus was always ready for a drink of water, and usually would not eat until it had had a drink. The water was given to it in a small shallow dish and it had two methods of drinking. The method most frequently employed was to run its lower jaw under the water, scoop up a little, and suck it down with a biting movement, as if it were "eating" the water. The other method which was not often used was to lap it up as a dog does. . . .

It spent nearly all its time in sleep, hanging on a rod I fixed in its box, or hanging from the edge of the box by its hind feet. Usually it woke about seven o'clock in the evening, and if let out then would fly about for some time. When going to sleep it hung itself up and commenced to shiver; its respirations, which during activity were about a hundred per minute, became slower and slower; its body relaxed—, the tremors ceased and it was fast asleep—all in a period of two minutes. Its sleep was extremely deep—more of a hibernation than an ordinary sleep—and its respiration seemed to occur about once in five minutes and often were so slight as to be undetectable. Even in its deepest sleep, auditory stimuli caused a response, a very slight noise being reacted to by a jerk of the head and body.

It cleaned itself by licking and scratching. The alar membrane and the interfemoral membrane came in for a good deal of the washing, during the course of which the former was stretched into all sorts of shapes. The back and sides were scratched with the hind feet, one of these at a time being run from behind forward with a rapid scratching motion.

In alighting it caught with the thumb-hooks while the wings were expanded, took hold with the feet, folded the wings, and turned head downwards.

That the guiding sense of bats on the wing is not sight but a superfine sense of touch—a sense which detects the presence of an object by the rebound of air without actually touching the object—seems to be definitely proven by experiments . . . and histological investigations. Nevertheless I thought it worthwhile to experiment for myself, and I found that Eptesicus was able to avoid objects, and even to dodge objects thrust suddenly in its path of flight, with its eyes sealed up with adhesive plaster as well as with eyes uncovered (Klugh, 1924).

Almost invariably, the first thing a big brown bat does on leaving its resting place in the evening is to quench its thirst by scooping up water in its mouth as it flies over some stream, lake, or puddle. It then proceeds in flight to capturing insects. No detailed studies of the food of this bat have been made in Wisconsin, but it probably is not essentially different from that of the species in West Virginia, where from Hanging Rock, Hampton County, W. J. Hamilton, Jr. (1933) reports on the examination of 2,200 fecal pellets found in the attic of Wilbur Frye late in August, 1931. Percentages by frequency of occurrences are used.

In all, about 300 wings were salvaged, and the best specimens of each kind were mounted for identification. Following is a list of the various orders of insects encountered, arranged in the order of their apparent abundance.

Coleoptera, 36.1; Hymenoptera, 26.3; Diptera, 13.2; Plecoptera, 6.5; Ephemeridae, 4.6; Hemiptera, 3.4; Trichoptera, 3.2; Neuroptera, 3.2; Mecoptera, 2.7; Orthoptera, .6.

Among the Coleoptera, beetles of the family Scarabaeidae occur most frequently. In general, we may say that this group, harboring the leaf chafers and May beetles, are on the whole injurious. Next in order occurred the family Elateridae, which includes such destructive forms as the wire worms. . . . Diptera were represented chiefly by muscids, a group which embraces the house fly. . . . It is rather surprising that no lepidopterous remains were encountered.

The big brown bat has been known to kill and feed upon smaller bats when kept in close confinement with them for a short time (Krutzsch, 1950).

There are few records of the big brown bat having been preyed upon by other vertebrates. Since this bat roosts commonly about buildings, cats, rats, and humans probably rate as its chief enemies.

Mr. Meyer of St. Peter related that he had actually seen cats scale walls offering footholds and catch hibernating bats. Following the November 11, 1940, storm, cats visited the Seven Caves at St. Peter, Minnesota, and carried away nearly all the frozen bat carcasses. . . . Rats, too, undoubtedly claim their toll of hibernating bats; for in several of the caves rat tracks were found. On March 2, 1939, I found remains of an *Eptesicus fuscus* in a rat tunnel in Seven Caves. The remains of another were noted at the entrance of a rat tunnel at one of the Stillwater caves on February 12, 1941 (Rysgaard, 1942: 255).

There are records of the sparrow hawk capturing and eating the big brown bat, one in July, 1870, in Chester County, Pennsylvania (Fisher, 1893: 123) and another in 1939 at Albany, New York (Stoner, 1939: 474). Great horned owls have been known to eat the big brown bat in Minnesota and Wisconsin. There apparently is also at times a high mortality among this species caused by storms or freezing.

Among the external parasites reported from *Eptesicus fuscus* are the mite *Spinturnix americana*, the fleas *Eptescopsylla chapini* and *Myodopsylla insignis*, and the bug *Cimex pilosellus*. The trematode *Plagiorchis microcanthus* has been reported by Rysgaard (1942: 256) as inhabiting the small intestine of *Eptesicus* in Minnesota. Rabies occurs.

Economically, the big brown bat is undoubtedly on the credit side, since it feeds exclusively on insects, the majority of which are probably harmful to human interests. It probably destroys a few useful insects, such as lady bugs, but otherwise has no obnoxious habits except for occasionally irritating some people by its noises or just by its presence. When such is the case, methods of control may be practiced as described in the account of the little brown bat.

Specimens examined from Wisconsin.—Total 34, as follows: *Brown County:* Green Bay, 5 (NPM). *Buffalo County:* Fountain City, 2 (MM). *Crawford County:* Crystal Cave, 1 (UWZ). *Dane County:* Madison, 7 (UWZ). *Dodge County:* Beaver Dam, 1 (UWZ). *Fond du Lac County:* Eden, 2 (UWZ). *Grant County:* Potosi (10 mi. S. S. E.), 1; Snake Cave (Potosi), 2 (UWZ). *Milwaukee County:* Milwaukee, 6 (1 CNHM; 5 MM). *Richland County:* Bogus Bluff, 1 (UWZ); Eagle Cave, 2 (UWZ). *Sauk County:* Prairie du Sac, 2 (MM). *Trempealeau County:* Trempealeau, 1 (UWZ). *Walworth County:* Lake Geneva, 1 (CNHM).

Selected references.—Allen, G. M., 1939; Allen, Harrison, 1893; Jackson, H. H. T., 1953; Klugh, A. B., 1924; Miller, G. S., 1897 b; Rysgaard, G. N., 1942.

Genus **Lasiurus** Gray
Hairy-tailed Bats

Dental formula:

$$I\frac{1-1}{3-3},\ C\frac{1-1}{1-1},\ P\frac{2-2}{2-2},\ M\frac{3-3}{3-3}=32.$$

Lasiurus borealis borealis (Müller)
Red Bat

Vespertilio borealis Müller, Natursyst., Suppl., p. 20, 1776.
Vespertilio Noveboracensis Lapham, p. 337, 1853.
Lasiurus noveboracensis Strong, 1883, p. 438.
Lasiurus borealis Snyder, p. 125, 1902; Jackson, p. 33, 1908.
Nycteris borealis Hollister, p. 30, 1910; Cory, p. 470, 1912.
Lasiurus borealis borealis Schmidt, p. 105, 1931; Barger, p. 10, 1952.

Vernacular names.—Leaf bat, New York bat, New York red bat, northern red bat, red tree bat, and tree bat.

Identification marks.—A rather small bat, usually with conspicuous bright rufous or fulvous color, the hairs plumbeous at base, more or less tipped with whitish and producing a slight frosted effect over back and breast; body rather chunky; head somewhat short and heavy; ear

Mother red bat coiled around young ones. About ¾×.

broad, blunt, and rounded at tip, mainly naked inside and on the rims and tip, hair rather dense on basal two-thirds of dorsal surface; ear when laid forward reaches slightly more than halfway from the angle of the mouth to the nostril; tragus triangular, broad at base; anterior border nearly straight, posterior border strongly angular; tail moderately long, the interfemoral membrane extending to the tip of the tail, thickly furred on upper surface almost to extreme edge; hair fine and silky, on middle of back about 7 mm. long and on neck about 10 mm.

There is considerable variation in the intensity of the reddish color, which may range in different individuals from the normally bright rusty red to almost a pinkish yellow; the amount of "frosting"

Skins of bats of the genus Lasiurus. *Left,* L. B. borealis, *Potosi, Wisconsin. Right,* L. C. cinereus, *Kelley Lake, Wisconsin.* 1×.

also varies considerably. A yellowish white patch is on each shoulder. The paler specimens appear much more grayish yellow than the normally colored specimens. There is no seasonal variation in color, and so far as known no seasonal molt. Males on the average are darker and more reddish than females. This sexual difference in color is more pronounced in the young than in adults. "The most interesting thing about the young in both these cases was the pronounced difference in color between the males and the females, the pelage of the young males being dark red, while that of the young females was gray, with just a trace of red" (Dice, 1927).

The skull, small, rather heavily built, is broad, short, and deep, very different from that of any other small bat found in Wisconsin; nares opening large, the sides relatively widely spread in dorsal view. The red bat is so characteristically colored that it needs comparison with practically

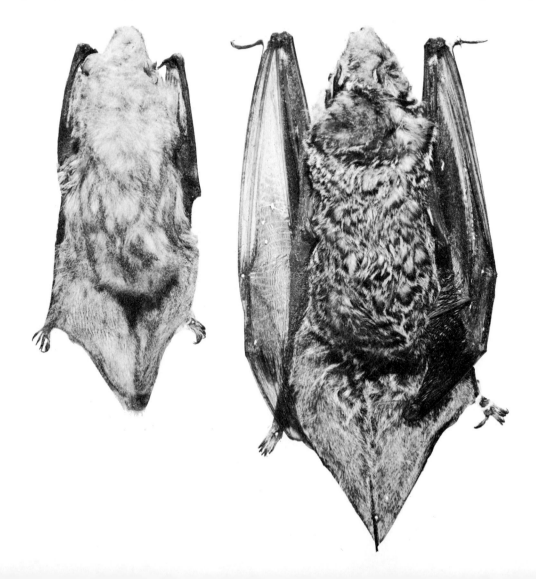

no other Wisconsin species. Its pelage is "frosted" and it is near the size of *Lasionycteris noctivagans,* but the color is always redder, never shows the blackish trend of the silver-haired bat, and the upper surface of the tail membrane is well furred. Compared with its closer relative, the hoary bat, it is contrastingly smaller and always more fulvous, reddish, or yellowish in color as compared to the grayish liver-colored tone of *Lasiurus cinereus.*

Measurements.—Total length of adults, 100 to 117 mm. (3.9 to 4.6 in.); tail, 45 to 52 mm. (1.9 to 2.0 in.); hind foot, 9 to 10 mm. (0.37 to 0.39 in.); forearm, 38 to 42 mm. (1.5 to 1.7 in.); ear length from notch, 10.5 to 13 mm. (0.4 to 0.6 in.); ear width, 10 to 11.5 mm. (0.4 to 0.5 in.); tragus height, 6.2 to 7.5 mm. (0.25 to 0.3 in.); wing spread, 290 to 325 mm. (11.4 to 12.8 in.). Weight, 8 to 13 grams (0.28 to 0.45 oz.). Skull length, 13.1 to 14.4 mm.; width, 9.2 to 10.4 mm.

Distribution in Wisconsin.—Occurs in all of the state; probably more plentiful in the southern half than in the northern.

Map 20. Distribution of LASIURUS BOREALIS. ● = *specimens examined.* ○ = *authentic records.*

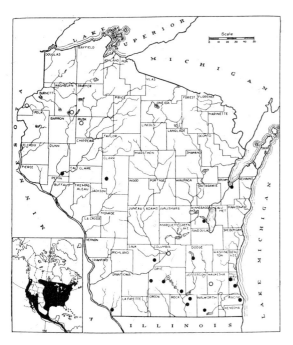

Habitat.—Wooded regions, showing preference for deciduous forests, open woodlands, and orchards, and for farmyards, city parks, streets, and yards if with trees or tall shrubs; seems to prefer vicinity of water.

Status and Habits.—The red bat is possibly the commonest bat in Wisconsin, for although in certain areas it may be outnumbered by the little brown bat, it is of wider distribution in the state. Certainly the combined population of these two species in Wisconsin is much greater than that of all the other species of bats, and would exceed the million mark. In the estimate of 110 flying bats of all species per acre that I made at Storr's Lake, town of Milton, Rock County, May 30, 1902, some 50 per acre were red bats. Nine miles southeast of Birchwood (Washburn County), in northwestern Rusk County, Mr. Francis Zirrer found them scarcely more than one to a square mile. "Walking 3 miles on the fire lane in the evening I remember seeing two or three only" (Letter to author, March 25, 1942). Probably more nearly an average over most of the midwest range of the species is the average of one bat per acre at Lewis, Iowa, as computed in 1939 (McClure, 1942: 430). Like most bats it has a rather wide home range for a small mammal, yet it has a smaller home range than some of the cave-dwelling bats. It frequently is seen flying six hundred to one thousand yards from its day resting place, and each individual seems to cover the same general area each evening, thus showing a trend for a home territory. Other than by watching for this species in flight in the evening, a person has little chance of seeing a red bat unless by good luck or diligent search one is found hanging from a leaf or twig of a tree or shrub.

This bat leaves its diurnal resting place at dusk, and at first usually flies high. Later it often flies low, sometimes within six or eight feet of the ground. On dark and cloudy days it is frequently seen flying early in the afternoon, and at times may come out even in bright sunlight. It is a strong and swift flier, as is attested by the number of red bats that have been seen flying far out to sea, sometimes up to five hundred miles from land, and by the fact that it has reached such distances from its normal range as the Galápagos Islands and Hawaiian Islands. It is most active on warm, humid nights. It seeks shelter, however, usually in foliage, during heavy rain. No winter records of red bats for Wisconsin are available, and so far as is known all individuals of this species migrate to more southern regions. Some of these may go far enough south so that they do not need to hibernate; others may stop at intermediate regions where winter conditions require them to hibernate for short periods. Migration starts with the beginning of cool weather, sometimes as early as the first week of September, when the bats may gather in rather loosely constructed flocks of scattered individuals and begin flight southward. At times red bats remain in southern Wisconsin until well into October, but before the middle of that month practically all have left the state. Their migration is probably mainly nocturnal, though in some localities, as for example in the District of Columbia (Howell, 1908: 37), they have been observed in migration during sunlight. A few of them may return as early as the middle of April, but red bats are not regularly seen until the middle of May, and do not become common until the last of May or middle of June.

Like all bats, *Lasiurus borealis* is awkward and clumsy when on a flat surface, but in flight it is swift though erratic. No accurate records have been made of its flight speed, but observational timing that I have made would indicate its ordinary straightaway flying speed near 40 miles an hour. It can progress fairly well in water by flapping its wings and making a hard effort, and can rise from the surface of water if its fur has not become too wet.

It frequently is heard to give a sharp chirp when in flight, especially when it dives and swirls. Its squeaks or chirps are so high-pitched as to be inaudible to many human ears. When touched or otherwise irritated it almost always will respond with a high-pitched rasping chatter, and sometimes will utter a sharp squeak. The red bat seems to be more muscular than some of the other species. It can readily puncture one's skin when it bites, but the needle-like teeth cause no serious or permanent harm. Possibly because of its more or less solitary habits, it does not appear so amiable with its own kind or with other species as the colonial little brown bat. Yet, as with most bats, it can be tamed and will come at call for food. It too has the special vibration senses mentioned for other bats, but its solitary

habits may tend to inhibit the use of such "radar" sensitivity. Its normal life span in the wild possibly is somewhat less than that of some bats because of its migratory and tree-roosting habits, and is probably near 5 years, with a potential longevity of near 12 years.

The red bat mates somewhat earlier than is known for other species of bats, and copulation in the Wisconsin area may occur between the first of August and the last of September. Sufficient reliable observations indicate that copulation begins while the bats are in flight, though in later stages of the act the pair may come to ground.

An instance of the copulation of this species in the air was recorded many years ago as having occurred in Massachusetts during the month of October. Many recent writers, however, having no corroboration of the incident, and realizing that other bats mate in a different manner, have declined to accept the original observation as correct. There is, nevertheless, no doubt of the truth of it. In the late afternoon of August 6, 1911, Mr. Henry Thurston, of Floral Park, Long Island, saw two Red Bats join in flight. One of them made several attempts to light upon the other and, finally succeeding, they remained together about half a minute, flying unsteadily the while, with all four wings beating. On the following evening at the same place Mr. Thurston shot two when they were apparently attempting the act of coalition. This pair came into Mr. Murphy's hands next day. . . . On August 23, at Floral Park, Mr. Murphy saw two Red Bats act in a similar manner, although in this case they remained joined only a few moments, and passed out of sight as they parted. Other observers, among whom Dr. A. K. Fisher of Washington is one, have since then related to him instances from their experience confirming the deduction that aerial copulation is the rule with this species (Murphy, R. C., and J. T. Nichols, 1913: 11).

In another case,

on the evening of August 20, 1947, Swan Creek Park, Allegan County, Michigan, . . . as darkness was rapidly closing in, a single bat, as it seemed, suddenly tumbled onto the bank of the pond not more than five feet away squeaking loudly. . . . There lay on the bank a red bat which appeared to have one or more of its kind attached to it . . . but when the animals were turned over . . . it was discovered that a male was clasped on the back of a female. Since this position undoubtedly had made it impossible for either to fly effectively, it seemed likely that the male had attached himself to the female in mid-air. . . . The male held his position by hooking the enlarged nail of the fore limb over the front edge of the female's wing, with the posterior end of his body curved underneath the rear of hers. . . . The male buried his head in the fur of the female's neck and attempted sexual contact. The penis of the male was protruded but complete sexual contact was not observed (Stuewer, 1948: 180–81).

Just as dawn was breaking September 6, 1944, Dr. Ned Dearborn found on a pier in the James River, at Hilton, Virginia, a pair of red bats in copulation (Dearborn, 1946: 178). This pair could have made first contact in flight.

Inasmuch as the mother usually gives birth to her young the last of May or during June, this would give an apparent gestation period of about eight months. It is not known, but seems quite possible that as in the case of the little brown bat, spermatozoa survive in the uterus throughout the winter and fertilization takes place in the spring after the ovulation. This would give an actual gestation period of 80 to 90 days. Three young at a birth is usual, sometimes only two, not infrequently four. They are born completely hairless, eyes closed, and weigh about one-half gram each. They are able to make a weak chattering noise soon after birth; they cling to the fur of their mother, chiefly by their hind feet, but also by their teeth and thumb claws, for about three or four weeks, by which time the weight of each one has grown to four or five grams, or nearly half the weight of the mother, and their combined weight is greater than that of the mother. They have grown rapidly, their eyes have opened, and their fur is short but dense and well grown. Their combined weight at this age is so great as frequently to pull the mother and her family to the ground when she attempts flight with them, and she usually leaves them clinging to a sheltering tree branch until they are able to fly, which is at the tender age of five or six weeks. One litter a year is the rule. The sex ratio is about equal, with a slight tendency toward male preponderance. Mammary glands are four.

Essentially a tree bat, this species spends its resting hours hanging from a leaf of a tree or shrub, usually solitary or a mother with her young. Rarely are two adults found hanging together. Its daytime shelter is low in the tree, usually between 5 and 20 feet above ground, sometimes as high as 40 feet. It is well concealed by the leaves, but experience in searching for it will soon make it easy for a person to locate it by its bright yellow-red color contrasted against the green foliage. In Wisconsin, although they seem partial to the American elm and oaks, they also use as shelters many other kinds of trees and shrubs, more particularly apple, ash, birch, box elder, hawthorn, hazel, jack pine, maple, Norway spruce, sumac, and wild crab. Occasionally it may roost on the bark of trees. Rarely does it enter a tree cavity to roost, and very rarely a building. It has never been found in caves in Wisconsin. On one occasion Walter L. Hahn found more than two hundred skulls of the red bat amid masses of fallen stone in Shawnee Cave, at Mitchell, Indiana (Hahn, 1909: 635), which might or might not point to their inhabiting the cave.

Like other Wisconsin bats, the red bat catches insects while on the wing, and drinks by dipping water into its mouth as it flies over the water surface. It also may obtain some of its food from foliage and even from near the ground, since remains of crickets (*Gryllus*) have been found in its food. It consumes many flies (Diptera) of various genera, and is known to eat bugs, beetles, cicadas, and other insects. It frequently may be observed in flight catching insects under street lights. Ravenous in its feeding, it nevertheless is cleanly, and when resting frequently washes itself by licking its fur and rubbing itself with its wing.

Very few enemies molest the red bat, though probably a few are captured by hawks, owls, and domestic cats. There is a record of a sparrow hawk having eaten one, and also a record for the great horned owl. The remains of a red bat, together with those of various insects and a mole, were found in the stomach of a Virginia opossum killed in the Pisgah National Forest, North Carolina, January 8, 1930 (Sperry, 1933: 152). The species, because of its roosting habits, is more exposed to weather than some bats, and undoubtedly storms and other conditions take a considerable toll. In other states there are several records of its alighting in a thorny or berry bush only to suffer death by being thus trapped. Burdocks late in the summer seem particularly hazardous to the red bat, where it may be caught in the burs when it swoops for an insect or alights for resting. Barb-wire accidents are rare.

I have to report another type of accident to a red bat (*Lasiurus borealis*). In July or August, 1932, I found a partly mummified body hanging from the top wire of a barbed wire fence, along a well-travelled road in Maryland, a few miles north of Washington, D. C. Its interfemoral membrane had been pierced by one of the sharp wire points or barbs about half an inch from the end of its tail, on the left side, close to the vertebrae. A slit, three-eighths of an inch long, had been torn but the remaining bit of the membrane had held firm and the poor creature's speed and later struggles had drawn it tightly into the clefts between the transfixing barb and the wires coiled on either side, so that I had to use considerable force to free it.

The bat probably was not attempting to hang up in such a place, nor does it seem probable that human hands had hung it there. This seems a more likely interpretation: The bat was flying low over the field and turned toward the road. It rose to clear the fence and depressed its tail (its horizontal rudder) to descend immediately into the roadway. The barb which caught it slanted downward toward the field, so that the tail and interfemoral membrane must have been depressed while the animal was still rising and moving forward (Johnson, P. B., 1933: 157).

The parasites of this species are not well known but include fleas of the genus *Eptescopsylla* and the bug *Cimex pilosellus*. Trematodes of the genus *Lecithodendrium* and cestodes of the genus *Taenia* have been reported as internal parasites, and a protozoan parasite of the genus *Distoma* has also been found. Rabies was found in *Lasiurus seminola* in Florida (Courter, 1954).

Economically, this bat is one of our truly beneficial mammals, since it is entirely an insect eater and has none of the obnoxious traits of some other bats of roosting in houses and other buildings.

Specimens examined from Wisconsin.—Total 57, as follows: *Brown County:* Allouez, 1 (NPM). *Clark County:* Foster Township, 1 (UWZ). *Dane County:* Albion, 1 (USNM); Madison, 6 (UWZ); Vermont, 4 (UWZ). *Dodge County:* Beaver Dam, 6 (3 CNHM; 3 UWZ). *Dunn County:* Meridean, 1 (JNC). *Grant County:* Potosi (10 mi. S. S. E.), 2. *Milwaukee County:* Milwaukee, 23 (21 MM; 2 UWZ); Wauwatosa, 1 (MM). *Racine County:* Racine, 1 (USNM). *Rock County:* Janesville, 3 (MM); Milton, 4 (1 MM; 3 UWZ). *Walworth County:* Delavan, 2 (1 MM). *Winnebago County:* Oshkosh, 1 (UWZ).

Selected references.—Allen, G. M., 1939; Allen, H., 1893; Gates, W. H., 1938; McClure, H. E., 1942; Miller, G. S., Jr., 1897; Murphy, R. C., and J. T. Nichols, 1913.

Lasiurus cinereus cinereus (Beauvois)
Hoary Bat

Vespertilio linereus (typographical error for *cinereus*) Beauvois, Catal. Raisonné Mus. de Peale, Philadelphia, p. 18 (p. 15 of English ed. by Peale and Beauvois), 1796.
Vespertilio pruinosus Lapham, p. 337, 1853.
Lasiurus pruinosus Strong, p. 438, 1883.
Lasiurus cinerea Snyder, p. 125, 1902.
Lasiurus cinereus Jackson, p. 33, 1908; Hollister, p. 142, 1908; Barger, p. 10, 1952.
Nycteris cinereus Hollister, p. 30, 1910; Cory, p. 472, 1912.

Vernacular names.—Frosted bat, gray bat, great hoary bat, great northern bat, northern bat, and twilight bat.

Identification marks.—The largest and most beautiful bat inhabiting Wisconsin, the hoary bat closely resembles the red bat (*Lasiurus borealis*) in general structure and stockiness, but is nearly three times as large by weight. Easily distinguished from all other Wisconsin bats by its large size (total length 5 inches or more), extensive wingspread (more than 14 inches), peculiar prevailing coloration of mixed grayish umber and chocolate brown heavily tinged with white, producing a hoary effect, especially on the back, and its large rounded ears conspicuously rimmed with blackish or dark umber. The head is broad; nose blunt; ear large and rounded, the outer side densely furred nearly to tip, the inner side with conspicuous patch of yellowish fur anteriorly; tragus rather large and heavy, broad basally, triangular, concave anteriorly, angular dorsally; tail medium in length, little more than 40 per cent of total length; interfemoral membrane extending to tip of tail, thickly furred on upper surface nearly to extreme edge; foot about half as long as tibia, thickly furred dorsally; calcar twice as long as foot, and somewhat shorter than free border of interfemoral membrane; fur long, very fine, and dense, longer on the neck than on the back and thus forming a ruff.

The general color of the upper parts is grayish umber overcast with grayish white, the hairs being plumbeous at base, light yellowish brown in the middle half, then umber brown just below the whitish tip. The face and cheeks are more yellowish, with little evidence of white hair tips; lips and edges of ears blackish. The under parts are more yellowish than the back; the chin and fore throat particularly yellowish and without white hair tips; chest umber and distinctly frosted; belly paler, yellowish, slightly frosted. Immature (one-third grown) darker in general color tone, but showing some white-tipped hairs. So far as known there is no seasonal variation in color, nor a seasonal molt. There is, however, considerable individual variation in color, a few specimens being very dark and having the whitish hair tips reduced.

The skull is relatively heavy and broad; the rostrum short and broad, the maxillary region flaring with wide nares opening; zygomatic arches widely spreading; broad interorbitally; brain case large.

Measurements.—Total length of adults, 130 to 150 mm. (5.1 to 5.9 in.); tail, 52 to 62 mm. (2.0 to 2.4 in.); hind foot, 11 to 14 mm. (0.43 to 0.56 in.); forearm, 46 to 56 mm. (1.8 to 2.2 in.); ear length from notch, 17 to 18.5 mm. (0.67 to 0.73 in.); ear width, 15.2 to 17.7 mm. (0.6 to 0.7 in.); tragus height, 9 to 9.5 mm. (0.35 to 0.37 in.); wing spread, 375 to 425 mm. (14.7 to 16.6 in.). Weight, 28 to 35 grams (1.0 to 1.25 oz.). Skull length, 17 to 18.2 mm.; width, 11.8 to 12.8 mm.

Distribution in Wisconsin.—Throughout the state in favorable habitats, probably more frequent in the northern half than in the southern.

Habitat.—Wooded regions, showing preference for coniferous forests; also woodlands, farmyards, city parks, and yards, particularly where spruce, hemlocks, or other coniferous trees grow.

Status and Habits.—The hoary bat is probably the rarest large bat in Wisconsin, as it is over most of its geographic range. To anyone familiar with the species it is readily identifiable either in hand or in flight, and to anyone unfamiliar with it, its peculiar characteristics immediately arouse attention. The few records clearly indicate it is nowhere common in Wisconsin, and there are probably not more than two thousand or so individuals in the state. It may be slightly exceeded in numbers by *Pipistrellus subflavus* in the state as a whole, as it certainly is in the southwestern part. As one might anticipate from its size and wing strength, the hoary bat has a rather wide home range, and may frequently

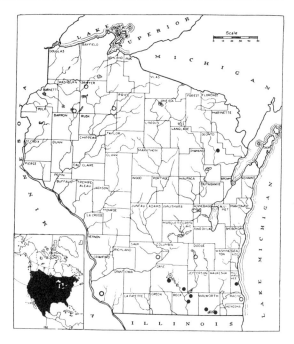

Map 21. Distribution of LASIURUS CINEREUS. ● = specimens examined. ○ = authentic records.

cruise a mile or farther from its resting place and return while searching for insects. Other than seeing it in flight or by chance finding one stranded on the ground or water, a person has little chance of seeing this species in life. It is difficult to locate in its resting places because of its color blending with its arboreal surroundings.

The hoary bat is usually the last to make its appearance in the evening, generally leaving its resting place well after sundown. It does sometimes come forth earlier, and there are records of its flying while the sun is shining. Harry H. Sheldon of our field party shot one during sunlight hours as it was flying among spruces and balsams near the west shore of Outer Island, Apostle Islands, July 6, 1919, but was unable to find it in the dense undergrowth where it dropped. This species appears to be active throughout the night, thus being more strictly nocturnal than some of our bats. It seems to prefer temperatures of between 45° F. and 60° F. for its active hours, but I have on several occasions observed them flying when the thermometer was above 70° F. There are no winter records of the hoary bat in Wisconsin, and all individuals are believed to migrate from the state by the middle of October. In the southern half of the state there appears to be an influx of individuals from the north beginning early in September, all of which have left for the south by about October 15, or the time of the first killing frost. The late Dr. Edgar A. Mearns told me some years ago that he had seen a flight of hoary bats in migration at Fort Snelling, Minnesota, while he was stationed there in 1889, but he did not have access to his notes to set the exact date. Just how far south they migrate is not established. There is a November record for Augusta, Georgia (Neill, 1952), and there are specimens in the U. S. Biological Surveys collection as of January 15 and February 16, 1912, Autaugaville, Alabama, and December 20, 1891, Brownsville, Texas. There are also spring records for Santo Domingo and Chihuahua, which may or may not represent the southernmost winter range of the species.

The hoary bat seems to be less awkward when on the ground or any solid surface than other species of Wisconsin bats, and can readily jump up and down, or jump into the air and take flight. It is a strong and rapid flier, and frequently makes swift forays straightaway for a mile or more and then returns, and may maintain on these excursions a speed close to 60 miles an hour. It never directly takes to water of its own volition, but can make fair progress in swimming by flopping around in a clumsy manner.

Dr. C. Hart Merriam has given us a glowing account of this bat as observed in the Adirondack Mountains, New York:

Imagine for the moment, sympathetic reader, that you are an enthusiastic bat hunter, and have chanced to visit some northern forest where this handsome species occurs. The twilight is fast fading into night, and your eyes fairly ache from the constant effort of searching its obscurity when suddenly a large bat is seen approaching, perhaps high above the tree-tops, and has scarcely entered the limited field of vision, when, in swooping for a passing insect, he cuts the line of the distant horizon and disappears in the darkness below. In breathless suspense you wait for him to rise, crouching low that his form may be sooner outlined against the dim light that still lingers in the northwest, when suddenly he shoots by, seemingly as big as an owl, within a few feet of your very eyes. Turning quickly,

you fire, but too late! He has vanished in the darkness. For more than a week each evening is thus spent, and you almost despair of seeing another Hoary Bat, when perhaps, on a clear cold night, just as the darkness is becoming too intense to permit you to shoot with accuracy and you are on the point of turning away, something appears above the horizon that sends a thrill of excitement through your whole frame. There is no mistaking the species —the size, the sharp, narrow wings, and the swift flight serve instantly to distinguish it from its nocturnal comrades. On he comes, but just before arriving within gunshot he makes one of his characteristic zig-zag side-shoots and you tremble as he momentarily vanishes from view. Suddenly he reappears, his flight becomes more steady, and now he sweeps swiftly toward you. No time is to be lost, and it is already too dark to aim, so you bring the gun quickly to your shoulder and fire. With a piercing, stridulous cry he falls to the earth. In an instant you are stooping to pick him up, but the sharp grating screams, uttered with a tone of intense anger, admonish you to observe discretion. With delight you cautiously take him in your hand and hurry to the light to feast your eyes upon his rich and handsome markings. He who can gaze upon a freshly killed example without feelings of admiration is not worthy to be called a naturalist. From its almost boreal distribution, and extreme rarity in collections, the capture of a specimen of the Hoary Bat must, for some time to come, be regarded as an event worthy of congratulations and record. Although I have been fortunate enough to shoot fourteen, I would rather kill another today than slay a dozen deer (Merriam, 1884 a: 78–79; 1884 b: 176–77).

The rasping chatter and shrill squeak of the hoary bat is not unlike that of the red bat, but is somewhat intensified, as might be expected, from its larger size. It acts pugnaciously when disturbed or harassed, as do all bats, particularly those of more or less solitary habits. Occasionally it gives a sharp chatter or sometimes a chirp when in flight, but usually only when it encounters another bat or some moving object. The hoary bat is muscular and strong, which seems to intensify its pugnacious disposition, and it will chatter and show its teeth on the least provocation. At times four or five may be in the same general area, but rarely is there more than one or two except during migration. Little observation has been made on its life span, but it probably has a life expectancy of 6 or 7 years and a potential longevity of 12 or 14 years.

Little is known about the breeding of the hoary

bat, but it probably mates in September or October, and the young are known to be born late in May or in June, thus giving an apparent gestation period of about eight months. It seems probable that as with some other bats spermatozoa survive in the uterus through the winter, fertilization taking place early in the spring after ovulation, giving an actual gestation period of about 90 days. During parturition the sexes remain isolated. Two is the usual number of young, though the mammae being four suggests that there may be at times three or four. The newborn hairless young has eyes closed and weighs nearly five grams. After about 10 or 12 days the eyes open. The hair has appeared and is dark reddish brown at first, turning to more nearly umber with a gray cast when the animal is two or three weeks old. The young clinging to the mother are carried around by her for nearly three weeks, by which time each weighs about nine or ten grams, or about one-third the weight of the mother. From Lewis, Cass County, Iowa, we have these observations:

On May 13, 1940, a hoary bat was noted clinging to the limb of Norway spruce. She used the roost almost every day. At some time in the two days before June 12 she gave birth to two young. By July 25 each was almost as long as her contracted body. By June 29 they were too large for her to carry when she was foraging, but they clung to her during the day. . . . On July 9 it was found that the family had broken up; probably the young had practiced flying before this date. On July 10 they were all back together again, but two days later they were gone (McClure, 1942: 233).

As I have elsewhere reported, "A female with two live young clinging to her was brought to me on the evening of July 27, 1903; it was found dead in a yard on the east side of the public park in Milton, Rock County. The young were over one-third grown" (Jackson, 1908: 33).

The hoary bat is essentially a coniferous tree bat, and during its resting periods usually hangs head downward from a twig or small branch of a pine, spruce, or hemlock. It sometimes resorts to a deciduous tree, and in some other states has been found in or clinging to a squirrel's nest. It has not been found in caves or rock crevices, nor as a voluntary inhabitant inside of buildings. Rarely, indeed, does it seek shelter behind blinds or similar structures. In a personal letter to me

of March 25, 1942, Francis Zirrer, Hayward, Wisconsin, writes of this species: "It came to my attention only on a farm on the Namakagon River, 5 miles north of Hayward; with the farm buildings set into a considerable grove of conifers (*Pinus strobus, resinosa,* and *banksiana*). During the summers of 1929–30–31–32 several took their daily abode behind loose tar paper under the eaves of a wooden building about 9 feet from the ground. They were new to me, and their large size and unusual color very surprising."

This bat feeds almost exclusively on insects which it captures while in flight, but inasmuch as it is a large bat and flies high and fast it is probable that more of the larger insects fall prey to it than to smaller bats. There is a record of its preying upon the Georgian bat in New York (Bishop, 1947: 293), and its size and strength make it possible for it to attack other species of small bats. After eating, it cleans itself by licking with its tongue and rubbing with its wings.

No important enemies are known for the hoary bat. More deaths apparently result from mothers falling to earth under the burden of heavy offspring than from any other single cause. It is not unlikely, however, that birds of prey may occasionally capture one. Some may succumb during the long migrations, but the hoary bat's strength and steady flight make it less vulnerable than its weaker cousins. There is little information on the parasites of *Lasiurus cinereus.* A protozoan of the genus *Distoma* has been found internally, and a few external parasites are known. Rabies has been reported.

Dr. Robert Cushman Murphy had the rare opportunity of having one of these bats in captivity for six weeks, and his observations throw light on the behavior of this species in confinement:

It was on the morning of August 19, 1911, that Mr. Murphy first made the acquaintance of a living Hoary Bat. He had been warbler hunting near Floral Park, Long Island, since sunrise, when, entering a copse of dense second growth about eight o'clock, he presently saw a gray oblong with no projections or irregularities, suspended about four feet above the ground from a chestnut sprout. A step nearer revealed the identity of the oblong. It hung from the toes with its wrists over its eyes, and little waves were crossing the soft fur in the morning breeze. He reached toward it cautiously, but its

ears were quick, and suddenly dropping to the
ground it lay with great wings spread to their fullest
extent while it raised its impish head with mouth
wide open, and chattered angrily as he threw his
hat over it. On the way home it was active and
pugnacious, continually attempting to bite, but it
calmed down when put into a box with door of fine
wire mesh. In this cage, after a few branches had
been introduced, it spent the greater part of the last
six weeks of its life.

It was an adult male, and was very fat. During
the first few days of its incarceration it made frequent tours all over the box, crawling laboriously
round and round the four sides, and back and forth
across the floor. Thereafter it hung head downward
on the wire door most of the time, but whenever the
door was faced toward a sunny window the bat
would soon crawl down, shuffle into the farthest
corner, and lie flat on the bottom of the cage. It
never would hang from the branching twigs tacked
up for it, and when placed upon one of them, it
would climb deliberately down, using its thumbs,
mouth, and feet as aids, and would return to the
wire netting. During its slumbers, which often en-
dured for hours without sign of life, its temperature
sank so low that it felt clammy and dead, but on
Mr. Murphy's enfolding it with his hands, respiration
would soon become perceptible, its body would
grow warm while the heart-beat quickened to a rapid
flutter, and within a few minutes the little beast
thus weirdly restored to activity, would shake its
wings, blink its tiny eyes, and grasping his fingers
with its thumbs, would gnaw his knuckles, *precisely
in the manner of a playful kitten.* It never attempted
to fly from the open hand even when it was most
active.

The coming on of evening seemed to have no
effect on rousing the captive to normal liveliness.
In fact, on only one occasion was it seen moving
about at night, and this was when two restless Red
Bats had been placed in the same cage. Both Red
Bats were dead next morning. A careful examination
showed no marks of violence on their corpses, and
no one was accused on circumstantial evidence, but
two more Reds, placed in the cage on another date,
were likewise dead on the morrow.

About nine o'clock in the morning the Hoary Bat
was usually, though not always, active of its own
accord, and at about this time of day was frequently
watched making its toilet, an elaborate operation. It
combed the fur of its head and neck with its sharp
curved claws by passing either hind foot over the
shoulder. Then it licked its back, flanks, and handsome collar, and the hairy patches on its wings,
spreading its black membranes repeatedly, and making grimaces with its mobile, curious nose and lips.

All this it would do either on the wire door or while
clinging upright on a proffered index finger. In the
latter position it also would drink water, taking two
or three laps with its tongue, then raising its mouth,
chicken-like, to swallow.

Within a few days after the capture, some meal
worms were procured to feed the unusual pet. It
paid no attention to the worm held before it until
the wriggling larva actually touched the face. Then
it snapped the insect from the fingers and began the
process of mastication, long and painful to behold!
No coaxing was needed after this. The bat reached
viciously for everything held before it, squeaking
the while in notes so high that they well might
have been above the range of some low-pitched
mortal ears, and fifteen good sized meal worms followed the first within ten minutes, a performance
which the bat equalled only once again, although
several times it ate ten at a meal. The brute's procedure was to seize a worm, pass it rapidly from
end to end through its teeth until all wriggling had
ceased, and then to chew it rapidly, thoroughly, and
loudly, with many an uncouth smack of the lips,
until the end of the victim gradually passed from
view. It would eat two worms at a time, one hanging from either side of its mouth, and would attempt
to seize even a third. Once satisfied, it would pay
no attention whatsoever to further profferings of
food. It would eat beetles whole, chopping the elytra
into tiny fragments. Moths it also devoured with
avidity, dropping the wings, however. If the victim
were large and powerful the bat would use its interfemoral membrane, thumb-joint, the sides of its body,
or its support to aid it in securing a better grasp.
House flies it would seize, but would immediately
spit them out again, and it never would touch a dead
insect. Invariably within a few minutes after eating
it exuded a few drops of dark yellow urine.

Several times the Bat was given the freedom of a
large room in order that its splendid flight might
be observed. When placed on the floor it would
spring into the air without the slightest difficulty,
and circle round the upper walls easily and gracefully, but as a rule after a few turns it dropped to
a piece of furniture and clung there (Murphy and
Nichols, 1913: 12–14).

Specimens examined from Wisconsin.—Total 18,
as follows: *Dane County:* Albion, 1 (UWZ); Madison, 1 (UWZ). *Dodge County:* Beaver Dam, 2
(UWZ). *Milwaukee County:* Milwaukee, 5 (MM).
Oconto County: Kelley Lake, 1. *Rock County:* Janesville, 3 (MM); Milton, 3 (UWZ). *Walworth County:*
Delavan, 1; Lake Geneva, 1 (CNHM).

Selected references.—Allen, H., 1893; Bishop, S. C.,
1947; McClure, H. E., 1942; Miller, G. S., Jr., 1897
b; Murphy, R. C., and J. T. Nichols, 1913; Provost,
E. E., and C. M. Kirkpatrick, 1952.

ORDER LAGOMORPHA
Hares, Rabbits, and Allies

This order was long recognized as the suborder Duplicidentata of the Rodentia, named thus on account of its two pairs of upper incisors the true rodents being of the suborder Simplicidentata with a single pair of upper incisors. Other characters also separate the two groups, and mammalogists now consider them distinct orders, regarding the resemblances between them as the result of parallel convergence rather than phylogenetic divergence (Gidley, 1912). Members of the Lagomorpha were native to most of the world except Australia, New Zealand, and Madagascar, but through the introduction of certain species by man the order has become represented practically worldwide. Distinguishing characters of the Lagomorpha that separate them from the Rodentia include four upper incisors, two of which are chisel-like as in the rodents, and a second pair small, nearly circular, and without cutting edge directly behind these; distance between the tooth rows of the lower jaws is less than the distance between the tooth rows of the upper jaws, so that only one pair of rows is opposable at the same time, and the motion of the jaws in mastication is lateral; premolars $\frac{3\text{-}3}{2\text{-}2}$, instead of $\frac{2\text{-}2}{1\text{-}1}$, or less as in the rodents; fibula always fused with tibia for more than half of its length, and articulate with calcaneum; testes in a scrotum anterior to penis; no baculum present.

The Lagomorpha embrace two living families, Ochotonidae and Leporidae, only the latter of which is represented in Wisconsin.

Family **Leporidae**
Hares and Rabbits

The family Leporidae has the entire geographic range of the order Lagomorpha. It is composed of nine currently recognized recent genera, of which two, *Lepus* and *Sylvilagus*, occur in Wisconsin. Wisconsin members of the genus *Lepus*, among other distinguishing characters, always have a hind foot length of more than 110 mm., flaring triangular supraorbital processes, and no interparietal, whereas members of the genus *Sylvilagus* always have a hind foot length of less than 110 mm., long and narrow supraorbital processes close to cranium or fused with it, and interparietal present.

Right, backs of left ears of lagomorphs. A. LEPUS T. CAMPANIUS, B. LEPUS A. PHAEONOTUS, C. SYLVILAGUS F. MEARNSII. ½×.

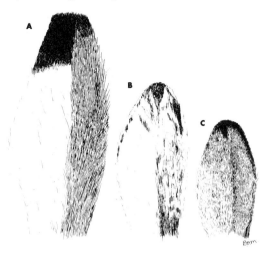

Skulls of lagomorphs. A. LEPUS T. CAMPANIUS, Buford, North Dakota, B. LEPUS A. PHAEONOTUS, Herbster, Wisconsin, C. SYLVILAGUS F. MEARNSII, Fountain City, Wisconsin. ½×.

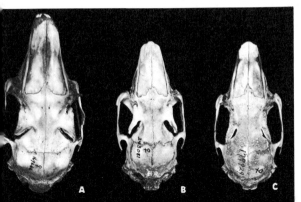

Underside left hind foot of (left) LEPUS T. CAMPAN-IUS, *(middle)* LEPUS A. PHAEONOTUS, *and (right)* SYLVILAGUS F. MEARNSII. ½×.

Genus **Lepus** Linnaeus
Hares

Dental formula:

$$I \frac{2-2}{1-1}, \ C \frac{0-0}{0-0}, \ P \frac{3-3}{2-2}, \ M \frac{3-3}{3-3} = 28.$$

Lepus townsendii campanius Hollister
White-tailed Jack Rabbit

Lepus townsendii campanius Hollister, Proc. Biol. Soc. Washington 28: 70, March 12, 1915.
Lepus campestris Cory, p. 265, 1912.
Lepus townsendii campanius Barger, p. 12, 1952.

Vernacular names.—Jack, jackass hare, jack rabbit, prairie hare, white jack, white jack rabbit, and white-tailed jack.

Identification marks.—A large, robust-bodied hare, total length more than 550 mm.; ears long and relatively narrow, length from notch to tip more than 90 mm.; tail large, more than 65 mm. long, all white above and below, or at most occasionally with dusky narrow stripe above which does not extend onto the rump; legs long and slender, the hind feet long, length more than 150 mm.

The general color in summer is pale buffish gray above; anterior half of outside of ear buff to buffy gray, the border tinged ochraceous; posterior half of outside of ear whitish with broad black patch extending to tip of ear; tail usually white above and below, sometimes with dusky line above, never extending to rump; under parts except throat near white or pale grayish. Color in winter in most Wisconsin individuals is pure white except for the black tips of the ears and the dark eyes, and sometimes a buffy tinge on upper parts, face, and feet. There are two molts annually.

The skull is large and relatively short, broad, and heavy; longest (length more than 88 mm.) and broadest (width more than 45 mm.) of the Wisconsin Leporidae; postorbital process flaring and not fused at posterior end with frontal, and the interparietal fused with parietal, both characters of the genus *Lepus*; orbits heavy, raised, making distinct depression in prefrontal region; premaxillary bone relatively long and narrow, extending anteriorly well beyond nasal, the tip clearly visible in superior view of skull; teeth rather heavy, the secondary incisors pronounced, the molariform series more than 15 mm. long.

Sexual variation is noticeable only in a slight tendency for females to be larger than males. Juvenile pelage is similar to that of adults except for a tendency for more underfur to show, thus producing a more blotched appearance, and the coloration of the feet, ears, and throat is duller. No color mutations or abnormalities have been recorded for this species.

Baby white-tailed jack rabbit, Manitoba. Photograph by H. and E. Pittman.

The white-tailed jack rabbit in any pelage easily can be separated from either the varying hare or the cottontail by size alone, the adult always being more than 550 mm. total length, ear from notch more than 90 mm. long, and molariform tooth row more than 15 mm. long, whereas in both the varying hare and the cottontail each is less in these respective measurements.

Measurements.—Total length, 575 to 670 mm. (22.6 to 26.4 in.); tail, 70 to 115 mm. (2.8 to 4.5 in.); hind foot, 148 to 172 mm. (5.8 to 6.8 in.). Weight, 5.8 to 9.5 pounds, the average about 8 pounds, very rarely to 14 pounds. Skull length, 88.8 to 102.5 mm.; width, 45.2 to 52.3 mm.

Distribution in Wisconsin.—Throughout the state in favorable habitats, except the northern tier of counties and Oneida, Oconto, and Milwaukee counties.

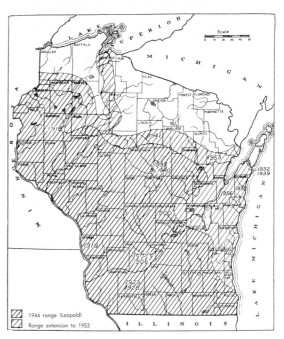

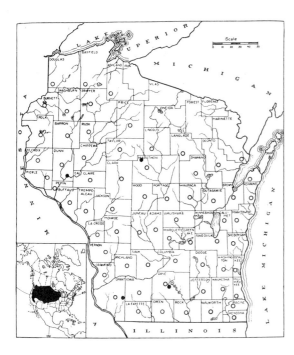

Map 22. *Distribution of* LEPUS TOWNSENDII. ● = *specimens examined.* ○ = *authentic records.*

Habitat.—Favors open fields such as rough plowed fields, stubble fields, pastures, grasslands, sand barrens and flats, and recently burnt-over lands; seldom in brushlands, and never in forests. Particularly favors plowed fields in winter.

Map 23. *Jack rabbit range extension and location and date of release. Dates indicate release in that county in that year. After Lemke, 1956, p. 137.*

Status and Habits.—The rather extensive population of white-tailed jack rabbits now in Wisconsin undoubtedly originated from introduced stock or plantings made chiefly during the early years of the twentieth century. Leopold (1947: 13) says of the Wisconsin jack rabbits: "The present jack rabbit population originated in part from plantings, but the bulk of it probably represents natural spread from the West." Possibly influenced by Leopold's statements, Hoffmeister (1948: 2) writes "*Lepus townsendii* apparently occurred natively and naturally in Grant and Iowa counties of extreme southwestern Wisconsin, and probably in Dunn County, west central Wisconsin. It seems safe to assume that the white-tailed jack rabbit, *Lepus townsendii campanius,* occurred natively in northwestern Illinois and northward through southwestern and west-central Wisconsin, west of the 89th parallel." There is no factual basis for the contention that *Lepus townsendii campanius* is a native of Wisconsin. We do know there were many introductions. The jack rabbit killed February 21, 1888, north of Platteville, in Grant County, and apparently considered by Leopold (1947: 2) as native, was probably introduced, otherwise why the comment that "jack rabbits were previously unknown in that locality." At one time, I too thought that the white-tailed jack rabbit was native to western Wisconsin, but my travels and inquiries in that part of the state, and the history of the species in Iowa and Minnesota, convince me that it is not indigenous to Wisconsin. It was not present in Sac County, northwestern Iowa, upon arrival of early settlers there in 1854, and did not appear until 1868 (Spurrell, 1917). In Minnesota, "it is only in the past 30 or 40 years that the species has invaded that part of the State east of the true original prairie" (Swanson, Surber, and Roberts, 1945: 97).

The occurrence of *Lepus townsendii campanius* Hollister as a native mammal in Wisconsin has always seemed to me more or less of a possibility. It was, therefore, not entirely a surprise when on August 13, 1918, I saw numerous tracks, which appeared to belong to this species, on the sand barrens north of the Chippewa River at Meridean, Dunn County, Wisconsin. Although careful search was made for the animals in the limited time at my disposal, none was seen. Returning to the village I made inquiry of several residents and learned that these jack rabbits were *not* native, but had been introduced from Minnesota about the year 1908 and that they had thrived very well. The next day, August 14, a mounted specimen in winter pelage, which had been collected on the sand barrens about 1912, was examined in the collection of Mr. John N. Clark, of Meridean, Wisconsin (Jackson, 1920).

The white-tailed jack rabbit has become rather common in suitable habitat in many parts of the state, and particularly in that area between Waushara, Portage, and western Shawano counties northwesterly to St. Croix and Polk counties. During 1951–52 there was an estimated hunting and trapping kill of 19,383 jack rabbits for the state, more than one-third of which came from seven counties, namely, Barron, Clark, Eau Claire, Marathon, Portage, Waushara, and Wood. This kill might indicate a possible population of 50,000 to 75,000 jack rabbits in the state. The white-tailed jack rabbit tends less to colonize than other American hares, which may account for its rapid dispersal from implantations. Its home range has not been accurately determined but probably is less than one-half mile radius, and often it may confine its activities to one large field.

It being an animal of the open country, one might suspect that the white-tailed jack could be easily seen, but its protective coloration of mostly gray-buff in summer like the soil and mostly white in winter like the snow tends to hide it effectively. It rests crouched low with ears flat against its shoulders, sometimes sheltered by a tussock of grass or a low shrub, often merely by a plow furrow or with no shelter, invisible until it moves. It usually will lie quietly until approached closely, often nearly stepped upon, then with a speedy jump will dash away at full speed, ears erect and moving to catch every sound. Sometimes it will jump high, nearly vertically, in order to detect its disturber. Its tracks as a rule are quite distinctive, much larger than those of the cottontail and much more widely spaced, and are sometimes conspicuous in dusty roads, sandy areas, or snow. Sometimes it makes clearly defined trails through prairie grass. Its presence is also announced by the many feces it leaves, large round somewhat flattened pellets, always larger than those left by the cottontail.

Scats or feces of white-tailed jack rabbit (upper figure) and cottontail rabbit.

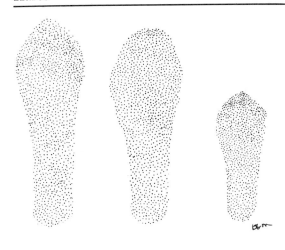

Tracks of right hind foot of (left) white-tailed jack rabbit, (middle) varying hare, and (right) cottontail rabbit. ½×.

Evening twilight is the chosen time for activity, and again at dawn, though it may be foraging at any time at night, particularly during moonlight hours. Rarely is it active in daylight unless disturbed from its resting place. It is active both winter and summer. In Wisconsin it is not known to migrate, but may change its home site when forced by food shortage, enemy pressure, or overabundance of its own kind. It is not highly gregarious, and overpopulation probably is the main cause of the rapid expansion of its range. It rarely progresses by walking. Its slow gait is a series of short hops of one to three feet. It runs in a series of high, bounding leaps of up to 12 feet in slower speeds, but low and longer leaps of up to 16 or 18 feet in higher speeds. Its fastest running speed seldom exceeds 36 miles an hour. One chased by a dog ran parallel with a moving train and as nearly as could be estimated was running 40 miles an hour (Bailey, 1927: 142). It will enter water when pursued or cornered, and swims by paddling with its front feet and leaping as best it can in the water, making rather fast progress.

This species is rather silent but, as with most hares, sometimes signals by thumping its hind feet on the gound. In winter its black ear tips on white body possibly identify it to members of its kind. At times when it is caught it calls with loud low-pitched squeals, three or four short notes in quick succession. Little need has it for an alarm note because it depends on its invisibility and silence for protection, and when approached lies close until almost trampled before bounding away at full speed with its white tail and buttocks showing conspicuously. Its senses of sight and hearing are acute. It moves its ears in different angles and directions, sometimes one ear forward and the other back, so as to hear from various directions. The sense of smell is also well developed, and the animal is frequently sniffing the air to detect odors. Although a hardy mammal, its potential longevity, so far as known, is only about eight years.

Mating in Wisconsin occurs about the middle of April or later, and is believed to be promiscuous. After a gestation period of about 30 days the young are born, well covered with fur and eyes open. The litter may consist of from two to six, four being close to the average number. Possibly a second litter sometimes may come later. The young one is active shortly after birth, and does some foraging for itself when about fifteen days old, but is not weaned until about one-fourth grown. When nearly half grown, or some two months old, it is entirely on its own, and at this age, unlike an old hare, may seek shelter in a burrow or under brush. The mammae are eight, two pectoral, four abdominal, and two inguinal.

No true nest or shelter is constructed by the white-tailed jack rabbit, and the young may be dropped on bare ground by the mother, or in one of the forms made and used by individual hares of both sexes as resting and hiding places. The hare does little in making a form, which often may be merely a soil-surface indication of where the animal has frequently rested or sometimes may suggest that a little pawing and scratching was done to make a satisfactory resting place. The size of the form depends some on the size of its maker, but it usually is 18 to 24 inches long, 8 to 12 inches wide, and may vary in depth from zero to rarely 6 or 8 inches, the majority being about 2 inches. There is no lining to the form other than such as may blow or drift into the hollow. Rarely a sheltered form may be dug into deep snow.

In summer, the white-tailed jack rabbit feeds chiefly on green vegetation such as growing grain, grass, clover, alfalfa, and the green shoots and leaves of various other wild and cultivated plants. In winter, its food is chiefly buds and other browse such as the tender tips, branches, and bark of many shrubs, including berry bushes and young fruit trees. It sometimes feeds on hay or straw scattered by the wind, or may even feed around hay or straw stacks, particularly if in a field away from buildings. It is cleanly after feeding, frequently lapping its body with its tongue and, catlike, rubbing its ears and head with its forefeet. It does not store food.

The ability of the jack rabbit to conceal itself and speedily escape when discovered protects it well from potential enemies. In its summer fur the young is even more concealed through its coloration than the adult. Occasionally, through stealth, a coyote or a fox catches a jack rabbit, and the great horned owl sometimes captures one. The larger hawks at times prey on jack rabbits, particularly on young ones. It is not infrequently killed by automobiles at night when it forages along roadsides. Hunting jack rabbits affords good sport, and several thousand are shot in the state each year by hunters.

External parasites that infest the white-tailed jack rabbit include the louse *Haemodipus setoni* and the fleas *Pulex irritans, Hoplopsyllus affinis,* and *H. lynx,* and probably ticks. Internally it is known to host the tapeworm *Taenia pisiformis,* but probably also has other tapeworms as well as flukes and roundworms. Tularemia or "rabbit disease" is known to occur in this species.

Even though the white-tailed jack rabbit feeds on many plants that are useful to man, it is not likely to become a serious economic problem in the state. Being nongregarious, it seldom occurs in a population concentrated enough to do serious damage to crops, in this respect having different habits from the black-tailed jack rabbit (*Lepus californicus*) of the Southwest. It is not apt to damage tree nurseries, since such environment usually is too densely wooded for it. It is an excellent game mammal, both from the standpoint of sport and food value, and hunting pressure should keep its numbers low enough to prevent serious crop damages. The meat of the white-tailed jack rabbit, unlike that of other species of jack rabbits, is tender and delicious. Appreciation of this hare as a game asset is evinced by the fact that it is protected as a game animal and that an estimated harvest of 23,699 was procured during the

1946–47 season (Scott, 1947 b: 4) and 19,383 during the 1951–52 season (Anon., 1952: 7). The pelts are practically worthless for use as clothing, being too fragile to withstand processing. Pelts have possible use for hatter's fur to be made into felt, and the white-tailed jack fur is classed as No. 1 for that purpose. The market for this fur, however, is too uncertain, the quantity available in Wisconsin insufficient, and the price of 25 to 50 cents a pelt too low to create a profitable industry.

Specimens examined from Wisconsin.—Total 4, as follows: *Dane County:* Madison (1 mi. W. of), 1 (AWS). *Dunn County:* Meridean, 1 (JNC). *Grant County:* Livingston, 1 (UWZ). *Marathon County:* Athens, 1 (UWZ).

Selected references.—Coues, E., 1876; Hall, E. R., 1951 a; Leopold, A., 1947; Lyon, M. W., Jr., 1904; Nelson, E. W., 1909; Palmer, T. S., 1897.

Lepus americanus phaeonotus J. A. Allen
Minnesota Varying Hare

Lepus americanus phaeonotus J. A. Allen, Bull. Amer. Mus. Nat. Hist. 12: 11, March 4, 1899.
Lepus americanus Lapham, p. 43, 1852; Lapham, p. 340, 1853.
Lepus Americana Strong, p. 440, 1883.
Lepus americanus phaeonotus Jackson, p. 25, 1908; Jackson, p. 88, 1910; Hollister, p. 26, 1910; Cory, p. 262, 1912; Schmidt, p. 117, 1931; Komarek, p. 209, 1932; Barger, p. 12, 1952.

Vernacular names.—In Wisconsin commonly called snowshoe hare, snowshoe rabbit, or simply snowshoe, sometimes varying hare. Other names include big rabbit, big white rabbit, brown jack rabbit, brown rabbit, bush rabbit, forest hare, northern hare, northern jack rabbit, snow rabbit, swamp jack rabbit, swamper, *wa–a–boos* (Chippewa), and white hare.

Identification marks.—A medium-sized hare, total length of adult more than 375 but less than 550 mm.; ears large, moderately long, from notch to tip less than 75 mm.; tail more than 30 but less than 55 mm. long; hind feet 110 to 150 mm. in length.

In summer pelage the upper parts are dull buffy to dark ochraceous, darkest and more mixed with black on the head and rump, and paling only slightly on the sides of body; sides of head clearer ochraceous buff than back; color of ears similar to that of back, darkening toward tips which are black; throat fulvous to rich cinnamon; chin and abdomen white; tail dusky above, pale gray to whitish below; feet ochraceous tawny above, soles dusky. In winter pelage pure white except the black tips of the ears. Base of hairs, or underfur, buffy gray both in summer and winter.

There are two molts annually, one in spring when the hare changes from white winter pelage to the brown of summer and the other in the autumn when the hare acquires its white pelage. The spring molt usually begins in March and is completed in about 80 days. The spring molting appears first on the forehead, progresses to the nose and over the body, and lastly to the ears and feet. The autumn molt usually begins between the last of September and the middle of October, and is completed by the end of December. Autumn molt begins on the ears and feet, spreads to the legs and ventral parts, and is last complete on the back. Details of molting have been described by Wallace Grange (1932 b).

The skull of *L. a. phaeonotus* is of medium size, averaging scarcely larger than that of *Sylvilagus*, the cottontail; always much smaller than that of *L. t. campanius*, being less than 88 mm. greatest length and less than 45 mm. greatest width; flaring postorbital process not fused at posterior end with frontal, and the interparietal fused with parietal as in *L. t. campanius;* premaxillary bone relatively short and broad, extending anteriorly scarcely beyond nasals, the tip invisible in superior view of skull; teeth moderate, secondary incisors normal, the molariform series less than 15 mm. long.

The female varying hare averages a trifle larger than the male, but in color and general appearance the sexes do not differ. There is considerable variation among individuals in color, and in the same animal Grange (1932 b: 103) has found "no less than 23 types of hairs, classified on color arrangement alone." Color or other mutations are rare. A male of another subspecies reported as totally black and the base of the hairs bluish-black was killed in Jefferson County, New York, in January, 1951, and another male reported as "black except for some dark brown-colored patches dorsally and a few white hairs in the axillary region of both forelegs" was killed in Lewis County, New York, August 20, 1951 (Gordon, 1954). There are also records of Melanistic specimens from Ontario, Prince Edward Island, and Quebec, Canada (Bird, 1955).

The varying hare in any pelage easily can be separated from the white-tailed jack rabbit by smaller size alone. From the cottontail, the varying hare can be distinguished always by its white pelage in winter and usually by its more general ochraceous color in summer; also by the absence of a distinct bright fulvous patch on the nape, the color of the nape and the back being continuous; larger hind foot; skull with heavier, less attenuate rostrum than in the cottontail; postorbital process flaring and not fused posteriorly to front-

Right, varying hare in summer, Minnesota. Photograph by L. B. Ritter.

Varying hare in winter. Copyright by H. H. Pittman.

al; interparietal fused with parietal, not fused in cottontail.

Measurements.—Total length, 380 to 520 mm. (15 to 20.5 in.); tail, 25 to 48 mm. (1.0 to 1.9 in.); hind foot, 112 to 150 mm. (4.4 to 5.9 in.). Weight, 2 lbs. 14 oz. to 4 lbs. 2 oz., rarely to 4 lbs. 6 oz., the usual weight about 3 lbs. 10 oz. Skull length, 73.5 to 85.5 mm.; width, 36.5 to 42 mm.

Distribution in Wisconsin.—Present general range north of line from northwestern Burnett County south-southeasterly through central Eau Claire County, western Jackson County to southwestern Monroe County, easterly to central Adams County, southwestern Wood County, northern Portage County, east to northeastern Brown County, and northern Manitowoc County. Formerly occurred in favorable habitats in central and southeastern Wisconsin as far south as Jefferson and Milwaukee counties.

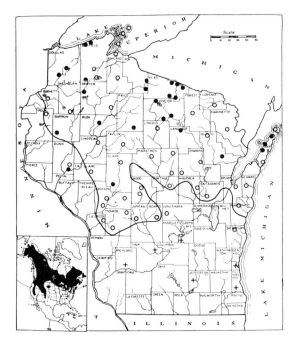

Map 24. Distribution of LEPUS AMERICANUS. ● = *specimens examined.* ○ = *authentic records since 1900.* + = *authentic records before 1900. Present main range north of solid line.*

Habitat.—Brushy woodlands and heavy forests, particularly of mixed conifers and hardwoods, and with forest floor of dense thickets, brush, and fallen logs; bogs and swamps, particularly those having growths of conifers, alders, and willows; old burns and cutover lands covered with fallen logs and limbs, and growths of young aspens, raspberry bushes, and other vegetation; heavy mature hemlock forest with ferns and fallen logs, and little brush (Crescent Lake); rarely in pure hardwood forest, unless interspersed with coniferous and other brush, and rarely in old stands of pine with bare forest floor. In northwestern Rusk County: "In the years of abundance evenly distributed throughout the woodlands; in the years of the disappearance, however, the remaining few retire to the bogs and marshes, where willows and similar shrubs grow plentifully" (F. Zirrer, Hayward, Wisconsin, in letter to author, March 25, 1942). The habitats frequented by the varying hare have been analyzed by Wallace Grange (1932 a: 3–4).

Status and Habits.—The varying hare a century ago inhabited tamarack and alder swamps in southern Wisconsin at least as far south as Jefferson and Milwaukee counties. Leopold (1945: 9) has compiled some of these records. Ludwig Kumlien in 1895 told me that five years previously he had collected a varying hare in the tamarack bogs southwest of Lake Mills in Jefferson County, explained to me its differences in appearance and habits from the cottontail, and suggested that I watch for it in the Lima Bog (Sec. 16, T 4 N, R 14 E, Rock County) where occasionally I was collecting mammal specimens, but I never heard of one in Rock County. I saw the Lake Mills mounted specimen in the Milton College collection many times between 1898 and 1904, but it was not there in May, 1947. The southern range of this hare has receded northward until there are few south of 44° 30' N. latitude except in scattered groups. A colony that inhabited Sheboygan Swamp, near Elkhart Lake, as late as 1918, may have been destroyed by flooding and the creation of the Broughton Sheboygan County Marsh Park in 1940. The varying hare is subject to cycles of abundance and scarcity which in some parts of its Canadian range are very pronounced, with peaks about every seven years, but cycles in this species in Wisconsin are not always clear. There was an apparent high in

1930–31 which seemed to coincide with a distribution leveling of the varying hare in the state. As indicated by game kill records (Scott, W. E., 1952: 12), there was a sharp decline in numbers to a period low in 1937, followed by a gradual increase to a moderate high in 1941, dropping to an extreme low game kill record of 26,854 in 1944 and 27,567 in 1945. In 1949 a new peak game kill of 310,132, or nearly half that of 1931, was reached, followed by a decline to less than half that number the next year. It would appear from these rather inadequate figures that the cycle of abundance in Wisconsin may be approximately once in ten years, and that at a high population there are considerably more than one million varying hares in the state. The cycle apparently does not coincide with that of the cottontail. This hare is not gregarious, and the normal population density in suitable habitat is seldom more than one or two per acre, though under specially favorable feeding conditions the number may greatly increase. Its home range is seldom more than a six to eight hundred foot radius, though under urge of food shortage, population pressure, or breeding instinct it may move two or three miles or more.

Unlike the cottontail, when flushed in the wild the varying hare slyly vanishes under the vegetative cover, unseen and unheard by its disturber. By remaining quiet and observant on a trail or road through its habitat, particularly evenings or mornings, a person may often glimpse one or more gamboling, feeding, or simply squatted in the trail resting. Its tracks are easily distinguished from those of the cottontail—the hind feet being not only longer but clearly showing a wide spread of the toes, particularly in evidence on snow, hence, the name "snowshoe rabbit." When the animal is running fast, the individual tracks may be five or six feet apart. The hops are shorter when the animal is sneaking away, the tracks made by the hind feet and front feet are closer together, and the space between tracks is sometimes less than 12 inches. Scats left often plentifully along the trail aid in marking the presence of the varying hare, the round scats averaging larger than those of the cottontail, the smallest being about as large as the largest cottontail scats. Gnawings on brush or other vegetation may lead to locating the presence of this hare, occasionally one of its resting places or forms, or

a place where it has rolled and bathed in the dust.

It is active both summer and winter, mostly early in the morning, late in the evening, and on moonlight nights, retiring to its resting place or form during the daytime, yet sometimes it rolls, stretches, and basks in the dust in the sunshine. On approach of danger, real or suspected, it quickly and quietly disappears under the vegetation with a series of short hops or a shambling walk, and it is very efficient at hiding. Under favorable conditions it can run about 25 miles an hour, although Terres (1941: 453) records a speed of 31 miles an hour on ice as clocked by a pursuing automobile. It would seem likely that slipping of the automobile tires may have caused an error in the mileage record. Its snowshoe feet enable it to run exceptionally well on crusted snow. It is agile, and can stand nearly erect on its two hind feet. It does not take to water freely, but swims fairly well for a short distance, even across a rapid stream.

Rather frequent thumping of the hind feet on the ground is indulged in by both sexes, and the surprisingly audible sound produced is probably an intercommunication or warning signal. The hares studied by Grange (1932 a: 14) made "a sort of grunting noise of displeasure at times and the females made use of a snort, seemingly a kind of reprimand or evidence of disgust most often used when a young hare that had been handled by a person was returned." When a hare is terrified, captured by an enemy, or injured, it frequently utters a shrill, bleating screech. The varying hare is not gregarious, the only ones really friendly with each other seemingly being the male and female at mating time. Males are particularly intolerant of each other, especially at breeding time, and frequently fight one another. During high cycles of abundance the density of population may become so great that gregariousness is forced on the hares, resulting in a food shortage and disease spread that may start the down cycle. Though in a measure solitary, this hare often gambols and plays, apparently for the mere pleasure of it. Its senses are all well developed except possibly that of taste. Hearing and sight are especially acute. Its normal longevity in the wild is less than four years; its potential longevity is about eight years.

The snowshoe hare is promiscuous in its breeding activities both in the wild and in captivity. First mating of the year begins early in March, is at its height by the last of the month, and may continue well into April. Ovulation takes place about ten hours after copulation. The gestation period is about 36 days. "The minimum gestation for which both copulation and parturition were accurately observed was 35 days, 20-1/2 hours, the maximum 37 days, 5-1/2 hours" (Severaid, 1942: 23). The first litter of leverets in the spring may appear by the middle of April, often before the mother has acquired her spring pelage. The doe may breed again on the day of parturition, and as many as four litters are possible during a breeding season, though the usual is two or three litters. The last litter may come as late as the last of August or possibly the first of September. Three appears to be the most frequent number of leverets in a litter and four next, the combined numbers comprising about two-thirds of recorded litters. Frequently the litter is of two leverets, sometimes only one. Very rarely is the number five or more, though in Minnesota out of 266 pregnant females examined C. M. Aldous found two with 7 embryos, one with 6 embryos, and six with 5 embryos (1937: 47). At birth the varying hare is covered with soft dense fur about three-fourths of an inch long, has the eyes open, and weighs about two and one-half ounces. It is very precocious, and crawls and hops when one day old, becomes quite active within a week, and when about ten days old begins to nibble grass, though still nursing until about four weeks old. Activities of the leveret until 65 days old have been described by Grange (1932 a: 8–10). It grows rapidly, and at three months old is about two-thirds grown and at about five months of age is an adult, though it does not breed until the following spring. The mammae are eight, two pectoral, four abdominal, and two inguinal.

No real nest is made by the varying hare, but it seems to have homing sense and often returns to rest at the same spot, ultimately packing the snow, soil, or grass or other vegetation into a form, part of which may be constructed by a few kicks of the hind feet. The form is nearly always in a sheltered spot under grass, brush, shrubbery, or a fallen log or tree, or sometimes even in a fallen hollow log or an old woodchuck burrow. I have seen several of these forms in the grass under red raspberry or blackberry bushes at the border of paper birch woods. Sometimes a varying hare will make its home under a log cabin or other cottage in the woods, and may maintain it there for several years. A mother hare may give birth to her offspring in one of her established forms, but it is believed that more often the young are dropped on the ground or grass and that any semblance of a hollow form is made by the kicking, tossing, and tumbling of the family. Apparently no sanitation is in vogue, for numerous feces may be found in the form and immediately around it.

The food of the varying hare in summer consists of many species of herbaceous plants such as clover, grasses, dandelion, strawberry, ferns, and others, and the more tender and succulent parts of aspen, willow, alder, hazelnut, and paper birch. In winter, when some of these foods are not regularly available, it feeds more on the bark and shoots of woody plants, including those above, and also pine, cedar, spruce, and sumac. At times, particularly when one is living under a cabin in the woods, it will feed on table refuse, eat some bread, and even taste meat, though it will not habitually eat meat. It consumes a few insects, probably taken accidently with the herbage, and likewise a slight amount of soil and fine gravel. During dry weather it drinks water, and at times it nibbles snow in the winter. It frequently washes its nose and chops with its paws, and rolls and tumbles in the dust for its bath.

Probably few of the larger predators would refuse a snowshoe hare, and among those known to prey upon it in Wisconsin are the coyote, wildcat, Canada lynx, red fox, both the short-tailed (*M. e. bangsi*) and the long-tailed (*M. f. noveboracensis*) weasel, great horned owl, snowy owl, bald eagle, and some of the larger hawks. Weasels kill not only numbers of young hares but also adults. As far back as the mound builders, man has killed varying hares for food and clothing. A few are killed at night by automobiles, others burn or smother in forest and brush fires, and continued wet and cold weather may cause the death of many young ones.

External parasites known to infect the varying hare include the rabbit tick *Haemaphysalis leporis-palustris*, the flea *Cediopsylla simplex*, and the mite *Haemogamasus hirsutus*. "The internal parasites include three trematodes, nine cestodes, fourteen nematodes, one acanthocephalan, and four dipterous larvae" (Erickson, 1944: 137). This hare is subject to tularemia, but possibly less so than the cottontail. A disease apparently peculiar to this species is "shock disease," characterized by a degeneration of the liver and insufficient storage of glycogen, yet with no apparent causative bacteria or parasites. What we know of the disease has been described (Green and Larson, 1938; Green, Larson, and Bell, 1939; Green, Larson, and Mather, 1938). Mild infections of the ringworm fungus have been reported in the snowshoe hare in Montana (Adams, Salvin, and Hadlow, 1956).

The snowshoe hare is an important game animal in Wisconsin, there being up to 600,000 killed in some years and seldom less than 100,000. It probably offers more sport in hunting than the cottontail, but as food it is not so highly esteemed by some. It has important value as a natural food for many fur-bearing animals. "Sometimes it does damage to forests by destroying young trees and new growth, particularly in forest nurseries, and when hares are abundant a serious loss may result. Methods of controlling this damage by use of repellents, traps, snares and otherwise have been partly devised and often are quite effective" (Mather, Gensch, and Barton, 1943). "Although often reported as a serious menace to forest stands, in other instances it has been cited as useful in thinning forest stands" (Cox, 1938). "Snowshoe hares can be raised in captivity, but production costs on an average of more than $1.25 a hare and other limiting factors make it impracticable as a commercial meat selling venture, but of possible value for game restocking purposes" (Severaid, 1942).

Specimens examined from Wisconsin.—Total 84, as follows: *Barron County:* Turtle Lake, 5 (UWZ). *Bayfield County:* Cable, 5 (UWZ). Herbster, 5; Orienta, 3. *Clark County:* Hewett Twp., 1 (UWZ). *Door County:* Fish Creek, 7 (UWZ); Liberty Grove, 1 (UWZ); Peninsula State Park, 4 (UWZ). *Douglas County:* Solon Springs, 8 (CNHM); Upper St. Croix River, T 44 N, R 13 W, 1 (UWZ). *Iron County:* Fisher Lake, 3 (UWZ); Mercer, 1 (UWZ). *Longlade County:* T 34 N, R 11 E, 5 (UWZ). *Oconto County:* Kelley Brook, 1 (MM). *Oneida County:* Rhinelander, 6 (2 CC; 3 UWZ); Woodruff, 2 (CNHM). *Price County:* Ogema, 1; *Rusk County;* Ladysmith, 9 (UWZ). *Vilas County:* Eagle River, 5; Lac Vieux Desert, 1 (CNHM); Mamie Lake, 1; Phelps, 7 (UWZ); Sayner, 2 (CNHM).
Selected references.—Aldous, C. M., 1937; Grange, W. B., 1932 a, 1932 b, 1953; MacLulich, D. A., 1937; Severaid, J. H., 1942.

Genus **Sylvilagus** Gray
Cottontails

Dental formula:
$$\text{I } \frac{2-2}{1-1}, \text{ C } \frac{0-0}{0-0}, \text{ P } \frac{3-3}{2-2}, \text{ M } \frac{3-3}{3-3} = 28.$$

Sylvilagus floridanus mearnsii (J. A. Allen)
Mearns' Cottontail

Lepus sylvaticus mearnsii J. A. Allen, Bull. Amer. Mus. Nat. Hist. 6: 171, May 31, 1894.
Lepus nanus Lapham, p. 340, 1853.
Lepus sylvaticus Strong, p. 440, 1883.
Lepus floridanus mearnsi Snyder, p. 124, 1902.
Sylvilagus floridanus mearnsi Jackson, p. 25, 1908; Jackson, p. 89, 1910; Hollister, p. 26, 1910; Komarek, p. 209, 1932.
Sylvilagus floridanus mearnsii Cory, p. 266, 1912; Schmidt, p. 116, 1931; Barger, p. 12, 1952.

Vernacular names.—In Wisconsin usually called cottontail or rabbit. Other names include bunny, common rabbit, cottontail hare, cottontail rabbit, cotton-tailed rabbit, gray rabbit, Molly cottontail, Peter rabbit, *pierre lapin* (French), *wa-a-boos* (Chippewa), and wood rabbit.

Identification marks.—A medium-sized rabbit, averaging somewhat smaller than the snowshoe hare, adult in total length more than 375 but less than 500 mm.; ears rather large, somewhat elongate, from notch to tip less than 70 mm.; tail more than 40 but less than 70 mm.; in all pelages buffy gray above and white below; hind feet much smaller than in *Lepus a. phaeonotus*, always less than 110 mm.

Color of upper parts pale buffy gray darkened by grayish and black hairtips; rump patch dark grayish; sides paler and more grayish than upper parts, with fewer black hair-tips; nape and legs cinnamon rufous; throat, dark ochraceous, the other under parts whitish. Color essentially similar at all seasons; the worn pelage often pale buffy gray sometimes with a slight pinkish-cinnamon cast. There are two molts annually. The spring molt may begin as early as the last of February, but usually begins in May and is completed by the last of June, although it sometimes may extend into August. The fall molt usually occurs in September or October, but occasionally is not completed until November.

The skull averages only slightly smaller than that of *Lepus a. phaeonotus*, and many skulls of the two species overlap in dimensions of length and breadth; postorbital process not flaring, fused

*Cottontail rabbit. U.S. Fish and Wildlife Service
photograph by W. M. Rush.*

at posterior end with frontal; interparietal not fused with parietal; teeth moderate.

The adult female cottontail averages about 2 per cent larger than the male, but in coloration is similar. The color of the young is quite similar to that of the adult, but the fur is more woolly and softer until the animal is about half grown. There is considerable individual variation not only in color, which may vary in the brown shades from pale buffy gray to ochraceous buff, but also in the length of ears and hind feet. Color mutations are rare, though Nelson (1909: 26) had seen an albinistic individual of *Sylvilagus f. mallurus* from unspecified locality. Ludwig Kumlien describes an interesting abnormal specimen of *S. f. mearnsii* that was shot September 10, 1890, in Sumner Township, Jefferson County, was mounted, and belonged to the Albion Academy Museum and Library Association:

It was of about medium length, perhaps slightly less than average, but the body was much slimmer than in a normal specimen. The head, neck, feet and tail did not differ in any way from an ordinary rabbit, but the rest of the body was covered with long silky ashy-blue hair, divided lengthwise dorsally, and falling gracefully down the sides, hanging like a fine fringe on either side. There was also a very distinct "part" on the ventral surface, the hair lying close to the body and pointing straight toward the sides. The hair on the under surface was not so luxuriant or soft as on the back, and of a lighter color.

The longest hairs of the back were slightly over four and one-half inches in length, and looked like very fine goat's hair, but of course, much finer and very soft and flossy. A more puzzling feature of this specimen was that the sex could not be determined; careful dissection showed rudimentary or imperfectly developed parts of both sexual organs (Kumlien, 1891: 89).

The cottontail can always be distinguished from the varying hare, and of course also from the white-tailed jack rabbit, by its shorter hind feet (always less than 110 mm. long), by the fact that its color never turns white in winter, and by a distinct fulvous patch on the nape; other characteristics are a skull with weaker, more attenuate rostrum than in the varying hare; postorbital process fused posteriorly to frontal; interparietal not fused with parietal. All native Wisconsin cottontails are referable to *S. f. mearnsii*. Other forms may have been introduced into the state

by sportsmen or by the State Game Department, but apparently animals from such introductions are soon killed or else absorbed by the native stock. To identify specimens of feral animals from such introductions might require difficult technical study.

Measurements.—Total length, 375 to 490 mm. (14.8 to 19.3 in.); tail, 40 to 70 mm. (1.6 to 2.8 in.); hind foot, 85 to 108 mm. (3.3 to 4.3 in.). Weight, 2 lbs. to 4 lbs. 8 oz., rarely to 5 lbs. 6 oz., pregnant female to 7 lbs.; the usual weight about 2 lbs. 8 oz. to 3 lbs. 4 oz. Skull length, 70 to 82 mm.; width, 33 to 40 mm.

Distribution in Wisconsin.—Found throughout the state; less plentiful in the more northern portions, particularly the heavily forested regions.

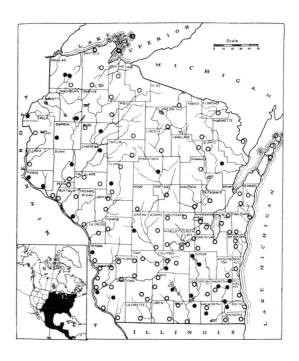

Map 25. *Distribution of* SYLVILAGUS FLORIDANUS. ● = *specimens examined.* ○ = *authentic records.*

Habitat.—Diverse and variable, always near cover suitable for concealment, never in dense forest nor in short grass prairie unless as a straggler. Sparse woodland with numerous thickets, brush piles, and fallen trees; uncultivated dry swampland abounding in tall grasses, sedges, and

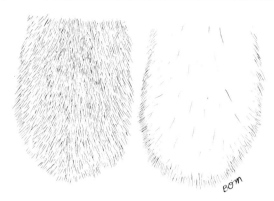

Tail of cottontail rabbit. Left, upper view; right, under view. ¾×.

brushy shrubs; tamarack swamps, particularly the drier grassy parts; grass and weed patches and thickets on farms, particularly along fences and stone walls, or in corn fields of advanced growth; hayfields of tall alfalfa, clover, or timothy; cut-over lands and slashings, or burns, especially where new vegetation has started; orchards and gardens, particularly if near patches or borders of weeds, tall grass, or brush, even in towns and villages, sometimes in cities.

Status and Habits.—With the northward movement of deforestation and agriculture in the state there has been a northward movement of habitat suitable for the cottontail, until now this species is found in favorable spots throughout the state. Just where the northern edge of its range was when the early explorers arrived is unknown, nor do we have a clear picture of its distribution movement. It was abundant in southern Wisconsin when early settlers arrived, and probably occupied forest borders throughout the deciduous forest regions. It occurred at least as far north as Kingston, Green Lake County, in 1846 (Muir, 1913: 181), though J. N. Clark of Meridean, Dunn County, wrote to Ned Hollister about the year 1902 that "the cottontail made its appearance in the county about 50 years ago, and the northern hare gradually disappeared." Nelson (1909: 172) tells us that this cottontail for the first time reached Gordon, Douglas County, during the fall of 1907, but that it was reported to have been common for some time just south of there although it was formerly unknown in this region. I found the cottontail on Madeline Island and Outer Island, Apostle Islands, Ashland County, in 1919 (Jackson, 1920 a: 64). The cot-

tontail in Wisconsin fluctuates in numbers from year to year, the variability in most parts of the state appearing to follow a cyclic pattern. As indicated by game harvest reports of the Wisconsin Conservation Department, there were high populations during the years 1932, 1942, and 1954, the cottontails taken during those years being 2,474,125, 1,397,308, and 1,311,392 respectively. During the low years of 1937 and 1948 cottontails taken were 528,911 and 382,186 respectively. This might indicate a population cycle of about ten or eleven years. We do not know the exact cause of these cycles, but weather and disease conditions, over-population, and hunting pressure may all be factors. The home range of the cottontail varies considerably with the amount of available food and cover; the male, whether immature or adult, tends to range farther than the female, and the adult ranges farther than the immature. The home range of an individual may be as small as one-half acre or less, or as large as 40 or more acres; the average range for males in Wisconsin is about 6 or 8 acres and that of females about 2 or 3 acres. A. O. Haugen (1942: 366) found that adult females had an average home range of 14.0 acres during winter and 22.5 acres during the breeding season in southern Michigan, a home range that is higher than shown by others in Iowa (Hendrickson, 1936), Missouri (Schwartz, 1941), and Connecticut (Dalke and Sime, 1941). When seeking a new homesite, a cottontail, particularly late in the winter or when released from confinement, may travel a mile or more. One cottontail to an acre of good habitat is a fairly high average, though this may increase to two or more an acre in much of the habitat, or be as low as one to three or more acres in times of scarcity. At the peak of a population there are probably at least five to six million cottontails in the state.

The presence and relative abundance of the cottontail in an area often is evident from the tracks and scats, particularly when snow is on the ground. The tracks are distinctive from those of the varying hare in that the hind-foot tracks are shorter and narrower, but often habitat alone will determine which species likely made the tracks. Feces of the cottontail are smaller than those of the varying hare, the largest of the former about equal in size to the smallest of the latter. Its toothmarks may be seen on shrubbery but are not always easily distinguished from those of

Resting place or "rabbit form" of Mearns cottontail.
Photograph by the author.

other mammals. The cottontail usually flushes readily from its hiding place, and bounds away often conspicuously ahead of its disturber. Beating brush or brush piles, poking into abandoned woodchuck holes, or hunting with a small

Gnawings of cottontail rabbit on sumach. 1×.

noisy dog, such as a beagle or beagle-terrier mongrel, will usually drive the rabbit from hiding. During extremely hot hours of summer the cottontail does not as a rule run far when flushed, but if cover is available is apt to move aside from the path of its disturber and remain quietly hidden. In many places it makes distinct runways leading to and from its feeding places and hiding cover.

Although the cottontail may be active at any time of day or night, particularly on moonlight nights, it is most active during the first three or four hours after sunrise and from two or three hours before sunset until one hour after sunset. It is about both winter and summer. Its usual slow locomotion is by short jumps or hops. Faster progress is made by longer leaps, the maximum speed being about 18 miles an hour, which, a cottontail does not maintain for more than one-half mile. In attempting escape, it depends more upon ducking and dodging than upon its speed, and often will travel a circuitous route and return to near its starting place. It does not take to water readily but is known to swim under duress.

Thumping of the hind feet is the most frequent, if not the only, method of intercommunication of the cottontail. Young rabbits when hungry or neglected often scream while in their nest. Vocally it is comparatively silent, though at times when the mother is with the young she may utter low grunts. Sometimes when attacked or in pain a cottontail will utter shrill and almost human baby-like cries, such as did an adult I saw being attacked by a barred owl near Storrs Lake, Rock County, July 28, 1902, and a young one attacked by a timber rattlesnake near Gotham, Richland County, August 21, 1920. The death scream of a rabbit is one of the most harrowing sounds of nature. The cottontail is solitary, and seldom are two or more found together, with the exception of young ones. It is wary and usually escapes by bounding away, though it may squat quietly or "freeze" and thus try to avoid detection. It is not entirely defenseless and can strike quick hard blows with its hind feet and often produce deep scratches with its toenails. Its hearing is acute, and its ears can be moved at will to catch sounds from various directions. Its sight is excellent, and the protruding construction of its eyes enables it to see at many angles at once, though often it is blind to objects directly ahead.

Its stamina and vitality are not strong, and it is easily killed. Predation, disease, and hunting pressure reduce its average life span in the wild to less than two years, though it has a potential longevity of eight or nine years.

Mating of the cottontail may occur in southern Wisconsin as early as the middle of February, though usually the first mating of the year does not take place until March. Sperms may form in the testes as early as the last of December, and live ones may be present as late as the first part of September. It appears that the oestrous usually does not begin until the last of January and ends by the last of August, the actual breeding season being thus limited by the female to a seven-month period. Mating is promiscuous. The gestation period in the wild apparently varies from 28 to 32 days, the normal being about 29 or 30 days. The first litter of the year may occur by the middle of March, but more often it is near the last of April. Two or three litters to each female usually are born each year, and possibly sometimes four. Usually three to six young constitute the litter, five being the most frequent number, sometimes only two, and rarely as many as seven or eight. Ten embryos approximately 25 days old on November 21, 1955, were reported at Madison by Lemke (1957). At birth the cottontail is naked and blind, weighs about an ounce, and is some four inches in total length, with ears about one-half inch long and tail scarcely longer than one-quarter inch. Though it receives little attention from its mother, except for nursing visits, it develops rapidly, and when two weeks old its eyes are open, the downy hair shows growth, and it is able to scamper and play outside the nest and to nibble foliage. When four or five weeks old it is weaned and independent. It may be considered mature when four months old. There is some evidence that young of early broods may breed the year of birth, but most cottontails do not breed until the spring following birth. The mammae are eight, two pectoral, four abdominal, and two inguinal.

The brooding nest is placed in a hollow or depression in the ground, about four or five inches in depth and of about the same diameter, dug or scratched by the mother. She lines the cavity first with grass and then with fur apparently plucked from her abdomen. Hamilton (1940 a: 107) in New York believed that in selecting the nesting site the female utilizes shallow depressions formed by mouse-hunting skunks or dislodged stones, or other ready-made holes that she may find. The well-concealed nesting form is made in a sheltered place in a grass or weed patch, hay field, or grain field, along a roadside, in scrubby open woodland or thicket, or even in a pasture or a berry patch. The cottontail also makes forms that it uses as hiding or resting places in grassy, herbaceous, or low bushy vegetation. The forms are a bedding place made by the cottontail scratching or trampling a shallow oval hollow in the soil, usually about six to eight inches in diameter by nine to eleven inches long, depending on the size of the cottontail. Some of the forms contain grass or leaves, a few may have fur in them, but fully half of them appear to have no lining. The cottontail uses these forms during inclement weather, lying protected by vegetation and facing away from the direction in which the rain or snow is coming (Dalke, 1942: 33). When the weather gets too stormy or too cold, the cottontail seeks shelter in a burrow or under a shock of grain, a brush pile or a stone wall, from which security it is often difficult to dislodge it.

The summer food of the cottontail is almost any kind of green vegetation. It does not eat hard ripe grain or dry straws at this season, nor does it dig or eat tubers and bulbous roots. Buds, sprouts, and tender shoots of many woody plants are eaten, and it nibbles at the stems of a few shrubby plants such as the blackberry, raspberry, and gooseberry. It seems to be especially fond of legumes, such as alfalfa, clover, peas, and beans, and consumes grass, dandelions, plantains, lettuce, and very many other plants. During winter, it resorts chiefly to tender parts of many species of shrubs and trees, and will gnaw away both the outer and the inner bark of smooth-barked trees sometimes two inches in diameter, often girdling the entire circumference of the trunk, and thus killing the plant. In a study of winter food of the cottontail in New York, it was found to feed on 71 species of plants, mostly trees and shrubs (Todd, 1927). A winter browse tally of 108 woody species, made near Madison, showed 41 per cent severely browsed, 8 per cent unbrowsed (McCabe, 1947: 33). There is considerable variation in the plant species eaten by the cottontail, which may be due to individual choice or seasonal or regional differences.

Whether adult or baby in the nest, the cottontail has many enemies that utilize it as food. It is prey for nearly all carnivorous mammals, birds, and reptiles, so much so that in years of low rabbit population there usually is a noticeable increase in predation on other animals, often followed by a decrease in population of flesh-eating mammals. High productivity of the cottontail usually well supplies this predatory food demand until the low cycle hits the species. It is the regular prey of the weasel, mink, skunk, grey fox, red fox, coyote, vagrant cat and dog, great horned and barred owls, larger hawks, and the black snake, blue racer, and timber rattlesnake. Young in the nest may be attacked by a weasel, skunk, or even by a short-tailed shrew, and in other cases may drown, be burned, or killed by farming or gardening operations. Wet weather often destroys many young, and during a wet breeding season leverets in more than half the nests may be destroyed. Young rabbits, under such conditions, may not drown outright but die through exposure to wet and cold. Cottontails are very vulnerable to highway traffic and are one of the commonest mammals run over by automobiles.

The cottontail in Wisconsin is host to the ticks *Haemaphysalis leporis-palustris* and *Dermacentor variabilis*, and to at least ten species of fleas, of which *Cediopsylla simplex, Odontopsyllus multispinosus, Ctenocephalides felis*, and identified species of the genera *Epitedia, Megabothris, Monopsyllus, Nosopsyllus, Orchopeas,* and *Thrassis* have been collected on it (Hass and Dicke, 1959). Five species of mites have been reported from it, namely *Trombicula lipovskyi, T. subsignata, T. sylvilaga, T. microti,* and *T. whartoni.* Among the endoparasites of the cottontail in Iowa are listed eight species of *Coccidia* and one *Sarcosporidia.* Larvae or grubs of botflies are sometimes present between the skin and the flesh. Species of helminth parasites as recovered from 97 cottontails from northern Minnesota included one fluke, six tapeworms, and nine roundworms (Erickson, 1947: 257).

The vitality of the cottontail is so low that it is easily killed by a slight gunshot wound, and sometimes fright, emaciation, or flea or tick infestation will cause its death. It is readily susceptible to several diseases, most of which are not transmissible to humans but a few of which are, most notably tularemia. This disease was discovered in ground squirrels in California in 1910 by Dr. George W. McCoy (1911) of the U. S. Public Health Service, who a year later reported it in other rodents and the black-tailed jack rabbit, and discovered the causative agent to be the bacterium *Pasteurella tularensis* (McCoy and Chapin, 1912). Dr. Edward Francis and his associates in the Public Health Service continued research and found that the disease is transmissible to man, gave it the name "tularemia," and established important information about it. Tularemia has been reported in every state except Vermont. It was first found in Wisconsin in 1928, and from then until 1946 a total of 459 human cases in 61 counties had been reported (Morgan, 1949: 6). It may occur anywhere in the state, particularly where there are cottontails or hares. It is now known to occur in fifty or more kinds of mammals or birds. Man usually becomes infected by handling rabbit carcasses or raw skins while dressing or preparing the rabbit for table or other use, though he may become infected by merely handling a tularemic animal. There is evidence that tularemia is carried by polluted water and insects, ticks, and other vectors. First symptoms of the disease in man may appear two or three days after infection. A painful ulcer may appear at the point where infection gained entrance, usually accompanied by headache, intermittent fever and chills, aching, swelling of lymph glands, general weakness, and exhaustion. Determination of the presence of tularemia usually is made by a blood test. Cure is often effected by use of the antibiotics streptomycin or chloromycetin, but in any event a physician should attend the patient. The mortality rate in humans has been about 5 per cent. The mortality rate in cottontails is 100 per cent. In rabbits, one of the most significant characteristics of the disease is the presence of yellowish or whitish flecks or spots varying in size from a pinpoint to 2 mm. in diameter on the liver and spleen and distributed throughout the tissue of these organs. Slightly infected animals may appear normal in all respects yet be potent carriers. Regard with caution and suspicion any wild rabbit that appears sick, or is slow, sluggish, or stupid, and do not shoot or handle it. "For safety's sake—rubber gloves should be worn when dressing rabbits—from the time the rabbits are shot until they are cooked. Be certain that the meat is thoroughly cooked, for undercooked flesh may be infectious. Under no conditions should rabbits be handled

if cuts or abrasions are present on the hands"
(McDermid, 1946: 11). This does not imply that
anyone should refrain from rabbit hunting. The
number of human tularemia cases in Wisconsin
is negligible in comparison to the thousands who
hunt rabbits.

Growths about the head of the cottontail, much
like horns in appearance and structure, occur
rarely. These primarily are caused by some irritation affecting the tissues, and may have their
origin from warts or from sebaceous cysts occurring in the skin. Such "horns" are of a pathological
nature, but are not malignant and do not directly
cause death, though they must be inconvenient
for the rabbit.

The leading game animal of Wisconsin, the
cottontail provides outdoor sport for thousands,
from the country boy to the city sportsman. In
years when the cottontail is plentiful the annual
kill seldom is less than one million rabbits, and
during the financial depression years of 1932 and
1933 the figure rose to nearly two and one-half
million each year. The value of the cottontail in
supplying a worry-lessening sport and millions of
pounds of delicious meat at such a harrowing
time cannot be estimated in terms of money. In
ordinary years rabbit meat is worth 50 to 75
cents a pound, and the annual total value to the
state well more than one million dollars but the
sport value of the rabbit is still unestimable. The
high rating of the cottontail as a game animal
warrants its protection and careful management.
The Wisconsin Conservation Department recognizes its value and attempts to increase its numbers in special areas by giving protection and
manipulating cover, food plants, and other habitat requirements (Truax, 1955). The Department judiciously does not import rabbits from
other states for transplant in Wisconsin, but
does make local transplants from areas overpopu-
lated by rabbits or where they may be pests to
hunting areas within the state. The cottontail
does not do well when raised in captivity. The
cottontail pelt has a low value of five to ten cents
a pound, and it takes about ten skins for a
pound. The skin is weak, and although the fur is
soft it wears poorly. It has little value for felt.
An economic advantage of the cottontail, often
overlooked, is that it serves as a buffer food
supply for predators that otherwise might prey
on domestic animals.

The cottontail may sometimes become a serious pest in a nursery, orchard, tree plantation,
garden, or farm crop land. It eats all sorts of
green herbage, being particularly partial to most
legumes, and in the absence of other conveniently
available food may in a short time materially
damage a garden, clover, or alfalfa crop. It often
is destructive to woody plants in the nursery,
orchard, tree plantation, or elsewhere, particularly in winter when it gnaws away the bark,
nips off young branches, shoots, and buds, and
cuts off seedlings (McCabe, 1947 a). Cottontails
may be kept out of a small garden by enclosing
the area in a tight chickenwire fence or electric
fence. Repellents somewhat effective in protecting garden crops, until washed off by rain, include blood meal in 40 parts to 1 part flour,
tobacco dust heavily dusted on plants that have
been sprayed lightly with water, or one tablespoon nicotine sulphate (Blackleaf 40) to one
gallon water, used as a spray. More effective, and
particularly useful on woody plants, are the commercial repellents Gordrite Z. I. P. (5 per cent
by weight solution in water) and Goulard and
Olena Rabbit Repellent heavily dusted on plants
that have been sprayed lightly with water
(Hayne, 1950). Rabbits may be trapped or easily
shot when legally permissible, and these often
are the most effective ways to prevent damage
to crops.

Specimens examined from Wisconsin.—Total 130,
as follows: *Barron County:* Turtle Lake, 7 (UWZ).
Buffalo County: Fountain City, 1. *Burnett County:*
Rush City Bridge (Benson), 2 (MM). *Chippewa
County:* Holcombe, 1. *Clark County:* Foster Town-
ship, 1 (UWZ). *Columbia County:* Okee, 1. *Dane
County:* Madison, 8 (UWZ). *Dodge County:* Beav-
er Dam, 40 (5 CNHM; 1 CU; 34 UWZ); Fox Lake,
4 (UWZ). *Douglas County:* Solon Springs, 1; Upper
Saint Croix Lake, 1 (MM). *Dunn County:* Colfax,
9 (UWZ). *Grant County:* Lancaster, 7 (MM);
Wyalusing, 4 (MM). *Jefferson County:* Sumner, 1
(MM). *Juneau County:* Camp Douglas, 3 (AMNH).
Marathon County: Rib Hill, 1. *Oconto County:* Kel-
ley Brook, 8 (MM). *Pierce County:* Maiden Rock, 1
(MM); Prescott, 5 (MM). *Racine County:* Roches-
ter, 3 (MM); Tischigan Lake, 1 (UWZ). *Rock
County:* Milton, 1 (UWZ). *Rusk County:* Lady-
smith, 2 (UWZ). *Vernon County:* Genoa, 5 (MM).
Walworth County: Delavan, 8 (2 MM). *Waukesha
County:* Delafield, 1 (UWZ); Menominee Falls, 1
(MM); Pewaukee, 2 (UWZ).

Selected references.—Dalke, P. D., 1942; Garlough,
F. E., Welch, J. F., and Spencer, H. J., 1942; Haugen,
A. O., 1942 b; McCabe, R. A., 1943; 1947 a; Morgan,
B. B., 1949.

ORDER RODENTIA

Rodents or Gnawing Mammals

Mammals of this order are for the most part small to medium size. Among the largest ones are the beaver and the South American agouti and capybara. Members of this order are complicated as to relationship and origin. The order contains many races and large populations. In fact living rodents are believed to be as numerous both as to races and individuals as all other living mammals. Rodents were originally absent from New Zealand, Antarctica, the extreme Arctic, and several oceanic islands, but are now practically worldwide in distribution and occur, often through unintentional introduction, wherever man has gone.

The order Rodentia may be defined as follows: Terrestrial and fossorial (occasionally arboreal or semiaquatic) placental mammals with both brain and placentation generalized in type; feet unguiculate; elbow joint always permitting free rotary motion of forearm; fibula never articulating with calcaneum; masseter muscle highly specialized, divided into three or more distinct portions having slightly different functions; caecum without spiral fold; dental formula not known to exceed

$$\text{I}\frac{1}{1}, \ \text{C}\frac{0}{0}, \ \text{PM}\frac{2}{1}, \ \text{M}\frac{3}{3} = 22 \ \text{permanent teeth};$$

incisors scalpriform, growing from persistent pulp, the enamel of the upper tooth not extending to posterior surface; distance between mandibular and maxillary toothrows approximately equal, both pairs of rows capable of partial or complete apposition at the same time, the primary motion of the lower jaw in mastication longitudinal or oblique (Miller and Gidley, 1918: 432).

The order Rodentia is currently divided into three suborders, namely the Sciuromorpha, containing some 60 genera of living forms; the Myomorpha, some 216 genera of living forms; and the Hystricomorpha, some 53 genera of living forms. In Wisconsin the Sciuromorpha are represented by the families Sciuridae, Geomyidae, and Castoridae; the Myomorpha by the families Cricetidae, Muridae, and Zapodidae; and the Hystricomorpha by the family Erethizontidae.

Key to the Families of Living Wisconsin Rodentia

a. Body more or less covered with sharp pointed quills; infraorbital foramen larger than foramen magnum. . . . . *Erethizontidae*

aa. Body covered with ordinary soft hair or fur; infraorbital foramen smaller than foramen magnum.

   b. Tail broad and flat dorsoventrally, scaly; total length of adult more than 3 feet; molars with 8 to 10 transverse ridges or cemented folds of enamel. . . . *Castoridae*

   bb. Tail not broad and flat dorsoventrally, variable; total length less than 3 feet; molars without 8 to 10 transverse ridges.

      c. Tail more or less bushy, hair on middle longer than diameter or fleshy part of tail at that point; postorbital processes well developed, conspicuous; molars with an internal heel from which 2 or 3 ridges pass to the outside margin of the tooth. . . . . *Sciuridae*

      cc. Tail not bushy, hair on middle shorter than diameter of fleshy part of tail at that point; postorbital processes absent or inconspicuous; molar pattern not as in Sciuridae.

         d. External fur-lined cheek pouches present; front feet longer than hind feet with long claws; 4 molariform teeth, in each lower jaw. . . . . . *Geomyidae*

         dd. No external fur-lined cheek pouches; front feet normal, not exceptionally long claws; 3 molariform teeth in each lower jaw.

           e. Hind feet long and kangaroo-like; tail very much longer (20 per cent longer) than head and body; infraorbital foramen broad and not a long narrow slit. . . . . *Zapodidae ee.* Hind feet normal; tail equal or less than length of head and body; infra-orbital foramen a long vertical slit.

   f. Tail nearly naked, the annulations clearly visible; upper molars with tubercles in 3 longitudinal rows. . . . . *Muridae*

   ff. Tail haired, the annulations nearly or completely invisible; upper molars with tubercles arranged in two longitudinal rows or of prismatic triangles. . *Cricetidae*

Family **Sciuridae**
Squirrels and Allies

The family Sciuridae ranges throughout most of the temperate and tropical regions of the earth. It is not found in the extreme north or south, nor in Australia, New Zealand, New Guinea, Madagascar, or the Pacific islands. It consists of about 42 genera exclusive of fossil forms, of which 7 occur in Wisconsin.

Genus **Marmota** Blumenbach
Woodchucks

$$I\frac{1-1}{1-1}, C\frac{0-0}{0-0}, P\frac{2-2}{1-1}, M\frac{3-3}{3-3}=22.$$

Marmota monax monax (Linnaeus)
Southern Woodchuck

Mus monax Linnaeus, Systema Naturae, edition 10, vol. 1, p. 60, 1758.
Arctomys monax Lapham, p. 339, 1853.
Arctomys monax Strong, p. 440, 1883; Snyder, p. 120, 1902.
Marmota monax Jackson, p. 19, 1908; Hollister, p. 25, 1910; Jackson, p. 88, 1910; Cory, p. 150, 1912.

Vernacular names.—In Wisconsin commonly called woodchuck or chuck, sometimes ground-hog. Other names include eastern marmot, eastern woodchuck, *kuk-wah-geeser* (Chippewa), marmot, monax, monk, moonack, *murmeltier* (German), *siffleur* (French-Canadian), whistle-pig or whistling pig, whistler, and woodshock.

Identification marks.—The heaviest Wisconsin member of the squirrel family, body short and thickset; head relatively broad; ears not prominent, rounded, short; tail well furred, moderately, bushy, rather short, about one-fourth or less of the total length of animal and less than twice the length of hind foot; legs short and strong, the hind feet with five toes, the front feet with four well-developed toes bearing slightly curved claws and a rudimentary thumb with small nail; pelage rather coarse, not dense.

Woodchuck, Fish Creek, Wisconsin. U.S. Fish and Wildlife Service photograph by the author.

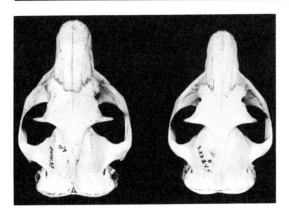

Skulls of woodchucks. Left, MARMOTA M. MONAX, *Platteville, Wisconsin; right,* M. M. RUFESCENS, *St. Croix Falls, Wisconsin.* ½×.

General color above dark grayish to brown, often considerably paled or grizzled by light buff hairtips; the basal part of hairs dark fuscous to deep mouse gray, next succeeded above by a band of pinkish cinnamon; top of head and face fuscous to clove brown; lower side of face, chin, and lips whitish buff; legs blackish fuscous, overlaid and mixed with burnt sienna, producing a distinct reddish-brown effect, particularly on the forelegs; feet blackish brown; general tone of under parts reddish brown, sometimes ochraceous buff, more or less mixed with tawny, ochraceous, and black hairs; tail clove brown to near black. There is one molt annually, usually in July, but sometimes molting is well advanced by June 1.

The skull is rather large and broad, flat and nearly straight in upper outline, constricted postorbitally, the occipital region scarcely depressed posteriorly, the rostrum considerably and gradually depressed anteriorly; brain case broad and somewhat flattened; interorbital region broad, depressed, and weakly concave between postorbital processes, which are relatively long and prominent, and extend at right angles to the anteroposterior axis of the skull; rostrum large and massive, nearly as broad apically as basally; maxillary tooth rows nearly parallel; incisors heavy, anterior faces ivory to pale yellow and somewhat roughened by faint longitudinal grooves.

The male woodchuck averages about 3 per cent heavier than the female, but there is no difference in coloration. The young soon acquire the pelage, which is quite variable in the amount of black or rufous in the darker parts and in the tones of buff or cinnamon in the paler parts. Albinism rarely occurs in the woodchuck. A tendency towards melanism is more frequent. The author found a totally melanistic specimen of *M. m. rufescens* washed upon the beach of Lake Superior west of Herbster, Bayfield County, in August, 1922, but the body may have drifted many miles, possibly even from the Canadian shore.

The woodchuck is the largest member of the squirrel family, and among Wisconsin rodents is exceeded in size only by the beaver with its broad, flat, scaly tail and the porcupine with its body and tail covered with sharp quills or spines. The total length of an adult of either *Marmota m. monax* or *M. m. rufescens* is between 21 and 26 inches, of which one-fourth or less is the brushy tail. The more southerly of the two, *Marmota m. monax,* averages larger than *M. m. rufescens,* has a correspondingly larger skull, and is of somewhat paler and more buffy color above, with the under parts buffy white or light

Left hind foot of woodchuck. Specimen from Mamie Lake, Wisconsin. 1×.

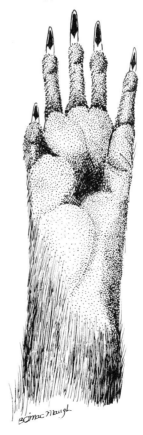

ochraceous, whereas in *rufuescens* the under parts usually are tawny with a distinct deep reddish tone, but sometimes mixed brown and buff with some red. Many of the individuals from areas where the two subspecies intergrade, approximately within 15 miles of latitude 44° N., are intermediate in characteristics and are difficult to assign to either race. A specimen from Trempealeau, for example, an immature male, approaches *M. m. monax* in size but is nearer *rufescens* in color. In most instances color appears to be a more pertinent and stable characteristic than size.

Measurements.—Total length of adults, 550 to 640 mm. (21.6 to 25.2 in.); tail 135 to 160 mm. (5.3 to 6.3 in.); hind foot, 82 to 92 mm. (3.2 to 3.6 in.). Weight, from about 5 lbs. when just out of hibernation in the spring to about 12 lbs. when prepared for hibernation in the fall. Skull length, 94 to 102 mm.; width, 60 to 69 mm.

Distribution in Wisconsin.—Southern part of the state from La Crosse, Sauk, Columbia, Dodge, Washington, and Ozaukee counties south to the Illinois state line.

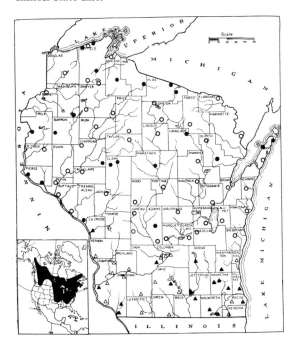

Map 26. *Distribution of* MARMOTA MONAX. *Solid symbols = specimens examined. Open symbols = authentic records.* ●, ○ = M. M. RUFESCENS. ▲, △ = M. M. MONAX.

Habitat.—The woodchuck is primarily a forest border mammal, and as such occurred throughout Wisconsin in early days, probably never in the heart of heavy, dense forest. It favors edges of brushy woodland, particularly near open fields along streams or lake banks, poorly cleared fence lines, railroads, and roads; also clearings, meadows, pastures, and grainfields, especially where near the crest or brow of a hill; attracted to old stumps, rocky outcrops, and piles; not infrequently near a barn or other outbuilding, an unoccupied house or shack, or a lumber pile (as near the depot at Danbury, Burnett County, May 28, 1919).

Status and Habits.—When the first white settlers arrived in Wisconsin the woodchuck was found in nearly all parts of the state. Its remains were present in the Indian mounds at Aztalan, Jefferson County (Somers, in Barrett, 1933: 386). Its numbers have varied in different parts of the state coincident with the whims and urge of man for its destruction on account of its interest as a sportman's target, but more on account of its economic damage, either real or fancied. In many of the intensive agricultural and dairying regions of the state, particularly in the southern parts, the woodchuck by 1950 had been almost extirpated.

In the year 1901 near Milton, Rock County, I could easily locate woodchucks or their holes in numbers, and in areas habitable to woodchucks there often was an average population of up to nearly 50 individuals to the square mile. Fifty years later, in May, 1951, in the same region, I searched diligently with experienced help over many miles before finding an occupied hole. The subspecies *monax* has been depleted more than *rufescens*, which with its more northerly range has had a more favorably protective environment. The woodchuck has legal protection in Wisconsin, as it does in some other states, without which it might become a scarce animal. There are a few places in northern and central Wisconsin where an average of 30 to 40 woodchucks a square mile may occur over a considerable area, and the average for the state as a whole is possibly not less than four or five to the square mile. In this low population of the woodchuck there are probably less than three hundred thousand of them in the state. The home range of the woodchuck is rather limited, usually within two or three hundred feet of its home burrow, though rarely an animal may wander six to eight hundred feet.

The chief evidence of the presence of a woodchuck is its characteristic hole. This cannot easily be mistaken as the work of any other animal, though it may sometimes be occupied by another species, such as a striped skunk, a cottontail, or even a fox or a badger. Although wary and not readily approached closely, it may be very conspicuous at some distance as it sits upright near its hole in an effort to view the intruder. When surprised amongst brush or grass, it clumsily scurries away and titters a loud chirping noise which once learned to be associated with the woodchuck is not apt to be mistaken. Tracks around the den entrance will indicate occupancy, and usually worn trails lead to it. The rather long blackish feces are distinctive but are seldom in evidence. The woodchuck may be active any hour of daylight, but is an early riser and is particularly busy gathering food early in the morning and again in the afternoon before sundown again prompts it to inactivity. It does not migrate, and in fact is rather sedentary and seldom moves its homesite far. It is a profound winter sleeper and spends from four to six months in hibernation. Late in the summer it becomes excessively fat from its ground-hoggish feedings.

Feces of woodchuck. Drawn by Mrs. MacMaugh from sketch by the author. 1×.

When cold weather arrives, sometimes as early as the last of September in the northern part of the state or possibly as late as the middle of November or even later in the southern counties, it retires to its underground hole, blocks the passage with soil, and goes into hibernation just about the time its food supply of green vegeta-

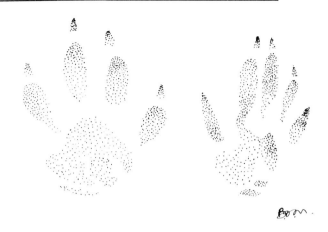

Tracks of woodchuck. Left, right forefoot. Right, right hind foot. 1×.

tion would fail it. Hibernation is very different from ordinary sleep or even winter dormancy. The woodchuck, coiled in a ball with its head passed between its forelegs and resting on its lower abdomen and the hind parts and tail wrapped over the head, with its eyes tightly closed and sunken, its vital functions low, appears lifeless. During hibernation its minimum heartbeats are 4 a minute and its low rectal temperature is 38° F., whereas during summer activity the heartbeats are 75 a minute and the temperature 90° F. (Benedict and Lee, 1938; Jackson, 1937 a; b;c). Extensive research has been conducted on hibernation and voluminous literature published, but as yet we do not know the exact cause for it. The woodchuck, excessively fat when it enters hibernation in the fall, awakens thin and weak in the spring, having lost about 30 to 40 per cent of its weight. During hibernation metabolism is low, and for four or five months the woodchuck in effect becomes a cold-blooded animal.

In view of the present knowledge, the most logical explanation of the cause of heat production and of the differences in heat production between warm-blooded and cold-blooded animals lies in the differences in the supply of oxygen and metabolites to the cells. This supply is regulated (1) by the nutritive state, i.e., the metabolites and oxygen in the blood, and (2) by the circulation and distribution of the blood to the tissues (Benedict and Lee, 1938: 239).

In southern Wisconsin the woodchuck usually emerges from hibernation during the first part of March, rarely as early as the last of February. One might possibly, certainly not probably, come out as early as "ground-hog day," February 2, but such an early date should not be anticipated. Records for winter appearance of the woodchuck in the north are not rare. One was found frozen dead in a trap set four days previously at the entrance to its burrow in Mercer County, Pennsylvania, January 1, 1928 (Holt, 1929), another was reported active at Orton, Dufferin County, Ontario, January 4, 1930 (E. R. S. Hall, 1930), and there are other December, January, and February records from northern states. Green vegetation is scarce when the woodchuck first appears in the spring—often snow is on the ground—and if the creature has difficulty procuring food and adjusting itself it may delay and retreat to its den before making a permanent appearance. And this regardless of whether or not it sees its shadow!

The normal gait of the woodchuck when undisturbed is a cumbersome waddling walk, with occasional pauses to nibble vegetation or to rise on its haunches to glance around for a possible enemy. In walking, its feet are wide spread and its body low hung, and it progresses possibly two miles an hour. When alarmed or chased it usually gallops, and may attain the speed of a running man, or about eight or nine miles an hour. It swims well for considerable distances, with its nose and the top of its head above water. W. T. Cox, in a letter to E. W. Nelson, reports that while he was ascending the Mississippi River just below Lynxville, Wisconsin, on July 26, 1926, he saw a woodchuck swimming across the river from the Iowa shore and that it had nearly reached the Wisconsin shore where the river was fully a half-mile wide. At times the woodchuck is abundant on some of the islands in the Mississippi River and occurs on islands in other rivers and small lakes. I did not find it on any of the Apostle Islands in Lake Superior nor on the islands about Door Peninsula, Lake Michigan, so possibly these waters are too rough for it. Although chiefly terrestrial, the woodchuck frequently climbs trees, especially if the animal is isolated from its burrow and pursued by man or dog, in which case it may climb to a height of 15 to 20 feet but more frequently only 8 to 12 feet. Rarely, it climbs trees to feed on foliage, just to sun itself, or to peer about. Once, in the

middle of March, 1902, north of Milton, Rock County, I found one in a cavity in a white oak of about one-foot diameter, the entrance to which was seven feet above ground. The animal was rather sluggish, and I wondered if it had hibernated there, particularly since there were no fresh scratch marks on the tree. It often basks in the sun, lying stretched flat on a log, stump, stone, inclining tree, or fence post, often four to eight feet above ground. When above ground it usually is easily dislodged.

Sentry duty is regulation for the woodchuck, and it is often seen standing nearly upright at the entrance to its burrow. Its vision is excellent. Sometimes it may quietly drop out of sight into its burrow, shortly to appear again for another peep. If one approaches it quickly and startles it, whether it be acting sentinel or scrambling through herbage, it will usually utter its loud shrill whistle, often following it with several short chuckling notes. The whistle may be heard for two or three hundred yards if the wind is favorable. Sometimes when a woodchuck whistles, others join in the alarm until a half dozen may be calling. Alarm or fear is also expressed by grinding its teeth, and pleasure may be indicated by a low grunt or bark.

The woodchuck is not a gregarious animal, and outside of the family group seldom are more than two or three seen near one another, and rarely do more than two adults live in the same hole. Once in a while a group of even a dozen or so may congregate in an especially favorable sunning place or place where food is particularly attractive. As a rule it is rather pugnacious, particularly the male with its own sex, and when cornered or harassed by a human will fight ferociously, displaying and using with effect its heavy incisors. A mature animal seldom plays except with its young offspring. Its strength, tenacity, and vitality are remarkable. One caught in a No. 1½ steel trap August 20, 1919, near Ogema, Price County, Wisconsin, held with its forelegs to the inside of its burrow with such tenacity that when H. H. Sheldon attempted to drag it out, using a board as a lever, the trap pulled from its hind foot and it escaped (MS. field report, Aug. 15–23, 1919). It will survive a severe injury, and often lives a long time after losing a leg, or even after internal injuries with a part of the viscera externally exposed (Hamilton, 1934: 95). Its curiosity often prompts it to peek from its hole for a look at man or dog, often to its destruction. It is sluggish as a rule in both physical and mental reactions, rates low in intelligence, and is easily trapped or shot. Its normal longevity is probably less than five years, possibly on the average less than three years in localities where it is heavily trapped or hunted. Its potential longevity is about ten years. One lived in the National Zoological Park, Washington, D. C., for nine years, three months (Mann, 1930: 303). Usually it does not live well in confinement, nor make a good pet.

The woodchuck breeds when one year old. Mating occurs from the first of March to early in April, possibly as late as the middle of April in northern Wisconsin. Copulation often occurs near the entrance to the den, sometimes in an exposed field nearby. The gestation period is about thirty days. One litter a year is produced by each pair. It may contain from two to seven kits, usually four to six, the average number being close to five, although litters of eight and nine have been recorded (Howell, 1915: 12). The litter of nine, which I observed, lived in a hole under a tobacco shed at the edge of a tobacco field (June, 1900, south of Milton, Wisconsin). At birth the woodchuck is blind, naked, and helpless, is about four inches long, of which one-half inch is tail, and weighs about one ounce. At the end of four weeks the kit has doubled its length, weighs some six times its birth weight, is covered with short hairs, and has eyes open. When five or six weeks old the kit is weaned and begins to wander from the burrow and shift for itself. Sometimes it wanders too far, and the mother will carry it in her mouth back to the burrow, holding it by the nape of the neck. The kit usually is supporting itself by the last of June, or at the age of eight weeks, by which time it weighs two pounds or more. It does not complete full growth until about two years old, but is sexually mature when one year old. The mammae are eight, four pectoral, two abdominal, two inguinal.

This efficient digger lives in a burrow which it excavates in the ground, usually on the side of a hill—especially near the top if in a meadow or a hay field—underneath a stump, the roots of a tree, a stone wall, or possibly an old building, or sometimes in an opening in cliffs. It has often

been stated, following the lead of C. Hart Merriam (1884 a: 148), that the burrows are of two principal types: the first type slopes at a moderate angle from the surface and has a mound of dirt near its entrance; the second is more or less vertical for several feet immediately below the surface, and no loose earth can be found in its neighborhood. Actually, when it starts digging its hole, the woodchuck always faces the surface of the ground with head and shoulders perpendicular to it, and thus when it digs on a slope the burrow inclines from the general ground level of the earth, and most of the soil removed accumulates at the entrance, whereas when it digs on level ground the burrow is vertical to the general ground level and a considerable amount of soil removed may fall back into the burrow. When a woodchuck burrows into a steep vertical bank, which it rarely does, it starts the hole horizontally inward, still perpendicular to the surface. Probably the burrow termed the second type by Merriam and others refers to the plunge hole, which is usually constructed on level ground, has no hill of soil at the entrance, and is dug from the inside of the burrow. The plunge or escape hole usually is well hidden in vegetation and is not used as a nesting place or regular resting place, nor for hibernation. The animal digs with its front feet and throws the dirt to the rear with its hind feet. It uses its heavy incisors for gnawing and tearing away roots and similar obstructions. The entrance to the burrow is slightly wider than high and is variable in size, not always in proportion to the size of its occupant. Possibly the length of time a burrow is occupied or its multiple use may cause an increase in the size of the entrance, which is usually between six and seven inches high and seven and eight inches wide. A large one that I measured at Milton, Rock County, was ten inches high and twelve inches wide. Hamilton (1934: 128) records one in New York 12 by 14 inches which housed a woodchuck weighing nearly 12 pounds. Usually there are two entrances to each burrow, often three, and sometimes four. The burrow varies in diameter but always narrows just inside the entrance. It goes directly inward for 2 to 4 feet, then inclines upward and generally extends more or less parallel to the surface for 15 to 30 feet, sometimes 50 feet or even farther, and frequently has

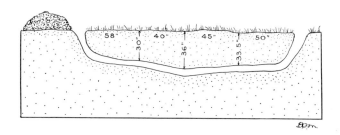

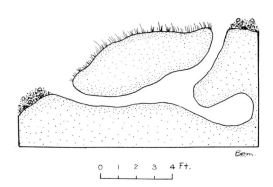

Diagram of woodchuck burrow on level ground. Copied from Fisher, 1893.

Diagram of woodchuck burrow on hillside. Drawn from field sketch by the author.

branch burrows. The passageway ordinarily is about two feet under ground, sometimes approaches within one foot of the surface, and rarely may be as deep as four or five feet under soil cover. A side gallery may lead to the nesting chamber, some 15 inches in diameter and

Woodchuck burrow in bank along road, Rock County, Wisconsin. Photograph by the author.

Woodchuck burrow in alfalfa field, Rock County, Wisconsin. Note observation hillock in front of hole. Photograph by the author.

about 8 inches high. The nesting material is rather scant and usually consists of vegetable material readily available, such as dried leaves, grasses, and weed stalks. Other branches may end in a blind chamber used as a latrine where the animal deposits and covers with soil its feces and urine. Dried urine mixed with soil may be brought outside the burrow for deposition, usually in the mound at the entrance to the hole. The hibernating chamber is similar to the nesting chamber, but is always plugged with soil by the animal to isolate it from the regular burrow, which may be occupied by a rabbit, skunk, or even a fox while the woodchuck is dormant.

Late afternoon is the heavy feeding time for the woodchuck, though it also feeds extensively in the morning. When it first appears from hibernation in the spring, green vegetation may be scarce, and it frequently resorts to the bark and buds of various trees and shrubs for food, and such early spring plants as the dandelion, chickweeds, sorrel, and plantains. It is particularly fond of legumes such as clover, alfalfa, vetch, beans, and peas. It eats sweet clover, growing buckwheat, oats, wheat, corn, and other grains and many grasses. It relishes ripe raspberries, blackberries, strawberries, cherries, and apples, and will feed upon beet and turnip tops, cabbage, kale, and cantaloupe. Once in a while it eats an insect or two, such as a grasshopper or a June bug (Gianini, 1925). It has been known to eat a nestling bird (Hatt, 1930: 640), and unverified claims have been made that it will pursue, kill and eat young chickens.

Man, the domestic dog, and the red fox, in the order named, are the chief enemies of the woodchuck, but even these have difficulty in capturing the prey because of the ease by which the woodchuck can quickly drop into its burrow. The timber rattlesnake also kills some, particularly young ones which at times it seeks in woodchuck burrows. The automobile kills only a very few on highways. External parasites include the louse *Enderleinellus saturalis,* the tick *Ixodes cookei,* and four species of fleas, *Oropsylla arctomys, Opisodasys pseudarctomys, Orchopeas wickhami,* and *Ctenocephalides canis,* of which the first is most common. Internal parasites include ten species of Protozoa (Gabel, 1954) and five kinds of helminths (Rausch and Tiner, 1948: 746; Tiner, 1951). Disease affects the life of the woodchuck but little. Malformed incisors sometimes occur in many species of rodents, and in the woodchuck seem to be especially frequent, occurring in more than 1 per cent of the individuals. The malformation is caused by a slight deflection of one or more of the incisors so that the tips do not meet and one or more of them grows unworn. Such a condition may cause serious malnutrition, or the incisor may even penetrate the skull and cause death. An interesting case of malocclusion caused by disease from a gunshot wound in a skull of *Marmota m. rufescens* found by W. E. Slagg on the shore of Sand Lake, Chippewa County, Wisconsin, in 1922, has been described by Professor George Wagner (1923):

The injury markedly altered the direction of growth of the right upper incisor, crowding it to the left. The apex of this tooth now lies to the left of the midline of the skull. This change in turn has forced a change in the direction of the growth of the left upper incisor, the tip of which now lies beyond the outline of the skull. . . . the position of the upper incisors has caused them to pass to the left of both lower incisors instead of opposing them. This in turn has forced the lower incisors to the right. As a result, with a closed mouth, these lower incisors must have come to bear on the upper lip of the right side.

Often severely condemned by farmers and truck gardeners as a damaging pest, the woodchuck in controlled numbers and places may be a useful asset. It is not known to be a vector of any human or animal disease. Not only does it directly supply an object for hunting and trapping in itself, but its numerous burrows are utilized as winter homes for rabbits, skunks, and other mammals that are game or fur species. An insufficient number of retreat burrows has shown a lowering of the population of cottontails. The woodchuck probably is hunted with a rifle more than any other small game mammal except possibly the gray squirrel, and in many states it rates high in the annual game kill. As food it is not the best, yet it is frequently eaten. If the glands in the upper part of the forelegs are removed as soon as possible after the animal has been bagged and it is properly cooked, it can be delicious. Marmot fur as used commercially comes from Eurasian animals. The fur of our woodchuck is too coarse and thin to be valuable. The skin is durable, and though not yet utilized for leather might serve that purpose. The animal has some curiosity value as the center of ground-hog day folklore. When too numerous in agricultural areas it does considerable damage to crops, particularly to clover, alfalfa, peas, and several vegetables. At the same time, however, it destroys some weeds. The large holes it digs are sometimes a menace to livestock and tractors that may fall into them, but the damage is usually mostly to the temper of the owner. When too numerous the woodchuck should be controlled. The best method of reducing its numbers is by hunting and trapping. Fumigation of its burrow with gas from carbon bisulphide, cyanide, or exhaust fumes from an automobile or tractor may also be utilized in summer when only the woodchuck occupies the den and other wildlife is not endangered. Fumigation should be used only under the supervision of a trained pest control expert and with the approval of a representative of the State Conservation Department.

Specimens examined from Wisconsin.—Total 48, as follows: *Dane County:* Madison, 2 (UWZ). *Dodge County:* Beaver Dam, 18 (UWZ). *Grant County:* Platteville, 1; Potosi, 1 (10 mi. S. S. E.); Wyalusing Township (T 6 N, R 6 W, Sec. 14), 1. *Jefferson County:* Lake Koshkonong, 1 (MM). *La Crosse County:* No locality, 1. *Milwaukee County:* South Milwaukee, 1 (MM). *Racine County:* Racine, 2 (USNM). *Rock County:* Milton, 3 (2 UWZ). *Sauk County:* Sumpter, 1 (MM). *Walworth County:* Delavan, 4 (2 CAS); Lake Geneva, 4 (UWZ). *Washington County:* Hubertus, 1 (MM). *Waukesha County:* Nashotah, 2 (UWZ); Pewaukee, 3 (UWZ); Waukesha, 2 (MM).

Selected references.—Benedict, F. G., and R. C. Lee, 1938; Fisher, W. H., 1893; Grizzell, R. A., Jr., 1955; Hamilton, W. J., Jr., 1934; Howell, A. H., 1915; Landis, C. S., 1951.

Marmota monax rufescens Howell
Rufescent Woodchuck

Marmota monax rufescens Howell, Proc. Biol. Soc.
Washington 27: 13, February 2, 1914.
Marmota monax rufescens Schmidt, p. 110, 1931;
Komarek, p. 207, 1932; Barger, p. 11, 1952.

Vernacular names.—Most of the common names
of the southern woodchuck.

Identification marks.—Similar to *Marmota monax monax* but averaging smaller; darker and
more richly colored, particularly the under parts,
which are distinctly dark reddish in tone.

Measurements.—Total length of adults, 510 to
600 mm. (20.1 to 23.6 in.); tail, 120 to 150 mm.
(4.7 to 5.9 in.); hind foot, 76 to 88 mm. (3 to
3.5 in.). Weight, from about 4 lbs. or less when
emerging from hibernation in the spring to about
10 or 11 lbs. when ready to hibernate in the fall.
Skull length, 88 to 97 mm.; width, 56 to 65 mm.

Distribution in Wisconsin.—Central and northern part of the state, north of and including
Trempealeau, Jackson, Juneau, Adams, Marinette, Green Lake, Fond du Lac, and Sheboygan
counties.

Habitat, Status, and Habits.—So far as known
essentially like those of *Marmota monax monax*
with which they are included.

Specimens examined from Wisconsin.—Total 46, as
follows: *Adams County:* Friendship, 1. *Ashland
County:* Mellen (8 mi. S. W.), 1. *Barron County:*
Turtle Lake, 4 (UWZ). *Bayfield County:* Grand-
view, 1; Herbster, 2; Orienta, 8. *Chippewa County:*
Stanley, 1. *Clark County:* Withee, 1; Worden Town-
ship, 1. *Door County:* Fish Creek, 4 (3 UWZ);
Newport, 2 (MM). *Iron County:* Mercer, 1 (UWZ).
Langlade County: T 34 N, R 11 E, 2 (UWZ).
Marathon County: Rib Hill, 1. *Oconto County:* Kel-
ley Lake, 1. *Pierce County:* Maiden Rock, 1 (MM);
Prescott, 3 (MM). *Polk County:* Saint Croix Falls, 3.
Trempealeau County: Trempealeau, 1. *Vilas Coun-
ty:* Conover, 1 (CNHM); Mamie Lake, 5. *Washburn
County:* Long Lake, 1.

Selected references.—Same as for *Marmota m.
monax*.

Genus **Citellus*** Oken
Ground Squirrels

Dental formula:

$$I \frac{1-1}{1-1}, \ C \frac{0-0}{0-0}, \ P \frac{2-2}{1-1}, \ M \frac{3-3}{3-3} = 22.$$

---

* In 1968 the Committee on Nomenclature of the
American Society of Mammalogists recommended the
use of *Spermophilus* as the generic name.

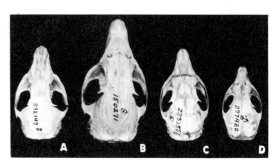

Skulls of ground squirrels and chipmunks. A. CITELLUS
T. TRIDECEMLINEATUS, *Danbury, Wisconsin,* B. C.
FRANKLINII, *Delavan, Wisconsin,* C. TAMIAS S.
GRISEUS, *Danbury, Wisconsin,* D. EUTAMIAS M.
JACKSONI, *Crescent Lake, Wisconsin.* ⅔×.

Citellus tridecemlineatus tridecemlineatus
(Mitchill)
Striped Ground Squirrel

Sciurus tridecem-lineatus Mitchill, Medical Reposi-
tory (N. S.) 6(21): 248, 1821.
Spermophilus tridecemlineatus Lapham, p. 44, 1852;
Snyder, p. 114, 1902.
Spermophilus tridecimlineatus Lapham, p. 339, 1853.
Spermophilus tridecem-lineatus Strong, p. 440, 1883.
Citellus tridecemlineatus Jackson, p. 18, 1908; Jack-
son, p. 87, 1910; Hollister, p. 24, 1910; Cory, p.
138, 1912.
Citellus tridecemlineatus tridecemlineatus Schmidt,
p. 111, 1931; Barger, p. 11, 1952.

Vernacular names.—In Wisconsin commonly
called gopher or striped gopher. Other names include *citelle* (French), federation squirrel or flag
squirrel (13 stripes and several "stars" suggest
U. S. flag), grass chippie, grass runner, grass
whistler, leopard ground squirrel, leopard squir-

Striped ground squirrel and burrow.

rel, little striped gopher, picket pin, prairie ground squirrel, prairie squirrel, prairie striper, small striped gopher, sod runner, striped citellus, striped gopher, striped prairie squirrel, striped spermophile, striper, stripsie, thirteen-lined ground squirrel, thirteen-striped citellus, thirteen-striped ground squirrel, streaked gopher, and whistle sneak.

Identification marks.—A comparatively small ground squirrel, some ten or eleven inches in total length, rather slender, with color pattern gay and strikingly striped above, head somewhat conical and narrow; ears small, rather broad and fleshy, inconspicuous, the tips not appearing above occiput; eyes large; nose rather slender; cheek pouches of moderate size; tail moderately long, a little more than one-third total length, flattened, and slightly bushy; legs short, feet rather large, the claws on the four toes of forefeet long and slender, those on the five toes of the hind feet shorter and stronger; fur dense and rather coarse, particularly in summer pelage, moderate in length.

Left hind foot of striped ground squirrel. From specimen from Wauzeka, Wisconsin. 1×.

In the fresh summer pelage the general basic color of the upper parts is dark brown, which conspicuously sets off the 13 long stripes of yellowish buff, all of which are continuous lines over the shoulders, but five of the uppermost alternate with solid pale lines and break into a series of blotches or spots; actually the effect of this viewed mid-length the animal is 13 pale stripes and 12 dark ones; crown and frontal region dark brown, finely streaked with pale cinnamon; nose, eye ring, cheeks, and sides of neck near cinnamon buff; under parts, throat, chest, abdomen, and legs, near cinnamon buff; tail above fuscous black bordered with buff; below more russet along midline, more or less bordered with fuscous black, and edged with cinnamon buff. Spring or post-winter pelage is much paler in general, the dark stripes near chestnut brown, the pale stripes and ventral parts nearer creamy buff. There appears to be only one delayed molt a year. The faded paler and more chestnut fur of post-hibernation is shed without indication of molt line during May or the first few days of June, and is gradually replaced over the entire body by the new shorter and stiffer hair of darker hue from June until September or even later. The hair apparently continues to grow, soften, and become paler and more reddish while the animal is in winter sleep.

The skull is rather narrow and weak with narrow brain case, gently curved above and laterally, with zygomatic arches not widely spreading; postorbital processes short and slender; rostrum rather long, tapering, and depressed anteriorly; interorbital breadth between 7.2 and 9.2 mm.; upper maxillary tooth rows diverging slightly anteriorly; upper incisors medium length, rather stout, the front surfaces pale to deep yellow in color.

Males average about 5 per cent larger than females, but there is no sexual variation in color. The color pattern and tones of the adult are assumed early by the young one, and except for smaller size, shorter hair, relatively larger feet, and thinner tail it is a good replica of its parent. There is some individual variation in color but except in spring and late in summer it is not pronounced. Color mutations, except albinism, are rare in the species. Hoffmeister and Hensley (1949) describe a specimen of this species taken in Urbana, Illinois, July 4, 1947, in which the color pattern, but not the color, is retained in an albino in which the eyes and claws were pink and the skin lacked pigmentation. The pattern was retained apparently because the hairs in the paler stripes and spots of the albino grew longer by 23 per cent than hairs elsewhere on the back and thus caused less of the pinkish color of the skin to show. There is also an albino specimen from Delavan Lake, Walworth County, in the Chicago Academy of Science. Three melanistic specimens have been described from one locality in Ohio (Goslin, 1959).

The striped ground squirrel may be distinguished from any other Wisconsin mammal by the number of dark brown and pale cinnamon stripes running lengthwise of the upper part of its body, and by the fact that none of these stripes extends on the face or cheek as in the chipmunks. When running, a striped ground squirrel can usually be distinguished from a chipmunk in that it carries its tail straight out behind whereas a chipmunk holds its tail vertically. The skull of the striped ground squirrel is smaller than that of any other Wisconsin squirrel except *Tamias, Eutamias,* and *Glaucomys.* Members of the genus *Citellus* have five upper cheek teeth on each side instead of four as in *Tamias.* The skull is always longer and narrower than that of *Eutamias,* always more than 34 mm. long and 20 mm. greatest width. Compared with that of either species of *Glaucomys* the skull of *Citellus tridecemlineatus* has the postorbital processes attenuate and more posteriorly placed, being posterior to middle of orbit whereas those of *Glaucomys* are near midorbit; prefrontal region more rotund and less depressed; the rostrum is longer, less attenute, the length of the nasal bones always more than 13 mm.; first upper molariform tooth about half the size of second molariform tooth, whereas in *Glaucomys* it is minute; upper incisor heavier in *Citellus,* the color of the front pale orange as contrasted to dark mahogany orange in *Glaucomys.*

Measurements.—Total length, 230 to 300 mm. (9 to 11.7 in.); tail, 75 to 110 mm. (3 to 4.3 in.); hind foot, 35 to 41 mm. (1.4 to 1.6 in.). Weight of adult from a low of about 110 grams (3.9 oz.) in May to a high of about 270 grams (9.5 oz.) in September when the animal has accumulated fat before hibernation. Skull length, 40.8 to 45.8 mm.; width, 22.8 to 26.4 mm.

Distribution in Wisconsin.—Occurs throughout the state in favorable habitats. Less plentiful in extreme northern part, particularly in Vilas, Forest, and Florence counties.

Habitat.—Dry meadows, grassy fields, pastures, golf courses, grassy fence rows between cultivated fields, along highways and railroad right-of-ways; parks, cemeteries, and campuses; abandoned fields, open jack pine barrens, and

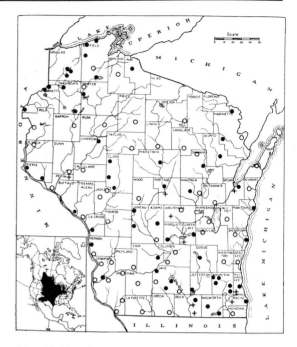

Map 27. Distribution of CITELLUS TRIDECEMLINEATUS.
⊜ = *specimens examined.* ○ = *authentic records since 1900.* + = *authentic records 1900 or before.*

sometimes even in open woodland, particularly if with grassy soil cover; very rarely and only accidentally in dense forest or on low wet ground.

Status and Habits.—The striped ground squirrel in early days in Wisconsin was probably confined closely to the southern half of the state, except possibly toward the western boundary where it may have extended farther northward in the prairie openings on tops of the bluffs and in sandy regions with sparser woodland. Moses Barrett (1873) records it as everywhere abundant when he settled upon what is known as the "Indian Lands" of central Wisconsin (probably western Waushara County) in the autumn of 1850; John Muir (1913: 77) found it at his old home in Kingston Township, Green Lake County, in 1846; William Canfield (1870; 38) mentions it as occurring in Sauk County; and there are early records for several of the more southerly counties such as Racine, where Hoy collected several specimens in 1853 (Baird, 1857: 318), and Milwaukee (Lapham, 1852: 44). Reports made to the Division of Ornithology and Mammalogy, precursor to the U. S. Biological Survey, show that this species occurred near Grantsburg, Burnett County; Durand, Pepin County; and Plover, Portage County, before 1886.

We do not have a complete picture of its march northward in the state, but it rapidly entered cutover lands and clearings and followed road and railway right-of-ways until it is now found in favorable habitat in every county, though very sparingly in some of the more northern ones. On September 9, 1908, I saw three striped ground squirrels and many of their burrows in what appeared to be an isolated colony a short distance east of Iron River, Bayfield County, and M. H. Hall told me that "only a year ago (1907) we saw the first one" (Jackson, 1910: 87–88), though actually it would seem hardly possible for the numbers to increase so much in only one year. Before the year 1920 the species was found in favorable habitat in most parts of the northern counties but had not ingressed the northern islands of Lake Superior (Jackson, 1920 a) or Lake Michigan. There is no predictable cycle of abundance with the striped ground squirrel. It may build a considerable population locally, but never approaches the immense numbers sometimes present in colonies of some other ground squirrels of the western United States, and its many natural enemies and man usually hold its numbers in check. It is impossible to get a near accurate estimate of its total number in the state, but based on small-area counts made in Rock and Grant counties where the population of adults in selected areas averaged from 1.2 to 8 animals per acre and accepting the minimum count for its habitable area of about ten million acres would suggest some ten million or more striped gophers in Wisconsin. There appears to be more of this species in the state than of any other mammal larger than a mouse. Its home range is somewhat restricted and rarely exceeds three acres, or a radius of about two hundred feet.

Feces of striped ground squirrel. Drawn by Mrs. MacMaugh from sketch made in Wisconsin by the author. 1×.

Probably the best way to locate a striped ground squirrel is to hunt for the animal itself on a bright day or look for the entrances to its burrows. On first sight the spermophile may appear like an upright six-inch wooden peg. One may with silence and caution approach an individual squirrel to within 12 or 15 feet before it ducks into its burrow. Even then, it may slyly reappear for another peek at the intruder, particularly if he whistles an imitation of its call note. Often it will scurry through the grass and dive into its hole, uttering its sharp rolling chirp as it does so, and if one withdraws a few feet and remains quiet, it probably will come entirely out of its burrow. It is strictly diurnal, prefers bright sunshine and balmy warm weather, and is loathe to expose itself on cold, dark, or rainy days. It does not migrate, but often extends its range into new and favorable habitats, frequently, it appears, making comparatively rapid progress in extending its distribution. It is a true hibernator

Position of striped ground squirrel during hibernation. Adapted from photograph by Wm. J. Hamilton, Jr.

and usually enters hibernation during October to remain torpid for five or six months until the last of March or the beginning of April. The latest I have seen them out of their burrows in the autumn in Wisconsin was November 1, 1903, at Milton. Engels (1932) records one active on a golf link near Green Bay on December 25, 1931. Much research has been made upon hibernation of this species, which is one of the most complete among mammals. The animal becomes fat by the last of September, having nearly doubled its spring weight, becomes torpid, and curls itself into a ball in its deeper nest, after solidly plugging with soil the entrances to the burrow. The arched back is uppermost, the nose turned under the body and touching the pelvic region. Bodily functions are reduced to a minimum, and bodily temperature nearly lowers to that of the air about the animal. Sometimes it does not survive the winter. One in Kingston Township, Green Lake County, about 1846, was "frozen solid in its snug grassy nest, in the middle of a store of nearly a peck of wheat it had carefully gathered. . . . Nothing I could do in the way of its survival was of any avail. Its life had passed away without the slightest struggle" (Muir, 1913: 135-36). This animal may not have been frozen dead when found, because suddenly warming and trying to exercise a cold and stiff hibernating animal will kill it. Several accounts of hibernation in *Citellus tridecemlineatus* have appeared (Hoy, 1875; Johnson, G. E., 1928; 1929 a; 1929 b; 1930; 1931 b; Johnson and Hanawalt, 1930; Lyman, 1954; Wade, 1930; 1948). The hibernating state has been well summarized by Johnson (1928: 28–29) as follows:

Baby striped ground squirrels, about ready to shift for themselves.

1. A torpid Citellus tridecemlineatus is rolled up, somewhat stiff, and is cold to the touch.

2. As contrasted with a rate of about 100 to more than 200 respirations a minute in active ground-squirrels the respiration rate in deeply torpid animals at external temperatures below 10° C. may average

from one-half to four a minute normally. Some records were made of no respiration for five minutes in animals long in hibernation.

3. Heart beats in animals awake and active usually ranged from 200 to 350 a minute. In forty-two torpid animals with body temperatures below 10° C. the average was 17.4 beats a minute, and the lowest was five beats a minute.

4. Ground-squirrels not in hibernation may have temperatures ranging from about 32° to about 41°, but a range of 35° to 39° is more common in a warm, and a range 32° to 36° C. is more prevalent in a cold room. High room temperatures produced a body temperature of 42.3° C. The minimum body temperature in hibernation appears to be between 0° and 2° C. The body temperature in deep hibernation is usually within 3°, is often within 1°, and may rarely be within 0.3° C. of the surrounding temperature.

5. Loss of weight in ground-squirrels may approach 40 per cent in a winter of hibernation. The daily loss appears to be about 0.30 per cent in nature and about 0.40 or 0.50 per cent in the refrigerator.

The rather short legs of this species compel a slow and somewhat awkward gait, and its maximum running speed is about eight miles an hour. Where it has no access to a burrow or other shelter, a man can with some effort outrun one. It is exceedingly quick in starting, and makes a flashing dive into its burrow, promptly disappearing from sight while uttering its daring birdlike call. It is proficient with its hind legs, often stretching and standing erect when on the lookout for danger. When foraging it usually walks, and only when frightened or disturbed does it run in its lumbering gallop. It does not enter water voluntarily, and swims very weakly when forced into it, as did one for 12 feet across an eight-inch-deep roadside puddle near Holcombe, Chippewa County, July 30, 1918. It seldom climbs even an inclining post or tree. An unusual instance of its climbing occurred on August 29, 1940, about eight miles east of Solon Springs, Douglas County, when one was observed about five feet above ground and about 18 inches from the trunk of a white oak sapling. Upon seeing its observer, it quietly flattened itself along the limb, and when approached leaped to the ground and ran to a burrow (Morrissey, 1941). The chirp or alarm note of this ground squirrel, though shrill, is truly musical. A rapid trill or quavering whistle, it can best be described as a long drawn-out *chur-r-r-r-r* in a high key, gradually descending in pitch toward the end.

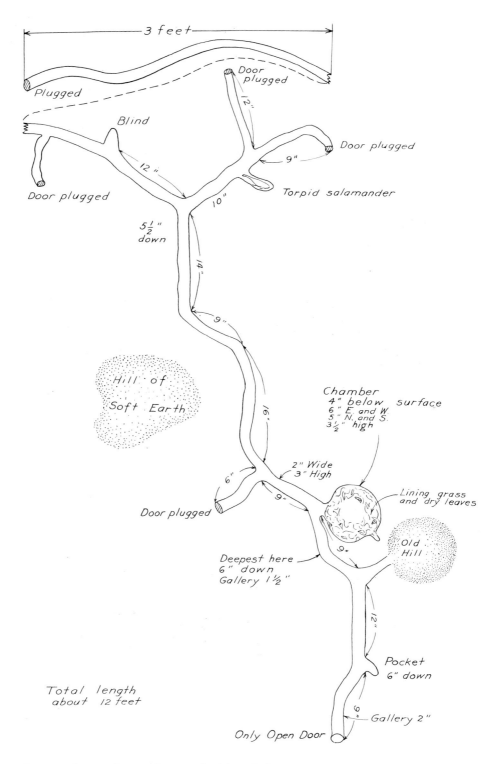

Burrow of striped ground squirrel. Adapted from Seton, 1909, p. 400.

Favorable environment or food abundance may bring these squirrels together in scattered small colonies, but the species cannot be considered truly gregarious. It is not a sociable animal, and in fact is inclined to be pugnacious rather than friendly with its own kind. It frequently chases another animal, yet with little evidence of a playful mood. Males, particularly, fight one another, their battles often resulting in a bobbed tail or other slight injury. A person careless in handling one may receive a severe and painful bite, though it is seldom infectious. The muscles of the long slender body and the short legs, as well as those of the jaws, are strong and sinewy. Sight appears to be more highly developed than any of the other senses, touch is moderately acute, while hearing and smell appear to be weak. Longevity of the striped ground squirrel is not positively known but is probably not more than four or five years. Of 27 specimens at various times in the National Zoological Park, one lived as long as two years.

Breeding activities of this race in southern Wisconsin are probably not essentially different from those in eastern Nebraska, where Dr. Otis Wade studied the species. Possibly the breeding season is a week or two later in northern Wisconsin.

1. In the region of Lincoln, Nebraska, the rutting season of *Citellus tridecemlineatus* extends over a period of about a month and corresponds roughly to the month of April, breeding activities being at their height the last two weeks of that month.

2. The rutting impulse of the males occurs only in the spring some three or four weeks following emergence from hibernation and lasts for a period of two to four weeks, more commonly for the shorter time. At this time the testes are much inflamed and swollen.

3. After having produced a litter, females are not known to breed a second time in the same season. In all cases observed females have refused to mate after having given birth to young.

4. The rutting impulse of the female appears to last for a longer time than it does in the male provided the female does not become pregnant in the meantime.

5. The gestation period is practically a lunar month—between twenty-seven and twenty-eight days.

6. The characteristic stripes are distinct, and the anterior portion of the body, at least, is clothed in downy hair when the young are twelve days old.

7. At twelve days of age the young make the typical ground squirrel "call" or "trill" when disturbed. The fore legs can also be used at this time for locomotion but the hind legs cannot and the posterior part of the body is simply dragged along.

8. When twenty days old the hind legs are strong enough to support the hind parts and the young squirrels can walk.

9. The eyes begin to open when the young are twenty-six days old and are fully open by the twenty-eighth day.

10. The young squirrels can take care of themselves when about six weeks old (Wade, 1927: 275).

The number of young at birth is usually eight to ten, eight and nine being the most common numbers, and very rarely as few as five or as many as thirteen. The mammae are ten, four pectoral, two abdominal, four inguinal.

The burrow of the striped ground squirrel is shallow, nearly circular in cross section, and comparatively simple. It is somewhat less than two inches in diameter and usually goes straight down for about five or six inches, then slants for a few inches before continuing in a rather crooked horizontal course. The burrow seldom descends more than two feet below the surface, and generally is within one foot of it. The tunnel used for home purposes, in which the animal rears its young or spends its winter, may be 15 or 20 feet long, and sometimes has branch passages. Very short burrows, three to six feet in length, are frequently dug in addition to the nesting burrow. These short tunnels are used as retreats into which the animal can dodge on approach of danger. Sometimes such a temporary burrow is made under a shock of grain in a grain field, at times it may enter a pocket gopher burrow. Each burrow usually has only one entrance, although not infrequently the long nesting tunnel may have two. The opening is apt to be on smooth bare ground, yet often it is hidden by a bunch of grass or a weed. The animal leaves no telltale mound of earth near its hole. As it digs it throws back the soil with its forefeet and then kicks it on farther back with its hind feet, thus scattering the soil evenly over the surface of the ground. Often it leaves the burrow and in similar actions further scatters the soil on the surface. Sometimes the squirrel plugs the burrow with soil after it enters, particularly when it retires for hibernation. The nest is built well inside the burrow, sometimes to one side of the tunnel, sometimes directly in the passageway or at a bend, frequently at the far end of the burrow. It is composed chiefly of dry grasses, is sphere-shaped, and fills a cavity six or eight inches in diameter. Seeds may be stored in the burrow for summer food, but apparently nothing is eaten after the animal once enters hibernation in the fall. Defecation is usually done outside the burrow.

Although structurally a true rodent, the striped ground squirrel is more or less omnivorous in food habits. Though it eats and apparently relishes many vegetable items such as grass, herbs, grain and other seeds, roots, and berries, it is also fond of insects and other animal matter. Probably during the summer insects constitute a considerable portion of its food. Grasshoppers seem to be especially relished by it. I have often seen a striped ground squirrel jump clear off the ground and capture a grasshopper on the wing with its forefeet, clip off the head, wings, and feet with its teeth, and then devour the body, beginning at the anterior end. I have also seen this animal dig for June beetles—both the larva and the adult—and cutworms. It is known also to eat crickets and various caterpillars, and at times to capture and consume a young bird or a mouse, or possibly a bird's egg if it can break the shell. Besides various grains, of which it seems to prefer corn, it also eats such other vegetable matter as grass and weed seeds, berries, green acorns, green garden peas and beans, sugar beets, cucumbers, and melons. It drinks very little water, probably acquiring what it needs from succulent vegetation or animal food, though it may supply some through interbody chemical action in the form of metabolic water (Babcock, S. M., 1912). It stores considerable quantities of hard grain and seeds in its burrow, which it gathers and carries in its cheek pouches, placing it in the pouch without use of the feet. It apparently consumes only a small part of the stored grain. Its bathing consists of dust baths, probably more to relieve irritation from insect pests than as a matter of cleanliness.

Among the mammal enemies of the striped ground squirrel are the red and gray foxes, weasels, the prowling domestic cat, and especially the badger, which persistently digs for this species as one of its favorite preys. Four species of hawks, the marsh hawk, Cooper's hawk, red-tailed hawk, and sparrow hawk, regularly prey

upon this ground squirrel, and in some areas it constitutes as much as 25 per cent of the summer food of the marsh hawk. Owls do not bother it because it is out only during bright sunny weather. One was followed into its burrow and attacked by a shrike in Green Lake County about the year 1846 (Muir, 1903: 196). Some species of snakes often penetrate the burrows to feed on both adults and young. Heavy summer rains affect it little, since its burrows are usually well drained on high ground. It is often killed by automobiles. External parasites known to infest it include the lice *Enderleinellus saturalis* and *Neohaematopinus laeviusculus* and the fleas *Thrassis fotus, Oropsylla bruneri,* and *Epipedia wenmanni.* Internally, it is host to at least eleven kinds of protozoans (Doran, 1954); two cestodes, *Hymenolepis diminuta* and *Choanotaenia spermophili;* four nematodes, *Rictularia citelli, Spirura infundibuliformis, Physaloptera sp.,* and *Trichinella spiralis;* and one horny-headed worm, *Moniliformis clarki.*

Economically, the striped ground squirrel has both good and bad habits. Dr. P. R. Hoy of Racine long ago wrote: "The striped gopher is abundant and slightly destructive. It is beneficial in destroying meadow mice and insects, etc. I have made the striped gopher a study for 30 years, and *know* they are beneficial" (letter to U. S. Division of Ornithology and Mammalogy, about 1888). During midsummer months, or more than half the time of its active existence, it feeds extensively on harmful insects, and at this time a large portion of its food is insects. It destroys many weed seeds, not scattering them as may birds. This species is pretty, interesting to watch, and makes a nice pet. I have often heard a horticulturist remark that he liked to have it around even if it does do a little damage to crops. Sometimes, however, this ground squirrel may become too abundant and do noticeable damage to some crops. Its chief offense in the corn belt is in digging out newly planted or sprouting seed corn, particularly near the edge of a field; the animal seldom enters the field more than 20 or 25 feet. Complaint is also sometimes made about its burrows, which really should not be very troublesome to anyone. At times it does damage to commercial crops of peas, cucumbers, melons, and other vegetables. It may store a small quantity of wheat, oats, or other grain in the fall, but most of this is from wasted grain scattered on the ground.

If the ground squirrel becomes too troublesome as a pest it may be controlled effectively by poisoning, fumigation, trapping, or shooting. The most effective means of control where it is numerous over a large area is poisoning. The following formula is suggested for preparation of the poisoned grain:

Dry gloss starch, 1 heaped tablespoonful
Strychnine (alkaloid) powdered, 1 ounce
Baking soda, 1 ounce
Corn syrup, ½ cupful
Glycerine, 1 tablespoonful
Clean whole corn kernels, 16 quarts

Dissolve the dry starch in a little cold water and add three-fourths of a pint of boiling water. Boil, stirring constantly, until a clear paste is formed. Mix together the powdered strychnine and baking soda, sift into the hot starch, and stir to a creamy mass. Add the corn syrup and glycerine, and stir thoroughly. Pour this mixture over the corn and thoroughly mix so that each kernel is evenly and thoroughly coated. Spread and dry the poisoned grain. Early in the season put three to six kernels of the poisoned grain into each ground squirrel hole near the cultivated field or area it is desired to control. It is important to get the poisoned kernels well down in the hole and leave none scattered on the ground, in order not to endanger useful wildlife, birds, and domestic stock or poultry. Another poison sometimes used is calcium cyanide, a tablespoonful of which is placed in the burrow, and the entrance then covered with soil. Any poison is highly dangerous and should be stored and used with extreme caution. The striped ground squirrel may also be destroyed by attaching one end of a hose to the exhaust pipe of an automobile or tractor, inserting the other end into the burrow, and running the motor, thus generating carbon monoxide gas into the burrow. The striped ground squirrel is easily trapped in a snap rat trap, offers a good target for a .22 calibre rifle or even an air gun, and usually can be driven from its burrow by a few buckets of water. Anyone shooting, trapping, or otherwise hunting ground squirrels on land other than their own should first procure permission from the landowner.

Specimens examined from Wisconsin.—Total 233, as follows: *Adams County:* Friendship, 2; *Bayfield County:* Herbster, 2; Iron River (4 mi. N.), 1 (WHD); Namakagon Lake, 2 (1 MM); Orienta, 2. *Brown County:* Bay Settlement, 3 (UND); Benderville, 1 (UND). *Burnett County:* Danbury, 2; Rush City Bridge, 1 (MM); Yellow River (Mouth), 12 (MM). *Buffalo County:* Fountain City, 1 (MM). *Chippewa County:* Holcombe, 2. *Clark County:* Foster Township, 2 (UM); Hewett Township, 5 (3 AMNH; 2 UWZ); Worden Township, 1 (UM). *Crawford County:* Wauzeka, 1. *Dane County:* Madison, 4 (UWZ); Roxbury, 4 (UWZ); Verona, 3 (UWZ). *Dodge County:* Beaver Dam, 50 (3 AMNH; 33 UWZ). *Douglas County:* Solon Springs, 2; T 44 N, R 12 W, 1 (F&FH); Upper Saint Croix Lake, 14 (MM). *Green Lake County:* Green Lake, 4. *Iron County:* Upson, 1 (WHD). *Jefferson County:* Sumner, 1 (USNM). *Juneau County:* Camp Douglas, 2 (1 AMNH); Mather, 2. *La Crosse County:* La Crosse, 2. *Manitowoc County:* Point Beach State Forest, 1 (UWZ). *Marathon County:* Rib Hill, 6. *Marinette County:* Cataline, 3 (MM); Three Falls (on Thunder River, 15 mi. W. of Cravitz), 2 (UND); Twining Lake, 1 (UWZ); Timms Lake, 1 (UWZ); *Marquette County:* Endeavor, 2. *Milwaukee County:* Fox Point, 1 (UWZ); Lake Township, 2 (UWZ); Lindwerm, 1 (MM); Milwaukee, 5 (MM). *Oconto County:* Kelley Lake, 1. *Pierce County:* Maiden Rock, 4 (MM); Prescott, 17 (16 MM). *Portage County:* Stevens Point, 1. *Racine County:* Racine, 7 (4 USNM). *Rock County:* Milton, 1 (UWZ). *Sauk County:* Devils Lake, 1. *Sawyer County:* Hayward, 1 (CMNH). *Shawano County:* Keshena, 2 (CAS). *Sheboygan County:* Terry Andrae State Park, 3 (UWZ). *Vernon County:* Genoa, 2 (MM). *Walworth County:* Delavan, 4 (2 MM; 1 CMNH); Delavan Lake, 19 (CAS); Lake Geneva, 1 (CAS). *Washburn County:* Long Lake, 1; T 41 N, R 13 W, 1 (UWZ). *Waukesha County:* Delafield, 2 (UWZ); Hartland, 2 (UWZ); Muskego Lake, 2 (MM); Nashotah, 3 (2 USNM; 1 UWZ); Sunny Slope, 1 (MM); Waukesha (6 mi. E.), 1 (WND). *Waupaca County:* Saint Lawrence Township, 1 (UWZ).

Selected references.—Bailey, V., 1893 b; Evans, F. C., 1951; Howell, A. H., 1938; Johnson, G. E., and V. B. Hanawalt, 1930; Wade, O., 1927; 1930.

Citellus franklinii (Sabine)
Franklin's Ground Squirrel

Arctomys franklinii Sabine, Trans. Linnaean Soc. London 13: 537, 1822.
Spermophilus grammurus Lapham, p. 44, 1852; Lapham, p. 339, 1853.
Spermophilus parryi Lapham, p. 339, 1853.
Spermophilus Franklini Strong, p. 440, 1883.
Spermophilus franklini Snyder, p. 115, 1902.
Citellus franklini Jackson, p. 18, 1908; Hollister, p. 139, 1909; Hollister, p. 24, 1910; Cory, p. 144, 1912; Schmidt, p. 111, 1931; Barger, p. 11, 1952.
Citellus franklinii Barger, p. 43, 1952.

Vernacular names.—In Wisconsin commonly called gray gopher. Other names include Franklin's spermophile, gray-cheeked squirrel, gray ground squirrel, gray souslik, line-tailed squirrel, prairie squirrel, and scrub gopher.

Identification marks.—Larger and chunkier of the two Wisconsin ground squirrels, or spermophiles, total length of adult more than 14 inches; coloration coarsely spotted or blotched and not striped; superficially resembles a small gray squirrel with a shorter and less bushy tail, and much smaller ears; legs rather short and feet large; claws of forefeet relatively shorter and heavier than those of *Citellus tridecemlineatus;* fur rather short and coarse.

The general summer color of the upper parts and sides is a mixture of brownish gray and blackish, with the head and neck slightly darker, the midback somewhat more suffused with brownish, and the whole more or less flecked or obscurely spotted in parts of some individuals at times, showing a tendency toward transdorsal lining of the dark and pale flecking; eyelids, lower cheeks, chin, throat, and inner sides of legs buffy white; under parts buffy white, often more or less mixed with blackish hairs; tail grayish in general tone, coarsely flecked above on basal one-third and finely flecked below on basal two-thirds, the apical two-thirds above and below bordered and tipped with creamy white with a subterminal band of near black. There is one molt annually which occurs slowly during the early part of summer.

The skull is long and narrow for a sciurid, somewhat flattened in superior outline; rostrum relatively long, not deeply depressed anteriorly; postorbital processes prominent; auditory bullae rather large, the auditory meatus clearly visible in superior view of the skull; broad interorbitally compared with *C. tridecemlineatus,* between 11 mm. and 13 mm.; upper incisors comparatively

Hind foot of Franklin's ground squirrel. From specimen from Cass Lake, Minnesota. 1×.

short, rather heavy, the front surfaces deep yellow to dull orange in color.

There is no appreciable sexual variation in size or color. The young appear to be somewhat darker than older animals, and show less suffusion of the brownish color dorsally. Individuals shortly out of hibernation in winter pelage late in April or in May are usually somewhat paler than when in full summer pelage.

Franklin's ground squirrel may be distinguished externally from other Wisconsin ground squirrels or chipmunks by its much larger size, the absence of longitudinal stripes, and its much larger skull (more than 50 mm. in greatest length). It is superficially similar to a gray tree squirrel (*Sciurus carolinensis*) but differs in the mottled or flecked coloration of its back, its shorter (about two-thirds as long) and much less bushy tail, its short ears not rising above the occiput, and its very different skull with interorbital breadth less than 13 mm. instead of more than 16 mm.

Measurements.—Total length of adults, 360 to 400 mm. (14.2 to 15.7 in.); tail, 130 to 155 mm. (5.1 to 6.1 in.); hind foot, 51 to 57 mm. (2.0 to 2.2 in.). Weight of adult from a low of about 280 grams (9.8 oz.) in June to a high of about 710 grams (25.4 oz.) in September. Skull length, 52.1 to 56.1 mm.; width, 30.1 to 32.3 mm.

Franklin's ground squirrel, from an old painting by Ernest Thompson Seton.

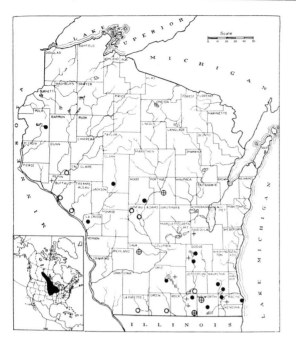

Map 28. *Distribution of* CITELLUS FRANKLINII. ● =
specimens examined. ○ = *authentic records since
1900.* + = *authentic records 1900 or before.*

Distribution in Wisconsin.—General range
southern and western parts of the state, in northerly distribution including Polk and Clark counties to the west, Wood, Portage, and Winnebago
counties centrally, and Waukesha and Milwaukee
counties easterly.

Habitat.—Dense grassy and shrubby near-dry
marshland; dense marsh grass bordering sloughs;
grassy borders of tamarack bogs; "in brush consisting of poplar, soft maple, and jack pine, in
which there were a few open spaces grown up
to sweet fern and blueberries" (Schmidt, 1931:
111); fields of growing grain and along old
grassy fence lines—when grain or hay is cut the
squirrel takes its abode in taller grass along fences
or in old pastures, but may return when new
growth is sufficiently high (Jackson, 1908: 18);
sometimes in fairly heavy woods, particularly of
Norway or jack pine, if sufficient undercover of
ferns, grass, or low shrubs is present; rarely in
the vicinity of barns or farm houses. Sheltering
cover of tall grass or other herbage is a necessary
condition for its habitat, and it is not found in
closely grazed or mowed pastures, fields, lawns,

or cemeteries where the striped ground squirrel
might be common.

Status and Habits.—Franklin's ground squirrel
was found not uncommonly in southern Wisconsin
when the first white settlers arrived. It was recognized as quite distinct from the striped ground
squirrel by its coloration as well as its large size,
but was confused with other large species such
as the Rocky Mountain form *Citellus variegatus
grammurus* and the Alaskan *Citellus parryii*, under both of which it was listed by Lapham (1853:
339). That same year (1853) Dr. P. R. Hoy sent
seven specimens to Dr. Spencer Baird at the
U. S. National Museum, Washington, where the
animal was correctly identified as *Citellus franklinii.* Two of these specimens still remain in the
National Museum collection. The species apparently has not considerably extended its range
northward in the state, as has the striped ground
squirrel. As early as 1886 it was known as far
northeasterly at Plover, Portage County, where it
also was seen by the author in 1918. It may become common at times in isolated small colonies,
but tends to shift its homesite and may be present
one day, gone the next, and back again in a few
weeks, another year, or several years. Within one
of these colonies may live 50 to 100 individuals
on eight or ten acres of suitable habitat, giving
an average population density of about eight
animals to one acre, often less, very rarely more.
The home range of each individual apparently is
limited to a radius of about 150 to 200 feet. The
gray gopher cannot be considered a common
mammal in the state, yet it is probably more
plentiful than records indicate. I hesitate to estimate its numbers, but in the state as a whole
there is probably not one Franklin's ground squirrel to a hundred striped ground squirrels.

Usually it is difficult to catch sight of this
ground squirrel, for as one approaches, it skulks
away under the vegetative cover and slips into
its burrow, sometimes uttering its alarm chirp,
but more often silently scampering into its hole.
Here it is apt to remain for several minutes before coming into the open again, and once
alarmed does not sit upright "picket-pin style" to
view the surroundings as do some other ground
squirrels. When a person attempts to imitate its
call it seems to scamper all the faster into its
hole. Often its presence may be detected by the
numerous runways leading to its burrows, which

are larger than those of the striped ground squirrel but much smaller than those of the woodchuck. Like most ground squirrels, it is strictly diurnal, though it does not restrict its activity to sunny days as does the striped ground squirrel. It usually enters hibernation by the last of September and comes from it the first part of April, thus having as a rule a somewhat longer hibernation period than the striped ground squirrel, although the hibernation of the two animals in most respects is similar.

The Franklin's ground squirrel, though rather slow in motion, is adept at concealing itself and at getting away without being clearly observed. It travels with its midback curved upward, sometimes walking but usually in a sluggish lope. Its maximum speed is near eight miles an hour. It frequently climbs into bushes and up trees, almost as efficiently as a gray squirrel. I have frequently seen them 20 to 30 feet up in trees, and Ned Hollister "once shot one from a considerable height in a tamarack tree, mistaking it for a gray squirrel" (Hollister, 1909: 139). Unlike the striped ground squirrel, it will voluntarily enter water, and swims fairly well. Its call note is somewhat similar to that of the striped ground squirrel, but is a trifle lower in pitch and usually much louder. This truly beautiful note is often given apparently as a conversational note among themselves while the animals are feeding, but is not so frequently employed when the animal is suddenly disturbed by an enemy, or suspects danger.

Semigregarious and somewhat sociable, the gray gopher lives in small rather compact colonies, usually of less than one hundred individuals, though often in favorable habitat other colonies may be nearby. It is not inclined to be pugnacious with its own kind, nor does it appear to fight the striped ground squirrel. Different types of habitat usually keep the two species isolated from each other, even though colonies of each may be within a few hundred feet. It seems to rely on sight more than its other senses, and hearing and smelling appear to be weak. Its span of life is unknown, but its potential longevity is probably near five or six years.

Each female has only one litter annually; mating takes place from the last of April to the middle of May. After a gestation period of about 28 days, the five to eight—most frequently six or seven—young are born between the last of May and the middle of June. At birth the young one is naked and blind. It develops rapidly, shows signs of hair growth as downy fuzz at 10 days old, opens its eyes at 27 days, and by the latter part of July or first of August is half grown and foraging for itself outside its burrow. The mammae are ten, four pectoral, two abdominal, four inguinal.

The burrow of Franklin's ground squirrel is more complicated than that of the striped ground squirrel, being longer and more branched, and usually contains several openings. It is commonly placed in tall grass or weeds, or under a brush heap, log, stone pile, or sloping bank, or is otherwise concealed. The opening is some three inches in diameter, and a noticeable quantity of soil is usually thrown out and left in a little mound in front of each entrance, though all openings may not be so conspicuously indicated. The burrow is about three to eight feet underground. The nest is scantily made of herbaceous material and is placed well within the burrow at some point above the lower level, usually in a side branch.

This true rodent does not confine its food to vegetable matter, but eats more than 30 per cent animal matter. The vegetable food includes seeds and foliage of a great variety of weeds, grasses, and grains and other crop plants. It is particularly fond of newly planted corn and other grains, and also eats corn when it is nearly ripe. Herbage of clover, timothy, thistle, nettle, cocklebur, June grass, plantain, dandelion, strawberry, and other plants are among its food, as are also seeds or fruit of elderberry, chokeberry, strawberry, blackberry, basswood, and nightshade. Sometimes, when it has access to them, it eats garden vegetables such as peas, beans, cabbage, lettuce, squash, carrots, potatoes, and, of course, newly planted sweet corn. It does not habitually cut the stalks of plants to reach its food, but pulls down the stems of grain or grass until it can reach the fruited tip. It gathers much of its food from the surface of the ground. Animal matter eaten includes a considerable number of insects, adult and larvae, particularly beetles, grasshoppers, crickets, and caterpillars. Birds, particularly young ones, are sometimes consumed, birds' eggs, even as large as ducks' eggs, not infrequently, and occasionally young mice or young rabbits may fall victim to this ground squirrel. It is also known to eat frogs and toads, and may even eat its own kind when it finds one dead or helpless.

Wariness of this species limits the predation upon it by its enemies, which probably have little effect on its numbers. Mammals known to be its enemy are the badger, coyote, mink, long-tailed weasel, skunk, and possibly rarely the house cat. The red-tailed hawk preys upon it. It seldom falls victim to the automobile, for it does not often cross a highway and is never out at night to be blinded by lights. External parasites known to infest it include the lice *Enderleinellus saturalis* and *Neohaematopinus laeviusculus* and a flea of the genus *Orchopeas*. Internal parasites include the protozoans *Eimeria franklinii* and *Trypanosoma hixsoni*, the cestode *Hymenolepis diminuta*, and the nematodes *Capillaria chandleri* (type specimen of which was collected from small intestine of *Citellus franklinii* at Madison), *Citellinema bifurcatum*, *Physaloptera masino*, *Rictularia citelli*, and *Weinlandia citelli*.

This species is not common enough in the state to be of any particular economic importance, yet where it locally becomes abundant it may do considerable damage to crops by consuming newly planted corn and by burrowing under corn shocks and eating ears. Where it invades grain fields, it may destroy considerable grain, and sometimes it eats garden vegetables, particularly legumes, cabbage, and lettuce. Where its burrows are numerous they may become a nuisance, but cannot be considered dangerous to livestock or other animals. At the Delta Duck Hatchery on the south shore of Lake Manitoba, Canada, during 1938, 1939, and 1940, Franklin's ground squirrel was found to be nearly as destructive of wild duck nests as the crow, destroying 19 per cent of the nests, but such predation upon duck nests was considered a local problem in certain places at certain times, and it was felt that control in wild marsh areas was too costly and too harmful to beneficial forms of wildlife to be practical (Sowls, 1948: 135). This squirrel destroys many harmful insects, and in general the good it does in most cases more than balances the harm. It makes an interesting pet, but is rather short-lived. In cases where it becomes a pest, its numbers may be reduced by any of the methods suggested for the striped ground squirrel.

Specimens examined from Wisconsin.—Total 45, as follows: *Clark County:* Hewett Township, 1

(AMNH). *Dane County:* Madison, 5 (2 AWS; 3 UWZ). *Dodge County:* Beaver Dam, 19 (UWZ); Lowell, 1 (MM). *La Crosse County:* No locality, 1 (UWZ). *Polk County:* Big Horseshoe Lake, 1 (UWZ). *Racine County:* No locality, 1 (MM); Tischigan Lake, 1 (MM); Racine, 2 (USNM). *Rock County:* Milton, 1 (UWZ). *Walworth County:* Delavan, 9 (2 CAS; 3 MM). *Waukesha County:* No locality, 1 (MM); Vernon, 1 (MM). *Wood County:* Cranmoor, 1 (MM).

Selected references.—Bailey, V., 1893 b; Howell, A. H., 1938, pp. 21–22, 133–35, col. pl. 6; Lyon, M. W., Jr., 1936, pp. 182–87; Seton, E. T., 1929, vol. 4, pp. 249–57, pl. 25; Sowls, L. K., 1948; Wood, F. E., 1910 a, pp. 528–33.

Genus **Tamias** Illiger
Big Chipmunks

Dental formula:

$$\text{I}\,\frac{1-1}{1-1},\ \ \text{C}\,\frac{0-0}{0-0},\ \ \text{P}\,\frac{1-1}{1-1},\ \ \text{M}\,\frac{3-3}{3-3}=20.$$

Tamias striatus griseus Mearns
Gray Chipmunk

Tamias striatus griseus Mearns, Bull. Amer. Mus. Nat. Hist., 3 (2): 231, June 5, 1891.
Sciurus Striatus Lapham, p. 44, 1852.
Sciurus striatus Lapham, p. 339, 1853.
Tamias striatus Strong, p. 439, 1883.
Tamias striatus griseus Snyder, p. 115, 1902; Jackson, p. 17, 1908; Hollister, p. 24, 1910; Jackson, p. 87, 1910; Cory, p. 130, 1912; Schmidt, p. 111, 1931; Barger, p. 11, 1952.
Tamias striatus lysteri Komarek, p. 207, 1932; Barger, p. 11, 1951.

Vernacular names.—In Wisconsin most commonly called chipmunk. Other names of general application include big chipmunk, chipmuck or chipmuk, chipper, chippie, chipping squirrel, common chipmunk, eastern chipmunk, fence mouse, ferrididdle, ground hackie, ground squirrel, *gwen-geesh* (Chippewa), hackie, monke or munk, mouse squirrel, striped chipmunk, striped ground squirrel, and striped squirrel. Of more specific application to *T. s. griseus* are the names gray eastern chipmunk, gray striped chipmunk, and Mearns' chipmunk.

Identification marks.—A small and rather heavy set ground squirrel, some 9.5 to 11 inches in total length, of which about two-fifths or less is the flattened, well-haired tail; ears prominent, slightly rounded at apex, about one-half inch base to tip; provided with two comparatively large cheek pouches that open between the lips and the molars and extend backward along the cheek and the neck beneath the outer skin; beautifully marked by two pale and three dark stripes on the sides of the face, and on the upper body parts by five blackish and four pale stripes, extending only to the rusty rump, the inner or uppermost pale stripes being much broader than the others and always distinctly grayish; fur dense, moderately fine.

In full summer pelage the top of the head and dark facial stripes are near russet; light facial stripes pale buffy; ears brownish; dorsal bands extending only to anterior part of rump, the dark ones near black, the two broad upper pale ones near smoke gray, shading posteriorly into tawny; inferior dorsal pale stripes creamy white; rump hazel; paling on thighs to ochraceous tawny; sides of jaws and flanks pale ochraceous buff; under parts of head and body creamy white; tail above fuscous black overlaid with pale gray, beneath ochraceous tawny bordered with fuscous black and edged with pale gray. Winter pelage, on account of wear and fading, generally somewhat paler throughout. There is only one molt annually, which usually begins in the latter part of June and may extend into July or even August.

A specimen of *T. s. ohionensis* in the University of Wisconsin Zoological Museum collected by the author at Milton, Rock County, July 26, 1907, is in fresh summer pelage, while another collected on the same date is still in worn winter pelage, with new hair coming on the anterior part of the abdomen and throat and on cheeks and forehead.

The skull of *Tamias* is rather flat and comparatively narrow; brain case shallow; relatively broad interorbitally, slightly arched, and somewhat depressed frontally; rostrum moderately elongate, becoming rather attenuate and slightly depressed anteriorly; infraorbital foramen large,

Left hind foot of TAMIAS S. GRISEUS. *Specimen from Long Lake, Washburn County, Wisconsin.* 1×.

relatively and actually larger than in *Citellus tridecemlineatus;* upper incisors short, moderately stout, and but slightly recurved; the only ground squirrel lacking the upper third premolar—in other words the only one having only four upper molariform teeth on each side.

No variation in size or color between the sexes is evident. For a mammal so diversely marked there is also little individual or age variation in color. Half-grown young have markings and color essentially like the old ones. Albino individuals rarely have been recorded. A breeding female specimen (No. 274,695, Biol. Surveys coll., U. S. Nat. Mus.) of *Tamias s. ohionensis* collected May 26, 1945, at Horicon Refuge, Dodge County, shows albinism, or white spotting on the nose and ears, and a few white hairs scattered on the tail. Lapham (1852: 44) reports a "beautiful

Gray chipmunk. Photograph by George Socha, Birge Hall, University of Wisconsin, Madison. Sept. 1959.

albino specimen has recently been found at Oconomowoc."

This species may be distinguished from any other Wisconsin mammal by its size and extent of striping. Only the chipmunks (*Tamias* and *Eutamias*) have two pale and three dark stripes on the sides of the face, those on *Tamias* being less contrasting in color, and only members of these two genera have five dark and four pale stripes down the back and sides. In *Tamias* the stripes all terminate on the anterior border of the chestnut colored rump and the upper two pale stripes are much wider than the other stripes. Members of this genus are the only ground squirrels with four (instead of five) molariform teeth on each side in the upper jaw, and the only squirrels with such dentition having a maximum skull width of less than 42.5 mm.

Measurements.—Total length, 240 to 273 mm. (9.5 to 10.8 inches); tail, 92 to 115 mm. (3.6 to 4.5 inches); hind foot, 36 to 39 mm. (1.4 to 1.5 inches). Weight of adult from a low of about 85 grams (3.2 oz.) to 115 grams (4.1 oz.) in October. Skull length, 40 to 42.4 mm.; width, 22.2 to 24 mm.

Distribution in Wisconsin.—Approximately the northern two-thirds of the state, north of and including most of Buffalo, Trempealeau, and Monroe counties, and all of Juneau, Adams, Marquette, Green Lake, and Fond du Lac counties, except northeastern Brown, Kewaunee, and Door counties occupied by *T. s. peninsulae,* and possibly also excepting Calumet, Manitowoc, and Sheboygan counties, from which no specimens have been examined.

Habitat.—Open forests, particularly where hardwoods occur; brushland and cut-over land; rocky wooded bluffs, particularly of limestone outcrops; wooded or brushy fence lines, around stone walls, brush piles, rubbish heaps, old buildings, and log cabins; sometimes around gardens, village yards, and parks when shelter is available.

Status and Habits.—The big chipmunk (*Tamias*) was undoubtedly found in favorable habitat throughout the state when the early settlers arrived, though it was often overlooked on account of its seclusive habits. Writing of its occurrence in the "Indian Lands," probably in southwestern Waushara County, Moses Barrett (1873: 695) said "not a single specimen of the common striped squirrels or chipmunk (*Tamias Striatus*)

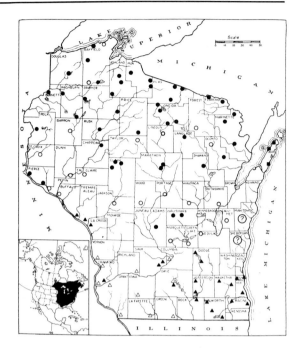

Map 29. *Distribution of* Tamias striatus. *Solid symbols = specimens examined. Open symbols = authentic records.* ●, ○ = T. s. griseus, ■ = T. s. peninsulae, ▲, △ = T. s. ohioensis.

appeared anywhere in the region" when he first arrived in 1850.

I well remember the first specimen of a chipmunk which I saw after two or three years residence in that section. I met him about five miles in the direction of Fox river on his emigrating tour northward. He had taken up his temporary residence under the roots of an old stump, on the top of which he was perched uttering his characteristic "chib" a note which the other species never produce. He was soon followed by numerous others and the two species lived together for a while as far as I could observe, without any discord. The four-lined squirrels [i.e. *Eutamias*], however, soon became less numerous and in a short time were so scarce that it was difficult to obtain specimens and they have long since entirely disappeared from that region (Barrett, 1873: 695).

In many places in Wisconsin, however, I have found both the big chipmunk (*Tamias*) and the least chipmunk (*Eutamias*) comparatively common and apparently living in harmony. Concentrations of abundance may be in different environments, the large chipmunk (*Tamias*) more common in deciduous areas, the least chipmunk (*Eutamias*) more frequent in coniferous areas, yet neither species is confined to the particular habitat. I have on occasion procured a specimen of each species on the same stump or log on successive days. In particularly favorable areas the population of *Tamias* may reach as high as twenty or more per acre, but the average number active in good environment seldom exceeds six or eight, and more frequently averages two or three individuals per acre (Blair, 1941: 8, northern Michigan; Burt, 1940: 47, southern Michigan). Possibly some three million acres in the state are favorable for this species, and if so we might have five million or more *Tamias* in Wisconsin. Its home range usually covers only one or two acres, but at times one may cover three acres, or a maximum radius of about two hundred feet from the homesite.

Tracks of TAMIAS. *Left, right forefoot. Right, right hind foot.* 1×.

Feces of TAMIAS. *Drawn by Mrs. MacMaugh, from field sketch by author.* 1×.

Although this chipmunk is well known in regions where it occurs, it may at times be difficult to observe on account of its quiet, seclusive, and retiring habits. At other times it may attract attention by its distinctive call or song. When disturbed it may run over logs, stumps, and brush, its tail erect and the whole animal quite conspicuous. Its burrows usually are well hidden and difficult to locate, its tracks and feces are not often too evident or well defined except on soft snow, and it makes no regular runways.

Sometimes numbers will gather about an occupied camp or cabin, become quite tame, beg for food, eat at one's feet, and even while eating let their backs be stroked by a finger, as they did for Vernon Bailey at Basswood Lake, Ashland County, in July, 1921, and for myself at Rib Hill, Marathon County, in July, 1918. It may be out any time during daylight hours when the weather is above freezing, but is most active early in the forenoon and late in the afternoon. It does not become excessively fat in autumn and does not regularly hibernate, though it may be dormant for considerable periods and is quite inactive outside its home in winter, utilizing food it has extensively stored within its burrow. Instances of an eastern chipmunk being wholly dormant in winter have been reported (Abbott, 1884: 59; Robinson, 1923: 257). Likewise, occasional instances of its activity in winter have been reported, especially on milder days late in January or early in February. Results of experiments by J. A. Panuska (1959) indicate that this species appears to be a somewhat deeper hibernator than has been commonly believed. The animal usually begins engaging in its spring activities about the first half of March, the males usually becoming active a few days before the females. In the autumn it retires to its burrow soon after continuous freezing begins, usually about the first or second week of November, though sometimes it may remain active until the last of November.

Rather slow and quiet in most of its undisturbed normal movements, it may become exceedingly quick if alarmed or threatened with danger. When foraging it usually walks slowly, meandering here and there to investigate some small object, sometimes almost darting into a trot for a foot or two, and if frightened hustling back to its burrow or shelter in a rapid trot or sometimes a gallop. Its slow walking speed is less than two miles an hour, its trot about four or five miles an hour, and its maximum speed galloping about ten or eleven miles an hour. When it gallops, its leaps may range from 15 to 24 inches on level ground, but when it jumps from a log or other elevation it may cover 30 inches or more. Although primarily terrestrial, it climbs well, and I have frequently seen one 20 to 40 feet up a tree where it had climbed to procure food or to escape danger. I have seen them in smooth-barked trees such as hickory, aspen, and paper birch, as well as in rough-barked species such as bur oak, hackberry, and black walnut. It prefers to keep its feet dry, yet when circumstances require it can swim well.

It has three distinctive notes or songs: a slowly uttered though often long continued low *chuck-chuck-chuck,* which appears to be a mild warning to its kind that danger may be near; a slightly higher pitched *kuk-kuk-kuk* often continued for many minutes, which seems to be simply a song and often uttered when it does not apprehend danger; and a high-pitched and rather musical continuous and excited chirp which is employed when the animal is aroused and running from danger toward its burrow with its tail upright and flipping. Frequently it watches from the top of a stump or post as if on sentry duty, and the chirping and the flipping tail may serve as a danger signal.

Active, alert, and bright, the gray chipmunk is an independent little squirrel that does not depend too much upon its relatives. In fact, except for its immediate family, it is rather pugnacious towards its kinsfolk, and does not tend to be gregarious. Sometimes in the autumn a family may remain together, or even take in one or two transients for the winter siesta. Usually, however, the older animal gathers and guards its own food supply, and spends its winter alone. Although thus showing a lack of sociability with its own kind, it may become very friendly with man, and around summer resorts and cottages often comes to eat food passed to it, sometimes taking food from a hand. Its curiosity often overcomes its timidity. It is more agile and playful than either of our true ground squirrels (*Citellus tridecemlineatus* and *C. franklinii*) but much less so than the least chipmunk (*Eutamias*). Its body is rather stocky and muscular, compensating somewhat for its lack of agility. Its senses are acute, those of sight and hearing particularly so. Normal longevity is probably not more than three or four years, though potential longevity is about eight years. One lived in captivity in the London Zoological Garden from April 8, 1891, to April 13, 1898.

The gray chipmunk breeds when one year old. Spring mating occurs from about March 20 to about April 15, and second or summer mating may take place between the last of June and the last of July. The gestation period is approximately 31 days. Two to seven young, usually four or five, are born in each litter. The animal is born naked with eyes closed, and develops slowly in its early days, but after about 30 days its eyes are open, and ten days later it rambles on its own outside the den. When it is eight weeks old it is two-thirds grown and begins to shift for itself. The mammae are eight, two pectoral, four abdominal, two inguinal.

The home is in a burrow which may be short and simple or extensive and complex. A burrow that has been used for several years is usually more extensive. In their studies of eastern chipmunk burrows at Waupaca, Wisconsin, J. A. Panuska and N. J. Wade differentiated burrows "into two types: *simple systems,* often consisting merely of a tunnel with a slightly widened terminal end, or of two tunnels leading into the one small chamber; and *extensive systems,* consisting of a more complex plan of tunnels with one or more large living or storage chambers (more than five inches in diameter and typically ten inches or over)" (Panuska and Wade, 1956: 25).

The investigations revealed a scarcity of leafy nests and food storage in the summer, an absence of accumulated feces within the system, some extensive systems with only one entrance, and a distinct preference on the part of the chipmunk to dig under or around (rather than over) large rocks or tree roots. There was considerable variation in the diameter of the burrows located on different levels of a single system. An unusually large nesting chamber, twenty-four inches by seventeen inches, is described (Panuska and Wade, 1956: 30).

Simple burrow and nest of Tamias. *From field sketch made at Bowers Lake, Rock County, Wisconsin, October 3, 1898, by the author.*

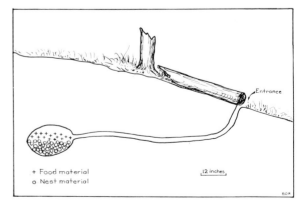

+ Food material
o Nest material

12 inches

Vernon Bailey excavated a chipmunk burrow at Elk River, Minnesota, July 4, 1920, which he found to be about 20 feet in length and from 1 to 3 feet below the surface. It had several branches and openings and four or five storage and nest cavities. A large old nest about 18 feet from the entrance, composed mainly of oak leaves, rested on a foundation of stored food supplies, consisting of about 8 quarts of the previous year's acorns, a pint of old moldy corn, and a handful of the previous years hazelnuts. The cavity would have held about a bushel. A smaller storage chamber at one side of the burrow contained a handful of freshly stored corn and about a pint of the previous year's acorns. At one side and about a foot below the nest cavity was a much-used toilet; the nest and storage chambers were clean and sweet (Howell, 1929: 4).

A burrow that the author excavated near Milton, Rock County, October 3, 1898, had the entrance near the end of a log on the gentle slope of a hill. The burrow was about two inches in diameter, extended nearly vertically downward for about ten inches, then followed nearly horizontally into the slope for about eight feet to the upper center of the nest, or about nine feet from the entrance hall to the nest and storage chamber. The chamber, shaped like a flattened sphere was about 18 inches in diameter and 14 inches deep, the ceiling being about 33 inches below the soil surface. The entire lower half or more was filled with about ten quarts of stored food consisting of about six quarts of hazelnuts and acorns, one quart of corn and oats, and three quarts of dry berries and fruit, mostly nannyberry (*Viburnum*), black raspberry, black cherry, and linden. There were no feces in the burrow and no evidence of a defecation chamber as described by Vernon Bailey (in Howell, 1929: 4). The burrow apparently had never seen winter use, which may account for the absence of feces.

The principal food of this chipmunk consists of nuts, fruit, seeds of woody plants (maple, oak hazel, basswood, hickory, beech, elm, box elder, wild and cultivated cherries, blackhaw, nannyberry, arrowwood, Virginia creeper, and prickly ash), some cultivated grains such as corn, wheat, and oats, seeds of weeds and grasses, wild fruits and berries, among them raspberry, strawberry, blueberry, wintergreen, gooseberry, barberry, and legumes, and occasionally mushrooms and various other fungi. Animal matter is not regularly eaten, although the big chipmunk is known to capture and consume considerable quantities of insects, particularly cicadas and grasshoppers. It is also reported to have eaten young mice, young birds and birds' eggs, and even a salamander, a frog, and a small snake. At Fish Creek, Door County, July 23–24, 1917, I found individuals of *Tamias s. peninsulae* feeding extensively on two species of land snails, *Pyramidula alternata* and *Helicina occulata*. Food for storage is carried in the cheek pouches to the burrow. The cheek pouches of a specimen that I collected at Friendship, Adams County, contained three pits of cultivated plums and 66 fruits of basswood (*Tilia americana*). This species frequently drinks at springs and other convenient watering places, and during winter may leave its burrow to drink or eat snow.

It is preyed upon by several birds, including the marsh, Cooper's, and red-tailed hawks, and even though it is strictly diurnal a number are consumed by the barred owl and great horned owl. In Michigan remains of three of them have been reported in the nest of a goshawk (Porter, 1951). Among mammals, weasels, minks, and

Complex burrow and nest of TAMIAS. *Modified from Allen, 1938, p. 32.*

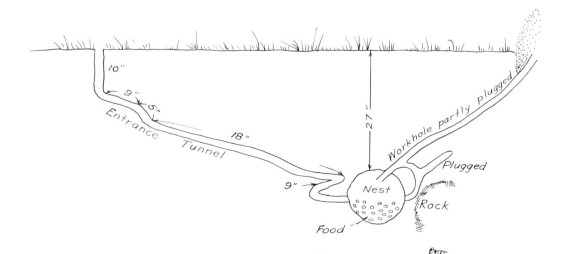

foxes get many, and the predatory house cat is an important enemy. Snakes also kill a few, and many fall victim to the boy or the irresponsible gunner. Forest and brush fires undoubtedly destroy a few, as may also floods. Rarely is one run over by an automobile.

External parasites that infest it include the louse *Haplopleura erratica* and the fleas *Megabothris acerbus, M. vison, Ceratophyllus gallinae, Orchopeas wickhami, Ctenophthalmus,* and *Pseudagyrtes.* Internal parasites include the trematode *Scaphiostomum pancreaticum,* the cestode *Hymenolepis diminuta,* the nematodes *Trychostrongylus sp., Rictularia halli, Spirura michiganensis, Trichuris madisonensis,* and *Capillaria tamiastriata,* and the horny-headed worms *Moniliformis clarki* and *Macracanthorhynchus hirundinaceus.*

The gray chipmunk is not especially detrimental to crops in Wisconsin, remaining as it does largely on uncultivated land and feeding upon native wild seeds, nuts, and berries. Corn and other grain that it eats are scattered kernels which it gathers from the ground near the border of a field. It is never apt to need special control measures. It is a beautiful little mammal, of intense interest around summer resorts and camps as well as in the wilderness, and one we will always want with us.

Specimens examined from Wisconsin.—Total 109, as follows: *Adams County:* Friendship, 2. *Ashland County:* Bear Lake, 1 (UWZ), Mellen, 1 (WHD); Mellen (8 mi. S. W.), 1. *Bayfield County:* Herbster, 6; Iron River, 1 (WHD); Namakagon Lake, 3 (2 MM). *Burnett County:* Danbury, 2; Yellow River (mouth), 6 (MM). *Chippewa County:* Holcombe, 2. *Clark County:* Thorp Township, 1 (AMNH); Withee, 1; Worden Township, 7 (1 AMNH; 1 UM; 3 UWZ). *Douglas County:* Solon Springs, 2. *Florence County:* Spread Eagle Lake, 2 (CNHM); T 40 N, R 16 E, 1 (UWZ). *Iron County:* Fisher Lake, 1 (UWZ); Mercer, 1 (MM); Upson (4 mi. N.), 1 (WHD). *Juneau County:* Camp Douglas, 5 (1 AMNH: 2 CNHM; 2 USNM). *Langlade County:* Elcho, 1 (UWZ). *Marathon County:* Rib Hill, 3; Wausau, 2 (CMMH). *Marinette County,* Cataline, 5 (MM); Cravitz, 2 (NPM); Timms Lake, 1 (UWZ). *Oconto County:* Kelley Lake, 2. *Oneida County:* Crescent Lake, 1; Lake Tomahawk, 4 (CNHM); Rhinelander, 2 (1 UWZ); Woodruff, 1. *Pierce County:* Maiden Rock, 10 (MM); Prescott, 6 (MM). *Polk County:* North Hudson, 1 (MM); Saint Croix Falls, 2. *Price County:* Ogema, 1. *Rusk County:* Ladysmith, 1 (UWZ). *Sawyer County:* Connors Lake, 1 (F&FH); Hayward (6 mi. S.), 2 (CNHM), *Shawano County:* Keshena, 3 (CAS). *Vilas County:*

Lac Vieux Desert, 1 (CNHM); Lake St. Germain, 5; Mamie Lake, 1. *Washburn County:* T 41 N, R 13 W, 1 (UWZ). *Waushara County:* Plainfield, 1; Wild Rose, 2.

Selected references.—Allen, E. G., 1938; Harper, F., 1927; Howell, A. H., 1929; Mearns, E. A., 1891; Panuska, J. A., and N. J. Wade, 1956; Yerger, R. W., 1955.

Tamias striatus ohionensis Bole and Moulthrop
Ohio Chipmunk

Tamias striatus ohionensis Bole and Moulthrop, Sci. Publs. Cleveland Mus. Nat. Hist. 5 (6): 135, September 11, 1942.

Vernacular names.—Most of the common and general names of the gray chipmunk. More specifically sometimes called brown chipmunk, Ohio brown chipmunk, or Ohio striped chipmunk.

Identification marks.—Differs from *T. s. griseus* in its duller and more brownish color with darker under parts; averages slightly smaller than *griseus* with slightly shorter tail and relatively narrower skull.

Measurements.—Total length, 233 to 265 mm. (9.1 to 10.4 inches); tail, 90 to 100 mm. (3.5 to 3.9 inches); hind foot, 35 to 37 mm. (1.4 to 1.5 inches). Skull length, 40.3 to 41.2 mm.; width, 20.6 to 22.9 mm.

Distribution in Wisconsin.—Southern part of the state northward in Mississippi Valley to southern Buffalo County, and elsewhere northward to include Sauk, Columbia, Dodge, Washington, and Ozaukee counties.

Habitat, Status, and Habits.—So far as known essentially like those of *Tamias striatus griseus.*

Specimens examined from Wisconsin.—Total 87, as follows: *Buffalo County:* Fountain City, 1. *Crawford County:* Wauzeka, 2. *Dane County:* Madison, 6 (UWZ); *Dodge County:* Beaver Dam, 17 (16 UWZ); Fox Lake, 4 (UWZ). *Jefferson County:* Lake Mills, 1 (UWZ); Sumner, 1 (MM). *La Crosse County:* La Crosse (4 mi. S. of), 3. *Milwaukee County:* Granville, 1 (MM); Lake Township, 4 (MM); Milwaukee, 4 (MM); Whitefish Bay, 5 (UWZ); *Racine County:* Racine, 1 (USNM); Tischigan Lake, 14 (1 MM; 13 UWZ). *Rock County:* Milton, 2 (UWZ). *Sauk County:* Devils Lake, 1; Sumpter, 1 (MM). *Trempealeau County:* Trempealeau, 1. *Walworth County:* Delavan, 2 (1 CAS); Lake Geneva, 1 (CAS); Whitewater, 1 (CMNH). *Waukesha County:* Hartland, 3 (UWZ); Keesus Lake (near Merton), 1 (MM); Nashotah, 8 (6 USNM; 2 UWZ); New Berlin, 2 (MM).

Selected references.—Same as for *Tamias s. griseus,* and also Bole and Moulthrop, 1942, pp. 135–37.

Tamias striatus peninsulae Hooper
Peninsula Chipmunk

Tamias striatus peninsulae Hooper, Occas, Papers
Mus. Zool., Univ. Michigan, No. 461: 1, September
15, 1942.
Tamias striatus lysteri Komarek, p. 207, 1932; Barger, p. 11, 1951.

Vernacular names.—Most of the common and
general names of the gray chipmunk. More specifically, sometimes has been called Lyster's
chipmunk or northeastern chipmunk.

Identification marks.—Slightly smaller than *T.
s. griseus*, color very pale and coppery; rostrum
relative to other Wisconsin forms rather short and
broad.

Measurements.—Total length, 232 to 260 mm.
(9.1 to 10.2 inches); tail, 92 to 112 mm. (3.6 to
4.4 inches); hind foot, 34 to 38 mm. (1.3 to 1.5
inches). Skull length, 39 to 42.1 mm.; width, 21.6
to 23 mm.

Distribution in Wisconsin.—Door Peninsula,
southward into Kewaunee County and northeastern Brown County, and possibly into Manitowoc
County.

Habitat, Status, and Habits.—So far as known
essentially like those of *Tamias striatus griseus*.

Specimens examined from Wisconsin.—Total 7, as
follows: *Brown County:* Benderville, 2 (UND);
Red Banks, 1 (NPM). *Door County:* Ellison Bay,
1; Fish Creek, 2 (1 UWZ); Newport, 1 (MM).

Selected references.—Same as for *Tamias s. griseus*, and also Hooper, 1942.

Genus **Eutamias**
Little Chipmunks

Dental formula:

$$\text{I } \frac{1-1}{1-1}, \quad \text{C} \frac{0-0}{0-0}, \quad \text{P} \frac{2-2}{1-1}, \quad \text{M} \frac{3-3}{3-3} = 22.$$

Eutamias minimus jacksoni Howell
Wisconsin Least Chipmunk

Eutamias minimus jacksoni Howell, Journ. Mammal.
6 (1): 53, February 15, 1925.
Tamias quadrivittatus Strong, p. 440, 1883.
Eutamias quadrivittatus neglectus Jackson, p. 17,
1908.
Eutamias borealis neglectus Hollister, p. 139, 1909:
Hollister, p. 24, 1910; Cory, p. 135, 1912.
Eutamias minimus jacksoni Schmidt, p. 111, 1931;
Komarek, p. 207, 1932; Barger, p. 11, 1952.

Vernacular names.—In Wisconsin most commonly called little chipmunk. Other names include *ah-kwin-quis* (Chippewa), four-lined chipmunk, four-striped squirrel, Jackson's chipmunk,
Lake Superior chipmunk, least chipmunk, little
chipmunk, little northern chipmunk, little striped
chipmunk, long-tailed chipmunk, northern chipmunk, and western chipmunk.

Identification marks.—Smallest of the Wisconsin ground squirrels, quite slender in form, some
7.7 to 8.5 inches in total length, of which more
than two-fifths is the flattened well-haired tail;
ears prominent, about one-half inch base to tip,
and somewhat pointed at tip; provided with two
comparatively large cheek pouches; exquisitely
marked by two pale and three very dark stripes
on the sides of the face and on the upper body
parts and by five blackish and four pale stripes
extending to the base of the tail, all the stripes
being nearly the same width; fur dense, fine,
rather silky.

In full summer pelage the general coloration is
as follows: top of head brownish drab; dark facial
stripes blackish sayal brown, pale facial stripes
creamy white; postauricular blotches pale smoke
gray; all dorsal stripes extending posteriorly to
base of tail, the five dark stripes black, the median stripe extending anteriorly to the crown;
median pair of pale dorsal stripes grayish drab
mixed with sayal brown; the outer hair creamy
white; sides bright ochraceous tawny; tail above
fuscous black mixed with ochraceous tawny, beneath bright ochraceous tawny; under parts of
head and body white. The winter pelage is
slightly paler throughout, the upper parts only

*Wisconsin least chipmunk, stuffing its pockets with
rolled oats. Photograph by Vernon Bailey.*

Left hind foot of EUTAMIAS M. JACKSONI, *specimen from Holcombe, Wisconsin.* 1×.

slightly less tawny than in summer pelage. There are two molts annually, the winter pelage being replaced by the summer fur during the latter part of June, in July, or early in August. The summer coat is worn only two or three months, the winter pelage being acquired by the last of September or early in October.

The skull of *Eutamias* is slightly curved, not especially flattened above, and comparatively narrow; the brain case suborbicular, distinctly arched, and noticeably depressed in frontal region; rostrum relatively short and heavy, considerably depressed anteriorly; upper third premolar present, thus making five upper molariform teeth on each side.

There is no sexual variation in size or color, nor is any considerable individual variation apparent. One-third grown young appear in markings and color essentially like the old animals except for a slightly duller tone. I have no record of either an albinistic or a melanistic individual of *E. m. jacksoni.*

This species is apt to be confused in Wisconsin only with *Tamias*, than which it is much smaller (total length always less than 225 mm.); hind foot less than 33.5 mm. in length, and width of longitudinal stripes about subequal and extending to base of tail. Tail more than 40 per cent of total length. The least chipmunk is the only squirrel in Wisconsin having a greatest skull width of less than 19 mm.

Measurements.—Total length of adults, 196 to 219 mm. (7.7 to 8.5 inches); tail, 82 to 100 mm. (3.2 to 3.9 inches); hind foot, 29 to 33 mm. (1.1 to 1.3 inches). Weight of adult from 35 grams

(1.2 oz.) to 51 grams (1.8 oz.). Skull length, 31.5 to 33.3 mm.; width, 17.7 to 18.6 mm.

Distribution in Wisconsin.—Northern and central parts of the state from northern Burnett County southeast to northeastern Chippewa County, south to central Jackson County and western Juneau County (Camp Douglas), east formerly to southwestern Waushara County, thence northeasterly to central Oconto and southern Marinette counties.

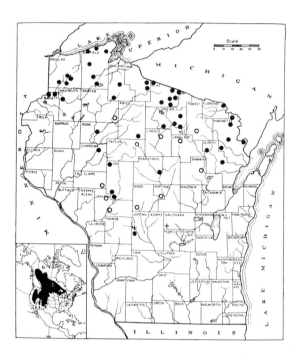

Map 30. *Distribution of* EUTAMIAS MINIMUS. ● = *specimens examined.* ○ = *authentic records since 1900.* + = *authentic records 1900 or before.*

Habitat.—Often coniferous or mixed coniferous and hardwood forests, particularly if with ground cover of brushes, stumps, and fallen logs; burns and slashings with rocks, limbs, upturned stumps, and trunks of trees, especially if covered with dense thicket of vines, bushes, and briars; lake shores, roadsides, and even sandy beaches among rocks, logs, and stumps; often around abandoned buildings; rarely in low wet places at edge of woods (McAllister, Marinette County, August 1, 1917).

Status and Habits.—The range of the least chipmunk in Wisconsin probably is not greatly different from what it was a century ago, though the species has apparently disappeared from some parts of the southern edge of its former distribution, especially toward the southeast. In the "Indian Lands, north of the Fox River," in what is now southwestern Waushara County, "in 1850 it was very common. On the immigration of the chipmunk (*T. striatus*) a few years later, it became less numerous and finally disappeared" (Barrett, M., 1873: 695). The cause of its disappearance, however, was undoubtedly not the ingression of the larger gray chipmunk. In personal notes sent to me by Ned Hollister in October, 1920, in regard to Eagle River, Vilas County, he predicted that *Tamias* would entirely replace *Eutamias* in that region before many years. The least chipmunk, however, is still common there. In an exceptionally favorable habitat such as a rocky outcrop covered with logs and berry brambles the population may exceed 30 or more per acre. Normally in a well-populated area the average population seldom exceeds 12 to 15 per acre, yet if any are present in favorable habitat the average number per acre is seldom less than 5 or 6. The least chipmunk (*Eutamias*) occupies somewhat more than half the distribution area of *Tamias* in Wisconsin, but is usually much more abundant where found, so that in the state as a whole its total population is probably as great or greater than that of *Tamias*. Its home range usually covers less than one acre, and often it is within a radius of 40 or 50 feet from the homesite.

The least chipmunk is not apt to remain long undiscovered where it occurs, though the uninitiated might easily mistake it for its larger cousin, the gray chipmunk. It is more active and noisy when disturbed than the gray chipmunk, and runs excitedly with its long tail vertical, usually calling in a series of rapid high-pitched chippers. Sometimes it is difficult to locate the least chipmunk by its notes because of their ventriloquial tendency. It is often active during the warmer winter days and may leave its tracks—the smallest of the squirrel tracks—in soft snow. Sometimes one may discover its food caches in logs or stumps, but its burrow is so well hidden as to be seldom observed. Although timid and shy, it soon makes itself known.

No sooner is the camp made than these little chipmunks make their appearance. At our camp on North Pelican Lake in the summer of 1906 no chipmunks were visible when we landed our boat-load of supplies, but within a few days they were present in dozens. They must investigate everything and one even entered my suitcase, left partly open, and remained there for several minutes. When we broke camp two of them entered the loaded boat. After the boat was launched they jumped into the water, though with considerable hesitation, and swam ashore (Jackson, 1908: 17–18).

It may be active any time of day but seems to delight in the most sunny hours of midday—though an animal of more northern climate it appears to prefer warm days. It enters a winter sleep that appears not to be very deep, and it frequently feeds upon its winter food supply, stored mostly above ground in stumps, logs, and other hideouts. It may begin its semihibernation by the last of October if the ground becomes frozen or there is a heavy snow, but it usually does not take its winter naps until the first part of November. It usually becomes fully active again by the middle of March. Once awake it is one of the quickest and most active of our mammals, and though it may perch on a stump, limb, branch, or post momentarily to peep at the surroundings, it is soon off again in its quick nervous manner, dashing here and there in its combined gallop and running gait. Its wakeful hours are seemingly too precious for it to rest or walk, though it will sometimes quietly perch for a few minutes while eating. It seldom runs any considerable distance in one of its spurts, yet in these excited sprints of 30 or 40 feet it may attain a speed of 15 miles an hour. It climbs well, especially in berry bushes, and I have seen one climb to 20 or more feet in a white cedar or a jack pine on several occasions. It does not like to enter water, but will do so of its own volition, and swims well for distances of up to at least 60 feet.

Sometimes in its rare moments of quiet resting on a log or stump it will utter a series of *chirp-chirp-chirp-chirp*, often for several seconds. If danger approaches or the chipmunk becomes frightened, the note becomes a nervous, rapid, and rather high-pitched *chit-chit-chit-chit-chit*. If the danger continues to approach, the chipmunk usually scampers away, uttering a continuous birdlike chipper. A lowly uttered *kek–kek–kek* is apparently used as a call note to its own kin. When very excited it often flips its tail, which may indicate fear or serve as a danger signal.

This active sprite is always alert, sensitive, quick as a flash, and of nervous temperament. It is timid and wild when first approached, but once its fears are subdued it usually becomes quiet, gentle, and tame. With its own kind it is usually friendly, though with some individuals it may be ugly and scrappy. It appears to be more gregarious than the gray chipmunk, and often gathers in numbers, particularly at a favorite food station, where it often plays with its companions. It delights in jumping for food tied to a string, and swinging and playing thereon while consuming the bait. Its sight, hearing, and sense of touch are acute. Its enemies and accidents probably keep its normal life span to less than four years, though its potential longevity is believed to be about eight years.

It breeds when slightly less than one year old, or in the spring of the year following its birth. Mating occurs about 10 to 20 days after the chipmunk becomes regularly active in the spring, but the actual time may vary with seasonal weather conditions. Usually breeding activities are well under way by April 1, and may continue in some cases until near the end of April. The young, four to seven in number—most frequently five or six, and in more than half the litters five—are usually born during May after a gestation period of approximately 30 days. One litter a year to each female is normal, though it is believed that a second litter may be reared if the first one is lost soon after birth. The new-born is naked, has its eyes closed, is about two inches long, and weighs about 2.3 grams. Its eyes open some 28 days after birth, and when it is 40 days old it is fairly well haired and explores outside its nest. When two months old it is two-thirds grown and on its own. The mammae are eight, two pectoral, four abdominal, two inguinal.

The summer nest is frequently made in a hollow tree or stump, in an old woodpecker's hole, in a hollow or rotting log, among rocks, or in such other location as will give protection from ground moisture below and rain and dew above. Rarely is a nest built in a tree, yet one apparently made of grass containing at least three young chipmunks and their mother was found about 18 feet above ground in a 25-foot-tall black spruce

in the middle of July, 1929, in Cook County, Minnesota (Orr, 1930). The winter nest is usually underground at the end of a comparatively short tunnel. The nest cavity is globular and small, seldom more than eight inches in diameter, and may or may not have a small storage place at its far end and underneath it. Small amounts of food are also placed in or under hollow logs or stumps, in cavities in trees, among rocks, or in almost any conceivable protected place. The nest may be made of rabbit, squirrel, deer, or other cottony down from thistles, aspens, and willows, and from other pods and catkins; the inner bark of trees and shrubs; grass, usually in small pieces; and fine shreds of fibrous plant material. The nest is frequently repaired and renewed. Stuart Criddle has described a winter home of the little northern chipmunk, very close relative of the Wisconsin least chipmunk, that he examined near Treesbank, Manitoba, Canada.

The winter home is very hard to find. In my efforts to locate them I have put out food and nest making materials in the hope that one of the chipmunks making use of them would lead me to its home, but they have never done so. I have had much better luck in following their tracks made on soft snow and some interesting homes have been found in this way. A typical example was found on the 8th of November 1934 in a thick wood at the foot of a willow bush, part of which had been broken and bent down. This was used by the chipmunk in getting to and from the mouth of a tunnel which led to the entrance of the home. The hole curved sharply to the right and in a length of twenty-five inches reached the store and nest chamber eleven inches down. The chamber was 5-3/4 inches high and 6-1/2 inches across. The winter store of cherry kernels and rye which weighed 528.5 gm. was beneath and well up on three sides of the nest which was made of finely shredded grass lined with rabbit fur (Criddle, S., 1943: 84).

The food of the least chipmunk consists mostly of seeds, small fruits, and thin-shelled nuts, rarely a trace of green leafy material, and sometimes considerable animal matter, particularly insects. It consumes many blueberries, blackberries, and especially red raspberries, and at Solon Springs, Douglas County, in July, 1919, was reported to have done some damage to the few strawberries cultivated there. Individuals observed at Lakewood, Oconto County, August 14, 1917, ate the pulp of the red raspberries, but put the seeds in their cheek pouches. The pouches of a male collected at Lakewood that day contained 172 red raspberry seeds and 16 timothy hay seeds.

Pouches of a female from Kelley Lake, Oconto County, August 8, 1917, contained 29 seeds of the smartweed *Polygonum convolvulus.* At Crescent Lake, Oneida County, type locality of *Eutamias m. jacksoni,* they were observed September 6, 1917, feeding upon wheat, oats, wild cherries, and plums that they gathered from the ground in an orchard. Cheek pouches of a male collected there on that date contained 23 pits of pin cherry (*Prunus pennsylvanica*), and those of a female 84 kernels of wheat. Hazelnuts (*Corylus rostrata*) are regularly eaten and stored by the least chipmunk. Animal matter eaten consists of grasshopper eggs, and sometimes adult grasshoppers and crickets; beetles of various species, both adult and larval; larvae of moths and butterflies; a very few ants, bees, flies, and spiders; and traces of bird feathers (Aldous, 1941). No animal matter or juicy or pulpy fruit parts is placed in the cheek pouches, and only such fruit pits, seeds, nuts, and other dry food as is to be stored is thus carried. Cheek pouches give a very different picture of the food from that which is disclosed by actual observation of the animal or examination of its stomach contents. The least chipmunk often drinks from small natural water containers, but does not bathe. It, however, frequently takes a dust or sand bath, and washes itself by use of its fore paws.

The least chipmunk is so quick and active that it is not easily captured by many species of animals. The marsh hawk and the red-tailed hawk occasionally catch one, and the weasel, mink, red fox, and domestic cat prey upon it. One was seen August 28, 1917, being chased by a male short-tailed weasel (*Mustela erminea bangsi*) near Mamie Lake, Vilas County, and was given lease of life only because the weasel was needed for a specimen. A boy may occasionally shoot one, but it is such an amusing mammal it is seldom molested by man. It sometimes is killed by an automobile, and fire and water undoubtedly destroy a few. External parasites to which it is host include the tick *Ixodes marxi* and the mite *Trombicula harperi.* Internal parasites include the nematodes *Citellinema bifurcatum, Rictularia* sp., and *Syphacia eutami,* and a horny-headed worm, *Moniliformis* sp. It has no known diseases in

Wisconsin, but the species has been found infected with tularemia in Wyoming and other northwestern states.

The little harm that this chipmunk can do is more than offset by its attractiveness and usefulness. Although it may rarely do some slight damage to cultivated berries, most of the berries it consumes are wild and uncultivated, and the grain it stores or eats is gathered as loose scattered grain from the ground. Beneficially, it destroys many weed seeds, and above all is valuable in that it affords many of us great pleasure in watching the beautiful little sprite go through its many antics and display its close friendship. Its tameness often causes it to become an interesting pet, either running free or confined in a suitable cage. Even crude lumberjacks and iron ore miners tend to love the least chipmunk. A Polish lumberjack at Lakewood, Oconto County, in August, 1917, told me that the stripes down the back of the chipmunk were made by Paul Bunyan's cat! Probably this folklore originated from a story that has been written about the Asiatic chipmunk, an animal somewhat similar to our least chipmunk, in which the bear is said to be responsible for the stripes.

When winter came the bear emptied his belly, relying on the fat he had accumulated during the summer to keep him alive through the long winter with-out eating, and retired into the lair he had prepared for himself. The frost came and he closed up the entrance with moss, dug himself into the soft bed he had got ready while the autumn weather still held, and fell asleep.

Just by the lair in the hollow of a tree lived a yellow chipmunk. All summer and autumn he had been collecting seeds from the grass and storing them up in its dwelling for the winter.

The bear slept without waking, while the chipmunk would wake up, eat some seeds and go to sleep again.

The winter went on and on until at last the sun returned to spring again. The chipmunk woke up and saw through a chink in his hole that it would be a late spring that year. He looked at his store of food and decided to cut down his meals.

Meanwhile the bear slept on without a care in his snow-covered lair, just occasionally turning over sleepily onto the other side.

The second half of the winter passed, the sun began to give more warmth and the snow melted. The chipmunk slept sounder in its warmed hole; but the bear got woken by the drops coming into his lair and had to move out.

Though the lair was gradually thawing and the ground round it was getting dry, deep snow still lay in the shade in dells and deep inside the forest. Where was he to find food? He tried going into the forest but found nothing, and only brought back weariness and increased gnawings of hunger.

So the bear stopped going into the taiga. He decided to wait for really warm weather that would melt all the snow and bring the world to life again. He lay day and night by his swamped lair and grumbled angrily: he was racked with hunger and his empty belly rumbled.

The chipmunk heard him and made his presence known. The bear came up to the hole and tried to turn the stump over with its paw, but it was a big one and more than he could manage.

"Who's that?", asked the chipmunk from the hole.

"It's me", said the bear. "I've got my lair near here".

"What's worrying you, bear?"

"It's the water; it's got into my nest and forced me out. I'm hungry in the daytime and frozen at night. I'm frozen because I've eaten nothing since the autumn. I want food and there's nothing to eat".

The chipmunk listened to the bear, was sorry for him and brought what food he had left out of his nest.

His neighbour ate it, satisfied his hunger and by way of thanks stroked the chipmunk's back with his paw, taking off strips of skin with the claws.

The chipmunk's back healed, but to this day instead of being an even yellow his fur and that of his descendants has brown stripes down the back! (Asharov, 1928).

Specimens examined from Wisconsin.—Total 216, as follows: *Ashland County:* Bear Lake, 4 (UWZ); Mellen (8 mi. S. W.), 1. *Bayfield County:* Basswood Lake, 1; Cornucopia (8 mi. S.), 1 (WHD); Herbster, 9; Iron River (4 mi. E.), 1 (WHD); Namakagon Lake, 2; Orienta, 1. *Burnett County:* Namakagon River (mouth), 1 (MM); Yellow River (mouth), 5 (MM). *Chippewa County:* Holcombe, 3. *Clark County:* Dewhurst Township, 13 (5 AMNH; 6 UWZ); Hewett Township, 1 (UWZ); Thorp Township, 1 (AMNH). *Douglas County:* Saint Croix Dam, 6 (MM); Solon Springs, 5; T 44 N, R 12 W, 1 (F&FH); Upper Saint Croix Lake, 4 (MM). *Florence County:* Florence, 2. *Iron County:* Fisher Lake, 2 (UWZ); Mercer 5 (2 MM). *Juneau County:* Camp Douglas, 57 (37 AMNH: 2 CC; 7 CNHM; 2 MCZ; 5 USNM). *Marathon County:* Rib Hill, 3. *Marinette County:* Cataline, 3 (MM); Cravitz (16 mi. W.), 2 (NM); McAllister, 1; No locality, 10 (MM); Pembine, 1 (MM); *Oconto County:* Kelley Brook, 5 (MM): Kelley Lake, 2; Lakewood, 5; *Oneida County:* Crescent Lake (type locality), 7; Hutchinson Lake, 1 (F&FH); Moen Lake, 1 (CC);

North Pelican Lake, 1 (CC); Rhinelander, 7 (1 CC; 5 UWZ). *Price County:* Ogema, 8. *Rusk County:* Ladysmith, 1 (UWZ). *Vilas County:* Conover, 1 (CNHM); Divide, 1 (MM); Lac Vieux Desert, 7 (CNHM); Lake St. Germain, 4; Mamie Lake, 13; Robinson Lake, 3 (UWZ); Sayner, 1 (UM); Trout Lake, 1 (UWZ). *Washburn County:* T 41 N, R 13 E, 1 (UWZ).

Selected references.—Aldous, S. E., 1941; Criddle, S., 1943; Howell, A. H., 1925, 1929; Jackson, H. H. T., 1957 b; Manville, R. H., 1949.

Genus **Sciurus** Linnaeus
Large Tree Squirrels

Dental formula:

$$I\frac{1-1}{1-1}, \quad C\frac{0-0}{0-0}, \quad P\frac{2-2}{1-1} \text{ or } \frac{1-1}{1-1}, \quad M\frac{3-3}{3-3}=22 \text{ or } 20$$

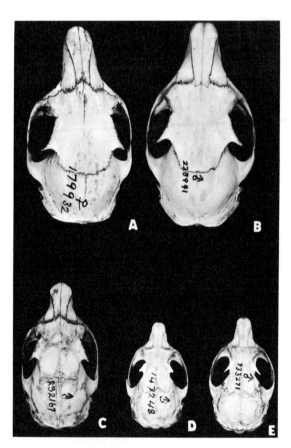

Skulls of tree squirrels. A. SCIURUS C. HYPOPHAEUS, *Fountain City, Wisconsin, B.* S. N. RUFIVENTER, *Endeavor, Wisconsin, C.* TAMIASCIURUS H. MINNESOTA, *St. Croix Falls, Wisconsin, D.* GLAUCOMYS V. VOLANS, *Delavan, Wisconsin, E.* G. S. MACROTIS, *Connors Lake, Wisconsin. About* ⅘×.

Sciurus carolinensis hypophaeus Merriam
Minnesota Gray Squirrel

Sciurus carolinensis hypophaeus Merriam, Science 7
    (167): 351, April 16, 1886.
Sciurus leucotis Lapham, p. 44, 1852; Lapham, p.
    339, 1853; Snyder, p. 119, 1902.
Sciurus niger Lapham, p. 339, 1853; Strong, p. 439,
    1883.
Sciurus migratorius Strong, p. 439, 1883.
Sciurus hypophaeus Snyder, p. 119, 1902.
Sciurus carolinensis hypophaeus Jackson, p. 15, 1908;
    Hollister, p. 23, 1910.
Sciurus carolinensis leucotis Jackson, p. 14, 1908;
    Hollister, p. 23, 1910; Jackson, p. 86, 1910; Cory,
    p. 116, 1912; Schmidt, p. 110, 1931; Komarek, p.
    206, 1932; Barger, p. 11, 1952.

Vernacular names.—In Wisconsin usually called
gray squirrel. Other names include *ah-ji-duh-mo*
(i.e. tail in the air, Chippewa), black squirrel
(for black color phase), bushy tail, cat squirrel,
dark-bellied squirrel, Merriam's gray squirrel,
Merriam's squirrel, migrating squirrel, northern
gray squirrel, stump ear, and timber squirrel.

Identification marks.—A rather large tree squirrel, 18 to 21.3 inches in total length, of which
8.5 to nearly 10 inches is the bushy well-haired
tail; ears prominent, rising well above the occiput, tapering at the apex, about one inch base to
tip, the inside dusky brown (not ochraceous or
orange, as in *Sciurus niger rufiventer*); no cheek
pouches; plainly colored with no distinct stripes
or spots, general tone dark gray above, often a

small median streak of whitish on belly, frequently under parts entirely dusky brownish; fur dense
and moderately soft.

The color is variable both in summer and winter, particularly the extent of the white on the
under parts. Some animals, particularly in summer pelage, are dark with a brownish gray tinge
over the entire under parts, a color variation apparently not always directly associated with melanistic or albinistic mutants. In winter the upper
parts are iron gray mixed slightly with fulvous
and heavily frosted with white hair-tips; color of
upper parts encroaching more or less onto under
parts, usually leaving a small median streak of
white on the belly and sometimes white on the
throat, or throat and chest sometimes yellowish
brown (possibly in some cases from nut stain);
tail buffy at base of hairs, next a broad band of
black, tipped with white, in effect producing in
superior view a dark buffy gray tail bordered
slightly with white; whitish tufts of fur behind
ears prominent in full winter pelage; eye ring
dirty white. In summer pelage the color tone is
slightly darker and more fulvous, the white of
the under parts may become a grayish tone
mixed or washed with fulvous; distinct wash of
fulvous along each flank; ears are brownish gray

Minnesota gray squirrel.

Bom

Left hind foot of gray squirrel. Specimen from St. Croix Falls, Wisconsin. 1×.

without tufts; the entire color change from winter to summer is apparently caused by wear and stain of the winter fur. There appears to be one molt annually which may begin in some instances by the middle of March, but usually in April, and possibly in breeding females not until late in June or early in July. Winter pelage is usually acquired by the middle of September, but the fur is not in winter fullness until October or November. Molting begins on top of the head and proceeds gradually rearward and downward, but often in late stages the fur over the entire body appears to be shedding and renewing at once.

The skull is moderately long and broad—more than 58 mm. and less than 67 mm. long, and between 33 mm. and 36 mm. broad; brain case high anteriorly, rounded to considerable depression posteriorly; frontals rather high posteriorly, depressed and somewhat flattened anteriorly; least interorbital constriction broad, 17.5 mm. to 21 mm., rostrum somewhat short, only slightly narrowed anteriorly; nasals somewhat narrow, rather short, and not extending backward to extreme posterior border of premaxillae, thus the latter bones forming an anteriorly convex suture outline with the frontals; upper molariform teeth

five on each side, the first one (upper third premolar) minute and inconspicuous, the second (upper fourth premolar) triangular and well developed, the third to the fifth (upper first, second, and third molars) near quadrate; incisors long and moderately heavy, the frontal surface deep orange in color.

There is no apparent sexual variation in size or color. Young in first pelage appear to average somewhat paler and more grayish than adults. There is individual variation in size of more than 7 per cent from a normal average in total length and length of skull. Considerable color variation occurs, particularly in the extent of encroachment of the dark of the upper parts on the under parts and the variation in the intensity of the darkness. It was primarily because of this encroachment of the color of the back and sides upon the belly that Merriam (1886 b) was prompted to name the race *hypophaeus*, from the Greek meaning "below, black."

In many Wisconsin localities, gray squirrels with dark under parts occur along with those having comparatively white under parts, in some localities one type predominating, in other localities the other type, and in many others only one color phase appears usually to occur, particularly if it is the white-bellied form. The proportion of dark-bellied squirrels appears to be higher in the northwestern part of the state than in the southeastern. Based on available summer specimens, Racine County shows 18 white bellied and 4 dark bellied; Walworth County, 8 white and 3 dark; Columbia County, 7 white and 2 dark; Sauk County, 5 white and 7 dark; Camp Douglas, Juneau County, 1 white and 10 dark; Buffalo County, 2 white and 8 dark; Maiden Rock, Pierce County, 4 white and 14 dark; Prescott (only 28 miles northwest of Maiden Rock in Pierce County), 8 white and 2 dark. A series of 7 that I collected at Long Lake, Washburn County, August 5 to 8, 1918, were divided 3 white and 4 dark, and the two color phases were found mated August 6 in male No. 228,945 (white) and female No. 228,946 (dark), Biological Surveys Collection, National Museum.

This tendency towards excessive dichromatism in *S. c. hypophaeus* is a very unsatisfactory and unreliable characteristic by which to separate the subspecies from the northeastern gray squirrel *Sciurus carolinensis pennsylvanicus* Ord (formerly called *Sciurus carolinensis leucotis* Gapper by many authors), as is also the slightly larger average size of *hypophaeus*. Distinctive color differences between the two in both winter and summer pelages heretofore not appreciated or overlooked are the generally darker upper parts of *hypophaeus;* the darker tail, particularly noticeable in the shorter white tips to the individual hairs and thus producing a much less frosted tail; the base of tail hairs much more grayish and less tawny or cinnamon; the brown tinge on the flanks darker and less ochraceous, the cheeks, temporal region, and ears brownish gray, often in winter distinctly iron gray, never yellowish ferruginous or ochraceous as in *S. c. pennsylvanicus.*

During the past century the black color phase of *S. c. hypophaeus* was often reported as frequent or even abundant in many Wisconsin localities, but as pointed out by Schorger (1949 b: 209), "Today the black squirrel is very rare south of Baraboo and Reedsburg. North of the latitude of these places it is nowhere abundant, but may be considered fairly common locally." Many of these black squirrels are jet black and apparently purely melanistic, but others are blackish in general appearance from the dark under parts and abundant black hairs mixed with the gray ones over the body. Both black squirrels and normal gray squirrels may occur in the same litter. Speculation has been rife as to why the black phase becomes rare or entirely disappears with increased human population, but it might be explained by the fact that the black squirrel is a more conspicuous target than the gray squirrel, and is more sought by the hunter.

A white phase or possibly in some cases a pure albino is sometimes reported, and "appears to occur most frequently in regions where there is melanism" (Schorger, 1949 b: 204). The white phase of *Sciurus carolinensis* has become temporarily dominant at a very few localities. A pair of these squirrels, one cream colored, the other white, was taken to Olney, Illinois, where there were no gray squirrels in 1902, turned loose in the park, protected, and fed. This pair became the ancestors of a population estimated at 650 in 1950. A small colony of white phase gray squirrels existed from 1875 to 1880 in southwestern Waupaca County, Wisconsin (Carr, 1890).

The Minnesota gray squirrel is somewhat small-

White mutant gray squirrels at Olney, Illinois. Courtesy Ernst Z. Bower.

er than the western fox squirrel, the largest individuals of the former being about the size of the average of the latter; the under parts are never bright orange fulvous as in the fox squirrel; the tips of the hairs of the tail are white, not orange; the skull, nearly the size of that of the fox squirrel, has five molariform teeth on each side of the upper jaw, the anterior one a tiny peg always absent in the fox squirrel. I have never seen an adult gray squirrel from Wisconsin that did not have this minute upper cheek tooth, though in some regions (Michigan, Missouri) it has been reported absent in 1 per cent or less of the skulls. Its color and larger size readily separate it from the red squirrel (*S. hudsonicus*).

In color sometimes very superficially similar to Franklin's ground squirrel, but never with the mottled or flecked coloration on its back; tail always longer and bushier; ears higher; different cranially, the interorbital breadth always more than 16 mm.

Measurements.—Total length of adults, 460 to 540 mm. (18.1 to 21.3 inches); tail, 217 to 252 mm. (8.5 to 9.9 inches); hind foot, 68 to 74 mm. (2.7 to 2.9 inches). Weight of adult from about 16 to 28 oz. Skull length, 60.8 to 66.5 mm.; width, 33 to 36 mm.

Distribution in Wisconsin.—Most of the state in favorable habitats, but less frequent in the extreme northern part.

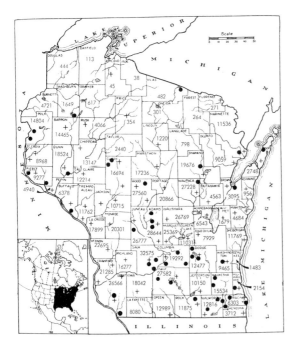

Map 31. Distribution of SCIURUS CAROLINENSIS. ● = *specimens examined.* + = *authentic records before 1900. Figures are estimated kill by counties, 1955-56.*

Habitat.—Hardwood forests, or occasionally mixed coniferous-hardwood forests, particularly those with nut-bearing trees, and preferably those with bushy undergrowth and in river bottoms, near water courses or lakes, or bluffs or slopes along such waters; sometimes in small woodlots

or along wooded fence rows; frequently seen in wooded parks and residential sections of cities and villages.

Status and Habits.—The gray squirrel has probably occurred in all counties of the state during the past century, but it has frequently shifted in local populations, and is without doubt now much more plentiful in the northern counties than at any time during the nineteenth century. "The increase northward has been induced by agriculture and the replacement of conifers by hardwoods" (Schorger: 1949 b: 204). Yet a hundred years ago there were undoubtedly very many more gray squirrels in the state as a whole than now because of the vast deciduous forests covering more than half the area of the state and the reportedly dense populations of gray squirrels in many areas. About 1852 to 1856 at some localities they were mentioned as "thousands of squirrels" and "woods full of squirrels" (in 1856 at Jefferson and Green Bay, and at Milwaukee and Neenah, *vide* Schorger, 1949 b: 228). Gray squirrel populations at that time, and even today, are believed by some to have intensity cycles of about once in five years, Their numbers fluctuate considerably, whether cyclic or not.

During the years 1901 and 1902 gray squirrels became so scarce throughout most of the northeastern United States that there was concern that this species and the fox squirrel might be exterminated. The naturalists G. O. Shields, David S. Jordan, Ernest T. Seton, and W. T. Hornaday went so far as to suggest a completely closed season on squirrels throughout their range. Times have changed. Based on an estimated kill of 795,452 during the 1955-56 season (Wisconsin Conservation Department, Activities Progress Rept. No. 86, p. 11, May, 1956) there possibly were three to four million gray squirrels in Wisconsin at the beginning of the 1955 hunting season. Although the gray squirrel may travel individually or in groups distances of four miles or more in search of food, its usual home range is small, generally within one thousand feet of its nest, and often less than four or five hundred feet. It becomes quite fixed to its homesite, and ear-tagged individuals released more than a mile from the place at which they were trapped have been retrapped within a few feet of the spot where first captured within one to four days. Populations of 20 or more to an acre of woodland may occur, but a more common number is about one pair to an acre.

Indications of the presence of this squirrel may often be confused with those of the fox squirrel, because tracks and other signs are quite similar. One can depend sometimes upon the habitat: if one finds gnawed nut or acorn shells, fallen branch tips, particularly of oaks, fresh claw marks on trees, or nesting holes or open leaf nests in trees, he may readily suspect that a gray squirrel is nearby, particularly if it is in a heavily wooded area. Sometimes the squirrel may utter a scolding bark, or be heard as it climbs a tree, and thus be located. More often the best chance of seeing it is to wait quietly and look and listen.

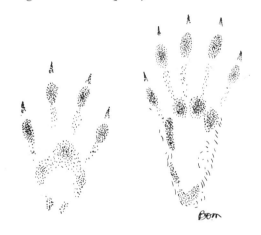

Tracks of gray squirrel. Left, right fore foot track. Right, right hind foot track. 1×.

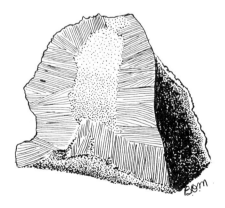

Gnawing of gray squirrel on leg bone of beef.

The gray squirrel is adept at hiding behind a tree trunk or limb, often peeking out with only its head visible, yet sooner or later its curiosity gets the best of it, and it begins to examine the intruder. In winter snow its tracks may be conspicuous, often in paths leading to or from nests and favored feeding spots. Scats, while more or less distinctive, are seldom found in the forests, except, sometimes, beneath a nesting tree.

It is strictly diurnal, and its most active period seems to be late in the afternoon to early in the evening, from about three hours to less than one hour before sundown. It is frequently out at dawn, and may sometimes be active all day, particularly during its nut-harvesting time and in winter. It dislikes rainy or too cold weather, though it is often out on cloudy days. It is active all winter, though during cold or stormy weather may remain snug in its nest for three or four days at a time until hunger or curiosity drives it forth. For its winter home it prefers a hollow tree or similar protection from the weather, and sometimes several squirrels may occupy the same cavity. At other times scarcity of such tree cavities may force it to an open nest. In northwestern Rusk County, "when the winter is very cold and snowy the gray squirrels burrow long tunnels under snow spending the cold season under the roots of the trees, hollow stumps and other underground shelters. Where food is available a number of them congregate in a small space, and the snow is undermined with tunnels over a considerable area" (Francis Zirrer, in letter to author, March 15, 1942). It does not become dormant, but often sleeps soundly, though sometimes it may be aroused enough to peek from its nest by a few sharp raps on the trunk of the nesting tree. With continued rapping it generally retires deep into its nest, though at other times it may leave.

Feces of gray squirrel. Drawn by Mrs. MacMaugh from rough sketch by the author. 1×.

Gray squirrels emigrate from time to time, sometimes in more or less of a mass movement, at other times singly or in small groups, yet always apparently in the same general direction. The maximum distance covered in such an emigration is unknown, but it probably never is more than a few miles. It has been said that in some places along the Mississippi River the squirrels in the spring swim across the river from the Wisconsin shore and that they return from the Minnesota to the Wisconsin side in the fall. An extensive emigration is not likely while the squirrels are breeding, and most such movements are in the fall. The governing factor that starts the emigration impulse is probably lessened food supply, which is usually the result of weather conditions or overpopulation. Schorger (1949 b; 227-34) has recorded emigrations in Wisconsin in 1842, 1847, 1852, 1855, 1856, 1857, 1866, 1871, 1873, 1878 (movement over much of the state), 1883 ("last year of great abundance and extensive movement"), 1888, 1895, 1897, 1903, 1905, 1907, 1914, 1925, and 1946. An emigration of gray squirrels not yet recorded occurred at Lake Chetek, Barron County, during the last 20 days of September, 1935. This information has been furnished by A. R. Webb, Whitehall, (letter to the author, October 23, 1935), who saw only single voyagers, no pairs or flocks, swimming across Lake Chetek from the north shore to the south shore, a distance of a quarter to a half mile. One afternoon he saw "at least dozen single squirrels crossing." Food on the south shore appeared no more plentiful than on the north shore. In small inlets and bays, Webb saw at least 20 carcasses of drowned squirrels, and reasoned that waves and winds exhausted them before they could swim across. All of them "seemed perfectly healthy; fat, sleek, full tailed." On a return visit in October, Webb saw no gray squirrels.

Its gait when it forages or seeks nuts that it has buried is most frequently an ambling walk, hither and thither, the animal sniffing the ground as it progresses. Often it hops short distances when foraging, and hops to and from its feeding places, frequently stopping to sniff or investigate some object. When alarmed or pursued its best speed is about 20 miles an hour, made in a leaping run, each leap covering three to five feet. In deep loose snow it is slow and clumsy and can often be caught by hand. It is an excellent climber, ascending to the top of an 80-foot tree in less than 20 seconds. It jumps from limb to limb and tree to tree, lies flat concealed on top of a limb, or sits pertly upright thereon, hangs by the hind claws head downward as it peeks from behind a tree trunk, and descends head down almost as rapidly as it ascends. It often lies flat on its abdomen on a limb or on the ground, not only for concealment but as a means of keeping cool in hot weather. One in a tamarack tree near Dousman, Waukesha County, July 24, 1922, jumped from a limb about 12 feet high and, feet spread flying-squirrel fashion, sailed directly over my head and landed fully 18 feet from the base of the tree. It swims well for distances of up to about two miles in quiet water, riding the surface with the head and rump out of water and the tail floating behind, paddling with all four feet. Its swimming often ends in drowning when attempted in rough water. Though disliking rainy weather, it has no aversion to entering water for a drink or to swim to some chosen spot.

The gray squirrel goes about its affairs rather quietly until disturbed by any noise or intrusion not to its liking, when it utters its harsh warning call, often termed a "bark," that continues as long as the individual is disturbed. Sometimes there is no intruder, the squirrel apparently "barking" merely to vent its pleasure or displeasure. Eyes alert and tail vibrant with a flip for each note, it utters a gutteral *qwa-ak, qwa-ak, qwa-ak, qwa-ak, qwa-ak, ak-ak-ak-ak-ak-ak-ak-ak-ak*, often repeated many times. If its displeasure is intensified it may quicken and intensify its barking, probably at the same time changing its location. Slight annoyances such as someone holding tightly to food offered it, patting it lightly with a stick while it is in its nest, or suddenly clapping one's hands near it, will often cause it to utter a short bark, sometimes of only two or three notes. Young ones from a week to two months old when disturbed utter a loud sharp squeak that can be heard 50 or more feet away. Its tail not only indicates excitement, but also is used as a "wig-wag" signal, and is employed as a balancer when the animal is climbing and jumping, as a cover under and behind which the animal feels it is hiding, as a shield from rain, sun, wind, and cold, and as a float when it is swimming.

It is timid and alert in its wild home, but when habitually around friendly people as in public parks, villages, or city suburbs it soon becomes friendly and will take food from a hand or even hop upon a knee. It is very playful with its kinsfolk, particularly the young of the year, with each other and with their mother. Though friendly and playful, the gray squirrel nevertheless is irritable and pugnacious, and quickly resents any infringement on its assumed rights by dashing at the perpetrator with ugly "barking" and attacks with claws and teeth. Some 20 years ago in Chevy Chase, Maryland, I so tamed a wild gray squirrel that it would sit up in front of me and eat from my right hand while simultaneously our huge cat sat two feet away from it eating from my left hand, a frequent occurrence for about two months. One day both had apparently had their fill, the cat having started quietly toward the house, when savagely and without warning the squirrel jumped on the cat's back and began pummelling and clawing the cat, the meantime "barking" furiously. The cat rolled over on its back to be rid of its tormentor and went on its way stoically, but never would eat with a squirrel again. The gray squirrel makes an interesting and friendly pet, yet before two years old may show flashes of its quick temper.

Its senses of touch, sight, hearing, smell, and taste are all well developed, the animal depending particularly upon smell and hearing in many of its activities. Its normal longevity in the wild is probably less than five years. Its potential longevity is about twelve years.

The gray squirrel breeds when one year old, the young females of the spring litter breeding late the following winter, but young of later litters usually do not breed until the second winter. Mating is promiscuous, and males often fight fiercely among themselves for the attention of a female. A female in its first year usually has only one litter, but two litters a year is usual after she is two years old. The early mating in Wisconsin occurs during February, sometimes during the latter half of January, and a second mating frequently occurs during June, sometimes about the last of May. The young are two to five in number, usually four and often only three, and are born after a gestation period of 40 days, or the last of March or first of April for the first litter, and the latter part of July or first of August for the second litter. The gray squirrel weighs about 15 grams (one-half ounce) at birth, and

is naked and pinkish in color; its eyes and ears are closed, and its head and feet are proportionally large. Growth is slow during early life. The ears open after about 28 days, and the eyes after about 32 days. Some 10 days after its eyes open, or when it is about six weeks old, it is well covered with hair. When two months old it has been weaned and is about half grown, and the hair is furry and the tail bushy. The spring litter usually stays with the mother until she has a second litter, and individually may seek new quarters or stay in the old nest, the mother building a new home. The second litter during its first winter often remains with its mother. A young squirrel is not an expert nest builder, and often has trouble until it gains experience. It drops twigs and branches before it properly places them, and when the nest is finally completed it often tumbles to the ground because of poor placement. A mother gray squirrel is attentive to its young ones, and if its nest is too much disturbed will move its family one by one to a new nest. To carry its offspring the mother grasps it with its teeth by the lower chest, the baby curling around the parent's head. The mammae are eight, four pectoral, two abdominal, two inguinal.

For its winter home it seems to prefer the hollow trunk of a tree where, protected from bad weather, it builds a cozy nest of bark and plant fibers. Often it uses such a cavity in which to rear its young. At other times, it builds a large nest of leaves and tips of branches in a crotch or among the branches of a tree, especially the juvenile. The leaf nest is a ball-like rainproof house with a nesting room in the center. The squirrel enters through an inconspicuous hole in the side. Leaf nests are seldom lower than 25 feet above ground. Sometimes the leaf nest is constructed upon an old nest, or upon an abandoned hawk's or crow's nest. Rarely, a nest is used for several years, the meantime occasionally being repaired or relined. More often the nest is abandoned after a year or two. It may be clean and without strong odor or trace of feces, yet an occupied nest soon becomes vile with fleas, lice, and mites. Leaf nests may be constructed at any season when needed by a squirrel, but the peak of activity in nest building by the young squirrel is shortly after it leaves the home nest. This peak is usually from June to October. In Wisconsin a great many more gray squirrels live in open leaf nests than in hollow trees, probably not always from choice but because hollow trees are sometimes scarce and are often occupied by other animals such as the raccoon, opossum, or barred owl.

Its chief food is vegetative and consists of many kinds of nuts, including acorns; seeds; fruits, particularly seedy fruits of trees such as of the maple, elm, hornbeam, hackberry, arrow-wood and other species of Viburnum, cherry, mulberry, and thorn apple; buds, particularly of maple, elm, and oak; fungi; inner bark and sap, particularly of maple and elm; occasionally corn and other grains (eating only the germinal part and discarding the remainder); sometimes underground fleshy parts of plants. It eats a small amount of animal food such as insects, including weevils, caterpillars, and insect galls, and certain individual squirrels may plunder a bird's nest for the eggs or young birds. The robin, wood thrush, and red-eyed vireo seem to be particularly vulnerable to raiding by the gray squirrel in Wisconsin. It gnaws bones to wear its incisors, and possibly also to procure mineral food. It will return many times to the same bone over a period of several weeks, and sometimes hides a bone at the base of a tree or in a hollow limb (Allan, 1935).

It is wasteful in feeding, often dropping and discarding considerable portions of apparently good food. It stores nuts for future use by burying them shallowly in the soil in scattered spots throughout its home range, seldom placing more than one nut in a digging, and never more than two or three. Frequently during an autumn of a good crop of acorns or other nuts a single squirrel may bury several hundred. During winter it often burrows in the snow to hide surplus food. When the squirrel needs food it wanders over its storage plot, sniffing here and there, until its acute sense of smell enables it to locate a hidden store. The squirrel finds only part of the nuts it has stored, and often another squirrel also fares on the storage. Nuts that are not discovered are well planted, and in the spring usually germinate and grow, frequently into trees. The gray squirrel drinks a great deal of water, which when not directly obtainable it may acquire from tree sap or green vegetation. Though it seldom avoids water, it

does not regularly bathe in it but prefers to keep itself clean by dust or sand baths.

The gray squirrel is not frequently killed by natural enemies because of its alertness and ability to escape, and its diurnal and arboreal habits. The red fox, gray fox, coyote, and bobcat sometimes catch one, as does the red-tailed hawk and the barred owl. A pickerel or a muskellunge sometimes captures one while it is swimming in a lake or river. A raccoon or an opossum may attempt to prey upon the young squirrels in the nest or in a hollow tree, but are usually dispersed by the mother squirrel. The red squirrel and the gray squirrel are always antagonistic to each other, the red usually the master but without seriously harming its gray cousin other than to drive it away. Yarns are told that the red squirrel deliberately emasculates the gray squirrel during combat, thus to reduce the gray squirrel increase! The myth, of course, is without credence.

Human activities other than legitimate hunting destroy the gray squirrels. The species is particularly vulnerable to forest fires. The illegal and dastardly practice of "smoking out" squirrels from a hollow tree has not only directly killed many squirrels not salvaged, but has also started many fires (Burke, 1954). Occasionally one is killed by short-circuiting electric wires as it climbs among them. The automobile kills a considerable number.

Many kinds of parasites infest the gray squirrel. External ones include the lice *Enderleinellus longiceps, Hoplopleura sciuricola,* and *Neohaematopinus sciurinus;* the mites *Sarcoptes scabiei* and *Euhaemogamasus ambulans;* the fleas *Orchopeas wickhami, Opisocrostis bruneri, Stenopenia americana, Conorhinopsylla stanfordi, Pulex irritans,* and *Echidnophaga gallinacea;* the chigger *Trombicula whartoni;* and the ticks *Haemolaelaps megaventralis, H. glasgowi,* and *Dermacentor variabilis.* Internal parasites include a few protozoans; two species of cestodes, *Hymenolepis diminuta* and *Cittelotaenia pectinata;* eight species of nematodes, *Ascaris lumbricoides, Bohmiella wilsoni, Capillaria americana, Citellinema bifurcatum, Heligmodendrium hassalli, Physaloptera sp., Rictularia halli,* and *Trichostrongyllus calcaratus;* and two horny-headed worms, *Moniliformis clarki* and *Macracanthorhynchus hirundinaceus.*

The most serious disease of the gray squirrel is

mange or scabies, caused by the mange mite which burrows into the skin causing scabs to form and the hair to fall out. Mange appears in squirrels every year but it seems to be most virulent during periods of dense population. Mange in its most severe form may entirely dehair a squirrel, in which case the animal will most surely die. In milder cases only a part of the hair is lost, but nevertheless the squirrel is weakened and subjected to wet, cold, and other hardships. Rabies is known to infect the gray squirrel at times, and a few cases of tularemia have been reported. Fibromas in the form of skin tumors have been diagnosed in gray squirrels from Maryland, New York, and other eastern states.

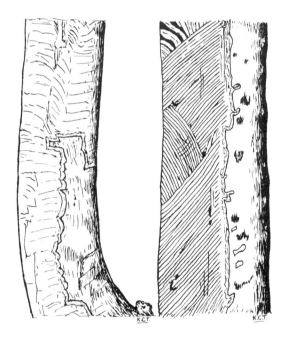

Gnawings of gray squirrel on maple (left) and of red squirrel on pin cherry. 1×.

Important as a game animal, attractive as a part of our forest wildlife, interesting as a feature of the city parks, friendly as a playfellow in our dooryard, and useful as a planter of nuts and seeds of forest trees, the gray squirrel may well be rated one of the most valuable of the Wisconsin mammals. As game it supplies sport to more people over a larger area of the state than any other mammal except the cottontail rabbit. It affords teenagers a commendable and healthful

outlet for their pent-up energy. It offers a potential meat supply in Wisconsin of about four hundred thousand pounds a year, and is exceeded in this among wild mammals of the state only by the deer, cottontail rabbit, snowshoe hare, and in some years the fox squirrel. It thrives in many public parks in the state, and has replaced or nearly replaced the fox squirrel in such places as Madison, Milton, Neenah, and other cities and towns where the fox squirrel was formerly the dominant squirrel. Probably in such cases the gray squirrel has not actually driven out the fox squirrel but has invaded its territory because of slight changes in environmental conditions. Where squirrels are desired it is well to provide nesting houses if sufficient hollows in trees are not available for them. A nesting box may be constructed from a nail keg or a hollow log, or by making it from one-inch lumber. Such a box, preferably made with a peaked roof, should contain about three cubic feet of space, should have an entrance hole about three inches in diameter located near the top, and should be placed at least 15 feet from the ground in a tree. Food and water often need to be supplied, and sometimes nesting material. Gray squirrels make interesting pets that can be kept in captivity in either large or small cages.

The American gray squirrel introduced into the British Isles, South Africa, and other areas has become a serious pest (Middleton, 1930; Bartholomew, 1933). In Wisconsin as a native forest animal, it seldom becomes a nuisance, except where plentiful in cities or towns. It may at times

A somewhat squirrel-proof bird feeder.

feed extensively on grain, particularly corn, when the field is near woodland. It may be destructive in a garden, not only by feeding upon particular vegetation, but even more by scratching and digging which kills plants and exposes bulbs and seeds. Occasionally a gray squirrel becomes a pest by occupying an attic, an area between walls, or some other space in a building. Rarely it may enter a house down a chimney. Birdwatchers frequently find it an annoyance around bird-feeding trays, where it may not only consume most of the food but also frighten the birds. Sometimes it gnaws an electric wire and causes a short circuit.

Control of gray squirrels in some local instances may be desirable. Squirrels should not be killed, trapped, or molested in conflict with state or local laws or regulations. If drastic control measures are necessary the local state game officer should be contacted. The best method of control for small numbers of squirrels is to live-trap the animals and release them in a woodland at least three miles away. Or they may be given to the management of a public park or an estate. Where dozens of the animals are feeding on corn near a woodland, shooting the squirrels with a small calibre rifle is most satisfactory. Squirrels may also be caught in choker rat traps. Nut meats are excellent trap bait. Squirrels may be driven from a house by use of napthalene flakes or paradichlorobenzene crystals (paracide by trade name) put liberally in the spaces occupied by the animals, and then securely closing all openings with half-inch to one-inch wire mesh. In small gardens use of paracide, tobacco dust, nicotine sulphate spray, or some of the commercial "dog scram" products will prevent considerable damage. A bird-feeding tray can be constructed squirrel proof by suspending it from a tree or placing it on a smooth iron post and having a sloping metal cover over it.

Specimens examined from Wisconsin.—Total number 217, as follows: *Adams County:* Adams Center, 1 (UWZ); Friendship, 1; Monroe Center, 1 (UWZ). *Brown County:* Green Bay, 1 (NPM). *Buffalo County:* Fountain City, 10 (8 MM). *Clark County:* Thorp, 1 (UWZ); Worden Township, 3 (2 AMNH; 1 UWZ). *Columbia County:* Fall River, 5 (MM); Okee, 1 (UWZ); Pardeeville, 9 (MM). *Dane County:* Madison, 4 (UWZ); Vermont, 1 (UWZ). *Dodge County:* Beaver Dam, 9 (UWZ); Fox Lake 3 (UWZ); Randolph, 2 (UWZ). *Door County:* Fish Creek, 4 (UWZ). *Dunn County:* Meridean, 2 (UWZ). *Grant*

County: Lancaster, 3 (MM); Rutledge, 3 (MM). *Jefferson County:* Palmyra, 5 (MM). *Juneau County:* Camp Douglas, 11 (10 AMNH; 1 CNHM). *Marinette County:* Peshtigo (near), 2 (UWZ). *Milwaukee County:* Wauwatosa, 1 (MM). *Pierce County:* Maiden Rock, 18 (MM); Prescott, 30 (MM). *Polk County:* Osceola, 4 (MM); Saint Croix Falls, 1. *Racine County:* Burlington, 10 (MM); No locality, 5 (MM); Racine, 6 (USNM); Rochester, 12 (MM). *Rock County:* Milton, 3 (1 MM; 2 UWZ). *Sauk County:* Devils Lake, 1; Sauk City, 6 (MM); Sumpter, 5 (MM). *Shawano County:* Keshena, 2 (CAS). *Vilas County:* Phelps, 2 (UWZ). *Walworth County:* Delavan, 6 (2 CAS; 1 MM); East Troy, 6 (MM); Honey Creek, 1 (MM). *Washburn County:* Long Lake, 7. *Washington County:* West Bend, 1 (MM). *Waukesha County:* Golden Lake, 1 (MM); No locality, 2 (MM); Oconomowoc, 3 (MM). *Waupaca County:* Clintonville, 1 (MM). *Wood County:* Auburndale, 1 (MM).

Selected references.—Brown, L. G., and L. E. Yeager, 1945; Middleton, A. D., 1930; Schorger, A. W., 1947; 1949 b; Seton, E. T., 1922; Zimmerman, F. R., 1939.

Sciurus niger rufiventer
Geoffroy-Saint-Hilaire
Western Fox Squirrel

Sciurus rufiventer Geoffroy-Saint-Hilaire, Catalogue des mammifères du Museum National d'Histoire Naturelle, Paris, p. 176, 1803.
Sciurus Vulpinus Lapham, p. 44, 1852.
Sciurus vulpinus Lapham, p. 339, 1853.
Sciurus Sayi Strong, p. 439, 1883.
Sciurus ludovicianus Snyder, p. 118, 1902.
Sciurus niger rufiventer Jackson, p. 16, 1908; Hollister, p. 23, 1910; Cory, p. 109, 1912; Schmidt, p. 110, 1931; Komarek, p. 206, 1932; Barger, p. 11, 1952.

Vernacular names.—In Wisconsin usually called fox squirrel. Other names include big red squirrel, hickory squirrel, *sinko* (Potawatomi), upper Mississippi Valley fox squirrel, and yellow-bellied squirrel.

Western fox squirrel in University Woods, Madison, Wisconsin.

Left hind foot of western fox squirrel. Specimen from Janesville, Wisconsin. 1×.

Identification marks.—The largest Wisconsin tree squirrel, 20 to 22.2 inches in total length, of which 8.6 to 10.4 inches is the well-haired tail; ears prominent, somewhat rounded at the apex, relatively broad basally, more than one inch base to tip, the inside ochraceous or near orange (not dusky brown as in *S. c. hypophaeus*); no distinct stripes or spots, but rather brightly colored in a general orange-fulvous tone, the back and sides much suffused with grayish, but the entire under parts, feet, and ears nearly clear orange fulvous, the cheeks nearly so, though sometimes suffused with tawny; fur dense and moderately soft.

Variation in color is only slight and consists chiefly in intensity of the fulvous, on the abdomen and cheeks, and in the degree of fulvous mixture and darkness on the upper parts. The under parts, particularly in the abdominal region and especially in worn winter pelage, sometimes pales almost to creamy orange. The intensity of the fulvous on the cheeks varies with an admixture of grayish tawny, which is never sufficient to hide the fulvous. The under side of the tail in all Wisconsin specimens I have examined has been clearly of orange fulvous tone. Winter color is

essentially like summer, except in a few cases where apparently wear of the pelage has produced a paler color to the under parts. One molt annually appears normal, which usually begins about April 10 to May 1, rarely earlier but occasionally later, and is generally completed by the middle or last of June. The hair continues growth the last of summer and early in autumn, and the winter pelage is longer and heavier than the summer.

The skull is comparatively large, between 62.5 and 70 mm. long, and between 35 and 40 mm. broad; brain case rather flat, shallow, somewhat broad posteriorly; frontals slightly elevated on posterior half; distinct interorbital notch; infraorbital foramen small; upper molariform teeth four on each side, one premolar and three molars, pm³ always absent.

There is no sexual variation, although in some series the females seem to average very slightly larger than the males. Young of the year in first pelage average somewhat paler than adults, and their orange and fulvous tones tend to be more creamy. Individual variation in size is about 8 per cent from normal in total length and length of skull. Mutants with black bellies rarely occur, though accounts would indicate that a century ago a fox squirrel with a black belly was not rare. I have seen no entirely black fox squirrel from Wisconsin. A specimen from Milwaukee in the Milwaukee Museum is blackish all over but a trifle flecked with yellowish hairs. Albinos are rare, the only entirely white specimen examined being one from North Lake, Waukesha County, in the Milwaukee Museum.

Measurements.—Total length of adults, 510 to 565 mm. (20 to 22.2 inches); tail, 218 to 265 mm. (8.6 to 10.4 inches); hind foot, 70 to 78 mm. (2.8 to 3.1 inches). Weight of adult from about 24 to 32 ounces, exceptionally heavy ones sometimes weighing to 38 ounces. Skull length, 62.5 to 70 mm.; width, 35 to 40 mm.

Distribution in Wisconsin.—Most of the state in favorable habitats; less common in the northern third; scarce north of latitude 46° N.; exceedingly rare or absent in Iron, Vilas, and Florence counties.

Habitat.—Prefers open hardwood woodlands and groves, particularly of hickory and oak, preferably in the higher rolling agricultural country; occasionally in sparse hardwood forests; less fre-

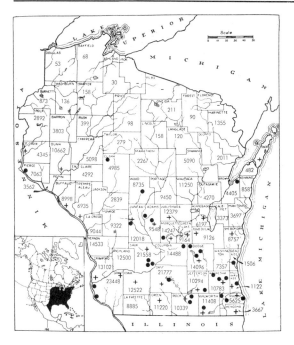

Map 32. Distribution of Sciurus niger. ● = *speci-mens examined.* + = *authentic records before 1900. Figures are estimated kill by counties, 1955-56.*

quently in hardwood timber along streams; occa-sionally in wooded city parks.

Status and Habits.—The fox squirrel has oc-curred in the more open oak and hickory groves of the southern third of the state since early set-tler days. Records for Racine and Milwaukee counties in 1836, Waushara County in 1850, Jef-ferson County in 1856, Winnebago County in 1859, Green County in 1869, Marquette County in 1877, and Trempealeau County in 1883, have been summarized (Schorger, 1949 b: 199–200). With agricultural advancement and increase of oak groves there has been a gradual extension of the range of this squirrel northward. Possibly some of this has been encouraged by artificial introductions, but in the main it has been natural. Abundance of individuals at a given locality may vary considerably from year to year. In most counties of the state it is less abundant than the gray squirrel, as it probably always has been. During the 1955–56 hunting season the estimated fox squirrel kill was 456,890 (Wisconsin Conser-vation Dept., Activities Progress Rept. No. 86, p. 11, May, 1956). Based upon this number there

probably were between two and two and one-half million fox squirrels in the state at the be-ginning of the 1955 hunting season. The fox squirrel not infrequently makes trips a half mile to a mile from its home. During food shortage some individuals may have a home range of 20 or more acres. Normally its home range is three or four acres. A high population density is about one fox squirrel to two acres. Long emigrations may occur late in summer or in autumn when a squirrel not infrequently travels 8 to 10 miles from its home, or rarely 15 or 20 miles, and does not return. Such emigrations usually involve the young of the year.

Tracks and other signs of the fox squirrel, though averaging larger than those of the gray squirrel, may easily be confused with those of the latter. Its barking or scolding note can sometimes be distinguished after one has learned the notes of both species by comparison. It is as a rule more easily seen than the gray squirrel, and is readily identified by its fulvous or orange coloring. It hides behind limbs and lies flat on top of them as does the gray squirrel, but its larger size and brighter color make it more conspicuous.

Even more strictly diurnal than the gray squir-rel, this species prefers clear days when the temperature is between 35° and 50° F. It is most active from 8 to 10 A.M., and again from 12 noon

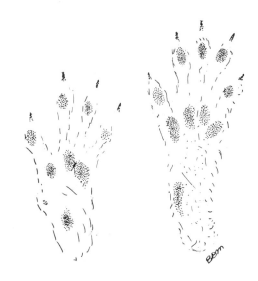

Tracks of fox squirrel. Left, right fore foot track. Right, right hind foot track. 1×.

to 3 P.M. The peak of activity seems to be from 9 to 10 A.M. Very few fox squirrels are active before eight in the morning or after five in the evening, even during the summer months of long daylight. It does not hibernate. During severe cold or stormy winter weather it spends long periods snug in its nest until hunger drives it to search for its hidden food. It seems to be less inclined to emigrate than the gray squirrel, though it often does so, either individually or in mass, often in company with gray squirrels.

Except when alarmed or irritated the fox squirrel is slow and sedate in its movements. When foraging it usually walks or progresses with short jumps or hops, sniffing here and there for hidden nuts or other food. Its maximum speed when galloping is about 18 miles an hour. It spends much time on the ground, and although a good climber it is more cumbersome in the tree tops and in jumping from tree to tree than the gray squirrel. It swims well for a mile or two in smooth water, but has more aversion to entering water than the gray squirrel.

The barking note of the fox squirrel is of lower pitch and more gutteral than that of the gray, and sometimes the two species can be identified by the difference. The call usually has fewer final short notes and ends in a drawn-out, shrill *qwa-a-a-a*. It sometimes utters a snarl when angry. A nestling young squirrel gives a sharp shriek when irritated. Its tail is employed to portray excitement and as a "wig-wag" signal, and has all the uses of that of the gray squirrel.

This squirrel is somewhat solitary in habits and does not tend to colonize. One or two pairs may occupy a small woodlot, and range possibly a mile to a woodlot occupied by other fox squirrels. Such intermingling is accepted in a friendly way, but does not result in groups or colonies. Sometimes in winter as many as four or five fox squir-

Feces of fox squirrel. Drawn by Mrs. MacMaugh from field sketch by author. 1×.

rels may occupy the same nest, particularly if in a hollow tree. In the wild the fox squirrel is less timid and alert than the gray squirrel. It adapts itself to city parks and suburban areas, but often fluctuates in numbers in such habitats and at times may be replaced by the gray species. It is improbable that in such instances the gray squirrel forcibly drives out the fox squirrel. More likely unfavorable food or other living conditions have forced out the fox squirrel, and the gray squirrel is a replacement.

It frequently has been said that the fox squirrel does not make a good pet. I have found that it makes an excellent one. When a boy in the 1890's I reared many from tiny hairless weaklings to old animals. Some of the babies were fed milk from a bottle or a spoon, while others I entrusted to a domestic cat to suckle and raise, after I had relieved her of some or all of her kittens. In the "University Woods" at Madison from the summer of 1908 to February, 1910, I frequently had different squirrels take food from my hand. Sometimes an old pet squirrel will bite a person quite severely, as did one that bit my nose, probably unintentionally, while it was trying to extract a piece of walnut from between my teeth. A pet squirrel seems to be more contented in a smaller cage than a huge one, but it should always be provided with a wheel on which it can run and exercise. Its normal longevity in the wild is probably less than four years. Its potential life span is about fifteen years.

It breeds when one year old; the yearling born in the spring breeds early the following spring. Young born late in the summer ordinarily do not breed until the second winter. A yearling female usually has only one litter; after she is two years old, two litters a year is the rule. Mating occurs in January and February, and again during the latter part of May and in June. The young are one to six in number, usually four, frequently three or five, and are born after a gestation period of 44 days. An instance of seven foetuses has been reported (Hoover, 1954). The youngster is naked at birth, with eyes and ears closed, and head and feet proportionally large. Its ears open after about 25 days, and its eyes after about 32 days. When two months old it ventures out of the nest and begins to climb around the tree, and a week or two later may scamper on the ground. It is dependent on its mother until three months old, and young ones born late in the season may stay in family groups for several weeks longer. The mammae are eight, two pectoral, four abdominal, two inguinal.

Although the fox squirrel sometimes makes its nest in a hollow tree, in Wisconsin it more frequently constructs a conspicuous nest of small branches and leaves in a crotch or on the branch of a tree some 30 or more feet above ground, even though hollow trees suitable for a nest are common. The nest is more or less globular in shape, made of sticks and leaves, and lined with shredded inner bark, leaves, and other fine material. The entrance on one side is about three inches in diameter. A nest made early in the spring, late in autumn, or in winter usually contains many more sticks and less leaves than one made during the summer when foliage is lush. Smaller poorly built temporary nests or resting nests are often built, particularly for winter use. Frequently during winter, however, the fox squirrel will avail itself of a hollow tree for protection. It prefers an entrance hole just large enough to admit it to the cavity, and in order to maintain a proper size it frequently gnaws the border of the hole to remove new growth of the tree. It usually nests in an oak or a hickory. Preference seems to lean toward the oak, possibly because the smoother hard bark of the hickory makes it more difficult for the squirrel to climb. A nest in a barn in eastern Iowa has been described (Sherman, 1926).

The favorite food of the fox squirrel appears to be hickory nuts, although it eats many other kinds of nuts, particularly acorns, walnuts, and hazelnuts. Many kinds of wild fruits, buds, and seeds are also eaten, particularly during the spring and summer when nuts are not available. It stores nuts for winter use, burying individual nuts and acorns here and there over a wide area. Autumn is a busy time for the fox squirrel in gathering, burying, and hiding food for winter. It sometimes eats soft unripe corn or even ripe grain, but is usually too busy gathering nuts when the crop is good to bother with hard corn on the cob. Sometimes early in the spring it taps an elm or a maple by gnawing into it, and consumes the sap and tender inner bark. It catches a few insects, such as grasshoppers and cicadas. It seldom bothers birds or their nests or eggs. It eats little meat in the wild, yet fox squirrels

that I have had in captivity ate parts of the bodies of mice and other animals I had prepared for specimens, and particularly ate the brains ravenously.

Few natural enemies capture the fox squirrel, even though it often frequents open places and is not shy. Its habit of midday activity protects it from most nocturnal enemies. Both the great horned owl and the barred owl occasionally capture one, usually a youngster taken from its nest or near it. The red-tailed hawk and roughleg hawk also have been known to capture a fox squirrel. Both the dog and the house cat sometimes catch one, and these domestic mammals frequently chase and harass squirrels. A considerable number are run over by automobiles, and a few are killed by forest or brush fires.

External parasites that infest the fox squirrel include the lice *Enderleinellus longiceps* and

Nest of fox squirrel in young burr oak, Clear Lake, Rock County, Wisconsin. Photograph by author.

Neohaematopinus sciurinus; the mites *Euhaemogamasus ambulans* and *Sarcoptes scabei* (mange mite); the flea *Orchopeas wickhami;* the chigger *Trombicula whartoni;* and the ticks *Haemolaelaps megaventralis* and *Dermacentor variabilis.* Internal parasites include the protozoan *Eimeria sciurorum;* the cestode *Choanotaenia sciurola;* ten species of nematodes, of which *Bohmiella wilsoni, Enterobius sciuri, Heligmodendrium hassalli, Physaloptera massino,* and *Trichostrongylus calcaratus* have been found in Wisconsin; and one horny-headed worm, *Macracanthorhynchus hirundinaceus.*

As with the gray squirrel, scabies caused by the mange mite is the most serious of its diseases. The little understood shock disease may also occur, and rabies has been reported. Sometimes excessive growth of incisors from lack of hard objects upon which to gnaw may cause serious trouble and even death.

The fox squirrel rates high as a game animal that can be hunted in many parts of the state and by many people, both young and old. As a meat supply it has-the same potential as the gray squirrel, about four hundred thousand pounds annually. It is an interesting mammal in many city parks and residential streets. Though it has been stated that it does not make as interesting a pet as the gray squirrel, I have personally found it an excellent pet, and more tractable and less erratic than its gray cousin. It sometimes is troublesome in a garden, and often indulges too freely in soft unripe corn on the cob. Sometimes it damages trees by bark-stripping. It is less apt to be a pest around houses and barns than the gray squirrel, though it sometimes attempts to build a nest in a house or barn (Sherman, 1936). Methods of control are the same as for the gray squirrel.

Specimens examined from Wisconsin.—Total number 158, as follows: *Adams County:* Friendship, 1 (MM); Strongs' Prairie, 1 (UWZ). *Brown County:* Sauble Point, 1 (NPM). *Clark County:* Worden Township, 1 (AMNH). *Columbia County:* Cambria, 1 (UWZ). *Dane County:* Madison, 6 (UWZ). *Dodge County:* Beaver Dam, 59 (55 UWZ); Burnett, 2; Fox Lake, 1 (UWZ). *Grant County:* Cassville, 1 (UWZ); Wyalusing, 1 (MM). *Jefferson County:* Palmyra, 2 (UWZ). *Juneau County:* Camp Douglas, 1 (CNHM). *Marquette County:* Endeavor, 1. *Milwaukee County:* Milwaukee, 3 (2 MM; 1 USNM). *Ozaukee County:* Saukville, 1 (MM). *Pierce County:* Prescott, 1 (MM). *Racine County:* Honey Creek,

1 (MM); Racine, 3 (USNM); Rochester, 43 (MM). *Rock County:* Janesville, 6; Milton, 5 (1 CNHM; 4 UWZ); No locality, 1 (MM). *Sauk County:* Honey Creek, 1 (MM); No locality, 3 (MM); Prairie du Sac, 1 (UWZ); Sumpter, 1 (MM). *Walworth County:* Delavan, 2 (1 CAS). *Waukesha County:* Brookfield, 1 (MM); North Lake, 1 (MM); Pewaukee, 4 (UWZ). *Wood County:* Pittsville, 1 (MM).

Selected references.—Allen, D. L., 1942 b, 1944; Brown, L. G., and L. E. Yeager, 1945; Hicks, E. A., 1949; Schorger, A. W., 1949 b; Zimmerman, F. R., 1939.

Genus **Tamiasciurus** Trouessart
Red Squirrels

Dental formula:

$$I\frac{1-1}{1-1}, C\frac{0-0}{0-0}, P\frac{2-2}{1-1}, \text{ or } \frac{1-1}{1-1}, M\frac{3-3}{3-3}=22 \text{ or } 20.$$

Tamiasciurus hudsonicus minnesota (Allen)
Minnesota Red Squirrel

Sciurus hudsonicus minnesota Allen, Amer. Nat., 33 (392): 640, August, 1899.
Sciurus Hudsonicus Lapham, p. 44, 1852; Lapham, p. 339, 1853.
Sciurus Hudsonius Strong, p. 439, 1883.
Sciurus hudsonius loquax Snyder, p. 120, 1902.
Sciurus hudsonicus loquax Jackson, p. 16, 1908; Cory, p. 122, 1912; Schmidt, p. 110, 1931.
Sciurus hudsonicus minnesota Hollister, p. 138, 1909; Hollister, p. 23, 1910; Komarek, p. 206, 1932.
Tamiasciurus hudsonicus loquax Barger, p. 11, 1952.
Tamiasciurus hudsonicus minnesota Barger, p. 11, 1952.

Vernacular names.—In Wisconsin usually called red squirrel or chickaree. Other names include boomer, chatterbox or chatterer, common red squirrel, *gid-a-mon* (Chippewa), hackee, Hudson Bay squirrel, pine squirrel, tree hackee, and *zee-sin-ko* (Potawatomi).

Identification marks.—The smallest Wisconsin true tree squirrel (the flying squirrels excluded), 11.7 to 13.8 inches in total length, of which 4.7 to 6 inches is bushy tail; ears moderate size, but prominent, somewhat pointed, usually conspicuously tufted with fur in winter pelage, the inside ochraceous gray; the bright reddish surface of the tail, white eye ring, and white under parts, combined with its small size, distinguish it.

In summer pelage the upper parts and sides are in general tone snuff brown, the head slightly darker and grayer; a narrow black line about three inches long on the flank separates the upper parts from the white under parts; legs and feet tawny; tail above reddish brown, bordered

Young red squirrel eating cedar seeds. Courtesy A. Brooker Klugh.

Red squirrel holding a small piece of wood. Courtesy A. Brooker Klugh.

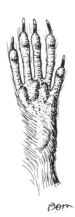

Left hind foot of red squirrel. Specimen from Rhinelander, Wisconsin. 1×.

with black and cinnamon buff; tail below smoke gray mixed with cinnamon, bordered with black tipped with cinnamon. In winter pelage much brighter color, the black lateral line lacking or barely present, and distinct fulvous ear tufts usually present; fulvous of back bright and concentrated into broad mid-dorsal stripe extending from frontal region to rump, the upper surface of tail being only slightly darker and less vivid; sides mixed buffy and fuscous, in general effect ochraceous gray slightly and finely flecked with fuscous; under parts whitish, without vermiculations but sometimes tinged with creamy white. There are two molts annually. The spring molt occurs in May or June, and is usually completed by the middle of the latter month. Winter fur may begin to appear as early as July 5 and 11 (young male and female, Rib Hill, Marathon County, 1918), but as a rule it does not begin until the middle of August or in September. By the middle of October, particularly in northern Wisconsin, most red squirrels have acquired full winter coat.

The skull is moderately broad, more than 44 mm. and less than 50 mm. long, and between 24 mm. and 29 mm. broad; superior outline of the skull is rather flat; zygomata only slightly expanded or arched, being nearly parallel to the axis of the skull; postorbital processes rather short for a squirrel; least interorbital constriction relatively broad, about 14 to 16 mm.; rostrum distinctly short, rather broad; anterior upper premolar (pm³) usually absent, and when present is minute and nonfunctional, and covered by the crown of pm⁴.

Although the red squirrel differs markedly from other Wisconsin tree squirrels in size and color, and differs little from them in cranial features, it is distinctly different in certain anatomical features, particularly in its reproductive organs.

This species differs much more fundamentally from the sciurid type, such as *S. carolinensis*, than any other studied. The striking differences in the male are: Minute Cowper's glands opening into the urethra in the bulb, no penile duct, no bulbar gland, a true urethral diverticulum in the bulb, a long filiform penis, and no os penis. The seminal vesicles are excessively large. Anal glands are present. The female also differs from other Sciuridae examined in having an unusually long coiled vagina during oestrous (Mossman, Lawlah, and Bradley, 1932: 119).

More recently Layne (1952: 457) reports that he found a minute baculum or os penis in *Tamiasciurus* collected in New York.

No sexual variation in size or color is evident. There is some individual variation in color both in summer and in winter pelage, which is mostly evident in intensity of coloration, probably often caused by fading of worn pelage. There is a variation of about 8 per cent from the average in total length of individuals from the same locality. Color mutations are infrequent. Melanism is extremely rare, and partly or completely white individuals are occasionally reported, though I have seen neither variation in a Wisconsin specimen.

After careful comparisons of many skins in both winter and summer pelages and of many skulls I conclude that all Wisconsin red squirrels are referable to *Tamiasciurus hudsonicus minnesota*, and none to *T. h. loquax*. The original description of *T. h. murii*, type locality Moorhead, Minnesota, published posthumously (Howell, 1943), includes only comparisons with *T. h. loquax* and does not mention *T. h. minnesota* of which it is a synonym. Characters there given as separating *murii* from *loquax* are in general the same as actually separate *minnesota* from *loquax*. The Minnesota red squirrel differs from the eastern *loquax* in its slightly larger size and particularly in its larger hind foot which averages about 10 per cent larger than in *loquax*. In both summer and winter pelages the red of the upper parts and tail is slightly paler and brighter in *minnesota* than in *loquax*, and, particularly in winter fur, the tops of the feet are much darker gray in *minnesota*.

Measurements.—Total length of adults, 297 to 350 mm. (10.9 to 13.8 inches); tail, 120 to 152 mm. (4.7 to 6 inches); hind foot, 46 to 54 mm. (1.8 to 2.1 inches). Weight of adult about 7 to 10 oz. Skull length, 44.3 to 48.4 mm.; width, 24.4 to 28.2 mm.

Distribution in Wisconsin.—In pioneer days probably found in favorable environment throughout the entire state, but possibly scarce or absent in southwestern Wisconsin from Rock County west to Grant County. Now found in suitable habitat throughout the northern two-thirds of the state from Vernon, northern Richland, Sauk, Marquette, Outagamie, and Brown counties northward to the state line; in southeastern Wisconsin in Jefferson, Washington, Ozaukee, Milwaukee, Waukesha, Racine, and Kenosha counties; northward along Lake Michigan to Door Peninsula and Washington Island. The red squirrel is now very rare in Winnebago County and the area extending southwesterly through Rock County to Grant County. It is said to occur in Iowa County, south of the Wisconsin River.

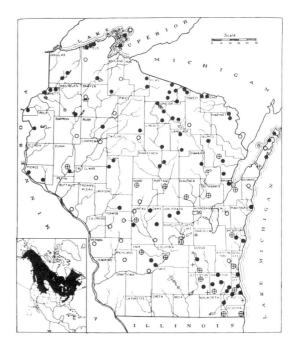

Map 33. *Distribution of* TAMIASCIURUS HUDSONICUS. ● = *specimens examined.* ○ = *authentic records since 1900.* + = *authentic records 1900 or before.*

Habitat.—Chiefly in coniferous forests or mixed forests of coniferous and deciduous trees; frequently in pure stands of deciduous trees, particularly if in wet terrain.

Status and Habits.—The red squirrel during the middle of the past century probably ranged throughout the state, except possibly that portion of southwestern Wisconsin from Dane and Rock counties west to the Mississippi River, from where we have no records. It became scarce south of the Fox River before the twentieth century and disappeared entirely from many parts of this region, though it is yet not uncommon locally towards Lake Michigan from Kenosha County northward. Though its population varies, in most parts of northern Wisconsin it is abundant, possibly even more so than in earlier days. As with many rodents, there appears to be a cycle of population, which in the case of the red squirrel seems to be of about eight to ten years. At a peak there may be four or five million red squirrels in the state. Under normal conditions the population in a favorable habitat will be about two to four squirrels per acre, though in cases of excessive abundance as many as ten or twelve adults may occupy a single acre of ground on a limited area. Its home range is rather limited, being usually within a radius of five or six hundred feet from the homesite, though in times of food shortage it may range three or four times that distance.

When one enters the domain of a red squirrel it almost always lets its presence be known by a scolding chatter, a display of its anger at the intrusion. One may possibly spy the squirrel perched on a limb stamping its feet and jerking its tail as it chatters. The faster and louder it chatters, the faster it stamps and jerks. If it suspects it is seen, it dodges to the far side of the tree, continues to chatter, and then likely hides or dashes away through the tree tops. It usually announces itself and is easily observed. One seldom has to depend upon finding its tracks or feces in order to detect its presence. Its storage piles of cones are always a tattletale sign.

The red squirrel is active all through the winter months, though it may become less so during the severest weather when it may stay in its nest for two or three days at a time. Very rarely, indeed, is it active at night, but between sunrise and sunset it is full of energy and life. Usually it rests during the early part of the afternoon, at which time it flattens itself on top of a limb or just squats down on a limb with its tail over its back. It does not migrate, and seldom emigrates any considerable distance to change its residence.

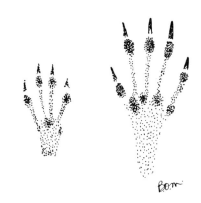

Tracks of red squirrel. Left, track of right fore foot. Right, track of right hind foot. 1×.

Although it is primarily arboreal, it is also at home on the ground. It is particularly agile among trees, and jumps from limb to limb and tree to tree with grace and ease, moving at such a rate of speed that at times the eye can barely follow the animal. It can hang by its claws from small twigs, and even a 40-mile-an-hour gale may not dislodge it from its fragile support. Its position, whether head down or head up, back down or back up, matters not to the animal. Distances of eight or ten feet are spanned in one of its leaps from tree to tree. As it lands, it grasps tiny twigs in its forepaws, and is on its way again. Rarely does it miss its hold and tumble to the ground. "George Bateman, manning the Flambeau tower, surprised a squirrel on his first trip up the tower this spring. The animal jumped a hundred feet to the ground and scampered away, apparently unhurt" (Clarence A. Winstrom, in Activities Progress Rept., Wisconsin Conserv. Dept., No. 45, p. 2, April 23, 1952). In traveling over ground, the red squirrel may walk, but ordinarily it progresses by a series of graceful bounds. In winter it frequently tunnels in the snow, leaving no trace of the tunnel on the surface except the entrances. Its maximum running speed is about 14 miles an hour.

The red squirrel swims well, and I have often seen it swimming in the lakes and rivers of northern Wisconsin. In August 13, 1906, I saw a red squirrel in North Pelican Lake, Oneida County, swimming from one point of land to another fully one-quarter-mile distant, and it was so skillful in swimming that at a distance I mistook it for a mink. I intercepted its route by pulling my canoe in front of the squirrel. Not to be daunted, it hopped on the canoe and ran along the gunwale towards its objective point, a tamarack grove. I quickly swerved the canoe around, when lo, the squirrel also reversed its direction on the boat and ran toward the opposite end, still bent on the forest beyond. Thus I swerved the canoe several times, and each time the squirrel stuck to its original destination, the tamaracks, until finally I felt I had tormented it enough and allowed it to jump off the end of the canoe and pursue its watery course (Jackson, 1932 a: 22). It swims with head well up, shoulders and foreback nearly submerged, and rump and tail high.

Sometimes the red squirrel communicates with another, its call then being a rolling *tcher-r-r-r-r-r-r*. This note is long continued and may last for five seconds or more, starting with a high pitch but lowering toward the end when it becomes slower and not so loud. Sometimes at the end of its call it uses its tail as a flash signal. It often utters a call note in early morning, a *kak-kak-kak*, repeated at intervals of 15 to 60 seconds, a note that seems not particularly loud at close range but has a carrying distance of fully one-quarter mile.

Although extremely agile and active most of its wakeful hours, it spends considerable time resting in a crotch or on a limb of a tree. One so active should require some rest. Sometimes it rests basking in the sun, particularly in winter and spring. Its senses are well developed. Its strong sense of touch is shown by the dexterity it displays in handling both large and small objects in its paws. Seldom does it drop anything it wants.

Adults play not only with the young, but also **with each other. In** the wild it is usually wary, but seldom becomes panicky. Its curiosity is intense. It must investigate every new object. "Surprise, fear, curiosity, attention, anger, contentment, all have their characteristic attitudes." (Klugh, 1927: 30; 1929: 521). Its normal longevity in the wild is probably near six or seven years. Its potential longevity is somewhat more than ten years.

The red squirrel is promiscuous in its mating, which begins about the middle of January and may continue until late in September, with two distinct breeding seasons. There are two peaks of mating, a spring one in March and a summer peak in July. Mating that takes place late in August or in September is apt to be by young born early in that year. The gestation period is about 38 days. The blind and naked baby squirrels first appear in the nest late in April, during May, or early in June. A second litter may appear late in August or in September. The number of young in a litter varies from two to seven, but usually is four or five. The pink, naked skin of the baby soon begins to show signs of downy fuzz growth, but the animal is a month old before it is covered with hair. A week or two later its eyes are open, it is one-third grown, and it leaves the nest for short periods of play. The mother still cares for it, and should her baby wander too far she grasps it between the forelegs with her mouth and carries it to safety, with the youngster entwining its legs and tail about the mother's neck. Sometimes the young ones take over the home nest and mother seeks new quarters while the youngsters learn to shift for themselves. More often the family group remains intact until the youngsters leave to care for themselves. The mammae are eight, four pectoral, two abdominal, and two inguinal.

In the dense coniferous forest when the red squirrel is common it usually makes its home in a nest that it builds in the branches of a tree, for in such regions hollow trees are scarce. In forests where there are hollow trees or woodpecker holes it takes advantage of them as a shelter for its home, and less frequently builds outside nests. One was observed carrying leaves for a nest into a hole about 30 feet up in a basswood tree on the bottomlands of Roche a Cri Creek near Friendship, Adams County, May 16, 1918. Rarely does a red squirrel nest in a hole in the ground or in a fallen log. Still less frequently does it nest in a building, though in June, 1922, a pair reared three young ones in the attic of the Antlers Hotel at Herbster, Bayfield County. When the nest is built in the branches of a tree it is usually placed near the trunk, about 5 to 10 feet from the top and 30 to 60 feet above ground. It is composed of twigs, leaves, and cones on the outside of the nest, with a thick lining of inner bark and other fine material on the inside. The single entrance is on the side. The whole is quite bulky and may be one and one-half to two feet through. When the nest is made in a hollow log or a woodpecker's hole the cavity is merely lined with fine plant material until it is snug and warm.

In the pine, spruce, and balsam regions one of the chief foods of the red squirrel is the seed of these trees, as well as of hemlocks, tamaracks, and white cedars, which it procures by tearing open the cones. Soft inner bark and buds, blossoms, and tender leaves of several kinds of trees, particularly maples, aspens, willows, and birches, are also consumed. Diseased bark of the pine tree found at the canker caused by blister rust is often gnawed and eaten. Also on its menu are wild and cultivated strawberries, wintergreen berries, blueberries, and wild red cherries. Hazelnuts are relished, and acorns and beechnuts are eaten. Fungi of several varieties are often consumed. Mushrooms are usually tucked away in the fork of a branch or behind a piece of bark, but may be hung from a branch, hidden in a stump, or buried in the ground. Not only does it store mushrooms, but it also gathers and stores quantities of cones, nuts, seeds, and other edibles. It does not store hard food items such as nuts and cones singly as do the gray and the fox squirrels, but places them in stumps, logs, hollow trees, or other convenient places, a central cache often containing a bushel or more of food. It may have one or several such storage places. Each squirrel selects some particular spot for a dining place, which it may use for many weeks. Litter and leavings accumulate in the spot, particularly when the squirrel is eating seeds from cones. Piles of cone scales and cores are frequently a foot high and several feet in diameter. The red squirrel accepts certain animal matter as food. It is known to feed upon insects and snails, and destroys numbers of scale insects. It is sometimes predatory upon birds and vertebrate animals, and has been known to destroy eggs and young of several species. It seldom attacks a mammal, but has been recorded as killing young of the cottontail and gray squirrel (Hamilton, 1934). It often drinks sap as a food from branches of trees. Water it frequently drinks from small pools or melted snow, and at times it even eats snow. After eating anything sticky, or after drinking, it licks its forefeet and rubs them repeatedly over its face and nose, often thus cleaning itself for several minutes.

Natural enemies seldom capture a red squirrel. The marten, in the days of its more frequent oc-

currence, was credited with being a chief enemy of this species. Nowadays very few are killed by any mammal. Among birds, the goshawk (Zirrer, 1947: 91) and red-tailed hawk occasionally capture one, and less frequently the Cooper's hawk. A very few are taken by barred and great horned owls. The pickerel and the muskellunge among fish not infrequently capture a red squirrel when it ventures to swim in their waters. The red squirrel is seldom molested by man, since it is not considered as game. Automobiles kill a few, but not as many as they do gray or fox squirrels. Forest fires may cause heavy mortality.

Among external parasites known to infest the red squirrel are three kinds of lice, one mite (*Euhaemogamasus horridus*), two fleas, two chiggers, and two ticks. A red squirrel (No. 226, 921 USNM) that I collected August 14, 1917, at Lakewood, Oconto County, had an enlarged female tick (*Ixodes hexagonus*) attached to its neck. Internal parasites that infest the red squirrel include one fluke (*Fibricola nana*), one tapeworm (*Andrya primordialis*), and six species of roundworms, among which *Citellinema bifurcatum* is a common parasite. Little is known about the diseases of the red squirrel, but it is probably subject to tularemia, and possibly to rabies. Its isolation from many other mammals might tend to keep it free from diseases.

As a food for human consumption or as an animal for sport hunting, except with a camera, the red squirrel has little value. Nor is its fur of any particular use to mankind. It is a forest dweller of beauty and vivacity that will not be driven from the earth by man's greed. About the only value it has is the enjoyment it gives us in watching it. It also helps forest growth by planting acorns, nuts, and seeds of forest trees. It eats large quantities of nuts and the seeds of evergreen trees, and competes somewhat with the gray squirrel and the fox squirrel for food. It does a little damage to trees by gnawing and peeling the bark. Locally it may become bothersome by making its home in the attic of a building. Bird lovers frequently make much ado over the damage that the red squirrel does to birds, especially by robbing birds' nests of eggs and young. No doubt such damage may occur at times. The number of birds destroyed, however, is probably greatly overestimated, and it is likely that only certain squirrels acquire the habit of robbing nests.

Specimens examined from Wisconsin.—Total 244, as follows: *Adams County:* Friendship, 2; Monroe Center, 1 (UWZ). *Ashland County:* Bear Lake, 1 (UWZ); Madeline Island, 1; Stockton Island, 1. *Bayfield County:* Herbster, 9; Namakagon Lake, 1; Orienta, 1; Port Wing, 2. *Brown County:* Bairds Creek, 1 (NPM): Duck Creek, 1 (NPM). *Burnett County:* Benson (Rush City Bridge), 5 (MM); Danbury, 5; Namakagon River (mouth of), 2 (MM); Yellow River (mouth of), 3 (MM). *Clark County:* Thorp, 1 (UWZ); Worden Township, 6 (4 AMNH; 2 UWZ). *Dodge County:* Beaver Dam, 11 (2 CNHM; 9 UWZ). *Door County:* Clarks Lake, 1; Detroit Harbor, 1 (MM); Ellison Bay, 1 (MM). *Douglas County:* Saint Croix Dam, 2 (MM); Solon Springs, 7 (CNHM). *Dunn County:* Meridean, 1. *Florence County:* Richardson Lake, 1 (UWZ); Sec. 26, T 40 N, R 16 E, 1 (UWZ). *Iron County:* Fisher Lake, 2 (UWZ); Mercer, 3 (MM). *Jackson County:* Millston, 1 (UWZ). *Jefferson County:* Hebron, 1. *Juneau County:* Camp Douglas, 28 (24 AMNH; 3 CNHM; 1 WHD). *Langlade County:* Antigo, 1 (UWZ); T 34 N, R 11 E, 6 (UWZ). *Lincoln County:* Merrill, 1 (UWZ). *Manitowoc County:* Point Branch State Forest, 1 (UWZ). *Marathon County:* Rib Hill, 6; Wausau, 1 (UWZ). *Marinette County:* Cataline, 14 (MM); No locality, 2 (MM); Pembine, 1 (MM). *Milwaukee County:* Fox Point, 1 (UWZ); Granville, 1 (MM); Milwaukee, 5 (MM); Oak Creek, 2 (UWZ). *Oconto County:* Kelley Brook, 1 (MM); Lakewood, 2; Morgan, 1 (NPM). *Oneida County:* Crescent Lake, 2 (1 UWZ); Moen Lake, 2 (UWZ); Rhinelander, 2 (1 UWZ); Tomahawk Lake, 1 (CNHM); Woodruff, 1 (CNHM). *Pierce County:* Maiden Rock, 7 (MM); Prescott, 1 (MM). *Polk County:* Nevers Dam, 1 (MM); St. Croix Falls, 4. *Price County:* Ogema, 4. *Racine County:* Rochester, 3 (2 MM; 1 UWZ). *Rusk County:* Ladysmith, 2 (UWZ). *Sauk County:* Prairie du Sac, 2 (MM); Sumpter, 1 (MM). *Shawano County:* Keshena, 3 (CAS). *Sheboygan County:* Elkhart Lake, 1; Sheboygan Falls, 1 (MM). *Vilas County:* Conover, 1 (MM); Eagle River, 2; Lac Vieux Desert, 3 (CNHM); Lake St. Germain, 2; Mamie Lake, 10; Phelps, 16 (UWZ); Robinson Lake, 1 (UWZ); Sayner, 2 (CNHM). *Washburn County:* Long Lake, 4. *Waukesha County:* Golden Lake, 1 (MM); Keesus Lake, 2 (MM); Muskego Lake, 2 (MM); New Berlin, 2 (MM); Pewaukee, 4 (UWZ). *Waushara County:* Hancock, 2 (UWZ); Wild Rose, 2.

Selected references.—Allen, J. A., 1898 a; Hatt, R. T., 1929; Jackson, H. H. T., 1932 a; Klugh, A. B., 1927, 1929; Layne, J. N., 1954; Mossman, H. W., 1940.

Genus **Glaucomys** Thomas
Flying Squirrels

Dental formula:

$$I \frac{1-1}{1-1}, \quad C \frac{0-0}{0-0}, \quad P \frac{2-2}{1-1}, \quad M \frac{3-3}{3-3} = 22.$$

Glaucomys volans volans (Linnaeus)
Southern Flying Squirrel

[Mus] volans Linnaeus, Systema naturae, ed. 10, vol. 1, p. 63, 1758.
Pteromys volucella Lapham, p. 44, 1852; Lapham, p. 339, 1853; Strong, p. 439, 1883.
Sciuropterus volans Snyder, p. 118, 1902; Jackson, p. 19, 1908; Hollister, p. 24, 1910; Cory, p. 102, 1912.
Glaucomys volans volans Barger, p. 11, 1952.

Vernacular names.—In Wisconsin usually called little flying squirrel, or in parts where the big species *sabrinus* is unknown, simply flying squirrel. Other names include asapan and assapanick (colonial), eastern flying squirrel, fairy diddle, glider squirrel, *sha-ka-skan-da-way* (Chippewa), small eastern flying squirrel, smaller American flying squirrel, and white-bellied flying squirrel.

Identification marks.—The two species of flying squirrels that occur in Wisconsin are both characterized by the presence of the flying membrane or fold of skin that extends along the flank from the fore limb (wrist) to the hind foot (ankle); the body is flat, and particularly so when the squirrel extends its legs and the skin attached to them; ears moderately large, particularly the auricular openings; eyes large, conspicuous, the lids edged black; plainly colored, with no distinct stripes or spots. The southern flying squirrel (*volans*) is 8.3 to 10 inches in total length, of which 3.2 to 4.3 inches is the flat softly furred tail; the fur is soft and dense.

In summer pelage the upper parts and sides are drab, overcast with pinkish cinnamon to snuff

Left hind foot of southern flying squirrel. Specimen from Elk River, Minnesota. 1×.

brown, the base of hairs slate-colored; sides of face gray, sometimes washed with pinkish buff; eye ring near fuscous; ears pale brown; under parts, including chin and suborbital region, white with a slight creamy tinge, the hairs white to the base; tail above similar to back but less overcast with pinkish, beneath light pinkish cinnamon; forefeet pale brownish gray; hind feet hair-brown; under parts of both fore and hind feet creamy white. Winter pelage similar to summer, but general tone of upper parts paler; feet paler, the toes and inner borders of the hind feet whitish. Apparently one complete molt occurs annually, usually beginning in September or early in October, and completed by the last of November. Winter fur is carried until March or later, but during spring and summer the winter pelage usually shows distinct signs of wear. The head, nape, and rump are the first parts to show signs of wear.

The skull is rounded and comparatively small, being less than 36, but more than 33.5 mm. long,

Southern flying squirrel, White River Refuge, Arkansas. U.S. Fish and Wildlife Service photograph by Peter J. Van Huizen.

and between 20 and 21.9 mm. broad; brain case depressed posteriorly; postorbital processes broad at base, tapering abruptly to a point; interorbital region decidedly longer than broad; rostrum short, sharply marked off from the broad interorbital region; nasals abruptly depressed at tip.

Males and females are essentially the same size, with no sexual color variation. There is slight individual variation, expressed mostly in paleness or darkness, or sometimes in the depth of a reddish cast. I have seen only one color variation that could be accepted as a mutation, that in specimen No. 3372, Milwaukee Public Museum, collected June 30, 1919, at Pewaukee, Waukesha County. This individual has pure white fur.

This species of flying squirrel can be distinguished from its relative *Glaucomys sabrinus* by the color of its under parts, the hairs of the breast and belly being white to the skin, whereas in *sabrinus* the hairs are plumbeous basally; the tail is much paler and more pale buffish below, not deep grayish buff and darker apically as in *sabrinus;* the feet are much paler above; *volans* is much smaller than *sabrinus*, shown particularly in the hind foot which is always less than 35

mm. long; skull of *volans* less than 36 mm. in greatest length, that of *sabrinus* 36 mm. or more in greatest length.

Measurements.—Total length of adults, 210 to 255 mm. (8.3 to 10 inches); tail, 81 to 110 mm. (3.2 to 4.3 inches); hind foot, 28 to 33 mm (1.1 to 1.3 inches). Weight of adult about 2.5 to 3.5 oz. Skull length, 33.5 to 35.6 mm.; width, 20 to 21.9 mm.

Distribution in Wisconsin.—Approximately the southern two-thirds of the state in suitable habitat, from about southern Polk County southeasterly to Outagamie and Manitowoc counties and south to the Illinois-Wisconsin boundary line.

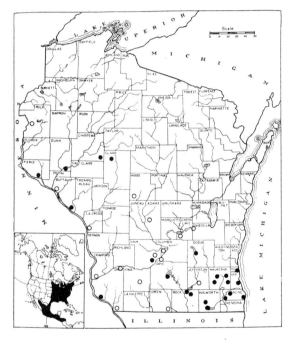

Map 34. Distribution of GLAUCOMYS VOLANS. ● = *specimens examined.* ○ = *authentic records.*

Habitat.—Forests and groves of deciduous trees, including old orchards; also woodlands of mixed hardwoods and conifers, particularly where hardwoods predominate.

Status and Habits.—Probably the southern flying squirrel is more plentiful within its range in Wisconsin than records indicate. Often its presence in a neighborhood is not suspected on account of its rather seclusive habits. Possibly, also,

its range extends farther northward in Wisconsin, particularly in the east, than records indicate. The general population of the species in the state has probably varied but little since the days of early settlers, except as brought about by a reduction in woodland area and particularly in old trees containing holes. It appears to be less common than either the fox squirrel or the gray squirrel. A considerable area of favorable habitat may average nearly two flying squirrels to an acre. Often it is less than two and seldom more. In cases of winter concentrations a single acre may have 20 or 30 individuals in one or two holes, with many bordering acres apparently void of the animals. It may range a radius of a mile or more in woodland from its homesite, though more often its range is within one thousand yards. A flying squirrel was trapped January 21, 1947, in the attic of Dr. J. T. Curtis, who lived a half mile from the University of Wisconsin Arboretum in Madison; it was marked by toe-clipping and released a half mile inside the Arboretum. Six days later the toe-clipped individual was again caught in the attic trap, a return distance of one mile in a straight line. "If we assume that the animal traveled through the trees, the distance would then be 1¾ miles and at one point it would have had to cross 250 yards of treeless terrain. If a straight line course was pursued, the treeless distance would be about ¼ mile" (McCabe, 1947 b).

It is not always easy to detect the presence of a flying squirrel in an area, though when it inhabits a building it may announce itself by its scampering or even by sailing into full view. It has been my experience that knocking heavily on the trunks of old trees that contain suitable cavities such as woodpecker holes, particularly during

Feces of southern flying squirrel. Drawn by Mrs. MacMaugh from field sketch by the author.

spring and summer, will dislodge any flying squirrel from the cavity, or at least cause it to peek from the hole to learn what is making the disturbance. One may sometimes locate a flying squirrel by listening in old woodland at night for the animal's chippering note and then observing its "eyes shine with a reddish-orange light when a flashlight is held in such a way as to reflect the light to the observer" (Sollberger, 1940: 284). One may also sometimes locate them at night by hearing them feeding in nut trees, or by finding hickory nut or acorn shells on the ground. Such nuts in most cases have been opened by a single nearly oval opening, though this is not always a sure sign. Traps to catch the animals alive may be baited with nut meats and placed on trees, or if the animal is needed lifeless a choker rat trap may be used. The flying squirrel, however, is protected in Wisconsin.

Although the flying squirrel may rarely be out and active on a cloudy day or shortly before sunset, it is one of the most strictly nocturnal of Wisconsin mammals. I have found that it rarely leaves its nest before the sun is well down, and does not become active in searching for food until dusk is well advanced. F. H. King (1883: 37) believed that there were two periods of activity in his captive flying squirrels, one beginning about 10:45 P.M. and the other about 3:30 A.M., each period lasting from an hour to an hour and a half. My experience both with captives and wild animals is that an individual is active all night. It is more active during summer and on temperate nights than during cold weather. In extremely cold weather, below freezing, it is essentially inactive. My observations indicate that under these conditions it is somewhat sleepy and sluggish, yet in no sense dormant. So far as known, it does not hibernate.

We call it flying squirrel, but it does not really fly. Its chief method of locomotion is by climbing high in a tree, then leaping with all legs extended and its patagium or lateral membrane outstretched, gliding in a descending curve towards another tree. At the end of its glide it swings sharply upward and lands head up on a neighboring tree. It climbs this tree to take another glide from near its top, and thus moves onward. The squirrel has considerable control of its gliding, and can not only quite accurately aim its course at the origin, but can make sharp turns

of nearly 90 degrees while it parachutes. Glides may be of any length from a few feet to as much as 150 feet or more. On the ground it runs awkwardly, seldom exceeds five miles an hour, and is easily overtaken by a running man. At best it swims poorly, if it does so at all.

Its mode of communication to its fellows usually is a weak chirp, sometimes almost a twitter, repeated often. When the squirrel is excited or alarmed it may intensify this note. At times, particularly when it is feeding, it utters a soft "*kuk-kuk,*" higher pitched, not so loud, and not so often repeated as the "*kok-kok-kok*" of the red squirrel, and, of course, heard chiefly at night. When an animal is irritated, distressed, or in pain it frequently utters a sharp shriek.

The southern flying squirrel is quite gregarious, particularly in winter. Possibly this may be on account of a shortage of warm retreats or in order for it to keep warm by the close contact of several individuals in a small space. Sometimes the same hollow is occupied by a small group for several successive winters. Eight to 15 animals is not unusual in such a wintering colony. In a hollow burr oak near Beaver Dam, Dodge County, in the winter of 1890, W. E. Snyder (1897 b) found 22 adult flying squirrels. It is generally friendly and easily tamed. Usually one disturbed in its nest or captured in the wild will make no attempt to bite if it is gently handled, and particularly if its captor talks low or hums to it. Sometimes it may be more pugnacious, or frightened, if handled too roughly, or held too tightly, and then it will bite. Its teeth can penetrate the bare skin or even pass through a thin glove and draw blood. It cannot bite through a thick leather or heavy canvas glove. Its nip may be bothersome and temporarily painful, but is unlikely to be serious. It plays and frolics a great deal, not only with its fellows but by itself. Thus it makes an interesting pet, though its nocturnal habits may make it difficult to observe and enjoy. In a cage it jumps and glides, but if supplied with a wheel it will spend many hours running thereon. Its senses of sight, hearing, and touch are very acute. Physically it is delicate and not tenacious. A slight wound, a little pressure on the body, or a light blow may kill it. Its normal longevity in the wild is probably less than five years. Its potential longevity is possibly near eight years.

Mating begins about the middle of February or during March for the first litter. Mating for a second litter usually occurs in June or July. The gestation period is about 40 days. I found three newly born young in a nest near Milton, Rock County, April 18, 1903. The young one is born blind, hairless, weighs about three or four grams, and is about two and one-half inches long. Data from Sollberger (1943: 66), who made a detailed study of the breeding habits of this species, indicate that the youngster doubles in weight by the end of its first week. At the end of six weeks its total length has tripled and its weight increased tenfold. At two weeks of age "the body, except for the abdomen, is almost completely clothed with hair." The eyes usually open at four weeks of age, and the body is then completely covered with hair. When the young one is two months old it is almost adult size in length, and has attained about two-thirds of its adult weight. Almost up to this time it has been nursed by its mother, though when six weeks old it forages a little for itself. The male takes no part in caring for the young. The number of young varies from two to six, three or four being the most frequent numbers, and three more often than four. The mammae are eight, two pectoral, four abdominal, two inguinal.

It usually makes its nest in a hole in a dead or decaying tree, sometimes only four or five feet from the ground, at other times high up. It seems to have little preference as to the kind of tree, though most nests are located in poplars, maples, or oaks, probably because these trees more frequently have cavities than some others. A cavity made by a woodpecker is preferred, but sometimes a natural cavity is chosen. The cavity must be large enough for the squirrel and its nesting material. The nest is composed of fine plant material, usually leaves and shredded bark, and is lined chiefly with finely shredded inner bark. Not infrequently it builds a nest in a loft or attic, or in a box put up for bird nesting. It may also sometimes make an outside nest in a tree, usually at an elevation of less than 20 feet. An open nest is an oval ball about 12 inches long and 8 or 10 inches in diameter, usually with bark strips and leaves on the outside and shredded bark interiorly. Larger nests occupied by a flying squirrel have been found, but the twig and leafy construction on the outside suggests an abandoned gray squirrel's nest has been utilized. Outside nests are extremely unusual in Wisconsin. They occur mostly in second growth or in areas where suitable cavities are not available. A flying squirrel, however, may occupy a loft or attic when many tall cavities are nearby. At Durward's Glen, Columbia County, about 1895, Dorward (1901: 70) says, "My nearest and most persistent squirrel neighbors—no less in fact than joint tenants with me of the building are the flying squirrels." The animal is very cleanly about its nest, and almost without exception goes several feet away to urinate or defecate. It apparently uses one place to deposit its stool for several days.

The food of the southern flying squirrel in the wild in Wisconsin consists chiefly of hickory nuts, beechnuts, black walnuts, acorns (especially of the white and burr oaks), seeds of hackberry, maple, and wild cherry, fruits of viburnum, grape, and apple (both wild and cultivated); buds and blossoms of several trees, particularly maple, and maple sap. It is also known to eat insects such as moths, beetles, and perhaps others. It sometimes eats young birds and birds' eggs. It holds its food in its forefeet when eating. It washes its face after eating by lapping it with its tongue and rubbing with its forefeet while sitting up. It stores a few nuts and acorns singly, slightly buried in the ground, and places many, along with seeds and fruit pits, in caches in hollow trees. In regard to its carnivorous trend, H. L. Stoddard (1920 a: 95) writes:

On April 6, 1914, an adult female flying squirrel (*Glaucomys volans*) was captured with her two young and placed in a roomy cage in the workshop with a section of tree trunk containing a flicker's hole as a nest. Two or three days later a fine male yellow-bellied sapsucker was captured unhurt, and placed in the same cage where he made himself at home on the stump. I was greatly surprised the next morning to find his bones on the bottom of the cage, picked clean. This strong, hardy woodpecker in perfect health had been killed and eaten during the few hours of darkness, by the old mother flying squirrel, though she had other food in abundance.

Partly on account of its nocturnal and arboreal habits the southern flying squirrel is molested by few natural predators. A prowling domestic cat will frequently catch one, and seems to be its chief mammalian enemy. The barred and the great horned owls kill one now and then. The automobile kill of this species is insignificant, nor does modern man hunt it for food or fur. Probably man lessens its numbers at times unwittingly by clearing away dead or "wolf" trees, and thus destroying nesting sites. A forest fire undoubtedly takes its toll.

External parasites known to infest the southern flying squirrel include three lice, *Hoplopleura trispinosa*, *Neohaematopinus sciuropteri*, and *Enderleinellus replicatus*; one mite, *Euhaemogamasus ambulans*; some eight or more kinds of fleas; and one chigger, *Trombicula microti*. Among internal parasites are three protozoans, *Eimeria glaucomydis*, *E. sciurorum*, and *Trypanosoma denysi*, and the roundworms *Capillaria americana*, *Citellinema bifurcatum*, *Enterobius sciuri*, and *Syphacia thompsoni*.

The southern flying squirrel is almost harmless so far as damaging crops is concerned. Sometimes it gathers enough nuts from a nut-tree orchard to become an economic factor in the failure of the crop. This is particularly the case with pecan and filbert nut groves. It does not damage farm crops in general. Occasionally it may occupy the loft of a dwelling house and thus become a nuisance. On the whole, its interesting and friendly habits and its beauty of form and action make it a desirable neighbor.

Specimens examined from Wisconsin.—Total number 50, as follows: *Buffalo County:* Fountain City, 1 (MM). *Chippewa County:* Stanley, 1 (MM). *Clark County:* Worden Township, 1 (CNHM). *Dane County:* Madison, 4 (UWZ). *Dodge County:* Beaver Dam, 9 (1 CC; 1 MVZ; 7 UWZ). *Dunn County:* Meridean, 2 (1 JNC; 1 UWZ). *Grant County:* Cassville, 1 (MCZ). *Jefferson County:* Lake Koshkonong, 1 (CC). *Milwaukee County:* Fox Point, 1 (MM); Milwaukee, 4 (MM). *Pierce County:* Maiden Rock, 1 (MM). *Racine County:* Racine, 2 (USNM); Rochester, 1 (MM); Wind Lake, 1 (MM). *Rock County:* Milton, 2 (UWZ). *Sauk County:* Sumpter, 1 (MM). *Walworth County:* Delavan, 1; Williams Bay, 2 (CM). *Waukesha County:* Delafield, 1 (UWZ); Elm Grove, 2 (MM); Nashotah, 8 (UWZ); No locality, 1 (MM); Pewaukee, 2 (1 MM; 1 UWZ).

Selected references.—Hatt, R. T., 1931; Howell, A. H., 1918; King, F. H., 1883; Perkins, G. H., 1873; Sollberger, D. E., 1940, 1943.

Northern flying squirrel, U.S. Fish and Wildlife Service photograph by Walter P. Taylor.

Glaucomys sabrinus macrotis (Mearns)
Northern Flying Squirrel

Sciuropterus sabrinus macrotis Mearns, Proc. U. S. Nat. Mus., vol. 21, p. 353, November 4, 1898.
Pteromys sabrinus Lapham, p. 339, 1853.
Pteromys Hudsonius Strong, p. 439, 1883.
Sciuropterus sabrinus Jackson, p. 19, 1908; Hollister, p. 24, 1910; Cory, p. 106, 1912.
Glaucomys sabrinus macrotis Schmidt, p. 111, 1931; Komarek, p. 206, 1932; Barger, p. 11, 1952.

Vernacular names.—In Wisconsin usually called northern flying squirrel or big flying squirrel, or in parts where the little species *volans* is unknown, simply flying squirrel. Other names include asapan or assapanick (colonial), avola (early explorers, trappers, and traders), Canadian flying squirrel, large flying squirrel, larger American flying squirrel, Mearns flying squirrel, and *so-gus-con-ta-wa* (Chippewa).

Identification marks.—In general form and appearance the northern flying squirrel is somewhat similar to the southern flying squirrel. It is larger in size, which is particularly noticeable in its longer tail and larger feet, is slightly more reddish in color of the upper parts, and has the bases of the hairs on the under parts always slate color instead of white as in *volans.*

In summer pelage the color of the upper parts (tips of hairs) is cinnamon or pale orange cinnamon, shading on the sides to pinkish buff; sides of face, under ears, top of nose, and sides of neck pale smoke gray; under parts whitish, shaded and overcast with light pinkish cinnamon, the base of hairs plumbeous or slate-color; tail above hair-brown to near snuff brown, below dusky pinkish cinnamon; forefeet above drab, hind feet

Left hind foot of northern flying squirrel. Specimen from Mamie Lake, Vilas County, Wisconsin. 1×.

above mouse gray; under parts of both fore and hind feet drabish. Winter pelage similar to summer, but tone of upper parts slightly paler. Young up to half grown are darker and more grayish than the adult. Apparently one molt occurs annually, which begins early in the autumn and is completed by the last of November. There is no apparent size or color variation associated with sex, and but slight individual variation in size or color. I have seen no color mutations in the northern flying squirrel.

The skull of *G. sabrinus* is larger than that of *G. volans,* the greatest length 36 mm. or more and the greatest width between 21.9 and 23.5 mm.; frontal region more elevated; braincase slightly more rotund; upper molariform tooth row (in Wisconsin specimens) more than 7 millimeters. This species can be separated from *Glaucomys volans* by the color of the underparts, the hairs of the breast and belly always being plumbeous or slate color at the bases; the tail is always much darker below and the feet darker above than in *volans;* hind foot more than 35 mm. long; skull more than 36 mm. in greatest length.

Measurements.—Total length of adults, 263 to 315 mm. (10.4 to 12.4 inches); tail, 115 to 150 mm. (4.5 to 5.9 inches); hind foot, 37 to 40 mm. (1.5 to 1.6 inches). Weight of adult about 4 to 7.5 ounces. Skull length, 36.5 to 39.2 mm.; width, 21.9 to 23.5 mm.

Distribution in Wisconsin.—The northern part of the state, chiefly in Canadian Life Zone from northern Burnett, northern Clark, northern Outagamie, and Kewaunee counties northward to the state line. Lapham (1853: 339), on authority of Dr. Hoy, records it from Winnebago County.

Habitat.—Heavily wooded areas of mixed conifers and deciduous trees of mature growth, preferably in moist forests with many fallen large decaying and mossy logs. Sometimes in pure stands of arborvitae and spruce or balsam fir forests. Especially favors hemlock-maple or hemlock-gray birch timber. Rarely in pure hardwood forest.

Status and Habits.—The author has carefully studied many specimens of *Glaucomys sabrinus* from the Great Lakes region and the Canadian north and concludes that all Wisconsin specimens are referable to *G. s. macrotis.* Howell (1918: 34) identified two specimens from Burnett and Douglas counties of Wisconsin as *G. s.*

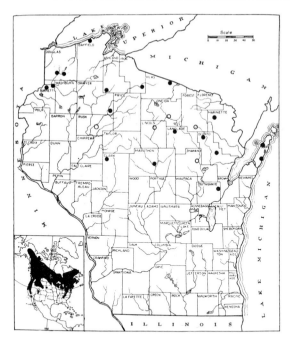

Map 35. *Distribution of* GLAUCOMYS SABRINUS. ● = *specimens examined.* ○ = *authentic records.*

sabrinus. These same two specimens and others from northwestern Wisconsin differ slightly if at all from specimens from Door County, extreme eastern Wisconsin, or specimens from intermediate points. None of these approaches the large size of hind foot or skull of *G. s. sabrinus,* nor do any show the preceptible darker color characteristic of *G. s. sabrinus.* As in the case of the southern flying squirrel, probably the northern flying squirrel is more plentiful within its range than records indicate. My experience, however, has been that its presence in a given area is more easily detected. It often appears to be more abundant in a given tract of forest than would be *volans* in its homeland, yet actually it probably is no more plentiful. Possibly about three or four per acre is a normal population in favorable habitat. Reduction of favorable habitat has probably reduced its population since early settler days.

Knocking on a tree trunk will usually dislodge a northern flying squirrel from its nest, or at least cause it to peek to see what is happening. It is not so noisy in its call notes as the southern flying squirrel, but is much more easily trapped, particularly on the ground or on a fallen log. Its

tracks in the snow are often discernible where it has jumped some distance from a tree to land on the ground and hop to another tree. The paired hops are about eight inches apart. Sometimes its large furry tail is found where it has been left uneaten by a prowling cat or other carnivore.

The northern flying squirrel is nocturnal, and unless disturbed remains in its nest during daylight hours. It is active during all seasons of the year. Its fresh tracks and other signs may sometimes be seen in the snow during subzero weather, though usually at such times it remains in its nest more than during mild weather. It is not known to hibernate. Lively individuals of this species have been found in nests or hollows in trees felled by woodsmen during zero weather in Oneida, Forest, and Vilas counties. Its chief method of locomotion is by volplaning in much the same manner as the southern flying squirrel. Unlike the southern form, however, it spends considerable time on the ground, hopping in short leaps along fallen logs or humus-covered soil. Its maximum running speed is about eight miles an hour.

It is less vociferous than its southern relative, but sometimes utters a chirp when communicating to its fellows. This chirp is softer and lower pitched than the chirp of *volans.* I have never heard it utter a *"kuk-kuk-kuk"* alarm note such as is common to many other squirrels. When in pain it squeaks loudly. It is somewhat gregarious, particularly in winter when as many as eight to a dozen have been found together in a tree cavity. At other seasons of the year it is not gregarious with its own kind, but is rather confiding and friendly with humans. I know of one that was caught by hand as it sat eating on a log. It sometimes fights viciously and bites its captor, but is seldom really pugnacious. Once captured, it is easily tamed, and makes a docile and interesting pet. Though strictly nocturnal, it will often come in search of food into the light of a campfire or of a cabin lamp. It is not as lively as *volans,* but is possibly less sensitive and more virile physically. It seldom indulges in true play, though frequently its antics and behavior might be interpreted as such. Its normal longevity in the wild is probably less than four years.

Mating may occur as early as the last week of March or as late as May 20. The gestation period is believed to be about 40 days, and the young are born between May 1 and June 30, rarely as late as the first week of July. There appears to be only one litter a year. Two or three young appears to be the usual number, most frequently three. Rarely are there four or five in a litter. The youngster at birth is hairless; the eyes and ears are closed by membrane; the flying membrane or patagium is visible as a fold of loose skin; the weight is about five or six grams; the total length about 2.8 inches. The young ceases nursing when about two months old, by which time it has foraged more or less for itself outside the nest for about two weeks. When ten weeks old it is essentially full grown and pretty much on its own. The mammae are eight, two pectoral, four abdominal, two inguinal.

The nest, utilized as a resting place and home during winter, is usually in a tree cavity, such as large woodpecker hole or a natural cavity. The nest may be anywhere from the surface of the ground to 50 or 60 feet up, usually in a poplar, birch, or hemlock. Occasionally the squirrel builds its nest in a cabin where an entrance hole has been left, and it is particularly apt to occupy the attic or upper rooms of a deserted log house. The nest is made of shredded fiber and lined with finely shredded inner bark, fur, or feathers. A nest in a hole or cavity in a tree or in a loft is frequently used as a breeding place. Often, however, the summer or breeding nest may be built in the open 5 to 35 feet from the ground in a spruce, balsam, hemlock, tamarack, white cedar, or possibly some other conifer. It is usually constructed close to the trunk of the tree and well below the tree top. A completed nest is about 12 inches in diameter, and is composed of small twigs and coarse strips of bark externally, the material gradually becoming finer and somewhat leafy toward the interior, which is lined with finely shredded inner bark and sometimes sphagnum, lichens, or other soft material. This type of nest has one entrance near the trunk of the tree, and in some instances a second one at the top of the nest. The outside nest is rarely used in winter, and then only when suitable tree cavities are not readily available to the squirrel. At times an abandoned crow's nest or that of a red squirrel is remade and utilized by a flying squirrel.

The northern flying squirrel is almost omnivorous. Nuts and seeds in wide variety constitute much of its food, and in Wisconsin it consumes quantities of hazelnuts and beechnuts, and spruce, balsam, and maple seeds. It eats many wild fruits such as the pin cherry, June berry, huckleberry, mountain ash berry, berries of various viburnum species, and others. Mushrooms and other fungi it relishes. Late in winter and during spring it feeds extensively upon buds of trees. It catches and eats some insects, particularly moths and beetles. Sometimes it eats young birds. It has an avid taste for raw meat, fresh, dried, or putrid. Its attempt to eat meat bait at traps set for carnivorous animals frequently causes it to be trapped, usually to the disgust of the trapper. It seems to procure water mostly from green vegetation and moisture on its food.

Most wild carnivorous animals hunt in the more open places, which offers some measure of protection to the northern flying squirrel, truly a forest animal. The feral and prowling house cat is its most frequent enemy, though undoubtedly others are captured by foxes and weasels, and by the marten in the days when it was more plentiful. Among birds the great horned owl and the goshawk catch one now and then. Forest fires kill many, and no small number are accidentally caught in traps set for fur animals. Very few are killed by automobiles, though probably more than of the smaller species. One has been reported killed in Mackinac County, upper peninsula of Michigan, by entangling itself on a barbed wire fence (Findley, 1946).

External parasites include the lice *Hoplopleura trispinosa, Microphthirus uncinatus,* and *Neohaematopinus sciuropteri;* the mite *Euhaemogamasus ambulans;* the fleas *Opisodasys pseudarctomys* and *Orchopeas wickhami;* and the chigger *Trombicula microti.* Internal parasites that have been found are the flatworms *Catenotaenia pusillo* and *Andrya sciuri* and the roundworms *Citellinema bifurcatum* and *Syphacia thompsoni.*

Practically no serious harm is done by the northern flying squirrel. It may become a nuisance sometimes by making its home in a cabin or in the attic of a house. Trappers also complain that at times it becomes a nuisance by entering traps that are baited with meat and set for fur animals. It has real value, however, as food for carnivorous fur animals when mice and many other animals are buried under deep snow.

Specimens examined from Wisconsin.—Total number 27, as follows: *Ashland County:* Bear Lake, 3 (1 CNHM; 2 UWZ). *Bayfield County:* Herbster, 2. *Burnett County:* Deer Lake, 1 (MM); Namakagon River (mouth of), 1 (MM). *Clark County:* Worden Township, 1. *Door County:* Clarks Lake, 1; Fish Creek, 2 (UWZ). *Douglas County:* Gordon, 1 (UWZ); Moose River (junction with St. Croix River), 1 (MM). *Iron County:* Manitowish, 1 (MM).

Langlade County: T 34 N, R 11 E, 2 (UWZ). *Marathon County:* Rib Hill, 3. *Marinette County:* Coleman Lake Club, 2 (MM). *Oconto County:* Kelley Brook, 1 (MM). *Outagamie County:* Oneida, 1 (MM). *Sawyer County:* Connors Lake, 1. *Vilas County:* Mamie Lake, 3.

Selected references.—Coventry, A. F., 1932; Cowan, I. M., 1936; Howell, A. H., 1918; Mearns, E. A., 1898; Seton, E. T., 1929, vol. 4, pp. 386–94.

Family **Geomyidae**
Pocket Gophers

The family Geomyidae is confined to North America. It consists of nine genera exclusive of fossil forms, of which one (*Geomys*) occurs in Wisconsin.

Genus **Geomys** Rafinesque
Eastern Pocket Gophers

Dental formula:

$$I \frac{1-1}{1-1}, \ C \frac{0-0}{0-0}, \ P \frac{1-1}{1-1}, \ M \frac{3-3}{3-3} = 20.$$

Geomys bursarius bursarius (Shaw)
Mississippi Valley Pocket Gopher

Mus bursarius Shaw, Trans. Linnaean Soc. London, vol. 5, p. 227, 1800.
Geomys bursarius Lapham, p. 44, 1852; Lapham, p. 340, 1853; Strong, p. 440, 1883; Jackson, p. 24, 1908; Hollister, p. 26, 1909; Jackson, p. 88, 1910; Cory, p. 239, 1912.
Geomys bursarius bursarius Schmidt, p. 116, 1931; Barger, p. 11, 1952.

Vernacular names.—In Wisconsin generally called pocket gopher; sometimes simply gopher, though the term gopher in this state usually refers to the striped ground squirrel. Other names include *gaufre* (French, meaning honey-combed, from which the name gopher was derived), pouched gopher, miner, prairie gopher, prairie pocket gopher, red gopher, and Shaw or Shaw's pocket gopher.

Identification marks.—A heavily built rat-sized mammal some 10 or 12 inches in total length, of which about three-tenths is tail; head rather broad and flat, the face somewhat truncate in nasal region; ears and eyes decidedly small and inconspicuous; deep fur-lined cheek pockets extending backward under the skin on the outside of the mouth to the shoulders; mouth opening

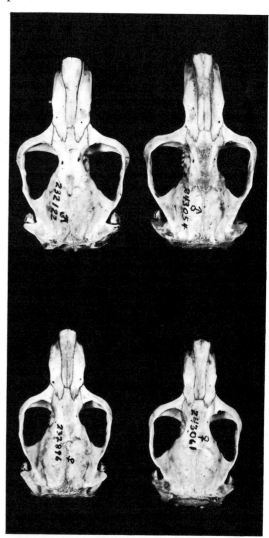

Skulls of pocket gophers. Left side, upper and lower, GEOMYS B. BURSARIUS. *Right side, upper and lower,* G. B. WISCONSINENSIS.

very small, and divided by a modified diaphragm between incisors and cheek teeth; tail comparatively short, nearly naked; legs short; feet sinewy, but not fleshy; forefeet with long, sharp, heavy claws; pelage short, fine, smooth, and glossy. It has no gall bladder.

The general color above is drabbish liver brown to light chestnut brown; under parts somewhat paler than upper parts; terminal parts such as feet, lips, and tip of tail whitish. The winter pelage may average a shade darker than summer fur, but the difference is scarcely noticeable. There are two molts annually, usually in May and September. Molting occurs in a series of waves of hair replacement beginning on top of the nose and proceeding posteriorly, the edge of the molt on the back almost always in advance of the molting on the under parts. Often as many as five or six molt waves occur before the molting is completed, and sometimes three or four dorsal molt lines are discernible on a gopher.

The skull is heavy and angular, essentially flat above from occiput to near anterior ends of nasals; zygoma robust widespread, the anterior border abruptly angular to the lateral arches and to the rostrum; frontal without postorbital process; rostrum prominent, long and heavy, the sides nearly parallel; nasals long, relatively narrow, and in upper view only slightly broader anteriorly; audital bullae small, angular, not inflated, length about twice width; teeth even, hypsodont, no tubercles evident in functional adult teeth; incisors large and heavy; upper incisor with large distinct groove down the middle

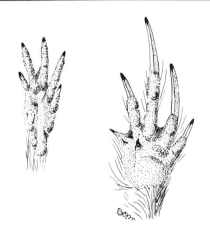

Left hind foot (left), and left fore foot (right), underside of pocket gopher, G. B. WISCONSINENSIS. *1×.*

Lower face of pocket gopher, GEOMYS BURSARIUS, *showing grooved incisors and openings to cheek pockets. 1×.*

Pocket gopher, GEOMYS BURSARIUS, *from old painting by Ernest Thompson Seton.*

of its anterior surface and also a slight groove on the inner side.

Adult males are larger than adult females, the difference amounting to nearly 15 per cent in most linear measurements and 25 or 30 per cent in weight. I have never found a female as big as any adult male. An unusual sexual dimorphism in *Geomys bursarius* was discovered by Dr. F. L. Hisaw of the University of Wisconsin, who found that males possess a normal rodent pelvis and normal pubic symphysis, as does the female until the time of bearing her first litter. At that time, under the influence of a hormone secreted by the ovary, her pubic symphysis becomes absorbed, thus enlarging the birth canal. This absorption persists throughout the life of the female (Hisaw, 1925). The skull of the adult male is not only larger than that of the female but tends to be more angular, has a more developed saggital crest, and a tendency towards longer rostrum and nasals. There is some individual color variation in the intensity and reddishness of the brown shade. What may be a color mutation, an approach towards albinism, appears in some of the specimens from near Brule and west of Iron River in the collection of the University of Illinois Museum of Natural History. Out of 38 skins from this region 8 show considerable white on the face, nose, and throat. Eleven others show a touch of white on the nose and throat, and one has a few white hairs in the mid-dorsal region. Blackish hair mixed with the white indicates possibly an unstable mutation. No specimens that I have seen have in any way suggested an approach towards the blackish pocket gopher of Illinois and Indiana, *Geomys b. illinoensis* Komarek and Spencer.

This species can be easily identified by its plain liver-brown coloration without stripes or spotting, its compact heavy build with a relatively short and essentially naked tail, heavy claws on the forefeet, and especially by the large fur-lined cheek pockets opening on either side of the mouth and the prominently grooved upper incisors set in an angular skull that is more than 40 mm. in greatest length. The subspecies *Geomys bursarius bursarius* can be distinguished from *Geomys bursarius wisconsinensis* only by skull characteristics, explained under that subspecies.

Measurements.—Total length, adult males, 260 to 325 mm. (10.4 to 12.8 inches); tail, 75 to 95

mm. (2.9 to 3.8 inches); hind foot, 34 to 37 mm. (1.4 to 1.5 inches). Weight, adult males, 270 to 350 grams (9.5 to 12.4 oz.). Skull length, adult males, 50.5 to 53.5 mm.; width 31.4 to 32.3 mm. Total length, adult females, 240 to 270 mm. (9.4 to 10.6 inches); tail, 65 to 82 mm. (2.6 to 3.2 inches); hind foot, 31 to 34 mm. (1.2 to 1.3 inches). Weight, adult females, 220 to 260 grams (7.8 to 9.2 oz.). Skull length, adult females, 43 to 45.2 mm.; width, 25.3 to 26.8 mm.

Distribution in Wisconsin.—Extreme northwestern part of the state from northern Pierce County (Prescott) to north central Bayfield County and eastern Douglas County; apparently confined to drainage area of the eastern side of Saint Croix River and of Brule River, Iron River, and possibly others flowing into Lake Superior.

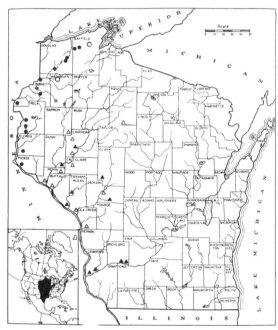

Map 36. Distribution of Geomys bursarius. *Solid symbols = specimens examined. Open symbols = authentic records.* ●, ○ = G. b. bursarius. ▲, △ = G. b. wisconsinensis.

Habitat.—Sandy soil or loose soft loam in open or semi-open locations such as pastures and dry meadows; cultivated land, particularly clover, alfalfa, and grain fields; undisturbed railway and highway roadsides; old fields and sometimes gardens; and burned cutover and partly forested areas.

Status and Habits.—The pocket gopher *Geomys bursarius* was mentioned in the earlier lists of mammals of Wisconsin (Lapham, 1852, 1853; Strong, 1883) as occurring in the state, but no specimens seem to have been available or recorded. In his extensive monograph of the pocket gophers, Merriam (1895: 120) included southern Wisconsin "east nearly to Lake Michigan (Winnebago and Fond du Lac, Wisconsin)" as within the range of this species. His two specified Wisconsin localities were undoubtedly based on a previous statement that "the gopher is common in portions of Wisconsin, being in fact very numerous in Winnebago and Fond du Lac counties, as I have myself ascertained" (Allen, J. A., 1870: 192). Dr. Allen possibly confused the name "gopher" as given for the striped ground squirrel commonly called "gopher." Merriam (1895: map 4) indicated these as "specimens examined" on his distribution map of *Geomys*, but does not list them under the heading "Specimens examined" (*ibid.*, pp. 122–23). He further indicates on the map a record from Madison. I have traced this record and find it is based on a letter from a Mr. Morse, Madison, written in 1893, stating that he had "kept a gopher in captivity for two years." Again the striped ground squirrel was the mammal. I never heard of a pocket gopher near Madison, and a pocket gopher would in all probability not live two years in captivity under ordinary care. I have found no authentic record of the occurrence of the pocket gopher in Wisconsin east of longitude 90° west. Lone Rock, Richland County, type locality of *G. b. wisconsinensis*, is only 12 miles west of this meridian. Ogema, Price County, where the experienced naturalist Harry H. Sheldon saw mounds August 23, 1919, is two hundred miles north of Lone Rock and 15 miles west of longitude 90°. It is quite probable, however, that *Geomys* does occur east of the ninetieth meridian in Wisconsin, for the presence of this animal is not always easily detected. Northward it occurs to within 15 miles of Lake Superior at Brule, Douglas County, and Iron River and Ino, Bayfield County (Jackson, 1910: 88; Davis, 1955). The subspecies *wisconsinensis* apparently spread northward from the Driftless Area, north of the lower Wisconsin River. It has not been found south of this river. The subspecies *bursarius* apparently ingressed Wisconsin from the west, and so far as known is confined in Wisconsin to that part drained by the Saint Croix River and its tributaries, and has not yet been found in that part of Douglas County west of the Saint Croix River. The home range of an individual pocket gopher has not been determined. Its general travels are subterranean and often in the same burrows. It may travel many miles in a year, yet at the end of that time it may be within four hundred feet or less of where it started. Intensive cultivation and other soil disturbances tend to limit its distribution.

Pocket gopher mounds are the telltale evidence of the presence of this species in an area. The animal remains underground to such an extent that it is rarely seen unless caught in a trap. Its mounds, however, are easily recognized when one is familiar with them. They can be seen several hundred feet away under favorable conditions. I have often traced the distribution of pocket gophers by their mounds along a railroad or highway. Time of day matters not to the pocket gopher in its activities. It is active winter as well as summer, and does not hibernate. During cold weather when the ground is frozen it usually works in tunnels below the frost line. In milder weather it often works near the surface, and may even throw dirt plugs into the snow and thus form only a partly completed mound. The animal is able to run forward or backward with equal facility. In its burrow it acts much like a shuttle in a shaft. The tail appears to serve as a guiding tactile organ when the gopher runs backward. On the surface of the ground it most frequently runs forward, but it is rather awkward and pro-

Mound of pocket gopher, G. B. WISCONSINENSIS, near Gotham, Wisconsin September 13, 1922. U.S. Fish and Wildlife Service photograph by author.

gresses at a speed of not more than four miles an hour. It cannot swim, and flounders miserably in water and soon drowns.

No means of communication between individuals is evident. When an animal is disturbed or an intruder enters its tunnel, it will fight viciously, the meantime uttering frequent angry hisses. We speak of "pocket gopher colonies," yet it is colonial only to the extent that it is inhibited in area expansion by soil conditions. It is, in fact, a solitary, surly mammal, and except at time of breeding only one individual occupies a tunnel. It is physically strong, particularly in the fore parts. Its sense of touch is highly developed; the other senses are apparently below normal for a rodent. Its longevity is unknown, but probably

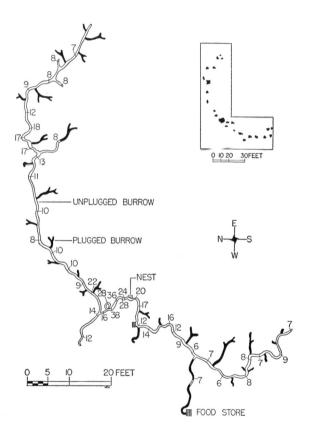

its normal life span is nearly as long as its potential longevity. Probably most pocket gophers live to be five or more years old.

So far as known the pocket gopher has only one litter annually. Mating takes place early in the spring, sometimes by the latter part of March, but more frequently during April or May. The male seeks the female in the burrow, but failing in this may leave the burrow and travel above ground in his search for a mate. The gestation period is not known. The young are two to six in a litter, three or four being the more usual. At birth the youngster is about two inches long and weighs about six or seven grams. It is void of hair. Its skin is pinkish, loose, and wrinkled; its eyes and ears are closed. Its cheek pouches are represented by slight furrows each about 5 mm. long. It may emit sharp squeaks soon after birth. It is nursed until nearly half grown, during which time the mother may traverse a tunnel system covering five to eight thousand square feet. When about half grown and weened, each young one digs for itself. It starts new tunnels of its own, which eventually become closed behind it, and its solitary life begins.

The pocket gopher spends practically all its life under the surface of the ground in burrows or tunnels of its own making. The main tunnel is usually about ten inches beneath the surface, and may be many yards long. In times of extended cold weather, when the ground is frozen deep, the gopher digs below the frost line to depths of three feet or more. A study and description of a tunnel system of the pocket gopher that aptly fits the Wisconsin form has been made by Smith, parts of which follow:

On the morning of November 29, 1947, one-fourth mile south and two miles west of Lawrence, Douglas Co., Kansas, I trapped a female pocket gopher (*Geomys bursarius majusculus* Swenk) and began excavating its burrow to ascertain the nature of the winter quarters of this animal. The external measurements of the gopher were: total length, 260 mm.; length of tail, 80 mm.; length of hind foot, 32 mm.

Parts of five consecutive days were devoted to excavating the burrow. I am convinced that the female was the only pocket gopher living in the burrow. . . .

The mounds above ground were typically fan-shaped. None was directly over the main burrow, but each was to one side of it, at the end of an inclined, lateral tunnel. The arrangement of the

Drawing, looking down on the burrow of the pocket gopher. Numerals are measurements in inches of depth below the surface of the ground of the burrow. Drawing at upper right shows the mounds of earth on the surface of the ground. After Smith, 1948, Courtesy E. R. Hall.

mounds of earth indicated that they all were associated with a single burrow, as later was proven to be the case. There was no sign of another burrow of a pocket gopher within a thousand yards. All of the burrow was excavated. It consisted of only one main tunnel. This was open but there were many short, lateral branches, which had been used in the past but which now were plugged with soil. These laterals from the main burrow may have been dug in an underground search for food; at any rate, the greater number of the laterals did not reach the surface of the ground. The floor of the main burrow for the most part was between six and nine inches below the surface of the ground. The greatest depth was thirty-eight inches; this was in the vicinity of the nest. The oval burrow, throughout, was remarkably consistent in the dimensions of its cross-section, being three inches wide and four and a half inches high. The total length of the main burrow was two hundred and six feet. More than seventy cubic feet of earth had been removed to make this one main burrow. . . . one gopher it is thought . . . moved all of this soil in less than one year.

The bottom of the nest was twenty-four inches below the surface of the ground. In inches the nest measured $7 \times 3\frac{1}{2} \times 6\frac{1}{2}$ and was constructed entirely of the cut stems, approximately one and a half inches in length, of the three kinds of wild grass which were abundant in the area. . . . The nest was free of fecal material and appeared to lack parasites and commensals, but did contain five small pieces of bone which bore toothmarks of pocket gopher size.

All fecal material was found in short, plugged-up tunnels approximately nine inches in length that originally branched from the main burrow, after the tunnel was almost full of feces, the gopher, plugged the remaining part with soil. As a result, the main tunnel was free of fecal material.

There were food stores at two places along the tunnel. One store was a mere enlargement of the end of a side tunnel, and the other store was in a pocket in one side of the main tunnel. This pocket opened into the main tunnel, but the larger food store was farther from the nest, at the end of the side tunnel. It had two earth plugs separating it from the main burrow (Charles F. Smith, 1948).

The Pocket Gophers, in working their way through the earth in the construction of their tunnels, use the powerful upper incisors as a pick to loosen the ground. At the same time the fore feet are kept in active operation, both in digging and in pressing the earth back under the body, and the hind feet are used also in moving it still further backward. When a sufficient quantity has accumulated behind the animal, he immediately turns in the burrow and by

bringing the wrists together under the chin, with the palms of the hands held vertically, forces himself along by the hind feet, pushing the earth out in front. When an opening in the earth is reached the earth is discharged through it, forming a little hillock (Merriam, 1895: 16).

The food of the pocket gopher consists of roots, tubers, and such green herbage and leaves as it may be able to locate around an opening to its burrow or drag into the burrow by a hold on the roots of the plant. Food material is cut by the teeth into small pieces, which are placed in the pouch and carried into storage.

These cheek pouches are used exclusively in carrying food, and not in carting dirt as often erroneously supposed. The animals are great hoarders and carry away to their storehouses vastly more than they consume. The cheek pouches reach back as far as the shoulder and are so attached that they can not be completely everted without rupture of their connections. . . . As a rule one pouch was filled at a time, though not always, and the hand of the same side was used to push the food in. . . . A piece of potato, root, or other food is seized between the incisor teeth, and is immediately transferred to the fore paws, which are held in horizontal position, the tips of the claws curving toward one another. . . . The piece is then pressed rapidly across the side of the face with a sort of whipping motion which forces it into the open mouth of the pouch. Sometimes a single rapid stroke with one hand is sufficient; at other times both hands are used, particularly if the piece is large. . . . The most remarkable thing connected with the use of the pouches is the way they are emptied. The fore feet are brought back simultaneously along the sides of the head until they reach a point opposite the hinder end of the pouches; they are then placed firmly against the head and carried rapidly forward. In this way the contents of the pouches are promptly dumped in front of the animal (Merriam, 1895: 18–19).

On account of its subterranean habits, the pocket gopher has few natural enemies. Among the mammals in Wisconsin, weasels are probably its only significant enemy. The house cat has been said to capture one rarely. Great horned owls and long-eared owls are also known enemies. The bull snake (*Pituophis sayi*) enters the burrows of pocket gophers and destroys many of them (Hisaw and Gloyd, 1926). Fires and automobiles destroy practically no pocket gophers. Water from melting snow, however, may flood

*Bull snake killing pocket gopher. After Hisaw and
Gloyd, 1926, p. 201.*

its burrows and cause the death of the animal
through drowning or exposure. External parasites
known to infest it include one species of louse
and three of fleas. Internal parasites known are
one protozoan and one flatworm.

In Wisconsin the pocket gopher most frequently inhabits waste ground, and there cannot be
called a menace. In fact in such situations it often
does more good than harm by turning over the
soil and mixing vegetable matter with it as it
works. In meadows, pastures, and other places it
may become a nuisance by throwing up mounds
which often bury and destroy hay or pasturage
and which give an annoying roughness to the
terrain. It consumes and stores quantities of
grass in such an area. It may be injurious to fruit
and other trees by gnawing the roots. It also may
ravage truck crops, including potatoes, beets,
turnips, parsnips, carrots, cabbages, and aspara-
gus roots. At times it may tunnel under a shock
of corn or grain, cutting up the straw and stalks,
devouring or carrying off the grain, and filling
the shock full of soil.

There are several methods of controlling
pocket gophers (Crouch, 1942), but in most cases
the best way is to trap them. Several special
traps have been devised for catching pocket

gophers, most of which perform well. A small
(No. 0) steel trap is also effective. No bait is
necessary. An unplugged doorway is sufficient to
tempt the animal to try to plug it and spring
the trap. If the steel trap is used it should be
placed level with the bottom in the tunnel so
that the gopher must cross the pan from one direction or the other. If most any one of the special
traps is used it is better to use two traps in each
setting with the trips together and the jaws at
alternate ends so that the gopher must bump the
trigger while over the jaws of the trap. After
placing the trap, the whole burrow should be
covered with cardboard, and dirt piled over it
to exclude light.

Specimens examined from Wisconsin.—Total 74, as
follows: *Bayfield County:* Iron River (4 mi. E. of),
1 (UI); Iron River (5 mi. W. of), 2 (UI); Iron
River (7 mi. W. of), 14 (UI). *Burnett County:* Dan-
bury, 2; Meenon Township, 1 (UWZ); Rush City
Bridge, 1 (MM); Yellow River (mouth of), 2 (MM).
Douglas County: Brule (3 mi. S., 3 mi. W. of), 21
(UI); Saint Croix Dam, 1 (MM); Solon Springs (3
mi. E., 3 mi. N. of), 5 (2 UI). *Pierce County:* Pres-
cott, 7 (6 MM). *Polk County:* Dresser, 12 (UI;)
Saint Croix Falls, 4 (2 UI). *Saint Croix County:*
River Falls (6 mi. N. E. of), 1 (UI).

Selected references.—Bailey, V., 1895; Crouch,
W. E., 1942; Johnson, C. E., 1926; Merriam, C. H.,
1895; Mossman, H. W., and F. L. Hisaw, 1940;
Scheffer, T. H., 1940.

Geomys bursarius wisconsinensis Jackson
Wisconsin Pocket Gopher

Geomys bursarius wisconsinensis Jackson, Proc. Biol. Soc. Washington 70: 33, June 28, 1957.

Vernacular names.—Same as those of *G. b. bursarius.*

Identification marks.—In general, external appearance of proportions, size, and color not readily distinguishable from *G. b. bursarius.* Certain cranial characters clearly separate the two races. The premaxilla in *wisconsinensis* in superior view is narrower and somewhat concave posteriorly, whereas in *bursarius* it is nearly flat or slightly convex posteriorly. The rostrum is somewhat narrower. Premaxilla distinctly and evenly incurved laterally anterior to premaxillary root of zygoma, whereas in *G. b. bursarius* the edge of the premaxilla is nearly straight anterior to root of zygoma. Inner borders of premaxillae diverge posteriorly and thus widen the distance between their posterior tips. The most conspicuous difference between the two subspecies results from this wider space between the posterior ends of the premaxillae, and is reflected in the broader anterior lobe of the frontal, which is about as broad as it is long in *wisconsinensis*, whereas in *G. b. bursarius* it is only about one-half as broad as it is long.

Measurements.—(Including two males and four females from type locality, Lone Rock, Wisconsin.) Total length, adult males, 277 to 297 mm. (11.1 to 11.9 inches); tail, 80 to 92 mm. (3.2 to 3.7 inches); hind foot, 35 to 37 mm. (1.4 to 1.5 inches). Skull length, adult males, 52.6 to 54.1 mm.; width, 31.2 to 31.7. Total length, adult females, 230 to 270 mm. (9.2 to 10.8 inches); tail, 68 to 85 mm. (2.7 to 3.4 inches); hind foot, 31 to 34 mm. (1.2 to 1.4 inches). Skull length, adult females, 42.5 to 44.5 mm.; width, 25.4 to 26.2 mm.

Distribution in Wisconsin.—Mississippi watershed from Chippewa River drainage to the north bank of the lower Wisconsin River, south of latitude 45° 30′ N. and west of longitude 90° W.

Habitat, Status, and Habits.—So far as known essentially like those of *Geomys bursarius bursarius.*

Specimens examined from Wisconsin.—Total 38, as follows: *Buffalo County:* Fountain City, 4 (MM). *Chippewa County:* Anson, 4. *Clark County:* Mentor Township, 2 (UWZ). *Crawford County:* Prairie du Chien, 1; Wauzeka, 9 (UI). *Dunn County:* Meridean, 3 (UWZ). *Jackson County:* Millston, 2 (1 AWS; 1 UWZ). *Richland County:* Gotham, 1 (UI); Lone Rock, 8. *Trempealeau County:* Arcadia, 4 (UI).

Selected references.—Same as for *Geomys b. bursarius,* and also Jackson, H. H. T., 1957 a.

Family Castoridae
Beavers

Beavers formerly occurred throughout most of the wooded regions of the temperate parts of the Northern Hemisphere. The genus *Castor* is the only living form.

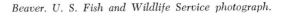

Beaver. U. S. Fish and Wildlife Service photograph.

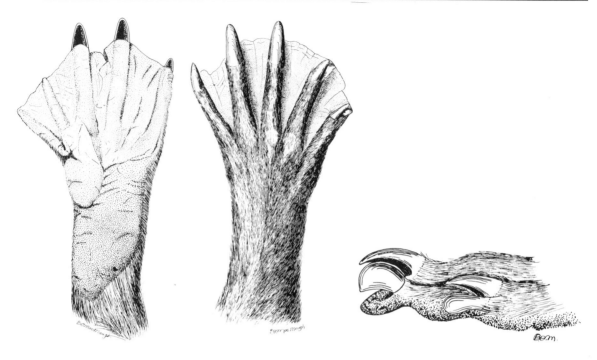

Left hind foot of beaver. Left, underside. Center, upper side showing combing claws. Specimen from Grand View, Wisconsin. ½×. Right, combing claws of the beaver. 1×.

Genus **Castor** Linnaeus
Beavers

Dental formula:

$$I\ \frac{1-1}{1-1},\quad C\ \frac{0-0}{0-0},\quad P\ \frac{1-1}{1-1},\quad M\ \frac{3-3}{3-3} = 20.$$

Castor canadensis michiganensis Bailey
Michigan Beaver

Castor canadensis michiganensis Bailey, Proc. Biol. Soc. Washington, 26: 192, October 23, 1913.

Castor fiber Lapham, p. 44, 1852; Lapham, p. 339, 1853; Strong, p. 439, 1883; Snyder, p. 126, 1902.

Castor Canadensis Hoy, p. 256, 1882.

Castor canadensis Jackson, p. 19, 1908; Hollister, p. 139, 1909; Hollister, p. 24, 1910; Cory, p. 159, 1912.

Castor canadensis canadensis Komarek, p. 207, 1932.

Castor canadensis michiganensis Barger, p. 11, 1952.

Vernacular names.—In Wisconsin usually called beaver. Other names include *ah-mik* (Chippewa), American beaver, Canadian beaver, golden beaver, and woods beaver.

Identification marks.—Largest of Wisconsin rodents; the body heavy, low, compact; eyes and ears small; nostrils and mouth valvular; tail broadly flattened horizontally, naked, leathery, scaly, the base fully furred and muscular; forefeet moderate with strong digging claws; hind feet large, fully webbed, the three outer toes straight and with normal claws, the two inner toes curved toward the body with nails—particularly those of the second claw—specialized and cleft for use in combing the fur; fur silky, dense, waterproof, and durable, the over hairs long and moderately coarse.

The color of the upper parts is deep burnt umber or seal brown, becoming slightly chestnut on the head and cheeks; under fur or base of hairs smoke gray or almost blackish; under parts somewhat paler than the back; ears, rhinarium, feet, and tail are near black.

The skull is large and massive, that of the adult more than 120 mm. long and 85 mm. broad; flat in superior outline; jugal broad, more than 18 mm. in greatest diameter; cheek teeth rootless, high crowned, with cross ridges of enamel; length of upper molar series about 28 to 30 mm.; incisors heavy, near 8 mm. broad, dark orange chestnut on anterior surface.

So far as known there is no sexual variation in

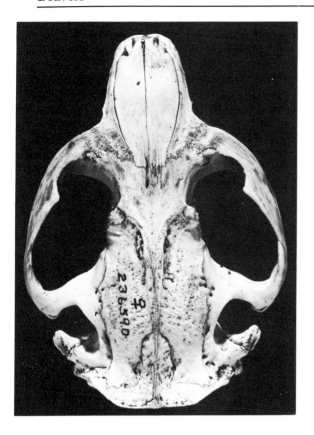

Skull of beaver, CASTOR C. MICHIGANENSIS, *Basswood Lake, Bayfield County, Wisconsin.* ¾ ×.

color or cranial characters. Nor do any color differences appear between young and adults. Slight individual variation is evident at times in size and color, but such color variations usually appear only in the shade of brown, or in the extent of paleness or darkness. Color variations or mutations of black, silvering, and white have been recorded (Jones, 1923).

Measurements.—Total length of adults, 900 to 1,170 mm. (35.4 to 46 inches); tail, 300 to 440 mm. (11.8 to 17.3 inches); scaly portion of tail about 9 to 12 inches long and 4.5 to 6.5 inches broad; hind foot, 165 to 185 mm. (6.5 to 7.3 inches). Weight of adult Wisconsin beaver is normally 45 to 60 pounds. A 2-year-old normally weighs about 30 pounds; an 8-year-old about 60 pounds. Heavier beavers have been recorded, mostly from the southwestern part of the state, as follows: 69.5 pounds (Anon., 1949 a); 72 pounds (Scott, 1951); 78.5, 80, and 87 pounds

(Schorger, 1953); and 94 pounds, probably the same beaver reported as 87 pounds by Schorger (Anon., 1952 b). W. T. Gray, then a Wisconsin state game warden located at Ashland, informed U. S. Biological Survey fieldmen that in March, 1921, he took 19 beavers, mostly in Bayfield County. The smallest weighed 25 pounds, and the greater part weighed 45 to 47 pounds. One not weighed that contained eight embryos he estimated at 100 pounds. The largest, a fat old male, weighed 110 pounds (Vernon Bailey, original manuscript, field report, Iron River, Wisconsin, July 5 to August 5, 1921). Skull length, 120 to 140 mm.; width, 85 to 100 mm.

Distribution in Wisconsin.—In early days, previous to about 1800, found throughout the state. Nearly extirpated by about 1900. At present found throughout the state except in Brown, Kewaunee, and Winnebago counties, and in that part of southeastern Wisconsin south of Dodge and Ozaukee counties and east of Rock County.

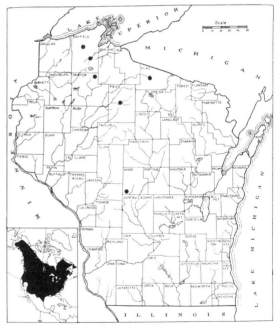

Map 37. Distribution of CASTOR CANADENSIS. ● = *specimens examined.*

Habitat.—Lakes and streams in wooded areas, usually remote from too much human activity.

Status and Habits.—When white man first set foot in Wisconsin the beaver was common in suitable habitat throughout the state. Its high value as fur and its use for food and other purposes caused intensive trapping and netting which gradually reduced it nearly to the point of extinction in the state by the year 1900. Numbers varied at irregular periods correlated with supply, demand, and prices. Often the stockpiles became glutted with beaver pelts, with the result that prices dropped and beavers in the wild had a short period to increase their population. There apparently were no regular cycles of abundance, as are common with most rodents. The population gradually decreased. The beaver probably was entirely extirpated from southern Wisconsin by the year 1825. "The last beaver killed, in the southern part of Wisconsin, was in 1819, on Sugar Creek, Walworth county, a very large one. (S. Juneau, Esq.)" (Lapham, 1853: 339 n.). There were relicts of beaver dams and ponds in Green, Walworth, and Rock counties as late as 1900, and several meadows and marshes in these counties as late as 1950 suggested beaver formation. Beavers were extirpated in the central part of the state by about the year 1890. In some of the northern counties, notably within the region north of a line from southwestern Douglas County to extreme southeastern Marinette County, a

few small isolated colonies existed in 1900. There probably were not more than five hundred beavers in the entire state then, though statements that there were only four or five colonies are ultraconservative.

In the year 1901 the first serious efforts were made to protect the animal. Rigid protection was established about 1905. A completely closed

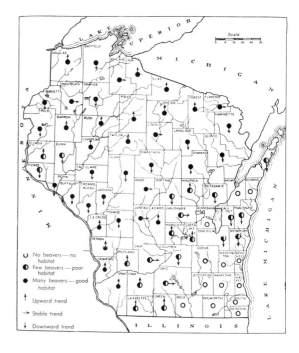

Map 38. *Beaver population trends, 1950-1952. From Wisconsin Wildlife Research, vol. 11, no. 4, p. 57. January, 1953. Colonies in 1950, number 3229, in 1952, —2956.*

Left, track of right hind foot of beaver. Right, track of right fore foot of beaver. ½×.

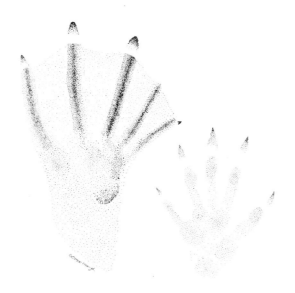

Feces of beaver. Adapted in part from Seton, 1929, vol. 4, p. 631. About 1×.

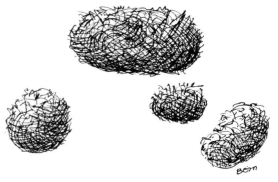

season began about 1908. The beaver was responsive. Its colonies increased in number and size, and its range expanded. Within ten years frequent and often unwarranted complaints were being entered about the damage done by beavers, and about the abundance of the animals. Early in September, 1919, the Wisconsin Conservation Commission conducted a preliminary survey to determine what could be done in the way of a study of the economic status, habits, and life history of the beaver in Wisconsin. The late Professor George Wagner, University of Wisconsin, and I made this brief study and reported thereon. Kaiser Jacoubek of the commission was with us at a few of the colonies visited. The complaints against beavers rested mainly on three charges: (1) Flooding meadows and agricultural lands and destroying trees by flooding; (2) Flooding highways (including roads, railroads, paths, and bridges); (3) Injuring trees by gnawing. In spite of these complaints, however, the general sentiment was that the beaver deserved protection. The animal was treated as an interesting asset of the country.

In the early 1920's there was instituted the practice of trapping live beavers in trouble areas and transplanting them to places within the state where they would find suitable habitat with less chance of becoming a nuisance. A few beavers were also transferred to the states of New York and Pennsylvania, where they formed the basic stock for the present large population of beavers there. The first beaver stocked in Pennsylvania came from Wisconsin and was released June 14, 1917. Due to the restocking within Wisconsin, and also the extensive spreading of old colonies and the establishment of new ones, beavers were found in 50 of the 71 counties in 1936, and in 18 counties they were sufficiently numerous to permit trapping. In 1954 they were present in 56 counties. Even under control and trapping management there is considerable annual variation in the number of beaver colonies and in beaver population in the state. In 1950 the estimated number of colonies was 3,239; in 1952 it was 2,956. A general average of somewhat more than three thousand colonies and some twenty-five to thirty thousand beavers might approximate the numbers. Population pressure, particularly the location of other nearby colonies, has a limiting effect on the home range of a colony. An average colony area includes about six to ten acres of water with a land range of rarely more than three or four hundred yards.

The beaver does not announce itself vocally. It is seldom heard except when it slaps the water surface with its tail. Its presence is usually easily detected by its structures, trails, and other evidences of activities. A beaver house, particularly one well out in a pond, is a conspicuous object. The dam is usually visible, and sometimes can be detected by the sound of trickling water before it is seen. Large chips of wood and fallen trees often tell of the work of the animal. Tracks and tail marks occur on land, but rarely are the feces located, since these are deposited in water. Frequently, well-worn trails made by beavers may be found leading from one pond to another, or to a favored patch of woodland. A beaver living in a burrow with an underwater entrance in a bank and no lodge may be more difficult to locate. Air bubbles under the ice near the entrance

Beaver swimming. Courtesy Norman McClintock.

of the shelter hole may indicate occupancy by a beaver. Air bubbles are sometimes frozen in the ice. Scent mounds are not easily found, but are a characteristic and dependable sign that to a keen nose can be detected by the musky odor. The scent mound is a small pile of mud, grass, and sticks shoved together, upon which the beaver deposits through the anus a few drops of castoreum, a bitter, orange-brown, pungent oil from the musk glands.

The animal is active throughout the year, though rather sluggish and less active in winter. It is seldom out in full daylight, but begins its routine work day about dusk and continues through until dawn. It does not migrate, but will leave a locality on account of food shortage, and often emigrate several miles to a more favorable home. Young beavers in the second year habitually leave the parental colony to emigrate, usually down the same stream, and establish themselves by pairs in new colonies. A beaver may sometimes travel 30 miles to establish a new home. Major travel is mostly by swimming, at which the beaver is past master. It can remain under water for ten to twelve minutes. On land it shambles along clumsily, and can be easily overtaken by a man walking rapidly.

The principal signal sound of the beaver is a loud slap of the tail on the surface of the water. This sound is recognizable for a distance of a half mile or more. It is a danger signal to all other beavers within hearing. Scent from the castor glands as deposited on a mound or other place is not a warning signal. It is a guidance that a beaver has been there. The scent may attract other animals besides beavers. The gnawing or scraping of the beaver teeth on wood can be heard five or six hundred feet away on a still night. The adult beaver makes no true vocal sound. The youngster, however, from birth until some six months old, is vociferous. It has many cries, whines, and soft plaintive sounds, and other more vigorous tones of protest and anger. Such baby notes are sometimes answered by the mother beaver with a low gruntlike sound, usually repeated three or four times.

Although the beaver is rated by many as one of the most intelligent mammals, it actually should not be classed too highly. Its special adaptations and unusual instincts and habits make it appear more mentally active than it actually is.

On the other hand, it is by no means stupid. It is colonial only to the extent that the parents and young under breeding age remain together. It is very quiet and does not fight its fellows. Its rare displeasure is expressed with a slap of the tail on the ground or by a grunted "ugh-ugh-ugh." A strange beaver coming to a colony, however, is apt to be treated as an enemy and attacked. In the wild it is timid and wary. When one is captured, particularly if young, it soon becomes tame and gentle with affectionate handling. It remains nervous and wary nevertheless, and is easily startled by a sudden noise or quick approach. The young beaver is active and playful, and demands much attention from its parents. Old animals also engage in play, and sometimes are quite frolicsome around the scent mound. The beaver is strong in bone, sinew, and muscle, and has many structural adaptations for its peculiar life. Its sight is not the best, but its senses of hearing, smell, and touch are excellent. The potential longevity of the beaver is about 14 years. One lived to be 12 years old in the National Zoological Park, Washington, D. C. (Mann, 1930: 303).

The beaver is monogamous, and a pair is believed to mate for life. The breeding season begins about the last of January and extends to the latter part of February. Young reach sexual maturity and breed in the second year, or when about 21 months old. The gestation period is about 120 days. The one litter a year may consist of one to eight kits, four or five being the more frequent number. There is one record of ten embryos. Six young is the maximum a mother can sufficiently nurse. The mammae are four, all pectoral. The beaver is born with its eyes open and the body furred. At birth it is an advanced youngster that with some variations is about one foot long and weighs about one pound. Development is rapid. It ceases regular nursing usually when less than a month old. It grows rather slowly during its first few months, and may weigh only 6 or 7 pounds when three months old. When nine months old it will weigh 12 to 15 pounds, and when a year old may weigh from 25 to 30 pounds. The youngster remains with the family colony until it is a year or two old and sexually mature. In the spring exodus the widowers are usually first to go, then the bachelors, and finally the two-year-olds of both sexes.

The colony is the center of home life of the beaver. It is an assemblage of unusual activities and structures upon which much has been written, yet about which there is still much to learn. Those interested in more detailed accounts of the life and habits of the beaver than are given in the summary descriptions that follow are referred to the publications listed under "Selected references."

Among the animal's more important habits or activities are felling trees, building a dam and making a pond, constructing a lodge or house, and making canals. The felling of trees is accomplished by gnawing around the base of the trunk until it is so thin that the tree falls of its own weight. It is no skill of the beaver that causes the trees to fall toward the pond or stream. Trees growing along banks by nature incline toward the water, and fall in that direction. Others fall with the wind or in the direction they lean. A beaver seldom travels more than three hundred feet to its timber supply, which pref-

Left (top), a well-constructed beaver dam, Spring Creek, Vilas County, Wisconsin, August, 1917. Photograph by the author. (Bottom), beaver repairing broken dam. Flashlight photograph courtesy George Shiras, III.

Below, diagram of beaver burrow and den in bank. Drawn by Mrs. MacMaugh from field sketch by the author.

Nest

1" – 6'

erably is aspen or poplar, though sometimes it may be other soft woods such as birch or willow. The trees it gnaws are usually comparatively small ones with trunks two to eight inches in diameter, though often it fells much larger trees. A black willow measuring 33 inches across the stump was felled by beavers in the Mississippi River bottoms near La Crosse, Wisconsin, though clumps of young willows were nearby (Anon., 1953). After the tree is felled the beaver cuts off the branches and cuts the trunk into such sections as it can manipulate. Trunks or branches more than six inches in diameter are seldom cut into sections. Sometimes a stick six inches in diameter and six feet long, or one two inches in diameter and twelve feet long, is dragged or floated to the lodge or dam. More often, however, the sticks are one or two inches thick and five or six feet long. Larger sticks are used in lodge or dam construction; smaller ones for food.

Many beavers that inhabit lakes and deep streams live in holes in the banks, and have no need of a dam. When a beaver takes abode on a small stream or shallow pond with an outlet, it immediately sets to work to build one. The dam deepens the water above it sufficiently for safe cover, storage of food, and freedom from ice. Six feet of water usually is sufficient, and often only an additional two or three feet will add enough. The beaver makes the dam by piling sticks across the channel pond, then shoving mud onto them from above. It continues this process until there is a huge ridge of sticks with an upper sloping surface of mud. Mud is dredged from the bottom of the pond and the pond deepened as well as the dam built upward. A break in a fresh beaver dam quickly attracts the owners, and they pack mud, sticks, and grass into it until the flow stops. A huge beaver dam 12 feet high and 40 rods long was on Taylor's Creek, Bayfield County,

Beaver dam and pond, near Engadine, Michigan.

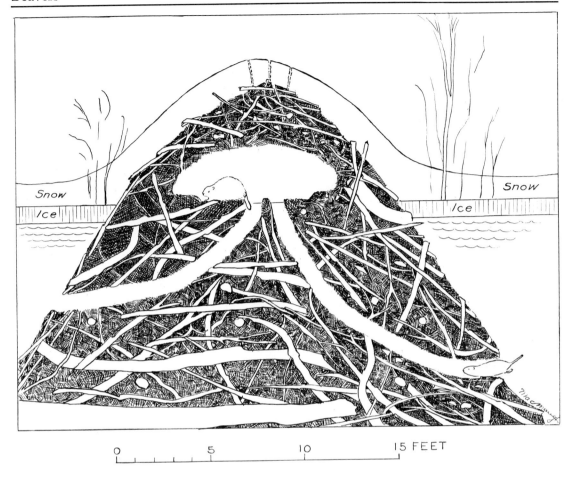

Beaver lodge with two entrances, diagrammatic.

Wisconsin, in 1919 (Barber, 1919). When a beaver starts to build a dam it sometimes takes advantage of a natural obstruction in a stream, such as a low corduroy bridge or a fallen tree.

Beaver ponds may vary in size from an acre or less to ten acres or more. The average Wisconsin beaver pond is about six acres. A canal is often dug by the beaver from the shore of the pond to a feeding ground or timber. Such a canal is deep and wide enough so that the animal can swim freely and carry branches from inland to the lodge. A canal may be several hundred feet long.

In a few cases a beaver may live in a burrow leading from under water into a bank to a nest chamber above the water level. Sometimes a beaver will pile sticks over such a burrow as if to imitate a beaver house. In most cases, however, the beaver builds a large house partly or entirely surrounded by water. A large house is normally about five or six feet high and fifteen or twenty feet wide at the water level. Smaller houses only three or four feet high and eight or ten feet in diameter are often occupied. The giant house at Taylor's Creek, Bayfield County, described by Barber (1919), was 16 feet high and 40 feet wide. This house later had to be destroyed, and Warden W. T. Gray of Ashland, who is six feet tall, said he could stand upright in the room inside and that there were beds for about eight beavers in the room. The walls were four feet thick. The inside of an ordinary lodge consists of one room, two or three feet high and three to five feet wide. As many as eight or ten beavers, perhaps more, may occupy a single lodge. The opening to a lodge is always under water. Methods of construction of the beaver

Beaver trails on steep banks made by Wisconsin beavers introduced into Herkimer County, New York. Left, branching trails. Middle, up and over. Right, return to the Pond. Photographs by Vernon Bailey.

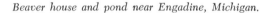

Beaver house and pond near Engadine, Michigan.

lodge have been described in detail by Bailey (1926 a; 1927 b).

The natural food of the beaver includes a wide range of plants. In summer it is largely sedges, rushes, water grasses, lily pads and roots, a variety of roots and tubers of water plants, and some bark, leaves, and twigs of bushes and trees from the shore. In winter it feeds chiefly upon green branches it has stored under water near the beaver house or bank den in water deep enough to ensure that the food will be available all winter. The beaver brings the wood to the storage place and piles and tucks it under until the mass rests on the bottom and only the surface branches stick out. Woods most frequently cut for food in Wisconsin are aspen, poplar, alder, willow, mountain maple (*Acer spicatum*), white birch, pin cherry, ash, box elder, and hazel. One acre of average size aspens will feed a colony of seven beavers for a year.

Natural enemies of the beaver in the wild are few. Among mammals, other than man, its enemies in Wisconsin are probably limited chiefly to the coyote, red fox, bobcat, and otter, and among birds to the great-horned owl and the goshawk. The beavers killed are probably all young animals, and except for the few possibly taken by the otter are all captured on land. An adult beaver is a worthy antagonist for any of these enemies. A beaver in the water can kill a dog of its own size. The muskrat is a commensal of the beaver in that it occasionally lives in beaver lodges and eats leavings of the beaver. Some persons consider it an enemy of the beaver because sometimes it does damage by tunneling into beaver lodges or through beaver dams. Rarely, a beaver is killed or trapped by a falling tree it has cut. One held by a cottonwood tree which had dropped on its right hind foot was found on an island in Wisconsin River near the Dane County-Iowa County boundary line, October 27, 1951 (Ellarson and Hickey, 1952). A very few are killed by automobiles.

Underwater entrance to beaver house after the pond has been drained being examined by W. T. Cox at Gresham Lake, Vilas County, Wisconsin, July 15, 1927. Photograph by Vernon Bailey.

Beaver canal, Marquette County, Michigan, October, 1928. Photograph by Vernon Bailey.

Few external parasites appear to infest the beaver. Internally, it is host to at least six kinds of protozoans and worms. It is subject to the diseases tularemia and pseudotuberculosis, and is also known to have ringworm fungus, rabies, and lumpy jaw. A beaver epidemic in north central Wisconsin in 1952 and 1953 was attributed to a tularemia-like disease. "In each of the 83 beaver colonies . . . from *two* to *nine* beaver carcasses were found floating in the water near the lodge, for a total of 290 dead beaver" (Knudsen, 1953 c: 21).

Like any other animal, the beaver has its good as well as its bad traits. Generally, however, those people who condemn the beaver would not like to see it extirpated. Often it is for personal gain that individuals want the privilege of capturing the animal. Now that the taking of beavers is under the rein of the State Conservation Depart-

ment, reason and not alibi determines the course to be taken. Among the complaints about the beaver are that the animal floods meadows, roads, and even bridges, that it cuts or otherwise kills good timber trees, and that it is harmful to forest plantations. In such cases the Conservation Department handles the matter judiciously. Another complaint is that the beaver ruins trout streams. This may or may not be true. The subject needs much more research. I have often found my very best brook trout fishing near a beaver dam, not only in Wisconsin but in several other states. In a very few cases in beaver ponds water had become too warm for trout, but I had no proof that it would not have been too warm without the beaver dam.

Most of the assets of the beaver are well known. It is valuable as a fur bearer. Its castoreum, produced by a pair of glands in the anal region, is used in the manufacture of perfume, and was formerly used as a medical sedative and antispasmodic. It is valuable in water conservation. Its dams and workings have widespread recreational interest. It is of historical interest for its place in the early history of Wisconsin and the northwest, when its pelt, with a value of one "plus," was the basis of monetary exchange. It plays an important role in conservation of humus and soil. Many of our low prairies are a result of beaver activities over a long period.

Beavers are able to aggrade all smaller valleys below the size of navigable rivers and having been

Top, beaver cutting tree. Flashlight photograph courtesy George Shiras, III. Bottom, beaver eating bark from green aspen stick. Courtesy Norman McClintock.

A pair of beaver pods or castors partly dried but full of castoreum. About ½ ×. Photgraph by Nelson H. Kent.

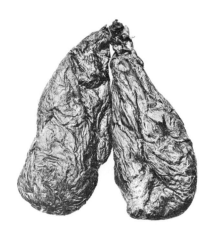

active for many thousands of years have accomplished an enormous amount of aggrading work and are important physiographic agents. Their work is characterized by complete aggrading of valley floors, originally in small descending steps, which disappear in time and leave a gently graded, even valley plain horizontal from bank to bank. The fine silt gathered in the beaver pools has produced the rich farm land in valleys of the wooded areas across the northern half of North America (Ruedemann and Schoonmaker, 1938: 525).

Beaver farming has been suggested as a possible beaver control and conservation measure, but it has not always proven practicable (Bailey, 1922: 16–18; Grange, 1947).

Specimens examined from Wisconsin.—Total 11, as follows: *Bayfield County:* Basswood Lake (10 mi. S. E. of Iron River), 2; Grand View, 2. *Price County:* Phillips, 3 (MM). *Sawyer County:* T 42 N, R 5 W, 1 (UWZ). *Vilas County:* Gresham Lake, 1; Nebish Lake, 1 (UWZ). *Wood County:* Babcock, 1 (WBG).

Selected references.—Bailey, V, 1927 b; Conibear, F., and J. L. Blundell, 1949; Dugmore, A. R., 1914; Johnson, C. E., 1927; Martin, H. T., 1892; Mills, E. A., 1913; Morgan, L. H., 1868; Warren, E. R., 1927.

Family Cricetidae
Deer Mice, Harvest Mice, Muskrat, Voles, and Others

Members of the family Cricetidae have been found in Eurasia, North and South America, and Africa (fossil in Madagascar), and often occur in huge populations. It consists of more than one hundred recognized genera exclusive of fossil forms, of which six occur in Wisconsin. Members of two currently recognized subfamilies occur in Wisconsin.

Key to the Subfamilies of Wisconsin Cricetidae

a. Ears moderately large, prominent; upper molars with tubercles arranged in two longitudinal rows. . . . . *Cricetinae*
. . . .(*Reithrodontomys, Peromyscus*)
aa. Ears small, inconspicuous; upper molars with the enamel in prismatic triangles, often growing from persistent pulp. . . . . *Microtinae*
. . . . (*Synaptomys, Clethrionomys, Microtus, Ondatra*)

Subfamily Cricetinae

Genus Reithrodontomys Giglioli
American Harvest Mice

Dental formula:
$$\text{I} \frac{1-1}{1-1}, \ \text{C} \frac{0-0}{0-0}, \ \text{P} \frac{0-0}{0-0}, \ \text{M} \frac{3-3}{3-3} = 16.$$

Reithrodontomys megalotis pectoralis Hanson
Hanson's Harvest Mouse

Reithrodontomys megalotis pectoralis Hanson, Field Mus. Nat. Hist. Publ. 564, Zool. Series 29 (14): 205–209, October 26, 1944.
Reithrodontomys megalotis pectoralis Barger, p. 11, 1952.

Vernacular names.—When recognized in Wisconsin usually called harvest mouse. Also known as pectoral harvest mouse and prairie harvest mouse.

Identification marks.—A small slender mouse with relatively large ears, prominent eyes; tail length a trifle less than that of head and body, and about four times the length of the hind

Skulls of harvest mouse and deer mice. A. REITHRODONTOMYS M. PECTORALIS, La Crosse, Wisconsin, B. PEROMYSCUS M. GRACILIS, Herbster, Wisconsin, C. P. M. BAIRDII, Milton, Wisconsin, D. P. L. NOVEBORACENSIS, Platteville, Wisconsin.

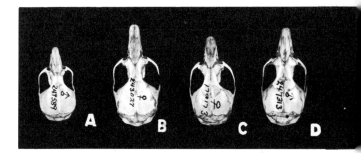

Harvest Mouse

Canadian Deer Mouse

Prairie Deer Mouse

Woodland Deer Mouse

Lemming Mouse

Red-backed Mouse

Meadow Vole

Prairie Vole

Pine Mouse

foot; legs and feet rather weak; forefoot with four clawed toes and small thumb; hind foot with five clawed toes; fur rather long, soft and silky.

The general color tone of the upper parts is buffy brown, produced by mixed light ochraceous buff and blackish; flanks more clearly buff; under parts white or near whitish, with a buffy pectoral spot between the forelegs in about 80 per cent of the specimens; tail bicolorous, dark hair-brown above, dirty whitish below; feet white.

Opposite page, side views of heads of cricetine rodents, drawn from Wisconsin specimens. 1×.

Hind feet, underside, of cricetine rodents, drawn from Wisconsin specimens. 1½×.

There are apparently at least three distinct pelages by the time the mouse assumes its adult coat, which have been classified as a juvenile, a subadult or postjuvenile, and an adult pelage. "After each of those pelages a partial or complete molt intervenes; the juvenile fur is lost and is synchronously replaced by the subadult fur and later the subadult pelage is replaced by the adult coat" (Hooper, 1944: 13). There appears to be one fall molt annually in the adult animal. The process of molting is described by Hooper (1944: 13).

The skull is smoothly rounded, moderately inflated, and without prominent ridges or processes; audital bullae somewhat inflated, longer than broad, obliquely situated with anterior ends in-

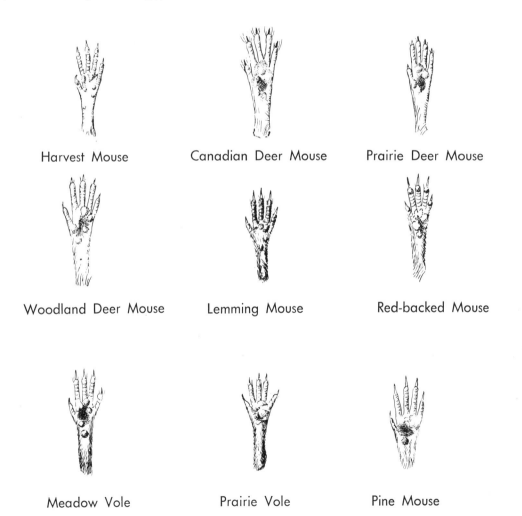

Harvest Mouse   Canadian Deer Mouse   Prairie Deer Mouse

Woodland Deer Mouse   Lemming Mouse   Red-backed Mouse

Meadow Vole   Prairie Vole   Pine Mouse

Skins of harvest mouse and deer mice. A. REITHRO-
DONTOMYS M. PECTORALIS, *La Crosse, Wisconsin,*
B. PEROMYSCUS M. GRACILIS, *Herbster, Wisconsin,*
C. P. P. M. BAIRDII, *La Crosse, Wisconsin,* D. P. L.
NOVEBORACENSIS, *Potosi, Wisconsin. About* ⅗×.

clined toward median line; zygomata slender; anterior palatine foramina large, long narrow slits,
terminating about at anterior end of molariform
tooth row; posterior border of palate truncate,
terminating at posterior end of tooth row; molars tuberculate, the tubercles arranged in two
longitudinal series; upper incisors with a deep
longitudinal groove near the middle of the tooth.

The harvest mouse can be distinguished from
the house mouse (*Mus musculus*) by its more
slender tail, which does not taper noticeably and
which shows no trace of annulations or scales; by
its white feet and under parts; and by the longi-

tudinal groove down the front surface of each
upper incisor. The grooved upper incisor will
also distinguish the harvest mouse from any of
the white-footed or deer mice (*Peromyscus*). The
prairie white-footed mouse (*Peromyscus m. bairdii*) often occurs in the same habitat, and might
possibly be mistaken for the harvest mouse.

Measurements.—Total length of adults, 120 to
150 mm. (4.7 to 5.9 inches); tail, 55 to 70 mm.
(2.2 to 2.8 inches); hind foot, 15 to 17 mm. (.6
to .7 inches); ear from notch, 10.5 to 12 mm.
Weight, 14.2 to 19 grams. Skull length, 19.9 to
22.2 mm.; width, 10.2 to 11.5 mm.

Distribution in Wisconsin.—In so far as known,
limited to the driftless region or its immediate
borders, from western Columbia and western
Dane counties to northern Juneau County, to La
Crosse County. Limits of range unknown.

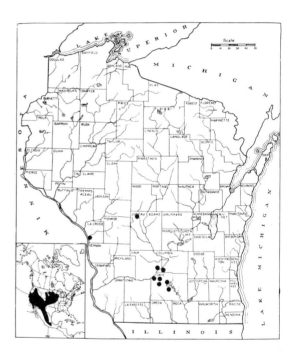

Map 39. Distribution of REITHRODONTOMYS MEGA-
LOTIS. ● = *specimens examined.*

Habitat.—More or less open grassy places; neglected fields overgrown with grasses or sedges;
weedy and grassy borders of cultivated tracts;
grain fields, particularly with ripened grain,
shocks of grain, or stubble. In the West Point

(Columbia County) concentration of this race Hanson (1945) collected 26 specimens distributed in various cover types. These included grain stubble, four caught Sept. 21–28, 1941; blue grass-sweet clover, four caught Oct. 2–11, 1941; alfalfa, nine caught Sept. 23–Oct. 5, 1941; *Carex stricta* bog, one caught Oct. 16–19, 1941; smartweed-foxtail, five caught Oct. 16–19, 1941; shortgrass prairie relic, one caught Oct. 17–20, 1941; sandy field, one caught Oct. 7–10, 1941; and juniper bluff, two caught Oct. 15–18, 1941.

Status and Habits.—The first specimens of the harvest mouse from Wisconsin were collected by Vernon Bailey of the U. S. Biological Survey on the sandy prairie and bottom lands south of La Crosse, July 14 and 16, 1930. Most of these six specimens were trapped along the edges of a sandy oat field or caught by hand under the grain shocks as the bundles were loaded in the field. Bailey noted that the specimens "seemed even darker than those on the Minnesota side of the river" (original field report). In 1936, Frances Hamerstrom procured a specimen at Sprague, Juneau County. In the fall of 1941 Harold C. Hanson found the species in West Point Township, Columbia County, and at Prairie du Sac, Sauk County. He collected 36 specimens, which he later described as *Reithrodontomys megalotis pectoralis* (Hanson, 1944 a). His chief diagnostic characteristic was the buffy pectoral spot between the forelegs, which occurs in about 80 per cent of the specimens. Statements of doubt have been cast on the validity of the form: "*R. m. pectoralis* may prove to be inseparable from *R. m.* dychei" (Hooper, 1952: 218); and "we find no way of distinguishing between specimens of '*pectoralis*' and *dychei*" (Hoffmeister and Warnock, 1955: 164). I have carefully compared Wisconsin specimens with specimens from eastern Kansas (near topotypes of *R. m. dychei*) and find that not only does *pectoralis* show the average difference from *dychei* in the presence of the pectoral spot, but it also averages a shade darker in color of comparable pelages. Its tail is also less pronounced bicolorous, the under side being darker and more grayish than in *dychei*. Adult individuals of *pectoralis* average slightly larger than similarly aged individuals of *dychei*. The differences between the two forms are slight, but inasmuch as the pectoral spot holds in more than 80 per cent of the specimens examined and

the other differences in even a higher percentage, and inasmuch as the variations can be assigned a geographic range, I am recognizing the subspecies *pectoralis*. I have made no attempt to identify such intermediate specimens as might occur in the bordering states of Minnesota, Iowa, and Illinois.

The population of harvest mice in an area appears to reach a high early in autumn, for both Bailey in La Crosse County and Hanson in Columbia County encountered concentrations of the species in September. The former did not estimate the density per acre, but Hanson (1945: 120) estimated the maximum in the foxtail-smartweed cover type as 2.4 per acre, running to a minimum of 0.3 per acre in the sandy field type. The home range is probably seldom more than one acre.

That the harvest mouse is difficult to find in Wisconsin is evident from the few areas where it has been discovered and from the fact that it was unknown in the state until September, 1930. It has probably been in these areas for centuries. A good way to locate this species is to find a likely habitat and search for the animal by examining bunches of grass and shocks of grain, observing the animal when it runs. "It would appear that the harvest mice like a partial over-head canopy and a relatively herb-free, hard packed ground surface that permits freedom of movement" (Hanson, 1945: 119). Trapping in suspected habitats is possibly the best way to locate the species, though it might require many trap nights.

The harvest mouse is active throughout the year, but more so early in the fall and late in the summer when it is busy gathering grain and other seeds for storage. During extremely cold winter weather it confines itself mostly to its nest, but does not hibernate. It seems to be active at any time of day or night. Its usual method of locomotion is a walk or slow trot, and at best it makes slow speed and can usually be overtaken by a man in a short distance. It climbs well, especially small objects such as grain, weed, or coarse grass stalks.

It has few calls or signals, but has been heard to utter a series of rolling birdlike squeaks that could be considered a song. Its small size and relative seclusiveness keep it concealed, yet it does not appear to be particularly wild or timid when approached. It could hardly be called

Nest of harvest mouse, La Crosse, Wisconsin, October 6, 1930. About ½×.

colonial in habits, though limitation of its habitat may make it appear so. It often scampers about as if in play. Although it appears to have normal strength for a small mouse, its life span is probably less than four or five years.

Throughout the year is the breeding time of this harvest mouse, though breeding is more active from April to October than during the winter. The gestation period is about 23 days. The baby at birth weighs 1 to 1.5 grams, is about 7 to 8 mm. long, is hairless with pinkish skin, and its eyes and ears are closed. The youngster can faintly squeak when one day old, the eyes open when it is 11 days old, and it is weaned when about 24 days old. It is fully grown in four or five months, but may sometimes breed when the female is only three months old, and regularly when four months old. The interval between litters may be less than 30 days. The number of young in a litter varies from one to six, but most frequently the number appears to be three or four. The mammae are six, two pectoral, four inguinal.

No runways are made by the harvest mouse, but sometimes it may utilize those made by other mice. It prefers the bare places for activity where runways are not essential. It makes a substantial nest on the ground, or probably more frequently

above the ground in mattocks of grass or weeds, vines, bushes, grain shocks, or even low trees. Cracks or surface openings in the ground are sometimes used for nesting sites. Sometimes a deserted bird's nest is used as a base for the mouse's nest. The nest is made of fine grass, fine grain, or sedge leaves, woven into a neat ball about three and one-half inches in diameter. The inside has a soft lining of fine soft grass and fibers, plant down, and sometimes even a few feathers. One entrance hole about one-half inch in diameter is on the side.

The food of this mouse consists mostly of seeds of various plants such as grass, alfalfa, clover, ragweed and other weeds, and grain. A little green vegetation may sometimes be consumed, as are also some fruits. It stores food, but not in large quantities. One or two caches of a quart or two of seeds is usually the maximum.

One might suspect that a mouse that inhabits more or less open places would have many animals preying upon it, particularly hawks and owls. Possibly this harvest mouse has more enemies than we know, but the only proven enemy is the long-eared owl. Records of this owl freely taking the harvest mouse at Sauk Prairie, Sauk County, in 1942, have been recorded (Hanson, 1945: 120). Undoubtedly weasels and some of the other small predators occasionally catch one.

Most of the food of this species is procured from wild plants of little or no value to man. Rarely does it feed on grain in the shock, and usually then for only a short period while the grain is being harvested. More rarely, when other foods are scarce, it will climb stalks of oats or wheat, pull down the seed head, and consume the grain. It undoubtedly does more good in destruction of weed seeds than it does harm in eating grain. In Wisconsin this mouse is not abundant enough to be of any real economic importance.

Specimens examined from Wisconsin.—Total 28, as follows: *Columbia County:* West Point, 3 (CNHM). *Dane County:* Madison, 8 (Picnic Point, 3; U. W. Arboretum, 5) (UWZ); Mazomanie, 1 (AWS); Middleton (4 mi. W. of), 5 (AWS); Pheasant Branch, 1 (AWS). *Juneau County:* Sprague, 1 (F&FH). *La Crosse County:* La Crosse, 6. *Sauk County:* Sauk Prairie, 3 (CNHM).

Selected references.—Hanson, H. C., 1944 a, 1945; Hoffmeister, D. F., and J. E. Warnock, 1955; Hooper, E. T., 1952; Howell, A. H., 1914.

Genus **Peromyscus** Gloger
White-footed Mice

Dental formula:

$$\text{I}\ \frac{1-1}{1-1},\ \ \text{C}\ \frac{0-0}{0-0},\ \ \text{P}\ \frac{0-0}{0-0},\ \ \text{M}\ \frac{3-3}{3-3} = 16.$$

Peromyscus maniculatus gracilis (Le Conte)
Woodland Deer Mouse

H [*esperomys*] *gracilis* LeConte, Proc. Acad. Nat. Sci. Philadelphia, vol. 7 (1854–55), p. 442, 1855.

Peromyscus canadensis Jackson, p. 20, 1908.

Peromyscus maniculatus gracilis Hollister, p. 25, 1910; Cory, p. 193, 1912; Schmidt, p. 115, 1931; Komarek, p. 208, 1932; Barger, p. 11, 1952.

Vernacular names.—In Wisconsin usually called simply deer mouse or white-footed mouse. Other names include Canadian deer mouse, Canadian white-footed mouse, LeConte's deer mouse, long-tailed deer mouse, peromyscus mouse, *quay-non-wit-wa-go-no-chi* (Chippewa), and white-bellied wood mouse.

Identification marks.—A medium-sized mouse, the adult averaging about 180 mm. in total length; ear large, measuring 19 to 21 mm. from notch; eyes prominent; tail relatively long, about 48 per cent of total length and about four times the length of the hind foot; tail finely haired but not bushy; fur soft and dense.

In fresh autumn or winter pelage the general color of the upper parts varies from near russet to dull cinnamon, the mid-dorsal area more or less mixed with blackish; more russet on the rump and flanks, more grayish on the shoulders and occiput; general tone of sides raw umber; ears dark, almost blackish, narrowly edged with whitish; under parts white; feet white; tail blackish above, white below. Worn pelage of summer somewhat paler and more cinnamon, the dorsal area particularly faded. The juvenile in its first full pelage is usually somewhat darker, particularly on dorsal area, than the adult. There is one molt annually, which usually occurs in August but may begin as early as June. The process of molting has been described by Osgood (1909: 19–21).

The skull is smoothly rounded, but little ridged and thin walled; interparietal well developed; zygoma slender, depressed to level of palate; anterior palatine foramen long, slitlike. Dentition rather weak; molars tuberculate, the tubercles

Woodland deer mouse, Marquette County, Michigan. Courtesy Norman McClintock.

in two longitudinal series; upper molars three-rooted, lower two-rooted.

In many carefully measured adult specimens males average very slightly larger than females. There is a range of individual variation in size of about 5 per cent from a mean, which is much less than the average sexual size variation indicated. Color variations are essentially normal. I have seen no variation in Wisconsin that could be considered a mutant. White-spotting has occasionally been reported in northern Michigan, but whether the spots were mutations or were caused by disease or parasites is not known. Dice (1936) found that mice of this race indicated growth in body size after the second year of life, but that there was no pronounced color change in the older mice. White side, a recessive mutation, appeared in offspring of hybrids of *P. m. gracilis* and *P. m. bairdii* (McIntosh, 1956).

Among the Wisconsin mice any members of the genus *Peromyscus* may be separated from *Reithrodontomys* by the smooth front of the upper incisor, which is longitudinally grooved in *Reithrodontomys;* also in the larger ear, though in some specimens a large ear of *R. m. pectoralis* (just under 12 mm.) may approach in size a small ear (just over 12 mm.) of *P. m. bairdii.* The house mouse (*Mus*) differs from any Wisconsin *Peromyscus* in that the tail is scarcely haired and shows a ringed scaliness lacking in *Peromyscus;* the under parts have a buffish or yellowish tinge, and are not pure white as in *Peromyscus,* with the exception of mutant individuals; the dental formula is the same, but the tubercles on the upper molars of the house mouse (*Mus*) are arranged in three longitudinal rows, not in two rows as in *Peromyscus.*

Peromyscus maniculatus gracilis is not known to intergrade directly with *P. m. bairdii,* and the two subspecies are more differentiated from each other in general appearance than either is from *P. leucopus noveboracensis.* Intergradation occurs indirectly through several western subspecies. Compared with *P. l. noveboracensis,* the tail of *P. m. gracilis* averages longer, is more distinctly penciled, and more sharply bicolorous; the pelage is softer; the ears are relatively and actually larger, measuring 18.5 to 21 mm. from notch to tip, whereas in *noveboracensis* this ear length is less than 18 mm.; skull more slender, and molar teeth relatively smaller. A character mentioned by Burt (1946: 207)—that "the skull may be set apart from that of *P. m. bairdii* and *P. leucopus* by the position of the anterior border of the zygomatic plate which, when the skull is viewed from the side, does not cover the infraorbital foramen" —does not hold in the many Wisconsin specimens I have examined. From the subspecies *bairdii,* the adult of *gracilis* can always be separated by its longer tail (more than 70 mm. long, *bairdii* less than); strikingly larger ear (*gracilis* 18.5 mm. or more, *bairdii* less than 15 mm.); and longer skull (*gracilis* 25 mm. or more; *bairdii* less than 25 mm.).

Measurements.—Total length of adults, 168 to 206 mm. (6.6 to 8.1 inches); tail, 77 to 108 mm. (3.0 to 4.3 inches); hind foot, 19 to 22.5 mm. (.7 to .9 inches); ear from notch, 18.5 to 21 mm. (.7 to .8 inches). Weight, 18 to 31 grams. Skull length, 25 to 27.8 mm.; width, 12.3 to 13.9 mm.

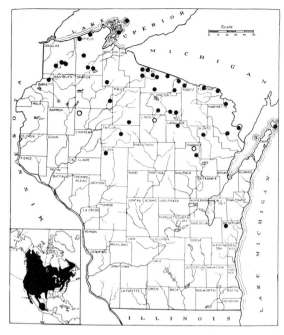

Map 40. Distribution of PEROMYSCUS MANICULATUS GRACILIS, *in Wisconsin, with insert showing range of the species.* ● = *specimen examined.* ○ = *authentic records.*

Distribution in Wisconsin.—Northern part of the state from Burnett County to northern Clark County, easterly to Green Bay and Door County (Washington Island). Formerly, in 1917, Sheboygan Swamp, Sheboygan County.

Habitat.—Northern woodland of coniferous, deciduous, or mixed tree growth, particularly in log-strewn timber or along river or lake banks; sometimes spruce-cedar swamps (Marinette County), old cabins, abandoned lumber mills (Orienta), and brush-covered limestone rocks (Washington Island).

Status and Habits.—The woodland deer mouse as an inhabitant of forested areas has been common in northern Wisconsin since the days of the first explorers. It was not recognized in reports on Wisconsin mammals until the present author (1908: 20–21) listed specimens of his own collecting under the name *Peromyscus canadensis.* The species is locally very abundant in some localities, probably exceeding in numbers in some local areas either *P. m. bairdii* or *P. l. noveboracensis* in their densest populations. At night they almost took over our crude camp on Outer Island in July, 1919, and frequently scampered over our sleeping bags and sometimes over our faces. They did not bother our food supply seriously, probably because we left exposed a liberal supply of rolled oats for them. They carried away some of our cotton and tow for nesting material. Every specimen taken on Outer Island was fully adult, the young of the year apparently not being sufficiently developed to shift for themselves. Population density appears to be somewhat variable from year to year, but with no apparent cycle of abundance. A normal population in favorable habitat may run about five or six individuals to the acre over a considerable area. Condensed populations around particularly favorable food and home conditions may reach a maximum of more than 30 or 40 animals per acre. Manville (1949a: 38) in northern Michigan found that the home range may vary from 500 to 1,500 square yards (0.11 to 0.31 acre) for adult males, from 600 to 1,200 square yards (0.12 to .0.25 acre) for adult females, and from 500 to 1,300 square yards (0.11 to 0.27 acre) for juveniles of both sexes. As estimated by Blair (1942: 29), however, in Alger County, Michigan, the average home range of adult males was 2.31 acres with a maximum of 5.64 acres, and that of females 1.39 acres with a maximum of 3.28 acres.

Trapping, and watching, listening, and waiting at dusk are the best means of detecting the presence of a deer mouse. It leaves fairly distinctive tracks in snow, sand, or dust, but they cannot easily be identified from those of some other mice. Occasionally one will appear when "squeaked up," for often it responds to an ordinary bird call. A flare from a flashlight does not usually frighten it, and the animal is often exposed to vision by that means. An experienced ear can often detect the patter of feet of a deer mouse and distinguish it from the slower and heavier tread of microtine mice, which also seldom get off the ground or fallen logs. In a newly established camp in a woodland or along a lake shore, a little grain, rolled oats, bread, or cracker crumbs will usually soon bring several nighttime deer mouse visitors. This mouse is active the year around, even in cold weather. It does not migrate, but may emigrate several hundred yards to establish a new home, particularly the juveniles. Its activities begin at dusk and continue throughout the night. Occasionally it is out in

daylight, even at midday. Its customary gait when searching for food is an indeterminate walk; when startled it usually runs or scampers; in snow or on soft ground, or when badly frightened, it gallops. It can climb fairly well, especially a tree, or shrub with rough bark, but spends most of its time on the ground or on fallen logs or branches. Its maximum speed is about five miles an hour.

The woodland deer mouse is sociable and not overly quarrelsome with its own kind, yet cannot be called colonial or gregarious. Its means of communication are chiefly by stamping or drumming its forefeet and by a vocal call that sounds like a buzzing, not unlike that of a bumblebee but of short duration. Sometimes it is regularly repeated. Sharp squeals or squeaks of protest are sometimes given. It does not regularly engage in play. It is extremely alert and sensitive to quick sounds and movements, but is not particularly keen-sighted. "It is to be noted that at least some peromyscus can hear ultrasonic sounds within the same general frequency range that is used by bats for echo location. It is not yet known, however, whether a peromyscus can produce ultrasonic sounds over the range of frequencies that it can hear" (Dice and Barto, 1952: 111). It makes an interesting pet, but is not especially friendly. It is quiet and cleanly in its habits when confined. The cage should be provided with soft nesting material, food, and water, and if possible with a wheel upon which the mouse can run. The normal longevity of life expectancy in the wild is probably less than four years. The potential longevity is eight years four months (Dice, 1933: 147).

The regular breeding season insofar as known begins about the last of April and continues at least until the middle of August; several females containing embryos were trapped in that month in several localities in northern Wisconsin. If food and warmth are available it will breed all winter. The gestation period seems to be somewhat variable, but is believed to be about 25 to 27 days. The young range from one to seven in a litter, the usual number being four or five. The baby is naked, with eyes closed. Indications of hair growth appear on the dorsal region on the second day after birth. In about 14 or 15 days the eyes open. The young one is usually weaned when about 30 days old. Four or five litters usually are raised by one female during the breeding season. The mammae are six, two pectoral, four inguinal.

The nest is placed in some natural opening in or close to the ground, in an old stump or log, a crevice among rocks, back of a loose piece of bark on a tree, or in a similar shelter. Sometimes it selects an abandoned burrow of a chipmunk or some other mammal. Often it will make its nest in a sheltered spot in a cabin or similar structure. It apparently does not construct its own burrow. Few nests of *P. m. gracilis* have been examined critically. The nest is composed of grass, leaves, and other plant material, and lined with finer herbage and shredded plants.

The food of the woodland deer mouse consists of various seeds, small nuts, many small fruits, and a considerable number of insects, many of which are in the larval or chrysalis stage. Among seeds or fruits known to be eaten by it are those of beaked hazelnut, Juneberry (*Amelanchier*), basswood, pin cherry, hemlock, hard maple, blueberry, wintergreen, yellow clintonia, and partridge berry. It stores some food such as seeds and nuts, but not in great quantity. It probably procures most of its water from its food.

Without doubt this mouse is preyed upon by some species of predatory mammals, as well as by some hawks and owls. Its woodland habitat and chiefly nocturnal habits may afford some protection to it. It appears to be rather vulnerable to heavy rain, and in fact any thorough soaking of the fur, particularly in cold weather, is apt to kill it. It sometimes falls into a water hole and drowns. A forest fire is quite destructive. Two species of lice, a mite, a tick, and a flea are known to infest it. It is also sometimes the victim of the botfly, and scars caused by this fly are not uncommon. At least four species of worms are among its internal parasites.

By and large the woodland deer mouse is of little economic importance. Some foresters claim that it destroys seeds of many forest trees. Many of the seeds it stores may grow; many more are eaten or stored in hollow logs or trees where they will never reach the soil. The relation of this race of mouse to forests is a question open to research. At times around a camp, cabin, or ranger station

it may become quite a nuisance. Metal-covered food boxes and cupboards will protect food from it. When it becomes too numerous and annoying it is easily trapped or poisoned. From late in summer through most of November in 1910, Clarence Birdseye, then of the U. S. Biological Survey, lived in one of the log buildings of an abandoned hunting camp at an island in the Tahquamenon River, Luce County, Michigan. He says:

During the first three weeks of my stay I caught 16 white-footed mice in this cabin, and during the next 6 weeks took 45 more. They seem to be equally abundant in other occupied shacks, and one morning I counted 8 which had jumped into a big kettle of water and been drowned. The trapper outside of whose cabin this kettle was, kept a cat and a dog, both of which killed many mice; and he poisoned many more with a mixture of pork grease and strychnine (Clarence Birdseye, in ms. report, November, 1910).

Specimens examined from Wisconsin.—Total 173, as follows: *Ashland County:* Bear Lake, 2 (UWZ); Madeline Island, 1; Outer Island, 14. *Bayfield County:* Basswood Lake (10 mi. S. E. of Iron River), 1; Herbster, 8; Namakagon Lake, 1; Orienta, 5; T 44 N, R 7 W, Sec. 13, 1 (F&FH). *Burnett County:* Namakagon River (mouth of), 9 (MM). *Clark County:* Thorp Township, 3 (1 AMNH). *Door County:* Washington Island, 3. *Douglas County:* Saint Croix Dam, 6 (MM); Solon Springs, 2; Upper Saint Croix Lake, 11 (7 MM; 4 CNHM). *Florence County:* Spread Eagle Lake, 4 (CNHM); T 40 N, R 16 E, Sec. 26, 1 (UWZ). *Iron County:* Fisher Lake, 13 (UWZ); Mercer, 5 (MM). *Langlade County:* Elcho, 1 (UWZ). *Marinette County:* Cataline, 2 (MM); McAllister, 1; No locality, 2 (MM). *Oconto County:* Lakewood, 10. *Oneida County:* Crescent Lake, 3; Moen Lake, 2 (UWZ); North Pelican Lake, 1 (UWZ); *Price County:* Long Lake, 1 (MM); Ogema, 1. *Sawyer County:* Connors Lake, 7 (2 F&FH). *Shawano County:* Keshena, 14 (CAS). *Sheboygan County:* Sheboygan Swamp (near Elkhart Lake), 2. *Taylor County:* North Twin Lake, 1 (F&FH). *Vilas County:* Divide, 4 (MM); Eagle River, 9 (2 MM); Lac Vieux Desert, 11 (CHNM); Lake St. Germain, 1; Lynx Lake (T 43 N, R 7 E, Sec. 19), 4 (2 F&FH); Mamie Lake, 4; Robinson Lake (near Nelma), 1 (UWZ); T 42 N, R 8 E, Sec. 26, 1 (F&FH).

Selected references.—Dice, L. R., 1936; Blair, W. F., 1941 b; Manville, R. H., 1949 a; Moody, P. A., 1929; Osgood, W. H., 1909; Svihla, A., 1932.

Peromyscus maniculatus bairdii (Hoy and Kennicott)

Prairie Deer Mouse

Mus bairdii Hoy and Kennicott, in Kennicott, Agricultural Report U. S. Commissioner of Patents 1856, p. 92, 1857.
Hesperomys Bairdii Strong, p. 438, 1883.
Hesperomys Michiganensis Strong, p. 439, 1883.
Peromyscus bairdi Snyder, p. 116, 1902; Hollister, p. 140, 1909.
Peromyscus michiganensis Jackson, p. 21, 1908.
Peromyscus maniculatus bairdi Hollister, p. 25, 1910; Cory, p. 190, 1912.
Peromyscus maniculatus bairdii Schmidt, p. 115, 1931; Barger, p. 11, 1952.

Vernacular names.—In Wisconsin usually called deer mouse or white-footed mouse; sometimes called long-tailed field mouse or prairie white-footed mouse. Other names include Baird's deer mouse, Baird's white-footed mouse, Michigan deer mouse, Michigan prairie mouse, Michigan white-footed mouse, Michigan wood mouse, and prairie mouse.

Identification marks.—Smallest of the three races of *Peromyscus* that occur in Wisconsin, the adult usually less than 160 mm. in total length, ear smallest of the Wisconsin deer mice, measuring from notch to tip 15 mm. or less; tail sharply bicolorous, rather short for *Peromyscus*, usually less than 65 mm. long and near 40 per cent of total length; hind foot small, less than 20 mm.

In fresh winter pelage the general color of the upper parts is near russet, heavily mixed with blackish, the dark generally concentrated in a mid-dorsal longitudinal band; sides heavily mixed with black, usually distinctly paler than back; sides of face about same color as flanks, the occiput somewhat paler; under parts' creamy white, often showing an indistinct russet line separat-ing the creamy white color from the brownish of flanks; ears dark fuscous, with narrow creamy margin; tail sharply bicolorous, dark fuscous above, creamy below; feet whitish below ankles. Summer pelage usually more brownish or reddish, with the dorsal dark area reduced. Young are darker and more grayish than adults. There is one molt annually, which occurs during the summer.

The general description of the skull as given for *P. m. gracilis* applies to *P. m. bairdii*. The skull of *bairdii* is much smaller than that of *gracilis* and measures 22.5 to 24.5 in greatest length. It averages smaller than that of *P. l. noveboracensis*, though a few large skulls of *bairdii* may be as long as a few small skulls of *noveboracensis*.

Means of identification of *P. m. bairdii* as compared with *Mus musculus, Reithrodontomys,* and *P. m. gracilis* have been indicated under *gracilis*. Separation of *P. m. bairdii* from certain specimens of *P. l. noveboracensis* is sometimes more difficult, although in adult individuals the smaller size, shorter tail, smaller ear, and smaller hind foot will determine its identity. Color alone cannot be used for sure identification. Cranial characters that separate *bairdii* from *noveboracensis* are the lesser cranial breadth; shorter length of maxillary tooth row (average length 3.2 mm. as against 3.5 in *noveboracensis*); incisive foramina open and evenly curved (constricted anteriorly in *noveboracensis*).

Measurements.—Total length of adults, 134 to 161 mm. (5.3 to 6.3 inches); tail, 48 to 69 mm. (1.9 to 2.7 inches); hind foot, 17 to 19.5 mm.

Prairie deer mouse. Photographed by George Socha.

(.7 to .8 inches); ear from notch, 12 to 15 mm. (.5 to .6 inches). Weight, 16 to 24 grams. Skull length, 22.5 to 24.5 mm.; width, 11.4 to 12.7 mm.

Distribution in Wisconsin.—Southern two-thirds of the state from the Illinois-Wisconsin boundary to northern Door County, central Oconto County, northern Clark and Dunn counties, and Saint Croix County.

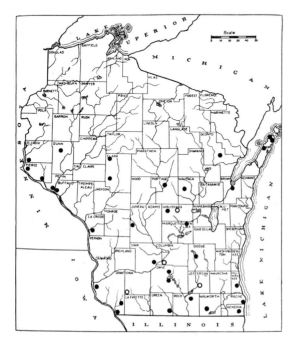

Map 41. *Distribution of* PEROMYSCUS MANICULATUS BAIRDII, *in Wisconsin.* ● = *specimens examined.* ○ = *authentic records.*

Habitat.—Open places, more especially in drier and well-drained areas, such as hay or grain fields, dry meadows, prairies, cultivated fields, grassy fence lines, and sandy beaches; usually more plentiful in sparse grassy cover, but frequently found in nearly bare land or with some cover of vines or brush; seldom found within a woodland border or under cover of trees.

Status and Habits.—In some favorable places in the state the prairie deer mouse may at times become very numerous. It apparently has extended its range northward following the trend of woodland destruction and open field development through agricultural activities. It was undoubtedly present in early days in the prairies

and along sandy beaches such as occurred along Lake Michigan and the lower Wisconsin River. It is quite possible that specimens taken near the northern tip of Door Peninsula 50 years ago were descendants of members of the race that had inhabited the sand beaches there for several centuries. The population of the prairie deer mouse in an area may vary from year to year, but there is no evidence of cycles of abundance. A normal population during midsummer in a favorable year may average ten per acre in a favorable habitat. Such an area has a lesser population in spring, and it is again reduced early in the autumn. In some fields where grain or corn is left in shocks the number of these mice may reach a concentration of 30 or more per acre. It has a large home range for a small mammal, and normally covers in its activities two or three acres, and sometimes as many as five or six acres.

Trapping with ordinary snap mousetraps, or carefully searching out the nesting and running places are the means of detecting the presence of this species. Sometimes its tracks—imprints of the four toes almost in a tiny square, with a track at each corner—tell the presence of this mouse or one of its kin, but the tracks are not always clearly seen. If one uptilts boards, clumps of earth, or like cover in a prospective habitat, one is apt to uncover a runway, a nest, or even a mouse itself. It is active both summer and winter. It is only rarely out during daylight, being rather strictly nocturnal. It seldom walks, traveling most of the time in a gallop. It is quick in movement and starts like a flash, yet once in motion is a comparatively slow runner. Its maximum speed is about 5.7 miles an hour, and if it does not have shelter near it can readily be captured by hand. I have collected many specimens by hand, captured under corn or other grain shocks. The only call note I have heard it utter is a series of short high-pitched squeaks, almost a song, or sometimes only a single squeak or two. The male sometimes "drums" with its fore paws.

This mouse is not gregarious and does not live in colonies. It becomes abundant in a given area only because food and other environmental conditions fit it. In confinement as a pet it is only moderately sociable, but not wild or vicious. It does not indulge in play, yet is extremely active in running on a wheel when one is supplied. Its senses of hearing and touch are well developed.

Its normal life span in the wild is probably not more than two or three years, and its potential longevity near six years.

The breeding season begins about March 1 and extends through November. Possibly there is an occasional litter in the winter months. A female may have three or four litters a year, possibly more. Whether or not she is served by the same male for each litter is unknown. The male is driven from the nest as soon as the young are born. The young vary from two to nine in a litter, the more frequent numbers being four to six. The gestation period is about 25 days. The eyes open when the baby is about 14 days old. When about 25 days old the youngster is weaned. The mammae are six, two pectoral, four inguinal.

The prairie deer mouse dislikes elevation above the ground and always builds its nest slightly under ground or on the surface. Sometimes it has a small tunnel leading to the nest, and at other times only a crude runway. The nest is usually placed under some object such as a board, slab, fallen limb, old pasteboard carton, shock of grain, or almost any conceivable cover. At Milton, I once found a nest in an old boat lying in a trash pile. Often the nest in an open field is simply in a burrow in the ground. The nest is usually rather large, some ten inches in diameter, and externally is composed of coarse plant stems. It has a single entrance to the inside bed of soft, downy material, which is frequently the down of milkweed or thistle, but sometimes contains hair or feathers. There seems to be little sanitation in the nest. Frequently an old nest is left under the same board or cover where a new nest has been built.

The principal foods of the prairie deer mouse are seeds, grain, fruits, and available vegetable food. Sometimes quantities of insects are eaten by this mouse, but it may be on occasions when there is a shortage of vegetable food. It stores small quantities of food, usually in its nest, or nearby. It drinks very little water. It frequently cleans itself by licking its fur from its nose to the tip of its tail. It often wallows in sand or dust, possibly more to rid itself of fleas and other parasites than for cleanliness.

Various predators feed upon the prairie deer mouse. Mammals known to prey upon it are the striped skunk, weasel, raccoon, red fox, and coyote. The domestic cat catches many. The marsh hawk preys upon it, as does the sparrow hawk. Among owls that prey upon it are the saw-whet, short-eared, long-eared, barred, and great horned. Snakes undoubtedly capture a few.

The prairie deer mouse is of little importance economically to man. Its food is mostly seeds of weeds, grass, and waste grain that it gathers on the ground. At times it consumes considerable numbers of injurious insects. Along the Mississippi River in Grant County, Wisconsin, complaint was made by melon growers that this mouse ate seeds planted during spring, and that later when the melons were ripe it ate through the rind into the melon to get the seeds inside. Not infrequently, in shocks of corn or other grain left standing in a field, it will do considerable damage.

Specimens examined from Wisconsin.—Total 236, as follows: *Brown County:* DePere, 1 (NPM). *Buffalo County:* Nelson, 1. *Clark County:* Thorp Township, 2 (UWZ); Tioga, 1 (UWZ). *Dane County:* Blooming Grove, 2 (UWZ); Madison, 11 (UWZ); West Port Township, 1 (UWZ). *Dodge County:* Beaver Dam, 72 (11 AMNH; 35 CNHM; 26 UWZ). *Door County:* Ellison Bay, 4; Fish Creek, 2; Newport, 3 (MM). *Dunn County:* Wheeler, 1. *Grant County:* Platteville, 1; Potosi (10 mi. S. S. E. of), 1; Wyalusing, 2 (MM). *Green County:* Broadhead, 1 (F&FH). *Green Lake County:* Berlin (3 mi. W. of), 1 (WHD). *Juneau County:* Camp Douglas, 2. *Kenosha County:* Kenosha, 2 (CAS). *La Crosse County:* La Crosse, 4. *Milwaukee County:* Milwaukee, 2 (MM). *Oconto County:* Kelley Brook, 4 (MM). *Pepin County:* Pepin, 1. *Pierce County:* Maiden Rock, 1 (MM); Prescott, 38 (MM). *Racine County:* Racine, 3 (1 AMNH). *Rock County:* Milton, 6 (1 CNHM; 4 UWZ). *Saint Croix County:* River Falls, 10 (WHD). *Sauk County:* Prairie du Sac, 41 (MM). *Walworth County:* Delavan, 8 (2 AMNH; 2 CAS; 1 NPM). *Waupaca County:* Saint Lawrence Township, 6 (UWZ). *Waushara County:* Plainfield, 1 (F&FH).

Selected references.—Blair, W. F., 1940; Dice, L. R., 1932 a, 1932 b; Howard, W. E., 1949; Osgood, W. H., 1909; Svihla, A., 1935.

Peromyscus leucopus noveboracensis
(Fischer)

Northern White-footed Mouse

[*Mus. sylvaticus*] δ *noveboracensis* Fischer, Synopsis
Mammalium, p. 318, 1829.
Mus leucopus Lapham, p. 340, 1853.
Hesperomys leucopus Strong, p. 438, 1883.
Peromyscus leucopus Snyder, p. 117, 1902.
Peromyscus leucopus noveboracensis Jackson, p. 21,
    1908; Hollister, p. 25, 1910; Cory, p. 185, 1912;
    Schmidt, p. 115, 1931; Komarek, p. 208, 1932;
    Barger, p. 11, 1952.

Vernacular names.—In Wisconsin often called
deer mouse, white-footed mouse, or wood mouse.
Other names include jumping mouse, northern
deer mouse, northern white-footed mouse, vesper
mouse, wood gnome, woods mouse, woodland
deer mouse, and woodland white-footed mouse.

Identification marks.—A medium-sized mouse,
the adult averaging about 175 mm. in total
length; ear medium, measuring from notch to tip
15 to 18 mm.; tail rather long compared with
that of other mice in southern Wisconsin, the
length usually from 72 to 84 mm. and near 44
per cent of total length; hind foot medium, 20
to 22 mm.

In full winter pelage the upper parts are cinnamon rufous to almost fulvous, mixed considerably with dusky down the middle of the back
and with dusky hairs scattered on the sides;
under parts creamy white; feet white; tail bicolorous, dusky brown above creamy below. Summer pelage duller and more grayish than winter
fur. Young in first pelage much more grayish.
There is one molt annually during the summer.
White spotting and "yellow" mutations sometimes occur. A yellow mutant male that I collected at Turtle Lake, Walworth County, August
24, 1922, is clear creamy buff above from tip of
nose to tip of tail and the normally white under
parts show a slight wash of creamy buff.

Tracks of white-footed mouse in mud. Natural size.

*White-footed mouse, P. L. NOVEBORACENSIS, with nest
exposed. U. S. Fish and Wildlife Service photograph by Donald A. Spencer.*

There is little overlapping of the geographic range of *P. l. noveboracensis* and *P. m. gracilis*, but within this area or elsewhere *P. l. noveboracensis* may be distinguished from *gracilis* by its average shorter tail with less pronounced pencil, and more especially by the size of the ear, which always measures less than 18 mm. from notch to tip; also the skull is more slender and the molar teeth smaller.

Often a specimen of *P. l. noveboracensis* in winter pelage can be distinguished from *P. m. bairdii* by its more fulvous color, but usually color alone is not determinate. An adult individual of *noveboracensis* is larger than *bairdii*, and has a longer tail and larger ear and hind foot. Cranially, *noveboracensis* may be separated from *bairdii* by its greater cranial breadth; length of maxillary tooth row greater (average 3.5 mm. as against 3.2 in *bairdii*); incisive foramina constricted anteriorly (open and evenly curved in *bairdii*).

Measurements.—Total length of adults, 158 to 192 mm. (6.3 to 7.6 inches); tail 70 to 88 mm. (2.8 to 3.5 inches); hind foot, 20 to 22 mm. (0.8 to 0.9 inches); ear from notch, 15 to 18 mm. (0.6 to 0.7 inches). Weight, 18 to 30 grams. Skull length, 24.2 to 27.4 mm.; width, 12.3 to 14 mm.

Distribution in Wisconsin.—Approximately the southern three-fourths of the state from the Illinois-Wisconsin boundary line northward to the tip of Door Peninsula, southern Oconto, southern Price and southern Washburn counties, and northern Burnett County (mouth of Yellow River).

Habitat.—Woodlands and forests, often densely brushy areas such as fence lines, sometimes more open grassy areas that border woodland; seldom more than fifty feet from woods, though rarely it may wander up to eight hundred or one thousand feet from timber (weed patches, July 15, 1912, Fountain City); prefers deciduous woods, more especially oak-hickory; sometimes excessively common in rocky ravines with perpendicular walls of limestone containing many cavities (Prescott, Pierce County).

Status and Habits.—The northern white-footed mouse probably has always been the most abundant mammal in the deciduous forests of Wisconsin, fluctuating in abundance only as it has been affected by availability of food, disease, and other environmental causes. Like some other

southern forms it has tended to advance its range slightly northward as the more southern biota, particularly deciduous vegetation, also moved northward. It apparently has not followed as extensively as some other hardwood inhabitants, such as the gray squirrel, and has not approached such prairie forms as *Citellus tridecemlineatus* or *Peromyscus m. bairdii*. A normal population is about 3 or 4 adults to the acre, which under favorable conditions may reach 20 or more. In June, 1912, I found this species excessively abundant, as had Herbert L. Stoddard four years previously, in a rocky ravine with perpendicular limestone walls containing many cavities south of Prescott, Pierce County. Here the mice lived one family above another in the ledges, like city apartment dwellers. One could hardly estimate the population, but Stoddard trapped more than two hundred of them in a few days. One hundred per acre of horizontal ground would be a very modest estimate. The normal home range of this species is about one-quarter acre, but sometimes an individual, particularly a male, may range over an acre or more.

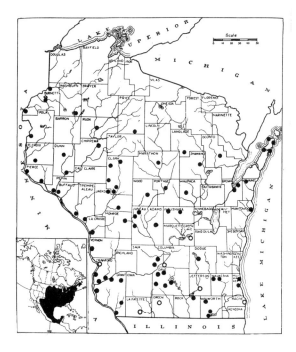

Map 42. Distribution of PEROMYSCUS LEUCOPUS.
● = *specimens examined.* ○ = *authentic records.*

Methods of detecting the presence of the northern white-footed mouse are essentially the same as with *P. m. gracilis*. This species, like its more northern relative, is active the year around, but appears to be more strictly nocturnal, seldom appearing until well after sundown and retiring before dawn. Even when disturbed during the daytime it is reluctant to run out into the light and seeks shelter under some protecting object. Its principal mode of locomotion when going any considerable distance is a gallop, though often when searching for food it walks or trots. When it walks it usually drags its tail, but when running it holds its tail well above ground. When the animal runs or gallops in deep, light snow the tail usually leaves a trail on the surface, as it does when the mouse walks. Its maximum running speed is about seven miles an hour. It is a proficient climber, and spends no small part of its time in trees.

The northern white-footed mouse has excellent sense of hearing, and also is very sensitive to touch. Its sight is good during the darker hours, but in sunlight the animal seems noticeably blinded. Its large eyes are well adapted to its nocturnal habits. Its usual method of communication is by a series of rapid taps with its finger tips on some smooth hard surface. The resulting sound is a sharp prolonged buzzing that can be almost exactly imitated by drawing one's fingernail over a wire screen. It varies somewhat in tempo, volume, and tone, depending on the object upon which the mouse is drumming. It also utters less frequently a clear birdlike whistle. The normal longevity or life expectancy in the wild is about three to four years, yet probably a majority of the white-footed mice live for a considerably shorter time. Potential longevity is about eight years.

Mating occurs the latter part of February or early in March, and the first litter is born between the middle and the last of April. The gestation period is variable, and has been reported as from 22 to 37 days (Svihla, 1932: 17). The usual period is between 23 and 25 days. The young vary in number from one to seven, usually three to six, with four the most frequent number. The young female may breed when only ten weeks old, but her first litter is small, usually only two or three. The species is prolific, and as many as four broods may be raised between April and

November. The mouse at birth weighs about 1.5 to 2 grams, and is hairless and blind. The eyes open in about 12 to 14 days, and the baby is usually weaned when about 24 to 28 days old. When it is five weeks old it must shift for itself. The mammae are six, two pectoral, four inguinal.

The northern white-footed mouse seemingly builds its nest wherever convenient. It apparently never digs its own burrow, nor makes a trail, though it is ready and eager to utilize burrows and trails of other mammals. It seems to prefer a tree site for its nest, usually about 6 to 8 feet from the ground, but some I have found in abandoned squirrels' nests have been fully 20 feet above ground. The nest may be in the open in an abandoned bird's nest or squirrel's nest, or even built by the mouse itself among the dense branches of a thorn apple, grape vine, or wild crabapple. Often the nest is built in a hollow tree or limb, with an entrance hole barely large enough to admit the mouse. Another favorite site is under an old stump or log. Old stone quarries, stone walls, and weathered limestone cliffs or caves containing small cavities are also favored nesting sites. The nest is composed of almost any available soft material, such as grass, leaves, or other vegetation, or even fur, feathers, or cloth. The nest is usually about ten or twelve inches in diameter and six or eight inches deep. It has one entrance hole on the side near the top. Frequently two or more nests are built by one individual, who may vacate one nest for another for a while, and return to the first one after a few days or weeks. Both male and female work in constructing the home. There is little or no sanitation, the feces being dropped inside the nest or nesting cavity.

The principal food of the northern white-footed mouse is seeds of various plants such as grasses, weeds, clover, small fruits, and grain. Nuts, particularly acorns and hazelnuts, and even hickory nuts, are eaten extensively. Some green herbage is consumed. A few insects and insect eggs and larval are eaten. Water is obtained chiefly from its food, though I have seen an individual lap water from a tiny woodland pool of rainwater. It stores considerable quantities of hard food, mixing nuts, seeds, grain, and fruit pits together in several small caches of a quart or two each. The storage place may be near the nest, or in any protected place, such as a small cavity in a tree, behind a piece of bark, in a hole under a rock, or in a crevice in a stone wall or cliff. After eating it thoroughly washes itself with its tongue from tip of nose to tip of tail. Of this subspecies, Nicholson (1941: 206) says:

When eating an acorn, the wood-mouse usually removes the cap, cuts the acorn in two around the middle on the mid-line, and then removes the meat from each half shell. Occasionally, the acorns are opened by shredding the shell down on all sides from the apex. . . . The red acorn, one of the most bitter, is apparently used for food as readily as any of the others.

Hickory nuts are always opened in the following manner: two holes are gnawed in the sides of the nut, opposite to each other. The openings usually occupy a little more than a quarter of the surface of each side. The openings are always made on the sides, crossing the longitudinal split in the nut; thus, when the openings are finished, the edge of the two halves of the kernel are exposed on both sides. Through these relatively small openings, the mice are able to obtain every bit of the food in each side of the nut. The mice eat both thin-shelled and hard-shelled nuts, both bitter and sweet nuts, all seemingly with the same readiness.

Owls are an important enemy of this nocturnal mouse, and there are many records of its capture by the saw-whet, screech, long-eared, barred, and great horned owls in Wisconsin. The red-tailed hawk captures this mouse occasionally. Weasels, skunks, and both the gray and the red fox are among its enemies. The black snake and the rattlesnake frequently prey upon this mouse. A rattlesnake which I collected at Devils Lake, Sauk County, the evening of August 26, 1918, had fur of this species in its stomach. Many parasites, both internal and external, infest *P. l. noveboracensis*. Among the more serious of these pests appear to be the scab mite (*Sarcoptes scabei*) and the botfly (*Cuterebra*). No special diseases are known, though it is probably susceptible to tularemia. Both food balls and hair balls have caused death in this species (Horner, 1950).

This mouse is seldom harmful to man's interests. Sometimes it enters shocks of corn or other grain that are stacked near a woodland border, and may make its abode and feeding place there for some time if the shocks are allowed to remain. Occasionally, particularly in autumn, it may enter buildings in or near woodland and become a slight nuisance for a while. It does not take freely, however, to human companionship or food, and one can get rid of it easily. As an asset, it destroys many weed seeds, and also many insects, especially in the form of cocoons, larvae, and eggs. It is an important food item for many fur animals.

Specimens examined from Wisconsin.—Total 537, as follows: *Adams County:* Friendship, 4. *Brown County:* Green Bay, 2 (NPM); Point Sauble, 2 (NPM). *Buffalo County:* Chippewa River (mouth of), 3; Fountain City, 4 (2 MM); Nelson, 1. *Burnett County:* Meenon Township, 1 (UWZ); Rush City Bridge (Benson), 7 (MM); Yellow River (mouth of), 10 (MM). *Chippewa County:* Holcombe, 2. *Clark County:* Dewhurst Township, 6 (5 AMNH; 1 UWZ); Foster, 1 (UWZ); Hewitt Township, 2 (1 AMNH; 1 UWZ); Withee, 1; Worden Township, 1 (UWZ). *Crawford County:* Bridgeport, 1; Lynxville, 4; Wauzeka, 5. *Dane County:* Madison, 12 (UWZ); Mazomanie, 1 (UWZ); Roxbury, 1 (UWZ); Vermont, 1 (UWZ); Verona, 3 (UWZ). *Dodge County:* Beaver Dam, 29 (14 CNHM; 15 UWZ). *Door County:* Ellison Bay, 5 (2 MM); Fish Creek, 8 (4 MM; 3 UWZ); Newport, 3 (MM); State Game Farm, 4 (UWZ). *Dunn County:* Meridean, 1; Wheeler, 1. *Grant County:* Castle Rock, 1 (UWZ); Platteville, 8 (2 AMNH); Potosi (10 mi. S. S. E.), 3; Rutledge, 5 (MM); Woodman, 2; Wyalusing, 27 (MM). *Jackson County:* Merrillan, 2; Millston, 2 (UWZ). *Juneau County:* Camp Douglas, 20 (13 AMNH; 3 CNHM); T 18 N, R 3 E, 2 (F&FH); T 19 N, R 3 E, 1 (F&FH). *La Crosse County:* La Crosse, 2. *Langlade County:* Antigo, 2 (UWZ). *Manitowoc County:* Two Rivers, 1. *Marathon County:* Rib Hill, 9. *Milwaukee County:* Milwaukee, 12 (3 MM; 9 UWZ); Whitefish Bay, 9 (UWZ). *Monroe County:* Tomah, 2 (UWZ). *Oconto County:* Kelley Lake, 5. *Pepin County:* Pepin 2. *Pierce County:* Maiden Rock, 23 (MM); Prescott, 161 (159 MM). *Polk County:* Osceola, 1 (MM). *Portage County:* Stevens Point, 4. *Rock County:* Milton, 6 (5 UWZ). *Rusk County:* Ladysmith, 3 (UWZ). *Saint Croix County:* River Falls (6 mi. N. E. of), 1 (WHD). *Sauk County:* Devils Lake, 2; Prairie du Sac, 26 (MM). *Shawano County:* Keshena, 2 (CAS). *Trempealeau County:* Trempealeau, 1. *Vernon County:* Genoa, 4 (MM). *Walworth County:* Delavan, 20 (7 AMNH; 2 CAS; 2 CNHM; 9 MM); Turtle Lake, 4; Williams Bay, 1 (UWZ). *Washburn County:* Long Lake, 7. *Waukesha County:* Hartland, 2 (UWZ); Nashotah, 12 (UWZ). *Waupaca County:* Saint Lawrence Township, 11 (UWZ). *Waushara County:* Plainfield, 1 (F&FH); Wild Rose, 1. *Wood County:* Wisconsin Rapids (10 mi. W. of), 1 (WHD).

Selected references.—Dice, L. R., 1937 b; Horner, B. E., 1954; Nicholson, A. J., 1941; Osgood, W. H., 1909; Snyder, D. P., 1956; Thomsen, H. P., 1945.

Subfamily **Microtinae**

Genus **Synaptomys** Baird
Lemming Mice

Dental formula:

$$I\frac{1-1}{1-1}, \quad C\frac{0-0}{0-0}, \quad P\frac{0-0}{0-0}, \quad M\frac{3-3}{3-3}=16$$

Synaptomys cooperi cooperi Baird

Cooper's Lemming Mouse

Synaptomys cooperi Baird, Mammals, Rept. Explor. and Surveys Railroad to Pacific, vol. 8, part 1, p. 558, July 14, 1858.

Synaptomys cooperi fatuus Cory, p. 237, 1912.

Synaptomys cooperi cooperi Komarek, p. 209, 1932; Barger, p. 11, 1952.

Vernacular names.—Bog lemming, bog mouse, Cooper lemming mouse, Cooper's lemming, Cooper's lemming vole, lemming mouse, lemming vole, and southern bog lemming.

Identification marks.—A rather small, robust mouse with short neck, rather massive head, and short ears almost concealed by the long dense fur; tail very short (under 25 mm.), about equal to one-fifth of head and body length, and indistinctly bicolorous; feet short, but rather heavy, the hind foot 20 mm. or less long; four toes on forefoot, five toes on hind foot.

In color of fresh pelage the upper parts are grizzled, a mixed gray, brown, and blackish, producing a general color tone of grizzled cinnamon-brown; under parts soiled whitish, pale grayish, or cream color wash over slate color or plumbeous base of hairs; grayish of under parts usually encroaching upon flanks and sides of throat and cheek, sometimes halfway to ear; tail indistinctly bicolorous, dark cinnamon-brown above, slightly paler below. There appears to be only one molt annually, which occurs gradually between spring and autumn.

Skulls of voles. A. SYNAPTOMYS C. COOPERI, *Rib Hill, Wisconsin,* B. S. C. GOSSII, *Lynxville, Wisconsin,* C. CLETHRIONOMYS G. GAPPERI, *Mercer, Wisconsin,* D. MICROTUS P. PENNSYLVANICUS, *Rib Hill, Wisconsin,* E. M. O. OCHROGASTER, *Lynxville, Wisconsin,* F. M. P. NEMORALIS, *Lynxville, Wisconsin,* G. M. P. SCHMIDTI, *Worden Township, Clark County, Wisconsin.*

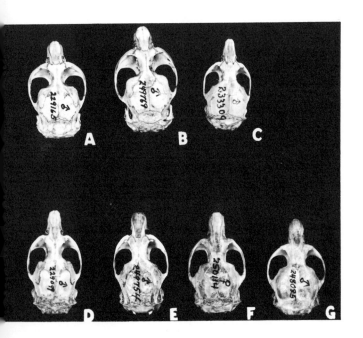

Enamel patterns of the third molars of the left upper jaws of A. SYNAPTOMYS COOPERI B. CLETHRIONOMYS GAPPERI, C. MICROTUS PENNSYLVANICUS, D. MICROTUS OCHROGASTER, E. MICROTUS PINETORUM, F. ONDATRA ZIBETHICUS. About 5×.

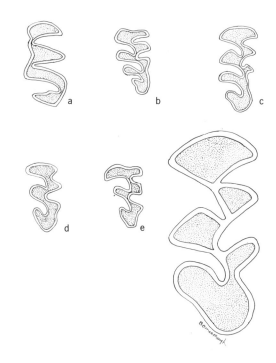

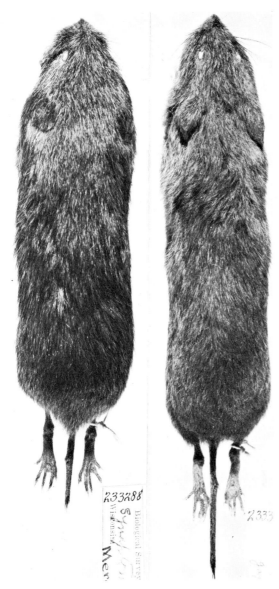

Skins of lemming mouse and red-backed mouse. Left, SYNAPTOMYS C. COOPERI, *Mercer, Wisconsin. Right,* CLETHRIONOMYS G. GAPPERI, *Mercer, Wisconsin.*

The skull is moderately massive and robust; the brain case is rather long; the outline of the postorbital almost right-angled; few ridges on brain case; the rostrum is depressed and very short, comprising only about 25 per cent of the total length of the skull; zygomatic processes heavy;

interorbital ridges prominent, particularly in adults. The upper incisors have longitudinal grooves on the outer edges; the molars are rootless and grow from a persistent pulp throughout life. The enamel pattern of the molars is characterized by the extreme depth of the re-entrant angles on the lingual side of the lower teeth and the buccal side of the upper ones, and is of a type different from any other Wisconsin microtine.

Sexual variation in *Synaptomys* occurs to the extent that old males may sometimes be distinguished from females by whitish hairs growing from the center of the hip glands, peculiar to males of the genus. Young animals tend to be darker than older ones, particularly on the under parts. I have never seen a mutant specimen from Wisconsin. Manville (1955) reported one from southern Michigan as fully albino.

The lemming mouse externally is quite distinctive to the trained eye. It is the only Wisconsin mouse with a tail less than 25 mm. long except the pine mouse (subgenus *Pitymys*). It differs from pine mice in the grizzled appearance of the upper parts and in the gray frosted under parts, which in *Pitymys* are velvety clear reddish brown above and buffy below. The skull may be distinguished from that of any other Wisconsin short-tailed mouse by the molar pattern and by the longitudinal groove on the outer side of each upper incisor. The *Synaptomys c. cooperi* may be distinguished from *S. c. gossii* by characters explained under the latter form.

Measurements.—Total length of adults, 114 to 134 mm. (4.5 to 5.3 inches); tail, 19 to 24 mm. (.7 to .9 inch); hind foot, 18 to 20 mm. (.7 to .8 inch); ear from notch, 9.5 to 12.5 mm. (.4 to .5 inch). Weight of adult, 24 to 40 grams. Skull length, 24.6 to 27.2 mm.; width, 14.0 to 16.8 mm.

Distribution in Wisconsin.—Northern two-thirds of the state; known to occur northward from southern Polk County, Jackson County, southern Adams County, and northern Sheboygan County; not known from Door Peninsula, but possibly occurs there.

Habitat.—Somewhat variable but usually in low bogs or damp meadows, sometimes (particularly in southern part of its Wisconsin range) in dry sandy fields; occasionally in hemlock or wet deciduous woods. It usually prefers a moderately grassy environment of such species as cotton grass, blue grass, and timothy.

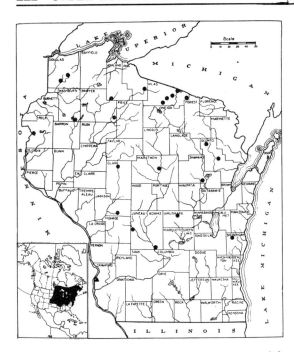

Map 43. *Distribution of* Synaptomys cooperi. *Solid symbols = specimens examined.* ● = S. c. cooperi. ▲ = S. c. gossii.

Status and Habits.—Three studies of the lemming mouse (Howell, 1927; Hall and Cockrum, 1953; Wetzel, 1955) do not agree on the classification of essentially the same Wisconsin material. All three include *S. c. cooperi* in northern Wisconsin. Howell lists *S. c. stonei* Rhoads for the more southern parts of the state. Most of these *stonei* specimens of Howell are called *S. c. saturatus* Bole by Hall and Cockrum. Wetzel assigned all specimens from Wisconsin to *S. c. cooperi* except those from parts of the Driftless Area of southwestern Wisconsin, which he identified as *S. c. gossii* (Coues). Wetzel's treatment of *Synaptomys* is ultraconservative, yet is the best possible with material available. My grouping of the forms in Wisconsin follows his rather closely. Members of this species may conceivably be more numerous in the state than specimens and records indicate. The first known from Wisconsin were collected in Vilas County, in August, 1910, by Wilfred H. Osgood. Half of the seventy specimens available have been collected since then by myself. In about four days nine were trapped at Kelley Lake, Oconto County, and in the same

period of time seven were procured at Wild Rose, Waushara County. Thus at times, at least in certain places, the lemming mouse certainly is not uncommon. The nine taken at Kelley Lake were captured within an area of about one-half acre of sphagnum bog, and consisted of three adult males, three adult females, one immature male, and two juvenile males. Two females contained three embryos each. I did not trap to exhaustion of the population, and in this particular bog there must have been a population of not less than 25 individuals per acre. Populations fluctuate, and the animal appears to be very local in distribution except in times of peak abundance. Near East Lansing, Michigan, in December, 1942, lemming mice

were especially numerous in a 3- or 4-acre opening beside a stream bottom which was grown up to largetooth aspen . . . and quaking aspen . . . . In this area, and during mid-day, these animals could be seen running along the snow surface as they moved between tunnels. It was not uncommon to have four or five in view at one time on an area less than 100 feet square. The small clearing in which they were particularly active was grown up to Saint John's wort, dewberry, wormwood, milkweed, mullein, ragweed, and bluegrass (Linduska, 1950: 51).

A population of 35 individuals per acre has been reported for central Illinois (Hoffmeister, 1947: 192). The normal home range of an individual is small, usually within a radius of about two hundred feet, though rarely it is up to nearly twice this distance.

Rarely does one have the opportunity to see this animal alive in the wild, though at times it may be seen running from burrow to burrow in broad daylight, particularly in winter. Usually it stays well within its tunnels, whether in bog or sand. Sometimes its presence in sandy areas may be detected by a pile of dried grass stems two and one-half to three inches long at the entrance to the burrow. In a boggy habitat it is often necessary to dig here and there and expose the runways in the sphagnum under the dead roots of conifers. Here piles of grass stems cut in pieces two to three inches long, and the abundance of small greenish slender fecal pellets about the size of small grains of rice indicate lemming mice have been present. The animal is active both winter and summer, and appears to be roving in daytime about as frequently as at night. Night and day might well be much alike in its dark under-sphagnum runways. Its principal mode of locomotion is running. It is slow and cautious in its movements, and starts running when startled, usually in a quick dart, yet its actual running speed is only about six or seven miles an hour. It seldom if ever climbs above the surface of the ground, and runs under an object, not over it. It swims moderately well, dog-fashion.

The lemming mouse tends to be colonial, probably chiefly because of its small home range and limited habitat rather than a tendency to be gregarious. It seems to be a highly nervous animal, and reacts quickly when frightened. In captivity it often appears to die from nervousness or worry. It, however, shows no signs of fear when handled and displays little tendency to bite. It often quarrels with its own kind and attempts to bite another, sometimes uttering a sharp squeak as it does so.

Breeding is believed to occur from early March until November. Females collected May 22, 1919, at Saint Croix Falls, Polk County, and June 26, 1918, at Lake St. Germain, Vilas County, and two collected August 10 and 12, 1917, at Kelley Lake, Oconto County, each contained three embryos. This variation in time of pregnancy, and the varying ages of young encountered during the summer and fall, would indicate that a female normally gives birth to about three litters each year, or possibly four. The gestation period is unknown, but is probably near 21 days. My experience indicates that in Wisconsin the number in a litter is most frequently three, sometimes four, and rarely two or five kits. The mammae are six, four pectoral, two inguinal.

The runways of the lemming mouse usually do not extend great distances, but are more frequently a complicated series of short passages, mostly under the surface, but sometimes on top of the ground under grass, logs or similar covering. In a bog habitat at Kelley Lake, Oconto County, the runways were exposed by my digging them open in the sphagnum under roots of dead tamarack, jack pine, and black spruce, and the mass of roots of live leather leaf (*Chamaedaphne calyculata*). Most of the specimens taken here were trapped well under the sphagnum, sometimes a foot below the surface. In southwestern Adams County most of the runways were in dry grass at the border of a dry sandy field. One specimen was caught at the entrance to a small burrow in this field. At the entrance was a pile of dried grass stems cut into lengths about three or more inches long. The burrow connected with numerous underground ridged burrows that had all the characteristics of pine-mouse burrows, except for the grass-stem cuttings. I would not have suspected *Synaptomys*. The nest is usually made by enlarging a section of the burrow to a diameter of six or eight inches, and lining the cavity with grass and weed stems. The nest is rather loosely constructed, has two to four entrances, and is lined with the finer grasses and sometimes bits of fur or feathers. Nests sometimes are built under stumps or logs. Speaking of *S. c. gossii* at Lawrence, Kansas, Burt (1928: 213–14) says, "In winter the nests may be found from four to six inches below the surface of the ground, while in summer the mice often build above the ground. . . . A large nest built above the ground and constructed wholly of dry grass, that was found October 30, 1925, was eight inches in diameter. The blue grass had grown up and fallen over, so that the nest was entirely concealed." I have never seen traces of a nest above ground in Wisconsin.

The food of this mouse consists almost exclusively of the stems, leaves, and seeds of grass. Cotton grass (*Calamagrostis canadensis*) appears to be its favorite grass in the northern bog habitats, and the blue grass in more southerly open-field habitats. Although primarily a grass eater, this mouse may sometimes eat other vegetable matter such as fungi, roots, and possibly bulbs. If it consumes any animal food it is an insignificant amount. It makes small stores of food, and often has considerable cut grass in its runways.

Insufficient data are available to determine what the important enemies of the lemming mouse are. It is well protected in its runways, but no doubt one is captured now and then by a hawk or an owl, and undoubtedly the weasel preys upon it. There are several records of its capture by the long-eared owl. One species of louse, *Hoplopleura acanthopus*, has been recorded from it.

The lemming mouse lives chiefly in places unsuitable for agriculture, and cannot be considered a species harmful to man. Possibly, its only use is for food for fur animals and as a buffer against predators that might prey on useful animals.

Specimens examined from Wisconsin.—Total 63, as follows: *Adams County:* Wisconsin Dells (3 mi. N.), 3. *Ashland County:* Bear Lake, 12 (UWZ). *Clark County:* Withee, 1. *Douglas County:* Moose and Saint Croix Rivers (junction), 1 (MM); Solon Springs, 1 (CNHM). *Iron County:* Mercer, 2 (1 MM). *Jackson County:* Millston, 3 (UWZ). *Juneau County:* Camp Douglas, 1. *Marathon County:* Rib Hill 2. *Oconto County:* Lakewood, 1; Kelley Lake, 9. *Polk County:* Saint Croix Falls, 2 (1 UWZ). *Sawyer County:* Connors Lake, 2 (1 F&FH). *Shawano County:* Keshena, 2 (CAS). *Sheboygan County:* Elkhart Lake (Sheboygan Swamp), 2. *Vilas County:* Conover, 3 (CNHM); Lac Vieux Desert, 1 (CNHM); Lake St. Germain, 4; Robinson Lake, 1 (UWZ); Sayner, 1 (CNHM). *Washburn County:* Long Lake, 2. *Waushara County:* Wild Rose, 7.

Selected references.—Hall, E. R., and E. L. Cockrum, 1952; Hoffmeister, D. F., 1947; Howell, A. B., 1927; Quick, E. R., and A. W. Butler, 1885; Stegeman, L. C., 1930; Wetzel, R. M., 1955.

Synaptomys cooperi gossii (Coues)
Goss Lemming Mouse

Arvicola (Synaptomys) gossii Coues, in Coues and Allen, Monographs of North American Rodentia (U. S. Geol. and Geograph. Surv. Terr., Rep., vol. 11, Washington), p. 235, August, 1877.

Vernacular names.—Goss lemming vole; Kansas lemming mouse.

Identification marks.—Differs but little in color from *S. c. cooperi,* possibly averaging a little paler and brighter. Larger both in body measurements and skull than *S. c. cooperi,* and those of "*gossii* as compared to *cooperi* tend to be proportionately larger. The exceptions include equal or near equal widths of upper incisors and nasals of *gossii,* with generally smaller nasal to upper incisor ratios for *cooperi* . . . and higher skulls for *gossii* (height of skull to condylobasilar length index of .43 for specimens examined)" (Wetzel, 1955: 17). The upper incisor in *gossii* is wider (about 1.9 mm.) than that of *S. c. cooperi* (about 1.6 mm.).

Measurements.—No 249,769, Biological Surveys Collection, U. S. National Museum, adult male from Lynxville, Crawford County: Total length, 129 mm.; tail, 22 mm.; hind foot, 19 mm.; ear from notch, 14 mm. Weight, 42 grams. Skull length, 27.7 mm.; width, 17.2 mm.; height, 10.3 mm.

Distribution in Wisconsin.—Known only from Lynxville, Crawford County, but probably occurs in other places in southwestern Wisconsin, and possibly in southeastern parts of the state.

Habitat, Status, and Habits.—So far as known, essentially like those of *Synaptomys c. cooperi.* It has fewer bog areas as habitat in southern Wisconsin than *cooperi* has in the north, and probably occurs more frequently in dry hillside fields.

Specimens examined from Wisconsin.—Total 4, as follows: *Crawford County:* Lynxville, 4.

Selected references.—Same as for *Synaptomys c. cooperi;* and also Burt, W. H., 1928; Fichter, E., and M. F. Hansen, 1947.

Genus **Clethrionomys** Tilesius
Red-backed Mice

Dental formula:

$$\text{I}\frac{1-1}{1-1}, \quad \text{C}\frac{0-0}{0-0}, \quad \text{P}\frac{0-0}{0-0}, \quad \text{M}\frac{3-3}{3-3}=16$$

Clethrionomys gapperi gapperi (Vigors)
Gapper's Red-backed Vole

Arvicola gapperi Vigors, Zoological Journ., vol. 5, p. 204, 1830.
Evotomys gapperi Snyder, p. 116, 1902; Jackson, p. 22, 1908; Hollister, p. 25, 1910; Cory, p. 208, 1912.
Clethrionomys gapperi gapperi Schmidt, p. 114, 1931; Komarek, p. 208, 1932; Barger, p. 12, 1952.

Vernacular names.—In Wisconsin commonly called red-backed mouse. Others names include boreal red-backed mouse, Gapper's red-backed mouse, redback mouse, red-backed vole, redbacked wood mouse, red wood mouse, and *wá-mik-wá-wá-go-no-chi* (Chippewa).

Identification marks.—A small mouse with moderately large head, ears long enough to project above the fur, and small eyes; tail slender, medium in length (32 to 42 mm.), about equal to one-third of head and body length, blackish above and gray below; feet medium length (hind foot, 18 to 20 mm.), dirty buffy white to grayish in color.

Color rather conspicuous; upper parts from forehead to base of tail a broad stripe of bright chestnut, slightly intermixed with a few black hairs; nose and sides of head and body grayish, washed or suffused with pale buff or ochraceous; under parts whitish, often washed with pale buff.

Red-backed mouse against the natural background of the forest floor, New York State. About ¾×. U. S. Fish and Wildlife Service photograph by Donald A. Spencer.

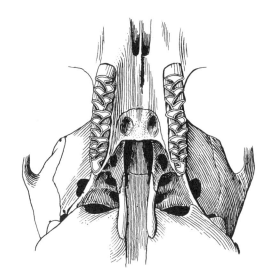

Palate of CLETHRIONOMYS GAPPERI, about 6×. Note smooth posterior edge of palate.

Summer pelage is darker and more dusky than winter fur.

The skull is comparatively weak, rather smooth, without conspicuous ridges or angularity; cranium narrow, smooth, rounded; audital bullae inflated, elongate round; zygoma relatively slender and zygomatic processes moderate; interorbital region rather broad, the ridges inconspicuous; posterior border of bony palate with straight edge, terminating in a thin shelf, without median posterior projection. Dentition rather weak; the upper incisors without grooves, pale orange in color; molars in adult animals with distinct roots; molariform tooth row short (about 5 mm.).

Males and females are similar in size and color. Young animals tend to be darker than adults and usually less ochraceous. There is considerable individual variation in color, particularly in the intensity of the chestnut red on the upper parts. The species has a mutant in some localities and is dichromatic, there being the ordinary chestnut phase and a grayish brown phase. I have never seen a specimen in the grayish brown phase from Wisconsin. Miller (1897 a: 16) reports such variants from several localities in Canada, including the north shore of Lake Superior, Ontario.

The red-backed mouse is easily identified externally by its descriptive color name. It is the only Wisconsin mouse with a short tail and a distinct reddish color ribbon down the back from head to base of tail, and with contrasting pale grayish under parts. The skull is narrower than that of any other Wisconsin microtine except for a few small pine mice, and in ratio of length to breadth is always narrower. The skull can always be distinguished from that of any other Wisconsin microtine species by the straight posterior border of the palatine shelf.

Measurements.—Total length of adults, 134 to 150 mm. (4.5 to 6.0 inches); tail, 32 to 42 mm. (1.2 to 1.6 inches); hind foot, 18 to 20 mm. (.7 to .8 inch); ear from notch, 14 to 16 mm. (.5 to .6 inch). Weight of adult, 22 to 36 grams. Skull length, 22.5 to 24.8 mm.; width, 12.0 to 13.6 mm.

Distribution in Wisconsin.—Northern, central, and eastern parts of the state from Burnett, Rusk, eastern Jackson, and northern Waushara counties northward to state line and eastward to Door County; southward in vicinity of Lake Michigan to southern Milwaukee County; accidental (one specimen) in Dodge County. Chiefly in tamarack bogs in southern part of range.

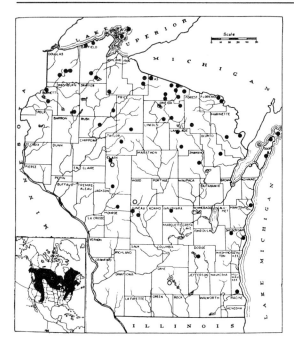

Map 44. *Distribution of* CLETHRIONOMYS GAPPERI.
● = *specimens examined.* ○ = *authentic records.*

Habitat.—Woodland and forests, both conifer, deciduous and mixed, preferably those somewhat moist and strewn with mossy logs or matted tall grass; sometimes in low places in dry white birch woods; less watery places and among arbor vitae (Sheboygan Swamp) in tamarack swamps.

Status and Habits.—The red-backed vole is probably much more plentiful in the state than records and observations indicate, though it is usually less common than the woodland deer mouse where the two species occur in the same habitat. "The home ranges of fifteen individuals . . . varied from 600 to 1100 square yards (0.12 to 0.23 acre) for adult males, and 600 to 1,000 square yards (0.12 to 0.21 acre) for adult females, and from 500 to 700 square yards (0.10 to 0.15 acre) for juveniles of both sexes. Additional captures would probably have increased the size of these calculated home ranges" (Manville, 1949 a: 47). Over a favorable habitat of several square miles, this vole may average only one or slightly more to the acre. In special places, however, over an area of a few acres, the population often reaches four or five per acre, and may reach more than twice that number.

Tracks of this species are not too distinctive. It is, however, the only Wisconsin mouse to my knowledge that will frequently and deliberately sit on its buttock in the snow to eat, and thus leave a "form" marked in the snow where it sat down. Its feces are black, small (smallest of our mice), and quite similar to those of the house mouse. This vole is active both winter and summer, and, although it is chiefly nocturnal, it is often active during daylight. Hopping is its usual mode of locomotion, though it runs a great deal, particularly under logs, debris, and vegetation. On the morning of July 11, 1917, at Clark Lake, Door County, I watched a red-backed vole from 6:10 A.M. till 6:32 A.M., when it disappeared. Its actions were exceedingly quick and agile, entirely different from those of the comparatively cumbersome meadow vole (*Microtus pennsylvanicus*). It ran as much on top of the moss-covered logs as along the sides and under them. Not infrequently, it would jump six or eight inches over minor obstructions. At no time did it utter a sound. It picked up seeds of undetermined species, sat on its haunches, and ate them. Once it ran under a chain fern (*Woodwardia*) and nibbled for some twenty seconds at its green leaves. The red-backed vole climbs inclined logs and trees, but seldom attempts an upright climb. Its maximum running speed is probably scarcely more than five miles an hour. It swims only moderately well.

The red-backed vole does not form colonies and is not gregarious. Possibly it is too nervous and irritable to tolerate companions other than members of its own family. It is comparatively silent most of the time, but when it encounters trouble or opposition it scolds with a sharp rolling squeak, well described by Manville (1949 a: 44) as "a shrill chattering 'churr-r-r.'" Manville further says:

This vole has a very nervous temperament and is extremely liable to shock. This is illustrated by a common reaction when a vole is first caught and marked by ear-punching. During this operation the animal was grasped with the thumb and index finger by the nape of the neck, its body cradled in the palm of the hand. The process did not appear to distress either deermice or chipmunks handled in the same manner. But fifteen voles, when thus handled, apparently became unconscious after struggling for a few seconds. In one case there was even some bleeding from the mouth. The voles which reacted in this way represented both sexes and both adults and juveniles in nearly equal numbers. After marking, the animals were placed on the ground. They recovered consciousness after one or two minutes and dashed for cover. There appeared to be no permanent aftereffects, for each of these individuals, in apparent good health, was recaptured on subsequent days.

Longevity in the wild in this species probably is less than three years, and potential longevity not more than five or six years. Its low longevity may account in part for its apparently slow increases in numbers and its often comparatively low population compared with some other species of mice.

In Wisconsin the red-backed vole may mate as early as March, but most of the first mating of the year occurs toward the last of the month or in April. Three or four litters may be raised between then and October. The young vary in number from three to eight. My field observations in Wisconsin indicate that five is the most frequent number, often six, and seldom only three or four. The smaller numbers are more frequent in lit-

ters born late in summer or in autumn. The mammae are eight, four pectoral, four inguinal. A female still nursing young may sometimes be pregnant. Svihla (1930: 490) summarizes the breeding of this species as follows:

Red-backed mice of the genus *Evotomys* were found to breed in captivity. The period of gestation varies from seventeen to nineteen days, with seventeen days as the more usual and perhaps normal period. The young are blind and hairless at birth, weighing on the average but 1.9 grams. Hair appears in four days. The eyes open in fifteen days (in one instance in eleven days). The young may be weaned in seventeen days if another litter follows—immediately; otherwise nursing may continue for at least three weeks. Both males and females are sexually mature at about four months of age; the females bear young at that time. At least two litters of young, numbering two to five, may be raised by one female within a year.

Inasmuch as nests of this vole had never been adequately described, our field party made especial effort to study them, both in sphagnum of spruce-tamarack swamps and in heavy timber, in August, 1919, at Ogema, Price County. Abundant runways were easily found by turning over fallen trees in the swamp. It was difficult to follow the little passages, however, as they would either suddenly come to the surface or be lost deep under the sphagnum moss, sometimes disappear-

Exposed runway of red-backed mouse, Ogema, Wisconsin, August 20, 1919. Photograph by H. H. Sheldon.

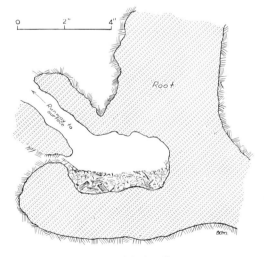

Nest of Red-backed Mouse

Nest of red-backed mouse. Drawn from original photographs and nest material from Ogema, Price County, Wisconsin.

ing into the seepage water that lay in a thin sheet
between the soil and the moss. Many square rods
were turned over in the swamp without finding
a nest among the plentiful runways. At the edge
of the swamp in an aspen woodland, where the
sphagnum was firm and not wet, we finally located a number of well-defined entrances encircling an isolated bunch of moss about six feet in
diameter, and apparently entering at its base.
Most of the entrances appeared to be in use. A
search finally revealed a nest, not at the terminal
of the main runway, but at the end of a branch
passage about ten inches long located among the
rootlets of small trees. The nest, some three inches
in diameter, was merely a small carpet, consisting chiefly of grass stems and a few particles of
dead leaves and moss, the entire bulk of which
would be no larger than a man's thumb.

In a heavily timbered section bordering a small
stream near Ogema, a runway was opened, at
the entrance to which a specimen pregnant with
six embryos had been caught. The runway led
from one large elm to another and continued on
to the remains of a rotten stump, under which the
nest was located at a depth of 18 inches. The
runway overall was 14 feet long, and for most of
the distance was only 3 inches below the surface.
At each tree there were several branch passage-
ways that dropped 12 to 18 inches beneath the
surface. The nest was situated on top of the soil
underneath a root of the stump. It was four inches
in diameter and about one inch deep, slightly
hollowed and without cover other than the log
above. It was composed of small pieces of dry
leaves, bark, hazelnut shells, hemlock cones,
twigs, dry sphagnum, and green moss, the last
two items being around the upper outside of the
nest.

The food of the red-backed vole is mostly
vegetable matter. Hamilton (1941: 259), on the
basis of an examination of stomach contents collected between March and December in New
York, states:

Nearly three-fourths of the food is composed of
green vegetation usually too finely ground for identification. In addition to this, the starchy pastelike
mass of nuts and seeds often occupies the larger
share of the stomach. Seeds of *Rubus, Amelanchier,*
and *Vaccinium* have been found in the stomachs.
These mice do not eat insects so frequently as do the
deer mice, slightly more than 10 per cent of the

stomachs containing insect remains. Of those eaten,
remains of ground beetles, adult flies, and lepidopterous larvae have been recognized. In addition, centipedes and spiders are consumed. A single stomach
contained the remains of a snail.

In Wisconsin I have known this species to consume hazel-nuts and beechnuts; hemlock, spruce,
and maple seeds; and the fruit or seeds of pin
cherry, shadbush, black alder, silky dogwood,
mountain ash, blueberry, partridge berry, and
clintonia. It also eats the bark of many varieties
of trees and shrubs, and nibbles at many kinds
of green vegetation and fungi. It sometimes
makes slight storages of food in the autumn, but
relies for most of its subsistence on constant har-
vesting. It often runs back into its burrow to consume its food after procuring a morsel, and may
soon reappear for more. This habit may give one
the impression that it is storing food when it is
actually seeking protection in its burrow while
eating the food.

Forest and undercover habitat may somewhat
protect this vole from certain potential enemies,
but is undoubtedly captured at times by hawks
and owls, and by predatory mammals such as
weasels, skunks, foxes, and feral house cats. External parasites appear not to be plentiful on this
species, yet at least seven species of mites and
chiggers, one louse, one tick (*Ixodes*), and four
species of fleas are known to infest it. Internally,
the protozoan *Oxyuris obvelata* and the cestode
Andrya primordialis infest it.

Economically, this vole is of little importance.
It certainly does no essential harm to agriculture,
and its activities in gnawing twigs and bark of
forest trees is negligible. Some of its natural
pruning might benefit the trees. It has some little
value as a destroyer of insects.

Specimens examined from Wisconsin.—Total 250,
as follows: *Ashland County:* Bear Lake, 4 (UWZ);
Outer Island, 3; Stockton Island, 6. *Bayfield County:*
Herbster, 8; Namakagon Lake, 5; Orienta, 1; T 44 N,
R 7 W, 1 (F&FH). *Burnett County:* Danbury, 3;
Meenon Township, 1 (UWZ); Yellow River
(mouth of), 3 (MM). *Clark County:* Hewett Town-
ship, 4 (3 AMNH; 1 UWZ); Thorp Township, 3
(AMNH). *Dodge County:* Beaver Dam, 1 (UWZ).
Door County: Clark Lake, 7; Ellison Bay, 1; Wash-
ington Island, 1. *Douglas County:* Moose and Saint
Croix rivers (junction), 5 (MM); Solon Springs, 25
(CNHM); Upper Saint Croix Lake, 2 (MM). *Flor-
ence County:* Florence, 2; Spread Eagle Lake, 4
(MM). *Forest County:* Crandon, 1. *Iron County:*

Fisher Lake, 13 (UWZ); Mercer, 8 (5 MM). *Jackson County:* Millston, 1 (UWZ). *Juneau County:* Mather, 1; T 19 N, R 3 E, 3 (F&FH). *Langlade County:* Antigo, 3 (UWZ); Elcho, 1 (UWZ). *Manitowoc County:* Point Creek State Forest, 1 (UWZ). *Marinette County:* McAllister, 1; No locality, 1 (MM). *Milwaukee County:* Oak Creek, 1 (UWZ). *Oconto County:* Kelley Lake, 2. *Oneida County:* Crescent Lake, 18; Rhinelander, 6 (3 UWZ); Three Lakes, 1 (UWZ). *Price County:* Ogema, 11. *Rusk County:* Ladysmith, 4 (UWZ). *Sawyer County:* Connors Lake, 1. *Shawano County:* Keshena, 16 (CAS). *Sheboygan County:* Elkhart Lake (Sheboygan Swamp), 4; Terry Andrae State Park, 2 (UWZ). *Taylor County:* Chaquamagon National Forest, 1 (F&FH). *Vilas County:* Conover, 5 (CNHM); Divide, 2 (MM); Lac Vieux Desert, 7 (CNHM); Lake St. Germain, 4; Mamie Lake, 14; Phelps, 2 (UWZ); Robinson Lake, 5 (UWZ); Sayner, 10 (CNHM). *Waushara County:* Wild Rose, 9. *Washburn County:* Long Lake 1.

Selected references.—Bailey, V., 1897; Blair, W. F., 1941 a; Hall, E. R., and E. L. Cockrum, 1953; Manville, R. H., 1949 a; Miller, G. S., Jr., 1896; Svihla, A., 1930.

Genus **Microtus** Schrank
Meadow Mice

Dental formula:

$$I\frac{1-1}{1-1}, \quad C\frac{0-0}{0-0}, \quad P\frac{0-0}{0-0}, \quad M\frac{3-3}{3-3} = 16.$$

In his work on the genera and subgenera of voles and lemmings, Miller (1896: 9) recognized 12 subgenera of the genus *Microtus,* and included among them *Pedomys* (type *Microtus austerus*) and *Pitymys* (type *Microtus pinetorum*). Bailey (1900: 11) and others followed this logical arrangement. Later Miller (1912 b: 228) considered *Pitymys* of generic rank, in which he was followed by many mammalogists, including the present writer (Jackson, 1941) and Miller and Kellogg (1955: 609). Miller and Kellogg, however, also recognize *Pedomys* as a distinct genus and use the name *Pedomys ochrogaster ochrogaster* (Wagner) for the prairie vole (1. c., p. 608), explaining their decision in footnote 45: "Regarded as a valid genus by Ellerman. The families and genera of living rodents, vol. 2, p. 620, March 21, 1941. Subsequently regarded as a valid subgenus of *Pitymys* by Ellerman, op. cit., vol. 3, pt. 1, pp. 111, 130, March, 1949. See also Ellerman and Morrison-Scott, Checklist of Palaearctic and Indian mammals 1758 to 1946, Publ. Brit. Mus. (Nat. Hist.), p. 681, Nov. 19, 1951."

Skins of MICROTUS P. PENNSYLVANICUS, *left.* M. O. OCHROGASTER, *middle.* M. P. SCHMIDTI, *right.* ½×.

In my opinion neither *Pitymys* nor *Pedomys* are sufficiently differentiated to warrant their recognition as genera. Each of the other ten subgenera of *Microtus* as outlined by Miller in 1900 is as fully worthy of generic rank as *Pitymys* and *Pedomys,* yet all have been retained as subgenera only. The utility and value of animal classification is lost when every subgenus and every species is brought to generic rank. I am therefore using the generic name *Microtus* for both the prairie vole and the pine mouse, as have also Hall and Cockrum (1953: 445, 448).

Microtus pennsylvanicus pennsylvanicus
(Ord)
Meadow Vole

Mus pennsylvanica Ord, in A new universal geography, originally compiled by William Guthrie, 2nd Amer. ed., vol. 2, p. 292, 1815.
Arvicola riparius Lapham, p. 340, 1853; Strong, p. 439, 1883.
Arvicola hirsutus Lapham, p. 340, 1853.
Microtus pennsylvanicus Snyder, p. 117, 1902; Jackson, p. 22, 1908; Hollister, p. 25, 1910; Cory, p. 214, 1912.
Microtus pennsylvanicus pennsylvanicus Schmidt, p. 112, 1931; Komarek, p. 208, 1932; Barger, p. 12, 1952.

Vernacular names. — Most frequently called meadow mouse in Wisconsin. Other names include beaver meadow mouse, bob-tailed Susie, bull mouse, common meadow vole, eastern meadow mouse, field mouse, ground vole, marsh meadow mouse, marsh monk, marsh mouse, meadow mike, Ord meadow mouse, Pennsylvania meadow mouse, and vole.

Identification marks.—A medium-sized, or moderately large, heavy-set mouse, with rather small ears nearly concealed in the long loose fur, and with small black beady eyes; external gland on hip in adult male prominent; tail medium in length (42 to 56 mm.), about equal to two-fifths of head and body length, scantily haired, dark brown above, somewhat paler below, being scarcely bicolorous; legs short; hind foot rather large (20 to 23 mm.), usually with six, rarely five, plantar tubercles; fur texture rather fine and silky.

Color in summer pelage: upper parts dull chestnut brown, occasionally brighter and almost yellowish chestnut darkened down the back with blackish hairs; under parts dusky gray, sometimes tinged with cinnamon; tail dusky brown above, very slightly paler below, not distinctly bicolorous; feet dark brown. Winter pelage usually duller and more grayish; tail more nearly bicolorous. Young dark, almost plumbeous. One rather prolonged molt annually, sometime between May and September.

The skull is moderately heavy, rather long, slightly angular, and little ridged; audital bullae

Meadow mouse, MICROTUS PENNSYLVANICUS, *from life. About* 1×. *Fish and Wildlife Service photograph.*

moderately large and rounded; incisors smooth, projecting considerably in front of nasals; anterior palatine foramina long (more than 5 mm.), not constricted posteriorly, and extending two-thirds of the distance between first molars and incisors; posterior border of palate with median projection. Dentition moderately heavy; the upper incisors without grooves, deep yellow in color; molars in adult animals rootless, growth being continuous from a persistent pulp; upper molariform tooth row relatively long (about 7.2 mm.); posterior (third) upper molar with an anterior crescent, three closed triangles, and a posterior loop with two inner lobes, in effect four inner and three outer salient angles. Rarely, a tendency for development of a fifth inner salient may be indicated.

There is essentially no sexual variation in size or color. Individual variation in color consists mostly in the shade and brightness of the chestnut of the upper parts, and in the occasional tendency for a buffish overcast on the under parts. Mutations in color are not infrequent and have been recorded as yellow, buff with pink eye, black or melanistic, albino, and also white and white spotted. Specimens of a yellow mutant from Alderly, Dodge County, Wisconsin, and two albinos from Madison and one from Lake Koshkonong have been reported (Owen and Shackleford, 1942). A peculiar color mutant is reported from near Ann Arbor, Michigan, with "back and sides, drab-gray at the tips of the hairs and white at the bases; belly, pale smoke-gray; nose and extending up between and slightly above the eyes, drab; dorsal streak on tail hair brown," (Svihla, R. D. and A., 1928).

The meadow vole (*M. p. pennsylvanicus*) is

Two meadow mice in a natural habitat of rank grass.
U. S. Fish and Wildlife Service photograph.

not apt to be confused with any other Wisconsin mouse except the prairie vole (*M. o. ochrogaster*). Externally, nearly every specimen of *pennsylvanicus* of comparable age can be separated from *ochrogaster* in Wisconsin by its larger size (160 mm. or more in total length), longer hind foot (20 to 23 mm. long), and particularly by its longer tail (more than 40 mm.) and its distinctly grayish ventral parts, seldom showing a slight cinnamon cast and never, in normal fur, a dense cinnamon wash. The skull of *pennsylvanicus* can always be separated from that of *ochrogaster* by the posterior upper molar, which in *pennsylvanicus* has four inner and three outer salient angles, whereas in *ochrogaster* it has three inner and three outer salient angles.

Measurements.—Total length of adults, 160 to 188 mm. (6.3 to 7.4 inches); tail, 42 to 56 mm. (1.7 to 2.2 inches); hind foot, 20 to 23 mm. (0.8 to 0.9 inches); ear from notch, 11 to 16 mm. (0.4 to 0.6 inches). Weight of adult, 36 to 56 grams. Skull length, 26.1 to 28.6 mm.; width, 14.5 to 15.8 mm.

Distribution in Wisconsin.—Entire state in suitable habitats.

Habitat.—Chiefly lowland fields and meadows, grassy marshes, along rivers and lakes, and similar areas with rank growths of grass, sometimes in flooded marshes or on high grasslands near water; orchards and open woodland if ground

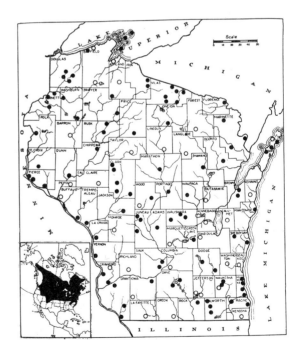

Map 45. *Distribution of* MICROTUS PENNSYLVANICUS.
● = *specimens examined.*   ○ = *authentic records.*

cover is of grassy or weedy growth; sometimes in grain, hay, pea, bean, and soybean fields; frequently in shocks of corn or other grain; occasionally in runways in sphagnum bogs.

Status and Habits.—The meadow vole in times of its peak abundance is probably the second most abundant mammal in the state, being exceeded possibly only by the mole shrew, *Blarina brevicauda.* If the meadow vole occupied in considerable numbers more environmental niches than it does, such as, for example, heavy timberland, flower and vegetable gardens, or dry sandy areas, it would outnumber any other mammal in the state. In many favorable habitats at a peak population it may easily reach two hundred or more individuals per acre over a con-

siderable area. Population peaks in this species appear to occur in cycles of about once in four years. It is indeed a very rough estimate to place the peak population in the state as possibly 75 million meadow voles and the low as possibly 5 million voles. The home range of a meadow vole is usually less than one-tenth acre. During intense populations the mice tend to wander in search of food, and because of population pressure, an individual then may travel farther. The male tends to range farther than the female. Wisconsin has never suffered a severe mouse plague such as occurred in Humboldt Valley, Nevada, in 1907, "when it was estimated that on many large ranches there were from 8,000 to 12,000 mice to each acre" (Piper, 1909: 5).

Increased population is fostered by three reproductive factors: (1) An acceleration of the breeding rate; (2) an increased number of young per litter; (3) the lengthening of the reproductive season, which allows for greater number of litters per year.

Causes responsible for a decrease in numbers of mice may be abiotic, such as climatic influences, or biotic, such as diseases, predators, etc. It appears that murine epizootics occurring when mice have reached the peak of their abundance, are the primary causative agent reducing mouse populations. Plagues of mice are often accompanied by disease of an epidemic nature among these animals (Hamilton, 1937 b: 789).

Though they are often abundant, the presence of the meadow vole is not always easily detected. The usual indication of its presence is a labyrinth of runways that covers the surface of the ground. These runways are constructed by the mice themselves, are about one and one-half inches in diameter, and run in a crisscross network under cover of dead grass. Sometimes little piles of cut grass stems, or scattered cut grass stems and blades, are in evidence. It leaves few tracks, but on wet mud its track may appear,

Tracks of meadow mouse trotting. About 1×. *Photograph by Vernon Bailey.*

Post-winter runways of M. **pennsylvanicus**, *Clear Lake, Rock County, Wisconsin, April 29, 1951. Photograph by the author.*

although it is not always readily identified except by location. Likewise, the feces are sometimes difficult to separate from those of some other mice. Sometimes its gnawings on trees and shrubs are identifiable. It is active both summer and winter. It sometimes shifts its homesite a short distance from lowland marsh to slightly higher bordering grassy areas for winter occupancy. It emigrates only at peaks of abundance when overpopulation or food shortage forces it to move. It operates on a twenty-four-hour schedule, but is inclined to be more nocturnal in the summer and more diurnal in the winter and on cloudy days in any season. Its peaks of activity are at dusk and dawn. The meadow vole was particularly active in its runways in November and December (in Virginia) from 6:00 to 7:30 and from 9:30 to 11:00 in the morning; and from 1:00 to 2:00 and from 3:30 to 5:00 in the afternoon (Don A. Spencer, in U. S. Dept. Agric., Biol. Surv. press release, Sept. 22, 1935). Its chief mode of locomotion is running, and in its runways it can reach a speed of about five or six miles an hour. It is an excellent swimmer, and often enters water freely, and even dives.

This species is colonial if for no other reason than that habitat, food supply, and high breeding potential tend to concentrate the population.

Meadow mice are by no means dumb, as some have asserted, though to our gross ears they may appear so. The young have many forms of minute whimpering, whining, crying sounds which seem to have a meaning to their mother. As she leaves the nest, and perhaps interrupts their meal, there is a fine little complaining jumble of whimpers from the very young, to which she pays no attention. If one tumbles out of the nest and lies wriggling helplessly on the floor it cries with a vigor that brings a quick parental response, and is carried back and replaced in the nest. If it falls far enough to be slightly hurt but not to be greatly injured a sharp squeal of pain sets the mother frantic to find and help it.

The adults and older young have little talky squeaks and sharp cross squeaks, and savage squeals, and in a fight a blur of squeaks and squeals and gutteral growls, not far different from a dog fight on a very small scale. Then there are chatterings of teeth at each other and stampings and scratching on the ground when rivals meet, all of which, and probably much more that we miss, have an evident meaning to them. A stranger or friend is recognized, either by voice, odor, sight, or other token, as quickly as we recognize a friend or foe.

In their home life these mice are sociable, friendly, playful, and happy among the members of a well-fed family or colony, but are savage fighters in the case of rival males and females in defense of young, or among strangers. When hungry or without comfortable nests or living conditions, they become cross and quarrelsome, will fight among themselves, even to the death, and will eat those killed, especially young.

They are fond of meat at any time, have no scruples against cannibalism, and will generally kill and eat newly born young not protected by the mother. Being ready fighters and always on the defensive, they will usually bite anything that catches or touches them, but can be safely handled, either by catching them firmly in the hand from above or by letting them run over the hands or arms or from one hand to another. They are not easily so tamed as to be gentle and safe to play with, but, unlike many of the native mice of other groups, are not timid and nervous" (Bailey, 1924: 525).

Life expectancy of this vole in the wild is less than one year. Potential longevity is not known, but probably is near five years.

The meadow vole breeds throughout the year, though the main breeding season is from March until November. At Milton, Rock County, "I have observed young of *pennsylvanicus* in the nest in every month of the year except February, and I have no doubt but that they breed in this month" (Jackson, 1903: 9). The number of young in a litter varies from two to nine, six or seven being the more usual numbers, though the first litters of a female are usually four or less. The mammae are eight, four pectoral, four inguinal. Mating is usually promiscuous. Most males are

Nest of meadow mouse, Dousman, Wisconsin, July 24, 1922. Photograph by the author.

Litter of eight young M. P. PENNSYLVANICUS *a few hours old. About* 1×. *Photograph by Vernon Bailey.*

highly polygamous. First mating may occur when the female is only half grown or about 25 days old, and young males mate when 45 days old. Breeding activities are practically continuous, the female mating immediately after the birth of the young.

The young are hairless and weigh only about 3 grams each when born, with closed eyes and ears and no trace of teeth. They grow rapidly, however, gaining after the first few days about 1 gram a day until over half grown. Their dark colored fur begins to appear as a soft velvet in five or six days, their incisor teeth about the fifth, the molar teeth about the seventh, and their eyes and ears open on or near the eighth day. As soon as their eyes are open they are quick to run and hide if disturbed, and a few days later are out of the nest searching for food, following the trails, and, if in cages, running on the wheels, playing and pushing for their rights.

When about 12 days old, the young are weaned, but they remain with their mother, occupying the old nest and holding together in friendly family relations until time for the next installment of young, when the mother seeks or builds a new nest and leaves her previous family to care for itself. If food were abundant, they would remain contentedly together for an indefinite time but for the disturbing sexual forces which before they are full grown impel the females to seek new homes for prospective offspring and the males to wander constantly in search of one mate after another (Bailey, 1924: 530).

Runways in the grass are very characteristic of the meadow vole. The runway is constructed

by the mouse parting and pushing aside the stems of grass, and tramping down the pathway. In later stages many of the grass stems are cut away and the runway becomes more open and exposed until grasses along the side overlap and hide it. Runways in constant use often become sunken paths lower than the surface of the ground. The nest may be built on the surface of the ground along one of these runways, or a few inches above ground in a tussock of grass. Meadow voles have occupied marsh wrens' nests for raising young (Low, 1944). On June 14, 1900, near Milton, Rock County, I found a song sparrow's nest containing three fledglings nearly ready to leave the nest. On July 1, I chanced by the same place and saw a meadow vole scurry from the nest through a runway. Upon examining the nest, I found it contained six young meadow voles about one week old. The young were fully exposed to view, scarcely a grass blade covering the nest. The following day the nest was vacant (Jackson, 1903: 7–8). A pair had a nest in hay stored in a barn at Crescent Lake, Oneida County, September 8, 1917, where the young were frequently heard "squeaking" and the old ones occasionally seen running on the dirt floor or in the hay. The nest is usually on the surface of the ground, and when underground is rarely more than eight or nine inches below the surface. It is a bulky globular affair about five or six inches in diameter and three or four inches deep, with one or two entrances. It is composed of diverse vegetative material, but generally of dry grass, sedge, and weed leaves, and lined with plant down or finely shredded plant material. The nest is usually enclosed, but sometimes is not covered. A nest containing five hairless young was openly exposed on top of tussock in a marsh near Dutchman Lake, Waukesha County, July 23, 1922. Within an hour after I had examined this nest the parent had removed the young and the nest was deserted, though I had not touched it. The nest is kept clean while in use, and abandoned when it becomes old and dirty, or is disturbed.

This vole subsists chiefly upon fresh grass, sedges, and other herbage, and also grains and seeds in variety. From May until August, green and succulent vegetation constitutes a major portion of its food. In autumn it frequently enters shocks of corn or other grains standing in a field and eats both foliage and grain seeds. In winter it sometimes eats the bark and roots of shrubs and small trees, and may extend its gnawings on a trunk to the height of the deepest snow available. It is quite fond of certain bulbs and tuberous roots, but does not consume such quantities of these as the pine mouse. It is particularly fond of legumes, both roots, stems, foliage, and green fruit. In the cranberry region it feeds extensively on cranberries, gathering quantities of the berries but eating only the seeds. Several piles containing a quart or two of seeded cranberries gathered by the meadow vole were found at Mather, Juneau County, in May, 1918. It consumes but little animal matter, less then 5 per cent of its total general food being of animal nature. Such animal matter is chiefly that of other small mammals and birds found dead, of which a large part is of its own kind. It drinks quantities of water. When eating, it sits up, and often stands to gnaw a grain stalk or the bark of a tree.

It has no pronounced storage habit, but occasionally lays away small caches of surplus seeds or particles of tubers. It is a prodigious eater, and in the wild normally consumes about 60 per cent of its own weight daily. When kept in captivity it often eats its own weight daily.

Hawks and owls of several species take heavy toll of the meadow vole. Especially predaceous upon it in Wisconsin are the screech, short-eared, and long-eared owls (Errington, 1932; Stoddard, 1922), and the marsh, sparrow, and red-tailed hawks (Errington, 1933). The rough-legged hawk has been known to prey upon it in this state (Wright, E. G., 1945). Other birds such as shrikes, gulls, and herons often prey upon it. It falls prey to nearly every kind of predatory mammal, and is particularly vulnerable to the three kinds of weasels, the mink, striped skunk, badger, red and gray foxes, coyote, and shrew, particularly the mole shrew. The family cat catches many voles. The farm dog, by following furrows during spring plowing and searching grain shocks in autumn and winter, destroys many. Among snakes, the blue racer, fox snake, rattlesnake, and garter snake destroy many. Muskellunge and pickerel among fishes often prey upon the meadow vole. A vole makes excellent bait for pickerel, muskellunge, and largemouth bass.

Floods and high water and forest and brush fires have little effect on the welfare of the meadow vole, though sudden floods sometimes drown the young in the nest. Rarely, a vole gets trapped or snared by plant stalks. Sometimes one falls into a basement window pit and cannot escape. Occasionally one is carried along with the crop and is mechanically baled with the straw or hay. Rarely, one is killed by an automobile.

A great many parasites, both internal and external, infest the meadow vole. Possibly one reason that the number of parasites appears to be excessive is that this vole has been easy to obtain and study. It would appear, however, that it is especially open to parasitism when, for example, sometimes 25 per cent or more are infested with the cestode *Andrya macrocephala*, and each animal possibly carries four or five other kinds of internal parasites and as many kinds of external ones. The presence of some of these parasites and the resultant diseases to the animals in one of the causes of the cyclic reduction in population so necessary in a species of such reproductive capacity.

Economically, the meadow vole in uncontrolled abundance is a pest. It does considerable damage to growing grain, is often destructive in orchard and forestry plantings, and may consume considerable harvestable grain and hay. "As few as 10 mice per acre on a 100-acre meadow could take 11 tons of grass, or 5½ tons of hay a year!" (Hine, 1950: 17). In many ways, however, it is useful to mankind. It destroys many weeds, particularly weed grasses. It serves as food for certain fur animals and other predators and thus forms a buffer species that protects more useful ones. While in some regions it has become a near menace, in Wisconsin it has never been a really serious pest problem. In small orchards, gardens, or home grounds, the simplest method of reducing meadow vole numbers is by the use of small wooden-based snap traps. These should be set in the runways at right angles to them, so that the vole will pass directly over the trigger. A properly set trap need not be baited. Bait of rolled oats, apple, or peanut butter may sometimes increase the mouse catch. In more destructive vole infestations it may be necessary to resort to poisoning or other methods, several of which have been devised and made available to the public. Details of control methods can always be procured from the Fish and Wildlife Service, U. S. Department of the Interior, Washington 25, D. C., or by consulting literature (Eadie, 1954: 135–146; Garlough and Spencer, 1944: 6–15; Hine, 1950: 18–19).

Specimens examined from Wisconsin.—Total 567, as follows: *Adams County:* Friendship, 4. *Ashland County:* Bear Lake, 1 (UWZ); Madeline Island, 2; Outer Island, 8; Stockton Island, 1. *Bayfield County:* Orienta, 7. *Brown County:* Allouez, 4 (NPM); Preble Township, 5 (NPM). *Buffalo County:* Fountain City, 12 (11 MM). *Burnett County:* Meenon Township, 1 (UWZ); Namakagon River (mouth), 1 (MM); Yellow River (mouth), 5 (MM). *Chippewa County:* Holcombe, 6. *Clark County:* Dewhurst Township, 1 (AMNH); Foster Township, 3 (1 AMNH; 2 UWZ); Hewett Township, 4 (1 AMNH; 3 UWZ); Thorp Township, 2 (1 AMNH; 3 UWZ); Worden Township, 6 (1 UWZ). *Crawford County:* Lynxville 4; Wauzeka, 3. *Dane County:* Blooming Grove, 2 (UWZ); Madison, 8 (UWZ). *Dodge County:* Alderley, 1 (UWZ); Beaver Dam, 164 (69 CNHM; 95 UWZ). *Door County:* Fish Creek, 3; Newport, 1 (MM); State Game Farm, 1 (UWZ). *Douglas County:* Gordon, 1 (MM); Solon Springs, 7 (CNHM); T 44 N, R 12 W, 1 (F&FH); Upper Saint Croix Lake, 1 (MM). *Dunn County:* Meridean, 2. *Florence County:* Spread Eagle Lake, 4 (CNHM). *Grant County:* Platteville, 5 (2 AMNH); Potosi (10 mi. S. S. E), 1; Woodman, 1. *Green Lake County:* Green Lake, 12. *Iowa County:* Arena, 1 (UWZ). *Iron County:* Fisher Lake, 14 (11 UWZ); Mercer, 2 (1 MM). *Jackson County:* Millston, 1 (UWZ). *Juneau County:* Beaver Creek, 2 (F&FH); Camp Douglas, 2; Mather 1; T 19 N, R 3 E, 3 (F&FH). *La Crosse County:* La Crosse, 4. *Manitowoc County:* Point Beach State Forest, 2 (UWZ). *Marathon County:* Rib Hill, 9. *Marinette County:* Cravitz, 2 (NPM); McAllister, 1; No locality, 1 (MM); Timm's Lake, 4 (UWZ). *Milwaukee County:* Fox Point, 1 (UWZ); Milwaukee, 34 (30 MM; 4 UWZ); Oak Creek, 1 (UWZ); Whitefish Bay, 1 (UWZ); Williamsburg, 1 (MM). *Oconto County:* Kelley Brook, 1 (MM); Kelley Lake, 1. *Oneida County:* Crescent Lake, 5. *Pierce County:* Big River, 1 (MM); Maiden Rock, 1 (MM); Prescott, 14 (MM). *Polk County:* Saint Croix Falls, 2. *Portage County:* Stevens Point, 3. *Price County:* Ogema, 6. *Racine County:* Racine, 12; Tischigan Lake, 4 (UWZ). *Rock County:* Milton, 7 (6 UWZ). *Rusk County:* Cedar Rapids, 1 (UWZ); Ladysmith, 1 (UWZ). *Saint Croix County:* River Falls (6 mi. N. E.), 1 (WHD). *Sauk County:* Devils Lake, 1; Prairie du Sac, 14 (MM). *Sawyer County:* Connors Lake, 1; T 38 N, R 3 W, 2 (F&FH). *Shawano County:* Keshena Falls, 1 (CAS). *Sheboygan County:* Elkhart Lake, 3; Terra Andrae State Park, 1 (UWZ). *Trempealeau County:* Trempealeau, 1. *Vernon County:* Genoa, 4 (MM). *Vilas County:* Conover, 2 (CMNH); Lake St. Germain, 5; Mamie Lake, 2; Phelps, 26 (UWZ); Robinson Lake, 1

(UWZ); Sayner, 2 (CNHM). *Walworth County:* Delavan, 28 (6 CAS; 1 MM); Delavan Lake, 1 (CAS); Turtle Creek Marsh, 1 (MM); Turtle Lake, 2; Whitewater, 1 (CAS). *Washburn County:* Long Lake, 3; T 41 N, R 13 W, 1 (UWZ). *Waukesha County:* Hartland, 3; Nagowicka Lake, 3 (MM). *Waupaca County:* Saint Lawrence Township, 4 (UWZ). *Waushara County:* Hancock, 1 (UWZ); Saxeville, 1; Wild Rose, 5. *Wood County:* Wisconsin Rapids (10 mi. W.), 1 (WHD).

Selected references.—Bailey, V., 1900, 1924; Hamilton, W. J., 1937 b; Hatt, R. T., 1930 a; Hine, R., 1950; Lantz, D. E., 1907.

Microtus ochrogaster ochrogaster (Wagner)
Prairie Vole

Hypudaeus ochrogaster Wagner, in Schreber, Die Saugthiere, Suppl., vol. 3, p. 592, 1842.
Arvicola austerus Strong, p. 439, 1883.
Microtus austerus Snyder, p. 118, 1902.
Microtus ochrogaster Jackson, p. 23, 1908; Hollister, p. 25, 1910; Cory, p. 218, 1912; Schmidt, p. 112, 1931; Barger, p. 12, 1952.

Vernacular names.—Probably most frequently called prairie mouse or short-tailed prairie mouse in Wisconsin, when distinguished from the meadow vole. Other names include prairie meadow mouse, prairie meadow vole, prairie short-tailed mouse, prairie vole, and upland mouse.

Identification marks.—The prairie vole in general form is similar to the meadow vole, but averages about 5 per cent shorter in total length. The external gland on the hip is absent or inconspicuous; eyes and ears about as in *pennsylvanicus*; tail shorter, both relatively and actually, than in *pennsylvanicus* (length 30 to 40 mm.), about equal to one-third head and body length, scantily haired, brownish above, cinnamon below, somewhat bicolorous; hind foot small (17.5 to 20 mm.), usually with five, rarely six, plantar tubercles; fur texture rather coarse.

Color of upper parts in general tone brownish gray with a flecked or grizzled appearance due to the mixture of blackish and ochraceous buffy tips of the long hairs; side paler; under parts washed with cinnamon or ochraceous, whence the specific name *ochrogaster* was derived. Summer and winter pelage essentially similar, except that the cinnamon wash on the under parts is usually heavier in winter. One molt occurs annually, usually during summer, but molting may occur at any time of the year.

The skull is high, narrow, somewhat arched;

premaxilla extends well back of nasal; audital bullae small and narrow; incisive foramen wide posteriorly; molars with wide re-entrant angles; upper molariform tooth row medium in length (about 6.8 mm.); posterior (third) upper molar with an anterior crescent, two closed triangles, and a posterior loop with two inner lobes, in effect three inner and three outer salient angles.

There is slight individual variation in the intensity of the yellow or ochraceous, both on the upper parts and, more particularly, ventrally. Color mutants are apparently uncommon, though several cases of white spotting have been reported from Kansas and Nebraska, and one "dirty white color" from Kansas (Cockrum, 1953).

Microtus ochrogaster can be readily separated from *Microtus pennsylvanicus* in nearly every instance by one or a combination of the following characteristics: usually five (instead of six) plantar tubercles; coarse pelage, grizzled color dorsally and fulvous or ochraceous wash ventrally; shorter tail (less than 40 mm.); and shorter hind foot (20 mm. or less). It can always be separated cranially in that the third upper molar has two closed triangles, whereas in *pennsylvanicus* there are three. The prairie vole may be distinguished from the pine mouse (*Microtus pinetorum*) by its more grizzled and less reddish color, its coarser, less velvety fur, larger eyes and ears, longer tail, and relatively narrower and higher skull. This species may easily be separated from the red-backed mouse by its color, and cranially in that the palate does not terminate abruptly posteriorly in a bony shelf. From *Synaptomys cooperi*, it differs in its longer tail (30 to 40 mm.) and in its smooth upper incisors (grooved in *S. cooperi*).

Measurements.—Total length of adults, 136 to 160 mm. (5.3 to 6.3 inches); tail, 30 to 40 mm. (1.2 to 1.6 inches); hind foot, 17.5 to 20 mm. (0.7 to 0.8 inches); ear from notch, 11 to 14 mm. (0.4 to 0.5 inches). Weight of adult, 32 to 50 grams. Skull length, 24.3 to 28.1 mm.; width, 13.8 to 15.8 mm.

Distribution in Wisconsin.—Southern and southwestern parts of the state from southern Dunn and Clark counties, northeastern Waushara County, and Dodge County, south to eastern Racine County and southwestern Grant County.

Habitat.—Dry and growing grassy areas along fence lines and in open fields; sandy prairies

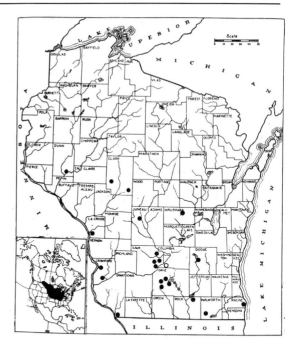

Map 46. Distribution of MICROTUS OCHROGASTER. ● = specimens examined. ○ = authentic record.

and slopes, especially if weed or grass grown; harvested small-grain fields; abandoned farm fields or poorly cultivated fields; seldom in sparsely wooded areas, as in "woods of jack pine and black oak" in Dewhurst Township, Clark County (Schmidt, 1931: 112). Its preferable habitat seems to be native prairie sod, of which there is very little left in Wisconsin. It avoids marshes and wet places.

Status and Habits.—The prairie vole is not as widely distributed in the state as the meadow vole, and where found does not appear to be so abundant. Limitation of suitable habitat for it in the state and apparent dominance of the meadow vole may in part account for its comparatively small population. Also, Wisconsin is the northeastern border of its geographic range. It is extremely local in habit, a given small area sometimes indicating a population of twenty or more to an acre, whereas within a few hundred yards an area apparently as favorable for them will have none. Its relative abundance does not appear to be cyclic. The home range of an individual is seldom more than one-fifth acre, and usually between that and one-tenth acre.

One can usually detect the presence of this vole by locating a suitable habitat and then searching for its runways. These are similar to those of the meadow vole, but are usually deeper in the soil, and more frequently run underground. Cut grass stems sometimes indicate its presence, but this species leaves fewer cut stems than does *pennsylvanicus*. One can depend little on feces or tracks for detecting its whereabouts. It is active both summer and winter, and both day and night. It appears, however, to be crepuscular in its habits, and is most active from dawn until well after sunrise, and between sunset and dark. Its chief mode of locomotion is creeping or a trotting run, both in and out of its burrow. Its maximum running speed is about five miles an hour, though the quick dart it can make into its burrow or runway would lead one to anticipate a faster running speed. It dislikes water, either as rain or as a puddle, and one I once kept could not be forced to enter it. This same individual, when placed on a bare kitchen table 30 inches high, would run around and around the edge of the table for hours, but never attempt to jump to the carpeted floor below. On the other hand, one kept by Hahn (1908 b: 571) in Indiana "showed a surprising ability to climb, going up the vertical sides of the box and clinging to them while attempting to gnaw out, or running along the under surface of the screen wire which formed the top."

The prairie vole is probably more colonial than the meadow vole, though the colonies it forms are never large either in number of animals or area covered. Possibly this tendency toward colonialism is psychological, for this species appears to be much less pugnacious than the meadow vole. It often leaves favorable habitat unoccupied.

In Foster Township [Clark County] those mice which were living on the flat plain extending out from the bases of the sandstone mounds were concentrated in a few of the large knolls formed by the uprooting of trees. In one knoll two adult males, one adult female, and two young were caught. In another knoll two adult males, two adult females, and four young were caught. Both of these knolls were riddled by the burrows of both old and young mice. In none of the adjacent knolls were there any burrows or other signs of mice. On the slope of the sandstone mound with a thicker covering of grass, most of the knolls showed signs of burrowing, and the knolls were connected by a network of runways under the grass (Schmidt, 1931: 113).

The expected life span in this species in the wild is short, probably less than a year. Potential longevity is unknown but is probably about four or five years.

Reproduction may occur throughout the year, with a low during December, January, and February, and a peak in July, August, and September. Young first breed when about 30 days old. Each female usually has three or four litters a year. The young may be two to six in number, but most litters are of three or four with an average nearer three. The gestation period is near 21 days. The youngster weighs about three grams or slightly less at birth. When about 30 days old it is sexually mature and about half to two-thirds adult weight.

The prairie vole spends most of its time in a network of runways and tunnels that it makes itself. Newer runways may be slightly exposed, but by constant use and some digging, scratching, and gnawing by the vole the runway soon becomes a tiny rut about one and one-half inches in diameter. Trampled grass may cover parts of the bare soil forming the floor of the runway. Usually more of the trails are underground as tunnels than on the surface as sunken paths. Sometimes in clover or alfalfa fields where the vole may run, it does not make the customary runway (Jameson, 1947: 136) but travels here

Nest of M. O. OCHROGASTER, *Clark County, Wisconsin. The nest is in a hollow next to a knoll. Sand from a hole entering the knoll may be seen at the left. Courtesy Frank J. W. Schmidt.*

and there among the small plant stems. When
the ground is covered with fallen leaves it may
even make its runway on top of the ground
under the leaves. The underground tunnels are
usually only two to four inches beneath the surface of the soil, though such a tunnel may drop
to a depth of eight or nine inches near a nest.
A large runway system may extend over 160
square yards. It may be utilized by more than
one family of voles, and may connect with an
adjoining runway system. A little hillock, knoll,
abandoned ant hill, or grassy mound makes a
favorite home. Such a mound is often honey-
combed with little holes from which the animal's
runways wind away through the grass. If a
mound is not handy, the holes on level ground
are scattered along the runways that connect the
burrows. The entrance to the burrow is clean
cut, about one and one-half inches in diameter,
and drops nearly straight downward. The nest
usually is placed in the burrow, though occasionally it is on the surface of the ground. A
chamber is dug by the vole for the subterranean
nest. Often a small pile of earth and pieces of
cut grass at the entrance of a burrow indicate a
nest within. When the vole builds a nest on the
surface it usually scratches a slight hollow for
its reception. A nest found near Devils Lake,
Sauk County, August 28, 1918, was built in such
a hollow on the surface of the ground where a
shock of barley recently had stood. The nest was
made of dry barley blades, and measured externally five and one-half inches long by four
inches broad, and was three inches deep. It was
covered. Its walls were about one inch in diameter, and the single entrance was seven-eighths
of an inch in diameter. This nest was short. The
nest is usually about seven to eight inches long,
four to five inches wide, and three and one-half
to four inches deep. It is always made of grass-
like plants, the inside usually of finer material.
Defecation is outside of the nest, but not infrequently in the runways.

The food of the prairie vole is primarily stems
of grass and herbaceous rootlets. It also consumes some tubers, small fruits, and at times the
bark of trees and shrubs. It does not make extensive stores of food for winter use, though
sometimes during an abundance of a choice food
it may store a considerable quantity of it. "One

underground food store-room, for example, was
crammed with 5- or 6-inch clippings of bluegrass. Another, found in a hollow stump in a
bluegrass meadow, contained about a gallon of
the yellow fruits of the horse nettle (*Solanum
carolinense*)" (Fisher, 1945: 436).

The prairie vole falls prey to hawks and owls
less frequently than many other mice. A few are
captured, particularly by the long-eared owl and
the marsh and red-tailed hawks. The least
weasel persistently preys upon the prairie vole,
and if this species of weasel were more plentiful
it would be a highly dangerous enemy. Other
species of weasels also prey upon this vole, as do
also the coyote, red and gray foxes, striped
skunk, and house cat. The rattlesnake and the
fox snake among reptiles catch a few. Heavy
rains are often highly destructive of the prairie
vole, and particularly vulnerable are the young
in the nest.

This species is annoyed by a considerable
number of external parasites, including five species of fleas, one louse, and six mites (Jameson,
1947: 138–44). Internally it is infested by several
kinds of trematodes, cestodes, and nematodes.

Economically, this vole usually is not important in the state. It has limited distribution, seldom occurs in great numbers, and often occupies
waste or sandy lands of little use agriculturally.
It may at times do serious damage locally to corn
or other grain left in shocks in the field. It
seldom is a pest in gnawing the bark on fruit
trees or forest plantations. When it does become
pestiferous, methods of control as described for
the meadow vole are usually effective.

Specimens examined from Wisconsin.—Total 79, as
follows: *Clark County:* Dewhurst, 2 (AMNH); Foster Township, 8 (2 UWZ). *Crawford County:* Lynxville, 5; Wauzeka, 4. *Dane County:* Cross Plains, 2
(1 AWS; 1 UWZ); Madison, 1 (AWS); Mazomanie,
3 (AWS); Pheasant Branch, 1 (AWS); Pine Bluff,
2 (AWS). *Dodge County:* Beaver Dam, 1 (UWZ).
Dunn County: Meridean, 3. *Grant County:* Potosi
(10 mi. S.S.E.), 1. *Juneau County:* T 18 N, R 3 E,
1 (F&FH). *La Crosse County:* La Crosse 6. *Racine
County:* Racine, 14 (3 USNM). *Rock County:* Milton, 7 (6 UWZ). *Sauk County:* Baraboo, 1; Devils
Lake, 1; Prairie du Sac, 6 (MM); Sumpter, 2
(MM). *Walworth County:* Delavan, 5 (4 AMNH).
Waushara County: Saxeville, 3 (1 UWZ).

Selected references.—Bailey, V., 1900; Calhoun,
J. B., 1945; Decoursey, G. E., Jr., 1957; Fisher, H. J.,
1946; Jameson, E. W., Jr., 1947; Martin, E. P., 1956.

Microtus pinetorum scalopsoides
(Audubon and Bachman)
Northern Pine Mouse

Arvicola scalopsoides Audubon and Bachman, Proc.
  Acad. Nat. Sci. Philadelphia, vol. 1, p. 97, 1841.
Arvicola pinetorum Strong, p. 439, 1883.
Microtus pinetorum scalopsoides Hollister, p. 31,
  1910; Cory, p. 222, 1912.

Vernacular names.—Where recognized in Wisconsin commonly called pine mouse or mole mouse. Other names include apple mouse, mole-like mouse, molelike pine vole, molelike vole, mole meadow mouse, mole pine mouse, pine vole, and potato mouse.

Identification marks.—The pine mouse is a small, thickset burrowing microtine with short legs, very short tail, and small eyes and ears; feet small, the hind foot about three-fourths as long as the tail; plantar tubercles five; flank gland high on either hip in male; fur smooth, glossy, silky or velvety, resembling that of a mole except for color, and of the type that repels the soil and comes out of the ground clean and shiny.

M. p. scalopsoides has the upper parts dull brownish chestnut, slightly darkened by dusky tipped hairs; flanks paler; under parts washed with buff over plumbeous base of hairs; feet brownish gray; tail brownish sooty above, dark grayish below. Winter pelage is slightly darker than summer fur. As with most burrowing mammals, there are two molts annually. The darker winter pelage is usually replaced in April or May. The slightly paler summer pelage is usually replaced in September or October.

The skull is flat, short, and wide, with brain case quadrate posteriorly; audital bullae small; molariform tooth row rather short, the series and individual teeth comparatively narrow; upper third molar with two closed triangles; lower third molar with three transverse loops.

There is no apparent sexual variation of color, size, or proportions. Adult males have a small elongate gland on the upper part of each hip. Young animals are more grayish than adults. Individual variation appears to be very little. Hatt (1930: 323) reports a specimen of *scalopsoides* from Long Island, New York, as "a case of restricted yellow ('black-eyed yellow,' 'fawn' or 'cream') mutation." Schantz (1960) reports an albino from Thomasville, Georgia.

Pine mouse, MICROTUS P. SCHMIDTI, *in cage eating slice of potato, Worden Township, Clark County, Wisconsin, August 1928. Courtesy Frank J. W. Schmidt.*

The pine mouse (*Microtus pinetorum*) may be distinguished externally from any other mouse by the combined characters of its short, velvety, molelike fur; its short tail, scarcely longer than its small hind feet; small ears (11 mm. or less measured from notch of ear) nearly concealed in the fur; and the auburn or chestnut uniform cast of upper parts. In size and length of tail *M. pinetorum* is about like *Synaptomys c. cooperi*, but it differs strikingly in color and fur texture, and has smooth fronts (no grooves) of upper incisors. It differs from the red-backed mouse not only in color and texture of fur, but also in much shorter tail (less than 25 mm.), and cranially in its much flatter and relatively broader skull without posterior palatal shelf. From either *M. pennsylvanicus* or *M. ochrogaster* it is separable not only by color but by smaller size (total length less than 135 mm.), shorter tail length (less than 25 mm.), and by its relatively broader and flatter skull.

Measurements.—Total length of adults, 110 to 132 mm. (4.3 to 5.2 inches); tail, 18 to 25 mm. (0.7 to 1.0 inches); ear from notch, 7 to 9 mm.

(0.3 to 0.4 inches); hind foot, 16.5 to 18 mm. (0.6 to 0.7 inches). Weight of adult, 24 to 30 grams. Skull length, 22.5 to 25.4 mm.; width, 13.5 to 15.5 mm.; upper molariform tooth row, 6.2 to 6.6.

Distribution in Wisconsin.—Known only from Dane and Columbia counties, but may be anticipated to occur in scattered colonies in other favorable habitats in southern Wisconsin.

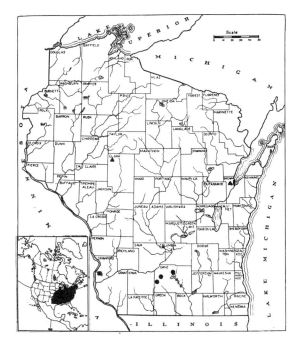

Map 47. Distribution of MICROTUS PINETORUM. *Solid symbols = specimens examined.* ● = M. P. SCALOPSOIDES. ▲ = M. P. SCHMIDTI. ■ = M. P. NEMORALIS.

Habitat.—Variable, not necessarily in pinelands; in Wisconsin chiefly red oak and white oak grazed woodlots, with friable top soil; also sandy fields and brush land. Elsewhere:

Few small eastern mammals exhibit such diverse habitat selection as the pine mouse. Its very name is a misnomer, for, although the type of *Pitymys pinetorum* was taken in the pine woods of Georgia, the northern race is usually a creature of the deciduous woods. In Indiana, according to Hahn (1908), it lives in the rocky hills, about the caves, in the heavy woods where the carpet of dead leaves is several inches thick, and in the fields. Copeland (1912) took 6 specimens of a small colony on the

very summit of Mt. Greylock, Massachusetts, at 3505 feet elevation. They were trapped beneath the spreading roots of the rather open growth of spruce and yellow birch, in the midst of a Canadian environment. Saunders (1932) found them abundant in dry beech woods and in moist banks of a wooded ravine in Middlesex County, Ontario. Poole (1932) found them most abundant in light sandy alluvial soils supporting a scattered growth of trees and shrubs, and large numbers resort to the apparently inhospitable muck and culm of the coal region of the lower Schuylkill Valley of Pennsylvania. Poole has also found a colony on the north slope of the Kittatiny ridge in Pennsylvania at 700 feet elevation, neighbors to *Clethrionomys* and *Sorex fumeus*. I have collected this mouse in the virgin hemlock stands of the Tionesta Forest of Pennsylvania, have noted its numerous tunnels in the sandy soils of Long Island, a few feet above sea level, trapped it in the maple-beech association at Ithaca, New York, and once caught an individual in a sphagnum swamp choked with winter berry (*Ilex verticillata*). To find *Pitymys* in wet ground was a real surprise, for most writers have emphatically stated that the pine mouse avoids swamp lands (Hamilton, 1938: 164).

Status and Habits.—More than fifty years ago I wrote:

The two preceding species [i.e. *pennsylvanicus* and *ochrogaster*] are actually known to occur in the state, but a third, *Microtus pinetorum*, must occur in southern Wisconsin, yet, so far, has evaded all efforts of mammalogists to obtain him. In regard to this species, Dr. C. Hart Merriam [then chief of the U. S. Biological Survey] wrote me under date of May 22, 1902: "There appears to be no reason why it should not occur there [Wisconsin], although as yet we have seen no specimens." Strong reports it from the state, but gives no records nor data; hence his note is valueless (Jackson, 1903: 8–9).

It was not until August 25, 1925, that the first specimen of a pine mouse from Wisconsin was procured by F. J. W. Schmidt in Worden Township, Clark County, and recorded under the name *Pitymys pinetorum scalopsoides* (Schmidt, 1927). During the following five years this enthusiastic young naturalist collected and recorded 34 specimens under the subspecific name *scalopsoides* from Worden Township (Schmidt, 1931: 113). Ten years later some of the specimens collected by Schmidt became the basis for the subspecies *schmidti*, with type locality as Worden Township, Clark County, Wisconsin (Jackson, 1941). The writer has seen less than 50 specimens of pine mice from Wisconsin, of which considerably more than half are referable to *schmidti* and from Clark County. A young male apparently killed and dropped by an owl (the talon marks showed on each side of the mouse's breast), found March 26, 1944, by E. G. Wright, in Brown County, is referable to *schmidti*. Worden Township, Clark County, would appear to be the only locality in Wisconsin where the pine mouse is not rare. The species, however, has probably been overlooked in many localities, and probably has a much more general distribution in the southern half of the state than the records indicate. The specimen of *M. p. nemoralis* was a lucky find, being caught in a trap set for other species. Persistent effort has pro-

Tracks of pine mouse trotting. About 1×. *Photograph by the author.*

duced four specimens from Dane County, which with two from West Point Township, Columbia County, constitute the available material referable to *M. p. scalopsoides*. Possibly when many additional specimens from various localities in the state are available we will have a different picture of the relationships of the various forms.

The pine mouse lives in a rather compact colony, and in some localities has been known to reach a high population. We have no records of dense populations in Wisconsin. The colonies of *schmidti* in Clark County probably indicate the highest population in the state. No estimate of number of animals per acre was made there. The home range of the pine mouse, like that of most true burrowing mammals, is small, seldom more than two hundred feet in diameter.

The presence of the pine mouse is usually difficult to detect. It may leave no evidence of its whereabouts except the small molelike ridges, and these are often indistinct or hidden under leaves. It is difficult to trap by any means, but is usually most easily captured by making a pitfall in its runway. An open two-quart jar or a gallon crock sunk in the pit makes a better trap. An open posthole often acts as a temporary trap for this vole. Its presence can sometimes be detected by the gnawing and bark-girdling it has done to shrubs and trees, usually lower on the stem than work done by other voles.

The pine mouse is active both summer and winter, at any time of the day or night, and in any kind of weather. It scampers in runways it has already formed, but is continually digging new runways, either main ones or branches, so that digging almost appears to be its main form of locomotion. Its fastest running gait is four miles an hour. It does not dig or tunnel as fast as the mole, yet in moderately packed loam it can dig and raise 15 inches of ridge in one minute.

As with many mammals, temperament and behavior vary with individuals. The pine mouse, however, usually is not disposed to be tame or friendly, and when kept in captivity, usually lives only a few weeks.

"A young mouse 80 mm. in length, was kept alive for three days. When picked up by the back of the neck it did not struggle and when held in the hand it did not try to bite. It often sat down and combed its whiskers with its front claws. I tried to

Mound of pine mouse, Worden Township, Clark County, Wisconsin. The dirt is brought up under the leaves without breaking through them. Moles and pocket gophers deposit the soil on top of the leaves. Courtesy Frank J. W. Schmidt.

get some tracks by putting ink on its feet, but it ran along on its front feet dragging its hind feet along behind with the soles up. When its feet were dry it ran about the same as *Microtus pennsylvanicus*. It never tried to jump out of its cage. A nearly full-grown mouse spent most of its time, when not sleeping, trying to jump out of its cage, which was eight inches high. At the end of sixteen days it succeeded in jumping out, and I then had to put it in a different cage. Unlike the young mouse it had a vicious temperament and would jump at one's fingers trying to bite them (Schmidt, 1931: 114).

Sometimes the pine mouse may breed during the winter months. Most of the mating, however, occurs between the last of February and the last of September. There may be as many as three or four litters by a female during the season. The gestation period is twenty days. Young are born naked and blind. The baby is weaned after about the third week and is essentially mature when 40 days old. The usual litter consists of three young, though occasionally two or four are born, and rarely only one.

This species is a burrower of only slighter degree than the mole or the pocket gopher. In mellow soil its little burrow extends two or three inches below the surface in an interminable network with numerous openings to the surface of the soil. Sometimes the burrow reaches depths of 12 inches if the soil is mellow. The nest may be in an enlargement of a side branch of a tunnel, under a root or stump, or, rarely, on the sur-

face of the soil. It is somewhat globular in shape, composed chiefly of dry leaves and grasses, and has two or three entrances leading to tunnels. Writing of nests and burrows of *M. p. schmidti* in Clark County, Schmidt (1931: 113-114) says:

Two nests were located in pine mouse burrows two inches below the surface. There were no young in these nests but traps set at the entrances of the nests caught both adults and half grown young. These nests had an outside measurement of 100 mm., and were constructed of maple leaves. Two young mice 83 mm. in length built a nest of leaves and moss in their cage.

Burrowing is carried on from the surface to a depth of eight or ten inches according to the amount of loam overlying the clay. The surface burrows are constructed just below the leaves, and they often form a network covering several square rods. From these burrows under the leaves other burrows penetrate the soil. Dirt brought up from below is left under the leaves in piles four or more inches in diameter and two or three inches high. As the leaves form a tough layer the dirt rarely breaks through above the leaves. This distinguishes the mounds from those of *Condylura cristata*, which are piled up on top of the leaves or grass. In diameter the burrows of pine mice are 30 to 35 mm. wide and 25 to 30 mm. high. Pine mice burrow both day and night. . . . Mice caught shoving out dirt were always coming out head first, indicating that the dirt is pushed out ahead of the mouse.

The pine mouse feeds chiefly upon roots, tubers, bulbs, and the bark of trees and shrubs. It eats little green vegetation, seeds, or fruit, though it apparently relishes apples and pears. It stores considerable quantities of food, such caches usually consisting of fleshy roots and tubers.

In one burrow a pile of tubers of dutchman's breeches was found. Mice kept in captivity ate the tubers of dutchman's breeches, but preferred a white tuber about one inch long and one fourth inch in diameter not yet identified. Rootstalks of solomon's seal and wild ginger were not eaten. One mouse was kept a month on a diet of potatoes, and was in good health when I killed it. It was offered water several times but always refused to drink (Schmidt, 1931: 113).

The chief enemies of the pine mouse are snakes and shrews, particularly the mole shrew, which can enter its burrows and prey upon the occupants. The least weasel probably is an enemy, and the striped skunk sometimes digs open a mouse burrow and captures both young and adults. Hawks and owls seldom find the pine mouse, which keeps too well under ground for their keen eyes. Continuous rain and high water often drown many pine mice in their burrows.

Pine mice have their share of ectoparasites. During the early spring of 1936, when their numbers in parts of the lower Hudson Valley of New York were unusually high, I examined several dozen that were heavily infected with mites, ticks, fleas, and especially lice. The most abundant mite, *Laelaps microti* (Ewing) occasionally numbered close to 1000 per mouse. A number of undetermined Parasitoidea were collected. Lice, *Hoplopleura,* of two apparently undescribed species, were so abundant at this time that every one of the longer hairs appeared to support an individual. The louse nits on the vibrissae, facial hairs and rump literally numbered in the thousands. A few fleas, *Ceratophyllus* sp., have been recovered from trapped mice. These fleas sometimes persist on the animal for 20 hours or more after death.

It is rather well established that microtine populations, after attaining excessive numbers, are drastically reduced by murine diseases. This was most evident in the spring of 1936, coincident with an epizootic among *Microtus.* Pine mice collected at Croton Falls, New York, and received in the laboratory at Ithaca, were suffering from a skin malady, causing great patches of fur and epidermis to slough away, leaving large glabrous patches on the head, shoulders and flanks. . . . This condition was attended by slight pustular excrescences, accompanied by redness and a general eczematous condition. Several weeks after the onset of these symptoms, a hard dry crust commenced to form about the eyes, eventually drawing the lids together and causing blindness. General weakness of the hind quarters accompanied these latter symptoms, eventually developing into complete paralysis and eventual death (Hamilton, 1938: 169).

Potentially, the pine mouse could be a serious liability where it occurs in numbers on agricultural land. All colonies so far located in Wisconsin are fortunately on more or less waste land. Populations have apparently been low, except possibly those of *schmidti* in Worden Township, Clark County. In places where the pine mouse is common it often does serious damage to orchards and gardens, both vegetable and flower. It may destroy many fruit trees by eating the bark from the roots and base of the trees, usually in

winter and often undetected by the owner until it is too late. In its shallow burrow it may enter a garden or flower bed, where it will feast on roots and bulbs unnoticed until serious losses have occurred. The pine mouse is rather difficult to trap, yet trapping may prove a useful measure in halting damage. Other simple methods of control are effective, and instructions may be obtained by writing the Fish and Wildlife Service, U. S. Department of the Interior, Washington 25, D. C. Detailed instructions for its control may also be found in various publications (Eadie, 1954; Garlough and Spencer, 1944; Hine, 1950; and others).

Specimens examined from Wisconsin.—Total 6, as follows: *Columbia County:* West Point Township, 2 (UWDEZ). *Dane County:* Cross Plains, 1 (AWS); Vermont, 2 (UWZ); West Port Township, 1 (UWZ).

Selected references.—Bailey, V., 1900; Benton, A. H., 1955; Hamilton, W. J., Jr., 1938; Hall, E. R., and E. L. Cockrum, 1953; Schmidt, F. J. W., 1927.

Microtus pinetorum nemoralis Bailey
Woodland Pine Mouse

Microtus pinetorum nemoralis Bailey, Proc. Biol. Soc. Washington, vol. 12, p. 89, April 30, 1898.
Pitymys pinetorum nemoralis Barger, p. 12, 1952.

Vernacular names.—About as for the northern pine mouse.

Identification marks.—Largest of the pine mice (*Microtus pinetorum*); color similar to that of *scalopsoides* but averaging slightly paler brown; skull large and massive; upper tooth row heavy, long, more than 6.6 mm. in alveolar length.

Measurements.—Adult female from Lynxville, Crawford County, Wisconsin: Total length, 133 mm. (5.2 inches); tail, 22 mm. (0.9 inches); hind foot, 19 mm. (0.7 inches); ear from notch, 8 mm. (0.3 inches). Weight, 36 grams (including two embryos). Skull length, 27.1 mm.; width, 16.0 mm.; upper molariform tooth row, 6.8 mm.

Distribution in Wisconsin.—Known only from one specimen trapped at Lynxville, Crawford County.

Habitat.—So far as known in Wisconsin essentially like that of *M. p. scalopsoides.* The Lynxville specimen was collected July 31, 1930, under leaves and grass close to an old brush heap on a dry hillside 50 feet above high-water level of the Mississippi River, where there were many burrows and runways under the leaves.

Status and Habits.—Included under *Microtus pinetorum scalopsoides.*

Specimens examined from Wisconsin.—Total 1, as follows: *Crawford County:* Lynxville, 1.

Selected references.—Same as for *M. p. scalopsoides.*

Microtus pinetorum schmidti (Jackson)
Schmidt's Pine Mouse

Pitymys pinetorum schmidti Jackson, Proc. Biol. Soc. Washington, vol. 54, p. 201, December 8, 1941.

Pitymys pinetorum scaloposoides Schmidt, p. 113, 1931.

Pitymys pinetorum schmidti Barger, p. 12, 1952.

Vernacular names.—About as for the northern pine mouse.

Identification marks.—The subspecies *schmidti* differs from both *scalopsoides* and *nemoralis* in its decidedly more grayish, less rufescent, coloration in specimens of comparable age and season, in its shorter upper molariform tooth row, and in its relatively higher skull. It averages considerably smaller than *M. p. nemoralis* (total length near 130 mm.), which shows in its smaller skull (greatest length 25.5 mm. or less).

In color, *schmidti* has the upper parts mummy brown, or a trifle paler and more grayish, fading on the flanks and legs to the drab gray or pale drab gray of the under parts. Immature (post-nursing young) are distinctly more grayish than young of the other subspecies.

Measurements.—Total length of adult, 115 to 128 mm. (4.5 to 5.0 inches); tail, 20 to 24 mm. (0.8 to 0.9 inches); hind foot, 16.5 to 18 mm. (0.65 to 0.7 inches); ear from notch, 10 to 10.5 mm. (0.4 inches). Weight, 24 to 30 grams. Skull length, 23.4 to 25.5 mm.; width, 14.0 to 16.0 mm.; upper molariform tooth row, 5.7 to 5.9 mm.

Distribution in Wisconsin.—Known only from Worden Township, Clark County, and one specimen from Bairds Creek, Brown County.

Habitat.—"Pine mice were found only in the hardwood forests of the Colby loamy clay area. No traces of them could be found in cultivated fields, pastures or orchards" (Schmidt, 1931: 113).

Status and Habits.—Included under *Microtus pinetorum scalopsoides.*

Specimens examined from Wisconsin.—Total 27, as follows: *Brown County:* Bairds Creek, 1 (NPM). *Clark County:* Worden Township, 26 (3 AMNH; 3 CNHM; 6 UWZ).

Selected references.—Same as for *Microtus p. scalopsoides,* and also Jackson, H. H. T., 1941; Schmidt, F. J. W., 1931: 113-14.

Genus Ondatra Link
Muskrats

Dental formula:

$$I\frac{1-1}{1-1}, \quad C\frac{0-0}{0-0}, \quad P\frac{0-0}{0-0}, \quad M\frac{3-3}{3-3}=16.$$

Ondatra zibethicus zibethicus (Linnaeus)
Common Muskrat

[Castor] zibethicus Linnaeus, Systema naturae, ed. 12, vol. 1, p. 79, 1766.

Fiber zibethicus Lapham, p. 44, 1852; Lapham, p. 340, 1853; Snyder, p. 121, 1902; Jackson, p. 23, 1908; Hollister, p. 25, 1909; Cory, p. 225, 1912.

Fiber Zibethicus Strong, p. 439, 1883.

Ondatra zibethica zibethica Schmidt, p. 116, 1931; Komarek, p. 208, 1932; Barger, p. 12, 1952.

Vernacular names. — In Wisconsin usually called muskrat. Other names include kit (young muskrat in trapper language), mouse (baby muskrat in trapper language), mud cat, mushrat, musk beaver, musquash, mussascus, and *wo-jush* (Chippewa).

Identification marks.—A large robust microtine, with small ears, scarcely extending beyond the fur; eyes small; tail long (205 to 275 mm.), compressed laterally, covered by small scales, and very thinly haired; legs short; feet large, both front and hind modified for swimming; feet and toes fringed by short stiff hairs; hind feet partly webbed; fur dense and fine, waterproof; strongly developed perineal glands (about 50 mm. long) between skin and abdominal muscular wall, secreting a powerful musk; plantar tubercles five.

Muskrat, ONDATRA Z. ZIBETHICUS. *U. S. Fish and Wildlife Service photograph.*

Color of upper parts in winter mummy brown, darkest on head, the general tone of the mid-back glossy and sometimes blackish because of sprinkling of black guard hairs; color of sides somewhat paler, less mixed with blackish; much paler and somewhat more grayish on the under parts, approaching tawny and shading to whitish or pale gray on the throat, lower abdomen, and inner side of legs; small line on chin, nasal pad, and tail blackish; feet dark brown. Worn summer pelage is paler and duller throughout. There is believed to be only one molt a year, which takes place in the summer.

The skull resembles that of a large skull of *Microtus*; angular, heavy zygomata, and long rostrum; audital bullae large; upper incisors smooth, not grooved; all molars are rooted; third upper molar with anterior and posterior enamel loops and two or three closed triangles.

Males and females average nearly the same weight, and there is no sexual variation in color. Also, there is little individual variation in color except for paleness or darkness, and such changes as may be caused by molting or other seasonal conditions. Color mutations are not infrequent,

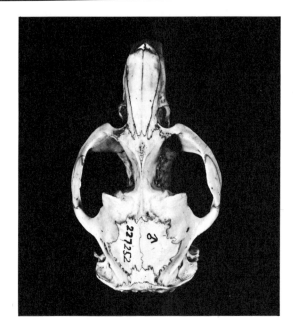

Skull of ONDATRA Z. ZIBETHICUS, *Mamie Lake, Vilas County, Wisconsin.*

usually appearing as melanism or albinism, or less frequently as a yellow or fawn mutant. Several white muskrats have been reported from Wisconsin. A white muskrat was discovered by boys in a swimming pool and captured in 1937 at Antigo (Anon., 1937 h), and one was trapped by Lon Jacobs in a creek south of the town of Lake Geneva in the fall of 1952 (Jacobs, 1953).

The muskrat can hardly be confused with any other Wisconsin mammal. Its size (about that of a small cat), tiny ears and eyes, dense and fine brown fur, and above all its scaled tail essentially void of hairs and laterally flattened, clearly identify it. The skull is of the microtine type, between 60 and 70 mm. in greatest length; it has flat surfaced molars with crowns of folded enamel loops surrounded by dentine, producing angular pattern; length of upper molar tooth row, 15 to 17 mm.

Measurements.—Total length of adults, 480 to 635 mm. (18.9 to 25.0 inches); tail, 205 to 275 mm. (8.0 to 10.8 inches); hind foot, 74 to 88 mm. (2.9 to 3.5 inches); ear from notch, 20 to 25 mm. (0.8 to 1.0 inches). Weight of adult, 900 to 1,500 grams. Skull length, 61.5 to 69.0 mm.; width, 36.8 to 42.8 mm.

Muskrat feet, underside. ⅘×. *U. S. Fish and Wildlife Service photograph.*

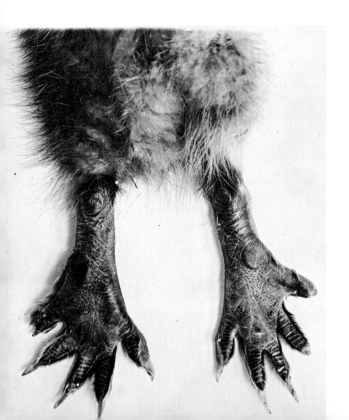

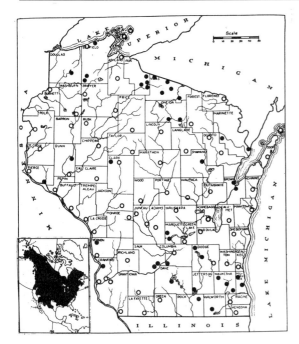

Map 48. *Distribution of* ONDATRA ZIBETHICUS. ● =
specimens examined. ○ = *authentic records.*

Distribution in Wisconsin.—Entire state in suitable habitats.

Habitat.—Marshes, lakes, ponds, slow-running
streams, and almost any place that has water.

Status and Habits.—Since the days of the earliest explorers and settlers in Wisconsin, the
muskrat has been found throughout the state.
Malhiot reported trappers' pelts in 1804 from Lac
du Flambeau (Vilas County) and Pelican Lake
(Oneida County) (Malhiot, 1910: 192, 202). T.
L. Kenny reported "2,500 skins first quality" at
"Prairie du Chien Factory" in the year 1821
(Thwaites, 1911 a: 230), and in 1825 it was
trapped at Lake Shawano (Thwaites, 1911 a:
376). Other reports indicate its occurrence in
numbers throughout the state up to the present
time. It has varied in population, though somewhat irregularly. It apparently does not conform
to regular cyclic increases and decreases in
numbers as do some of the smaller microtines.
The muskrat certainly has no cycles where waters are under control in muskrat management.
"The capacity for accommodation of environment for muskrats is hard to define, under that
name or 'threshold of security' or 'biological

base' or some other. It may show a noteworthy
resistance to change, irrespective of many ordinary seasonal or year-to-year variations in water,
food, and weather, but environmental changes
may be of sufficient magnitude to affect a muskrat population" (Errington, 1951: 277). If one
considers the recent average trapper catch as
six hundred thousand annually and the take as
about half the muskrat population, then there
should be on the average considerably more than
one million muskrats in the state. In a favorable
deep-water area a muskrat population may reach
as high as 25 animals per acre, though in shallow-
water marshes it is seldom more than 15 or 20
muskrats per acre. An average population of one
animal to two acres of marsh, or about three
hundred animals per square mile, is about optimum. Along creek and river banks the population seldom exceeds 15 or 16 muskrats for each
mile of flowage.

Although common in many places, the muskrat is not frequently seen unless special search
is made for it. Clear evidence of its existence in
a neighborhood is the conspicuous house that it
builds in a marsh. Less conspicuous are piles of
cut sedges and cattails, or floating fragments of
them. Trails through the marsh vegetation are
often clearly visible. Holes in the bank with
underwater entrances are less conspicuous. Sometimes a telltale trail or path on the bank or
through vegetation in the water will guide one
to a muskrat's bank home. Muskrat tracks are
quite easily recognized by one who has acquaintance with them, and frequently are abundant
and well marked in the mud where a muskrat
has been. Sometimes tracks appear distinctly in
a dusty trail or road, and they usually show the
mark left by the rat's dragging tail. Occasionally
one may be seen resting on a log or swimming
in the water. It is a quiet mammal, both vocally

Muskrat feces. About 1×. *Adapted from Seton,
1929, vol. IV, p. 631.*

and in locomotion, and seldom attracts a human's attention by any noise. When suddenly aroused, it may enter water with a loud splash, a warning to its companions that an enemy is near.

It is active at all seasons of the year. It is chiefly nocturnal, though sometimes it is active in the daytime, particularly during cloudy weather. Even on bright days it sometimes basks in the sunshine on a log in the water or on its house. Emigrations of muskrats sometimes occur, and in such cases the animal seldom travels overland more than 20 miles from its old home. Movements are often caused by density of population or overcrowding, but may also be brought about by freezing or drought conditions. Movements are most frequent in early spring, next most frequent in autumn. Emigrations at Madison, Dane County, New Glarus, Green County (Schorger, 1939), in Dodge County (Snyder, 1897 a), and at other places in Wisconsin have occurred. It may travel on top of snow and ice during a warm spell in winter. Although the muskrat may take these overland movements under duress, its chief mode of locomotion is by swimming. It is an excellent swimmer and diver, and can travel 180 feet under water without

Tracks of muskrat. Left, left fore foot. Right, left hind foot. 1×.

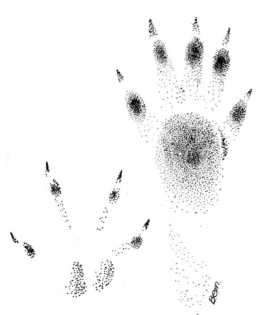

coming up for air. It can remain under water for 15 minutes. It swims with its body under water and only its head above. It can swim backward dog-paddle fashion for 20 or 30 feet, as well as forward, frog or dog fashion, an indefinite distance. It is not a rapid swimmer, about three miles an hour being its limit. Even this is as fast as it can run on land.

The muskrat is not a friendly animal and is only slightly socially inclined among its own kind. It is colonial only to the extent that an environment may offer favorable habitat for several animals. A house may be shared by four or five muskrats during winter, rarely as many as nine or ten. During summer a house is usually occupied only by one family. Its chief mode of communication to its fellows is probably by secreting the musk from its scent glands when it defecates. It usually drops into the water with a splash when suddenly alarmed. It utters a light squeaking note when disposed to be friendly, but when irritated it squeals loudly. On the whole it has an unfriendly and irritable disposition. It plays but little, even with its young. When cornered it will fight vigorously, with dashing charges at the intruder, often making a hissing noise. Its sight, hearing, and sense of smell are poor, but it has an uncanny sense of direction. Considering its size, it is not a muscularly strong mammal, and is not tenacious of life. In the wild its expected longevity is about three or four years. Potential longevity is probably near seven years. One kept in the National Zoological Park lived two and one-half years (Mann, 1930: 303).

"The breeding season of the muskrat in southern and central Wisconsin is from about the first week in April to the middle of June, with occasional animals sexually active as early as the middle of February and as late as the middle of August" (Beer, 1950: 155). The average litter number in Wisconsin is between seven and eight. The number of young in a litter may vary from four to nine, though sometimes as few as two constitute the litter, and as many as sixteen have been reported. The gestation period is about 29 days. A single pair will raise at least two, and sometimes as many as three or four, litters in a year, and under very favorable conditions may raise 16 to 20 young in one season. When two weeks old the young one can swim and dive, and begins to feed on green vegetation. The young muskrat grows rapidly, but ordinarily does not become sexually mature during the year of its birth. The mammae are usually eight, four pectoral, four inguinal.

In the broader expanses of marsh or water that have gently sloping banks, and particularly if there be abundant vegetation, muskrats build their familiar houses. Heaps of aquatic vegetation and mud, hollowed above the water on the inside for a nest cavity, and with runways for exit and entrance extending beneath the surface, are their homes. These houses may be small in the summer, but are enlarged during autumn for winter protection, and sometimes become huge domelike affairs eight or ten feet in diameter and as high as four feet above the water's

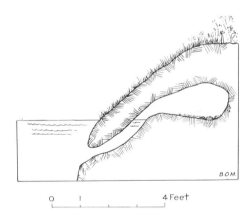

Diagram of section of muskrat bank den, from rough sketch made by the author at Cranberry River, Bayfield County, Wisconsin.

Diagram of cross section of muskrat house from rough sketch made by the author at Storrs Lake, Rock County, Wisconsin.

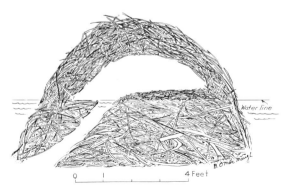

surface. Rumor has it that one can predict the severity of the winter to follow by the size of the muskrat houses! Needless to say, muskrats can foretell the weather no better than humans, and the size of the house depends largely on the amount of available vegetation. Along bodies of water with steeper shores and less abundant aquatic vegetation, muskrats make their homes in holes in the bank. The entrance to such a home is usually below the surface of the water but the tunnel goes upward into the bank to a dry and cozy nesting place several feet back from the water (Jackson, 1931 a: 45).

Stanley A. Apel, State Conservation Warden, photographed a large muskrat house along the Kickapoo River, Crawford County, in the winter of 1946–47. The house measured 41 inches in height from ice level and was 31 feet in circumference (Anon., 1947 e).

The chief foods of the muskrat are various aquatic plants, among the important ones being cattail (*Typha latifolia*), arrowhead (*Sagittaria graminea*), spike rush (*Eleocharis aricularis*), water bullrush (*Scirpus subterminalis*), pickerel weed (*Pontederia cordata*), and large-leaved pondweed (*Potamogeton amplifolius*). On the last named, Francis Zirrer found it feeding in the region of Hayward during the winter of 1943–44. One animal he observed gnawed holes in the ice from below for air and exit. On one occasion Zirrer observed a muskrat eating *Potamogeton* as it sat on the ice near one of these holes. The muskrat also eats other water plants such as the white water lily, lotus, and even the leaves and bark of the black willow along the

Muskrat house in Storrs Lake, Rock County, Wisconsin, August 29, 1922. U. S. Fish and Wildlife Service photograph by the author.

Mississippi River. It sometimes eats wild rice, It indulges but little in animal food, but has been known to eat clams, snails, and crayfish. At Crescent Lake, Oneida County, in September, 1917, I found many gnawed and broken clam shells discarded by muskrats feeding along the shore of the lake and the bank of Crescent Creek.

Few predators harass the muskrat, but it has abundant other enemies, particularly in parasites and diseases. Large hawks and, more particularly, large owls occasionally capture a muskrat. Among mammals the mink is its most persistent enemy, though the red fox and the otter have been known to feed upon it. Snapping turtles and predatory fish such as the muskellunge and northern pike frequently capture one, particularly the young one. A few are killed by automobiles, and floods and droughts cause the death of a few. "Oil in which D. D. T. is sprayed on marshes in which muskrats are living is likely to have a more deleterious effect on the animals than the D. D. T." (Wragg, 1954: 13).

Hale (1954 d: 18) tells us that "at least 22 different parasites and diseases, including tularemia, have been found among Wisconsin muskrats." For the whole of North America 24 kinds of trematodes alone have been reported as occurring in the muskrat (Doran, 1955 b). External parasites are also numerous. A form of hemorrhagic epizootic, called Errington's disease in recognition of its discoverer, often causes serious losses in a muskrat population (Errington, 1946; McDermid, 1946).

The muskrat, economically, is one of our most valuable native mammals. It has always been popular with Wisconsin people. The muskrat

Yellow domestic cat mothering one kitten and five baby muskrats. Courtesy of Stanley C. Arthur.

group in Milwaukee Museum, by Carl Akeley, 1890, I am told by Dr. W. C. McKern, is the oldest "habitat group" as it is now understood. The group is six feet long by four feet deep, and has the painted background of a true habitat group. The muskrat is not without its faults. It sometimes molests corn and other crops and causes minor damage. It may at times cause serious damage by tunneling and weakening dams, dikes, levees, railway embankments, and the banks of irrigation and drainage ditches and canals. In one notable and unique instance in April, 1904, the floodwaters of Saline River in southern Illinois invaded Equity Mine by way of muskrat burrows and threatened the lives of about one hundred miners. It has become a particular threat to dykes in Holland.

The muskrat was established in 1905 on an estate near Prague, Bohemia, where it was hoped it would help supply the demand for fur. The colony, however, increased more rapidly than was anticipated, and from this nucleus the animals spread into Bavaria, Saxony, and Silesia. In their adopted countries the animals have become decidedly harmful to growing crops, and the fur of the species in its new environment is of low standard. The problem now in these countries is how to rid themselves of their adoption. The best policy always is to foster and protect useful animals that may be native to a country, rather than to introduce foreigners (Jackson, 1931: 48; see also Ahrens, 1921; Middleton, 1931; Mohr, 1933; Ulbrich, 1930).

The average annual muskrat catch in Wisconsin will run close to 500,000 pelts. In 1953 it was 1,240,516 pelts. It is seldom less than 300,000 skins. An average pelt value of 90 cents on an average crop of 500,000 is $450,000 for muskrat skins alone in the state. Many other values could be added.

Although the cash value of an individual muskrat pelt is low compared with that of many other fur-bearers, such as minks, otters, martens, and foxes, yet in the aggregate the immense numbers marketed produce a distinct financial asset to the region of the animal's domain. The total catch in North America will approximate an average of about 15,000,000 muskrats annually. Figure them at an average price of eighty cents a pelt, which is reasonably low, and you can estimate an asset to the country of $12,000,-000 a year. But that is not all. We should bear in mind that muskrats inhabit for the most part only low or marsh land that is not suitable for cultivation,

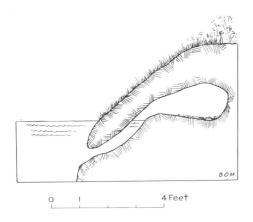

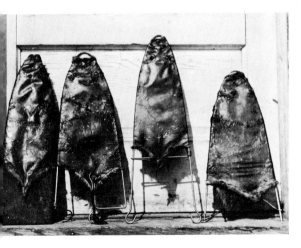

Muskrat pelts stretched fur inside over a board or wire frame to dry.

and that from a national standpoint the profit is clear gain.

As a result of their realization of the value of certain marsh lands for raising muskrats, aided and encouraged by the investigations of the United States Biological Survey [and the Wisconsin Conservation Department], men are now practicing muskrat farming. To establish a muskrat farm, a large area that includes marsh land with suitable vegetation and otherwise favorable for muskrats is fenced. A breeding supply of the animals should already inhabit the marshes. Ditches are frequently constructed to allow easier access to certain parts of the farm and to drain areas where the water may be too deep for maintaining a good growth of aquatic plants. An effort is made to obtain the best possible breeding and living conditions for the animals, which are allowed to live as in nature, and special effort is made to protect the animals from their natural enemies and poachers. At the proper season when the fur is prime, about December, January, and February in most localities, the surplus animals are trapped, and their pelts carefully dried, stretched with fur inside over board or wire frames. The trapping of muskrats on these farms is usually subject to the same state law restrictions as the trapping of the animal in wild.

Should we follow the pelts, sent in by the trapper or fur farmer, from the fur trader or dealer until they are worn in a coat by "My Lady", we should find that not only does the muskrat have an intrinsic value in its fur, but that it is an important economic factor in production of work. Many large industries are more or less dependent upon this little mammal for success. The tanner transfers the raw pelt into soft leather. Then the plucker and the dyer may have a chance at the tanned skin. Sometimes the fur is made directly into garments, but generally the long or guard hairs are "plucked" out. At other times the fur may be clipped to produce a somewhat silvery effect, or it may be dyed a glossy black. . . . Special cutters shape the skins for garments, and special fur workers tailor the finished product. The final money distribution value of the muskrat will average not less than $100,000,000 annually, a no mean sum to be added to our resources and one that can continue indefinitely with proper protection of the source.

The flesh of the muskrat is esteemed as food by many. A few who have partaken pronounce it unfit to eat on account of a musky flavor. Personally, I

Oil and musk glands of the muskrat. A. Adult male, ventral view, B. Adult male, right side view, C. Adult female, ventral view in situ showing external aperture. About 1×.

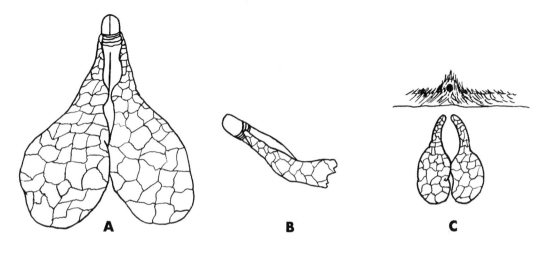

A   B   C

A prime unplucked muskrat pelt.

have never been able to detect this muskiness when the flesh has been carefully prepared and cleaned, and find the meat very palatable. Unfortunately, the name muskrat in itself taints the meat as both musky and ratty for the finicky, and causes unwarranted prejudice against it. In its habits and natural relationships the muskrat is far removed from the rats as we know them. In some of our eastern markets, more particularly in Baltimore, Washington, and Philadelphia, muskrats are on sale during the winter, usually under the name of "marsh rabbits". The sales, however, do not begin to utilize the possible supply from the animals trapped for fur, and by the nonconsumption of this meat there is an economic waste equivalent in food value to about eight thousand cattle annually.

The muskrat has held an important position in the development of American history. The early colonists, following the Indian methods, soon learned to use it for food. Not only were muskrats used as fresh meat, but, particularly in the region of the upper Mississippi Valley, the flesh was dried or salted, and stored for winter use. Muskrat fur in those days was appreciated as now, and in many sections was a valuable commodity in trade. In an old account with the trading post at Lac du Flambeau, now in Wisconsin, dated April 12, 1805, we get an interesting side light on the comparative value of fur pelts at that time. The statement, as translated from the French, reads:

		"Plus"
2	Large bear skins at 2 "plus" each	4
1	Small do	1
7	Otter skins at 2 "plus" each	14
3	Fisher skins	3
3	Beaver skins	3
4	Marten skins	2
20	Muskrat skins at 10 for a "plus"	2
	For grease	2

This would make ten muskrat pelts the equivalent of one beaver or two martens. In 1821, a sale of 2,500 first-quality muskrat skins at the Prairie du Chien Factory, Wisconsin, brought fifty-five cents each, a price only a little below that of 1930. Probably no fur during a period of over a century has maintained a more uniform actual selling price, but as compared with some other furs of colonial days the price is now relatively lower (Jackson, 1931 a: 46–48; see also Dozier, 1953; Field, 1948; Mathiak, 1953; Mathiak and Linde, 1954).

Specimens examined from Wisconsin.—Total 152, as follows: *Bayfield County:* Clear Lake, 1 (MM); Eau Claire Lake, 1 (MM); Herbster, 1. *Brown County:* Green Bay, 3 (2 CNHM; 1 NPM); Long Tail, 1 (MM). *Clark County:* Worden Township, 1. *Columbia County:* Okee, 1. *Crawford County:* Ferryville, 1. *Dane County:* Madison, 3 (1 AWS; 2 UWZ). *Dodge County:* Beaver Dam, 27 (3 CNHM; 1 MVZ; 23 UWZ); Lake Emily, 1 (MM). *Douglas County:* Upper Saint Croix Lake, 1 (MM). *Dunn County:* Colfax, 12 (UWZ). *Iron County:* Cedar Lake, 1 (UWZ); Fisher Lake, 1 (UWZ). Mercer, 15 (UWZ); Turtle Lake, 1 (UWZ). *Jefferson County:* Lake Koshkonong, 1 (USNM). *Marinette County:* Marinette, 1 (UWZ); Thunder Mountain, 1 (NPM). *Marquette County:* Endeavor (Buffalo Lake), 10; Oxford, 1 (UWZ). *Milwaukee County:* Milwaukee 1 (MM); Wauwatosa, 2 (MM). *Oneida County:* Crescent Lake, 3; North Pelican Lake, 1 (UWZ). *Pierce County:* Maiden Rock, 1 (MM). *Racine County:* Tischigan Lake, 1 (MM). *Rock County:* Milton, 2 (UWZ). *Sauk County:* Honey Creek, 1 (MM); Prairie de Sac, 7 (MM). *Shawano County:* Keshena, 4 (CAS). *Vernon County:* Coon Valley, 1. *Vilas County:* Conover, 1 (CNHM); Crab Lake, 1; Eagle River, 4 (1 CNHM); Mamie Lake, 7; Sayner, 1 (CNHM). *Walworth County:* Delavan, 16 (2 MM). *Waukesha County:* Golden Lake, 1 (MM); Pewaukee Lake, 9 (4 MM; 5 UWZ); Muskego Lake, 2 (MM).

Selected references.—Dozier, H. L., 1953; Errington, P. L., 1941; Field, W. H., 1948; Hollister, N., 1911 c; Johnson, C. E., 1925 a; Mathiak, H. A., 1953 a.

Family **Muridae**
Old World Rats and Mice

The family Muridae was originally confined to the Old World south of the Arctic region, but members of the genera *Rattus* and *Mus* are now everywhere distributed through human agencies. Only these 2 genera occur in Wisconsin, although at lease 90 genera, exclusive of fossil forms, are usually included in the family.

Genus **Rattus** G. Fischer
Old World Rats

Dental formula:

$$I\frac{1-1}{1-1}, \quad C\frac{0-0}{0-0}, \quad P\frac{0-0}{0-0}, \quad M\frac{3-3}{3-3} = 16.$$

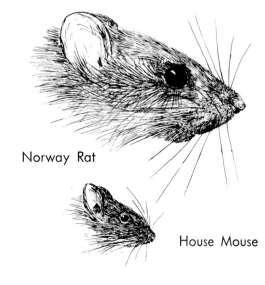

Norway Rat

House Mouse

Woodland Jumping Mouse   Jumping Mouse

Heads of Muridae and Zapodidae. 1×.

House Mouse

Jumping Mouse

Woodland

Jumping Mouse   Norway Rat

Hind feet of Muridae and Zapodidae. 1½×.

Rattus norvegicus (Berkenhout)
Norway Rat

Mus norvegicus Berkenhout, Outlines of the natural history of Great Britain, vol. 1, p. 5, 1769.

Mus decumanus Lapham, p. 340, 1853; Strong, p. 438, 1883; Snyder, p. 117, 1902.

Mus norvegicus Jackson, p. 20, 1908.

Epimys norvegicus Hollister, p. 25, 1910; Cory, p. 180, 1912.

Rattus norvegicus Komarek, p. 208, 1932; Barger, p. 12, 1952.

Vernacular names.—In Wisconsin commonly called rat. Other names include barn rat, brown rat, common rat, dock rat, domestic rat, gray rat, Hanoverian rat (in England, because this kind of rat reached England the same year as the Hanoverian Monarchy), house rat, oriental rat, sewer rat, wharf rat, and white rat (of commerce).

Identification marks.—The Norway rat is too well known to need detailed description. It is on the average about 16 inches long from tip of nose to tip of tail, and is of rather slender build; ears prominent and naked, rather short, if depressed not reaching to the angle of the eye; tail moderately long but not longer than head and body, nearly naked, scaly, bicolorous at base; pelage coarse; mammae twelve. Skull more than 35 mm. long; upper molars with tubercles (cusps) in three longitudinal rows.

The color of the upper parts is brownish or grayish, darker in the middle of the back, and everywhere mixed more or less with black hairs; underparts grayish brown or pale gray; tail dark grayish above, very slightly paler below, not distinctly bicolorous; feet above dirty white.

There appears to be no sexual variation in size or color. Individual variation in size of adults is considerable, but the color of rats in general throughout the state is quite stable. The species has been very flexible regarding color mutants, and the albino of this species is the commercial white rat. Melanistic mutants also occur, and occasionally piebald or blotched gray-black and white.

Measurements.—Total length of adults, 340 to 450 mm. (13.4 to 17.7 inches); tail, 150 to 210 mm. (5.9 to 8.3 inches); hind foot, 38 to 44 mm.

Norway or brown rat, from mounted specimen in corn crib, Washington, D. C. U. S. Fish and Wildlife Service photograph by Silver and Blake.

(1.6 to 1.7 inches). Weight of adult, 275 to 450 grams, rarely to 600 grams. Skull length, 42.4 to 45 mm.; width, 20.5 to 22.2 mm.

Distribution in Wisconsin.—Throughout the state, particularly near human habitations.

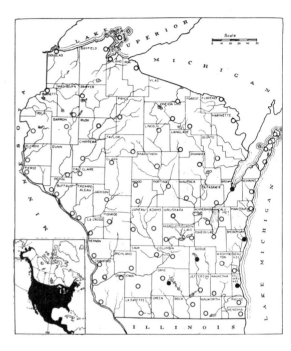

Map 49. Distribution of RATTUS NORVEGICUS. ● = *specimens examined.* ○ = *authentic records.*

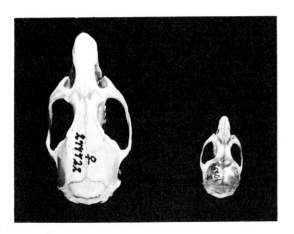

Skulls of Muridae. Left, RATTUS NORVEGICUS, *Camp Crowder, Missouri. Right,* MUS MUSCULUS, *Washington, D. C.*

Habitat.—Chiefly found about buildings on farms, in villages and cities, and near other human settlements; frequently found in fields, especially in summer; occasionally found along beaches and at summer resorts and recreation centers.

Status and Habits.—The Norway rat is an oriental intruder into the United States, and is not a native of Norway as its name might imply. It is believed to have first invaded Europe from Asia in 1727, when hordes of them are said to have swam the Volga River. About the same time, it arrived in England on ships from Asia. The first Norway rats to be introduced into the United States probably came in ships from England at about the time of the American Revolution. Since then the species has been constantly imported into the United States from all parts of the world, until it now is found in every state of the Union and in all United States territories. It is not known when the first Norway rat arrived in Wisconsin. Lapham (1853: 340) mentions the occurrence of the brown rat in Wisconsin and specifies the locality as Racine. It occurred in Wisconsin much earlier than the year 1853, possibly near the beginning of the nineteenth century. The railroad reached Milton, Rock County, in 1852, but Ezra Goodrich, a pioneer of that village, told me in the nineties that "the brown rat was in Milton before the railroad came." On account of more sanitary conditions, better building construction, and constant warfare by man against it, the Norway rat is ap-

parently less abundant in the United States, and also in Wisconsin, then it was at the beginning of the twentieth century. Even so, it is estimated that there are between 150 and 175 million rats in the United States. On that basis we probably entertain not less than 2 million Norway rats in Wisconsin. The species is more or less colonial, and often under favorable food and shelter conditions may reach a dense population. The town of Middleton, Dane County, in 1950 became so overrun with rats that special measures were adopted to eradicate the pest, and the village became rat free the next year. During the year 1900 I was assigned to destroy the rats in and around a slaughterhouse and pigyard near Milton. The building was in a field, four hundred yards from any other building or road. My first catch in a cage trap was 22 rats one night. The next day I devised two dropping-board traps over a barrel one-third full of water. All three traps worked, and within five days I had caught or drowned more than 200 rats. The remaining few were later caught in steel traps. The entire area was less than one-half acre, or about the home range of one rat. The home range of the brown rat is about 150 feet in diameter in Baltimore, Maryland (Dr. David E. Davis, Johns Hopkins University, at a meeting of the American Society of Mammalogists, Higgins Lake, Michigan, August 26, 1947).

The presence of a rat is easily detected. The animal, though timid, is not usually very seclusive, and often it peeks from its hole or around a corner, runs alongside a foundation, or otherwise makes itself conspicuous. Often it betrays

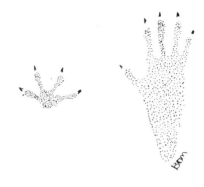

Tracks of Norway rat. Left, track of right fore foot. Right, track of right hind foot. 1×.

its presence by scampering rather noisily over the floor, or if numbers are present the occasional squealings are a telltale sign. When a rat is around it soon leaves its marks by gnawings, feces, and despoiled food. It is active winter and summer. It is slightly more nocturnal than diurnal, but is often active all day. It seldom migrates unless forced away by food shortage or some other factor. It more often starves, or dies of disease. Its major migrations are for the most part accidental, by boat, truck, or train. Its movements are rather cumbersome, and its usual running gait is only about one or two miles an hour, yet it can continue almost indefinitely. It seldom attempts to climb, and does poorly as a climber. It swims and dives well, and can swim across a river of considerable width. Though able to swim, it does not favor watery areas, and usually makes quick exodus from a flooded place. Its normal longevity is probably about two or three years. Its potential longevity is near five years.

The prolificacy of the species tends to maintain a high population of Norway rats. The female may have young when only four months old. The number of litters for each female is usually six to eight annually, and may reach as high as eleven or twelve. Each litter contains six to eight young, and sometimes a dozen or more. The mammae are twelve, six pectoral, two abdominal, four inguinal. The gestation period is 21 to 22 days.

We have numerous records of startling local increases in the numbers of rats under favorable conditions, which prove that the high reproductive potential, when undisturbed, becomes an actuality, but as these are always followed by an equal or greater decrease, the rat population as a whole is maintained at a remarkably constant level.

The high reproductivity of rats is not sufficient in itself, therefore, to allow an indefinite increase in their numbers. It does, however, enable them to recuperate quickly from any unusual depletion in their numbers and is the important factor in the maintenance of rats at their high position in the relative abundance of mammals (Silver, 1924 a: 67).

The nest is a rather crude assemblage of soft material placed well under shelter in a trash pile or dump, under a building or wood pile, in a straw or hay stack, or where similar protection is afforded. It is always on or very near the ground. The rat makes burrows in the gound and trails on the surface, particularly under cover of old boards and the like. It seldom builds its nest in a burrow.

Although the rat, being a true rodent, is primarily fitted to feed upon vegetable matter, it actually is omnivorous. It is fond of garbage and food refuse, and is always attracted to a low open garbage pail. It feeds upon food stores wherever they may be found near the ground. It often visits a poultry house, and may destroy eggs in nests accessible to it. It will catch and kill baby chicks. In fact, it eats almost anything.

Fortunately for humans, the rat has many enemies. Almost every kind of bird and mammal dislikes the rat, and fights it. With some it is mostly fight and protest, because the rat can viciously fight back and often quickly find shelter. Nevertheless, hawks and owls, and weasels and other carnivores frequently catch one, or worry it to death. Some house cats are excellent "ratters," yet others are afraid of a big rat. Mrs. F. L. Larkin (1949) tells of 12 or 15 bluejays attacking a large rat and killing it in Milwaukee. Bluejays were nesting in the vicinity. Occasionally a rat is run over by an automobile, particularly in the autumn, but not many are killed by cars. The chief enemies of the rat are the many parasites that infest it and the diseases that infect it. Many of these same parasites transmit disease to man, such as the oriental rat flea (*Xenopsylla cheopis*), the principal vector from the Norway rat to humans of murine typhus fever (Good and Kotcher, 1949). Other diseases of the rat, such as tularemia, are directly transmitted to man. Still others, such as rat-bite fever and Haverhill fever, are communicated to man by the bite of the rat (Jellison, 1949).

About the only good thing that can be said of the Norway or brown rat is that it is the ancestor of the albino or white rat, which came from it as a mutation ages ago. The white rat has not only proven to be a clean and adaptable pet, but it is valuable for zoological and medical experiments and tests in all biological laboratories. Most mammals, unlike man, do not look back on their ancestry for stimulus and support. If they did, the white rat would have little to admire. One of the worst names a person can call another is a "rat." Of all mammals, the Norway rat is the greatest pest to mankind. It has long been known not only as a destroyer of crops, buildings, and storage supplies, but as a factor in the spread of disease. The tenth-century physician Avicenna wrote that when rats died in numbers or migrated there was danger of an outbreak of plague. As far back as the beginning of the Christian era a connection between human life and rats was realized. Rats are now recognized as vectors of such human and animal diseases as leprosy, typhus in various forms, paratyphoid, glanders, spotted fever, cholera, tuberculosis, tularemia, dysentery, foot and mouth disease, rabies, rat-bite fever, Haverhill fever, epidemic jaundice (Weil's disease), trichinosis, and mange. The only answer to a malicious enemy is to destroy it as completely as possible, and take preventative measures against its return or increase. It has been said that five cents worth of poison or other protection will return five dollars if used to keep rats out of a storehouse. One rat will destroy five to ten dollars worth of grain a year. The same five cents might also save human lives. The owner of a building destroyed by fire gets little consolation from the knowledge that the rat which short-circuited the electric current was probably killed. Many methods of rat destruction have been formulated. One of the better of the poisons, but one which must be used with caution, is Warfarin, discovered by Dr. Karl Paul Link of the University of Wisconsin. It is sold under various trade names. Directions for its use may be procured from the Wisconsin Alumni Research Foundation, Madison, Wisconsin. Anyone interested in rat control or destruction may write for bulletins to the Fish and Wildlife Service, U.S. Department of the Interior, Washington 25, D. C. Reference to certain publications may also give the needed aid (Dykstra and Jones, 1955; Mills, 1953; Silver, Crouch, and Betts, 1942; Silver and Garlough, 1941).

Specimens examined from Wisconsin.—Total 40, as follows: *Brown County:* Green Bay, 1 (NPM). *Dane County:* Madison, 3 (UWZ). *Dodge County:* Beaver Dam, 26 (2 CNHM; 24 UWZ). *Milwaukee County:* Milwaukee, 9 (8 MM; 1 UWZ). *Sheboygan County:* Terry Andrae State Park, 1 (UWZ).

Selected references.—Donaldson, H. H., 1924; Greene, E. C., 1935; Lantz, D. E., 1909; Silver, J., W. E. Crouch, and M. C. Betts, 1942; Silver, J., and F. E. Garlough, 1941; Wyman, W., and others, 1910.

Genus **Mus** Linnaeus
Old World Mice

Dental formula:

$$\text{I}\frac{1-1}{1-1}, \quad \text{C}\frac{0-0}{0-0}, \quad \text{P}\frac{0-0}{0-0}, \quad \text{M}\frac{3-3}{3-3} = 16.$$

Mus musculus domesticus Rutty
House Mouse

Mus domesticus Rutty, Essay Nat. Hist. County Dublin, vol. 1, p. 281, 1772.
Mus musculus Lapham, p. 44, 1852; Lapham p. 340, 1853; Strong, p. 438, 1883; Snyder, p. 117, 1902; Jackson, p. 20, 1908; Hollister, p. 24, 1910; Cory, p. 176, 1912; Schmidt, p. 116, 1931; Komarek, p. 208, 1932.
Mus musculus musculus Barger, p. 12, 1952.

Vernacular names.—Commonly called house mouse or simply mouse. Other names include common mouse, gray mouse, pantry mouse, singing mouse, and white mouse (albino form).

Identification marks.—A small mouse, almost too well known to need description. Recognized by its slender tapering tail, the length of which is about equal to that of the head and body (about half the total length), and which is almost hairless, scaly, and shows annulations; ear moderately large, naked or nearly so; nose rather pointed; fur somewhat coarse.

The color of the upper parts is brownish or mixed yellowish brown and black with a grayish cast; color of upper parts gradually grading into buffy gray of under parts without sharp contrasting mark, the under parts very rarely showing any white; tail not bicolorous, dusky above, very slightly paler below. Young are essentially like adults in color. The skull is characteristic of *Muridae*, never more than 25 mm. in greatest length; molars with three longitudinal rows of tubercles.

The sexes are similar in size and color. Young are essentially like the adult except for smaller size. Individual variation is slight. Color varia-

House mouse. About ¾×. U. S. Fish and Wildlife Service photograph.

tion may appear at times in "whitish" or "yellow" belly, which may indicate ancestry from some other race of *musculus* than true *domesticus*. Mutations in color, particularly white or albino, are not unusual. The commercial "white mouse" sold for pets and laboratory use is an albinistic mutation. Other mutations, some producing psychic effects such as the dancing mouse, occur. Various phases of genetics and variations in the mouse have been the subjects of intensive research (see Grüneberg, 1943, and Snell, 1943, and references in bibliographies therein).

About the only Wisconsin mammals with which the house mouse might be confused are the genera *Peromyscus* and *Reithrodontomys*. From both of these the house mouse may be distinguished by its scantily haired tail showing scale annulations and its darker, more buffy under parts, which are never white except in abnormal specimens. The harvest mouse (*Reithrodontomys*), particularly the young, is sometimes more difficult to separate. Structure of the teeth will always separate the house mouse (*Mus*). In *Mus* the molars have three longitudinal rows of tubercles, whereas in *Peromyscus* and *Reithrodontomys* the molars have only two longitudinal rows of tubercles. Moreover, the incisors of *Reithrodontomys* are grooved, whereas the incisors of both *Mus* and *Peromyscus* are smooth.

Measurements.—Total length of adults, 160 to 200 mm. (6.3 to 7.9 inches); tail, 78 to 94 mm. (3.0 to 3.7 inches); hind foot, 17 to 20 mm. (0.7 to 0.8 inches). Weight of adult, 15 to 24 grams. Skull length, 20.4 to 22.5 mm.; width, 10.4 to 11.5 mm.

Distribution in Wisconsin.—Throughout the state.

Habitat.—In and around houses, stores, warehouses, granaries, barns, and other buildings; frequently in fields and meadows, particularly in summer; rarely in wet marshes.

Status and Habits.—The exact time of the introduction of the house mouse into America is not certain. It was a pest in England at the beginning of the seventeenth century. It came with the early settlers, possibly about the time of the American Revolution or earlier. Likewise we have no records as to when the first house mice were introduced into Wisconsin. It may have been in the storehouses of Green Bay and Prairie du Chien by the close of the eighteenth

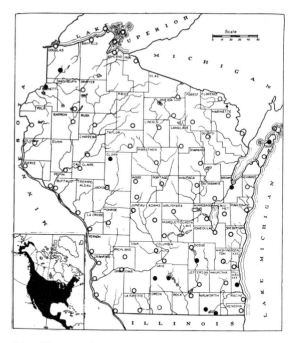

Map 50. *Distribution of* Mus musculus. ● = *specimens examined.* ○ = *authentic records.*

century. It is mentioned as present at Milwaukee in the first mammal list of Lapham (1852: 44). It occurred at Milton, Rock County, as early as 1842, soon after the founding of the settlement. It has reached an apparently near stable population throughout the nation as a whole. Local populations vary in accord with spurts for mouse control and eradication. House mice over Wisconsin, as throughout the nation, are about twice as abundant as Norway rats. They occupy a much more extensive habitat. They dwell in every story of tall buildings, whereas the Norway rat is a basement and first floor operator. Wisconsin is host to possibly four of five million house mice during most years. The house mouse does not confine itself to one runway or one corner, and in this sense it is not territorial. It does, however, once it has become established, cling closely to a small general region, whether in a field, yard, barn, or house. It seldom travels more than 50 feet from its established home. Occasionally it may reach a dense population. From January 7 to December 24, 1942, in a room (42 x 21 feet) of the agronomy seedhouse, University of California, Davis, 235 house mice were

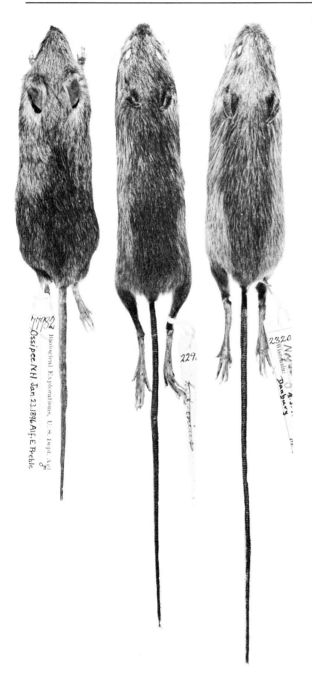

Skins of house mouse and jumping mice. Left, Mus
musculus, *Ossipee, New Hampshire. Middle,*
Zapus h. intermedius, *Rib Hill, Wisconsin. Right,*
Napaeozapus i. frutectanus, *Danbury, Wiscon-*
sin. ¾×.

caught. The mice disappeared by June, 1943, and
a new population began to develop in November, but did not approach the concentration of
the previous winter (Evans, 1949: 362).

Although the house mouse usually keeps out
of sight, it often announces itself by its persistent gnawing and scampering in the partitions
of a building, and by its characteristic little black
pellets left on shelves and elsewhere. It is active
the year round. It does most of its pilfering at
night, particularly during early evening. Sometimes it forages in daylight. It runs rather than
gallops from place to place, but when foraging
usually walks, wandering here and there, usually close to objects, and stopping and sniffing
for food evidences as it progresses. In its food-
searching it walks slowly, only a few inches a
minute. When it runs, its maximum speed is
about eight miles an hour. It climbs rough surfaces fairly well, and can easily jump upward
eight inches. It is a moderately good swimmer
for only a few feet, but soon drowns when it
falls into water.

The house mouse is not truly a colonial species. Often many individuals may be found in
a small area, but with no colony organization.
It has no flash signals, no sentries, no warning
calls, and no odor posts. Yet an experienced human can often detect the presence of house mice
by their peculiar odor. It squeaks when hurt, but
otherwise utters few sounds. On occasion, however, a so-called singing mouse has been reported. Pathological condition, inheritance, and other
causes have been suggested to explain why a
house mouse "sings." Actually we do not know.
The song has been said to resemble that of a
cricket, but is more prolonged. Others say it is
a musical chitter. A review of the subject and
an excellent bibliography up to the time of its
publication is presented by Dice (1932 b: 193):

Singing house mice have been recorded in many
parts of the world, and both males and females have
this rare habit. However, from the published descriptions, it appears that several different sorts of
vocal performances have been described as songs.

The song of a male from Detroit . . . was under
control of the animal and apparently was not caused
by any diseased condition of the vocal apparatus.

The singing habit of this mouse was not inherited,
but a weak "chitter" which appeared in the descendants was inherited, though the character was
so weak that its mode of inheritance could not be

determined. A somewhat similar chitter has been found in some other domestic house mice and in some deer mice (*Peromyscus*).

". . . Perhaps the house mouse and deer mouse have a normal song of very high pitch, which song in rare individuals is lowered sufficiently in pitch to be heard by human ears.

Singing mice have been reported in Wisconsin. Mrs. Charles Ewer, Marshfield, reported to the Wisconsin Conservation Department that she had one or two of them in her cellar and that the singing resembled that of a canary (Anon., 1937 b).

Chicago, Ill. May 15.—Some friend, whose name is unknown, has sent me a clipping from a newspaper published at Beaver Dam, Wis., mentioning the capture of that rare animal, a singing mouse. The item reads in full as follows:

Fox Lake has one of those rare creatures known as a singing mouse. It looks just like any other mouse and acts like them, except that it sings very much like a canary bird. It has a very sweet little chirp and quite a vocabulary of sounds, and when everything is still and quiet, he fills the store with beautiful melody. The mouse is at the Annex store, and was captured in a trap by Sam Tarrant. The boys had heard him for some days around the shelves, but did not know what it was. Finally he was seen sitting on the edge of a box of starch, singing away for dear life. Sam set a trap for him, and succeeded in getting him into it in a day or so. It was a catch-em-alive trap, and the little fellow was not injured. He is now fixed out in a nice cage, and taking life easy with plenty to eat and best of care. In return, when all is quiet and not too many around, the mouse sings away to his heart's content. Sam is very proud of his little warbler. We have heard of singing mice before, but this is the first one we ever saw or heard, and it is quite a curiosity (Hough, 1897).

Unlike its near relative, the Norway rat, the house mouse is easily tamed and makes an acceptable and friendly pet. It often plays, and delights in running a wheel or merry-go-round, as do many of our native mice. It is rather short-lived, normally living less than two years. Its potential longevity is six years.

The female house mouse reaches sexual maturity when about eight weeks old. The number of young in the early litters is lower than the average for adults, which is five or six. Rarely are there as few as three in a litter, and there

may occasionally be as many as ten. Mating takes place and young are born in every month of the year, though there appears to be a slight peak in the breeding during April and May, and again in August and September. The average gestation period is 18 to 19 days. The mammae are ten, four pectoral, two abdominal, four inguinal.

No distinct runways or trails are made by the house mouse, but in fields and meadows it sometimes follows runways made by other species of mice. Its nest is well hidden, behind rafters, in a woodpile or storage bin, in a cupboard drawer, or in a similar hiding place. It is a loose structure of rags, paper, or other soft material with an innner nest of finer shredded paper, rags, grass, or whatever soft material is available. Where nesting sites and material are scarce, house mice have been reported to occupy communal nests (Orr, 1944).

Omnivorous in food habits, the house mouse will eat almost anything, cooked or raw, animal or vegetable. It is not a heavy feeder, and a few crumbs dropped here and there on pantry shelves is enough to attract and support several house mice. It sometimes eats insects, such as roaches and flies, but probably does not catch them. In the Pacific Northwest in 1937, 1938, and 1939, Linduska (1942) found that the house mouse fed on weevils in stored "weevily" seed. This species frequently drinks water, and also relishes milk, either fresh or sour, when it is left available in open dishes. It frequently cleans itself by licking and pawing, but is filthy in food habits in that its feces and dirty tracks cover what it leaves.

The favorite abode of the house mouse— around buildings—tends to limit attacks upon it by predacious animals. Some house cats are good mousers and destroy or frighten away many mice. In fields and open places, weasels and skunks destroy house mice. Hawks and owls occasionally catch them, particularly the red-tailed hawk and the long-eared, screech, barred, and great-horned owls. I have seen near Milton a house mouse impaled on a thorn apple spike by a shrike or butcherbird. The house mouse has many parasites, both external and internal, a summarized account of which has been presented by Dr. Walter E. Heston, National Cancer Institute (in Snell, 1943: 349–79). The house mouse is subject to many diseases—bacterial, parasitical, and virus. These have been listed and described with a bibliography of 341 titles by Dr. John H. Dingle, Harvard Medical School (in Snell, 1943: 380–474).

Mainly because it is a smaller mammal, the house mouse is not such a serious pest as the Norway rat. Also, it is easier to control. As with the rat, however, it has its chief value in its albino variety, which under the name "white mouse" is sold commercially. The white mouse has not only a minor value as a pet for children, but is an ideal subject for biological, genetical, and medical research. It is used extensively in laboratories and research centers. Its value as an insect destroyer is too small to give a credit count. As a pest, it not only consumes and destroys with filth large quantities of food products, but it also does damage by gnawing furniture, storage boxes, and buildings. Probably its annual damage in Wisconsin is well over a million dollars. An intangible damage is its carrying and spreading of human diseases. It has carried murine typhus in Mississippi (Smith, W. W., 1954) and other places. "*Rickettsia akari*, the causative agent of rickettsialpox was recovered from the tissues of a naturally infected mouse (*Mus musculus*) trapped at the site of the outbreak of the disease [in New York City]" (Huebner, Jellison, and Armstrong, 1947: 780). Rickettsialpox is carried by the rodent mite *Allodermanyssus sanguineus* Hirst.

When present in small numbers it is easily eliminated by trapping with ordinary small wooden-base snap traps. The trap should be set at right angles against some object where the mouse runs. Bait is not always necessary. A good bait, however, is peanut butter. Others are cooked bacon, nut meats, rolled oats, cake, or soft candy. Mouse-proofing a building by eliminating all possible entrances is essential for permanent eradication. In a warehouse or other large building, when mice are troublesome it may be necessary to resort to poison or other methods of eradication. In such circumstances it would be well to write for instructions to the U. S. Fish and Wildlife Service, Washington 25, D. C., or to your State Agriculture Extension Office. Details for control or eradication of minor infestations may be found in "Control of house mice," Wildlife Leaflet 349, U. S. Fish and Wildlife Service.

Specimens examined from Wisconsin.—Total 46, as follows: *Brown County:* DePere, 2 (NPM). *Burnett County:* Yellow River (mouth), 1 (MM). *Clark County:* Worden Township, 1. *Dane County:* Madison, 2 (UWZ); western part of Dane County, 2 (UWZ). *Dodge County:* Beaver Dam, 10 (1 CNHM; 9 (UWZ). *Door County:* Fish Creek, 1. *Douglas County:* Saint Croix Dam, 3 (MM). *Milwaukee County:* Milwaukee, 12 (10 MM; 2 UWZ). *Walworth County:* Delavan, 4 (3 CAS; 1 MM); Lake Geneva, 8 (CNHM).

Selected references.—Dice, L. R., 1932; Evans, F. C., 1949; Grüneberg, H., 1943; Laurie, E. M. O., 1946; Snell, G. D., 1943; Strecker, R. L., and J. T. Emlen, 1953.

Family **Zapodidae**
Jumping Mice

Members of the Zapodidae are found in the northern parts of both hemispheres. The family includes three currently recognized genera of living forms, of which *Zapus* and *Napaeozapus* occur in Wisconsin.

Genus **Zapus** Coues
Jumping Mice

Dental formula:

$$I\frac{1-1}{1-1}, \quad C\frac{0-0}{0-0}, \quad P\frac{1-1}{0-0}, \quad M\frac{3-3}{3-3} = 18.$$

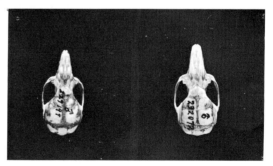

Skulls of Zapodidae. Left, ZAPUS H. INTERMEDIUS, *Rib Hill, Wisconsin.* **Right,** NAPAEOZAPUS I. FRU-TECTANUS, *Danbury, Wisconsin.*

Zapus hudsonius hudsonius (Zimmerman)
Hudsonian Meadow Jumping Mouse

Dipus hudsonius Zimmerman, Geographische Geschichte d. Menschen und vierfüssigen Thiere, vol. 2, p. 358, 1780.
Meriones americanus Lapham, p. 44, 1852; Lapham, p. 339, 1853.
Jaculus Hudsonius Strong, p. 438, 1883.
Zapus hudsonius Snyder, p. 116, 1902; Jackson, p. 24, 1908; Hollister, p. 140, 1909; Hollister, p. 26, 1910; Cory, p. 247, 1912.
Zapus hudsonius hudsonius Schmidt, p. 115, 1931; Komarek, p. 208, 1932; Barger, p. 12, 1952.

Vernacular names.—In Wisconsin usually called jumping mouse or jumping jack. Other names include Canadian jumping mouse, Hudson Bay jumping mouse, Hudsonian jumping mouse, jumper, long-legged mouse, meadow jumping mouse, northern jumping mouse, and *qua-quash-go-dwa-wa-go-no-chi* (Chippewa).

Identification marks.—A small or medium-sized mouse; rather slender body; short ears (about 12 to 14 mm. from notch); an exceedingly long and tapering tail (about 1.4 times length of head and body, or about 60 per cent of total length of mouse); tail scantily haired, showing annulations; hind foot long (about one-third length of head and body); foreleg and foot relatively short; fur slightly coarse, not velvety but soft to touch.

Color of upper parts tawny olive to cinnamon buff, with heavy admixture of black hair forming

Meadow jumping mouse, Zapus hudsonius. *About ½×. Photograph copyright by H. and E. Pittman.*

a dorsal band from face to rump; sides paler than upper parts, less admixture of black hairs, usually producing an appearance of fine but scanty streaking of black; lateral line from chin to thigh ochraceous buff; under parts whitish, usually washed ochraceous buff; ears dark, near seal brown, edged with ochraceous buff; tail rather sharply bicolorous, grayish brown above, whitish below; feet dirty white. Fall and early spring pelage is often duller and more suffused than fresh summer fur.

The sequence of molt for *Zapus* has been ascertained from examination of the study skins. In all species of this genus there seems to be only one annual molt in adults. In the young of the year this molt occurs after August first and before hibernation. All individuals of a single population do not molt at any one time; females continue to molt later in the autumn than do males; some individuals begin to molt as early as mid-June and others show molt as late as the end of October; approximately three weeks are required for an individual to complete its molt (Quimby, 1951: 74); readiness for molt and early stages in molt can be detected (in museum specimens) by greater thickness of the skin. Hairs lost accidentally are quickly replaced, regardless of the condition of the molt.

In *Zapus hudsonius,* new hair appears simultaneously on the anterior dorsal surface of the nose and on the mid-dorsal surface between the scapulae. The molt proceeds anteriorly from the shoulders and posteriorly from the nose. At the same time that the head is covered, new hair appears on the sides of the body from the forelegs to the cheeks. New pelage then appears posteriorly, and molt continues as a wave from these points over the sides and back with the rump receiving new hair last (Krutzsch, 1954: 374).

Skull essentially mouselike; brain case high and rounded; infraorbital foramen large; antorbital foramen oval, large; zygoma broadly expanded anteriorly. Dentition of 18 teeth, a tiny upper premolar making 4 cheek teeth in each upper tooth row; enamel of molars much folded; upper incisors compressed, curved, and deeply grooved.

There is no pronounced secondary sexual variation, and individual variation is possibly less than normal for a rodent. Color mutations are rare, though white spotting has been reported. Three of six specimens collected by Dr. A. W. Schorger between September 23 and October 7,

1950, on an area of about five acres at the western end of Six Mile Creek marsh, town of Springfield, Dane County, had white tailtips. The white portions measured as follows: male, 6 mm.; male, 4 mm.; female, 12 mm. (Schorger, 1951).

Members of the genus *Zapus* can usually be distinguished externally from *Napaeozapus* by the shorter tail (140 mm. or less), never tipped with white except in an abnormal specimen, and the generally more tawny olive coloration of the upper parts. There are four upper molariform teeth in *Zapus*; only three in *Napaeozapus*. A member of the genus *Zapus* is the only Wisconsin mammal having a total of 18 teeth.

"From *Zapus hudsonius intermedius*, *Z. h. hudsonius* differs in: color darker, more tawny dorsally; sides averaging darker, more black-tipped hairs . . . braincase averaging broader; audital bullae broader and less inflated . . . mastoid region averaging broader; incisive foramina averaging shorter" (Krutzsch, 1954: 444).

Measurements.—Total length of adults, 214 to 227 mm. (8.5 to 9.0 inches); tail, 115 to 140 mm. (4.5 to 5.5. inches); hind foot, 29 to 32 mm. (1.1 to 1.2 inches). Weight of adult, 10 to 15 grams in spring to 28 grams in autumn when fat before hibernation, or when females are pregnant. Skull length, 21.5 to 23.3 mm.; width, 10 to 11.1 mm.

Distribution in Wisconsin.—Northern part of the state, north of and including Douglas County, northern Taylor County, and Langlade and Oconto counties.

Habitat.—Meadows, shrubby fields, brushland, and thickets along the edge of woods; usually in a moist grassy situation, and preferably near a stream or lake. At Crescent Lake, Oneida County, said to occur occasionally around barns. In Grant County, seven were taken in hazel brush pasture, five in cornfield, and three in the hemp (S. H. Richards, Wisconsin Wildlife Research, Quart. Prog. Rept., 6 [3]; 86, October, 1947).

Status and Habits.—Seldom does one find this species so abundant as some other kinds of mice. It is local in distribution, however, and at a particularly favorable spot may show its presence in considerable numbers. It is more plentiful in the northern and central parts of the state than in the southern parts. Although not subject to cycles of abundance, it has a varying population in any area from year to year. It may reach a high of

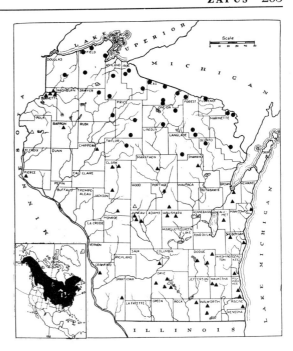

Map 51. *Distribution of* ZAPUS HUDSONIUS. *Solid symbols = specimens examined. Open symbol = authentic record.* ● = Z. H. HUDSONIUS. ▲, △ = Z. H. INTERMEDIUS.

an average of ten per acre in August one year, and the following June drop to an average of less than one per acre on the same area. The peak of abundance does not seem to occur at the same time as peaks in other species. On the George Reserve, in southern Michigan, "It is interesting, and possibly significant, that the peak of jumping-mouse abundance in 1939 followed by one year the 1938 peak of meadow vole abundance in the same ecological association" (Blair, 1948 b: 407). The home range is ordinarily only an acre or two, but sometimes is as extensive as three or four acres.

The jumping mouse cannot often be located by its tracks, trails, or feces, for it leaves few such traces. Only by chance encounter in its haunts may a person really expect to find one. When startled, it bounds away in hops two or three feet long, resembling somewhat a slender frog except for the long tail. Usually it stops after a leap or two to see if it is being pursued, and a keen eye may then locate it. Sometimes one can easily capture it by quickly slipping a hand over it. It is chiefly nocturnal in habits, but not infrequently is out in the daytime, particularly on a cloudy day. It is entirely inactive in cold weather, and hibernates from the first heavy frosts early in the fall until it awakens with the warmer weather late in spring. Late in the summer a thin oily fat is deposited in the mouse until the animal weighs about twice its normal spring weight. This fat supplies nutriment for the long winter sleep, usually carrying the animal through until about the last part of April or the first of May. It usually hibernates in a nest about 2 feet or more underground at a temperature seldom above freezing. It sleeps curled in a ball, feet close together and tail wrapped around the body. It awakens when it is slightly warmed, but falls back into dormancy quickly when the temperature is lowered below freezing. Several accounts of *Zapus* in hibernation have been written (cf. Clough, 1955; Eadie, 1949; Preble, 1899: 8–9; Quimby, 1951: 81–85; Sheldon, 1938 a).

Although called jumping mouse, this species in ordinary progression when not alarmed moves by a series of short hops of two to eight inches. Occasionally it creeps through the grass on all fours, a method of locomotion it must necessarily employ in a burrow. Some reliable writers have stated that it will jump "6 or 8 feet" or "10 to 12 feet." I measured the distance jumped by a startled one at Rib Hill, Marathon County, in

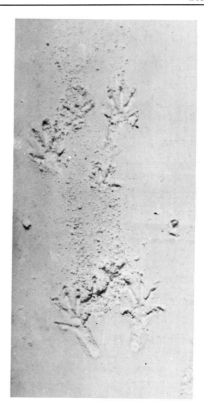

Tracks of meadow jumping mouse, hopping on plaster. About 1×.

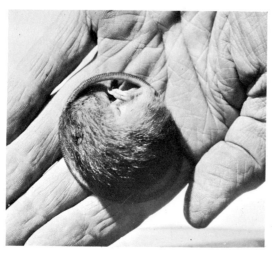

Meadow jumping mouse in hibernation, April 5, 1926.

July, 1918, as 6 feet 8 inches. Quimby (1951: 72) says:

> Many observations do not substantiate the longer jumps. The writer has never seen one jump farther than about 3 feet. On several occasions fully mature mice were released and pursued on level ground to ascertain their jumping ability. Many observations were made under more or less natural conditions. The greatest jumps were made initially when [the animal was] suddenly startled while in a squatting position. The first jump normally covered a distance of 2 to 3 feet and occasionally exceeded 3 feet by a few inches. Subsequent leaps were shorter but more rapid. A jumping mouse in full retreat always progressed by rapid jumps of about one foot.

Its fastest progression is about eight miles an hour. It digs burrows with its forefeet, passing the dirt backward with both fore and hind feet. It is a poor climber, but sometimes ascends a few inches up herbaceous stalks. It is an excellent swimmer for a short distance, and dives well, but becomes exhausted after five or ten minutes in the water.

Like most solitary mammals, the jumping mouse is a silent animal. It sometimes makes a squeaking note when disturbed, and the young ones particularly are apt to squeak when annoyed. It sometimes fights with another jumping mouse, but on the whole is rather amiable. It appears to play by jumping around in an open space. On several occasions I have tramped down the grass over a space six or eight feet in diameter, hidden myself nearby, and watched for a *Zapus* to come out and dance in the clearing. Several times I have been rewarded by seeing one use the space, apparently as a dancing area. I have also learned that setting unbaited snap mousetraps here and there in such an area is an excellent way to capture specimens. Except for its jumping ability, *Zapus* does not appear to be a physically robust animal. Its normal life span in the wild is probably about two years. Its potential longevity is possibly near five years.

One litter a year is probably normal for the jumping mouse in Wisconsin, although it is probable that a female may sometimes have two litters or possibly three. Young of early litters may sometimes breed that year, but usually a female does not mate until the spring after her birth. The gestation period is approximately 18 days. The first litter of the year appears about the last of May or first of June. Young may vary in number from three to eight, but four to six seem to be the more usual numbers. The mammae are eight, four pectoral, two abdominal, two inguinal.

The young were successfully raised in captivity. At birth they are helpless and devoid of hair. The eyes and ears are closed. Hair appears about the 9th day; the incisors erupt about the 13th day and the external auditory meatus opens about the 19th day. By the third week, they are readily recognized as jumping mice. The eyes open between the 22nd and 25th days. Weaning is gradual and begins about the same time the eyes open. The juvenile pelage is replaced by adult pelage during the 4th week (Quimby, 1951: 93).

The winter nest is usually placed deep underground. The summer nest is only a few inches underground, or it may be on the surface of the ground, well concealed by grass or other vege-

tation. Not infrequently it is in the base of a hollow tree or stump, or in a fallen log. It is a globular affair of grass or leaves about five or six inches in diameter, with a small entrance on the side. A Wisconsin nest has been described thusly:

Mr. Karl W. Kahmann of Hayward, Wisconsin found the nest of a jumping mouse in that locality containing 5 young about July 28, 1941. Concerning this nest he wrote " . . . they (the young) were taken from a nest placed at ground level on the inside of a large red oak, which, while living is rotted to a shell of about 4 inches thick and is open for a distance of at least 10 feet high and 18 inches wide, facing north. The tree has a diameter of about 2 feet at stump height.

"The nest was sunken among the rotted wood and debris at the ground and was composed of grasses, plant fibers, and rootlets, and was a globular structure about 6 inches in diameter with an indefinite entrance hole near the top.

"The parent (one of them) was in the nest and left when disturbed."

Mr. Kahmann further stated, "I would say that this nest was rather unusual as to location and have found several while plowing our garden of a similar construction but underground at a depth of about 6 inches from the top of the nest" (Quimby, 1951: 80–81).

Examination of stomachs of the jumping mouse has revealed little except a fine white pulp of well-masticated seeds. In the wild it probably feeds almost exclusively on seeds, grass, grains, and weeds. Quimby (1951) made extensive studies on the food habits of jumping mice in captivity in the laboratory and found that seeds of grasses, the fleshy fruits of various plants, and insects were, in general, heavily utilized. It drinks considerable water, both in the wild and in captivity. It is a cleanly mouse that frequently washes itself by rubbing its front feet over itself from nose to tip of tail, sometimes wetting the front feet before starting the process. It rarely stores food. As an early and intense hibernator it would have little use for such stores.

Its quick jump saves the jumping mouse from some predators. Weasels, foxes, the mink, and the domestic cat have been known to capture adult jumping mice, and the striped skunk digs out a nest of young ones now and then. Among birds, the short-eared owl, barn owl, and the marsh hawk capture it. Snakes, especially rattlesnakes, and even frogs sometimes catch one. Predatory fishes, particularly the northern pike, muskellunge, and black bass, are apt to snap one up quickly when it enters their waters. A few undoubtedly meet death from floods and fires, and others are caught in farming machinery such as plows, mowers, and combines.

As to parasites of the jumping mouse:

All jumping mice handled were examined for external parasites. They quite frequently harbored fleas of two species, *Megabothris quirini* and *Megabothris wagneri* (Identified by Dr. A. L. Burroughs) and occasionally a larval tick, *Dermacentor variabilis*. One snap-trapped specimen had a hole in the throat region from which a bot-fly presumably emerged. Three others had such holes in the inguinal region. Hamilton (1935) reports having found a louse on a *Zapus*, and Sheldon (1938) reports finding a number infested by larva of the bot-fly, *Cuterebra fontinella*. Erickson (1938) examined 18 *Zapus hudsonius* and found 3 to be parasitized. Nematodes of the genera *Subulura* and *Spirocerca*, a dipterous larva *Cuterebra* sp., and a fluke of the genus *Notocotylus* were found (Quimby, 1951: 74–75).

The jumping mouse is rarely sufficiently abundant to be of any importance economically. It sometimes cuts down possibly up to 1 or 2 per cent of the grass in limited areas in a meadow. Its damage to growing grain is negligible.

Specimens examined from Wisconsin.—Total 72, as follows: *Ashland County:* Bear Lake, 4 (UWZ); Mellen (8 mi. S. W.), 1. *Bayfield County:* Basswood Lake (10 mi. S. E. of Iron River), 1; Herbster, 4; Orienta, 1; Washburn (Brink's Camp), 1 (AMNH). *Douglas County:* Solon Springs, 9. *Florence County:* T 40 N, R 16 E, 1 (UWZ). *Forest County:* Crandon, 1; Richardson Lake (T 34 N, R 14 E), 1 (UWZ). *Iron County:* Mercer, 2; Upson (4 mi. N.), 3 (WHD); Upson (5 mi. W.), 1 (WHD). *Langlade County:* Antigo, 2 (UWZ). *Marinette County:* Brown's Spur, 1 (MM); Cataline, 1 (MM); Cravitz, 4 (NPM). *Oconto County:* Lakewood, 1. *Oneida County:* Crescent Lake, 2; Hutchinson Lake (T 38 N, R 10 E), 1 (F&FH). *Price County:* Omega, 2; T 37 N, R 2 W, 4 (2 F&FH). *Sawyer County:* Connors Lake, 1; Ghost River, 1 (UWZ); T 38 N, R 3 W (essentially Connors Lake), 2 (F&FH). *Taylor County:* North Twin Lake, 1 (F&FH). *Vilas County:* Conover, 1 (CNHM); Divide, 1 (MM); Lake St. Germain, 9; Mamie Lake, 3; Robinson Lake, 3 (UWZ); T 42 N, R 8 E, 2 (F&FH).

Selected references.—Hamilton, W. J., Jr., 1935; Krutzsch, P. H., 1954; Lyon, M. W., Jr., 1936: 276–81; Preble, E. A., 1899; Quimby, D. C., 1951; Sheldon, C., 1938 a.

Zapus hudsonius intermedius Krutzsch
Intermediate Meadow Jumping Mouse

Zapus hudsonius intermedius Krutzsch, Univ. Kansas, Mus. Nat. Hist. Publs., vol. 7, no. 4, p. 447, April 21, 1954.

Vernacular names.—Most of the common and general names of the Hudson Bay jumping mouse.

Identification marks.—Differs from *Napaeozapus* and *Zapus hudsonius hudsonius* in characters indicated under *Zapus h. hudsonius*.

Measurements.—Total length of adults, 213 to 233 mm. (8.5 to 9.2 inches); tail, 115 to 134 mm. (4.5 to 5.3 inches); hind foot, 29 to 32 mm. (1.1 to 1.2 inches). Weight about as in *Z.h. hudsonius*. Skull length, 21.9 to 23.7; width, 10.3 to 11.2 mm.

Distribution in Wisconsin.—That part of the state south of and including Burnett, Marathon, Shawano, and southern Oconto counties.

Habitat, Status, and Habits.—So far as known essentially like those of *Zapus hudsonius hudsonius.*

Specimens examined from Wisconsin.—Total 117, as follows: *Barron County:* Big Sand Lake (T 36 N, R 12 W), 1. *Brown County:* Green Bay, 2 (NPM); Preble, 1 (NPM). *Burnett County:* Danbury, 1; Namakagon River (mouth of), 2 (MM); Saint Croix River (above mouth of Namakagon River), 1 (MM); Yellow River (mouth of), 8 (MM). *Calumet County:* Chilton, 1 (UWZ). *Chippewa County:* Holcombe, 3. *Clark County:* Hewett Township, 3 (UWZ); Withee, 4; Worden Township, 4 (2 UWZ). *Crawford County:* Lynxville, 1. *Dane County:* Madison, 5 (UWZ); Springfield Township, 6 (AWS); Vermont, 4 (UWZ); West Port Township, 1 (UWZ). *Dodge County:* Beaver Dam, 22 (5 CNHM; 17 UWZ); Horicon Refuge, 2; Theresa, 1 (MM). *Grant County:* T 5 N, R 1 W, 1 (UWZ). *Jackson County:* Millston, 2 (UWZ). *Juneau County:* Beaver Creek, 3 (F&FH); Mather, 1; Necedah, 1 (F&FH). *Manitowoc County:* Point Beach State Forest, 3 (UWZ). *Marathon County:* Rib Hill, 8. *Milwaukee County:* Milwaukee, 1 (MM); Oak Creek, 1 (MM). *Ozaukee County:* Mequon, 1 (MM). *Pierce County:* Prescott, 1 (MM). *Portage County:* Almond, 1 (UWZ); Stevens Point, 3. *Racine County:* Racine, 1 (USNM). *Rock County:* Milton, 2 (1 MM). *Sauk County:* Devils Lake, 1. *Shawano County:* Keshena, 2 (CAS). *Sheboygan County:* Elkhart Lake (Sheboygan Swamp), 1; Terry Andrae State Park, 2 (UWZ). *Walworth County:* Delavan, 2 (1 CAS); Turtle Lake, 1. *Waukesha County:* Dousman, 1; Waterville, 2 (MM). *Waushara County:* Plainfield, 1 (F&FH); T 20 N, R 8 E, 1 (F&FH).

Selected references.—Same as for *Zapus h. hudsonius.*

Genus **Napaeozapus** Preble
Woodland Jumping Mice

Dental formula:

$$I\frac{1-1}{1-1}, \quad C\frac{0-0}{0-0}, \quad P\frac{0-0}{0-0}, \quad M\frac{3-3}{3-3}=16.$$

Napaeozapus insignis frutectanus Jackson
Wisconsin Woodland Jumping Mouse

Napaeozapus insignis frutectanus Jackson, Proc. Biol. Soc. Washington, vol. 32, p. 9, February 14, 1919.
Napaeozapus insignis frutectanus Schmidt, p. 116, 1931; Barger, p. 12, 1952.

Vernacular names.—When distinguished from *Zapus hudsonius* usually called woodland jumping mouse. More frequently confused with *Z. hudsonius* and given the same vernacular names. Sometimes called Jackson jumping mouse (Soper, Journ. Mammal., 27: 149, August 1946).

Identification marks.—Most colorful of the Wisconsin mice, its general pattern being similar to that of the meadow jumping mouse. Broad dorsal stripe extending from snout to base of tail clay color much mixed with blackish, decidedly darker than sides and remainder of upper parts which are clay color scantily mixed with coarse blackish hairs; ventral parts from chin to base of tail creamy white; ears essentially like dorsal stripe, narrowly edged with between pinkish buff and pale pinkish buff; tail distinctly bicolorous nearly to tip, between olive-brown and chaetura drab above, whitish below, the terminal 20 mm. whitish both above and below.

The woodland jumping mouse (*Napaeozapus*) can be distinguished from the meadow jumping mouse (*Zapus*) by the paler but brighter clay color of the flanks, which sets out in sharper contrast; also by the dorsal stripe; in *Napaeozapus* the terminal 18 to 22 mm. of the tail are white both above and below, and the tail averages longer. The skull of *Napaeozapus* averages a trifle longer and narrower than that of *Zapus*, but can always be distinguished by its three (not four) upper molariform teeth, or a total of 16 rather than 18 teeth.

Measurements.—Total length of adults, 225 to 252 mm. (9.0 to 10.0 inches); tail, 142 to 154 mm. (5.5 to 6.0 inches); hind foot, 31 to 33 mm. (1.2 to 1.3 inches). Weight of adult, 16 to 26 grams in spring to 32 grams in autumn when fat before hibernation, or in pregnant females. Skull length, 21.6 to 23.8 mm.; width, 11.8 to 12.9 mm.

Distribution in Wisconsin.—Northern part of the state north of northern Burnett, northern Clark, and central Oconto counties. Not known from Door Peninsula.

Woodland jumping mouse, NAPAEOZAPUS INSIGNIS.

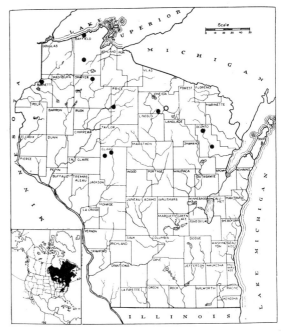

Map 52. Distribution of NAPAEOZAPUS INSIGNIS. ● = *specimens examined.* ○ = *authentic record.*

Habitat.—Along creeks or in small, low damp openings, usually in grassy brushland or second growth predominantly alder or paper birch, or sometimes in mixed timber of arbor vitae, maple, aspen, or paper birch. The type-specimen was trapped in a grassy paper-birch thicket near the bank of Crescent Creek, Oneida County. The woodland jumping mouse, so far as known, is never found in open meadows, fields, or marshes far from brushland or woods, as is the meadow jumping mouse.

Status and Habits.—Cory suspected that *Napaeozapus* occurred in Wisconsin when he wrote, "the Woodland Jumping Mouse may be looked for in northern Wisconsin, for although it has not as yet been found within our limits, it has been taken in northwestern Michigan" (Cory, 1912: 253). I trapped an adult male among small paper birches about 35 feet from a grassy ditch, August 7, 1917, at Kelley Lake, Oconto County. This was the first specimen record (no. 226,994, U. S. Nat. Mus., Biol. Surv. Coll.) for Wisconsin. I collected another near the same spot August 9, 1917. The next week three were caught in low mixed forest along McCaslin Brook, near Lakewood, Oconto County. The type-specimen of *frutectanus* was trapped September 6, 1917, at Crescent Lake, Oneida County. It would appear that the species is not common in Wisconsin, because even with some knowledge of its habits and special effort to procure specimens, less than a score are known to have been collected. A concentrated population may some time be encountered in Wisconsin, as happened in Alger County, Michigan, where 52 were trapped from August 25 to September 22, 1940 (Blair, 1941 a: 683). The population in a limited area seldom reaches more than an average of one per acre. The home range has been variously estimated as from one to nine acres. A home range of one and one-half acres, as accepted by Manville (1949: 69), is probably within reason.

Methods of detecting the woodland jumping mouse are much the same as with the meadow jumping mouse. Once the mouse is located it often may be easily captured by quietly placing one's hand over it. It is chiefly nocturnal, and hibernates deeply, as does *Zapus*. As far as known its methods of locomotion and its speed are about the same as those of the meadow jumping mouse. One might imply, however, from its longer hind feet and tail, that it can leap farther.

Carolyn Sheldon (1934: 291) thought *Napaeo-*

zapus displayed a colonial type of distribution at Lake Kedgemekooge, Nova Scotia. I have found it a rather solitary mammal in Wisconsin. Preble (1956: 198) failed to find evidence of colonialism in his studies in the Presidential Range, New Hampshire. Although solitary in habits, it is not pugnacious among its kind or with humans. It can be kept in captivity, and becomes tame quickly. Of its senses, hearing seems to be particularly well developed. The normal life span in nature is about two years. The potential life span is about five years.

The woodland jumping mouse normally raises only one litter of young a year. Rarely, a second breeding may occur, but we have no proved record of such. Young of the year do not breed until the following spring. The gestation period is between 20 and 23 days. Young are two to six in number, possibly sometimes up to eight. The more frequent number appears to be five. The mammae are eight, four pectoral, two abdominal, two inguinal.

The nest is usually placed underground, usually without sign of trail or runway to the entrance of the burrow, which is often closed by the animal when it is in the burrow. An unusual location of a nest of *N. i. insignis* made of leaves and dry grasses placed low in a brush pile at Tarn, Maine, was described by Stupka (1934). Of *Napaeozapus i. abietorum* at Lake Nipigon, Ontario, L. L. Snyder (1924) writes:

About midnight on the night of June 16–17 (1923) my wife called my attention to a thumping against the canvas of our tent wall. . . . Securing a flashlight I stepped out the front of the tent into a screened-in portion . . . A small object could be distinctly seen jumping rapidly up and down, against

Woodland jumping mouse, NAPAEOZAPUS INSIGNIS, *in hibernation, November 15, 1925.*

the canvas and away from it. Not until it leaped away beyond my vision did I realize it was a jumping mouse. In a moment it could be heard returning, this time with short quick jumps. It came . . . to within three feet of where I was lying prone. In an instant it had disappeared into a small hole near the first tent stake. Hastily securing another flashlight . . . I returned to my post and for more than an hour watched the mouse make trips to and from the hole. It was carrying into the hole some material which it had secured back of the tent. As nearly as could be ascertained the material was carried in the mouth and seemed to be supported by the front feet. While the animal was laden its jumps were short and slightly labored, being not more than two feet in length, but after it emerged from the hole one leap usually carried it to the end of the tent, which was seven feet long.

. . . Mr. J. R. Dymond and myself started excavation [on July 3]. By probing the ground near the tent stake we discovered a spot which seemed soft although the surface appearance was not different from that of the rest of the area. This spot proved to be the entrance to the tunnel. The tunnel was found to have a very gradual descent and to follow a semicircular course. At a point fourteen inches from the opening the dry leaves of a nest were seen. Uncovering the nest, we proceeded cautiously in the hope of catching the adult mouse, but with one leap it cleared the nest and before we could give chase had reached the shelter of the shrubs forty feet to the west at the foot of the knoll. The course taken by the fleeing mouse was direct and unwavering and we estimated that it cleared from ten to twelve feet at a jump.

. . . we found [the nest] to be composed of the soft dry leaves of wild sarsaparilla and aspen poplar, entirely filling a rounded chamber in the tunnel which measured six inches long, five inches wide and four and one half inches high. Removing the top of the nest we discovered five sluggish young jumping mice, naked and blind. They appeared to be about one week old.

. . . the tunnel extended past the nesting chamber for nineteen inches where it turned to the left and then downwards, ending blindly. Throughout this extent the tunnel ran about parallel with the surface of the ground, being about five and one half inches below the surface.

Under *Napaeozapus insignis insignis,* Hamilton (1941 b: 260–61) writes:

The food habits have been casually studied by several investigators. Saunders (1921) notes its fondness for alder cones. Sheldon (1938) records various insects and berries eaten by captive specimens. A number of stomach analyses of *Napaeozapus,* reported in an earlier paper (Hamilton, 1935) showed that insect larvae, enchytrid worms, various beetles, and adult flies were eaten. In addition the seeds of mitrewort (*Mitella diphylla*) and the green fruit of May apple (*Podophyllum peltatum*) were eaten.

Forty additional stomachs have been examined since my last report. The results suggest that insect larvae, particularly lepidopterous and dipterous forms, are taken in considerable quantities. In addition, spiders, small soil worms, centipedes and various small invertebrates are consumed. Blueberries, raspberries, quantities of small seeds and tiny nuts, and small green leaves are eaten. Fragments of *Asplenium* fronds have been recognized in stomachs of these mice.

Weasels are probably the most important mammalian enemy of the woodland jumping mouse. Foxes and skunks sometimes capture one, and a domestic cat catches one occasionally. A few fall victim to birds of prey such as the red-tailed hawk and the great horned owl. Rarely is one killed by an automobile. It has its internal and external parasites as do all mice, but they are not well known. The red mite or chigger *Trombicula harperi* is often found on it. Botfly larvae are not infrequent. The nematode *Citellinoides zapodis* occurs internally.

Economically, the woodland jumping mouse is a harmless mammal, beautiful and graceful, interesting to behold by those who may be favored with the opportunity. It is too scarce to do appreciable damage to crops or forests. Its insect-eating habit may do some good.

Specimens examined from Wisconsin.—Total 14, as follows: *Bayfield County:* Basswood Lake (10 mi. S. E. of Iron River), 1; Herbster, 1. *Burnett County:* Danbury, 1. *Clark County:* Withee, 1; Worden Township, 1 (AMNH). *Oconto County:* Kelley Lake, 2; Lakewood, 3. *Oneida County:* Crescent Lake, 1 (type-specimen). *Price County:* T 37 N, R 2 W, sec. 9, 2 (F&FH). *Sawyer County:* Teal Lake, 1 (AWS).

Selected references.—Jackson, H. H. T., 1919 a; Preble, E. A., 1899; Preble, N. A., 1956; Sheldon, C., 1934; 1938 b; Snyder, L. L., 1924.

Family **Erethizontidae**
American Porcupines

The family Erethizontidae is confined to the Western Hemisphere. It contains four genera exclusive of fossil forms. Three genera are confined to Central and South America, and the other, *Erethizon*, is confined to North America.

Genus **Erethizon** F. Cuvier
American Porcupines

Dental formula:

$$I\frac{1-1}{1-1}, \quad C\frac{0-0}{0-0}, \quad P\frac{1-1}{1-1}, \quad M\frac{3-3}{3-3} = 20.$$

Erethizon dorsatum dorsatum (Linnaeus)
Canada Porcupine

[*Hystrix*] *dorsata* Linnaeus, Systema naturae, ed. 10, vol. 1, p. 57, 1758.
Hystrix Hudsonius Lapham, p. 44, 1852; Lapham, p. 340, 1853.
Hystrix dorsata Strong, p. 440, 1883.
Erethizon dorsatum Snyder, p. 126, 1902; Jackson, p. 24, 1908; Hollister, p. 26, 1910; Cory, p. 254, 1912; Komarek, p. 209, 1932.
Erethizon dorsatum dorsatum Schmidt, p. 116, 1931; Barger, p. 12, 1952.

Canada porcupine. U. S. Fish and Wildlife Service photograph by Leo K. Couch.

Vernacular names.—In Wisconsin usually called porcupine or porky. Other vernacular names include black-haired porcupine, hedgehog, *ogog* (Chippewa), *okak* (Potawatomi), porcupette (young porcupine), porkepick (seventeenth century explorers, from the French *porc-épic*), porky hog, prickle cub, prickle pig, quill pig, quills, sliver cat, and urson.

Identification marks.—A large, thickset rodent (total length about 30 to 40 inches), with small head, moderately small ears, and blunt, hairy nose; tail short and thick, heavily armed with quills above and stiff bristles below; feet heavy, with naked soles; four toes on forefeet, five on hind feet, all with strong curved claws. Pelage distinctive and of three kinds of hair: long, soft, woolly hair, long coarse hair, and highly specialized spines or quills. The quills are slender and sharply pointed, and provided with several fine barbs at the free end; the other end, loosely attached to the skin, is also narrow; the main shaft of the quill is thick, stiff, and hollow. The under parts of the animal are without quills.

Summer fur of upper parts is dark chocolate or seal brown, glossy, and sometimes nearly black; tips of some long hairs, particularly on shoulders, whitish; quills are whitish or yellow-

ish white with dark tips; quills exposed chiefly on tail, rump, and head. The under parts are deep chocolate or seal brown. Winter pelage is darker and duller than summer fur, the hair being longer, particularly on the shoulders, and only the longer quills showing on head, rump, and tail.

Skull heavy; somewhat swollen interorbitally; rostrum short and broad, the nasal bone also short and broad; no postorbital processes; upper incisors and anterior portions of premaxillaries projecting well beyond tip of nasals anteriorly; supraoccipital relatively narrow dorsoventrally; foramen magnum relatively deep, audital bullae large, rotund; infraorbital foramen larger than foramen magnum; palate narrow and short, extending posteriorly to anterior border of last molar. Dentition of 20 teeth, four molariform teeth in upper jaw; molar enamel pattern intricately folded; incisors heavy, projecting anteriorly, deep orange or almost ochraceous in color.

Males and females are about the same size and color. Young animals have weaker quills than adults and are somewhat darker in color. Winter fur tends to grow longer, and often nearly obscures the quills. Color mutations occasionally produce albinos. An albino female collected near Mamie Lake, Vilas County, October 25, 1926, is in the Milwaukee Museum. Another

from Wisconsin was kept alive at the State Fur Farm, Poynette, a photograph of which has been published (Ferguson, 1939: 31). Other albinos have been reported from the state.

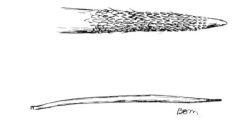

Porcupine quills. Above, point of quill about 10×. Below, small quill about natural size.

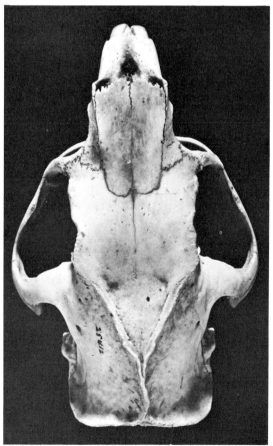

Skull of ERETHIZON DORSATUM, *Hinckley, Minnesota.*

Canada porcupine, in long winter pelage with hairs raised to expose quills on the back. Copyright by H. H. Pittman.

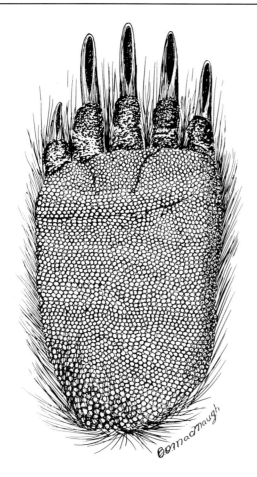

Left hind foot of porcupine, under side. 1×. *Mamie Lake, Wisconsin.*

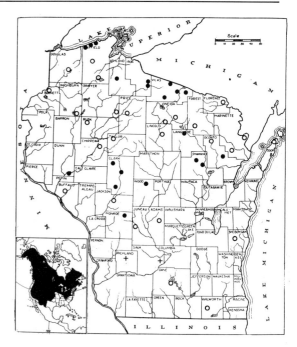

Map 53. Distribution of ERETHIZON DORSATUM. ● = *specimens examined.* O = *authentic records since 1870.* + = *authentic records before 1870.*

The porcupine is so easily identified by its size and peculiar quill pelage that comparison with any other mammal is hardly necessary. The skull is exceeded in size among Wisconsin rodents only by that of the beaver. It averages only slightly larger than that of the woodchuck, and superficially somewhat resembles it in upper view. The skull of the porcupine, however, has many characteristics that separate it from the woodchuck's skull, such as its lack of postorbital processes, its short and broad rostrum with protruding incisors, its huge infraorbital foramen, and the presence of only 20 teeth instead of 22 (in *Marmota*).

Measurements.—Total length of adults, 740 to 1,030 mm. (29 to 40 inches); tail, 148 to 184 mm. (5.8 to 7.2 inches); hind foot, 76 to 90 mm.

(3.0 to 3.5 inches). Weight of adult, 12 to 25 pounds, the average about 18 pounds; records as heavy as 43 pounds. Skull length, 92 to 111 mm.; width, 62 to 79 mm.

Distribution in Wisconsin.—Probably once occupied all the timbered areas of the state. Now found regularly only northerly from Burnett, Rusk, Clark, and Shawano counties, and northern Door County. Erratic and casually rare in southern half of state.

Habitat.—Forests of almost any kind, but preferably with some coniferous growth.

Status and Habits.—The porcupine was one of the conspicuous mammals which soon drew the attention of the early settlers of the northern states. Josselyn (1672: 17–18) mentions it in his *New Englands Rarities Discovered:*

The *Porcupine* in some parts of the Country Eastward, towards the *French,* are as big as an ordinary Mongrel Cur; a very angry Creature and dangerous, shooting a whole shower of Quills with a rouse at their enemies, which are of that nature, that wherever they stick in the flesh, they will work through in a short time if not prevented by pulling of them

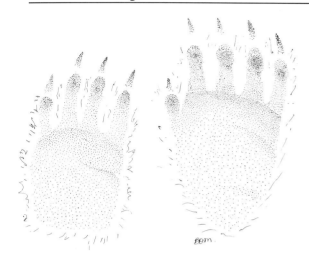

Tracks of porcupine. Left, right fore foot. Right, right hind foot. ½×.

out. The *Indians* make use of the Quills, which are hardly a handful long, to adorn the edges of their birchen dishes, and weave (dying some of them red, others yellow and blew) curious bags or pouches, in works like *Turkie-work*.

Of course, Josselyn was inaccurate about the quills being shot and about the "angry Creature," but he was correct about the Indians utilizing the animal. In Wisconsin as early as 1662 the quills were used for decoration. "The speech being finished, they interested us to be at the feast. We goe presently back againe to furnish us with wooden bowls. . . . We had a role of porkepick about our heads, which was as a crowne" (Anon., 1888: 88). Numerous accounts indicate that not only were the quills used for ornaments and pins by the Indians and the early explorers and settlers in Wisconsin, but also that the flesh was an important meat, rating along with duck and venison (Green Bay, 1822; Ellis, 1876: 220). I have found the flesh of a young porcupine delicious, although a camp hand told me it tasted like a Christmas tree.

The porcupine was probably never as common in the extreme southern part of the state as in the northern two-thirds. Today it is often locally common in many of the most northern counties. It practically reached extirpation in areas south of 44° north latitude by 1870. The few recent records are probably of stragglers, or possibly of animals imported by man. In She-

boygan Swamp, on September 24, 1917, the author saw tracks, feces, and gnawings of porcupines, in an area where the animal was probably native. "A specimen of a half-grown porcupine was brought in Friday evening from the Hollister Woods. . . . The animal is not common in this section and has doubtless wandered in from the north" (*Delavan Enterprise*, September 5, 1918, p. 5). The Hollister Woods were also known as the "Big Woods," and were 5 miles west of Delavan, Walworth County. Ned Hollister sent me a note with the clipping: "Although this is a new record for Walworth County I see no reason to question it, as the animal could hardly be misidentified. It probably came in by way of the Whitewater bluff country. . . . I should guess they are recent *immigrants* rather *survivors* in the Delavan Woods, at this time" (Hollister to author, October 3, 1918).

Ordinarily if a porcupine is in an area for long it is easily found. The heavy tracks with long claw marks in the snow or soil are distinctive. Badger tracks are somewhat similar, but the badger is not likely to be in the same habitat. Fresh gnawings on trees, old buildings, or almost anything wooden are good indicators of a porcupine nearby. Feces, though sometimes resembling those of a deer, are quite characteristic.

Dung of porcupine at "porcupine house," Herbster, Wisconsin, August 15, 1922. U. S. silver half-dollar (1.2 inches in diameter) used for comparison to show size of feces. U. S. Fish and Wildlife Service photograph by the author.

Feces are often deposited in a huge pile, or may be scattered promiscuously under a tree. The porcupine is an amiable and unsuspicious mammal that can easily be observed and studied. Often, especially during the winter, it may be found well up in a tree, either resting or gnawing the bark. At other times it meanders on the ground, particularly during the summer months. Or it may be resting on a log at the edge of a lake, or on the branch of a small tree along a bank.

It is often as active by day as by night, though primarily it is nocturnal. It usually weathers out the winter in the high branches of a tree. Sometimes, however, if a rocky ledge or an old abandoned frame building is available, several may assemble in it, moving out to feed when hunger prompts them. The porcupine travels in a slow swaggering walk, and seldom attempts to run. Its fastest gait is about two miles an hour. The more snow, the less tendency it has to travel, and it moves about very little when the weather is below zero degrees Fahrenheit. It climbs well, but deliberately, arm over arm. My observations are that it clumsily descends a tree backward, arm over arm also. It will voluntarily enter water to swim a creek or small river. It does not swim well, nor does it appear to enjoy swimming. With body nearly all submerged, the rump spines held high, it paddles dog-fashion at a rate of about two miles an hour.

Such diverse sounds are made by the porcupine that it is difficult to classify them. Probably they are just involuntary self expressions on the part of the individual, rather than communications to fellow beings. Anger and fear are often indicated by a chattering of the teeth, sometimes associated with a slight low hiss. Slight discomfort may cause the animal to grunt slightly, or continue a gruntlike crying whimper in low pitch. If the discomfort is increased to pain, the animal may issue a raucous grunt, almost a low-pitched shreak. When searching for food or locating danger, a porcupine sniffs the air vigorously, often producing a noise that may be heard 10 to 15 feet away. The mating sound, sometimes called a song, is a rather low-pitched meowing which at times may be heard many yards away. I encountered a young one about two-thirds or more grown near Nemakagon Lake, Bayfield County, the evening of May 30, 1919.

It was gnawing the staves of an old salt pork barrel lying along the road. I tested the animal somewhat for sound and found that its hearing, though fair, was not of the best. A high-pitched note, or squeak, it would practically ignore. A lower-pitched note, a low voice no louder than the squeak, would slightly attract its attention. Jarring the earth with my foot, even lightly, caused the animal to look and bristle its quills. A gnawing sound such as it was making itself did not worry it in the least. It appeared that this animal was more sensitive to vibration than sound. Sight also appears to be poorly developed. On the other hand the porcupine is extremely sensitive to touch and smell. Its reaction to touch, either directly or through vibrations, is exemplified by the manner in which it quickly erects its quills and flops its tail around in defense when thus disturbed. True, it will sometimes attempt to back into an adversary and smack it with its tail, but usually its attack is first provoked by contact. Only too well do I remember a teamster racing a team of horses downhill on our way to Eau Claire Lakes, Bayfield County, in 1909. Near the bottom of the hill, the horses ran into a porcupine, and for nearly two hours three of us pulled quills from the front legs of the irritated horses. Once a quill has entered the flesh it travels through the tissue at a rate which in one case was timed at 1.05 mm. an hour (Shadle and Po-Chedley, 1949). A quill puncture causes little pain if the quill is promptly removed. Grasp the quill with pliers and pull it out, but do not break it and leave part in the flesh. That may cause intense irritation. As a precaution, treat the puncture with an antiseptic.

The literature contains little on the play reactions of the porcupine. Two main types, solitary play and collective play, were observed. *Solitary play* may be, (1) defensive reaction type, (2) exercise dance type, (3) climbing and gnawing type where sound and resonance seem to be of some satisfaction. *Collective play* might be (1) offensive charging, seizing, wrestling, holding, biting, (2) defensive biting, striking, wrestling, etc., (3) chasing something as a pup or kitten would. The typical play reaction of youth may be in evidence from birth until animals are well over a year old. The *exercise dance* common to mature, caged porcupines may be carried out through the remainder of life in confinement. *Individual variation of expression* in behavior pattern as well as in voice is marked" (Shadle, 1944: 149).

Breeding habits of the porcupine have been studied in detail by Dr. Albert R. Shadle and his associates at the University of Buffalo, and the results covered in various papers (cf. Shadle, 1944, 1946, 1948, 1950 a, 1951, 1952; Shadle and Ploss, 1943; Shadle, Smelzer, and Metz, 1946; Mirand and Shadle, 1953). An earlier study was made by Struthers (1928). The following notes on breeding habits are from Shadle (1950 a):

The courting reactions of the porcupines are very unusual and extremely interesting. The males are very aggressive and go about their curious courting antics with great seriousness and vigor. They vocalize or, as I call it, "sing" a great deal in their wooing. It is quite humorous to see one of these ardent males following a female about as he sings to her in a high falsetto voice. Rubbing noses and touching each other's face and head with the forepaws, a kind of fondling gesture, are also part of his amorous courtship period.

I have watched courting pairs in the woods. The female usually sits well up in a tree watching the male as he sits patiently waiting several feet lower down on the bole of the same tree or out on a limb. If the female is in an amorous mood, she quietly watches the male as he hesitantly inches toward her from time to time. If she resents his attention, she may be very short-tempered and squall so loudly and viciously as he moves towards her that she can be heard a half-mile away.

The breeding of porcupines in our laboratory has occurred as early as September, with the peak of the breeding season in October and November, but it has also occurred as late as December and January. The secret of having them breed readily in captivity is not yet solved, but we are working toward a solution.

Usually within four to six hours after breeding, the female tends to lose interest in the male and may even become antagonistic to him. After a time, each animal may tend to go its own way.

Only recently has the gestation period been definitely determined. The only three exact gestation figures known, 209, 217, 205 days, indicate the gestation period to be approximately seven months (average 210 days which is considerably longer than the supposed sixteen weeks). These three periods were obtained for young porcupines bred and born since 1944 in our Vivarium. In spite of the statements in literature that there are one to four young per birth, a single young is born at a time. If twins do occur, they are very rare: in several thousand pregnancies reported, there was not a single case of twins.

In Mammalogy, we often have a certain name which definitely refers to a particular animal of a very early age. The term kitten, pup, whelp, lamb, etc. immediately orients one's thoughts to the very young of the animal under consideration. To speak of the new born porcupine as a "baby porcupine" or a "young porcupine" is awkward, indefinite, and unsatisfactory. I am therefore proposing and using here the term "porcupette" to mean a "small porcupine still in the nursing stage." The term would cover the early life of the individual until it is approximately four months old, as judged by laboratory observations on nursing porcupines.

From data collected at the University of Buffalo Vivarium, the porcupette shows the following points at birth: Birth weight usually varies from 12 to 20 oz. The hair coat is generally long, thick, and black or gray—being longer and thicker in more northern forms. The spines are ¼ to 1 inch or longer and cover most of the dorsal portion of the head, body and tail, and they are perfectly functional as soon after birth as they dry out and sometimes even while still wet. The eyes are open and are thoroughly functional in locating moving objects, the animal responding to the movement of other animals or things in its range of vision. The erection of quills as a defense appears perfectly executed. The reaction of turning its head away from and its tail toward a moving object is displayed within minutes to hours after birth. The defense tail stroke which drives tail quills into an adversary is well performed from the first hours. The crowding reaction by which the porcupine withdraws his feet and rolls to one side, thus pushing side quills into an adversary, is well timed and very well done. The reaction to protect the head by sticking it into a corner, or under something, is well developed and functional within minutes to hours after birth.

The reaction to the call of the mother or the chatter of her teeth is very positive in the porcupette and it appears to orient itself quite readily and accurately to the noises made by the mother. The legs and feet are quite functional almost immediately after birth, and although the gait is rather wobbly and uncertain the first day or two, it is remarkable how well the little animal can move about and follow its mother. In a day or two, it may even begin to climb like the adults. The porcupette is inclined to go into a dark area to sleep.

The porcupette tries to click its teeth together the first day, but due to the small size of the teeth, the lack of strength in the jaw muscles, and probably some protection of the tooth surfaces by surrounding tissues, at first you may hear little or no sound, although the rapid movement of the jaws is perfectly performed and is readily seen. By holding the porcupette up to one's ears, as it performs this reaction, one can sometimes hear the faint clicking of the little teeth during the first day or two. It rapidly grows stronger and in three to five days, the young animal will click its teeth in response to the mother's clicking or that of someone imitating her. At this time the sound can be heard a few feet away.

The porcupette does not immediately eat leaves, bark, etc., and many days pass before he begins to take an appreciable amount of such solid material. Meanwhile, he continues to nurse frequently, with only small amounts of milk taken at a time. Bottle-fed young at first may take only 3 to 5 cc. of milk, but soon take as much as 10, 20 or more at a time. Still later they feed readily on bread and milk. The statements that they are almost on their own from birth and are weaned by the mother in ten days are not true. Lactation and nursing continue for many weeks and we have had cases lasting as much as four months and longer.

The mother usually shows little or no concern or definite affection for her offspring. She may or may not follow it about as it walks away from her. She does not seem to draw or hold her porcupette to her as it nurses; only once have I seen a mother draw the nursing young to her with the front paws. She generally squats on her haunches and tail, bending forward until a crease in her belly brings the two nipples of each side within an inch or so of each other. In this position with her forelegs hanging limply at her sides, she passively permits the porcupette to nose about her belly until it locates the nipples. The latter, having found nourishment, tugs briefly at one nipple, shifting every few seconds to another, moves back to the first one, or on to the fourth, and the third nipples, etc. In this hit and miss way, it eventually obtains all the nourishment it wants or, having exhausted the milk supply, it wanders off to play or to sleep. In the case of some porcupettes this erratic procedure gives way to a fairly definite nursing pattern in which they seize the nipples in a rather well established sequence which is repeated over and over with only an occasional variation. This nursing pattern is often accompanied by a markedly rhythmic series of actions, and it frequently is also accompanied by considerable noise, such as sucking sounds, smacking of the lips, and soft cooing sounds and grunts somewhat similar to the nursing human infant.

The mammae are four, two pectoral, two abdominal.

No elaborate trails or runways are made by the porcupine, though it often follows roads, lanes, trails, and paths made by other mammals. In the autumn it wears trails through the woodland to and from its feeding ground. It seldom goes in a straight line, but usually wanders from side to side in an undetermined manner. It gathers no nesting material. It often accepts as a den a shelter under the roots of an upturned tree, under a leaning stump or a windfall, or in a hollow log. Permanent dens, occupied by one to several individuals, are made in rock ledges in some localities, but I have never found such a den in Wisconsin. In this state, however, one to several porcupines may occupy as a denning site an old tumbled-down frame or log building, and retain it as a more or less permanent residence from which to meander for food. Usually, however, the porcupine here spends most of its time, especially during winter, in a tree, either solitary or in a group of as many as five or six in a large tree. Here it eats and rests, clinging to, sitting upon, or lying draped over, a branch. If it has a den, it may occupy it only intermittently or abandon it entirely.

Food of the porcupine is seasonal. At all seasons it feeds upon the inner bark, branches, and leaves of trees. During winter, bark and branches of trees, and especially wood that has had contact with salt, is its chief food. Many kinds of trees are victims of its attack—for example, the conifers, balsam fir, hemlock, black spruce, white spruce, arbor vitae, white pine, red pine, jack pine, and tamarack. Among deciduous trees supplying the porcupine with food are the willow, beech, hard maple, soft maple, mountain maple, striped maple, quaking aspen, big-leaved aspen, yellow birch, sweet birch, and paper birch. In summer it may feed some on bark and leaves of trees, but it also forages on the ground, particularly along shores and water banks, and eats quantities of wild plant roots, leaves, and stems, hazelnuts, beechnuts, and other nuts, and fruits. It may also stray into a graden or field and consume corn and other crops. It is especially fond of pond lilies. On June 18, 1918, I saw one feeding on pond lily pads (*Nymphaea advena*) along Spring Creek, Vilas County, and the same day saw another, well out in a sphagnum bog near Spring Lake, feeding upon *Nymphaea* pads in a swampy bay. At all seasons it is especially fond of salt, and any object that has salt or a salty solution such as perspiration on it is apt to be gnawed and eaten. Bone is also regularly gnawed by the porcupine.

The porcupine has few natural enemies.

Among mammals known to have attacked it are the bobcat and domestic dog. It can well be conceived that one attack for an individual animal might give sufficient learning. A dog soon learns to treat a porcupine with respect. Porcupine hair and bone fragments have been found in a pellet of the great horned owl in Maine (Curtis and Kozicky, 1944: 143). Forest and brush fires kill more porcupines than any other natural cause. Many are killed by automobiles (Stoner, 1940). An awkward animal like the porcupine is likely to meet accident, as did one that caught its head in a tin can (Anon., 1947). Another at Itasca Park, Minnesota, apparently slipped while climbing a double-stemmed tamarack tree and was caught sideways just behind the forelimbs in the V of the trunks about one foot above ground (Marshall, 1951 b).

An abundance of parasites infest the porcupine, chiefly, so far as known, of only a few species. External parasites include the louse *Eutrichophilus setosus* and the ticks *Ixodes cookei* and *Dermacentor andersoni*. Internally, flatworms are often a serious parasite, including the two species *Shizotaenia erethizontis* and *S. laticephaea*. Four kinds of roundworms occur:

Dipetalonema arbuta, Dirofilaria subdermata, Molinema diacantha, and *Wellcomia evoluta.*

Exaggeration and prejudice often prevent a dispassionate consideration of the good and bad habits of the porcupine. Its economic status in Wisconsin is neutral. It does little damage to established forests, but locally may damage forest plantations. Its damage to farm crops is negligible. Not infrequently, however, it becomes an exasperating nuisance by committing minor destructive acts that to the individual person involved may prove a hardship. Its liking for salt causes many of its overt acts. It delights in gnawing handles of tools such as axes, hammers, and spades. Leather, particularly of a garment recently worn, attracts it. On a field collecting trip near Palmer Lake, Vilas County, in July, 1919, one of our party placed a beautiful leather jacket in a canoe cached for about five hours at the edge of the lake. When we returned, the jacket was in shreds, partly devoured and completely ruined. At many camps in the woods left for a time unoccupied, it has eaten doors, floors, tables, boxes, chairs, and particularly toilet seats, slop pails, and cooking utensils. Walter Scott (1941) tells of the remains of an aluminum

A pair of porcupines in top of pin cherry tree where they have eaten away much bark, Marquette County, Michigan, October 15, 1923. Photograph by Vernon Bailey.

Gnawings of porcupine on pin cherry. 1×.

kettle in the Rhinelander Lumbering Museum that had been almost entirely consumed when it was left through the winter in a small lumber camp in Taylor County. It is often destructive to cached canoes, oars, and paddles, but much of the destruction could be eliminated by properly caching the items on suspension chains. It is also charged with gnawing and damaging synthetic automobile tires.

On June 19, 1918, one blunderingly upset a Robin's nest in an aspen near our cottage at Bent's Camp, Mamie Lake. The nest contained four young robins about a week old, and the porcupine seemed loathe to have anything to do with the young birds, much less with the adults which were fighting him. The porcupine apparently accidentally tipped the nest in climbing the tree. It happened about 9:15 A.M. on a bright clear day. When the nest was readjusted, one young robin having died, the old bird renewed household duties and continued to occupy the nest until the morning of June 24, when we left.

The nuisance behavior of the porcupine affects comparatively few persons, and in Wisconsin it has never resulted in general or serious economic loss. The animal is approachable and interesting, attractive to thousands who like the outdoors and its wildings. It is a good photographic subject. It is an asset to many resort owners, some of whom encourage its presence to attract tourists. In these respects it has educational and esthetic value. It is edible, a young one being especially tasty. It is one of the few mammals that can be procured easily without trap or gun, and thus may offer a food resource to a person lost or stranded in a forest wilderness.

Extensive control of the porcupine is rarely necessary. Methods may be procured from the U. S. Fish and Wildlife Service, Washington 25, D. C., or the Wisconsin Conservation Department, Madison, Wisconsin. See also methods of control listed by Spencer (1950).

Specimens examined from Wisconsin.—Total 43, as follows: *Ashland County:* Mellen (8 mi. S. W.), 2. *Bayfield County:* Herbster, 2; Orienta, 1; Port Wing, 1. *Clark County:* No locality, 1 (UWZ); Worden Township, 1. *Dunn County:* Meridean, 1 (JNC). *Iron County:* Fisher Lake, 2 (UWZ); Mercer, 3 (UWZ). *Langlade County:* T 35 N, R 11 E, 9 (UWZ). *Monroe County:* Warren, 1 (UWZ). *Oconto County:* Kelley Lake, 1. *Shawano County:* Keshena, 1 (CAS); Neopit, 2 (CAS). *Vilas County:* Mamie Lake, 8 (1 MM); Phelps, 2 (UWZ); Rummeles, 1 (CNHM); Sayner, 3 (CNHM). *Wood County:* Marshfield, 1 (WES).

Selected references.—Batchelder, C. F., 1948; Curtis, J. D., and E. L. Kozicky, 1944; Po-Chedley, D. S., and A. R. Shadle, 1955; Sackett, L. W., 1913; Shapiro, J., 1949; Spencer, D. A., 1950.

ORDER CARNIVORA

Carnivores or Flesh-eaters

Mammals of this order are essentially flesh-eaters. Bears, raccoons, and some of the foxes feed also on vegetable matter and are in a sense omnivorous, and in the bears and raccoons the teeth are somewhat modified toward an omnivorous habit. They are found throughout the world, except Australia, and in Wisconsin vary in size from the least weasel, *Mustela rixosa*, to the black bear, *Euarctos americanus*. The four limbs are well developed and of moderate length, usually with five toes on each foot (four on hind foot of Canidae and Felidae), each digit provided with a claw. The braincase is large, the brain highly developed and showing many convolutions. Auditory bullae and zygomatic arches complete. The mandibles articulate closely with the cranium and allow only vertical movement. The incisors always are small and the canines heavy, long, and sharp, usually projecting well beyond the other teeth and adapted for seizing prey. The fourth upper premolar and the first lower molar (except in *Euarctos* and *Procyon*) enlarged and modified as cutting teeth, called carnassials or sectorials.

The Carnivora embrace eleven living families, five of which are represented in Wisconsin:

Key to the Families of Living Wisconsin Carnivora

a. Feet plantigrade; larger cheek teeth with crowns relatively flat, only slightly cuspidate without conspicuous cutting edges.
    b. Size large (more than 100 lbs.); tail short, inconspicuous, uniform blackish color; skull length more than 150 mm.; teeth 42. . . . . *Ursidae*
    bb. Size medium (less than 100 lbs.); tail relatively long, conspicuous, with series of buff and blackish rings and dark tip; skull length less than 150 mm.; teeth 40. *Procyonidae*
aa. Feet chiefly digitigrade; larger cheek teeth with crowns relatively cuspidate with more or less conspicuous cutting edges.
    b. Claws not retractile or only partly so, not completely concealed in fur; hindmost cheek teeth with crushing surfaces.
        c. Tail with mane of stiff hairs on upper surface; no specialized anal musk glands; total number of teeth 42. . . . . *Canidae*
        cc. Tail without mane of stiff hairs; specialized anal musk glands well developed; total number of teeth 38 or less. . . . . *Mustelidae*
    bb. Claws completely retractile, completely concealed in fur; cheek teeth without crushing surfaces. . . . . *Felidae*

Family Canidae

Wolves, Coyotes, and Foxes

The family Canidae is practically worldwide in distribution. It contains about a dozen living genera, three of which occur in Wisconsin.

Because of the economic importance of most Canidae, it often becomes necessary to identify juveniles or very immature individuals. Most of these can be identified, although it is often difficult, sometimes impossible, to distinguish between some wild species and the domestic dog. The following synopsis, modified from Vernon Bailey (1909), is inserted here as an aid to such identifications:

Synopsis to Juvenile Wisconsin Canidae

Wolf pup:
    Muzzle blackish at birth, fading in a month or 6 weeks to grayish.
    Head grayish in decided contrast to black of back, nose, and ears.
    Ears black at tips, fading to grayish in a month or 6 weeks.
    Tail black, fading to gray with black tip.

Coyote pup:
    Fur short and rough, little or no mustache.

Timber Wolf

Coyote

German Shepherd

Collie

Gray Fox

Red Fox

B.Ô'macmaugh

Side views of heads of canids.

Muzzle tawny, or yellowish brown, becoming more yellowish with age.

Head yellowish gray, not strongly contrasted with rest of body.

Ears dark brown at tips and back, soon fading to yellowish brown.

Tail black, fading to gray with black tip.

Red Fox pup:

Fur soft and silky, mustache long.

Muzzle blackish.

Head dusky with sides of face light yellowish.

Ears large, nearly the whole back of ears bright black at all ages.

Eyes and ears relatively larger and nose pad smaller than in coyote or wolf.

Tail dusky, tip white at all ages.

Gray Fox pup:

Muzzle blackish.

Head grayish, face back of eyes sharply pepper and salt gray.

Ears large, back of ears dusky at tip, fulvous at base.

Eyes and nose pad small.

Tail with tip black at all ages.

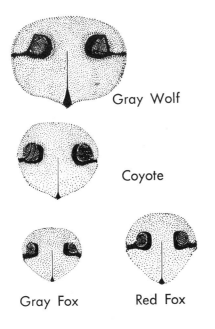

Nose pads of canids. 1×.

Genus **Canis** Linnaeus
Wolves and Coyotes

Dental formula:

$$I\frac{3-3}{3-3}, \quad C\frac{1-1}{1-1}, \quad P\frac{4-4}{4-4}, \quad M\frac{2-2}{3-3} = 42.$$

Canis latrans thamnos Jackson
Northeastern Coyote or Brush Wolf

Canis latrans thamnos Jackson, Proc. Biol. Soc. Washinton 62: 31, March 17, 1949.

Lupus latrans Lapham, p. 339, 1853.

Canis latrans Strong, p. 436, 1883; Jackson, p. 27, 1908; Hollister, p. 141, 1909; Hollister, p. 27, 1910; Cory, p. 322, 1912; Schmidt, p. 117, 1931; Komarek, p. 205, 1932.

Canis latrans thamnos Barger, p. 11, 1952.

Vernacular names.—Known as coyote throughout Wisconsin; commonly called brush wolf, especially in the northern half of state, and frequently called prairie wolf, particularly in the southern half of state. Other names include American jackal, barking coyote, coy-dog (nickname for coyote-dog cross), kyute, little wolf, and *mush-quo-de-ma-in-gon* (Chippewa).

Identification marks.—In general form and appearance the coyote suggests a rather large grayish collie dog or a small pale-yellowish German shepherd dog, with drooping tail; large erect pointed ears opening forward; eyes medium, the pupil round and iris yellow; slender, pointed muzzle; tail rather bushy, length less than one-third total length of animal; feet of medium size; four toes on each hind foot, five on each front foot, the first short and rudimentary but bearing a well-developed claw; claws blunt and nonretractile; fur moderately long, the guard hairs rather harsh and coarse.

Color of normal adult individual in fresh autumn pelage: muzzle near snuff brown, sometimes near cinnamon-brown; forehead and cheeks paler, mixed with gray and black; crown more mixed with tawny, becoming more ochraceous on nape and back of ears; upper parts from neck to tail coarsely mixed buffy gray and black, the general tone gray to cinnamon gray, with much blackish down the midline; tail above like back, tipped with black, and paler below with little or no black; color of upper parts extending down fore and hind legs; forelegs and feet lined with black on upper surface; under parts buffish, mixed with deep gray and a few blackish hairs on throat; chin grayish. Summer pelage is usually somewhat more buffy than winter fur. There is one molt annually, which in Wisconsin ordinarily starts about June and continues throughout most of the summer, the full fresh coat usually being acquired by October.

The skull is moderately low, rather slender and elongate, more than 160 mm. long and less than 210 mm., the greatest breadth more than 90 mm. and less than 112 mm.; interorbital and frontal region rather flat, slightly sloping anteriorly; postorbital processes heavy, distinctly convex above; rostrum long and moderately narrow, slightly depressed in prefrontal region; sagittal ridge well developed and prominent, particularly in adult males; audital bullae relatively long, the ratio of length to width about 10:7.5, the posterior borders widely diverging; teeth moderate in size, the canines long and rather slender, antero-posterior diameter at base less than 11 mm.; in anterior view of skull with lower jaw attached, the tips of the upper canines fall below a line drawn through the anterior mental foramina.

Males average larger than females, with correspondingly larger skulls which are more angular, tend to have the sagittal and other ridges more prominent, and have heavier dentition. Young coyotes in fuzzy fur before the guard

hairs develop are dark cinnamon gray above, the head pale brownish, snout and back of ears darker brown, under parts paler with a white elongate patch on throat and one on chest, the scantily haired tail the same color as upper parts. The skull goes through a process of development, the stages of which may be classed artificially as juvenile, immature, young, young adult, adult, and old adult. The juvenile of about four months has sutures more or less open, the coronal suture much arched posteriorly, milk dentition being dropped, and the first permanent dentition starting. The old adult (more than three years old) has coronal and sagittal sutures anastomosed, the sagittal ridge well developed and widening, the maxillo-nasal suture anastomoed, as are also the sutures at the base of the skull, and dentition complete and usually much worn (Young and Jackson, 1951: 250–51). There is considerable individual variation in size, color, and even cranial characteristics, but apparently less than in the wolf. Color mutations such as albinism and melanism are rare in the coyote, and I have no record of such in Wisconsin. On the other hand, nonhereditary abnormalities caused by injury, particularly to a foot, the tail, or the mouth or teeth, are not infrequent, though again I have no record of such in Wisconsin.

The adult coyote can be distinguished from either the red fox or the gray fox by color and size in that its total length is more than 1,050 mm.; tail vertebrae less than one-third of the

Northeastern coyote. Courtesy Wisconsin Conservation Department.

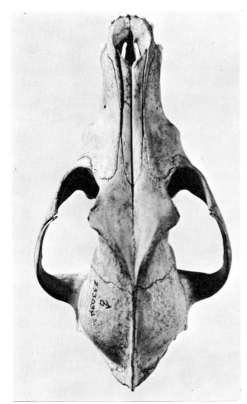

Skull of northeastern coyote, CANIS L. THAMNOS, *type specimen, Basswood Island, Ashland County, Wisconsin. About* ½ ×.

Right side upper tooth row of C. L. THAMNOS, *type specimen.*

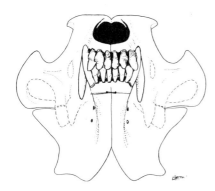

Anterior view of coyote skull, from Basswood Island, Wisconsin. ½ ×.

total length; nose pad more than 19 mm. wide; pupil round; skull in greatest length more than 160 mm. and in width more than 90 mm.; infraorbital foramen large, and clearly shows in superior view of skull; upper surface of postorbi-

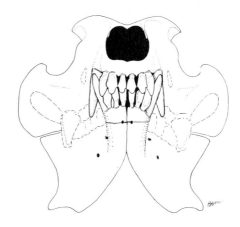

Anterior view of German shepherd dog skull. ½ ×.

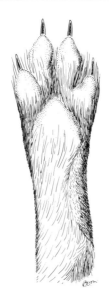

Left hind foot of coyote, CANIS L. THAMNOS. ½×.

tal process convex. As compared with the east-ern wolf (*Canis lupus lycaon*), the coyote is always smaller, less than 1,400 mm. in total length; in normal posture or when running car-ries the tail down low, not up as does the wolf and domestic dog; hind foot shorter, less than 240 mm.; skull less arched, less than 210 mm. in greatest length; upper canine tooth relatively narrower, less than 11 mm. in antero-posterior diameter at base. Color and color pattern, size, general proportions, and tail carriage usually distinguish the coyote from a domestic dog. The skull of *Canis l. thamnos* is most doglike of all coyotes, but may be distinguished by the long slender upper canines, the tips of which in an-terior view of skull with lower jaw attached fall below a line drawn through the anterior mental foramina, whereas in the dog the tips of the up-per canines fall well above such a line; incisors of the coyote usually much smaller than those of domestic dog; premolars, both upper and lower, relatively widely spaced in coyote.

It has been attempted to measure proportionally and explain statistically the average broader and shorter rostrum of the domestic dog as compared with that of the coyote. "This index or ratio is the *palatal width* (between inner margins of alveoli of upper, first premolars) *divided by the length of the upper molar tooth row* (anterior margin of alveolus of first premolar to the posterior margin of the last

molar alveolus). To identify a skull in the field and without a ruler the reciprocal of this ratio is used; the length of the upper molar teeth row divided by the palatal width between the upper first premolars. If the molar tooth row is 3.1 or more times that of the palatal width, the specimen is a coyote; but if less than 2.7 times it is a dog. Skulls can be differ-entiated even when flesh is present" (Howard, W. E., 1949, p. 171). Howard's method . . . in the Great Lakes States where the native coyote (*C. l. thamnos*) has a relatively short and broad rostrum . . . would probably not accurately separate more than 80 or 90 percent of the skulls" (Young and Jackson, 1951: 242–44).

A hybrid of the domestic dog and coyote, the "coy-dog" essentially is a dog in most character-istics, though sometimes it may display such coyote characteristics as to be difficult to identify except by careful comparison.

Measurements.—Total length of adult, 1,125 to 1,320 mm. (44.3 to 52 in.); tail, 295 to 390 mm. (11.6 to 15.4 in.); hind foot, 180 to 220 mm. (7 to 8.7 in.). Weight of adult, 25 to 42 pounds; average weight of adult male about 32 to 35 pounds; very rarely to 53 pounds. Skull length, 175 to 208 mm.; width, 92 to 110 mm.

Distribution in Wisconsin.—May occur in any of the less densely settled parts of the state; most plentiful in the northern half, north of about 44° 30′ N. Lat., except towards the Mississippi and lower St. Croix rivers where fewer occur; not un-common in central and south-central Wiscon-sin; rather infrequent in the southern parts of the state.

Habitat.—Prefers woodland borders and brushy areas, particularly hardwood second-growth that follows cutover or burned forests; sometimes dry marshes and prairies when interspersed with thickets of bushes or high herbaceous growth; often follows trails or old lumber roads through fairly dense woodland; rarely in meadows, cul-tivated fields, or areas removed from cover pro-tection, except to travel or forage.

Status and Habits.—Many records for wolves in Wisconsin are not clear as to whether the ani-mal was a coyote or a timber wolf; other rec-ords, even though only "wolf" is mentioned, have sufficient notes on habits to identify the animal; and still others clearly specify that the animal was a prairie or brush wolf, or a timber or gray wolf. The coyote was undoubtedly present in southern Wisconsin when the early explorers

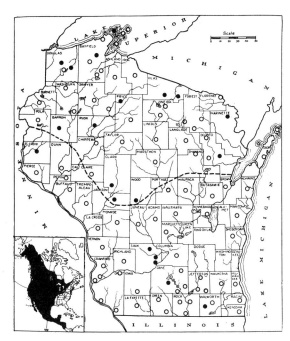

Map 54. Distribution of CANIS LATRANS. ● =
specimens examined. ○ = *authentic records. Coyotes now more abundant north of heavy broken
line.*

arrived, but how far north in the state it then
ranged is unknown, though the present preferred
habitat of the subspecies *thamnos* in brushland
and forest borders and openings might lead one
to believe that a few then occured also in the
northern part of the state. In recent years it has
been much more plentiful in the northern than
in the southern half of the state, yet everywhere
it is subject to fluctuation in population, which
sometimes seems to be cyclic and possibly correlated with population cycles of mice and rabbits. In a "bill for sundry Articles" from T. L.
McKenney in 1821, proceeds of Prairie du Chien
Factory include "80 Wolf skins in Pack No. 85
from P. du Chien same invoice 30c . . . $24.00"
(Thwaites, 1911: 231), and it is probable that
most of these wolves were coyotes. In a locality
near the present town of Lodi, Columbia County, in September, 1832, "the sight of a prairie
wolf was not an uncommon thing" (Whittlesey,
1855: 76), and in 1834 near Darlington, Lafayette County, accounts say, "Still more annoying
were the wolves. Every clear summer evening,
after sundown, we could hear their whoo-oo-o-oo,

in the distance, which would be answered from
another direction, and again from another, until the whole horizon seemed to be alive with
their howls" (Rodolf, 1900: 353). S. M. Palmer,
writing about Mineral Point as of 1836, says,
"Among the other evidences of the rude and
primitive condition of the town was the almost
unceasing howling and barking of the wolves
during the night, around and within its very
borders, sounding at times as though the town
was invested by scores of the brutes, much to
the annoyance and alarm of timid strangers"
(Palmer, 1872: 302). About that same time, coyotes were apparently common near Janesville
and Milwaukee (Janes, 1872: 429), in Walworth
County (Baker, C. M., 1872: 451), and near
Kenosha (Quarles, 1933: 310). The "prairie wolf"
occurred at Racine, and a specimen is recorded
by Lapham (1853: 339). Levi St. John, in the
vicinity of Janesville in 1856, said "wolves have
left" (Guernsey and Willard, 1856: 173), and
it seems possible that following hard winters
about that time coyotes may have become reduced in numbers throughout southern Wisconsin. They apparently soon increased again, and
many newspaper items told of their occurrence
and of pending wolf hunts.

A grand wolf hunt will come off Monday the 17th
of December, 1863. There will be a line formed,
commencing at the mouth of Spring Brook, on Rock
River above Silas Hurd's, in the town of Fulton,
extending up said brook to the Janesville road, near
J. B. Kidders; thence along said road to the mouth
of the ravine below Chapins lime kiln, in the town
of Janesville. Said line will be formed and ready to
march at 10 o'clock A.M. There will also be a line
formed on the west side of the river to act in con-
junction with the first. The center will be the Stoughton lot, on Rock River, in the town of Fulton, under
the superintendence of Capt. Isaac Miles. . . . We
invite all to take part, for the wolves are troublesome
(*Janesville Daily Gazette*, Dec. 7, 1863).

Other records indicate that the coyote was not
scarce in southern Wisconsin during the period
from 1865 to 1885, or even later. "Another prairie wolf has been caught within the city limits
of Milwaukee" (*Janesville Gazette*, Jan. 4, 1866);
and that same year, 1866, the skull of a prairie
wolf from Columbia County, Wisconsin, was presented to the Museum of Essex Institute, Salem,
Massachusetts (Proc. Essex Inst. 5 [1]: 7, 1866),
and a grand circle wolf hunt was conducted

March 15 in Green County, the closing-in ground north of the Juda depot, on land of S. Witmer (*Janesville Gazette*, March 13, 1866). Other reports of coyote occurrence among the many are for Beloit (*Evansville Review*, Evansville, Wisconsin, Feb. 19, 1873), Sun Prairie, Dane County (*Wisconsin Tobacco Reporter*, Edgerton, Nov. 12, 1880), Palmyra (*Wisconsin Tobacco Reporter*, Nov. 19, 1880), Juda (*The Latest News*, Juda, Green County, May 15, 1880, and Oct. 29, 1881), Walworth County (*Wisconsin Tobacco Reporter*, March 18, 1881), Stoughton (*Wisconsin Tobacco Reporter*, June 10, 1881), and Fort Atkinson (*Wisconsin Tobacco Reporter*, May 30, 1884). Possibly before the year 1900 there were as many coyotes in southern Wisconsin as in northern Wisconsin, if not more. In recent years, however, the coyote population in the northern part of the state has been many times as great as that in the southern part, as illustrated by wolf bounty claims for the 1950–51 fiscal year, in which 278 were paid in Price County as against 2 in Sauk County and none in many of the southern counties. In 1878 the state paid bounties on 9,734 wolves, though probably some of these were not wolves, and possibly some were not killed in Wisconsin. In the average high year, about 3,600 coyotes are killed in Wisconsin, which might indicate a peak abundance of 20,000 to 25,000 coyotes in the state. Population density seldom reaches an average of more than one a square mile, and usually much less. The home range is usually determined by food availability, and may extend over trails and roads a distance of eight to ten miles, but is normally within a radius of three miles from the den.

The presence of coyotes in any neighborhood in the far west can usually be determined by their yapping or howling at night. In frontier days coyotes yapped and howled in Wisconsin, but in recent years they seldom do in our state, either north or south. Possibly they have learned through experience that howling is not a good protective trait, possibly those that howl have been eliminated by hunter pressure, or more likely the habitat and environment have changed so as to eliminate the howling urge. Seldom is one seen, for they have become much more shy and slyer than their western brothers. There is no certainty of attracting a coyote into view by call notes, though by cleverly making a squeak-call, a howl-call, or a distress-call, or a combination of these calls, a coyote may be decoyed to within a few yards of the caller (Alcorn, 1946: 122). It sometimes will come to a bait, especially if a prepared scent is used. This scent is made as follows:

Put into a bottle the urine and gall of . . . a coyote . . . and also the anal glands, which are situated under the skin on either side of the vent and resemble small pieces of bluish fat. . . . To every 3 ounces of the mixture add 1 ounce of glycerin, to give it body and to prevent too rapid evaporation, and 1 grain of corrosive sublimate to keep it from spoiling. Let the mixture stand several days, then shake well and scatter a few drops on weeds or ground 6 or 8 inches from the place where the trap is set (Young, 1930: 8).

The coyote track, left in the dust, mud, or wet snow, is similar to that of a dog but is more elliptical, more elongate, and the imprint of the side toe is relatively longer. Tracks may be encountered along old roads and trails, or near a coyote feeding spot. At times a place where a coyote has wallowed is found, but unless hairs or tracks are present the identity of the maker may not be determined. The feces of the coyote are more generally broken into smaller parts than those of the domestic dog, and sometimes

Coyote howling.

Track of right fore foot of coyote. 1×.

Track of right fore foot of domestic dog. 1×.

Coyote feces. ½×.

show remains of food that a dog probably would not eat, but on the whole they are difficult to distinguish from the dog's feces.

Unless driven from its home by enemies or food shortage, the coyote is resident wherever found. It is chiefly nocturnal in habits, though in wilder regions may be out during daylight hours, particularly at dawn or early in the evening. It is active both summer and winter. It usually travels in the proverbial "dog trot," and sometimes under pressure gallops, though making little more speed than with its fastest trot. When trotting normally, the speed of the coyote is less than 20 miles an hour, and its fastest speed seldom exceeds 30 miles, although there is record of its running 35 miles an hour in Oregon (Cottam, 1945) and 43 miles an hour in Utah (Zimmerman, R. S., 1943). Its endurance when running, particularly when galloping, is

not great, and it tires rather easily, usually depending for escape upon keeping hidden by dodging and worming its way through rocks or vegetation. It swims fairly well dog-fashion.

The characteristic call of the coyote, one of the symbols of western prairies and of southern Wisconsin in pioneer days, is a high-pitched vibrant yapping howl that usually ends in a long, broken shrill scream. It is most often given about twilight or dawn, but may be heard any time of night and, very rarely, in the daytime. The coyote also utters a short high-pitched bark, and when in distress a shrill screaming howl. At play with its pups and sometimes while feeding, it has a purrlike whine. Through voice and signs such as a urine post, it is quite conversant with its fellow beings. When enemies are suspected, it watches like a sentry, and usually sneaks away undetected.

The coyote is a more or less sociable animal, and aside from gathering in the family group they often assemble in groups of three or four for feeding or for stalking game, at breeding time, or apparently merely to howl and play. Sometimes these gatherings may contain a dozen or more animals. It frequently plays by romping and tussling one with another, even those fully grown, and several times in Arizona, Idaho, and Oklahoma I have watched such play even near midday. Compared to some other carnivores, the coyote is not physically strong, yet its cunning, wits, and grit give it the full value of its muscles. Its capacity to withstand injury, pain, and other hardships is tremendous (Young and Jackson, 1951: 98–106). Its senses are all highly developed, except possibly that of taste. Sight, hearing, and smell are exceptionally acute, and it has constant use for them. The average longevity of the coyote in Wisconsin is probably less than 6 or 8 years, though normal life expectancy for the animal at large is near 12 years and the life potential about 18 years. There is a record of a coyote living 18-1/2 years in the National Zoological Park, Washington, D.C.

In areas where the coyote is not abundant it may have one mate for life, and in any event a pair often remains together for several years. More often, however, it stays with a mate a few years only, and often not more than a single year. Breeding in Wisconsin occurs chiefly during February, and after a gestation period of 60 to 63 days the young are born in April. Rarely do births occur later, and even more rarely earlier. The sex ratio is about 50:50. One litter each year is the rule, consisting of 4 to 8 young, usually 5 to 7, though it is not uncommon to find litters of 9 to 12 and females have been known to have as many as 17 and 19, (Young and Jackson, 1951: 81). Some of these excessively large litters may have been offspring of more than one female. The mammae are ten, four pectoral, four abdominal, two inguinal. At birth the pup is lightly covered with yellowish-brown, short, rough fur; the eyes open after about ten days. At about four weeks old the fur has become fuzzy and more yellowish, and the whelp frequently rambles and plays just outside the den. When about eight or nine weeks old it is weaned. By the last of July or in August the pup is half-grown and is shifting more or less for itself, though the family group may stay together until well into autumn. It becomes sexually mature and may breed when one year old. The coyote will breed with the domestic dog, crossing either male dog with female coyote or male coyote with female dog, and produce fertile offspring. Such crosses are not uncommon when the animals are in captivity, but also occur in the wild, particularly where the coyote is scarce or where it has been introduced outside its normal range and does not have ready mating with its own kind. Dog-coyote hybrids, or "coy-dogs," have been found

in the wild in Illinois, Kansas, Maine, New York, Pennsylvania, and other states. One is on record from Wisconsin: a scalp and skull (No. 177, 837, Biol. Surv. coll., U. S. Nat. Mus.) from Dane County, submitted Dec. 16, 1911, by J. A. Frear, then Secretary of State for Wisconsin.

The den is made in a concealed place, usually in a hole in the ground but sometimes in a crevice among rocks, at the base of a cliff, or under a stump. Sometimes the coyote digs its own burrow, but more frequently it enlarges the burrow of a woodchuck, badger, skunk, or fox. The entrance, some 10 inches high and 12 to 14 inches in diameter, usually is hidden by vegetation, but sometimes it is readily found by following the converging tracks and trails of the coyote, observing the accumulation of feces, and searching for a conspicuous mound apt to be found at the entrance. Often there are two or three entrances to one of the longer burrows, which may be 20 to 30 feet long, though most of the burrows are much shorter. The burrow seldom is more than 3 or 4 feet underground, and the nest consists merely of an enlargement to about 3 feet in diameter, no lining or nest material being used. The parent coyote leaves the burrow to defecate and urinate. The same den is frequently used by a coyote for many years, if not by the same individual, then by others. Pups taken away from the den may or may not cause desertion of the den for a year or two, but it is finally reoccupied if coyotes are in the region.

The food of the coyote, as summarized from stomach analyses by Sperry (1941), fecal analyses by Dearborn (1932), and general studies by others, is by volume about 98 per cent animal matter, of which mammals constitute about 94 per cent; birds 3 per cent; other vertebrates (reptiles, amphibians, fishes) 0.1 per cent; and invertebrates, mostly insects, about 1 per cent. Vegetable matter, mostly wild fruit, constitutes less than 2 per cent annually, but during the months from July until October may amount to as much as 5 or 6 per cent of all food eaten. Food habits research has not been extensive on the coyote in Wisconsin, the studies of Sperry (1941) involving only 7 stomachs from this state and 88 from Michigan out of 8,339 examined, and those of Dearborn (1932) 78 feces from Michigan. We know that normally on an annual basis, rabbits, both cottontail and snowshoe, constitute 30 to 35 per cent of the coyote's food, and rodents about 20 to 30 per cent, among which are the field mouse (*Microtus*), red-backed vole (*Clethrionomys*), ground squirrel (*Citellus*), woodchuck, pocket gopher (*Geomys*), muskrat, and porcupine, and apparently smaller numbers of the gray squirrel, flying squirrel (*Glaucomys*), and other miscellaneous rodents, moles, and shrews. In the Michigan studies, domestic sheep were 1.08 per cent of the fecal contents and white-tailed deer 9.5 per cent (Dearborn, 1932: 27), but it is probable that some of this was eaten as carrion. The coyote is a scavenger, particularly attracted to carrion, which Sperry (1941: 6, 11) estimated was 25 per cent by volume in the stomach contents he examined. Some domestic sheep (12.92 per cent, Sperry, 1941: 30) and deer (3.58 per cent, Sperry, 1941: 35) are consumed, but none of the Wisconsin coyote stomachs contained sheep remains. Sheep and deer, particularly fawns, occasionally are attacked by the coyote, and in early Wisconsin days raising sheep was often abandoned on account of prairie wolf depredation. Birds consumed are about equally divided among domestic poultry, game birds, and possibly more miscellaneous small birds, chiefly ground dwellers. In catching mice and other small prey, the coyote pounces on the animal with its feet, noses it, and proceeds to eat. Larger prey it usually rushes and attacks from the front, killing by a quick jab of its canines to the neck or throat of the animal, and cutting the jugular blood vessels. It is a ravenous feeder, and voraciously tears apart its prey, eating any or all parts, but preferring softer pieces such as the heart, liver, and lungs. Sometimes it kicks soil over food it has left, and it may return several times to the feeding station. Often the coyote hunts in pairs, or even in groups of three or four individuals, whether the food sought be larger prey or small mice and ground squirrels.

In the early days when the timber wolf and the puma were more frequent they probably preyed some upon the coyote, but nowadays man is about its only enemy. There are records of a buck white-tailed deer trampling a coyote to death. "Downed by wind near Wood Lake in Vilas County, a 18,000-volt power line electrocuted a deer, and then a coyote lost its life when it touched the dead animal. A Minocqua utility employee found the carcasses while repairing the line" (Conservation Volunteer [Saint Paul] 14: 44, October, 1951). Mechanical devices, however, seldom cause the accidental death of a coyote, and rarely is one struck by an automobile.

External parasites of the coyote include the lice *Heterodoxus spiniger* and *Trichodectes canis;* the mange mite *Sarcoptes scabei;* the ticks *Ixodes scapularis* and *Dermacentor variabilis;* and the fleas *Oropsylla arctomys, Arctopsylla setosa, Cediopsylla simplex, Echidnophaga gallinacea,* and *Pulex irritans.* Internal parasites (mostly from Erickson, 1944: 365) include the flukes *Alaria mustelae, Nanophyetus salmincola,* and *Opisthorchis pseudofelineus;* the tapeworms *Mesocestoides kirbyi, Multiceps multiceps, Taenia hydatigena, T. krabbei, T. laruei, T. laticollis, T. pisiformis,* and *T. rileyi;* the roundworms *Ancylostoma caninum, Dioctophyme renale, Molineus patens, Passalurus nonanulatus, Physaloptera rara, Protospirura muris, P. numidica, Rictularia splendida,* and *Toxascaris leonina;* and the thorny-headed worm *Oncicola canis.* Several diseases besides those caused by parasites affect the coyote, among them being distemper, rabies, and tularemia. Tumors and abscesses, particularly about the mouth, are not infrequent in the coyote.

Much heated argument, written and spoken, has been made about the economic status of the coyote and needs and methods for control of the animal. It became the subject for an all-day debate in a "Symposium on Predatory Animal Control," May 21, 1930, at the annual meeting of the American Society of Mammalogists in New York City, but even there the explosion of pent emotions did not settle the controversial problem (Adams, 1930; Dixon, 1930; Goldman, 1930; Hall, 1930; Henderson, 1930; Howell, A. B., 1930). General agreement was that the coyote at times was useful in destroying noxious rodents, that at other times it might be harmful by preying upon stock, poultry, and game animals, and that it should not be exterminated. It was not determined how much control should be operated, or the methods, though the bounty system seemed not in favor. In Wisconsin, during normal seasons when it has an abundance of wild food such as mice and rabbits, the coyote does more good than harm by its destruction of rodents. It also consumes a quantity of carrion, to its credit. The number of rabbits it kills has little effect on the game supply, and the very few deer it consumes acts only as a slight check on the deer population, increasing in many parts of the state to a deer irruption problem. When its natural wild food is plentiful the coyote seldom molests domestic animals. Occasionally a coyote breaks loose from normal habits (as does also the domestic dog) and acquires habits of killing livestock. Such an animal should be destroyed. When the coyote becomes too abundant or when its wild food supply becomes scarce, it may turn to killing livestock, particularly sheep, and then special control measures may be necessary.

The pelt, sometimes used for trimming or caps, has little commercial value, seldom bringing more than two or three dollars each, and the coyote population is not sufficiently or selectively reduced by the trapping for its fur. Catching the individual animal that is doing the killing is the only effective way to stop damage from coyotes. The bounty system in effect off and on in Wisconsin for more than a century has proved expensive and ineffective. The coyote-proof pasture involves expensive fencing with frequent patrol and repairs, and provides for what may be only a passing trouble for a limited area (Jardine, 1909; McAtee, 1939). The operation of state or federal predator control men who trap or poison the coyote in the field is not practicable in Wisconsin, where coyote depredations are minor and populations low in comparison with some of the western states. Iowa, Missouri, and other states where conditions are somewhat similar to those in Wisconsin have been rather successful in the control of the coyote through the State Extension Service or equivalent agency. Extension employees conduct schools to give trappers and farmers specific direction in catching coyotes and other predators. Farmers who have livestock or poultry destroyed by predators notify the county agent, who arranges demonstrations in the neighborhood where damage is occurring. The coyote is not difficult to catch in a No. 3 or 4 steel trap if the trapper carefully selects the site near a trail, uses proper bait or scent, leaves no trace of the work or scent of man on or near the trap, and employs other necessary precautions. Methods of trapping and den hunting have been amply described (Young, 1941; Young and Jackson, 1951: 184–99).

Specimens examined from Wisconsin.—Total 37, as follows: *Ashland County:* Basswood Island, Apostle Islands, 1 (type specimen). *Barron County:* No locality, 1. *Bayfield County:* Moquah National Forest, 8 (AMNH). *Clark County:* Hewett Twp., 1 (AMNH). *Dane County:* No locality, 1. *Douglas County:* Brule River cedar swamp, 1 (MM); No locality, 2 (UWZC). *Jackson County:* No locality, 1 (UWZC). *Marinette County:* Pembine, 1 (CNHM). *Oconto County:* Kelley Brook, 1 (MM). *Price County:* T 40 N, R 2 W, 1 (UWZC). *Rusk County:* Ladysmith, 4 (UWZC). *St. Croix County:* No locality, 1. *Sauk County:* Baraboo, (6 miles south of), 1 (UWZC); Prairie du Sac, 1 (MM); between Reedsburg and Wisconsin Dells, 2 (UWZC). *Vilas County:* Eagle River, 3; Lake St. Germain, 1. *Walworth County:* Delavan, 1. *Wood County:* Babcock, 4 (UWZC).

Selected references.—Hamlett, G. W. D., 1938; Jackson, H. H. T., 1949; Sperry, C. C., 1941; Whiteman, E. E., 1940; Young, S. P., 1941; Young, S. P., and H. H. T. Jackson, 1951.

Canis lupus lycaon Schreber
Eastern Wolf

Canis lycaon Schreber, Die Saugthiere, Theil 2, Heft 13, pl. 89, 1775.
Lupus occidentalis Lapham, p. 43, 1852; Lapham, p. 339, 1853.
Canis lupus Strong, p. 436, 1883.
Canis griseus Jackson, p. 27, 1908.
Canis occidentalis Hollister, p. 27, 1910.
Canis nubilus Cory, p. 313, 1912; Komarek, p. 205, 1932.
Canis lupus lycaon Barger, p. 11, 1952.

Vernacular names.—In Wisconsin commonly called gray wolf or timber wolf. Other names include big gray wolf, big wolf, black wolf (for the black color phase), common wolf, deer wolf, large gray wolf, *mä-in-gon* (Chippewa), *m'whä* (Potawatomi), northern timber wolf, and wolf. In the southwestern United States this species is often called the lobo, and in early days on the Great Plains it was called the loafer or buffalo wolf.

Identification marks.—General form and appearance suggests a huge gray German shepherd dog; color and markings somewhat similar to the coyote; size much larger, the total length of adults more than 1,350 mm., hind foot more than 225 mm., and the weight of comparable specimens averaging about twice that of the coyote; head rather broad; ears moderate and less conspicuous than in the coyote; muzzle relatively broader than in the coyote, the nose pad broader, more than 30 mm. in diameter; tail less than one-third of total length, bushy, bland on dorsal surface rather short, marked by narrow patch of coarse black-tipped hairs; feet and claws heavy, the heel pad of front foot more than 30 mm. in diameter; pelage moderately dense, somewhat coarse.

There is some variation in the extent of black tips to the hairs and the intensity of the cinnamon color. In full fall or winter pelage the upper parts are generally grayish, more or less overlaid with black from nape to rump; head mixed with ochraceous or cinnamon; under parts whitish to pale buff, with occasional scattered dark hairs, becoming more clearly whitish on inguinal region; ears cinnamon to tawny; chin and upper throat variable from white to blackish; outer parts of legs cinnamon buff to cinnamon, the forelegs with a more or less conspicuous black line, rarely absent; feet buffy; tail grayish above, suffused with black, buffy below, the tip blackish. There is no seasonal variation in color except for the fading, paling, and sometimes more reddish color of the old pelage in the spring, and early in summer. There is one slow molt annually; in Wisconsin it usually begins in May or June, and may not be completed until September or October.

The skull is moderately elongate, more than 210 mm. in greatest length and more than 112 mm. in greatest breadth; interorbital and frontal region somewhat inflated, moderately sloping anteriorly; postorbital processes heavy, prominent, convex above; rostrum moderately long, rather heavy, distinctly depressed in prefrontal region; sagittal ridge prominent, highly developed posteriorly, particularly in adult males; audital bullae large, prominent and relatively rather long, the ratio of length to width about 10 to 7, the posterior borders widely diverging; teeth rather large, the canines moderately long and heavy, antero-posterior diameter at base more than 12 mm.; in anterior view of skull with lower jaw attached, the tips of the upper canines fall above a line drawn through the anterior mental foramina.

Males average about 10 per cent larger than females, with larger and more angular skulls which have the sagittal and other ridges more developed, and have larger teeth. The wolf pup in fuzzy fur after birth before the guard hairs

Eastern timber wolf from Wisconsin in captivity. Courtesy Wisconsin Conservation Department.

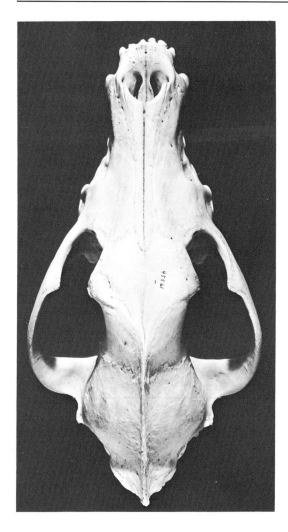

Skull of eastern timber wolf, C. L. LYCAON, *Elk River, Minnesota.* ½×.

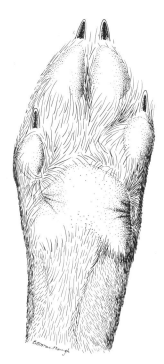

Left hind foot of timber wolf, CANIS L. LYCAON. ½×.

appear is blackish except for the head, which is over the entire upper parts dirty gray. At about six weeks of age the muzzle, ears, and tail except for the tip begin to change to grayish, and in a week or two the other upper parts begin to turn grayish. There is much individual variation in size, color, and cranial features. Color variations have ranged from a very pale gray to near blackish, but wolves in Wisconsin during the past several years seem to have maintained a fairly stable gray coloration. I have never seen a color mutation from Wisconsin.

The eastern wolf is readily distinguishable from its near relative, the brush wolf or coyote, in that it is much larger at comparable ages, the adult always more than 1,400 mm. in total length; in normal posture or when running it carries the tail up or horizontal, as does the domestic dog, not low down as does the coyote; hind foot longer, more than 250 mm.; skull much more arched, higher, more than 210 mm. in greatest length; upper canine tooth relatively broader, more than 12 mm. in antero-posterior diameter at base. Rarely a domestic dog may have the size and external appearance of an eastern wolf; the skull of the dog is relatively broader and shorter, more dished frontally; the rostrum in particular is relatively wider, as measured through the infraorbital foramina being more than 20 per cent of total length of skull and as measured across the first upper molars being more than 32 per cent of total length of skull; the canines of the domestic dog are usually shorter than those of the wolf and not so heavy. Positive identification is sometimes difficult, and can be made only by careful measurements and actual comparison of specimens.

Measurements.—Total length of adult, 1,490 to 1,650 mm. (58.6 to 64.8 in.); tail, 390 to 480 mm.

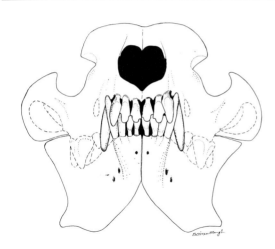

Anterior view of wolf skull, from Eagle River, Wisconsin. ½×.

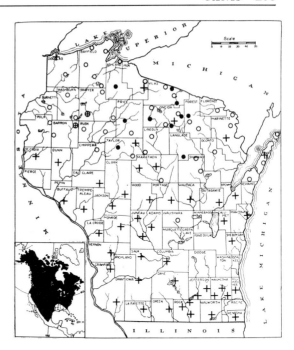

Map 55. *Distribution of* CANIS LUPUS. ● = *specimens examined.* ○ = *authentic records 1900 or later.* + = *records before 1900.*

(15.3 to 18.9 in.); hind foot, 255 to 290 mm. (10 to 11.4 in.). Weight of adult, 65 to 100 pounds, average weight of adult male about 75 to 85 pounds, rarely to 105 pounds. Skull length, 230 to 268 mm.; width, 120 to 142 mm.

Distribution in Wisconsin.—Formerly throughout the state, especially in timbered areas. Now rare, and except possibly for occasional wanderers, confined to wilderness cut-over areas of northern parts of the state, particularly in the counties of Ashland, Bayfield, Florence, Forest, Iron, Oneida, and Price.

Habitat.—Wilderness areas of forests and heavily wooded cut-over lands, sometimes inhabiting trails, old roads, and borders for travelling and searching prey.

Status and Habits.—The eastern wolf is making its last stand in the United States in northern parts of Michigan, Wisconsin, and Minnesota, but it has little chance of survival in Wisconsin where its numbers are reduced probably to less than 50. The winter population density now on known wolf ranges probably is not more than "approximately one wolf per 40 or 50 square miles" (Thompson, 1952: 430), whereas in the early part of the nineteenth century there may have been one to every two or three square miles, a total state population, say in the year 1835, of possibly twenty or twenty-five thousand. A small pack of timber wolves may have a home range of 150 to 250 square miles, depending greatly upon habitat limitations. Under present

conditions in northern Wisconsin the home range is usually less than 150 square miles, that of the female believed to be some 10 or 15 miles less than that of the male. Emigration over many miles that may have taken place in earlier days is now prevented through isolation of the wilderness ranges by broad areas of human disturbances.

Many of the old statements about "wolves," particularly in southern Wisconsin, may have referred to coyotes or brush wolves, yet many clearly refer to the timber wolf. Early records for the southern half of the state include Manitowoc County, 1827 (Fonda, 1868: 230); Rock County, 1837 (Pratt, 1855: 141); Walworth County, 1837 (Baker, 1872: 451); Kenosha County, 1839 (Quarles, 1933: 310); Jefferson County, 1842 (Cartwright and Bailey, 1875: 155); Milwaukee County, 1853 (Lapham, 1853: 339); Vernon County, 1855 (Mather, 1896: 331); and Grant County, 1857 (*Janesville Daily Free Press,* February 9, 1857). Old newspaper reports indicate that from about 1873 to 1884, especially during the severe winters of 1880–81 and 1881–

82, timber wolves were not uncommon in parts of southern Wisconsin (Dane, Green, Jefferson, Rock, Waukesha, and Walworth counties), but that their occurrence in these parts terminated about 1885 or shortly thereafter. The most recent record I have for central Wisconsin is of a large one "killed one and one-half miles from Wautoma by Chester Wilcox" (*The Journal Telephone*, Milton Jct., Wisconsin, November 30, 1916).

The eastern wolf is an elusive mammal that does not make its presence in a region generally known, particularly in the recent years of its continued persecution and decreasing numbers. Its howl is distinctive, a deep, prolonged dismal wail, quite different from the high-pitched yapping of the coyote. Wolf tracks are not always easily distinguishable from dog tracks. The wolf's track is more elongated and relatively narrower, more elliptical and less nearly circular, than that of the dog; the impressions of the two anterior toes are less spread than those made by a dog, and the toenail prints are more prominent. The imprint is always much larger than that made by a coyote, or by most dogs. The feces are similar to those of a dog, except that they show indications of deer hair and other undigested items not apt to be eaten by a dog. The tracks and feces may be found along game trails that the wolf frequents.

Almost strictly nocturnal, the big wolf, unlike the coyote, is very seldom out in daylight unless forced there by ravenous hunger or other extreme cause. It is active all night, in all kinds of weather. It does not truly migrate. When on extensive wolf range, such as no longer exists in Wisconsin, it may roam long distances from its home area, and may emigrate one or two hundred miles to escape starvation food shortages or other disturbing conditions. It is active both summer and winter. Its running gait is about 18 to 20 miles an hour, which in a long chase slows to half that speed. When pressed it may reach a speed of 28 miles an hour for a short distance. It cannot run as fast as the coyote, but has greater endurance. It swims well, of course treading water dog-fashion, and may even enter water in search of its prey.

Young and Goldman (1944: 77–78) have classified the voice of the wolf into five distinct vocal sounds:

Tracks of timber wolf. Above, right fore foot. Below, right hind foot. ½×.

The first in our classification is a high, though soft, and plaintive sound similar to the whine of a puppy dog, and is used mostly at or near the opening of the wolf den, particularly when the young whelps are out playing around. It seems to indicate solicitude for the offspring, and is made mostly by the adult female. As the pitch of the whines varies so much, it seems ventriloquial.

The second is a loud, throaty howl, seemingly a call of loneliness. It is best heard in zoological parks where either the male or the female wolf is confined alone; and when a sudden loud noise such as the sound of a whistle, a clap of thunder, or the clang of a fire-bell causes the animal to give voice. This

Wolf tracks, Wyoming, 1909. Photograph by Vernon Bailey.

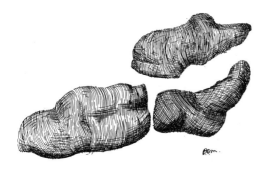

Feces of timber wolf. ½×. Drawn after Seton, 1929, vol. 1, p. 384.

long, lonesome-sounding howl is also uttered during the breeding season (December, January, and February).

The third sound is a loud, deep gutteral, though not harsh, howl, apparently the call of the chase, that generally is given by an adult male and is answered by other wolves on the hunt for food. It might be termed a call for assembling a group of wolves of the same vicinity. The gutteral howl may at times be followed by a loud bark or two similar to that of a Newfoundland dog.

The fourth call is that of the chase, made after starting prey, as a deer or moose. The utterance is not quite so throaty or gutteral as the third, and consists of several short, deep barking sounds rapidly made, very similar to that of a pack of hounds on a very hot chase.

The fifth call is that of the kill. A bulldog of the heavier breed makes a similar sound when in hard combat with a rival. It is a deep snarl produced by

exhaust of air through the wolf's partially opened mouth as it hangs on with teeth sunken into the flesh of its victim.

Early settlers' accounts of wolves howling referred as a rule to the second type as given by Goldman and Young, a howling that might occur at any time of night, but more frequently during the first hours. Less often were heard the calls of the chase, and seldom the call of the killing—the most terrifying and bloodcurdling of all—or the whines of the mother wolf at the den. Wolf puppies in their den whine and whimper much as domestic dog puppies in an effort to attract attention to their real or seeming troubles. Wolves declare their presence to other wolves and mark their ownership by use of their urine for an odor post, much as does the domestic dog. It is always watchful and closely alert to its surroundings, but does not actually stand sentry, except sometimes near its den.

The disposition and temperament of the timber wolf might well be described as that of a wild, untampered dog; it investigates everything, viciously fights and antagonizes those it does not like, and befriends and mollycoddles those of its choosing. It snarls and shows its teeth when angry, throws its ears back and its tail between the hind legs when defeated or depressed, and laps objects with its tongue and wags its tail when happy or pleased. It is temperamental, and may be a raging fury one minute and docile and friendly with its own kind the next. It is wary, and usually quickly retreats with suspicious glances from any human intruder without his knowledge, particularly in the recent years of its low population, restricted range, and abundant food supply. Several stories are written of wolves attacking humans during the early years in Wisconsin, some of which may have been fiction, others with some basis of fact. Many records of wolves following persons on foot or on horseback are told, but whether the wolves would have attacked we do not know.

The Grant County Herald learns that Mr. W. T. Patton, resident of the town of Ellenboro, while returning home from Lancaster on the evening of Monday last, just beyond Mr. Rowdens, was met in the road by five large wolves. They refused to give the road and from appearances of the plainest kind were about to attack him, but he beat them off with an axe handle, which he fortunately carried in his hand. The circumstance affords a hint to those who travel afoot and alone to be on guard, as the wolves are just about starved enough to attack a man with wilful savageness (*The Janesville Daily Free Press*, February 9, 1857).

And from Douglas County:

Within a few days past, quite a number of wolves have been showing themselves along the mail route, between this place and the Bay de Noquette. A trapper was followed ten miles by about a dozen of the crafty, ravenous, howling creatures, and only escaped with his life by running at a 2, 40 pace and keeping up a perpetual fire from his gun, until he reached a station on the route, when they stopped, turned, and put off into the forest again (From *Lake Superior Journal*, in *Janesville Daily Gazette*, February 4, 1862).

Uncle Dave Cartwright, in his trip by foot from Madison to northwestern Wisconsin in 1856, says:

After we passed the Black River Falls, we stayed at night at a private house, where we found that we were needed to help care for a stranger who had lost an arm by accidental discharge of his gun. Being near the house he crept in and was cared for there. The wolves had tracked the blood on his way to the house, and the man would doubtless have been devoured by them, had not the inmates of the house happened to hear him just in time to save him (Cartwright and Bailey, 1875: 236).

Other equally reliable accounts of wolves attacking man in Wisconsin are on record. To my knowledge, however, only one unprovoked attack by an eastern wolf on man in America has been fully substantiated. This is the case of Mike Dusiak, Canadian Pacific Railway section foreman, who, while patrolling his section of the railway between Devon and Poulin, Ontario on December 29, 1942, travelling at about ten miles an hour on a speeder, was grabbed by the left arm and hit so hard by a wolf that he and the speeder were pulled from the track. The wolf circled him, and with an axe in each hand Dusiak fought fiercely for about half an hour, when a freight train came along and the crew killed the wolf and rescued the man (Peterson, 1947: 294).

Wolves frequently assemble in packs, composed sometimes of the family group, or less frequently of a group of unmated males, such packs in olden days sometimes being composed of 20 or more individuals, but nowadays seldom comprising half that number. The wolf is a serious stoic, less playful than the coyote, though the mother plays with the pups, and the pups, until half-grown, play together. Sinewy, strong, and possessing great endurance, the wolf is not only actually but also comparatively a much more powerful animal than the coyote. Its senses are highly developed, particularly those of sight, hearing, and smell. The normal longevity is about 12 years and the potential longevity near 18 years. A male gray wolf, *Canis lupus nubilus*, lived in the National Zoological Park, Washington, D. C., 16 years, 3 months, 5 days (Hollister, 1923: 93).

The wolf is believed to be monogamous, and in Wisconsin remains mated through the season of caring for the young. Probably some pairs remain mated for life, possibly most pairs. Mating does not occur until the wolf is in its third year. Coition usually takes place in February or March, and after a gestation period of 63 days the pups or whelps are born in April or May. One litter each year is the rule, consisting of four to ten young, usually seven or eight, sooty in color except for brownish-gray heads. The mammae are ten, four pectoral, four abdominal, two inguinal. The eyes are closed for nine days after birth, and when open show their gray-blue color. The she-wolf, bitch, or dam nurses and cautiously watches over her offspring. The father (often called dog or dog-wolf) helps provide food for the family and acts as lookout or sentinel. The whelps begin to shift for themselves when about two or three months old, but often continue together as a family unit for a year or more. They usually leave the brood den by the last of summer, though they may return to it for shelter. The timber wolf will breed with the domestic dog and produce fertile offspring from either dog or wolf mother. Numerous such hybrids in the wild have been recorded from the western United States, Canada, and Alaska (Young and Goldman, 1944: 180–210), and others have been bred in captivity. Many Eskimo dogs have a high percentage of wolf blood in them, as do also some Indian dogs. The Wisconsin naturalist Ludwig Kumlien, in his observations at Cumberland Sound, Baffin Island, Arctic Canada, in 1877, noted wolf-dog crosses: "It often happens that the Eskimo dogs and wolves interbreed; the female dog is especially liable to cohabit with a wolf, and the progeny are considered much superior beasts, but are very hard to manage. I have seen Eskimo dogs that corresponded hair for hair with the Arctic wolf" (Kumlien, 1879: 53).

The breeding den is in a burrow, usually in a natural cavity or hollow in a bank or side of a hill, or sometimes in a large hollow log, under an old stump, or under wind-drifted debris and brush, always in a wilderness situation. There is no attempt at nest-building, the resting place having only accumulated dirt, leaves, and such other material as may be present, more or less molded into form by repeated circling and tramping by the occupant. The den is occupied only as long as the whelps need its protection, though it may be entered at other times when a wolf wants safe retreat. The same breeding den, or one nearby, is usually occupied each year by the same pair of wolves throughout their lives, though sometimes, apparently for sanitary reasons, a pair may occupy three or four different dens during one breeding season. Apparently the parent wolves do not defecate or urinate in the den, but the entrance may sometimes be well polluted by such action.

The white-tailed deer is the chief food of the timber wolf in Wisconsin, and except possibly in times of low deer or high wolf populations probably always has been. In early days the timber wolf was known to attack the bison, the elk, the caribou, and the moose among big game animals. In a study made by Daniel Q. Thompson on wolf ranges in Oneida and Iron counties, representing analyses of 435 timber wolf scats collected from the spring of 1946 to the summer of 1948, the frequency of occurrence of animal matter was: deer, 97 per cent of the scats; snowshoe hare (*Lepus*), 5 per cent; meadow vole (*Microtus*), 2 per cent; red-backed vole (*Clethrionomys*), 0.9 per cent; cottontail (*Sylvilagus*), 0.7 per cent; June beetle (*Phyllophaga*), 0.5 per cent; bird (egg shell), 0.5 per cent; and eastern chipmunk (*Tamias*), 0.2 per cent. Late in the summer and in the fall of 1946 meadow voles appeared in 15 per cent of the scats during an abundant rodent population. Ten types of vegetable matter were found: grass in 25 per cent of the scats; balsam fir, 11 per cent; hemlock, 8 per cent; white cedar, 3 per cent; leatherleaf (*Chamaedaphne*), 3 per cent; black spruce, 2

per cent; Labrador tea (*Ledum*), 2 per cent; pine, 1 per cent; and aspen and goldenrod (gall) in single scats. Rind (from garbage, wrapping cord, cotton cloth, and metal scraps) was found in single scats (Thompson, 1952: 433). This probably represents a fair perspectus of food habits of the timber wolf in its reduced numbers in wilderness habitat. More snowshoe hares and cottontails might show in wolf scats during periods of abundance of these mammals, and particularly during a scarcity of deer. In its present scarcity, and with an abundance of other food, the timber wolf rarely attacks domestic stock. In earlier days in Wisconsin, however, it frequently caused serious damage to stock, particularly to sheep and young cattle, and numerous early accounts attest to their havoc. Near Sullivan, Jefferson County, in the winter of 1842–43: "The wolves were then more numerous than I have ever known them to be elsewhere. We had to keep all our young stock shut up to keep them from the wolves. It was not uncommon for these fierce creatures to chase a dog to the door of the house, which by the way was not furnished with doors, only blankets stretched across the door-way (Cartwright and Bailey, 1875: 157). Timber wolves fight wildcats on sight, much as domestic dogs fight house cats. Andrew Berg, near Odanah, Ashland County, was hunting and, "attracted by snarling and howling, forced his way into a thicket, where the wolf was battling a wildcat. As Berg appeared the wolf had the cat by the neck and was about to make an end of him. One shot finished the wolf, and the wildcat, too weak to run, was easily dispatched" (*The New North*, Rhinelander, Wisconsin, 33 [7]: 2, January 14, 1915). The timber wolf frequently watches for prey, but except for pouncing on smaller animals seldom attacks from a standing position. Its usual attacking method is to follow the prey, close in on it, rush it, and strike viciously. It literally eats its prey alive, but may return several times to a kill until nearly the whole carcass is devoured. Records indicate that in Wisconsin a single wolf attacks more often than a pack of wolves. In days when the wolf was more plentiful in this state a pack probably at times followed a buffalo or elk herd and attacked when opportunity or urge arose, as they are known to have done in other regions. In its attack it hits with tremendous strength, usually with loud bloodcurdling growls. Sometimes, particularly with larger mammals, it attacks the hocks, thus hamstringing the victim, but more often it snaps for the throat or nose, and once its jaws set, it hangs viciously until the prey is down. N. A. Coleman saw a wolf attack a deer on his farm on the shores of Clearwater Lake, northeastern Oneida County, in December, 1914, after hearing a peculiar noise in a large tract of woods. "Without stopping to secure a gun Mr. Coleman hurried to the woods and upon entering the densest part saw a large half famished wolf attacking a deer. Just as Mr. Coleman approached the animals, the wolf buried its fangs into the deer's throat and with a quick jump hurled the deer to the ground. When Mr. Coleman was within ten feet of the animals the wolf got up and ran away" (*The New North*, Rhinelander, Wisconsin, December 31, 1914). The wolf drinks often, lapping water like the domestic dog. It frequently licks itself and wallows, but is not a very cleanly animal.

Other than man, the wolf has no natural enemies that affect its welfare. The few now killed in Wisconsin are taken for bounty. Even such conditions as severe storms, extreme cold weather, and forest fires probably do not cause much loss in the wolf population. External parasites that infest it include the lice *Trichodectes canis* and *Linognathus setosus*; the mange mite *Sarcoptes scabei*; the ticks *Dermacentor variabilis*, *Amblyomma americana*, and *Ixodes kingi*; and the flea *Pulex irritans*. Internal parasites for the species (*Canis lupus*) include the fluke *Alaria americana*; the tapeworms *Echinococcus granulosus*, *Multiceps packii*, *Taenia hydatigena*, and *T. pisiformis*; and the roundworms *Ancylostoma caninum*, *Dioctophyme renale*, *Dirofilaria immitis*, *Filaroides osleri*, *Physaloptera rara*, *Toxocara canis*, and *Uncinaria stenocephala* (Erickson, 1944: 366–67). Among diseases occurring in the timber wolf in the wild are arthritis (Cross, 1940 a), distemper (Grinnell, 1904: 287), cancer (Pocock, 1935: 680), rabies (Young, 1948: 233), and possibly tularemia.

The Eastern wolf is now so rare in Wisconsin as to be of little economic importance. The few that possibly remain are in remote wilderness areas void of settlements and domestic livestock. Predation by so few wolves on the deer herd could be an asset to man and the deer rather than a liability.

Long investigation [on big game types, Superior area, Minnesota] indicates that the great majority of the killings are of old, diseased or crippled animals. Such purely savage killings are assuredly not detrimental to either deer or moose, for without the constant elimination of the unfit the breeding stock would suffer. Furthermore, the wolf is a natural stimulus to a herd's alertness and injects the primitive element of danger without which most big game animals lose much of their natural charm (Olson, 1938: 335).

Wolf predation tends to reduce the problem of deer irruptions with their attendant destruction of browse and starvation of deer. There is little chance of the wolf ever again becoming so plentiful in Wisconsin as to seriously harm livestock as it did in the early days. Wolf fur has low value in the market, seldom bringing more than ten dollars a pelt. The bounty for a wolf may pay even more than its pelt value, but bounty as a system of predator control should be abolished. The wolf is difficult to trap or hunt, but only slightly more so than the coyote, and methods, somewhat similar, have been described (see Young, 1941; Young and Goldman, 1944: 286–368).

Specimens examined from Wisconsin.—Total 13, as follows: *Ashland County:* No locality, 2 (1 MM, 1 UWZ). *Forest County:* Hiles Twp., 1 (UWZ). *Langlade County:* Antigo, 1 (CNHM). *Oneida County:* Rhinelander, 1 (MM); Sec. 31, T 37 N, R 5 E, 1 (UWZ); Three Lakes, 1 (MM). *Price County:* Price County, 1. *Taylor County:* Perkinstown, 1. *Vilas County:* Eagle River, 1; near Michigan line, 2 (CNHM); No locality, 1 (UWZ).

Selected references.—Goldman, E. A., 1937; Olson, S. F., 1938; Stenlund, M. H., 1955; Thompson, D. Q., 1952; Young, S. P., 1941; Young, S. P., and E. A. Goldman, 1944.

Genus **Vulpes** Oken
Foxes

Dental formula:

$$I\frac{3-3}{3-3}, \quad C\frac{1-1}{1-1}, \quad P\frac{4-4}{4-4}, \quad M\frac{2-2}{3-3}=42.$$

Vulpes fulva fulva (Desmarest)
Eastern Red Fox

Canis fulvus Desmarest, Mammalogie, vol. 1, p. 203, 1820.
Vulpes fulvus Lapham, p. 43, 1852; Lapham, p. 339, 1853; Strong, p. 436, 1883; Snyder, p. 122, 1902; Jackson, p. 26, 1908; Hollister, p. 140, 1909; Hollister, p. 27, 1910; Cory, p. 305, 1912.
Vulpes fulvus argentatus Snyder, p. 123, 1902.
Vulpes fulva fulva Komarek, p. 205, 1932; Barger, p. 11, 1952.

Vernacular names.—Black fox (color phase), colored fox, cross fox (color phase), red fox, *renard* (French), *Fuchsroth* (German), Sampson or scorched fox (color and pelage-condition phase), silver fox (color phase), silver-gray fox (color phase), *wa-a-gush* (Chippewa), and yellow fox.

Identification marks.—In general suggests a small dog, much smaller than an average Collie; rather long, slender legs; pointed nose; prominent erect ears; long bushy tail or "brush," always with white tip, discernible even in young one day old; eyes moderate in size, the pupils elliptical; legs rather long; feet relatively small, four digits on hind feet and five on forefeet; claws rather long and sharp; fur long, fine, and dense.

Color of normal individual: face and occiput rusty or yellowish fulvous, usually mixed with whitish; upper parts bright yellowish red or fulvous, darker on the median line, the rump more or less grizzled with whitish; cheeks, chin, throat, and band down under parts whitish; feet blackish; outside of ears blackish, inside whitish; tail fulvous profusely mixed with black, nearly producing a blackish patch on upper surface near base, the tip of tail always distinctly whitish.

There is no seasonal variation in color except for the increased richness in full winter pelage. There is one molt annually, which begins the last of April or early in May; shedding of old hairs may not fully be completed until early in September, and new fur growth may not be completed until early in November (Bassett and Llewellyn, 1949).

The skull is low and slender, less than 160 mm. long; interorbital and frontal region flat, the frontal sinuses scarcely inflated; postorbital processes weak, slightly concave above; rostrum long and narrow, very slightly depressed below frontal region; sagittal crest often developed but usually not into a conspicuous ridge, narrowly diverging anteriorly into the temporal ridges which enclose a narrow V on top of skull; audital bullae prominent, relatively long, the ratio of length to width about 10:7 (in *Urocyon* about 8:7), the posterior borders not widely diverging; teeth relatively small, the canines rather long and slender, the upper incisors lobed.

Males average slightly larger than females, but

Red fox, Wisconsin. Courtesy Wisconsin Conservation Department.

there are no other variations that can be associated with sex. Young red foxes are dark, sometimes nearly blackish, the color soon changing
to yellowish or grayish brown and then to the
adult coloration. Color variation is extensive, not
only in the darkness or paleness of the general
fulvous tone, but in the tendency towards color
mutations, particularly melanism. Melanism may
occur rarely in the wild animal, producing either
an entirely black fox, a silver fox in which the
black is frosted with white hairs or white-tipped
black hairs, or a cross fox with a dark cross on
the neck, shoulders, and back. The three color
phases, red, silver or black, and cross, may occur
in the same litter. Rarely, a red fox lacks some
or all of the guard hairs, and the woolly animal
may be called a Sampson fox or, less frequently,
a scorched fox. The black or silver phase occurs
more frequently in the northern half of Wisconsin than in the southern half. Wisconsin records
of black or silver foxes taken in the wild include
Door County, 1867 (*Janesville Gazette*, December 5, 1867); Fifield, Price County, 1882 (F. J.
Fraenkle, report to Wisconsin Conservation Department, June 26, 1937); Beaver Dam, Dodge
County, 1890 (Snyder, 1902: 123); Atkins, Forest County, 1911 (*New North*, Rhinelander,
January 12, 1911); Crandon, Forest County, 1912
(*New North*, Rhinelander, January 11, 1912);
Ashland, 1921 (Orig. report, August 11, 1921,
Vernon Bailey); and Big Sand Lake, Menominee

Indian Reservation, 1927 (Komarek, 1932: 205).
A red fox of the Sampson fox phase, on which
bounty had been paid for a "wolf pup" at Eagle
River, Vilas County, was submitted to the U. S.
Biological Survey by N. L. Kinney in October
1921, for identification. When bred under control
in captivity, the red fox displays many other
variants such as blue platinum, fawn, full silver,
pale silver, pale platinum, pearl, platinum, silver
buff, silvery red, white faced, and white with
black marks. Pure albinos seem not to occur, and
the few completely white pups are dead at birth
or die shortly thereafter.

The white tip to the tail will distinguish the
red fox from any other wild, native dog-like
mammal. A domestic dog, however, may sometimes have a white tip to the tail. All specimens

Skull of Vulpes f. fulva, *Highlandville, Iowa.*

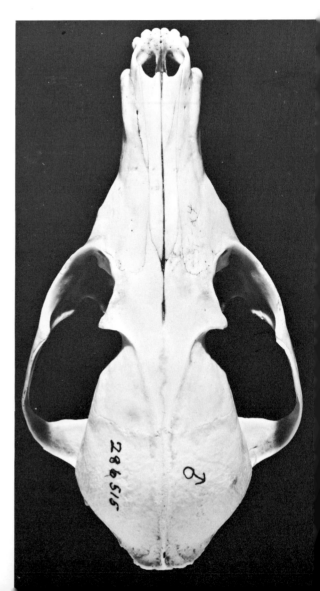

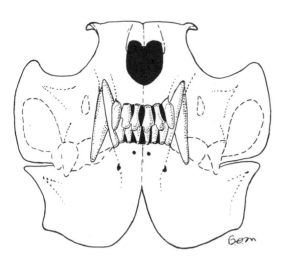

*Anterior view of red fox skull, from Highlandville,
Iowa.* 1×.

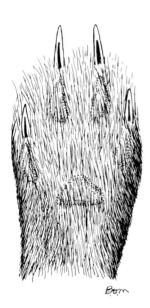

Left hind foot of red fox, VULPES FULVA. 1×.

from Wisconsin are referred to the typical subspecies *fulva*, although a few from the northwestern part of the state show a slight trend
towards *V. f. regalis* in size and color.

Measurements.—Total length of adults, 975 to
1,050 mm. (38.4 to 41.3 in.); tail, 330 to 405 mm.
(13 to 16 in.); hind foot, 160 to 175 mm. (6.3
to 7 in.). Weight of adult, 9 to 13 pounds, rarely
to 15 pounds. Skull length, 134 to 156 mm.;
width, 69 to 79 mm.

Distribution in Wisconsin.—Entire state in favorable habitats; more plentiful in western, central, and northeastern parts.

Habitat.—Hilly farmland of mixed woodlots,
brushland, cropland, and pasture, and stream and
lakeside bottoms; occasionally wanders into
towns and urban areas; avoids dense forests.

Status and Habits.—The population of red
foxes in the state has varied; top abundance
seems to occur in cycles of eight to ten years,
such peaks having been reached in about the
years 1915, 1925, 1936, 1945, and 1953. Low
populations occurred in 1920, 1932, and 1940.
"Since 1944–45 red foxes have remained at a
relatively high, stable level" (Richards and Hine,
1953: 31). Native red foxes inhabited Wisconsin
when the first settlers arrived, though probably
in lesser numbers than now, and were reported
in the Green Bay fur sales as early as 1814

(Thwaites, 1910 b: 357). Settlement and agriculture have offered them increased habitat, for
red foxes prefer the more open places to heavy
timber, and often wander into urban areas, even
into larger cities. "A red fox . . . was captured
in October [1899] in a chicken pen at Wells and
Twenty-fifth Streets [Milwaukee], which is a
thickly populated district" (Bennetts, 1900: 63),
and the animal had probably been at large in
that district for more than a month. At the peak
of these population cycles there may be 150,000
red foxes in the state, possibly more; however,
food shortage, disease, hunting pressure, and
other factors may within a year or two reduce
the number to less than 10 per cent of the high.
The paying of bounties by state and counties
over a period of 75 years has had little effect on
wild fox populations, and has proven a useless
waste of public funds. A population density over
any considerable area of six or more red foxes
to one square mile is high, but may occur in
parts of Dunn, Grant, Iowa, Monroe, Sauk, Trempealeau, and other western counties. A red fox,
when hunted or pursued, may travel 10 to 20
miles from its den, but ordinarily its home range

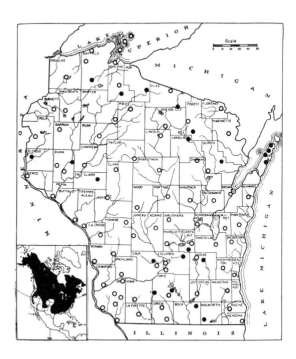

Map 56. *Distribution of* VULPES FULVA. ● = *specimens examined.* ○ = *authentic records.*

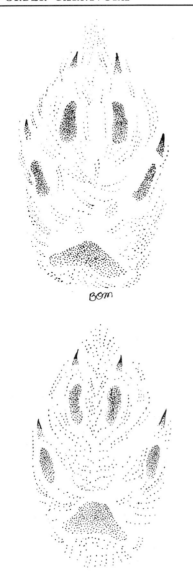

Tracks of red fox. Above, right fore foot. Below, right hind foot. 1×.

it an easy animal to observe. Sometimes it can be called into sight by imitating the squeaks of a mouse or the cry of a rabbit in distress. Often when being trailed a fox will make a zigzag circle and backtrack out of curiosity to see what is following it, when it may be observed. The track of the red fox is something like that of a small dog, but the footprint is narrower and the claw imprint usually shows clearly. The tracks always are in nearly straight alignment, evenly spaced when the animal is walking, paired when the animal is loping. Characteristic feces may tell of the presence of a red fox in an area. If a pair of foxes is in a neighborhood the den can be located by diligent search. The animal often follows trails and paths, and even lanes and roads, and thus reveals his whereabouts.

The red fox is resident wherever found, and seldom emigrates to another region unless forced by food shortage. It is active both winter and summer, and although principally nocturnal, it may at times be active on sunny days, and frequently is quite active on moonlight nights and at twilight. The normal gait of a fox is a spritely walk, slowed to scarcely any movement at times when the animal is cautiously following its prey, occasionally breaking into a running trot or, when maximum speed is developed, into a gallop that may attain 32 miles an hour if the animal is being pursued, but the normal maximum is about 28 miles an hour. Rather averse to water, the red fox is nevertheless a fairly good swimmer, and will voluntarily swim a half mile or more across a stream or lake. Quite naturally, because of its structure and relationships, it swims dog-fashion, nose slightly elevated and tail floating directly backward; it progresses at about four or five miles an hour.

Feces of red fox. Adapted from Scott, 1943; 435.

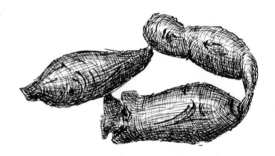

is within a radius of one mile, rarely extending to two or three miles.

The presence of a fox in a region, particularly if it has a den, can be detected by the initiated by the characteristic fox odor, and one experienced with foxes can usually determine from this odor whether the animal is a red fox or a gray fox. A red fox may occasionally be seen in broad daylight, and its inherent curiosity often makes

Noise making is not habitual with the red fox, and its principal sound is a rather high-pitched howl that consists of a few short yaps or barks followed by a long gurgling *ya—a—a—a—a—r*, and sometimes ending in a near scream or screech. When heard in the wilds on a still winter night this call has been described as "a long, loud, anguished, spine-tingling, hair-raising shriek of varied pitch and blood-curdling quality which tore the bitter cold night to shreds and left it shuddering" (Seagers, 1944: 13). There is considerable intercommunication among individuals, especially in the family, by soft low screeches or rolling whines, and in times of anger and fighting, shrill screams are employed. Odor posts where urine is deposited are used occasionally for intercommunication. "Examples of good scent posts in the study area were rocks, fence posts, mullen stalks, ends of logs, trunks of small apple or thornapple trees, ant hills, and small stumps" (Richards and Hine, 1953: 18). Signals apparently are not flashed. The animal sometimes acts as a sentry to protect its young. It is in no sense a gregarious or sociable animal, and seldom are two or three seen together except in a family group or when they have gathered at a food-concentration area. The red fox has a mild temper for a carnivore. It frequently plays, and, particularly at twilight or on moonlight nights, gambols and rolls, whimpers and chirrs, and chases other foxes in apparent fun. All of its senses are well developed, and it has especially acute sight, hearing, and smell. Its alertness, cunning, and curiosity are proverbial. One day in September, 1907, as I was walking among the sand dunes along the shore of Lake Michigan in Lake County, Illinois, a few miles south of Kenosha County, Wisconsin, I spied a red fox slowly following about 40 yards behind me. When I walked slower, it walked slower; when I stopped, it stopped, and sometimes tried to hide behind a shrub; when I retreated a few steps, it did likewise. We continued our game for more than 20 minutes, when it suddenly disappeared among the dunes. Southwest of Ellison Bay, Door County, on August 5, 1922, I saw a red fox being trailed by two dogs. The fox backtracked 20 or 30 feet, jumped 5 or 6 feet onto a rocky ledge, squatted into a flattened posture, watched the dogs run past to its right, then slowly meandered up the hill, occasionally glancing back over its shoulder to see if the disillusioned dogs would follow, which they did not. The normal longevity is probably less than 8 years, depending a great deal upon hunting and trapping pressure. The potential longevity is near 15 years.

The red fox is monogamous and is believed sometimes to remain mated for life. Coition usually takes place from the middle of January to the last of February, but rarely may occur as early as the last of December. The gestation period is about 53 days, and most of the kits, whelps, or pups are born between March 10 and April 20. There is normally only one litter each year, consisting of two to ten young, usually five or six. The mammae are eight, two pectoral, four abdominal, two inguinal. At birth the young are lightly covered with dull-gray fine hair but display the distinctive white tip to the tail. The eyes are closed for nine days after birth. Growth is fairly rapid, and when the pups are about three weeks old they play outside, particularly in the morning and evening. They are carefully watched by the parents, sometimes both father and mother guarding them, at other times only the male, or more often only the vixen. The youngsters are weaned when about two months old. Food is brought to the young by the parents, and often the bare front entrance to the den is scattered with remains of rabbits, mice, and other animals. The pups usually leave the den shortly after they are four months old, at which time they are nearly three-fourths grown and their permanent dentition is replacing the milk teeth. The youngster has become essentially mature when six months old, and may breed the following winter.

The breeding or family den is nearly always in a burrow, often the deserted hole of a woodchuck or some other animal, and is most frequently located in more open land such as a pasture, fence border, or even a cultivated field, sometimes in pastured brushland, but rarely deep in heavy woodland. Dens are more frequent on the higher slopes or the summits of hills than in lower valleys, and also appear to be more frequent in looser sandy and loamy soils than in heavy clay. The red fox is not a natural burrowing animal, but does sometimes dig its own burrow, and nearly always has to enlarge a pilfered burrow. The burrow ordinarily may be 15 or 20 feet long, and sometimes reaches a length of 40 feet or more, with the den at least 3 feet beneath the surface. The entrance is 12 to 15 inches high and 8 to 11 inches wide, and there are two or more to each den, usually opening in different directions, thus favoring safe exit of the fox from an enemy. The nest is merely a widening of the burrow lined with grass. Rarely, two vixens, each with a family, may occupy the same burrow. William G. Sheldon cites several instances in New York of two litters occupying the same den. "Pups of two sizes were observed at a den near Townsend, New York, on May 5, 1948. This den had 27 holes and the forest floor was smooth by fox activity. From the amount of sign so early in the spring it is likely that at least two litters occupied the den site. Several experienced trappers said they had never seen another den of such size and with so much 'sign' " (Sheldon, 1950: 36). Supplementary dens are made, and one may be occupied by a family driven from its former home. Infrequently, a red fox may make its den in a hole or cleft in a rocky ledge or cliff, or even under an abandoned building. During inclement weather, particularly if wet, a red fox may sleep in a den, but in pleasant weather it prefers a lair amongst long grass or brush in the open. The inside of the burrow is kept well cleaned of feces and food remnants, but the outside may be very messy.

Although there may be variation in the diet of the red fox in different areas and through individual food preferences, nevertheless anywhere in Wisconsin the dominant food is mammals, which on a yearly basis may run as high as 90 per cent, and rarely less than 50 per cent, of the food consumed. Of the mammals eaten by the red fox, the cottontail rabbit is most important and sometimes constitutes 60 per cent or more of the winter food and a considerable percentage of the summer diet. Many snowshoe rabbits are also eaten in regions where they abound. Mice of many species, but more especially meadow voles (*Microtus*), are consumed, sometimes constituting half of the food of the fox, particularly in the summer and fall. Other mammals eaten less frequently include the striped ground squirrel, chipmunk, woodchuck, fox squirrel, gray squirrel, porcupine, Norway rat, muskrat, skunk, weasel, opossum, mole, and shrew. It has been known to eat small pigs,

lambs, whitetail deer, and even domestic cats, but it is probable that such food in most cases was found as carrion. It does not relish shrews, and often leaves them untouched after killing them. Birds constitute a comparatively small portion of the food, being probably not more than 5 to 10 per cent on a yearly average. There is possibly little selection of birds on the part of the red fox, those available when the fox is hungry and cannot readily procure mammals being captured. Species that appear to be particularly vulnerable in Wisconsin include ground-feeding birds such as the redwing blackbird, cardinal, meadowlark, flicker, crow, catbird, mourning dove, bobwhite quail, pheasant, ruffed grouse, and domestic chicken. Some chickens may be picked up as carrion, especially during winter. Insects, particularly grasshoppers and beetles, are eaten, and rarely a snake or a frog. Fruit is eaten, such as June berry (*Amelanchier*), blueberry, mulberry, strawberry, gooseberry, plum, grape, apple, and wild black cherry; a few acorns and hickory nuts are consumed, and considerable corn and a trifling amount of other grains are eaten. The red fox hunts by stealthy approach, creeping low, stopping to stretch its head high to peek and sight its prey, then pouncing with forefeet on the mouse, rabbit, or other prey, and biting it back of the head if it be large or merely nipping or nosing it if it be small, before consumption. It never runs its prey any distance, and rarely waits by a trail for its prey unless it senses its presence nearby. It seems to prefer as food the forequarters and body of its larger victims, and has small liking for the hindquarters, which it often buries lightly in the soil as it does other surplus food. It frequently drinks from pools or other standing water, lapping the water dog-fashion. Occasionally it washes itself by licking its fur, but performs most of its cleaning by rolling in sand or dust.

The red fox has few natural enemies in Wisconsin. Occasionally a coyote may catch one, and formerly the timber wolf and lynx, and possibly also the fisher and wolverine, when more were in the state, captured a red fox now and then. A few are known to die from the effects of quills of porcupines they have tried to devour. Many are trapped, both for fur and riddance purposes, but the fashion trends for platinum, silver, and other trade-color mutants of foxes reared in captivity reduces the trapping pressure on wild red foxes. Fox hunting is good sport, but is not one of the favored pastimes in Wisconsin. Never in this state do we have the organized fox chase, with its gaily attired hunters and barking hounds, that was originated in Europe and is now sometimes held in the eastern United States. In that we are fortunate. Very rarely is a red fox killed by an automobile, or by other accidental means.

External parasites known to infest the red fox include the louse *Felicola vulpis*; the mites *Otodectes cynotis* (the troublesome ear mite) and *Sarcoptes scabei* (the mange mite); the ticks *Ixodes hexagonus* and *I. marxi;* and the fleas *Ctenocephalides canis, Hoplopsyllus affinis, Pulex irritans, Cediopsylla simplex, Oropsylla arctomys,* and *Megabothris wagneri.* Internal parasites found in the red fox are many, 11 species of trematodes or flukes, 6 species of cestodes or tapeworms, and 17 species of nematodes or roundworms being reported by Erickson (1944: 366–67). A flagellate protozoan of the genus *Trichomonas* has also been reported (Morgan, 1944). Besides parasites, many of which cause disease, the red fox in the wild is reported to have died from septicemia, tularemia, a distemper-like disease, and rabies. To rabies it is highly susceptible, and there are records of fox rabies epizootics for many states. Referring to Wisconsin, Richards and Hine wrote, "there have been two 'highs' in the incidence of rabies in the state since 1918, the first occurring in 1928 and the second in 1940, and the trend is again rising. The two periods of peak fox populations occurred during years in which there was a very low incidence of rabies" (Richards and Hine, 1953).

Although often severely condemned and popularly disliked, particularly by farmers, the red fox is more of an economic asset than a liability. It destroys vast numbers of mice, supplies fur of considerable value, offers recreation in fox hunting and trapping, and is an interesting bit of life on the landscape. The fur is used chiefly for collars, neckpieces, and trimmings, often for capes and throws, and sometimes for coats. The normally colored wild red fox has a much lower value as fur than the mutant cross, black, and

silver types which are reared in captivity, and which in the highly developed "platinums" and other types have brought fantastic prices of several thousand dollars a pelt. Prices and sales depend greatly on demands controlled by whims of fashion, and the once flourishing fox-raising industry of the state is not now doing so well because of fashion trends towards mink and other furs. This low market value of fox pelts has also in effect lowered the take of wild red foxes in the state, which reduction, however, may have been offset in part by bounties paid by state and county.

It is important to point out that although a higher bounty resulted in a higher kill in Wisconsin, the bounty was not essential to insure a harvest of foxes. In Wisconsin foxes have been taken in considerable numbers without a bounty, even when fur prices were low. . . . However, at the present time, the red fox population has remained at a high level following peak densities in 1944–45. The annual harvest of foxes in Wisconsin is apparently removing only the annual surplus (Richards and Hine, 1953: 67, 71).

In some years of high fox fur prices the value of sales from both trapped and ranch-reared foxes in the state has been upward of one million dollars annually.

In times of low mouse or rabbit populations, or of high red fox population, an individual fox may resort to preying upon domestic animals, particularly chickens, occasionally a lamb. Sometimes even when other food is plentiful, a "renegade" fox may prey on chickens or other domestic animals. Such individuals are seldom numerous, and can usually be controlled by trapping or hunting. The red fox is clever but may be trapped in water, den, or baited sets if carefully concealed and free from human odors. "Killer of game" is a charge brought against the red fox, yet the effect of red fox predation on game animals is negligible. The red fox is highly susceptible to rabies, and has been condemned as a carrier of this disease, yet any warm-blooded animal is susceptible. To endeavor extensively to hunt foxes to wipe out the disease tends only to spread it. The primary vectors are dogs and cats, and the first "clean-up" should be made on feral and stray dogs and cats, followed by vaccination of all others.

Specimens examined from Wisconsin.—Total 42, as follows: *Ashland County:* Butternut, 1 (UWZ). *Bayfield County:* Drummond, 1 (UWZ). *Columbia County:* Cambria, 1 (UWZ). *Dane County:* Madison, 1 (UWZ); western Dane County, 5 (UWZ). *Dodge County:* Burnett Corners, 1 (UWZ). *Door County:* Baileys Harbor (near), 1 (UWZ); Fish Creek, 3 (1 NPM; 2 UWZ); Liberty Grove, 1 (UWZ); Peninsula State Park, 2 (UWZ). *Dunn County:* Colfax, 3 (UWZ). *Eau Claire County:* No locality, 1. *Forest County:* Crandon, 1. *Green Lake County:* Manchester, 1 (UWZ). *Iron County:* Mercer, 2 (UWZ). *Langlade County:* T 34 N, R 11 E, 2 (UWZ). *Oconto County:* Kelley Brook, 5 (MM). *Rock County:* Milton, 2 (UWZ). *Saint Croix County:* No locality, 1. *Sauk County:* Baraboo, 3 (UWZ). *Vilas County:* Eagle River, 2. *Walworth County:* Delavan, 2.

Selected references.—Garlough, F. E., 1945; Hine, R. L., 1953; Murie, A., 1936; Richards, S. H., and R. L. Hine, 1953; Scott, T. G., 1947, and Seagears, C. B., 1944.

Genus **Urocyon** Baird
Gray Foxes

Dental formula:

$$I\frac{3-3}{3-3}, \quad C\frac{1-1}{1-1}, \quad P\frac{4-4}{4-4}, \quad M\frac{2-2}{3-3}=42.$$

Urocyon cinereoargenteus ocythous Bangs
Wisconsin Gray Fox

Urocyon cinereoargenteus ocythous Bangs, Proc. New England Zool. Club, vol. 1, p. 43, June 5, 1899.

Vulpes Virginianus Lapham, p. 339, 1853; Strong, p. 436, 1883.

Urocyon cinereoargenteus ocythous Jackson, p. 26, 1908; Hollister, p. 140, 1909; Hollister, p. 27, 1910, Jackson, p. 89, 1910; Cory, p. 303, 1912; Barger, p. 11, 1952.

Urocyon cinereoargenteus Komarek, p. 205, 1932.

Urocyon cinereoargenteus cinereoargenteus [printer's error for *Urocyon cinereoargenteus cinereoargenteus*] Barger, p. 11, 1952.

Vernacular names.—Gray fox, maned fox, southern fox, tree fox, virgin fox, Virginia fox, and wood fox.

Identification marks.—The gray fox averages slightly shorter in total length than the red fox, but being a little more robust in body may weigh as much or slightly more; head a trifle shorter and broader than in *Vulpes*, and legs and feet somewhat shorter; ear prominent, erect; eye moderate in size, the pupil elliptical; nose point-

Wisconsin gray fox. Courtesy Wisconsin Conservation Department.

ed, but somewhat shorter than in red fox; tail bushy, tipped with blackish, a distinct mane of short bristles or stiff hairs down the median dorsal surface, particularly prominent in the middle third; claws medium; fur dense, but coarser than that of red fox.

Color of upper parts from forehead to rump grizzled; individual guard hairs tipped black or whitish, the black tipped subterminably whitish, and the whitish in either case bordered below by black which may continue to base of hair or in most cases assume buffy color of underfur; nose blackish above, a strip of blackish extending around eye rims; upper side of ear ferruginous, the lower (inner) side near white; upper part of tail basally like back, the black dominating

on the apical three-fourths in long hairs that suggest a black mane, and terminating in a black tip; lower chest and flanks, region of vent, under side of tail, and inner side of hind leg, tawny; chest and abdomen distinctly whitish in median

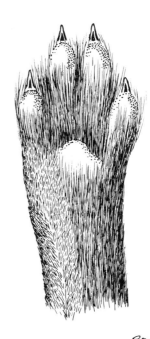

Left hind foot of gray fox, UROCYON C. OCYTHOUS. 1×.

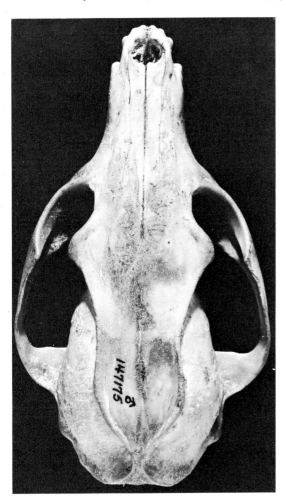

Skull of UROCYON C. OCYTHOUS, *Delavan, Wisconsin.*

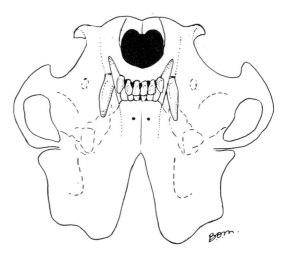

Anterior view of skull of gray fox, from Delavan, Wisconsin. 1×.

parts; side of neck from under ear to foreleg and band across lower throat rather deep ferruginous or reddish brown; under side of nose, lower lip, lower side of cheek, and throat near white; upper lip and chin near black. There is no seasonal variation in color. One annual molt occurs over a rather prolonged period in summer.

The skull is low, moderately slender (ratio of length to breadth about 7:4), less than 130 mm. long, flat; postorbital process short, but rather heavy, with pronounced longitudinal depression on interior dorsal surface; rostrum short, moderately heavy, scarcely depressed below frontal and occipital region; maxillary short, about even with end of nasal posteriorly; nasal short, the length less than 45 mm.; no or very short sagittal crest developed posteriorly, the temporal ridges well developed and forming a conspicuous U or lyrate form, the open end anterior; audital bullae prominent, relatively rather short and broad, the ratio of length to width about 8:7 (in *Vulpes* about 10:7); teeth relatively small, the upper incisors not lobed.

The only sexual variation is that males average slightly larger than females (up to about 10 per cent in weight). Color pattern appears clearly in the young as soon as the guard hairs develop, the very young being less marked in their soft plumbeous underfur. Color mutations are rare in *Urocyon*, though black variants have been recorded (Jones, S. V. H., 1923: 174).

The gray fox can readily be separated from the red fox by the distinctive grizzled color of the upper parts, the reddish legs and feet, the black tip to the tail, and the distinctive black mane on the upper part of the tail. The skull of the gray fox is distinguished from that of *Vulpes* and all other Wisconsin canids by the lyrate form of the temporal ridges; the upper incisors are not lobed as in *Vulpes*. Smaller size alone will distinguish the gray fox from either the wolf or the coyote, each of which has a black tip to the tail. All specimens of *Urocyon* from Wisconsin are referred to *Urocyon cinereoargenteus ocythous*, there seeming to be no trenchant differences among those from southeastern Wisconsin, those from near Platteville, the type-locality, and those from the upper Mississippi Valley. I have examined the type-specimen of *ocythous* in the Museum of Comparative Zoology, Harvard University, Cambridge, Massachusetts, and it ap-

pears to be greatly faded and paler than other specimens I have examined and not a true representative of the color of this subspecies.

Measurements.—Total length of adults, 950 to 1,040 mm. (37.3 to 40.9 in.); tail, 310 to 390 mm. (12.2 to 15.3 in.); hind foot, 130 to 145 mm. (5.1 to 5.7 in.). Weight of adult, 10 to 14 pounds, rarely to 15.5 pounds. Skull length, 119.1 to 128.9 mm.; width, 65.9 to 73.8 mm.

Distribution in Wisconsin.—Entire state in favorable habitats; most plentiful in southwestern counties bordering the Mississippi and lower Wisconsin rivers, less common easterly and centrally in the state; scarce in extreme northern and northeastern Wisconsin, where it has probably ingressed in recent years.

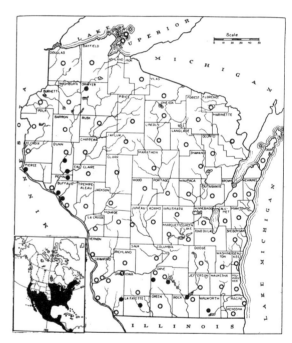

Map 57. *Distribution of* Urocyon cinereoargenteus.
● = *specimens examined.* ○ = *authentic records.*

Habitat.—Hardwood or mixed hardwood-coniferous forests, brushlands, and dense weed patches, particularly in rough, hilly terrain; sometimes in heavy woods on bottomlands; favors vicinity of streams and lakes.

Status and Habits.—The distribution of the gray fox in Wisconsin in the early part of the nineteenth century is not clear, but the species probably then occurred in woodlands in the southern part of the state. In a bill of sale of pelts of Jac Porlier sold by Jean Baptiste Berthelot to Mons Pothier at Green Bay on July 11, 1814, is listed one "virgin fox" (also five red foxes), which probably did not come from near Green Bay but from the vicinity of Prairie du Chien, where Berthelot also maintained a post. The pelt may or may not have been from a gray fox. The species occurred at Racine about 1850 (Lapham, 1853: 339) and later near Milton, where I saw pelts in 1895; the type-specimen was collected in Grant County, January 25, 1896. Many reports and records were made during the years 1900 to 1910 from parts of the state that would indicate its range at that time covered its present areas of denser population along the Mississippi and Wisconsin rivers, as well as southeastern Wisconsin. During the last 50 years there seems to have been a tendency for the gray fox to invade the northern part of the state, yet in all parts north of a line from southwest Douglas County to Sheboygan County it is still not common. The gray fox is somewhat cyclic in population density, reaching a peak about once in ten years. Even in those parts of the state where it is most abundant, it is outnumbered by the red fox, and the total population in the state might be some seventy-five thousand in high years. The gray fox may attain a population density of three or four to a square mile. Its home range ordinarily is less than that of the red fox, seldom being more than a mile in diameter, and often half that distance.

Not having the curiosity of the red fox to watch or follow every newcomer into its haunts, or perhaps being more secretive in its curiosity, the gray fox is less often observed in the wild than the red fox. It can be called by one's squeaking like a mouse, and there are several records of its being decoyed by a crow call. The tracks of the gray fox are shorter and relatively broader than those of the red fox, and are closer spaced. They are similar to tracks made by a large house cat, except that they are larger and the claw marks show. The feces in most cases are difficult to distinguish from those of the red fox, but usually are heavier and more creased into adhesive individual pellets.

Although the gray fox is chiefly a night prowler, starting activities at twilight and continuing

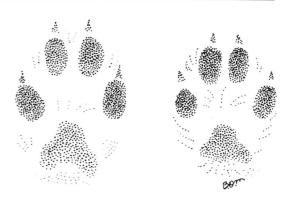

Tracks of gray fox. Left, right fore foot. Right, right hind foot. 1×.

until dawn, it frequently is out during the day, often in full sunlight. Ordinarily, though, it sleeps concealed in a hollow tree or log or other den or cover during the daytime, and is most active the first half of the night. It is active both summer and winter, though seemingly preferring warmer weather, as one might surmise from its southern origin. Its usual gait is the proverbial "fox trot," though sometimes under strain it will gallop rather clumsily. It may attain a speed of 28 miles an hour, but 18 or 20 miles is more normal, and it cannot continue such speed for more than an hour or so. It is the only Wisconsin mammal of the dog tribe that regularly climbs trees. Not only does it jump upon limbs of low-hung trees and hop from branch to branch as it ascends, but it is also known to "shin up" or climb cat-fashion for 20 feet trees with limbless trunks a foot in diameter, and then hop from limb to limb to 40 feet elevation, either to escape enemies or capture prey. It swims rather clumsily, dog-fashion, with nose somewhat raised and tail afloat, but is rarely seen in water.

Apparently the gray fox does less yapping and barking than the red fox, and its call is less sonorous, lower pitched, and not so loud, though in some respects similar. It utters at times a purring grunt when contented, but on the whole seems to be a rather quiet animal. It urinates on weeds, rocks, tree trunks, and other objects to create scent posts as a means of communication to its kin, but does not stand sentry duty nor flash signals. In disposition it appears to be a little surly, and it is not a playful animal. It is muscular and strong, quick in action, yet not endowed with great endurance. Its eyes, nose, and ears function well. Its potential longevity is 14 years or more, its normal in the wild probably less than 6 years, and in captivity in zoological parks it usually lives less than 8 years.

Mating usually takes place from the middle of February to the last of March, and after a gestation period of about 51 days the three to five blind and near naked young are born. The kit's eyes open when it is nine days old, and the fuzzy fur soon appears. The mother apparently tends the youngsters alone until they are about two or three weeks old, when the male may bring some food for the family. When about three months old, the cubs begin to hunt for themselves, but the family remains more or less together until autumn, when the young are nearly full grown. The mammae are eight, two pectoral, two abdominal, and four inguinal.

The home of the gray fox is a den concealed in brushland or woodland, and may be in or under a hollow log or stump, in the base of a hollow tree, in a natural crevice among rocks, rarely in a burrow under a stump or rock pile, and very rarely if ever in a burrow in an exposed field or meadow. A den containing four young in a discarded milk can has been described in Pennsylvania in the year 1943. A scant nest is composed of leaves, grass, fur, and any available soft material scratched together by the fox. There is little evidence of sanitation around the den, though usually the entrance is not so messed with bones and waste food as in the case of the red fox, and the entrance is more direct and without the play platform. Winter protection or shelter from an enemy may be sought in any convenient hollow log, stump, or tree, or in a hole among rocks.

The gray fox, though primarily carnivorous, has a varied diet that includes some fleshy fruits, corn, and acorns along with the more favored rabbits, rodents, insects, and a very few birds. Winter food shows an increase in the percentage of rabbits and mice eaten, whereas late in spring and in summer more insects and berries appear in the diet, though even in winter many larval insects are consumed and fallen apples and acorns are frequently eaten. Weasels and some other species of mammals are killed and not always eaten (Latham, 1952). Food items found in the stomachs of 55 gray foxes taken between December 22, 1930, and March 17, 1931, and between December 14, 1931, and February 16, 1932, mostly in Wisconsin but partly in Iowa, were, in frequency of occurrence: cottontail, 80 per cent; meadow mouse, 18 per cent; apple, 16 per cent; domestic chicken, 11 per cent; deer mouse, 9 per cent; mouse and carrion, 4 per cent each; woodchuck, fox squirrel, muskrat, unidentified mammal, ruffed grouse, bobwhite, blue jay, small bird, grapes, and haw berry, 2 per cent each (Errington, 1935: 193). Prey remains found at 18 gray fox dens, April to July, 1948, in Wisconsin were in frequency of occurrence: cottontail, 78 per cent; mole (*Scalopus*), 40 per cent; catbird and unidentified song birds, 33 per cent each; ruffed grouse, 28 per cent; woodchuck, 22 per cent; fox squirrel, chipmunk (*Tamias*), domestic chicken, and flicker, 11 per cent each; skunk (*Mephitis*), gray squirrel, deer mouse, Norway rat, pheasant, and redwing blackbird, 6 per cent each (Richards and Hine, 1953: 46). The gray fox also sometimes molests eggs of ruffed grouse, bobwhite, and other ground nesting birds, often eating the entire clutch (Nelson and Handley, 1938: 78). Unwanted food items may be left with little concealment, and so far as known food is never hidden or covered for storage. The gray fox drinks frequently, lapping water like a dog. It seldom bathes, instead wallowing in sand, dust, grass, or leaves to keep clean or relieve skin irritation, though it frequently licks itself.

Very few predators molest the adult gray fox, and man usually only destroys it as a suspected pest or for its rather low-value fur. The bobcat, coyote, great horned owl, and possibly some of the larger hawks prey on the cubs when the chance is offered. Practically none are killed by automobiles. It is subject to tularemia, and seems to have rabies more than the red fox.

External parasites of the gray fox include the louse *Felicola quadraticeps*; the ticks *Ixodes cookei*, *I. ricinus*, and *I. scapularis*; the fleas *Oropsylla simplex*, *O. arctomys*, *Ctenocephalides felis*, *C. canis*, *Echidnophaga gallinacea*, and *Pulex irritans*; and rarely the ear mite *Otodectes cyanotis*. Among the internal parasites reported are the fluke *Alaria arisaemoides*; the tapeworms *Diphyllobothrium latum*, *Mesocestoides litteratus*, *M. variabilis*, *Multiceps serialis*, *Taenia pisiformis*, and *T. serrata*; the roundworms *Ancylostoma caninum, Crenosoma vulpis, Physaloptera prae-putialis, Spirocerca lupi,* and *Toxocara leonina*; and the thorny-headed worm *Pachysentis canicola.*

The gray fox on the whole is not a bad citizen in Wisconsin. It is a good mouser and an interesting mammal. Its fur is not highly esteemed, being shorter and less elegant and lustrous than that of the red fox, though actually it wears as well and the hide is stronger. The pelt of a gray fox usually sells for about half the price of an ordinary red fox pelt, or about one or two dollars, rarely as high as four dollars. In total annual cash value to the state, even including a questionable credit of monies paid for bounty, the gray fox does not rate high. Its value is mostly intangible. On the debit side it does some damage to game and a little to poultry; "cottontails and grouse, for example, were taken more frequently by gray than by red foxes. . . . though considerable predation by . . . gray foxes occurred

on certain prey species, there was no evidence that prey populations suffered" (Richards and Hine, 1953: 56). It is more of a wildwood species than the red fox, and thus probably comes less frequently in contact with domestic animals. When one does become a pest, it is more easily trapped than the red fox, and can be eliminated. Rabies is sometimes carried by the gray fox, but killing foxes has little effect on rabies prevention.

Specimens examined from Wisconsin.—Total 19, as follows: *Buffalo County:* Alma, 2; Wabasha Flats, 2. *Dane County:* Madison, 2 (UWZ); western Dane County, 2 (UWZ). *Dunn County:* Menomonie, 1 (UWZ); Meridean, 2 (1 JNC; 1 UWZ). *Pepin County:* Lima, 1 (UWZ). *Pierce County:* Prescott, 1 (MM). *Lafayette County:* Darlington, 2 (UWZ). *Rock County:* Edgerton, 1 (UWZ). *Sawyer County:* Hayward, 1 (CAS). *Walworth County:* Delavan, 2.

Selected references.—Bangs, O., 1899; Chaddock, T. T., 1939; Garlough, F. E., 1945; Nelson, A.L., and C. O. Handley, 1938; Richards, S. H., and R. L. Hine, 1953; and Seagears, C. B., 1944.

Family **Ursidae**
Bears

Members of the family Ursidae occur in Europe, Asia, North America, and northern South America. It contains eight living genera, one of which occurs in Wisconsin.

Genus **Euarctos** Gray
Black Bears

Dental formula:

$$I\frac{3-3}{3-3}, \quad C\frac{1-1}{1-1}, \quad P\frac{4-4}{4-4}, \quad M\frac{2-2}{3-3}=42.$$

Euarctos americanus americanus (Pallas)
Black Bear

Ursus americanus Pallas, Spicilegia Zoologica, fasc. 14, p. 5, 1780.
Ursus Americanus Lapham, p. 43, 1852; Lapham, p. 338, 1853; Strong, p. 437, 1883.
Ursus cinnamonum Strong, p. 437, 1883.
Ursus americanus Snyder, p. 126, 1902; Jackson, p. 30, 1908; Hollister, p. 29, 1910; Jackson, p. 89, 1910; Cory, p. 397, 1912.
Euarctos americanus Komarek, p. 206, 1932.
Euarctos americanus americanus Barger, p. 10, 1952.

Vernacular names.—American black bear, bear, brown bear (for brown color-phase), bruin (Dutch adjective from brown), bruno, cinnamon bear (for tawny color-phase), common black

bear, cranberry bear, cub (usually applied to young), *mu-ko* (Potawatomi), *muk-wa* (Chippewa), sun bear or yellow bear (for cinnamon color-phase).

Identification marks.—The largest carnivore now found in Wisconsin and one of the largest Wisconsin mammals, being exceeded in size only by some of the larger hoofed animals, the black bear is so familiar as to scarcely need description. About the size of a huge hog but more rangy, it is a bulky, thick-set, massive mammal; moderate-sized head with facial profile rather straight and but slightly curved; ears prominent and rounded; eyes small; nose tapering, with broad rhinarium and large nostrils; tail exceedingly short, inconspicuous, well haired; feet broad and plantigrade, five-toed; claws relatively short for a bear, the front ones much curved; fur harsh and coarse.

The general normal color both above and below is black or very dark brown, except for a cinnamon-brown patch across the muzzle, and sometimes a white blotch on the throat. The spring fur later may become somewhat faded and raggy. Molting occurs in April or May, new fur being sometimes fully acquired by the mid-

Bruin stands to take a look, Minnesota.

as molar in front of it; upper carnassial (PM⁴) smaller than first molar, with a broad crown dividing elongated cusps, lacks inner tubercle and its supporting root; other three upper premolars small, single rooted, and inconspicuous, may be deciduous; canine teeth heavy, 17 mm. or more in antero-posterior diameter at basal enamel line.

The male bear averages considerably larger than the female, the difference being fully 10 per cent by weight. Sexual difference is also shown in the size of the skull and in the tendency to more angularity in the skulls of males. There is little variation in the color of the animal as age advances, but the skull and teeth show distinct changes. The black bear does not reach full maturity until the sixth year, during which there are changes in the skull and dentition; at this age

Skull of Euarctos a. americanus, *Bayfield County, Wisconsin.* ⅖×.

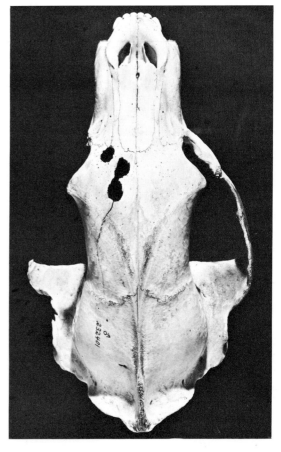

dle of June. September or October sees the bear in its full fresh coat, much darker than the worn spring coat, and in Wisconsin usually glossy black.

The skull is large—largest and widest of Wisconsin carnivores; upper profile gently rounded, the frontal region not sharply depressed, but rather flattened; audital bullae inconspicuous, flat and depressed, little inflated; nares large, exposing well-developed turbinate bones; lower jaw short and moderately heavy. Teeth not so trenchant as those of other carnivores (except *Procyon*), but have rather blunt crowns, the true molars with broad tuberculate crowns; length of last upper molar about one and one-half times width, and about one and one-half times as long the frontal region of the skull has reached its maximum of bulging, and thereafter it becomes more flattened and the sagittal more developed. Bears in their second year still show some of the milk dentition, the permanent dentition being fully acquired at two years of age. Considerable individual variation is displayed in the teeth, particularly in the number and relation of the accessory cusps and the shape and proportions of the upper and lower fourth premolars and the last upper molar. The brown and the cinnamon color phases of the black bear, though not common in Wisconsin, frequently occur in the northwestern United States. Cubs representing all three color phases—black, brown, and cinnamon—have occurred in the same litter, and each retains its general coloration through life. There is a record for Assiniboine River, Canada, of "an old she bear that was perfectly white," and which had four cubs, "one white, with red eyes, and red nails, like herself; one red [brown ?], and

two black" (Stanley, P. C., 1921: 74). There is also a record of white spotting in the black bear.

The black bear is so distinctive both in flesh and in skull as to need critical comparison with no other Wisconsin mammal.

Measurements.—Total length, adult males, 1,375 to 1,780 mm. (54 to 70 in.); tail, 90 to 125 mm. (3.5 to 5 in.); hind foot, 215 to 280 mm. (8.5 to 11 in.). Weight, adult males, 250 to 500 pounds, rarely 600 pounds or more, normally 300 to 400 pounds. Skull, adult males, length, 270 to 298 mm.; width, 158 to 185 mm. Total length, adult females, 1,270 to 1,475 mm. (50 to 58 in.); tail, 80 to 115 mm. (3 to 4.5 in.); hind foot, 190 to 240 mm. (7.5 to 9.5 in.). Weight, adult females, 225 to 450 pounds. Skull, adult females, length, 255 to 285 mm.; width, 148 to 172 mm.

Distribution in Wisconsin.—In early days (about the year 1840) found in every county in

Left hind foot of black bear. ½×.

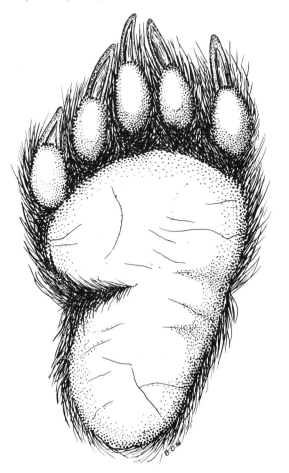

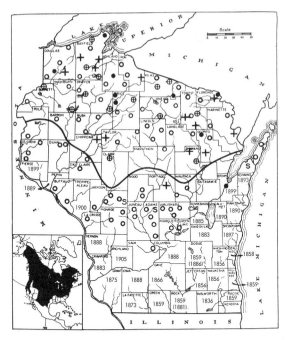

Map 58. *Distribution of* EUARCTOS AMERICANUS. ● = *specimens examined.* ○ = *authentic records since 1935.* + = *authentic records between 1915 and 1935.* S = *a few bears were stocked. Year* = *last general appearance in the county. (Year)* = *last appearance of stray or wanderer in the county. Southern limit of present range in Wisconsin indicated by solid line. Information from many sources including Wisconsin Conservation Department.*

the state, though less frequently in the regions of the prairie and oak openings of the southern counties. Now confined chiefly to the northern third of the state west of the mouth of Green Bay, rarely straggling as far south as northern Sauk County in central Wisconsin.

Habitat.—Heavily wooded areas and dense brushland, particularly if partly of deciduous species.

Status and Habits.—The black bear maintained a dwindling population as settlement progressed in the state and was extirpated in the extreme southeastern counties by the year 1860. In central and western parts of southern Wisconsin it continued until the late 1880's or 1890's, and in some regions (Sauk and Richland counties) until well after 1900. Human pressure such as excessive hunting and general prejudice against bears was chiefly responsible for their disappearance, though their early absence from the southern counties may have been on account of low population in their original numbers. Within a few miles of the early fur post of Green Bay, where bears had been continuously hunted, they existed occasionally until as late as 1899. They vanished from Door Peninsula only a year or two later, but have since been replaced in small numbers by cubs released in Door County in 1942 by the State Conservation Department. Between 1937 and 1942 black bears were also liberated in Adams, Jackson, and Wood coounties, but not all, if any, of the recent records for bears in central Wisconsin can be attributed to these transplants. Black bears have fluctuated in numbers in their main range in Wisconsin, and locally at times have become quite numerous. Their general trend, however, was to decline in numbers until they reached a low about the year 1915. Legal protection through a closed season, enacted first in 1917, permitting hunting only from November 11 to 30, and better control of forest fires, allowed the bears to increase until now there are probably at least three or four thousand in the state. With this recent increase in population of bears in their main range, there was also an expansion of their range southward in the state, so that some areas void of black bears for a number of years now are inhabited by them. Bears tend to wander considerable distances, and individuals, particularly males, have a normal range from their homes of ten or more miles,

Black bear in good blueberry brushland, Minnesota. Photograph by Christiansen Studio.

and may cover an area of five or six hundred square miles. A female with cubs normally may range at least four or five miles from her home site. There is some evidence of old bears wandering distances up to 80 miles or possibly more from their established range. The early history of the black bear in Wisconsin has been studied by A. W. Schorger (1949 a), and the recent status of the species in the state by W. E. Scott (1947 c).

Being wary and timid, and as a rule solitary except for the mother with her cubs, the black bear is seldom seen in the wild. Around campsites and cabins in the woods it may make itself known by nightly visits to garbage cans or other food supplies. Wherever it goes it leaves large tracks, quite similar to those of a chubby barefooted boy, but wide through the toes and usually showing claw marks. Such tracks are clearly distinctive when made in snow, mud, or wet sand, but in other surfaces may be hard to distinguish. Where bears have been some time resident they make trails and paths through the forest to and from their feeding places. Overturned logs, diggings around trees and stumps, and the mauling of berry patches often indicate to the trained eye where bears have been. Gnawings and claw marks on trees, most conspicuous on aspens and birches, are indicators of bear inhabitants. Some of these claw marks are made when the bears climb the trees, but others are made by them when standing on their hind feet and reaching up to claw. Such clawed trees are sometimes called measuring trees. Experienced woodsmen can also detect the presence of a bear by identifying its dung.

Although nocturnal in habits, the black bear usually does not wait for full darkness before it leaves its lair, but sallies forth as soon as the sun begins to set and remains out until near daylight. Sometimes it ventures forth in full daylight. It travels at least a half mile from its home before foraging, and more often goes several miles. Most of its regular activities occur during some eight months between the middle of March and the end of November. From about the last of November or sometime in December, the bear dozes in a dormant or semidormant condition until well into March or April. Winter life is solitary except when a female and its cubs stay together. It does not truly hibernate in the physiological sense where metabolism and body temperature drop to a low level, and the heartbeat and respiration become greatly slowed. It is rare indeed that a bear cannot easily be aroused from its winter slumbers, though it may act very drowsy. A bear may alter its position several times during a winter. Ordinary conversation seldom disturbs it. Its sleepiness should not be trusted too far, however, for if prodded or tormented, it may become very pugnacious. There are records of bears wandering about in cold midwinter weather, but it seems probable that such animals were insufficiently nourished when they went to sleep. Such an animal may even establish a new home. Usually by the last of November the bear has fed so bounteously that it is heavy with fat, and for several days preceding its winter sleep it may not eat. The winter bed is just large enough snugly to accommodate its incumbent, that of an adult bear being about four feet in diameter. These winter dens are usually dug under an overturned tree, most often at the roots. The cavity is shallow and lined with leaves, moss, and bark. Often other sites are selected for the winter den, such as a sheltered cave in rocks, a hollow tree or stump, a dense thicket, or a stand of small conifers. Generally the animal is exposed and be-

comes partly covered with snow. When the bear awakes in the spring and wanders forth it nearly always has an excellent fur coat and appears well nourished. In fact, it may not show a tendency to eat heavily for several days. Sometimes, however, a bear that was in poor condition in the fall emerges from its sleep ragged, thin, and hungry.

The bear walks with a deliberate lumbering gait, toes inward and soles flat on the ground, and with much side-swinging of head and body. Its progression is more rapid than it appears. It runs with a gallop, and normally will travel about 32 miles an hour for short distances. It is claimed, however, that a badly frightened pursued black bear may in one hour be 35 miles from the spot where first sighted or disturbed. It frequently stands erect on its hind feet, particularly for observation purposes, and can walk several steps in this position. It climbs well and with surprising speed, beginning its ascent by standing full length at the base of the tree, then reaches high with its forefeet and grasps the tree with claws and legs in a series of bounds. Smaller saplings it cannot master as a rule. It is a good swimmer and seems to enjoy water.

Like most animals of solitary habits, it has no regular call notes. It bellows and bawls when in pain, and growls at other bears or other animals when things are not to its liking. A mother is frequently communicating with her cubs by voice signals. She warns them of danger by a loud "woof-woof," and calls them by a peculiar whimpering sound. When inquisitive, she will rise on her haunches, sniff loudly, and look, and

Black bear in winter lethargy, sufficiently awake to have eyes open. Courtesy Wisconsin Conservation Department.

soon her cubs learn to take the same precaution. The cubs, when nursing and often when asleep, utter a doleful whimpering or moaning sound which probably has some significance to the mother. Bears give no flash signals, have no odor posts, and place no sentries. Their clawings and rubbings on trees are construed by some to be challenge or warning signals to other bears.

Black bear tracks in light snow. Courtesy National Park Service.

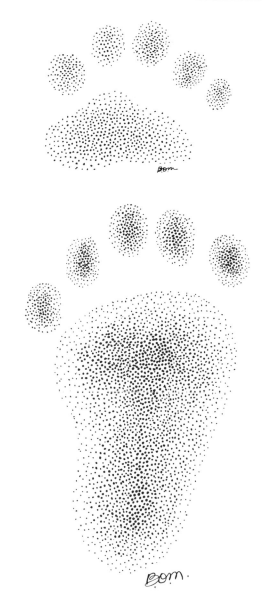

Tracks of black bear. Above, right fore foot. Below, right hind foot. About ½×.

The black bear is by nature a solitary animal, though occasionally a number may be seen together, particularly during the mating season or when a mother is with her young. On the whole, its animal disposition is calm, and it goes about its affairs attending pretty much to its own. As a rule it is not friendly with its kind, and members of the same sex, whether male or female, will usually engage in dispute, if not combat. It also dislikes interference from other animals, yet at times breaks from its routine and seems actually to play with members of other species. Almost invariably a black bear flees from a human being and disappears, often unsuspected by the intruder. Records anywhere of its unprovoked attack on a human are rare. One such occurred

July 7, 1948, at Mission Hill in the Marquette National Forest, 30 miles northwest of Sault Ste Marie, Michigan, when a bear seized a three-year-old girl, the daughter of a forest ranger, while she was playing on the back steps of a lookout cabin, and dragged her body five hundred feet into the woods. The child apparently died instantly. The bear was shot shortly thereafter, and appeared to be in normal health except that it was very thin. There may have been extenuating circumstances in this case that caused such unusual actions by the bear (Whitlock, 1950). In contrast to this is a newspaper item from Amberg, Marinette County, Wisconsin. "Margaret, 8-year-old daughter of Mr. and Mrs. George Frisque, while on her way to school encountered a large bear a short distance from her home. The bear ambled off into the swamp when she screamed" (*Journal-Telephone*, Milton, Wisconsin, May 20, 1926).

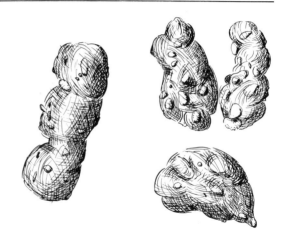

Feces of black bear. About ¾ ×.

Black bear cub. Courtesy Wisconsin Conservation Department.

The cubs are very playful, not only individually and among themselves, but with their mother, who frequently plays with her offspring, but gives one a lusty cuff with her forepaw when it gets obstreperous. In appearance soft and flabby, the bear nevertheless is strong and powerful, especially in its limbs and shoulders. Its sight is poor, and hearing only moderately acute. Its sense of smell is highly developed, the mass of turbinate bones in its nasal cavity offering extensive surface for the olfactory nerve endings. The potential longevity of the black bear is near 30 years. Normal longevity or life expectancy is relatively high, probably near 25 years. Black bears not infrequently have survived in zoological parks for more than 20 years.

Mating occurs in June or early in July, and since the black bear is not sexually mature until

Bear Cub. Photograph by Dean Tvedt. Courtesy Wisconsin Conservation Department.

three years old its first mating comes at approximately three and one-half years of age. Black bears normally breed only every other year. The gestation period is about 225 days, and the young are born in January or early in February, while the mother is still in her winter sleepiness. Two young is the most frequent number in a litter, three almost as often, one in about one litter out of seven, four in about 10 per cent of the litters, and five exceedingly rare. Schorger mentions one record of six in a litter from near Peshtigo, Wisconsin, and gives the average number of cubs per litter as 2.4 from records of 284 litters taken from Wisconsin newspapers (Schorger, 1949 a: 165). At birth the young one is about six to eight inches long, weight 7 to 12 ounces, has eyes closed, and is covered so sparingly with a fine but stiff hair that it is essentially naked. The first few days after birth it develops slowly, but if sufficiently nourished by the mother, growth thereafter is rapid. In about 25 days the eyes open and the baby is covered with short fuzzy hair with a faint brownish cast, even though the youngster may be destined to be a black adult. The mother is very attentive to her young and fights gallantly for their protection. When too disturbed, she often moves her cubs to a new location, carrying each by the nape of the neck. She may move her home several hundred feet, even though her winter sleep is not finished. The cubs are quite active by the time they wander with their mother from their winter home about the last of March. Before they are three months old, they begin to play by themselves, watched and guarded by their mother. The young remain with the mother for a year or longer, usually sleeping with her their first winter, or sometimes having individual dens nearby. The cub is able to care for itself when six months old. At two months the cub weighs 5 to 6 pounds; at twelve months, 40 to 75 pounds; at two years, 90 to 150 pounds; at three years, 125 to 200 pounds; at four years, 175 to 250 pounds; at five years, 225 to 300 pounds; at six years, 275 to 350 pounds. The mammae are six, four pectoral and two inguinal.

Summer nests or shelters consist merely of a concealed place scratched in the ground amongst dense shrubbery, by a log, tree, or rock, or under the branches of a fallen tree. The resting place may or may not be lined with small bits of vegetation. Often it appears that the bear had simply lain down in a hidden spot. Rarely, a bear will rest in a crotch of a tree. The den or nest is fairly neat, and though the owner does not habitually clean it, it usually goes some distance from its home to defecate or urinate.

The black bear is omnivorous in its diet, and will eat almost anything, though much of its food is vegetable matter. When it first emerges from its winter slumbers it may have trouble finding sufficient vegetable food, and at that time preys on small mammals, and may even attack domestic stock, especially young pigs and sheep. Some bears may acquire this habit and become habitual stock killers. It is an expert fisherman, and will watch for fish, jump into the water, and grasp a fish in its mouth. Black bears do not "slap" fish from the water as does the big Alaskan brown bear. Mice and squirrels fall prey to it, and it will eat carrion and garbage. Two yearling bears knocked off a 16 inch cover on a garbage pit near Trout Lake, Vilas County, and gorged themselves until they could not get out (Anonymous, 1949: 21). A bear will tear logs and rotten wood and dig open ant hills to feed on eggs, larvae, and parent ants, and it is proverbially fond of honey. It may also disturb birds' nests, as it is fond of eggs, whether fresh or incubated. During the season it eats quantities of fruit such as strawberries, dwarf dogwood, serviceberries, Juneberries, elderberries, raspberries, apples, and wild grapes, and it is particularly fond of blueberries. It picks quantities of small berries from the bushes by use of its lips and tongue, sometimes without pulling off many leaves or twigs, though it often breaks down branches and tramples an area when feeding. At other times it browses on the berry bushes, eating leaves and twigs as well as berries. Mrs. William Brumstad, picking blueberries with her two boys at Squash Lake, near Woodboro, Oneida County, in August, 1905, returned to pick up a three gallon pail of berries which she had cached and found a big black bear sitting on its haunches eating the berries from the pail, holding it with both forepaws. Grass, roots, and, rarely, fungus are eaten. When nuts are available in the autumn, the bear feeds extensively on acorns, beechnuts, and hazelnuts. By the last of November it is very fat as a rule, and ready for the winter siesta. It is not particularly cleanly about its eating. It drinks frequently, and seems to enjoy water, often wallowing and bathing in shallow pools that by their regular use become recognized as bear wallows.

The black bear is little molested by predators. Wolves sometimes capture cubs, and in days when pumas were in Wisconsin they undoubtedly captured a cub now and then. Man is the worst enemy of the black bear, and if regulations for its protection had not been passed, we would no longer have this interesting mammal in Wisconsin. Steel beartraps should be outlawed, not so much for their danger to the bear as for their danger to man. Forest fires sometimes destroy black bears. There is a record of a bear being seriously injured when hit by a truck in Minnesota. Accounts of rare accidents where a motorcycle or an automobile hits a bear usually show the riders to be the ones injured. We know of no diseases that menace the bear, though not infrequently dental caries cause it trouble, particularly with the molars. A tick, genus *Dermacentor*, and a flea, *Chaetopsylla setosa*, have been found as external parasites, and internally the round worm *Trichinella spiralis*.

The black bear fills an important niche as a game animal in the state, there being 1,276 killed during the hunting season of 1950–51 and 1,094 during 1951–52. Its value, however, is not merely as game but as an interesting species that is a part of the early history of Wisconsin. Not only were the meat, hides, and fur utilized, but bear fat or oil was one of the essential items, both among the Indians and early settlers. It was used as a frying grease and for other culinary purposes, as well as to burn for lighting purposes. It was also used as a liniment or ointment for limbering stiffened joints and muscles, or for other pains. "The Ottawas had built another fort somewhere on Chequamegon Point. In travelling towards this Ottawa fort, on the half-rotten ice, Radisson gave out and was very sick for eight days, but by rubbing his legs with hot bear's oil and keeping them well bandaged, he finally recovered [1652]" (Verwyst, 1895: 434). One use of bear fat during the fourth voyage of Radisson, 1661–62, is of interest: "The young men that indeavoured to gett a pryse, indeavoured to clime up a great post, very smooth, and greased with oyle of bear" (Anonymous, 1888: 91). Many people pronounce bear meat delicious; many others dislike it. The meat is rich and fatty, and that of older animals is apt to be tough and

Trap for catching bears alive. Courtesy National Park Service.

Beehive damage by bear. Photography by Clifford Freeman. Courtesy Wisconsin Conservation Department.

strong-flavored. For the Christmas trade in 1873 in Chicago, ten thousand pounds of bear meat sold at eight cents a pound wholesale, but at this time game brought higher prices in the Cleveland, Detroit, and New York markets. Bear meat, like pork, should be well cooked before eating to avoid danger of trichinosis. Bearskins have no special value nowadays, but in early times were used extensively for bedding and clothing, and quantities were shipped from Green Bay. Indians bore honor to visitors by placing bearskins on which the visitors were to walk or sit.

They have especial veneration for the Bear; as soon as they slay one of these animals, they make a Feast, accompanied by singular ceremonies. The Bear's head, painted with all sorts of colors, is placed during the repast upon a raised place, and there receives the homage of all the Guests, who celebrate in song the praises of the Animal, meanwhile cutting its body into pieces and regaling themselves thereon. Not only do these Savages have, like all the others, the Custom of preparing themselves for their grand Hunts by fasting, which the Outagamis extend even to ten consecutive days; but besides, while the Hunters are in the field, the Boys are often compelled to fast; the dreams which they have during this abstinence are noted, and good or evil auguries for the success of the Hunt are drawn from them. The object of these fasts is to appease the tutlelary Spirits of the Animals whom they are to hunt; and it is claimed that they make known through dreams, whether they oppose or are favorable to the Hunters [1721, from Charlevoix's Journal] (Thwaites, 1902: 416).

Effigy mounds representing the bear exist on the northern shore of Lake Mendota, Dane County, and along Fox River in Green Lake County.

Bears at times do considerable damage to livestock, particularly to sheep, pigs, and calves. An "outlaw" attack on stock is often the result of a bear having acquired destructive habits. Such a bear may singly kill several sheep or pigs in a few nights. Damage by bears to apiaries is also high, and in some years may amount to a third of all damage by bears in the state. Since 1939, in proven cases of bear damage, the state of Wisconsin reimburses the loser, and up to June 30, 1950, had paid $65,042.01 for such damage. Douglas County leads in damage claims, followed by Bayfield, Ashland, Sawyer, Langlade, and Florence counties. Bears occasionally do damage to orchards, cranberry and other berry crops, and rarely to corn, but it is comparatively small. A secure high fence with an overhang of electrically charged wires is a good protection against bears molesting stock or fruit crops.

Specimens examined from Wisconsin.—Total 11, as follows: *Ashland County:* Cayuga, 1 (UWZ). *Bayfield County:* Bayfield (near Sand River, 7 mi. N. W.), 1. *Brown County:* De Pere, 1 (UWZ). *Douglas County:* T 44 N, R 13 W, 1 (UWZ). *Florence County:* Northeastern Florence County (west of Spread Eagle Lake), 3 (CNHM). *Oconto County:* Lakewood, 1 (UWZ). *Price County:* T 39 N, R 2 W, 1 (UWZ); T 40 N, R 2 W, 1 (UWZ). *Vilas County:* Eagle River, 1.

Selected references.—Matson, J. R., 1946; Merriam, C. H., 1896 a; Schorger, A. W., 1949 a; Scott, W. E., 1947 c; Underwood, W. L., 1921; Wright, W. H., 1910.

Family **Procyonidae**
Raccoons and Allies

Members of the family Procyonidae are found in North and South America and in northern India. Nine living genera are known, of which one occurs in Wisconsin.

Genus **Procyon** Storr
Raccoons

Dental formula:

$$I\frac{3-3}{3-3}, \quad C\frac{1-1}{1-1}, \quad P\frac{4-4}{4-4}, \quad M\frac{2-2}{2-2} = 40.$$

Procyon lotor hirtus Nelson and Goldman
Upper Mississippi Valley Raccoon

Procyon lotor hirtus Nelson and Goldman, Jour. Mammalogy 11 (4): 455, November 11, 1930.
Procyon lotor Lapham, p. 43, 1852; Lapham, p. 338, 1853; Strong, p. 457, 1883; Snyder, p. 122, 1902; Jackson, p. 29, 1908; Hollister, p. 29, 1910; Cory, p. 392, 1912.
Procyon lotor lotor Schmidt, p. 117, 1931; Komarek, p. 205, 1932.
Procyon lotor hirtus Barger, p. 10, 1952.

Raccoon curiosity up a tree. Courtesy Wisconsin Conservation Department.

Vernacular names. — In Wisconsin usually called coon or raccoon. Other names include *A-spû-n* (Potawatomi), blanket coon (by fur dealers, because of the long underfur of this subspecies), *chat sauvage* (French settlers), *espan* (Swedish), *Es-see-ban*, (Chippewa), racoon, *Waschbär* (German), and western raccoon.

Identification marks.—The raccoon, about the size of a huge cat, is easily distinguished from all other Wisconsin mammals by the conspicuous blackish mask across the eyes and down onto cheeks in corners of mouth, and by the moderately long, well-haired tail, ringed with blackish and dull yellowish. The body is somewhat robust; head broad; ears medium, erect, somewhat pointed; eyes medium, conspicuous; nose short, pointed; tail shorter than body, cylindrical, bushy, annulated with five to seven rings; feet both fore and hind with five prominent nonretractile claws, the soles naked and those of hind feet plantigrade; fur long, dense, and rather fine.

The color of the upper parts is grizzled gray, brownish, and blackish, there being considerable variation, particularly in the amount of black; the underfur dull grayish brown; sides paler than upper parts; under parts dull grayish brown, tinged with yellowish gray or white; black band across the forehead and through the eyes, and extending across cheeks; rest of face yellowish gray; tail alternately banded brownish gray and blackish, with five to seven dark rings, terminating in a dark tip. Winter fur is usually longer, glossier, and more intense in color. Molting occurs once a year over an extended period in summer.

The skull is broad, massive, and rounded, the rostrum broad and obtuse; audital bullae medium, inflated on inner side; bony palate extending well posterior to back molars; dentition relatively heavy, the incisors with crowns more or less grooved; canines grooved, oval in cross section; molariform teeth broad, tuberculate, with weak, rounded cusps.

Adult males average slightly larger than females. There is considerable individual variation in color, particularly in the amount of black or reddish brown in the hair, and color mutations sometimes appear. During the winter of 1858–

59, in the Gilbert Creek region, Dunn County, David Cartwright says: "We caught two black coons. I have never seen any others like them" (Cartwright and Bailey, 1875: 245). There are other reports of "black" raccoons, but such animals generally show the usual paler rings on the tail and the facial markings. White raccoons are rarities, and albinos are even scarcer. A beautiful albino raccoon was kept at the Wisconsin State Experimental Game and Fur Farm, Poynette, in 1938 (Ferguson, 1939: 32). "Prairie du Chien—White raccoon fur promises to be a valuable Wisconsin product in the future, according to Frank A. Garvey, fur farm proprietor operating near here. Garvey has several pens of the white animals" (Anonymous, 1937: 13). Rarely, white-spotted or blotched raccoons have been reported.

Measurements.—Total length of adults, 700 to 960 mm. (27.5 to 37.8 in.); tail, 225 to 275 mm. (8.9 to 10.8 in.); hind foot, 110 to 125 mm. (4.3 to 4.9 in.). Weight of adults 12 to 30 pounds, rarely 40 pounds or more, normally 14 to 24 pounds. G. H. King, La Grange, Walworth County, had killed over two hundred raccoons to June, 1886, and gave the average weight as 18 to 20 pounds for old ones ("Badger," 1886: 560). An abnormally huge raccoon has been recorded from the drainage of the Chippewa River:

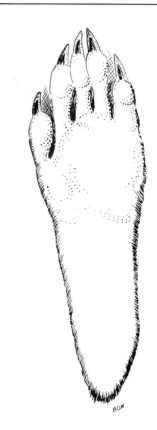

Left hind foot of raccoon. 1×.

Raccoon feeding on snails. U. S. Fish and Wildlife Service photograph.

On November 4, 1950, a raccoon hunter, Albert K. Larson of Route 2, Nelson, Wisconsin, shot a male raccoon (*Procyon lotor hirtus*) in T. 24 N., R. 12 W., Buffalo County, Wisconsin, which was weighed in on an accurate platform before witnesses at 62 pounds, 6 ounces. Another less accurate hanging spring scales recorded 59 pounds, 6 ounces. When this data was double-checked with the trapper he also reported the following gross measurements on this specimen: 4 feet 7 inches, length from tip of nose to tip of tail; 17¼ inches wide across back on specimen in the flesh. The trapper stated the specimen was very fat and judged to be about three years old (Scott, W. E., 1951: 363).

Oliver J. Valley records one from Grant County, Wisconsin, weighing 54 pounds (in Whitney and Underwood, 1952: 12). Skull length, 115 to 128 mm.; width, 72 to 82 mm.

Distribution in Wisconsin.—All of the state in favorable habitats; in varying abundance, but less abundant in the extreme northern part.

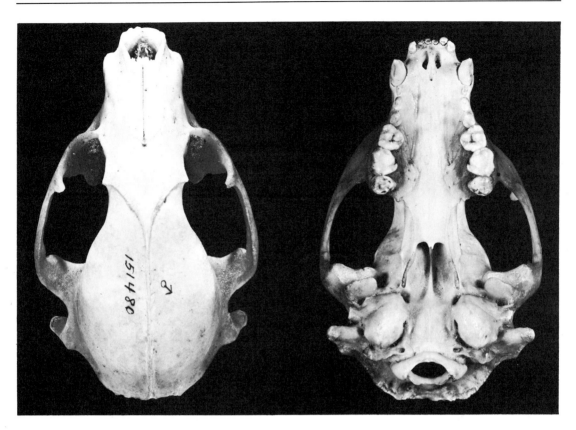

Skull of Procyon l. hirtus, *Delavan, Wisconsin.*
⅕×.

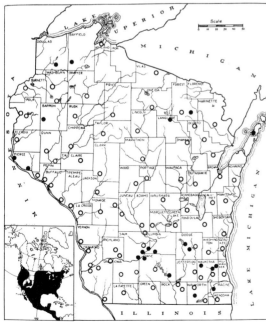

Map 59. *Distribution of* Procyon lotor. ● = *speci mens examined.* ○ = *authentic records.*

Habitat.—Forests and wooded areas, particularly old hardwood timber with hollow trees, and especially near water.

Status and Habits.—The raccoon was one of the peculiarly American animals that attracted the attention of the early settlers, not only in Wisconsin but in Virginia and other eastern pioneer colonies. "*There* is a beast they call Aroughcun much like a badger [i.e. the European badger, genus *Meles*], but vseth to live on trees as squirrels doe" (Smith, Captaine [John], 1612: 13). This early Indian name, "aroughcun," was transliterated into the common name "raccoon." There are many records of raccoons for various parts of Wisconsin as observed by early settlers at the beginning of the nineteenth century and earlier. Thus, in referring to the squaw *O-chaown*, who lived at Little Kaukaulin, Green Bay region, in the latter part of the eighteenth century, we are informed that "She was a great huntress . . . and was quite successful in killing bear, raccoons, and other game" (Grignon, A., 1857: 259). Its numbers in the state have varied without cyclic routine, chiefly from hunting and trapping pressure, though through reduction of suitable habitat, there may be fewer in the state today than a hundred years ago. Yet on account of their adaptability, they have persisted where some other carnivores have been extirpated, and often in a favorable environment become actually abundant. Individual raccoons have a normal home range of about 2 miles, though rarely one may wander 20 miles or farther, probably not to return to its homesite. Where food is plentiful a family may stay within a mile of its den. Population densities under favorable conditions may reach as high as one hundred per square mile. In exceptionally dense populations, raccoons have been known to average more than one per acre. Normally, in well-inhabited woodland, 15 to 20 per square mile is more likely. The total population of raccoons in the state as estimated on trapper and hunter license returns, may average sixty thousand or more.

The raccoon leaves evidence of its presence by its tracks, particularly in the mud along waterways and in dirt paths and roads. These tracks, baby-like and usually showing the full form of the foot since the raccoon walks flatfooted, are quite characteristic, and once known are not easily mistaken for those of any other animal. Sometimes one may be seen sunning itself on the limb of a tree, but as a rule it is not often observed in daytime. Scats may be found in raccoon territory, since this species makes no effort to cover its dung. Scratchings or chewings around an opening may indicate an occupied den, and a heavy rap on a tree may bring the masked face of a curious raccoon to the entrance, particularly if the occupant is a young animal. A harsh shrill whistle imitating the fright scream of the raccoon may call raccoons from a tree or den. Paths leading here and there made by raccoons may often be detected leading from the den.

Nocturnal in habits, a raccoon normally comes out of its den shortly after dusk, and is active till morning. Many, however, linger in their dens until later, some not emerging till near morning, and others, possibly not hungry or disinclined to leave a warm, snug bed, may forego going out

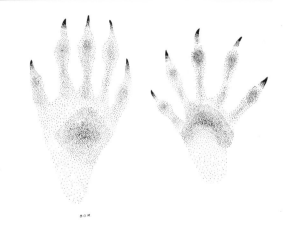

Raccoon tracks. Left, right hind foot. Right, right fore foot. ½×.

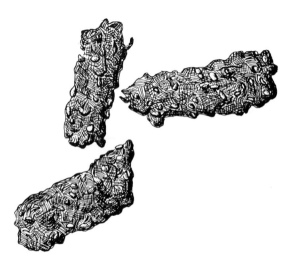

Feces of raccoon. 1×.

on a particular night. Not infrequently, it is out in the daytime, not so much to actively travel about as to lounge in some tree branch to sun itself. Warm weather suits it, and in summer it is more active than in winter, when during severe weather it usually becomes torpid or somewhat dormant, though it does not go into deep hibernation. This period of dormancy may come by the middle of December, and seldom lasts past the first of March. Warm days during the winter may stimulate the animal to become active. A raccoon may sometimes wander 50 or 60 miles from its former home to establish a new one, but there is no true seasonal migration. During the summer of 1950, an "invading army of raccoons made itself at home on the shores of Lake Geneva," Walworth County, and it appeared that the animals would settle permanently (Anonymous, 1951: 38). No evidence was presented, however, to indicate that this "army" migrated to the area or that it represented anything other than a population increase in the region.

The raccoon is deliberate and rather slow in movements, but when occasion demands can be exceedingly quick and rapid. It walks with feet plantigrade, and with a somewhat slow and lumbering gait. It runs with dexterity and determination, yet makes rather slow progress and soon tires. At maximum speed it seldom exceeds 15 miles an hour, and could easily be overtaken by dog or even man except for its cleverness in dodging and in obscuring its trail by taking to water or running on hard ground; it also often escapes by climbing high in a tree. It climbs well, either outside a tree or within its hollow trunk, and has the strength to withstand great stress or weight when clinging to a tree. Although fond of a watery habitat, it is only a fair swimmer; however, it takes apparent delight in wading, frequently with its body half submerged.

Socially inclined, the raccoon is somewhat gregarious, and may be encountered hunting in small groups of three to six, such groups often apparently consisting of a single family. A "coon tree" is more apt to hold five or six animals in a cavity than one or two, except during the nesting season. The call note is often uttered from spring until fall, and might well be termed a song. By some it has been likened to the call of the screech owl, but to me it sounds louder, harsher, and of higher pitch, more like a long tremulous whistle; on a quiet night and with favorable wind, it may be heard for a mile. Other than the song, which is seldom uttered, the raccoon produces several noises, such as a harsh growl or snarl when it is fighting or severely irritated, a rasping scream when it is suddenly and badly frightened, a loud purr sometimes to express pleasure, low grunts often repeated that seem to indicate a warning, particularly to its offspring, and a hissing sound as a sort of scolding cry. Young raccoons utter a plaintive, musical "orr-orr-orr" when begging food, cry and whimper plaintively when hungry or deserted, and squeal loudly when roughly handled or violently disturbed. The raccoon, so far as I

know, has no odor post, unless possibly its latrines established often near its den may serve as such. Sentries are not maintained, though the scream of a single raccoon may warn all others within hearing.

Individual raccoons vary greatly in disposition and temperament, although most tend to become more sullen and temperamental as they get older. As a rule the raccoon is not ferocious or combative, and prefers to seek safety in flight and concealment rather than fight. When cornered, however, it fights desperately, and being tough and muscular is a worthy opponent for an enemy considerably larger than itself. Young raccoons play frequently, either several together or by themselves; older animals often play alone, but seldom in groups. Curiosity is a strong trait of the raccoon, and it investigates and snoops into everything to satisfy this urge. It learns from trying to satisfy this curiosity, yet seldom mimics other animals, and seems to learn little by imitating. The senses, mental characteristics, and psychology of the raccoon have been investigated by several researchers (Cole, L. W., 1907, 1912; Cole, L. W., and F. M. Long, 1909; Davis, H. B., 1907; Whitney, L. F., 1933). "In the rapidity with which it forms associations the raccoon seems to stand almost midway between the monkey and the cat, as shown by numerical records for these animals. In the complexity of the associations it is able to form it stands nearer the monkey" (Cole, L. W., 1907: 261). Of the senses, touch apparently is the one most highly developed in the raccoon, particularly in the soles of the feet, and the animal when active is continuously feeling and searching with its forepaws for objects it might desire, and others that it might try to avoid. Sight is good, particularly in the dark. The raccoon hears well, but often pays little attention to loud sounds to which it has become accustomed. Unusual noises, especially if quick and snappy like the report of a gun or clap of the hands, attract it immediately. Possibly the vibrations from a knock on a tree hiding a raccoon may in part cause the reaction of the animal in exposing itself, but it appears that sound is important also. The associated senses of smell and taste appear less acute. The normal longevity of a wild raccoon is between 5 and 6 years, and the potential longevity near 10 or 12 years. There is a record of one living in a zoological park for nearly 14 years.

The raccoon may breed when one year old, and has one litter a year. Mating normally occurs from the last week of January to the middle of March. The young number two to seven, the average and usual number being four, though three or five are frequent, and they are born in April or May after a gestation period of 63 to 65 days. Females that have not conceived during the regular breeding season may mate again from April till June, and have young in June, July, or August. The new-born young has blackish skin and is well covered with mixed yellowish and grayish fur except on the belly and inner sides of legs which are scantily haired, and indistinct darker areas show where the facial mask and tail rings will appear prominently later. The eyes are closed, and open after about 20 days. At birth the raccoon weighs near three ounces, but it grows rapidly and when weaned at 10 to 12 weeks old weighs three or four pounds. The young ones remain with their mother until well into autumn, and often stay with her until she mates again. Mammae six: pectoral, two; abdominal, two; inguinal, two.

The den of the raccoon is usually in a hollow tree, and a limb seems to be preferred to the main trunk, though either may be utilized. Trees with rough bark, being easier for the animal to climb, are preferred, and tree species commonly selected in Wisconsin include burr oak, white oak, black oak, red maple, sugar maple, American elm, basswood, cottonwood, river birch, black walnut, and white ash. The entrance to the cavity may be anywhere from ground level to 60 or more feet above the surface, though the majority of raccoon dens in Wisconsin are between heights of 15 and 40 feet. The den cavity, if for rearing the young, preferably is a foot or slightly more in diameter, and the nest material consists simply of accumulated rotten wood and debris, no nesting material being added by the raccoon. When a suitable denning site is not available in a hollow tree, a home may be made in a fallen log, old stump, muskrat house, deserted building, barn loft or haymow, cavern in a rocky ledge, cave, or abandoned mine. In southwestern Wisconsin many dens are in abandoned mines or in clefts in limestone outcrops. Rarely, indeed, does a raccoon make its home in the ground, such as in a woodchuck burrow, if other sites are available. The raccoon makes little effort to clean its den; it drops its dung anywhere outside the nest, yet seems to have more or less established places as well as latrines not far from the den.

The raccoon has a varied diet and is as omnivorous as any Wisconsin mammal. Although a carnivore in structure and relationships, it apparently eats more plant than animal food. Its diet depends in no small degree on the food to its liking most readily available, and hence varies not only seasonally but with the habitat and environment in which it finds itself. A long list of known foods eaten by wild raccoons in Wisconsin or nearby regions includes the fruits of many plants, such as black cherry, chokecherry, pin cherry, currant, wild grape, hawthorn, wild plum, apple, tomato, cantaloupe, watermelon, wild crab, blackberry, raspberry, strawberry, blueberry, dogwood (various species), dwarf cornel, common elder, gooseberry, hackberry, shadbush, mulberry, nannyberry, and pokeweed; nuts such as acorns, hickory nuts, hazelnuts, and beechnuts; field corn, sweet corn, oats, ragweed and smartweed seeds, grass (possibly accidentally), and the tender shoots and buds of many trees and other plants. The animal matter may rarely and seasonally in some areas be as high as 70 per cent of the food volume, particularly where crayfish, snails, or insects are abundant, but more often the percentage of animal matter is less than that of plant material, constituting 30 to 40 per cent of the food. Animals eaten include crayfish, snails, clams, and a few earthworms; many insects, chiefly grasshoppers, crickets, beetles, wasps, bees, and moths; fish, particularly shallow water species like small bullheads; a few frogs; turtles, both eggs and immature; a few birds and some birds' eggs, even occasionally chicken eggs; and small mammals such as mice and shrews, rarely muskrat or squirrel that may have been in some cases found dead by the raccoon. Of the vegetable food, corn, fruit, and acorns rank high; of the animal food, crayfish and insects. The raccoon's penchant for corn was recognized by the early American settlers: "The *raccoon* liveth in hollow trees, and is about the size of a *Gib Cat*; they feed upon Mass, and do infest our *Indian* Corn very much" (Josselyn, J., 1672: 114). When feeding, the raccoon seldom eats directly from the ground, but gathers the food in its paws and transfers it to its mouth, sometimes sitting on its haunches. It stands or sits on its hind feet when pulling down ears of corn from the growing plant, sometimes eating nearly all the kernels from the ear, but more often only those from the terminal third or half. When hunting for crayfish or other prey in water, it feels under stones and rocks with its forefeet, and catches most of its food in its paws. A wild raccoon may dip its aquatic food in water a few times during the course of its eating, but it does not habitually dunk its food, and it is doubtful if it actually washes any of it. It likes to play, and likes to handle objects in water during its play, food and otherwise. It is such a rapacious and greedy eater that one might surmise it would not waste time in washing its food.

Man is the principal enemy of the raccoon, and his hunting and trapping annually cause the greatest part of the mortality. An insignificant number of young raccoons may be captured by bobcats and great horned owls. Forest fires kill raccoons and destroy their homesites, though storms seem less destructive of them. Very few are killed by automobiles. The species is subject to several diseases, among which are tuberculosis, pneumonia, dog distemper, infectious enteritis, and raccoon encephalitis. None of these diseases is of special significance to raccoons in the wild, except possibly distemper and encephalitis. The last named also has seriously affected raccoons in captivity in some parts of Wisconsin. This disease causes inflammation of the brain and produces paralysis of the hindquarters, spasms and convulsions, and finally coma. Rabies is not common in the raccoon, although several cases have been reported from Illinois, Iowa, and other states, two cases of which were as close to Wisconsin as Dubuque County, Iowa.

External parasites known from the raccoon include the biting lice *Trichodectes procyonis* and *Suricatoecus octomaculata*, the sucking louse *Polyplax spinulosa*; the ticks *Ixodes marxi* and *cookei*, and *Dermacentor variabilis*; and the fleas *Trichopsylla lotoris* and *coloris*, *Orchopeas wickhami* and *howardi*, *Odontopsyllus multispinosus*, *Ctenocephalides felis*, and *Cediopsylla simplex*. The many internal parasites include the roundworms *Uncinaria lotoris* (intestine) and *Trich-*

inella spiralis (muscles), the tapeworms *Mesocestoides lotoris* and *Diphyllobothrium latum*, and a fluke (*Clinostomum*).

The value of the raccoon both for clothing and food was recognized by the earliest American settlers, and it still ranks high, varying from time to time according to fashion whims and styles and food fancies. "Their flesh is somewhat dark, but good food roasted. Their Fat is excellent for Bruises and Aches. Their Skins are esteemed a good deep Fur, but yet as the *Wild Cats* somewhat coarse" (Josselyn, 1672: 17). At Green Bay, Prairie du Chien, and other fur posts, hundreds of raccoon skins were handled in the early years of the nineteenth century. There are many amusing accounts bearing on the utility of raccoons in these early days, such as one related as occurring at "Millwackie" in 1803:

On Christmas eve my invitations were extended to my friends. I had secured the fattest raccoon the Indians could tree; and defied any one to procure a fatter one, for there was no lean about it. Towards sun-set, I set my cook to chop any quantity of venison for stuffing. My raccoon was unusually large, weighing about thirty-two pounds, requiring a large quantity of stuffing to fill it out plump. In the meantime I had the pepper in a piece of deer skin, pounding it into pulverized form, cutting up onions, and a little cedar leaves, to give my viand a pleasant taste. No coonship's body, I am sure, was ever so cram-full before. About eight o'clock, it was stitched up, and ready for placing on the spit early the next morning. Then where should it be placed for safety during the night to prevent it from freezing? Of course by the fire. I went to bed and my mind was on the raccoon subject all night. But what was my mortification, when I got up at daylight to hang my coon up to roast, to find it putrid, and stinking. Oh, misery! sympathize with me for my lost labor, and with my friends for their lost dinner, I had no cook book. So ended my second attempt at cooking. Of course, I went without my dinner, and got laughed at by my half-famished friends (Anderson, T. G., 1882: 154).

Raccoon meat is dark, and the abundant fat is strong in odor and flavor. Nevertheless, it has good food values, being high in vitamin contents and delicious in taste—particularly if a young animal—when properly prepared before cooking. The scent glands under the legs and along the spine near the rump should be carefully removed, as should most of the fat, and the meat parboiled before final cooking. Full food use is not made of the annual Wisconsin raccoon take, which will average fully 180,000 pounds. The fur skin take varies greatly from year to year, depending largely upon demand. The take dropped from 26,192 in 1943 to a low of 15,740 in 1945, and fluctuated from 16,337 to 24,364 in the following years. Raccoon skins and fur have high wearing quality, but fashion does not always select for wear. Long-haired furs are not in demand now, and although the Upper Mississippi Valley raccoon has the longest and finest fur of any form, it is not in style. Clipped and dyed, our Wisconsin raccoon fur is truly luxurious. Aside from the value of raccoons for fur, oil, and food, they provide excellent sport for night hunting, with or without dogs. The raccoon also has some use as a laboratory animal and as a pet. There are nearly two hundred persons in Wisconsin raising raccoons. The State Experimental Game and Fur Farm raises them for restocking depleted areas in the wild.

The raccoon is sometimes harmful to human interests. Its greatest havoc is probably to growing field corn, and it is even more fond of sugar corn. At times it destroys other crops such as melons and tomatoes, and is occasionally reported to kill chickens. None of these depredations, however, is of really serious proportions. An electric fence will discourage raccoons from entering a field or garden, and a well-made scarecrow will keep them 50 or 60 yards away. Repellents, both in spray and dust form, I have found ineffective.

Specimens examined from Wisconsin.—Total 46, as follows: *Barron County:* Turtle Lake, 1 (UWZ). *Bayfield County:* Sandbar Lake (18 mi. S. of Iron River), 1 (UWZ). *Columbia County:* Lodi, 1 (UWZ); Okee, 1. *Dane County:* Roxbury, 3 (UWZ); Stoughton, 1 (UWZ). *Dodge County:* Beaver Dam, 4 (UWZ); Oak Grove, 1 (UWZ). *Douglas County:* Gordon, 6 (UWZ). *Forest County:* Laona, 1 (NPM). *Langlade County:* Post Lake, 1 (UWZ). *Pierce County:* Maiden Rock, 2 (MM); Prescott, 1 (MM). *Racine County:* Waterford Township, 1 (UWZ). *Sauk County:* Merrimac (4½ mi. N. W.), 4 (UWZ); Prairie du Sac, 1 (MM); Troy Township, 3 (MM). *Walworth County:* Delavan, 6. *Waukesha County:* Dousman, 2 (MM); Duplainville, 1 (UWZ); Pewaukee, 3 (UWZ); Waukesha, 1 (MM).

Selected references.—Cole, L. W., 1907; Giles, L. W., 1940; Goldman, E. A., 1950; Hamilton, W. J., 1936; Stuewer, F. W., 1943 b; Whitney, L. F., and A. C. Underwood, 1952.

Family **Mustelidae**
Martens, Weasels, Badgers, Skunks, Otters, and Allies

The family Mustelidae is large, varied, and widely distributed, and is found in all continents except Australia, particularly in temperate regions. It contains about 22 living genera, of which 11 are found in North America and 7 in Wisconsin.

Genus **Martes** Pinel
Martens and Fishers

Dental formula:

$$I\frac{3-3}{3-3}, \quad C\frac{1-1}{1-1}, \quad P\frac{4-4}{3-3}, \quad M\frac{1-1}{2-2}=36.$$

Martes americana americana (Turton)
American Marten

[*Mustela*] *americanus* Turton, Linnaeus, System of Nature, vol. 1, p. 60, 1806.
Mustela Martes Lapham, p. 43, 1852.
Mustela martes Lapham, p. 338, 1853.
Mustela americana Strong, p. 436, 1883; Jackson, p. 29, 1908; Hollister, p. 28, 1910; Cory, p. 381, 1912.
Martes americana Barger, p. 59, 1952.

Vernacular names.—American sable, *la fouine* (French), marten, pine marten, ranger's cat, sable, and *tha* (Chippewa).

Identification marks.—A weasel-like mammal about three-fourths the size of a small house cat, with body long and rather slender; head somewhat heavy; ears prominent, broad and rounded; eyes small; nose short and pointed; tail about one-third total length of animal, bushy, cylindrical; legs somewhat short; feet with five toes each, claws slender, semi-retractable, soles densely furred; fur fine, soft, silky, dense.

Color rich yellowish brown to ochraceous brown, or sometimes tawny above; darker on legs and tail; top of head brownish to almost cream color; ears edged with whitish; under parts usually slightly darker and warmer in tone than upper parts, with an irregular splotch of ochraceous or creamy white on throat and chest. In summer the pelage may become thinner and coarser, but otherwise it is similar to the winter pelage. One

Pine marten. Experimental Farm. Poynette, 1955. Photograph by Dean Tvedt. Courtesy Wisconsin Conservation Department.

molt occurs annually, late in summer or early in fall, and the new fur is usually complete by mid-October.

The skull is smooth and rounded dorsally, not angular; brain case only moderately flattened; frontal region slightly depressed; rostrum moderately elongate and slender; palate somewhat elongate, the palatilar shelf extending beyond last molar about one-fourth the length of entire tooth row; audital bullae moderately inflated, prominent, rounded.

There is no sexual variation in color, though individual color variation is considerable, particularly in the tone of brownish on the back and in the intensity and extent of the yellowish or orange on the throat, chest, and abdomen. Immature individuals are apt to be quite reddish. Males average some 12 per cent larger than females. Variations in color that approach mutations have been reported in wild martens in North America, such as almost black, slate, light yellow, silver sprinkled, and nearly white (Jones, S.V.H., 1923).

Measurements.—Total length, adult males, 600 to 675 mm. (23.5 to 26.5 in.); tail, 190 to 220 mm. (7.4 to 8.7 in.); hind foot, 90 to 98 mm. (3.5 to 3.9 in.). Weight, adult males, 2.2 to 3.2 pounds. Skull, adult males, length, 78 to 90 mm.; width, 45 to 52.5 mm. Total length, adult fe-

males, 540 to 580 mm. (21.2 to 22.8 in.); tail, 180 to 200 mm. (7 to 7.9 in.); hind foot, 78 to 88 mm. (3 to 3.5 in.). Weight, adult females, 1.6 to 2.2 pounds. Skull, adult females, length, 69.7 to 76 mm.; width, 38 to 45 mm.

Distribution in Wisconsin.—Originally probably occurred in most wooded areas of Wisconsin, particularly where there were dense coniferous forests, except possibly in the southern part. Now probably absent from the state except as stocked.

Habitat.—Forests and heavy woodland, particularly of old and dense conifer growth; sometimes wandering short distances into brushland and meadows in summer. Apparently favors forests of cedar, balsam, spruce and hemlock.

Status and Habits.—In the spruce and pine forests of Wisconsin until the middle of the nineteenth century, the marten was not uncommon, and in the early days of the territory it may have maintained a population peak average of one to each square mile of forest over many areas. Even at that time there is some evidence that the marten population was cyclic, increasing to a maximum once in about ten years, which may have been incident to a fluctuation in one of its chief

Skull of Martes a. americana, *Manitoba.*

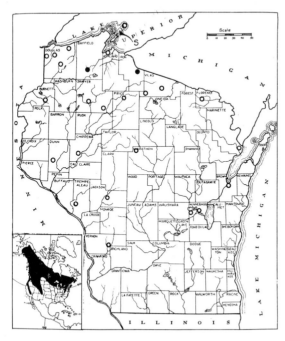

Map 60. *Distribution of* Martes americana.
● = *specimens examined.* O = *authentic records.*
S = *stocked.*

Left hind foot of marten. 1×.

foods, rabbits, as suggested by Schorger (1942: 26). During a winter season, a marten may have a home range of five to eight miles, and in Idaho "it appears that it moves over a 10 to 15 mile square area" (Marshall, 1951: 901). During the summer it is less roving. Commercial value of marten fur and the ease of trapping the animal were the causes for the extirpation of the species in Wisconsin. Destruction of habitat has undoubtedly contributed. From the early fur sale records, one cannot always determine exact localities where martens were trapped, but there is evidence that they occurred in numbers at Lac du Flambeau, Vilas County, where 153 pelts were received by Malhiot in 1804 and 1805 (1910: 192–233), although many of these came from other areas as far north as Lake Superior; Michel Curot reported pelts from the Yellow River, Burnett County, in 1803–1804 (Curot, 1911). More than six hundred pelts were received at Green Bay 1814–16 (Thwaites, 1910 a: 357; 1910 b: 376, 429), and upward of one thousand in 1821 (Thwaites, 1911: 193), many of which probably came from nearby. C. Grignon had marten pelts from Village de la Laine (not far from Winneconne, Winnebago County) in 1820 (Thwaites, 1911: 149), and the following year mentioned ten or eleven martens as having been procured at La Poehigans (Poygan Lake, Winnebago County) (Thwaites, 1911: 194). In 1821, P. Grignon wrote to Augustin Grignon "that Peaulette at the Menominee . . . had 875 Martens (Thwaites, 1911: 193), many of which probably came from the Wisconsin side of the Menominee River. James Reed trapped martens in Trempealeau County, probably in the present township of Arcadia, after 1853 (Anonymous, 1948: 25). Fred Mather trapped one near the Kickapoo River, Vernon County, in October 1855 (Mather, 1896: 331; 1897: 331). David Cartwright trapped 18 martens during the winter of 1958-59 in the Gilbert Creek region, Dunn County, and in 1870 trapped 10 in St. Croix River valley, probably in Burnett County (Cartwright and Bailey, 1875: 245, 272). Hoy recorded it as in Racine County about this same year (Hoy, 1874: 121). By this time, however, the marten was becoming scarce, and "a shipment of furs from Chippewa Falls, Wisconsin, in 1871, stated to have been one of the largest ever sent from the place, contained but 60 marten skins" (Schorger, 1942: 27). There was a specimen in the Milwaukee Museum collected in Ashland County in 1880. F. Joseph Fraenkle, Fifield, reported to Walter E. Scott, State Conservation Department, June 26, 1937, that John Rivers caught a marten in that vicinity in 1880. Charles B. Cory wrote in 1912 that he had been informed "that Martens are still to be found in the counties of northern Wisconsin named below . . . based upon personal knowledge or the testimony of realiable hunters and trappers," and the counties he named were Marinette, Florence, Price, Iron, Bayfield, Douglas, and Marathon (Cory, 1912: 383). "One marten was also taken in 1922 by Sig Tucsulla of Radisson, Sawyer County according to Sam Ruegger of that place" (Scott, 1939: 27). "During the past few years I have made special inquiry at the Apostle Islands. In 1934, a fisherman from Madeline Island, stated that a Frenchman spent a winter on Outer Island during the World War and trapped several marten" (Schorger, 1942: 27). None of our expedition saw signs of martens on Outer Island during our field work there in July and September, 1919. The first official state report of fur trapped in Wisconsin was for 1917-18, and shows 48 martens (Barber, 1918: 17). Subsequent reports were 10 martens for 1919-20, and 21 for 1921-22. "The last mar-

ten recorded as taken in Wisconsin is one reported by federal wardens as shipped out from Maple, Douglas County in 1925" (Scott, 1939: 27). The marten occurred in southeastern Sawyer County as late as the winter of 1939-40, as reported to Walter E. Scott, Wisconsin Conservation Department, by John Helsing, Jr., Winter, Wisconsin, April 30, 1940: "Hervis Brothers saw signs of 4 or 5." W. R. Spellum, Viroqua, Wisconsin, on February 24, 1940, also wrote Walter Scott in regard to the occurrence of a marten in SE Sec. 24, T 37 N, R 4 W, Sawyer County, in the general region of Hervis Brothers' observations, on November 27 and 29, 1930:

The place . . . is some distance back from the river . . . There is no water at this place except a small creek across the logging road north and some 200 yds. from the place I saw the marten . . . I was sitting on a deer crossing on watch and had the chance to observe this animal in pursuit of a red squirrel for perhaps ten minutes and from 50 feet away to as close as 15 feet when he effected his capture and ate the squirrel. The second case was within 1/4 mile of this same area and an aminal tried for a partridge but missed (in a tree) and I was able to see it at very close range again. There is no doubt in my mind as to identification and I am sure you can credit it.

In an effort to re-establish the marten in Wisconsin, five animals from near Kalispell, Montana, were released on Stockton Island, Ashland County. November 19, 1953 (Jordahl, 1954), and a second stocking was made in 1956.

During summer and fall, indications of the marten's presence are hard to detect. Its rather

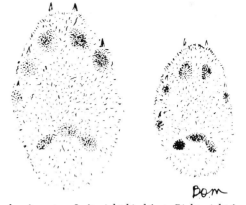

Tracks of marten. Left, right hind foot. Right, right fore foot. 1×.

broad tracks in soft snow in winter and spring are quite distinctive, each footprint being about three-fourths of an inch wide. Ordinarily it is wary, yet if a person is quiet, a marten may continue its activities within a few feet of the observer, and may even be called closer by one's squeaking like a mouse. It has no fixed trails or runways, though it sometimes "plows through soft fresh snow and may tunnel in snow when approaching prey, or perhaps in play" (Marshall, 1951: 800). It runs by a series of jumps, whether on ground or in trees, and appears to spend as much time on the ground as in the trees, particularly during the summer when it may seek the more open forests and brushlands. It seems to dislike water, but will cross a stream or other water barrier. Daybreak and twilight are its active times, although it may be active during the day, particularly if dark. It does not hibernate or migrate.

The marten employs scant voice communication, and makes little noise in the wild. It sometimes utters a soft purrlike grunt or cooing sound while with its young. When captured, or surprised in captivity, it may through fright or irritation chatter, snarl, growl, hiss, or even sharply screech or scream. It employs little or no communication with its kind, maintains no sentries, and flashes no signals. Before and during the mating season, however, both sexes establish odor posts by frequently rubbing their abdominal scent glands on tree branches or other objects.

Although active, energetic, and extremely curious, the marten is primarily a solitary animal, and seldom associates with others of its kind except during the breeding season. When two of them meet, it is the occasion for a snarling and hissing fight. This pugnacious disposition is displayed by a marten when captured. Nevertheless, a wild captive marten, when treated kindly, may soon become rather docile, though always displaying a nervous temperament. Taken when young or born in captivity, a marten may become a tame pet. It scarcely ever indulges in play, unless its continuous running and jumping can be called such. Its senses are well developed, especially those of smell, sight, and hearing, and its muscles, particularly those of the shoulders and hips, are strong. The potential longevity is probably near 15 years, and the normal longevity in the wild possibly less than 6 years.

There are records of the American marten living in captivity for 11 years.

The marten is polygamous, and mating occurs in June, July, or August, usually in July. It does not mate until its second summer, and may bear young in its third year. Most of the courting and copulation occurs on the ground. The gestation period is from 260 to 275 days. The young are born between the last of March and the middle of May, the greatest number of births being in April. Two to four constitute the usual number of young in a litter, a little less than three being near average, and rarely there may be one or five. The mammae are six, two pectoral and four inguinal. At birth the young one is hairless, with closed eyes, and weighs about 30 to 40 grams (1.1 to 1.4 ounces). It develops rapidly, however, and when three months old may weigh 900 to 1000 grams, or almost as much as its parent, and is well furred.

The marten has no fixed place of abode, but may have its young in one den one year and in another place another year, and in its predatory search for food may change its resting place frequently. Its daytime den is in a hollow tree or stump, or often in or under a fallen log on the ground. "In the Boise [Idaho] study area, of sixteen marten tracked to dens thirteen had used down logs and three holes in stumps. There appeared to be little regularity in the use of dens —the main point being the proximity of the kill" (Marshall, 1951: 900). The mother alone is believed to make the nest for her young, and selects a hollow tree, stump, or log, the cavity of which is lined with leaves, grass, moss, and other vegetation. It makes little attempt at sanitation, though it is cleanly about its nest, and usually deposits its dung in a pile away from the nest.

No verified data are available on the food of the marten in Wisconsin, but it probably ate small animals such as red squirrels, snowshoe hares, flying squirrels, mice, and a few grouse and small birds, and not infrequently nuts, berries, and some grass. In northwestern Montana in the winters of 1941–42 and 1942–43, Marshall (1946) found the principal food of the marten to be red squirrels, northern flying squirrels, red-backed mice, and snowshoe hares, with a few other items, including deer carrion and ruffed grouse. In the Rocky Mountain region of Canada, Cowan and Mackay (1950) found that annually mice comprised two-thirds of all food of the marten (red-backed mice one-fourth), in winter constituting 80 per cent and in summer 59 per cent of all food. It hunts in tangled covers, dense thickets, or among old snags, and captures its prey by pouncing upon it. It diligently searches every nook and cranny for food. The marten never voluntarily bathes, nor does it indulge in dust baths. It cleans occasionally by licking itself with its tongue, and delights in sun baths.

Wild enemies of the marten were apparently few in Wisconsin, though a few may have been captured by the coyote, timber wolf, wildcat, and the great horned owl. It was easily trapped, and man has been its primary enemy. Few serious diseases are known for the marten in the wild, though it is reported to have had rabies. Among external parasites of the marten, a louse, *Trichodectes retusus,* and a flea, *Orchopeas caedens,* have been recorded, and internal parasites include the roundworms *Dioctophyme renale, Ascaris columnaris,* and *Soboliphyme baturini.*

The marten has been extirpated in Wisconsin and many other regions because of the high value of its fur. Introductions of a few animals in the denser forests of the state, and their rigid protection, might re-establish the species here, but only as an interesting element of the fauna. It does not seem probable that in Wisconsin it could ever become a fur producer in the wild again. Experiments in raising martens have not shown that it can be raised in captivity for fur purposes. In the wild it does little harm, the small number of game and beneficial animals it captures being offset by the destructive ones among its prey.

Specimens examined from Wisconsin.—Total 2, as follows: *Bayfield County:* Drummond, 1 (UWZ); *Iron County:* Fisher Lake, 1 (UWZ).

Selected references.—Ashbrook, F. G., and K. B. Hanson, 1930; Markley, M. H., and C. F. Bassett, 1942; Marshall, W. H., 1951; Scott, W. E., 1939: 26–27; Seton, E. T., 1929, vol. 2: 481–516; Yeager, L. E., 1950.

Martes pennanti pennanti (Erxleben)
Fisher

[*Mustela] pennanti* Erxleben, Systema Regni Animalium, vol. 1, p. 470, 1777.

Mustela Canadensis Lapham, p. 43, 1852; Lapham, p. 338, 1853.
Mustela Pennantii Strong, p. 436, 1883.
Mustela pennanti Cory, p. 387, 1912.
Martes permanti permanti [printer's error for *Martes pennanti pennanti*] Barger, p. 12, 1952.

Vernacular names.—Black cat, black fox, fisher cat, fisher marten, fisher weasel, *ocheeg* (Potawatomi), pekan, pekan marten, pekan weasel, Pennant's cat, Pennant's marten, *tha-cho* (Chippewa), and wood shock.

Identification marks.—The fisher is similar in structure and body proportions to the marten, but is nearly twice as large, fully four times as heavy, and of different color. The head is somewhat broad and flat, narrowing to a rather pointed face and nose; ears rounded, low and broad, relatively smaller than in the marten; tail relatively a little longer than in the marten, more tapering, though bushy; feet strong, moderately large, five toed, provided with heavy, curved claws; fur dense, coarse, yet luxurious and glossy.

The general color tone is very dark brown to blackish brown, darker on rump and lower back, with a grizzled frosting of whitish or pale gray over top of head, neck, and shoulders; under parts dark brown, occasionally with one or a few whitish spots on the throat, and frequently a white blotch on the belly; tail, feet, and nose blackish. Winter color is essentially the same as in summer. There probably is one molt a year, early in the autumn.

The skull is similar to that of the marten, except that it is larger, the smallest skull of an adult fisher being larger than the largest skull of an adult marten; in the adult male fisher the sagittal crest is highly developed, posteriorly forming a vertical plate sometimes 20 mm. high, such a sagittal plate never being present in the marten; the audital bullae are flatter than in the marten, and the external auditory meatus relatively longer; teeth much larger and heavier than in the marten.

Sexual variation in the fisher shows chiefly that the adult male is 15 to 18 per cent larger than the adult female, and the skull of any mature animal more than 110 mm. in greatest length or 62 mm. in greatest breadth is almost certainly that of a male, and any skull of a mature fisher less than these dimensions is equally certain to be that of a female. Age variation shows in the usual tooth wear and closing of cranial sutures, and, slightly in the female but conspicuously in the male, in the development of a sagittal ridge. There is some individual variation in the color of the back, which varies from almost black to pale gray, though the gray seems more frequent in males and particularly older individuals. Rarely, a rufous color may appear. Mutations of fawn color, white, and "mottled" have been recorded.

Measurements.—Total length, adult males, 910 to 1,020 mm. (35.8 to 40.1 in.); tail, 334 to 400 mm. (12.8 to 15.7 in.); hind foot, 122 to 143 mm. (4.8 to 5.6 in.). Weight, adult males, 7 to 13 pounds, rarely possibly up to 18 pounds. Skull, adult males, length, 112 to 125 mm.; width, 63 to 82 mm. Total length, adult females, 800 to 880 mm. (31.4 to 34.6 in); tail, 300 to 360

mm. (11.8 to 14.1 in.); hind foot, 112 to 120 mm. (4.4 to 4.7 in.). Weight, adult females, 4 to 6.5 pounds. Skull, adult females, length, 98 to 106 mm.; width, 52 to 61 mm.

Distribution in Wisconsin.—Formerly, until about the year 1850, probably over most of the state in favorable wooded habitats, but soon extirpated from the southern half, and now probably does not exist anywhere in Wisconsin as a native animal.

Habitat.—Heavy forests, preferably of mixed hardwoods and conifers on lowlands near streams or lakes; sometimes pure hardwood stands, more rarely pure coniferous ones.

Status and Habits.—Judging from records of early fur sales, the fisher was never as common as the marten in Wisconsin, even though one allows for the greater difficulty in trapping the fisher. Nineteenth-century records include Lac-du Flambeau (1804); St. Croix River, Burnett

Fisher from southern Alberta in San Diego Zoo. Courtesy Mrs. Belle Benchley.

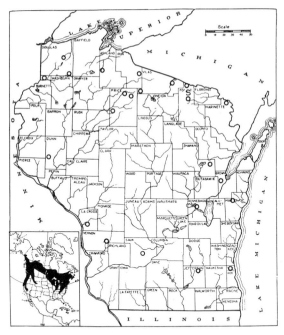

Map 61. Distribution of MARTES PENNANTI. O = *authentic records.* S = *stocked.*

County (1804); Lac Vieux Desert, Vilas County (1805); Green Bay (1814); Winneconne, Winnebago County (1820); Between Green Bay and Lake Shawano, Shawano County (1823); La Crosse (1842); Milwaukee (before 1852); Watertown, Jefferson County (before 1852); Sauk County (before 1870); headwaters of Brule River, Douglas County (1890); and between Iron Mountain, Michigan, and Pembine, Wisconsin, in Marinette County (1900). Extracted from the many records for the first half of the twentieth century, as provided by the Wisconsin State Conservation Department, and the reports of W. E. Scott (1939: 26–27), and letters to the author and A. W. Schorger (1942: 28), the following seem authentic: Brunsweiler River, Sec. 27, T 44 N, R 4 W, Ashland County (1920); Fifield, Price County, near Oneida County line (1921); Coch-

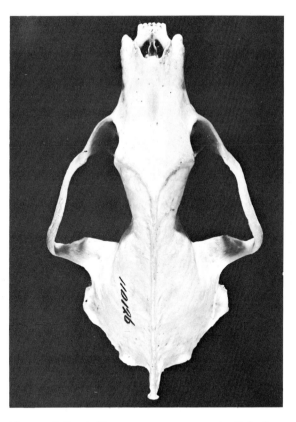

Above, skull of MARTES P. PENNANTI, ♂, *Oxford House, Manitoba.* ¾×.

Left, left hind foot of fisher. ¾×.

ran Lake, Price County (1922); northern part of Forest County, near Michigan line (1923); Popple River, Forest County (1923); Headwaters of Brule River, Douglas County (1928); Totogatic River, southeastern Douglas County (1932); and Sec. 6, T 37 N, R 2 W, Elk, Price County (1939). From about the year 1915 through the early twenties, the otter was protected in Wisconsin whereas the fisher was not, and trappers' reports often indicated fishers captured which were most likely otters. Thus, in the season 1917–18 there were reported 559 fishers, but no otters (Barber, 1918: 17). W. E. Barber, then commissioner, State Conservation Commission, wrote to me on February 7, 1921:

In regard to looking up the Fisher, about which you wrote me sometime ago, will say that our trappers' reports show that a number of Fisher have been caught during the past year, but upon writing the trappers it seems that some of them have the idea that the otter is the same animal as the Fisher; that the otter being a fish eater, he has taken the name of Fisher. I doubt if we have any Fisher in Wisconsin.

A forty-thousand-acre "Fisher Wildlife Man-

Tracks of fisher. Above, right fore foot. Below, right hind foot. ⅗×. Adapted from Seton, 1909, p. 936.

agement Area" under the supervision of the Wisconsin Conservation Department, in cooperation with Nicolet National Forest, has been established in that forest to protect the fisher. Here trapping is prohibited except for water sets for beaver and otter during the open season. The area is a wilderness consisting chiefly of heavy hardwoods and large swamps within the Pine River watershed in Forest County. This management area has been stocked with fourteen fishers, six males and eight females. These were transplanted from the Adirondack Mountains, New York, seven during the winter of 1955–56, and seven during the winter of 1956–57. Additional stocking is planned (cf. Bradle, 1957.)

The fisher seems to have a greater tendency to repopulate an area from which it has been extirpated than does the marten, which may result from its wandering habits. A fisher has a normal home range 8 to 15 miles in diameter, and during winter may wander 40 to 100 miles in four to twelve days, often in a more or less circuitous route, returning to near the homesite, or, less frequently, it may wander out of its general home range and inhabit new territory.

The tracks of the fisher are distinctive, appearing much like huge marten tracks with the marks of the individual pads plainer. The fisher does not make distinct trails or runways, but in its travels across country it usually "moves in a rather straight line," "may travel in one direction for more than a mile" and "seems to be aware of its destination as evidenced by the fact that its tracks often lead directly to the site of a den" (De Vos, 1952: 11). "Short cuts across points in the lake and crossing of creeks are made at definite places, where frequently used trails can be seen" (De Vos, 1952: 12). The fisher is active both summer and winter, and does not hibernate or truly migrate. Normally nocturnal, it nevertheless is often active by day, sometimes in bright sunshine.

The fisher, when hunting or when traveling crosscountry, normally walks, often in a nearly straight line for many yards, and frequently on fallen logs. When frightened or when chasing its prey, it may run in a series of bounds or jumps, landing on all four feet after each jump. Its maximum speed has not been determined, but probably does not exceed 15 miles an hour. It swims well, and is not so averse to water as its cousin the marten; though it is not an aquatic animal, it likes to travel very close to the water. It climbs well, but does not habitually travel through the treetops by jumping from tree to tree, although sometimes doing so.

It has no call notes, but is said to make a kind of "put, put, put" noise, low and soft, which cannot be heard more than a few feet. At mating time, "they make a peculiar kind of noise which sounds a little like the grunt of a buck Rabbit" (Seton, 1929, vol. 2: 461). An angry fisher will snarl, growl, and hiss, show its teeth, and hunch up its back like an angry cat. In temperament and disposition it is tense and irritable, and it is solitary in habits. If two or more are found amicably together, it is a female with her young or a mated pair. It is a courageous fighter, and too sagacious to be easily trapped. It sometimes follows trap lines, and will steal the bait without getting caught, or eat any animal already in the trap. The fisher's normal longevity is probably near 8 or 10 years, and its potential longevity near 15 years. There is record of a fisher living in a zoological garden for more than 9 years.

The fisher may breed when one year old. Mating occurs late in March or in April, sometimes as late as the first part of May. The female mates within a week or two after giving birth to the young, usually born between March 15 and April 15. The gestation period is about 352 days. The young are one to five in number, two or three being usual in a litter. They are slow to develop, it being several weeks after birth before their eyes open, and three or four months before they are weaned. Functional mammae are four, all inguinal.

The fisher is not particular in its requirements for the site of a den. Hollow trees or logs, openings in rocky ledges, actually any kind of a hole may serve the purpose. In the study area both more or less prominent and temporary dens appeared to be used. The pekan may shift occasionally between more permanent dens. . . . One trapper confirmed this discontinuous use of dens by stating that a fisher will change its main dens occasionally throughout the year. This man also dug out a much utilized den and found that it was lined with leaves, apparently placed there by the occupant. . . . Temporary dens in the study area were listed in their frequency of usage: (a) holes under large boulders, (b) dens dug in the snow, (c) hollow logs, and (d) brushpiles. The dens in the snow and under brush-

piles are generally just used overnight or for a few hours during the day. . . . Two temporary dens were situated in deserted beaver houses (De Vos, 1952: 14–15). The fisher very rarely digs a burrow.

The fisher feeds primarily on small mammals such as the snowshoe hare, porcupine, various wild mice, particularly the red-backed mouse (*Clethrionomys*), shrews, red squirrels, and chipmunks, but hares and porcupines appear to be its main prey. Hair and fragments of larger mammals have been found in feces and stomach contents of fishers, including the deer, moose, and red fox, which probably indicates carrion feeding. It occasionally captures grouse or other birds, rarely catches fish, and sometimes eats insects. During summer and early in the autumn it consumes many wild fruits such as mountain-ash berries, pin cherries, highbush cranberries, cranberries, blueberries, and salmon berries, and at times eats other vegetable matter, including leaves and lichens. On the whole the fisher is quite omnivorous.

Other than man, the fisher has few enemies, and it seems to be troubled little by disease or parasites either in the wild or in captivity. Among its internal parasites there have been recorded three roundworms, *Soboliphyme baturini*, *Uncinaria stenocephala*, and *Ascaris devosi*, and one tapeworm, *Mesocestoides variabilis*. External parasites are the tick *Ixodes cookei* and the flea *Oropsylla arctomys*.

The fisher is an asset to any wilderness area. It rarely becomes so numerous as to be unduly destructive of other useful species, and the high value of its fur makes control measures unnecessary. Single pelts often bring $75 to $100, and several have brought more than $300 each. It can be reared in captivity, but the few attempts to raise it as a commercial enterprise have not proven successful. Some of these efforts have been made in Wisconsin. "New Holstein—A group of 13 fisher is held at the Associated Fur farm here, representing one of a half dozen attempts being made in the United States and Canada to raise these fur animals commercially" (Anonymous, 1937 e: 45).

Specimens examined from Wisconsin.—None.
Selected references.—Bradle, B. J., 1957; De Vos, A., 1952; Hamilton, W. J., and A. H. Cook, 1957; Lowe, L. D., 1930; Scott, W. E., 1939; Seton, E. T., 1929, vol. 2: 452-79.

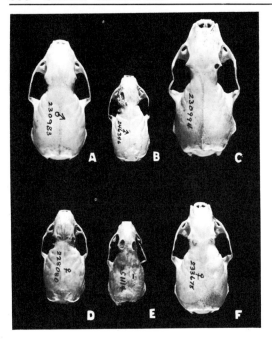

Skulls of weasels. A. M. E. BANGSI, *Mamie Lake, Wisconsin,* B. M. R. ALLEGHENIENSIS, *Roanoke, Indiana,* C. M. F. NOVEBORACENSIS, ♂, *Mamie Lake, Wisconsin,* D. M. E. BANGSI, *Mamie Lake, Wisconsin,* E. M. R. ALLEGHENIENSIS, ♀, *McFarland, Wisconsin,* F. M. F. NOVEBORACENSIS, *Mamie Lake, Wisconsin.* ¾×.

Tails of weasels. Left, MUSTELA F. NOVEBORACENSIS. *Middle,* M. E. BANGSI. *Right,* M. R. ALLEGHENIENSIS. ¾×.

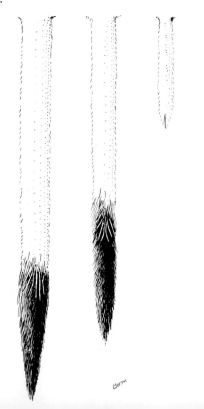

Genus **Mustela** Linnaeus
Weasels and Minks

Dental formula:

$$I\frac{3-3}{3-3}, \quad C\frac{1-1}{1-1}, \quad P\frac{3-3}{3-3}, \quad M\frac{1-1}{2-2}=34.$$

Mustela erminea bangsi Hall
Bangs' Short-tailed Weasel, or Ermine

Mustela erminea bangsi Hall, Jour. Mammalogy 26 (2): 176, July 19, 1945.
Mustela pusilla Lapham, p. 338, 1853.
Putorius cicognanii Strong, p. 437, 1883; Jackson, p. 28, 1908; Hollister, p. 28, 1910; Cory, p. 375, 1912.
Putorius Richardsonii Strong, p. 437, 1883.
Putorius cicognani Snyder, p. 125, 1902.
Mustela erminea bangsi Barger, p. 10, 1952.

Vernacular names.—In Wisconsin usually called weasel, and often when in white winter pelage called ermine. Other names include Bangs' ermine, Bonaparte or Bonaparte's weasel, brown weasel, *ching-gwus* (Chippewa), common weasel, ermine, ermine of the woods, *la belette de Bonaparte* (French), lesser weasel, little stoat, little weasel, short-tailed weasel, *s'kos* (Potawatomi), small weasel, and stoat.

Identification marks.—A medium-sized weasel; body lithe and slender; legs short; tail moderately short, average about 35 (30 to 42) per cent of head and body length, well haired, very slightly bushy; head rather narrow and elongate, gradually narrowing to the moderately blunt nose; ears moderately prominent, rounded, well haired; eyes medium, conspicuous; feet moderate size, five claws on each foot, small; fur rather short, moderately fine, not dense.

The color of the upper parts in summer pelage is dark brown, near burnt umber to slightly paler and more yellowish, near raw umber, slightly darker on the head and face, the dark brown extending on to the outsides of the legs and feet, base of hairs paler; tip of tail black above and below; under parts whitish, usually tinged heavily with yellow near straw yellow, sulphur yellow, or creamy buff, the color of the under parts extending onto the insides of fore and hind legs; chin and sometimes throat near white, the upper lip narrowly banded in white; toes usually tipped with whitish. Winter pelage entirely white, sometimes stained with yellowish, except for the black tip of the tail. The cause for this hereditary change in winter

Bangs' short-tailed weasel in white winter fur. Mounted specimen in Wisconsin Conservation Department Museum, Poynette. Courtesy of the Department.

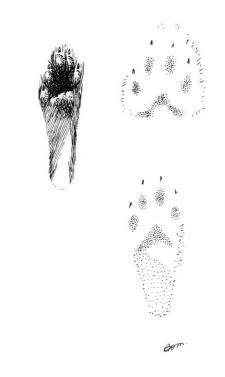

Left, left hind foot of M. E. BANGSI. *Right, tracks of* M. E. BANGSI, *above, fore foot; below, hind foot.*

to white fur is unknown, but it results in some protective coloration for the weasel.

In northern Wisconsin, the fall molt or change from brown to white pelage usually begins before November 1 and is in most cases completed by the last of that month. In rare cases, however, molt may be delayed until well into December. During stages of transition the fur may have a mixed brown and white appearance, the white hairs appearing over most of the body intermixed with the brown ones. The rump and shoulders may retain brown hairs longer than the rest of the body, though the hair on the tail is usually last to molt both in autumn and spring. It has been contended by some researchers that this color change may occur without molting as a direct replacement of pigment in the hair. Sufficient evidence to establish proof of this has not been produced. Spring molt rarely may begin as early as the middle of February, but usually starts about the middle of March, and is completed by the last of April.

The skull is rather elongate with smoothly rounded brain case, sagittal crest weakly de-

veloped; frontal region scarcely inflated, rather flat; zygomata slender, weak, moderately arched; rostrum short, swollen posteriorly, nearly truncate vertically; audital bullae large, flattened, the inner sides nearly parallel, no tubular meatus; teeth moderate in size, sharp.

Although there is no evident sexual variation of color or proportions in this species, except possibly for a relatively longer tail in the male, there is a pronounced sex difference in size, the male averaging 30 to 35 per cent greater in dimensions than the female and 50 per cent heavier. Old males develop a slight sagittal ridge. The skull of the male weasel averages relatively wider than that of the female. Young animals tend to average a trifle darker than adults. On the whole there is little individual variation in color, and the only mutation reported is that of an albino *Mustela erminea* (Jones, S. V. H., 1923: 176).

This weasel can be distinguished from *Mustela f. noveboracensis* by these characteristics: smaller size; relatively and actually shorter tail, in *M. c. bangsi* being about 40 (32 to 43) per cent of head and body length, whereas in *M. f. nove-boracensis* it is about 50 (44 to 55) per cent of head and body length; black tip of tail nearly 50 per cent of tail vertebrae length, whereas in *noveboracensis* about 40 per cent or less of tail vertebrae length; in summer pelage *bangsi* usually shows whitish on the insides of the hind feet, whereas *noveboracensis* shows brownish. When the sex is known, these two weasels are easily separable. When the sex is not known, the male *bangsi*, particularly the skull, is not always easily distinguished from the female *noveboracensis*. Size of skull alone, particularly greatest breadth, will distinguish the two weasels when sex is known. The least weasel, *M. r. alleghenien-sis*, differs from *M. e. bangsi* not only in its smaller size but in that its tail is only about 25 per cent of head and body length and has no black tip, or at most only two or three black hairs.

Measurements.—Total length, adult males, 277 to 341 mm. (10.9 to 13.4 in.); tail, 70 to 100 (2.8 to 4 in.); hind foot, 37 to 44 mm. (1.5 to 1.7 in.). Weight, adult males, 90 to 170 grams (3.1 to 6 oz.). Skull, adult males, length, 39 to 45.6 mm.; width, 20.3 to 23.5. Total length, adult females, 240 to 260 mm. (9.4 to 10.2 in.); tail, 42 to 68 mm. (1.6 to 2.7 in.); hind foot,

28 to 33 mm. (1.1 to 1.3 in.). Weight, adult females, 42.5 to 71 grams (1.8 to 2.8 oz.). Skull, adult females, length, 35.6 to 37.5 mm.; width, 17.1 to 17.9 mm.

Distribution in Wisconsin.—Probably occurs in suitable habitats throughout the state. Much more plentiful in the northern half of the state, where it outnumbers *Mustela f. noveboracensis,* than in the southern half, where *noveboracensis* is the more common weasel.

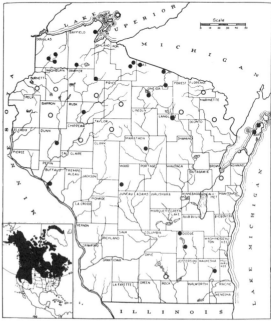

Map 62. *Distribution of* MUSTELA ERMINEA. ● = *specimens examined.* ○ = *authentic records.*

Short-tailed weasel or ermine in summer fur. Courtesy Mrs. Donald R. Murdock.

Habitat.—Principally woodlands and brushlands, but occasionally more open country, especially around stone walls, woodpiles, barns, and old buildings.

Status and Habits.—Except for cycles of scarcity and abundance, and fluctuations in demands for its pelt for the fur market, the short-tailed weasel has maintained a rather stable populations, though it has never been an abundant species. Based on trapping reports indicating an average annual catch of some 30,000 weasels in the state, of which 20,000 might well be this species, there possibly are about 125,000 short-tailed weasels in Wisconsin, mostly in the northern half of the state. In favorable habitat this weasel may reach a population of about 20 per square mile, or sometimes considerably more under especially favorable food conditions. Its home range usually is between 30 and 40 acres. At times, possibly due to food scarcity, it may change its home range and travel 2 or 3 miles in one night.

The short-tailed weasel may be in one's vicinity undetected for some time, yet sooner or later its curiosity will bring it forth from behind some log or stone pile, and a sharp squeak imitating a mouse or chipmunk will draw it near. The tracks, when discovered, are distinctive, particularly in snow, and its kills are often telltale marks, the plunder sometimes being left partly eaten and sometimes being stored, often several animals in one place. Some people can detect a weasel by the fetid odor from its scent glands. The dung is elongate and usually contains hair of mammals devoured. In any of these methods of detecting the presence of this species, it is always difficult to be certain whether the weasel leaving the sign is *M. e. bangsi* or *M. f. noveboracensis*. Although primarily nocturnal, this species frequently is active in the daytime, and I have seen it pursuing its prey on bright, warm days. It is active both summer and winter, and does not hibernate or migrate, though it may move its home base a few miles on account of food shortage or other habitat defects.

Its normal gait when pursuing prey or covering distances in the open is a galloping bound, with the back somewhat arched and the hind feet landing at each leap only a very short distance behind the forefeet. When attempting speed, each leap may be five or six feet or more, yet the maximum speed attained is not more than eight miles an hour, and in a straightaway a weasel can usually be "run down" by an active man, though it is expert at dodging. It climbs small trees with rough bark, sometimes to a height of 10 or 15 feet. It will enter water, and even try to pursue its prey there, but it is not a good swimmer, paddling rather clumsily with the arched back well out of water.

The short-tailed weasel has a variety of calls. One is a repeated short grunt or low chatter. When satisfied or content it may purr softly, and if very excited or alarmed it may issue a shrill sharp note, almost a screech, or when less ex-

cited it may give a series of soft sharp barks. It frequently hisses when searching and nosing for signs of its prey or other objects. It is not known to have sentries or signal posts, though the pungent odor from its glands may have some significance, probably sexual.

Fearless and ferocious, the ermine in fighting or hunting its prey is quick in every movement of its lithe, muscular body. It has extreme curiosity, and will watch with deliberation and quietness objects or actions that may attract its interest. Then, with almost lightning quickness, it may attack ferociously, even animals many times its own size, or it may discreetly continue its watchful curiosity, with muscular twitches and jerks indicating each urge to charge. Parents play with their young ones; young play among themselves, but adults are not known to do so. Senses of smell, hearing, and sight are all well developed, and a weasel can follow its prey under snow or through thickets chiefly by the sense of smell. Its life span is unknown, but its normal longevity is probably near five or six years and its potential longevity may be as high as ten years.

Only one litter is reared each year, there being from four to nine young in each litter, with six and seven the more common numbers. Details of the breeding habits of this species are not well known. The male probably is not sexually mature until a year old. It is not sexually active after September 1 (Wright, P. L., 1942 a: 344). The female may be sexually mature when three or four months old. There appears to be a delay in implantation of the embryo which results in a long gestation period. So far as known, breeding normally takes place in July or August and the young are born from the middle of April to early in May, indicating a gestation period of about 255 days. The young when first born is blind and very slightly covered with fine hair. It develops rapidly, and at two weeks of age begins to show a "heavy brown mane in marked contrast to the rest of the scantily, white furred animal" (Hamilton, 1933 b: 323). Hamilton further tells us that at 35 days the young has opened its eyes, and that at 45 days "the brown fur of the dorsum obscures any trace of the mane, which is no longer distinct, and . . . the youngsters are quite active, and play with one another much after the fashion of young kittens" (Hamilton, 1933 b: 324–25). Both parents care for the young. The mammae are eight, four abdominal and four inguinal.

The nest is usually underground, frequently beneath tree roots or under a stump, log, woodpile, or stone wall. Often there are three or four tunnels or runways into the nest proper. The breeding nest consists primarily of fragments of leaves and grass intermixed with much fur from mammals the weasel has captured. Food fragments are commonly scattered on the surface or stored in the runways, and although the old weasels ordinarily do not urinate or defecate in the nest, they have favored places nearby used for this.

Fully 50 per cent of the yearly food of the short-tailed weasel consists of mice, and during the winter and late in fall and early in spring the percentage of mice may be considerably higher. More than half of the mice captured are of microtine forms of the genera *Microtus* and *Clethrionomys,* while a considerable proportion of the others are of the genus *Peromyscus.* An adult male was killed unwittingly by one of Wallace Grange's helpers on April 24, 1951, in a garage on Sandhill Game Farm, Babcock, where it had been feeding on mice. Rabbits are very rarely eaten, and then only the kits. Wild birds constitute about 5 per cent of its food, but this weasel rarely molests domestic fowl. Rarely, frogs, snakes, and fish are tasted. Shrews are eaten, particularly in the winter, and during the summer a considerable number of chipmunks of both Wisconsin species are captured, especially of the least chipmunk. A least chipmunk that ran "chippering" out of the brush near Mamie Lake, Vilas County, the afternoon of August 28, 1917, was being chased by a short-tailed weasel. The chipmunk was shot, whereupon the weasel grasped it in its mouth and started away. A shot at the weasel caused it to drop its prey, and it escaped in the brush. A No. 1 steel trap, baited by hanging the chipmunk over it, was set, and the following morning the weasel was found dead in the trap, caught by the right forefoot.

Weasels have . . . a highly successful manner in the securing and killing of their catch. A rapid dash, and the bird or mouse is grabbed over the back of the skull, the fore legs encircle the animal as though hugging it, and the hind legs are brought up to scratch wildly at the captive. . . . If a large

animal, as a rat, the weasel usually lies on its side, while the diminishing struggles of the rodent continue, but if a mouse or a small bird, the weasel is apt to crouch over its prey (Hamilton, 1933 b: 332).

The weasel frequently drinks water in small amounts.

Very few animals seem to be persistent enemies of the short-tailed weasel. Among raptorial birds known to have attacked it are the rough-legged hawk, goshawk, bald eagle, barred owl, great horned owl, and snowy owl. There are records of both red and gray foxes preying upon it in Pennsylvania (Latham, 1952: 516), and the domestic cat will occasionally kill one. The road kill by automobiles is rather high when one takes into consideration the comparative scarcity of the mammal.

The parasites of this weasel are not well known. Lice and ticks probably are found on it, and it harbors in considerable numbers the fleas *Ceratophyllus vison* and *Nearctopsylla brooksi.* Internal parasites include the nematodes *Dracunculus medinensis, Molineus patens,* and *Physaloptera maxillaris;* the cestode *Taenia taeniaformis;* and the trematodes *Alaria mustelae* and *A. taxideae.*

Economically, the short-tailed weasel, sustained in its normal population, is valuable to man. Its prey consists largely of mice, most of which are detrimental to man's interests, and the number of birds it captures is negligible. Rarely does this species molest chickens, and when an individual is found doing so it can easily be killed. Its habits do not bring it constantly in contact with domestic fowl. It seldom catches rabbits, and its effect on game birds can be discounted. The annual fur value of ermine from the state will approximate twenty thousand dollars or more, varying greatly from year to year.

Specimens examined from Wisconsin.—Total 66, as follows: *Ashland County:* Bear Lake, 2 (UWZ). *Bayfield County:* Cable, 1 (UWZ); Washburn, 1 (AMNH). *Buffalo County:* Wabasha Flats, 1. *Dodge County:* Beaver Dam, 19 (UWZ); Fox Lake, 1 (UWZ). *Door County:* Ellison Bay, 1 (MM); Fish Creek, 2 (UWZ). *Douglas County:* Gordon, 1 (UWZ); Moose and Saint Croix rivers (junction), 2 (MM); Solon Springs (6 mi. S.W.), 1 (UWZ). *Dunn County:* Colfax, 2 (UWZ). *Iron County:* Fisher Lake 4, (UWZ); Mercer, 1 (UWZ). *Langlade County:* Post Lake, 3 (UWZ). *Marathon County:* Wausau, 1 (UWZ). *Oneida County:* Tomahawk Lake, 1 (CNHM). *Rusk County:* Ladysmith, 1 (UWZ).

Vilas County: Eagle River, 1 (MM); Mamie Lake, 17; Oxbow Lake, 1. *Waukesha County:* Pewaukee, 1 (UWZ). *Wood County:* Babcock, 1 (WBG).

Selected references.—Aldous, S. E., and J. Manweiler, 1942; Hall, E. R., 1945, 1951 b; Hamilton, W. J., Jr., 1933 b; Merriam, C. H., 1896 b; Wright, P. L., 1942 a.

Mustela rixosa allegheniensis (Rhoads)
Allegheny Least Weasel

Putorius allegheniensis Rhoads, Proc. Acad. Nat. Sci. Philadelphia, 1900, p. 751, March 25, 1901.
Putorius rixosa allegheniensis Jackson, p. 29, 1908; Hollister, p. 28, 1910; Cory, p. 378, 1912.
Mustela rixosa allegheniensis Barger, p. 10, 1952.

Vernacular names.—Alleghenian least weasel, dwarf weasel, least stoat, least weasel, mouse-hunter, mouse weasel, and pigmy weasel.

Identification marks.—A tiny weasel, smallest of Wisconsin carnivores, 6.5 to 8 inches long including tail, which is 1 to 1.5 inches long, or less than 20 per cent of total length or 25 per cent of head and body length; body slender, about .8 inch in diameter.

The color of the upper parts in summer fur is rich chocolate brown, near broccoli brown, or hair brown, tending slightly toward raw umber, but with less yellowish or reddish tone than in the larger weasels (*bangsi* and *noveboracensis*), and often extending well down on each side on to ventral parts, sometimes meeting midventrally; under parts white, often brown blotched or rarely the same brown as the upper parts; tail brown above and below, with no black tip, though occasionally there may be a few scattered black hairs near the tip. The normal winter pelage is entirely white, except in some specimens there are a few scattered black hairs at the tip of the tail. Very rarely the summer color may be retained through the winter. The time of molting appears to be rather irregular, but full winter pelage usually is acquired by the middle of November, though sometimes it is delayed until January or February. Full summer pelage may be expected by the last of March or the early part of April.

The skull of *M. r. allegheniensis* is almost a miniature of that of *M. e. bangsi*, although skulls of large male *allegheniensis* may nearly overlap in size those of small female *bangsi*. In skulls of approximately equal size, comparison will show that in the skull of *allegheniensis* the brain case

is relatively narrower through the mastoid processes, is less flattened or compressed above, has a more distinct sagittal ridge, and has more prominent postorbital processes.

There is little variation in color in this weasel, other than in the extent of distribution of the brown of the upper parts onto the under parts. Males average larger than females, but only by about 10 per cent in total length and other linear measurements. Small size, length of tail, and absence of black tip to tail will readily distinguish *M. r. allegheniensis* from *M. e. bangsi* or *M. f. noveboracensis*. Any adult weasel in the state with total length less than 225 mm., tail vertebrae length less than 40 mm., and with no black tip to tail is *M. r. allegheniensis*. The skull of the male least weasel sometimes approaches that of the female ermine in size and appearance, but the skull of *allegheniensis* is always less than 34 mm. in greatest length, whereas that of *bangsi* is always more than 34 mm. A novel method of distinguishing pelts of *M. r. allegheniensis* from those of *M. erminea* and *M. f. noveboracensis* has been described:

Fairly regularly the tail of small pelts of least weasels and Bonaparte weasels would be missing and positive identification became difficult. It was discovered that the fur of the least weasel would fluoresce under ultra-violet light producing a vivid lavender color. The fur of the other two species remained a dull brown under the ultra-violet light. Thus, identification is positively and simply made, immediately (Latham, 1953: 385).

Measurements.—Total length, adult males, 189 to 206 mm. (7.4 to 8.1 in.); tail, 30 to 38 mm. (1.2 to 1.5 in.); hind foot, 21 to 23 mm. (0.8 to 0.9 in.). Weight, adult males, 41 to 50 grams (1.4 to 1.8 oz.). Skull, adult males, length 31.5 to 32.8 mm.; width, 15.8 to 17.5 mm. Total length, adult females, 172 to 188 mm. (6.8 to 7.4 in.); tail, 24 to 33 mm. (1 to 1.3 in.); hind foot, 19

Least weasel, MUSTELA RIXOSA, *in winter pelage in natural habitat, North Dakota. Courtesy A. K. Momb, North Dakota Game and Fish Department.*

to 21 mm. (0.7 to 0.8 in.). Weight, adult females, 37 to 41 grams (1.3 to 1.4 oz.). Skull, adult females, length, 30.2 to 30.5 mm.; width, 14.7 to 15.9 mm.

Distribution in Wisconsin.—Occurs locally over most of southern Wisconsin south of latitude 45° N. May possibly occur in northern Wisconsin, though there are no records from there or from the northern peninsula of Michigan.

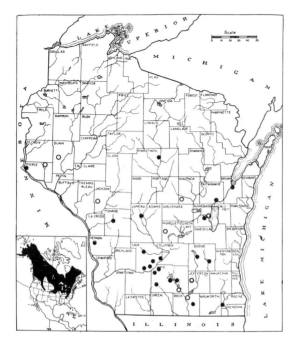

Map 63. Distribution of MUSTELA RIXOSA. ● = *specimens examined.* ○ = *authentic records.*

Habitat.—"High marsh with ground-water level at or very near the surface during a good part of the year" (Beer, 1950: 149). It also inhabits meadows and grassy fields, and has at times been found around houses, woodpiles, and brush heaps.

Status and Habits.—The least weasel is a rare mammal throughout most of its range—and Wisconsin is no exception—or else it is exceedingly difficult to collect. At times in scattered areas there are indications of cycles of increased populations, but the species seldom approaches being common. From Madison, Wisconsin, Dr. A. W. Schorger, in a letter to me dated March 12, 1946, says: "This winter I secured two Least Weasels that were drowned in the raceway of the local

fish hatchery. Judging from the tracks in the snow, this species is locally common but infernally difficult to trap." Its home range is usually less than two acres. Unless its tracks are well known, the presence of this tiny weasel in a locality is apt to go unnoticed. Rarely, a dog or a cat may capture one, and more rarely one is killed by an automobile. A few have been discovered by being plowed out of their underground nests. Probably less than 1 per cent of the weasels in Wisconsin are of the species.

The least weasel is active both summer and winter, and although primarily nocturnal, it frequently hunts in the daytime. It neither hibernates nor migrates, though it may move from area to area to find available food. Its ordinary gait is a slow gallop or jump, though it frequently walks, and when following a runway will either walk or run. Though quick in movements, it travels rather slowly, probably never exceeding five or six miles an hour.

So far as known this weasel is comparatively silent, and inasmuch as it is nongregarious, it has little need for intercommunication. It is known to utter a shrill squeal when irritated, and at such times may discharge a fetid glandular odor as do other weasels. Its major senses of hearing, sight, touch, and smell are highly developed, and though small of body it is strong and muscular.

Possibly the least weasel may sometimes have two litters of young in a year, though this is probably not the usual thing, nor has it actually been proven. One can suspect it, however, considering data from various localities in the United States and Canada: "November, May, and June are the only months in which young least weasels have not been reported. . . . the data now available suggest that, in the United States, young least weasels may be born in every month of the year" (Hall, 1951: 178). Mammary gland development on specimen No. 249,874, Biological Surveys collection, taken at Madison, Wisconsin, June 24, 1930, by Paul Errington, indicates that the animal was nursing young at the time. These young were probably born in June, if not in May. The gestation period is not known. The number in a litter may vary from three to six, with four or five the more usual number. "A female with litter of ten small young" brought to P. O. Fryklund, Roseau, Roseau County, Minnesota, August 12, 1932 (Swanson and Fryklund, 1935: 121), may well have had two litters rather than one containing ten youngsters. The young are born blind and hairless, pinkish in color tone from the blood circulation, and with some dark pigmentation showing from the covered eyes. Little is known about the development of the young, but records would indicate that when the animal is little more than three months old it has attained near adult size and is well furred. The mammae are six, two abdominal and four inguinal.

The nest is in a shallow burrow made by a mouse, vole, mole, pocket gopher, or some other small mammal, and most often has been found underground in a field or meadow. Nests also have been found in a hole in a creek bank in a meadow in southwestern Pennsylvania (Sutton, 1929: 254), in a clover stack in Manitoba (Criddle, 1947), and in a corn shock in Wisconsin. The nest is usually that of a mouse or other animal that the weasel probably killed as prey, and is often made exteriorly of the grass, brushes, and other vegetation gathered by the original owner, and then lined with fur gathered from the many victims of the weasel. Often secondary nests are established that may be used as retreats or minor storage places. In a nest used continuously for some time, the lining of fur may approach an inch in thickness and become matted and packed almost to a felt. In this main nest the weasel sleeps, rears its young, and brings it food to eat. Frequently, remains of its food are left around the nest, and dung is deposited in a pile nearby.

The food of the least weasel consists chiefly of mice, and in Wisconsin, voles constitute a large percentage of its prey, though many other mice, such as wood and deer mice (*Peromyscus*), and possibly a very few moles (*Scalopus*) and shrews may be included. There are no positive accounts of its feeding upon birds or insects. Its method of capturing its prey is by pursuit in the victims' runways, either underground or through surface runways. It attacks by jumping at the prey, and kills by biting into the neck and the back of the head of the prey. It may kill more than it needs, but stores most of its captures that are not immediately consumed.

In Wisconsin there are records of *M. r. allegheniensis* having been eaten by the great horned owl (Errington, Hamerstrom, and Hamerstrom, 1940: 839) and the American rough-legged hawk, and it is probably eaten by other species of large owls and hawks. The long-tailed weasel, domestic cat, the red and the gray fox, and other predatory mammals prey upon it. The remains of a least weasel were found in pellets of a barn owl in Virginia (Handley, 1949: 431), and the remains of one were found in the nest of a long-tailed weasel in Iowa (Polderboer, Lee, and Hendrickson, 1941: 118). It is not infrequently destroyed by a plow digging into its nest, and rarely by being hit by an automobile.

The least weasel is undoubtedly host to some species of lice, ticks, and fleas, but such parasites have not been determined. Two species of roundworms, *Molineus patens* and *Physaloptera maxillaris*, have been found in it.

Although the least weasel has practically no commercial value from the sale of its fur or otherwise, it is nevertheless a distinct economic asset, since all of its habits are beneficial—or at least not harmful—to humans. It feeds primarily on mice, and should it catch a baby chicken, which it is not known to do, it would be such a small chick as to have little value.

Specimens examined from Wisconsin.—Total 38, as follows: *Brown County:* De Pere, 1 (NPM). *Dane County:* Christiana Township, 1 (UWZ); McFarland, 1; Madison, 11 (3 AWS; 7 UWZ); Mazomanie, 1 (MM); Mount Horeb, 1 (UWZ); Roxbury, 1 (MM). *Dodge County:* Beaver Dam, 1 (UWZ); Horicon Marsh, 1 (UWZ), *Juneau County:* Necedah, 1 (F&FH). *Marathon County:* Wausau, 1 (UWZ). *Monroe County:* Sparta, 1 (UWZ). *Outagamie County:* Grand Chute, 1 (UWZ). *Pierce County:* Prescott, 1 (MM). *Racine County:* Burlington, 1 (MM). *Rock County:* Janesville (McArthur Game Farm, 5 mi. E.), 4 (MM). *Sauk County:* Honey Creek, 1 (MM); Merrimac, 1 (MM); Reedsburg, 2 (UWZ); Sumpter, 2 (MM); Troy Township, 1 (MM). *Vernon County:* Stoddard, 1 (UWZ). *Winnebago County:* T 18 N, R 15 E, 1 (UWZ).

Selected references.—Beer, J. R., 1950; Hall, E. R., 1951 b; Polderboer, E. B., 1942, 1948 b; Swanson, G., and P. O. Fryklund, 1935; Swenk, M. H., 1926.

Mustela frenata noveboracensis (Emmons)
New York Long-tailed Weasel

Putorius noveboracensis Emmons, Quadrupeds of Massachusetts, p. 45, 1840.
Putorius Noveboracensis Lapham, p. 43, 1852; Lapham, p. 338, 1853.
Putorius noveboracensis Strong, p. 437, 1883; Snyder, p. 125, 1902; Jackson, p. 29, 1908; Hollister, p. 28, 1910; Cory, p. 366, 1912.
Putorius vulgaris Strong, p. 437, 1883.
Mustela frenata noveboracensis Barger, p. 10, 1952.

Vernacular names. — Big stoat, *ching-gwus* (Chippewa), ermine weasel, large brown wea-

Long-tailed weasel in summer. Photograph by William T. Shaw.

Long-tailed weasel in winter, Wyoming. U. S. Fish and Wildlife Service photograph by A. P. Nelson.

sel, large ermine, large weasel, long-tailed weasel, New York State weasel, New York weasel, and *s'kos* (Potawatomi).

Identification marks.—A large weasel; body slender; legs short; tail relatively long, averages about 50 (44 to 55) per cent of head and body length, well haired; ears distinct, rounded, well haired; five small claws on each foot; fur not dense, moderately fine, and rather short.

The color of the upper parts in summer is dark brown, much as in *M. e. bangsi,* near burnt umber or raw umber, slightly darker on the face and nose, the brown extending down on the basal portion of the tail above and below, and on the legs usually to the tips of the toes, the foot and toes above sometimes being whitish; tip of tail black, above and below; under parts whitish, tinged more or less heavily with yellowish. Winter pelage normally entirely white, sometimes stained with yellowish, except the black tip of the tail. In the southern half of the state, particularly during mild winters, many of the long-tailed weasels retain the brown coloration of summer; others may partly change toward the white pelage and remain mottled or blended a mixed brown and white throughout the winter. Males tend to retain their brown coats more than females, the majority of the females usually turning white. The fall molt usually begins by mid-October and is completed by mid-November. The spring molt usually starts about the

first of March, and full summer fur is normally acquired by April 1.

The skull of the adult *M. f. noveboracensis* in general proportions is more angular than that of *M. e. bangsi,* has more prominent and more pointed postorbital processes, and is distinctly larger. Skulls of adults of the same sex can always be distinguished by the greater size of *noveboracensis.*

Sexual variation exists in that the male averages 30 to 35 per cent greater in dimensions than the female and nearly twice as heavy. As with the short-tailed weasel, the young average a shade darker than adults. There is little individual variation in color, confined chiefly to the intensity and darkness of the yellow tone on the under parts.

This species is easily separable from the mink by its bicolor contrast of upper and lower parts, whereas in the mink the under parts are essentially as dark as the back, except for white spots or blotches on the throat. The long-tailed weasel is separable from the short-tailed weasel in that its tail is about 50 (44 to 55) per cent of head and body length, whereas in the short-tailed weasel it is about 40 (32 to 43) per cent of head and body length. When the sex is unknown, the female *M. f. noveboracensis,* particularly the skull, is not always easily distinguished from a male *M. e. bangsi.* Size of skull alone will separate the two species when the sex is known. Several specimens of *noveboracensis* from the state, particularly from western Wisconsin, display in size and color an approach toward the weakly marked subspecies *M. f. spadix*.

Measurements.—Total length, adult males, 350 to 431 mm. (13.8 to 17 in.); tail, 115 to 150 mm. (4.5 to 5.9 in.); hind foot, 40 to 51 mm. (1.6 to 2 in.). Weight, adult males, 170 to 245 grams (6 to 8.7 oz.). Skull, adult males, length, 44.3 to 50.8 mm.; width, 23.5 to 27.8 mm. Total length, adult females, 285 to 340 mm. (11.2 to 13.4 in.); tail, 85 to 123 mm. (3.3 to 4.8 in.); hind foot, 30 to 40 mm. (1.2 to 1.6 in.). Weight, adult females, 85 to 130 grams (3 to 3.5 oz.). Skull, adult females, length, 39.1 to 43.5 mm.; width, 19.7 to 23 mm.

Distribution in Wisconsin.—Occurs in suitable habitats throughout the state. Apparently more plentiful in the southern half of the state than in the northern part, where it is outnumbered by *M. e. bangsi*.

Habitat.—Woodland, brushland, open timber about ridges and fields, brushy field borders, and prairies, especially near creeks, lakes, and other water.

Status and Habits.—The long-tailed weasel is subject to cycles of population, as are most mammals, but on the whole it apparently has maintained relatively stable numbers in the state since early days. Based on the average number of weasels reported on trappers' returns, one can roughly estimate the population of long-tailed weasels in Wisconsin as possibly sixty to seventy-five thousand a majority of which are south of latitude 45° north. Population density in some areas may reach 15 to 18 individuals to a square mile, but over many other areas is less than one animal. The home range is about 30 or 40 acres, often less when food is readily available.

Only by chance is one apt to see a long-tailed weasel, but it is always curious over a person's presence and will often quietly show itself, and a squeak or low sharp whistle will cause it to dodge in and out of its hiding place to peek at the source of the noise. I have often "squeaked" a weasel to within three or four feet of me, sometimes when I was not even certain one was around but where the environment looked right. Long ago, one June day in 1895, another boy and myself were sitting on a pile of cordwood at the edge of a woodland near Milton, Rock County, eating our lunch, when a long-tailed weasel became interested in us, watched our every move, and approached within a few inches. We watched each other for nearly an hour, and though he would touch none of our lunch offered him, he continued to peek at us from various parts of the woodpile. In winter, its tracks in the snow may betray its presence, and pellets of regurgitated fur are characteristic, though seldom found. Feces, likewise, are not always visible, it being the habit of this weasel usually to deposit its dung near the nest underground. Tracks or dung left by a female *noveboracensis* may be difficult to separate from signs left by a male *bangsi*.

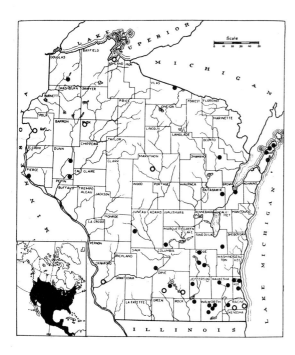

Map 64. *Distribution of* MUSTELA FRENATA. ● = specimens examined. ○ = authentic records.

Feces of M. F. NOVEBORACENSIS *from specimen sent by Francis Zirrer, Hayward, Wisconsin.* 1×.

This species is frequently active during daylight, although it is generally considered nocturnal. Probably the state of its hunger and the time of activity of its prey help determine its own time of maximum activity; chipmunks and ground squirrels, for example, are diurnal, whereas most mice and the flying squirrel are nocturnal. It is active both summer and winter, and seldom moves its abode except in the case of food shortage, and then only for distances of less than four or five miles. Its movements and gaits are similar to those of the short-tailed weasel, but being a larger animal, the distances of its leaps and the height of them are greater, though its maximum running speed is probably no faster. It climbs trees, particularly when chasing its prey, but does so with some difficulty, most frequently by spiralling around the trunk, and may ascend to a height of 15 to 20 feet, yet never appears free and at home in such a situation. It is a slow swimmer and tends to avoid getting thoroughly wet, though it likes to splash and play in shallow water.

The New York weasel has few methods of communication, but frequently utters a hissing sound when angered or excited. It has been observed rubbing and dragging its body over surfaces, possibly to leave scent from its glands. When tormented or captured, it frequently utters a sharp shriek. Its senses are well developed, and those of smell and hearing are especially acute. Its sight is excellent, and its curiosity will often prompt it to come forth to investigate a slight noise, when it will often stand erect with head at right angles to the body in order to see the object of disturbance. It will attack aggressively and ferociously any animal that interferes with its attempts to capture its prey, and there are many instances where one has viciously attacked a person who has tried to capture it or to interfere with its hunting (Wight, H. M., 1932; Oehler, C., 1944). Its length of life is unknown, but it probably does not differ greatly from that of the short-tailed weasel.

One litter of four to nine young ones is born each year between mid-April and mid-May, usually about the last week of April. The more usual number in a litter is six to eight young. Philip L. Wright (1942 a, 1947, 1948 a, 1948 b), studying the subspecies *longicauda* and *oribasus* at the University of Montana, has given us information on breeding habits and reproduction in this species. Males remain sexually immature during the first summer, and females three or four months old as well as old ones are bred by the adult males, during July or August. The length of the gestation period ranges from 205 to 337 days, the average being 279 days (Wright, 1948 a: 342), the embryo remaining quiescent through delayed implantation until the last 27 days of pregnancy, when development is more rapid (Wright, 1948 b: 602). The young are born with scarcely a trace of pale hairs on the head, and shoulders are without pigment except for the eye spots, showing only the pinkish color from the blood. Eyes, closed at birth, open in about 35 days. Development is on the whole rapid, the youngster at three months being essentially mature and two-thirds or more grown. The male assists in the care of the young ones, at least during their early period of growth. The mammae are eight, four abdominal and four inguinal.

The nest site or den is well hidden and is generally in the burrow of a chipmunk, ground squirrel, pocket gopher, or mole, though sometimes it may be in a hole or crevice in or under a stump, in a stone wall, among rocks, or even in a haystack. Rarely, it makes its den around barns. A more or less typical nest of the closely related subspecies *spadix* has been described from near Ames, Iowa:

The first den excavated was located in a weed patch. It was an old mole run that had been used by at least two weasels during the winter months. The nest was an enlargement of one of the runs about six inches below the surface of the ground and about two feet from the entrance of the burrow. The nest cell was nine inches in diameter and had four burrows radiating from it. This nest chamber was filled with grasses packed in a layer-like formation. In the center of this mass was a nest hollow lined with patches of mouse and shrew fur. Beneath this layer of fur and at the sides of the nest were skins, various bones, and skulls of partially eaten mice and shrews. The presence of scats in the nest mass indicated that the weasels had defecated in the nest. At intervals layers of clean grass had been laid over the filth of the former bed, thus giving the nest a stratified appearance. A mass of scats was found packed into one of the radiating tunnels, and some mouse and shrew remains were found stored in two other tunnels. (Polderboer, Kuhn, and Hendrickson, 1941: 117).

The long-tailed weasel probably is the most relentless, persistent, fearless, and rapacious of carnivores in the pursuit of its prey. Its food consists chiefly of mammals, mice of the genera *Microtus* and *Peromyscus* constituting more than half of its diet, though around farm buildings it may consume large numbers of house mice and brown rats. It catches numbers of rabbits, mostly those a few weeks old, near 12 per cent of its food being rabbits. In a chase it is seldom able to capture a rabbit or hare more than half grown, but in a confined space may kill a large one occasionally. It catches chipmunks and ground squirrels, eats shrews of the genera *Sorex* and *Blarina,* and at times consumes a common mole or a star-nosed mole. Wild birds are seldom molested, but when mice and rats have become scarce, a long-tailed weasel frequently has entered a poultry house and killed a considerable number of fowls, and at times it attacks young poultry in the farm yard. Polderboer (1948 a) records its predation on three-day-old pigs at Marion, Iowa. Insects constitute a very insignificant part of its food, rarely more than 5 per cent, usually less. Its method of attacking its prey is essentially the same as that of the short-tailed weasel. It has been claimed that this weasel habitually "sucks the blood" of its victims, and preferably eats the brains, but evidence is not conclusive. Sometimes it may, other times it does not. Apropos the killing technique and the blood-sucking habit are the following observations made in Dane County, Wisconsin:

The following observations were witnessed by Prof. G. M. Longenecker, Mr. Donald McBeath, and myself. On June 3, 1935, we were driving very slowly along an unfrequented road on the University Arboretum near Madison. From the grass 20 feet ahead of us at the side of the road a cottontail rabbit, about one-third grown, appeared and came hopping toward us. On his trail and about 10 feet behind him was a weasel. I hurriedly stopped the car and we all leaned out of the open windows, but barely in time to see the action, which took place when the cottontail was directly alongside the car and 4 feet away. At this spot he turned again into the grass and just then the weasel overtook him. Evidently sensing our presence, the latter struck the rabbit on the run, and without any pause continued out of sight into the dense growth. The cottontail squealed, collapsed, and lay kicking, a small patch of blood showing at the base of its skull. The in-

credible swiftness of the action is still vivid in our minds.

The weasel returned several times within 4 feet of the expiring rabbit to size up the situation, then finally moved in to its kill. The rabbit squealed a second time, evidently as he received the final *coup de grace.* Then came the blood-licking, the weasel sucking or licking the wound and the blood which had spilled on the rabbit's fur. This lasted several minutes, but was conducted with such swift dexterity that it was hard for the eye to follow the details.

Apparently the weasel was not satisfied with our presence, for he picked up his prey and loped off about 15 feet to the base of a roadside tree. This was an amazing feat. The rabbit must have weighed twice as much as the weasel. One might liken it to a terrier loping off with a sheep, but there was no indication that the load placed the slightest strain on the weasel's speed or strength.

The blood-sucking now continued, but not in plain sight. One of us, in an effort to see, made a slight noise, which caused the weasel to rear up for a look around. By this action one could clearly see that his snowy chin and throat were entirely free of blood stains, another evidence of the skill with which the whole job was executed. The situation evidently was unsatisfactory to the weasel, for again he picked up the rabbit and with effortless bounds disappeared into a dense path of nettles (Leopold, A., 1937).

A number of predators are known to attack the long-tailed weasel, though its quick actions and pugnacious behavior probably often save its life. In Wisconsin there are several records of its having been eaten by the great horned owl (Errington, Hamerstrom, and Hamerstrom, 1940). Elsewhere, the black snake and the rattlesnake have preyed upon it, and among raptorial birds the rough-legged hawk, goshawk, and barred owl are included. The domestic cat sometimes catches one, and the dog rarely. In Pennsylvania both the gray and the red fox prey upon it (Latham, 1952: 516). Automobiles kill a few on the highways (Steinke, 1953). The species also is sometimes endangered by heavy rains.

Fleas are common on the long-tailed weasel, and several species have been reported, including *Ceratophyllus faciatus, C. vison, Neotrichodectes mephitidis,* and others. The ticks *Dermacentor variabilis* and *Ixodes cookei* and the lice *Trichodectes retusus* and *T. kingi* also are found. Internal parasites include the trematode *Alaria taxideae,* cestodes of the genus *Taenia,* and the nematodes *Filaroides martis, Physaloptera max-illaris, Skrjabingylus nasicola* (Erickson, 1946: 502), and *Capillaria mustelorum.*

Economically, *Mustela frenata noveboracensis* is more of an asset than a liability, though it has characteristics that make it a little less desirable citizen than either of the two other Wisconsin weasels, the short-tailed and the least. It destroys quantities of field mice, and kills more brown rats and house mice than either of the others, but it also kills more rabbits, which in many instances might be marked as a debit. Moreover, individuals of this species are more prone to attack domestic poultry. However, such action may often come only after it has cleaned out a rat population around the farmyard which may have destroyed more poults than the weasel. Its prime winter fur when white has as high a value as that of the ermine, but the number of white pelts is less in proportion to the weasel population since many long-tailed weasels are brown throughout the winter. Select long-tailed weasel pelts, however, bring a higher price in the fur market than select short-tailed weasel pelts, the high reaching sometimes up to $3.50 a pelt, though ordinarily the trapper may anticipate not more than $1.00 for each weasel skin. The estimated total harvest of all weasels in Wisconsin for the 1949–50 fur season was 19,223, with total value of $16,147.32, or an average pelt value of 84 cents (Scott, W. E., 1950).

Specimens examined from Wisconsin.—Total 135, as follows: *Brown County:* Green Bay, 1 (NPM). *Dane County:* Madison, 2 (UWZ). *Dodge County:* Beaver Dam, 54 (UWZ); Rolling Prairie, 1 (UWZ); Trenton Township, 1 (UWZ). *Door County:* Fish Creek, 5 (UWZ); Peninsula State Park, 4 (UWZ); State Game Farm, 14 (UWZ); Whitefish Bay, 1 (MM). *Douglas County:* Gordon, 1 (UWZ). *Dunn County:* Colfax, 4 (UWZ); Meridean, 1 (UWZ). *Fond du Lac County:* Spruce Lake, 1 (MM). *Jefferson County:* Lake Mills, 1 (UWZ). *Juneau County:* Camp Douglas, 1 (AMNH). *Marquette County:* Briggsville, 1 (MM). *Milwaukee County:* Hales Corners, 1 (MM); Milwaukee, 6 (MM); North Milwaukee, 2 (MM). *Oconto County:* Kelley Brook, 1 (MM). *Outagamie County:* Oneida, 1 (MM). *Pierce County:* Prescott, 2 (MM). *Racine County:* Waterford, 2 (UWZ). *Rock County:* Milton, 4 (2 MM; 2 UWZ). *Sauk County:* Prairie du Sac, 1 (MM). *Vilas County:* Mamie Lake, 4. *Walworth County:* Delavan, 7; Elkhorn, 1 (UWZ); Lanes Mill, 6 (UWZ); Lauderdale Lake, 1 (CAS). *Waukesha County:* Nashotah Lake, 1 (MM); Pewaukee, 2 (UWZ).

Selected references.—Hall, E. R., 1951; Hamilton, W. J., Jr., 1933 b; Pearce, J., 1937; Polderboer, E. B., L. W. Kuhn, and G. O. Hendrickson, 1941; Wright, P. L., 1947, 1948 a.

Mustela vison letifera Hollister
Upper Mississippi Valley Mink

Mustela vison letifera Hollister, Proc. U. S. Nat. Mus. 44: 475, April 18, 1913.
Putorius Vison Lapham, p. 43, 1852.
Putorius vison Lapham, p. 338, 1853; Strong, p. 437, 1883; Jackson, p. 28, 1908.
Lutreola vison Snyder, p. 125, 1902; Hollister, p. 28, 1910.
Putorius vison lutreocephalus Cory, p. 361, 1912.
Mustela vison letifera Schmidt, p. 117, 1931; Barger, p. 10, 1952.
Mustela vison Komarek, p. 206, 1932.

Vernacular names.—In Wisconsin, commonly called mink. Other names include American mink, *ching-woose se* (Chippewa), common mink, minx, Mississippi Valley mink, *n'pshikwä* (Potawatomi), vison, and water weasel.

Identification marks.—The largest member of the genus *Mustela* in Wisconsin, adult males varying from 23 to 27.5 inches in total length and adult females from 18 to 22.6 inches, with the characteristic weasel-like body and proportions, but with rather bushy tail; fur of dark brown color both on back and ventral parts, though often scarcely if any darker than the upper parts of any of the Wisconsin weasels; under parts always dark brown except for white blotches on chin and throat, and sometimes broken white streaks or blotches on mid-line of chest and belly; tail not only more bushy but also darker than in the weasels, almost black above and below and becoming even more blackish near tip; tail about one-third of total length, very slightly tapering; fur dense and glossy, adapted to aquatic life.

The general color of this mink is almost uniform dark rich brown, nearest burnt umber or chocolate, becoming nearly black at tip of tail; under parts scarcely a shade paler than upper parts, rarely as pale as Prout's brown; chin whitish, and occasionally there are white spots, blotches, or streaks on the throat, chest and belly. The mink never turns white in winter, but retains the dark color throughout the year. The spring molt usually begins in March or April, and the shorter summer fur is acquired by the latter part of April or in May. Under natural conditions in the wild the mink usually sheds its sum-mer fur late in August or early in September, and in Wisconsin it may acquire the full glossy, dense winter coat by the last of October.

The skull is moderately strong, somewhat flattened, with short, broad rostrum and evenly spreading zygomatic arches; lambdoidal ridge well developed in adult, and usually extending posteriorly almost as far as posterior border of condyle, thus almost obscuring foramen magnum in superior view; auditory bullae moderately inflated, about 1.5 times as long as wide; bony palate extends a considerable distance posterior to back molars, the extension nearly as great as the depth of the palatal notch; upper molari-form or cheek teeth four on each side, medium in size, the posterior one depressed medially postero-anteriorly into somewhat hourglass pro-file, shorter than third molariform tooth.

There is a distinct sexual variation in size, the males averaging something more than 10 per cent larger in dimensions than the females. Age changes only slightly the appearance of the mink during growth, though extremely old animals may show a slight grizzling, and young ones are usually a shade paler than adults. There is con-siderable variation individually in the shade of brown, and worn fur always shows a paleness on account of fading. The amount of white spot-

Young mink. Experimental Farm, Poynette, 1938. Photograph by Dorothy Ferguson. Courtesy Wis-consin Conservation Department.

Mink, MUSTELA VISON, *in eastern Oregon. Courtesy Harry H. Sheldon.*

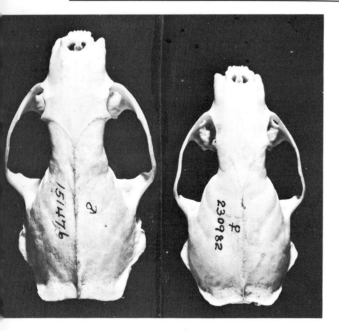

Skulls of M. v. letifera. *Left, Delavan, Wisconsin. Right, Mamie Lake, Wisconsin.*

Left hind foot of mink. 1×.

ting on the under parts varies, and there are records of wild minks being classed as "white spotted," "mottled," and "silvering" variants. Albino minks in the wild have been reported, as have also "drab" and the more expected variation, "nearly black."

By crossbreeding and selection, particularly with the Yukon mink (*Mustela vison ingens*) as a standard stock, mink farmers have produced many mutants and other variants that may not occur in the wild mink, and that have acquired such descriptive trade names as Aleutian, ambergold, blue iris, gunmetal, natural dark, pastel, platinum, sapphire, snowhite, steelblu, two-tone, white, and winterblu, some of the names having further color descriptions by divisions into light, medium, and dark.

The mink cannot easily be confused with any other Wisconsin mammal. The dark chocolate color above and below, except for white chin and throat marks, and the moderately bushy tail slightly tapering are distinctive. The smallest female mink is larger than the largest male New York weasel, and the skull of the mink always has a length of more than 54 mm. and a width of more than 29 mm., whereas any weasel skull measures less. The otter is somewhat similar in color to the mink but is much larger, has tail heavy at base tapering apically, a different type of pelage, and noramlly no white spots or blotches on the under parts.

Measurements.—Total length, adult males, 580 to 700 mm. (22.8 to 27.5 in.); tail, 190 to 230 mm. (7.5 to 9.0 in.); hind foot, 68 to 80 mm. (2.7 to 3.1 in.). Weight, adult males, 1.9 to 3.6 pounds. Skull, adult males, length 65.2 to 72.4 mm.; width, 36.2 to 43.6 mm. Total length, adult females, 460 to 575 mm. (18.1 to 22.6 in.); tail, 150 to 190 mm. (5.9 to 7.5 in.); hind foot, 60 to 70 mm. (2.4 to 2.8 in.). Weight, adult females, 1.5 to 2.4 pounds.

Distribution in Wisconsin—All of the state in favorable habitats, and occurring regularly in every county, its abundance in a degree apparently being measured by the amount of such habitat. A few of the specimens from northeastern Wisconsin show in smaller size and darker coloration a slight trend toward the northeastern form, *M. v. vison*, yet are more nearly like *M. v. letifera*, to which subspecies all Wisconsin minks are referred.

Habitat.—Banks of lakes, marshes, rivers, and other waterways, particularly if forested, log-strewn, or bushy. Sometimes in shallow water cattail marshes, if broken by stumps, logs, or old muskrat houses.

Status and Habits.—Except as affected by trapping pressure and demand for pelts, the mink probably has maintained a comparatively stable

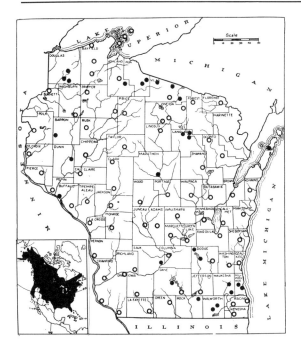

Map 65. Distribution of MUSTELA VISON. ● = specimens examined. ○ = authentic records.

miles in one night, and even find itself in an unusual habitat, as witness one captured behind a refrigerator in a saloon on Ninth Street, Milwaukee, in 1899 (Bennetts, 1900: 64).

The mink is not an excessively shy mammal, and where it occurs commonly one may be glimpsed occasionally at dusk, often it will watch an intruder with curiosity for several seconds. Its inquisitive watching may be prolonged by one's squeaking or chirping like a mouse or bird. Persons adept at locating minks can sometimes determine its presence in a neighborhood by the fetid odor from its scent glands, from

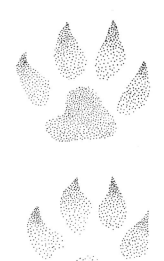

Tracks of mink. Above, right fore foot. Below, right hind foot. 1×.

Mink feces. Adapted after Seton, 1929, vol. 2, p. 701.

population in the state since the days of the early fur markets. Mink pelt receipts at Green Bay from 1800 to 1820 apparently were fewer than marten pelts, but the price was about the same, frequently the mink pelts being the higher. As long as the environment was not too much disturbed, minks continued in fair numbers, and they may possibly have increased in numbers during some recent years. For example, trapper license reports for mink show an increase in the catch from 26,155 in 1943 to 43,898 in 1944, followed by a gradual increase to 49,762 by 1947. The year 1948 showed a noticeable decline to 12,908, followed by 35,060 in 1949, 28,234 in 1950, and a drop to 19,537 in 1951. On the basis of these reports, one might estimate an average population of not far from 160,000 to 180,000 wild minks in Wisconsin. Normally, the home range of the mink is only a short distance for a carnivore, the female seldom going more than one-fourth mile from its den and usually confining its activities to an area of 30 or 40 acres, while the male may double the area and distance covered by its smaller mate. At times, particularly during food shortages, the mink may travel considerable distances, as far as 15 or 18 which a liquid discharge is often made when the animal is irritated, injured, or greatly excited. To most people this scent is more disagreeable than that of the skunk. The dung is fairly characteristic. The best way to determine the presence of a mink is to select a proper habitat and then search for tracks in wet sand, mud, or snow. They do not make regular runways, but sometimes may follow those of muskrats or other animals. Mink, though primarily nocturnal, seem to be more active at dawn and at dusk, and not infrequently may be active on cloudy days and sometimes on clear days, yet in winter "tend to be inactive during cold periods following precipitation" (Marshall, 1936: 388). It is active during all seasons of the year, but appears to be less so in winter than in other seasons. Its usual locomotion is by a series of bounds or leaps, each 10 to 16 inches long, and even though it moves only a short distance, it will frequently do so by a single bound. It runs slowly and can be overtaken by a man on foot, its fastest speed not exceeding eight miles an hour. At times when traveling it will slide or toboggan down a snow bank. It swims well, moving quickly in the water, but seldom attempts to swim distances of more than 80 or 100 yards unless hard pressed. It can dive to depths of 15 or 18 feet, and may alertly swim under water for a distance of 75 to 100 feet, usually submerged less than a foot. Its ordinary progression in water is about 100 feet a minute, or a little more than one mile an hour, which, however, under urge may increase to nearly two miles an hour. In New York, it has been seen in "what appeared to be a knot floating down stream but [was] in reality a mink curled up and apparently asleep. Motion on the part of the men [observers] always awoke the animal and caused it to dive and sometimes appear on the bank some distance up stream" (Gianini, 1927: 244). It frequently climbs around logs and stumps, and may rarely climb small trees to a height of about ten feet.

Not particularly unfriendly among its own kind, the mink nevertheless should be classed as a solitary animal, as it occurs in a group only in the case of a mother and her young. The female will sometimes tolerate the male for a short time while her young are with her. When adult minks of either sex come together at any time other than the mating season, it is the

occasion for a fight that consists mostly of much shrieking, snarling, and tumbling, but probably very few injuries. A fetid odor is discharged by the anal scent glands during any such fight. It is not so pugnacious as the New York weasel when captured, and can be confined and to a small degree tamed. It is a bundle of nervous activity, strong in muscle, and extremely hard to kill. One should not expect to shoot a mink in the wild and recover it, as I have learned from many examples. Harry H. Sheldon, one of our field men, reporting from Solon Springs, Douglas County, on August 8, 1919, says:

I saw a mink hunting along upturned roots of trees, logs, etc., at edge of water. It disappeared among the roots and I rowed up to within good range and commenced to squeak. He came out at once and stood with paws upon log and hind feet in water, his head and throat being concealed by a limb. The shot to his under parts brought forth a great deal of commotion and screaming, but he escaped, undoubtedly mortally hurt. It had been eating crawfish as I found several fresh remains, the claws and parts of the shell were in quantities close to where I had shot at it. The strong odor from the scent sac was to me more disagreeable than that of the skunk and must have been expelled in no small quantities.

The sense of smell in the mink is acute, those of hearing and sight moderate. It is not as playful as the otter, nor possibly as the weasels, but adults sometimes engage in gymnastics that appear to be play, and the mother and kits frequently play together. The life span of the wild mink is not accurately known, but its potential longevity may be near eight or nine years, and its life expectancy is probably not more than three or four years.

The mink is a promiscuous breeder, and during the mating season a male may visit two or more females and a female may receive two or more males, and may share her den with the male (Marshall, 1936: 388). The mating season may begin as early as the last of January, more often in February, and extends through March, and at times well into April. The period of gestation is variable, from 40 to 75 days, the fluctuation probably due to variations in delayed implantation of the blastocysts. The average gestation period is 51 days. It is known that regardless of date of breeding, embryonic attachment is only for 30 to 32 days, the fertilized ova being free during the early stages of impregnation (Enders, 1952: 739). The young are born in April or May, and are three to six in number, usually four; a litter of ten has been reported, but this may have been two litters combined. The mammae are six, two abdominal, four inguinal. The kit is naked at birth, with eyes closed, and is pale pinkish in color. Growth is rapid, and when the kit is about 25 days old its eyes are open and it is covered with a sleek coat of short hair. At five or six weeks it is being weaned and accepts food from the wild that its mother provides, and when eight weeks old it attempts to capture small animals for itself. The mother and youngsters usually stay together as a family until autumn, when the family separates and each member is on its own. There is one litter a year.

The den is near water and may be in a hole under tree roots, a stump, or a log, sometimes in a hollow log, a crevice in a rock, or a cranny in a drain, bridge, or pier, not infrequently in an abandoned or pilfered muskrat house, and occasionally in a hole in the steep bank of a creek, river, or lake. A great majority of the dens in Wisconsin are made in abandoned burrows of the muskrat or some other mammal, although the mink may dig its own burrow. The burrow is 8 to 12 or more feet long, 4 or more inches in diameter, and 2 or 3 feet under the surface, always with one or more entrances just above the water level, and occasionally with a steep entrance to the soil surface above. The male has his own den, and does not build such a complete nest as the female, which has a nesting and brooding enlargement of the burrow a few feet back from the water-side exit. The nesting den is 10 to 12 inches in diameter, and is lined with grass, plant fibers, feathers, and fur to make a snug home for the kits. Feces and urine of the adult are usually deposited outside the den or burrow. An interesting comment on mink behavior comes to me from Mr. Francis Zirrer:

Here three miles west of Hayward a mink visits in summer the nearby pond to prey on water birds and other animals. The pond is one of those "bottomless" basins of water set in a floating, shaky, sphagnum-tamarack-spruce bog. Since it is not so easy to negotiate the rim of the floating bog from the side of the water, and the mink apparently does not deposit its droppings into the water, the animal burrows a tunnel through the matted vegetation commencing at the water level and emerging at the top 4 or 5 feet from the rim. There it deposits its droppings and returns, not the same way, however; another similar tunnel, a few feet further, leads back to water. The piles of droppings are bluntly cone-shaped, about 2 inches high and wide, and composed of slate-colored dirt, hair, feathers and bones. The animal uses this for weeks at a time, for some of these piles are fresh, others appear older, and some are washed out so that nothing but hair, feathers and bones remain. The most remarkable are the bones, some of them an inch and a half long and so sharp that one cannot understand how they pass through the intestine of such a comparatively small animal (Zirrer, F., in letter to H. H. T. Jackson, March 25, 1942).

Unlike the weasels, the mink does not habitually store its food. Sometimes it will kill several animals, however, and eat part of each one and leave the remains. In its attack it is as ferocious and persistent as the weasel, and once it has found its prey the animal of its choice has little chance of escape. Stories and pictures of minks and weasels hanging by their jaws to birds in flight until they were brought down to earth dead, seemed fantastic lies to me as a small boy. It may sometimes happen, however. About 9:00 A.M. November 27, 1908, as I rounded a hilly point and came in full view of a part of a marsh at Storrs Lake, one mile east of Milton, Rock County, I saw lying belly down on the soft mud a big mallard drake, apparently dead. I approached cautiously, and discovered that the duck was dead, but also found tracks of a large mink around the bird, leading across the mud flat, through a narrow strip of the marsh, and onto dry ground where I could not follow them farther. I did not see the mink, though it might have left when it detected my coming. There were no duck tracks anywhere, and no tracks indicating that a mink had entered the area. A large hole and blood stains at the upper left base of the neck showed where the mink had attacked the bird. All evidence clearly indicated that the mallard flew for many yards from open water with the mink dangling from its neck. The mallard was preserved as a specimen and sent to the late R. D. Hoyt, Seven Oaks, Florida. One should not conclude from this incident that the mink regularly preys upon wild ducks. Birds are a comparatively small item in the diet of the mink, usually less than 10 per cent by volume at any season of the year, a considerable proportion of which may be domestic fowls.

There is often a distinct difference between the winter diet, in which mammals rate sometimes as high as 90 per cent of the volume of food eaten, and that of summer, when crayfish may be dominant in the food. As based upon food studies of the mink in the lower peninsula of Michigan (Dearborn, 1932: 32–33) and at Horicon Marsh, Wisconsin (Stollberg and Hine, 1952: 18–19), the winter food of minks, by volume, consists of: mammals, 32 to 93.5 per cent; birds, 0 to 20 per cent; snakes, 0 to 1.6 per cent; frogs, 0 to 14 per cent; fish, 3.5 to 26 per cent; crayfish, 0 to 9.5 per cent; insects, 0 to 2.3 per cent; and debris, 2 to 5 per cent. Of the mammals eaten in winter, muskrats constituted by volume 24.5 to 66 per cent; cottontail rabbits, 1 to 14.8 per cent; field mice (Microtinae), 9.5 to 35 per cent; deer mice (*Peromyscus*), 1.1 to 5 per cent; red squirrels, 0 to 1.7 per cent; jumping mice (*Zapus*), 0 to 0.6 per cent; moles, 0 to 1.1 per cent; shrews, 0.6 to 15 per cent; and there were traces of house mice, brown rats, and varying hares. Summer food of minks in southern Michigan, as reported by volume, includes: mammals, 19.64 per cent; birds, 0.89 per cent; snakes, 0.61 per cent; frogs, 5.75 per cent; fish, 2.87 per cent; crayfish, 68.22 per cent; and insects, 2.02 per cent (Dearborn, 1932: 31). Of the mammals eaten in summer, meadow mice constituted 56.8 per cent; muskrats, 22.3 per cent; varying hares, 9.75 per cent; short-tailed shrews (*Blarina*), 5.23 per cent; long-tailed shrews (*Sorex*), 1.74 per cent; and common moles, 4.18 per cent. In Carter Caves, Carter County, Kentucky, it was found that two minks collected in the caves had been eating bats, either *Myotis lucifugus* or *Myotis sodalis,* and it was surmised that the minks caught a few bats as they accidentally fell from their ceiling clusters to the floor or stream below (Goodpaster and Hoffmeister, 1950).

Very few enemies are known to prey upon the mink, though it possibly now and then may be attacked by a red fox or a bobcat. The great horned owl sometimes kills one—in a study of the contents of pellets and stomachs of this bird in the northcentral part of the United States, two minks were represented (Errington, Hamerstrom, and Hamerstrom, 1940: 793). Automobiles kill a few, there having been seen dead on the roads in Wisconsin by one observer an average of one mink in about 8,500 miles of country driving (Steinke, 1953: 8). Man traps many of them for their fur.

External parasites of the native wild mink include the biting louse *Trichodectes retusus*; the ticks *Ixodes kingi* and *I. cruciarius;* the fleas *Ceratophyllus vison, Oropsylla arctomys, Orchopeas wickhami, Nosopsyllus faciatus,* and *Nearctopsylla genalis*; and grubs of flies of several species. Internal parasites of many kinds occur in the wild mink, and apparently even more in the domesticated one, particularly when not under proper care. Many species of roundworms, tapeworms, and flukes, as well as protozoa, have been reported from the mink (Erickson, 1946: 501; Gorham and Griffiths, 1952: 31–35). Little is known of diseases in the wild mink, although tularemia and abscesses have been reported. Twenty or more diseases, infections, and poisonings may occur in domesticated mink stock (Gorham and Griffiths, 1952: 6–26).

An individual mink may locally do considerable damage to poultry, particularly chickens and ducks, and unless controlled it may continue its attacks until an entire flock is annihilated. Sometimes it enters a poultry house or coop to attack the fowls, or it may attack the birds in farmyards, poultry pens, or duck ponds. Such raids on poultry are not as frequent as with the weasels. The mink kills numbers of fish, which in the wild has little economic effect, but when it raids ponds in a fish hatchery, it may cause serious damage to fish culture. Its killing of many muskrats may be of real economic value when the muskrats are damaging dikes, drainage ditches, or embankments, but usually is tolerated or condoned only because its own pelt is more valuable for fur than that of the muskrat. Its harmfulness is more than compensated for by the good it does in killing mice, and by its bearing a pelt among the most valuable for fur. Wild mink trapped in Wisconsin produce in favorable years a total sale value of near $500,000. In the year 1950 the estimated total trappers' harvest in Wisconsin of 28,234 minks had a fur value of $551,692.36, and in 1951 the 19,537 pelts had a value of $402,184.64. Minks have been raised in captivity for the production of fur since the middle of the nineteenth century, but only in recent years has mink raising become a major industry. Wisconsin now leads all states in the number of mink farms and in sales of ranch minks, averaging more than one hundred thousand pelts annually. Ranch mink and trapped mink pelts combined have in normal years an annual sale value of more than $2,500,000 in the state.

Specimens examined from Wisconsin.—Total 103, as follows: *Ashland County:* Glidden, 1 (MM). *Barron County:* Turtle Lake, 5 (UWZ). *Buffalo County:* Wabasha Flats, 7. *Dane County:* Madison, 2 (UWZ). *Dodge County:* Beaver Dam, 13 (UWZ); Fox Lake, 2 (UWZ). *Door County:* Fish Creek, 6 (UWZ). *Douglas County:* Saint Croix River, 2 (UWZ); T 42 N, R 14 W, 1 (UWZ); T 44 N, R 13 W, 1 (UWZ). *Dunn County:* Colfax, 8 (UWZ). *Iron County:* Fisher Lake, 1 (UWZ); Mercer, 2 (UWZ). *Langlade County:* Post Lake, 3 (UWZ); T 33 N, R 12 E, 3 (UWZ); T 34 N, R 11 E, 1 (UWZ). *Marathon County:* Mosinee, 1 (UWZ). *Milwaukee County:* Milwaukee, 2 (MM); Wauwatosa, 1 (MM). *Rock County:* Milton, 1 (MM). *Sauk County:* Merrimac (5½ mi. N. W.), 1 (UWZ). *Vilas County:* Crab Lake, 2; Eagle River, 1; Mamie Lake, 1. *Walworth County:* Delavan, 10; Elkhorn, 1 (UWZ). *Waukesha County:* Duplainville, 1 (UWZ); Golden Lake, 2 (MM); Muskego Lake, 6 (MM); Pewaukee Lake, 15 (UWZ).

Selected references.—Enders, R. K., 1952; Errington, P. L., 1943; Gorham, J. R., and H. J. Griffiths, 1952; Hollister, N., 1913; Marshall, W. H., 1936; Stollberg, B. P., and R. L. Hine, 1952.

Genus **Gulo** Pallas
Wolverines

Dental formula:

$$I\frac{3-3}{3-3}, \quad C\frac{1-1}{1-1}, \quad P\frac{4-4}{4-4}, \quad M\frac{1-1}{2-2} = 38.$$

Gulo luscus luscus (Linnaeus)
Wolverine

[*Ursus*] *luscus* Linnaeus, Systema Naturae, ed. 12, vol. 1, p. 71, 1766.
Gulo luscus Lapham, p. 43, 1852; Lapham, p. 338, 1853; Hoy, p. 256, 1882; Strong, p. 437, 1883; Hollister, p. 141, 1909; Hollister, p. 28, 1910; Cory, p. 353, 1912; Barger, p. 12, 1952.

Vernacular names.—American glutton, carcajou or karkajou, common wolverine, devil bear, glutton, Indian devil, *nag-gwy-gway* (Chippewa), skunk-bear, wolverene (secondary spelling for wolverine), and woods devil.

Identification marks.—A large, muscular member of the weasel tribe, the heaviest North American mustelid with the exception of the sea otter (*Enhydra*); general form and proportions quite bearlike; head broad, heavy, rounded; ears short, only slightly pointed, not prominent; eyes medium, forward-looking; nose broad and truncate, in effect almost that of a bulldog; tail rather short, about one-fifth total length, bushy; legs short and sturdy; feet semiplantigrade, relatively large, five-toed, provided with strong, curved, semiretractile claws; under fur not dense but soft, the long guard hairs abundant and rather coarse.

The general color is dark brown to almost black, paler (near buff) on the cheeks, face, and forehead, with two yellowish gray broad stripes extending from the upper shoulder region dorsad along the sides and meeting across the rump, thus producing a conspicuous dark color-patch in middle of back; throat and breast usually and belly occasionally with a few irregular white blotches; tail and feet dark. Details of molting have not been observed, but it probably has two molts annually, one in spring and one in fall.

Skull largest and widest of Wisconsin mustelids, heavily built, upper profile distinctly arched medially in postfrontal region, the prefrontal and maxillary regions being somewhat depressed; sagittal crest and lambdoidal ridge prominent, particularly in the adult male, the posterior extension reaching considerable distance (12 mm. in some skulls) beyond occipital condyles; audital bullae large and conspicuous,

Wolverine near Juneau, Alaska. U. S. Fish and Wildlife Service photograph by Henry Harmon.

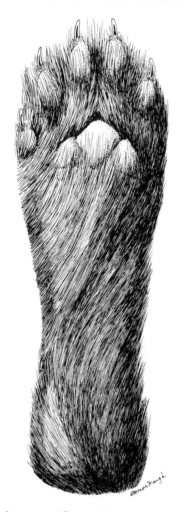

Left hind foot of wolverine. ⅗×.

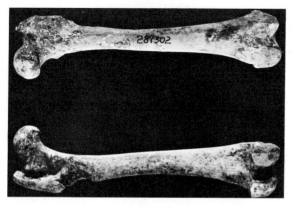

Left femur or leg bone of GULO L. LUSCUS *from Bogie's Cave, Richland County, Wisconsin. Above, anterior view. Below, posterior view. About* ⅗×.

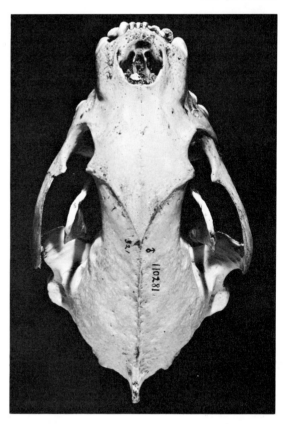

Skull of GULO L. LUSCUS, *Itasca County, Minnesota. About* ⅗×. *Lower jaw attached.*

but not much inflated; nares large, placed well superiorly at angle of about 45° with horizontal axis of skull, the turbinals small, conspicuous, and many; lower jaw short and heavy, so firmly matriculated in the bony hinge to the cranium that in most specimens it cannot readily be separated. The dental formula is the same as that for the marten and fisher, but the teeth are not only considerably larger but are relatively wider and heavier and tend to be less hypsodont.

The male wolverine averages 10 per cent or more larger than the female, the skull not only being larger but also more angular with more pronounced sagittal and lambdoidal ridges. There is little age variation, although young wolverines are paler in color and display less pattern. Maturity in physical form is reached about the third year. There is some individual variation in the paleness or darkness, and in the intensity of coloration, particularly of the "saddle mark" on the back. Apparently mutations have been re-

corded as "dark brown" and "almost black" specimens, and one sure mutation as an albino individual (Jones, S. V. H., 1923: 176).

Measurements.—Total length, adult males, 960
to 1,070 mm. (37.8 to 42.1 in.); tail, 200 to 220
mm. (7.9 to 8.7 in.); hind foot, 173 to 205 mm.
(6.8 to 8.1 in.). Weight, adult males, 30 to 42
pounds. Skull, adult males, length, 166 to 174
mm.; width, 99.5 to 105 mm. Total length, adult
females, 725 to 947 mm. (28.5 to 37.3 in.); tail,
170 to 200 mm. (6.7 to 7.9 in.); hind foot, 170
to 180 mm. (6.7 to 7.1 in.). Weight, adult females, 22 to 28 pouns. Skull, adult females,
length, 132.6 to 149.7 mm.; width, 87.2 to 96.2
mm.

Distribution in Wisconsin.—Formerly, until
about the year 1870, possibly occurred sparingly
over most of the state in favorable wooded habitats, but now probably does not exist anywhere
in Wisconsin.

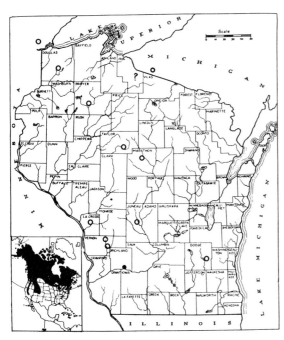

Map 66. *Distribution of* GULO LUSCUS. ● = *specimen examined.* ○ = *authentic records.*

Habitat.—Forests and heavily wooded areas,
sometimes wandering into more open country.

Status and Habits.—Although there are several authentic records of the occurrence of the
wolverine in Wisconsin, only two fragmentary

specimens from the state are known. One of
these is a left femur bone of an apparently adult
female, and the other the distal joint end of a
left femur of a young animal (both accessioned
under No. 287,302, U. S. National Museum)
found by the author August 21, 1920, among
bones of the raccoon, bobcat, and other animals
mixed with the surface soil on the floor of Bogie's
Cave (sometimes called Bogus Cave), Sec. 35,
T 9 N, R 1 E, about two and one-half miles west
of Gotham, Richland County. The deposit was
some 60 feet inside the entrance to the cave
where very little daylight penetrated, and the
bones appeared to be remains of animals that
died there or, less likely, that had been skinned
by trappers and the bodies left (Jackson, 1954:
254). Bogie's Cave is about 25 miles southeast
of Kickapoo River, Vernon County, where Fred
Mather and his trapper companion, Antoine
Gardapee, took two wolverines in October and
December, 1855 (Mather, 1896: 330, 349). Although the locality has been recorded as Bad
Axe River (Schorger, 1946: 90) and was called
such by Mather in his original account, he further states:

As near as I can make out from the map of
Wisconsin in a school atlas of to-day we were on the
fork of the Bad Ax River in what is now Vernon
county, and just north of Readstown; but there was
no town, village or settlement on the river that we
saw or heard of when we went up it in 1855. At
any rate we were near the main forks of the river,
and our cabin was between the streams (Mather,
1896: 371).

Other parts of Mather's account clearly indicate that they ascended what is now known as
the Kickapoo River and came back by the same
route. The site of their cabin camp probably was
in or near Sec. 35, T 12 N, R 3 W, opposite the
mouth of the stream now called Elk Creek.
Two mounted specimens in the Milwaukee Museum that were labeled "Wisconsin" were recorded by me with the comments, "but as there
are no other data we consider the record unsatisfactory" (Jackson, 1908: 14). Later, Cory
says these specimens "may or may not have been
actually taken in the state" (Cory, 1912: 355).
They probably came from Colorado.

The Wisconsin Historical Society has a letter written July 5, 1876, by Charles Mann to A. L. Kumlien,
Busseyville, Wisconsin, asking him what he would

charge to mount the skins of two wolverines from Colorado. Mann was corresponding secretary of the Natural History Society of Wisconsin, predecessor to the Museum. It therefore seems very improbable that the Museum's specimens are of Wisconsin origin (Schorger, 1946: 90).

At the meeting of the Wisconsin Academy of Sciences, Arts, and Letters, July 19, 1870, the following donation to the Museum was acknowledged: "A wolverine (*Gulo luscus* Sabine) killed in Juneau County, and presented by Hon. J. T. Kingston, of Necedah." (Trans. Wis. Acad. Sci., 1: 186, 1872). The collections of the Academy were destroyed in the burning of the State Capitol, February 27, 1904. . . . The Medford (Wis.) *News,* June 8, 1876, mentions that among the animals presented for bounty in Taylor County, since January 1, was one wolverine (Schorger, 1948: 295).

Elsewhere, Schorger (1942: 29) cites a newspaper record for the spring of 1870 for Big Rib River, Marathon County. One was recorded by

Hoy (1882: 256) as taken in La Crosse County that same year, and Hoy further states that they "are occasionally taken in the timber." There may be some doubt about the validity of the 1870 La Crosse County record, since many newspapers in the state mentioned the Big Rib River wolverine simply as trapped "in the pinery."

Another good record comes from Chief Warden Barney Devine and George Ruegger of Radisson in their report that a Mr. Sig Tucsulla trapped a wolverine in the vicinity of Radisson, Sawyer county, in 1922. Other records for Wisconsin are as follows: July, 1883 (Weekly Telephone [Fairfield]) "Lawn Keyes, Burnett, killed a wolverine on Horicon Marsh a few days since, weighing 31-1/2 pounds" (Scott, W. E., 1939: 26).

There are records for Gogebic County, Michigan (Burt, 1946: 144), and St. Louis County, Minnesota (Johnson, C. E., 1923: 54), both of which adjoin Wisconsin. The wolverine probably was always scarce in Wisconsin. I have found no positive records of commercial sales of its pelt,

Tracks of wolverine. Left, right hind foot. Right, right fore foot. ¾×.

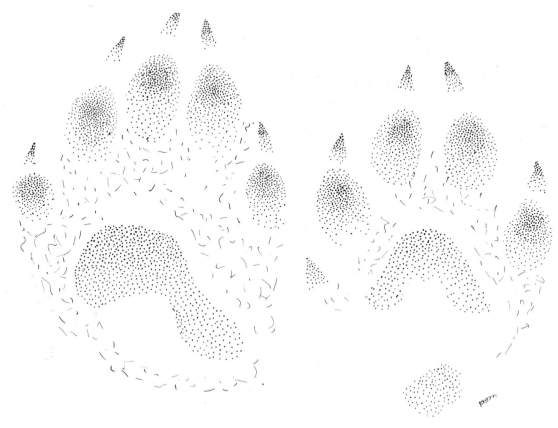

though it may have been so highly prized by the natives as not to be bartered. An individual wolverine may travel great distances, and although there is no research information on its home range, it is believed to be extensive, at least 30 to 50 miles in diameter.

Nearly all of our knowledge of the habits of the wolverine is from observations outside of Wisconsin. The animal is solitary, seldom being found in the wild with another of its kind, except the mother with her kits or a mated pair. It is wary, and is seldom seen except when trapped. Its tracks are quite distinctive when clearly marked, being somewhat like those of a wolf or huge dog, but relatively wider, and usually showing the presence of the fifth toe, the heavy hairiness of the sole, and the characteristic divisions of the sole-pad of the forefoot. In heavy snow or very soft ground or muskeg the belly of the animal may drag a furrow, but otherwise the animal makes no trails or runways except at the entrance to its den. Its habit of plundering trap lines and fouling traps and trapped animals with urine, feces, and scent from its anal glands announces its presence to those familiar with the animal.

Although primarily nocturnal, the wolverine is frequently out during daylight hours. Cold weather and snow do not bother it, and it is active throughout severe winters as well as during milder seasons. It is known to wander alone many miles from its old home, and may rarely establish a new one, but it does not truly migrate. Usually it keeps its home within a few miles of the place of its birth. Its usual gait is a sort of gallop or series of jumps, much like that of a mink or weasel, but at times it walks in a lumbering movement. It is chiefly terrestrial in its activities, yet climbs fairly well, ascending trees by climbing the trunk from the base (Grinnell, G. B., 1921), or rarely by jumping from the ground to a low bough (personal letter to the author from A. H. Twitchell, Flat, Alaska, March 27, 1927). Swimming apparently is not to its liking, and though slow in the water, it progresses firmly and steadily. It also runs slowly and heavily, and although no careful studies have been made of its speed, it probably does not exceed ten miles an hour. It can be overtaken by a fast human runner.

Possibly the chief means of communication be-

tween wolverines is through urine and the anal scent glands, the scent and urine being deposited on objects, particularly near food left by the animal, possibly more of an ownership signal than real communication. Except for grunts and growls when it is irritated, the animal in the wild is rather quiet. One that I observed in the National Zoological Park, Washington, D. C., on June 2, 1928, was uttering a low-pitched, slow, not loud grunt that was not unpleasant to the human ear. The wolverine has a bad reputation as to disposition, based perhaps on a lack of real knowledge regarding its habits and behavior. It is as a rule not aggressive, but will attack and fight when molested, particularly the female with her young. Most mammals, even larger carnivores, retreat to safety when a wolverine appears, which may be due to fear of the fighting power of the wolverine or to dislike of its fetid odor. The result is the same in either case, for often the intruder profits by enjoying the food left by the vanished. It is easily treed by a barking dog, yet when cornered will outfight any dog. Trappers and explorers have told many stories about wolverines following a trap line for miles and fouling both traps and trapped animals by its glandular secretions, urine, and excrement, eating such bait and trapped animals as it fancied, and even destroying traps. Other trappers, however, have maintained that a wolverine may follow a trap line and eat squirrels or other meat used for bait, but does not molest trapped martens or destroy traps (A. J. Cardisky in Grinnell, Dixon, and Linsdale, 1937: 262). Probably the strength and sagacity of the wolverine have been greatly exaggerated, but it is without doubt physically powerful for its size and has tremendous endurance. It is no more mentally alert than others of its tribe, such as the fisher or the marten, but its inquisitiveness, persistence, endurance, and strength make it appear cunning. It is not especially difficult to trap, yet sometimes escapes from a trap because its large foot may not provide a good trap hold, and it may gnaw or pull itself free. Of its senses, those of smell and hearing are well developed, that of touch moderately so, but its sight is poor. Longevity of the wolverine is unknown, but its life expectancy in the wild is probably not more than 8 to 10 years and its potential longevity possibly near 18 years.

Reproduction of the wolverine, based on specimens procured in Alaska, has been studied by Wright and Rausch (1955: 354–55):

Adult females taken in October, November, and January showed unimplanted blastocysts in their uteri and inactive corpora lutea in their ovaries. A late-January and an early-February specimen had implanted embryos of 22 and 68 mm. crown-rump length, respectively. Two early-April specimens were lactating but not pregnant. . . . The wolverine has a long period of gestation like many of the other mustelids. The breeding season is not precisely known, but it probably occurs in mid-summer.

The wolverine is blind at birth and has slight if any indication of hair. Its first fur is pale creamy buff, much paler than that of the adult animal. The baby develops rather rapidly, and when five or six months old parts company with its mother, brothers, and sisters, and shifts for itself. When one year old, it is nearly full grown. There is one litter a year. The mammae are eight, four abdominal and four inguinal.

The wolverine makes little provision for a nest, and is content to find shelter in a shallow cave or rock cleft, or under a rock, bank, or fallen tree, where by pawing and twisting it makes a depression 24 to 30 inches in diameter and about 6 inches deep, sometimes lining it scantily with leaves, grass, and bits of fur. The nest site is usually evident by tracks leading to it. There appears to be no special sanitation, though the occupant as a rule leaves the den to urinate or defecate.

The name "glutton" is often applied to the wolverine on account of its habits of consuming ravenously quantities of almost anything. It is primarily a meat eater, and captures most of its prey, though it is also an extensive scavenger and eats quantities of carrion. Either through choice or on account of meat shortage, it sometimes eats quantities of wild berries. In Wisconsin, the wolverine probably chiefly preyed upon such animals as snowshoe and cottontail rabbits, beavers, woodchucks, squirrels, chipmunks, and mice of various species, as well as rarely upon birds such as grouse and waterfowl. It may possibly have killed a white-tailed deer very rarely, for in other regions it has been known to attack and kill a reindeer and a small moose. Its method of attack is to pounce on the back of its prey. Its slowness of gait would not allow it to "run down" a deer, but it might pounce from a hidden position. Fawns undoubtedly were sometimes killed by the wolverine.

Man is the only important enemy of the wolverine. Not only do trappers catch the wolverine for the value of its fur, but they and other woodsmen take especial delight in killing it on account of its reputation as a robber and fouler of traps and caches, and because of its other reputed misdemeanors. Bears, pumas, and other carnivores much larger than the wolverine are reported to leave food or prey without putting up a fight on its approach. Sometimes a wolverine may be killed by quills from a porcupine it has devoured. The life and feeding habits of the wolverine are such that one might expect the animal to have many parasites, both external and internal. No information is at hand on the external parasites. Internal parasites include the fluke *Opisthorchis felineus*; the tapeworms *Bothriocephalus* sp. and *Taenia twitchelli*; and the roundworms *Dioctophyme renale* and *Soboliphyme baturini* (Erickson, 1946: 503).

The wolverine was never plentiful enough to have any pronounced economic effect on the welfare of the state. It is an interesting mammal that we wish was still a part of our fauna. Its food habits were nearly neutral, as much on the beneficial as the detrimental side. It produced a durable, luxuriant, and beautiful fur that seldom reached the fur trade, the pelt being so highly prized locally as not to enter commercial channels. The fur is said to be one of the few that will not cover with frost when breathed upon in freezing weather. I have never seen mentioned the sale of a wolverine pelt in any of the bills of lading of the early fur sales in Wisconsin.

Specimens examined from Wisconsin.—Total 2, as follows: *Richland County:* Bogie's Cave (sometimes called Bogus Cave), 2 1/2 miles west of Gotham, in Sec. 35, T 9 N, R 1 E, 2 (one left femur and one part of left femur recovered from deposit of cave floor).

Selected references.—Grinnell, G. B., 1926; Grinnell, J., J. S. Dixon, and J. M. Linsdale, 1937: 251–70; Jackson, H. H. T., 1954; Schorger, A. W., 1942: 29; 1946; Scott, W. E., 1939: 26.

Genus **Taxidea** Waterhouse
American Badgers

Dental formula:

$$I\frac{3-3}{3-3}, \quad C\frac{1-1}{1-1}, \quad P\frac{3-3}{3-3}, \quad M\frac{1-1}{2-2} = 34.$$

Taxidea taxus jacksoni Schantz
Jackson's Badger

Taxidea taxus jacksoni Schantz, Jour. Mammalogy
    26 (4): 431, February 12, 1946.
Meles Labradorica Lapham, p. 43, 1852; Lapham,
    p. 338, 1853.
Taxidea Americana Hoy, p. 256, 1882; Strong, p. 437,
    1883; Snyder, p. 122, 1902.
Taxidea taxus Jackson, p. 28, 1908; Hollister, p. 141,
    1909; Hollister, p. 27, 1910; Cory, p. 348, 1912;
    Komarek, p. 206, 1932.
Taxidea taxus taxus Schmidt, p. 117, 1931.
Taxidea taxus jacksoni Barger, p. 11, 1952.

Vernacular names.—In Wisconsin usually
called badger; other names include American
badger, *Americanische Dachs* or simply *Dachs*
(German), *blaireau d'Amerique* or *brairo*
(French), caracajou (in the mid-nineteenth century, possibly used carelessly in confusing the
badger with the wolverine), common badger,
gray badger, *mat-ten-usk* (Potawatomi), *me-suk-
ka-ko-che-se* (Chippewa), *siffleur* (French), and
Wisconsin badger.

Identification marks.—The badger is a heavy,
stout mammal, about as large as a medium-sized
dog, with broad, low body, and short muscular
neck; a large member of the weasel tribe with
conspicuous whitish cheek marks and stripe
from nose to shoulders; head moderate, broad
basally, only slightly flattened, tapering gradually anteriorly; ears rounded, small, upright, the
auditory opening conspicuously large; eyes rather small; nose moderately pointed, the rhinarium small, about one inch wide and one-half inch
deep; tail brushy and short, about one-sixth
total length and about 1.3 times length of hind
foot; legs short; feet heavy, five-toed; claws
heavy, particularly on forefeet, the midclaw on
forefoot more than 1.3 inches long; fur, soft bristles, very strong and elastic, long and shaggy,
particularly on upper parts. Upper parts with
base of hairs near clay color broadly banded
with clove brown or blackish and tipped slightly with cream color or grayish, producing a mixed
clay color heavily infused with blackish and
lightly grizzled or frosted; median cream-colored
or near white stripe from nose over occiput to
shoulders, whitish irregular band from cheeks to
postorbital region; black patch in front of each
ear over temporal region, and broadly blackish
on sides of nose, around eyes, and on latero-
frontal region; ears clove brown or blackish exteriorly, with cream color edge, and whitish interiorly; tail slightly darker in basal color than
back, the tip clove brown or blackish; fore and
hind feet clove brown to blackish; chin and

*Badgerland badger, Wisconsin. Courtesy Wisconsin
Conservation Department.*

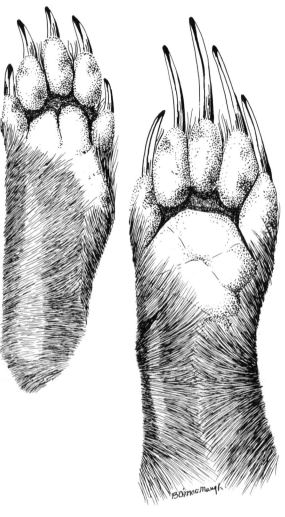

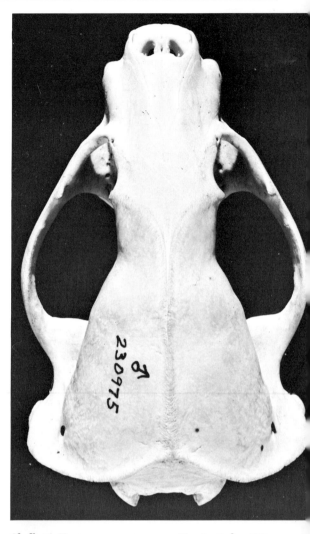

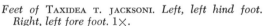

Feet of TAXIDEA T. JACKSONI. *Left, left hind foot. Right, left fore foot.* 1×.

Skull of TAXIDEA T. JACKSONI, *Mamie Lake, Wisconsin.* 1×.

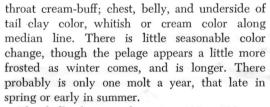

throat cream-buff; chest, belly, and underside of tail clay color, whitish or cream color along median line. There is little seasonable color change, though the pelage appears a little more frosted as winter comes, and is longer. There probably is only one molt a year, that late in spring or early in summer.

The skull is heavy and massive, 110 to 130 mm. long; brain case rather angular, broad posteriorly and narrower anteriorly, the occipital region wide and truncate, the posterior part of skull almost as broad as zygomatic width; facial angle and maxillary region moderately depressed; audi-

tal bullae large, highly inflated; infraorbital foramen rather large, near triangular in anterior view; bony palate extending beyond last molar, its length nearly equal to one-half that of upper molariform tooth row; last upper molar triangular, narrowing posteriorly, usually with two rows of cusplets extending nearly parallel interoposteriorly.

There is sexual variation in that the male averages about 5 per cent larger than the female. Young animals of the year are somewhat darker that adults, and extremely old adults tend to become more frosted in coloration. Besides the usually heavy wear on the teeth, the skull of a very old *Taxidea* has the sagittal crest well developed, averaging sometimes 10 mm. in height over its posterior half, and the lower mandible usually is locked permanently with the cranium at its articulations in the glenoid fossae, as in some other carnivores when senile.

The flat massive body, the short black legs, the median white stripe over the head and shoulders, the white cheek patches, and the black temporal spots will serve to distinguish this animal in the flesh. The skull of an adult may be distinguished by these combined characters: more than 100 mm. in length, bony palate extending beyond last molar a distance nearly 50 per cent of molariform tooth row, triangular last upper molar, infraorbital foramen triangular in anterior view (not oval in outline as in *Lutra*), and four molariform teeth above and five below (as in *Mephitis* and *Spilogale*, which are much smaller skulls).

Measurements.—Total length of adults, 710 to 800 mm. (28 to 31.5 in.); tail, 120 to 150 mm. (4.3 to 5.9 in.); hind foot, 95 to 128 mm. (3.7 to 5 in.). Weight, 14 to 26 pounds; an adult male (type-specimen of *Taxidea t. jacksoni*) from four miles east of Milton, Rock County, weighed 23 lbs. 6 oz. (Jackson, 1908: 28). Skull length, 110 to 132 mm.; width, 76 to 90 mm.

Distribution in Wisconsin.—Irregular in abundance and distribution throughout the state, found more plentifully in the northern and western parts, and usually rather scarce in the counties bordering Lake Michigan.

Habitat.—Preferably grasslands, sandy fields, and pastures, but also found in sparse brushland and open woodlots, particularly along bases of hills, and in open farmland.

Status and Habits.—Wisconsin, the Badger State, is not so nicknamed because a large number of wild badgers is found therein.

Miners need food and shelter. Those from Southern Illinois went home to winter; those from the east could not, but dodged the cold in such dug-outs as they could hurry up. The eastern men were hence nicknamed Badgers, as if burrowing in similar holes with those animals. This jocose appellation became the badge of all the Wisconsin tribe; and it will remain indelible forever (Butler, J. D., 1888: 79).

Another version, told to me at Platteville, has it that these miners were dubbed "badgers" on account of their digging and burrowing activities

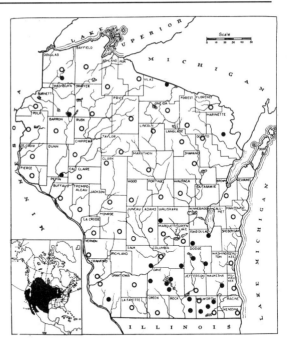

Map 67. Distribution of TAXIDEA TAXUS. ● = specimens examined. ○ = authentic records.

in making holes and tunnels to procure lead and zinc ore. Badgers are not common in most of Wisconsin, though fairly regular and not scarce in some of the western and central counties, and at times showing trends toward becoming more plentiful in some of the southern and eastern parts. "During the eighteen months from August, 1900 until February, 1902, badgers were quite common in certain sections of Rock County; between these two dates there were nine badgers captured within a radius of eight miles of Milton" (Jackson, 1908: 28). Trappers' reports to the State Conservation Department show that in the 25 year period from 1928 to 1952, inclusive, an average of 825 badgers were taken annually, the low number being 190 in 1952, and the high 4,606 in 1939. Low trappers' take is correlated with low fur price. The figures might lead one to estimate a variable population of from five to twenty thousand badgers in the state. The population is never concentrated, and an average density of one badger to two or three square miles over a considerable area would be heavy. The home range of a badger is usually less than twelve hundred feet from its den, though in cases of food shortage or disturbances, it will emigrate to a new location.

A badger usually makes known its presence in a region by its conspicuous home burrow, and by the many big holes it digs and the piles of fresh soil it throws up in burrowing for rodents and other animals. The hole is horizontally elliptical in cross section, some 12 to 15 inches broad and 6 or 8 inches high. Tracks are often seen at entrances to burrows, and though the large foot pads may leave only an indistinct impression in

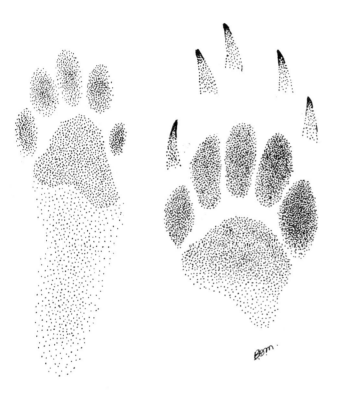

the fresh soil, the marks left by the long front claws are characteristic. Telltale tracks also may be left in soft snow, and in deeper snow a broad shallow trough may be evident where the animal has plowed through. Rarely, a badger is encountered while it forages in daytime, when its sluggish actions may offer a chance for observation.

Chiefly nocturnal in habits, the badger is nevertheless often active in daytime, even in full sunshine, and I have several times encountered an animal afield near mid-day. It seems to dislike excessively hot weather, yet is more active in summer than in winter. It does not hibernate, but in Wisconsin sometimes retires to its den for two or three weeks at a time during cold spells, and may even temporarily plug its burrow from within during severe winter weather. It walks slowly, with body low hung and legs wide apart; when running at its best it rises as high as its short legs and shallow body will permit, very rarely breaking into a gallop, usually progressing at an awkward pace that can barely exceed six miles an hour. The badger is such an efficient excavator that its digging may be considered a method of locomotion. In burrowing it uses the forelegs and mouth to loosen the soil, throws it back with the forelegs, and kicks it out behind with the hind legs, sometimes sending the soil a distance of eight to ten feet. A man with a spade can hardly catch up with a burrowing badger, but five or ten gallons of water thrown in the hole will usually stop the animal's activities and allow one to extract it. Coarse gravel or stones greatly impede its burrowing. Although primarily a land dweller, the badger swims well for a mile or more, tail erect and feet paddling dog fashion, and it can even dive.

Tracks of badger. Left, right hind foot. Right, right fore foot. 1×.

Feces of Wisconsin badger. 1×.

Being a rather solitary animal the badger has little need for intercommunication and has no known vocal signals, though it has been said that it "can utter most alarming vocalizations" and "strange cries . . . in the night" (Texas Fish and Game 8 [4]: 24, March, 1953). The badger growls and snarls when it is harassed, and often makes a hissing noise by heavily breathing through its upturned nostrils. It may even squeal when attacked or in a fight, and when thus angry the long hair parts in the middle line along the back, alternately rises and falls, and fluffs up, the animal meanwhile growling, snarling, hissing, and gnashing its teeth. The badger occasionally grunts, but more often when contented than when angry. It can emit a very foul and fetid odor from the anal glands—its tail aloft as with the skunk when it does so—but it cannot throw the scent. Males also have abdominal glands that have a disagreeable fetid stench. Possibly these abdominal glands may have signal-making use. Belligerent, stubborn, strong, energetic, and persistent as a fighter, the badger can master any animal its size, and, moreover, its tough hide and elastic dermal tissue offers almost a protective armament against dogs and similar carnivores. It will snarl and growl, and make advances at a human, but much of its aggressiveness here seems to be bluffing, and it will gradually back away and finally turn heels and scamper away if pressed too hard. When it enters a burrow in retreat or defense, it usually backs in, thus facing any enemy that might follow it. Though apparently ugly in temperament, it indulges in play, not only the youngsters among themselves, but older animals as well. In captivity it plays with articles in its den, such as dishes, balls, and bones, tossing an object hither and yon and batting it around as would a domestic kitten. Often a badger will romp and play with some other mammal that it has accepted as a friend, such as a domestic puppy or kitten, a bear cub, or a raccoon. Senses are all well developed, those of smell and hearing especially so. Its great endurance often wanes

in intense heat, and when it is hot from excessive exercise it sometimes sprawls out in a puddle of water. Its normal longevity in the wild in Wisconsin is probably not more than 4 or 5 years, but its potential longevity is fully 15 years, and one individual in the National Zoological Park, Washington, D. C., lived to be 15 years and 5 months old.

Little detail is known of the breeding habits of the badger. Mating probably occurs late in August or during September. There is a delay of at least two months in implantation, during which time the monodermic blastocysts lie free in the uterine lumen, implantation and resumption of embryonic development taking place about February (Hamlett, 1932: 300). The young are born from late in April to early in June, the time from inception to birth being approximately eight months, though the active gestation period is possibly less than nine weeks. The one litter annually consists of one to five young, two or three being the usual number. The animal is born with eyes closed and body scantily covered with hair somewhat paler than that of the adult; the color pattern shows clearly. When four weeks old its eyes open; when about half grown—near eight weeks old—it is weaned. The mother carries food to the youngster until it is nearly three-fourths grown (early in autumn), when it shifts

Young badgers, Dane County. Photograph by Dean Tvedt. Courtesy Wisconsin Conservation Department.

for itself and the family scatters. The mother is faithful and guards her offspring desperately. The mammae are eight, four pectoral, two abdominal, and two inguinal.

The brooding nest of the badger is a grass- and herb-lined chamber some 24 to 30 inches in diameter placed 2 to 6 feet underground at the end of a burrow 8 to 30 feet long. The homesite has one entrance, which usually has scant cover of growing herbs or grass to hide it, and frequently is placed near the base of a hill or on an elevated plain. The large size of the entrance, its elliptical shape, and its shallowness tend to identify the owner. Many holes are dug by the badger to procure food, and some of these may be used as rest dens or temporary hideouts, but the nest burrow shows the effects of more use and longer occupancy, and is more energetically guarded by the owner. Little sanitation is practiced around the burrow, and although the badger ordinarily leaves its den to defecate, it may not go far, and makes no effort to remove scats from near the entrance.

Meat and eggs, fresh or decayed, and a small amount of vegetable matter, constitutes the food of the badger. It digs for most of its prey, following by scent and hearing ground squirrels, woodchucks, and other rodents and cottontails in their burrows.

Ground squirrels (67.67 percent), mice (45.55 percent), cottontail (25.49 percent) and insects (27.10 percent) were major food items in central Iowa. Of less importance were birds, pocket gophers, and snakes. Traces of plant material were found in the scats. The most frequent prey, the striped ground squirrel, was taken in greatest numbers in summer when the least number of mice were consumed. Insects, especially various ages of bumblebees, May beetles, and larger ground beetles were eaten in greatly increased proportions during the summer months (Snead and Hendrickson, 1942: 390).

In South Dakota the badger has been found to feed extensively on rattlesnakes, particularly those snakes in hibernation (Jackley, 1944). It sometimes stores food for winter or emergency use, will eat carrion, and is easily baited to a trap by scattering pieces of meat nearby. It frequently drinks water. It is cleanly about its eating, and washes itself by frequent lapping with its tongue. Sometimes it wallows in water, but apparently more for cooling than cleansing purposes.

Few wild animals will attack the badger, since it is a match for anything near its size; hence it has few natural enemies. Two or more large domestic dogs may attack a badger and kill it, but even such a pack more often comes out second best. Man is responsible for the death of most of the badgers killed in Wisconsin, mostly in the normal trapping and hunting for the fur, but some are killed wantonly through sheer dislike of the badger because of inconveniences it may cause by its diggings, or damage it is suspected of doing to poultry or stock. Considering the relative scarcity of this mammal in the state, a comparatively large number are killed by automobiles. External parasites include the louse *Trichodectes interrupto-fasciatus*; the ticks *Ixodes kingi*, *Dermacentor variabilis*, and *D. andersoni*; and the fleas *Pulex irritans* and *Oropsylla arctomys*. Among internal parasites are the fluke *Alaria taxideae;* the tapeworms *Fossor angertrutrudae* and *Taenia taxidiensis*; and the roundworms *Ascaris columnaris*, *Molineus patens*, *Physaloptera maxillaris* and *P. torquata*, and *Trichinella spiralis*. The badger is susceptible to rabies and tularemia.

The badger, emblem of the Badger State, has not only sentimental value but is a useful animal in that it spends a large part of its time unearthing and devouring injurious rodent pests, thus saving quantities of grain and other crops from destruction. It is one of the most beneficial and least harmful of Wisconsin mammals. Its destruction of domestic poultry and stock is negligible. Badger burrows are sometimes made in inconvenient places that may cause injury to cattle and horses and damage to tractors and automobiles. A badger easily may be stopped from digging by a few pails of water, and if a little ammonia or nicotine sulphate is added, a single pailful will make it stop digging and sometimes move its place of operations. The fur when prime is beautiful, though rather coarse, and wears fairly well. It has little sale value, however, the price ranging from about fifty cents to a rare high of seven or eight dollars, and is used chiefly for trimming. Hair of the American badger (*Taxidea*) is used but little for bristles in shaving brushes, the bulk of the supply for that purpose coming from the European badger (*Meles*).

Specimens examined from Wisconsin.—Total 28, as follows: *Columbia County:* Columbus, 1 (UWZ). *Dane County:* Madison (1 mi. E.), 1 (UWZ); Madison (1 mi. S.), 1 (UWZ); Oregon, 1 (UWZ); western Dane County, 1 (UWZ). *Dodge County:* Beaver Dam, 3 (UWZ); Horicon, 1 (UWZ). *Douglas County:* Gordon, 1 (UWZ). *Dunn County:* Meridean, 1 (JNC). *Fond du Lac County:* Fond du Lac, 1 (MM); Waupun, 1 (UWZ). *Grant County:* Hurrican (T 4 N, R 3 W), 1 (mounted in Badger Bank, Cassville). *Marinette County:* Wausaukee, 1 (NPM). *Rock County:* Emerald Grove, 1 (USNM); Milton, 4 (1 MC; 1 MM; 1 UWZ). *Sauk County:* Badger Village, 1 (UWZ). *Vilas County:* Mamie Lake, 1. *Walworth County:* Delavan, 1; East Troy, 1 (MM); Lanes Mill, 1 (AMNH). *Washburn County:* Nobleton, 1 (UWZ). *Waukesha County:* Waukesha, 1 (CNHM). *Waushara County:* Coloma, 1 (BG).

Selected references.—Bradt, G. W., 1947; Errington, P. L., 1937; Hamlett, G. W. D., 1932; Hall, E. R., 1927; Schantz, V. S., 1946; and Snead, E., and G. O. Hendrickson, 1942.

Spotted skunk, SPILOGALE. *Oregon animal in the picture that looks much like the Wisconsin animal. U. S. Fish and Wildlife Service photograph.*

Genus **Spilogale** Gray
Spotted Skunks

Dental formula:

$$I\frac{3-3}{3-3}, \quad C\frac{1-1}{1-1}, \quad P\frac{3-3}{3-3}, \quad M\frac{1-1}{2-2}=34.$$

Spilogale putorius interrupta (Rafinesque)
Prairie Spotted Skunk

Mephitis interrupta Rafinesque, Annals of Nature 1: 3, 1820.
Spilogale interrupta Barger, p. 10, 1952.

Vernacular names.—Civet, civet cat, four-striped skunk, hydrophobia cat, little polecat, little skunk, little spotted skunk, little striped skunk, spotted skunk, and tree-climbing skunk.

Identification marks.—A moderately sized, conspicuously marked black and white mammal of the weasel tribe, closely related to *Mephitis,* but much smaller and slenderer, and having four narrow white stripes on anterior part of back instead of two broader ones and starting independently from a black occiput instead of conjunctively from an anterior white patch; head short; ears rather small; eye moderate, placed

rather anteriorly; nose short, somewhat truncate, the rhinarium and nostrils small; tail hairy and bushy, the length of tail vertebrae about 35 to 38 per cent that of total length of animal, the length of tail to tips of hairs usually about equal to head and body length; legs rather short; feet moderate in size, the pads on both hind and front feet being divided into four tubercles at the base of the toes; claws slender and sharp, the fore ones relatively long; fur rather long, soft and silky.

General color of entire animal black with conspicuous white markings as follows: a white spot or blotch on the forehead between the eyes, one temporal on each side between the eye and the ear, one on each side of the rump, and one on each side of the dorsal base of the tail; two inner parallel white stripes from occiput to middle of back, and two outer broader white stripes from near base of ear to mid-dorsal region of flank, sometimes reduced to separated spots; lateral white stripe extending from behind foreleg almost to rump, where it curves upward onto back; white dorsal stripes continued as spots on rump, meeting transverse white bands, extending from in front of hips; tip of tail usually white, sometimes only a few white hairs, sometimes black; under parts, legs, and feet black. There is no essential seasonal variation in color. It is believed to have one molt annually, late in spring or early in summer.

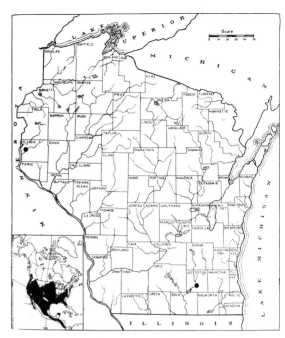

Map 68. *Distribution of* Spilogale putorius. ● = *specimens examined.*

Skull about two-thirds the length of that of *Mephitis*, flat, rostrum only slightly lower than plane of upper surface; lambdoidal crest moderately developed, sagittal crest weakly developed; audital bullae moderate in size, not elongated, considerably inflated medially; postorbital processes obscure, nearly obsolete; zygomata rather evenly arched and rounded; infraorbital foramen medium, rather elongate dorso-ventrally, opening above anterior half of premolar four; posterior border of bony palate nearly on line with posterior borders of upper molars; dentition moderately heavy; antero-posterior diameter of upper molar less than lateral width.

There is some sexual variation, males averaging slightly longer than females, seldom exceeding 5 per cent longer in total length, but averaging nearly 25 per cent heavier. Individual color variation appears to be restricted to the extent of white stripes and spots, which wear of the fur affects but little since the white extends to base of hairs. Color pattern of the young at birth prevails throughout the life of the animal. Mutations as such are unknown.

Measurements (mostly Iowa specimens).— Total length, adult males, 470 to 550 mm. (18.5

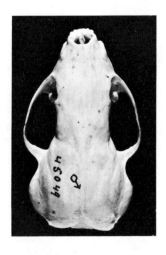

Left, skull of Spilogale p. interrupta, *Gladbrook, Iowa. Right, left hind foot of spotted skunk. Adapted from Seton, 1929, vol. 2, p. 395, and specimen from Iowa.* 1×.

to 21.7 in.); tail, 178 to 220 mm. (7.1 to 8.6 in.); hind foot, 48 to 52 mm. (1.9 to 2 in.). Weight, adult males, 0.8 to 2.8 pounds. Skull, adult males, length, 48 to 56 mm.; width, 32 to 35.3 mm. Total length, adult females, 445 to 482 mm. (17.5 to 19 in.); tail, 165 to 200 mm. (6.5 to 7.9 in.); hind foot, 43 to 47 mm. (1.7 to 1.9 in.). Weight, adult females, 0.7 to 1.4 pounds. Skull, adult females, length, 45 to 54 mm.; width, 31.5 to 33 mm.

Distribution in Wisconsin.—Known only by two specimens, the first one from the east side of Bass Lake, in Sec. 25, T 30 N, R 19 W, St. Croix County, trapped by L. L. Bailey of Hudson, Wisconsin. Through the efforts of State Conservation Warden Lawrence Hope, the skin was procured and is now in the University of Wisconsin Zoological Collections, number 12965. The record was first officially announced by N. R. Barger (1951: 28), and later in the same year was reported in more detail by W. E. Scott (1951), although mention of it in state newspapers appeared early in 1947 (Anonymous, 1947 a). The second specimen was trapped in Jefferson County in 1955, and was first recorded by Frank A. Iwen (1958).

Habitat.—Apparently variable in the nearby states of Iowa and Minnesota: grain and hayfields, tall grass, bushes and scrub openings, weed patches and weedy fence rows, hedge rows, stone walls, grain stacks, farm yards, old buildings, and dry rocky gulches and stream banks.

Status and Habits.—The spotted skunk probably did not occur in Wisconsin very long before the capture of the first specimen in 1946, and although "Mr. Bailey (*fide* Lawrence Hope) stated at the time that tracks of a second individual were seen" (Barger, 1952: 30), only one other specimen has been taken in the state since then. In my rather intensive field work conducted over considerable periods from 1908 to 1947 along the Wisconsin side of the Mississippi River I have made repeated inquiries about spotted skunks and "civet cats" and have never been able to find anybody that knew of the occurrence of the species on the Wisconsin side of the river, though occasionally a person would remark that it occurred on the Iowa side. I have searched especially for it over almost every mile of the bluffs and bottoms along the Wisconsin side of

the Mississippi River and never saw any "sign" that could belong to *Spilogale*. Possibly the Jefferson County specimen had ingress by way of Rock River Valley from Illinois. Apparently the species has been able to cross the St. Croix River, possibly at some point just north of Stillwater, Minnesota. It is not uncommon in the southern half of Minnesota, and occasionally is found in the northwestern part of the state. In the eastern half of Iowa it may reach a winter population density of 13 to the square mile (Crabb, 1948: 218). Both the male and the female spotted skunk were found to have a home range in winter of approximately one-quarter section, but during spring the home range of the male expanded to two to four sections (Crabb, 1948: 232).

The presence of a spotted skunk in a neighborhood may often be detected by the odor, which to one familiar with skunk odors is quite different from that of the striped skunk, being sharper and more pungent.

The tracks are of several types depending upon the speed the animal is making and the method of travel. While hunting the animal may be walking. The hind feet are then placed exactly in the print of the front feet and steps are made at five or five and one-half inch intervals depending upon the particular individuals. By far the most common gait in the field while hunting is a bounding gait. Here the front and hind feet work in pairs after the manner of weasel and mink. The distance between tracks may vary from nine to fourteen inches depending upon the rate of progress and size of the animal. Another track frequently made results from a gallop-

Tracks of spotted skunk. Left, right fore foot. Right, right hind foot. Adapted from Seton, 1929, vol. 2, p. 401. 1×.

ing gait. In this the tracks are more like those of the striped skunk in that the front feet tracks do not register perfectly with those of the hind feet. This gait, as the others may be used at varying rates of speed and with different distances between tracks ranging from seven to ten inches (Crabb, 1948: 207–208).

Tracks of a spotted skunk made in wet sand or snow usually show more distinct claw marks of forefeet, are more widely separated than those of the striped skunk, and are always smaller. Feces may be scattered anywhere along their runways, and according to Crabb (1948: 207), cow paths, dry washes in fields, fence lines, and even low gravestones are likely places to find scats. The scat is about one inch long and one-eighth inch in greatest diameter, differing from that of the striped skunk in being about three-fourths as long and one-half as wide and in having as a rule more tapering ends.

Although the spotted skunk is more active in summer than in winter, it does not have a dormant or sleeping period as does the striped skunk. It is nocturnal, possibly more so than the striped skunk. It is not sluggish, and is quick and graceful in most of its movements, quite weasel-like, though it runs comparatively slowly. It climbs well, sometimes ascending trees 20 feet or more, and often climbing fence posts and stumps, and scampering around rafters in buildings. It is averse to water and swims poorly.

A comparatively silent animal, the spotted skunk when angry may utter a hissing snarl, and when feeding or sniffing expectantly for food may issue a series of low grunts. It is not gregarious, rather independently going about its affairs without regard to others of its kind. It deliberately makes no odor posts or latrines, but often unconsciously leaves its stench. It appears to be less disposed to discharge its scent than *Mephitis*, or at least gives warning by more frequent tail upheavals before it "shoots." It has a peculiar "handstand" habit that has been described by A. H. Howell (1920), C. E. Johnson (1921 c), and Alex Walker (1930). The observations of Dr. Johnson were made on the form *interrupta* at Lawrence, Kansas, on December 28, 1920, at 11 A.M.:

The skunk, which was proceeding at a rather slow, deliberate trot, suddenly threw up its hind quarters into the air and actually ran a few steps on its fore

legs. Its body seemed almost perpendicular and the hind legs were spread apart but were also drawn up somewhat toward the flanks; the tail was erect but drooped more or less over the back and sides and twitched threateningly. . . . in the relatively short time . . . I induced about a dozen of these reactions. . . . A number of times this little beast actually charged me as I stepped in front of it. . . . The last time, however, I held my ground as the skunk bristled and charged directly at me. When within probably 8 or 9 feet of me it stopped abruptly and elevated its rear end, standing perfectly balanced on its fore legs for what seemed at least a couple of seconds. . . . My companion . . . declared afterwards that whenever the skunk rose upon its fore feet a fine spray of vapor could be seen issuing from the vent (Johnson, C. E., 1921 b).

Alex Walker, who had numbers of Oregon spotted skunks under observation at various times over a period of several years, had "seen the 'hand-stand' reactions hundreds of times without having once noted any attempt on the part of the animals to throw scent from that position" (Walker, 1938: 228). Walker considers the "handstand" reaction to be mostly bluff or done in a spirit of playfulness, and explains that during the actual act of discharging the scent the spotted skunk assumes but one attitude, a horseshoe-shaped position with both head and rear facing the object of its attention. So far as known the fluid is chemically about the same as that of *Mephitis* and produces the same effects. To me it seems more acrid and pungent, a characteristic odor that can be identified as that of a *Spilogale*. The spotted skunk possibly does not have its senses more highly developed than the striped skunk, yet it is more active, agile, and alert in every way. It can be raised in captivity, and though it does not make as docile a pet, it is more playful and more interesting to watch than its big brother, and can learn acrobatic tricks. Its longevity is unknown, but individuals have lived in captivity for more than four years; possibly about ten years is its potential longevity.

Little is known of the mating of the spotted skunk, which occurs once a year late in winter or early in the spring, in the latitude of Wisconsin probably in March or early in April. The gestation period, not accurately known, is probably between 60 and 70 days, and the young are born usually between the first of May and the middle of June. They may be from two to six in number, generally three or four, the latter apparently being the most frequent number in a litter. The baby at birth is about four inches in total length, weighs about ten grams or one-third ounce, has eyes closed, and is hairless, though the hair has already begun to form within the skin and shows clearly the black and white color pattern to follow. The eyes open in about 30 days, and development is rapid, so that by mid-August the youngsters are more than half grown, though still foraging with the mother. "Evidently the spotted skunk may attain full size in slightly more than three months" (Crabb, 1944: 219). The mammae are ten, four pectoral, four abdominal, and two inguinal.

Three requirements for the selection of a denning site seem to be exclusion of light, protection against weather, and protection against enemies (Crabb, 1948: 211). The spotted skunk, however, is very adaptable and may lodge or den in almost any conceivable dry shelter, including natural sites such as a hole in a rock ledge; a hollow tree, log, or stump; under a fallen log, stump, or windfall; or in a deserted or confiscated burrow of some other mammal such as a woodchuck or a ground squirrel. Man-made sites frequently are utilized, especially old or loosely constructed buildings, particularly corncribs, graneries, barns, and outbuildings, and sometimes houses; other sites include woodpiles, boardpiles, rock or stone piles, and junk piles; strawstacks and haystacks, particularly long-standing rotting ones; and hollow tiles, drainpipes, and loose bridge abutments. There is more or less community use of dens, especially in the winter, and sometimes five or six animals may be found in one den. A female with her young, however, is always mistress and owner of her own home. Material consisting of grass, hay, and other dry leaves is usually accumulated in the den to form a nest, yet often in a resting den, particularly if in a stump, hollow tree, or fallen log, there may be no nest. Feces are not generally deposited within the den itself, but are commonly dropped anywhere nearby along the trails and paths leading to and from the nest. There are no established latrines.

Although a carnivore in physical characteristics, the spotted skunk is omnivorous in habits, and frequently eats grain such as corn when animal food is scarce, and is fond of many fruits.

Eight striped skunks adopted by cat on Franklin Farm near Portage, June, 1937. Photograph by Eugene Sanborn. Courtesy Wisconsin Conservation Department.

Basing his conclusions on a study of 834 scats found from March 18, 1939, to March 1, 1940, in southeastern Iowa, Crabb (1941 b: 363) found that winter foods were largely of mammal origin, cottontail rabbits appearing in 54.26 per cent of the 75 scats, and that corn was important, appearing in 25.75 per cent. Spring food was also predominantly mammal, native field mice appearing in approximately 80 per cent of 330 spring scats, and insects in 47.57 per cent of the scats. Summer food was predominantly insects, which were found in 92.35 per cent of 254 scats, while mammals occurred in only 34.97 per cent, plant material (mostly fruit) in 26.72 per cent, and birds and birds' eggs in 11 per cent, birds being eaten more frequently at this period than at any other time. Fall food, like summer food, consisted mainly of insects, which were found in 80.46 per cent of 185 scats; mammals appeared in 58.32 per cent, fruits such as grapes, mulberries, and ground cherries in 36.18 per cent, and birds in only 3.78 per cent, fewer during this period than at any other time.

During this investigation insects seemed to be the preferred food with members of the families Carabidae and Scarabaeidae being taken most frequently. Small mammals were a regular and important item in the diet. Norway rats were eaten freely when other food was difficult to obtain. Cottontail carrion and chicken carrion were taken freely during the winter when they were available. Birds appeared infrequently in the diet (Crabb, 1941 b: 363).

The spotted skunk does not store or cache food, though it frequently returns to food that it has left uneaten.

The spotted skunk has few wild enemies, although it is likely that the great horned owl and probably also the barred owl occasionally capture one. Man is the chief enemy, and not only traps them for the fur but also kills them out of pure wantonness. Domestic dogs kill many, even though this skunk is sometimes able to escape by climbing a tree or fence post. Cats capture only a few. Automobiles kill many, but the small size and quick actions of this species hold its relative mortality from this cause lower than that of the striped skunk. It is subject to rabies, so much so as to be called hydrophobia cat or hydrophobia skunk in many places, particularly in the southwest. There is at least one record of rabies in this species in Minnesota. It probably is also susceptible to tularemia. External parasites include the biting lice *Trichodectes osborni* and *Neotrichodectes mephitidis;* the fleas *Echidnophaga gallinacea* and *Ctenocephalides felis;* and the tick *Ixodes cookei.* Internal parasites are the fluke *Alaria taxideae;* the tapeworms *Mesocestoides latus* and *Oochoristica oklahomensis;* and the roundworms *Ascaris columnaris, Crenosoma mephitidis, Physaloptera maxillaris,* and *Skrjabingylus chitwoodorum* (Erickson, A.B., 1946: 503).

In the economy of man the spotted skunk is decidedly more beneficial than harmful. It consumes quantities of noxious insects and mice. At times it has been known to be an important factor in the control of brown rats (Crabb, 1941 a). It has a pelt of beautiful and fairly durable fur, which may bring as much as 65 cents each to the trapper, but ordinarily sells for only 25 or 30 cents apiece. Possibly the mere fact that it is skunk keeps the price low. In Minnesota more than ten thousand pelts of spotted skunks were reported taken in 1943 (Swanson, Surber, and Roberts, 1945: 68). On the debit side, the spotted skunk has the same offensive spray from its two anal glands as the striped skunk, the results and methods of treatment being similar. The spotted skunk sometimes molests chickens

—particularly young chicks and eggs—and other poultry, but it is believed that the habit usually is acquired by the individual skunk and is not a trait of the population as a whole. In such a case the individual should be destroyed. Likewise an animal should be removed when it becomes obnoxious by making its den in or around human habitation. By and large, however, it is a nice mammal to have around.

Specimens examined from Wisconsin.—Total 2, as follows: *Jefferson County:* Fort Atkinson, 1 (UWZ). *St. Croix County:* Bass Lake, Sec. 25, T 30 N, R 19 W, 1 (UWZ).

Selected references.—Crabb, W. D., 1941 b, 1944, 1948; Iwen, F. A., 1958; Johnson, C. E., 1921 b; Scott, W. E., 1951; Van Gelder, R. G., 1959.

Genus **Mephitis** Geoffroy and Cuvier
Striped Skunks

Dental formula:

$$\text{I}\frac{3-3}{3-3}, \quad \text{C}\frac{1-1}{1-1}, \quad \text{P}\frac{3-3}{3-3}, \quad \text{M}\frac{1-1}{2-2} = 34.$$

Mephitis mephitis hudsonica Richardson
Northern Plains Skunk

Mephitis americana var. *hudsonica* Richardson, Fauna Boreali-Americana, part 1st, Quadrupeds, p. 55, 1829.
Mephitis Americana Lapham, p. 43, 1852; Lapham, p. 338, 1853.
Mephitis mephitica Strong, p. 437, 1883.
Mephitis sp. Snyder, p. 121, 1902.
Mephitis hudsonica Jackson, p. 28, 1908; Hollister, p. 27, 1910; Cory, p. 340, 1912; Komarek, p. 206, 1932.
Mephitis mesomelas avia Hollister, p. 141, 1909; Hollister, p. 27, 1910; Cory, p. 343, 1912.
Mephitis mephitis minnesotae Schmidt, p. 117, 1931.
Mephitis mephitis hudsonica Barger, p. 10, 1952.
Mephitis mephitis minnesota Barger, p. 10, 1952.
Mephitis mephitis avia Barger, p. 10, 1952.

Vernacular names.—In Wisconsin, commonly called skunk. Other names include American polecat, big skunk, common skunk, large striped skunk, lined skunk, mephitic weasel, northern skunk, plains skunk, polecat, *shi-gak* (Potawatomi), *ski-kog* (Chippewa), smell-cat, stink-cat, *Stinktier* (German), striped pussy cat, striped skunk, two-striped skunk, and wood pussy.

Identification marks.—This well-known carnivore, an aberrant type of the weasel tribe, is about the size of a house cat, has a large stocky body particularly heavy rearward; head relatively small; ears small, rounded; eyes small, somewhat anteriorly placed; nose rather slender, the nostrils somewhat laterally placed; tail long and bushy, about 35 per cent of total length of animal; legs short; feet heavily palmate, plantigrade; fore claws long, hind claws moderate; fur long, loose, and glossy, the under fur dense and fine, the long guard hairs coarse and flabby. Characteristic are two well-developed scent glands capable of discharging a pungent and malodorous fluid.

A pair of anal glands . . . lie on either side of the rectum, and are imbedded in a dense, gizzard-like mass of muscle which serves to compress them so forcibly that the contained fluid may be ejected to the distance of four or five metres (approximately 13 to 16-1/2 feet). Each sac is furnished with a single duct that leads into a prominent nipple-like papilla that is capable of being protruded from the anus, and by means of which the direction of the jet is governed (Merriam, 1883: 76).

General color glossy black or deeply blackish above and below, with narrow white stripe from base of nose to back of forehead; triangular white patch on top of head, the base forward and the apex rearward, and extending in broad stripe posteriorly over shoulders, dividing anterior part of back into two distinct white stripes enclosing a black median patch and extending posteriorly usually to the base of the tail or onto it, sometimes terminating on the rump, or rarely on the midback; tail black and white of varying proportions, often ending in a mixed black and white tapering brush, sometimes in a blunt black brush, and sometimes with a white pencil; underfur often more grizzled. Winter pelage is longer and glossier than worn summer pelage, which sometimes fades into a dull brownish tinge. Molting occurs once a year, late in summer or early in autumn.

The skull is of heavy structure, highly convex superiorly, and distinctly high in frontal region; rostrum deep and truncate; infraorbital foramen small; palate short, the posterior margin nearly on line with posterior borders of upper molars; palatal notch large, deep, and wide; audital bullae small, slightly inflated; teeth rather heavy, the upper molar somewhat rectangular in outline.

The male is somewhat larger than the female, averaging about 10 per cent heavier and 6 to 8 per cent longer in body and skull length. There is essentially no change in color as age advances, but the skull shows differences, particularly in the development of the sagittal ridge. Individual variation in the extent and pattern of the stripes is considerable, as is also the amount of white in the tail and its distribution. Entirely black individuals sometimes occur. Brown or drab mutations are not rare, silvering seldom occurs, and albinos are scarce. A beautiful albino skunk from Wisconsin was kept in 1937

Striped skunk, MEPHITIS MEPHITIS, *Washington. U. S. Fish and Wildlife Service photograph by Victor B. Scheffer.*

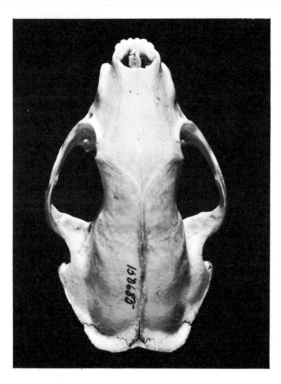

Skull of MEPHITIS M. HUDSONICA, ♂, Eagle River, Wisconsin. 1×.

Left hind foot of striped skunk. Drawn from Wisconsin specimens.

at the State Experimental Game and Fur Farm, near Poynette (Anonymous, 1939 b: 30).

Externally, the striped skunk cannot be mistaken for any other Wisconsin mammal. The skull of a large male mink might be as long as that of a female striped skunk but would be narrower through zygomatic arches, less inflated frontally, and with bony palate extending at least 5 mm. beyond molars, audital bullae more than 10 mm. in antero-posterior diameter, and last upper molar noticeably wider than long. The skull of Spilogale is always decidedly smaller and less inflated frontally than that of Mephitis. All specimen of Mephitis from Wisconsin that I have examined are referable to M. m. hudsonica. There is great variation in characters that may be of taxonomic importance and have been so considered (Howell, 1906) but this variation cannot be assigned either to any particular geographic range or any other grouping. About 10 per cent of the specimens from southeastern Wisconsin (Racine, Walworth, and Rock Counties) show some trend in characters toward M.

m. avia, but on the whole are nearer to hudsonica.

Measurements.—Total length, adult males, 630 to 760 mm. (24.8 to 29.9 in.); tail, 220 to 280 mm. (8.6 to 11.0 in.); hind foot, 72 to 82 mm. (2.8 to 3.2 in.). Weight, adult males, 5.5 to 10 pounds, excessively fat ones in autumn sometimes up to 14 pounds. Skull, adult males, length, 69.9 to 84.6 mm.; width, 42.0 to 54.4 mm. Total length, adult females, 540 to 650 mm. (21.2 to 25.5 in.); tail, 200 to 265 mm. (7.9 to 10.4 in.); hind foot, 69 to 76 mm. (2.7 to 3.0 in.). Weight, adult females, 4 to 9 pounds, excessively fat ones sometimes up to 12 pounds. Skull, adult females, length, 68.0 to 76.8 mm.; width, 42.0 to 46.4 mm.

Distribution in Wisconsin.—Occurs in favorable habitats throughout the state.

Habitat.—Brushland and sparse woods; grassy and weedy fields and pastures, especially along brushy borders; under woodpiles, rockpiles, and buildings; most common along brushy borders of lakes and streams and in thickets in gulches and at the base of cliffs.

Status and Habits.—The striped skunk is the most widely distributed and most common carnivore in Wisconsin, and though it has had periods of lowered population on account of trapping pressure during high fur prices or disease, it has never become actually scarce. The average population is probably more than three hundred thousand skunks in the state, which at a peak may reach more than twice that number. Winter density in favorable habitats is often sixty or more individuals per square mile. In autumn a skunk may wander a few miles to find a suitable winter denning place, but ordinarily its home range is within a radius of one-half mile.

The presence of a skunk in a neighborhood may often be announced by "skunk odor," yet one cannot always depend on this greeting as the skunk may have no pronounced odor unless it has been molested. Then too, the odor from a spot where a skunk discharged its secretion or was killed even many months before may be carried by wind for a mile or more. If a person watches just before dusk in good skunk habitat, one of the animals may come along and show little fear of the observer, who can watch the skunk without danger of malodorous results so long as motion and noise are restrained. At Prescott, Pierce County, on the evening of June 19, 1912, I watched one for several minutes as it

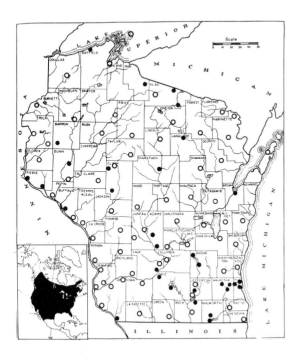

Map 69. Distribution of MEPHITIS MEPHITIS. ● = *specimens examined.* ○ = *authentic records.*

bolted along, digging here and there for insects, until I finally lost it in the darkness. These little diggings, one or two inches deep and three or four inches across, made both by the claws and nose of the animal, are characteristic signs, as are also the dung and the distinctive tracks. The skunk often follows trails, roads, and paths made by other animals, but does not itself make runways. Skunk burrows usually show tracks or detached hairs, and often emit a characteristic skunk odor.

Night is the active time of the striped skunk, though it usually starts its movements at dusk and may not retire till sunrise. It is much more active in summer than in winter, particularly the females and young. True hibernation does not occur. Preparation for winter dens is made the last of October or early in November, and the skunks bed together in groups of about 8 to 12 individuals, with seldom more than one male to a group. Young go into winter sleep before adults, and usually awake a little later in the spring. Males may be rather active in winter, and sometimes take a sleeping den alone. Adults become more or less active by the last of February, and by the end of March both adults and young are quite active. The skunk may roam a considerable distance in the fall in search of a denning site, but no migration occurs.

It is sluggish in movement, usually plodding along in a slow ambling walk at about a mile an hour, sometimes lumbering into a slow trot at about three or four miles an hour, and rarely breaks into a fast trot at five or six miles an hour. It does not climb trees, but can hop upstairs in an old building, and will climb a yard or so on a wire mesh. It is not particularly fond of water, but can swim well for a distance up to three or four hundred feet, though it seems to tire easily. A family bathing in the Wisconsin River between Sauk City and Spring Green in the summer of 1921 saw a mother skunk and her four young swimming toward them from an island on the other side of the stream; when the skunks saw the bathers, all turned about and swam back to the island (Cole, H. E., 1921).

The striped skunk is a comparatively silent animal, seemingly without any loud call note, yet occasionally utters various low grunts, growls, snarls, squeals, twitters, and chatters. It often utters a series of low grunts while feeding, evi-

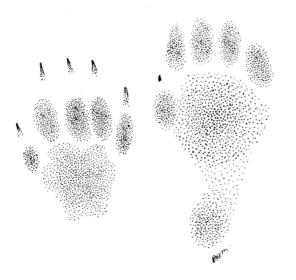

Tracks of striped skunk. Left, right fore foot. Right, right hind foot.

Feces of striped skunk. Adapted from Seton, 1929, vol. 2, p. 304 and specimens.

dently an expression of pleasure. It has no odor posts as such. Its contrasting black and white coloration acts as a warning signal to most animals, and the raising of its tail in a threatening manner gives a true warning flash. In my experience, a skunk does not like to throw its scent, and ordinarily will not do so unless pressed. A young skunk is more prone to use its scent glands than an old one. I was attempting to photograph a half-grown female skunk July 12, 1918, south of Rib Hill, Marathon County, and had a string tied to her foreleg to keep her quiet. One of my field assistants thought the string was not just proper, and though often warned never to do so, made a quick movement with a stick to adjust the string and jabbed the skunk in the ribs. I got the full benefit of the glandular discharge on the right side of my face and body, including some in my eye. I photographed the skunk in this action, and afterwards petted it without further incident before I prepared it for a specimen (No. 228935, B. S. coll., U.S.N.M.). The amber-colored fluid is thrown in a spray often so fine as to be unnoticeable except for the overpowering odor, and the animal takes care not to get the fluid on itself. Rarely does a skunk caught in a steel trap throw its fluid unless it is roughly handled by the trapper or is otherwise annoyed. If struck a quick sharp blow with a club back of the shoulders or shot

so as to break the spinal column, a skunk loses control of the posterior muscles so that it cannot discharge the scent. The dead animal may then be handled and skinned with no unpleasantness, unless one should carelessly cut or squeeze one of the scent glands. If shot in the head, a skunk will nearly always throw a full discharge of the fluid. Ether or chloroform may be used (Wilke, 1942). Holding a skunk with the tail stretched backward will not prevent a discharge unless the shoulders and rump are held taut at the time, and not always then. Do not try it!

The chemical responsible for skunk scent is butylmercaptan, a sulphur-alcohol compound that like all volatile suphur compounds is malodorous. Pure butylmercaptan in considerable internal doses produces unconsciousness, lowering of body temperature, slowing of pulse, lowering of blood pressure, and a general paralyzing of the central nervous system. Skunk fluid has been said to have a lasting deleterious effect if sprayed into the eyes, but this is not true. One's eyes will smart and burn for a moment, sometimes possibly for nearly an hour, and one will become blinded with tears from the skunk spray, but the pain is soon gone and there is no lasting trouble. A skunk instinctively knows its peculiar defensive powers, and has an easygoing, indifferent attitude toward humans and other animals. Only one affected with rabies will voluntarily chase or attack a man, dog, or other enemy. It is a stolid, plodding mammal, slow and indifferent; though rather muscular in appearance, it does not have correlated muscular strength. Neither adults nor young engage in play. Most of its major senses are weak—its hearing and sight are poor, its senses of smell and taste are only moderate, but its sense of touch is acute. Its potential longevity is seven or eight years, and its life expectancy in the wild is probably between two and three years.

The skunk is polygamous, and mating takes place in the den from late in February until the last of March, the young being born between May 1 and June 15. Normally there is only one litter annually, though there is record of a captive skunk producing two litters in a year, one on May 16 and a second on July 28, in 1952 (Shadle, 1953). The gestation period is 62 to 64 days. The cubs or kits are two to ten in a litter, the usual number being six or seven, and are born with eyes and ears closed, and with skin pinkish and thinly covered with very short fine hair that plainly discloses the color pattern of the animal. The youngsters develop rapidly, but in their early weeks are subject to hazards, such as having a male skunk enter the den and kill some of them, sometimes his own offspring. Even the mother on occasion may kill some of the kits in her excitement during the first few days after their birth, but she later becomes an excellent and attentive mother. She cuddles her babies and carries them by grasping the skin of the napes of their necks. Eyes and ears of the cub open at 30 days old, and about this time the youngster can assume the posture of discharging the scent fluid and can emit a small amount of it. Mother keeps the family together, and at dusk they parade out to hunt, she in the lead and her little skunklets lined single file behind her. Sometimes the youngsters leave the family group early in the fall, but usually most of the group dens together, except some of the males who may shift for themselves. Reproduction in the skunk has been described by Wight (1931), and development of young in captivity by L. C. Stegeman (1937). The mammae are normally fourteen, four pectoral, six abdominal, and four inguinal. Sometimes there is a reduction, particularly in the pectoral and inguinal mammae, to as low as ten functional mammae.

Generally the skunk makes its home in a burrow which it may dig itself in a bank or brush patch, or sometimes in a hayfield or pasture. More often it occupies a burrow dug by a woodchuck or some other mammal. The burrow may have one entrance, but is more likely to have two openings, and at times may have as many as three, four, or even five. Sometimes the den is in a cave or opening among rocks, and again under an old stump or a fallen log, or the skunk may take shelter in a hollow down log, or under an outbuilding. Burrows will average 18 to 20 feet long, though one recorded for Michigan was 56 feet and 4 inches in length (Allen and Shapton, 1942: 64). Side burrows and blind pockets are not infrequent. Burrows reach an average maximum depth of three to four feet below ground surface, rarely more than five feet, and those less than 20 inches underground are apt to have no nest or be unoccupied. Usually there is only one nest to each burrow, infrequently two, and rarely three (Allen and Shapton, 1942: 64). The nest is in a den, a widening of the burrow 12 to 15 inches in diameter and lined with dry leaves and grass.

Many and diverse foods enter the diet of the striped skunk. On the average by bulk, annually 40 to 50 per cent of a skunk's food consists of insects, a lesser amount in the winter, and a greater amount in the summer. Usually more than half of the insects eaten are grasshoppers and crickets, but large quantities of beetles, both adult and larvae, are consumed, and also a considerable number of caterpillars, cutworms, bugs, bees, and wasps. About 10 to 20 per cent of the food consists of mammals, mostly mice of the genera *Microtus* and *Peromyscus,* and a few *Zapus, Mus,* and others; short-tailed shrews, moles, striped ground squirrels, and chipmunks are eaten, as are parts of some of the larger mammals such as red, gray, and fox squirrels, woodchucks and cottontail rabbits. Possibly a considerable portion of the food utilized from larger mammals is procured as carrion. Birds, reptiles, and amphibians are seldom eaten, though broken birds' eggs are sometimes consumed, as are turtle eggs dug from the underground nest. Nearly 30 per cent of the skunk's food is vegetable matter, in summer consisting mostly of fruits such as dogwood, raspberry, blackberry, wild grape, wild cherries, gooseberry, and wild plums; and grains; in winter, grains, grasses, leaves, and buds are eaten. Food habits of the skunk in Michigan have been studied by Ned Dearborn (1932: 37–42), and in New York by W. J. Hamilton (1936 b). Much of the prey captured by the skunk is procured by its digging in the soil or tearing apart ground nests of mice, and of wasps and other insects. Often the skunk hunts much as does the domestic cat, by lying in wait or slowly stalking its intended prey, and then pouncing upon it. It is too slow to pursue animals for capture. A skunk may roll small prey, such as a hairy caterpillar or a toad, on the ground with one or both forepaws in order to remove hair or other objectionable matter before eating it (Schmidt, K. P., 1936). After eating, like most carnivores, it licks its chops, possibly as a cleaning move but more probably to get the last taste of the delicacy.

Except for the great horned owl and barred owl, the skunk has no essential enemy other than man, who not only kills many for their pelts, but destroys others through prejudice or ignorance, or to protect against predatory damage. The larger carnivores, such as the wildcat and the coyote, soon learn from experience not to molest a skunk. A dog will molest a skunk once, but usually after the one experience of burning eyes and smelly coat is satisfied to leave black and white animals alone. Skunks are heavy victims of automobiles, particularly during fall just before they den for the winter. Harold Steinke (1953), in 153,089 miles of driving over a period of six years in Dane, Columbia, Outagamie, Waupaca, and Winnebago counties, counted 82 skunks that had been killed on the road. In many regions the number would be much higher. The skunk seems to be readily susceptible to disease, and of those transmissible to humans, rabies has occurred not infrequently and tularemia at least twice (Morgan, 1949: 8) in this species in Wisconsin. A skunk is not likely to bite a person unless it is being handled and irritated or has rabies, and anyone attacked and bitten by a skunk should be cautious and if necessary take at once the Pasteur treatment.

Among the external parasites of this skunk are the biting louse *Trichodectes mephitidis;* the ticks *Dermacentor variabilis, Ixodes kingi,* and *Amblyomma americana;* and the fleas *Oropsylla arctomys, Cediopsylla simplex, Ctenocephalides felis,* and *Pulex irritans.* Internal parasites are many, among them the flukes *Alaria taxideae* and *A. minnesotae, Sellacotyle mustelae;* the tapeworms *Mesocestoides latus* and *M. variabilis,* and *Oochoristica mephitis* and *O. peduculata;* the roundworms *Ascaris columnaris* and *A. dasypodina, Crenosoma mephitidis* and *C. microbursa, Chlamydoprocta itascensis, Filaria martis, Physaloptera maxillaris, Skrjabingylus chitwoodorum,* and *Strongyloides papillosus* (Erickson, 1946: 502). The horny headed worm *Moniliformis clarki* also occurs. The roundworm *P. maxillaris* occurs in the stomachs of more than 50 per cent of wild Wisconsin skunks. The threadlike roundworm *S. chitwoodorum* infests the frontal region of the skull, and may cause a severe swelling and absorption of bone so that the skull is disfigured and misshapen.

Economically, the usefulness of the skunk far exceeds its harmfulness. Its fur is of good texture, durable, and of reasonable cost, and when popular may produce sales of raw fur in the state up to $100,000 annually, a large part of which goes as pin money to farmers and farm boys. Prejudice against skunk fur tends to keep its popularity down. Skunks usually are abundantly fat, and oil from this fat is an excellent rubbing oil. Chippewa Indians not only used the oil for rubbing but took it as a purgative for worms. Skunk meat for some might be difficult to relish, yet properly cooked it is clean, white, and delicious, in taste and texture between pork and chicken. The chief asset of the skunk, however, is its high value as a destroyer of mice, rats, and noxious insects such as cutworms, grasshoppers, squash bugs, and potato beetles, of which it consumes a prodigious amount. It also has value as a harmless and interesting pet. Many are now sold in city pet stores after they have been deodorized by cutting out the two scent glands, a simple operation on a young skunk for a skilled hand or a veterinarian. Methods of deodorizing skunks have been described by Vernon Bailey (1937) and others. Some prefer to leave the glands intact.

I have had several skunks at various times, for pets, and last year brought up two from very early infancy with various experiences some of which are colorful and amusing. In the course of their *up bringing* I was a "bulls eye" for more than one shot, and I thought it might interest you to know that upon applying a cloth or sponge saturated with *turpentine* to the affected areas, the odor immediately vanished. I should know, because more than once I was anointed from the top of my head to my feet (Marie Anne Jordan, Newton Highlands, Massachusetts, in letter to the author, March 4, 1939).

The skunk's interesting method of defense has given the animal an undeservedly bad reputation. The glandular extract and odor, however, can be removed. If in one's eyes it will cause a smarting and burning sensation, which may be relieved by washing the eyes in clear luke-warm water, followed by using a boracic acid eyewash. Turpentine sponging will remove the odor from skin or clothing, but in most instances this is too severe treatment. To remove skunk odor from any live mammal, bathe the animal by using tincture of green soap; wipe dry; then sponge the animal with a solution of three tablespoons sodium perborate, trisodium phosphate, or a good detergent in a small basin of warm water; if odor still remains, sponge the animal with chlorine disinfectant or chlorine water, using the solution as recommended on the container. A good commercial dry cleaning will eliminate the odor from clothing. Skunk odor also can be removed from clothing or fur by sprinkling thereon Labarraque's solution—active ingredient chlorinated soda—in proportion of one part to three parts water. A smelly dead skunk should be liberally powdered with calcium chloride and buried. Stench remaining on a place where a skunk has been killed or has sprayed the ground, a building, or other object can usually be quenched by washing or soaking the spot with chlorinated water. Skunks may be a valuable asset in catching rats and mice while housing themselves under a barn or other outbuilding, but if not wanted they can often be driven away by the use of repellents such as naphthalene, paradichlorobenzine, and nicotine sulphate, scattered in and about the den. After the skunks have left, all openings should be closed.

Even though the skunk is generally valuable to agriculture, occasionally one acquires the habit of killing poultry, and may be quite persistent and destructive. Such an animal should be removed or eliminated. It is not a climber, and

limits its predatory attempts on poultry to those birds on the ground or low floors. Many skunks will not attack a live chicken, but will act only as a scavenger on birds. Often the skunk is blamed for predation by rats or other mammals. It may do a little damage to ground-nesting wild birds and their eggs, but birds form a negligible part of its food. Skunks eat bees, and have been known to eat dead and dormantly chilled honey bees outside a hive. It has been claimed that they will aggravate bees in a hive and eat the insects as fast as they leave, badly depleting the hive. The skunk also may make holes in lawns and golf greens, and the indignant owner is apt to condemn the skunk, not realizing that the trespasser is a friend digging holes to destroy cutworms and other larvae. Most of this damage by skunks can be prevented by skillful management. Install proper fencing on the chicken range, have well-constructed chicken houses, and keep the entrances closed at night. Raise bee hives 24 to 30 inches above the ground, or place a temporary skunk-proof fence around groups of hives. If as a final resort it is necessary to dispose of the skunk, it will be an easy animal to trap either in a baited box trap or a No. 1-1/2 steel trap. Above all, do not wantonly destroy skunks.

Specimens examined from Wisconsin.—Total 139, as follows: *Adams County:* Dells of the Wisconsin (3 mi. N. of Wisconsin Dells), 1. *Barron County:* Turtle Lake, 2 (UWZ). *Bayfield County:* Herbster, 4. *Brown County:* Green Bay, 10 (CNHM). *Buffalo County:* Wabasha Flats, 2. *Clark County:* Howett Township, 1 (UWZ); Worden Township, 1. *Dane County:* Madison, 1 (UWZ); Mazomanie, 1 (UWZ). *Dodge County:* Beaver Dam, 17 (UWZ); Fox Lake, 1 (UWZ). *Dunn County:* Colfax, 6 (UWZ). *Grant County:* Potosi (10 mi. S. S. E.), 1. *Iron County:* Fisher Lake, 2 (UWZ). *Jefferson County:* Fayville Grove, 1 (UWZ). *Langlade County:* T 34 N, R 11 E, 1 (UWZ). *Marathon County:* Rib Hill, 3. *Milwaukee County:* Cudahy, 1 (MM); Milwaukee, 1 (UWZ); Wauwatosa, 1 (MM). *Pierce County:* Maiden Rock, 3 (MM); Prescott, 12 (MM). *Rock County:* Milton, 2 (1 MM). *Sauk County:* Prairie du Sac, 2 (MM). *Vilas County:* Eagle River, 9; Mamie Lake, 5. *Walworth County:* Delavan, 35 (6 MM; 2 UWZ); Fontana, 1. *Waukesha County:* Duplainville, 1 (UWZ); Pewaukee, 5 (UWZ); Waukesha, 6 (3 MM; 3 UWZ).

Selected references.—Allen, D. L., 1939; Hamilton, W. J., Jr., 1936 b; Howell, A. H., 1901; Kelker, G. H., 1937; Shaw, W. T., 1928; Stegeman, L. C., 1937.

Genus **Lutra** Brisson
Otters

Dental formula:

$$I\frac{3-3}{3-3}, \quad C\frac{1-1}{1-1}, \quad P\frac{4-4}{3-3}, \quad M\frac{1-1}{2-2} = 36.$$

Lutra canadensis canadensis (Schreber)
Canada Otter

Mustela lutra canadensis Schreber, Säugthiere, p. 126 b, 1776.

Lutra Canadensis Lapham, p. 43, 1852; Lapham, p. 338, 1853; Strong, p. 437, 1883.

Lutra canadensis Snyder, p. 123, 1902; Jackson, p. 27, 1908; Hollister, p. 27, 1910; Jackson, p. 89, 1910; Cory, p. 330, 1912.

Lutra canadensis canadensis Komarek, p. 205, 1932; Barger, p. 10, 1952.

Vernacular names.—In Wisconsin, commonly called otter; other vernacular names include American otter, common otter, *Fischotter* (German), fisher (partly for deliberate falsification), *ku-tet-tahx* (Potawatomi), land otter, *loutre* (French-Canadian), *neeg-keek* (Chippewa), North American otter, river otter, and waterdog.

Identification marks.—A large, slender member of the weasel family, the largest that now occurs regularly in Wisconsin, usually lighter in weight and slighter in body than the wolverine, but longer in total length; body lithe and elongate, yet solid and muscular; head comparatively small, broad and distinctly flattened; ears small, rounded; eyes small, somewhat anteriorly placed; nose broad and rather flat; tail long, about one-third of total length of animal, sometimes called the "pole," thick and muscular, very heavy at the base, tapering gradually to the tip; legs both fore and hind short; feet large and broad; toes webbed; claws short; underfur rather short, dense, and soft, intermixed with long

Canada otter from Michigan in standing position, National Zoological Park, Washington, D. C. Photograph by Vernon Bailey.

silky guard hairs, the whole being impervious to water.

The general color tone is rich dark brown, near chocolate or seal brown, usually a shade paler on the under parts, and often with a distinct grayish or vinaceous mixture on the lips, chin, and throat. Studies of skins in various seasons of the year and from many localities indicate that there may be two molts a year, one in spring and one in fall, with the molting extending over a long period. Winter pelage is essentially the same as that of summer.

The skull is 3.9 to 4.5 inches in greatest length, actually rather small for the body size of the animal, broad and flat; parietals somewhat rounded and swollen; rostrum flat, shorter than wide; audital bullae small and depressed, the auditory meatus narrow in antero-posterior diameter; infraorbital foramen large, near oval in anterior view (not triangular in outline as in *Taxidea*), wider (lateral dimension) than deep (dorso-ventral diameter); dentition moderate, the incisors and premolars rather small; only Wisconsin carnivore having total of 36 teeth, and only one having five molariform teeth on each side of both upper and lower jaw; upper molar large and rectangular.

Canada otter. Courtesy Wisconsin Conservation Department.

In adult otters the male averages about 5 per cent larger than the female in basic measurements, and sometimes in mated pairs the male may appear to be nearly one-third larger than a younger mate. The tail of the juvenile is relatively shorter than that of the adult, but the general appearance except for size is similar. The sutures of the skull close early, and the molariform teeth usually become greatly worn by the time the animal nears maturity at about one year's age. The fur of a senescent otter may become white-tipped or frosted, but otherwise there is not extensive color variation except in intensity or in paleness or darkness of the brown. White and albino variations have been recorded, as well as other variations such as black, slate, mottled, silvering, and grizzled (Jones, 1923: 174, 176), though one might suspect the last two to be on account of old age.

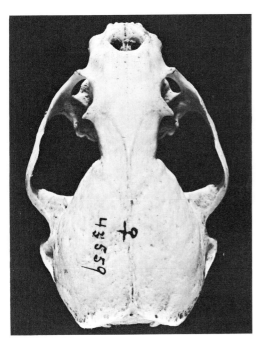

Skull of LUTRA C. CANADENSIS, *Elk River, Minnesota.* ¾×.

Measurements.—Total length of adults, 900 to 1,220 mm. (35.4 to 48.0 in.); tail, 300 to 475 mm. (11.8 to 18.7 in.); hind foot, 112 to 133 mm. (4.4 to 5.2 in.). Weight, 15 to 25 pounds, rarely to 30 pounds in males. Skull length, 100 to 115 mm.; width, 66 to 79 mm.

Distribution in Wisconsin.—Formerly occurred not uncommonly in favorable habitat throughout Wisconsin, but reduced nearly to extirpation by the early years of this century. Now under protection again, it occurs throughout the state, regularly in some areas, but only rarely as a straggler in others, particularly in the southeastern counties.

Habitat.—Chiefly along rivers, larger creeks, sloughs, and lakes.

Status and Habits.—The otter has continued in varying abundance and distribution in Wisconsin since the days of early settlement when it was found throughout the state in favorable habitats. In later years in many counties in the southern part of the state where it was supposed to have been extirpated, a few may have existed, unknown on account of their secretive habits. There was an otter slide on the southeast side of Lake Koshkonong in section 34, T 5 N, R 13 E, Jefferson County, in July, 1901 (Jackson, 1908: 27), and the writer saw tracks of one along Otter Creek, in section 5, town of Milton, T 4 N, R

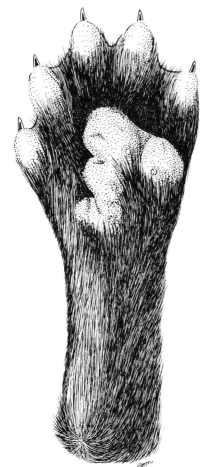

Left, left hind foot of Canada otter. From specimens from Michigan and Minnesota. ¾×.

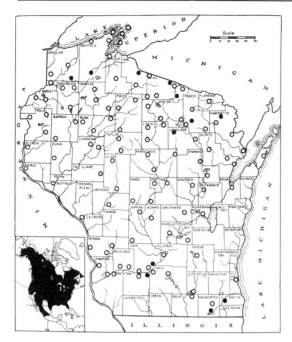

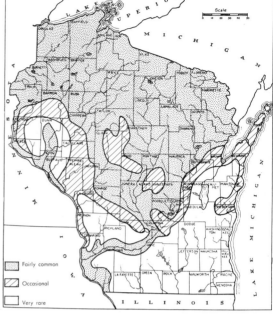

Map 70. Distribution of LUTRA CANADENSIS. ● =
specimens examined. ○ = *authentic records.*

*Map 71. Relative abundance of otter, 1951-1953.
Copied after Knudsen, 1956 a, p. 147.*

13 E, Rock County, in June, 1902, some two
miles from the slide on Lake Koshkonong. "Otter
Creek [Rock County] took its name from the
number of otter slides along its banks at the
time of its surveying" (Smith, 1856: 41). "Otter"
has been used as a name for creeks in Dunn,
Eau Claire, Forest, Iowa, and Sauk counties, and
for lakes in Chippewa, Forest, Langlade, Lincoln, Polk, Taylor, Vilas, Walworth, and Waupaca
counties. Scattered and infrequent reports of
the otter in southern Wisconsin continued until
the time of its legal protection by the state
about the year 1915, by which time the species
was becoming increasingly uncommon also in
the northern parts of the state. Even with the
prohibition against the taking of otters, some
continued to trap them, reporting the take as
"fishers," which were then unprotected. The protective measure, however, was effective, and
there has been an increase in the number of otters in Wisconsin since that time. Though it may
never be a common mammal, the presence of an
occasional otter may be expected in any county,
even in the southeastern ones, and it is now of
regular occurrence in its favorite watery habitats
in the northern and western two-thirds of the

state. If one might hazard an estimate, there are
probably not less than three thousand otters in
the state today, and probably more. The otter
is a great wanderer, and a family may travel
100 miles or more seeking a more favorable living place. Even from an established den a lone
otter, particularly a male, or a pair, may travel
20 to 30 miles and return after an absence of
several days. The home range of a mother tending her nestlings is seldom greater than a mile
or so.

An otter goes about its own business, spends
a great deal of its time in the water, and is con-
sequently seldom seen by the casual observer.
Yet to anyone who knows its habits it cannot remain hidden for long, for its tracks and feces
are quite distinctive and may be seen in the
sand and mud at the borders of waters, and its
slides are even more characteristic. An otter
slide is made by the animal sliding down a slope,
forming as it were a furrowed trail in the particular spot. These slides may be only a few feet
or several yards long, though in soil they are
seldom longer than 40 feet, and usually 12 to 18
feet. Slides also may be found in snow, often
on a slight slope where the animal slid as a

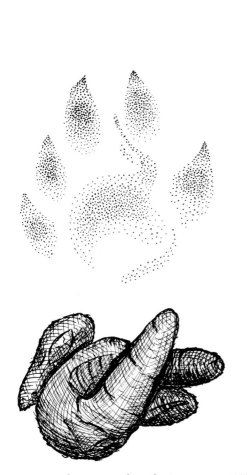

Tracks of Canada otter. Left, right fore foot. Right, right hind foot.

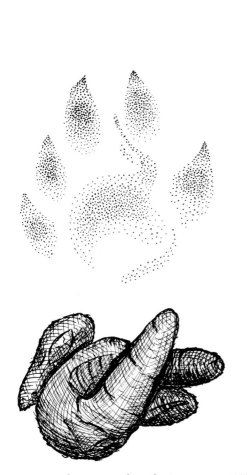

Feces of Canada otter. Adapted after Seton, 1929, vol. 2, p. 701.

part of its progression, and the slide then is a part of the track. Snow slides often show three deeper parallel furrows, a middle one made by the tail, and one on each side made by the legs. Under favorable conditions of either snow slickness or slope of surface, an otter slide on snow may be 50 or 60 feet long. A shallow depression is sometimes evident where an otter has twisted and rubbed in the sand or other soil, but it does not habitually return to the same spot and does not make a clear-cut wallow.

The otter may be active any time of day or night, and although generally considered nocturnal, it is more crepuscular, and is often diurnal in its activities. It may emigrate because of food shortage or environmental conditions, but does not migrate. It does not hibernate, and is

extremely tolerant of most weather conditions, though extreme heat seems to bother it more than extreme cold. Its short legs and long body are not well adapted to rapid movement on land. It runs with a lope or canter, and if there is ice, snow, or a very smooth soil surface it will take three or four leaps, then slide 15 to 25 feet, its forelegs laid back against its sides. On soil surface it seldom runs more than eight or ten miles an hour, but on snow or ice where it can slide, it may progress at a speed of 15 or 16 miles an hour.

Before each jump the body was bent up like a hairpin (resembling a doubled up inch worm) and the tail was raised slightly above horizontal. In springing forward from this position, it straightened its body and tail, thus raising its front feet off the snow, and in the same motion shoved forward with its hind feet. The motion of the tail, body, and hind feet were coordinated for propulsion. Its body barely cleared the ice or snow in the jump. It was not possible to determine how the hind legs changed from this position to the doubled up position ready for the first jump after the glide. But from our observations it was deduced that at the end of a glide the front feet dug into the snow and the body doubled up so that the hind feet naturally came into position for the next jump (Severinghaus and Tanck, 1948).

Canada otter in sliding position. Drawn from photographs, field notes, and specimens.

The otter is most expert and graceful in the water, swimming and diving with ease, agility, and speed. When swimming on the surface it holds its head high, well out of water; the mid-back may also be exposed slightly, and both fore and hind legs are rearward. It paddles some with the hind feet, but progression is made chiefly through sinuous movements and twisting and writhing of the body and tail. An undulating motion through the water is frequent, as is also a spiral motion, the animal rolling over and over as it speeds ahead. Its maximum speed on the surface is six or seven miles an hour, and under water it can do nearly as well. It can remain submerged for nearly two minutes, and regularly swims for considerable distances under ice, obtaining its oxygen from air bubbles under the ice or from open holes in it. On February 24, 1939, Ben Gustavson, a commercial fisherman of Bayfield, pulled up a set line from 42 feet of water 500 feet from the shore of Basswood Island, Apostle Islands, Ashland County, and found bait missing from several hooks, but a large otter had been caught on one hook and had drowned (Waskow, 1939: 61; Scott, 1939: 371). At Fish Bay, Baranof Island, Alaska, in April, 1949, an otter was found drowned in a fish net at a depth of 60 feet, and at a later date two otters were taken from a net at the same depth in Deep Bay, Baranof Island (Scheffer, 1953: 255).

The only loud notes of the otter are a savage snarling growl when it is angry or disturbed and a shrill whistle when it is in pain, or sometimes at mating time. At other times when angry the more usual note is a hissing bark, which may be modified into a clear distinct hiss. When at play or galloping from place to place, it frequently emits a low purring grunt, probably a pleasure reaction, and an oft-repeated birdlike musical chirp, evidently a call note. Even in its movements it is not noisy. It swims with scarcely a ripple and dives with little splashing, quite in contrast to a muskrat or beaver. Mild tempered as a rule, an otter can nevertheless put up a vigorous and fierce fight. On land it is equal to any of its native opponents of comparable size; in water it is master of all. A dog in fair fight is a poor match for an otter. Females appear to be more aggressive than males, not only in defense of the young but also in family squabbles. A lone male confined with two or more females in a short time will show a head and face battle-marked with bite wounds.

The otter may have some purpose in its many antics and strange performances or there may be some use for these in response to instinct, but certainly to our weak human insight they have all the appearances of play. . . . Go to any zoological park and toss a small white stone or peanut into the otter pool, and immediately the animals commence "playing" with it. They carry the object on their noses or heads, and jostle it around with all the appearance of great glee. They gallop and chase each other in a sort of "play tag" manner, with no apparent show of anger. But more interesting is their habit in the wild of "sliding down hill". Not only do they "run and slide" in their method of progress, but they select certain places where by continuously sliding they create the so-called "otter-slide". . . . Often the slides are worn deep into chute-like troughs by the many coasting trips made by the otters as they slide down the steep slopes head foremost (Jackson, 1931 b: 47).

An otter will frequently tumble and roll and act "kittenish," apparently for sheer fun. It is strong and muscular, showing especial strength in neck, body, and tail muscles. Its senses are acute, particularly those of smell and touch. We are told that "otters can follow other otters by scent even though the trail is many weeks old" (Liers, 1953: 120). The life potential may be near 21 years, with the life expectancy possibly not more than 8 years.

Information on breeding habits of the otter in the wild is incomplete and conflicting. Study of its breeding habits in semi-wild captivity has been made by Liers (1951: 4–8), who tells us that in Minnesota otters breed in winter and early spring. Copulation usually takes place while the animals are in the water, either above or below the surface, though they have been known to mate on land. In the wild in Wisconsin the otter probably usually mates in the spring or summer, and the young are born the following year between January and May. The gestation period is about ten months, animals in captivity in Minnesota varying from 9 months, 18 days to 12 months, 15 days (Liers, 1951: 6). Mating may occur soon after the female gives birth to her cubs or kittens, and usually within two months after whelping time. The litter, one a year, consists of two to four cubs, sometimes only one, rarely five or six. The animal at birth is slightly covered with short fur, has eyes closed, and is about eight inches in total length. The eyes open after 30 to 38 days. "When the cubs are five to six weeks old they begin to play with one another and with their mother, and when ten to twelve weeks old the mother first permits them to exercise and play outside of the nest" (Liers, 1951: 7). The male usually joins the family after

the cubs leave the nest, and is attentive to the young. The cubs play with each other and with the parents much like domestic kittens. Swimming and food hunting are taught them by the parents, and the young at first are even reluctant to enter the water. At one year of age the otter is nearly full grown, and at two years it is sexually mature. The mammae are four, all inguinal.

The den of the otter is well hidden, and most apt to be located in a bank along a stream or lake, always with the main entrance under water and usually below the ice line. At times an abandoned beaver lodge is utilized for the otter home, and again it may be under a big stump with its many tunnels and ramifications, or even in a hollow log. An inhabited den in the sandstone cliffs on the southeast side of Madeline Island, Apostle Islands, Lake Superior, that I examined in July, 1919, was said to have been inhabited by otters off and on for many years. The den may be simple, with short tunnels, or it may be very extensive and complicated, as the one on Madeline Island appeared to be. A complicated

Diagrammatic sketch of otter hole and den.

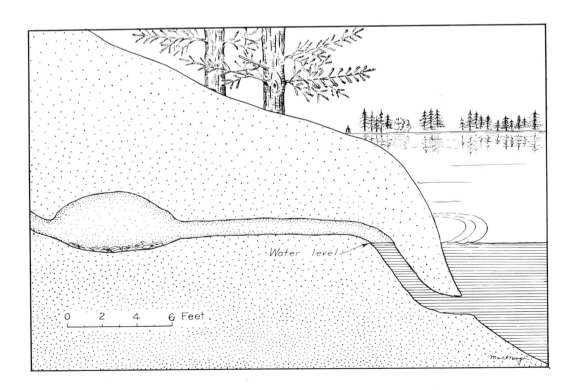

burrow near Lenola, New Jersey, in 1893 was reported to be over two hundred feet long, containing a den "big enough to hold a horse and cart" (Rhoads, 1903: 160). When traveling, if an otter cannot find a hole, vacant beaver lodge, or muskrat house in which to lodge, it may make a temporary nest of grass near water. It defecates and urinates outside the den, but the young otter under about two months old does not go outside the shelter to eliminate, and the mother does not clean the den by removing feces of her babies.

The otter has a somewhat varied diet, but feeds almost exclusively on animal matter, chiefly aquatic. So swift and sure is it in the water that it is able to capture the most agile species. It catches fish by direct pursuit, and when it has obtained its quarry, takes the food to dry land to eat it. It often plays with its prey after bringing it to land, much as a cat might play with a captured mouse. One that I watched on Cranberry River, Bayfield County, August 12, 1922, came to a flat place on the bank of the stream with a ten-inch river chub (*Nocomis*) grasped in its mouth, and played with it, tossing the fish in the air, then using its flat head or nose to catch it on its downward flight, or to butt it into the air again, and thus continued for some five minutes. Then it ate the fish piecemeal, beginning at the head. Liers (1953: 105) says that "ninety per cent of the otter's food was crawfish." It is true that particularly during the spring and summer months in Wisconsin the otter eats quantities of crayfish as its dominant food, yet during fall and winter when crayfish are more difficult to capture, it may feed more on fishes. A large percentage of the fish it captures, even when feeding in trout or other game-fish streams and lakes, are non-game or forage fishes, and it also consumes frogs, mud puppies, and clams, as well as water beetles, water bugs, caddis flies, and other insects. A research examination of 95 stomachs of otters taken early in the spring on trout waters in Michigan in 1940 and 1941 showed the following percentage composition by volume: forage fishes, 35.9 per cent; amphibians, 25.2 per cent; game and pan fishes, 22.7 per cent; crayfish, 7.4 per cent; miscellaneous vertebrates, 4.5 per cent; fish remains, 3.9 per cent; and insects, 0.4 per cent (Lagler and Ostenson, 1942: 250). Rarely, a muskrat, young beaver, or duck

may enter into the otter's diet. It rarely, if ever, molests domestic poultry. Parts of land vertebrates found among its food remains probably were eaten as carrion.

Except for man, the otter has few serious enemies. Possibly a bobcat, coyote, great horned owl, or bald eagle may sometimes attempt to catch an otter kit, but the young are so carefully guarded by the mother that one is rarely captured by any predator. Sometimes an otter is caught accidentally in a fishnet, and there are a few records of one being caught on a set line. A tick, *Ixodes hexagonus*, has been found on it. Internal parasites known to infest it are a fluke, *Euparyphium melis*, and a roundworm of the genus *Physaloptera*.

Otter fur is the best wearing of any Wisconsin fur, and by many is also considered the most beautiful. At the beginning of the nineteenth century an otter pelt at the Green Bay fur depots was worth two beaver pelts (two plus) and sold in cash for $3.00 to $5.00. Otter pelts in the sales, however, were always fewer than beaver pelts, there being generally only 25 to 40 per cent as many. Indians utilized otter skins for headgear and decorations, and a dried otter skin with head and tail preserved, made into the form of a pouch, was sometimes used by the Winnebago medicine man for a medicine bag. In reference to otters in Virginia, Captain John Smith says , "*they have many Otters*, which, as the Beavers, they take with snares, and esteeme the skin as great ornaments; and of all these beasts they use to feede, when they catch them" (Smith, J., 1612: 14). For a few years after 1915 there was a closed season on otters in the state, but more recently trapping has been allowed in some areas. Reports indicate that trappers took 178 otters in 1935; 226 in 1936; 310 in 1937; 154 in 1938; 142 in 1939; 444 in 1940; 188 in 1941; 203 in 1942; 117 in 1943; 135 in 1944; 171 in 1945; 291 in 1946; 484 in 1947; 4 in 1948; 324 in 1949; 472 in 1950; 497 in 1951; and 461 in 1952. An otter pelt now sells for $20.00 to $40.00, the average price being about $25.00. It is doubtful if the otter can maintain its numbers in the state under such a heavy take. Some fishermen blacklist the otter because they believe it eats game fish. It does eat a few game and pan fish, but it destroys nearly twice as many forage fish. It is an interesting mammal to have around, is on the whole not injurious, and has a valuable pelt that possibly might be produced by raising the animals in captivity. It deserves careful protection.

Specimens examined from Wisconsin.—Total 11, as follows: *Bayfield County:* Drummond, 1 (UWZ). *Douglas County:* Gordon, 1 (UWZ). *Forest County:* Crandon, 1 (UWZ). *Iowa County:* Arena, 1 (MM). *Iron County:* Fisher Lake, 1 (UWZ). *Langlade County:* T 33 N, R 12 E, 1 (UWZ). *Marinette County:* White Hill Lodge (south of Dunbar), 1 (MM). *Racine County:* Waterford, 1 (UWZ). *Sauk County:* Prairie du Sac, 1 (MM). *Vilas County:* Eagle Lake, 1 (CNHM); Spring Creek (T 43 N, R 9 E, Sec. 21), 1 (HHTJ).

Selected references.—Hooper, E. T., and B. T. Ostenson, 1949; Jackson, H. H. T., 1931 b; Kaukl, M. O., 1950; Lagler, K. F., and B. T. Ostenson, 1942; Liers, E. E., 1951, 1953.

Family **Felidae**
Cats and Allies

The family Felidae is widely distributed and is found to the limits of tree growth or beyond in all continents except Australia. It contains about 22 genera and subgenera, of which two have occurred in Wisconsin.

Genus **Felis** Linnaeus
True Cats

Dental formula:

$$I\frac{3-3}{3-3}, \quad C\frac{1-1}{1-1}, \quad P\frac{3-3}{2-2}, \quad M\frac{1-1}{1-1} = 30.$$

Puma in zoo, Spokane, Washington, November, 1930. Photograph by Charles L. Sheely.

Felis concolor schorgeri Jackson
Wisconsin Puma

Felis concolor schorgeri Jackson, Proc. Biol. Soc. Washington 68: 149, Oct. 31, 1955.
Felis concolor Lapham, p. 339, 1853; Hoy, p. 256, 1882; Strong, p. 436, 1883.
Felis couguar Hollister, p. 141, 1909; Hollister, p. 26, 1910; Cory, p. 280, 1912.
Felis concolor cougar Barger, p. 11, 1952.

Vernacular names.—In former days in Wisconsin usually called panther, cougar, or catamount. Other names include American lion, American panther, couguar, cuguar, deer killer, *mishibijin* (Chippewa), mountain lion, painter, and puma.

Identification marks.—Excepting the jaguar

(*Felis onca*), the puma is the largest American cat, and the subspecies *schorgeri* is among the largest pumas. Adult males measure from 7.5 to 8.5 feet from tip of nose to tip of tail, of which about 35 to 40 per cent is tail; the body is rather long and slender; head broad, short, rotund, and somewhat small in comparison with body size; ears well developed, erect, short, rounded, not tufted with long hairs; nose blunt, the rhinarium pinkish, narrowly bordered by blackish that extends onto the lips; the nares pinkish; tail long, cylindrical, well haired, but not bushy; legs relatively short, muscular; feet large, with four digits on hind feet and five on forefeet; claws curved and strong; fur moderately soft and rather short.

The only native Wisconsin cat with the color unspotted in the adult animal. Seasonal and sexual variations in color are not evident, though there is considerable individual variation. The general color of the adult, so far as known, is tawny cinnamon buff varying rarely to grayish buff, paler on the feet, upper lips, chin, supraorbital region, throat, and underparts, which is sometimes nearly white; back of head, nape, and median dorsal strip considerably darker, intermixed with black-tipped hairs; tail above similar to back, below pale buffy nearly to tip which is blackish above and below; ears externally, hairs on soles and sides of the base of the nose near black. Young to about six months old, ground color near pale cinnamon or pinkish buff, the body and head conspicuously marked with dark brown or near black blotches, and the tail banded with same color. An annual molt occurs usually in spring, the molting process being slow and gradual, and seldom showing distinct molting marks.

The skull is relatively rather short and broad, the greatest width being near two-thirds the greatest length of more than 185 mm.; frontal region high and arched, though less so in *schorgeri* than other forms; rostrum broad, the nasal bones particularly wide anteriorly; complete dentition 30, the only native cat having 30 teeth, the same as the domestic cat; cheek teeth four on each side, the first and the last simple, tiny.

The male puma averages about 15 per cent larger than the female, but there are no sexual color differences. The skull of the male is not only larger and more massive than that of the female but in the adult animal also has more

prominent sagittal and lambdoid ridges. Dentition relative to size of the animal is about the same in both sexes. Individual color variation may range on the upper parts from reddish brown through tawny or brown to grayish phases, and any intermediate colors. There seems to be a tendency in extreme variations for males to be gray, whereas females tend toward reddish, but evidence is insufficient to fix this as a rule. Verified records of color mutations such as albinism and melanism are unknown in the puma in North America, although Halloch "heard of a black panther being shot near Gordon last Winter—a case of melanism in *felis concolor*" (Halloch, 1884: 81). Abnormalities, particularly as displayed in the skull, are not infrequent, and usually appear to have been caused by injuries.

Measurements.—Total length of adult, 1,800 to 2,590 mm. (71 to 102 in.); tail, 700 to 900 mm. (28 to 35 in.); hind foot, 254 to 295 mm. (10 to

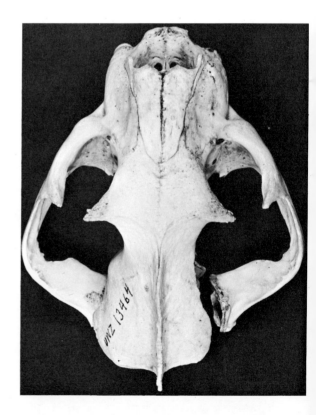

Skull of FELIS C. SCHORGERI, *type specimen, no. 13464, University of Wisconsin Zool. Museum. Photograph by University of Wisconsin Photographic Laboratory. Courtesy John T. Emlen.* ½×.

11.5 in.). The Appleton specimen measured in the flesh "7 feet 2 inches in length" (Schorger, 1938: 252). Weight of adult variable, 80 to 210 pounds; average male about 160 pounds, average female about 135 pounds. Skull length, 185 to 228 mm.; width, 125 to 160 mm. Skull of type specimen (adult male from Appleton, Wisconsin): zygomatic width, 151.5 mm.; height of cranium, 73.8 mm.; interorbital breadth, 43.3 mm. postorbital processes (width), 75.6 mm. width of nasals (at anterior tips of frontals), 22.6 mm.; width of palate (across interpterygoid fossa) 28.7 mm.; maxillary tooth row alveolar length, 65.0 mm.; upper carnassial crown length, 24.2 mm.; upper carnassial crown width, 13.2 mm.; lower carnassial crown length, 19.2 mm.; lower carnassial crown width, 15.2 mm.

Distribution in Wisconsin.—Believed to be extirpated in Wisconsin. In early times (before 1870) probably occurred not infrequently throughout most of the state in favorable habitats, particularly in the valleys of the Mississippi River and its tributaries and of the Fox River.

Habitat.—Forests and forest borders, especially in rough, hilly, and rocky terrain, seeming to prefer the headwaters of streams; sometimes prairies and grasslands in search of food.

Status and Habits.—The puma probably was not rare in Wisconsin in early days. The earliest mention I know was in June, 1673, below or near the mouth of the Wisconsin River, probably in what is now Grant County, when the Louis Jolliet exploration party "saw a few monsters: big catfish, a spadefish, a panther" (DeVoto, 1952: 118). Since then until well into the nineteenth century and possibly later there were several reliable records of its occurrence in Wisconsin, some of which have been mentioned by W. E. Scott (1939: 27) and A. W. Schorger (1942: 31–32). Carver, speaking of the "Tyger of America," says, "I saw one on an island in the Chipeway River, of which I had a very good view, as it was no great distance from me. It sat up on its hinder parts like a dog; and did not seem either to be apprehensive of our approach, or to discover any ravenous inclinations. It is however very seldom to be met with in this part of the world" (Carver, 1838: 273). This was in 1767, probably in May or June, and likely on the lower stretches of the Chippewa where wooded islands are frequent in what is now Pepin County. Other records include Blue Mounds, Dane County, 1839 (Locke, cited by Schorger, 1942: 31); Pewaukee Township, Waukesha County, 1839 (Marcy, 1888 b: 523); island in Mississippi River, opposite Trempealeau Mountain, Trempealeau County, possibly in Minnesota, 1839 (Fonda, 1868: 269); Green Lake County, 1840 (Schorger: 1942: 31); and four miles west of Fond du Lac County, 1857 (*Janesville Daily Gazette*, March 19, 1857, "From *Fond du Lac Journal*"). On November 22, 1857, Samuel P. Hart killed the type specimen of *F. c. schorgeri* near Appleton (Schorger, 1938; Jackson, 1955). Other early records include Tomah, Monroe County (Scott, 1939: 25), and between Appleton and Menasha, Winnebago County, 1859 (*Janesville Morning Gazette*, November 14, 1859). "Benjamin Bones of Racine shot one on the headwaters of the Black River, December, 1863" (Hoy, 1882: 256), probably in Clark County, and the same year one was killed with a tomahawk by James A. Reed near Dodge, Trempealeau County (Anon., 1948: 25). One was trapped by Sam Warren near Bloomfield, Waushara County, November 7, 1866 (From *Wau-*

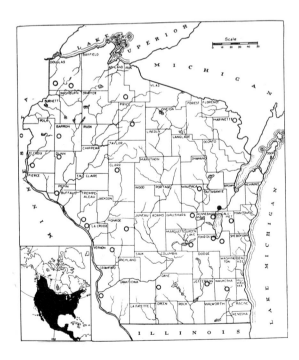

Map 72. *Distribution of* FELIS CONCOLOR. ● = specimen examined. ○ = *authentic records.*

shara Argus in *Janesville Gazette*, November 19, 1866); one killed near Brillion, Calumet County, in March, 1867 (*Janesville Gazette*, March 13, 1867); one on the upper St. Croix River, probably in Saint Croix County, during the winter of 1867–68 (*Prescott Journal*, May 2, 1868); one in the town of Empire, Fond du Lac County, late in March, 1868 (*Janesville Gazette*, April 3, 1868); one killed near Westby, Vernon County, 1870 (Cory, 1912: 282); one seen running wild in Clark County, September, 1878 (*Clinton Independent*, Clinton, Wisconsin, September 18, 1878); one shot near Gordon, Douglas County, 1883 (Hallock, 1884: 81); one killed near Butternut, Ashland County, in February, 1884 (*Ashland Press*, March 8, 1884); and one seen near Clintonville, Waupaca County, in the fall of 1884 (Hough, 1895: 509). One was seen by different persons near Tamarack River in Sec. 16, T 44 N, R 14 W and near Gordon, Douglas County, 1897 (letter from Geo. A. Bubar, Minneapolis, to W. E. Scott, October 25, 1939); one was seen in the vicinity of Prentice, Phillips, and Fifield, Price County, and near Butternut and Glidden, Ashland County, 1898 (Loomis, 1898: 114). "Herrick brothers—captured a panther measuring nine feet from tip to tip" near Turtle Lake, Barron County, spring of

1903 (Anon., 1903: 101). One was killed in Douglas County about 1905, and two seen near Kremlin, Marinette County, January 2, 1909 (Cory, 1912: 282). A large cat that from descriptions was evidently a puma was reportedly seen and heard several times by different observers from June 4 to well into autumn, 1945, in the region where corners of Dunn, Barron, Polk, and St. Croix counties adjoin, definite localities being Reeve in Barron County, Boyceville and Connorsville in Dunn County, and Clear Lake in Polk County (Anon., 1947 b: 31). This animal probably was not native and may have escaped from a traveling show. Many animals which either escaped or were released as unwanted pets by automobile travelers have thus found their way into strange country, and it is probable that any record of a puma in Wisconsin since 1920 is of such an animal. A native puma, particularly the male, ranges widely and may travel at times 25 or 30 miles from its homesite, or emigrate 50 or more miles during food shortage. Unpredictable, however, is the behavior of a fugitive puma, which may establish at once a small home range, or may, through fear, immediately travel many miles from the place of its release.

This species is a seclusive and retiring animal that seldom shows itself and rarely makes any noise that might announce its presence. Yet its occurrence in a region where it is rare or long

Tracks of puma. Left, right fore foot. Right, right hind foot. ¾×. Drawn from casts of feet of Wisconsin specimen.

absent is more often suspected by the inexperienced from a chance view of the individual or by hearing it "scream" than by the more reliable method of the experienced in finding its scratch hills or its tracks. The scratch hills, which may be isolated or may be grouped several in a small place, are small mounds of soil five to eight inches in diameter and three to six inches high scratched by the puma to cover its dung or urine. Usually puma tracks are evident near the scratch mounds, and the large, rather broad tracks showing no claw marks may elsewhere betray the puma in the vicinity, or more rarely its covered and partly devoured prey may be found.

The puma is nocturnal, but not infrequently it prowls early in the evening or late in the morning, and it may even sometimes be out at midday. It is active both summer and winter, and remains in a general region until pressed to emigrate on account of food shortage or human interference. Its locomotion is usually by walking in rather long strides; often in pursuing its prey or when harassed by dogs or men following, it gallops or lopes in long graceful leaps, sometimes of 25 feet or more, always the acme of artistic elegance in its movements. It does not trot. It is primarily a terrestrial creature, yet easily ascends to near the top of a tall tree by first jumping to a lower branch and then springing from branch to branch. It descends with less ease in the same manner. It most often climbs a tree when pursued. It is rather averse to water, yet may voluntarily enter a lake or river, and swims well for at least a mile or more. The running speed of the puma has not been determined accurately, but for a short distance its speed is about that of a hound, probably near 30 miles an hour.

Much dispute has arisen as to the nature of the "scream" of the puma, and whether it actually does scream, but the fact has been established that it does sometimes make a loud, terrifying shrill noise (Young and Goldman, 1946: 83-93), or even roar (McCabe, 1949 a). I have heard this call in Fish Creek Canyon and the Sierra Ancha Mountains, Arizona, and to me it sounded not unlike the moonlight call of a backyard tomcat, intensified some twentyfold. Tame pumas and those in zoological gardens utter all the notes of the domestic cat—the caterwaul, the

mew, the purr, and the spits and hisses, usually greatly intensified, though I have heard a yearling puma mew and purr as gently as a domestic kitten. The puma covers with soil its urine and sometimes its dung, and though it may not be intended as an odor post, it often becomes one.

It is solitary in its habits, and seldom does more than a pair or a mother with her young ones occur together. Although not ill-tempered in general demeanor, when adult males approach each other growls and spits are in order, and a fight soon follows if neither retreats. Curiosity is dominant, and a puma will frequently follow another animal, even a man, apparently purely out of curiosity and with no urge to attack. The kits are as playful as domestic kittens, and continue very playful until about three years old. The adult also often plays with small objects, batting them with its paws hither and yon in great gusto. Its lithe and sinewy body is endowed with great strength, vitality, and endurance, yet when running or in any hurried activity it seems to exhaust easily. It will fight when cornered, but prefers to run away when possible, and usually takes to a tree when followed by a human or a dog. Few authentic cases are known of the puma attacking man. The case of a 13 year old boy who was sent on an errand to a neighboring ranch about 11:30 A.M., December 17, 1924, near Malott, Washington, first reported in journals by F. S. Hall (1925) and W. L. Findley (1925), has been summarized by S. P. Young:

He took a short-cut along a trail through a coulee, and when he failed to return a search revealed his remains. Tracks of the boy and of a puma in the light snow told the story. It was apparent that the cat had been following the boy, keeping to one side of the trail in the brush. When the boy saw the animal he had become frightened and ran to the base of a small tree with the apparent intent of climbing it to avoid the animal. However, at this point he was struck down and partly devoured. The opinion formed by those inspecting the scene of the attack was that the puma had leaped at least 10 feet in its attack on the boy. A general hunt followed but without success, owing to the obliteration of the tracks and other signs by the large number of persons who took up the pursuit, seeking the liberal bounty that was offered. About a month later a grown female Puma about 3 years old was taken in a coyote trap by a local rancher, some 4 1/2 miles from the point where the boy was killed. Its stomach

Baby puma. Photograph by Boysen Studio.

. . . contained a small undigested mass, which upon examination in the Food Habits Laboratory of the Biological Survey proved to consist of hair from the boy's head, two bits of blue jeans, and a part of a pocket from his overalls, containing an empty brass cartridge shell which he was known to have carried as a pocket-piece. It is probable that if the boy had not run no attack would have been made, as these animals have often been known to follow people, as previously mentioned, apparently out of curiosity," (In Young and Goldman, 1946:100).

All five major senses of the puma are well developed, those of sight and smell being especially keen, and that of hearing also excellent. The normal longevity of the puma is probably near 12 years, the potential longevity about 18 years. One procured when six weeks old lived

Half-grown pumas in a pine tree, Montana. Photograph by Jacob Neitzling.

in the National Zoological Park, Washington, D. C., from April 21, 1921, to December 27, 1938, or 17 years and 8 months.

Evidence indicates that the puma is monogamous, though it is known that sometimes at mating time two or more males will fight for one female. Sometimes a female in heat may hunt the male. The same pair may mate together year after year, but this is not necessarily so. Usually a female has one litter every two or three years, though rarely she may bear young two years in succession. The puma does not breed until its third year, and may mate at any season, though most matings appear to be from December to March. The gestation period is recorded as 91 to 97 days, with more records for 96 days. The cubs or kittens are one to five in number, usually one to three, with the average something more than two. There is one record of a litter of six in Utah. The animal at birth is some ten inches long and 14 or 16 ounces in weight, and is covered with short, soft fur, dull buff in color with darker blotches on the body and bands on the tail and legs which usually disappear at about six months of age, though sometimes showing indistinctly until the animal is nearly a year old. The eyes, closed at birth, open after nine or ten days. The kittens gain a pound or more a week until near maturity, and when two months old weigh about 10 pounds, and when six months about 40 pounds. The kittens are weaned at ten or twelve weeks of age when they are able to ramble of their own accord, at which time the mother leads them to the kill she has made. At this stage the mother and young may establish a new den near the kill, and wander as a family from kill to kill and from den to den for several months until the youngsters are forced out or voluntarily leave to shift for themselves. The mammae are eight, four pectoral (upper two nonfunctional), two abdominal, two inguinal.

The den or lair of the puma in Wisconsin probably was in most cases under a low-branched tree, an overhanging bank, or a tree root, or in a dense clump of bushes. There was no attempt at nest building, the accumulated windblown grasses and leaves providing sufficient bedding after the puma had scratched a place to lie down. Food was rarely brought to the den, and feces and urine were deposited at some distance and usually covered with soil.

The puma is a fresh meat eater and a big-game hunter that seems to prefer deer to any other prey. It captures, among other wild mammals, the porcupine, cottontail rabbits, and varying hare in considerable numbers, and occasionally other rodents and small carnivores. At times it will kill an elk. It seldom molests birds. Of the domestic stock, it seems to prefer horses, especially colts, and, next in order, cattle, though it also will attack sheep and pigs. Of the puma in Clark County woods in 1878 it was written, "it has already killed a cow and two yearling calves" (*Clinton Independent*, September 18, 1878). In making its kill, the puma does not run its prey and attack from below as does the wolf, but captures it by lying in wait or stealthily creeping upon it and then making a quick rush and springing on the back or side of the prey. It often consumes the entire animal, but any remains are usually covered with soil, leaves, or debris; the puma may return after two or three days for further feeding. Sometimes the prey which is left may be consumed by other carnivores.

In Wisconsin the puma had no natural enemies other than man. External parasites believed to infest the species in North America include the louse *Trichodectes felis*; the ticks *Dermacentor variabilis*, *Ixodes ricinus*, and *I. cookei*; and the flea *Arctopsylla setosa*. Internal parasites include the nematode *Physaloptera praeputialis* and the cestodes *Echinococcus granulosus*, *Taenia taeniaformis*, and *T. lyncis*. Rabies is the only disease known to affect the puma seriously.

The puma has little economic value except as an object for hunting and trapping sport, and as an aid in reducing excess deer populations when hunting does not control the surplus. Its pelt has little value except as a trophy. We might like to have a few in the wilderness areas of Wisconsin and may regret its passing from our fauna, but its presence in any numbers in a dairying country could not be tolerated. When its natural food of deer, rabbits, and porcupines is scarce, farmers have heavy losses from its depredations on domestic stock.

Specimens examined from Wisconsin.—Only 1, as follows: *Outagamie County:* Appleton (near), 1 (type specimen, UWZ, No. 13,464).

Selected references.—Anonymous, 1947 b; Jackson, H.H.T., 1955; Schorger, A. W., 1938; Scott, W. E., 1939 b; True, F. W., 1891; Young, S. P., and E. A. Goldman, 1946.

Genus **Lynx** Kerr
Lynxes and Bobcats

Dental formula:

$$I\frac{3-3}{3-3}, \quad C\frac{1-1}{1-1}, \quad P\frac{2-2}{2-2}, \quad M\frac{1-1}{1-1} = 28.$$

Lynx canadensis canadensis Kerr
Canada Lynx

Lynx canadensis Kerr, Animal Kingdom, vol. 1: systematic catalogue between pp. 32 and 33, and p. 157, 1792.
Lyncus borealis Lapham, p. 43, 1852; Lapham, p. 339, 1853.
Lynx Canadensis Strong, p. 436, 1883.
Lynx canadensis Snyder, p. 126, 1902; Jackson, p. 25, 1908; Hollister, p. 26, 1910; Cory, p. 287, 1912.
Lynx canadensis canadensis Komarek, p. 205, 1932; Barger, p. 11, 1952.

Vernacular names.—Usually called lynx in Wisconsin, and in colonial days often called *loup cervier* (French Canadian). Other names include *be-jew* or *pe-zu* (Chippewa), catamount, gray wildcat, *le chat* (French Canadian), *loupcervier*, lynx cat, and *pichu* (French Canadian).

Identification marks.—A rather large cat, about twice the weight of a big domestic cat, with comparatively short and robust body; prominent tufts of hair on the ears and ruffs on the cheeks and below the jaws; very short furry tail with black tip all around; long limbs and especially large broad feet; eyes prominent; nose short and broad; fur, particularly in winter, long, fine, and silky. In full autumn or winter pelage the general color of the upper parts is pale

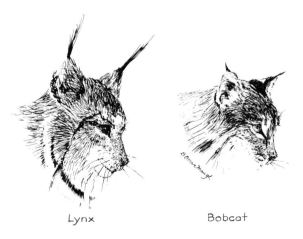

Lynx   Bobcat

Side view profile of heads of Canada lynx and bobcat.

grizzled buff gray, more or less mixed with buffish
or pale brown, the top of the head more brownish; inside of ears grayish white, the tips of the
ear tufts and lines down margin black; cheeks and
nose grayish; ruff on cheeks and throat dark,
a mixture of blackish, gray, and brown; under
parts pale, grayish white or grayish buffy white,
sometimes with a few spots of blackish, especially
on inside of legs; tail pale buffy gray with tip
black all around. The worn pelage late in spring
is more buffy than the winter fur. The fresh summer pelage is darker and more brownish than

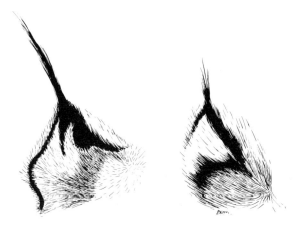

Ears of Canada lynx and bobcat, drawn from Lake
States specimens. ⅗×.

Tails of bobcat, left, and Canada lynx, right. ⅗×.

Basilar parts of skulls of Lynx rufus, left, and Lynx
canadensis, right, to show differences in shape of
presphenoid bones and in placement of anterior
condyloid foramina. ⅗×.

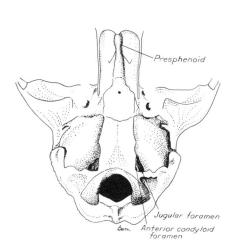

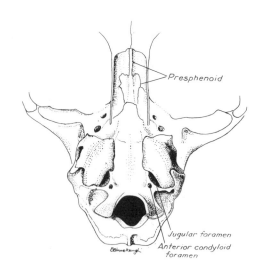

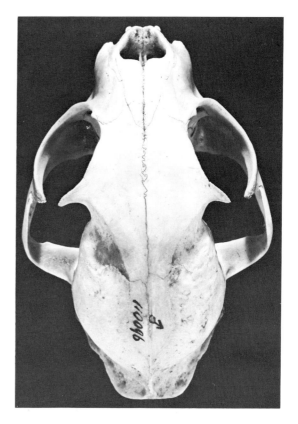

Skull of LYNX C. CANADENSIS, *Oxford House, Manitoba.* ¾×.

Left hind foot of Canada lynx. 1×.

Canada lynx. Photograph by W. J. Banks. Courtesy of W. A. Swallow, editor, Our Dumb Animals.

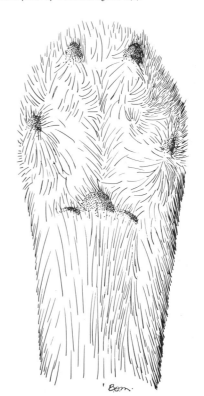

full winter fur. Apparently there is only one molt a year which occurs late in spring. The difference between summer and winter fur and coloration is due to continuous growth of the hair during autumn, the long silky hair with grayish tips being acquired by late in autumn or early in winter. The immature lynx is paler and more buffy than the adult, and is spotted and dashed with darker brown and blackish.

The skull of the lynx is low and broad, much smaller than that of the puma (always less than 160 mm. broad), and has one less upper premolar on each side, a total of 28 teeth as in the bobcat. The skull of the lynx is usually larger than that of the bobcat, though occasionally a small lynx skull may be smaller than a large bob-cat skull; relatively and actually smaller audital bullae; broader interorbitally, usually more than 30 mm. (always less than 30 mm. in the bob-cat); flatter in facial area (prefrontal and pos-terior maxillo-nasal region) and less compressed laterally; presphenoid wide posteriorly, more than 6 mm. in greatest width; anterior condyloid foramen separate from foramen lacerum poste-rius (comfluent foramina in bobcat); condyle of ramus shorter in extero-interior diameter; denti-tion heavier; length of upper carnassial more than 16 mm.

The male lynx averages slightly larger than the female, possibly about 5 per cent, and in old individuals tends to develop a more pro-nounced saggital ridge. The more or less spotted young drop the spots from the upper parts as the fur develops, and attain adult pelage their first winter. Thereafter no color change associated with age of the animal occurs other than the occasional paling and raggedness of extreme senility. Individual variation is normal, though what may be mutations have been mentioned as "drab-blue" and "fawn or yellow" (Jones, S. V. H., 1923).

The lynx is apt to be confused only with the bobcat, from which it differs in the solid black all around tip of tail, longer ear tufts, and huge feet, twice as long as the tail. Skull characters previously mentioned are also distinctive.

Measurements.—Total length of adult, 875 to 1,000 mm. (34.5 to 39.2 in.); tail, 100 to 120 mm. (3.9 to 4.7 in.); hind foot, 215 to 250 mm. (8.4 to 9.8 in.). Weight of adult, 16 to 35 pounds, occasionally heavier. The specimen UWZ No. 14,607, adult female from Hurley, Iron County, Wisconsin, weighed 8390 grams (18.5 pounds). An adult male from Spring Green, Sauk County, weighed 27 pounds when shot (Schorger, 1947: 186). Skull length, 122 to 146 mm.; width, 92 to 108 mm.

Distribution in Wisconsin.—Formerly probably throughout the entire state in wooded areas, ap-parently more frequently in the northern half of the state, though never common. Now very rare and erratic in distribution.

Habitat.—Heavy and dense forests and wood-lands.

Status and Habits.—The Canada lynx has never been common in Wisconsin, and fur rec-ords early in the nineteenth century indicate that only a few of its pelts were sold each year, though its fur was highly desirable. In 1803–1804, Michel Curot (1911: 410) purchased a few in the region of Yellow Lake and the St. Croix River, Burnett County; in 1804, Victor Malhiot (1910: 221) procured some at Lac du Flambeau, Vilas County; and in 1814 and 1816 lynx pelts were procured near Green Bay (Thwaites, 1910 c: 429). Numerous records of the Canada lynx occurring in various parts of the state were made available in newspapers or reports until about 1880, a few of which may have referred to the bobcat or even the puma, but many of which were authentic. Recognition of the differences in the three species seems to have been surprisingly common. Possibly the extensive lumbering oper-ations and forest disturbances during the last years of the nineteenth century may have been a contributing factor to the near extirpation of the lynx during that period. It will always be a rare mammal in Wisconsin, yet comparatively recent records from widely separated localities such as Middleton, Dane County, 1907, Spring Green, Sauk County, 1946 (Schorger, 1947),

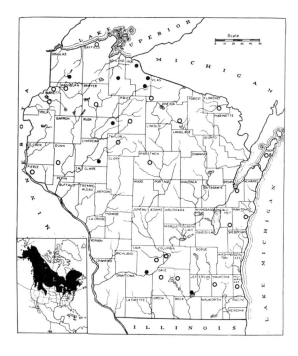

Map 73. *Distribution of* Lynx canadensis. ● = *specimens examined.* ○ = *authentic records.*

Chippewa County, 1908 (Scott, W. E., 1951), and Hurley, Iron County, 1954 (John T. Emlen, Jr., in litt. April 6, 1955) indicate that a few might continue to be with us.

I have accepted as reliable two recent records reported by Doll, Balser, and Wendt (1957):

There have been other unverified reports recently. Dewey Yeager, Conservation Department trapper, and John Waggoner reported jumping and running a lynx on January 22, 1956, in Washburn County; the animal was not captured. This was in T41 and 42N, R12W. Donald Balser, game manager with the Conservation Department at Cornell, reported seeing lynx tracks in the Chequamegon National Forest in Taylor County (about twenty miles southeast of the Rusk County record) during the latter part of November, 1955. It seems probable that a low remnant population has persisted and, with the increased forest cover in northern Wisconsin, may be slowly increasing throughout the area.

In Canada, where the lynx sometimes is not uncommon, it has cycles of abundance. "Hudson's Bay Company and some other records provide a record of lynx (*Lynx canadensis*) fur collections for 206 years. . . . The cycle in lynx furs is very violent and regular and has persisted unchanged for the whole period. Its average period is about 9.6 years" (Elton and Nicholson, 1942: 243). The lynx may wander many miles to new country, and particularly during the winter may travel 50 miles or more over a favored route, yet near its established breeding home it usually confines its range to a radius of less than 5 miles.

A Canada lynx may inhabit a neighborhood for a long time unknown to human dwellers. Any kill of game or small domestic stock left uneaten by a lynx may be suspected to be the discard of some other predator, unless the unmistakable big, round, evenly spaced tracks are evident. Feces, claw marks, scratches, and other signs usually are unidentifiable, especially from those of the wildcat. The lynx, active both summer and winter, is almost strictly nocturnal, though sometimes it is out mornings or during the daytime if hungry. It is not a fast runner, and usually when traveling faster than a walk, runs in a near trot, rarely breaking into a clumsy gallop. It travels well on snow, particularly if slightly crusted, its large feet acting, as it were, like snowshoes. Its fastest running speed probably is not more than 12 miles an

Tracks of Canada lynx. Left, right fore foot. Right, Right hind foot. ½ ×.

hour, though it has never been accurately determined. It jumps exceedingly well, and from a standing posture or a slow walk can leap 15 or more feet. It takes to water voluntarily and swims well, with its head and shoulders well out of water.

The lynx is a solitary animal that rarely assembles in a group, and then of only three or four animals, probably a mother and young. It has most of the vocal attributes of a house cat—purrs lightly, hisses through bared teeth and with upturned nose in defense, growls when distressed or disturbed, mews to its kittens, and, especially during the mating season, utters a terrific yowl or cry. In writing of one that came to Durward's Glen, Caledonia Township, Columbia County, previous to 1880, Dorward (1901: 116) tells us that it "tarried quite a while within easy gunshot, screaming in a blood-curdling manner all the time," and that it "was too dark to see it, but the scream was considered sufficient identification." The lynx has a rather sullen disposition. It is extremely inquisitive, and frequently will follow a person in the wilderness for many miles, with no intent to attack. David Cartwright, referring to the Gilbert Creek region, Dunn County, in December, 1858, writes: "We found that a lynx had followed my track for several miles after I had left the deer the night before" (Cartwright and Bailey, 1875: 243). Muscular and agile, the lynx nevertheless tires easily and frequently rests crouched in a convenient location. Its endurance, however, against cold, famine, and injury are phenomenal. Its senses are well developed, especially that of sight, hence the expression "lynx-eyed" and the north Eurasian legend that the European lynx had the ability to see through thick stone walls. Its potential longevity possibly is near 15 to 18 years. The longevity record for the National Zoological Park is 11 years and 4 months (Mann, 1930: 303).

Mating takes place in January or February, and after a gestation period of about 62 days the one to four—rarely five—young are born in March or April. The only description we have of a newly born lynx is that published by C. Hart Merriam:

"It was dropped" writes Mr. [Montague] Chamberlain, "on the 20th March, 1883, when the mother had been in captivity about a month. She gave birth to five (5) kittens, but this was the only one rescued from her unmotherly jaws. When the first was born she at once prepared to clean it, and seemed fond of it. After a short time, however, it gave vent to a weak squeal, which caused her to eye it curiously for a moment, when another squeal was delivered. This settled the kitten's doom—it was at once devoured. The mother did not exhibit any tenderness towards the other four, and the keeper made two unsuccessful efforts before he was able to get one away from her. The kitten lived two days, and then died from injuries received in its removal from the cage. Its 'mew' was something like that of a domestic kitten, but stronger and harsher; it was almost fierce and very penetrating. The general strength of the animal was greater than that of a domestic kitten. Two hours after birth it stood firmly on its feet and turned around in its box, but it did not show any inclination to fight when teased. The eyes were open at birth." (Merriam: 1886:10).

More recent observations indicate that normally the young are born with closed eyes that open in about nine or ten days. The kitten is much more brownish than the adult and is streaked and blotched on the upper parts and blotched and spotted on the flanks and under parts, the markings gradually disappearing until adult pelage is acquired at about nine months of age. There is only one litter a year, and the young one becomes sexually mature at the end of its first year. The mammae are four, two abdominal and two inguinal.

The den where the young are reared is in a hollow tree, stump, or log, and sometimes under fallen timber. The nest consists of leaves, bark, and similar vegetative matter pawed and trampled into form by the parent. Similar dens are sometimes occupied as shelters, but as a rule the lynx prefers to rest crouching on top of a rock, log, or knoll where it has vantage to attack its prey or escape a possible enemy.

Rabbits, particularly snowshoe rabbits, are the chief prey of the lynx, normally constituting probably 90 per cent of its food. It also captures grouse and squirrels, and is a natural enemy of the red fox, which it kills and consumes. Rarely, it eats porcupine, but is sometimes killed by the quills when it does. It seldom consumes deer, and its wilderness habitat gives it little contact with domestic stock. Prey usually is consumed where killed, and any remains are left uncovered. The predator may return to the quarry for other meals as long as the flesh is not putrid, but it prefers fresh meat. The lynx is one of our most strictly carnivorous mammals and never eats vegetable matter except rarely to chew a little grass. There are records of its attacking its own kind, and a case of cannibalism occurred in northern Ontario in March, 1951, when a large lynx attacked and killed one of two young lynxes that were hunting snowshoe rabbits, and ate the flesh from the hind legs and as far forward as the kidneys (Elsey, 1954). It attacks its prey by patiently lying crouched in waiting and giving a tremendous leap onto its victim, and never follows its prey for more than two or three jumps.

Enemies of the lynx other than man are negligible. Probably many kinds of parasites infect it, as with most carnivores, among which are the external parasites *Ceratophyllus dentatus*, *C. labiatus*, and *C. petriolatus*, *Foxella ignotus*, and *Hoplopsyllus glacialis*, and the internal parasites *Taenia laticollis* and *T. rileyi*.

The lynx is a potential fur producer. Its pelt brings $20 to $25 on the fur market, and sometimes, as in 1922, choice pelts bring as high as $80 each. It is so rare now in Wisconsin as to have little economic importance, and the few trapped are taken along with wildcats for bounty payment. It is not a regular domestic stock killer, and no forester would oppose its disposing of snowshoe rabbits that are so harmful to forest nursery stock. It is comparatively easy to trap. Any protection given the lynx would favor the wildcat.

Specimens examined from Wisconsin.—Total 11, as follows: *Ashland County:* Cayuga, 3 (UWZ). *Chippewa County:* Sec. 27, T 28 N, R 6 E, 1

(WCDG). *Douglas County:* Gordon, 1 (UWZ). *Iron County:* Fisher Lake, 1 (UWZ); Hurley, 1 (UWZ); Mercer, 1 (UWZ). *Jefferson County:* No locality, 1 (UWZ). *Rusk County:* Ingram, 1 (UWZ). *Sauk County,* 1 (UWZ).

Selected references.—Cory, C. B., 1912: 287-91; Elton, C., and M. Nicholson, 1942; Jordahl, H. C., 1956; Merriam, C. H., 1886; Schorger, A. W., 1947; and Seton, E. T., 1921, vol. 1: 161–209, pls. 33–36.

Lynx rufus superiorensis
Peterson and Downing
Lake Superior Bobcat

Lynx rufus superiorensis Peterson and Downing, Contrib. Royal Ontario Mus. Zool. and Palaeontol. No. 33, p. 1, April 8, 1952.
Lyncus rufus, Lapham, p. 43, 1852; Lapham, p. 339, 1853.
Lynx rufus Strong, p. 436, 1883; Komarek, p. 205, 1932.
Lynx ruffus Jackson, p. 25, 1908; Hollister, p. 26, 1910; Jackson, p. 89, 1910; Cory, p. 291, 1912.
Lynx rufus rufus Barger, p. 11, 1952.

Vernacular names.—In Wisconsin now most frequently called bobcat or wildcat. Other names include bay lynx, catamount, lynx cat, *loupcervier* (French), *pichou* or *pichu* (French Canadian), and red lynx.

Identification marks.—In general appearance something like an overgrown domestic tabby or tiger house cat with a short tail and sideburn cheek whiskers; actually about twice the body size and weight of an ordinary domestic cat. Body rather short; ears conspicuous but with small ear tufts; eyes prominent, pupils elliptical; tail about one-fourth total length of animal, the whitish of underparts extending to tip; feet relatively small; fur only moderately long, rather fine.

Lake Superior bobcat from Wisconsin. Courtesy of Wisconsin Conservation Department.

Bobcat, the Rocky Mountain race. Photograph by Charles T. Vorhies.

The color of the upper parts is grayish to brownish, spotted and blotched, and darker along the mid-dorsal from head to base of tail; under parts and inside of legs whitish, conspicuously marked with irregular spots and blotches of blackish, with conspicuous black bar on inside of front leg; tail above like upper parts, with black tip and black bars, below whitish to tip. There is a tendency for the full winter fur to be more grayish and darker than the worn spring and summer pelage, which often has a reddish tone. So far as known there is one molt annually, which begins early in summer.

The skull of the bobcat is usually smaller than that of the Canada lynx, though sometimes a large bobcat has a skull as large as that of a small lynx. Compared with the skull of the Canada lynx, that of the bobcat has relatively and actually larger audital bullae; is narrower interorbitally, always less than 30 mm.; is more inflated in facial area (prefrontal and posterior maxillo-nasal region) and more compressed laterally; presphenoid narrower posteriorly, less than 6 mm. in greatest width; anterior condyloid foramen confluent with foramen lacerum posterius (separate in Canada lynx); condyle of ramus longer in extero-interior diameter; dentition weaker; length of upper carnassial less than 16 mm.

The male bobcat averages about 10 per cent longer than the female, and weighs about 30 per cent more. There is no sexual color difference nor any color change associated with age. As with

most carnivores the old individuals tend to develop a more pronounced saggital ridge, particularly the males. Individual variation in color is rather wide, not only in the extent and intensity of redness or grayness, but also in the darkness and extent of the dark mid-dorsal streak and the degree and style of spottedness on the upper parts. What may be color mutations have been described as "light blue," "red and paler," and "almost white" (Jones, 1923: 174–76). A case of true melanism in a Florida bobcat has been described and illustrated (Ulmer, 1941).

The bobcat can easily be distinguished from the Canada lynx by characters previously mentioned. All Wisconsin bobcats are here ascribed to *Lynx rufus superiorensis* Peterson and Downing, though it is possible that the race that formerly occurred in the extreme southern part of the state may have been nearer in essential characters to *L. r. rufus*, with which form all Wis-

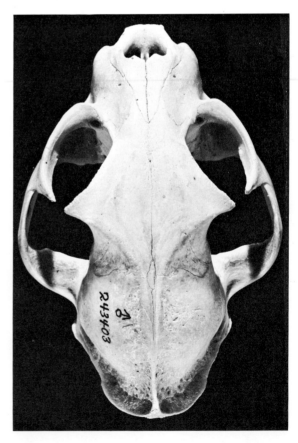

Skull of Lynx r. superiorensis, *Champion, Michigan.* ¾×.

consin specimens were usually identified until *L. r. superiorensis* was described as having different cranial characters:

Skull characters. in adults, *Lynx rufus superiorensis* differs from *L. r. rufus* in the shape of the dorsal contour of the cranium, that of *rufus* being a more-or-less symmetrical curve, while in the new race the symmetry is usually interrupted by a more inflated supra-orbital region. When fully adult skulls of the two races are placed on their dorsal surfaces on a flat, level table, the palate of *superiorensis* usually lies in a horizontal plane while that of *rufus* inclines forward (Peterson and Downing, 1952:1).

Other ways in which *superiorensis* differs from *rufus* is in having a relatively smaller upper third molar, a relatively narrower third upper premolar, and a narrower zygomatic width.

Measurements.—Total length of adult, 800 to 1,015 mm. (31.5 to 40 in.); tail, 130 to 180 mm. (5.1 to 7.1 in.); hind foot, 155 to 197 mm. (6.1 to 7.8 in.). Weight of adult, 15 to 35 pounds, occasionally as heavy as 40 pounds; average male about 24 pounds; average female about 16 pounds. Skull length, 120 to 143 mm.; width, 84 to 107 mm.

Distribution in Wisconsin.—In early days (about the year 1850) found throughout the state. Now found chiefly north of latitude 45° N., most commonly in the region from Sawyer County east to Marinette County. Occasionally found farther south, except in the extreme southeastern section.

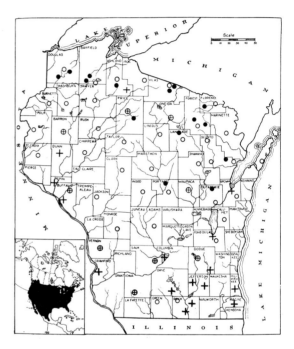

Map 74. Distribution of LYNX RUFUS. ● = *specimens examined.* ○ = *authentic records since 1900.* + = *authentic records before 1900.*

Habitat.—Wilder sections of brushy and woodlands country, particularly in swamps and rocky areas.

Status and Habits.—Like its near relative the Canada lynx, the wildcat is subject to cycles of abundance that approach a high population about once in ten years. Recent peaks of the cycle came in 1936–38 and again in 1946–47. Several old records indicate that there may have been a high in the cycle in southern Wisconsin about 1867. It has been suggested that possibly in early days the Canada lynx was more abundant in northern Wisconsin than the bobcat.

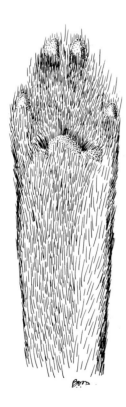

Left hind foot of bobcat. ¾×.

Possibly this may have been true in some heavily forested areas, but old records of fur sales in Green Bay show a ratio of 40 or 50 wildcat pelts sold to one lynx pelt, even though the latter brought a much higher price. During a food shortage or when seriously disturbed the bobcat may wander or emigrate 50 miles or more from its homesite, but ordinarily its home range is seldom more than a mile or two. Today in Wisconsin in a heavy population of bobcats they seldom average as many as one to five square miles. In years of cycle peak there are possibly some 2,500 or 3,000 bobcats in the entire State.

Solitary and retiring, the Lake Superior bobcat is seldom seen by humans as it keeps watchful and alert for enemies and slinks away at approaching danger. It leaves signs, however, such as claw marks on trees, scratches in the soil, feces, and the more easily identified tracks. It is active summer and winter, and is almost strictly nocturnal, though sometimes it is out during daylight. It usually moves in a stealthy walk; sometimes it trots, but when trying to speed it has a bounding gallop of leaps six to eight feet long. It is not a fast runner, and at its best makes only 12 to 15 miles an hour. It dislikes water, yet when forced into a lake or river swims moderately well.

The bobcat utters most of the calls of a domestic cat—increased in intensity and shrillness —and becomes especially noisy during a bobcat fight at night. Generally, however, it is a quiet animal. It does not act as sentry, except to watch its young, and has no odor posts. When cornered or harassed, a bobcat shows its ugly disposition—it scowls, snarls, and spits defiance with its teeth bared; its hair ruffled, and its eyes flashing. It sometimes indulges in play with its kittens, but otherwise plays little if any as an adult, except to maul its prey if small or box it if large before eating it. The kittens frequently play among themselves. Quick, active, and sinewy, the bobcat appears physically strong, and has an exceptional musculature of more than five hundred muscles, yet like many cats it has a comparatively low endurance. Its major senses are highly developed, especially that of sight. Like most cats, it can see in darkness, but not

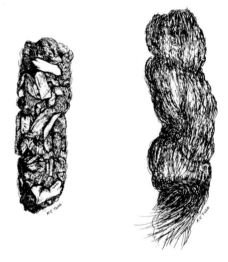

Bobcat feces. Left figure shows varying hare bones and some vegetation that was probably consumed with the hare. Right figure shows deer hair. Drawn from Pollack, 1909, pl. 16. ¾×.

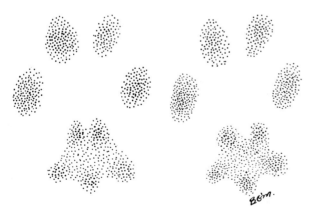

Tracks of bobcat. Left, right fore foot. Right, right hind foot. 1×.

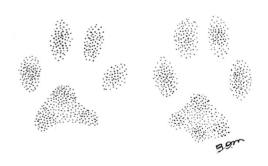

Tracks of domestic cat. Left, right fore foot. Right, right hind foot. 1×.

in total darkness; it has exceptionally sensitive vibrissae and a sense of balance. Its potential longevity is probably between 18 to 21 years, with a normal in the wild possibly reduced to 8 to 10 years. The longevity record for the National Zoological Park is 15 years 10 months (Mann, 1930: 303). A male raised in a private zoo in New Jersey weighed 30-1/2 pounds at the time of its death, and was 25 years old (Carter, 1955).

Mating usually occurs in March, sometimes during the last part of February, although rarely, for unknown reasons, it is delayed to as late as June. After a gestation period of about 62 days, the blind furred young are born, from one to four in number, usually two. The eyes of the young open when it is 9 or 10 days old. It is weaned in about 60 or 70 days, but stays with the mother until autumn or early in the winter, sometimes not leaving its parent until January or even February when it is by weight about three-fourths grown. It is mature and essentially full grown when one year old. One litter a year is the rule. The mammae are four, two abdominal and two inguinal.

The den is made in a crevice among rocks or in a hollow tree, stump, or log, and the nest is a shallow lining of leaves, moss, and other vegetation pawed and scratched into shape by the bobcat. The den is sometimes occupied as a shelter, but when resting the bobcat more often lies quietly concealed under a shrub or grass.

The natural food of the bobcat is rabbits, cottontails and varying hares usually constituting 50 per cent or more of its diet in frequency of occurrence and 40 per cent or more in volume. Deer at times is one of its significant food items, part of which comes from carrion or dead animals rather than its own kills. As long ago as 1844, at Sullivan, Jefferson County, it was reported, "we had a deer hanging in the woods; a wild cat came to eat it" (Cartwright and Bailey, 1875: 160). The bobcat undoubtedly may kill a few deer fawns during summer, and occasionally grown deer during winter in deep snow or when the deer are weakened from lack of food. The effect of the bobcat on deer population as a whole is slight. Other items known to be eaten in frequency of more than 1 per cent are squirrels, porcupines, mice, muskrats, skunks, and grouse. Unusual food contents of stomachs have

Lake Superior bobcat, swimming in lake near Ely, Minnesota.

included red fox, gray fox, house cat, mink, opossum, and crow. The bobcat tends to retire from farm land, but sometimes kills domestic animals, particularly calves and sheep, and rarely poultry. Its method of attack is to sneak up on its prey. Sometimes it lies in wait; often it follows trails and runways until it encounters its victim. It eats voraciously and furiously, growling and hissing at anything that interferes with it. It usually eats the hinder parts of larger prey first, and usually turns the skin inside out. Like our domestic cat, it washes itself after each meal.

Man is the worst enemy of the bobcat. Inasmuch as this species is easy to trap or to hunt with dogs, once an individual is located it is readily killed. The great horned owl is reported occasionally to kill a young bobcat, but it is not a serious enemy. Among the external parasites known to infest the bobcat are the mange mite *Neotedres*; the lice *Felicola felis* and *F. subrostratus*; the ticks *Dermacentor andersoni* and *D. variabilis*; and the fleas *Orchopeas wickhami, Cediopsylla simplex, Odontopsyllus multispinosus, Hoplosyllus lynx, Echidnophaga gallinacea,* and *Stenocephalides felis*. Internal parasites include the flatworms *Taenia laticollis, T. lyncis,* and *T. macrocystis,* and *Toxocara cati;* the roundworms *Filaria fasciata, Physaloptera rara,* and *P. praeputialis,* and others of the genera *Ascaris* and *Toxascaris*. The bobcat has been known to have rabies (Young, 1948: 233).

The fur of the bobcat is used for jackets and trimmings. Its sale value is low, a pelt seldom netting the trapper as much as two dollars. The bobcat has slight value in its preying on rabbits when over abundant and in catching a few rodents. On the other hand, it destroys many rabbits when they may be wanted as game mammals. In former years when cattle and sheep were allowed to graze as range animals, the bobcat not infrequently killed a few calves and numbers of sheep and lambs. Nowadays it will seldom approach a farmyard to kill stock. In moderate numbers it is not obnoxious. When it does become a pest it is easily captured in a No. 2 steel trap, particularly when catnip oil is used as an attraction. Methods of trapping have been explained by Young (1941 a). As a pet the bobcat is not to be recommended, although a few that were captured as tiny youngsters have become almost as docile as house cats.

Specimens examined from Wisconsin.—Total 24, as follows: *Ashland County:* Cayuga, 3 (UWZ). *Bayfield County:* Cable, 2 (UWZ); Drummond, 1 (UWZ). *Douglas County:* Gordon, 1 (UWZ); junction of Moose and St. Croix rivers, 1 (UWZ). *Florence County:* No locality, 1 (UWZ). *Forest County:* Laona, 1 (NPM); North Crandon, 2 (MM). *Langlade County:* T 34 N, R 11 E, 3 (UWZ). *Oconto County:* Lena, 3 (MM). *Outagamie County:* Black Creek, 1 (MM). *Portage County:* Dewey Twp., 1 (UWZ). *Price County:* No locality, 1 (MM). *Vilas County:* No locality, 1 (CNHM); Mamie Lake, 2.

Selected references.—Barger, N. R., 1948 d; Peterson, R. L., and S. C. Downing, 1952; Pollack, E. M., and W. G. Sheldon, 1951; Rollins, C. T., 1945; and Young, S. P., 1941 b; 1958.

ORDER ARTIODACTYLA

Even-toed Hoofed Mammals

This order covers such diverse forms as the deer, ox, goat, sheep, antelope, camel, pig, and hippopotamus. Most of the species are strictly vegetarian and graze or browse for their food. The order has representatives on all the continents except Australia. Functional toes are four, the first or inner digit being suppressed, or by reduction or even complete suppression the toes may be only two in number. Third and fourth digits of each foot almost equally developed, their terminal phalanges flattened on their inner or contiguous surfaces so that each is not symmetrical in itself, but when the two are placed together they form a figure symmetrically disposed to a line drawn between them. The calcaneum has articular facet for the lower end of the fibula, thus permitting flexibility of the hind foot, and thus allowing the mammals of this order to arise rear end first instead of front end first. The molar and premolar teeth are not alike, the former being double lobed and the latter single lobed. The last lower molar of both first and second dentition almost always triple lobed, the first tooth of the upper molariform series always without a milk predecessor.

The order Artiodactyla contains nine living families, two of which are represented as native to Wisconsin.

Key to the Families of Living Wisconsin Artiodactyla

a. Boney outgrowths (antlers) from the frontal bones in the males annually developed and shed; large ante-orbital vacuity exposing inner bones. . . . . . . *Cervidae*

b. Boney outgrowths (horns) from the frontal bones, permanently covered with true horn and present in both sexes, not shed but present throughout life. No large ante-orbital vacuity exposing inner bones. . . . . *Bovidae*

Family **Cervidae**

Deer and Allies

The deer family ranges as a native over all the continents and larger land masses except Australia, New Zealand, and Africa south of the Sahara Desert. It is composed of some 17 genera exclusive of fossil forms, of which 4 have occurred in Wisconsin.

The striking characteristic of the deer family is the presence of antlers in the male (very rarely in the female in some genera). These are bony outgrowths which start as a soft pulpy growth from a pedicle on the frontal bone. The outgrowth is well supplied with blood vessels, and is protected by a tough skin which is covered with a dense pelage of stiff hairs, called "velvet." After about four to six months' growth, during which the antler is richly supplied with mineral matter, the supply of blood to it slows and finally ceases. The skin then dies and peels off or is rubbed off by the animal, leaving the antler bone bare, hard, and nerveless. The animal carries the antlers two or three months covering the rutting season. The antler then becomes loosened from the pedicle by a process of absorption of the bone at the base of the antler and it is shed. Antler formation and shedding is repeated with regularity each year. Details of the anatomical and histological processes, based largely on the European red deer, have been published by William Macewen (1920).

Genus **Cervus** Linnaeus

Typical Deer

Dental formula:

$$I\frac{0-0}{3-3}, \quad C\frac{1-1}{1-1}, \quad P\frac{3-3}{3-3}, \quad M\frac{3-3}{3-3} = 34.$$

Cervus canadensis canadensis Erxleben
American Elk

[*Cervus elaphus*] *canadensis* Erxleben, Systema
   regni animalis, p. 305, 1777.
Elaphus Canadensis Lapham, p. 44, 1852; Lapham,
   p. 340, 1853.
Cervus Canadensis Hoy, p. 256, 1882; Strong, p.
   437, 1883.
Cervus canadensis Jackson, p. 15, 1908; Hollister, p.
   137, 1909; Hollister, p. 23, 1910; Cory, p. 67, 1912.
Cervus canadensis canadensis Barger, p. 12, 1952.
Cervus canadensis nelsoni Barger, 12, 1952 (for the
   introduced Rocky Mountain elk).

Vernacular names.—In Wisconsin commonly
called elk. Other names include American red
elk, American stag, Canadian elk, Canadian wap-
piti, eastern elk, *mish-wa-wa* (Potawatomi), *o-
masch-koohs* (Chippewa), stag, wapiti. The
term Rocky Mountain elk is used for the introduced elk, *Cervus canadensis nelsoni.*

There has long been confusion over the names
elk and wapiti as applied to *Cervus canadensis.*
Europeans who first came to America knew
about the European moose (called "elk" in Europe) and also were familiar with the European
red deer (*Cervus elaphus*), a mammal somewhat
similar to the American elk. The names wapiti
and American elk are now so well established
that effort should not be made to change them.
Discussion of the confusion, however, is of interest, and is here supplied by E. T. Adney, Upper Woodstock, New Brunswick, who has made
an intensive study of the language of Indians of
the northeast, particularly of the Malecites:

In Long's vocabulary of Shawnee collected toward
the end of the 18th century *wapi* appears in *wap-i-ti*

which Long wrote down as *elk* (as the moose is still
called) but the meaning was a *white* elk (moose),
a sacred animal in that color—*wap-i-ti* being a con-
traction of *wap-i-ti-am-ul,* a white *ti-am-ul* or tutelary
which has replaced *mos,* indicating this animal was
once a tutelary of the Micmacs.

The European name *elk, olk,* etc. was abandoned;
or being abandoned in the latter half of the 18th
century, for the Indian name *mos;* with most re-
grettable consequences, that the words *wapiti* and
elk, left kicking around were applied to *Cervus
canadensis* of the Rocky Mountains, and on the
"evidence" of name purely, various pseudo-natural-
ists (as Madison Grant once called them) have
argued that *C. canadensis* occurred, even in settlement times, along the Atlantic slope. Hornaday,
Thompson Seton, Stone, in books have perpetuated
this inexcusable blunder; inexcusable for in the English edition of 1772 (?) of Per Kalm's Travels into
N. A., an editor's footnote states that *olk* of the
Swedish naturalist is the same animal "now called
moose-deer." In the figure of the arms granted to
Sir Humphrey Gilbert for Newfoundland, the crest
calls for "an elk passant" while the drawings distinctly shows palmations.

White weasel, the white or polar bear (*wab-i-sig-
wes, wabskw* respectively) appear in Malecite
myths in association with magic. Wicked medeulins,
sorcerers, turned themselves into a white weasel, or
a white otter, and no doubt also the white owl.

I especially desire to draw your attention to the
misuse of *wapiti* and *elk.* To bolster his "evidence"

*Bull elk. Vilas County, February 1944. Photograph
by Staber W. Reese. Courtesy Wisconsin Conservation Department.*

*Cow elk from Montana at Jerome Hunting and
Fishing Club reserve, Trude Lake, Wisconsin.
Photograph by L. A. Gehr.*

as to *canadensis*, Seton mistranslated Jacques Cartier's *cerfs et dains* as "stags and deer," stags meaning canadensis, for the French had named the moose *eland* and *originaux;* whereas *dain* is the common French for a *doe.* These were white-tailed deer and Cartier was only writing "bucks and does" as we would say "horses and mares". (E. T. Adney to the author, January, 1945).

Identification marks.—With the exception of the moose (*Alces*) the elk is the largest in weight of North American deer, and in total length from tip of nose to tip of tail it will average longer than the moose; neck maned; ears moderately prominent; facial gland well developed; nose naked; tail short (5.5 to 6.0 inches); metatarsal gland present below hock on outside of hind leg; males with large widely branched antlers, the main backward sweeping beam, sometimes four feet long, having a well-developed brow tine and normally five other tines in adults; younger males have smaller antlers with fewer tines; females antlerless; antlers shed in winter and renewed during spring and summer; a conspicuous upper canine tooth present in both males and females.

The general color of the head and neck is dark brown; sides and back pale brown or yellowish gray; large and conspicuous whitish or buffy patch on the rump. Winter fur longer and somewhat paler and more grayish than summer pelage. Young calves, or fawns, are brownish blotched with large spots of yellowish white or creamy buff. The cow and the calf are darker in body color than the bull elk. Two molts occur annually, one early in the summer (about June) that appears like a true molt, the other late in

the summer (about August) that appears gradually as the winter pelage replaces the old. The antlers are shed from the middle of April through March. By the end of May or in June the new antlers in the velvet are usually full length. By the last of August most of the velvet has been shed or rubbed from the antlers.

The non-palmate antlers, the greatest length of skull (less than 520 mm.), and the presence of upper canines will separate the skull of the elk from that of the moose. Greatest length of skull (more than 400 mm.) and greatest breadth (more than 160 mm.), the presence of upper canines, and no separation of the posterior nares cavity will separate an elk skull from that of a white-tailed deer (*Odocoileus*). The skull of the caribou (*Rangifer*) differs from that of the elk in that both male and female have antlers, the tips of which are somewhat palmate; the posterior nares are divided; upper canines, if present, are only narrow slivers anteriorly projecting.

Measurements. — Total length, adult males, 2,285 to 2,745 mm. (7.5 to 9 feet); tail, 140 to 157 mm. (5.5 to 6.1 in.); hind foot, 610 to 710 mm. (24 to 28 in.); height at withers, 1,425 to 1,730 (56 to 68 in.). Weight, adult males, 650 to 830 pounds. Skull, adult males, length, 490 to 525 mm.; width, 205 to 218 mm. Total length, adult females, 2,135 to 2,440 mm. (7 to 7.5 feet); tail, 114 to 125 mm. (4.5 to 5 in.); hind foot, 580 to 655 mm. (23 to 26 in.); height at

A group of elk, a bull, two cows, and a calf, Yellowstone Park, Wyoming, January, 1920. Photograph by M. P. Skinner.

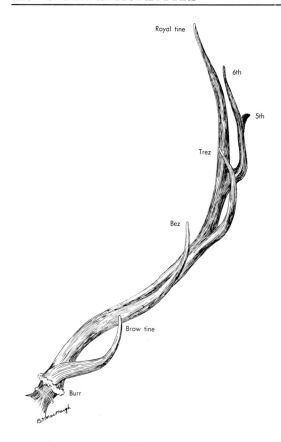

Left antler of American elk. ⅛×.

Bull elk from Montana in an ugly mood trying to knock free his shedding antlers, Trude Lake, Iron County, Wisconsin. Photograph by L. A. Gehr.

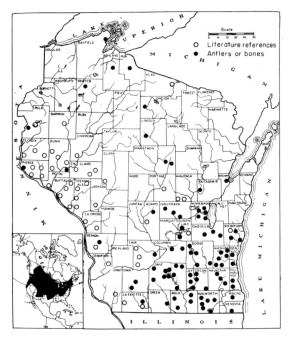

Map 75. Records of elk in Wisconsin. Copied after Schorger, 1954, p. 9. Insert map shows range of species.

withers, 1,220 to 1,425 mm. (48 to 56 in.). Weight, adult females, 500 to 650 pounds. Skull, adult females, length, 410 to 425 mm.; width, 165 to 190 mm.

Distribution in Wisconsin.—Now extirpated in Wisconsin; formerly probably occurred throughout the state in favorable habitats, perhaps more abundantly in the southern and western two-thirds of the state than to the northeastward.

Habitat.—Woodlands, forest borders and openings, bushland, and edges of grasslands and prairies, showing some preference for the vicinity of lakes, bogs, and marshes.

Status and Habits.—Just when the last native elk was killed in Wisconsin is unknown. Hoy (1882: 256) says they "were on Hay river in 1863, and I have but little doubt that a few still linger with us." Possibly a few remained in the state at that time (1882), but it is more probable that the elk was extirpated in Wisconsin before 1875. The eastern form (*C. c. canadensis*) is believed to have been exterminated. One fairly complete specimen of it from Potter County, Pennsylvania, is in the Philadelphia Academy of Natural Sciences (Bailey, 1937). David

Cartwright refers to "twelve or fifteen elk" at Menomonie (Red Cedar River) in 1856, and as of December, 1858, mentions seven elk tracked and seen near the Gilbert Creek camp. One was killed on the north branch of Ogalle River (Cartwright and Bailey, 1875: 244). For many years, certainly from 1898 until 1906, a mounted elk head hung on the wall in the zoological department at Milton College. No visible data were on it except the word "elk." One day Professor Ludwig Kumlien and myself took it from the wall to examine it. On the back of the shield was written simply "Cartwright." We both suspected it was the head of the original 1858 David Cartwright elk, inasmuch as he had been known to donate various objects of natural history to Milton College, and the pelage was faded. There also is a possibility that it came from Cartwright, a small town then existing in northwestern Chippewa County. In May, 1947, and again in May, 1951, I attempted to examine the specimen again, but was told each time by the professor in charge that he knew of no such elk, and that the only elk specimens in the college were a pair of antlers. Upon examining these, I could not be certain that they were from the "Cartwright" animal. A report from the same general region in the *Janesville Gazette* of December 10, 1866, reads:

The Dunn County News reports that a few days ago, while 2 hunters were standing in the road about 15 miles west of Menomonie, twelve elk, old and young, came into the road of a few rods from them. A dog caught one of the calves, the old ones rushed to the rescue, while the hunters shot down 9 of the animals and the other three made off with the hunters in close pursuit.

Lawrence Johnson, Boyceville, Wisconsin, in a letter to Walter E. Scott, Wisconsin State Game Department, dated October 24, 1939, wrote: "Father and uncles of elderly bartender in the village pursued a herd of elk from north of Connersville to vicinity of present village of Prairie Farm, Barron County. None killed. Date seen: Early 1880's. Seen by relatives of bartender in Boyceville." Probably the actual date was earlier than 1880. The animals, however, might well have been elk. The story of the elk in Wisconsin has been ably told by Dr. A. W. Schorger (1954). He considers that "the elk may not have become [extirpated in Wisconsin] until 1868" (p. 7).

Introductions of the Rocky Mountain elk (*C. c. nelsoni*) have been made in Wisconsin, chiefly by the State Conservation Department, but also to a lesser extent by individuals and game clubs such as the Jerome Hunting and Fishing Club, near Mercer, Iron County. At times there were indications of success, but all efforts ended in failure in establishment of elk again in Wisconsin. No elk are "wild" in Wisconsin so far as known at the present time. Staber W. Reese (1944) has reviewed the history and methods of the attempt to restore the elk to the Wisconsin fauna. Schorger (1954:8) summarizes Reese's paper and present conditions thus:

In 1913 a carload of elk from Yellowstone Park was shipped to Trout Lake. The sole survivors were two females. Later a bull elk was obtained and the herd increased slowly in the enclosure provided for it. A second carload of elk, all young, consisting of 32 cows and eight bulls, was obtained from Jackson Hole, Wyoming, in February, 1917. Although the animals arrived in good condition, 14 died during the winter. In August, 1932, the 15 elk remaining were released from the enclosure. They were not known to have ranged out of Vilas and Oneida Counties. At the present time not over two elk survive due to shooting by hunters and other causes.

The elk is chiefly nocturnal, though its favorite hours for activity are at twilight and at dawn. Rarely does it move or feed during the day. It has a home range of two to eight miles. Transplanted elk often travel many miles soon after introduction into a new area. A 21 month-old Rocky Mountain elk, marked with U. S. Biological Survey tag No. 223, was liberated in Giles County, Virginia, on February 18, 1935. It was shot on December 27, 1940 in Greene County, North Carolina; in a period of less than six years it had traveled some 225 miles in a direct line to the southeast (Jackson, 1941 a). The Rocky Mountain elk migrates several miles to its winter feeding grounds and returns to its mountain woods summer home in the spring. Such migrations are usually in scattered bands of fifty to a hundred animals, each a component of the whole herd which may number ten to twenty thousand elk. We do not know that the eastern elk performed such extensive migrations. There is reason to believe, however, that in smaller groups it engaged in a seasonal movement to and from its feeding grounds. The elk travels at only a moderate speed during these migrations; most of the time the animal walks. An elk, however, is a speedy animal when it is running, and in its trot-pacing gait can achieve 45 miles an hour. It is a graceful animal when it trots. When it gallops it appears extremely awkward, and its gait is slower.

The elk is the most highly social of any of the deer that have in recent times inhabited Wisconsin. It is colonial in habits, and there is little fighting in the herd except between bulls during the mating season. At this time one may hear the elk bugle, a shrill shriek descending the scale into a blasting bawl.

Elk calves give voice to a squealing call, to which the mother replies in a deeper voice. Adult elk express alarm, concern, or curiosity by a sharp bark. Adult bulls in rutting season, and cows in the spring during the period of parturition, give emotional expression by bugling, most highly specialized in the bulls. Elk calls, for the most part, are an expression of individual feeling and do not appear to be in the nature of direct, conscious communication (Murie, 1932:336).

Mating normally occurs during the last of September or early in October. The bull is sexually mature when 28 months old, but often loses to a stronger bull in the fierce battles that take place between the males for control of the harem. In nature one male elk usually serves about six to eight cows, but in game management practice one bull to twelve cows is more desirable. The gestation period is about eight and one-half months. One is the usual number of young, though rarely two are born, and there are a few records of three. The cow has only one litter a year and it usually comes during June.

Some seasonal preferences mark the food habits of the elk. It both grazes and browses. In the spring it grazes extensively on grasses, sedges, and weeds. During the summer and autumn it grazes some on grass and browses on shrubs and trees. During winter it procures most of its food by browsing on shrubs and trees.

Large predators such as the puma, wolf, and coyote occasionally captured an elk, particularly a calf, in the early days in Wisconsin, but the primary cause of its extirpation during its last stand was man. It was hunted persistently. It is easily approached and, once located, easily shot. Its flesh is among the most delicious of all large game animals. Whites and Indians both utilized the pelts for leather, which proved excellent for moccasins and gloves. The canine teeth of the elk were prized by Indian women, and sometimes an Indian woman's rank in her tribe was indicated by the number and size of the elk teeth she wore. In later years, when the elk tooth worn as a charm became an emblem of the Elks Lodge, the search for teeth brought about the wanton destruction of many elk, particularly in Montana, Wyoming, and Idaho. Elk were gone from Wisconsin then. The destruction was curtailed only when strict regulations were placed on the killing of elk and the Elks Lodge coöperated by discontinuing "real" elk teeth as the necessary emblem. Drowning and starvation are always possible factors in elk mortality. Parasites, either external or internal, are not particularly bothersome:

Summing up the effect of parasites on elk, it may be concluded that some parasitic species are scarce and mainly of academic interest; that others are fairly common but only occasionally serious and that the elk appear to be adjusted to their presence; that a few, such as the various horseflies, are very annoying but have no lasting effect and are taken "philosophically" by the elk; and that at least one, the winter tick, though not usually fatal to the elk, is certainly a drain on vitality and may be a contributing factor in some elk deaths (Murie, O. J., 1951: 171).

Economically, the unrestricted wild elk has no place in the agricultural parts of Wisconsin. A few might well be kept on refuges or other restricted areas for their scientific and esthetic interest. It is not likely that any introductions will develop sufficient population to allow hunting.

Selected references.—Graves, H. S., and E. W. Nelson, 1919; Murie, O. J., 1951; Reese, S. W., 1944; Rush, W. M., 1932; Schorger, A. W., 1954; Sheldon, Charles, 1927.

Roosevelt elk calves about two months old, Washington. Photograph by the author.

Genus **Odocoileus** Rafinesque
North American Deer

Dental formula:

$$I\frac{0-0}{3-3}, \quad C\frac{0-0}{1-1}, \quad P\frac{3-3}{3-3}, \quad M\frac{3-3}{3-3} = 32.$$

Odocoileus virginianus borealis Miller
Northern White-tailed Deer

Odocoileus americanus borealis Miller, Bull. New York State Mus. Nat. Hist., Albany, vol. 8, p. 83, 1900.

Cervus Virginianus Lapham, p. 44, 1852; Lapham, p. 340, 1853; Strong, p. 437, 1883.

Odocoileus virginianus Snyder, p. 126, 1902.

Odocoileus americanus borealis Jackson, p. 14, 1908.

Odocoileus virginianus borealis Hollister, p. 22, 1910; Jackson, p. 86, 1910; Cory, p. 64, 1912; Barger, p. 12, 1952.

Vernacular names.—In Wisconsin commonly called deer or whitetail. Other names include bannertail, common deer, flag deer, long-tailed deer, northern deer, northern Virginia deer, northern woodland white-tailed deer, *o-masch-kosh* (Chippewa), *psu-ksi* (Potawatomi), and Virginia deer. Potawatomi for buck is *iyá päo;* doe is *akó;* yearling deer, *wämskowä;* and forked-horn buck, *suakwona* (Skinner, A., 1926: 283).

Northern white-tailed deer, adult buck. Courtesy Wisconsin Conservation Department.

Identification marks.—The white-tailed deer is the only native hoofed mammal now found regularly in Wisconsin. Excepting a small caribou, it is the smallest of the deer tribe ever to occur in the state, a huge buck being smaller than an adult cow elk or moose, though it appears much larger in life than it actually is, particularly when it is running; a huge buck is rarely more than 42 inches high at the shoulders, and the doe usually less than 32 inches high; ears moderate, though conspicuous; nose naked; tail relatively long (10 to 14 in.), bushy, pure white below and on edges, dark on upper surface, a conspicuous white flag and identification mark when tail is raised and deer is running; small metatarsal gland (about 25 mm. long) margined with white hairs well below hock on outside of hind leg; hoofs narrow and pointed; males with widely branched antlers, the main beam (less than 30 inches long) first directed backward and then the axis curves forward, bearing several tines posteriorly, but with no brow tine; females antlerless; no canine teeth.

General color of the upper parts in summer, reddish tan, sometimes faded to almost yellowish brown; in winter grizzled medium gray, with dark markings on face and ears. Under parts, including throat, inner side of legs, and underside and edges of tail white or whitish at all seasons. The tail of the white-tailed deer is frequently called the "flag" and sometimes the "single." The fawn is reddish brown with white spots until the first winter pelage is assumed, or at the age of about five months. Two molts occur annually, one the latter part of May to June 20, when the red summer pelage is acquired, the other during September when the longer and heavier gray winter coat is assumed.

The antlers are grown and shed annually. The term "casting" has often been used for "dropping" antlers, and sometimes it is said the antlers "mew." Antlers are usually dropped or shed between the middle of December and the last of January, though sometimes they are retained somewhat later. The younger the animal usually the longer the antlers are in reaching growth

Skull of doe ODOCOILEUS V. BOREALIS, *Black River Falls.* ½×.

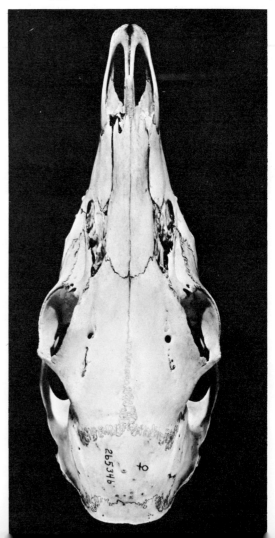

Left hind foot of buck white-tailed deer. Specimen from Eagle River, Wisconsin. ½×.

and the later they are carried. A buck is without its antlers until April or May, when new growth begins. Growth is rapid, and the antlers are completely grown in about 14 or 15 weeks. The antlers while in growth are plentifully supplied with blood vessels, and have a thick skin covered with velvet-like hair. The antlers gradually harden into a hard bone about five months after growth first started, the blood circulation in them stops, and the velvet sloughs and is rubbed away by the buck against brush, trees, and other objects. Very rarely, the antlers may retain the velvet sheathing until well into November. Frequent rubbing of the antlers continually polishes them until the time for shedding again in the winter.

The skull differs from that of any other species of the deer tribe that has occurred in Wisconsin by its small size (greatest length less than 380 mm.) and the complete division of the posterior nares by the middle vomer.

Secondary sexual variation is pronounced in the larger size and the presence of antlers in males. Very rarely, a doe has been reported with

an antler, usually small, greatly modified, and associated with sexual abnormality. Young are white-spotted dorsally, the spots disappearing when the animal completes its first molt at about five months of age. The size of the antler and the number of prongs is no true criterion as to the age of the animal. The age of a deer is best determined by a study of the teeth of the lower jaw. Methods for such determinations have been described by Severinghaus (1949), and abridged by Dahlberg and Guettinger (1956: 246–53). Abnormal color variations are infrequent except for albinistic individuals. Several "white" deer have been reported from various parts of Wisconsin in recent years. As long ago as 1883, a white fawn was seen in September, and a white buck and doe in October, near Marinette (Dane, 1884). Several other reports are in the files of the *Wisconsin Conservation Bulletin,* and a white deer was kept at the Wisconsin State Game Farm, Poynette, in the thirties (Ferguson, 1939).

Measurements.—Total length, adult males, 1,800 to 2,150 mm. (71 to 85 in.); tail, 280 to

Left antler of white-tailed deer. Specimen from Eagle River, Wisconsin. ¼×.

White-tailed deer with antlers in early pulpy velvet stage, June 10, 1932, Cass Lake, Minnesota. Photograph by Vernon Bailey.

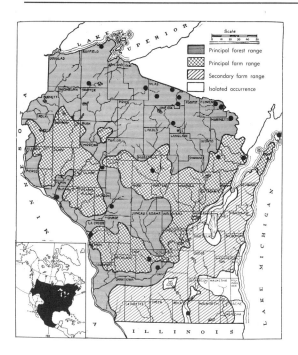

Map 76. *Distribution of* ODOCOILEUS VIRGINIANUS. *Classified range in Wisconsin copied from Dahlberg and Guettinger, 1956, p. 32, to which has been added solid circles to indicate scientific specimens examined.*

Map 77. *Probable deer densities prior to 1800. Copied from Dahlberg and Guettinger, 1956, p. 15.*

360 mm. (11 to 14 in.); hind foot, 510 to 538 mm. (20 to 21 in.); height at withers, 785 to 1,120 mm. (31 to 44 in.). Weight variable with food and other environmental conditions. The average buck will weigh about 240 pounds live weight, with variation from about 150 to 310 pounds, and excessively large bucks may weigh nearly 500 pounds. The largest buck recorded for Wisconsin had a calculated live weight of 491 pounds, and was killed in 1924 in Sawyer County by Robert Hogue of Hayward. Skull, adult male, length, 310 to 350 mm.; width, 120 to 145 mm. Total length, adult females, 1,600 to 2,000 mm. (63 to 79 in.); tail 255 to 325 mm. (10 to 13 in.); hind foot, 480 to 520 mm. (19 to 20.5 in.); height at withers, 700 to 840 mm. (27 to 33 in.). Weight of average doe about 160 pounds, varying from about 90 to 210 pounds. Skull, adult female, length, 260 to 290 mm.; width, 102 to 115 mm.

Distribution in Wisconsin. — Now found throughout the state in favorable habitat, but with isolated and irregular occurrence in the extreme southeastern part and in the Lake Winnebago region and the lower Fox River valley.

Habitat.—Somewhat variable; prefers woodland borders, and thrives in some agricultural areas. Sometimes common in old growth types of arborvitae, balsam fir, and mountain maple. During winter, when there is deep snow it often resorts to tamarack and spruce swamps, where it may congregate in large herds in "deer yards."

Status and Habits.—The status of the whitetail in Wisconsin has been a varying one locally, punctuated with increases and decreases from year to year and from county to county. In days of the early explorers the deer was found throughout the state, more plentifully in the southern part than in the northern, but everywhere it was a common big-game mammal. Differences in deer abundance between the northern parts and the southern were probably not nearly as great as assumed by some conservationists in later years. Explorers in northern Wisconsin in the seventeenth century commented on the numbers of deer and the ease of procuring them for food. Others failed to observe many. Deer had practically vanished from Wisconsin south of latitude 40° N. by 1860. A few have lingered in

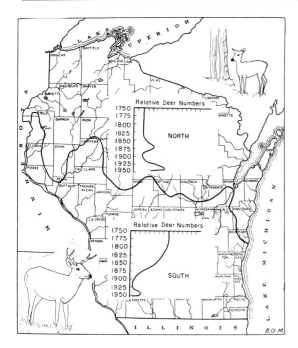

Map 78. Deer population changes, 1750 to 1950. Copied from Dahlberg and Guettinger, 1956, p. 28.

the Baraboo Hills and other parts of Sauk County since early days. Several records are cited for Sauk County: north of Baraboo River, 1854; near Reedsburg, 1875; and Spring Green, 1889 and 1892 (Schorger, 1953 b: 239). I saw three deer five miles east of Reedsburg in April, 1893; on September 19, 1909, I saw a doe and tracks of other deer near Devils Lake; and again in August, 1918, I observed several deer and many tracks in the same region. Cole (1922) says deer were established in the Baraboo Hills in 1921; in May, 1947, and again in May, 1951, I saw several deer in Sauk County. "At no times have the deer been exterminated in this county" (Schorger, 153 b: 239). The history of the white-tailed deer in early Wisconsin has been lucidly delineated by Schorger (1953 b) in a publication with considerable application to the history of humans in early Wisconsin. The later history, problems, and management of deer in Wisconsin are explained in detail in three easily accessible works, namely, those of Ernest Swift (1946 a), Otis S. Bersing (1956) and Burton L. Dahlberg and Ralph C. Guettinger (1956). The annual big game inventory, planned and initiated by the writer in 1938 and issued by the U. S. Fish

and Wildlife Service each year since then, gives estimates of the number of deer in Wisconsin (cf. Neuberger, 1946). In 1941 Wisconsin was estimated to have a population of 604,625 white-tails (Jackson, 1945: 14), and in 1947 the population had increased to more than 800,000.

If you should walk through the brush of a woodland inhabited by deer you might startle one and get a fleeting glimpse of its "flag"—the white underside of its raised tail. The presence of deer are easily determined by the tracks and

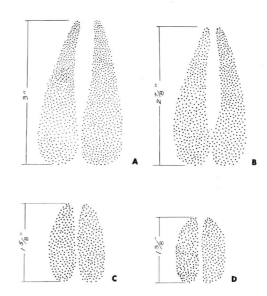

Tracks of white-tailed deer, domestic sheep, and domestic pig. A. right fore foot white-tail deer (male), B. right hind foot white-tail deer (male), C. right fore foot domestic sheep, D. right fore foot domestic pig. ½×.

Feces of white-tailed deer. 1×. Drawn in part from Seton, 1929, vol. 3, p. 40, and from Wisconsin specimens.

droppings. Tracks of large bucks may be recognized as such, but tracks of small bucks may look exactly like tracks of large does. The sex of the maker of small tracks cannot be determined by the imprints. Very quietly waiting while you are hidden in a secluded spot inhabited by deer is one of the best ways to see an animal. Such a method is often used by efficient deer hunters. The whitetail is a past master itself at hiding and sneaking away unseen. If suddenly startled, it takes off with a snort or grunt, tail erect, and is quickly out of sight. Or it—more especially the doe—may inquisitively watch a person for several minutes, sometimes uttering a wheezy whistle, before running. Its normal running speed is about 30 miles an hour, though

a maximum speed of 50 miles an hour has been reported. It can jump exceedingly well, clearing objects seven or eight feet high from a standing position. It swims fairly well, but enters deep water only when pressed. Daybreak and just before nightfall are its chief periods of activity. Moonlight nights also tempt it to activity. At one o'clock the moonlight night of August 12, 1919, a doe and fawn spent several minutes within 20 feet of me as I lay on a cot at Connors Lake, Sawyer County. No true migrations are performed by the whitetail. It goes to and from its feeding ground each day. During winters of heavy snow it sometimes travels a considerable distance to a feeding ground, often situated in a spruce or tamarack swamp. Sometimes many deer congregate to feed in a single area and create a "deer yard"—and often a serious food shortage for themselves.

The white-tailed deer is not strictly a colonial

White-tailed deer fawn. Courtesy Wisconsin Conservation Department.

animal, though it gathers in small groups. It is much less socially inclined than the elk. The winter deer-yard problem is a result of its colonial inclination. In summer during daylight hours whitetails often gather in a small group in protecting woods. They favor bogs and spruce swamps where I have often seen a group standing with their bodies within the conifers and their heads in the open, facing the cassandra swamp or other opening. Possibly this affords them protection from flies.

Young deer are gentle and affectionate, and older does usually so. An old buck, however, often develops an ugly disposition, particularly in the rutting season, and may fight anything. The senses of hearing and sight are both highly developed in the white-tailed deer. The sense of smell is also keen. Ofter a deer will show a repulsive reaction to some slight odor obnoxious to it. The expected life span of a deer in the wild varies greatly with protective conditions and other factors. The life span of a whitetail under normally protective conditions is about 10 or 12 years. Under ideal conditions a deer may be expected to live to be 15 years old. There are records up to nearly 20 years of age. In a wild herd that is subjected to hunting, few deer live more than 6 years. So far as known, length of life is the same in the male and the female.

The breeding or rutting season starts about the last week of October, when the bucks, previously indifferent to the does, begin to court them. The rutting season may sometimes last well into December. Breeding in Wisconsin reaches its peak during the last two weeks of November. Bucks often engage in severe fights, using both their antlers and hoofs, for possession of the doe. Sometimes the fight results in the death of one combatant, or even, rarely, in the death of both fighters, when their antlers become locked together. The gestation period is about 196 days. The fawns are born usually late in May or early in June, and may be from one to three in number, though three is rare. "An average of 1.6 fawns per breeding doe is indicated" in the Wisconsin studies (Dahlberg and Guettinger, 1956: 84). The fawn, which weighs six to eight pounds at birth, is born with white spots on its back and sides which disappear with the animal's first molt in the fourth or fifth month. The young doe normally breeds when it is about 19 months old, but breeding is known to occur in its first year.

The white-tailed deer is primarily a browsing animal and procures only a small portion of its food by grazing. Occasionally it grazes upon clover and other legumes, and rarely will associate with cattle grazing upon clover. When fed hay during winter starvation periods it often tramples it and refuses to eat, particularly timothy and bluegrass, but will usually eat alfalfa and clover hay if it becomes sufficiently hungry. A check list of trees and shrubs browsed by deer in Wisconsin appears in Dahlberg and Guettinger (1956; 254-55). Among first rating are yew, white cedar, hemlock, mountain ash, red maple, staghorn sumac, alternate-leaved dogwood, wintergreen, and wild cranberry. One hundred other food plants browsed by deer are also listed. About six or eight pounds of browse are consumed daily by the average-sized deer.

Natural predators are no longer a serious factor in deer destruction. The puma, timber wolf, and Canada lynx during their heyday probably captured many. The coyote, bobcat, and the red fox may now and then kill a fawn. The main destruction of Wisconsin deer comes from hunting, starvation, and accidents. Of the unwanted causes, starvation is probably the most serious. Dahlberg and Guettinger (1956: 121-22) list 13 types of fatal accidents in Wisconsin that have been verified, viz:

1) Killed by automobiles.
2) Killed by trains.
3) Entangled in fences.
4) Feet caught while reaching for browse.
5) Impaled on branches while running.
6) Falling over cliffs.
7) Falling into wells and silo pits.
8) Mired in muck around swamp edges.
9) Drowned while swimming or after pulling through ice.
10) Trapped on ice floes.
11) Struck by lightning.
12) Poisoned by herbicides.
13) Buck fighting.

Although Wisconsin deer are at times infested with various parasites, both internal and external, parasites have never been a serious factor in the destruction of deer in the state. "Since 1938, at least 14 kinds of parasites have been found on Wisconsin deer. None have caused serious losses so far" (Hale, 1953). Likewise, diseases have never seriously affected the whitetail in this state. Diseases and parasites of Wisconsin deer have been summarized by Dahlberg and Guettinger (1956: 256–58).

In that part of the United States and Mexico east of longitude 105 degrees the white-tailed deer is the most important big game animal. In Wisconsin it has always been economically important. Not only did the Indians use venison as food, but they utilized the tallow as a rubbing liniment, and applied it to body areas which had been frozen or burned. Antlers, hoofs, and teeth were used for ornamentation and as emblems. Deer hides were always in demand by Indians and explorers in the early 1800's, and their value was about half that of beaver. Not only were deer hides used for coats, capes, gloves, moccasins, blankets, and body cover, but they were sometimes skived thin, stretched, dried, and placed in windows, much as we use window glass. Skins of fawns were taken off nearly whole and sewed into sacks that had a capacity of about two bushels each. These fawn skin bags were used to gather wild rice and other grains, and nuts. Deer hides have always been in demand, and were especially so during World War II. The hunting value of deer in the state is always high, as is also their esthetic value. These two contending values have created serious political and management problems in the handling of Wisconsin deer. The record annual state kill is 167,911 deer in 1950. This figure could be within reason transferred to dollar value. There is no rational way of estimating dollar value of esthetics, pleasure, and education.

Deer also are capable of doing considerable damage, both to man's interest and their own, when they become too abundant. Complaints of harm are chiefly because of real or assumed damage to farm and garden crops, orchards, nurseries, and forest plantations. Many hundreds of deer are destroyed through starvation by exhaustion of their food supply in winter deer yards.

In Wisconsin the deer problem has been a particularly troublesome one not alone because our state is inhabited each year by more deer than almost any other, but also because of the multiple and varied selfish interests in the deer by different groups. Even though deer had become so numerous that they were literally "eating themselves out of house and home," the sportsmen clamored for more and more deer to shoot. City folk and other resorters lazying on their vacations wanted more and more deer to view at the doorstep of a hotel, cottage, or

camp, but objected to any shooting. Agriculturists feared that the deer would severely damage crops, and wanted fewer and fewer deer. Likewise, dairymen wanted fewer deer browsing in their pastures. As citizens, we were faced with a major problem that involved many factors—biological, ecological, historical, economic, sociological, legal, diplomatic.

Some quotations [from Dahlberg and Guettinger] are of interest: "The mistakes can be attributed to lack of specific information. There is no further excuse for continuing to make the same mistakes. . . . This report has its main value as a reference for facts about why Wisconsin has had deer problems, and what has been and can be done about them" (p. 9–10). "There is continued need for research, especially of habitat and manipulation" (p. 235). "However, we have high hopes that Wisconsin sportsmen will come to the support of deer management practices that will give them the largest possible return" (p. 238). The Wisconsin deer herd can well be maintained as one of the largest and healthiest in the nation (Jackson, 1956:183–84).

Specimens examined from Wisconsin.—Total 55, as follows: *Bayfield County:* Cable, 1 (UWZ); Cornucopia, 1 (UWZ). *Buffalo County:* Nelson, 1. *Chippewa County:* Boyd, 1 (fossil, UWZ). *Door County:* Rock Island, 1 (UWZ). *Florence County:* Florence, 1 (MM); Spread Eagle region, 16 (CNHM). *Iron County:* Fisher Lake, 1 (UWZ). *Jackson County:* Black River Falls, 6. *La Crosse County:* La Crosse, 1. *Marathon County:* Mosinee, 1 (UWZ). *Marinette County:* Cataline, 1 (MM); Peshtigo, 1 (USNM). *Oconto County:* Badger, 2 (MM). *Oneida County:* Rhinelander, 1 (UWZ). *Rock County:* Janesville, 1 (fossil, UWZ). *Sauk County:* Baraboo Bluffs, 5 (UWZ); Merrimac, 1. *Vilas County:* Eagle River, 4 (MM); Mamie Lake, 1; No locality, 1 (UWZ); Twin Lakes (Conover), 1 (MM); Trout Lake, 5 (MM).

Selected references.—Bersing, O. S., 1956; Dahlberg, B. L., and R. C. Guettinger, 1956; Gregory, T., 1930; Newsom, W. M., 1926; Rawley, E., J. B. Low, and E. O. Greaves, 1950; Schorger, A. W., 1953 b; Swift, E., 1946 a; Taylor, W. P., 1956.

Albino deer, near Boulder Junction, Vilas County, March 1950. Photograph by Staber W. Reese. (Picture of the week in Life Magazine, April 24, 1950.) Courtesy Wisconsin Conservation Department.

Genus **Alces** Gray
Moose

Dental formula:

$$I\frac{0-0}{3-3}, \quad C\frac{0-0}{1-1}, \quad P\frac{3-3}{3-3}, \quad M\frac{3-3}{3-3}=32.$$

Alces alces andersoni Peterson
Northwestern Moose

Alces americanus andersoni Peterson, Occas. Papers Royal Ontario Mus. Zool., No. 9, p. 1, May 25, 1950.
Cervus alces Lapham, p. 44, 1852; Lapham, p. 340, 1853; Strong, p. 437, 1883.
Alce Americanus Hoy, p. 256, 1882.
Alce americanus Hollister, p. 138, 1909; Hollister, p. 23, 1910.
Paralces americanus Cory, p. 74, 1912.
Alces americana americana Barger, p. 12, 1952.

Vernacular names.—Commonly known in Wisconsin as moose, a name of Indian origin. Other names include Anderson moose, black moose, common moose, eastern moose, *élan* (French explorers), flat-horned elk, moose deer, *muswa* (Chippewa), and *orignac, original,* and *oriniak* (French explorers and settlers).

Identification marks.—Largest of the native deer that inhabited Wisconsin, and, excepting the bison, largest of all recent mammals of the state; appearance huge and ungainly, withers higher than rump when animal stands; neck short; a slight mane on neck and shoulders; a strip of dewlap skin, called the "bell," six to ten inches long or more, hangs from the underside of the throat; ears large and conspicuous; eyes small and sunken; head long, massive, yet rather narrow; muzzle long, humped, the anterior end overhanging the lower lips; nose nearly completely haired; tail very short; no metatarsal gland; antlers on the male massive, broadly palmate; hair coarse and brittle. Color dark. The general tone of winter pelage is dark blackish brown, sometimes almost black; back, shoulders, neck, and head tend to be slightly paler than flanks; face sometimes grayish; lower belly and inner sides of legs whitish. The pelage early in summer is somewhat similar, but tends to become paler. Young of the year are plain reddish brown in color and are not spotted or blotched. There is little variation in color. One molt occurs annually in the spring.

The huge antlers of the moose are usually dropped in mature moose during December or January. Younger moose sometimes may not shed antlers until March or April. Antlers usually reach full new development late in August or in September, when the velvet sloughs and is rubbed off. The skull of the moose can be identified by its size (more than 500 mm. long) and by its long rostrum with short nasal bones. The spread of antlers of an adult northwestern moose is usually between 60 and 72 inches.

Bull moose, Idaho. Photograph by U. S. Forest Service.

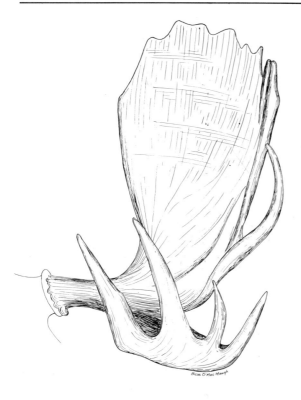

Above, left antler of moose. ⅛ ✕

Measurements.—Total length, adult males, 2,440 to 2,800 mm. (8 to 9.2 feet); tail, 76 to 110 mm. (3 to 4.3 in.); hind foot, 760 to 840 mm. (30 to 33 in.); height at withers, 1,780 to 1,920 mm. (70 to 75.5 in.). Weight, adult males, about 850 to 1,200 pounds. Skull, adult males, length, 560 to 595 mm.; width, 220 to 240 mm. Total length, adult females, 2,040 to 2,590 mm. (6.7 to 8.5 feet); tail, 90 to 122 mm. (3.5 to 4.8 in.); hind foot, 725 to 810 mm. (29.3 to 31.8 in.); height at withers, 1,730 to 1,830 mm. (68 to 72 in.). Weight, adult females, about 725 to 850 pounds. Skull, adult females, length, 540 to 575 mm.; width, 210 to 230 mm.

Distribution in Wisconsin.—Now extirpated in Wisconsin, except for possible wanderers from native stock in northeastern Minnesota or from introduced stock in the Upper Peninsula of Michigan. In early colonial days it occurred over most of the state north of latitude 44 degrees, wanderers occurring in woodland possibly even to the southern boundary; most frequent in northwestern part of the state.

Below, cow moose and calf in Yellowstone National Park. Courtesy George B. Saunders.

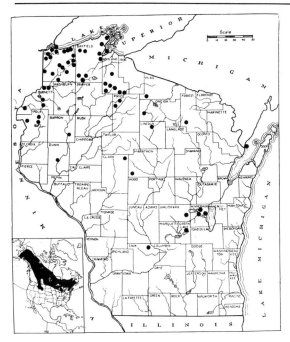

Map 79. Records of the moose in Wisconsin as given by Schorger (1957). Insert map shows range of the species in North America.

Habitat.—Forests, particularly in the vicinity of lakes and rivers.

Status and Habits.—The last native moose known to have been killed in Wisconsin drowned in Allouez Bay, at Superior, on September 11, 1921, after being roped and towed by a launch (McNaughton, 1922; Schorger, 1957: 7). Upon reading McNaughton's account of the incident I wrote to him for details. His reply in part follows:

Received your letter of March 10th relative to the capture of a stray Bull Moose in the waters of Allouez Bay, Sept. 11, 1921.

In reply, the moose was captured in Wisconsin in the waters of Allouez Bay, (not in Lake Superior). This was a bull moose about six years old, he had five points on one horn and seven points on the other, and weighed about seven hundred pounds.

Upon investigating the killing of this moose, I found that the moose came up along the south shore of Lake Superior and around the end of Allouez Bay, trotted up through the main street of Allouez, and entered the waters of Allouez Bay between the Great Northern Ore Docks and the Pittsburgh Coal Dock and started to swim across the bay headed for Wisconsin Point.

One W. E. Gaynor, of Superior, Manager for the Great Lakes Dredge and Dock Co., was out on Allouez Bay with some of the Dredge Company's officials in a launch, when they saw the moose swimming across the bay, they took after him with the launch, pursued and annoyed the moose until they tired him out. Gaynor then roped and lassoed the moose, tied him to the boat and towed him up the bay for a distance of a half a mile against a heavy sea, and finally drowned him. They then towed the moose ashore and hauled him out on the beach.

Mr. Gaynor's story was that he thought the moose was wounded or injured and exhausted and that he was trying to rescue it. The fact of the matter is Gaynor was trying to show off and thought he was acting smart and wanted to show the dredge officials who were from Chicago that he could rope a bull moose in Superior Harbor and tow it back to the State of Minnesota where he thought it belonged. I do not believe Gaynor had any intention of killing or drowning the moose.

Later reports of moose in Wisconsin are either doubtful records of native ones in the northwestern counties, or of wanderers into northeastern counties that were from stock introduced from Isle Royale into the Upper Peninsula of Michigan. One is reported to have escaped from a hunting club on Trude Lake, Iron County, in 1918. The status of the moose in Wisconsin has been reviewed briefly by Walter Scott (1939 b: 24-25) and in detail by A. W. Schorger (1957).

Bull moose swimming, British Columbia. Photograph by Joseph Wendle.

As with many ruminants, the chief periods of activity of the moose are at nightfall and day-break, with some activity at all hours of the day and considerable activity at all hours of the night. It does not usually travel great distances, and may stay for a period of a year or more within a home range of four to six miles radius. Often a single moose may be found within a home range of a mile or less for several months. In Wells Gray Park, British Columbia, it was found that the moose undertake annual migrations between winter and summer range. "Distance moved is 40 miles for some animals, while some may not migrate at all" (Edwards and Richey, 1957: 493). The moose is not a speedy animal. Its normal running gait is about 22 to 25 miles an hour, but when forced for a short distance it can travel 30 to 35 miles an hour. The moose is an excellent swimmer, enters water freely, and swims long distances.

The moose is not truly gregarious, and seldom gathers in groups of more than three or four, usually a mother with its young. Sometimes in non-rutting season a bull may be tolerated in the group. In winter as many as a dozen or fifteen may congregate, but they never create a yarding starvation hazard as do the white-tailed deer. Even though not colonial, the moose is not always unfriendly, either among its own kind or with other harmless big mammals. Moose and

A bull and a cow moose from Minnesota drop to their knees to feed from the ground, Jerome Hunting and Fishing Club, Trude Lake, Wisconsin. Photograph by L. A. Gehr.

deer often live together in the same general area. Several moose introduced from Minnesota were confined on the grounds of the Jerome Fishing and Hunting Club at Trude Lake, Iron County. When I was there in August, 1919, the bulls as well as the cows were very tame—in fact were pets—and thrived well. The moose is a stolid animal, and engages but little, if any, in play. The bull is ugly and fearless during the rutting season. He whistles and utters a hoarse bellow or heavy grunt to his rivals, clashes his antlers against trees and other objects, and charges at any moving object. He bellows for three or four weeks. His calls are imitated by hunters with a moose horn which the bull readily answers and approaches. It is said that the whistles of some diesel locomotives have sounded so much like a moose call that moose have attacked the trains and been killed. A moose cow with a calf will fight desperately. During the mating season the cow calls with a long low "moo," and the bull responds with his bellow. If two bulls respond, a fight follows. The calf whimpers and sobs when crying for food or when tormented. Sight in the moose is poor, as might be expected considering the small sunken eyes. The senses of hearing and smell are highly developed.

When the antlers are cleaned of the velvet and polished it is the beginning of the breeding season. This may be as early as the middle of September or in October, possibly sometimes later. One bull may mate with two or three cows, sometimes more. When fighting for the cow, the bulls come head on at a gallop and charge each other over and over again until one becomes master. Sometimes the antlers become interlocked, and both animals may die. At other times the defeated bull dies, and rarely both animals are killed. Young bulls under four or five years of age have little chance with the older animals. The gestation period is believed to be about eight months. One or two young constitute the litter, one apparently more frequently than two. Rarely, there may be three in a litter. The calf is wobbly at birth, and for a day or two afterwards. It grows rapidly, is weaned when about six or eight weeks old, and grows to a height of five feet at the withers within about six months after its birth. Even though weaned, the calf usually stays with its mother until a year old. It attains full growth when 15 to 18 months old.

The moose is essentially a browsing mammal that feeds chiefly on the leaves of trees and shrubs. It often reaches to a height of ten or eleven feet to obtain its food, which it grasps with its almost trunklike upper lip. It cannot readily take food from the ground without kneeling, even the fawns. In summer it often wades into lakes and swamps to feed upon aquatic vegetation, and it is particularly fond of pondweeds and waterlilies. Among the more important trees upon which it browses are the willows (particularly Bebbs willow), sugar maple, mountain maple, mountain ash, paper and yellow birches, pin cherry, beaked hazel, shadbush, and balsam fir. An adult moose requires about 50 or 60 pounds of food a day.

The timber wolf was probably about the only serious natural enemy the moose had to fear in Wisconsin. It was subjected to accidents, such as getting mired in a swamp or caught in a flood or storm, as are all wildlings. Little is known about parasites and diseases that plague the moose, some of those reported having been from animals in zoological gardens or in wildlife refuges. A few parasites have been reported from animals in the wild (De Vos and Allen, 1949).

Economically, the moose is of little importance now in Wisconsin. It will never become a game animal in the state again, and should a few become established, the animals will be of use only for their esthetic and scientific value.

Selected references.—Hickie, P. F., 1943; Hosley, N. W., 1949; Merrill, S., 1916; Murie, A., 1934; Peterson, R. L., 1955; Schorger, A. W., 1957.

Genus **Rangifer** Hamilton-Smith
Caribou

Dental formula:

$$I\frac{0-0}{3-3}, C\frac{0-0}{1-1}, \text{ or } \frac{1-1}{1-1}, P\frac{3-3}{3-3}, M\frac{3-3}{3-3} = 32 \text{ or } 34.$$

Rangifer caribou sylvestris (Richardson)
Western Woodland Caribou

Cervus tarandus var. *B. sylvestris* Richardson, Fauna Boreali-Americana, vol. 1, p. 250, 1829.
Rangifer tarandus Lapham, p. 44, 1852; Lapham, p. 340, 1853.
Rangifer caribou Hoy, p. 256, 1882; Hollister, p. 30, 1910; Cory, p. 81, 1912.
Rangifer caribou sylvestris Barger, p. 12, 1952.

Vernacular names.—Commonly called woodland caribou. Other names include American reindeer, *atick* (Ojibway), caribou, carribouck, khali-

Woodland caribou group in University of Kansas Museum. Cow at head of group, calf in central foreground, two adult bulls in rear. The three animals at the left are Minnesota specimens. Photograph by University of Kansas.

bu, maccarib, pawer, rain deer, reindeer, and Richardson's caribou.

Identification marks.—In size, the caribou is between a large deer and a small elk; antlers large, with more or less flattened prongs and forks of beams, usually with broad flat brow prongs extending between the eyes and over the nose; antlers of does usually smaller than those of bucks; nose rounded-truncate, not projecting beyond lower jaw, completely covered with short hair; ears rather small; tail short; feet large, the side toes well developed and the hoofs broad and rotund, the width about one and one-half times the length, the toes rather widely spaced.

The general body color is dark smoke gray or brownish gray; the color of the forehead, neck, abdomen, patch back of shoulder, under side of tail, and edging around the feet is white. Males and females are similar in color. Summer fur is somewhat darker than winter fur.

Measurements.—Total length, adult males, 1,840 to 2,260 mm. (6 to 7.4 feet); tail, 110 to 150 mm. (4.3 to 5.9 in.); hind foot, 550 to 670 mm. (21.6 to 26.4 in.); height at withers, 1,170 to 1,300 mm. (46 to 51 in.). Weight, adult males, about 355 to 400 pounds. Skull, adult males, length, 400 to 450 mm.; width, 170 to 188 mm. Total length, adult females, 1,660 to 2,030 mm. (5.4 to 6.7 feet); tail, 100 to 140 mm. (4 to 5.5 in.); hind foot, 500 to 600 mm. (20 to 23.6 in.); height at withers, 1,060 to 1,170 mm. (42 to 46 in.). Weight, adult females, about 195 to 260 pounds. Skull, adult females, length, 365 to 410 mm.; width, 150 to 170 mm.

Distribution in Wisconsin.—Now extirpated in Wisconsin. Former limits of range unknown, but confined to the northern part of the state, probably mostly in the vicinity of Lake Superior.

Habitat.—Forests and more particularly wooded swamps, bogs, and muskegs.

Status and Habits.—The woodland caribou in its primitive range inhabited only a comparatively narrow strip of the United States adjacent to its Canadian range. It apparently was never common in Wisconsin, but always more plentiful in northern Minnesota. A very few of the original stock survived under protection in Minnesota until early in the 1940's. They were augmented by ten animals from Saskatchewan in 1938. Swanson (1945: 100) says, "today we are not

sure that any remain in the State." I have examined some of the Minnesota specimens and they are referable to *Rangifer caribou sylvestris* (Richardson). There are no specimens of caribou available from Wisconsin, but it seems probable that the caribou here was the same form as occurred in Minnesota.

Following glaciation in the Great Lakes area, it would seem likely that the redispersal of caribou took place from both an unglaciated forested area of Wisconsin and a similar area south of the limits of glacial ice in northeastern United States. It also seems reasonable to suppose that the two presently-recognized races originated from these two areas (*R. c. caribou* in the east and *R. c. sylvestris* in the west) to give a redispersal pattern similar to that found by Peterson (1950) in moose (De Vos and Peterson, 1951:329).

Records of the occurrence of caribou in Wisconsin, particularly in the northwestern parts, from that of Schoolcraft in 1831 to the somewhat questionable ones of 1910 for White River, Ashland County, and Burnett County, have been reviewed by W. E. Scott (1939 b: 22–23) and A. W. Schorger (1942 b: 34–35). Inasmuch as

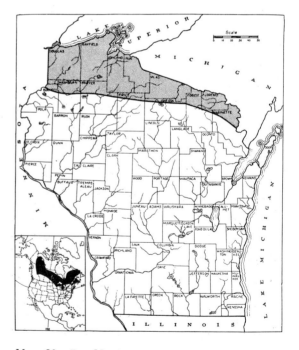

Map 80. *Possible former range of the woodland caribou,* RANGIFER CARIBOU SYLVESTRIS, *in Wisconsin, with insert showing range of the species.*

caribou were still known to be present in northern Minnesota in 1910 it is possible that the Wisconsin records for that year may be valid for a wild animal. Or they may be based on an escaped animal from the introduction of twenty Newfoundland caribou placed at Cedar Island Lodge, Brule, Douglas County, in 1906. All of these animals, however, were believed to have died by the end of one year and there is no record of any escape.

The woodland caribou is a wanderer but does not make extensive migrations as does its cousin, the barren ground caribou. It has winter protection in its forest home which the Arctic animal must travel hundreds of miles to find. It is more active by day than by night. It usually travels long distances in an easy trot. If greatly alarmed, it breaks into a cumbersome gallop which is little, if any, faster than its trot, and which soon tires the animal. It swims well and fairly rapidly for distances of three or four miles. The voice of the adult consists of a grunt. The fawn bawls. A clicking noise is made by the hoofs of the animal when it runs. "There is fairly general agreement on the Caribou's keen sense of smell, good hearing, and less well-developed vision. But perhaps the last-mentioned attribute does not so much constitute poor eyesight as lack of *perception* of *recognition*. In other words, is it not possible that the animal is merely deficient in interpreting what it may see clearly enough?" (Harper, 1955: 86). In the barren ground caribou the mean expected life span at birth was found to be 4.09 years; the apparent potential natural longevity was about 13 years (Banfield, 1955: 143).

The rutting season is the last of September or October. Males fight fiercely for the does. One buck will serve ten to fifteen does. The gestation period is about 31 weeks, and the number of young is usually one or two. The fawn is fulvous brown in color, normally without spots, but sometimes mottled with pale irregular blotches.

The food of the caribou consists chiefly of lichens and mosses. It occasionally eats other green vegetation both by browsing and grazing. It often "paws" in the snow to uncover mosses and other plants upon which it feeds.

Selected references.—Dugmore, A. A. R., 1913; Grant, M., 1903; Harper, F., 1955; Riis, P. R., 1938; Scott, W. E., 1939 b: 22–23; Schorger, 1942 b: 34–35.

Family **Bovidae**
Oxen, Sheep, Goats, and Antelopes

Members of the Bovidae are found on all the continents except South America and Australia. The family reaches its highest development in Africa and India. It is composed of about 54 genera exclusive of fossil forms, of which only one (*Bison*) has occurred in Wisconsin.

Genus **Bison** Hamilton-Smith
Bison

Dental formula:

$$I\frac{0-0}{3-3}, \quad C\frac{0-0}{1-1}, \quad P\frac{3-3}{3-3}, \quad M\frac{3-3}{3-3} = 32.$$

Bison bison bison (Linnaeus)
Plains Buffalo

[Bos] bison Linnaeus, Systema Naturae, ed. 10, vol. 1, p. 72, 1758.
Bison Americanus Lapham, p. 44, 1852; Lapham, p. 340, 1853.
Bos Americana Hoy, p. 256, 1882.

Bison. Vilas County, March, 1944. Photograph by Staber W. Reese. Courtesy Wisconsin Conservation Department.

Bison bison Hollister, p. 23, 1910; Cory, p. 87, 1912.
Bison bison bison Barger, p. 12, 1952.

Vernacular names.—Commonly called buffalo or bison. Other names include American bison, American buffalo, American wild ox, *boeuf* (French explorers), *boeuf sauvage* (French explorers), buffle or bufle (early explorers, from the French *boeuf*), *chei-ki-ka-ra-cha-da* (Winnebago), *ed-jier-ay* (Chippewa); *mus-ku-te-a pi-shakiu* (Menomini, literally prairie buffalo, Skinner, 1926: 283), North American buffalo, *pkotc-p'sh$_e$ k$_e$* (Potawatomi, literally wild buffalo, Skinner, *ibid.*), plains bison, prairie beef, and prairie buffalo.

Identification marks.—The buffalo is a powerful and huge member of the cattle tribe, the largest mammal to inhabit Wisconsin in historic times; the withers are high, there being a hump on the shoulders produced by the unusually long spines of the vertebrae; head carried low, nares naked; head, neck, and foreparts massive, covered with especially long woolly hair; tail moderately long, with a tuft of long hair at the tip; true horns on both males and females, rising sidewise and upwards, and in older animals turning inward.

White bison (right) along with normal colored bison cow. National Bison Range, Moiese, Montana. U. S. Fish and Wildlife Service photograph by E. P. Haddon.

The general color is dark brown, sometimes almost blackish brown, with a trend to being paler on the upper parts and palest on the shoulders. Summer pelage is more faded on upper parts and body, and contrasts with dark brown of head. Color of female is similar to male but more uniformly dark brown. New-born calves are reddish in color, and they retain this natal coat until about three months old, when it is shed and replaced by the dark brown coat of the adult.

Males are much larger than females, being about 80 per cent larger by weight and about 50 per cent longer in total length. Color mutations are unusual. Very rarely does an albino or partial albino with white pelage occur. Such mutations have been known in recent years and were occasionally reported in the days of early western exploration. Some tribes of Indians were said to have looked upon a white buffalo as sacred.

The skull of the buffalo, with its solid bone horn cores attached as a permanent part of the skull, can be confused only with the skull of the domestic cow. It is usually larger and more massive than that of the domestic cow and has a heavier and longer upper molar series, and the premaxillary bone does not extend back to the nasal bone.

Measurements.—Total length, adult males, 3,050 to 3,800 mm. (10 to 12.5 feet); tail, 550

to 815 mm. (22 to 32 in.); hind foot, 585 to 660 mm. (23 to 26 in.); height at withers, 1,675 to 1,830 mm. (66 to 72 in.). Weight, adult males, about 1,600 to 2,000 pounds. Skull, adult males, length 491 to 570 mm.; width, 271 to 343 mm. Total length, adult females, 1,980 to 2,280 mm. (6.5 to 7.5 feet); tail, 430 to 535 mm. (17 to 21 in.); hind foot, 460 to 555 mm. (18 to 22 in.); height at withers, 1,420 to 1,625 mm. (56 to 64 in.). Weight, adult females, about 900 to 1,100 pounds. Skull, adult females, length, 445 to 510 mm.; width, 245 to 310 mm.

Distribution in Wisconsin.—Now extirpated in the state, except for about 25 to 30 individuals in zoological parks and wildlife refuges. Formerly in western Wisconsin south of latitude 46° and southern and eastern Wisconsin north to about latitude 43° 30'.

Habitat.—Prairies, dry marshes, and borders and openings of deciduous forests.

Status and Habits.—Two buffaloes killed by Sioux Indians on the Trempealeau River in 1832 are believed to have been the last wild buffaloes in Wisconsin. Not only were they the last for this state, but they were also the last seen east of the Mississippi River. The species was never as abundant in Wisconsin as in parts of the western Great Plains, yet in the latter part of the eighteenth century there were undoubtedly many thousands of them on the prairies of the state. They were greatly utilized, especially for food and clothing, and were persistently hunted and killed until exterminated. Dr. A. W. Schorger (1937 b) has given us an excellent historical review of the bison in Wisconsin.

On the western plains as of 1832 there were

still millions of buffaloes. They were constantly hunted by Indians, explorers, and settlers, and by every conceivable method.

The American bison roamed the prairies and plains of the United States and Canada in herds that in pioneer times certainly aggregated more than 50,000,000 animals. By the close of the nine-

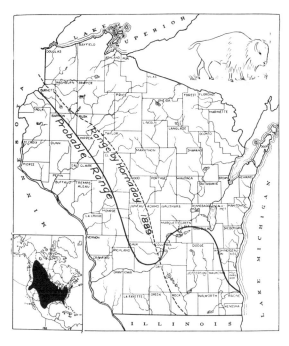

Map 81. *Range of* BISON *in Wisconsin, as copied from Schorger, 1937, p. 122. Insert map shows former range of the species.*

Bison cows and calves in Lamar Valley, Wyoming, about 1925. The last "wild" herd in the United States. Photograph by M. P. Skinner.

teenth century, the population had probably reached its low at a total of about 800 animals. The American Bison Society estimated 1,917 living animals in 1908. Shortly afterwards, through the efforts of that Society, the National Bison Range was established under the administration of the Biological Survey on land formerly a part of the Flathead Indian Reservation, Montana. It was stocked October 17, 1909, with 37 bisons, all but one from a private herd at Kalispell, Montana. This was really the beginning of the upbuild of the American bison population. Today there are more than 5,000 [6,200 in 1957] bisons in the United States, mostly confined to ranches, parks, and refuges, and another possible 30,000 on refuges in Canada, a total of not less than 35,000. Nineteen bisons from the National Bison Range were introduced into the Big Delta region, near Fairbanks, Alaska, and had in 1941 increased to more than 200 animals. In this region they are given free range. Modern civilization and agricultural practices in most localities in the United States no longer make possible the free-ranging of vast migrating hordes of big-game animals. We can, nevertheless, save a species from extinction as witness the bison! (Jackson, 1944:80; 1945:263).

The buffalo is a highly gregarious mammal. Its extreme colonization threatened its existence as a species. It migrated in a slow movement of

Bison tracks on Sandhill Game Farm, Babcock, Wisconsin. April 26, 1951. About 1/12×. Photograph by the author.

immense herds from the north toward the south in the autumn, and returned northward in the spring. These migrations or wanderings covered distances of two to four hundred miles. On its home range it left deeply worn paths or trails in the soil, and dropped huge flats of soft dung. These feces thoroughly dried became known as "buffalo chips," and were frequently used as fuel by Indians and white settlers. The buffalo is almost strictly diurnal in its general activities. It has great endurance and can run 40 to 50 miles without pause and can tire any horse. It is of uncertain temperament and may attack horse or man without provocation. A man on foot is almost a sure target for attack, and man on horseback sometimes may be attacked. Seldom if ever does a buffalo attempt an attack on a man in an automobile. There are many instances where a bison has charged and killed or seriously injured a man. Records in zoological parks and observations on animals on national wildlife refuges and private estates indicate that the normal longevity of the buffalo is about 12 to 15 years. The potential longevity, however, is at least 23 to 25 years, and there are records of individuals living 30 or more years.

Buffalo cows ordinarily mate when they are two years old and bear their first calves when three years old. Instances of two-year-old heifers producing calves have been recorded but are not common. Calves are usually born singly, cases of multiple births being rare. The cows are irregular breeders; they do not bear calves every year, but retain their fecundity to a rather advanced age. Cows 26 years old have been known to produce strong, well-developed calves. Bulls reach breeding age at about four years, but are not fully mature until eight years old. The breeding season normally occurs during July and August, but under artificial conditions induced by confinement and semidomestication, individuals may breed during all seasons. Mature bulls are dangerous during the rutting period. The gestation period is between 270 and 280 days. Calves are usually born during April, May, or June, although births have been recorded in all months. The calf weighs between 30 and 40 pounds at birth. It grows rapidly, and when one year old will weigh about three to four hundred pounds, and at two years old may weigh up to about six hundred pounds. The cow continues to grow until six or seven years old, and the bull until nine or ten years old.

Cattalo is the name applied to the hybrid off-spring which results from crossing American bison with domestic cattle. Cattaloes are believed to inherit the hardy characteristics of their bison parents and, to a considerable extent, the excellent beef of domestic cattle. Several breeders have attempted to develop herds of cattaloes, but none has succeeded in establishing one of commercial importance. Cattalo production is still in the experimental stage. Anyone venturing to engage in it should look upon it purely as an experiment that requires patience, intelligence, and hard work, backed by capital resources. He might succeed, but should not be too optimistic. Deaths from disease or accident may occur in his stock among both parents and offspring. Mating indifference and general sterility of the hybrids, more especially in the males, will prevail and hinder production.

A major retarding factor in cattalo production is the high mortality among cows and calves at the time of parturition. Crossing a buffalo bull with a small type of domestic cow would be certain to result in failure. A domestic bull and a buffalo cow preferably should be used in such an experiment. One Montana breeder who conducted experiments in the production of cattaloes a number of years ago abandoned the venture after two years, claiming that the loss in cows was too great for him to continue in the busi-ness. Another cattleman lost 30 cows while attempting to raise cattaloes, but later had somewhat better results when he selected a different type of cow.

The foraging habits of buffaloes are, in many ways, similar to those of domestic cattle. Buffaloes graze principally on grasses, seemingly preferring them to weeds or shrubs. On southern ranges, buffalo grass (*Buchloe dactyloides*) and grama (*Bouteloua gracilis* and *B. hirsuta*) provide excellent pasturage. The shorter grasses appear to be preferred to the taller and coarser species. On northern ranges, in addition to buffalo grass and grama, wheatgrass (*Agropyron* sp.), bluegrass (*Poa* spp.) and the smaller fescues (*Festuca* spp.) are readily eaten. Buffaloes graze closely, and because of their habit of compact herding, they may rapidly deplete a pasture inadequate to their needs. It is estimated that two buffaloes require about as much pasture as three domestic cattle (Jackson and Rouse, 1942: 2).

Aside from man and the wolf, the buffalo had other natural enemies such as confront many wild animals. In the case of the buffalo, prairie fires were no small hazard, yet sleet, snow, and ice probably killed even more. Many buffaloes were drowned in crossing rivers. Sometimes a rampaging herd would push many of its own members over a steep bluff or cliff to their de-

The bison hunt. From photograph of painting by Carl Bodmer in Reise in das Innere Nord-Amerika in den Jahren 1832 bis 1834, by Maximilian, Prince of Wied.

struction. The buffalo is a hardy animal, however, and is comparatively free from diseases and parasites.

Some parasites that affect cattle also affect buffaloes. Ox warbles, the larvae of botflies of the family Oestridae, are frequently found in buffaloes, although heavy or troublesome infestations are not common. Buffaloes may also become infested with ticks in localities in which these parasites occur. Gnats and other flies cause considerable annoyance to buffaloes during the summer. Swarms of flies gather about the flanks of the animals and by their repeated biting, abraded areas several square inches in size may develop. These areas quickly heal when no longer irritated by the flies. Moist places where the animals may wallow and become coated with mud afford temporary relief from these pests.

Internal parasites commonly found in buffaloes include lungworms (*Dictyocaulus hadweni* and *D. viviporus*), stomach worms (*Haemonchus contortus*), and intestinal worms (*Oesophagostomum radiatum*). Heavy infestations of lungworms may lead to a verminous form of pneumonia and cause death. Stomach and intestinal worms, when abundant, have a debilitating effect, causing emaciation and anemia. Yearlings seem to be most frequently affected and they seldom recover from severe attacks. Animals weakened by these parasites readily succumb to pneumonia or other secondary infections (Jackson and Rouse, 1942:6).

The buffalo is one of the most useful native quadrupeds that ever inhabited the United States. It supplied food, clothing, and shelter for hundreds of thousands of natives for centuries. Buffalo meat was utilized fresh and dried as pemmican. Dried dung was used as fuel and to smolder as an insect repellent. Hides were used for robes, both for clothing and bedding, and for making boats, tepees, shields, rawhide ropes, and sheets for winding the dead. Many ornamental articles were made from the bones, and the horns were made into spoons and other utensils. Sinews were utilized for bowstrings and for binding the arrow point into the arrow shaft. Tallow was molded into large balls and kept for waterproofing and other purposes, and buffalo marrow was preserved in buffalo bladders. White man carried buffalo utilization and waste to the point of near extermination of the species. Be that as it may, the buffalo was foredoomed to great reductions in number with the expansion of agriculture and other human developments. The buffalo is a fine big-game animal and has high utility value. There is, however, no place for it in any considerable numbers in an agricultural region.

Selected references.—Allen, J. A., 1877 a; Branch, E. D., 1929; Garretson, M. S., 1938; Hornaday, W. T., 1889; Roe, F. G., 1951; Schorger, A. W., 1937 b.

BIBLIOGRAPHY

BIBLIOGRAPHY

An asterisk (°) before a title denotes a general work.

"A. B. C."
  1884. [Note on albino deer near Marinette, Wisconsin.] Amer. Field 22(25):584. December 20.
ADAMS, CHARLES C.
  °1926. The economic and social importance of animals in forestry. Roosevelt Wildlife Bull. 3 (4):505–699.
  °1930. Rational predatory animal control. Journ. Mammal. 11(3):353–62. August 9.
ADAMS, LOWELL, S. B. SALVIN, and W. J. HADLOW.
  1956. Ringworms in a population of snowshoe hares. Journ. Mammal. 37(1):94–99. March.
AHRENS, THEODOR G.
  1921. Muskrats in central Europe. Journ. Mammal. 2(4):236–37. November 29.
ALCORN, J. R.
  1946. On the decoying of coyotes. Journ. Mammal. 27(2):122–26. May 14.
ALDOUS, C. M.
  1936. Food habits of Lepus americanus phaeonotus. Journ. Mammal. 17(2):175–76. May 14.
  1937. Notes on the life history of the snowshoe hare. Journ. Mammal. 18(1):46–57. February 11.
ALDOUS, SHALER E.
  1937. A hibernating black bear with cubs. Journ. Mammal. 18(4):466–68. November 22.
  1941. Food habits of chipmunks. Journ. Mammal. 22(1):18–24. February 14.
ALDOUS, SHALER E., and J. MANWEILER.
  1942. The winter food habits of the short-tailed weasel in northern Minnesota. Journ. Mammal. 23(3):250–55. August 13.
ALDRICH, JOHN W.
  1957. Investigations of woodcock, snipe, and rails in 1956. U. S. Fish and Wildlife Service, Special Sci. Rept.—Wildlife no. 34, 85 pp., illus. (Mimeographed). January.
ALDRICH, THOMAS B.
  1896. A chemical study of the anal glands of the *Mephitis mephitica* (common skunk) with remarks on the physiological properties of this substance. Journ. Exper. Med. 1:323–40.
ALLAN, PHILIP F.
  1935. Bone cache of a gray squirrel. Journ. Mammal. 16(4):326. November 15.
ALLEN, ARTHUR A.
  1921. Banding bats. Journ. Mammal. 2(2):53–57, pls. 4–5. May.
ALLEN, DURWARD L.
  1937. The skunk: A boon or pest? Michigan Conservation 7(4):3, 9–10. December.
  1938. Notes on the killing technique of the New York weasel. Journ. Mammal. 9(2):225–29. May 12.
  1939. Winter habits of Michigan skunks. Journ. Wildlife Management 3(3):212–28. July.
  1944. Michigan fox squirrel management. Michigan Dept. Conserv., Game Div., publ. no. 100, 404 pp., illus. Dated October, 1943; issued in December, 1944.
ALLEN, DURWARD L., and WARREN W. SHAPTON.
  1942. An ecological study of winter dens, with special reference to the eastern skunk. Ecology 23(1):59–68, illus. January.
ALLEN, ELSA G.
  1938. The habits and life history of the eastern chipmunk, Tamias striatus lysteri. New York State Mus. Bull. no. 314, pp. 1–122, illus. September.
ALLEN, GLOVER M.
  °1920. Dogs of the American aborigines. Bull. Mus. Comp. Zool 63(9):431–517, 12 pls. March.
  °1939. Bats. Harvard Univ. Press, Cambridge. 368 pp., illus.
  °1942. Extinct and vanishing mammals of the Western Hemisphere with the marine species of all oceans. Amer. Comm. International Wildlife Protection, Special publ. no. 11, pp. xv + 620, illus. December 11.
ALLEN, HARRISON.
  °1893. A monograph of the bats of North America. U. S. Nat. Mus. Bull 43, pp. ix + 198, pls. 38.
ALLEN, J. A.
  1870. Notes on the mammals of Iowa. Proc. Boston Soc. Nat. Hist. 13:178–94. February 1.
  °1874. Geographical variation in color among North American squirrels, with a list of the species and varieties of the American Sciuridae occurring north of Mexico. Proc. Boston Soc. Nat. Hist. 16:276–94. February 4.
  1876 a. Description of some remains of an extinct species of wolf and an extinct species of deer from the lead region of the Upper Mississippi. Amer. Journ. Sci. and Arts, 3rd series, vol. 11, pp. 47–51. June.
  °1876 b. The American bisons, living and extinct. Mem. Mus. Comp. Zool., vol. 4, no. 10, pp. 1–246, illus.
  °1877 a. History of the American bison (*Bison americanus*). 9th Ann. Rept. U. S. Geol. Surv. Terr., pt. 3, pp. 441–587. June.
  °1877 b. *In* Coues, Elliott, and Joel Asaph Allen, 1877. Monographs of North America Rodentia. J. A. Allen author of No. 2, Leporidae, pp. 265–378; No. 3, Hystricidae, pp. 379–98; No. 4, Lagomyidae, pp. 399–414; No. 6, Castoridae, pp. 427–54; No. 9, Sciuridae, pp. 631-940. August.

1894 a. On seasonal change of color in the varying hare (*Lepus americanus* Erxl.). Bull. Amer. Mus. Nat. Hist. 6:107–28. April 14.

1894 b. On the mammals of Aransas County, Texas, with descriptions of new forms of Lepus and Oryzomys. Bull. Amer. Mus. Nat. Hist. 6(6): 165–98. May 31.

1898 a. Revision of the chickarees, or North American red squirrels (subgenus Tamiasciurus). Bull. Amer. Mus. Nat. Hist. 10:249–98. July 22.

1898 b. Nomenclatorial notes on North American mammals. Bull. Amer. Mus. Nat. Hist. 10:449–61. November 10.

1899 a. Descriptions of five new American rodents. Bull. Amer. Mus. Nat. Hist. 12(2):11–17. March 4.

1899 b. The North-American arboreal squirrels. Amer. Nat. 33(302): 635–42. August.

ALTMANN, MARGARET.
1956. Patterns of herd behavior in free-ranging elk of Wyoming, *Cervus canadensis nelsoni*. Zoologica, vol. 41, pt. 2, no. 8, pp. 68–71. September 17.

AMES, H. T.
1921. Wolves and foxes plentiful. Wisconsin Conservationist 3(1):15–16. March.

ANDERSON, RUDOLPH MARTIN.
°1949. Methods of collecting and preserving vertebrate animals. Nat. Mus. Canada, Bull. no. 69, Biol. Ser. no. 18, pp. v + 162, illus. March 22.

ANDERSON, RUDOLPH M., and A. L. RAND.
1944. Notes on chipmunks of the genus *Eutamias* in Canada. Canadian Field-Nat. 57(7 & 8): 133–35. January 24.

ANDERSON, THOMAS G.
1882. Personal narrative of Captain Thomas G Anderson. Early experiences in North-West fur trade—British capture of Prairie du Chien, 1814. Repts. and Collections State Hist. Soc. Wisconsin for years 1880, 1881, and 1882, 9:137–206.

ANONYMOUS.
1867. Additions to the Museum and Library during January, February and March, 1866. Proc. Essex Institute 5(1):6–12. (Coyote skull from Columbia Co., Wis.)

1888. The fourth voyage of Radisson. Wisconsin Hist. Coll., vol. 11.

1897 a. Wisconsin deer. Forest and Stream 49 (21):407. November 20.

1897 b. Wolves in Wisconsin. Forest and Stream 49(21):407. November 20.

1897 c. Albino deer. Forest and Stream 49(23): 448. December 4.

1903. [Wolves and panther in Wisconsin.] Amer. Field 60(5):101. August.

1909. One of the few remaining beaver dams in Wisconsin. Wild Life 2(3):11, halftone only.

1921. Around the state and elsewhere. Wisconsin Conservationist 2(6):23–24. January.

1932. Rare fisher found. Delavan (Wis.) Republican. November 23.

1936. Bull moose. Wisconsin Conserv. Bull. 1(11): 12. November.

1937 a. Big game inventory of the United States, 1937. U. S. Dept. Agric., Bur. Biological Survey, Leaflet BS–122, pp. 13 (mimeographed). January. [H. H. T. Jackson.]

1937 b. [Singing mice.] Wisconsin Conserv. Bull. 2(3):25. March.

1937 c. [White raccoons raised.] Wisconsin Conserv. Bull. 2(4):13. April.

1937 d. Cat adopts skunk family. Wisconsin Conserv. Bull. 2(6):3, illus. June.

1937 e. Half century of deer hunting. Wisconsin Conserv. Bull. 2(9):10–11. September.

1937 f. Wisconsin moose. Wisconsin Conserv. Bull. 2(10):25. October.

1937 g. Timber and brush wolves. Wisconsin Conserv. Bull. 2(10):30. October.

1937 h. [Attempt to raise fishers commercially at New Holstein, Wis.] Wisconsn Conserv. Bull. 2(10):45. October.

1937 i. [White muskrat at Antigo.] Wisconsin Conserv. Bull. 2(10):45. October.

1938. Distribution of Wisconsin deer. Wisconsin Conserv. Bull. 3(6):28. June.

1939 a. Solon Springs bear. Wisconsin Conserv. Bull. 4(2):45, illus. February.

1939 b. State fur farm oddities. Wisconsin Conserv. Bull. 4(3):30–32, illus. March.

1939 c. Fur production. Wisconsin Conserv. Bull. 4(4):49–50. April.

1939 d. Wildlife shifts. Wisconsin Conserv. Bull. 4(7):41. July.

1939 e. Record deer antlers taken. Wisconsin Conserv. Bull. 4(8):9. August.

1939 f. Big-game inventory of the United States, 1938. U. S. Dept. Interior, Bur. Biological Survey, Wildlife Leaflet BS–142, pp. 11 (mimeographed). August. [H. H. T. Jackson.]

1939 g. Wisconsin raccoon. Wisconsin Conserv. Bull. 4(10):56. October.

1939 h. Status of the American bison in the United States and Alaska, 1939. U. S. Dept. Interior, Bur. Biological Survey, Wildlife Leaflet BS–148, pp. 10 (mimeographed). December. [H. H. T. Jackson.]

1940 a. A record trophy for 1939. Wisconsin Conserv. Bull. 5(1):21. January. (Second largest Wisconsin deer antlers.)

1940 b. Fight victims. Wisconsin Conserv. Bull. 5(2):67, illus. February. (Deer with locked horns, near Park Falls, Wis.)

1940 c. Wisconsin mammals scarce. Outdoor Life 85(4):99. April. (As reported from article by W. E. Scott, Wisconsin Conserv. Bull. 4(10):21–28, Oct., 1939.)

1940 d. Big-game inventory of the United States, 1939. U. S. Dept. Interior, Fish and Wildlife Service, Wildlife Leaflet BS–175, pp. 11 (mimeographed). November. [H. H. T. Jackson.]

1941 a. Bear pictures. Wisconsin Conserv. Bull. 6(5):16–17. May.

1941 b. [Skunk queries and answers.] Wisconsin Conserv. Bull. 6(5):36. May.

1941 c. Hints on the care of opossums. U. S. Fish

and Wildlife Serv., Wildlife Leaflet 187, 2 pp. (mimeographed). May.

1941 d. Mink raising. U. S. Dept. Interior, Fish and Wildlife Service, Wildlife Leaflet 191, 10 pp. (mimeographed). May.

1941 e. Directions for poisoning thirteen-striped ground squirrels. U. S. Dept. Interior, Fish and Wildlife Service, Wildlife Leaflet 195, 2 pp. (mimeographed). July.

1941 f. Raising badgers in captivity. U. S. Dept. Interior, Fish and Wildlife Service, Wildlife Leaflet 203, 2 pp. (mimeographed). November.

1942 a. Big-game inventory of the United States, 1940. U. S. Dept. Interior, Fish and Wildlife Service, Wildlife Leaflet 207, 10 pp. (mimeographed). January. [H. H. T. Jackson.]

1942 b. Battling deer. Wisconsin Conserv. Bull. 7(12):18. December.

1943 a. Wildlife as meat. Wisconsin Conserv. Bull. 8(3):9. March.

1943 b. Majority report of the Citizens' Deer Committee to the Wisconsin Conservation Commission. Wisconsin Conserv. Bull. 8(8):19–22. August.

1943 c. Moose? Wisconsin Conserv. Bull. 8(10):15. October.

1944 a. More about deer. Pennsylvania Game News 14(12):4–5, 26–27, illus. March. (Wisconsin deer problem.)

1944 b. Six points of deer policy. Wisconsin Conserv. Bull. 9(11): 10. October.

1945. Marathon opossum. Wisconsin Conserv. Bull. 19(4):18. April.

1946 a. Big-game inventory of the United States, 1943. Wildlife Service Leaflet 283, 11 pp. (mimeographed). February. [H. H. T. Jackson.]

1946 b. Raising deer in captivity. U. S. Fish and Wildlife Service, Wildlife Leaflet 289, 9 pp. (mimeographed). June. [H. H. T. Jackson.]

1946 c. The deer problem. Wisconsin Conserv. Bull. 11(7):18. July.

1946 d. Deer feeding. Wisconsin Conserv. Bull. 11(8–9):28–30. August.

1947 a. Capture prairie spotted skunk. The New North (newspaper, Rhinelander, Wis.), Thursday, January 2.

1947 b. Mountain lions? Wisconsin Conserv. Bull. 12(3):31. March.

1947 c. Deer in 1882. Wisconsin Conserv. Bull. 21(4):5. April.

1947 d. Fox cooperation. Wisconsin Conserv. Bull. 12(5):22, illus. May.

1947 e. Bear damage. Wisconsin Conserv. Bull. 12(6):16. June.

1947 f. Giant muskrat house. Wisconsin Conserv. Bull. 12(8):11. August.

1947 g. Hunting regulations. Wisconsin Conserv. Bull. 12(9):18, map. September.

1947 h. "Canned" porcupine. Wisconsin Conserv. Bull. 12(12):16, illus. December.

1948 a. The rabbit hazard. Wisconsin Conserv. Bull. 13(1):7. January.

1948 b. The fox decline. Wisconsin Conserv. Bull. 13(3):29–39. March.

1948 c. James Reed's Trempealeau. Wisconsin Conserv. Bull. 13(4):23–25. April.

1949 a. Those beaver were blanket size. Wisconsin Conserv. Bull. 14(5):29. May.

1949 b. Now bears get stuck after dining. Wisconsin Conserv. Bull. 14(12):21, illus. December.

1950 a. Wisconsin's oldest deer lived to be nearly 20. Wisconsin Conserv. Bull. 15(7):21–22, illus. July.

1950 b. Use of warfarin for the control of rats and mice. U. S. Dept. Interior, Fish and Wildlife Service, processed circular, no number, 4 pp., illus. August 7.

1951. Raccoons move in on resort area. Wisconsin Conserv. Bull. 16(1):38. January.

1952 a. Last bull elk killed. Wisconsin Conservationist 1(5):3. January.

1952 b. Wolf drags trap in chase of four dogs. Wisconsin Conservationist 1(6):6. February.

1952 c. 94-pound beaver. Wisconsin Conservationist 1(8):5. April.

1952 d. Game and fur harvest report. Hunting 1951–52; Trapping 1950–51. Wisconsin Conserv. Dept., 13 pp. (mimeographed). June.

1952 e. Control of skunks. U. S. Fish and Wildlife Service, Wildlife Leaflet 181, 2 pp., revised. September.

1952 f. This "Battle to Death" showed new angles. Wisconsin Conserv. Bull. 17(9):27–28, illus. September.

1952 g. *Bulletin* cover picture: Fearless raccoon. Wisconsin Conserv. Bull. 17(11):10, and 1st cover. November.

1953 a. Deer hunting 1952 season. Wisconsin Conserv. Bull. 18(1):11–13. January.

1953 b. Deer management struggle marks 10th anniversary. Wisconsin Conserv. Bull. 18(3):35. March.

1953 c. These were eager beavers—They felled 33-inch tree. Wisconsin Conserv. Bull. 16(7):28, illus. July.

1953 d. Control of house mice. U. S. Dept. Interior, Fish and Wildlife Service, Wildlife Leaflet 349, 4 pp., illus. October.

1954. Deer in Kenosha County. Wisconsin Conserv. Bull. 19(8):21. August.

1955. Deer weighing 240 dressed taken in Florence County. Wisconsin Conserv. Bull. 20(3):26. March.

1956 a. Deer kill rises sharply; herd has grown fast. Wisconsin Conserv. Bull. 21(1):31. January.

1956 b. Twelve deer killed in record accident. Wisconsin Conserv. Bull. 21(5):32. May.

ANTHONY, HAROLD E.

°1925. The capture and preservation of small mammals for study. Amer. Mus. Nat. His., Guide Leaflet no. 61, 53 pp., illus. November.

°1928 a. Field book of North American mammals. G. P. Putnam's Sons, New York. Pp. xxv + 625, 48 pls. (32 colored).

°1928 b. Horns and antlers. Their occurrence, de-

velopment and functions in the Mammalia. Part
I [Horns]. Bull. New York Zool. Soc. 31:178–
216. December.

°1929. Horns and antlers. Their occurrence, development, and functions in the Mammalia.
Part II [Antlers]. Bull. New York Zool. Soc.
32(1):2–40, illus. January.

APEL, H. B.
1943. The muskrat. Wisconsin Conserv. Bull.
8(1):30–31. January.

ARLTON, A. V.
1936. An ecological study of the mole. Journ.
Mammal. 17(4):349–71. November 16.

ARMSTRONG, RUTH ALISON.
1950. Fetal development of the northern white-
tailed deer (Odocoileus virginianus borealis
Miller). Amer. Midland Nat. 43(3):650–66, illus.
May.

ASDELL, S[YDNEY]. A[RTHUR].
°1946. Patterns of mammalian reproduction. Comstock Publishing Co., Ithaca, N.Y. pp. xii + 437,
12 pls.

ASHAROV, M.
1928. Tungus tales. Why the chipmunk has dark
stripes on its back. Siberian Hunter and Fur-
Trader, no. 3, In I. M. Zalesskii and M. D.
Zverev, 1935, The chipmunk (Eutamias asiati-
cus), pp. 80–102, figs. 33–43, publ. in Russian by
All-Union Cooperative United Publishing House,
Moscow, Leningrad. Translation No. 141; J. D.
Jackson, 1943, for Bureau of Animal Population,
Oxford Univ., England.

ASHBROOK, FRANK G.
1927. Mink raising. U. S. Dept. Agric. Leaflet no.
8, 6 pp., illus. October. Revised February, 1928.

ASHBROOK, FRANK G., and KARL B. HANSON.
1927. Breeding martens in captivity. Journ. Heredity 18:498–503, illus. November.
1930. The normal breeding season and gestation
period of martens. U. S. Dept. Agric. Circ. no.
107, pp. 1–6. February.

ATWOOD, EARL L.
1941. White-tailed deer foods of the United States.
Journ. Wildlife Management 5(3):314–32. July.

AUDUBON, JOHN J., and JOHN BACHMAN.
°1842. Descriptions of new species of quadrupeds
inhabiting North America. Journ. Acad. Nat.
Sci. Philadelphia, ser. 1, vol. 8, pp. 280–323.
°1845–54. The viviparous quadrupeds of North
America. Vol. 1, 389 pp.; vol. 2, 334 pp.; vol. 3,
348 pp. New York.

B., S. J.
1884. Wisconsin notes. Amer. Field 21(9):205.
March 1. (Foxes, wild cats, wolves in Dunn
County in 1883.)

BABCOCK, H. L.
1914. Food habits of the short-tailed shrew, Blarina
brevicauda. Science (n.s.) 40 (1032):526–30.
October 9.

BABCOCK, S. M.
°1912. Metabolic water: Its production and role
in vital phenomena. Univ. Wisconsin, Agric.

Exper. Station, Research Bull. no. 22, pp. 87–181.
March.

BAILEY, BERNARD.
1922. Some random notes on mammals of Minnesota. Journ. Mammal. 3(4):259. November 2.
1929. Mammals of Sherburne County, Minnesota.
Journ. Mammal. 10(2):153–64. May 9.

BAILEY, ROBERT A.
1946 a. Reading rabbit population cycles from
pines. Wisconsin Conser. Bull. 11(7):14–17.
July.
1946 b. Squirrel damage. Wisconsin Conserv. Bull.
11(8–9):5. August.

BAILEY, VERNON.
1893 a. Notes on some of the spermophiles and
pocket gophers of the Mississippi Valley. Ann.
Rept. Dept. Agric. for year 1892, pp. 185–93,
pls. 1–5, colored.
1893 b. The prairie ground squirrels or spermophiles of the Mississippi Valley. U. S. Dept.
Agric., Div. Ornithology and Mammalogy Bull.
no. 4, 69 pp., 3 colored plates, 4 maps. August
17.
1895. The pocket gophers of the United States.
U. S. Dept. Agric., Div. Ornithology and Mammalogy, Bull no. 5, 47 pp., illus. August 17.
°1897. Revision of the American voles of the genus
Evotomys. Proc. Biol. Soc. Washington 11:113–
38, pl. 3. May 13.
°1900. Revision of American voles of the genus
Microtus. North Amer. Fauna no. 17, 88 pp., 5
pls. June 6.
1907 a. Wolves in relation to stock, game, and the
national forest reserves. U. S. Dept. Agric.,
Forest Service Bull. no. 72, pp. 1–31, illus. January 19.
1907 b. Directions for the destruction of wolves
and coyotes. U. S. Dept. Agric., Biol. Survey
Circ. no. 55, pp. 1–6. March 13.
1907 c. Destruction of deer by the Northern timber wolf. U. S. Dept. Agric., Biol. Survey Circ.
no. 58, pp. 1–2, illus. May 4.
1908. Destruction of wolves and coyotes. Results
obtained during 1907. U. S. Dept. Agric., Biol.
Survey Circ. no. 63, pp. 1–11, illus. April 29.
1909. Key to animals on which wolf and coyote
bounties are often paid. U. S. Dept. Agric., Biol.
Survey Circ. no. 69, pp. 1–3, illus. May 22.
1913. Two new subspecies of North American beavers. Proc. Biol. Soc. Washington 26:191–94.
October 23.
°1921. Capturing small mammals for study. Journ.
Mammal. 2(2):63–68. May 2.
1922. Beaver habits, beaver control and possibili-
ties in beaver farming. U. S. Dept. Agric., Bull.
1078, pp. 1–31, illus. October 18.
1923. The combing claws of the beaver. Journ.
Mammal. 4(1):77–79, pl. 9. May 9.
1924. Breeding, feeding, and other life habits of
meadow mice (Microtus). Journ. Agric. Research 27(8):523–38, pls. 1–3. February 23.
1926 a. How beavers build their houses. Journ.

Mammal. 7(1):41–43, pls. 5–9. February 15.

1926 b. Construction and operation of the Biological Survey beaver trap. U. S. Dept. Agric., Bur. Biol. Survey, Misc. Circ. 69, pp. 1–4. June.

°1927 a. Biological Survey of North Dakota. North Amer. Fauna no. 51, 226 pp., illus. January 8.

1927 b. Beaver habits and experiments in beaver culture. U. S. Dept. Agric., Tech. Bull. 21, pp. 1–40, 14 pls. October.

1927 c. How beavers build their houses. Ann. Rept. Smithsonian Inst. for 1926, publ. 2895, pp. 357–60, illus. November.

°1932. Trapping animals alive. Journ. Mammal. 13(4):337–42. November.

°1933. Cave life in Kentucky. Notre Dame University Press. 265 pp., illus. (Reprinted from Amer. Midland Nat. 14(5):385–635.)

1937 a. A typical specimen of the eastern elk from Pennsylvania. Journ. Mammal. 18(1):104. February 14.

1937 b. Deodorizing skunks. Journ. Mammal. 18(4):481–82. November 22.

1940. The home life of the big wolves. Nat. Hist. 46(2):120–22, illus. September.

BAIRD, SPENCER F.

°1857. Reports of explorations and surveys to ascertain the most practicable and economical route for a railroad from the Mississippi River to the Pacific Ocean, vol. 8, pt. 1, Mammals. 757 pp., 60 pls.

BAKER, CHARLES M.

1872. Pioneer history of Walworth County. Rept. & Collections State Hist. Soc. of Wisconsin for the year 1869, 1870, 1871 and 1872, vol. 6, pp. 436–75.

BANFIELD, A. W. F.

1954. Tularemia in beavers and muskrats, Water Lakes National Park, Alberta, 1952–53. Canadian Journ. Zool. 32–139–43.

1955. A provisional life table for the barren ground caribou. Canadian Journ. Zool. 33:143–47.

BANGS, OUTRAM.

1899. A new gray fox from the upper Mississippi Valley. Proc. New England Zool. Club 1:43–44. June 5.

BANKS, W. J.

1947. Wildcat of the North. Our Dumb Animals 80(9):18. September.

BARBEHENN, KILE R.

1955. A field study of growth in Microtus pennsylvanicus. Journ. Mammal. 36(4):533–43. December 12.

BARBER, W. E.

1918. Wild life conservation. In Bien. Rept. State Conserv. Comm. Wisconsin for fiscal years ending June 30, 1917, and June 30, 1918, pp. 15–35, illus.

1919. Interesting facts concerning the beaver. Wisconsin Conservationist 1(4):2–3, illus. September.

1920 a. A beaver dam of huge proportions. Scien-

tific American 122(7):167. February 14.

1920 b. A giant beaver dam. Literary Digest 64 (11):30. March 13.

1921 a. Tragedy of the north woods. Wisconsin Conservationist 2(6):6, illus. January.

1921 b. The blood-stained trail of the white-tailed deer in Wisconsin. Wisconsin Conservationist 3(1):1–2. March.

1922 a. Deer still plentiful in Wisconsin. Wisconsin Conservationist 3(6):16. January.

1922 b. Again, our fur-bearing animals. Wisconsin Conservationist 4(1):11. March.

BARGER, N. R.

1944. How was the deer season, 1943? Wisconsin Conserv. Bull. 9(4):3–5. April.

1946 a. Animals taken under bounty. Wisconsin Conserv. Bull. 11(8–9):16–18. August.

1946 b. The raccoon (Procyon lotor hirtus). Wisconsin Conserv. Bull. 11(10–11):19, illus. October.

1947 a. Red fox (Vulpes fulvus). Wisconsin Conserv. Bull. 12(1):29–30, illus. January.

1947 b. Canada porcupine (Erethizon dorsatum dorsatum). Wisconsin Conserv. Bull. 12(2):24–25, illus. February.

1947 c. Opossum (Didelphis virginiana virginiana). Wisconsin Conserv. Bull. 12(3):24–25, illus. March.

1947 d. Little flying squirrel (Glaucomys volans volans). Wisconsin Conserv. Bull. 12(4):28–29, illus. April.

1947 e. The little brown bat (Myotis lucifugus lucifugus). Wisconsin Conserv. Bull. 12(6):27–28, illus. June.

1947 f. Northern white-footed mouse or deer mouse (Peromyscus leucopus noveboracensis). Wisconsin Conserv. Bull. 12(10):46, illus. October.

1947 g. A peak in Wisconsin beaver harvest. Wisconsin Conserv. Bull. 12(11):11–15. November.

1947 h. The chipmunk. Wisconsin Conserv. Bull. 12(11):29–30, illus. November.

1947 i. Badger (Taxidea taxus taxus). Wisconsin Conserv. Bull. 12(12): 32, illus. December.

1948 a. The skunk. Wisconsin Conserv. Bull. 13(1):16–17, illus. January.

1948 b. The gray fox Urocyon cinereoargenteus (species). Wisconsin Conserv. Bull. 13(3):27–28, illus. March.

1948 c. Prairie mole. Wisconsin Conserv. Bull. 13(4):26–27, illus. April.

1948 d. Bobcat-wildcat (Lynx rufus rufus). Wisconsin Conserv. Bull. 13(5):29–30, illus. May.

1948 e. Minnesota varying hare—snowshoe hare (Lepus americanus phaeonotus). Wisconsin Conserv. Bull. 13(9):24–25, illus. September.

1948 f. Gray wolf-timber wolf (Canis lupus lycaon). Wisconsin Conserv. Bull. 13(1):26, illus. October.

1948 g. Common muskrat (Ondatra zibethica zibethica). Wisconsin Conserv. Bull. 13(11):25–26, illus. November.

1948 h. Mississippi Valley mink (Mustela vison

letifera). Wisconsin Conserv. Bull. 13(12):28, illus. December.

1949 a. Northern Virginia deer (*Odocoileus virginianus borealis*). Wisconsin Conserv. Bull. 14 (1):35–36, illus. January.

1949 b. Thirteen-lined ground squirrel (striped gopher) (*Citellus t. tridecemlineatus*). Wisconsin Conserv. Bull. 14(2):31–32, illus. February.

1949 c. Red squirrel (*Tamiasciurus hudsonicus loquax*). Wisconsin Conserv. Bull. 14(3):39–49, illus. March.

1949 d. White-tailed jack rabbit (*Lepus townsendi campestris*). Wisconsin Conserv. Bull. 14(4):39, illus. April.

1949 e. Field mouse (*Microtus pennsylvanicus pennsylvanicus*). Wisconsin Conserv. Bull. 14 (5):37–38. May.

1949 f. Mearn's cottontail (*Sylvilagus floridanus mearnsi*). Wisconsin Conserv. Bull. 14(9):31–32, illus. September.

1949 g. Black bear (*Euarctos americanus americanus*). Wisconsin Conserv. Bull. 14(11):32–33, illus. October.

1949 h. Short-tailed shrew. Wisconsin Conserv. Bull. 14(11):33, illus. November.

1949 i. Rufescent woodchuck (*Marmota monax rufescens*). Wisconsin Conserv. Bull. 14(12):26–27, illus. December.

1950 a. Otter (*Lutra canadensis canadensis*). Wisconsin Conserv. Bull. 15(1):33, illus. January.

1950 b. Northern gray squirrel (*Sciurus carolinensis leucotis*). Wisconsin Conserv. Bull. 15(3):38–39, illus. March.

1950 c. Coyote (*Canis latrans latrans*). Wisconsin Conserv. Bull. 15(4):32–33, illus. April.

1950 d. Canadian beaver (*Castor canadensis canadensis*). Wisconsin Conserv. Bull. 15(5):34–35, illus. May.

1950 e. Western fox squirrel (*Sciurus niger rufiventer*). Wisconsin Conserv. Bull. 15(9):33–34, illus. September.

1950 f. Bonaparte's weasel (*Mustela erminea bangsi*). Wisconsin Conserv. Bull. 15(10):39–40, illus. October.

1950 g. Franklin ground squirrel (*Citellus franklini*). Wisconsin Conserv. Bull. 15(11):35–36, illus. November.

1950 h. Meadow jumping mouse (Zapus *hudsonius hudsonius*). Wisconsin Conserv. Bull. 15 (12):28, illus. December.

1951 a. The elk (*Cervus canadensis canadensis*). Wisconsin Conserv. Bull. 16(1):33–34, illus. January.

1951 b. Star-nosed mole (*Condylura cristata*). Wisconsin Conserv. Bull. 16(3):29–30, illus. March.

1951 c. New York weasel (*Mustela frenata noveboracensis*). Wisconsin Conserv. Bull. 16(4):34–35, illus. April.

1951 d. Prairie spotted skunk (*Spilogale interrupta*). Wisconsin Conserv. Bull. 16(5):28. May.

1952. Wisconsin mammals. Wisconsin Conserv. Dept., publ. 351-51, 56 pp., illus. March.

BARGER, N. R., ELTON E. BUSSEWITZ, EARL L. LOYSTER, SAM ROBBINS, AND WALTER E. SCOTT.
1942. Wisconsin birds: A preliminary check list with migration charts. Wisconsin Society of Ornithology, Madison. 32 pp., map.

BARRETT, MOSES.
1873. On the migration of certain animals as influenced by civilization. Amer. Nat. 7(11):693–95. November.

BARRETT, S. A.
1933. Ancient Aztalan. Bull. Public Mus. City Milwaukee 13:1–622, illus. April 24.

BASSETT, CHARLES F., and LEONARD M. LLEWELLYN.
1949 a. The molting and fur growth pattern in the adult silver fox. Natl. Fur News 21(7):12, 24–25, illus. August.

1949 b. The molting and fur growth pattern in the adult mink. Amer. Midland Nat. 42(3):751–56.

BATCHELDER, CHARLES FOSTER.
1930. The voice of the porcupine. Journ. Mammal. 11(2):237–39. May 9.

1948. Notes on the Canada porcupine. Journ. Mammal. 29(3):260–68. August 31.

BAUMGARTNER, LUTHER L.
1943. Pelage studies of fox squirrels (Sciurus niger rufiventer). Amer. Midland Nat. 29(3):588–90. May.

BAUMGARTNER, LUTHER L., and STEPHEN E. POWELL.
1949. Zinc dimethyldithiocarbamate-cyclohexylamine complex as a deer repellent applicable to agricultural crops, Cont. Boyce Thompson Inst. 15(7):411–20, illus. June.

BEARD, DANIEL B., FREDERICK C. LINCOLN, VICTOR H. CAHALANE, HARTLEY H. T. JACKSON, and BEN H. THOMPSON.
°1942. Fading trails. Macmillan Co., New York. pp. xv + 279, illus.

BEARD, ELIZABETH B.
1953. The importance of beaver in waterfowl management at the Seney National Wildlife Refuge. Journ. Wildlife Management 17(4):398–436, illus. October.

BEBB, WILLIAM.
1934. Source of small birds eaten by the coyote. Journ. Mammal. 15(4):320–21. November 15.

BECKER, E. R.
1926 a. The flagellate fauna of the caecum of the striped ground squirrel, *Citellus tridecemlineatus* with special reference to *Chilomastix magna* sp. nov. Biol. Bull. 51:287–98.

1926 b. *Endamoeba citelli* sp. nov. from the striped ground squirrel *Citellus tridecemlineatus* and the life history of its parasite *Sphaerits endomoebae* sp. nov. Biol. Bull. 51:444–54.

BECKER, GEORGE.
1947. Bounty questions. Wisconsin Conserv. Bull. 12(3):11. March.

BEDDARD, FRANK EVERS.
°1902. Mammalia. Cambridge Nat. Hist. Series. 605 pp., illus.

BEER, JAMES R.
1948 a. Molt pattern as an age criterion in musk-

rats. Wisconsin Conserv. Bull. 13(1):21. January.

1948 b. Muskrats "aged" at a glance. Wisconsin Conserv. Bull. 13(8):13–14, illus. August.

1950 a. The reproductive cycle of the muskrat in Wisconsin. Journ. Wildlife Management 14(2): 151–56. April (May).

1950 b. The least weasel in Wisconsin. Journ. Mammal. 31(2):146–49. May 30.

1953. The screech owl as a predator on the big brown bat. Journ. Mammal. 34(3):384. August 17.

1955 a. Survival and movements of banded big brown bats. Journ. Mammal. 36(2):242–48. May.

1956. A record of a silver-haired bat in a cave. Journ. Mammal. 37(2):282. June 12.

BEER, JAMES R., and A. GLENN RICHARDS.
1956. Hibernation of the big brown bat. Journ. Mammal. 37(1):31–41. March 1.

BEER, JAMES R., CHARLES F. MACLEOD, and LOUIS D. FRENZEL.
1957. Prenatal survival and loss in some cricetid rodents. Journ. Mammal. 38(3):392–402. August 23.

BEER, JAMES R., and ROLAND K. MEYER.
1951. Seasonal changes in the endocrine organs and behavior patterns of the muskrat. Journ. Mammal. 32(2):173–91. May.

BEER, JAMES R., and WAYNE TRUAX.
1950. Sex and age ratios in Wisconsin muskrats. Journ. Wildlife Management 14(3):323–31. July.

BELITZ, A. F.
1919–20. On the trail of the white-tail. Wisconsin Conservationist 1(5):1, November, 1919; 1(6): 5–6, January, 1920; 2(1):33–34, March, 1920; 2 (3):7–8, July, 1920.

BELL, J. F., and W. S. CHALGREN.
1943. Some wildlife diseases of the eastern United States. Journ. Wildlife Management 7(3):270–78. July.

BELLROSE, FRANK C.
1950. The relationship of muskrat populations to various marsh and aquatic plants. Journ. Wildlife Management 14(3):299–315. July.

BELLROSE, FRANK C., and JESSOP B. LOW.
1943. The influence of flood and low water levels on the survival of muskrats. Journ. Mammal. 24(2):173–88. June 8.

BENDRICK, BEN.
1952. Beaver turn law-makers—they open musky refuge. Wisconsin Conserv. Bull. 17(12):26. December.

°BENEDICT, FRANCES A.
1957. Hair structure as a generic character in bats. Univ. California Publ. Zool. 59(8):285–548. October 10.

BENEDICT, FRANCIS G., and ROBERT C. LEE.
1938. Hibernation and marmot physiology. Carnegie Inst. of Washington Publ. no. 497, 239 pp., 2 pls. June 22.

BENNETTS, W. J.
1900. The wild animal life of a large city. Bull. Wisconsin Nat. Hist. Soc. 1(1):63–64. February

27.

BENTON, ALLEN H.
1955. Observations on the life history of the northern pine mouse. Journ. Mammal. 36(1):52–62. February 28.

BERSING, OTIS S.
1945. The hunters' report of the 1944 deer kill. Wisconsin Conserv. Bull. 10(10):3–11, illus. October.

1946. The 1945 deer kill. Wisconsin Conserv. Bull. 11(8–9):6–15, maps. August.

1947 a. Bow hunting for deer in Wisconsin 1946. Wisconsin Conserv. Bull. 12(2):10–11. February.

1947 b. The 1946 deer hunting season. Wisconsin Conserv. Bull. 12(9):4–12, map. September.

1948 a. Bow and arrow deer hunting in Wisconsin, 1934–1947. Wisconsin Conserv. Bull. 13(4): 7–16, illus. April.

1948 b. The 1947 deer season. Wisconsin Conserv. Bull. 13(10):11–12. October.

1956 a. A century of Wisconsin deer. Wisconsin Conservation Dept., Madison, 184 pp. May 29.

1956 b. Wisconsin black bear. Wisconsin Conserv. Bull. 21(10):25–28. October.

BESANDY, C. D.
1957. Bushytail business. Wisconsin Conserv. Bull. 22(10):17–19. October.

BIRD, RALPH D.
1933. A three-horned wapiti (Cervus canadensis canadensis). Journ. Mammal. 14(2):164–66, illus. May 15.

1955. Melanism in the varying hare, Lepus americanus Erxleben. Canadian Field-Nat. 69(1):11. December.

BISHOP, SHERMAN C.
1923. Note on the nest and young of the small brown weasel. Journ. Mammal. 4(1):26–27, pl. 5. February 9.

1947. Curious behavior of a hoary bat. Journ. Mammal. 28(3):293–94. August 20.

BISSONETTE, THOMAS HUME.
1942. Anomalous seasonal coat-color-changes in a small male Bonaparte's weasel (Mustela cicognanii cicognanii Bonaparte). Amer. Midland Nat. 28(2):327–33, illus. September.

BISSONETTE, THOMAS HUME, and EARL ELMORE BAILEY.
1944. Experimental modification and control of molts and changes of coat-color in weasels by controlled lighting. Ann. New York Acad. Sci. 45(6):221–60, illus. April 7.

BLAIR, W. FRANK.
1940 a. Home ranges and populations of the jumping mouse. Amer. Midland Nat. 23(1):244–50. January.

1940 b. Notes on home ranges and populations of the short-tailed shrew. Ecology 21(2):284–88. April.

1940 c. Home ranges and populations of the meadow vole in southern Michigan. Journ. Wildlife Management 4(2):149–61. April.

1940 d. A study of the prairie deer-mouse populations in southern Michigan. Amer. Midland Nat.

24(2):273–305. September.

1941 a. Some data on the home ranges and general life history of the short-tailed shrew, red-backed mouse, and woodland jumping mouse in northern Michigan. Amer. Midland Nat. 25(3):681–85. May.

1941 b. The small mammal population of a hardwood forest in northern Michigan. Univ. Michigan, Contributions Lab. Vertebrate Genetics, no. 17, pp. 1–10. November.

1942. Size of home range and notes on the life history of the woodland deer-mouse and eastern chipmunk in northern Michigan. Journ. Mammal. 23(1):27–36. February.

1948. Population density, life span, and mortality rates of small mammals in blue-grass field associations of southern Michigan. Amer. Midland Nat. 40(2):395–419. September.

BLOSSOM, PHILLIP M.
1932. A pair of long-tailed shrews (Sorex cinereus cinereus) in captivity. Journ. Mammal. 13(2):136–43. May 11.

BOLE, B. PATTERSON, JR., and PHILIP N. MOULTHROP.
1942. The Ohio Recent mammal collection in the Cleveland Museum of Natural History. Sci. Publs. Cleveland Mus. Nat. Hist. 5(6):83–181. September 11.

BRADLE, BERNARD J.
1957. The fisher returns to Wisconsin. Wisconsin Conserv. Bull. 22(11):9–11, illus. November.

BRADT, GLENN W.
1939. Breeding habits of the beaver. Journ. Mammal. 20(4):486–89. November 14.

BRANCH, E. DOUGLAS.
°1929. The hunting of the buffalo. Appleton and Co., 240 pp., illus.

BRECK, LLOYD.
1908. In wild Wisconsin. Forest and Stream 71:297. August 22.

BRECKENRIDGE, W. J.
1929. Actions of the pocket gopher (Geomys bursarius). Journ. Mammal. 10(4):326–29. November 11.

1946. Weights of a Minnesota moose. Journ. Mammal. 27(1):90–91. March 14.

BROWN, CHARLES E.
1921. The lynx effigy at Devils Lake. Wisconsin Conservationist 3(1):7. March.

BROWN, LEE P.
1923. Fire and its effect on wild life. Journ. Mammal 4(3):195–96. August 10.

BROWN, LOUIS G., and LEE E. YEAGER.
1945. Fox squirrels and gray squirrels in Illinois. Bull. Illinois Nat. Hist. Survey 23(5):449–536. September.

BRYANT, MONROE D.
1945. Phylogeny of Nearctic Sciuridae. Amer. Midland Nat. 33(2): 257–390, illus. March.

BUCKNER, C. H.
1957. Home range of Synaptomys cooperi. Journ. Mammal. 38(1):132. February 25.

BUNN, LOWELL.
1956. States favor either-sex deer hunts. Wisconsin Conserv. Bull. 21(12):10–13. December.

BURKE, F. M.
1954. Smoked squirrel in the hide. Wisconsin Conserv. Bull. 19(10):13. October.

BURT, WILLIAM HENRY.
1928. Additional notes on the life history of the Goss lemming mouse. Journ. Mammal. 9(3):212–16. August 9.

1940. Territorial behavior and populations of some small mammals in southern Michigan. Misc. publ. Mus. Zool., Univ. Michigan, no. 45, 58 pp., 2 pls. May 8.

1943. Changes in the nomenclature of Michigan mammals. Occas. Papers Mus. Zool., Univ. Michigan, no. 481, 9 pp. November 10.

°1946. The mammals of Michigan. Univ. of Michigan Press, 288 pp., 13 pls.

°1957. Mammals of the Great Lakes Region. Univ. of Michigan Press. pp. xv + 246, illus.

°1954. The subspecies category in mammals. Systematic Zoology 3:99–104.

BURT, WILLIAM HENRY, and R. P. GROSSENHEIDER.
°1952. A field guide to the mammals. Houghton Mifflin Co., Boston. pp. xxiv + 200, illus. (many colored).

BUSS, IRVEN O.
1941. Sex ratios and weights of muskrats (Ondatra zibethica zibethica) from Wisconsin. Journ. Mammal. 22(4):403. November 13.

1946. Pheasants, fox, and quail. Wisconsin Conserv. Bull. 11(4):8–15.

BUSS, IRVEN O. and HERMAN E. BUSS.
1947. Deer hunting records from central Bayfield County 1930–1946. Wisconsin Conserv. Bull. 12 (1):5–11. January.

BUTLER, JAMES D.
1888. Tay-cho-pe-rab, the Four Lake Country, first white foot-prints there. Rept. and Collections State Hist. Soc. Wisconsin for years 1883, 1884 and 1885, vol. 10, pp. 64–89.

BUTSCH, ROBERT STEARNS.
1954. The life history and ecology of the redbacked vole, Clethrionomys gapperi gapperi Vigors in Minnesota. Ph.D. thesis, Univ. of Michigan. 161 pp. (Abstract in Wildlife Review no. 78, p. 35.)

BUTTERFIELD, ROBERT T.
1954 a. Traps, live-trapping, and marking of raccoons. Journ. Mammal. 35(3):440–42. August.

1954 b. Some raccoon and groundhog relationships. Journ. Wildlife Management 18(4):433–37. October.

CABRERA, ANGEL.
°1922. Manual de Mastozoologia. Madrid. 440 pp., illus.

CAGLE, FRED R., and LENDELL COCKRUM.
1943. Notes on a summer colony of Myotis lucifugus lucifugus. Journ. Mammal. 24(4):474–92, illus. November 17.

CAHALANE, VICTOR H.
1932. Age variation in the teeth and skull of the white-tail deer. Cranbrook Inst. Sci., Sci. Publ. no. 2, 14 pp., 8 pls. November.
°1947. Mammals of North America. Macmillan Co., New York. pp. x + 682, illus. June.

CALHOUN, JOHN B.
1945. Diel activity rhythms of the rodents, *Microtus ochrogaster* and *Sigmodon hispidus hispidus.* Ecology 26(3):251–73. July.
1948. Mortality and movement of brown rats (*Rattus norvegicus*) in artificially supersaturated populations. Journ. Wildlife Management 12 (2):167–72. April.

CAMPBELL, BERRY.
1939. The shoulder anatomy of the moles. A study in phylogeny and adaptation. Amer. Journ. Anatomy 64(1):1–39, illus. January.

CANFIELD, WILLIAM H.
1861. Sketches of Sauk County. Third sketch. A. N. Kellogg, Baraboo. 40 pp., 3 maps.

CARHART, ARTHUR HAWTHORNE.
°1946. Hunting North American deer. Macmillan Co., New York. pp. viii + 232, pls. 18.

[CARR, CHARLES F.]
1890. Albino squirrels. Wisconsin Naturalist 1(3): 48. October.

CARTER, T. DONALD.
1955. Remarkable age attained by a bobcat. Journ. Mammal. 36(2):290. May.

CARTWRIGHT, DAVID W., and MARY F. BAILEY.
1875. Natural history of western wild animals and guide for hunters, trappers, and sportsmen. Toledo. 280 pp., illus.

CARVER, JONATHAN.
1838. Carver's travels in Wisconsin. Harper and Brothers, New York. 376 pp., 5 pls., 2 maps. (A reprint of "Travels through the interior parts of North America in the years 1766, 1767, and 1768," third edition, London, 1781.)

CASSODAY, DOROTHY.
1942. Animal tracks. Wisconsin Conserv. Bull. 7 (8):8–11, illus. August.

CHADDOCK, T. T.
1938. Some facts concerning cottontails imported into Wisconsin. Wisconsin Conserv. Bull. 3(4): 49–52. April.
1939 a. Epithelial papillomas reported in deer. Wisconsin Conserv. Bull. 4(2):31–32. February.
1939 b. Report on grey and red fox stomach examinations. Wisconsin Conserv. Bull. 4(9):53–54. September.
1940. Chemical analysis of deer antlers. Wisconsin Conserv. Bull. 5(6):42. June.

CHAMBERLAIN, E. B.
1929. Behavior of the least shrew. Journ. Mammal. 10(3):250–51. August 10.

CHAPMAN, FLOYD B.
1938. Exodus of Norway rats from flooded areas. Journ. Mammal. 19(3):376–77. August 18.

CHASE, A. C.
1945. Sport hunting for foxes. Wisconsin Conserv.

Bull. 10(5–6):10. May.

CHITTY, DENNIS, and HELEN CHITTY.
1942. The snowshoe rabbit enquiry, 1939–40. Canadian Field-Nat. 56(2):17–21. February.

CHITTY, DENNIS, and MARY NICHOLSON.
1943. The snowshoe rabbit enquiry, 1940–41. Canadian Field-Nat. 57:64–68. May.

CHITTY, DENNIS, and H. N. SOUTHERN, eds.
°1954. Control of rats and mice. Oxford Univ. Press. 3 vols., 824 pp., 16 pls., text figs.

CHITTY, HELEN.
1944. The snowshoe rabbit enquiry, 1941–42. Canadian Field-Nat. 57(7 and 8):136–41. January 24.
1946. The snowshoe rabbit enquiry, 1942–43. Canadian Field-Nat. 60(3):67–70. June.
1948. The snowshoe rabbit enquiry, 1943–46. Journ. Animal Ecology 17(1):39–44. May.
1950. The snowshoe rabbit enquiry, 1946–48. Journ. Animal Ecology 19(1):15–20. May.

CHRISTENSEN, EARL M.
1959. A historical view of the ranges of the white-tailed deer in northern Wisconsin forests. Amer. Midland Nat. 6(1):230–38. January.

CHURCHER, CHARLES S.
1959. The specific status of the New World red fox. Journ. Mammal. 40(4):513–20. November 20.

CLARK, FRANK H.
1935. Linkage relations of Zavadskaia shaker in the house-mouse (*Mus musculus*). Proc. Nat. Acad. Sci. 21(5):247–51. May.
1936. The oestrous cycle of the deer-mouse, *Peromyscus maniculatus.* Contrib. Lab. Vertebrate Genetics, Univ. Michigan, no. 1, pp. 1–7, pl. 1. May.

CLEFISCH, AUGUST J.
1943. Skunk trapping. Wisconsin Conserv. Bull. 8(2):15. February.

CLOUGH, GARI C.
1955. Repeated hibernation in a captive meadow jumping mouse. Journ. Mammal. 36(2):301–2. May.

CLOUGH, GARRETT C.
1960. Arctic shrew in southern Wisconsin. Journ. Mammal. 40(2):263. May 20.

COCKRUM, E. LENDELL.
1949. Longevity in the little brown bat, *Myotis lucifugus lucifugus.* Journ. Mammal. 30(4):433–34. November 21.
1953. Aberrations in the color of the prairie vole, Microtus ochrogaster. Trans. Kansas Acad. Sci. 56(1):86–88.
1954. Non-geographic variation in cranial measurements of wild-taken *Peromyscus leucopus noveboracensis.* Journ. Mammal. 35(3): 362–76. August.
°1955. Laboratory manual of mammalogy. Minneapolis. pp. 175, illus.
1956. Homing, movements, and longevity of bats. Journ. Mammal. 37(1):48–57. March 1.

COGSHALL, ANNETTA STOW.

1928. Food habits of deer mice of the genus Peromyscus in captivity. Journ. Mammal. 9(3):217–
21. August 9.

COLE, H. E.
1921. A swimming skunk. Wisconsin Conservationist 3(4):6. September.
1922. Wild life in Baraboo Hills. Wisconsin Conservationist 3(6):9. January.

COLE, LEON J.
1922. Red squirrels swimming a lake. Journ. Mammal 3(1):53–54. February 8.

COLE, LEON J., and RICHARD M. SHACKELFORD.
1943. White spotting in the fox. Amer. Nat. 77(4):
289–321, illus. July.
1947. Fox hybrids. Trans. Wisconsin Acad. Sciences, Arts and Letters 38:315–32. December 31.

COLE, L. W.
1907. Concerning intelligence of raccoon. Journ.
Comparative Neurology and Psychology 17(3):
211–61. June.
1912. Observations on the senses and instincts of
the raccoon. Journ. Animal Behavior 2(5):299–
309. September.

COLE, L. W., and F. M. LONG.
1909. Visual discrimination in raccoons. Journ.
Comp. Neurology and Psychology 19(6):657–
83. December.

COMSTOCK, H. S.
1956. The bear was a menace to Dennis. Wisconsin Conserv. Bull. 21(10):29–30. October.

CONAWAY, CLINTON H.
1952. Life history of the water shrew (Sorex palustris navigator). Amer. Midland Nat. 48(1):219–
48, illus. July 2.
1958. Maintenance, reproduction and growth of
the least shrew in captivity. Journ. Mammal.
39(4):507–12. November 20.
1959. The reproductive cycle of the eastern mole.
Journ. Mammal. 40(2):180–94, illus. May 20.

CONIBEAR, FRANK, and J. L. BLUNDELL.
1949. The wise one. Wm. Sloane Associates, New
York. pp. 265, illus.

CONINX-GIRARDET, BERTA.
1927. Beiträge zur Kenntnis innersekretorischer
Organe des Murmeltieres (Arctomys marmota
L.) und ihrer Beziehungen zum Problem des
Winterschlafes. Acta Zoologica 8:161–224, pls.
1–5.

CONNOR, PAUL F.
1959. The bog lemming Synaptomys cooperi in
southern New Jersey. Publ. Mus. Michigan State
Univ. Biol. series 1(5):161–248, 4 pls. July 24.

CONSTANTINE, DENNY G.
1958. An automatic bat-collecting device. Journ.
Wildlife Management 22(1):17–22, illus. January.

CONWAY, RALPH C.
1949. "Whitney" demonstrates deer life. Nat'l. Humane Review 37(6): 10–11, 26, illus. June.

COPELAND, MANTON.
1912. Notes on the mammals of Mt. Greylock,
Massachusetts. Proc. Biol. Soc. Washington
25:157–62.

CORBIN, DUANE L.
1955. How to miss deer. Wisconsin Conserv. Bull.
20(6):9–11. June.

CORY, CHARLES B.
1912. The mammals of Illinois and Wisconsin.
Field Mus. Nat. Hist. Publ. 153, Zool. Series
11, 505 pp., illus.

COTTAM, CLARENCE.
1945. Speed and endurance of the coyote. Journ.
Mammal. 26(1):94. February 27.

COTTAM, CLARENCE, and C. S. WILLIAMS.
1943. Speed of some wild mammals. Journ. Mammal. 24(2):262–63. June 8.

COUCH, LEO K.
1927. Trapping and transplanting live beavers.
U. S. Dept. Agric. Farmers' Bull. no. 1768, pp.
1–18, illus. March.

COUES, ELLIOTT.
1876. Habits of the prairie hare. Bull. Essex Institute 7(1875):73–85.
°1877. Fur-bearing animals: A monograph of
North American Mustelidae. U. S. Geol. Surv.
Terr. Misc. publ. no. 8, pp. 348, pls. 20.

COUES, ELLIOTT, and JOEL ASAPH ALLEN.
°1877. Monographs of North American Rodentia.
Rept. U. S. Geol. Surv. Terr. vol. 11, pp. x +
1091, pls. 5. August.

COURTER, ROBERT D.
1954. Bat rabies. U. S. Dept. of Health, Education,
and Welfare, Public Health Repts. 69(1):9–16.
January.

COVENTRY, A. F.
1932. Notes on the Mearns flying squirrel. Canadian Field-Nat. 46(4):75–78. April.

COWAN, IAN McTAGGART.
1936. Nesting habits of the flying squirrel, Glaucomys sabrinus. Journ. Mammal. 17(1):58–60.
February 14.

COWAN, IAN McTAGGART, and R. H. MACKAY.
1950. Food habits of the marten (Martes ameri-
canas) in the Rocky Mountain region of Canada.
Canadian Field-Nat. 64(3):100–104. June

COX, W. T.
1938. Snowshoe hare useful in thinning forest
stands. Journ. Forestry 36(11):1107–9. November.

CRABB, WILFRED D.
1941 a. Civits are rat killers. Farm Sci. Reporter,
Iowa State College. pp. 12–13. January.
1941 b. Food habits of the prairie spotted skunk
in southeastern Iowa. Journ. Mammal. 22(4):
349–64, illus. November 13.
1944. Growth, development and seasonal weights
of spotted skunks. Journ. Mammal. 25(3):213–
21, illus. September 8.
1948. The ecology and management of the prairie spotted skunk in Iowa. Ecological Monographs 18(2):201–32, illus. April.

CRAM, WILLIAM EVERETT.
1924. The red squirrel. Journ. Mammal. 5(1):37–
41. February 9.

CRAMER, H. T. J.
1948. Harvest of deer in Wisconsin. Trans. 13th

North Amer. Wildlife Conference, pp. 492–508.

CREED, WILLIAM A.
1958. Let's show blackie some respect! Wisc. Conserv. Bull. 23(6):18–20. June.

CRIDDLE, STUART.
1932. The red-backed vole (Clethrionomys gapperi loringi Bailey) in southern Manitoba. Canadian Field-Nat. 46:178–81. November.
1938. A study of the snowshoe rabbit. Canadian Field-Nat. 52(3): 31–40. March.
1939. The thirteen-striped ground squirrel in Manitoba. Canadian Field-Nat. 53(1):1–6. January.
1943. The little northern chipmunk in southern Manitoba. Canadian Field-Nat. 57(4–5):81–86.
1947. A nest of the least weasel. Canadian Field-Nat. 61(2):69. April.
1950. The Peromyscus maniculatus bairdii complex in Manitoba. Canadian Field-Nat. 64(5):169–77. October.

CROSS, E. C.
1940a. Arthritis among wolves. Canadian Field-Nat. 54(1):2–4, January.
1940b. Periodic fluctuations in numbers of the red fox in Ontario. Journ. Mammal. 21(3):294–306. August 13.
1941. Colour phases of the red fox (Vulpes fulva). Journ. Mammal. 22(1):25–39. February 14.

CROUCH, H. B.
1936. The animal parasites of the woodchuck (Marmota monax Linn.) with special reference to protozoa. Iowa State College Journ. Sci. 11: 48–50.

CROUCH, W. E.
1942. Pocket gopher control, U. S. Dept. Interior, Fish and Wildlife Service, Conserv. Bull. 23, pp. ii + 20, illus.

CUNNINGHAM, G. W.
1897. Still-hunting deer in Wisconsin. Forest and Stream 49(21):405–6. November 20.

CUROT, MICHEL.
1911. A Wisconsin fur-traders journal, 1803–1804. Journal Falle Avoine, River Jaune. Edited by Reuben Gold Thwaites. Coll. State Hist. Soc. Wisconsin 20:396–471.

CURTIS, JAMES D., and EDWARD L. KOZICKY.
1944. Observations on the eastern porcupine. Journ. Mammal. 25(2):137–46. May 26.

CURTIS, JOHN T.
1959. The vegetation of Wisconsin. Univ. of Wisconsin Press. 657 pp., illus.

DAHLBERG, BURTON L.
1948. Deer management research report. Wisconsin Wildlife Research, Quarterly Progress Repts. 7(3):1–12. October.
1949. Winter deer-range conditions, 1949. Wisconsin Conserv. Bull. 14(6):21–24. June.
1950. The Wisconsin deer problem and the 1949 hunting season. Wisconsin Conserv. Bull. 15(4): 3–7. April.

DAHLBERG, BURTON L., and R. C. GUETTINGER.
1949. A critical review of Wisconsin's deer problem. Wisconsin Conserv. Bull. 14(11):6–9.

1956. The white-tailed deer in Wisconsin. Wisconsin Conservation Dept., Technical Wildlife Bull. no. 14, pp. 282, illus. July 19.

DAHLBERG, BURTON L., and JAMES B. HALE.
1950. Preliminary report on the 1949 deer season. Wisconsin Conserv. Bull. 15(1):7–8. January.

DALKE, PAUL D.
1942. The cottontail rabbits in Connecticut. Connecticut State Geol. and Nat. Hist. Surv. 65:1–97, illus.

DALKE, PAUL D., and PALMER R. SIME.
1941. Food habits of the eastern and New England cottontails. Journ. Wildlife Management 5(2):216–28. April.

DANE.
1884. White deer. Amer. Field 21(2):37. January 12.

DAVIS, DAVID E.
1949. The weight of wild brown rats at sexual maturity. Journ. Mammal. 30(2):125–30. May 26.

DAVIS, DAVID E., JOHN T. EMLEN, JR., and ALLEN W. STOKES.
1948. Studies on home ranges in the brown rat. Journ. Mammal. 29(3):207–25. August 29.

DAVIS, DAVID E., and JOHN E. WOOD.
1959. Ecology of foxes and rabies control. Publ. Health Repts. 74(2):115–18. February.

DAVIS, H. B.
1907. The raccoon: A study in animal intelligence. Amer. Journ. Psychol. 18(4):447–87. October.

DAVIS, WAYNE H.
1955. Northern extension of range of pocket gopher east of the Mississippi. Journ. Mammal. 36(1): 142–43. February 28.
1959. Taxonomy of the eastern pipistrel. Journ. Mammal. 40(4):521–31. November 20.

DAVIS, WAYNE H. and WILLIAM Z. LIDICKER, JR.
1955. Myotis sodalis in Wisconsin. Journ. Mammal. 36(4):567. December 15.

DAVIS, WILLIAM B.
1938. A heavy concentration of Cryptotis. Journ. Mammal. 19(4):499–500. November 14.

DEAKIN, ALAN, G. W. MUIR, A. G. SMITH, and A. S. MacLELLAN.
1943. Hybridization of domestic cattle and buffalo (Bison americanus). Progress Rept. of Wainwright Experiment, 10 pp., mimeographed.

DEARBORN, NED.
*1932. Foods of some predatory fur-bearing animals in Michigan. Univ. of Michigan School of Forestry and Conserv., Bull. no. 1, pp. 52, pls. 4.

DeBOER, STANLEY G.
1947. The deer damage to forest reproduction survey. Wisconsin Conserv. Bull. 12(10):3–23, map. October.
1953. And the browse came back! Wisconsin Conserv. Bull. 18(1):3–10. January.

DeCOURSEY, G. E., JR.
1957. Identification, ecology and reproduction of Microtus in Ohio. Journ. Mammal. 38(1):44–52.

DEERWESTER, THERMAN.
1941. Cooperative snowshoe hare control project. Wisconsin Conserv. Bull. 6(4):19–20. April.

DePUY, PERCY L.
1957. The coyote and his menu. Nature Mag. 50 (3):132–35, illus. March.

DESMAREST, A. G.
°1820. Mammalogie, ou description des espèces de mammifères. 1re partie, les ordres des Bimanes, Quadrupèdes et des Carnassiers, viii + 1–276 pp., 1820; 2e partie, les ordres des Rongeurs, des Edentés, des Pachydermes, des Ruminans, et des Cétacés, viii, 277–556.

DE VOS, ANTON.
1952. The ecology and management of fisher and marten in Ontario. Ontario Dept. Lands and Forests, Toronto. pp. 90, illus. December.

DE VOS, ANTON, and A. E. ALLEN.
1949. Some notes on moose parasites. Journ. Mammal. 30(4):430–31. November 21.

DE VOS, ANTON, and STANLEY E. GUENTHER.
1952. Preliminary live-trapping studies of marten. Journ. Wildlife Management 16(2):207–14. April.

DE VOS, ANTON, and RANDOLPH L. PETERSON.
1951. A review of the status of woodland caribou (Rangifer caribou) in Ontario. Journ. Mammal. 32(3):329–37, maps. August.

DE VOTO, BERNARD.
1952. The course of empire. Houghton Mifflin, Boston, pp. xxii + 647.

DICE, LEE RAYMOND.
1922. Some factors affecting the distribution of the prairie vole, forest deer mouse, and prairie deer mouse. Ecology 3(1):29–47. January (March).
1927 a. How do squirrels find buried nuts? Journ. Mammal. 8(1):55. February 9.
1927 b. Notes on the young of the red bat (Nycteris borealis borealis). Journ. Mammal. 8(3):243–44. August.
1931. The occurrence of two subspecies of the same species in the same area. Journ. Mammal. 12(3):210–13. August 24.
1932 a. Variation in a geographic race of the deermouse, Peromyscus maniculatus bairdii. Occas. Papers Mus. Zool. Univ. Michigan, no. 239, pp. 1–26. April. 8.
1932 b. The songs of mice. Journ. Mammal. 13(3):187–96. August 9.
1932 c. The prairie deer mouse. Bull. 2, Cranbrook Inst. Sci., pp. 8, pls. 5. November.
1933. Longevity in Peromyscus maniculatus gracilis. Journ. Mammal. 14(2):147–48. May 15.
1936. Age variation in Peromyscus maniculatus gracilis. Journ. Mammal. 17(1):55–57. February 14.
1937 a. Additional data on variation in the prairie deer-mouse, Peromyscus maniculatus bairdii. Occas. Papers Mus. Zool. Univ. Michigan, no. 351, pp. 1–19. April. 2.
1937 b. Variation in the wood-mouse, Peromyscus leucopus noveboracensis, in the northeastern United States. Occas. papers Mus. Zool. Univ.

Michigan, no. 352, pp. 32. April 17.
1937 c. The common names of mammals. Journ. Mammal. 18(2):223–25. May 12.
°1943. The biotic provinces of North America. Univ. of Michigan Press. pp. viii + 78.

DICE, LEE RAYMOND, and ELIZABETH BARTO.
1952. Ability of mice of the genus Peromyscus to hear ultrasonic sounds. Science 116:110–11. August 1.

DICE, LEE RAYMOND, and ROBERT M. BRADLEY.
1942. Growth in the deer-mouse, Peromyscus maniculatus. Journ. Mammal. 23(4):416–27. December 30.

DILGER, WILLIAM C.
1948. Hibernation site of the meadow jumping mouse. Journ. Mammal. 29(3):299–300. August 31.

DIXON, JOSEPH S.
1930. Fur-bearers caught in traps for predatory animals. Journ. Mammal. 11(3):373–77. August 9.

DOLL, ARTHUR D., DONALD S. BALSER, and ROBERT F. WENDT.
1957. Recent records of the Canada lynx in Wisconsin. Journ. Mammal. 38(3):414. August 23.

DONALDSON, HENRY H.
°1924. The rat: data and reference tables. Second edition, revised and enlarged. Memoir of the Wistar Institute of Anatomy and Biology, No. 6, pp. xiv + 469; 212 tables, 72 charts and 13 figures in text.

DORAN, DAVID J.
°1954 a. A catalogue of the Protozoa and helminths of North American rodents. I. Protozoa and Acanthocephala. Amer. Midland Nat. 52 (1):118–28. July.
°1954 b. A catalogue of the Protozoa and helminths of North American rodents. II. Cestoda. Amer. Midland Nat. 52(2):469–80. October.
°1955 a. A catalogue of the Protozoa and helminths of North America rodents. III. Nematoda. Amer. Midland Nat. 53(1):162–75. January.
°1955 b. A catalogue of the Protozoa and helminths of North American rodents. IV. Trematoda. Amer. Midland Nat. 53(2):446–52. April.

DORNEY, ROBERT S.
1954. Ecology of marsh raccoons. Journ. Wildlife Management 18(2): 217–25. April.

DORNEY, ROBERT S., and ALAN J. RUSCH.
1953. Muskrat growth and litter production. Tech. Wildlife Bull no. 8, Wisconsin Conserv. Dept., 32 pp. October.

DORWARD, WILFRID J.
1901. Annals of the Glen. Privately published. Pp. 137, 24 unnumbered pls.

DOUGHERTY, ELLSWORTH C., and E. RAYMOND HALL.
1955. The biological relationships between American weasels (genus Mustela) and nematodes of the genus Skrjabingylus Petrov, 1927 (Nematoda: Metastrongylidae), the causative organisms of certain lesions in weasel skulls. Revista Iberica de Parasitologia. Granada, Spain. Tomo extra-

ordinario, pp. 531-576, illus. March.

DOUGLAS, M. H.
1902. Coon chatter. Recreation 16(3):223-24. March.

DOZIER, HERBERT L.
1953. Muskrat production and management. U. S. Dept. Interior, Fish & Wildlife Service, circ. 18, pp. ii + 42. February.

DUGMORE, A RADCLIFFE.
1913. The romance of the Newfoundland caribou. London and Philadelphia. Pp. viii + 191, pls. 65 (1 colored), 39 figs., 1 folding map.
1914. The romance of the beaver. Heinemann, London, pp. 1-225, illus.

DUNNAM, E. E.
1924. The common garden mole in Iowa. Iowa Agric. Exper. Sta., Circ. no. 88, 44 pp., illus. January.

DYKSTRA, WALTER W., and JOHN C. JONES.
1955. Conquer filth—to assure cleaner food. Wisconsin Alumni Research Foundation, Madison, 8 pp., illus. April.

DYMOND, J. R.
1936. Life history notes and growth studies on the little brown bat, Myotis lucifugus lucifugus. Canadian Field-Nat. 50(7):141-49, illus.

EADIE, W. ROBERT.
1944. Short-tailed shrew and field mouse predation. Journ. Mammal. 25(4):359-64.
1949a. Hibernating meadow jumping mouse. Journ. Mammal. 30(3):307-8. August 30.
1949b. Predation on Sorex by Blarina. Journ. Mammal. 30(3):308-9. August 30.
1954a. Skin gland activity and pelage descriptions in moles. Journ. Mammal. 35(2):186-96.
*1954b. Animal control in field, farm, and forest. Macmillan Co., New York, pp. viii + 257.

EADIE, W. ROBERT, and W. J. HAMILTON, JR.
1956. Notes on reproduction in the star-nosed mole. Journ. Mammal. 37(2):223-31. June 12.

EADS, R. B., and G. C. MENZIES.
1949. A new flea from the pocket gopher. Journ. Parisitology 35(2):171-74. April.

EDWARDS, R. YORKE, and RALPH W. RICHEY.
1957. The migration of a moose herd. Journ. Mammal. 37(4):486-94. January 14.

ELDER, WILLIAM H., and LYLE K. SOWLS.
1942. Body weight and sex ratio of cottontail rabbits. Journ. Wildlife Management 6(3):203-7.

ELLARSON, ROBERT S., and JOSEPH J. HICKEY.
1952. Beaver trapped by tree. Journ. Mammal. 33(4):482-83.

ELLERMAN, J. R.
*1940-49. The families and genera of living rodents. With a list of named forms (1758-1936) by R. W. Hayman and G. W. C. Holt, Publ. by British Museum. Vol. 1 (Rodents other than Muridae), xxvi + 689 pp., 189 figs., June 8, 1940; Vol. 2 (Family Muridae), xii + 690 pp., 50 figs., March 21, 1941; Vol. 3, part 1 (additions and corrections), 210 pp., March, 1949.

ELLERMAN, J. R., and T. C. S. MORRISON-SCOTT.
*1951. Checklist of Palaearctic and Indian mammals 1758 to 1946. Publ. by British Museum. 810 pp., 1 folding map. November 19.

ELLIS, ALBERT G.
1876. Fifty-four years' recollections of man and events in Wisconsin. Report and Collections State Hist. Soc. Wisconsin for the years 1873, 1874, 1875, and 1876; vol. 7, pp. 207-68.

ELSEY, C. A.
1954. A case of cannibalism in Canada lynx (Lynx canadensis). Journ. Mammal. 35(1):129. February 10.

ELTON, C. S.
1953. The use of cats in farm rat control. British Journ. Animal Behavior 1(4):151-55. October.

ELTON, CHARLES, and MARY NICHOLSON.
1942. The ten-year cycle in numbers of the lynx in Canada. Journ. Animal Ecology 11(2):215-44. November.

ELY, ALFRED, and others.
*1939. North American big game. Charles Scribner's Sons. pp. 533, illus.

EMLEN, JOHN T., JR.
1950. How far will a mouse travel to a poisoned bait? Pest Control 18(8):16-20.

EMLEN, JOHN T., JR., RUTH L. HINE, WILLIAM A. FULLER, and PABLO ALFONSO.
1957. Dropping boards for population studies of small mammals. Journ. Wildlife Management 21 (3):300-14. July.

EMLEN, JOHN T., JR., ALLEN W. STOKES, and DAVID E. DAVIS.
1949. Methods for estimating populations of brown rats in urban habitats. Ecology 30(4):430-42. October.

EMLEN, JOHN T., JR., ALLEN W. STOKES, and CHARLES P. WINSOR.
1948. The rate of recovery of decimated populations of brown rats in nature. Ecology 29(2):133-45, illus. April.

ENDERS, ROBERT K.
1952. Reproduction in the mink (Mustela vison). Proc. Amer. Philos. Soc. 96(6):691-755, illus. December.

ENDERS, ROBERT K., and JAMES R. LEEKLEY.
1941. Cyclic changes in the vulva of the marten (Martes americana). Anat. Record 79(1):1-11, pls. 2. January 25.

ENGELS, WILLIAM L.
1932. Mid-winter activity in a striped spermophile. Journ. Mammal. 13(2):164-65. May 11.

EREKSON, ALMA.
1947. Genetic problems in breeding foxes and mink. Nat. Fur News 19(1):11-13, 33-35, illus. February.

ERICKSON, ALBERT W.
1959. The age of self-sufficiency in the black bear. Journ. Wildlife Management 23(4):401-5. October.

ERICKSON, ARNOLD B.
1938a. Parasites of some Minnesota rodents. Journ. Mammal. 19(2):252-53. May.
1938b. Parasites of some Minnesota Cricetidae and Zapodidae, and a host catalogue of hel-

minth parasites to native American mice. Amer. Midland Nat. 20(3):575–89.

1944 a. Helminth infections in relation to population fluctuation in snowshoe hares. Journ. Wildlife Management 8(2):134–53, pl. 7. April.

1944 b. Helminths of Minnesota Canidae in relation to food habits and a host list and key to the species reported from North America. Amer. Midland Nat. 32(3):358–72. September.

1946. Incidence of worm parasites in Minnesota Mustelidae and host lists and keys to North American species. Amer. Midland Nat. 36(2):494–509. September.

1947. Helminth parasites of rabbits of the genus *Sylvilagus*. Journ. Wildlife Management 11(3):255–63. July.

ERRINGTON, PAUL L.

1932. Food habits of southern Wisconsin raptores. Part 1, Owls. Condor 34(4):176–86. July.

1933. Food habits of southern Wisconsin raptores. Part 2, Hawks. Condor 35(1):19–29. January.

1935 a. Wintering of field-living Norway rats in south-central Wisconsin. Ecology 16(1):122–23. January.

1935 b. Food habits of Mid-West foxes. Journ. Mammal. 16(3):192–200. August.

1936. Notes on food habits of southern Wisconsin house cats. Journ. Mammal. 17(1):64–65. February.

1937 a. Food habits of Iowa red foxes during a drought summer. Ecology 18(1):53–61. January.

1937 b. Summer food habits of the badger in northwestern Iowa. Journ. Mammal. 18(2):213–16. May 12.

1937 c. The breeding season of the muskrat in northwest Iowa. Journ. Mammal. 18(3):333–37. August 14.

1937 d. Habit requirements of stream-dwelling muskrats. Trans. Second North Amer. Wildlife Conference, pp. 411–16. December.

1937 e. Drownings as a cause of mortality in muskrats. Journ. Mammal. 18(4):497–500. November 22.

1938. Observations on muskrat damage to corn and other crops in central Iowa. Journ. Agric. Research 57(6):415–22. September 15.

1939 a. Reactions of muskrat populations to drought. Ecology 20(2):168–86. April.

1939 b. Observations on young muskrats in Iowa. Journ. Mammal. 20(4):465–78. November 14.

1943. An analysis of mink predation upon muskrats in north central United States. Iowa Agric. Exper. Sta. Research Bull. 320:799–924, illus. June.

1946. Special report on muskrat disease. Excerpted from the Quarterly Report, Iowa Cooperative Wildlife Research Unit, July-September, 1946, pp. 34–51. Mimeographed.

1951. Concerning fluctuation in populations of the prolific and widely distributed muskrat. Amer. Nat. 85(824):273–92. October.

ERRINGTON, PAUL L., FRANCES HAMMERSTROM, and F. N. HAMMERSTROM, JR.

1940. The great horned owl and its prey in north-

central United States. Iowa Agric. Exper. Station Bull. 277:757–850. September.

ERRINGTON, PAUL L., and THOMAS G. SCOTT.

1945. Reduction in productivity of muskrat pelts on an Iowa marsh through depredations of red foxes. Journ. Agric. Research 71(4):137–48. August 15.

EVANS, E. F.

1941. Eulogy of a pet deer. Wisconsin Conserv. Bull. 6(1):26–28. January.

EVANS, FRANCIS C.

1949. A population study of house mice (*Mus musculus*) following a period of local abundance. Journ. Mammal. 30(4):351–63. November 17.

1951. Notes on a population of striped ground squirrel (*Citellus tridecemlineatus*) in an abandoned field in southeastern Michigan. Journ. Mammal. 32(4):437–49. November 21.

EVERMANN, B. W., and A. W. BUTLER.

1894. Preliminary list of Indiana mammals. Proc. Indiana Acad. Sci., for 1893, pp. 124–39. August.

EVERMANN, B. W., and HOWARD WALTON CLARK.

1911. Notes on the mammals of the Lake Maxinkuckee region. Proc. Washington Acad. Sci. 13(1):1–34. February 15.

FARRIS, EDMOND J., and JOHN Q. GRIFFITH, JR., eds.

*1949. The rat in laboratory investigation. J. B. Lippincott Co., Philadelphia. Second edition. pp. xvi + 542, pls. 2, 177 text figs.

FEENEY, W. S.

1941. Deer management research project. Wisconsin Wildlife Research, Quarterly Progress Reports, 1 (2):1–12. July.

1942. Famine stalks the deer. Wisconsin Conserv. Bull. 7(9):8–10, illus. September.

1943 a. Deer management research project. Wisconsin Wildlife Research, Quarterly Progress Reports, 3(1):1–9. April. Mimeographed.

1943 b. Wisconsin deer today and tomorrow. Wisconsin Conserv. Bull. 8(8):11–19, illus. August.

1944 a. Deer management research. Wisconsin Wildlife Research, Progress Rpts., 3(2):3–9. April.

1944 b. The present status of Wisconsin's deer herd and deer range. Wisconsin Conserv. Bull. 9(6):4–5. June.

1944 c. Deer management research. [A report of progress.] Wisconsin Wildlife Research, Progress Repts., 3(3):1–13. June. Also vol. 4(1):1–18, October, 1944.

FERGUSON, DOROTHY.

1939. State Fur Farm oddities. Wisconsin Conserv. Bull. 4(3):30–32 (half-tones only). March.

FICHTER, EDSON.

1950. Watching coyotes. Journ. Mammal. 31(1):66–73. February 25.

FICHTER, EDSON, and MERLE F. HANSEN.

1947. The Goss lemming mouse, *Synaptomys cooperi gossii* (Coues), in Nebraska. Bull. Univ. Nebraska State Mus. 3(2):1–8. September.

FIELD, WILLIAM H.
1948. Muskrats and muskrat farming. Wisconsin Conserv. Bull. 13(8):9–13. August.

FINLEY, WILLIAM L.
1925. Cougar kills a boy. Journ. Mammal. 6(3): 197–99. August 10.

FINLEY, WILLIAM L., and IRENE FINLEY.
1942. The flying squirrel. Outdoor American 7(9): 4–5. September.

FISHER, A. K.
1885. The star-nosed mole amphibious. **Amer.** Nat. 19(4):895. September.

FISHER, HERBERT J.
1946. Notes on voles in central Missouri. Journ. Mammal. 26(4):435–37. February 12.

FISHER, WILLIAM HUBBELL.
1893. Investigations of the burrows of the American marmot (*Arctomys monax*). Journ. Cincinnati Soc. Nat. Hist. 16:105–23, pls. 6–10. October.

FITCH, HENRY S., and LEWIS L. SANDIDGE.
1957. Aspects of reproduction and development in the prairie vole (*Microtus ochrogaster*). Univ. Kansas Publs., Mus. Nat. Hist. 10(4):129–61, illus. December 19.
1958. Home ranges, territories, and seasonal movements of vertebrates on the Natural History Reservation. Univ. Kansas Publs., Mus. Nat. Hist. 11(5):63–326, illus. December 12.

FITCH, HENRY S., and LEWIS L. SANDIDGE.
1953. Ecology of the opossum on a natural area in northeastern Kansas. Univ. Kansas Publ., Mus. Nat. Hist. 7(2):305–38, illus. August 24.

FLAKAS, KENNETH G.
1951. Parasites of game. Wisconsin Conserv. Bull. 16(8):11–12. August.

FLAWS, THOMAS.
1939. Amberg note. Wisconsin Conserv. Bull. 4(3):33. March (Bobcat).

FLOWER, WILLIAM HENRY, and RICHARD LYDEKKER.
°1891. An introduction to the study of mammals living and extinct. London. pp. xvi + 754, illus.

FONDA, JOHN H.
1868. Early reminiscences of Wisconsin. Report and Collections of the State Historical Soc. of Wisconsin for the year 1868, vol. 5, pp. 205–84. (First published in Prairie du Chien Courier [newspaper], Spring, 1858).

FOSTER, C. ARTHUR.
1947. On tail color in Napaeozapus. Journ. Mammal. 28(1):62. February 17.

FOSTER, MARK A.
1934. The reproductive cycle in the female ground squirrel, Citellus tridecemlineatus (Mitchill). Amer. Journ. Anat. 54(3):487–511, illus. May 15.

FOX, CHARLES PHILIP.
1955. Hitch-hiking babies. Wisconsin Conserv. Bull. 20(3):27–31, illus. March. (Opossum.)

FOX, IRVING.
°1940. Fleas of eastern United States. Iowa State College Press. 191 pp., illus.

FREEMAN, CLIFF, ED MANTHEI, and ED SEALANDER.
1959. Black bear blitz. Wisconsin Conserv. Bull. 24(7):12–14, illus. July.

FRILEY, CHARLES E., JR.
1949 a. Age determination, by use of the baculum, in the river otter, *Lutra c. canadensis* Schreber. Journ. Mammal. 30(2):102–10. May 26.
1949 b. Use of the baculum in age determination of Michigan beaver. Journ. Mammal. 30(3):261–67. August 20.

FRYXELL, F. M.
1926. Squirrels migrate from Wisconsin to Iowa. Journ. Mammal. 7(1):60. February 15.

G., F.
1884. [Note on deer and wolves at Westboro, Wisconsin.] Amer. Field 21(5):110. February 2.

G., F. E.
1895. A curiously marked deer. Forest and Stream 45(21):445. November 23.

GABEL, J. RUSSEL.
1954. The morphology and taxonomy of the intestinal Protozoa of the American woodchuck, Marmota monax Linnaeus. Journ. Exper. Zool. 94(3):473–540, pls. 4. May.

GALE, GEORGE.
1867. The Upper Mississippi Valley: or, Historical sketches of the mound-builders, the Indian tribes, and the progress of civilization in the North-West; From A. D. 1600 to the present time. Galesville, Wis. 460 pp., illus.

GARDINER, A. H.
1920. A specific whitetail. Wisconsin Conservationist 1(6):9. January.

GARLOUGH, F. E.
1945. Capturing foxes. Fish and Wildlife Service, U. S. Dept. Interior, Circ. no. 8, 11 pp., illus.

GARLOUGH, F. E., and DONALD A. SPENCER.
1944. Control of destructive mice. U. S. Dept. Interior, Fish and Wildlife Service, Conserv. Bull. no. 36, pp. 37, illus.

GARLOUGH, F. E., J. F. WELCH, and H. J. SPENCER.
1942. Rabbits in relation to crops. U. S. Dept. Interior, Fish and Wildlife Service, Conserv. Bull. 11, pp. 20, illus.

GARRETSON, MARTIN S.
°1938. The American Bison. The story of its extermination as a wild species and its restoration under federal protection. Publ. by New York Zool. Soc. 254 pp., 47 pls.

GATES, WILLIAM H.
1938. Raising the young of red bats on an artificial diet. Journ. Mammal. 19(4):461–64. November 14.

GAUGHRAN, GEORGE R. L.
1954. A comparative study of the osteology and myology of the cranial and cervical regions of the shrew, *Blarina brevicauda*, and the mole, *Scalopus aquaticus*. Misc. Publ. Mus. Zool., Univ. Michigan, no. 80, pp. 82, pls. 23. February 26.

GEOFFROY-SAINT-HILARE, E.
1803. Catalogue des mammifères du Museum National d'Histoire Naturelle. Paris. 272 pp.

450 **BIBLIOGRAPHY**

GIANINI, CHARLES A.
 1925. Tree climbing and insect eating wood-chucks. Journ. Mammal. 6(4):281–82. November 14.
 1927. An unusual habit of the mink. Journ. Mammal. 8(3):244. August 9.
GIDLEY, JAMES W.
 1912. The lagomorphs an independent order. Science, n.s., 36(922):285–86. August 30.
GIER, H. T.
 1948. Rabies in the wild. Journ. Wildlife Management 12(2):142–53. April.
GILE, P. L., and J. O. CARRERO.
 1918. The bat guanos of Porto Rico and their fertilizing value. Porto Rico Agric. Exper. Sta. Bull. no. 25, pp. 1–66. July 8.
GILES, LEROY W.
 1940. Food habits of the raccoon in eastern Iowa. Journ. Wildlife Management 4(4):375–82. October.
GILMAN, H.
 1873. The caribou on Lake Superior. Amer. Nat. 7:751.
 1876. Sensitiveness to sound in the shrew. Amer. Nat. 10:430–31. July.
GOBLE, FRANS C.
 1942. Skrjabingylus chitwoodorum from the frontal sinuses of Mephitis nigra in New York. Journ. Mammal. 23(1):96–97. February 14.
GOEHRING, HARRY H.
 1955. Observations on hoary bats in a storm. Journ. Mammal. 36(1):130. February 28.
GOIN, OLIVE B.
 1943. A study of individual variation in Microtus pennsylvanicus pennsylvanicus. Journ. Mammal. 24(2):212–23. June 8.
GOLDMAN, EDWARD A.
 1930. The coyote—archpredator. Journ. Mammal. 11(3):325–34. August 9.
 1937. The wolves of North America. Journ. Mammal. 18(1):37–45. February 11.
 1950. Raccoons of North and Middle America. North Amer. Fauna 60, 153 pp., illus. November 7.
GOOD, NEWELL E., and EMIL KOTCHER.
 1949. Louisville, Kentucky, Publ. Health Reports 64(8):229–37. February 25.
GOODPASTER, WOODROW, and DONALD F. HOFFMEISTER.
 1950. Bats as prey for mink in Kentucky cave. Journ. Mammal. 31(4): 457. November 21.
GORDON, DAVID C.
 1954. Melanism in the varying hare, Lepus americanus virginianus. Journ. Mammal. 35(1):122. February 1.
GORHAM, J. R., and H. J. GRIFFITHS.
 1952. Diseases and parasites of minks. U. S. Dept. Agric., Farmers' Bull. no. 2050, 41 pp., illus. November.
GOSLIN, ROBERT M.
 1959. Melanistic ground squirrels from Ohio. Journ. Mammal. 40(1):145. February.

GOTTSCHANG, JACK I.
 1957. Juvenile molt in Peromyscus leucopus noveboracensis. Journ. Mammal. 37(4):516–20. January 14.
GRANGE, WALLACE B.
 1932 a. Observations on the snowshoe hare, Lepus americanus phaeonotus Allen. Journ. Mammal. 13(1):1–19, pls. 1–2. February 9.
 1932 b. The pelages and color changes of the snowshoe hare, Lepus americanus phaeonotus Allen. Journ. Mammal. 13 (20):99–116, pls. 7–8. May 11.
 1947. Practical beaver and muskrat farming. Sandhill Game Farm, Inc., Babcock, Wisconsin, 52 pp., illus.
 °1949. The way to game abundance. Charles Scribner's Sons. pp. 365, illus.
 1953. Those of the forest. Flambeau Publishing Co., Babcock, Wisconsin. pp. 314, illus.
GRANT, MADISON.
 1903. The caribou. Seventh Annual Rept. New York Zool. Soc. (1902), pp. 175–96, 32 pls., map.
GRAVES, HENRY S., and E. W. NELSON.
 1919. Our national elk herds: a program for conserving the elk on national forests about the Yellowstone National Park. U. S. Dept. Agric. Circ. 51, 34 pp., illus.
GREELEY, FREDERICK, and JAMES R. BEER.
 1949. The pipistrel (Pipistellus subflavus) in northern Wisconsin. Journ. Mammal. 30(2):198. May 26.
GREEN, DORR D.
 1947. Albino coyotes are rare. Journ. Mammal. 28(1):63. February.
GREENE, EUNICE CHACE.
 °1935. Anatomy of the rat. Trans. Amer. Philosophical Soc., vol. 28, new series, pp. xi + 370, illus.
GREEN, R. G., and C. A. EVANS.
 1940 a. Studies on a population cycle of snowshoe hares on the Lake Alexander Area. I. Gross annual censuses, 1932–1939. Journ. Wildlife Management 4(2):220–38. April.
 1940 b. Studies on a population cycle of snowshoe hares on the Lake Alexander Area. II. Mortality according to age groups and seasons. Journ. Wildlife Management 4(3):267–78. July.
 1940 c. Studies on a population cycle of snowshoe hares on the Lake Alexander Area. III. Effect of reproduction and mortality of young hares on the cycle. Journ. Wildlife Management 4(4):347–58. October.
GREEN, R. G., and C. L. LARSON.
 1938. A description of shock disease in the snowshoe hare. Amer. Journ. Hygiene 28(2):190–212.
GREEN, R. G., C. L. LARSON, and J. F. BELL.
 1939. Shock disease as the cause of the periodic decimation of the snowshoe hare. Amer. Journ. Hygiene 30 (3, Sect. B):83–102.
GREEN, R. G., C. L. LARSON, and D. W. MATHER.
 1938. The natural occurrence of shock disease in hares. Trans. 3rd North Amer. Wildlife Conference, pp. 877–81. November.

GREGORY, TAPPAN.
1930. Deer at night in the north woods. Chas. Thomas, Springfield, Illinois. pp. 211, pls. 45.
*1939. Eyes in the night. Thos. Y. Crowell Co. pp. 243, illus.
GREGORY, WILLIAM K.
*1910. The orders of mammals. Bull. Amer. Mus. Nat. Hist., vol. 85, pp. 350.
GRIFFIN, DONALD R.
1940 a. Migrations of New England bats. Bull. Mus. Comp. Zool., Harvard College, 86(6):217–46, pls. 1–5. January.
1940 b. Notes on the life histories of New England cave bats. Journ. Mammal. 21(2):181–87. May 16.
1945. Travels of banded cave bats. Journ. Mammal. 26(1):15–23. February 27.
1950. Measurements of the ultrasonic cries of bats. Journ. Acoustical Soc. of America 22(2):247–55. March 28.
1951. Audible and ultrasonic sounds of bats. Experientia 7(12):448–53, illus. Basil, Switzerland. December 15.
1953. Bat sounds under natural conditions, with evidence for echolocation of insect prey. Journ. Exper. Zool. 123(3):435–66, illus. August.
GRIFFIN, DONALD R., and ROBERT GALAMBOS.
1941. The sensory basis of obstacle avoidance by flying bats. Journ. Exper. Zool. 86(3):481–506. April 5.
GRIFFIN, DONALD R., and ALVIN NOVICK.
1955. Acoustic orientation of neotropical bats. Journ. Exper. Zool. 130(2):251–300, illus. November.
GRIGNON, AUGUSTIN.
1857. Seventy-two years recollections of Wisconsin. Third Ann. Rept. & Collections State Hist. Soc. Wisconsin for year 1856. 3:197–295.
GRIMMER, W. F.
1937. The 1937 bear season. Wisconsin Conserv. Bull. 2(10):4–6. October.
1939 a. Roadside zoos. Wisconsin Conserv. Bull. 4(1):45–46. January.
1939 b. Highlights of the 1939 game seasons. Wisconsin Conserv. Bull. 4(10):16–20. October.
GRINNELL, GEORGE BIRD.
1920. As to the wolverine. Journ. Mammal. 1(3):182–84. August 24.
1921. The tree-climbing wolverine. Journ. Mammal. 2(1):36–37. February 10.
1926. Some habits of the wolverine. Journ. Mammal. 7(1):30–34. February 15.
GRINNELL, JOSEPH, JOSEPH S. DIXON, and JEAN M. LINSDALE.
*1937. Fur-bearing mammals of California, their natural history, systematic status, and relations to man. Vol. 1, pp. i–xii, 1–376, col. pls 1–7; vol. 2, pp. i–xiv, 377–777, col. pls. 8–13. Univ. of California Press, Berkeley. August.
GRIZZELL, ROY A., JR.
1955. A study of the southern woodchuck, Marmota monax monax. Amer. Midland Nat. 53(2):257–93. April.

GRÜNEBERG, HANS.
*1943. The genetics of the mouse. University Press, Cambridge, England. pp. xii + 412, pls. 14.
GUERNSEY, ORRIN, and JOSIAH F. WILLARD, eds.
1856. History of Rock County and Transactions of the Rock County Agricultural Society and Mechanics' Institute. Janesville.
GUETTINGER, RALPH C.
1950. Wisconsin deer hunting prospects—1950. Wisconsin Conserv. Bull. 15(10):11–13. October.
1951. Sex and age ratio studies in Wisconsin deer. Presented at 13th Midwest Wildlife Conference, Minneapolis, December 12–14, 1951, 3 pp.
1952. Wisconsin deer seasons—A review. Michigan Conservation 21(6):10–12. December.
GUILDAY, JOHN E.
1948. Little brown bats copulating in winter. Journ. Mammal. 29(4):416–17. December 31.
1950. Winter fetus in the little brown bat, Myotis lucifugus. Journ. Mammal. 31(1):96–97. February 25.
GUILFORD, H. M.
1938. Rabies prevalent. Wisconsin Conserv. Bull. 3(11):30–31. November.
GUNDERSON, HARVEY L., and JAMES R. BEER.
1953. The mammals of Minnesota. Minnesota Mus. Nat. Hist., Univ. of Minnesota, Occas. Papers no. 6, pp. xii + 190, illus. Univ. of Minnesota Press, Minneapolis. October.
GUTHRIE, MARY J.
1933 a. Notes on the seasonal movements and habits of some cave bats. Journ. Mammal. 14(1):1–19. February 14.
1933 b. The reproductive cycles of some cave bats. Journ. Mammal. 14(3):199–216. August 17.
HAAS, GLENN E., and ROBERT J. DICKE.
1959. Fleas collected from cottontail rabbits in Wisconsin. Trans. Wisconsin Acad. Sci., Arts and Letters 48:125–33. December 23.
HABECK, JAMES R.
1959. A vegetational study of the central Wisconsin winter deer range. Journ. Wildlife Management 23(3):273–78. July.
1960. Tree-caching behavior in the gray squirrel. Journ. Mammal. 41(1):125–26. February 20.
HABECK, JAMES R., and J. T. CURTIS.
1959. Forest cover and deer population densities in early northern Wisconsin. Trans. Wisconsin Acad. Sci., Arts and Letters 48:49–56. December 23.
HAHN, WALTER LOUIS.
1908 a. Some habits and sensory adaptations of cave-inhabiting bats. Biol. Bull. 15:135–93.
1908 b. Notes on the mammals and cold-blooded vertebrates of the Indiana University Farm, Mitchell, Indiana. Proc. U. S. Nat. Mus. 35:545–81. December 7.
*HAINES, R. WHEELER.
1958. Arboreal or terrestrial ancestry of placental mammals. Quart. Rev. Biol. 33(1):1–23, illus. March.

HALE, JAMES B.
1949. Aging cottontail rabbits by bone growth. Journ. Wildlife Management 13(2):216–25. April.
1950 a. Nutria versus muskrat. Wisconsin Conserv. Bull. 15(4):15–16. April.
1950 b. Is it coyote or dog? Wisconsin Conserv. Bull. 15(7):16–17. July.
1953. Wildlife research notes. Wisconsin Conserv. Bull. 18(1):16. January.
1954 a. Wildlife research notes. Wisconsin Conserv. Bull. 19(5):28. May.
1954 b. Wildlife research notes. Wisconsin Conserv. Bull. 19(7):18. July.
1954 c. Wildlife research notes. Wisconsin Conserv. Bull. 19(10):30. October.
1954 d. Deer hunting prospects—1954. Wisconsin Conserv. Bull. 19(11):3–6. November.
1954 e. Wildlife research notes. Wisconsin Conserv. Bull. 19(11):18–19. November.
1955. Wildlife research notes. Wisconsin Conserv. Bull. 20(8):18. August.
1956 a. Wildlife research notes. Wisconsin Conserv. Bull. 21(5): 17. May.
1956 b. [Wisconsin jackrabbits.] Wisconsin Conserv. Bull. 21(7):23. July.
1956 c. Deer-hunting diary—1956. Wisconsin Conserv. Bull. 21(10):9–11. October.
HALL, E. RAYMOND.
1927. The muscular anatomy of the American badger. Univ. California Publ. Zool. 30(8):205–19, illus. July 28.
1930. Predatory mammal destruction. Journ. Mammal. 11(3):362–72. August 9.
1936. Mustelid mammals from the Pleistocene of North America with systematic notes on some recent members of the genera Mustela, Taxidea, and Mephitis. Carnegie Inst. Washington publ. no. 473, pp. 41–119, pls. 1–5. November 20.
1942. Gestation period of the fisher with recommendations for the animals protection in California. California Fish and Game 28(3):143–47. July.
1943. Cranial characters of a dog-coyote hybrid. Amer. Midland Nat. 29(2):371–74, illus. March.
1945. A revised classification of the American ermines with description of a new subspecies from the western Great Lakes region. Journ. Mammal. 26(2):175–82. July 19.
1951 a. A synopsis of the North American Lagomorpha. Univ. Kansas Publ., Mus. Nat. Hist. 5(10):119–202, illus. December 15.
1951 b. American weasels. Univ. Kansas Publ., Mus. Nat. Hist. 4:1–466, pls. 1–41. December 27.
°1957. Vernacular names for North American mammals north of Mexico. Univ. Kansas, Mus. Nat. Hist., Miscl. publ. no. 14, pp. 1–16. June 19.
HALL, E. RAYMOND, and E. LENDELL COCKRUM.
1952. Comments on the taxonomy and geographic distribution of North American microtines. Univ. Kansas Publ., Mus. Nat. Hist. 5(23):293–312. November 17.

1953. A synopsis of the North American microtine rodents. Univ. Kansas Publ., Mus. Nat. Hist. 5(27):373–498, illus. January 15.
HALL, E. RAYMOND, and WALTER W. DALQUEST.
1950. A synopsis of the American bats of the genus Pipistrellus. Univ. Kansas Publ., Mus. Nat. Hist. 1(26):591–602. January 20.
HALL, E. RAYMOND, and KEITH R. KELSON.
1952 a. Comments on the taxonomy and geographic distribution of some North American marsupials, insectivores, and carnivores. Univ. Kansas Publ., Mus. Nat. Hist. 5(25):319–41. December 5.
1952 b. Comments on the taxonomy and geographic distribution of some North American rodents. Univ. Kansas Publ., Mus. Nat. Hist. 5(26):343–71. December 15.
°1959. The mammals of North America. 2 vols. pp. xxx + 1083 + 158 index, illus. Ronald Press, New York. March 31.
HALL, E. R. S.
1930. Groundhog active in winter. Canadian Field-Nat. 44:198. November.
HALL, F. S.
1925. Killing of a boy by a mountain lion. Murrelet 6(2):33–37, illus. May.
HALL, MAURICE C.
°1919. The adult taenoid cestodes of dogs and cats, and of related carnivores in North America. Proc. U. S. Nat. Mus. 55:1–94, illus.
HALLOCK, CHARLES.
1884. The big woods of Wisconsin. Amer. Field 22(4):80–81. July 26.
HALLORAN, ARTHUR F.
1957. Live and dressed weights of American bison. Journ. Mammal. 38(1):139. March.
HAMERSTROM, F. N., JR., and JAMES BLAKE.
1939. Winter movements and winter foods of white-tailed deer in central Wisconsin. Journ. Mammal. 20(2):206–15. May 15.
HAMILTON, WILLIAM J., JR.
1928. Weasels eat shrews. Journ. Mammal. 9(3):249–50. August 9.
1929. Breeding habits of the short-tailed shrew, Blarina brevicauda. Journ. Mammal. 10(2):125–34, pls. 10–12. May 9.
1930. The food of the Soricidae. Journ. Mammal. 11(1):26–39. February 11.
1931 a. Habits of the short-tailed shrew, Blarina brevicauda (Say). Ohio Journ. Sci. 31(2):97–106. March.
1931 b. Habits of the star-nosed mole, Condylura cristata. Journ. Mammal. 12(4):345–55, pl. 13. November 11.
1933 a. The insect food of the big brown bat. Journ. Mammal. 14(2):155–56. May 15.
1933 b. The weasels of New York: Their natural history and economic status. Amer. Midland Nat. 14(4):289–344. July.
1934 a. The life history of the rufescent woodchuck Marmota monax rufescens Howell. Annals Carnegie Mus. 23:85–178, pls. 15–20. July 5.
1934 b. Red squirrel killing young cottontail and

young gray squirrel. Journ. Mammal. 15(4): 322. November 15.

1935. Habits of jumping mice. Amer. Midland Nat. 16(2):187–200.

1936 a. The food and breeding habits of the raccoon. Ohio Journ. Sci. 36(3):131–40. May.

1936 b. Seasonal foods of skunks in New York. Journ. Mammal. 17(3): 240–46. August.

1937 a. Activity and home range of the field mouse, *Microtus pennsylvanicus pennsylvanicus* (Ord). Ecology 18(2):255–63. April.

1937 b. The biology of microtine cycles. Journ. Agric. Research 54(10):779–90. May 15.

1937 c. Growth and life span of the field mouse. Amer. Nat. 71(5): 500–507. October.

1938. Life history notes on the northern pine mouse. Journ. Mammal. 19(2):163–70. May 12.

*1939 a. American mammals: Their lives, habits and economic relations. McGraw-Hill Book Co., New York. pp. xii + 434.

1939 b. Observations on the life history of the red squirrel in New York. Amer. Midland Nat. 22 (3):732–45. November.

1940 a. The summer food of minks and raccoons on the Montezuma Marsh, New York. Journ. Wildlife Management 4(1):80–84. January.

1940 b. Breeding habits of the cottontail rabbit in New York State. Journ. Mammal. 21(1):8–11. February 15.

1940 c. The molt of Blarina brevicauda. Journ. Mammal. 21(4):457–58. November 14.

1940 d. The biology of the smoky shrew (*Sorex fumeus fumeus* Miller). Zoologica 25(4):473–92, pls. 1–4. December 31.

1941. The food of small forest mammals in eastern United States. Journ. Mammal. 22(3):250–63. August 14.

1942. The buccal pouch of Peromyscus. Journ. Mammal. 23(4):449–50. December 30.

*1943. The mammals of eastern United States. An account of Recent land mammals occurring east of the Mississippi. Comstock Publishing Co., Ithaca, N.Y. pp. 432; illus.

1944. The biology of the little short-tailed shrew, *Cryptotis parva*. Journ. Mammal. 25(1):1–7. February 18.

1946 a. Reproduction of the field mouse Microtus pennsylvanicus (Ord). Cornell Univ. Agric. Exp. Sta. mem. 237, pp. 1–23, illus. May.

1946 b. A study of the baculum in some North American Microtinae. Journ. Mammal. 27(4): 378–87. November 25.

1949 a. The bacula of some North American bats. Journ. Mammal. 30(2):97–102. May 26.

1949 b. The reproductive rates of some small mammals. Journ. Mammal. 30(3):257–60. August 20.

1950. Exploring the world of "Whistle Pig." Audubon Mag. 52(2):96–101, illus. March.

*1955. Mammalogy in North America. A century of progress in the natural sciences 1853–1953. California Academy of Sciences, San Francisco. pp. 661–68, illus.

HAMILTON, WILLIAM J., JR., and ARTHUR H. COOK.
1955. The biology and management of the fisher in New York. New York Fish and Game Journ. 2(1):13–35, map. January.

HAMILTON, WILLIAM J., JR., and RUSSELL P. HUNTER.
1939. Fall and winter food habits of Vermont bobcats. Journ. Wildlife Management 3(2):99–103. April.

HAMLETT, GEORGE WHITFIELD DELUZ.
1932. Observations on the embryology of the badger. Anat. Record 53(3):283–303, illus. August 25.

1938. The reproductive cycle of the coyote. U. S. Dept. Agric., Technical Bull. No. 616, pp. 12, illus. July.

HANAWALT, F. A.
1922. Habits of the common mole. Ohio Journ. Sci. 22:164–69. April.

HANDLEY, CHARLES O., JR.
1949. Least weasel, prey of barn owl. Journ. Mammal. 30(4):431. November 21.

HANSON, HAROLD C.
1944 a. A new harvest mouse from Wisconsin. Field Mus. Nat. Hist. Publ. 564, Zool. Series 29(14):205–90. October 26.

1944 b. The cottontail and the weather. Trans. Wisconsin Acad. Sci., Arts and Letters 35:91–97. December 10.

1945. Small mammal censuses near Prairie du Sac, Wisconsin. Trans. Wisconsin Acad. Sci., Arts and Letters 36:105–29.

HARPER, FRANCIS.
1927. The ways of chipmunks. Bull. Boston Soc. Nat. Hist. no. 43, pp. 3–9. April.

1930. Notes on certain forms of the house mouse (Mus musculus), particularly those of eastern North America. Journ. Mammal. 11(1):49–52. February 11.

1955. The barren ground caribou of Keewatin. Univ. Kansas Mus. Nat. Hist., Miscl. publ. no. 6, pp. 1–163, illus., map. October 21.

HARRIS, VAN T.
1952. An experimental study of habitat selection by prairie and forest races of the deermouse, Peromyscus maniculatus. Univ. Michigan, Contrib. Laboratory Vertebrate Biol. no. 56, pp. 53, pls. 2. May.

HARTMAN, CARL G.
1920. Studies in the development of the opossum Didelphis virginiana L. V. The phenomena of parturition. Anat. Record 19(5):251–61. October.

1922. A brown mutation of the opossum (*Didelphis virginiana*) with remarks upon the gray and black phases in this species. Journ. Mammal. 3(3):146–49. August 4.

1923. Breeding habits, development, and birth of the opossum. Ann. Repts. Smithsonian Inst., 121, pp. 347–63, 10 pls. June 25.

1952. Possums. Univ. of Texas Press, Austin. pp. 174, illus.

HATFIELD, DONALD M.
1939. Winter food habits of foxes in Minnesota. Journ. Mammal. 20(2):202–6. May 15.

HATT, ROBERT T.
1929. The red squirrel: its life history and habits. Bull. New York State College Forestry, Roosevelt Wild Life Annals 2(1):1–140, illus. July.
1930 a. The biology of the voles of New York. Bull. New York State College of Forestry 3 (2c): 505–623, illus. August.
1930 b. Color variations of Long Island mammals. Journ. Mammal. 11(3):322–23. August.
*1930 c. The relation of mammals to the Harvard Forest. Roosevelt Wildlife Bull. 5(4):625–71.
1931. Habits of a young flying squirrel (Glaucomys volans). Journ. Mammal. 12(3):233–38. August 14.
1938. Feeding habits of the least shrew. Journ. Mammal. 19(2):247–48. May 12.

HAUGEN, ARNOLD O.
1942 a. Home range of the cottontail rabbit. Ecology 23(3): 354–67. July.
1942 b. Life history studies of the cottontail rabbit in southwestern Michigan. Amer. Midland Nat. 28(1):204–44. July.

HAUGEN, ORLAND L.
1954. Longevity of the raccoon in the wild. Journ. Mammal. 35(3):439. August.

HAUSMAN, LEON AUGUSTUS.
*1920. Structural characteristics of the hair of mammals. Amer. Naturalist 54(635):496–523. December.
*1924. Further studies of the relationships of the structural characteristics of mammalian hair. Amer. Naturalist 58:544–57, pl. 1. November.

HAWKINS, ARTHUR S.
1937. Winter feeding at Faville Grove, 1935–1937. Journ. Wildlife Management 1(3–4):62–69.
1940. A wildlife history of Faville Grove, Wisconsin. Trans. Wisconsin Acad. Sciences, Arts and Letters 32:29–65.

HAYNE, DON W.
1950. A further test of cottontail repellents for garden use. Michigan Agric. Exper. Sta. Quart. Bull. 32(3):373–77. February.

HEIN, EDWARD N.
1937. Wisconsin deer. Wisconsin Conserv. Bull. 2(10):3. October.
1942. Wisconsin's caves. Wisconsin Conserv. Bull. 7(4):20–21. April.
1943. The forest balance. Wisconsin Conserv. Bull. 8(9):19–11. September.
1944. Remember Whitey? Wisconsin Conserv. Bull. 9(10):11, illus. October.
1949. The coming catastrophe in the Flagg. Wisconsin Conserv. Bull. 14(6):24–25. June.

HENDERSON, JUNIUS, and ELBERTA L. CRAIG.
*1932. Economic mammalogy. C. C. Thomas, Springfield, Illinois. pp. x + 397.

HENDERSON, WALTER C.
1930. The control of the coyote. Journ. Mammal. 11(3):336–50. August 9.

HENDRICKSON, GEORGE O.
1936. Summer studies on the cottontail rabbit (Sylvilagus floridanus mearnsi Allen). Iowa State College, Journ. Sci. 10(4):367–71. July.

HERMAN, CARLTON M., and JAMES R. REILLY.
1955. Skin tumors on squirrels. Journ. Wildlife Management 19(3):402–3. July.

HERMAN, ELMER F.
1943. A faunal survey of Sheboygan Marsh. Wisconsin Conserv. Bull. 8(10):9–11. October.

HICKIE, PAUL F.
1936. Isle Royal moose studies. Proc. North Amer. Wildlife Conference, February 3–7, 1936, pp. 396–98.
1943. Michigan moose. Michigan Dept. Conservation. pp. 57, illus. August 19.

HICKS, ELLIS A.
1949. Ecological factors affecting the activity of the western fox squirrel, Sciurus niger rufiventer (Geoffroy). Ecological Monographs 19(4): 287–302, illus. October.

HILL, R. G.
*1943. Good eating from woods and fields. Michigan State College Exten. Bull. 252, 24 pp.

HINE, RUTH.
1950. The field mouse: Characteristics and control. Wisconsin Conserv. Bull. 15(11):16–19. November.
1953 a. Dollars and sense for foxes. Wisconsin Conserv. Bull. 18(2):14–19. February.
1953 b. The ecology of small mammal communities in southern Wisconsin. Unpublished Ph.D. thesis on file in the University of Wisconsin Library.
1955. Rabies in Wisconsin. Wisconsin Conserv. Bull. 20(7):25–28. July.
1956. "Is it good to eat?" Wisconsin Conserv. Bull. 21(9):7–9. September.
1957. [Going deer hunting?] Wisconsin Conserv. Bull. 22(11):7. November.

HISAW, FREDERICK LEE.
1923 a. Feeding habits of moles. Journ. Mammal. 4(1):9–20. February 9.
1923 b. Observations on the burrowing habits of moles (Scalopus aquaticus machrinoides). Journ. Mammal. 4(2):79–88. May 9.
1925. The influence of the ovary on the resorption of the pubic bones of the pocket gopher, Geomys bursarius (Shaw). Journ. Exper. Zool. 42(4):411–41, illus. October 5.

HISAW, FREDERICK LEE, and FREDERICK E. EMERY.
1927. Food selection of ground squirrels, Citellus tridecemlineatus. Journ. Mammal. 8(1):41–44. February 9.

HISAW, FREDERICK LEE, and HOWARD K. GLOYD.
1926. The bull snake as a natural enemy of injurious rodents. Journ. Mammal. 7(3):200–205. August 9.

HITCHCOCK, HAROLD B.
1957. The use of bird bands on bats. Journ. Mammal. 38(3):402–405. August 23.

HITCHCOCK, HAROLD B., and KEITH REYNOLDS.
1942. Homing experiments with the little brown

bat, *Myotis lucifugus lucifugus* (Le Conte). Journ. Mammal. 23(3):258–67. August 14.

HOCK, RAYMOND J.
1951. The metabolic rates and body temperatures of bats. Biol. Bull. 101(3):289–99. December.

HOFFMEISTER, DONALD F., and JOHN E. WARNOCK.
1947. A concentration of lemming mice (*Synaptomys cooperi*) in central Illinois. Illinois Acad. Sci. Trans. 40:190–93.
1948. A specimen of the white-tailed jack rabbit, *Lepus townsendii*, from Illinois. Chicago Acad. Sci., Nat. Hist. Miscellanea no. 29, pp. 2. October 15.

HOFFMEISTER, DONALD F., and MAX HENSLEY.
1949. Retention of the "color" pattern in an albino thirteen-lined ground squirrel (*Citellus tridecemlineatus*). Amer. Midland Nat. 42(2):403–5, illus. September.

HOFFMEISTER, DONALD F., and JOHN E. WARNOCK.
1955. The harvest mouse (Reithrodontomys megalotis) in Illinois and its taxonomic status. Illinois Acad. Sci. Transactions 47:161–64. April.

HOLGER, WARREN.
1950. Where are the deer? Wisconsin Conserv. Bull. 15(10):13–15. October.

HOLLISTER, N.
1909 a. Notes on Wisconsin mammals. Bull. Wisconsin Nat. Hist. Soc. 6(3 and 4):137–42. April.
1909 b. The last records of deer in Walworth County, Wisconsin. Bull. Wisconsin Nat. Hist. Soc. 6(3 and 4):143–44. April.
1910. A check-list of Wisconsin mammals. Bull. Wisconsin Nat. Hist. Soc. 8(1):21–31. May 7.
1911 a. The generic name of the muskrat. Proc. Biol. Soc. Washington 24:13–14. January 28.
1911 b. Remarks on the long-tailed shrews of the eastern United States, with description of a new species. Proc. U. S. National Mus. 40:377–81. April 17.
1913. A synopsis of the American minks. Proc. U. S. National Museum 44:471–80. April. 18.
1915. A new name for the white-tailed jack rabbit. Proc. Biol. Soc. Washington 28:70. March 12.
1916 a. The generic names *Epimys* and *Rattus*. Proc. Biol. Soc. Washington 29:126. June 6.
1916 b. The type species of *Rattus*. Proc. Biol. Soc. Washington 29:206–7. September 22.
1923. Report on the National Zoological Park. Smithsonian Inst. Annual Report for 1922:88–103. Washington, D. C.

HOLMES, MARY E.
1888. The red fox at school. Amer. Nat. 22(255):267–70. March.

HOLT, ERNEST G.
1929. Midwinter record of the woodchuck in western Pennsylvania. Journ. Mammal. 10(1):80. February 11.

HOOPER, EMMET T.
1942. Geographic variation in the eastern chipmunk, *Tamias striatus*, in Michigan. Occas. Papers Mus. Zool., Univ. Michigan, no. 461, 5 pp. September 15.
1952. A systematic review of the harvest mice (genus *Reithrodontomys*) of Latin America. Miscl. Publ. Mus. Zool., Univ. Michigan, no. 77, pp. 255, pls. 9. January 16.
1958. The male phallus in mice of the genus *Peromyscus*. Misc. Publ., Mus. Zool. University of Michigan, no. 105, 24 pp., 14 pls. December 29.

HOOPER, EMMET T., and BURTON T. OSTENSON.
1949. Age groups in Michigan otter. Occas. Papers. Mus. Zool., Univ. Michigan, no. 518, 22 pp. March 23.

HOOVER, ROBERT T.
1954. Seven fetuses in western fox squirrel (*Sciurus niger rufiventer*). Journ. Mammal. 35(3):447–48. August 20.

HOPKINS, RALPH C.
1939 a. Wisconsin's large deer of 1938. Wisconsin Conserv. Bull. 4(10):49–51. October.
1939 b. Measuring deer antlers. Wisconsin Conserv. Bull. 4(12):36–40. December.

HORNADAY, WILLIAM T.
1889. The extermination of the American bison. Rept. U. S. Nat. Mus. 1886–1887, pp. 369–548, pls. 1–21.
1902. Spare the grey squirrel. Recreation 16(3):205. March.

HORNER, B. ELIZABETH.
1947. Paternal care of young mice of the genus Peromyscus. Journ. Mammal. 28(1):31–36. February 17.
1950. Trichobenzoars (hair balls) in *Peromyscus*. Journ. Mammal. 31(1):94–95. February 25.
1954. Arboreal adaptations of Peromyscus, with special reference to use of the tail. Contribs. Lab. Vertebrate Zool., Univ. Michigan, no. 61, pp. 84, pls. 7. February.

HORR, V. L.
1909. Notes on mink trapping. Wild Life 2(3):14–15. November.

HOSLEY, N. W.
1949. The moose and its ecology. U. S. Dept. Interior, Fish and Wildlife Service, Wildlife Leaflet 312, pp. 51, illus. October. (Processed.)

HOUGH, E.
1895. How fur is caught. Forest and Stream 45(22):464–65; (23):486–87; (24):509–10; (25):532–33; (26):558–59. December.
1897. Singing mice. Forest and Stream 48:446. June 5.

HOVIND, JAMES.
1948. Beaver trouble. Wisconsin Conserv. Bull. 13(7):15–18, illus. July.

HOVIND, RALPH B.
1953 a. Deer drives in Vilas County reveal substantial population of whitetails. Wisconsin Conservationist 2(4):4. January.
1953 b. Wildlife for the summer tourist. Wisconsin Conserv. Bull. 18(6):3–7. June.
1957. "Tourist deer." Wisconsin Conserv. Bull. 22(8):3–5, illus. August.

HOWARD, WALTER E.
1949 a. Dispersal, amount of inbreeding, and longevity in a local population of prairie deermice

on the George Reserve, southern Michigan. Contrib. Laboratory Vertebrate Biol., Univ. Michigan, no. 43, pp. 1–50, pls. 1–2. April.

1949 b. A means to distinguish skulls of coyotes and domestic dogs. Journ. Mammal. 30(2): 169–71. May 26.

HOWELL, A. BRAZIER.

1927. Revision of the American lemming mice (Genus Synaptomys). North American Fauna no. 50, 38 pp., 11 figs., 2 pls. August 5.

1930. At the cross-roads. Journ. Mammal. 11(3): 377–89. August 9.

HOWELL, ARTHUR H.

1901. Revision of the skunks of the genus Chincha. North Amer. Fauna no. 20, 62 pp., illus. December 28.

1906. Revision of the skunks of the genus Spilogale. North Amer. Fauna no. 26, 54 pp., 10 pls. November 24.

1908. Notes on diurnal migrations of bats. Proc. Biol. Soc. Washington 21:35–38.

1914. Revision of the American harvest mice. North Amer. Fauna no. 36, pp. 97, pls. 7. June 5.

1915. Revision of the American marmots. North Amer. Fauna no. 37, pp. 80, pls. 15. April. 7.

1918. Revision of the American flying squirrels. North Amer. Fauna no. 44, 64 pp., 7 pls. June 13.

1920. The Florida spotted skunk as an acrobat. Journ. Mammal. 1(2):88. March 2.

1925. Preliminary descriptions of five new chipmunks from North America. Journ. Mammal. 6(1):51–54. February 9.

1929. Revision of the American chipmunks (Genera Tamias and Eutamias). North Amer. Fauna no. 52, 157 pp., illus. November 20.

1938. Revision of the North American ground squirrels, with a classification of the North American Sciuridae. North Amer. Fauna no. 56, 256 pp., 32 pls. (11 color), 20 figs. (maps).

1943. A new red squirrel from Minnesota. Proc. Biol. Soc. Washington 56:67–68. June 16.

HOY, P. R.

1853. The striped ground squirrel, or prairie ground squirrel, of Wisconsin. Agric. Rept. for 1852, U. S. Patent Office Rept., part 2, pp. 68–70.

1874. Some of the peculiarities of the fauna near Racine. Trans. Wisconsin Acad. Sciences, Arts and Letters 2(1873–74):120–22.

1875. On hibernation as exhibited in the striped gopher. Proc. Amer. Asso. Adv. Sci. 24:148–50.

1882 a. The larger wild animals that have become extinct in Wisconsin. Trans. Wisconsin Acad. Sci., Arts and Letters 5(1877–81):255–57.

1882 b. Fauna of Wisconsin. In History of Walworth County, Wisc. Western Historical Co., Chicago. pp. 134–39.

HUBBARD, BEN W.

1940. Wisconsin white-tailed deer. Wisconsin Conserv. Bull. 5(10):10–11. October.

HUEBNER, ROBERT J., WILLIAM L. JELLISON, and CHARLES ARMSTRONG.

1947. Rickettsialpox—a newly recognized rickettsial disease. V. Recovery of Rickettsia akari

from a house mouse (Mus musculus). U. S. Public Health Repts. 62(22):777–80. May 30.

HUISH, MELVIN T., and DONALD F. HOFFMEISTER.

1947. The short-tailed shrew (Blarina) as a source of food for the green sunfish. Copeia, no. 3, p. 198.

HULL, MERLIN.

1917. Bounty laws. Information for the town chairman and descriptions of wolves and foxes. Secretary of State, Madison, Wisconsin. pp. 8.

HUNGERFORD, K. E., and N. G. WILDER.

1941. Observations on the homing of the gray squirrel (Sciurus carolinensis). Journ. Wildlife Management 5(4):458–60. October.

HUNT, E. S.

1909. Northern Wisconsin deer hunting. Wild Life 1(2):13–17, illus. February.

HUNT, GEORGE S.

1950. Aquatic activity of a snowshoe hare. Journ. Mammal. 31(2):193–94. May 30.

HYDE, J. B.

1957. A comparative study of certain tergeminal components in two soricid shrews, Blarina brevicauda and Sorex cinereus. Journ. Comp. Neurology 107(3):339–52. June.

INGRAM, WILLIAM MARCUS.

1942. Snail associates of Blarina brevicauda talpoides (Say). Journ. Mammal. 23(3):255–58. August 13.

IVOR, H. ROY.

1934. Notes on the rearing of captive young meadow jumping mice. Canadian Field-Nat. 47(1): 8–10.

IWEN, FRANK A.

1958 a. Another Wisconsin record of the prairie spotted skunk. Journ. Mammal. 39(2):296. May.

1958 b. Hoary bat the victim of a barbed wire fence. Journ. Mammal. 39(3):438. August 24.

JACKLEY, A. M.

1944. Badger—rattlesnake enemy, says expert. South Dakota Conserv. Digest 11(1):2–3, 16, illus. January.

JACKSON, HARTLEY H. T.

1902. A ramble in the marsh. Amer. Ornithology 2(2):69–71, illus. March.

1903 a. The meadow voles of southern Wisconsin. Milton College Review 4:6–10. February 14.

1903 b. About that skunk editorial. Oologist 22 (12):188–89 . December.

1908. A preliminary list of Wisconsin mammals. Bull. Wisconsin Nat. Hist. Soc. 6(1–2):13–34, pl. 3. April.

1910. The distribution of certain Wisconsin mammals. Bull. Wisconsin Nat. Hist. Soc. 8(2):86–90. October 6.

1914. The land vertebrates of Ridgeway Bog, Wisconsin: Their ecological succession and source of ingression. Bull. Wisconsin Nat. Hist. Soc. 12 (1–2):4–54, illus. October 31.

1915. A review of the American moles. North American Fauna no. 38, pp. 100, pls. 6. September 30.

1919 a. The Wisconsin Napaeozapus. Proc. Biol.

Soc. Washington 32:9–10. February 14.

1919 b. The Georgian bat, Pipistrellus subflavus, in Wisconsin. Journ. Mammal. 1(1):38. November 28.

1920 a. An apparent effect of winter inactivity upon distribution of mammals. Journ. Mammal. 1(2):58–64, map. March 2.

1920 b. The white-tailed jack rabbit, Lepus townsendii campanius, introduced into Wisconsin. Journ. Mammal. 1(3):186. August 24.

1921 a. A recent migration of the gray squirrel in Wisconsin. Journ. Mammal. 2(2):113–14. May 2.

1921 b. An inquisitive porcupine. Journ. Mammal. 2(4):238. November 29.

1922 a. Wolverine in Itasca County, Minnesota. Journ. Mammal. 3(1):53. February 8.

1922 b. Some habits of the prairie mole, Scalopus aquaticus machrinus. Journ. Mammal. 3(2):115. May 9.

1922 c. A coyote in Maryland. Journ. Mammal. 3(3):186–87. August 4.

1924 a. Against destruction of predatory animals. Parks and Recreation 7(6):658. July.

1924 b. Resolution on destruction of vermin and predatory animals. Science 59:548. June 20.

1925 a. The Sorex arcticus and Sorex arcticus cinereus of Kerr. Journ. Mammal. 6(1):55–56. February 9.

1925 b. Two new pigmy shrews of the genus Microsorex. Proc. Biol. Soc. Washington 38:125–26. November 13.

1925 c. Preliminary descriptions of seven shrews of the genus Sorex. Proc. Biol. Soc. Washington 38:127–30. November 13.

1926 a. An unrecognized water shrew from Wisconsin. Journ. Mammal. 7(1):57–58. February 15.

°1926 b. The care of museum specimens of recent mammals. Journ. Mammal. 7(2):113–18, pl. 13. May.

1926 c. Catching bats with gill-nets. Journ. Mammal. 7(3):231. August 9.

1928. A taxonomic review of the American long-tailed shrews (Genera Sorex and Microsorex). North Amer. Fauna no. 51, pp. 238, figs. 24, pls. 13. July 24.

1930 a. [Coyote in Wisconsin before 1875.] Journ. Mammal. 11(3):335. August 9.

1930 b. Fur farming and game raising old ideas. Journ. Mammal. 11(3):432–33. August 9.

1931 a. The muskrat, a trapper's treasure trove. Home Geographic Monthly 1(2):44–48, illus. February.

1931 b. The otter, playfellow of the wild. Home Geographic Monthly 1(6):44–48, illus. December.

1932 a. The red squirrel, chatterer of the spruces. Home Geographic Monthly 2(3):19–24, illus. September.

1932 b. The striped ground squirrel, chirper of the prairies. Home Geographic Monthly 2(5):19–24, illus. November.

1937a. Waking from winter sleep. [Radio talk,

Tuesday, Feb. 23, 1937, under the auspices of Science Service, over Columbia Broadcasting System.] Science Service, Washington, D. C. 5 pp. (Mimeographed). February 23.

1937 b. Animals soon waking from winter sleep: Science still puzzled by hibernation. Science Service Press Release, 2 pp. (Mimeographed.) February 23.

1937 c. Waking from a winter's sleep. Science Digest 1(3):83–85. May.

1938. Distribution of Wisconsin deer. Wisconsin Conserv. Bull. 3(6): 28. June. (Reprint.)

1939 a. Big-game inventory of the United States, 1937. U. S. Dept. Agric., Bur. Biological Survey, Leaflet BS-122, pp. 13 (mimeographed). January.

1939 b. A record black bear. Journ. Mammal. 20 (2):252–53. May 14.

1939 c. Big-game inventory of the United States, 1938. U. S. Dept. Interior, Bur. Biological Survey, Wildlife Leaflet BS-142, pp. 11 (mimeographed). August.

1939 d. Status of the American bison in the United States and Alaska, 1939. U. S. Dept. Interior, Bur. Biological Survey, Wildlife Leaflet BS-148, pp. 10 (mimeographed). December.

1940. Big-game inventory of the United States, 1939. U. S. Dept. Interior, Fish and Wildlife Service, Wildlife Leaflet BS-175, pp. 11 (mimeographed). November.

1941 a. Transplanted elk wanders. Journ. Mammal. 22(4):448. November 14.

1941 b. A new pine mouse, genus Pitymys, from Wisconsin. Proc. Biol. Soc. Washington 54:201–2. December 8.

1942. Big-game inventory of the United States, 1940. U. S. Dept. Interior, Fish and Wildlife Service, Wildlife Leaflet 207, pp. 10 (mimeographed). January.

°1944. Conserving endangered wildlife species. Trans. Wisconsin Acad. Sci., Arts and Letters 35:61–89, pls. 2. December 11.

°1945. Big-game resources of the United States, 1937–1942. U. S. Dept. of the Interior, Fish and Wildlife Service, Research Rept. 8, pp. 56, illus. January 25.

1946 a. Big-game inventory of the United States, 1943. Wildlife Service Leaflet 283, pp. 11 (mimeographed). February.

1946 b. Raising deer in captivity. U. S. Dept. Interior Fish and Wildlife Service, Wildlife Leaflet 289, pp. 9 (mimeographed). June.

°1947 a. Conserving endangered wildlife species. Smithsonian Rept. for 1945, pp. 247–72, 4 figs., 13 pls. January.

1947 b. Attitude in conservation. In Silent Wings, Wisconsin Society for Ornithology, pp. 19–24. May 10.

1949. Two new coyotes from the United States. Proc. Biol. Soc. Washington 62:31–32. March 17.

1953. Our flying mammals of the night. Audubon Mag. 55(2):74–77, illus. April.

1954. Wolverine (Gulo luscus) specimens from

Wisconsin. Journ. Mammal. 35(2):254. May 26.

1955. The Wisconsin puma. Proc. Biol Soc. Washington 68:149–50. October 31.

1956. Review of "A century of Wisconsin deer," by Otto S. Bersing, and "The white-tailed deer in Wisconsin," by Burton L. Dahlberg and Richard C. Guettinger, Wisconsin Acad. Review 3(4):183–84. October.

1957 a. An unrecognized pocket gopher from Wisconsin. Proc. Biol. Soc. Washington 70:33–34. June 28.

1957 b. The status of *Eutamias minimus jacksoni.* Journ. Mammal. 38(4):518–19. November 20.

1959. Wild mammal chase. Wisconsin Acad. Rev. 6(1):6–7, illus. Winter.

JACKSON, HARTLEY H. T., and CHARLES H. ROUSE.

1942. Care of buffaloes. U. S. Dept. Interior, Fish & Wildlife Service, Wildlife Leaflet 212, 8 pp. (mimeographed). February.

JACKSON, WILLIAM B.

1952. Populations of the wood mouse (*Peromyscus leucopus*) subjected to the applications of DDT and parathion. Ecological Monographs 22(4):259–81. October.

JACOBS, LOU.

1953. White muskrat. Wisconsin Conserv. Bull. 18 (10):28. October.

"JACOBSTAFF."

1894. Ways of the fisher. Forest and Stream 43:159. August 25.

JAEGER, ELLSWORTH.

°1948. Tracks and trail craft. Macmillan Co., New York. pp. 381, illus.

JAHN, LAURENCE R.

1959. Highway mortality as an index of deer population change. Journ. Wildlife Management 23(2):187–97. April.

JAMES, C. S.

1941. Fisher. Questions and answers. Amer. Fur Breeder 13(8):14–15. February.

JAMESON, E. W., JR.

1947. Natural history of the prairie vole (Mammalian genus Microtus). Univ. Kansas publs., Mus. Nat. Hist. 1(7):125–51. October.

1948 Myobiid mites (Acarina: Myobiidae) from *Condylura cristata* Linnaeus) and *Neurotrichus gibbsii* (Baird). (Mammalia: Talpidae). Journ. Parasitology 35(3):423–30. August.

1950 a. *Eubrachylaelaps debilis,* a new laelaptid mite (Acarina: Laelaptidae) parasitic on the deer mouse, *Peromyscus maniculatus* (Mammalia: Cricetidae). Journ. Parasitology. 36(1):62–64. February.

1950 b. The external parasites of the short-tailed shrew *Blarina brevicauda* Say. Journ. Mammal. 31(2):138–45. May 30.

JANES, HENRY F.

1872. Early reminiscences of Janesville. Report & Collections of the State Historical Soc. of Wisconsin for the years 1869, 1870, 1871, and 1872, vol. 6, pp. 426-35.

JARDINE, JAMES T.

1909. Coyote-proof pasture experiment, 1908. U. S. Dept. Agric., Forest Service circ. 160, pp. 40, illus. September 30.

JELLISON, W. L.

1949. Rat-bite fever in Montana. Public Health Repts. 64(52):1661–65. December 30.

JELLISON, W. L., GLEN M. KOHLS, W. J. BUTLER, and JAMES A. WEAVER.

1942. Epizootic tularemia in the beaver, *Castor canadensis,* and the contamination of stream water with *Pasteurella tularensis.* Amer. Journ. Hygiene 36(2):168–82. September.

JELLISON, W. L., and R. R. PARKER.

1945. Rodents, rabbits and tularemia in North America: Some zoological and epidemiological considerations. Amer. Journ. Tropical Medicine 24(4):349–62. July.

JOHNSON, ARTHUR M.

1922. An observation on the carnivorous propensities of the gray gopher. Journ. Mammal. 3(3):187. August 4.

JOHNSON, CHARLES EUGENE.

1921 a. A note on the habits of the timber wolf. Journ. Mammal. 2(1):11–15. February 10.

1921 b. Beaver "forms." Journ. Mammal. 2(3):171–72. August 19.

1921 c. The "hand-stand" habit of the spotted skunk. Journ. Mammal. 2(2):87–89. May 2.

1922. An investigation of the beaver in Herkimer and Hamilton counties of the Adirondacks. Roosevelt Wild Life Bull. 1(2):117–86, illus. August.

1923. A recent report of the wolverine in Minnesota. Journ. Mammal. 4(1):54–55. February 9.

1925 a. The muskrat in New York: Its natural history and economics. Roosevelt Wild Life Bull. 3(2):205–320, illus., 2 folding maps. March.

1925 b. The jack and snowshoe rabbits as swimmers. Journ. Mammal. 6(4):245–49. November 14.

1926. Notes on a pocket gopher in captivity. Journ. Mammal. 7(1):35–37. February 15.

1927. The beaver in the Adirondacks: Its economics and natural history. Roosevelt Wild Life Bull. 4(4):501–641, illus. July.

1932. Notes on a family of red bats in captivity. Journ. Mammal. 13(2)132–35. May 11.

1933. What are proper hibernating conditions for bats? Journ. Mammal. 14(4):366–68. November 13.

JOHNSON, DONALD E.

1951. Biology of the elk calf, *Cervus canadensis nelsoni.* Journ. Wildlife Management 15(4):396–410, pls. 12–13. October.

JOHNSON, GEORGE EDWIN.

1917. The habits of the thirteen-lined ground squirrel. Quart. Journ. Univ. North Dakota 7 (3):261–71. April.

1928. Hibernation of the thirteen-lined ground-squirrel, Citellus tridecemlineatus (Mitchell).

I. A comparison of the normal and hibernating states. Journ. Exper. Zool. 59(1):15–30. January.

1929 a. Hibernation of the thirteen-lined ground squirrel, Citellus tridecemlineatus (Mitchell). II. The general process of waking from hibernation. Amer. Nat. 63(685):171–80. March.

1929 b. Hibernation of the thirteen-lined ground squirrel, Citellus tridecemlineatus (Mitchell). III. The rise in respiration, heart beat and temperature in waking from hibernation. Biol. Bull. 57(2):107–29. August.

1930. Hibernation of the thirteen-lined ground squirrel, Citellus tridecemlineatus (Mitchell). V. Food, light, confined air, precooling, castration and fatness in relation to production of hibernation. Biol. Bull. 59(1):114–27. August.

1931 a. Early life of the thirteen-lined ground squirrel. Trans. Kansas Acad. Sci. 34:282–90.

°1931 b. Hibernation in mammals. Quart. Review Biology 6(4):439–61.

JOHNSON, GEORGE EDWIN, MARK A. FOSTER, and RUSSELL M. COCA.
1933. The sexual cycle of the thirteen-lined ground squirrel in the laboratory. Trans. Kansas Acad. Sci. 36:250–69, illus.

JOHNSON, GEORGE EDWIN, and VIRGINIA BRANDS HANAWALT.
1930. Hibernation of the thirteen-lined ground squirrel, Citellus tridecemlineatus (Mitchell). Amer. Nat. 64(692):272–84. June.

JOHNSON, M. S.
1926. Activity and distribution of certain wild mice in relation to biotic communities. Journ. Mammal. 7(4):245–77. November 23.

JOHNSON, PAUL B.
1933. Accidents to bats. Journ. Mammal. 14(2):156–57. May 15.

JOHNSON, T. N.
1957. The olfactory centers and connections in the cerebral hemisphere of the mole (Scalopus aquaticus machrinus). Journ. Comp. Neurology 107(3):379–426. June.

JONES, JOHN C.
1949. Squirrels can be pests. Pest Control 17(11):8–14, illus. November.

JONES, SARAH V. H.
°1923. Color variations in wild animals. Journ. Mammal. 4(3):172–77. August 10.

JORDAHL, HAROLD C., JR.
1954. Marten are back! Wisconsin Conserv. Bull. 19(2):26–28, illus. February.
1956. Canada lynx. Wisconsin Conserv. Bull. 21(11):22–26, illus. November.

JORDAN, DAVID S.
1902. Others appeal for the grey squirrel. Recreation 16(4):285. April.

JORDAN, JAMES S.
1948. A midsummer study of the southern flying squirrel. Journ. Mammal. 29(1):44–48. February 13.
1956. Notes on a population of eastern flying

squirrel. Journ. Mammal. 37(2):294–95. June 12.

JORGENSEN, ARTHUR W.
1951. Wisconsin wildlife. Wisconsin Conserv. Dept., publ. 613-50, pp. 64, illus.

JOSSELYN, JOHN.
°1672. New-England's rarities discovered: in birds, beasts, fishes, serpents, and plants of that country. London. pp. 114.

KABAT, CYRIL.
1953. Deer hunting prospects—1953. Wisconsin Conserv. Bull. 18(1):3–8, illus. October.

KABAT, CYRIL, NICHOLAS E. COLIAS, and RALPH C. GUETINGER.
1953. Some winter habits of white-tailed deer and the development of census methods in the Flag Yard of northern Wisconsin. Wisconsin Conserv. Dept., Tech. Wildlife Bull. no. 7, pp. 1–32, illus. August.

KABAT, CYRIL, and RUTH L. HINE.
1954. Operation wildlife research. Wisconsin Conserv. Dept., Wisconsin Wildlife no. 2, pp. 35, illus. September.

KARPULEON, FAY.
1958. Food habits of Wisconsin foxes. Journ. Mammal. 39(4):591–93. November 20.

KATZ, J. S.
°1939. An annotated bibliography of references concerning parasites of squirrels (Family, Sciuridae). Ohio Wildlife Research Station, Ohio State Univ., Release No. 13k, pp. 21 (processed). December 1.

KAUKL, MARVIN O.
1950. Game Farm otter. Wisconsin Conserv. Bull. 15(12):21–22, illus. December. Reprinted Amer. Nation. Fur & Market Journ. 29(9):7. March, 1951. Reprinted Central Furrier 35(5):18. June, 1951.

KEENER, JOHN M.
1952. The need for deer range management. Wisconsin Conserv. Bull. 17(11):7–10. November.
1955. The case of the timber wolf. Wisconsin Conserv. Bull. 20(11):22–24, illus. November.
1956. A new deal for deer and hunter. Wisconsin Conserv. Bull. 21(12):3–9. December.
1957. The 1956 deer season. Wisconsin Conserv. Bull. 22(2):8–11. February.
1959. Wisconsin's predator control program. Wisconsin Conserv. Bull. 24(6):3–10, illus. June.

KEENER, JOHN M., and JAMES B. HALE.
1957. The 1957 deer season. Wisconsin Conserv. Bull. 22(10):5–9. October.

KEENER, JOHN M., and DONALD R. THOMPSON.
1957. The deer unit: Surveys and management. Wisconsin Conserv. Bull. 22(8):6–10. August.

KELKER, GEORGE HILLS.
1931. The breeding time of the flying squirrel (Glaucomys volans volans). Journ. Mammal. 12(2):166–67. May.
1937. Insect foods of skunks. Journ. Mammal. 18(2):164–70. May 12.
1943. A winter wildlife census in northeastern

Wisconsin. Journ. Wildlife Management 7(2): 133–41. April.

KELLOGG, CHARLES E.
1937. Utility of jack rabbit and cottontail skins. U. S. Dept. Agric., Misc. publ. no. 289, 8 pp. November.

KELLOGG, CHARLES E., CHARLES E. BASSETT, and ROBERT K. ENDERS.
1948. Mink raising. U. S. Dept. Agric., Circ. no. 801, 42 pp., illus. September.

KELSON, KEITH R.
1946. Notes on the comparative osteology of the bobcat and the house cat. Journ. Mammal. 27 (3):255–64. August 14.

KENNICOTT, ROBERT.
°1857. The quadrupeds of Illinois, injurious and beneficial to the farmer. U. S. Patent Office Rept. (Agric.) for 1856, pp. 52–110, pls. 5–14.
°1858. The quadrupeds of Illinois, injurious and beneficial to the farmer. U. S. Patent Office Rept. (Agric.) for 1857, pp. 72–107.
°1859. The quadrupeds of Illinois, injurious and beneficial to the farmer. U. S. Patent Office Rept. (Agric.) for 1858, pp. 241–56.

KING, F. H.
1883. Instinct and memory exhibited by the flying squirrel in confinement, with a thought on the origin of wings in bats. Amer. Naturalist 17(1): 36–42. January.

KING, JOHN A.
1958. Maternal behavior and behavioral development in two subspecies of Peromyscus maniculatus. Journ. Mammal. 39 (2):177–90. May 20.

KING, OTIS M.
1950. An ecological study of the Norway rat and the house mouse in a city block in Lawrence, Kansas. Trans. Kansas Acad. Sci. 53(4):500–28, illus. December.

KINGSTON, J. T.
1879. Early exploration and settlement of Juneau Co. Report and Collections State Historical Soc. Wisconsin for the years 1877, 1878, and 1879, vol. 8, pp. 371–410.

KIPP, DUANE H.
1931. Wild life in a fire. Amer. Forests and Forest Life 37(6):323–25, 360, illus. June.

KIRK, GEORGE L.
1921. Shrews and weasels. Journ. Mammal. 2(2): 111. May 3.

KLEIN, HAROLD G.
1957. Inducement of torpidity in the woodland jumping mouse. Journ. Mammal. 38(2):272–74. May 27.

KLUGH, A. BOOKER.
1924. Notes on Eptesicus fuscus. Journ. Mammal. 5(1):42–43. February 9.
1927. Ecology of the red squirrel. Journ. Mammal. 8(1):1–32, pls. 1–5. February 9.
1929. Ecology of the red squirrel. Smithsonian Inst. An. Rep. for 1928, publ. 2981, pp. 495–524, pls. 5. November 18. (Reprinted from Journ. Mammal.)

KNUDSEN, GEORGE J.
1951. Wisconsin's eager beaver. Wisconsin Conserv. Bull. 16(12):11–15, illus. December.
1953 a. Beaver movement studies. Wisconsin Wildlife Research 12(1):139–47 (processed). April.
1953 b. Opus on opossum. Wisconsin Conserv. Bull. 18(6):21–24. June.
1953 c. Beaver die-off. Wisconsin Conserv. Bull. 18(9):20–23. September.
1954. General beaver damage summary, 1952–53. Wisconsin Wildlife Research 13(1):117–37 (processed). April.
1956. Preliminary otter investigations. Wisconsin Wildlife Research (Pittman-Robertson Quarterly Prog. Repts.), vol. 15, no. 2, pp. 131–47. (mimeographed). July.
1957 a. Preliminary otter investigations. Wisconsin Wildlife Research 15(4):51–69. Pittman-Robertson Quarterly Progress Reports. January.
1957 b. What's doin' with Bruin? Wisconsin Conserv. Bull. 22(9):12–14. September.
1959. The case of the beaver pond. Wisconsin Conserv. Bull. 24(4):3–6, illus. April.

KOMAREK, E. V.
1932. Notes on mammals of Menominee Indian Reservation, Wisconsin. Journ. Mammal. 13(3): 203–9. August 9.

KOMAREK, E. V., and DON A. SPENCER.
1931. A new pocket gopher from Illinois and Indiana. Journ. Mammal. 12(4):404–8, pl. 14. November 11.

KREFTING, LAURITS W., and JOSEPH H. STOECKELER.
1953. Effect of simulated snowshoe hare and deer damage on planted conifers in the Lake States. Journ. Wildlife Management 17(4):487–94. October.

KRUTZSCH, PHILIP H.
1954. North American jumping mice (genus Zapus). Univ. Kansas Publication, Mus. Nat. Hist. 7(4):349–472, illus. April 21.

KUMLIEN, LUDWIG.
1879. Contributions to the natural history of Arctic America, made in connection with the Howgate Polar Expedition, 1877–78. Bull. U. S. Nat. Mus. no. 15, pp. 179.
1891. A curious rabbit. Wisconsin Naturalist 1(6): 89. January.

LACEY, JAMES, CARL RYDBERG, W. A. ROLANDS, W. F. GRIMMER, G. S. HADLAND, and ALAN HANSON.
°1952. Safeguard your livestock from bears, wolves, coyotes, killer dogs. Univ. Wisconsin. Exten. Serv., College Agric. Circ. 411, 8 pp., unnumbered. April.

LAGLER, KARL F., and BURTON T. OSTENSON.
1942. Early spring food of the otter in Michigan. Journ. Wildlife Management 6(3):244–54, illus. July.

LANDIS, C. S.
1951. Woodchucks and woodchuck rifles. Greenberg: Publisher, New York. 402 pp., illus.

LANG, HERBERT.
1924. Position of limbs in the sliding otter. Journ.

Mammal. 5(3):216–17. August 11.

1925. How squirrels and other rodents carry their young. Journ. Mammal. 6(1):18–24, pl. 3. February 9.

LANGE, D.

1920. Notes on flying squirrels and gray squirrels. Journ. Mammal. 1(5):243–44. December 4.

LANTZ, DAVID E.

1907. An economic study of field mice (genus *Microtus*). U. S. Dept. Agric., Biol. Surv. Bull. 31:1–64, illus. October. 28.

1908. Deer farming in the United States. U. S. Dept. Agriculture, Farmer's Bull. 330, pp. 20, illus.

1909. The brown rat in the United States. U. S. Dept. Agric., Biol. Surv. Bull. 33:1–54, pls. 1–3. May 29.

1910. Pocket gophers as enemies of trees. Yearbook, U. S. Dept. Agric. 1901. Separate 506, pp. 290–18, pls. 8–10.

1917. Economic value of North American skunks. U. S. Dept. Agric., Farmer's Bull. 587, 24 pp., illus. Rev. ed. July.

LAPHAM, I. A.

1852. A systematic catlogue of the animals of Wisconsin. Prepared for the use of the University of Wisconsin, by I. A. Lapham of Milwaukee. 1851. Fourth Annual Rept. of the Board of Regents of the Univ. Wisconsin for year ending December 31, 1851, pp. 43–44. Madison.

1853. A systematic catalogue of the animals of Wisconsin. Trans. Wisconsin State Agric. Soc., vol. 2(1852), pp. 337–40.

[LAPHAM, I. A., Secy.]

1872. Second meeting of the Academy. Trans. Wisconsin Acad. Sci., Arts and Letters 1(1870–72): 186–88.

LARKIN, F. L.

1949. Norway rat killed by blue jays. Passenger Pigeon 11(4):182. December.

LARSEN, JAMES A.

°1957. Wisconsin's renewable resources. University of Wisconsin, Madison. January. pp. xiv + 160, illus.

LATHAM, ROBERT M.

1952. The fox as a factor in the control of weasel populations. Journ. Wildlife Management 16(4): 516–17. October.

1953. Simple method of identification of least weasel. Journ. Mammal. 34(3):385. August 17.

1955. The controversial San Juan rabbit. Trans. 20th North Amer. Wildlife Conference, pp. 406–14.

LAURIE, E. M. O.

1946. The reproduction of the house mouse (Mus musculus) living in different environments. Proc. Royal Soc. London, ser. B, Biol. Sci. 133(872): 248–81, illus.

LAWRENCE, BARBARA.

1946. Brief comparison of the short-tailed shrew and reptile poisons. Journ. Mammal. 26(4): 393–96. February 12.

LAWSON, PUBLIUS V.

1922. Thure Kumlien. Trans. Wisconsin Acad. Sci., Arts and Letters 20:663–86, pls. 62–64. March. (Quoting private paper by T. V. Kumlien "Even Buffalo horns were found by the early settlers" at Lake Koshkonong. P. 668.)

LAYNE, JAMES N.

1952. The os genitale of the red squirrel, *Tamiasciurus*. Journ. Mammal. 33(4):457–59. November 24.

1954. The biology of the red squirrel, *Tamiasciurus hudsonicus loquax* (Bangs), in central New York. Ecological Monographs 24(3):227–67. July 26.

LAYNE, JAMES N., and ALLEN H. BENTON.

1954. Some speeds of small mammals. Journ. Mammal. 35(1):103–04. February.

LAYNE, JAMES N., and W. J. HAMILTON, JR.

1954. The young of the woodland jumping mouse, Napaeozapus insignis insignis (Miller). Amer. Midland Nat. 52(1):242–47, illus. July.

LECONTE, JOHN.

1853. Descriptions of three new species of American Arvicolae, with remarks upon some other American rodents. Proc. Acad. Nat. Sci. Philadelphia 6 (1852–53): 404–15. October.

1855 a. Observations on the North American species of bats. Proc. Acad. Nat. Sci. Philadelphia 7 (1854–55):431–38. December.

1855 b. Description of two new species of Hesperomys. Proc. Acad. Nat. Sci. Philadelphia 7 (1854–55):442. December.

LEE, THOMAS G.

1902. On the early development of Spermophilus tridecemlineatus, a new type of mammalian placentation. Science 15(379):525.

1903. Implantation of the ovum in Spermophilus tridecemlineatus Mitch. Mark Anniv. Volume, art. 21, pp. 417–36, pls. 30–31.

LEIGHTON, ALEXANDER H.

1932. Notes on the beaver's individuality and mental characteristics. Journ. Mammal. 13(2): 117–26. May 11.

LEMKE, CHARLES W.

1952. How can we produce more cottontails? Wisconsin Conserv. Bull. 17(7):22–25. July.

1957. An unusual late pregnancy in a Wisconsin cottontail. Journ. Mammal. 38(2):375. May 27.

LEMKE, CHARLES W., and LOUIS OSHESKY.

1955. Alias: San Juan rabbit. Wisconsin Conserv. Bull. 20(11):9–11, back cover, illus. November.

LEOPOLD, ALDO.

°1931. Report on a game survey of the North Central States. Publ. at Madison, Wisconsin, by the Amer. Game Asso., Washington, D. C. pp. 299, illus.

1937. Killing technique of the weasel. Journ. Mammal. 18(1):98–99. February 15.

1939. The farmer as a conservationist. Amer. Forests 45(6):294–99, 316, 323. June.

1940. Wisconsin wildlife chronology. Wisconsin Conserv. Bull. 5(11):8–20. November.

1943. Deer irruptions. Wisconsin Conserv. Bull. 8 (8):3–11. August.

1944 a. What next in deer policy? Wisconsin Conserv. Bull. 9(6):3–4. June.

1944 b. Deer irruptions. Trans. Wisconsin Acad. Sci., Arts and Letters 35:351–66.

1945 a. Deer, wolves, foxes and pheasants. Wisconsin Conserv. Bull. 10(4):3–5. April.

1945 b. Wildlife explorations at Prairie du Sac. Wisconsin Conserv. Bull. 10(7–8):3–5. July.

1946. The deer dilemma. Wisconsin Conserv. Bull. 11(8–9):3–5. August.

1947 a. The distribution of Wisconsin hares. Trans. Wisconsin Acad. Sciences, Arts and Letters 37: 1–14. April. 10.

1947 b. Mortgaging the future deer herd. Wisconsin Conserv. Bull. 12(9):3. September.

LEOPOLD, ALDO, and HARRY G. ANDERSON.
1938. The 1936 cottontail scarcity in Wisconsin. Journ. Mammal. 19(1):110–11. February 13.

LEOPOLD, ALDO, LYLE K. SOWLS, and DAVID L. SPENCER.
1947. A survey of over-populated deer ranges in the United States. Journ. Wildlife Management 11(2):162–77. April.

LIERS, EMIL E.
1951. Notes on the river otter (*Lutra canadensis*). Journ. Mammal. 32(1):1–9, illus. February 20.

1953. An otter's story. Viking Press, New York, 191 pp., illus.

1958. Early breeding in the river otter. Journ. Mammal. 39(3):438–39. August 24.

LINCOLN, ROBERT PAGE.
1909 a. The rambler of the solitudes. Wild Life 1 (1):11–13. Autumn, 1908. January.

1909 b. The haunter of the stream. Wild Life 1(2):7–8. Winter, 1908–9. February.

1909 c. The fisher. Wild Life 1(4):10–11. July.

1909 d. The guardian of the water gate. Wild Life 2(1):6–7. September.

1909 e. The badger and the raccoon. Wild Life 2(2):13–14. October.

1909 f. The way of the fox. Wild Life 2(3):9–10. November.

LINDE, ARLYN F.
1954. Share-trapping on Horicon Marsh. Wisconsin Conserv. Bull. 19(12):8–11, illus. December.

LINDUSKA, J. P.
1942 a. Insect feeding by the house mouse. Journ. Mammal. 23(2):212–13. June 3.

1942 b. Winter rodent populations in field-shocked corn. Journ. Wildlife Management 6(4):353–63. October.

1950. Ecology and land-use relationships of small mammals on a Michigan farm. Game Division, Dept. Conservation, Lansing, Michigan. pp. x + 144, illus.

LINNAEUS, C.
°1758. Systema naturae, secundum classes, ordines, genera, species, cum characteribus, differentiis, synonymis, locis. Edition 10, tomus 1. Regnum animale, 821 pp.

°LITTLE, C. C.
1958. Coat color genes in rodents and carnivores. Quart. Rev. Biol. 33(2):103–37. June.

LOBUE, JOSEPH P., and REZNEAT M. DARNELL.
1958. An improved live trap for small mammals. Journ. Mammal. 39(2):286–90. May 20.

1959. Effect of habitat disturbance on a small mammal population. Journ. Mammal. 40(3): 425–37. August 20.

LONG, STEPHEN H., and EDWIN JAMES.
1823. Account of an expedition from Pittsburgh to the Rocky Mountains performed in the years 1819 and 1820. 2 vols. Philadelphia.

LOOMIS, CLARKE HELME.
1898. In the West with notebook and kodak. Field and Stream 4(2):112–15.

LOW, JESSUP, B.
1944. Meadow mice use wrens' nest. Journ. Mammal. 25(3):308. September 8.

LOWE, LESTER D.
1930. The first authentic report of fisher bred in captivity. Amer. Fur Breeder 11(12):34–36. June.

LOWRENCE, E. W.
1949. Variability and growth of the opossum skeleton. Journ. Morphology 85(3):569–93. November.

LOYSTER, EARL L.
1942. Archery deer season 1941. Wisconsin Conserv. Bull. 7(1):21–22. January.

1944 a. Winter deer food distribution. Wisconsin Conserv. Bull. 9(2):5. February.

1944 b. The 1943 archery deer season. Wisconsin Conserv. Bull. 9(2):17–18. February.

1948. Small-game damage on Wisconsin farms. Wisconsin Conserv. Bull. 13(7):19–22. July.

LULL, RICHARD S.
°1906. Volant adaptation in vertebrates. Amer. Nat. 40(476):537–66. August.

LYMAN, CHARLES PEIRSON.
1943. Control of coat color in the varying hare *Lepus americanus* Erxleben. Bull. Mus. Comp. Zool. 93(3):393–461, pls. 1–11. December.

1954. Activity, food consumption and hoarding in hibernation. Journ. Mammal. 35(4):545–52. November.

LYON, MARCUS WARD, JR.
°1904. Classification of hares and their allies. Smithsonian Misc. Coll. 45(1456):321–447, pls. 74–100. June 15.

1925. Bats caught in burdocks. Journ. Mammal. 6(4):280. November 14.

1936. Mammals of Indiana. Amer. Midland Nat. 17(1):1–384, illus. January.

MACEWEN, WILLIAM.
1920. The growth and shedding of the antler of the deer. Macclehose, Jackson and Co., Glasgow. pp. 109, illus.

MACKENZIE, H. W.
1937. To the citizens of Wisconsin interested in deer. Wisconsin Conserv. Bull. 2(9):3–11. September.

MacLulich, D. A.
  1937. Fluctuations in the numbers of the varying hare (*Lepus americanus*). Univ. Toronto Biol. Ser. no. 43, pp. 136, illus.

Malkiot, Victor Francois.
  1910. A Wisconsin Fur-Trader's Journal, 1804–05. Edited by Reuben Gold Thwaites. Coll. of State Hist. Soc. Wisconsin 19:163–233.

Mann, William M.
  1930. Wild animals in and out of the Zoo. Smithsonian Sci. Series, vol. 6, 374 pp., 107 pls.

Manville, Richard H.
  1949 a. A study of small mammal populations in northern Michigan. Misc. Publ. Mus. Zool., Univ. Michigan no. 73, 83 pp., 4 pls. August 16.
  1949 b. The fate of Morgan's beaver. Scientific Monthly 69(3):186–91, illus. September.
  1953. Longevity of the coyote. Journ. Mammal. 34 (3):390. August 17.
  1955. Dichromatism in Michigan rodents. Journ. Mammal. 36(2):293. May.
  1956. Hibernation of meadow jumping mouse. Journ. Mammal. 37(1):122. March 1.

Marcy, Randolph B.
  1888 a. Big game hunting in the wild west. IV. Wolves. Outing 11(4):291–99, illus. January.
  1888 b. Big game hunting in the wild west. VI. Feline animals. Outing 11(6):517–25, illus. March.

Markley, Merle H., and Charles F. Bassett.
  1942. Habits of captive marten. Amer. Midland Nat. 28(3):604–16. November.
  1943. Habits of captive marten. Amer. Fur Journ. 16(3):26, 28, 30 (September); 16(4):22, 24 (October); 16(5):42–46 (November).

Marshall, William H.
  1936. A study of the winter activities of the mink. Journ. Mammal. 17(4):382–92, illus. November 16.
  1946. Winter food habits of the pine marten in Montana. Journ. Mammal. 27(1):83–84. March 14.
  1951 a. Predation on shrews by frogs. Journ. Mammal. 32(2):219. May.
  1951 b. Accidental death of porcupine. Journ. Mammal. 32(2):221. May.
  1951 c. Pine marten as a forest product. Journ. Forestry 49(12):899–905, illus. December.
  1956. Summer weights of raccoons in northern Minnesota. Journ. Mammal. 37(3):445. August.

Martin, Alexander C., Herbert S. Zim, and Arnold L. Nelson.
  °1951. American wildlife and plants. McGraw-Hill Book Co., New York. pp. ix + 500, illus.

Martin, Edward P.
  1956. A population study of the prairie vole (Microtus ochrogaster) in northeastern Kansas. Univ. Kansas publs., Mus. Nat. Hist. 8(6):361–416. April 2.

Martin, F. R., and L. W. Krefting.
  1953. The Necedah Refuge deer irruption. Journ. Wildlife Management 17(2):166–76. April.

Martin, Horace T.
  1892. Castorologia, or the history and traditions of the Canadian beaver. Montreal and London. pp. 238, illus.

Martin, Lawrence.
  °1916. The physical geography of Wisconsin. Wisconsin Geol. and Nat. Hist. Survey, Bull. no. 36, Educational series no. 4, pp. 549, illus.

Mather, Deane, R. H. Gensch, and H. Allen Barton.
  1943. Report on the snowshoe hare repellent and poison studies conducted on the Nicolet National Forest in 1941 and 1942. U. S. Dept. Agric., Forest Service, Region 9, 36 pp.

Mather, Fred.
  1896. Men I have fished with. Antoine Gardapee. Forest and Stream 47, no. 17, pp. 329–31, October 24; no. 18, pp. 348–50, October 31; no. 19, pp. 370–71, November 7.
  1897. Men I have fished with. Forest and Stream Pub. Co., New York, 371 pp., illus. November 19.

Mathiak, Harold A.
  °1938. A key to hair of the mammals of southern Michigan. Journ. Wildlife Management 2(4):251–68. October.
  1949. Developments in muskrat research. Amer. Natl. Fur and Market Journ. 28(1):7–8. August.
  1952. Principles of level ditching for muskrat management. Wisconsin Conserv. Bull. 17(12):14–16. December.
  1953 a. Experimental level ditching for muskrat management. Wisconsin Conserv. Dept., Tech. Wildlife Bull. no. 5, pp. 35, illus. February.
  1953 b. Early muskrat season pays off. Wisconsin Conserv. Bull. 18(12):10. December.

Mathiak, Harold A., and Arlyn F. Linde.
  1954. Role of refuges in muskrat management. Wisconsin Conserv. Dept., Tech. Wildlife Bull. no. 10, pp. 16. September.

Matson, J. R.
  1946. Notes on dormancy in the black bear. Journ. Mammal. 27(3):203–12. August 14.
  1954. Observations on the dormant phase of a female black bear. Journ. Mammal. 35(1):28–35, illus. February.

Maynard, Charles J.
  1889. Singular effects produced by the bite of a short-tailed shrew, Blarina brevicauda. Contributions to Science 1(2):57–59. July.

McAtee, W. L.
  1939. The electric fence in wildlife management. Journ. Wildlife Management 3(1):1–13. January.

McCabe, Robert A.
  1943. Population trends in Wisconsin cottontails. Journ. Mammal. 24(1):18–22. February 20.
  1947 a. A winter rabbit browse tally on the University of Wisconsin Arboretum. Trans. Wisconsin Acad. Sciences, Arts and Letters 37:15–33. April 10.
  1947 b. Homing of flying squirrels. Journ. Mammal. 28(4):404. December 1.

1948. Live-trapping mink in the University of Wisconsin Arboretum. Wisconsin Conserv. Bull. 13(1):20–21. January.

1949 a. The scream of the mountain lion. Journ. Mammal. 30(3):305–6. August 20.

1949 b. Notes on live-trapping mink. Journ. Mammal. 30(4):416–23. November 21.

McCabe, Robert A., and Lloyd B. Keith.
1958. Effectiveness of expanded aluminum foil in preventing rabbit damage. Trans. Wisconsin Acad. Sci., Arts and Letters 46:305–14. January.

McCarley, W. H.
1954. Natural hybridization in the Peromyscus leucopus species group of mice. Evolution 8(4):314–23, illus. December.

McCoy, George W.
1911. A plague-like disease of rodents. U. S. Public Health Service Bull. no. 43(2):53–71.

McCoy, George W., and Charles W. Chapin.
1912. Further observations on a plague-like disease of rodents with a preliminary note on the causative agent *Bacterium tularense.* Journ. Infect. Diseases 10(1):61–72.

McDermid, A. M.
1939. Infectious gastro-enteritis in raccoon. Wisconsin Conserv. Bull. 4(3):21–22. March.

1946 a. Report on muskrat disease outbreak. Wisconsin Conserv. Bull. 11(8–9):21–22. August.

1946 b. Tularemia or rabbit fever. Wisconsin Conserv. Bull. 11(12): 10–11. October.

McHugh, Tom.
1958. Social behavior of the American buffalo (*Bison bison bison*). Zoologica 43(1):1–40, pls. 1–3. April 4.

McIntosh, William B.
1956. Whiteside, a new mutation in Peromyscus. Journ. Heredity 47(1):28–32. January.

McKeague, Harley T.
1944. Locked antlers. Wisconsin Conserv. Bull. 11(3):20. March.

McNair, George T.
1931. The deer mouse, Peromyscus, a valuable laboratory mammal. Journ. Mammal. 12(1):48–52. February 12.

McNaughton, James W.
1922. A stray moose. Wisconsin Conservationist 3(6):12, illus. January.

McWhorter, Tom.
1946. Bow hunting in Wisconsin. Texas Game and Fish 4(2):6, 16–17. January.

Mearns, Edgar A.
1891. Description of a new subspecies of the eastern chipmunk, from the upper Mississippi region of the Great Lakes. Bull. Amer. Mus. Nat. Hist. 3(2):229–33, June 5.

1898. Notes on the mammals of the Catskill Mountains, New York, with general remarks on the fauna and flora of the region. Proc. U. S. Nat. Mus. 21(1147):341–60.

Mease, J. A.
1929. Tularemia from opossums. Journ. Amer. Med. Asso. 92:1042. March 30.

Merriam, C. Hart.
°1883. The vertebrates of the Adirondack region, northeastern New York. First installment, chap. 1, Introduction; chap. 2, Mammals [part], Trans. Linnaean Soc. New York 1:5–106.

°1884 a. The vertebrates of the Adirondack region, northeastern New York. Second installment, chap. 2, Mammals [concluding part]. Trans. Linnaean Soc. New York 2:5–214.

°1884 b. The mammals of the Adirondack region, northeastern New York. Published by the Author, New York. 316 pp.

1886 a. Description of a newly-born lynx, *Lynx canadensis* (Desm.) Raf. Bull. Nat. Hist. Soc. New Brunswick, no. 5, pp. 10–13, 1 pl. April.

1886 b. Preliminary description of a new squirrel from Minnesota (Sciurus carolinensis hypophaeus sp. nov.). Science 7(167):351. April 16.

1888. Do any Canadian bats migrate? Evidence in the affirmative. Trans. Royal Soc. Canada 1887, sec. 4, pp. 85–87.

1889. The mink (*Lutreola vison*). Rept. of the Ornithologist and Mammalogist, C. Hart Merriam, M. D., for the year 1888, pp. 488–90. Ann. Rep. Dept. Agric. for year 1888, pp. 477–536.

°1892. The geographic distribution of life in North America with special reference to the Mammalia. Proc. Biol. Soc. Washington 7:1–64, map. April 13.

1895 a. Monographic revision of the pocket gophers, family Geomyidae (exclusive of the species of Thomomys). North Amer. Fauna no. 8, U. S. Dept. Agric. pp. 258, pls. 19, col. maps 4. January 31.

1895 b. Revision of the shrews of the American genera Blarina and Notiosorex. North Amer. Fauna no. 10, U. S. Dept. Agric. pp. 5–34, pls. 1–3. December 31.

1895 c. Synopsis of the American shrews of the genus Sorex. North Amer. Fauna no. 10, U. S. Dept. Agric. pp. 57–98, pls. 7–12. December 31.

1896 a. Revision of the lemmings of the genus Synaptomys, with descriptions of new species. Proc. Biol. Soc. Washington 10:55–64. March 9.

1896 b. Preliminary synopsis of the American bears. Proc. Biol. Soc. Washington 10:65–83. April 13.

1896 c. Synopsis of the weasels of North America. North Amer. Fauna no. 11, U. S. Dept. Agric. 45 pp., illus. June 30.

1897. Revision of the coyotes or prairie wolves with descriptions of new forms. Proc. Biol. Soc. Washington 11:19–33. March 15.

°1898. Life zones and crop zones of the United States. U. S. Dept. Agric., Biological Survey, Bull. no. 10, pp. 79, colored map.

1904. Jack rabbits of the *Lepus campestris* group. Proc. Biol. Soc. Washington 17:131–34. July 14.

Merrill, Samuel.
1916. The moose book. E. P. Dutton and Co., New York. 339 pp., illus. (2nd edition published in 1920).

METZGER, BRICE.
  1957. Partial albinism in *Myotis sodalis*. Journ. Mammal. 37(4):546. January 14.

MIDDLETON, A. D.
  1930. The ecology of the American grey squirrel (*Sciurus carolinensis* Gmelin) in the British Isles. Proc. Zool. Soc. London, 1930, part 3, pp. 809–43, illus. October.
  1931. Muskrats in Great Britain. A new danger to the country. The Field [London] 157 (4105):319, illus. August 29.

MIKULA, EDWARD J.
  1955. An efficient handling crate for whitetail deer. Journ. Wildlife Management 19(4):501–2, illus. October.

MILLARD, CLARENCE.
  1939. Raccoon experiment. Wisconsin Conserv. Bull. 4(3):28–29, illus. March.

MILLER, ERIC.
  °1928. A century of temperatures in Wisconsin. Trans. Wisconsin Acad. Sci., Arts and Letters 23:165–77. January.
  °1930. Monthly rainfall maps of Wisconsin and adjoining states. Trans. Wisconsin Acad. Sci., Arts and Letters 25:135–56.
  °1931. Extremes of temperatures in Wisconsin. Trans. Wisconsin Acad. Sci., Arts and Letters 26:61–68.

MILLER, GERRIT S., JR.
  1895. The long-tailed shrews of the eastern United States. North Amer. Fauna no. 10, U. S. Dept. Agric. pp. 35–56, pls. 4–6. December 31.
  1896. The genera and subgenera of voles and lemmings. North Amer. Fauna no. 12, 84 pp., 3 pls. July 23.
  1897 a. Notes on the mammals of Ontario. Proc. Boston Soc. Nat. Hist. 28(1):1–44. April.
  1897 b. Revision of the North American bats of the family Vespertilionidae. North Amer. Fauna no. 13, U. S. Dept. Agric. 144 pp., illus. October 16.
  1907. The families and genera of bats. U. S. Nat. Mus. Bull. 57, pp. 282, pls. 14.
  1912 a. The names of two North American wolves. Proc. Biol. Soc. Washington 25:95. May 4.
  °1912 b. List of North American land-mammals in the United States National Museum, 1911. U. S. Nat. Mus. Bull. 79, pp. xiv + 455. December 31.
  °1929. Mammalogy and the Smithsonian Institution. Smithsonian Rept. 1928, pp. 391–411, pl. 1. November 18.

MILLER, GERRIT S., JR., and GLOVER M. ALLEN.
  1928. The American bats of the genera Myotis and Pizonyx. U. S. Nat. Mus. Bull. 144, pp. viii + 218, pl. 1. May 25.

MILLER, GERRIT S., JR., and JAMES W. GIDLEY.
  1918. Synopsis of the subgeneric groups of rodents. Journ. Washington Acad. Sci. 8(13):431–48. July 19.
  °1943. Warm-blooded vertebrates. Part 2: Mammals. Smithsonian Scientific Series, no. 9, pp. 389, illus.

MILLER, GERRIT S., JR., and REMINGTON KELLOGG.
  °1955. List of North American Recent mammals. U. S. Nat. Mus., Bull. 205, pp. xii + 954. March 3.

MILLS, ENOS A.
  1913. In beaver world. Houghton Mifflin, Boston. 240 pp., illus.

MILLS, ERNEST M.
  1953. Rats–Let's get rid of them. U. S. Dept. Interior, Fish and Wildlife Service, Circ. 22, 14 pp., illus.

MILLS, KENNETH L.
  1949. Wisconsin mink ranching. Wisconsin Conserv. Bull. 14(8):17–19. August.

MINOR, FRED T., and JOHN HANSON.
  1939. Report of two deer yards in Douglas and Bayfield countries. Wisconsin Conserv. Bull. 4(5):18–24. May.

MIRAND, EDWIN A., and ALBERT R. SHADLE.
  1953. Gross anatomy of the male reproductive system of the porcupine. Journ. Mammal. 34(2):210–20. May 21.

MITCHILL, SAMUEL LATHAM.
  1821. Description of two mammiferous animals of North America. Med. Repository (n.s.) 6:248–49.

MIZELLE, JOHN D.
  1935. Swimming of the muskrat. Journ. Mammal. 16(1):22–25. February 14.

M'MURTRIE, H.
  °1831. The animal kingdom arranged in conformity with its organization. By the Baron Cuvier, and translated from the French, with notes and additions by H. M'Murtrie. 4 vols., New York. (Volume 1 includes the mammals.)

MOHR, CARL O.
  1940. Strange action of a house mouse. Journ. Mammal. 21(1):93–94. February 15.
  1946. Distribution of the prairie mole and the pocket gopher in Illinois. Journ. Mammal. 27(4):390–92. November 25.

MOHR, CHARLES E.
  1945. Sex ratios of bats in Pennsylvania. Proc. Pennsylvania Acad. Sci. 19:65–69.
  1953. A survey of bat banding in North America, 1932–1951. The American Caver, Bull. 14:3–13.

MOHR, ERNA.
  1933. The muskrat, Ondatra zibethica (Linnaeus), in Europe. Journ. Mammal. 14(1):58–63. February 14.

MOLL, A. M.
  1917. Animal parasites of rats at Madison, Wisconsin. Journ. Parasitol. 4:89–90.

MONTEZUMA [F. H. MAYER].
  1919. Buffalo chips. Outer's Recreation 61:17–20 (July); 91–94 (August); 179–81, 225 (September); 263–65 (October); 330–32, 384 (November).

MOODY, F. B.
  1916. Protection of beaver in Wisconsin. Amer. Forestry 22:220–24.

MOODY, PAUL AMOS.
    1929. Brightness vision in the deer-mouse, Pero-
    myscus maniculatus gracilis. Journ. Exper. Zool.
    52(3):367–405, illus. February.
    1941. Identification of mice in genus Peromyscus
    by a red blood cell agglutination test. Journ.
    Mammal. 22(1):40–47. February 14.
MOORE, JOSEPH C.
    1943. A contribution to the natural history of the
    Florida short-tailed shrew. Proc. Florida Acad.
    Sci. 6:155–66. December.
    1949. Notes on the shrew, Sorex cinereus, in the
    southern Appalachians. Ecology 30(2):234–37.
    April.
    °1959. Relationships among living squirrels of the
    Sciurinae. Bull. Amer. Mus. Nat. Hist. 118(4):
    153–206, illus. July 27.
MORGAN, BANNER BILL.
    1943. The Physaloptera (Nematoda) of rodents.
    Wasmann Collector 5(3):99–107. April.
    1944. Host list of the genus Trichomonas (Proto-
    zoa: Flagellata). Part II, Host-parasite list.
    Trans. Wisconsin Acad. Sci., Arts and Letters
    35:235–45.
    1945. The Physaloptera (Nematoda) of carnivores.
    Trans. Wisconsin Acad. Sci., Arts and Letters
    36:375–88.
    1949. Tularemia in Wisconsin. Trans. Wisconsin
    Acad. Sciences, Arts and Letters 39:1–19. Au-
    gust 1.
MORGAN, BANNER BILL, and E. F. WALLER.
    1940. A survey of the parasites of the Iowa cotton-
    tail (Sylvilagus floridanus mearnsi). Journ. Wild-
    life Management 4(1):21–26. January.
MORGAN, LEWIS H.
    °1868. The American beaver and his works. Lip-
    pincott, Philadelphia. 330 pp., illus.
MORRISSEY, THOMAS J.
    1941. Ground squirrel in an oak sapling. Journ.
    Mammal. 22(1):88. February 14.
MOSELEY, E. L.
    1928. Red bat as a mother. Journ. Mammal. 9(3):
    248–49. August 9.
MOSSMAN, ARCHIE S.
    1955. Light penetration in relation to small mam-
    mal abundance. Journ. Mammal. 36(4):564–66.
    December 12.
MOSSMAN, H. W.
    1931. Fading of color accidentally induced in cap-
    tive chipmunks. Journ. Mammal. 12(2):167–68.
    May 14.
    1937. The thecal gland and its relation to the re-
    productive cycle. A study of the cyclic changes
    in the ovary of the pocket gopher, Geomys bur-
    sarius (Shaw). Amer. Journ. Anat. 61(2):289–
    319, illus. July 15.
    1940. What is the red squirrel? Trans. Wisconsin
    Acad. Sci., Arts and Letters 32:123–34, pls. 1–2.
MOSSMAN, H. W., and F. L. HISAW.
    1940. The fetal membranes of the pocket gopher,
    illustrating an intermediate type of rodent
    membrane formation. Amer. Journ. Anat. 66(3):

    367–91, illus. May 15.
MOSSMAN, H. W., JOHN W. LAWLAY, and J. A. BRAD-
LEY.
    1932. The male reproductive tract of the Sciuridae.
    Amer. Journ. Anat. 51(1):89–155, illus. Septem-
    ber.
MOSSMAN, H. W., and L. A. WEISFELDT.
    1939. The fetal membranes of a primitive rodent,
    the thirteen-striped ground squirrel. Amer. Journ.
    Anat. 64(1):59–109, 10 pls. January.
MUELLER, H. C., and J. T. EMLEN, JR.
    1957. Homing in bats. Science 126(3268):307–8.
    August 16.
MUIR, JOHN.
    1913. The story of my boyhood and youth. Hough-
    ton Mifflin Co., Boston. 286 pp., illus.
MURIE, ADOLPH.
    1934. The moose of Isle Royale. Univ. Michigan
    Mus. Zool., Misc. publ. no. 25, 44 pp., 7 pls. July
    7.
    1936. Following fox trails. Mus. Zool., Univ. Michi-
    gan, Misc. publ. no. 32, 45 pp., 6 pls. August
    7.
MURIE, OLAUS J.
    1930. An epizootic disease of elk. Journ. Mam-
    mal. 11(2):214–22, pls. 13–14. May 9.
    1932. Elk calls. Journ. Mammal. 13(4):331–36.
    November 2.
    1951. The elk of North America. Wildlife Manage-
    ment Institute, Washington, D. C. pp. viii +
    376, pls. 29 (1 colored).
    °1954. A field guide to animal tracks. Houghton
    Mifflin Co., Boston. pp. xxii + 374, illus.
MURPHY, ROBERT CUSHMAN, and JOHN TREADWELL
NICHOLS.
    1913. Long Island Fauna and Flora — I — The Bats.
    Mus. Brooklyn Inst., Arts and Sciences, Science
    Bull. 2(1):1–15. June 21.
MURRAY, LEO T.
    1939. An albino Blarina from Indiana. Journ.
    Mammal. 20(4):501. November 14.
MUSKEEGO.
    1887. Wolves in Wisconsin. Forest and Stream
    28:48. February 10.
NAKAMURA, MITSURU.
    1950 a. Tularemia in the jumping mouse. Journ.
    Mammal. 31(2):194. May 30.
    1950 b. A survey of Pasturella tularensis in ani-
    mals of the Jackson Hole area. Zoologica 35(2):
    129–31. August 1.
NASON, EILEEN SINCLAIR.
    1948. Morphology of hair of eastern North Ameri-
    can bats. Amer. Midland Nat. 39(2):345–61.
    March.
NEGUS, NORMAN C.
    1958. Pelage stages in the cottontail rabbit. Journ.
    Mammal. 39(2): 246–52. May 20.
NEILL, WILFRED T.
    1952. Hoary bat in a squirrel's nest. Journ. Mam-
    mal 33(1):113. February.
NELSON, ARNOLD L.
    1934. Notes on Wisconsin mammals. Journ. Mam-

mal. 15(3):252–53. August 10.

NELSON, ARNOLD L., and C. O. HANDLEY.
1938. Behavior of gray foxes in raiding quail nests. Journ. Wildlife Management 2(3):73–78. July.

NELSON, BERNARD A.
1946. The spring molt of the northern red squirrel in Minnesota. Journ. Mammal. 26(4):397–400. February 12.

NELSON, E. W.
1909. The rabbits of North America. North Amer. Fauna 29, pp. 314, pls. 13. August 13.
1926. Bats in relation to the production of guano and the destruction of insects. U. S. Dept. Agric., Dept. Bull. no. 1395, pp. 1–12, illus. March.
°1930. Wild animals of North America. National Geographic Society, Washington, D. C. pp. 254, many col. pls. and figs.

NELSON, E. W., and E. A. GOLDMAN.
1930. Six new raccoons of the Procyon lotor group. Journ. Mammal. 11(4):453–59. November 11.

NEUBERGER, RICHARD L.
1946. The great American snout count. Saturday Evening Post 218(51):28–29, 92, 94, illus. June 22.

NEUSTADTER, LESLIE L.
1956. Tracks in the snow. Wisconsin Conserv. Bull. 21(12):19–21. December.

NEW, JOHN G.
1958. Dyes for studying the movements of small mammals. Journ. Mammal. 39(3):416–29. August 20.

NEWSOM, WILLIAM MONYPENY.
1926. Whitetailed deer. Scribner's Sons, New York. pp. xviii + 288, pls. 31, many text figs.
1937. Winter notes on the moose. Journ. Mammal. 18(3):347–49. August 14.

NICE, MARGARET M., CONSTANCE NICE, and DOROTHEA EWERS.
1956. Comparison of behavior development in snowshoe hares and red squirrels. Journ. Mammal. 37(1):64–74. March 1.

NICHOLS, DAVID G.
1944. Further consideration of the American house mice. Journ. Mammal. 25(1):82–84. February 18.

NICHOLSON, ARNOLD J.
1937. A hibernating jumping mouse. Journ. Mammal. 18(1):103. February 14.
1941. The homes and social habits of the woodmouse (Peromyscus leucopus noveboracensis) in southern Michigan. Amer. Midland Nat. 25(1):196–223. January.

NOBACK, CHARLES V.
1935. Observations on the seasonal hair moult in a New York State weasel (Mustela noveboracensis). Bull. New York Zool. Soc. 38(1):25–27, illus. February 19.

OBERHOLTZER, ERNST C.
1911. Some observations on moose. Proc. Zool. Soc. London, 1911, pp. 358–64.

OEHLER, CHARLES.
1944. Notes on the temperament of the New York weasel. Journ. Mammal. 25(2):198. May 26.

OEHMEKE, ARTHUR.
1945. Wolves and coyotes. Wisconsin Conserv. Bull. 10(9):9, illus. September.

OLIVE, JOHN R., and CHARLES V. RILEY.
1948. Sarcoptic mange in the red fox in Ohio. Journ. Mammal. 29(1):73–74. February 13.

OKEN, LORENZ.
1816. Okens Lehrbuch der Naturgeschichte. Part 3 (Zoologie), Sect. 2 (Fleischthiere), pp. xvi + 1270.

OLSON, SIGURD. F.
1938. A study of predatory relationship with particular reference to the wolf. Sci. Monthly 4:323–26, illus. April.

ORD, GEORGE.
1815. A universal geography, or a view of the present state of the known world. Originally compiled by William Guthrie, esq.; the astronomical part by James Ferguson. 2nd Amer. ed., 2 vols. Philadelphia.

O'REILLY, R. A., JR.
1949. Shrew preying on ribbon snake. Journ. Mammal. 30(3):309. August 20.

ORR, LESLIE W.
1930. An unusual chipmunk nest. Journ. Mammal. 11(3):315. August 9.

ORR, ROBERT T.
1944. Communal nests of the house mouse (Mus musculus Linnaeus). Wasmann Collector 6(2):15–17. November.
1958. Keeping bats in captivity. Journ. Mammal. 39(3):339–44. August 20.

OSBORN, DALE J.
1955. Techniques of sexing beaver, Castor canadensis. Journ. Mammal. 36(1):141–42. February 2.

OSBORN, HENRY FAIRFIELD.
°1910. The age of mammals. Macmillan Co., New York. 635 pp., illus.

OSGOOD, WILFRED H.
1907. Some unrecognized and missapplied names of American mammals. Proc. Biol. Soc. Washington 20:43–52. April 18.
1909. Revision of the mice of the American genus Peromyscus. North Amer. Fauna 28, pp. 285, pls. 8, map. 1. April 17.

OWEN, R. D., and R. M. SHACKLEFORD.
1942. Color aberrations in Microtus and Pitymys. Journ. Mammal. 23(3):306–14. August 13.

PACKARD, FRED M.
1949. Tufted titmice pull hairs from living mammals. Journ. Mammal. 30(4):432. November 21.

PACKARD, ROSS L.
1956. An observation on quadruplets in the red bat. Journ. Mammal. 37(2):279–80. June 12.

PALMER, RALPH S.
°1954. The mammal guide. Mammals of North America north of Mexico. Doubleday & Co., N. Y. 384 pp., illus.

PALMER, STRANGE M.
1872. Western Wisconsin in 1836. Rept. and Collections State Hist. Soc. of Wisconsin for the years

1869, 1870, 1871, and 1872, vol. 6, pp. 297–307.

PALMER, T. S.
1897. The jack rabbits of the United States. U. S. Dept. Agric., Div. Biological Survey, Bull. no. 8 (revised), pp. 88, pls. 6 and frontispiece.
°1904. Index generum mammalium: A list of the genera and families of mammals. North Amer. Fauna no. 23, 984 pp. January 23.

PANUSKA, JOSEPH ALLEN.
1959. Weight patterns and hibernation in *Tamias striatus*. Journ. Mammal. 40(4):554–66. November 20.

PANUSKA, JOSEPH A., and NELSON J. WADE.
1956. The burrow of *Tamias striatus*. Journ. Mammal. 37(1):23–31, illus. March 1.
1957. Field observations on *Tamias striatus* in Wisconsin. Journ. Mammal. 38(2):192–96. May 27.

PEARCE, JOHN.
1934. Albinism in the cinereous shrew. Journ. Mammal. 15(1):67. February 15.
1937. A captive New York weasel. Journ. Mammal. 18(4):483–88. November 22.
°1947. Identifying injury by wildlife to trees and shrubs in northeastern United States. U. S. Dept. Interior, Fish and Wildlife Service, Research Rept. 13, pp. 29, illus.

PEARSON, OLIVER P.
1942. On the cause and nature of a poisonous action produced by the bite of a shrew (*Blarina brevicauda*). Journ. Mammal. 23(2):159–66. June 3.
1944. Reproduction in the shrew (Blarina brevicauda Say). Amer. Journ. Anatomy 15(1):39–93. July.
1945. Longevity of the short-tailed shrew. Amer. Midland Nat. 34(2):531–46. September.

PEARSON, OLIVER P., and ROBERT K. ENDERS.
1944. Duration of pregnancy in certain mustelids. Journ. Exper. Zool. 95(1):21–35. February.

PERKINS, G. H.
1873. The flying squirrel. Amer. Nat. 7(3):132–39. March.

PETERSON, ARTHUR WARD.
1950. Backward swimming of the muskrat. Journ. Mammal. 31(4):453. November 22.

PETERSON, RANDOLPH L.
1947. A record of a timber wolf attacking a man. Journ. Mammal. 28(3):294–95. August 20.
1950. A new subspecies of moose from North America. Occas. Papers Royal Ontario Mus. Zool., no. 9, pp. 1–7. May 25.
1952. A review of the living representatives of the genus *Alces*. Contrib. Royal Ontario Mus. Zool. and Palaeont. 34:1–30, illus. October 15.
1953. Studies of the food habits of the habitat of moose in Ontario. Contrib. Royal Ontario Mus. Zool. and Palaeont. 36:1–49, illus. May 30.
1955. North American moose. Univ. of Toronto Press. pp. xii + 280.

PETERSON, RANDOLPH L., and STUART C. DOWNING.
1952. Notes on the bobcats (*Lynx rufus*) of eastern North America with description of a new race.

Contrib. Ontario Mus. Zool. and Palaeontol. 33: 1–23, illus. April 8.

PETRIDES, GEORGE A.
1949. Sex and age determination in the opossum. Journ. Mammal. 30(4):264–78. November 21.
1951 a. Notes on age determination in squirrels. Journ. Mammal. 32(1):111–12, illus.
1951 b. The determination of sex and age ratios in the cottontail rabbit. Amer. Midland Nat. 46 (2):312–36. September.

PIERCE, G. W., and DONALD R. GRIFFIN.
1938. Experimental determination of supersonic notes emitted by bats. Journ. Mammal. 19(4): 454–55. November 14.

PIKE, GALEN W.
1949. Food for deer and food for thought. Wisconsin Conserv. Bull. 14(7):22–24. July.

PIPER STANLEY E.
1909. The Nevada mouse plague of 1907–8. U. S. Dept. Agric., Farmers' Bull. 352, pp. 23, illus. March 20.

PO-CHEDLEY, DONALD S., and ALBERT R. SHADLE.
1955. Pelage of the porcupine, *Erethizon dorsatum dorsatum*. Journ. Mammal. 36(1):84–95, illus. February 25.

POCOCK, R. I.
1935. The races of *Canis lupus*. Proc. Zool. Soc. London, 1935, pt. 3, pp. 647–86, illus. September.

POHLE, HERMANN.
1920. Die Unterfamilie der Lutrinae. Archiv für Naturg., 85 Jahrg. (1919), Abt. A, Heft 9, pp. 1–247. November.

POILEY, SAMUEL M.
1949. Raising captive meadow mice (*Microtus p. pennsylvanicus*). Journ. Mammal. 30(3):317–18. August 30.

POLDERBOER, EMMETT B.
1942. Habits of the least weasel (*Mustela rixosa*) in northeastern Iowa. Journ. Mammal. 23(2): 145–47. June 3.
1948 a. Predation on the domestic pig by the long-tailed weasel. Journ. Mammal. 29(3):295–96. August 31.
1948 b. Late fall sexual activity in an Iowa least weasel. Journ. Mammal. 29(3):296. August 31.

POLDERBOER, EMMETT B., LEE W. KUHN, and GEORGE O. HENDRICKSON.
1941. Winter and spring habits of weasels in central Iowa. Journ. Wildlife Management 5(1): 115–19, pl. 7. January.

POLLACK, E. MICHAEL.
1951 a. Food habits of the bobcat in the New England states. Journ. Wildlife Management 15(2): 209–13. April.
1951 b. Observations on New England bobcats. Journ. Mammal. 32(3):356–58. August.

POLLACK, E. MICHAEL, and WILLIAM G. SHELDON.
1951. The bobcat in Massachusetts, including analyses of food habits of bobcats from other northeastern states, principally New Hampshire. Massachusetts Div. Fisheries and Game. 24 pp., illus. September.

POOLE, EARL L.
1932. A survey of the mammals of Berks County, Pennsylvania. Reading Publ. Mus. and Art Gallery, Bull. no. 13, pp. 1–74, illus. December.

PORTER, T. WAYNE.
1951. A second nest of the goshawk near Douglas Lake, Cheboygan County, Michigan. Jack-Pine Warbler 29(3). September.

PRATT, ALEXANDER F.
1855. Reminiscence of Wisconsin. First Annual Report and Collections of the State Historical Soc. of Wisconsin for the year 1854, vol. 1, pp. 127–45.

PRATT, LORING W.
1942. Bregmatic fontanelle bones in the genus Lynx. Journ. Mammal. 23(4):411–16. December 30.

PRAY, LEON L.
1921. Opossum carries leaves with its tail. Journ. Mammal. 2(2):109–10. May 2.

PREBLE, EDWARD A.
1899. Revision of the jumping mice of the genus Zapus. North Amer. Fauna 15, 42 pp., 1 pl. August 8.

PREBLE, NORMAN A.
1938. Sexual dimorphism in Napaeozapus. Journ. Mammal. 19(2):254. May 12.
1956. Notes on the life history of Napaeozapus. Journ. Mammal. 37(2):196–200. June 12.

PRINCE, LESLIE A.
1940. Notes on the habits of the pigmy shrew (Microsorex hoyi) in captivity. Canadian Field-Nat. 54(7):97–100. October.

PROVOST, ERNEST E., and CHARLES M. KIRKPATRICK.
1952. Observations on the hoary bat in Indiana and Illinois. Journ. Mammal. 33(1):110–13. February 15.

PRUITT, WILLIAM O., JR.
1951. Mammals of the Chase C. Osborn Preserve, Sugar Island, Michigan. Journ. Mammal. 32(4):470–72. November 21.
1953. An analysis of some physical factors affecting the local distribution of the short-tail shrew (Blarina brevicauda) in the northern part of the Lower Peninsula of Michigan. Misc. Publ. Mus. Zool., Univ. Michigan, no. 79, pp. 39, map. July 30.
1954 a. Aging in the masked shrew, Sorex cinereus cinereus Kerr. Journ. Mammal. 35(1):35–39. February.
1954 b. Notes on a litter of young masked shrews. Journ. Mammal. 35(1):109–10. February.
1954 c. Notes on the short-tail shrew (Blarina brevicauda kirtlandi) in northern lower Michigan. Amer. Midland Nat. 52(1):236–41. July.

QUARLES, JOSEPH V.
1933. Letters of Joseph V. Quarles. Wisconsin Mag. of History 16(3):297–320. March.

QUAY, WILBUR B.
1954. The Meibomian glands of voles and lemmings (Microtinae). Mus. Zool., Univ. Michigan, Misc. Publ. no. 82, pp. 17, pls. 3. March 17.
1959. Microscopic structure and variation in the cutaneous glands of the deer, Odocoileus virginianus. Journ. Mammal. 40(1):114–28, illus. February.

QUICK, EDGAR R., and A. W. BUTLER.
1885. The habits of some Arvicolinae. Amer. Nat. 19(2):113–18, pl. 2. February.

QUICK, HORACE F.
1953. Occurrence of porcupine quills in carnivorous mammals. Journ. Mammal. 34(2):256–59. May 21.

QUIMBY, DON C.
1944. A comparison of overwintering populations of small mammals in northern coniferous forest for two consecutive years. Journ. Mammal. 25(1):86–87. February 18.
1951. The life history and ecology of the jumping mouse, Zapus hudsonius. Ecological Monographs 21:61–95, illus. January.

QUIMBY, DON C., and J. E. GAAB.
1957. Mandibular dentition as an age indicator in Rocky Mountain elk. Journ. Wildlife Management 21(4):435–51, illus. October.

RADECKEL, ARTHUR.
1920. A Wisconsin skunk farmer. Wisconsin Conservationist 1(6):11 January.

RAFINESQUE, C. S.
1832. On the moles of North America and two new species from Kentucky. Atlantic Journal, and Friend of Knowledge 1(2):61–62. Summer.

RAMAGE, MARY C.
1947. Notes on keeping bats in captivity. Journ. Mammal. 28(1):60–62. February 17.

RASMUSSEN, A. T.
1921. The hypophysis cerebri of the woodchuck (Marmota monax) with special reference to hibernation and inanitation. Endocrinology 5(1):33–66. January.
1916. Theories of hibernation. Amer. Naturalist 50:609–25.
1923. The so-called hibernating gland. Journ. Morphology 38:147–205, illus.

RAUSCH, ROBERT.
1950. Observations on histopathological changes associated with starvation in Wisconsin deer. Journ. Wildlife Management 14(2):156–61, pl. 6. April (May).

RAUSCH, ROBERT, and EVERETT L. SCHILLER.
1949. Some observations on cestodes of the genus Paranoplocephala Tuehe, parasitic on North American voles (Microtus spp.). Proc. Helminthological Soc. Washington 16(1):23–31. January.

RAUSCH, ROBERT, and JACK D. TINER.
1948. Studies on the parasitic helminths of the North Central States. I. Helminths of Sciuridae. Amer. Midland Nat. 39(3):728–47. May.
1949. Studies on the parasitic helminths of the North Central States. II. Helminths of voles (Microtus spp.). Preliminary report. Amer. Midland Nat. 41(3):655–74, illus. May.

RAWLEY, EDWIN, JESSOP B. LOW, and ETHELYN O. GREAVES.
1950. Venison, its care and cooking. Utah State

Agric. College, Extension Bull. 200, pp. 1–21, illus.

READ, CLARK P.
1949 a. Studies on North American helminths of the genus *Capillaria* Zeder, 1800 (Nematoda). I. Capillarids from mammals. Journ. Parasitology 35(3):223–30, illus. June.
1949 b. Studies on North American helminths of the genus *Capillaria* Zeder, 1800 (Nematoda). II. Additional capillarids from mammals with keys to the North American mammalian species. Journ. Parasitology 35(3):231–39, illus. June.

REARDEN, JIM D.
1951. Identification of waterfowl nest predators. Journ. Wildlife Management 15(4):386–95. October.

RECTOR, L. E.
1949. The mole as a possible reservoir of poliomyelitis. Archives of Pathology 47(4):366–77. April.

REESE, STABLER W.
1944. Wisconsin's elk herd. Wisconsin Conserv. Bull. 9(4):6–10, illus. April.

RESLER, GEORGE W.
1950. The Wisconsin rabbit-trapping program. Wisconsin Conserv. Bull. 15(4):13–15. April.

REYNOLDS, HAROLD C.
1945. Some aspects of the life history and ecology of the opossum in central Missouri. Journ. Mammal. 26(4):361–79. February 12.
1952. Studies on reproduction in the opossum (*Didelphis virginiana virginiana*). Univ. Calif. Publs. Zool. 52(3):223–84, illus.

RHOADS, SAMUEL N.
1901. A new weasel from western Pennsylvania. Proc. Acad. Nat. Sci. Philadelphia, 1900, pp. 751–54. February 7.
1903. The mammals of Pennsylvania and New Jersey. Philadelphia. 266 pp., 9 pls., 1 map.

RICHARDS, STEPHEN H.
1948. Fox Research Report (Summer quarter, 1948). Wisconsin Wildlife Research Quarterly Progress Repts. 7(3):51–55. October.

RICHARDS, STEPHEN H., and RUTH L. HINE.
1953. Wisconsin fox populations. Wisconsin Conserv. Dept., Tech. Wildlife Bull., no. 6, 78 pp., illus. July.

RICHARDSON, JOHN.
*1829. Fauna Boreali-Americana. Part First, Quadrupeds. London. 346 pp., illus.

RICHTER, CURT P., and JOHN T. EMLEN, JR.
1946. Instructions for using antu as a poison for the common Norway rat. U. S. Publ. Health Repts. 61(17):602–7. April 26.

RIEGEL, J. A.
1937 a. The deer question. Wisconsin Conserv. Bull. 2(11):10–13. November.
1937 b. More about deer. Wisconsin Conserv. Bull. 2(12):22–26. December.

RIIS, PAUL R.
1938. Woodland caribou and—time. Parks and Recreation, part 1, 21(10):529–35, June; part 2, 21

(11):594–600, July; part 3, 21(12):639–45, August; part 4, 22(1):23–30, September. Illustrated.

ROBINSON, A. J.
1941. Torture and destruction. Wisconsin Conserv. Bull. 6(5):19–24, illus. May.

ROBINSON, WELDON B.
1943. The "humane coyote-getter" vs. the steel trap in control of predatory animals. Journ. Wildlife Management 7(2):179–89. April.

ROBINSON, WIRT.
1923. Woodchucks and chipmunks. Journ. Mammal. 4(4):256–57. November 1.

ROCKWELL, ROBERT B.
1912. Peculiar actions of a striped ground squirrel. Journ. Animal Behavior 2(3):218–21. June.

RODOLF, THEODORE.
1900. Pioneering in the Wisconsin lead region. Rept. and Collections State Hist. Soc. of Wisconsin 15:353–54.

ROE, FRANK GILBERT.
1951. The North American buffalo; a critical study of the species in its wild state. Univ. of Toronto Press. pp. viii + 957, frontispiece.

ROLLINS, CLAIR T.
1945. Habits, foods and parasites of the bobcat in Minnesota. Journ. Wildlife Management 9(2):131–45, pls. 4–5. April.

ROTH, ADOLPH R.
1938. Mating of beavers. Journ. Mammal. 19(1):108. February 13.

ROWAN, WILLIAM.
1950. Winter habits and numbers of timber wolves. Journ. Mammal. 31(2):167–69. May 30.

RUEDEMANN, RUDOLPH, and W. J. SCHOONMAKER.
1938. Beaver-dams as geologic agents. Science, n.s., 88(2292):523–25. December 2.

RUHL, H. D.
1949. Deer management designed to win support. Wisconsin Conserv. Bull. 14(6):27–28. June.

RUSH, WILLIAM M.
1932. Northern Yellowstone elk study. Montana Fish and Game Commission, Helena. 131 pp., illus. 1 fold. table, 1 fold. map. December.

RUSSELL, ERNEST.
1902. Others appeal for the grey squirrel. Recreation 16(4):284–85. April.

RUSTAD, ORWIN A.
1952. Carnivorous behavior in the muskrat. Journ. Mammal. 33(1):114. February.

RYBARCZYK, WILLIAM.
1949. Deer management means better hunting— or worse? Wisconsin Conserv. Bull. 14(6):26. June.

RYSGAARD, G. N.
1941. Bats killed by severe storm. Journ. Mammal. 22(4):452–53. November 13.
1942. A study of the cave bats of Minnesota with especial reference to the large brown bat, Eptesicus fuscus fuscus (Beauvois). Amer. Midland Nat. 28(1):245–67. July.

SABINE, JOSEPH.
1822. Accounts of the marmots of North America

hitherto known, with notices and descriptions of three new species. Trans. Linnaean Soc. London 13:579–91, illus.

SACKETT, LEROY WALTER.

1913. The Canada porcupine: A study of the learning process. Behavior Monographs 2(2), serial number 7, pp. iii + 84. June.

SAMPSON, FRANK W., and ALLEN BROHN.

1955. Missouri's program of extension predator control. Journ. Wildlife Management 19(2):272–80. April.

SANBORN, COLIN CAMPBELL, and DOUGLASS TIBBITS.

1949. Hoy's pygmy shrew in Illinois. Chicago Acad. Sci., Nat. Hist., Miscellanea no. 36, pp. 2. February 18.

SANBORN, ELWIN R.

1929. The growth of a wapiti antler. New York Zool. Soc. Bull. 32:25–33, illus.

SANBORN, T.

1872. Hibernation of the jumping mouse. Amer. Nat. 6:330–32.

SANDERSON, GLEN C.

1949. Growth and behavior of a litter of captive long-tailed weasels. Journ. Mammal. 30(4):412–15. November 21.

SATHER, J. HENRY.

1954. The dentition method of aging muskrats. Chicago Acad. Sciences, Nat. Hist. Miscellanea no. 130, 3 pp., illus. March 8.

SAUNDERS, ARETAS A.

1932. The voice of the porcupine. Journ. Mammal. 13(2):107–8. May 11.

SAUNDERS, P. B.

1929. Microsorex hoyi in captivity. Journ. Mammal. 10(1):78–79. February 11.

SAUNDERS, W. E.

1921. Notes on Napaeozapus. Journ. Mammal. 2 (4):237–38. November.

1932. Notes on the mammals of Ontario. Trans. Royal Canadian Inst. 18:271–309.

SAY, THOMAS.

1823. In Stephen H. Long and Edwin James. "Account of an expedition from Pittsburgh to the Rocky Mountains performed in the years 1819–1820."

SCHANTZ, VIOLA S.

1946. A new badger from Wisconsin. Journ. Mammal. 26(4):431. February 12.

1953. Additional information on distribution and variation of eastern badgers. Journ. Mammal. 34(3):388–89. August 17.

1960. Record of an albino pine vole. Journ. Mammal. 41(1):129. February 20.

SCHEFFER, THEO. H.

1910. The common mole. Kansas State Agric. College Exper. Sta. Bull. 168, pp. 36, illus. August 1.

1917. The common mole of the eastern United States. U. S. Dept. Agric., Farmers' Bull. 583, pp. 12. April.

1922. American moles as agricultural pests and as fur producers. U. S. Dept. Agric., Farmers' Bull. 1247, pp. 24. March.

1940. Excavation of a runway of the pocket gopher (Geomys bursarius). Trans. Kansas Acad. Sci. 43:473–74.

SCHEFFER, VICTOR B.

1953. Otter diving to a depth of sixty feet. Journ. Mammal. 34(2):255. May 14.

SCHMIDT, F. J. W.

1927. Pitymys pinetorum scalopsoides in Wisconsin. Journ. Mammal. 8:248. August 9.

1931. Mammals of western Clark County, Wisconsin. Journ. Mammal. 12(2):99–117. May 14.

SCHMIDT, KARL P.

1936. Dehairing of caterpillars by skunks. Journ. Mammal. 17(3):287. August 17.

SCHOOLEY, J. P.

1934. A summer breeding season in the eastern chipmunk, Tamias striatus. Journ. Mammal. 15(3):194–96. August 10.

SCHOONOVER, LYLE J., and WILLIAM H. MARSHALL.

1951. Food habits of the raccoon (Procyon lotor hirtus) in North-central Minnesota. Journ. Mammal. 32(4):422–28. November 21.

SCHORGER, A. W.

1937 a. House rat in bank swallow's nest. Journ. Mammal. 18(2):244. May 12.

1937 b. The range of the bison in Wisconsin. Trans. Wisconsin Acad. Sciences, Arts and Letters 30:117–30, illus. November.

1938. A Wisconsin specimen of the cougar. Journ. Mammal. 19(2):252. May 12.

1939 a. Wolverine in Michigan. Journ. Mammal. 20(4):503. November 14.

1939 b. Notes on the muskrat. Journ. Mammal. 20(4):506. November 14.

1940. A record of the caribou in Michigan. Journ. Mammal 21(2):222. May 16.

1942 a. The Canada porcupine in southern Wisconsin. Journ. Mammal. 23(1):97–98. February 16.

1942 b. Extinct and endangered mammals and birds of the upper Great Lakes region. Trans. Wisconsin Acad. Sciences, Arts and Letters 34:23–44.

1944. The validity of Bison bison pennsylvanicus. Journ. Mammal. 25(3):313–15. September 8.

1946. Records of wolverine for Wisconsin and Minnesota. Journ. Mammal. 27(1):90. March 14.

1947 a. The sense of smell in the short-tailed shrew. Journ. Mammal. 28(2):180. May 22.

1947 b. Canada lynx taken in Sauk County, Wisconsin. Journ. Mammal. 28(2):186–87. May 22.

1947 c. An emigration of squirrels in Wisconsin. Journ. Mammal. 28(4):401–3. December 1.

1948 a. Changing wildlife conditions in Wisconsin. Wisconsin Conserv. Bull. 13(6):53–60, illus. June

1948 b. Further records of the wolverine for Wisconsin and Michigan. Journ. Mammal. 29(3):295. August 31.

1949 a. The black bear in early Wisconsin. Trans.

Wisconsin Acad. Sci., Arts and Letters 39:151–94. August 1.

1949 b. Squirrels in early Wisconsin. Trans. Wisconsin Acad. Sci., Arts and Letters 39:195–247. August 1.

1950. Harvest mouse in Dane County, Wisconsin. Journ. Mammal. 31(3):363. August.

1951. *Zapus* with white tail-tip. Journ. Mammal. 32(3):362. August 23.

1953 a. Large Wisconsin beaver. Journ. Mammal. 34(2):260–61. May 14.

1953 b. The white-tailed deer in early Wisconsin. Trans. Wisconsin Acad. Sci., Arts and Letters 42:197–247. August 27.

1954. The elk in early Wisconsin. Trans. Wisconsin Acad. Sci., Arts and Letters 43:5–23. September 15.

1957. The moose in early Wisconsin. Trans. Wisconsin Acad. Sci., Arts and Letters 45:1–10. March 29.

SCHUETTE, H. A., and RALPH W. THOMAS.
1930. The composition of the fat of the silver black fox. Trans. Wisconsin Acad. Sci., Arts and Letters 25:113–16.

SCHUNKE, WILLIAM H., and IRVIN O. BUSS.
1941. Trends in the kill of Wisconsin whitetail bucks, 1936–1940. Journ. Wildlife Management 5(3):333–36, pl. 19. July.

SCHWARTZ, CHARLES W.
1941. Home range of the cottontail in central Missouri. Journ. Mammal. 22(4):386–92. November 13.

SCHWARTZ, CHARLES W., and ELIZABETH SCHWARTZ.
1956 a. Pine mouse (*Microtus pinetorum*). Missouri Conservationist 17(4):16–17, illus. April.

1956 b. Prairie meadow mouse (*Microtus ochrogaster*). Missouri Conservationist 17(5):15–17, illus. May.

SCHWARTZ, HAROLD.
1929. Tularemia from a muskrat. Journ. Amer. Med. Asso. 92:1180–81. April 6.

SCHWARZ, ERNST.
1945. On North American house mice. Journ. Mammal. 26(3):315–16. November 14.

SCHWARZ, ERNST, and HENRIETTA K. SCHWARZ.
1943. The wild and commensal stocks of house mouse, *Mus musculus* Linnaeus. Journ. Mammal. 24(1):59–72. February 20.

SCOTT, THOMAS G.
1937. Mammals of Iowa. Iowa State Journ. Sci. 12(1):43–97. October.

1939. Number of foetuses in the Hoy pigmy shrew. Journ. Mammal. 20(2):251. May 15.

1947. Comparative analysis of red fox feeding on two central Iowa areas. Agric. Exper. Sta., Iowa State College of Agric. and Mechanic Arts, Research Bull. 353, pp. 425–87, illus. August.

1955 a. Dietary patterns of red and gray foxes. Ecology 36(2):366–67. April.

1955 b. An evaluation of the red fox. Illinois Nat. Hist. Surv., Biol. Notes no. 35, pp. 1–16, illus. July.

SCOTT, THOMAS G., and WILLARD D. KLIMSTRA.
1955. Red foxes and a declining prey population. Southern Illinois Univ., Carbondale, Ill., Monograph ser. no. 1, pp. 123. June.

SCOTT, WALTER E.
1937–38. Conservation history. Wisconsin Conserv. Bull. 2(3):10–15; (4):14–20; (5):23–30 (6): 27–37; (9):26–31; 3(4):26–37.

1938 a. Wisconsin deer situation, September, 1938. Wisconsin Conserv. Bull. 3(10):40–46. October.

1938 b. Wisconsin's large deer. Wisconsin Conserv. Bull. 3(11):3–4. November.

1939 a. Swimming power of the Canadian otter. Journ. Mammal. 20(3):371. August 14.

1939 b. Rare and extinct mammals of Wisconsin. Wisconsin Conserv. Bull. 4(10):21–28, illus. October.

1939 c. Fifth archery deer season. Wisconsin Conserv. Bull. 4(12):32–35. December.

1941. Kettle eaten by porcupine. Journ. Mammal. 22(3):325–26. August 14.

1946. Fox cycle high in Crawford County. Wisconsin Conserv. Bull. 11(8–9):19–29, illus. August.

1947 a. Muskrat farms. Wisconsin Conserv. Bull. 12(2):16. February.

1947 b. The "Old North" returns. A study of wildlife in central Wisconsin with especial reference to recent hunting seasons. Wisconsin Conserv. Bull. 12(4):13–27, illus. April.

1947 c. Maps showing Wisconsin game statistics with license sales data. (Hunting 1946–47; Trapping 1945-46.) Wisconsin Conserv. Dept., 10 pp., maps. Processed. June.

1947 d. The black bear in Wisconsin. Wisconsin Conserv. Bull. 12(11):3–10, 3 maps. November.

1948. Deer facts and sympathies crash head-on in Wisconsin — Administrator's dilemma — Sportsmen's burden. Michigan Conservation 17(1):6–7, 12–13. November.

1949. Administrator's dilemma—sportsmen's burden. Wisconsin Conserv. Bull. 14(1):6–10. January.

1950. Estimated total harvest 1949–50 fur seasons on muskrat, mink, skunk and weasel. Activities Progress Rept., State Conserv. Comm. of Wisconsin, no. 29, fig. 3C, processed. August 31.

1951. Wisconsin's first spotted skunk, and other notes. Journ. Mammal. 32(3):363. August 23.

1952. Wisconsin game kill and license sales charts. Wisconsin Conserv. Dept., Game Management Div., 20 pp., charts.

SCOTT, WILLIAM BERRYMAN.
*1937. A history of land mammals in the Western Hemisphere. Second ed., revised. Macmillan Co. 786 pp., illus.

SEAGEARS, CLAYTON B.
1944. The fox in New York. Educational Bull., New York Conserv. Dept., 85 pp., illus. October.

SEALANDER, JOHN A.
1943. Notes on some parasites of the mink in southern Michigan. Journ. Parasitology 29(3):361–62. October.

SELKO, LYLE F.
1937. Food habits of Iowa skunks in the fall of 1936. Journ. Wildlife Management 1(3–4):70–76. October.
1938. Hibernation of the striped skunk in Iowa. Journ. Mammal. 19(3):320–24. August 18.

SETON, ERNEST THOMPSON.
1902. [Spare the grey squirrel.] Recreation 16 (3):205. March.
1907. The habits of wolves. Amer. Magazine 64 (6):636–45, illus. October.
°1909. Life-histories of northern animals. An account of the mammals of Manitoba. Vol. 1, pp. 1–673, pls. 1–46, maps 1–38; Vol. 2, pp. 675–1267 pls. 47–100, maps 39–68. October.
1920 a. Migrations of the gray squirrel (Sciurus carolinensis). Journ. Mammal. 1(2):53–58. March 2.
1920 b. Notes on the breeding habits of captive deermice. Journ. Mammal. 1(3):134–38. June 19.
1922. Bannertail. The story of a gray squirrel. Charles Scribner's Sons, New York. 265 pp., 8 pls.
1923. The mane on the tail of the gray-fox. Journ. Mammal. 4(3):180–82. August 10.
°1929. Lives of game animals. 4 vols., in 8 parts. Doubleday, Doran and Co., New York.

SEVERAID, JOYE HAROLD.
1942. The snowshoe hare: Its life history and artificial propagation. Maine Dept. Inland Fisheries and Game. 95 pp.
1945. Breeding potential and artificial propagation of the snowshoe hare. Journ. Wildlife Management 9(11):290–95. October.

SEVERINGHAUS, C. W.
1949. Tooth development and wear as criteria of age in white-tailed deer. Journ. Wildlife Management 12(2):195–216, pls. 4–7. April.

SEVERINGHAUS, C. W., and JOHN E. TANCK.
1948. Speed and gait of an otter. Journ. Mammal. 29(1):71. February 13.

SHACKLEFORD, RICHARD M.
1949. Six mutations affecting coat color in ranch-bred mink. Amer. Nat. 83(809):49–67. April.

SHADLE, ALBERT R.
1944. The play of American porcupines (Erethizon d. dorsatum and E. epizanthum). Journ. Comp. Psychol. 37(3):145–50. June.
1946. Copulation in the porcupine. Journ. Wildlife Management 10(2):159–62, pls. 12–13. April.
1947. Porcupine spine penetration. Journ. Mammal. 28(2):180–81. May 22.
1948. Gestation period in the porcupine, Erethizon dorsatum dorsatum. Journ. Mammal. 29(2):162–64. May 14.
1950 a. The North American porcupine up-to-date. Ward's Nat. Sci. Bull. 24(1):5–6, 11. September.
1950 b. Feeding, care, and handling captive porcupines (Erethizon). Journ. Mammal. 31(4):411–16. November 22.
1951. Laboratory copulations and gestations of porcupine, Erethizon dorsatum. Journ. Mammal. 32

(2):219–21. May.
1952. Sexual maturity and first recorded copulation of a 16-month male porcupine, Erethizon dorsatum dorsatum. Journ. Mammal. 33(2):239–41. May.
1953. Captive striped skunk produces two litters. Journ. Wildlife Management 17(3):388–89. July.
1955 a. Effects of porcupine quills in humans. Amer. Nat. 89 (whole no. 844):47–49. February.
1955 b. Removal of foreign quills by porcupines. Journ. Mammal. 36(3):463–65. August 30.
1956. The American beaver. Animal Kingdom [New York Zool. Soc.] 59(4):98–104; 59(5):152–56; 59(6):181–85.

SHADLE, ALBERT R., and WILLIAM R. PLOSS.
1943. An unusual porcupine parturition and development of the young. Journ. Mammal. 24(4):492–96. November 17.

SHADLE, ALBERT R., WILLIAM B. PLOSS and EUGENE M. MARKS.
1944. The extrusive growth and attrition of the incisor teeth of Erethizon dorsatum. Anat. Record 90(4):337–41. December.

SHADLE, ALBERT R., and DONALD PO-CHEDLEY.
1949. Rate of penetration of porcupine spine. Journ. Mammal. 30(2):172–73. May 26.

SHADLE, ALBERT R., MARILYN SMELZER, and MARGERY METZ
1946. The sex reactions of porcupines (Erethizon d. dorsatum) before and after copulation. Journ. Mammal. 27(2):116–21. May 14.

SHAPIRO, JACOB.
1949. Ecological and life history notes on the porcupine in the Adirondacks. Journ. Mammal. 30 (3):247–57. August 20.

SHARP, WARD M.
1958. Aging gray squirrels by use of tail-pelage characteristics. Journ. Wildlife Management 22 (1):29–34; illus. January.

SHAW, GEORGE.
1800. Description of the Mus bursarius. Trans. Linnaean Soc. London 5:227–28, plate 8.

SHAW, WILLIAM T.
1928. The spring and summer activities of the dusky skunk in captivity. With a chapter on the insect food of the dusky skunk by K. F. Chamberlain. New York State Mus. Handbook no. 4, 103 pp., illus. August.

SHEAK, W. HENRY.
1926. A study of the Virginia opossum. Bull. Wagner Free Inst. Sci. (Philadelphia) 1(5):39–45. October.

SHELDON, CAROLYN.
1934. Studies on the life histories of Zapus and Napaeozapus in Nova Scotia. Journ. Mammal. 15(4):290–300. November 15.
1938 a. Vermont jumping mice of the genus Zapus. Journ. Mammal. 19(3):324–32, illus. August 18.
1938 b. Vermont jumping mice of the genus Napaeozapus. Journ. Mammal. 19(4):444–53. November 14.

SHELDON, CHARLES.
1927. The conservation of the elk of Jackson Hole, Wyoming. A report [by the chairman, Commission on Conservation of the Jackson Hole elk] to Hon. Dwight F. Davis, the Secretary of War, Chairman of the President's Committee on Outdoor Recreation and Hon. Frank C. Emerson, Governor of Wyoming. Washington, D. C. 36 pp., illus. July.

SHELDON, WILLIAM G.
1949. Reproductive behavior of foxes in New York State. Journ. Mammal. 30(3):236–46. August 20.
1950. Denning habits and home range of red foxes in New York state. Journ. Wildlife Management 14(1):33–42. January.

SHERMAN, ALTHEA R.
1926 a. Periodicity in the calling of a chipmunk. Journ. Mammal. 7(4):331–32. November 23.
1926 b. Fox squirrels' nests in a barn. Journ. Mammal. 7(4):332. November 23.
1929. Summer outings of bats during fourteen seasons. Journ. Mammal. 10(4):319–26. November 11.

SHIELDS, G. O.
1902. Save the grey squirrels. Recreation 16(1):70. January.

SHIRAS, GEORGE, 3RD.
1920. A raccoon explores new country. How one of these pioneers visited a camp on the south shore of Lake Superior, and was encouraged to remain. Forest & Stream 90:10–11, 44. January.
1921. The wild life of Lake Superior, past and present. Nat. Geogr. Mag. 40(2):113–204. August.

SHORTEN, MONICA.
1951. Some aspects of the biology of the grey squirrel (Sciurus carolinensis) in Great Britain. Proc. Zool. Soc. London 121(2):427–59, pl. 1. August 31.

SHULL, A. FRANKLIN.
1907. Habits of the short-tailed shrew Blarina brevicauda (Say). Amer. Nat. 41(488):495–522, illus.

SIEGLER, HILBERT R.
1937. Winter rodent damage to game cover. Journ. Mammal. 18(1):57–61. February 11.

SILVER, JAMES.
1924 a. The reproductive potential of rats. Journ. Mammal. 5(1):66–67. February 8.
1924 b. Rodent enemies of fruit and shade trees. Journ. Mammal. 5(2):165–73. May.
1927. The introduction and spread of house rats in the United States. Journ. Mammal. 8(1):58–60. February 9.
1933. Hunting the den of the timber wolf. Northern Sportsman, 3(12):3–4, 14, April. Munising, Mich.
1935. Eliminating bats from buildings. U. S. Dept. Agric. Leaflet no. 109, pp. 5. September.

SILVER, JAMES, and A. W. MOORE.
1941. Mole control. U. S. Fish & Wildlife Service, Conserv. Bul. 14, pp. 17, illus.

SILVER, JAMES, W. E. CROUCH, and M. C. BETTS.
1942. Rat proofing buildings and premises. U. S.

Dept. Interior, Fish & Wildlife Service, Conserv. Bull. no. 19, pp. 26, illus.

SILVER, JAMES, and F. E. GARLOUGH.
1941. Rat control. U. S. Dept. Interior, Fish & Wildlife Service, Conserv. Bull. no. 8, pp. 27, illus.

SILVER, JAMES, and J. C. MUNCH.
1931. Red-squill powder in rat control. Leaflet 65, U. S. Dept. Agric., Washington, pp. 1–8, figs. 1–2. January, 1931.

SIMPSON, GEORGE GAYLORD.
1935. Note on the classification of recent and fossil opossums. Journ. Mammal. 16(2):134–38. May 15.
°1945. The principles of classification and a classification of mammals. Bull. Amer. Mus. Nat. Hist., vol. 85, pp. xvi + 350.

SIMPSON, SUTHERLAND ERIC.
1923. The nest and young of the star-nosed mole (Condylura cristata). Journ. Mammal. 4(3):167–70, pls. 17–20. August 10.

SKINNER, ALANSON.
1926. The Mascoutens or Prairie Potawatomi Indians. Part II. Notes on the material culture. Bull. Public Mus. City of Milwaukee 6(2):263–326, pls. 9–21. June 15.

SKINNER, MORRIS F., and OVE C. KAISEN.
1947. The fossil Bison of Alaska and preliminary revision of the genus. Bull. Amer. Mus. Nat. Hist. 89(3):125–236, pls. 8–26. October 31.

SLONAKER, JAMES ROLLIN.
1902. The eyes of the common mole, Scalops aquaticus machrinus. Journ. Comp. Neurology 12(4):335–66, pls. 18–20.
1920. Some morphological changes for adaptation in the mole. Journ. Morphology 34(2):335–73, illus. September.

SMITH, ALBERT E., and GEORGE J. KNUDSEN.
1955. Beaver control in Wisconsin. Wisconsin Conserv. Bull. 20(7):21–24. July.

SMITH, CHARLES F.
1948. A burrow of the pocket gopher (Geomys bursarius) in eastern Kansas. Trans. Kansas Acad. Sci. 51(3):313–15, illus.

SMITH, ELIZABETH.
1956. Pregnancy in the little brown bat. Amer. Journ. Physiol. 185(1):61–74. April.

SMITH, ISAAC T.
1856. Extract from the Journal of I. T. Smith, Esq. In History of Rock County and Transactions of the Rock County Agricultural Society and Mechanics' Institute. Edited by Orrin Guernsey and Josiah F. Willard. Janesville, Wisconsin.

SMITH, CAPTAINE [JOHN].
1612. A Map of Virginia with a description of the Countrey, the Commodities, People, Government and Religion. 109 pp.

SMITH, LAWRENCE F.
1943. Internal parasites of the red fox in Iowa. Journ. Wildlife Management 7(2):172–78. April.

SMITH, LUTHER.
1941. Observations on the nest-building behavior of

the opossum. Journ. Mammal. 22(2):201–2. May 13.

SMITH, SAM'L R.
1897. Locked deer horns. Forest and Stream 49 (16):303, illus. October 16. (Clear Lake, Vilas Co., Wisc.)

SMITH, WILLIAM W.
1954. The house mouse and murine typhus in Mississippi. U. S. Publ. Health Repts. 69(6):591–93. June.

SNEAD, EDWIN, and GEORGE O. HENDERSON.
1942. Food habits of the badger in Iowa. Journ. Mammal. 23(4):380–91. November 4.

SNELL, GEORGE D., ed.
°1943. Biology of the laboratory mouse. By the Staff of the Rosco B. Jackson Memorial Laboratory; with a chapter on the infectious diseases of mice by J. H. Dingle. 2nd ed. Blackiston Co., Philadelphia. pp. ix + 497, illus.

SNYDER, DANA P.
1954. Skull variation in the meadow vole (Microtus p. pennsylvanicus) in Pennsylvania. Ann. Carnegie Mus. 33:201–34. September 21.
1956. Survival rates, longevity, and population fluctuations in the white-footed mouse, Peromyscus leucopus, in southeastern Michigan. Misc. Publ. Mus. Zool. Univ. Michigan, no. 95, 33 pp. January 30.

SNYDER, L. L.
1921. An outside nest of a flying squirrel. Journ. Mammal. 2(3):171. August 19.
1923. A method employed by a black squirrel in carrying its young. Journ. Mammal. 4(1):59. February 9.
1924. Some details on the life history and behavior of Napaeozapus insignis abietorum (Preble). Journ. Mammal. 5(4):233–37, illus. November 15.
1929. Cryptotis parva, a new shrew for the Canadian list. Journ. Mammal. 10(1):79–80. February 11.

SNYDER, W. E.
1897 a. Overland journeys of Fiber zibethicus. Oregon Nat. 4:8. January.
1897 b. A full house. Oregon Nat. 4:9. January.
1897 c. Variation in the genus Sciurus. Oregon Nat. 4:10. January.
1902. A list, with brief notes, of the mammals of Dodge Co., Wisc. Bull. Wisc. Nat. Hist. Soc. 2(2):113–26. April.

SOLLBERGER, DWIGHT E.
1940. Notes on the life history of the small eastern flying squirrel. Journ. Mammal. 21(3):282–93. August 13.
1943. Notes on the breeding habits of the eastern flying squirrel (Glaucomys volans volans). Journ. Mammal. 24(2):163–73, illus. June 8.

SOMERS, A. N.
1933. In S. A. Barrett. Ancient Aztalan. Appendix F, pp. 384–88.

SOOTER, CLARENCE A.
1943. Speed of predator and prey. Journ. Mam-

mal. 24(1):102–3. February 20.

SOPER, J. DEWEY.
1921. Notes on the snowshoe rabbit. Journ. Mammal 2(2):101–8. May 2.
1944. Notes on the large short-tailed shrew at Fort Garry, Manitoba. Canadian Field-Nat. 58(3):104. June.

SOUTHERN, H. N., and E. M. O. LAURIE.
1946. The house-mouse (Mus musculus) in corn ricks. Journ. Animal Ecology 15(2):134–49, pls. 3–4. November.

SOUTHWICK, CHARLES H.
1954. Canine teeth in a Wisconsin white-tailed deer fawn. Journ. Mammal. 35(3):456–57. August.
1955. The population dynamics of confined house mice supplied with unlimited food. Ecology 36 (2):212–225, illus. April.

SOWLS, LYLE K.
1948. The Franklin ground squirrel, Citellus franklinii (Sabine), and its relationship to nesting ducks. Journ. Mammal. 29(2):113–37, illus. May 14.

SPENCER, DONALD A.
1950. The porcupine, its economic status and control. U. S. Dept. Interior, Fish and Wildlife Service, Wildlife Leaflet 328, pp. 1–7. (Processed.)

SPERRY, CHARLES E.
1933. Opossum and skunk eat bats. Journ. Mammal. 14(2):152–53. May 15.
1941. Food habits of the coyote. U. S. Dept. Interior, Fish and Wildlife Service, Wildlife Research Bull. 4, pp. iv + 70, pls. 3. July 11.

SPRULES, WILLIAM M.
1941. The effect of a beaver dam on the insect fauna of a trout stream. Trans. Amer. Fisheries Soc. 70(1940):236–48.

SPURRELL, J. A.
1917. An annotated list of the mammals of Sac County. Proc. Iowa Acad. Sci. 24:273–84.

STANLEY, PAUL C.
1921. Albinism in the black bear. Science (n.s.) 54(1386):74. July 22.

STEBLER, A. M.
1938. Feeding behavior of a skunk. Journ. Mammal. 19(3):374. August 18.
1940. The tracking technique in the study of the larger predatory mammals. Trans. Fourth Annual North Amer. Wildlife Conference, pp. 203–8.
1944. The status of the wolf in Michigan. Journ. Mammal. 25(1):37–43. February 18.

STEGEMAN, LeROY C.
1930. Notes on Synaptomys cooperi cooperi in Washtenaw County, Michigan. Journ. Mammal. 11(4):460–66. November 11.
1937. Notes on young skunks in captivity. Journ. Mammal. 18(2):194–202, illus. May 12.
1939. Some parasites and pathological conditions of the skunk (Mephitis mephitis nigra) in central New York. Journ. Mammal. 20(4):493–96. November 14.
1954. Notes on the development of the little brown

bat *Myotis lucifugus lucifugus.* Journ. Mammal. 35(3):432–33. August.

STEINKE, HAROLD.
1953. The automobile as a predator of wildlife. Wisconsin Conserv. Bull. 16(7):7–10. July.

STENLUND, MILTON H.
1955. A field study of the timber wolf (Canis lupus) on the Superior National Forest, Minnesota. Minnesota Dept. Conservation, Tech. Bull. No. 4, pp. 55, illus.

STILES, CHESTER W., and CLARA EDITH BAKER.
°1935. Key-catalogue of parasites reported for Carnivora (cats, dogs, bears, etc.) with their possible public health importance. Nat. Inst. Health Bull. no. 163, pp. 913–1223. March.

STILES, CHESTER W., and MABELLE O. NOLAN.
°1931. Key catalogue of parasites reported for Chiroptera (bats) with their possible public health importance. U. S. Public Health Service, Nat. Inst. Health Bull. 155, pp. 603–742.

STODDARD, H. L.
1920 a. The flying squirrel as a bird killer. Journ. Mammal. 1(2):95–96. March 2.
1920 b. Nests of the western fox squirrel. Journ. Mammal. 1(3):122–23, pl. 7. June 19.
1922. Notes on the diet of the long-eared owl. Year Book, Public Mus. City of Milwaukee, 1921, vol. 1, pp. 66–71, illus. July 20.

STOECKELER, J. H.
1955. Deer, mice, and hares damage young aspen and paper birch plantings in northeastern Wisconsin. U. S. Forest Service, Lake States Exper. Sta. (St. Paul, Minn.) Tech. Notes No. 441, 1 p. October.

STOECKELER, J. H., and G. A. LIMSTROM.
1942. Ecological factors influencing reforestation in northern Wisconsin. Ecological Monographs 12:191–212.

STOECKELER, J. H., R. O. STROTHMANN, and L. W. KREFTING.
1957. Effect of deer browsing on reproduction in the northern hardwood-hemlock type in northeastern Wisconsin. Journ. Wildlife Management 21(1):75–80, illus. January.

STOLLBERG, BRUCE P.
1948. The white-tailed deer (*Odocoileus virginianus borealis*) in Wisconsin. Pro Natura [Switzerland] 1(2):89–91, illus. October.

STOLLBERG, BRUCE P., and RUTH L. HINE.
1952. Food habit studies of ruffed grouse, pheasant, quail and mink in Wisconsin. Wisconsin Conser. Dept., Tech. Wildlife Bull. no. 4, pp. 22, illus.

STONE, WITMER, and WILLIAM EVERETT CRAM.
°1905. American animals. Doubleday Co., New York. 318 pp., illus.

STONER, DAYTON.
1939. Eastern sparrow hawk feeding on big brown bat. Auk 56(4):474. October.
1940. The Canada porcupine as a highway casualty. Journ. Mammal. 21(3):360–61. August 13.

STRECKER, R. L., and JOHN T. EMLEN, JR.
1953. Regulatory mechanisms in house-mouse pop-

ulations: the effect of limited food supply on a confined population. Ecology 34(2):375–85. April.

STRONG, MOSES.
1883. List of the mammals of Wisconsin. Geology of Wisconsin, Survey of 1873–1879, vol. 1, chap. 10, pp. 436–40.

STRUTHERS, PARKE H.
1928. Breeding habits of the Canadian porcupine (Erethizon dorsatum). Journ. Mammal. 9(4): 300–308, pls. 22–23. November 13.

STUEWER, FREDERICK W.
1942. Studies of molting and priming of fur of the eastern raccoon. Journ. Mammal. 23(4):399–404. December 30.
1943 a. Reproduction of raccoons in Michigan. Journ. Wildlife Management 7(1):60–73, pl. 3. January.
1943 b. Raccoons: their habits and management in Michigan. Ecol. Monographs 13(203–58, illus. April.
1948 a. A record of red bats mating. Journ. Mammal. 29(2):180–81. May 14.
1948 b. Artificial dens for raccoons. Journ. Wildlife Management 12(3):296–301, pl. 8. July.

STUPKA, ARTHUR.
1934. Woodland jumping mouse. Nature Notes from Arcadia 3:6. (Mimeographed.)

SURBER, THADDEUS.
1932. The mammals of Minnesota. (With a chapter on the vanished mammals of Minnesota, by Thomas S. Roberts.) Bull. Minnesota Dept. Conservation, Div. Game and Fish, 84 pp., illus.

SUTTON, GEORGE MIKSCH.
1929. The Alleghenian least weasel in Pennsylvanian. Journ. Mammal. 19(3):251–54. August 10.
1930. A wooly white-tailed deer. Journ. Mammal. 11(1):86–87. February 11.

SUTTON, R. W.
1956. Aquatic tendencies in the jumping mouse. Journ. Mammal. 37(2):299. June 12.

SVIHLA, ARTHUR.
1929. Number of mammae in muskrats. Amer. Nat. 63:573–74. November.
1930. Breeding habits and young of the red-backed mouse, Evotomys. Papers Michigan Acad. Sci., Arts and Letters 11:485–90.
1931 a. Change in color pattern in a captive red squirrel. Amer. Nat. 65(696):92–95. January.
1931 b. Habits of New York weasel in captivity. Journ. Mammal. 12(1):67–68. February 12.
1932. A comparative life history study of the mice of the genus *Peromyscus.* Univ. Michigan, Mus. Zool. Miscl. Publ. No. 24, pp. 39. July 8.
1935. Development and growth of the prairie deermouse, Peromyscus maniculatus bairdii. Journ. Mammal. 16(2):109–15. May 15.

SVIHLA, ARTHUR, and HOWARD S. BOWMAN.
1954. Hibernation in the American black bear. Amer. Midland Nat. 52(1):248–52. July.

SVIHLA, ARTHUR, and RUTH DOWELL SVIHLA.
1930. How a chipmunk carried her young. Journ.

Mammal. 11(3):314–15. August 9.

SVIHLA, RUTH DOWELL.
1931. Captive fox squirrels. Journ. Mammal. 12(2): 152–56. May 14.

SVIHLA, RUTH DOWELL, and ARTHUR SVIHLA.
1928. Occurrence of a mutant meadow-mouse. Science 67(1743):531. May 25.

SWANSON, GUSTAV.
1934. The little spotted skunk in northern Minnesota. Journ. Mammal. 15(4):318–19. November 15.

SWANSON, GUSTAV, and ARNOLD B. ERICKSON.
1946. Alaria taxideae n. sp., from the badger and other mustelids. Journ. Parasitol. 33(1):17–19. February.

SWANSON, GUSTAV, and CHARLES EVANS.
1936. The hibernation of certain bats in southern Minnesota. Journ. Mammal. 17(1):39–43. February 14.

SWANSON, GUSTAV, and P. O. FRYKLUND.
1935. The least weasel in Minnesota and its fluctuation in numbers. Amer. Midland Nat. 16(1): 120–26.

SWANSON, GUSTAV, THADDEUS SURBER, and THOMAS S. ROBERTS.
1945. The mammals of Minnesota. Minnesota Dept. Conserv., tech. bull. no. 2, pp. 108, illus.

SWENK, MYRON H.
1926. Notes on Mustela campestris Jackson, and on the American forms of least weasels. Journ. Mammal. 7(4):313–30. November 23.
1938. Distribution of Marmota monax in the Missouri Valley region. Journ. Mammal. 19(3):348–53. August 18.

SWIFT, ERNEST.
1937. First reports of 1937 deer season. Wisconsin Conserv. Bull. 2(11):7–9. November.
1940–41. Biography of a self-made naturalist. Wisconsin Conserv. Bull. 5(12):3–12; 6(1):41–52; 6(3):3–17; 6(4):3–8 (George Ruegger).
1946 a. A history of Wisconsin deer. Wisconsin Conservation Dept., Publication 323, pp. 96, illus. March.
1946 b. Deer as an outdoor problem. Wisconsin Conserv. Bull. 11(7):6–10. July.
1948. Wisconsin's deer damage to forest reproduction survey—final report. Wisconsin State Conserv. Dept., publ. no. 347, 24 pp., illus.
1949. Deer damage to forest reproduction survey. Wisconsin Conserv. Dept., Publ. no. 347, pp. 1–24.
1952. Deer herd control methods and their results. Wisconsin Conserv. Bull. 17(1):3–9. January.

SWITZENBERGER, D. F.
1950 a. A look at the fox bounty. Michigan Conservation 19(1):3–6, illus. February.
1950 b. Breeding productivity in Michigan red foxes. Journ. Mammal. 31(2):194–95. May 30.

SYLVESTER, WALTER R.
1949. The story of a Portage County deer yard. Wisconsin Conserv. Bull. 14(5):13–16. May.

TAUBE, CLARENCE M.
1947. Food habits of Michigan opossums. Journ.

Wildlife Management 11(1):97–103. January.

TAYLOR, WALTER P.
*1948. Outlines for study of mammalian ecology and life histories. U. S. Dept. Interior, Fish and Wildlife Service, Wildlife Leaflet 304, pp. 36, illus. (Processed.) April.
*1956. The deer of North America. The white-tailed, mule, and black-tailed deer, genus Odocoileus. Their history and management. Wildlife Management Institute. pp. xx + 668, illus.

TEERI, A. E., W. VIRCHOW, N. F. COLOVOS, and F. GREELEY.
1958. Blood composition of white-tailed deer. Journ. Mammal. 39(2):269–74. May 20.

TERRES, J. KENNETH.
1937. A chipmunk captures a mouse. Journ. Mammal. 18(1):100. February 11.
1939. Gray squirrel utilization of elm. Journ. Wildlife Management 3(4):358–59. October.
1940. Notes on the winter activity of a captive skunk. Journ. Mammal. 21(2):216–17. May 16.
1941. Speed of the varying hare. Journ. Mammal. 22(4):453–54. November 13.

TEST, FREDERICK H., and AVERY R. TEST.
1943. Incidence of dipteran parasitosis in populations of small mammals. Journ. Mammal. 24(4): 506–98. November 17.

THOMPSON, DANIEL Q.
1952. Travel, range, and food habits of timber wolves in Wisconsin. Journ. Mammal. 33(4): 429–42. November 19.

THOMPSON, DONALD R.
1953. Small game hunting prospects—1953. Wisconsin Conserv. Bull. 18(9):3–12. September.
1954. Small game hunting prospects—1954. Wisconsin Conserv. Bull. 19(9):3–12, maps. September.
1955. Small game prospects—1955. Wisconsin Conserv. Bull. 20(9):3–7, illus. September.
*1958. Field techniques for sexing and aging game animals. Wisconsin Conserv. Dept., Special Wildlife Rep. no. 1, 44 pp., illus. October.

THOMAS, CRAIG S.
1922. Are squirrels bird-enemies? Bird-Lore 24:206 7. August.

THOMSEN, HANS PETER.
1945. The winter habits of the northern white-footed mouse. Journ. Mammal. 26(2):138–42. July 19.

THWAITES, REUBEN GOLD, ed.
1902. French Regime in Wisconsin. 1721: Charlevoix visits Wisconsin; his description of the tribes. Collections State Historical Society of Wisconsin, vol. 16.
1910 a. Malhiot's Journal. See Malhiot, Victor Francois.
1910 b. Fur-Trade on the Upper Lakes, 1778–1815. Collections State Historical Society of Wisconsin 19:233–374.
1910 c. Fur-Trade in Wisconsin, 1815–1817. Collections State Historical Society of Wisconsin 19:375–488.
1911 a. The fur-trade in Wisconsin, 1812–1825. Collections State Historical Society of Wiscon-

sin 20:1–395.
1911 b. Curot's Journal. See Curot, Michel.
TINER, JACK D.
1951. A redescription of *Ascaris laevis* Leidy 1856 and notes on ascarids in rodents. Proc. Helminthological Soc. Washington 18:126–31.
1953. Fatalities in rodents caused by larvae *Ascaris* in the central nervous system. Journ. Mammal. 34(2):153–67. May 14.
1954. The fraction of *Peromyscus leucopus* fatalities caused by raccoon ascarid larvae. Journ. Mammal. 35(4):389–92. November.
TODD, JOHN B.
1927. Winter food of cottontail rabbits. Journ. Mammal. 8(3):222–28. August 9.
TRAINER, DANIEL O., JR.
1957. What about rabies? Wisconsin Conserv. Bull. 22(9):15–18. September.
TRAPIDS, HAROLD, and PETER E. CROWE.
1942. Color abnormalities in three genera of northeastern bats. Journ. Mammal. 23(3):303–5, illus. August 13.
TRUAX, WAYNE C.
1947. Muskrat management research. Wisconsin Conserv. Bull. 12(10):31–34, illus. October.
1950. The muskrat harvest on Horicon Marsh. Wiscon Conserv. Bull. 15(7):12–14, illus. July.
1955. Cottontails aplenty. Wisconsin Conserv. Bull. 20(8):3–5, illus. August.
TRUE, FREDERICK W.
1887. Some distinctive cranial characters of the Canada lynx. Proc. U. S. Nat. Mus. 10:8–0.
1891. The puma, or American lion: Felis concolor of Linnaeus. Rept. U. S. Nat. Mus. for 1889, pp. 591–608, pl. 94.
1896. A revision of the American moles. Proc. U. S. Nat. Mus. 19:1–111, pls. 4. December 21.
ULBRICH, JOHANNES.
1930. Die Bisamaratte: Lebensweise, Gang ihrer Ausbreitung in Europa, wirtschaftl. Bedeutg. u. Bekaempfg. pp. 137, illus.
ULMER, FREDERICK A., JR.
1940 a. Albinism in Blarina. Journ. Mammal. 21(1):89–90. February 15.
1940 b. A Delaware record of albinism in Blarina. Journ. Mammal. 21(4):457. November 14.
1941. Melanism in the Felidae, with special reference to the genus Lynx. Journ. Mammal. 22(3):285–88. August 14.
UNDERWOOD, WILLIAM LYMAN.
1921. Wild Brother. Atlantic Monthly Press, Boston. pp. xi + 140, 39 pls.
VALLEY, OLIVER J.
1948. 'Coon and 'Coonin'. Wisconsin Conserv. Bull. 13(9):15–18, illus. September.
VAN CLEAVE, HARLEY J.
*1953. Acanthocephala of North American mammals. Illinois Biol. Monographs 23(1–2):i–x; 1–179, illus.
VAN GELDER, RICHARD G.
1959. A taxonomic revision of the spotted skunks (genus *Spilogale*). Amer. Mus. Nat. Hist. 117(5):229–392, illus. June 15.

VERWYST, CHRYSOSTEM.
1895. Historic sites on Chequamegon Bay. Wisconsin Hist. Coll., vol. 13.
WADE, OTIS.
1927. Breeding habits and early life of the thirteen-striped ground squirrel, *Citellus tridecemlineatus* (Mitchill). Journ. Mammal. 8(4):269–76. November 11.
1930. The behavior of certain spermophiles with special reference to aestivation and hibernation. Journ. Mammal. 11(2):160–88, pl. 9. May 9.
1948. Rapid fat production by ground squirrels preceding hibernation. Nat. Hist. Miscellanea no. 28, 3 pp. October 12.
1950. Soil temperatures, weather conditions, and emergence of ground squirrels from hibernation. Journ. Mammal. 31(2):158–61. May 30.
WADE, OTIS, and PAUL T. GILBERT.
1940. The baculum of some Sciuridae and its significance in determining relationships. Journ. Mammal. 21(1):52–63, illus. February 14.
WAGGONER, DAVID W.
1946. The gray squirrel in western Vilas County. Wisconsin Conserv. Bull. 11(6):3–5. June.
1955. Hunting coyote and fox. Wisconsin Conserv. Bull. 20(12):15–18. December.
WAGNER, GEORGE.
1923. An odd malformation in a woodchuck. Journ. Mammal. 4(1):21, pl. 4. February 9.
WALKER, ALEX.
1930. The "hand-stand" and some other habits of the Oregon spotted skunk. Journ. Mammal. 11(9):227–29.
WALKER, ERNEST P.
1929. Evidence on the gestation period of martens. Journ. Mammal. 10(3):206–9, pl. 16. August 10.
1954. Shrews is shrews. Nature Mag. 47(3):125–28, illus. March.
WALLACE, A. F.
1922. Timber wolf. Wisconsin Conservationist 3(6):11. January.
WARD, HENRY L.
1904. A study of the variations of proportions in bats, with brief notes on some of the species mentioned. Trans. Wisconsin Acad. Sci., Arts and Letters 14:630–54, pls. 50–54 (graphs).
1905. The number of young of the red bat. Bull. Wisconsin Nat. Hist. Soc. 3:181–82.
1907. A weasel new to Wisconsin's fauna. Bull. Wisconsin Nat. Hist., Soc. 5:63–64.
1908. The American elk in southern Wisconsin. Bull. Wisconsin Nat. Hist. Soc. 6(3–4):145–46.
1909. Additional records of the Alleghenian least weasel in Wisconsin. Bull. Wisconsin Nat. Hist. Soc. 7:11–12.
1910. The brown bat in Wisconsin. Bull. Wisconsin Nat. Hist. Soc. 8:180–82. October.
1911 a. Additional Wisconsin record of Allegheny least weasel. Bull. Wisconsin Nat. Hist. Soc. 9:82.
1911 b. The status of Hoy's shrew in Wisconsin. Bull. Wisconsin Nat. Hist. Soc. 9:83–84.

WARREN, EDWARD R.
1927. The beaver: Its work and its ways. Monog. Amer. Soc. Mammal., no. 2. Williams and Wilkins Co., Baltimore. pp. xx + 177, pls. 47. April.

WASKOW, BEN F.
1939. Bayfield otter. Wisconsin Conserv. Bull. 4 (4):61. April.

WASKOW, BEN F., and GEORGE A. CURRAN.
1954. Deer hunting on the Apostle Islands. Wisconsin Conserv. Bull. 19(10):3–7. October.

WEGG, ROBERT T.
1939. Managing Wisconsin deer. Wisconsin Conserv. Bull. 4(4):20–23. April.

WEISS, SIEGFRIED.
1940. A simple deer repellent for conifer plantations. Journ. Wildlife Management 4(1):77–79. January.

WEITZ, CHAUNCEY A.
1941. Winter muskrat trapping. Wisconsin Conserv. Bull. 6(3):43–45. March.
1954. Preparation and care of pelts. Wisconsin Conserv. Bull. 19(12):12–14. December.

WELLS, L. J.
1935. Seasonal sexual rhythm and its experimental modification in the male of the thirteen-lined ground squirrel (Citellus tridecemlineatus). Anat. Rec. 62:409–47. July 25.

WELSH, STANLEY.
1939. Deer damage in the Brule Valley. Wisconsin Conserv. Bull. 4(5):41–46. May.

WEST, JAMES A.
1910. A study of the food of moles in Illinois. Bull. Illinois State Laboratory Nat. Hist. 9(2):14–22. October.

WETMORE, ALEXANDER.
1936. Hibernation of brown bat. Journ. Mammal. 17(2):130–31. May 14.
1952. The gray fox attracted by a crow call. Journ. Mammal. 33(2):244–45. May.

WETZEL, RALPH M.
1955. Speciation and dispersal of the southern bog lemming, Synaptomys cooperi (Baird). Journ. Mammal. 36(1):1–20. February 28.

WHITE, KEITH L.
1953. This marsh is managed for production. Wisconsin Conserv. Bull. 18(12):21–24. December.

WHITELAW, C. J., and E. T. PENGELLEY.
1954. A method for handling live beaver. Journ. Wildlife Management 18(4):533–34. October.

WHITEMAN, ELDON E.
1940. Habits and pelage changes in captive coyotes. Journ. Mammal. 21(4):435–38. November 14.

WHITLOCK, S. C.
1950. The black bear as a predator of man. Journ. Mammal. 31(2):135–38. May 30.
1948. Identification of wolf, coyote, dog. Michigan Conservation 17(10):6–7, 15, illus. October.

WHITNEY, LEON F.
'1931. The raccoon and its hunting. Journ. Mammal. 12(1):29–38. February 12.
1933. The raccoon—some mental attributes. Journ. Mammal. 14(2):108–14. May 15.

WHITNEY, LEON F., and ACIL B. UNDERWOOD.
1952. The raccoon. Practical Science Publ. Co., Orange, Conn. 177 pp., illus.

WHITSON, A. R., and O. E. BAKER.
*1912. The climate of Wisconsin and its relation to agriculture. Agric. Exper. Station, Univ. Wisconsin. Bull. 223, pp. 67, illus. July.

WHITTLESAY, CHARLES.
1855. Recollections of a tour through Wisconsin in 1832. First Annual Rept. and Collections State Hist. Soc. of Wisconsin for year 1854, vol. 1, pp. 64–85.

WIED [-NEUWEID, MAXIMILIAN A. P.], PRINCE OF.
1839–41. Reise in das Innere Nord-Amerika in den Jahren 1832 bis 1834. Bd. 1, illus., 1839; Bd. 2, illus., 1841; folios.

WIGHT, H. M.
1931. Reproduction in the eastern skunk (Mephitis mephitis nigra). Journ. Mammal. 12(1):42–47. February 12.
1932. A weasel attacks a man. Journ. Mammal. 13(2):163–64. May 11.

WILDE, S. A., C. T. YOUNGBERG, and J. H. HOVIND.
1950. Changes in composition of ground water, soil fertility, and forest growth produced by the construction and removal of beaver dams. Journ. Wildlife Management 14(2):123–28, pl. 2. April.

WILKE, FORD.
1942. Scentless skunk trapping. Wisconsin Conserv. Bull. 7(10):40. October.

WILLIAMS, CECIL S.
1938. Aids to the identification of mole and shrew hairs with general comments of hair structure and hair determination. Journ. Wildlife Management 2(4):239–50. October.

WILLIAMS, ESSIE W.
1923. Young gray squirrels at Hudson, Wisconsin. Journ. Mammal. 4(2):128. May 9.

WILSON, F. G.
1942. Snowshoe hare damage and control. Wisconsin Conserv. Bull. 7(12):4–7. December.

WILSON, HARRY.
1898. The economic status of the mole. Pennsylvania Dept. Agric. Bull. no. 31, pp. 42, illus.

WIMSETT, WILLIAM A.
1945. Notes on breeding behavior, pregnancy, and parturition in some vespertilionid bats of the eastern United States. Journ. Mammal. 26(1):23–35. February 27.

WIPF, LOUISE, and RICHARD M. SHACKELFORD.
1942. Chromosomes of the red fox. Proc. Nat. Acad. Sci. 28:265–68.

WISEMAN, GEORGE L., and GEORGE O. HENDRICKSON.
1950. Notes on the life history and ecology of the opossum in southeast Iowa. Journ. Mammal. 31(3):331–36. August.

WOEHLER, E. E.
1957. How about raccoon stocking? Wisconsin Conserv. Bull. 22(4):12–14. April.

WOERPEL, LES.
1952. Biologist charges wolf persecution. Wisconsin Conservationist 1(6):8. February.

WOOD, FRANK ELMER.
1910 a. A study of the mammals of Champaign County, Illinois. Bull. Illinois State Laboratory Nat. Hist. 8(5):i–iv, 501–613, pls. 26–28. May.
1910 b. On the common shrew-mole in Illinois. Bull. Illinois State Laboratory Nat. Hist. 9(1): 1–13. October.
WOODIN, HOWARD E.
1956. The appearance of a moose rutting ground. Journ. Mammal. 37(3):458–59. August.
WRAGG, L. E.
1954. The effect of D.D.T. and oil on muskrats. Canadian Field-Nat. 68(1):11–13. March.
WRIGHT, BRUCE S.
1953. Further notes on the panther in the Northeast. Canadian Field-Nat. 67(1):12–28, illus. January–March (June).
WRIGHT, EARL G.
1945. Mistaking the hawk. Passenger Pigeon 7(4): 127. October.
WRIGHT, PHILIP L.
1942 a. Delayed implantation in the long-tailed weasel (Mustela frenata), the short-tailed weasel (Mustela cicognani), and the marten (Martes americana). Anat. Rec. 83(3):341–53, illus. July 25.
1942 b. A correlation between the spring molt and spring changes in the sexual cycle in the weasel. Journ. Exper. Zool. 91(1):103–10. October 5.
1947. The sexual cycle of the male long-tailed weasel (Mustela frenata). Journ. Mammal. 28 (4):343–52, illus. December 1.
1948 a. Breeding habits of captive long-tailed weasels (Mustela frenata). Amer. Midland Nat. 39(2):338–44. March.
1948 b. Preimplantation stages in the long-tailed weasel (Mustela frenata). Anat. Rec. 100(4): 593–608, illus. April.
WRIGHT, PHILIP L., and ROBERT RAUSCH.
1955. Reproduction in the wolverine, Gulo gulo. Journ. Mammal. 36(3):346–55, illus. August 30.
WRIGHT, WILLIAM H.
1910. The black bear. Scribner's, New York. 127 pp., illus.
WYMAN, WALTER, and others.
1910. The rat and its relation to public health. Treasury Dept., Public Health and Marine-Hospital Service of the U. S., Washington. 254 pp., illus.
YEAGER, LEE E.
1936. Fox squirrel seriously damages elm tree. Journ. Mammal. 17(4):417–18. November 16.
1937. Cone-piling by Michigan red squirrels. Journ. Mammal. 18(2):191–94. May 12.
1943. Storing of muskrats and other food by minks. Journ. Mammal. 24(1):100–101. February 20.
1950. Implications of some harvest and habitat factors on pine marten management. Trans. 15th North Amer. Wildlife Conference, pp. 319–34.
YEAGER, LEE E., and WILLIAM H. ELDER.
1945. Pre- and post-hunting season foods of raccoons on an Illinois goose refuge. Journ. Wildlife Management 9(1):48–56. January.

YEAGER, LEE E., and R. E. RENNELS.
1943. Fur yield and autumn foods of the raccoon in Illinois river bottom lands. Journ. Wildlife Management 7(1):45–73. January.
YERGER, RALPH W.
1955. Life history notes on the eastern chipmunk, Tamias striatus lysteri (Richardson), in central New York. Amer. Midland Nat. 53(2):312–23. April.
YOAKUM, C. S.
1909. Some experiments upon the behavior of squirrels. Journ. Comp. Neurol. and Psychol. 19:541–68.
YOUNG, FLOYD W.
1936. The identification of the sex of beavers. Agric. Exper. Station, Michigan State College, Special Bull. 279, 8 pp., illus. November.
1937. Studies of osteology and myology of the beaver (Castor canadensis). Agric. Exper. Sta., Michigan State College, Section of Anatomy, memoir no. 2, pp. 84, illus. April.
YOUNG, HOWARD, ROBERT L. STRECKER, and JOHN T. EMLEN, JR.
1950. Localization of activity in two indoor populations of house mice, Mus musculus. Journ. Mammal. 31(4):403–10. November 22.
YOUNG, STANLEY P.
1927. Mountain lion eats kitten. Journ. Mammal. 8(2):158–60. May.
1940. Catniping our big cats. Western Sportsman 4(6):4–8, illus. May.
1941 a. Does the puma (mountain lion) scream? Western Sportsman 6(6):6–9, 24, illus. May.
1941 b. Hints on bobcat trapping. U. S. Dept. Interior, Fish and Wildlife Serv. Circ. no. 1, pp. 6, illus.
1941 c. Hints on wolf and coyote trapping. U. S. Dept. Interior, Fish and Wildlife Serv. Circ. no. 2, pp. 8, illus.
1945. Mountain lion trapping. U. S. Dept. Interior, Fish and Wildlife Serv. Circ. no. 6, 7 pp., illus.
1948. Fish and Wildlife Service in relation to rabies control. Proc. U. S. Livestock Sanit. Asso., 52nd Ann. Meeting, pp. 232–36. December.
1958. The bobcat of North America. Wildlife Management Institute, Washington, D. C. pp. xiv + 193, illus.
YOUNG, STANLEY P., and EDWARD A. GOLDMAN.
1944. The wolves of North America. Part I. Their history, life habits, economic status, and control, by Stanley P. Young. Part II. Classification of wolves, by Edward A. Goldman. Amer. Wildlife Inst., Washington, D. C. pp. xxi + 636, 15 figs., 131 pls. May 29.
1946. The puma, mysterious American cat. Part I. History, life habits, economic status, and control, by Stanley P. Young. Part II. Classification of the races of the puma, by Edward A. Goldman. Amer. Wildlife Inst., Washington, D. C. pp. xvi + 358, 6 figs., 93 pls. November 16.
YOUNG, STANLEY P., and HARTLEY H. T. JACKSON.
1951. The clever coyote. Part I. Its history, life habits, economic status, and control, by Stanley

P. Young. Part II. Classification of the races of the coyote, by Hartley H. T. Jackson. Wildlife Management Inst., Washington, D. C. pp. xv + 411, 28 figs., 81 pls. November 29.

YOUNG, VERNON A., and W. LESLIE ROBINETTE.
1939. A study of the range habits of elk on the Selway Game Preserve. Univ. Idaho Bull. 34 (1):1–48, illus.

ZIM, HERBERT S., and DONALD F. HOFFMEISTER.
*1955. Mammals, a guide to familiar American species. Simon and Schuster, New York. 160 pp., 218 color illus.

ZIMMERMAN, FRED R.
1937. Migration of little brown bats. Journ. Mammal 18(3):363. August 14.
1939. Squirrels need management. Wisconsin Conserv. Bull. 4(10):40–43. October.

ZIMMERMAN, R. SCOTT.
1943. A coyote's speed and endurance. Journ. Mammal. 24(3):400. August 17.

ZIRRER, FRANCIS.
1947. The goshawk. Passenger Pigeon 9(3):79–94. July (November).

INDEX

INDEX

This index was prepared by Emma M. Charters, formerly with U.S. Biological Surveys. Figures in **bold face** indicate principal mammal references; others, synonyms and secondary references to mammals, or references to nonmammalian items. References to illustrations are indicated by "fig." in parentheses following the page number.

A

Abies balsamea, 9
Abietorium, Napaeozapus insignis, 268
Abscesses, 289, 356
Acadian bat, 81
Acanthocephala, 112
Accipiter gentilis atricapillus, 9
Acer spicatum, 9
Acorns, 24, 174, 218, 304, 319, 326
Adney, E. T., 408
Agropyron, 431
Ah-ji-duh-mo, 155
Ah-kwin-quis, 149
Ah-mik, 192
Ah-pe-kwa-nah-djee, 75
Alaria americana, 298
  arisaemoides, 310
  minnesotae, 380
  mustelae, 289, 342
  taxideae, 342, 349, 368, 374, 380
Albinism, 87, 90, 115, 131, 144, 157, 240, 254, 258, 271, 313, 322, 375, 383, 420, 428
Albino Blarina brevicauda, 44 (fig.)
  deer, 420 (fig.)
Alce americanus, 421
Alces, 409
  alces andersoni, 9, **421**
  americana americana, 421
  americanus andersoni, 421
  Cervus, 421
Alder, 112
  black, 228
  speckled, 9
Alfalfa, 118, 128, 208, 419
Allegheniensis, Mustela rixosa, 338 (fig.), **343**
  Putorius, 343
  Putorius rixosa, 343
Allodermanyssus sanguineus, 261

Alnus rugosa, 9
Amblyomma americana, 298, 380
Amelanchier, 212, 228, 304
Americana, Alces americana, 421
  Antilocapra, 11
  antilope, 11
  Bos, 427
  Lepus, 108
  Martes, 328
  Martes americana, **328**
  Mephitis, 374
  Mustela, 328
  Taxidea, 363
American badger, 363
  beaver, 192
  bison, 428
  black bear, 311
  buffalo, 428
  glutton, 357
  jackal, 281
  lion, 389
  mink, 350
  opossum, 17
  otter, 382
  panther, 389
  polecat, 374
  red elk, 408
  reindeer, 425
  sable, 328
  stag, 408
  wild ox, 428
Americanische Dachs, 363
Americanus, Alce, 421
  Bison, 427
  Euarctos, 311
  Euarctos americanus, **311**
  Lepus, 108
  Meriones, 262
  Mustela, 328
  Paralces, 421
  Ursus, 311
Amorphacarus, 34
  hengererorum, 31, 34
Amphibians, 379, 388
Amphipods, 72
Amphisorex lesueurii, 32

Ancylostoma caninum, 289, 298, 310
Andersoni, Alces alces, 9, **421**
  Alces americanus, 421
Anderson moose, 421
Androlaelaps, 73
Andrya macrocephala, 235
  primordialis, 174, 228
  sciuri, 183
Anemia, 432
Antelope, pronghorn, 11
Antilocapra americana, 11
Antilope Americana, 11
Antler of American elk, 410 (fig.)
  moose, 422 (fig.)
  white-tailed deer, 415 (fig.)
Antrozous, 80
Ants, 51, 65, 153, 319
Apple mouse, 240
Aquaticus, Scalops, 61
Arachnids, 51
Arcticus Sorex, 33
  Sorex arcticus, 27 (fig.)
Arctomys franklinii, 138
  monax, 122
Arctopsylla setosa, 289, 395
Argentatus, Scalops, 61
  Vulpes fulvus, 298
Arrowhead, 249
Arrowwood, 147, 162
Arthritis, 298
Arvicola austerus, 7, 236
  gapperi, 224
  gossii, 224
  hirsutus, 229
  pinetorum, 240
  riparius, 229
  scalopsoides, 47, 240
  xanthognathus, 11
Asapan, 175, 181
Ascarids, 73
Ascaris, 405
  columnaris, 333, 368, 374, 380
  dasypodina, 380
  devosi, 337
  lumbricoides, 162

Ash, mountain, 9, 183, 228, 337,
     419, 425
   prickly, 147
Aspen, 112, 174, 297
   big-leaved, 276
   quaking, 276
Asplenium, 269
A-spu-n, 321
Assapanick, 175, 181
Atick, 425
Austerus, Arvicola, 7, 236
   Microtus, 229, 236
Austin, Oliver L., Jr., xi
Avia, Mephitis mephitis, 374
   Mephitis mesomelas, 374
Avola, 181

B

Baby mole, 43
   puma, 394 (fig.)
   striped ground squirrel, 134
      (fig.)
   white-tailed jack rabbit, 104
      (fig.)
Badger, 24, 137, 142, 235, 288,
      367 (fig.)
   Jackson's, **363**
Badgerland badger, 363 (fig.)
Bailey, Vernon, x
Bairdi, Peromyscus, 213
   Peromyscus maniculatus, 213
Bairdii, Hesperomys, 213
   Mus, 213
   Peromyscus maniculatus, 45,
      203 (fig.), 206 (fig.),
      209, 210, **213**, 217
Baird's deer mouse, 213
   white-footed mouse, 213
Balsam, 174, 183
Bangs' ermine, 338
Bangsi, Mustela erminea, 112, 153,
      338 (fig.), 343, 346
Bannertail, 413
Barber, W. E., 336
Barberry, 147
Barking coyote, 281
Barn rat, 253
Bass, black, 39, 266
   large-mouthed black, 53
Basswood, 141, 147, 212
Bat, 76 (fig.)
   big brown, **89** (fig.), 91 (fig.)
   Carolina, 11
   eastern long-eared, 77, **81**, 91
   Georgian, **86**, 91
   hoary, 78, 88, 89, **98**
   Indiana, **83**
   little brown, **75**, 77 (fig.), 88
   red, 78, **93**, 98, 100
   silver-haired, **84**, 86, 91
Bay lynx, 401

Bear, 311, 318 (fig.), 362
   black, **311**, 317 (fig.)
Bear tracks, 316 (fig.)
Bear trap, 320 (fig.)
Beaver, 191 (fig.), 192, 362,
      386, 388
   Michigan, **192**
Beaver burrow, 197 (fig.)
   canal, 201 (fig.)
   cutting tree, 202 (fig.)
   dam, 197 (fig.), 198 (fig.)
   eating bark, 202 (fig.)
   house, 200 (fig.), 201 (fig.)
   lodge, 199 (fig.)
   meadow mouse, 230
   mouse, 36
   pods or castors, 202 (fig.)
   swimming, 195 (fig.)
   trails, 200 (fig.)
Bee, 65, 153, 326, 379, 381
Beech, 147, 276
Beechnuts, 174, 179, 183, 228,
      319, 326
Beehive damage by bear, 320
      (fig.)
Beer, James R., 82
Bee shrew, 59
Beetles, 31, 39, 51, 54, 59, 66, 80,
      97, 141, 153, 179, 183,
      209, 304, 326, 379
   ground, 24, 51, 65, 228, 368
   June, 137, 397
   May, 65, 368
   water, 388
Be-jew, 395
Bellii, Vireo bellii, 10
Betula nigra, 10
Bewickii, Thryomanes, 10
Big chipmunk, 142
   flying squirrel, 181
   gray wolf, 290
   myotis, 75
   rabbit, 108
   red squirrel, 164
   short-tailed shrew, 43
   skunk, 374
   stoat, 345
   white rabbit, 108
   wolf, 290
Bill-mouse, 27
Birch, 174
   paper, 112, 276, 425
   river, 10
   sweet, 276
   yellow, 276, 425
Birds, 24, 34, 141, 147, 368, 373,
      374, 379
   ground-nesting, 381
Birds' eggs, 24, 319, 373, 379
Birdseye, Clarence, 212
Birge, E. A., ix, x
Bison, 297, 427 (fig.), 429 (fig.)

Americanus, 427
   bison, 428
   bison bison, **427**
   Bison bison, 427
   Bos, 427
Bison hunt, 431 (fig.)
Bison tracks, 430 (fig.)
Black and white shrew, 36
Black-backed shrew, 35
Black bear, 314 (fig.), 315 (fig.),
      317 (fig.)
   cat, 333
   fox, 299, 333
   mole, 68
   moose, 421
   squirrel, 155
   wolf, 290
Blackberry, 24, 118, 141, 152,
      326, 380
Blackbird, redwing, 304, 310
Black-haired porcupine, 270
Blackhaw, 147
Blaireau d'Amerique, 363
Blanket coon, 321
Blarina, 34, 37, 43, 349, 356
   brevicauda, 42, 43 (fig.), 232
   brevicauda brevicauda, 26
      (fig.), 39 (fig.), 40 (fig.),
      42, 55
   brevicauda kirtlandi, 39 (fig.),
      43, **55**
   brevicauda talpoides, 42
   talpoides, 42
Blow viper, 60
Blueberry, 147, 152, 174, 212,
      228, 269, 304, 319, 326,
      337
Bluegrass, 321
Blue racer, 119, 235
Blunt-nosed bat, 75
Bobcat, 34, 54, 162, 277, 310,
      327, 356, 359, 388, 398,
      401, 419
   Lake Superior, **401** (fig.)
   Rocky Mountain, 402 (fig.)
Bobcat feces, 404 (fig.)
Bob-tailed shrew, 43
Bob-tailed Susie, 230
Bobwhite, 310
Boeuf, 428
   sauvage, 428
Bogie's Cave, 6 (fig.)
Bog lemming, 220
   mouse, 220
Bohmiella wilsoni, 162, 169
Bonaparte's weasel, 338
Bonaparte weasel, 338
Boomer, 169
Borealis, Lasiurus, 85, 89, 93, 98
   Lasiurus borealis, 74 (fig.), **93**
   Lyncus, 395
   Nycteris, 93

Borealis (*cont.*)
    Odocoileus americanus, 413
    Odocoileus virginianus, **413**
    Vespertilio, 93
Boreal red-backed mouse, 224
Bos Americana, 427
    bison, 427
Botfly, 119, 212, 219, 266, 269,
    432
Bothriocephalus, 362
Bouteloua gracilis, 431
    hirsuta, 431
Boxelder, 147
Brachysorex harlani, 56
Brady, Maurice K., 58
Brain case capacity, 4 (fig.)
Brairo, 363
Brevicauda, Blarina, 42, 232
    Blarina brevicauda, 39 (fig.),
        40 (fig.), **42**, 55
Brevicaudus, Sorex, 42
Brown bat, 90
    bear, 311
    chipmunk, 148
    jack rabbit, 108
    myotis, 75
    rabbit, 108
    rat, 253
    weasel, 338
Bruin, 311, 312 (fig.)
Bruno, 311
Brush wolf, **281**, 293
Buchloe dactyloides, 431
Buffalo, 428
    plains, **427**
Buffalo wolf, 290
Buffle, 428
Bufle, 428
Bugs, 31, 39, 59, 80, 97, 379
    water, 388
Bullheads, 326
Bull mouse, 230
Bullrush, water, 249
Bull snake killing pocket gopher,
    190 (fig.)
Bumblebees, 368
Bunny, 113
Burrow of mole, 66 (fig.)
    pocket gopher, 188 (fig).
    striped ground squirrel, 135
        (fig.)
    Tamias, 146 (fig.), 147 (fig.)
Bursarius, Geomys, 184, 185
    (fig.)
    Geomys bursarius, **184**, 191
    Mus, 184
Bush rabbit, 108
Bushy tail, 155
Butcherbird, 260
Butterflies, 153

C

Caerulea, Polioptila caerulea, 10

Calamagrostis canadensis, 223
Californicus, Lepus, 108
Campanius, Lepus townsendii,
    103 (fig.), **104**, 109
Campestris, Lepus, 104
Canachites canadensis canace, 9
Canada lynx, 397 (fig.)
    otter, 382 (fig.), 386 (fig.)
    porcupine, 270 (fig.)
Canadensis, Castor, 192
    Castor canadensis, 192
    Cervus, 7, 408
    Cervus canadensis, **408**
    Cervus elaphus, 408
    Elaphus, 408
    Lutra, 382
    Lutra canadensis, **382**
    Lynx, 395
    Lynx canadensis, **395**
    Mustela, 333
    Mustela lutra, 382
    Peromyscus, 209, 210
Canadian beaver, 182
    deer mouse, 209
    elk, 408
    flying squirrel, 181
    jumping mouse, 262
    wapiti, 408
    white-footed mouse, 209
    Zone, 9, 37
Cancer, 298
Canis fulvus, 298
    griseus, 290
    latrans, 281
    latrans thamnos, 7, **281**, 283
        (fig.)
    lupus, 290
    lupus lycaon, 284, **290**
    lycaon, 290
    nubilus, 289
    occidentalis, 290
Cannibalism: Lynx, 400
Capillaria americana, 162, 180
    chandleri, 142
    mustelorum, 350
    tamiastriata, 148
Carabidae, 373
Caracajou, 363
Carcajou, 357
Cardinal, 304
Cariacus wisconsinensis, **7**
Caribou, 297, 409, 414, 425
    Barren Ground, 427
    Newfoundland, 427
    Rangifer, 425
    western woodland, **425**
Carolina bat, 90
Carolinensis, Sciurus, 139, 170
    Scotophilus, 11
Carribouck, 425
Carya illinoensis, 10
Castor canadensis, 192

canadensis canadensis, 192
canadensis michiganensis, **192**
fiber, 192
zibethicus, 245
Cat, domestic, 31, 60, 92, 97, 119,
    137, 142, 148, 153, 168,
    179, 183, 189, 228, 235,
    239, 250 (fig.), 256, 265,
    269, 304, 342, 345, 349,
    375, 405
Catamount, 389, 395, 401
Catbird, 304, 310
Catenotaenia pusillo, 183
Caterpillars, 31, 51, 137, 141, 162,
    379, 380
Catfish, 391
Cathartes aura septentrionalis, 10
Cat squirrel, 155
Cattail, 249
Cattalo, 431
Cave bat, 83
Cedar, 112
    northern white, 9
    red, 10
    white, 174, 297, 419
Cediopsylla simplex, 112, 119,
    289, 305, 327, 380, 405
Celtis occidentalis, 10
Centipedes, 51, 65, 228, 269
Centurus carolinus zebra, 10
Ceratophyllus, 244
    dentatus, 400
    faciatus, 349
    gallinae, 148
    labiatus, 401
    petriolatus, 400
    vison, 342, 349, 356
    wickhami, 73
Cervus alces, 421
    canadensis, 7, 408
    canadensis canadensis, **408**
    canadensis nelsoni, 408, 411
    elaphus canadensis, 408
    tarandus sylvestris, 425
    Virginianus, 413
    whitneyi, 7
Cestodes, 54, 73, 98, 112, 137,
    142, 148, 162, 169, 228,
    235, 239, 305, 342, 349,
    395
Chaetopsylla setosa, 319
Chamaedaphne, 297
Chat sauvage, 321
Chatterbox, 169
Chatterer, 169
Chauvesouris, 75
Chei-ki-ka-ra-cha-da, 428
Cherry, 162
    black, 326
    pin, 153, 183, 212, 228, 326,
        337, 425
    wild, 147, 174, 179, 304, 380

Chickaree, 169
Chickweed, 128
Chigger, 31, 162, 169, 174, 180, 183, 228
Ching-gwus, 338, 345
Ching-woose se, 350
Chipmuck, 142
Chipmuk, 142
Chipmunk, 142, 304, 310, 337, 348, 362, 379
    eastern, 297
    gray, **142**, 143 (fig.), 152
    least, 144, 145, 146, 342
    Ohio, **148**
    peninsula, **149**
    Wisconsin least, **149**
Chipper, 142
Chippie, 142
Chipping squirrel, 142
Chlamydoprocta itascensis, 380
Choanotaenia sciurola, 169
    spermophili, 137
Chokecherry, 141, 326
Cholera, 257
Chub, 388
Chuck, 122
Cicada, 97, 147, 168
Cicognani, Putorius, 338
Cicognanii, Putorius, 338
Cimex pilosellus, 80, 93, 98
Cinerea, Lasiurus, 98
Cinereoargenteus, Urocyon, 306
    Urocyon cinereoargenteus, 306
Cinereorargenteus, Urocyon ciner-
        eoargenteus, 306
Cinereus, Lasiurus, 88, 90, 95, 98
    Lasiurus cinereus, 74 (fig.), **98**
    Nycteris, 98
    Sorex, 36, 40
    Sorex arcticus, 27
    Sorex cinereus, 26 (fig.), **27**, 32
    Vespertilio, 98
Cinnamomum, Ursus, 311
Cinnamon bear, 311
Citelle, 130
Citellinema bifurcatum, 142, 153, 162, 174, 180, 183
Citellinoides zapodis, 269
Citellus, 289
    frankini, 138
    franklinii, 130 (fig.), **138**, 146
    parryii, 140
    tridecemlineatus, 130, 139, 143, 146, 217
    tridecemlineatus tridecemlinea-
        tus, **130**
    variegatus grammurus, 140
Citrea, Protonotaria, 10
Cittelotaenia pectinata, 162
Civet, 369
    cat, 369
Clams, 250, 326, 388

Clethrionomys, 225 (fig.), 241, 289, 297, 337, 342
    gapperi gapperi, 220 (fig.), 221 (fig.), **224**
Clinostomum, 327
Clintonia, 228
Clover, 112, 118, 128, 141, 208, 419
Coccidia, 119
Cocklebur, 141
Coffee tree, Kentucky, 10
Coleoptera, 31
Colored fox, 299
Common black bear, 311
    brown bat, 90
    chipmunk, 142
    deer, 413
    mink, 350
    mole, 61
    mole shrew, 43
    moose, 421
    mouse, 257
    opossum, 17
    otter, 382
    rabbit, 113
    rat, 253
    red squirrel, 169
    short-tailed shrew, 43
    shrew, 27
    shrew-mole, 61
    skunk, 374
    weasel, 338
    wolf, 290
    wolverine, 357
Companion bat, 83
Concolor, Felis, 389
Condylura cristata, 68 (fig.), 243
    cristata cristata, 61 (fig.), **68**
Conorhinopsylla stanfordi, 162
Construction of mound by mole, 66 (fig.)
Coon, 321
Cooperi, Sorex, 27
    Synaptomys, 220, 237
    Synaptomys cooperi, **220** (fig.), 224, 240
Cooper lemming mouse, 220
    shrew, 28
Cooper's lemming, 220
    lemming vole, 220
    shrew, 28
Copperhead, 53
Corylus rostrata, 9, 153
Cottontailed rabbit, 113
Cottontail gnawings, 117 (fig.)
Cottontail rabbit, 113, 114 (fig.)
Cougar, 389
    Felis concolor, 389
Couguar, 389
    Felis, 389
Cox, W. T., 126
Coy-dog, 281, 284, 288

Coyote, 24, 54, 112, 119, 142, 162, 215, 235, 239, 281, 293, 294, 310, 333, 388, 412, 419
    northeastern, **281**
Coyote feces, 287 (fig.)
    howling, 286 (fig.)
    skull, 283, (fig.)
Cranberry, 235
    highbush, 337
    wild, 419
Cranberry bear, 311
Crayfish, 24, 250, 326, 356, 388
Crenosoma mephitidis, 374, 380
    microbursa, 380
    vulpis, 310
Crickets, 31, 59, 97, 137, 141, 153, 326, 379
Cristata, Condylura, 68, 243
    Condylura cristata, 61 (fig.), **68**
Cristatus, Sorex, 68
Crossbill, red, 9
Cross fox, 299
Crow, 142, 304, 405
Crustacea, 51, 72
Cruzia tentaculata, 24
Cryptotis parva, 44, 56 (fig.)
    parva harlani, 10, **56**
    parva parva, 26 (fig.), 39 (fig.), 50, 57
Ctenocephalides canis, 129, 305, 310
    felis, 119, 310, 327, 374, 380
Ctenophthalmus, 148
    pseudogyrtes, 31, 34, 54, 73
    wenmanni, 73
Cuguar, 389
Cuterebra, 219
    fontinella, 266
Cutworms, 65, 137, 379, 381

D

Dachs, 363
Dandelion, 112, 118, 128, 141
Dark-bellied squirrel, 155
Dasypterus, 80
Decumanus, Mus, 253
Deer, 290, 395, 400, 405, 413, 426
    European red, 407
    northern white-tailed, **413**
    whitetail, 304
    white-tailed, 289, 297, 362, 409
Deer antlers in velvet, 415 (fig.)
Deer killer, 389
Deer mouse, 209, 213, 216
Deer wolf, 290
Dekayi, Sorex, 42
Dendroica coronata coronata, 9
Dermacentor, 319
    andersoni, 277, 368, 405
    variabilis, 24, 119, 162, 169,

Dermacentor variabilis (*cont.*) 266, 289, 298, 327, 349, 368, 380, 395, 405
Desmodus, 80
Devil bear, 357
Dictyocaulus hadweni, 432
Didelphis marsupialis virginiana, **17**, 18 (fig.)
  virginiana, 17
  virginiana virginiana, 17
Didelphus Virginiana, 17
Didelphys Virginiana, 17
Dioctophyme renale, 289, 298, 333, 362
Dioica, Gymnocladus, 10
Dipetalonema arbuta, 277
Diphyllobothrium latum, 310, 327
Diptera, 31, 97
Dipus hudsonius, 262
Dirofilaria immitis, 298
  subdermata, 277
Diseases: abscesses, 289, 356
  anemia, 432
  arthritis, 298
  cancer, 298
  cholera, 257
  distemper, 289, 298, 305, 327
  dysentery, 257
  encephalitis, 327
  enteritis, 327
  epidemic jaundice, 257
  Errington's disease, 250
  foot and mouth disease, 257
  Haverhill fever, 256
  hemorrhagic epizootic, 250
  hydrophobia, 80
  leprosy, 257
  lumpy jaw, 202
  mange, 163, 257
  murine, 244
  murine typhus, 261
  parasitical, 261
  paratyphoid, 257
  Pasteurella tularensis, 119
  pneumonia, 327, 432
  pseudotuberculosis, 202
  rabies, 80, 93, 98, 101, 163, 174, 202, 257, 289, 298, 305, 310, 311, 327, 333, 368, 374, 380, 395, 405
  rat-bite fever, 256
  Rickettsia akari, 261
  rickettsialpox, 261
  ringworm, 113, 202
  scabies, 163
  septicemia, 305
  shock disease, 113
  spotted fever, 257
  trichinosis, 257
  tuberculosis, 257, 327
  tularemia, 24, 108, 113, 119,

153, 163, 174, 202, 256, 289, 298, 305, 310, 356, 368, 374, 380
  tumors, 289
  typhus, 257
  typhus fever, 256
  virus, 261
  Weil's disease, 257
Distemper, 289, 298, 305, 327
Distoma, 98, 101
Dock rat, 253
Dog, domestic, 119, 128, 168, 235, 277, 374
  German shepherd, 281, 290
  grayish collie, 281
Dogwood, 319, 326, 380
  alternate leaved, 419
  silky, 228
Domestic rat, 253
Domesticus, Mus, 257
  Mus musculus, **257**
Doratopsylla blarinae, 31, 35, 39, 54, 60
Dorsata, Hystrix, 270
Dorsatum, Erethizon, 270
  Erethizon dorsatum, **270**
Dracunculus medinensis, 342
Duck, 388
  mallard, 355
  wild, 142
Dusky bat, 90
Dutchman's breeches, 243
Dwarf cornel, 326
  weasel, 343
Dychei, Reithrodontomys megalotis, 207
Dysentery, 257

E

Eadiea condylurae, 73
Eagle, bald, 112, 342, 388
Eagle Cave, 6 (fig.)
Early mammals, 5
Ears of bats, 74 (fig.)
  Canada lynx, 396 (fig.)
  lagomorphs, 103 (fig.)
Earthworms, 51, 59, 65, 72, 326
Eastern chipmunk, 142
  elk, 408
  flying squirrel, 175
  garden mole, 61
  Keen's bat, 81
  long-eared brown bat, 81
  long-eared little brown bat, 81
  long-eared myotis, 81
  marmot, 122
  moose, 421
  timber wolf, 291 (fig.)
  woodchuck, 122
Echidnophaga gallinacea, 162, 289, 310, 374, 405

Echinococcus granulosus, 298, 395
Ed-jier-ay, 428
Eimeria franklinii, 142
  glaucomydis, 180
  sciurorum, 169, 180
Elan, 421
Elaphe vulpina, 51
Elaphus Canadensis, 408
Elder, common, 326
Elderberry, 24, 141, 319
Eleocharis aricularis, 249
Elk, 297, 395, 408 (fig.), 409 (fig.), 410 (fig.), 414, 426
  American, **408**
  Roosevelt, 412 (fig.)
Elm, 147, 162, 168
Embryo of star-nosed mole, 72 (fig.)
Empidonax virescens, 10
Enamel pattern in muskrat, 220 (fig.)
  voles, 220 (fig.)
Encephalitis, 327
Enderleinellus longiceps, 162, 168
  replicatus, 180
  saturalis, 129, 137, 142
Enhydra, 357
Enteritis, 327
Enterobius sciuri, 169, 180
Epidemic jaundice, 257
Epimys norvegicus, 253
Epitedia, 119
  wenmanni, 137
Eptescopsylla, 98
  chapini, 93
Eptesicus, 80
  fuscus, 89
  fuscus fuscus, 74 (fig.), **89**
Erethizon dorsatum, 270
  dorsatum dorsatum, **270**
Ermine, **338**, 340 (fig.)
Erminea, Mustela, 54
Ermine of the woods, 338
Ermine weasel, 345
Errington, Paul L., 57
Errington's disease, 250
Espan, 321
Es-see-ban, 321
Euarctos americanus, 311
  americanus americanus, **311**
Euhaemogamasus ambulans, 162, 169, 180, 183
  horridus, 174
  leponyssoides, 54
Euhaemotopinus abnormis, 66
Euparyphium melis, 388
Euschongastia blarinae, 54
Eutamias, 132, 144, 145, 146
  minimus jacksoni, 7, 130 (fig.), **149**
  quadrivittatus neglectus, 149

Eutrichophilus setosus, 277
Evotomys gapperi, 224
Excrement of Blarina, 46 (fig.)
　　star-nosed mole, 70 (fig.)

F

Fairy diddle, 175
Fatuus, Synaptomys cooperi, 220
Feces of beaver, 194 (fig.)
　　black bear, 317 (fig.)
　　Canada otter, 385 (fig.)
　　cottontail, 106 (fig.)
　　coyote, 287 (fig.)
　　fox squirrel, 167 (fig.)
　　gray squirrel, 159 (fig.)
　　jack rabbit, 106 (fig.)
　　Mustela frenata noveboracensis,
　　　　347 (fig.)
　　porcupine, 273 (fig.)
　　raccoon, 324 (fig.)
　　red fox, 302 (fig.)
　　southern flying squirrel, 177
　　　　(fig.)
　　striped ground squirrel, 133
　　　　(fig.)
　　striped skunk, 378 (fig.)
　　Tamias, 145 (fig.)
　　timber wolf, 295 (fig.)
　　white-tailed deer, 417 (fig.)
　　Wisconsin badger, 366 (fig.)
　　woodchuck, 125 (fig.)
Federation squirrel, 130
Feet of bats, 75 (fig.)
　　cricetine rodents, 205 (fig.)
　　Muridae, 253 (fig.)
　　shrews, 26 (fig.)
　　Taxidea, 364 (fig.)
　　Zapodidae, 253 (fig.)
Felicola felis, 405
　　quadraticeps, 310
　　subrostratus, 405
　　vulpis, 305
Felis concolor, 389
　　concolor cougar, 389
　　concolor schorgeri, 7, **389**
　　couguar, 389
　　onca, 390
Fence mouse, 142
Ferns, 112
Ferrididdle, 142
Festuca, 431
Fiber, Castor, 192
　　zibethicus, 245
Fibricola nana, 174
Field mouse, 230
Filaria, 66
　　fasciata, 405
　　martis, 380
Filaroides martis, 350
　　osleri, 298
Filbert, 180
Fir, balsam, 9, 276, 297, 425

Fischotter, 382
Fish, 39, 342, 356, 388
　　mouse, 36
　　shrew, 36
Fisher, 304, **333**, 334 (fig.), 382
　　cat, 333
　　marten, 333
　　weasel, 333
Flag deer, 413
　　squirrel, 130
Flat-horned elk, 421
Flatworm, 183, 190, 277, 405
Fleas, 24, 31, 34, 39, 54, 60, 66,
　　80, 93, 98, 108, 112, 119,
　　129, 137, 142, 148, 162,
　　169, 174, 180, 183, 190,
　　212, 228, 239, 244, 256,
　　266, 289, 298, 305, 310,
　　319, 327, 333, 337, 342,
　　345, 349, 356, 368, 374,
　　380, 395, 405
Fledermaus, 75
Flicker, 179, 304, 310
Flies, 31, 97, 153, 228, 269, 356,
　　432
　　caddis, 39, 388
　　May, 39
Flukes, 80, 108, 119, 174, 266,
　　289, 298, 305, 310, 327,
　　356, 362, 368, 374, 380,
　　388
Flycatcher, Acadian, 10
Flying squirrel, 181
Foot and mouth disease, 257
Foot of black bear, 313 (fig.)
　　bobcat, 403 (fig.)
　　Canada lynx, 397 (fig.)
　　Canada otter, 383 (fig.)
　　coyote, 284 (fig.)
　　Eutamias minimus jacksoni,
　　　　150 (fig.)
　　fisher, 335 (fig.)
　　flying squirrel, 175 (fig.)
　　Franklin's ground squirrel, 139
　　　　(fig.)
　　gray fox, 307 (fig.)
　　gray squirrel, 156 (fig.)
　　ground squirrel, 131 (fig.)
　　Lepus, 104 (fig.)
　　marten, 330 (fig.)
　　mink, 352 (fig.)
　　Mustela erminea bangsi, 339
　　　　(fig.)
　　northern flying squirrel, 181
　　　　(fig.)
　　opossum, 17 (fig.)
　　pocket gopher, 185 (fig.)
　　porcupine, 272 (fig.)
　　raccoon, 322 (fig.)
　　red fox, 301 (fig.)
　　red squirrel, 170 (fig.)
　　striped skunk, 376 (fig.)

Sylvilagus, 104 (fig.)
Tamias, 143 (fig.)
timber wolf, 292 (fig.)
western fox squirrel, 165 (fig.)
white-tailed deer, 414 (fig.)
wolverine, 358 (fig.)
woodchuck, 123 (fig.)
Forest hare, 108
Formosus, Oporornis, 10
Forsteri, Sorex, 27
Forster's shrew, 28
Fossor angertrutrudae, 368
Four-lined chipmunk, 149
Four-striped skunk, 369
　　squirrel, 149
Fox, 24, 66, 108, 148, 183, 228,
　　265, 269, 288
　　eastern red, **298**
　　gray, 34, 54, 60, 119, 137, 162,
　　　　219, 235, 239, 282, 342,
　　　　345, 349, 405
　　red, 34, 54, 60, 112, 119, 128,
　　　　137, 153, 162, 215, 219,
　　　　235, 239, 250, 282, 308,
　　　　309, 311, 342, 345, 349,
　　　　356, 400, 405, 419
　　Wisconsin gray, **306**
Foxella ignotus, 400
Fox squirrel, 164
Franklini, Citellus, 138
　　Spermophilus, 138
Franklinii, Arctomys, 138
　　Citellus, 130 (fig.), **138**, 146
Franklin's ground squirrel, 139
　　(fig.)
　　spermophile, 139
Frenata, Mustela, 54
Frogs, 24, 59, 65, 72, 141, 147,
　　266, 304, 326, 342, 356,
　　388
Frosted bat, 98
Frutectanus, Napaeozapus insignis,
　　7, 9, 259 (fig.), 261 (fig.),
　　267
Fuchsroth, 299
Fulva, Vulpes fulva, **298**
Fulvus, Canis, 298
　　Vulpes, 298
Fumeus, Sorex, 28, 32, 35, 41,
　　241
　　Sorex fumeus, 27 (fig.), **32**
Fungi, 162, 174, 183, 223, 228
Fuscus, Eptesicus, 89
　　Eptesicus fuscus, 74 (fig.), **89**
　　Scotophilus, 89
　　Vespertilio, 89

G

Gapperi, Arvicola, 224
　　Clethrionomys gapperi, 220 fig.,
　　　　221 (fig.), **224**
　　Evotomys, 224

Gapper's red-backed mouse, **224**
Garden mole, 61
Gaufre, 184
Gavia immer, 9
Geomys, 289
  bursarius, 184, 185 (fig.)
  bursarius bursarius, **184**, 191
  bursarius illinoensis, 186
  bursarius majusculus, 188
  bursarius wisconsinensis, 7, 184
    (fig.), 185 (fig.), 186, 187
    (fig.), **191**
Georgianus, Scotophilus, 86
Georgia pipistrelle, 86
Giant blarina, 43
  mole shrew, 43 (fig.)
  short-tailed shrew, 43
Gid-a-mon, 169
Glanders, 257
Glaucomys, 132, 289
  sabrinus, 176
  sabrinus macrotis, 9, 154 (fig.),
    181
  sabrinus sabrinus, 182
  volans, 181
  volans volans, 154 (fig.), **175**
Gleditsia triacanthos, 10
Glider squirrel, 175
Glutton, 357
Glyptoporus, 80
Gnatcatcher, blue-gray, 10
Gnats, 432
Gnawings of cottontail rabbit, 117
  (fig.)
  gray squirrel, 159 (fig.), 163
    (fig.)
  porcupine, 277 (fig.)
  red squirrel, 163 (fig.)
Golden beaver, 182
Goldenrod, 297
Goodrich, Ezra, 255
Gooseberry, 118, 147, 304, 326,
  380
Gopher, 130, 184
Goshawk, 9, 147, 174, 183, 342,
  349
Gossii, Arvicola, 224
  Synaptomys, 224
  Synaptomys cooperi, 10, 220
    (fig.), 221, 222, 223, **224**
Goss lemming vole, 224
Gracilis, Hesperomys, 209
  Peromyscus maniculatus, 9, 203
    (fig.), 206 (fig.), **209**, 213,
    217, 218
Grammurus, Citellus variegatus,
  140
  Spermophilus, 138
Grapes, 24, 310, 373
  wild, 179, 380
Grass, 112, 118, 208, 218, 234
  ·blue, 223, 239

buffalo, 431
cotton, 223
fescue, 431
grama, 431
June, 141
Grass chippie, 130
Grasshoppers, 24, 59, 128, 137,
  141, 147, 153, 168, 304,
  326, 379
Grass runner, 130
Grass whistler, 130
Gray, W. T., 193
Gray badger, 363
  bat, 98
  chipmunk, 143 (fig.)
  eastern chipmunk, 142
  fox, 306
  gopher, 139
  ground squirrel, 139
  mouse, 257
  rabbit, 113
  rat, 253
  souslik, 139
  squirrel, 155
  striped chipmunk, 142
  wildcat, 395
  wolf, 290
Gray-cheeked squirrel, 139
Great hoary bat, 98
  northern bat, 98
Griseus, Canis, 290
  Tamias striatus, 130 (fig.), **142**,
    148, 149
Grosbeak, rose-breasted, 51
Ground cherry, 24
Ground hackie, 142
Groundhog, 122
Ground mole, 61
Ground mole rat, 43
Ground squirrel, 119, 142, 289,
  348, 368
  Franklin's, **138**, 158
  striped, **130**, 141, 184, 304, 368,
    379
Ground squirrel burrow, 130 (fig.)
Ground vole, 230
Grouse, 311, 362, 400, 405
  ruffed, 304, 310, 332
  spruce, 9
Grubs, 356
Gryllus, 97
Gull, 235
Gulo luscus, 357, 358 (fig.)
  luscus luscus, **357**
Gwen-geesh, 142
Gymnocladus dioica, 10

H

Hackberry, 10, 24, 162, 179, 326
Hackee, 169
Hackie, 142

Haemaphysalis leporis-palustris,
  112, 119
Haemodipus setoni, 108
Haemogamasus, 34
  alaskensis, 54, 80
  hirsutus, 112
Haemolaelaps glasgowi, 162
  megaventralis, 162, 169
Haemonchus contortus, 432
Hall, F. Gregory, x
Hanoverian rat, 253
Haplopleura erratica, 148
Hare, Minnesota varying, **108**
  snowshoe, 297, 332, 337
  varying, 9, 105, 109 (fig.), 115,
    116, 356, 395, 405
Harlani, Brachysorex, 56
  Cryptotis parva, 10, **56**
Harvest mouse, 203
Haverhill fever, 256
Hawberry, 310
Hawk, 31, 34, 39, 53, 97, 108,
  112, 119, 212, 223, 228,
  244, 250, 256, 260, 310
  American rough-legged, 60, 345
  Cooper's, 137, 147, 174
  marsh, 137, 147, 153, 215, 235,
    239, 265
  pigeon, 80
  red-shouldered, 60
  red-tailed, 137, 142, 147, 153,
    162, 168, 174, 219, 235,
    239, 260, 269
  rough-legged, 168, 235, 342, 349
  sharp-shinned, 80
  sparrow, 80, 93, 97, 137, 215,
    235
Hawthorn, 326
Hazel, 112, 147, 153, 174, 183,
  218, 228, 276, 319, 326
  beaked, 9, 212, 425
Heads of bobcat, 395 (fig.)
  Canada lynx, 395 (fig.)
  canids, 280 (fig.)
  cricetine rodents, 205 (fig.)
  Muridae, 253 (fig.)
  Zapodidae, 253 (fig.)
Hedgehog, 270
Helicina occulata, 147
Heligmodendrium hassalli, 162,
  169
Helminths, 129
Hemlock, 174, 212, 228, 276, 297,
  419
Hemorrhagic epizootic, 250
Herons, 235
Hesperomys Bairdii, 213
  gracilis, 209
  leucopus, 216
  Michiganensis, 213
Heterodon platyrhinus, 60
Heterodoxus spiniger, 289

Hibernation of jumping mouse, 264 (fig.)
Hickory, 147, 179, 218, 304, 326
Hickory squirrel, 164
Hirstionyssus, 54
Hirsutus, Arvicola, 229
Hirtus, Procyon lotor, **321**
Hollister, Ned, 273
Hoplopleura, 244
    acanthopus, 223
    sciuricola, 162
    trispinosa, 180, 183
Hoplopsyllus affinis, 108, 305
    glacialis, 400
    lynx, 108, 405
Hornbeam, 162
Hornets, 65
Horsefly, 51
Horse nettle, 239
House bat, 90
    mouse, 257 (fig.)
    rat, 253
Hoyi, Microsorex, 28, 40
    Microsorex hoyi, 7, **40**, 42
    Sorex, 7, 40
Hoy shrew, 40
Hoy's pygmy shrew, 40
Hoy's shrew, 40
Huckleberry, 183
Hudson Bay jumping mouse, 262
    squirrel, 169
Hudsonian jumping mouse, 262
Hudsonica, Mephitis, 374
    Mephitis americana, 374
    Mephitis mephitis, **374**
Hudsonicus, Sciurus, 157, 169
Hudsonius, Dipus, 262
    Hystrix, 270
    Jaculus, 262
    Pteromys, 181
    Sciurus, 169
    Zapus, 262
    Zapus hudsonius, 9, **262**, 266
Humeralis, Nycticeius, 11
Hydrobadistes, Sorex palustris, 7, 9, 26 (fig.), 27 (fig.), 28, **36**
Hydrophobia, 80
Hydrophobia cat, 369
Hylocichla guttata faxoni, 9
Hymenolepis christensoni, 80
    diminuta, 137, 142, 148, 162
Hymenoptera, 31
Hypophaeus, Sciurus, 155
    Sciurus carolinensis, 154 (fig.), **155**, 165
Hypothetical list, 11
Hypudaeus ochrogaster, 7, 236
Hystrix dorsata, 270
    Hudsonius, 270

I

Illinoensis, Geomys bursarius, 186
Indian devil, 357
Insects, 65, 72, 80, 97, 174, 215, 218
Insignis, Napaeozapus insignis, 268, 269
Intermediate pigmy shrew, 42
Intermedius, Zapus hudsonius, 259 (fig.), 261 (fig.), 263, **266**
Interrupta, Mephitis, 369
    Spilogale, 369
    Spilogale putorius, **369**
Intervectus, Microsorex hoyi, 7, 39 (fig.), 40 (fig.), **42**
Isopods, 72
Ixodes, 228
    angustus, 31
    cookei, 129, 277, 310, 327, 337, 349, 374, 395
    cruciarius, 356
    hexagonus, 174, 305, 388
    kingi, 298, 356, 368, 380
    marxi, 153, 305, 327
    ricinus, 310, 395
    scapularis, 289, 310

J

Jack, 104
Jackass hare, 104
Jack rabbit, 104
Jacksoni, Eutamias minimus, 7, 130 (fig.), **149**
    Taxidea taxus, 7, **363**
Jackson jumping mouse, 267
Jackson's chipmunk, 149
Jacoubek, Kaiser, 195
Jaculus Hudsonius, 262
Jaguar, 389
Jaundice, 257
Jay, blue, 256, 310
    Canada, 9
Jordan, Marie Anne, 381
Juglans nigra, 10
Jumper, 262
Jumping jack, 262
Jumping mouse, 216
Juneberry, 183, 212, 304, 319
June bug, 128
Juniperus virginiana, 10

K

Kalmia glauca, 38
Kansas lemming mouse, 224
Karkajou, 357
Keen bat, 81
    myotis, 81
Keenii, Myotis, 84, 87
Keen's bat, 81
    myotis, 81
Khalibu, 425

Kin-skee-sha-wah-wah-bee-gah-note-see, 43
Kirtlandi, Blarina brevicauda, 39 (fig.), 44, **55**
Kirtland's blarina, 55
    mole shrew, 55
    short-tailed shrew, 55
Kuk-wah-geeser, 122
Kumlien, Ludwig, 110, 411
Ku-tet-tahx, 382
Kyute, 281

L

La belette de Bonaparte, 338
Labradorica, Meles, 363
Labrador tea, 9, 297
Laelaps microti, 244
La fouine, 328
Lakes States blarina, 55
Lake Superior bobcat, **401** (fig.)
    chipmunk, 149
Lampropeltis doliata, 60
Land otter, 382
Lanius borealis, 53
    ludovicianus migrans, 53
Large blarina, 43
    bob-tailed shrew, 43
    brown bat, 90
    brown weasel, 345
    ermine, 346
    flying squirrel, 181
    gray wolf, 290
    mole shrew, 43
    short-tailed shrew, 43
    striped skunk, 374
    weasel, 346
Larger American flying squirrel, 181
Laricorum, Sorex arcticus, 26 (fig.), 27 (fig.), 32, **35**
Lasionycteris, 80
    noctivagans, 74 (fig.), **84**, 95
Lasiurus, 80
    borealis, 85, 89, 93, 98
    borealis borealis, 74 (fig.), **93**
    cinerea, 98
    cinereus, 88, 90, 95, 98
    cinereus cinereus, 74 (fig.), **98**
    noveboracensis, 93
    pruinosus, 98
    seminola, 98
Latrans, Canis, 281
    Lupus, 281
Laurel, swamp, 38
Leaf bat, 93
Least chipmunk, 149
    stoat, 343
    weasel, 343 (fig.)
Leatherleaf, 297
Le chat, 395
Lecithodendrium, 80, 98
LeConte's deer mouse, 209

Ledum, 297
  groenlandicum, 9
Leeches, 39
Legumes, 147, 419
Lemming mouse, 220
  vole, 220
Leopard ground squirrel, 130
Leopard squirrel, 130
Lepidoptera, 31
Lepomis cyanellus, 53
Leprosy, 257
Leptinus americanus, 54
Lepus, 297
  Americana, 108
  americanus, 108
  americanus phaeonotus, 9, 103
    (fig.), 104 (fig.), **108**,
    113
  californicus, 108
  campestris, 104
  floridanus mearnsi, 113
  nanus, 113
  sylvaticus, 113
  sylvaticus mearnsii, 113
  townsendii campanius, 103
    (fig.), **104**, 109
Lesser weasel, 338
Lesùeurii, Amphisorex, 32
  Sorex cinereus, 10, 26 (fig.), 27
    (fig.), 28, **32**
Letifera, Mustela vison, **350**
Leucopus, Hesperomys, 216
  Mus, 216
  Peromyscus, 216
Leucotis, Sciurus, 155
  Sciurus carolinensis, 155, 157
Lice, 66, 108, 129, 137, 142, 148,
    162, 168, 174, 180, 183,
    190, 212, 223, 228, 239,
    244, 266, 277, 289, 298,
    305, 327, 333, 342, 345,
    349, 368, 395, 405
  biting, 356, 374, 380
Lichens, 337, 427
Life zones, 8
  Canadian, 9 (fig.)
  Transition, 9
  Upper Austral, 10 (fig.)
Lined skunk, 374
Linereus, Vespertilio, 98
Line-tailed squirrel, 139
Linognathus setosus, 298
Listrophorus, 54
Little chipmunk, 149
  flying squirrel, 175
  mole, 43
  northern chipmunk, 149
  polecat, 369
  short-tailed shrew, 56 (fig.)
  skunk, 369
  sooty bat, 83
  spotted skunk, 369

stoat, 338
striped chipmunk, 149
striped gopher, 131
striped skunk, 369
weasel, 338
wolf, 281
Loafer, 290
Lobo, 290
Locust, honey, 10
Longicauda, Mustela frenata, 348
Long-legged mouse, 262
Long-tailed chipmunk, 149
  deer, 413
  deer mouse, 209
  field mouse, 213
  mole, 68
  shrew, 27, 28
  shrew-mouse, 28
  weasel, 346 (fig.)
Loon, 9
Loquax, Sciurus hudsonicus, 169
  Tamiasciurus hudsonicus, 169,
    171
Lotor, Procyon, 321
  Procyon lotor, 321
Lotus, 10, 249
Loupcervier, 395, 401
Loutre, 382
Loxia curvirostra minor, 9
Lucifugus, Myotis, 75, 76 (fig.),
    77 (fig.), 84, 85, 87, 356
  Myotis lucifugus, 74 (fig.), **75**
    (fig.), 82, 83
  Vespertilio, 75
Ludovicianus, Sciurus, **164**
Lumpy jaw, 202
Lung worms, 432
Lupus, Canis, 290
  latrans, 281
  occidentalis, 290
Luscus, Gulo, 357
  Gulo luscus, **357**
  Ursus, 357
Lutra canadensis, 382
  canadensis canadensis, **382**
Lutreocephalus, Putorius vison,
    350
Lutreola vison, 350
Lycaon, Canis, 290
  Canis lupus, 284, **290**
Lyncus borealis, 395
  rufus, 401
Lynx, 304, 395
  Canada, 112, **395**, 402, 419
Lynx canadensis, 395
  canadensis canadensis, **395**
  ruffus, 401
  rufus, 401
  rufus rufus, 401, 403
  rufus superiorensis, **401**
Lynx cat, 395, 401
Lysteri, Tamias striatus, 142, 149

Lyster's chipmunk, 149

M

Maccarib, 426
Machrina, Talpa, 61
Machrinus, Scalopus aquaticus, **61**
    (fig.), 62 (fig.)
McNaughton, James W., 423
Macracanthorhynchus hirundina-
    ceus, 148, 162, 169
Macrotis, Glaucomys sabrinus, 9,
    154 (fig.), **181**
  Sciuropterus sabrinus, 181
Ma-in-gon, 290
Majusculus, Geomys bursarius, 188
Mallurus, Sylvilagus floridanus,
    115
Maned fox, 306
Mange, 163, 257
Maple, 147, 162, 168, 174, 179,
    183, 228
  hard, 212, 276
  mountain, 9, 276, 425
  red, 419
  soft, 276
  striped, 276
  sugar, 425
Marmot, 122
Marmota monax, 122
  monax monax, 10, **122**, 123
    (fig.), 130
  monax rufescens, 123 (fig.),
    124, **130**
Marsh meadow mouse, 230
  monk, 230
  shrew, 36
Marten, 174, 183, 328
  American, **328**
Martes americana, 328
  americana americana, **328**
  Mustela, 328
  pennanti pennanti, **333**
  permanti permanti, 333
Masked shrew, 28
Mat-ten-usk, 363
Maulwürfe, 61
May apple, 269
Meadow jumping mouse, 262
    (fig.), 264 (fig.)
Meadowlark, 304
Meadow mike, 230
  mole, 43
  mouse, 230 (fig.), 231 (fig.)
  vole, 236, 263
Mearns' chipmunk, 142
  flying squirrel, 181
Mearnsi, Lepus floridanus, 113
Mearnsii, Lepus sylvaticus, 113
  Sylvilagus floridanus, 103 (fig.),
    104 (fig.), **113**
Megabothris, 119
  acerbus, 148

Megabothris (*cont.*)
  quirini, 266
  vison, 148
  wagneri, 266, 305
Melanism, 87, 109, 157, 254, 300,
    390
Meles, Labradorica, 363
Mephitica, Mephitis, 374
Mephitic weasel, 374
Mephitis, 310, 369, 370, 372
  Americana, 374
  americana hudsonica, 374
  hudsonica, 374
  interrupta, 369
  mephitica, 374
  mephitis avia, 374
  mephitis hudsonica, **374**
  mephitis minnesota, 374
  mephitis minnesotae, 374
  mesomelas avia, 374
Meriones americanus, 262
Merriam's gray squirrel, 155
  squirrel, 155
Mesocestoides kirbyi, 289
  latus, 374, 380
  litteratus, 310
  lotoris, 327
  variabilis, 310, 337, 380
Me-suk-ka-ko-che-se, 363
Michigan deer mouse, 213
  prairie mouse, 213
  white-footed mouse, 213
  wood mouse, 213
Michiganensis, Castor canadensis,
    192
  Hesperomys, 213
  Peromyscus, 213
Microdrili, 73
Microphthirus uncinatus, 183
Microsorex hoyi, 28, 40
  hoyi hoyi, **40**, 42
  hoyi intervectus, 7, 26 (fig.), 39
    (fig.), 40 (fig.), **42**
  hoyi thompsoni, 30
Microtus, 297, 304, 342, 349, 356,
    379
  austerus, 229, 236
  ochrogaster, 236, 240
  ochrogaster ochrogaster, 7, 45,
    220 (fig.), 231, **236**
  pennsylvanicus, 226, 229, 234
    (fig.), **237**, 240
  pennsylvanicus pennsylvanicus,
    45, 220 (fig.), **229** (fig.)
  pinetorum, 229, 237
  pinetorum nemoralis, 10, 220
    (fig.), 242, **244**, 245
  pinetorum scalopsoides, **240**,
    244, 245
  pinetorum schmidti, 7, 9, 220
    (fig.), 229 (fig.), 241, 242,
    245

xanthognathus, 11
Migrating squirrel, 155
Migratorius, Sciurus, 155
Millipedes, 51, 59, 65
Miner, 184
Mink, 39, 80, 119, 142, 147, 153,
    235, 250, 265, 350, 351
    (fig.), 405
  Upper Mississippi Valley, **350**
Mink feces, 353 (fig.)
Minnesota, Mephitis mephitis,
    374
  Sciurus hudsonicus, 169
  Tamiasciurus hudsonicus, 154
    (fig.), **169**
Minnesotae, Mephitis mephitis,
    374
Minnesota gray squirrel, 155 (fig.)
Minnows, 72
Minx, 350
Mishibigin, 389
Mish-wa-wa, 408
Mississippi Valley mink, 350
Mitella diphylla, 269
Mites, 54, 73, 93, 112, 119, 153,
    162, 169, 174, 180, 183,
    212, 228, 239, 244, 305
  ear, 310
  mange, 163, 169, 289, 298, 305,
    405
  red, 269
  scab, 219
Mitrewort, 269
Modewarp, 61
Mole, 43, 97, 304, 310, 356, 379
  common, 356
  prairie, **61** (fig.)
  star-nosed, **68** (fig.), 72 (fig.)
Mole-like mouse, 240
  pine vole, 240
  vole, 240
Mole meadow mouse, 240
  mouse, 43, 240
  pine mouse, 240
  rat, 43
  shrew, 43, 232, 235
Molinema diacantha, 277
Molineus patens, 289, 342, 345,
    368
Mollusks, 51, 72
Molly cottontail, 113
Monax, 122
  Arctomys, 122
  Marmota, 122
  Marmota monax, 10, **122**, 123
    (fig.), 130
  Mus, 122
Moniliformis, 153
  clarki, 137, 148, 162, 380
  moniliformis, 66
Monk, 122
Monke, 142

Monopsyllus, 119
Moonack, 122
Moose, 9, 362, 409, 414, 421
    (fig.), 422 (fig.), 423
    (fig.), 424 (fig.)
  northwestern, **421**
Moose deer, 421
Morax, Arctomys, 122
Morus rubra, 10
Moss, 31, 427
Moths, 31, 80, 153, 179, 183, 326
Mould-warp, 61
Mound of mole, 66 (fig.)
  pine mouse, 243 (fig.)
  pocket gopher, 187 (fig.)
  star-nosed mole, 70 (fig.)
Mountain lion, 389
Mourning dove, 304
Mouse, 31, 54, 141, 147, 245, 289,
    319, 362, 368, 381, 405
  Cooper's lemming, **220**
  deer, 206, 310, 345, 356
  field, 289, 350, 356, 373
  Goss lemming, 10, **224**
  Hanson's harvest, **203**
  harvest, 10
  house, 78, 206, **257**, 349, 350,
    356
  Hudsonian jumping, 9
  Hudsonian meadow jumping,
    262
  intermediate meadow jumping,
    266
  jumping, 356
  lemming, 221 (fig.)
  meadow, 47, 137, 310
  northern pine, 240
  northern white-footed, **216**
  pine, 52
  prairie deer, **213**
  red-backed, 221 (fig.), 240, 332,
    337
  Schmidt's pine, **245**
  white-footed, 52
  Wisconsin woodland jumping,
    267
  wood, 345
  woodland deer, 9, **209**
  woodland jumping, 9
  woodland pine, 10, **244**
  yellow-cheeked meadow, 11
Mouse-eared bat, 75
Mouse-hunter, 343
Mouse mole, 43
  squirrel, 142
  weasel, 343
M'possum, 17
Mud cat, 245
Mud puppies, 388
Mu-ko, 311
Muk-wa, 311

Mulberry, 24, 162, 304, 326, 373
  red, 10
Multiceps multiceps, 289
  packii, 298
  serialis, 310
Munk, 142
Murii, Tamiasciurus hudsonicus, 171
Murine typhus, 261
Murmeltier, 122
Mus, 379
  bairdii, 213
  bursarius, 184
  decumanus, 253
  domesticus, 257
  leucopus, 216
  monax, 122
  musculus, 45, 206, 213, 255 (fig.), 257
  musculus domesticus, **257**
  musculus musculus, 257
  norvegicus, 253
  pennsylvanica, 229
  rattus, 11
  sylvaticus noveboracensis, 216
  volans, 175
Musculus, Mus, 45, 206, 213, 255 (fig.), 257
  Mus musculus, 257
Mush-quo-de-ma-in-gon, 281
Mushrat, 245
Mushrooms, 174, 183
Musk beaver, 245
Muskellunge, 162, 174, 235, 250, 266
Muskrat, 250 (fig.), 251 (fig.), 289, 304, 310, 356, 386, 388, 405
  common, **245** (fig.)
Muskrat bank den, 249 (fig.)
  feces, 247 (fig.)
  feet, 246 (fig.)
  house, 249 (fig.)
  pelts, 251 (fig.), 252 (fig.)
Muskrat mouse, 36
Mus-ku-te-a pishakiu, 428
Musquash, 245
Mussascus, 245
Mustela americana, 328
  americanus, 328
  Canadensis, 333
  erminea, 54
  erminea bangsi, 112, 153, **338** (fig.), 343, 346
  frenata, 54
  frenata longicauda, 348
  frenata noveboracensis, 112, 338 (fig.), 339, 341, 343, **345**
  frenata oribasus, 348
  frenata spadix, 347
  lutra canadensis, 382
  martes, 328

pennanti, 333
Pennantii, 333
pusilla, 338
rixosa allegheniensis, 338 (fig.), **343**
vison, 350
vison letifera, **350**
Muswa, 421
M'wha, 290
Myobia, 34
  simplex, 31, 54
Myocoptes, 54
Myodopsylla insignis, 80, 93
Myonyssus jamesoni, 54
Myotis keenii, 84, 87
  keenii septentrionalis, 74 (fig.), 75 (fig.), 77, **81**, 91
  lucifugus, 75, 76 (fig.), 77 (fig.), 84, 85, 87, 356
  lucifugus lucifugus, 74 (fig.), **75** (fig.), 81, 82, 83
  sodalis, 74 (fig.), 75 (fig.), **83**, 356
  subulatus, 81

N

Nag-gwy-gway, 357
Nannyberry, 147, 326
Nanophyetus salmincola, 289
Nanus, Lepus, 113
Napaeozapus insignis abietorum, 268
  insignis frutectanus, 7, 9, 259 (fig.), 261 (fig.), **267**
  insignis insignis, 268, 269
Natrix, 53
Navigator, Sorex palustris, 38
Nearctopsylla brooksi, 342
  genalis, 54, 256
Neeg-keek, 382
Neglectus, Eutamias quadrivittatus, 149
Nelson, Edward William, x
Nelsoni, Cervus canadensis, 408, 411
Nelumbo lutea, 10
Nematodes, 24, 54, 73, 112, 137, 142, 153, 162, 169, 239, 266, 269, 305, 342, 350, 395
Nemoralis, Microtus pinetorum, 10, 220 (fig.), 242, **244**, 245
  Pitymys pinetorum, 244
Neohaematopinus laeviusculus, 137, 142
  sciurinus, 162, 169
  sciuropteri, 180, 183
Neosorex palustris, 36
Neotedres, 405
Neotrichodectes mephitidis, 349, 374

Nesting site of mole, 66 (fig.)
Nest of Blarina, 50 (fig.)
  fox squirrel, 168 (fig.)
  harvest mouse, 208 (fig.)
  meadow mouse, 233 (fig.)
  Microtus ochrogaster, 238 (fig.)
  red-backed mouse, 227 (fig.)
  star-nosed mole, 72 (fig.)
Nettle, 141
New York bat, 93
  red bat, 93
  weasel, 346
New York State weasel, 346
Niger, Sciurus, 155
Nightshade, 141
Nocomis, 388
Noctivagans, Lasionycteris, 74 (fig.), 84, 95
  Scotophilus, 84
  Vespertilio, 84
  Vesperugo, 86
North American buffalo, 428
  otter, 382
Northeastern chipmunk, 149
  coyote, 282 (fig.)
Northern bat, 98
  chipmunk, 149
  deer, 413
  deer mouse, 216
  gray squirrel, 155
  hare, 108
  jack rabbit, 108
  jumping mouse, 262
  red bat, 93
  skunk, 374
  timber wolf, 290
  Virginia deer, 413
  white-footed mouse, **216**
  white-tailed deer, 413 (fig.)
  woodland white-tailed deer, 413
Norvegicus, Epimys, 253
  Mus, 253
  Rattus, 11, **253**, 255 (fig.)
Norway rat, 254 (fig.)
Nose pads of canids, 281 (fig.)
Nosopsyllus, 119
  faciatus, 356
Notocotylus, 266
Noveboracensis, Lasiurus, 93
  Mus sylvaticus, 216
  Mustela frenata, 112, 338 (fig.), 339, 341, 343, **345**
  Peromyscus leucopus, 203 (fig.), 206 (fig.), 210, 213, **216** (fig.)
  Putorius, 345
  Vespertilio, 93
N'pshikwa, 350
Nubilus, Canis, 289
Nycteris borealis, 93
  cinereus, 98
Nycticeius humeralis, 11

Nymphaea advena, 276

O

Oak, 147, 162
  burr, 179
  pin, 10
  white, 179
Obscurus, Pipistrellus subflavus,
    87, 89
Occidentalis, Canis, 290
Ocheeg, 333
Ochrogaster, Hypudaeus, 236
  Microtus, 236, 240
  Microtus ochrogaster, 7, 45, 220
    (fig.), 231, **236**
  Pedomys ochrogaster, 229
Ocythous, Urocyon cinereoargen-
    teus, 7, **306**
Odocoileus, 409
  americanus borealis, 413
  virginianus, 413
  virginianus borealis, **413**
Odontopsyllus multispinosus,
    119, 327, 405
Oesophagostomum radiatum, 432
Oestridae, 432
Ogog, 270
Ohio brown chipmunk, 148
  striped chipmunk, 148
Ohionensis, Tamias striatus, 143,
    148
Okak, 270
Oke-pa-ku-kue, 28
O-masch-koohs, 408
O-masch-kosh, 413
Onca, Felis, 390
Oncicola canis, 289
Ondatra zibethica, 220 (fig.)
  zibethica zibethica, 245
  zibethicus zibethicus, **245**
Oochoristica mephitis, 380
  oklahomensis, 374
  peduculata, 380
Opassom, 17
Opassum, 17
Opisocrostis bruneri, 162
Opisodasys, 24
  pseudarctomys, 129, 183
Opisthorchis felineus, 362
  pseudofelineus, 289
Opornis formosus, 10
O'possum, 17
Opossum, 4 (fig.), 16 (fig.), 20
    (fig.), 23 (fig.), 162, 304,
    405
  Virginia, **17**, 97
Opossum embryos, 22 (fig.)
  feces, 23 (fig.)
  tracks, 21 (fig.)
Oppossum, 17
Orchopeas, 119, 142
  caedens, 333

howardi, 327
  wickhami, 129, 148, 162, 169,
    183, 327, 356, 405
Ord meadow mouse, 230
Oribasus, Mustela frenata, 348
Oriental rat, 253
Original, 421
Orignac, 421
Oriniak, 421
Oropsylla arctomys, 129, 289, 305,
    310, 337, 356, 368, 380
  bruneri, 137
  simplex, 310
Ortenburger, Arthur I., x
Orthoptera, 31
Otodectes synotis, 305, 310
Otter, 250, 354
  Canada, **382**
Otter den, 387 (fig.)
Outlaw attacks, 320
Ovenbird, 51
Owl, 31, 34, 39, 97, 212, 228, 244,
    250, 256, 260
  barn, 10, 57, 60, 265, 345
  barred, 60, 117, 119, 147, 162,
    168, 174, 179, 215, 219,
    260, 342, 349, 374, 380
  great horned, 24, 53, 60, 80, 93,
    97, 108, 112, 119, 147, 168,
    174, 180, 183, 189, 215,
    219, 260, 269, 277, 310,
    327, 333, 342, 345, 349,
    356, 374, 380, 388, 405
  long-eared, 60, 189, 215, 219,
    223, 235, 239, 260
  saw-whet, 215, 219
  screech, 54, 60, 219, 235, 260
  short-eared, 60, 215, 235, 265
  snowy, 112, 342
Ox warbles, 432
Oxyuris obvelata, 228

P

Pachysentis canicola, 311
Painter, 389
Palustris, Neosorex, 36
  Sorex, 35
  Sorex palustris, 27 (fig.), 28
Panther, 389
Pantry mouse, 257
Paralces americanus, 421
Parasites: Acanthocephala, 112
  Alaria americana, 298
    arisaemoides, 310
    minnesotae, 380
    mustelae, 289, 342
    taxideae, 342, 349, 368, 374,
      380
  Allodermanyssus sanguineus,
    261
  Amblyomma americana, 298,
    380

Amorphacarus hengererorum,
    31, 34
Ancylostoma caninum, 289,
    298, 310
Androlaelaps, 73
Andrya macrocephala, 235
  primordialis, 174, 228
  sciuri, 183
Arctopsylla setosa, 289, 395
Ascarids, 73
Ascaris, 405
  columnaris, 333, 368, 374,
    380
  dasypodina, 380
  devosi, 337
  lumbricoides, 162
Beetle, 66
Bohmiella wilsoni, 162, 169
Botfly, 119, 212, 219, 266, 269,
    432
Bothriocephalus, 362
Capillaria americana, 162, 180
  chandleri, 142
  mustelorum, 350
  tamiastriata, 148
Catenotaenia pusillo, 183
Cediopsylla simplex, 112, 119,
    289, 305, 327, 380, 405
Ceratophyllus, 244
  dentatus, 400
  faciatus, 349
  gallinae, 148
  labiatus, 400
  petriolatus, 400
  vison, 342, 349, 356
  wickhami, 73
Cestodes, 54, 73, 98, 112, 137,
    142, 148, 162, 169, 228,
    235, 239, 305, 342, 349,
    395
Chaetopsylla setosa, 319
Chiggers, 31, 162, 169, 174,
    180, 183, 228
Chlamydoprocta itascensis,
    380
Choanotaenia sciurola, 169
  spermophili, 137
Cimex pilosellus, 80, 93, 98
Citellinema bifurcatum, 142,
    153, 162, 174, 180, 183
Citellinoides zapodis, 269
Cittelotaenia pectinata, 162
Clinostomum, 327
Coccidia, 119
Comatacarus americanus, 54
Conorhinopsylla stanfordi, 162
Crenosoma mephitidis, 374,
    380
  microbursa, 380
  vulpis, 310
Cruzia tentaculata, 24

Parasites (*cont.*)
Ctenocephalides canis, 129, 305, 310
felis, 119, 310, 327, 374, 380
Ctenophthalmus, 148
pseudogyrtes, 31, 34, 54, 73
wenmanni, 73
Cuterebra, 219
fontinella, 266
Dermacentor, 319
andersoni, 277, 368, 405
variabilis, 24, 119, 162, 169, 266, 289, 298, 327, 349, 368, 380, 395, 405
Dictyocaulus hadweni, 432
viviporus, 432
Dioctophyme renale, 289, 298, 333, 362
Dipetalonema arbuta, 277
Diphyllobothrium latum, 310, 327
Dirofilaria immitis, 298
subdermata, 277
Distoma, 98, 101
Doratopsylla blarinae, 31, 35, 39, 54, 60
Dracunculus medinensis, 342
Eadiea condylurae, 73
Echidnophaga gallinacea, 162, 289, 310, 374, 405
Echinococcus granulosus, 298, 395
Eimeria franklinii, 142
glaucomydis, 180
sciurorum, 169, 180
Enderleinellus longiceps, 162, 168
replicatus, 180
saturalis, 129, 137, 142
Enterobius sciuri, 169, 180
Epitedia, 119
wenmanni, 137
Eptescopsylla, 98
chapini, 93
Euhaemogamasus ambulans, 162, 169, 180, 183
horridus, 174
leponyssoides, 54
Euhaemotopinus abnormis, 66
Euparyhium melis, 388
Euschongastia blarinae, 54
Eutrichophilus setosus, 277
Felicola felis, 405
quadraticeps, 310
subrostratus, 405
vulpis, 305
Fibricola nana, 174
Filaria, 66
fasciata, 405
martis, 380
Filaroides martis, 350
osleri, 298

Flatworms, 183, 190, 277, 405
Fleas, 24, 31, 34, 54, 60, 66, 80, 93, 98, 108, 112, 119, 129, 137, 142, 148, 162, 169, 174, 180, 183, 190, 212, 228, 239, 244, 256, 266, 289, 298, 305, 310, 319, 327, 333, 337, 342, 345, 349, 356, 368, 374, 380, 395, 405
Flies, 356, 432
Flukes, 80, 108, 119, 174, 266, 289, 298, 305, 310, 327, 356, 362, 368, 374, 380, 388
Fossor angertrutrudae, 368
Foxella ignotus, 400
Glyptoporus, 80
Gnats, 432
Grubs, 356
Haemaphysalis leporis-palustris, 112, 119
Haemodipus setoni, 108
Haemogamasus, 34
alaskensis, 54, 80
hirsutus, 112
Haemolaelaps glasgowi, 162
megaventralis, 162, 169
Haemonchus contortus, 432
Haplopleura erratica, 148
Heligmodendrium hassalli, 162, 169
Helminths, 129
Heterodoxus spiniger, 289
Hirstionyssus, 54
Hoplopleura, 244
acanthopus, 223
sciuricola, 162
trispinosa, 180, 183
Hoplopsyllus affinis, 108, 305
glacialis, 400
lynx, 108, 405
Hymenolepis christensoni, 80
diminuta, 137, 142, 148, 162
Ixodes, 228
angustus, 31
cookei, 129, 277, 310, 327, 337, 349, 374, 395
cruciarius, 356
hexagonus, 174, 305, 388
kingi, 298, 356, 368, 380
marxi, 153, 305, 327
ricinus, 310, 395
scapularis, 289, 310
Laelaps microti, 244
Lecithodendrium, 80, 98
Leptinus americanus, 54
Linognathus setosus, 298
Listrophorus, 54
Louse, 66, 108, 129, 137, 142, 148, 162, 168, 174, 180, 183, 190, 212, 223, 228,

239, 244, 266, 277, 289, 298, 305, 327, 333, 342, 345, 349, 368, 395, 405
biting, 356, 374, 380
Lungworms, 432
Macracanthorhynchus hirundinaceus, 148, 162, 169
Megabothris, 119
acerbus, 148
quirini, 266
vison, 148
wagneri, 266, 305
Mesocestoides kirbyi, 289
latus, 374, 380
litteratus, 310
lotoris, 327
variabilis, 310, 337, 380
Microphthirus uncinatus, 183
Mites, 54, 73, 93, 112, 119, 153, 162, 169, 174, 180, 183, 212, 228, 239, 244, 305
ear, 310
mange, 163, 169, 289, 298, 305, 405
red, 269
scab, 219
Molinema diacantha, 277
Molineus patens, 289, 342, 345, 368
Moniliformis, 153
clarki, 137, 148, 162, 380
moniliformis, 66
Monopsyllus, 119
Multiceps multiceps, 289
packii, 298
serialis, 310
Myobia, 34
simplex, 31, 54
Myocoptes, 54
Myodopsylla insignis, 80, 93
Myonyssus jamesoni, 54
Nanophyetus salmincola, 289
Nearctopsylla brooksi, 342
genalis, 54, 356
Nematodes, 24, 54, 73, 112, 137, 142, 153, 162, 169, 239, 266, 269, 305, 342, 350, 395
Neohaematopinus laeviusculus, 137, 142
sciurinus, 162, 169
sciuropteri, 180, 183
Neotedres, 405
Neotrichodectes mephitidis, 349, 374
Nosopsyllus, 119
faciatus, 356
Notocotylus, 266
Odontopsyllus multispinosus, 119, 327, 405
Oesophagostomum radiatum, 432

Parasites (*cont.*)
  Oestridae, 432
  Oncicola canis, 289
  Oochoristica mephitis, 380
    oklahomensis, 374
    peduculata, 380
  Opisocrostis bruneri, 162
  Opisodasys, 24
    pseudarctomys, 129, 183
  Opisthorchis felineus, 362
    pseudofelineus, 289
  Orchopeas, 119, 142
    caedens, 333
    howardi, 327
    wickhami, 129, 148, 162, 169,
      183, 327, 356, 405
  Oropsylla arctomys, 129, 289,
    305, 310, 337, 356, 368,
    380
    bruneri, 137
    simplex, 310
  Otodectes cynotis, 305, 310
  Ox warbles, 432
  Oxyuris obvelata, 228
  Pachysentis canicola, 311
  Passalurus nonanulatus, 289
  Physaloptera, 137, 162, 388
    masino, 142, 169
    maxillaris, 342, 345, 350,
      368, 374, 380
    praeputialis, 311, 395, 405
    rara, 289, 298, 405
    torquata, 368
    turgida, 24
  Plagiorchis microcanthus, 93
  Porrocaecum, 35
  Protomyobia, 34
    brevisetosa, 34
    claparedei, 31, 54
  Protospirura muris, 289
    numidica, 289
  Protozoa, 129, 162, 169, 180,
    190, 202, 228, 305, 356
  Pseudagyrtes, 148
  Pulex irritans, 108, 162, 289,
    298, 305, 310, 368, 380
  Rabbit tick, 112
  Rictularia, 153
    citelli, 137, 142
    halli, 148, 162
    splendida, 289
  Roundworms, 35, 54, 108, 119,
    174, 180, 183, 277, 289,
    298, 305, 310, 319, 327,
    333, 337, 345, 356, 362,
    368, 374, 380, 388, 405
  Sarcoptes scabiei, 162, 169,
    219, 289, 298, 305
  Sarcosporidia, 119
  Scaphiostomum pancreaticum,
    148
  Sellacotyle mustelae, 380

  Shizotaenia erethizontis, 277
    laticephaea, 277
  Siphonaptera, 73
  Skrjabingylus chitwoodorum,
    374, 380
    nasicola, 350
  Soboliphyme baturini, 333,
    337, 362
  Spinturnix americana, 93
  Spirocerca, 266
    lupi, 311
  Spiroptera, 66
  Spirura infundibuliformis, 137
    michiganensis, 148
  Stenocephalides felis, 405
  Stenopenia americana, 162
  Strongyloides papillosus, 380
  Subulura, 266
  Suricatoecus octomaculata, 327
  Syphacia eutami, 153
    thompsoni, 180, 183
  Taenia, 98, 349
    hydatigena, 289, 298
    krabbei, 289
    laruei, 289
    laticollis, 289, 400, 405
    lyncis, 395, 405
    macrocystis, 405
    pisiformis, 108, 289, 298, 310
    rileyi, 289, 400
    serrata, 289
    taeniaformis, 342, 395
    taxidiensis, 368
    twitchelli, 362
  Tapeworm, 80, 108, 119, 174,
    289, 298, 305, 310, 327,
    337, 356, 362, 368, 374,
    380
  Thrassis, 119
    fotus, 137
  Tick, 24, 31, 119, 129, 153, 162,
    169, 174, 212, 228, 244,
    266, 277, 289, 298, 305,
    310, 319, 337, 342, 345,
    349, 356, 368, 374, 380,
    388, 395, 405, 432
  Toxascaris, 405
    leonina, 289
  Toxocara canis, 298
    cati, 405
    leonina, 311
  Trematodes, 93, 98, 112, 239,
    250, 305, 342, 349
  Trichinella spiralis, 137, 319,
    327, 368
  Trichodectes canis, 289, 298
    felis, 395
    interrupto-fasciatus, 368
    kingi, 349
    mephitidis, 380
    osborni, 374
    procyonis, 327

    retusus, 333, 349, 356
  Trichomonas, 305
  Trichopsylla coloris, 327
    lotoris, 327
  Trichostrongyllus, 148
    calcaratus, 162, 169
  Trichuris madisonensis, 148
  Trombicula harperi, 153, 269
    jamesoni, 54
    lipovskyi, 119
    microti, 119, 180, 183
    subsignata, 119
    sylvilaga, 119
    whartoni, 119, 162, 169
  Trypanosoma denysi, 180
    hixsoni, 142
  Uncinaria lotoris, 327
    stenocephala, 298, 337
  Weinlandia citelli, 142
  Wellcomia evoluta, 277
  Worms, 202, 212, 432
    horny-headed, 137, 148,
      153, 162, 169, 380
    intestinal, 432
    stomach, 432
    thorny-headed, 289, 311
  Xenopsylla cheopis, 256
Parasitoidea, 244
Paratyphoid, 257
Parryi, Spermophilus, 138
Parryii, Citellus, 140
Partridge berry, 212, 228
Parus bicolor, 10
Parva, Cryptotis, 44, 56
  Cryptotis parva, 39 (fig.), 56,
    57
Passalurus nonanulatus, 289
Pasteurella tularensis, 119
Pawer, 426
Pawpaws, 24
Pecan, 10, 180
Pectoral harvest mouse, 203
Pectoralis, Reithrodontomys meg-
    alotis, 7, 10, **203**, 210
Pedomys, 229
  ochrogaster ochrogaster, 229
Pekan, 333
  marten, 333
  weasel, 333
Peninsulae, Tamias striatus, 147,
  149
Pennanti, Martes pennanti, **333**
  Mustela, 333
Pennantii, Mustela, 333
Pennant's cat, 333
  marten, 333
Pennsylvania meadow mouse,
  230
Pennsylvanica, Mus, 229
Pennsylvanicus, Microtus, 226,
  229, 237, 240

Pennsylvanicus (*cont.*)
  Microtus pennsylvanicus, 45, 220 (fig.), **229** (fig.)
  Sciurus carolinensis, 156, 157
Perisoreus canadensis canadensis, 9
Permanti, Martes permanti, 333
Peromyscus, 258, 345, 349, 356, 379
  bairdi, 213
  canadensis, 209, 210
  leucopus, 216
  leucopus noveboracensis, 203 (fig.), 206 (fig.), 210, 213, **216**
  maniculatus bairdi, 213
  maniculatus bairdii, 45, 203 (fig.), 206 (fig.), 209, 210, **213**, 217
  maniculatus gracilis, 9, 203 (fig.), 206 (fig.), **209**, 213, 217, 218
  michiganensis, 213
Peromyscus mouse, 209
Persimmons, 24
Personatus, Sorex, 27
Peter rabbit, 113
Pe-zu, 395
Phaeonotus, Lepus americanus, 9, 103 (fig.), 104 (fig.), **108**, 113
Pheasant, 304, 310
Phyllophaga, 297
Physaloptera, 137, 162, 388
  masino, 142, 169
  maxillaris, 342, 345, 350, 368, 374, 380
  praeputialis, 311, 395, 405
  rara, 289, 298, 405
  torquata, 368
  turgida, 24
Picea glauca, 9
  mariana, 9
Pichou, 401
Pichu, 395, 401
Pickerel, 39, 53, 162, 174, 235
Pickerel weed, 249
Picket pin, 131
Picoides arcticus, 9
Pierre lapin, 113
Pigmy bat, 86
  shrew, 40
  weasel, 343
Pike, northern, 250, 266
  walleyed, 39
Pine, 112, 174, 297
  jack, 276
  red, 276
Pine marten, 328, 329 (fig.)
  mouse, 240 (fig.)
  squirrel, 169
  vole, 240

Pinetorum, Arvicola, 240
  Microtus, 229, 237
  Pitymys, 241
Pink bat, 83
Pinus banksiana, 101
  resinosus, 101
  strobus, 101
Pipistrel, 86
Pipistrelle, 86, 89
Pipistrelle bat, 86
Pipistrellus subflavus, 76 (fig.), 86, 99
  subflavus obscurus, 87, 89
  subflavus subflavus, 74 (fig.), 77, **86**
Pituophis sayi, 189
Pitymys, 229
  pinetorum, 241
  pinetorum nemoralis, 244
  pinetorum scalopsoides, 245
  pinetorum schmidti, 7, 245
Pkotcp'sh, k, 428
Plagiorchis microcanthus, 93
Plains bison, 428
  skunk, 374
Planarians, 39
Plantain, 118, 128, 141
Platyrhinus, Sorex, 27
Playing possum, 20 (fig.)
Plum, wild, 380
Pneumonia, 327, 432
Poa, 431
Pocket gopher, 184, 185 (fig.), 289, 368
  Mississippi Valley, **184**
  Wisconsin, **191**
Podophyllum peltatum, 269
Pokeweed, 24, 326
Polecat, 374
Polioptila caerulea caerulea, 10
Polygonum convolvulus, 153
Polygyra, 51
Pondlily, 276
Pondweed, 425
  large-leaved, 249
Pontederia cordata, 249
Poole, Arthur J., x
Po-qua-na-ge, 75
Porcupette, 270
Porcupine, 271 (fig.), 277 (fig.), 289, 304, 337, 362, 395, 400, 405
  Canada, **270**
Porcupine quills, 271 (fig.)
Porkepick, 270
Porky, 270
Porky hog, 270
Porrocaecum, 35
Possum, 17
Potamogeton amplifolius, 249
Potato mouse, 240
Pouched gopher, 184

Prairie beef, 428
  buffalo, 428
  deer mouse, 213 (fig.)
  gopher, 184
  ground squirrel, 131
  hare, 104
  harvest mouse, 203
  meadow mouse, 236
  meadow vole, 236
  mole, **61** (fig.), 62 (fig.)
  mouse, 213, 236
  pocket gopher, 184
  short-tailed mouse, 236
  squirrel, 131, 139
  striper, 131
  vole, 236
  white-footed mouse, 213
  wolf, 281
Prickle cub, 270
Prickle pig, 270
Procyon lotor, 321
  lotor hirtus, **321**
  lotor lotor, 321
Protomyobia, 34
  brevisetosa, 34
  claparedei, 31, 54
Protonotaria citrea, 10
Protospirura muris, 289
  numidica, 289
Protozoa, 129, 162, 169, 180, 190, 202, 228, 305, 356
Pruinosus, Lasiurus, 98
  Vespertilio, 98
Prunus pennsylvanica, 153
Pseudagyrtes, 148
Pseudotuberculosis, 202
Psu-ksi, 413
Pteromys Hudsonius, 181
  sabrinus, 181
  volucella, 175
Pugnacity of shrews, 47
Pulex irritans, 108, 162, 289, 298, 305, 310, 268, 380
Puma, 289, 362, 389 (fig.), 394 (fig.), 412, 419
  Wisconsin, **389**
Pusilla, Mustela, 338
Putorius allegheniensis, 343
  cicognani, 338
  cicognanii, 338
  noveboracensis, 345
  Richardsonii, 338
  rixosa alleghaniensis, 343
  vison, 350
  vison lutreocephalus, 350
  vulgaris, 345
Pygmy bat, 86
  shrew, 40
Pyramidula alternata, 147
Pyrus americana, 9

Q

Quadrivittatus, Tamias, 149

Quail, bobwhite, 304
Qua-quash-go-dwa-wa-go-no-chi, 262
Quay-non-wit-wa-go-no-chi, 209
Quercus palustris, 10
Quill pig, 270
Quills, 270

R

Rabbit, 141, 290, 310, 342, 350, 395
  black-tailed jack, 108, 119
  cottontail, 24, 105, 109, 111, 113, 174, 288, 297, 304, 310, 311, 349, 356, 362, 368, 373, 379, 395, 405
  jack, 105, introduced
  Mearns' cottontail, **113**
  snowshoe, 288, 304, 362, 400
  white-tailed jack, **104**, 115
Rabbit disease, 108
Rabbit form, 117 (fig.)
Rabies, 80, 93, 98, 101, 163, 174, 202, 257, 289, 298, 305, 310, 311, 327, 333, 368, 374, 380, 395, 405
Raccoon, 4 (fig.), 162, 215, 321, 322 (fig.), 359
  Upper Mississippi Valley, **321**
Raccoon curiosity, 321 (fig.)
  tracks, 324 (fig.)
Ragweed, 208, 326
Rain deer, 426
Ranger's cat, 328
Rangifer, 409
  caribou, 425
  caribou sylvestris, **425**
  tarandus, 425
Raspberry, 24, 118, 147, 269, 319, 326, 380
Rat, 92, 381
  black, 11
  brown, 349, 350, 356, 374
  Norway, **253**, 260, 304, 310, 373
Rat-bite fever, 256, 257
Rattlesnake, 53, 219, 235, 239, 265, 349, 368
  timber, 117, 119, 129
Rattus norvegicus, 11, **253**, 255 (fig.)
  rattus, 11
Red-backed mouse, 224, 225 (fig.)
  vole, 224
  wood mouse, 224
Redback mouse, 224
Red bat, 93 (fig.)
  fox, 299 (fig.), 300 (fig.)
  gopher, 184
  lynx, 401

squirrel, 169, 170 (fig.)
tree bat, 93
wood mouse, 224
Regalis, Vulpes fulva, 301
Reindeer, 362, 426
Reithrodontomys, 213, 258
  megalotis dychei, 207
  megalotis pectoralis, 7, 10, **203**, 206 (fig.), 210
Renard, 299
Reptiles, 379
Richardsoni, Sorex, 33, 35
Richardsonii, Putorius, 338
  Sorex, 35, 38
Richardson's caribou, 426
  shrew, 35
Rickettsia akari, 261
Rickettsialpox, 261
Rictularia, 153
  citelli, 137, 142
  halli, 148, 162
  splendida, 289
Ringworm, 113, 202
Riparius, Arvicola, 229
River otter, 382
Robin, 162
Rocky Mountain elk, 408
Roosevelt elk, 412 (fig.)
Roundworm, 35, 54, 108, 119, 174, 180, 183, 277, 289, 298, 305, 310, 319, 327, 333, 337, 345, 356, 362, 368, 374, 380, 388, 405
Rubus, 228
Refescens, Marmota monax, 123 (fig.), 124, **130**
Ruffus, Lynx, 401
Rufiventer, Sciurus, 164
  Sciurus niger, 154 (fig.), 155, **164**
Rufus, Lyncus, 401
  Lynx, 401
  Lynx rufus, 401, 403
Runways of Microtus, 232 (fig.)
  red-backed mouse, 227 (fig.)

S

Sable, 328
Sabrinus, Glaucomys, 176
  Glaucomys sabrinus, 182
  Pteromys, 181
  Sciuropterus, 181
Saddle-backed shrew, 35
Saddle-back shrew, 35
Sagittaria graminea, 249
Salamander, 31, 34, 51, 58, 147
Salmonberry, 337
Sampson fox, 299
Sapsucker, yellow-bellied, 179
Sarcoptes scabiei, 162, 169, 219, 289, 298, 305
Sarcosporidia, 119

Saturatus, Synaptomys cooperi, 222
Say bat, 81
Sayi, Sciurus, 164
Say's bat, 81
Scabies, 163
Scalops aquaticus, 61
  argentatus, 61
Scalopsoides, Arvicola, 47, 240
  Microtus pinetorum, **240**, 244, 245
  Pitymys pinetorum, 245
Scalopus, 310, 345
  aquaticus machrinus, **61** (fig.), 62 (fig.)
Scaphiostomum pancreaticum, 148
Scarabaeidae, 373
Schmidti, Microtus pinetorum, 7, 9, 220 (fig.), 229 (fig.), 241, 242, **245**
  Pitymys pinetorum, 7, 245
Schorger, A. W., 344
Schorgeri, Felis concolor, 7, **389**
Scirpus subterminalis, 249
Sciuropterus sabrinus, 181
  sabrinus macrotis, 181
  volans, 175
Sciurus carolinensis, 139, 170
  carolinensis hypophaeus, 154 (fig.), **155**, 165
  carolinensis leucotis, 155, 157
  carolinensis pennsylvanicus, 156, 157
  hudsonicus, 157, 169
  hudsonicus loquax, 169
  hudsonicus minnesota, 169
  Hudsonius, 169
  hypophaeus, 155
  leucotis, 155
  ludovicianus, 164
  migratorius, 155
  niger, 155
  niger rufiventer, 154 (fig.), 155, **164**
  rufiventer, 164
  Sayi, 164
  striatus, 142
  tridecem-lineatus, 130
  vulpinus, 164
Scorched fox, 299
Scotophilus carolinensis, 11
  fuscus, 89
  Georgianus, 86
  noctivagans, 84
Scrub gopher, 139
Sea otter, 357
Sedges, 234
Sellacotyle mustelae, 380
Seminola, Lasiurus, 98
Septentrionalis, Cathartes aura, 10

Septentrionalis (*cont.*)
Myotis keenii, 74 (fig.), **75**
(fig.), 77, **81**, 91
Vespertilio gryphus, 81
Septicemia, 305
Serotine bat, 90
Serviceberry, 319
Sewer rat, 253
Shadbush, 228, 326, 425
Sha-ka-skan-da-way, 175
Sharp-nosed mouse, 28
short-tailed field mouse, 43
Shaw pocket gopher, 184
Shaw's pocket gopher, 184
Sheldon, Harry H., x, 354
Shi-gak, 374
Shizotaenia erethizontis, 277
laticephaea, 277
Shock disease, 113
Short-tailed prairie mouse, 236
shrew, 43
weasel, 338
Shrew, 28, 235, 304, 337, 342,
356
American pigmy, **40**
big-tailed, 34
cinereous, **27**, 38, 58
giant mole, **42**
Harlan's little mole, 10
Indiana cinereous, 10, **32**
Indiana little short-tailed, **56**
Lakes States mole, **55**
long-tailed, 356
mole, 243
northwestern pigmy, **42**
pigmy, 38, 58
short-tailed, 37, 52, 119, 356,
379
smoky, **32**, 35, 41
southern saddle-backed, **35**
Thompson's, 30
water, 9, 37 (fig.)
Wisconsin water, **36**
Shrew-mole, 61
Shrew mouse, 27, 28, 43
Shrike, 137, 235, 260
migrant, 53
northern, 53
Shrubs, 118
Siffleur, 122, 363
Silver fox, 299
Silver-gray fox, 299
Silvery mole, 61
Singing mouse, 257, 260
Sinko, 164
Siphonaptera, 73
Ski-kog, 374
Skins of bats, 75 (fig.)
deer mouse, 206 (fig.)
Eptesicus, 84 (fig.)
harvest mouse, 206 (fig.)
house mouse, 259 (fig.)

jumping mouse, 259 (fig.)
Lasionycteris, 84 (fig.)
Lasiurus, 94 (fig.)
lemming mouse, 221 (fig.)
long-tailed shrew, 27 (fig.)
Microtus pennsylvanicus, 229
(fig.)
mole shrew, 39 (fig.)
pigmy shrew, 39 (fig.)
Pipistrellus, 84 (fig.)
S'kos, 338, 346
Skrjabingylus chitwoodorum,
374, 380
nasicola, 350
Skulls of bats, 74 (fig.)
beaver, 193 (fig.)
chipmunks, 130 (fig.)
deer mouse, 203 (fig.)
Didelphis, 18 (fig.)
eastern timber wolf, 292 (fig.)
Erethizon dorsatum, 271 (fig.)
Euarctos, 312 (fig.)
Felis schorgeri, 390 (fig.)
German shepherd dog, 83
(fig.)
gray fox, 307 (fig.)
ground squirrels, 130 (fig.)
Gulo, 358 (fig.)
harvest mouse, 203 (fig.)
lagomorphs, 103 (fig.)
Lutra, 383 (fig.)
Lynx canadensis, 396 (fig.),
397 (fig.)
Lynx rufus, 396 (fig.), 402
(fig.)
marten, 330 (fig.)
Martes pennanti, 335 (fig.)
Mephitis, 376 (fig.)
moles, 61 (fig.)
Muridae, 255 (fig.)
Mustela vison letifera, 352
(fig.)
northeastern coyote, 283 (fig.)
Ondatra zibethicus, 246 (fig.)
pocket gophers, 184 (fig.)
raccoon, 323 (fig.)
shrews, 26 (fig.)
Spilogale, 370 (fig.)
Taxidea, 364
tree squirrels, 154 (fig.)
voles, 220 (fig.)
Vulpes fulva, 300 (fig.)
weasels, 338 (fig.)
white-tailed deer, 414 (fig.)
wolf, 293 (fig.)
woodchucks, 123 (fig.)
Zapodidae, 261 (fig.)
Skunk, 66, 119, 142, 219, 228,
260, 269, 288, 304, 310,
374, 405
Northern Plains, **374**
prairie spotted, **369**

striped, 54, 215, 235, 239, 244,
265
Skunk-bear, 357
Skunks adopted by cat, 373 (fig.)
Sliver cat, 270
Slugs, 65
Small eastern flying squirrel, 175
myotis, 75
Smaller American flying squirrel,
175
Small-footed myotis, 81
Small striped gopher, 131
weasel, 338
Smartweed, 153, 326
Smell-cat, 374
Snails, 24, 34, 39, 51, 54, 59, 65,
72, 147, 174, 250, 326
Snake, 24, 51, 137, 148, 215, 243,
265, 304, 342, 356, 368
black, 119, 219, 349
bull, 189
fox, 235, 239
garter, 39, 235
milk, 60
pine, 53
water, 53
Snow mole, 36
rabbit, 108
Snowshoe, 108
hare, 108
rabbit, 108
Snow shrew, 36
Soboliphyme baturini, 333, 337,
362
Social bat, 83
Sodalis, Myotis, 74 (fig.), 75
(fig.), **83**, 356
Sod runner, 131
So-gus-con-ta-wa, 181
Solanum carolinense, 239
Solomon's seal, 243
Sorex, 349, 356
arcticus, 33
arcticus arcticus, 27 (fig.)
arcticus cinereus, 27
arcticus laricorum, 26 (fig.), 27
(fig.), 32, **35**
brevicaudus, 42
cinereus, 36, 40
cinereus cinereus, 26 (fig.), **27**,
28 (fig.), 32
cinereus lesueurii, 10, 26 (fig.),
27 (fig.), 28, 32
cooperi, 27
cristatus, 68
Dekayi, 42
Forsteri, 27
fumeus, 28, 32, 35, 41, 241
fumeus fumeus, 27 (fig.), **32**
hoyi, 7, **40**
palustris, 35, 37 (fig.)

Sorex (*cont.*)
  palustris hydrobadistes, **7, 9,**
      26 (fig.), 27 (fig.), 28, **36**
  palustris navigator, 38
  palustris palustris, 27 (fig.)
  personatus, 27
  platyrhinus, 27
  richardsoni, 33, 35
  Richardsonii, 35
  richardsonii, 38
  thompsoni, 30
Sorrel, 128
Southern bog lemming, 220
  flying squirrel, **175,** 176 (fig.)
  fox, 306
Sowbugs, 34, 59, 65
Spadefish, 391
Spadix, Mustela frenata, 347
Sparrow, white-throated, 9
Spermophilus Franklini, 138
  grammurus, 138
  parryi, 138
  tridecemlineatus, 130
  tridecimlineatus, 130
Sphagnum, 38
Spiders, 31, 34, 65, 153, 228, 269
Spike rush, 249
Spilogale interrupta, 369
  putorius interrupta, **369**
Spinturnix americana, 93
Spirocerca, 266
  lupi, 311
Spiroptera, 66
Spirura infundibuliformis, 137
  michiganensis, 148
Spotted fever, 257
  skunk, 369 (fig.)
Spruce, 112, 174, 183, 228
  black, 9, 276, 297
  white, 9, 276
Squash bugs, 24
Squirrel, 319, 362, 400, 405
  black, 157
  flying, 169, 175, 289, 348
  fox, 158, 174, 304, 310, 379
  gray, 129, 169, 174, 217, 289,
      304, 310, 379
  gray tree, 139
  Minnesota gray, **155**
  Minnesota red, **169**
  northeastern gray, 156
  northern flying, 9, **181,** 332
  red, 157, 162, 178, 332, 337,
      356, 379
  southern flying, **175**
  striped ground, **130**
  western fox, 157, **164**
Squirrel-proof bird feeder, 163
      (fig.)
Stag, 408
Star-nose, 68
Star-nose mole, 68

Stenocephalides felis, 405
Stenopenia americana, 162
Stink bugs, 24
Stink-cat, 374
Stinktier, 374
Stoat, 338
Stonei, Synaptomys cooperi, 222
Strawberry, 112, 141, 147, 174,
      304, 319, 326
Streaked gopher, 131
Striatus, Sciurus, 142
  Tamias, 142, 151
Striped chipmunk, 142
  citellus, 131
  gopher, 130, 131
  ground squirrel, 133 (fig.), 142
  prairie squirrel, 131
  pussy cat, 374
  skunk, 374, 375 (fig.)
  spermophile, 131
  squirrel, 142
Striper, 131
Stripsie, 131
Strongyloides papillosus, 380
Stump ear, 155
Subflavus, Pipistrellus, 76 (fig.),
      86, 99
  Pipistrellus subflavus, 74 (fig.),
      77, **86**
  Vespertilio, 86
Subulatus, Myotis, 81
  Vespertilio, 81
Subulura, 266
Sumac, 112
  staghorn, 419
Sun bear, 311
Sunfish, green, 53
Superficial tunnel, 66 (fig.)
Superiorensis, Lynx rufus, **401**
Suricatoecus octomaculata, 327
Swamper, 108
Swamp jack rabbit, 108
Sylvaticus, Lepus, 113
Sylvestris, Rangifer caribou, **425**
  Rangifer tarandus, 425
Sylvilagus, 109, 297
  floridanus mallurus, 115
  floridanus mearnsi, 113
  floridanus mearnsii, 103 (fig.),
      104 (fig.), **113**
Synaptomys cooperi, 220, 237
  cooperi cooperi, **220,** 221
      (fig.), 224, 240
  cooperi fatuus, 220
  cooperi gossii, 10, 220 (fig.),
      221, 222, 223, **224**
  cooperi saturatus, 222
  cooperi stonei, 222
  gossii, 224
Syphacia eutami, 153
  thompsoni, 180, 183

T

Tabanus, 51
Tadarida, 80
Taenia, 98, 349
  hydatigena, 289, 298
  krabbei, 289
  laruei, 289
  laticollis, 289, 400, 405
  lyncis, 395, 405
  macrocystis, 405
  pisiformis, 108, 289, 298, 310
  rileyi, 289, 400
  serrata, 310
  taeniformis, 342, 395
  taxidiensis, 368
  twitchelli, 362
Tails of bobcat, 396 (fig.)
  Canada lynx, 396 (fig.)
  cottontail, 116 (fig.)
  weasel, 338 (fig.)
Talpa machrina, 61
Talpoides, Blarina, 42
  Blarina brevicauda, 42
Tamarack, 174, 276
Tamias, 132, 297, 310
  quadrivittatus, 149
  striatus, 142, 151
  striatus griseus, 130 (fig.),
      142, 148, 149
  striatus lysteri, 142, 149
  striatus ohionensis, 143, **148**
  striatus peninsulae, 147, **149**
Tamiasciurus hudsonicus loquax,
      169, 171
  hudsonicus minneosta, 154
      (fig.), **169**
  hudsonicus murii, 171
Tapeworm, 80, 108, 119, 174, 289,
      298, 305, 310, 327, 337,
      356, 362, 368, 374, 380
Tarandus, Rangifer, 425
Taxidea Americana, 363
  taxus, 363
  taxus jacksoni, 7, **363**
  taxus taxus, 363
Taxus, Taxidea, 363
  Taxidea taxus, 363
Teeth of Canis latrans, 283 (fig.)
  Eptesicus fuscus, 90 (fig.)
  shrews, 40 (fig.)
  Sorex, 27 (fig.)
Tennessee possum, 17
Tha, 328
Tha-cho, 333
Thamnos, Canis latrans, 7, **281,**
      283 (fig.)
Thirteen-lined ground squirrel,
      131
Thirteen-striped citellus, 131
  ground squirrel, 131
Thistle, 141

Thompsoni, Microsorex hoyi, 30
  Sorex, 30
Thornapple, 162
Thrassis, 119
  fotus, 137
Thrush, golden-crowned, 51
  hermit, 9
Thryomanes bewickii, 10
Thuja occidentalis, 9
Ticks, 24, 31, 119, 129, 153, 162,
      169, 174, 212, 228, 244,
      277, 289, 298, 305, 310,
      319, 337, 342, 345, 349,
      356, 368, 374, 380, 388,
      395, 405, 432
  larval, 266
  rabbit, 112
Tilia americana, 147
Timber squirrel, 155
  wolf, 290
Timothy, 141
Titmouse, tufted, 10
Toad, 141, 380
Toxascaris, 405
  leonina, 289
Toxocara canis, 298
  cati, 405
  leonina, 311
Tracks of badger, 266 (fig.)
  beaver, 194 (fig.)
  bison, 430 (fig.)
  black bear, 316 (fig.)
  bobcat, 404 (fig.)
  Canada lynx, 399 (fig.)
  Canada otter, 385 (fig.)
  cottontail, 107 (fig.)
  coyote, 287 (fig.)
  domestic cat, 403 (fig.)
  domestic dog, 287 (fig.)
  domestic pig, 417 (fig.)
  domestic sheep, 417 (fig.)
  fisher, 336 (fig.)
  fox squirrel, 166 (fig.)
  gray fox, 309 (fig.)
  gray squirrel, 159 (fig.)
  jack rabbit, 107 (fig.)
  marten, 331 (fig.)
  meadow jumping mouse, 264
      (fig.)
  meadow mouse, 232 (fig.)
  mink, 353 (fig.)
  muskrat, 248 (fig.)
  Norway rat, 255 (fig.)
  pine mouse, 242 (fig.)
  porcupine, 273 (fig.)
  puma, 392 (fig.)
  red fox, 302 (fig.)
  red squirrel, 172 (fig.)
  shrews, 46 (fig.)
  spotted skunk, 371 (fig.)
  striped skunk, 378 (fig.)
  Tamias, 145 (fig.)

timber wolf, 294 (fig.)
varying hare, 107 (fig.)
white-footed mouse, 216 (fig.)
white-tailed deer, 417 (fig.)
wolverine, 360 (fig.)
woodchuck, 125 (fig.)
Transition Zone, 9, 37
Tree bat, 93
Tree-climbing skunk, 369
Tree fox, 306
Tree hackee, 169
Trematodes, 93, 98, 112, 239,
      250, 305, 342, 349
Triacanthos, Gleditsia, 10
Trichinella spiralis, 137, 319, 327,
      368
Trichinosis, 257
Trichodectes canis, 289, 298
  felis, 395
  interrupto-fasciatus, 368
  kingi, 349
  mephitidis, 380
  osborni, 374
  procyonis, 327
  retusus, 333, 349, 356
Trichomonas, 305
Trichopsylla coloris, 327
  lotoris, 327
Trichostrongyllus, 148
  calcaratus, 162, 169
Trichuris madisonensis, 148
Tricolor shrew, 35
Tridecemlineatus, Citellus, 130,
      139, 143, 144, 217
  Citellus tridecemlineatus, 130
      (fig.)
  Sciurus, 130
  Spermophilus, 130
Tridecimlineatus, Spermophilus,
      130
Trombicula harperi, 153, 269
  jamesoni, 54
  lipovskyi, 119
  microti, 119, 180, 183
  subsignata, 119
  sylvilaga, 119
  whartoni, 119, 162, 169
Trouessart bat, 81
  little brown bat, 81
Trouessart's bat, 81
  little brown bat, 81
Trout, 53
  brook, 39
  rainbow, 39
Trypanosoma denysi, 180
  hixsoni, 142
Tuberculosis, 257, 327
Tularemia, 24, 108, 113, 119, 153,
      163, 174, 202, 256, 289,
      298, 305, 310, 356, 368,
      374, 380
Tumors, 289

Tunnel by mole, 66 (fig.)
Turkey vulture, 10
Turtle, 326
  eggs, 379
  snapping, 250
Twilight bat, 98
Twitchell, A. H., 361
Two-striped skunk, 374
Typha latifolia, 249
Typhus, 257
  fever, 256
Tyto alba pratincola, 10
U
Uncinaria lotoris, 327
  stenocephala, 298, 337
Upland mouse, 236
Upper Austral Zone, 10
  Mississippi Valley fox squirrel,
      164
Urocyon cinereoargenteus, 306
  cinereoargenteus cinereoargen-
      teus, 306
  cinereoargenteus cinereorar-
      genteus, 306
  cinereoargenteus ocythous, 7,
      306
Urson, 270
Ursus americanus, 311
  cinnamomum, 311
  luscus, 357

V

Vaccinium, 228
Varying hare, 108, 109 (fig.)
Vesper mouse, 216
Vespertilio borealis, 93
  cinereus, 98
  fuscus, 89
  gryphus septentrionalis, 81
  linereus, 98
  lucifugus, 75
  noctivagans, 84
  Noveboracensis, 93
  pruinosus, 98
  subflavus, 86
  subulatus, 81
Vesperugo noctivagans, 86
Vetch, 128
Viburnum, 162, 179, 183
Vireo, Bell's, 10
  red-eyed, 162
Vireo bellii bellii, 10
Virgin fox, 306
Virginia creeper, 147
  deer, 413
  fox, 306
  opossum, 17
  possum, 17
Virginiana, Didelphis, 17
  Didelphis marsupialis, 17, 18
      (fig.)
  Didelphis virginiana, 17

Virginiana (*cont.*)
 Didelphus, 17
 Didelphys, 17
Virginianus, Cervus, 413
 Odocoileus, 413
 Vulpes, 306
Vison, 350
 Lutreola, 350
 Mustela, 350
 Putorius, 350
Volans, Glaucomys, 181
 Glaucomys volans, 154 (fig.)
  175
 Mus, 175
 Sciuropterus, 175
Vole, 230, 345
 Gapper's red-backed, **224**
 meadow, 24, 51, 226, **229**, 238,
  263, 297, 304
 prairie, **236**
 red-backed, 289, 297
 yellow-cheeked, 11
Volucella, Pteromys, 175
Vulgaris, Putorius, 345
Vulpes fulva fulva, **298**
 fulva regalis, 301
 fulvus, 298
 fulvus argentatus, 298
 Virginianus, 306
Vulpinus, Sciurus, 164

W

Wa-a-boos, 108, 113
Wa-a-gush, 299
Wagner, George, 195
Walnut, black, 10, 179
Wa-mik-wa-wa-go-no-chi, 224
Wapiti, 408
Warbler, Kentucky, 10
 myrtle, 9
 prothonotary, 10
Waschbar, 321
Wasps, 326, 379
Waterdog, 382
Waterfowl, 362
Waterlily, 425
 white, 249
Water shrew, 36
 weasel, 350
Weasel, 34, 39, 54, 66, 80, 119,
 137, 147, 183, 189, 215,
 219, 223, 228, 235, 256,
 260, 265, 269, 304, 310,
 338, 339 (fig.)
 Allegheny least, **343**
 Bangs' short-tailed, **338**
 least, 239, 243, 350
 long-tailed, 112, 142, 345
 New York long-tailed, **345**
 short-tailed, 112, 153, 348, 350
Webb, A. R., 160

Weevils, 162
Weil's disease, 257
Weinlandia citelli, 142
Wellcomia evoluta, 277
Western chipmunk, 149
 fox squirrel, 164 (fig.)
 raccoon, 321
Wharf rat, 253
Wheatgrass, 431
Whistle-pig, 122
Whistler, 122
Whistle sneak, 131
Whistling pig, 122
White-bellied flying squirrel, 175
 wood mouse, 209
White bison, 428 (fig.)
 grubs, 65
 hare, 108
 jack, 104
 jack rabbit, 104
 mouse, 257
 rat, 253
White-footed mouse, 209, 213,
 216 (fig.)
Whitetail, 413
White-tailed deer, 418 (fig.)
 jack, 104
Whitneyi, Cervus, 7
Wild buffalo, 428
Wildcat, 112, 297, 333, 401
Wild crab, 326
 grape, 319, 326
 plum, 326
 rice, 250
Willow, 112, 174, 276
 Bebbs, 425
 black, 249
Wintergreen, 147, 174, 212, 419
Wireworms, 65
Wisconsin badger, 363
 gray fox, **306** (fig.)
 least chipmunk, **149** (fig.)
Wisconsinensis, Cariacus, 7
 Geomys bursarius, 7, 184
  (fig.), 185 (fig.), 186, 187,
  191
Wo-jush, 245
Wolf, 290, 319, 395, 412, 431
 brush, **281**, 284
 eastern, 284, **290**
 gray, 284
 prairie, 284
 timber, 284, 289, 304, 332, 419,
  425
 tracks, 295 (fig.)
Wolverene, 357
Wolverine, 304, **357** (fig.)
Woodchuck, 122 (fig.), 288, 289,
 304, 310, 362, 368, 379
 eastern, 10
 rufescent, **130**

 southern, **122**
Woodchuck burrows, 128 (fig.)
Wood fox, 306
 gnome, 216
Woodland caribou, 425 (fig.)
 deer mouse, 209 (fig.), 216
 jumping mouse, 267 (fig.), 268
  (fig.)
 white-footed mouse, 216
Wood mouse, 216
Woodpecker, 179
 northern three-toed, 9
 red-bellied, 10
Wood pussy, 374
 rabbit, 113
Woodshock, 122, 333
Wood thrush, 162
Woods beaver, 192
 devil, 357
 mouse, 216
Woolly shoat, 17
Worms, 51, 65, 72, 202, 212,
 432
 enchytrid, 269
 horny-headed, 137, 148, 153,
  162, 169, 380
 intestinal, 432
 soil, 269
 stomach, 432
 thorny-headed, 289, 311
Wren, Bewick's, 10
Wyandotte Cave bat, 83

X

Xanthognathus, Microtus, 11
Xenopsylla cheopis, 256

Y

Yellow bear, 311
Yellow-bellied squirrel, 164
Yellow clintonia, 212
 fox, 299
Yellowish-brown bat, 86
Yew, 419

Z

Zapus, 356, 379
 hudsonius, 262
 hudsonius hudsonius, 9, **262**,
  266
 hudsonius intermedius, 259
  (fig.), 261 (fig.), 263, **266**
Zebra, Centurus carolinus, 10
Zee-sin-ko, 169
Zibethica, Ondatra, 220 (fig.)
 Ondatra zibethica, 245
Zibethicus, Castor, 245
 Fiber, 245
 Ondatra zibethicus, **245**
Zirrer, Francis, 159, 355
Zonotrichia albicollis, 9